# Contents

 The Netherlands

 Belgium

 Luxembourg

 Germany

 Switzerland

 Austria

 Poland

 Czech Republic

 Hungary

 Slovenia

 Croatia

 Greece

 United Kingdom

 Ireland

# CampingCard ACSI 2019

This year you can take advantage of large discounts at no fewer than
**3,401 campsites** in 21 countries.

## Also of interest:

You can always have campsite information to hand, even without an internet connection, with the CampingCard ACSI app.
See page **26**.

Book your spot online, directly with the campsite. See page **22**.

Leave a review and have a chance to win a great prize! See page **13**.

You will find your discount card in part 2.

| | |
|---:|:---|
| 18 | in Norway |
| 35 | in Sweden |
| 66 | in Denmark |
| 391 | in The Netherlands |
| 56 | in Belgium |
| 26 | in Luxembourg |
| 345 | in Germany |
| 40 | in Switzerland |
| 91 | in Austria |
| 7 | in Poland |
| 16 | in The Czech Republic |
| 15 | in Hungary |
| 18 | in Slovenia |
| 79 | in Croatia |
| 40 | in Greece |
| 40 | in The United Kingdom |
| 14 | in Ireland |
| 1,494 | in France |
| 276 | in Spain |
| 23 | in Portugal |
| 311 | in Italy |

Check
# www.CampingCard.com/modifications
before you leave for the most up to date information.

# Validity of CampingCard ACSI

*The CampingCard ACSI card is valid for one calendar year and is non-transferable. We ask you therefore to complete the back of the card in full and sign it. A campsite has the right to ask you for additional identification.*

The information in this guide applies specifically to 2019. Each year new campsites join, other sites change the period in which the discount card is accepted or their rates. The details in this guide are therefore updated annually. Check www.CampingCard.com/modifications for the most up to date information. If you use the CampingCard ACSI app, the campsite information in this app is updated multiple times a year.

**Take note!** Only campsites which appear in this guide display the blue CC logo, and you will only get a discount on your overnight stay with your CampingCard ACSI discount card at these sites. See also 'Only campsites with the CC logo' on page 11.

Please also note that expired discount cards will not be accepted at campsites.

Visit: **www.CampingCard.com**

**ALMERIMAR 1 - Port** ✳  ⌖  G5  123  (A) N36°41.824' W002°47.635'  04711
(B) N36°41.689' W002°47.256'

Parking A

➡ **(A)** Calle de Varadero. Turn off A-7 at Junction 409 and follow sp 'Almerimar'. Follow road for 6.7km, then turn right at roundabout by Hotel Golf Almerimar, sp 'Puerto Deportivo'. At next roundabout turn left, sp 'Puerto Deportivo'. In 220m turn left into car park, then right along harbour wall to service point. **(B)** Obtain barrier pass (€20/CCI deposit) from lighthouse; Mon-Sun 9am-2pm/4-9pm. Exit port and turn right at 3 roundabouts. In 300m turn right, sp 'Escuela de Vela'. Use pass to enter. Service Point at far end.

🚐 75; €10/night inc service; €13/night inc 16amp elec; Long stay discounts
🔒 Custom; M/F WC/showers each require key, €5 deposit

ℹ **(A)** At lighthouse adj to sandy beach/marina; views. **(B)** Popular with families and dog owners. Behind sea wall; 4 bays have sea views. Both adj to marina, lined with lively bars, restaurants and commerce. English spoken. WiFi €3.50/24hrs, decreases to €30/1 month. 2 washing machines at marina, request map. Reinspected 2017.

Parking B

All The Aires Spain And Portugal entry above. All The Aires France map below.

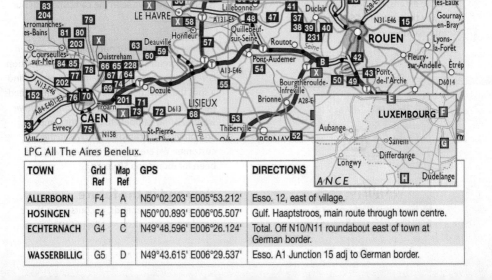

LPG All The Aires Benelux.

| TOWN | Grid Ref | Map Ref | GPS | DIRECTIONS |
|------|----------|---------|-----|------------|
| **ALLERBORN** | F4 | A | N50°02.203' E005°53.212' | Esso. 12, east of village. |
| **HOSINGEN** | F4 | B | N50°00.893' E006°05.507' | Gulf. Haaptstroos, main route through town centre. |
| **ECHTERNACH** | G4 | C | N49°48.596' E006°26.124' | Total. Off N10/N11 roundabout east of town at German border. |
| **WASSERBILLIG** | G5 | D | N49°43.615' E006°29.537' | Esso. A1 Junction 15 adj to German border. |

### How it all started

It was the summer of 1964. Teacher Ed van Reine drove his car and trailer from his home in the Netherlands, over Belgian and French roads, to the Spanish sun. Finally time for a holiday. Finally time to go camping again, driving around, looking for a nice place for the whole family to stay. The prospect was wonderful: a carefree time and a few weeks outside. But then, on arrival, disappointment ... Completo; most campsites were already full.

It must be possible to do things differently, Ed thought. He envisioned a European reservation system, and right there, while still on holiday, he thought up a way to avoid closed barriers. Upon his return he asked his teaching colleagues for help and compiled his first campsite guide with the most important information about the most popular campsites in Europe, like addresses and telephone numbers. It was the forerunner of the extensive book that is now before you. It was the birth of ACSI, Auto Camper Service International.

Ed could not have known then that his stencilled booklet would form the basis of an internationally operating publishing house and tour operator in the field of camping.

## It's all about quality

Anyone can collect and bundle information. That's why we do it differently. All campsites that would like to be included in our guides, on our websites and in our apps, are visited annually by an inspector. That was already the case in 1964 and it is still the case today. The inspectors – who were usually critical campers even before they became inspectors - are trained in-house and ensure that only the best campsites are allowed to use our well-known logo.

And that's what campsites want. ACSI stands for quality and our logo has become a quality mark. The inspection also ensures that the information is reliable: we have seen the campsite with our own eyes.

In other words, we put our products together with the greatest possible care. The information is very extensive and that helps campers to find a spot that suits them, their family or their needs perfectly. And that is precisely our mission: we want to bring campers to the right campsite, and provide the campsite with a satisfied customer. We are good at that, and we have been for more than 50 years.

## Now and in the future

That mission never ends, of course. But there are always new missions. Like in 1993, when

Ramon took over the management of the company from his father. He started working on increasing professionalism, making more use of computers, and he crossed the border. ACSI went international with multilingual products.

And then the next challenge presented itself. Could ACSI succeed in providing campsites with campers in the spring and autumn? They developed a discount system with an accompanying discount card, which is simple to use for both campers and campsite owners. Within ten years, CampingCard ACSI had become ACSI's most successful product. Today, nearly 700,000 campers use the discount card to travel across Europe.

Ramon's father's original idea - a reservation system - is now also taking shape. More and more campsites can be booked directly via our websites and apps. That is one of our next missions. We want to create an online place where campers can search, book and find information and inspiration. One address to get to know everything about the campsite, the region and the activities to do there. A starting point for everyone who loves camping.

## For every camper
Of course not everyone is the same. Different strokes for different folks. Not everyone wants a book and not everyone wants an app. Not everyone wants a large campsite with lots of amenities and not everyone wants a small, quiet campsite. We know that all too well. That's why we have products for every camper.

### Campsite guides
There are many campers who like to read a campsite guide on their lap, or to open one up on the kitchen table. So they can leaf through to find a place to camp. We have campsite guides for campers who go out especially in

low season. We also have a guide for campers who like to go camping in high and low season, with detailed information about campsites in the five most popular camping destinations: the United Kingdom, Ireland, France, Spain and Portugal.

### Websites
With the handy filters on our websites you will quickly find a campsite that meets your needs. And for more and more campsites you can now book a pitch or accommodation quickly and safely via the website or app. But there is more. We also write on the internet about beautiful destinations and new trends and we give camping tips. We do this on www.Eurocampings.co.uk/blog.

### Apps
For added convenience while on the road: our apps can be used without an internet connection and are very easy to use, thanks to the filter options. Motorhome owners can expand the campsite information with information on 9,000 motorhome pitches in Europe! Thanks to location information (GPS) you can always find a place to stay in the neighbourhood.

advantages: liability insurance, and discounts on almost all products in our webshop.

We have been organising group camping trips for 30 years. With ACSI Camping Tours we take caravan and motorhome owners on dream trips inside and outside of Europe. Thanks to our years of experience we know how to find the best unique spots. These tours are available for campers who speak Dutch, English and German.

Suncamp holidays is our online travel agency for camping holidays. The selection consists of top campsites with many facilities at popular destinations. On a number of these campsites you can book our SunLodges. We have developed these comfortable and luxurious accommodations ourselves.

Check www.ACSI.eu to find out more about our company and our products.

## Magazines

We like to write about camping and we like to inspire campers for their next holiday. We do not only do this online, we also love paper. We create various camping magazines, such as ACSI FreeLife, which appears in Dutch eight times a year, and Start2Camp (in Dutch).

## That's not all

With ACSI Club ID you can keep your passport with you, safely in your pocket. This membership card is a replacement proof of identity and is accepted at almost 8,800 campsites in Europe. But it has more

## All campsites inspected annually

Reliable and objective information does not come naturally. That's why we inspect all campsites in our guides, on our websites and in our apps every year. Did you know that we have to make changes to 95% of those campsites every year?

Our 319 inspectors receive tough training before they go out. They check the campsites for more than 220 amenities, but of course also for quality. They experience the atmosphere and talk to the campers that are there and to the campsite owner.

# A relaxed start to your holiday,
## by being sure you have your pitch already booked

- Search by availability
- Book quickly and easily, even when you are already on the road
- Stay overnight at advantageous CampingCard ACSI rates!
- Safe payment via credit card

For more information please visit:

# www.CampingCard.com/bookonline

# Your off-season discount card

*It couldn't be easier. Using your discount card you can enjoy bargain holidays in low season at top-quality campsites throughout Europe. And all that for just one of five fixed rates: 12, 14, 16, 18 or 20 euros per night.*

## The rates

The fixed rates of 12, 14, 16, 18 and 20 euros are lower than the minimum prices charged by the participating campsites in the low season. You can therefore be certain of big discounts on the overnight price! At least 10% - and in some cases as much as 60%. Some campsites offer an extra discount if you stay for a longer period. Campsites are just as attractive in the low season as in the high season; the owners guarantee the same standards of facilities and service and the main facilities are also available in the low season; you just pay less. You can therefore avoid the busy period and take advantage of your discount in early and late season!

## What do you have to do to enjoy your discount?

It couldn't be easier - take the CampingCard ACSI with you and present it to the receptionist when you arrive at one of the participating

campsites and take advantage of our preferential rates! Show your discount card again at the reception when you pay and you will be charged the advantageous CampingCard ACSI rate. You can see what is included in the rate in the 'Rate per overnight stay' section on page 24 of this guide, and you can see any supplementary charges there may be in the 'Not included in the overnight rate' section on page 25.

## Payment conditions

CampingCard ACSI may look like a credit or debit card but it is actually a discount card.
You show your CampingCard ACSI and you can stay on selected sites at advantageous rates. You don't usually have to pay in advance for a fixed number of nights; just pay when you depart.

However, ultimately the payment method is determined by the rules of the campsite, and that includes when you need to pay or provide a deposit. If for example you announce that you will be staying for just one night or want to reserve, the campsite may ask you to pay in advance or pay a deposit. The campsite reception will inform you of their policy in this matter.

## Reservation with CampingCard ACSI

On some campsites you can reserve in advance with CampingCard ACSI. A campsite has

then indicated facility 6A 'Reservation with CampingCard ACSI possible' in the campsite's information.

A reservation with your CampingCard ACSI is in fact considered a normal reservation, only the overnight rate is lower. In some cases you will have to pay a reservation charge and a deposit may be required. A reservation made well in advance by a CampingCard holder can cause problems for campsites. In such cases a campsite may have a policy not to accept your reservation. There are also some sites where reservation is never possible.

It is important when making a reservation to mention that you are a CampingCard holder. If you fail to do this there is a chance that you will have to pay the regular rate.

**Take note:**
ACSI annually inspects 9,900 campsites in Europe. Of these 9,900 campsites, 3,401 are participating in CampingCard ACSI in 2019.

You only have the right to a CampingCard ACSI discount if a campsite appears in this guide or on www.CampingCard.com. Also make sure to check whether the discount card will be accepted during the period you wish to stay at the campsite of your choice.

CampingCard ACSI sites can be recognised by the blue CC logo that you will see on a sticker at the reception or by a large flag near the reception. **Only campsites with a blue CC logo participate in CampingCard ACSI so you only have the right to a discount at these campsites.**

## Only campsites with the CC logo

All participating campsites featured in this guide have been individually inspected and approved by ACSI.

## 319 inspectors

Inspectors set off every year throughout Europe to visit campsites for the renowned ACSI campsite guides. This is how ACSI has been collecting the most reliable campsite information for the past 54 years. In 2018, 319 inspectors visited the campsites.

They inspect the campsites using a 220 point checklist and also pay attention to details that cannot easily be rated, such as surroundings, recreational facilities and the friendliness of the staff, etc.

The opinion of the campers themselves is of course of the utmost importance, so our inspection teams regularly ask campsite guests for their opinions of the campsite. You can let your opinion count after visiting a CampingCard site. See page 13 for more information.

## Probably the biggest advantage of camping in low season…

CampingCard ACSI is first and foremost a discount card for the low season. With it, you will pay a lower overnight rate.

Another advantage of camping outside the high season – and for some the biggest reason – is relaxation. You avoid congested roads, the sites are quieter, you rarely need to reserve a pitch and the staff have much more time and attention for you. Additionally, the local sights around your campsite are less busy.

In other words: everything you need for a relaxing and carefree holiday awaits you. We hope you will make the most of it!

# How to find a campsite?

*This CampingCard ACSI guide consists of two parts. Participating CampingCard ACSI campsites are described one by one in an 'editorial entry', which includes a description of the rate, the acceptance periods and the amenities.*

In this guide campsites have been arranged alphabetically by place name per country. An example: Zaton Holiday Resort in Zaton/Nin (Zadar) in Croatia can be found under Z for Zaton/Nin (Zadar).

Exceptions to this are the Netherlands, Germany, France, Spain and Italy. These countries are divided up into regions. Within a region you will find the campsite by place name. In the contents page of this guide and in the accompanying mini-atlas you will also see that the Netherlands, Germany, France, Spain and Italy are divided up into regions.

Using the general maps which precede the country information you will easily be able to find a campsite in your favourite holiday area!

## How to find a participating campsite

There are several possibilities:

**In this campsite guide:**
- Search for a campsite by place. Use the register at the back of the guide or the mini-atlas for this purpose.
- Search the country or region where you want to camp. For this you can use the table of contents in the front of the guide. Or use the mini-atlas. The CampingCard ACSI campsites are indicated by a blue logo, together with a number. The numbers in the

guide go upwards, so you can easily find the corresponding editorial entry and you will find the information for the campsite you are looking for.
- You can also search for a particular amenity. Using the fold-out cover at the front of this book, you can easily see if the campsite offers the facilities that are important to you.

**On the website:**
Website www.CampingCard.com.
Here, you can choose different ways to find a campsite. You can filter by holiday period, for example, or the availability of certain facilities, or by theme such as 'suitable for disabled people', 'naturist campsites' or 'winter sports'.

**In the app:**
The special CampingCard ACSI app. See also page 26.

**In the mini-atlas:**
Enclosed in this guide you will find a mini-atlas showing all the participating CampingCard ACSI campsites in Europe. In the mini-atlas you will see blue logos showing a number which corresponds to the blue logo and number in the editorial entry for each campsite.
The register in the mini-atlas is composed as follows: campsite number, campsite name, place name in alphabetical order, page number and sub-area on the page. In the Netherlands, Germany, France, Spain and Italy the campsites have been arranged in alphabetical place name order by region.

# Campsite reviews

# Give your opinion and have the chance to win an iPad!

Plenty of campers prefer to be prepared before going on holiday. You can help them by leaving a review. Because sometimes it's great, but sometimes you might be disappointed.

### Your campsite
How do you review a campsite? Go to www.CampingCard.com/ipad and find the campsite you stayed at using the search box.

### Your review
On the campsite page, you'll see a tab for 'Reviews'. Open the tab, and then click on 'Add a review'. Then let us know what you thought of the campsite!

### Your code
Under the review form, there's a box labelled 'promotional code'. Type **IPAD-2019-CCA** in there, and you'll be in with a chance of winning an iPad!

### Free ACSI Camping Cookbook
We really appreciate you taking the time to leave a review. So, after you've left your review, we'll send you an email with a link to download the free ACSI Camping Cookbook (pdf).

# Instructions for use

1. Place name - Postal code - Region

4. Campsite name and star ratings

5. Address

6. Telephone

7. Opening period

8. E-mail address

9. Facilities (see fold-out flap)

 Facilities open throughout the campsite's entire opening period

## Rieste, D-49597 / Niedersachsen

🔺 Alfsee Ferien- und Erholungspark*****
🏠 Am Campingpark 10
☎ +49 5 46 49 21 20
⏰ 1/1 - 31/12
@ info@alfsee.com

16ha 350T(110m²) 16A CEE

**1** ACD**F**HIJK**L**MOPQ
**2** ADFLMRT**U**VWXY
**3** AB**CF**HJK**L**M**NOPQ**RU**VW**Z
**4** **LN**(Q+S+T 6/4-27/10) (U+Y+Z 🔲)
**5** **AB**DEFGJKLNP**S**UWXYZ
**6** CDEG**H**K(N 2km)OSTUV

💬 The campsite is part of a large holiday plenty of amenities. The wonderful wellness Roman style is highly recommended. There good cycling in the vicinity.

🚗 A1 Osnabrück-Bremen, exit Neuenkirch Vörden, towards Alfsee. Campsite is signpo

ⒸⒸ €⒇ 3/1-5/4 28/4-29/5 24/6-3/7 27/8-2/10 28/10-20/12

10. Surface area of the campsite in hectares (1 ha = 10,000 m² (square metres) or approximately 2.5 acres)

11. Number of touring pitches (size of the pitches is shown in brackets)

12. Maximum loading available for electrical connections

13. Three pin Euro adaptor required (CEE)

14. Rate and (possible) extra discount

15. Acceptance period

16. Description

17. Route description

14

2. **†† Three children up to and including the age of 5 included**

NEW **New CampingCard ACSI campsite in 2019**

⊗ **Dogs not permitted**

⊙ **Campsite totally suitable for naturists**

⊙ **Campsite partially suitable for naturists**

⊼ **Winter sports campsite**

& **Amenities suitable for the disabled**

⊛ **Wifi zone on the campsite**

⊛ **Wifi coverage on at least 80% of the campsite**

✿ **Recognised by the environmental organisation in that particular country**

**iD** **ACSI Club ID accepted as an identity card**

3. 627 **Campsite number**

## 1. Place name, postal code and region

The place name and postal code of the campsite and the region in which it is located.

## 2. Three children up to and including the age of 5 included (possible) ††

You will find 657 campsites in this guide where (maximum) three children up to and including the age of 5 are included in the CampingCard ACSI rate. The symbol †† is shown in the editorial entry for these campsites. Take note: where a campsite displays this symbol they may still require you to pay tourist tax for children, as the campsite has to pay the tourist tax directly to the local authorities. Items such as shower tokens for children are not included.

## Dogs not allowed ⊗

The stay of one dog is included in the CampingCard ACSI rate, assuming dogs are allowed on the campsite. If you are bringing more dogs, it is possible that an extra payment will be required. At some campsites there is a limit to the number of dogs per guest and/or

18. Sectional map with the exact position of the campsite

19. GPS coordinates

some breeds are not permitted. You can find the number of dogs you are allowed to bring with you on the campsite on the campsite page on www.CampingCard.com. If you are in doubt if your dogs are permitted or not, please contact the campsite.

At campsites with the above symbol, dogs are not permitted at all.

## Wifi zone and/or wifi 80-100% coverage

If there is a wifi zone on the campsite, then there is a location on the campsite where you can access wireless Internet. In the editorial entry for these campsites you will see this symbol:

If there is 80-100% wifi coverage, then you can access wireless internet on most of the campsite. In the editorial entry for these campsites you will see this symbol:

## ACSI Club ID

On many campsites you can use the ACSI Club ID Card, this is a substitute identity card. When you can use the ACSI Club ID at a campsite, this is indicated in the facilities with the symbol. You will find more explanation of this Camping Carnet on page 30 of this guide.

## 3. Campsite number 627

The number in the blue CC logo refers to the number in the mini-atlas, included with this guide, which gives a good overview of where the campsite is located. See also: 'In the mini-atlas' on page 12.

## 4. Campsite name and star ratings

Here you can see the campsite name and possibly the number of stars. ACSI does not give stars or other classifications to campsites. Star ratings or other types of classification are awarded to the campsite by local or national organisations and are shown after the campsite name. Stars do not always indicate the quality but more often the comfort that a campsite offers. The more stars there are, the more amenities. The judgement of whether a campsite is good or not and whether you think it deserves two stars or four is something you must decide for yourself.

## 5. Address

The postal address of the campsite. You will find the postal address including the post code in the uppermost block of the editorial entry. Sometimes, in France and Italy for example, you will see that there is no postal address. You will discover that you will usually be able to find the campsite yourself once you have arrived in the town. To make it easier to find the campsite we have included a route description and the GPS coordinates in the editorial entry.

## 6. Telephone

The telephone numbers in this guide are preceded by a + sign. The + is the international access code (00 in the United Kingdom). The digits after the + denote the country where the campsite is located. For example: the phone number of a German campsite is shown as +49 followed by the area code with the 0 (in brackets) and the subscriber number. In most European countries, you should not dial the first zero of the area code after dialling the international access code. So for Germany you dial 0049 and then the area code, without the zero, followed by the subscriber's number. In general you do need to dial the zero in Italy.

## 7. Opening period

The periods advised by the campsite management during which the site will be open in 2019. TAKE NOTE: campsites do not offer the CampingCard ACSI discount for the entire period that they are open. For dates when the

CampingCard ACSI discount is available you will need to refer to the acceptance periods in the lower block of the campsite's editorial entry. See also: 'Acceptance period' on page 19.

The opening and acceptance data have been compiled with the greatest care. It is possible that circumstances may cause these dates to change after publication of this guide. Go to www.CampingCard.com/modifications before you leave to see whether there have been changes at your chosen campsite.

## 8. E-mail address @

The campsite's e-mail address. The e-mail address is especially useful to make a reservation or enquiries in the low season, when the reception may be staffed less frequently.

## 9. Facilities

CampingCard ACSI is a discount card for the low season. Participating campsites will ensure that the most important facilities will also be available and functioning in the acceptance period of the discount card.
You will find a complete summary of all the facilities that are included in this guide in the fold-out cover at the front of the guide. If you leave the cover folded out you can see precisely which facilities are available at each campsite. By the numbers 1 to 6 you will find six categories with facilities:
1 Regulations
2 Location, ground and shade
3 Sports and play
4 Water recreation / Shops and restaurants
5 Washing up, laundry and cooking / Washing and toilet facilities
6 Miscellaneous

The letters after the numbers relate to the facilities in each category. Some facilities have a period shown in brackets, showing the day and month. These are the dates that you can expect these facilities to be available.
If a small key  is shown, this facility can be used during the entire opening period of the campsite.

**Take note:**
- These are the facilities that are present at the campsite. This does not mean that all these facilities are available on standard pitches and can be used by CampingCard ACSI guests. For example, when there is a mention of facility 6S, this means that the campsite offers pitches with radio/tv access. In most cases, these pitches will be comfort pitches, which are not meant for CampingCard ACSI guests.

- If a swimming pool or other facility is right next to the campsite, and campsite guests are allowed to use those facilities, the letters of those facilities are also shown in the campsite information.
- Some facilities on the fold-out cover have a *. Facilities with a * that are in **bold** script in the campsite information are not included in the overnight rate at that campsite. There are two exceptions for CampingCard ACSI guests: in the CampingCard ACSI rate, one dog (assuming they are allowed on the campsite) and one warm shower per person per overnight stay are included, even if the facility is printed in bold and therefore belongs to the facilities at the campsite that require payment. Facilities without a * are never in bold, but this does not mean they are free of charge.

## 10. Surface area of the campsite

The surface area of the campsite is given in hectares. 1 ha = 10,000 m² (square metres) or approximately 2.5 acres).

## 11. Number of touring pitches

As a camper on the move, it is interesting to know how many overnight pitches a site offers. The size of the pitches is shown in brackets, in m². If it says > 100 m², then the pitches are larger than 100 m². < 100 m² means smaller than 100 m². Every campsite makes some of these touring pitches available for campers with CampingCard ACSI. A standard pitch is included in the CampingCard rate. See page 24 for more explanation.

## 12. Maximum loading available for electrical connections

With your CampingCard ACSI a connection with maximum 6A or power consumption to a maximum of 4 kWh per day, including the connection fee, is included in the overnight rate. If you use more, for example 5 kWh it is quite likely you have to pay a surcharge. You will find the minimum and maximum amperage available for the electrical connection for each campsite in the block with facilities. When the campsite information mentions 6-10A, this means that at this campsite there are pitches with an amperage of minimum 6 and maximum 10. This does not mean that 10A is included in the CampingCard ACSI rate.

State clearly on arrival at the campsite if you want a higher amperage than the included 6A, but be aware that you may have to pay a surcharge. Only when there is no lower amperage than 10A available at the campsite, you will not have to pay extra. Take note: on a connection that allows maximum 6A you cannot connect devices with a combined power consumption of more than 1380 Watt.

## 13. CEE

This indication means that you will need a three pin euro-adapter.

## 14. Rate and extra discount

A rate of 12, 14, 16, 18 or 20 euros is shown for each campsite. The rates offered by CampingCard ACSI are already low but could be even lower. Some campsites give an extra discount if you stay longer.

If, for example a campsite is showing '7=6' this means that you pay only 6 nights at the CampingCard ACSI rate for a 7 night stay. Be sure to indicate the number of nights you wish to stay when arriving or reserving. The campsite will make one booking for the entire period and will apply the discount. The discount may not apply if you decide to stay longer during your stay and thereby reach the required number of days.

Take note! If a campsite has several of these discounts you only have the right to one of these offers. For example: the special offers are 4=3, 7=6 and 14=12. If you stay for 13 nights you only have the right to one 7=6 discount and not to multiples of 4=3 or a combination of 4=3 and 7=6.

## 15. Acceptance period

Each campsite decides its own acceptance period and so defines its own low season. For dates when the CampingCard ACSI discount is available you will need to look at the acceptance periods in the lower blue block of the editorial entry for the campsite. The last date specified in a period is the date on which the discount is no longer valid. An acceptance period of 1/1 - 30/6 means that the first night you are entitled to a discount is the night from 1 January to 2 January, and the last night you are entitled to a discount is the night from 29 June to 30 June. So, on the night from 30 June to 1 July, you will pay the normal rate.

The opening and acceptance periods are compiled with the greatest care.

It is possible that circumstances may cause these dates to change after publication of this guide.

Check www.CampingCard.com/modifications to see whether we have been informed of any changes at the campsite of your choice.

## 16. Description

In this section you will get an idea of the layout of the campsite and its characteristics. Some examples: on the coast, by a lake, quiet family campsite, high specification of facilities, pleasant views, plenty of shade, privacy, pitches separated by shrubbery, stony ground, grass, terraced, etc.

## 17. Route description

The written directions in this route description will assist you in finding your way for the last few miles to the campsite entrance and will advise you which motorway exit to take and which signs to follow.

## 18. Sectional map

The sectional map shows where the campsite is located in its immediate surroundings. The precise location of the campsite is shown with the blue CampingCard ACSI logo.

## 19. GPS coordinates 🏕

If you make use of a navigation system the GPS coordinates are almost indispensable. ACSI has therefore noted the GPS coordinates in this guide. Our inspectors have measured the coordinates right next to the campsite barrier, so nothing can go wrong. Take care: not all navigation systems are configured for cars with a caravan so always read the route description that is included with each campsite and don't forget to watch out for the signs. The shortest route is, after all, not always the easiest one. The GPS coordinates are shown in degrees, minutes and seconds. Check when you enter the data into your navigation system that it is also configured in degrees, minutes and seconds. The letter N is shown by the first number. By the second number there is a letter E or W (right or left of the Greenwich meridian).

# Online booking

## Book your camping pitch via ACSI

Nothing is more irritating than finding a campsite, and then arriving there to find there's no space left. In the low season, that luckily won't happen too often, but for those who prefer to err on the side of caution, it's possible to reserve a space online at a growing number of campsites.

You can now easily book your camping pitch online, whether you're still at home, or already on the road, via www.CampingCard.com or the CampingCard ACSI app. You can see which campsites are bookable as they will have an orange 'Book now' button. You will book directly with the campsite and pay online. This will ensure the booking is definitive both for you and the campsite.

## Booking a campsite

Once you've found a bookable campsite that suits your tastes, just click on the orange 'Book now' button. Then select your preferred date of arrival and length of stay, click 'Book now' in the calendar, and take the following steps.

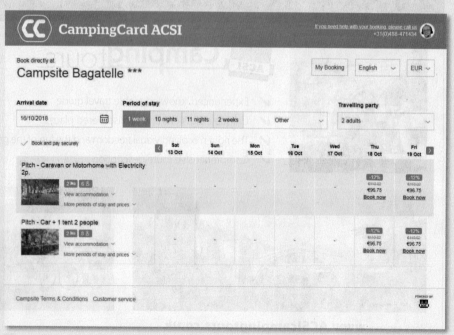

*Sample booking form*

1. Fill in the names of the people you're travelling with.
2. Select any extras.
3. Fill in any other details, and the details of your camping vehicle.
4. Choose your payment method.
5. Check your details, and click on 'Confirm booking'.

You will be redirected to the payment page, and pay the full booking amount immediately. Your booking is final, and is made under the terms and conditions of the campsite. If you cancel, this is also under the terms and conditions of the campsite.

## The advantages of booking online

- You can be sure that there will be space for you.
- All costs* will be clear in advance.
- Pay easily and safely using your credit card.

**Important:** don't forget to bring your CampingCard ACSI with you! Even if you book online, it's still necessary to show your discount card at the campsite reception. This is the only way you are entitled to camp at the reduced rate.

## More and more campsites bookable via ACSI

The number of campsites that you can book via ACSI is increasing all the time. So keep an eye on the website, and check the app regularly. For more information and a handy overview of all bookable CampingCard ACSI campsites, please visit www.CampingCard.com/bookonline.

*You'll pay the great value CampingCard ACSI rate, plus booking costs.*

# Rate per overnight stay

There are five CampingCard ACSI rates:

At campsites in countries which use currencies other than the euro, you will normally pay in that country's currency. In this case, the CampingCard ACSI rate is converted to that currency using the daily exchange rate that is valid at that moment (average of highest and lowest rate of that day). Please take into account that exchange rates can be subject to large changes.

## Inclusive

Participating campsites offer the following in the CampingCard ACSI rate on touring pitches:

- A camping pitch.*
- Overnight stay for 2 adults.
- Car & caravan & awning, or car & folding caravan, or car & tent, or motor home & awning.
- Electricity. A connection of maximum 6A or a consumption of maximum 4 kWh per day is included in the CampingCard ACSI rate. When a campsite only has pitches with a lower amperage, this lower amperage will apply. If you use excess, for example 5 kWh, it is possible that you might have to pay extra. See also 'Maximum loading available for electrical connections' on page 19.
- Hot showers. In campsites where showers are operated by tokens, CampingCard ACSI holders are entitled to one token per adult per overnight stay.**
- Maximum one dog staying on campsites which accept dogs. For a second

(or additional) dog you might have to pay extra.
- VAT.

\* Some campsites make a distinction between standard, luxury or comfort pitches. Luxury or comfort pitches are in general larger and equipped with their own water supply and drainage. CampingCard ACSI gives you the right to a standard pitch but it may occur that you are able to have a more expensive pitch at the CampingCard ACSI rate. The campsite has the right to decide this; you can NEVER insist on a luxury or comfort pitch.
Be aware also that some campsites have a different policy with regard to twin-axled caravans and mobile homes which are so large that they will not fit on a standard pitch.

\*\* As stipulated in the CampingCard ACSI terms and conditions, the campsite must allow the CampingCard ACSI holder one free shower per overnight stay. That means every CampingCard ACSI holder has a right to one shower token per person per night. If the campsite has a different "shower system", such as small change, a key or a sep-key, then the campsite must ensure that the charge for the CampingCard holder is reimbursed. Hot water in washing up sinks is not included in the price. Unused shower tokens cannot be exchanged for money.

# Not included in the overnight rate

In general the CampingCard ACSI rate is sufficient to pay for the overnight charge. The campsite may however make extra charges for a number of items:

- Tourist taxes, environmental taxes, waste disposal charges or local authority requirements are not included in the CampingCard ACSI rate. These taxes can differ greatly by country and region. In Switzerland and Austria in particular, and also in the Netherlands, you should be prepared for high charges for some of these taxes.
- Reservation and administration charges are not included in the CampingCard ACSI rate. You can read more about reserving with CampingCard ACSI on page 10.
- A campsite may make a surcharge for a luxury or comfort pitch (unless the campsite only has comfort pitches).
- Campsites make pitches available for two adults. The campsite may decide if more guests may stay on these pitches, apart from the two adults who can stay for the CampingCard ACSI rate (for example the guests' children or more adults), for payment of the regular rate per guest. If this is not allowed, then the camping group will be directed to pitches that are not meant for CampingCard ACSI users and for which the regular low season rates must be paid. However, at campsites which display the following symbol 👥, (a maximum of) three children up to and including the age of 5 are included in the CampingCard ACSI rate. Items such as shower coins and tourist tax (if applicable) for these children are not included.
- Extra services such as facilities for which the campsite makes a charge, such as a tennis court, can be charged to you at the applicable low season rate.
- Electricity, if more is consumed than is specified on page 24. See also 'Maximum loading available for electrical connections' on page 19.

# CampingCard ACSI app

## Now even more convenience with the CampingCard ACSI app

With the CampingCard ACSI app you have all campsite information at your fingertips! The app, which can also be used without an internet connection, includes all CampingCard ACSI campsites and has many handy functionalities and search filters. The campsite information in the CampingCard ACSI app is updated several times a year. The app is suitable for smartphones and tablets (Android and iOS) and for devices with Windows 10!

Are you going on holiday with a motorhome? You can now purchase information in the app about 9,000 motorhome pitches in Europe!

I think the CampingCard ACSI app is wonderful. I use it all the time – before and during my holiday. Works perfectly!

F. Heijsteeg

- **Search by name**
You can search by country, region, place, campsite number or campsite name. Fill in a search term and see where you can spend the night nearby on a map. The database is very extensive and contains more than 500,000 search terms!

- **Search in the area**
Is location awareness activated on your device? If so the app will identify your location and show the CampingCard ACSI campsites (and motorhome pitches if you have purchased the motorhome information for the app) that are close to you. If you prefer to search for a specific place on the map you can set your location on the map manually. Perfect if you're looking for a place to stay overnight.

- **Search filters**
The app contains really useful search filters. You can filter by more than 150 amenities, the CampingCard ACSI rates, periods of stay and stopover campsites.

- **View the campsite**
You will find comprehensive information about the grounds and the amenities for each

campsite. Check if it's suitable by looking at the photos, map resources and campsite reviews from other campers.

- **Favourites**

Have you found your perfect spot? Then add it to your list of favourites so you can quickly find it later. You'll also be able to find your favourites on the map.

- **Contacting the campsite**

Have you found the campsite you want to stay at? It's possible to book more and more campsites directly from the app. It's also possible to call the campsite to check availability. And you can even send the campsite an email from the app.

## Campsite reviews

It is also possible to review a campsite in the app. Even when there is no internet connection. The app will save the review and send it automatically when your device connects to the internet at a later time!

**Attention:**

In order to be able to take advantage of the low, fixed rates you will always need to show a physical, valid discount card at the reception. Showing only the app or campsite guide does not suffice.

Go to www.CampingCard.com/app for more information and an explanation on how to purchase access to the app.

## Information to hand, wherever you are, with the CampingCard ACSI app

- With more than 3,600 campsites that accept CampingCard ACSI
- Can be expanded to include 9,000 inspected motorhome pitches
- Find a place to spend the night in no time with the handy filters
- Free updates with modifications and new campsite reviews

**From just € 3.59**

## Your unique purchase code

In order to gain access to the CampingCard ACSI app you will need a unique purchase code. With this code, we can verify that you have a valid CampingCard ACSI. You will find the code on the back of your discount card, as pictured below:

To purchase the CC-app fill in the unique code below on www.CampingCard.com/app19

**1 2 3 4 5 6**

Please complete in capital letters

Name

Address

Town & postal code

Signature

Only valid on campsites with CC logo. Only a completely filled in card will be accepted. Published by ACSI Publishing BV. Valid from January 1st to December 31st 2019.

CC

# Comparison of ACSI apps

| | ACSI Campsites Europe app | CampingCard ACSI app | ACSI Great Little Campsites app |
|---|---|---|---|
| Price | Packages with campsite information from € 0.99 | App with campsite information: € 3.59 | App with campsite information: € 2.99 |
| Number of campsites | 8,100 | More than 3,600 | More than 2,000 |
| Type of campsite | All campsites in the ACSI Campinggids Europa | All campsites that accept CampingCard ACSI | Small campsites with max. 50 touring pitches |
| Information about 9,000 motorhome pitches | Can be purchased in individual country packages, and only in combination with campsite information. | Can only be purchased in combination with campsite information | Can only be purchased in combination with campsite information |
| Suitable for | Smartphone, tablet, laptop and computer | Smartphone, tablet, laptop and computer | Smartphone, tablet, laptop and computer |
| Can be used on three devices at the same time | ✓ | ✓ | ✓ |
| Free updates | ✓ | ✓ | ✓ |
| Can be used offline | ✓ | ✓ | ✓ |
| Search by country, region, town or campsite name | ✓ | ✓ | ✓ |
| Search on map/GPS | ✓ | ✓ | ✓ |
| Search by CC rate and CC acceptance period | | ✓ | |
| Total search filters | 250 | 150 | 150 |
| Book, call or mail campsite via app | ✓ | ✓ | ✓ |
| Read and submit campsite reviews | ✓ | ✓ | ✓ |
| Plan route | ✓ | ✓ | ✓ |
| More information | Eurocampings.co.uk/app | CampingCard.com/app | Greatlittlecampsites.co.uk/app |

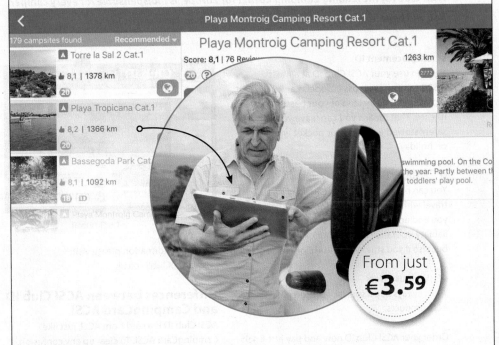

*ACSI Club ID, the leading Camping Carnet for Europe, is indispensable for every camper. You will benefit from it both during your camping holiday and at home!*

### ✔ Replacement ID

You can use your ACSI Club ID at almost 8,800 campsites across Europe as a replacement ID instead of your passport or ID card. That means you can leave your ID safely stowed away in your pocket when you're on holiday.

### ✔ Liability insurance

You can be sure of a carefree holiday if you travel with your ACSI Club ID. This card offers you and up to 11 people travelling with you liability insurance during your camping holiday, but also if you stay in a holiday home or a hotel!

### ✔ Various offers

You'll always pay a special, reduced price for ACSI products.

Order your ACSI Club ID now and pay just € 4.95 a year!

For more information please visit:
www.ACSIClubID.co.uk

## Differences between ACSI Club ID and CampingCard ACSI

ACSI Club ID is a card from ACSI, just like CampingCard ACSI. To clear up any confusion, we've compiled an overview of the differences.

| | **ACSI Club ID** | **CampingCard ACSI** |
|---|---|---|
| What | Camping Carnet: replacement ID for use at the campsite | Discount card for camping in the low season |
| Accepted for | Accepted as replacement ID at almost 8,800 campsites in 29 countries | Spend the night at 3,401 campsites in 21 countries at a fixed reduced rate |
| Extras | Liability insurance, membership discounts in the ACSI Webshop | Includes a guide listing all the campsites where you can use CampingCard ACSI |
| Purchase | Membership, you can purchase it on the ACSI Webshop | 'Individual' product, you can purchase it in bookshops, camping shops and on the ACSI Webshop. Subscription, you can order it on the ACSI Webshop |
| Validity | 1 year, until the expiry date (is automatically renewed every year) | Valid for 1 calendar year |
| Costs | € 4.95 per year | From € 12.95 per year |
| More information | www.ACSIClubID.co.uk | www.CampingCard.com |

# Norway

## General

Norway is not a member of the EU.

### Time
The time in Norway is the same as Amsterdam, Paris and Rome and one hour ahead of London.

### Languages
Norwegian, but English is widely understood and spoken.

### Ferry crossings
You can reach Norway via Copenhagen (Denmark) and Malmö (Sweden) using the Øresundbron bridge and there are popular ferry routes direct from UK ports.

## Border formalities

Many formalities and agreements about matters such as necessary travel documents, car papers, requirements relating to your means of transport and accommodation, medical expenses and taking pets with you do not only depend on the country you are travelling to but also on your departure point and nationality. The length of your stay can also play a role here. It is not possible within the confines of this guide to guarantee the correct and most up to date information with regard to these matters.

We advise you to consult the relevant authorities before your departure about:
- which travel documents you will need for yourself and your fellow passengers
- which documents you need for your car
- which regulations your caravan must meet
- which goods you may import and export

- how medical treatment will be arranged and paid for in your holiday destination in cases of accident or illness
- whether you can take pets. Contact your vets well in advance. They can give you information about the necessary vaccinations, proof thereof and obligations on return. It would also make sense to enquire whether any special regulations apply to your pet in public places at your holiday destination. In some countries for example dogs must always be muzzled or transported in a cage.

Make certain you assemble the information that is relevant to your specific situation.

For the most recent customs regulations you should get in contact with the authorities of your holiday destination in your country of residence.

## Currency
The national currency is the Norwegian krone (NOK). Exchange rate September 2018: £1 = 10.79 NOK.

### Credit cards
You can pay by credit card in most places.

## Opening times
### Banks
Banks are open weekdays until 15:30, on Thursdays until 17:00. Closed on Saturdays.

### Shops
Shops in Norway are open Monday to Wednesday and Friday from 10:00 to 17:00.

In most towns the shops are open on Thursdays until 19:00 and on Saturdays from 10:00 to 15:00. Wine, spirits and strong beer is only available in the special Vinmonopolet shops.

### Chemists, doctors
Doctors and chemists are available everywhere day and night via a special telephone number. 'Legevakt' is a local doctors' service for medical problems outside normal surgery hours.

## Communication
### (Mobile) phones
The mobile network works well in almost all of Norway, except in some remote nature reserves. There is a 4G network for mobile internet.

### Wifi, internet
Restaurants and bars often offer wifi.

### Post
Open Monday to Friday until 17:00 and on Saturday until 13:00.

## Roads and traffic
### Road network
Remember, all traffic in Norway drives on the right and overtakes on the left! Headlight deflectors are advisable to prevent annoying oncoming drivers. Norway uses the metric system, so distances are measured in kilometres (km) and speeds in kilometres per hour (km/h). The roads are good but sometimes very twisting, meaning your journey may take longer than planned. Mountain roads are narrow and winding and often steep. They are only usable from mid June to mid October due to snow. Take note: Norwegian police make strict checks on non-Scandinavian vehicles arriving in Kristiansand (Norway) from Hirtshals (Denmark) by ferry. The Norwegian automobile club (NAF) can be reached on tel. 08505. You can also call the two other breakdown services: Falken tel. 02222 and Viking tel. 06000.
Take a recent road map with you as all national roads were reclassified in 2010. Some roads may be closed in winter.

### Traffic regulations
Traffic from the right in Norway always has priority unless otherwise indicated. When driving on a roundabout you have priority over drivers wishing to enter it. Trams always have priority. Special regulations apply to mountain roads; the driver who can most easily move over or go back should give priority.
The maximum permitted alcohol level is 0.2 ‰. Watch out for wild animals on motorways in woods and mountain areas. Dipped headlights are mandatory during daytime. Only hands-

free use of phones in cars is permitted. You are not allowed to smoke when driving in built up areas. Winter tyres are mandatory in the winter season.

*Maximum speed*

| | Speed |
|---|---|
| (built up) | 80 |
| | 80 |
| < 3,5 т | 80 |
| > 3,5 т | 80 |
| (motorway) | 90-100 |
| | 80 |
| < 3,5 т | 90-100 |
| > 3,5 т | 80 |

### Caravans, motorhomes
Be aware that driving with a caravan can sometimes be difficult in the fjords and mountains. A good towing car is highly recommended. You are not permitted to dispose of waste water in the street. There are sufficient service stations on the most important roads throughout the country.

### Maximum allowed measurements of combined length
Height 4 metres, width 2.55 metres and length 19.50 metres (of which the trailer maximum 12 metres). On some secondary roads the permitted length is less than 19.50 metres.

### Fuel
Lead free petrol and diesel is easily available. It is best to fill up with LPG in the south and close to Oslo. The number of filling stations, particularly in Central and Northern Norway is limited, with the exception of Highway 6.

Fuel prices in Northern Norway are considerably higher.

### Filling stations
Filling stations are open from 07:00 to 23:00. It is possible to pay by credit card in many places.

### Tolls
You can pay for toll roads in Norway in 3 ways:
- Visitors' payment: for when you are staying less than 2 months in Norway.
- AutoPASS: if you will be staying longer than 2 months in Norway.
- Without AutoPASS.
More information ▸ *www.autopass.no* ◂ (also in English).

### Emergency numbers
- 112: police
- 110: fire
- 113: ambulance

## Camping
Toilet facilities are generally 'good' with standards still rising. Marked out pitches are a rarity. Supplies of provisions, amenities and recreation are low in comparison to popular camping countries. But there is countryside in abundance so it is ideally suited to walking, rock climbing and fishing.

In principal you can 'free' camp anywhere. You are not permitted to camp on cultivated ground (including pastures, meadows and newly planted woodland) without permission from the owner.

### Practical
If you are going camping in Norway, there is a chance that you will need a special card that you must show at reception. You can purchase this card at the relevant campsite.

- Make sure that you have a world adaptor with you.
- Take note: there are only limited opportunities for refilling gas bottles. It is better to take sufficient gas with you.
- Tap water is safe to drink.

## Fishing

All anglers above 16 years must be in possession of a national licence. A local licence may also be required, but that is only for fresh water fishing. Fishing licences are available at sports shops, kiosks, tourist information offices and campsites.

Anyone is allowed to fish freely on the coast, so also in the (fresh water) fjords.

## Aurdal i Valdres, N-2910 / Oppland

👫 🏊 ⛷ ♿ 📶 iD 1

🏕 Aurdal Fjordcamping og Hytter****
✉ Vestringslinna 252
☎ +47 61 36 52 12
🔑 1/1 - 31/12
@ post@aurdalcamp.no

7ha 122T(90m²) 16A

**1** ACDGIJKLMPQ
**2** ADKRSTWX
**3** BFHJKQUWZ
**4** N(Q+R+T+U+Z 1/5-1/10)
**5** ABDFGIJKLOPUW
**6** ADEGJ(N 3km)OSV

💬 A beautifully located campsite halfway between Oslo and Bergen. From the E16 you descend 2 km to the fjord so there is no sound disturbance from the road. The natural surroundings here are wonderful. The fjord is full of fish which you are allowed to catch for free. Excellent heated toilet facilities and a friendly clubhouse.

🚗 On the E16, turn off by the church in Aurdal (17 km south east of Fagernes), the campsite is then signposted. Campsite 2 km further on.

Nord-Aurdal
CC
Etnedal
E16
Sør-Aurdal

CC €20 1/1-21/6 18/8-31/12

📍 N 60°54'59'' E 09°23'22''

## Byglandsfjord, N-4741 / Agder

👫 ♿ 📶 iD 2

🏕 Camping Neset****
✉ Setesdalsvegen 2039
☎ +47 37 93 40 50
🔑 1/1 - 31/12
@ post@neset.no

7ha 260T 10-16A

**1** ACDGIJKLMOPQ
**2** ADIKLORSTUWX
**3** AHRUWZ
**4** N(Q 15/5-15/9)
     (R 15/5-30/9)
     (T+U+V+X 15/6-15/8)
**5** ABDEFGIJKLMNPQRUWZ
**6** CDEGK(N 2,5km)V

💬 On a gently sloping headland with free sunny pitches on grass. Next to the water and a spacious field. Special headland for motorhomes. Boats for hire. Communal barbecue on an idyllic rocky point in the lake. Chickens and rabbits can be petted on the site.

🚗 The campsite is located 13 km north of Evje, 3 km north of Byglandsfjord. The site is clearly marked with camping signs from route 9.

Longerak
CC
Byglandsfjord

CC €20 1/4-29/5 11/6-28/6 19/8-31/12

📍 N 58°41'20'' E 07°48'12''

## Engerdal, N-2440 / Hedmark

👫 ⛷ 📶 iD 3

🏕 Camping Sølenstua Camp & Hytter***
✉ Sundveien 1011
☎ +47 62 45 97 42
🔑 1/1 - 31/12
@ camping@solenstua.com

4ha 90T(100-120m²) 16A

**1** ACDGIJKLMOPQ
**2** BCRUWX
**3** BHUW
**4** (Q+R+T+U+V+W+X+Z 1/6-31/8)
**5** ABDGIJKLMNOPQUWZ
**6** EGJV

💬 Quiet campsite in beautiful countryside among woods, rivers and lakes. Moose and reindeer are at home here. Winter or summer, the friendly owners will take care of you. Good toilet facilities and cuisine. Renovated play equipment. Also perfect for the winter season. Wintersports: ski rental and reparation, cross-country skiing track from the campsite, total tracks 80 km, practice lift, large ski area at 2 km.

🚗 Campsite is signposted from the RV217.

Engerdal
CC
Granberget

CC €20 1/5-30/6 18/8-30/9

📍 N 61°50'07'' E 11°43'49''

## Fåberg, N-2625 / Oppland

**4**

🔼 Hunderfossen Camping***
📧 Fossekrovegen 90
☎ +47 61 27 73 00
🕐 1/1 - 31/12
@ camping@hunderfossen.no

18ha  450T(80-100m²)  16A

**1** ACDGIJKLM**P**Q
**2** CGKLRTWX
**3** B**FQUW**
**5** **AB**DFGIJKLMNO**PQ**RUWZ
**6** CFGH(N 3km)SV

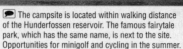

💬 The campsite is located within walking distance of the Hunderfossen reservoir. The famous fairytale park, which has the same name, is next to the site. Opportunities for minigolf and cycling in the summer.

🚗 From the E6 take exit 'Hunderfossen Family Park', over the bridge in Øyer. Well signposted in both directions.

Øyer
Gausdal
Follebu  E6
Lillehammer

CC € 20  1/4-28/6  18/8-30/9      📐 N 61°13'20''  E 10°26'19''

## Gaupne, N-6868 / Romsdal-Sognefjord

**5**

🔼 Pluscamp Sandvik***
📧 Sandvikvegen 20
☎ +47 99 20 61 10
🕐 1/1 - 31/12
@ sandvik@pluscamp.no

1ha  40T  10A

**1** ACDFIJKLMO**P**Q
**2** DEGKRSTUWXY
**3** AHKUWZ
**4** (**A** 15/5-30/9) (X 1/5-30/9)
**5** **AB**DEFGIJKLMNO**PQ**RUWZ
**6** EGKM(N 0,4km)STV

💬 Idyllic family campsite by the Sognefjord. Located in the middle of an old fruit garden with a view of the glacier. Situated between three national parks and a perfect basecamp for activities and attractions. You can join guided glacier activities like hiking, kayaking, rafting and more. Best of all is perhaps the beautiful mountain hikes you can do.

🚗 Well signposted in both directions on the RV55, in Gaupne with a view of the fjords.

Luster
Gaupne CC
Feigom
Hafslo

CC € 20  1/5-14/6  25/8-30/9      📐 N 61°24'02''  E 07°18'02''

## Heidal, N-2676 / Oppland

**6**

🔼 Jotunheimen Feriesenter****
📧 Heidalsvegen 2930
☎ +47 61 23 49 50
🕐 1/1 - 31/12
@ post@jotunheimenferiesenter.no

5ha  100T(80-100m²)  10A

**1** ACDFIJKLMOPQ
**2** CLRTWXY
**3** AHN**QUW**
**4** (Q 1/5-31/8) (R 1/7-31/8) (T+U+X 1/6-31/8)
**5** **AB**DGIJKLMNO**P**UWZ
**6** EGJ(N 3km)V

NEW

💬 Very quiet, well-maintained and hospitable campsite. Approximately 5 km from the touristy, beautiful "route 51". Flat grassy grounds and shaded, non-numbered pitches. Surrounded by very beautiful countryside, sporty trips from the campsite possible, including to the Bessegen, or fishing, rafting.

🚗 The campsite is located on route 257, 2 km from road 51 (Randsverk), 30 km from the E6 in Sjoa.

Lalm
Bjølstadmo
CC

CC € 20  1/5-27/6  25/8-30/9      📐 N 61°43'45''  E 09°07'15''

## Hovet i Hallingdal, N-3577 / Telemark-Buskerud

🎿 📶 **iD** **7**

🏔 Birkelund Camping
📧 Hovsvegen 50
☎ +47 45 29 78 41
🕐 1/1 - 31/12
@ informasjon@
   birkelund-camping.com

1,3ha 45T(90m²) 10A

**1** ACDGIJKLMPQ
**2** GRTUWX
**3** AHIJK**W**
**4** (B 1/6-31/8) N(Q+R+T 🚗)
**5** **AB**DFGIJKLMNO**P**UW
**6** ACEIK(N 3,5km)

💬 A quiet, well maintained campsite. Opportunities for trips out, walking and cycling (Fv50). Fly fishing, mountain biking, geocaching. Plenty of wintersports opportunities. Free internet. Free communal sauna. Dutch owners.

🚗 On route 50 from Hol to Aurland. 8 km past intersection with route 7. Easliy visible on the left of the road.

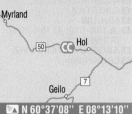

Myrland

Hol

Geilo

🅲🅲 €**18** 1/1-28/6  18/8-31/12

📍 N 60°37'08'' E 08°13'10''

---

## Koppang, N-2480 / Hedmark

🎿 ♿ 📶 **iD** **8**

🏔 Koppang Camping &
   Hytteutleie****
📧 Koppangveien 56
☎ +47 62 46 02 34
🕐 1/5 - 30/9
@ info@koppangcamping.no

5,5ha 100T(75-125m²) 10-16A

**1** AGIJKLM**P**Q
**2** CDGILNRSTWXY
**3** BHIJKNO**W**XZ
**4** (R 1/6-15/9)
**5** **AB**DFGIJKLMNO**P**RUWZ
**6** CEJ(N 2,5km)OTV

💬 A large and well equipped campsite with sunny and shaded pitches and a very large, level grassy field. Fishing, watersports, cycling, game safaris, walking, mountain biking, geocaching.

🚗 From the RV3 direction Koppang, via the FV30 turn left immediately before the large bridge.

Dølperstua

Stai

🅲🅲 €**20** 1/5-16/6  18/8-29/9

📍 N 61°34'19'' E 11°01'01''

---

## Lærdal, N-6887 / Romsdal-Sognefjord

♿ 📶 **iD** **9**

🏔 Lærdal Ferie og Fritidspark****
📧 Grandavegen 5
☎ +47 57 66 66 95
🕐 11/1 - 14/12
@ info@laerdalferiepark.com

2ha 100T(80-120m²) 16A

**1** ACDGIJKLMOPQ
**2** AEGLOQRVWX
**3** ABHJK**M**NUWY
**4** (R 15/5-15/9) (V 1/5-15/9)
   (Y 16/4-15/10) (Z 1/5-15/9)
**5** **AB**DFGIJKLMNO**P**UWZ
**6** EGHK(N 0,4km)TV

💬 Well maintained campsite. Unique and central on the Sognefjord. Excellent toilet facilities. Salmon centre within walking distance. Ideal for an active holiday with walking, cycling, climbing, glacier tours, fishing and sailing. The area is perfect for painting, drawing and photography and for anyone who loves nature or just wants to enjoy the relaxation.

🚗 From the E16 take route 5. Campsite located near the centre of Lærdal and close to the beach and playpark.

Amla

Naddvik

Lærdalsøyri

Ljøsne

E16

🅲🅲 €**18** 11/1-15/5  19/5-28/5  2/6-6/6  16/6-27/6  18/8-25/9  29/9-14/12  7=6, 14=11

📍 N 61°06'02'' E 07°28'13''

## Loen, N-6789 / Romsdal-Sognefjord

👬 📶 iD **10**

🔺 Tjugen Camping***
📧 FV723
☎ +47 57 87 76 17
🕐 15/4 - 15/10
@ camping@tjugen.no

2ha 60T(40-100m²) 10-16A

**1** ACDGIJKLMOPQ
**2** CJKLRTWX
**3** ABHJU**W**
**4** (**A** 10/6-1/10) (Q 15/6-20/8)
   (R 10/6-1/10)
**5** A**B**DFGIJKLMNO**P**RUWZ
**6** CEGK(N 2km)V

💬 Beautiful view from the campsite to the lively Loelva river and snowy mountain tops. Welcoming reception by a kind married couple. Recommended: cycling, Loen skylift, Via Ferrata, glacier visit Bødalsbreen, Kjenndalen and walk to Skålatoren (1848 m).

🚗 In the centre of Loen follow road FV723 to Lodalen/Kjendal. Campsite indicated 2 km further on the left side. This road starts at the Alexandra Hotel.

Flo
Stryn · Hjelle
CC
Olden

CC € **20** 15/4-23/6 18/8-15/10        🏞 N 61°52'05" E 06°52'36"

---

## Notodden, N-3677 / Telemark-Buskerud

👬 📶 iD **11**

🔺 Notodden Camping AS
📧 Reshjemveien 46
☎ +47 35 01 33 10
🕐 1/1 - 31/12
@ notcamp@
   notoddencamping.com

1ha 50T 10A

**1** ACDGIJKLMPQ
**2** FKLRWX
**3** AW
**5** A**B**DIJKLMNOPUWXY
**6** **J**(N 0,5km)

💬 Notodden Camping AS is located between the river Heddola, which is in a Unesco area, and a small airport that mainly supports gliding. The centre of Notodden in the east or Heddal Stabde, and features open air museum 'Heddal Bygdetum', in the west are about 3 km away.

🚗 E134 from Kongsberg-Seljord to centre Notodden over runway. First left.

Heddal · E134
CC · Notodden
Hjukse

CC € **20** 1/1-15/6 1/9-31/12        🏞 N 59°33'56" E 09°12'34"

---

## Olden, N-6788 / Romsdal-Sognefjord

👬 📶 iD **12**

🔺 Gryta-Camping***
📧 RV60/FV724
☎ +47 57 87 59 50
🕐 1/5 - 1/10
@ gryta@gryta.no

1,5ha 80T 10-16A

**1** ACDGIJKLMOPQ
**2** CDGJKLNORSTUWX
**3** ABDHKNU**W**Z
**4** (**A** 15/5-15/9) (Q+R 🕐)
**5** A**B**DFGIJKLMNO**P**RUWZ
**6** CEGIKV

💬 Uniquely situated on the Olden Lake with a view of the Briksdal glacier. A few pitches have shade. Free use of boat for fishing in the lake. The famous Briksdal Glacier is only 10 minutes from the campsite. Great walking and hiking in the mountains. Glaciers are visible from the campsite. You can see and hear the melting water flowing into the lake.

🚗 In Olden take route FV 724 dir. Briksal. Campsite after 12 km, 1st campsite left of the road after tunnel.

Olden
Sanddal
CC

CC € **18** 1/5-22/6 20/8-30/9        🏞 N 61°44'27" E 06°47'27"

## Rjukan/Miland, N-3658 / Telemark-Buskerud

🏔 Rjukan Hytte og Caravan Park
🏠 Gaustaveien 78
☎ +47 35 09 63 53
📅 1/1 - 31/10, 1/12 - 31/12
@ post@rjukanhytte.com

2ha 100T(90m²) 10A

**1** ACDG**I**JKLM**P**Q
**2** BCGKRSTWX
**3** AFHJ
**4** (Q+R 🔌)
**5** **AB**DFGIJKMNO**P**UW
**6** E**J**(N 5km)U

💬 Located between the hills and the mountains in the north of the Telemark province. A perfect base for a sportive/ active holiday. Panoramic view of the 'Gaustatoppen'. The spacious pitches are on a large field surrounded by old stone walls and exude real Nordic camping life.

🚗 Campsite located on route 37 between Rjukan and Miland and is well signposted.

Tinn
Dalsgrende

CC € 20 1/1-15/6 9/9-30/10 1/12-31/12

📍 N 59°54'09'' E 08°42'28''

## Seljord, N-3840 / Telemark-Buskerud

🏔 Seljord Camping****
🏠 Manheimstrondi 61
☎ +47 35 05 04 71
📅 1/1 - 31/12
@ post@seljordcamping.no

3ha 180T(90m²) 16A

**1** ACGIJKLM**P**Q
**2** ADGJKLRSTWX
**3** BHJKRU**WZ**
**4** (Q+R 23/6-10/8)
**5** **AB**DFGIJKLMNO**P**UW
**6** EGIK(N 1km)V

💬 Seljord Camping is a beautiful, quiet campsite located 1 km from Seljord. They have lovely pitches for motorhomes, caravans and tents. You may want to pitch close to the lake and enjoy the silence. You might be lucky enough to see 'Sjoormen' the sea monster.

🚗 E134, exit RV36 direction Seljord/Bø/Skien. The campsite is about 500 metres on the right.

Sundbøgrendi

Seljord
E134

Kviteseid

CC € 18 1/1-29/6 18/8-10/9 17/9-31/12

📍 N 59°29'13'' E 08°39'13''

## Skittenelv, N-9023 / Finnmark-Troms

🏔 Skittenelv Camping AS****
🏠 Ullstindveien 736
☎ +47 46 85 80 00
📅 15/5 - 30/9
@ post@skittenelvcamping.no

1,3ha 90T 10A

**1** ACDGIJKLMO**P**ST
**2** EGKLNORT
**3** AHJ**Q**UWY
**4** (**C**+**H** 20/6-20/8) J**N**(Q 🔌)
(R+T+U+V 20/6-20/8)
**5** **AB**DFGIJKMNOPQRUWYZ
**6** CEIKV

💬 Camping directly on the fjord near the pebble beach. Near Tromsø. Heated swimming pool with slide. Various possibilities for hiking, fishing and enjoying the view of the fjord. Four-star campsite with all modern conveniences, excellent toilet facilities and good free wifi.

🚗 Follow E8 as far as Tromsø. Campsite signposted before the bridge.

Oldervik

Movik

CC € 20 15/5-20/6 1/9-30/9

📍 N 69°46'39'' E 19°22'57''

## Tresfjord, N-6392 / Romsdal-Sognefjord

▲ Fagervik Camping
🏠 Fagervika, Tresfjord
☎ +47 99 29 07 22
🕒 15/3 - 15/10
@ info@fagervikcamping.no

👫 ♿ 🛜  **16**

2,4ha 50T(40-100m²) 8-16A

1 CDGIJKLMOPQ
2 BCDJKLNORUVWX
3 AWXZ
5 **AB**DFGIJMNOPUW
6 DEGK(N 2km)

💬 Camp right on the Fjord, extensive campsite next to the water. Cycle path along Fjord (20km). Equipment available for anglers, filleting contests on jetty. Charge for boat trailers (renting also possible). Camping pitch includes picnic table. Walking routes into mountains from campsite. Peace, space, enchanting countryside.

🚗 From Vikebukt head left before the new toll bridge to Tresfjord. From Vestnes head right before the new toll bridge and drive past Tresfjord.

Vestnes
E39
E136
CC
Tresfjord

CC €20 *15/3-23/6  19/8-15/10*

📷 **N 62°32'31'' E 07°08'58''**

## Vågå, N-2680 / Oppland

▲ Randsverk Camping
🏠 Fjellvegen 1972
☎ +47 97 50 30 81
🕒 3/5 - 6/10
@ post@randsverk.no

♿ 🛜 **iD** **17**

3ha 80T(80-100m²) 16A

1 ACDGIJKLMOPST
2 GRTUW
3 AHJNU**W**
4 (Q+R+W 🅿)
5 **AB**DFGIJMNO**PQR**UW
6 CDEJ(N 6km)OTV

💬 Open terraced campsite with extensive views and sunny pitches on the beautiful, tourist RV51 road close to Jotunheimen. Well maintained modern toilet facilities. Family showers and dining room/kitchen for campsite guests. Good cafeteria. Excellent base for hiking and cycling in the surrounding countryside. Glacier tours on your own or in organised groups from the campsite.

🚗 On the RV51 directly on the T-junction with the 257, 27 km south of Vågåmo.

Lalm
Bjølstadmo
Randsverk   257
CC
51

CC €20 *3/5-23/6  18/8-6/10*

📷 **N 61°43'49'' E 09°04'54''**

## Vang i Valdres, N-2975 / Oppland

▲ Bøflaten Camping****
🏠 Tyinvegen 5335
☎ +47 90 60 04 89
🕒 1/1 - 31/12
@ info@boflaten.com

⛷ ♿ 🛜 **iD** **18**

3ha 150T(90m²) 16A

1 ACGIJKLMPQ
2 CDGKORSTWXY
3 AHJNR**W**XZ
4 (A+Q+R 🅿)
5 **AB**DFGIJKLMNO**P**QRUW
6 EGJL(N 2km)

💬 Bøflaten campsite is situated by a large lake with beautiful views of the Jotunheimen national park. Large camping pitches with electrical hook-ups. Marked out walking and cycling routes right from the campsite and a varied selection of bikes and canoes are available for rent, with supervised activities. The site has a climbing park and places to grill the fish you caught. Free internet.

🚗 Along the E16 Fagernes-Lærdal, in Vang signposted along the E16.

Neset
CC E16
Vang

CC €20 *1/1-21/6  26/8-31/12*

📷 **N 61°07'50'' E 08°32'40''**

# Sweden

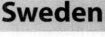

## General
Sweden is a member of the EU.

### Time
The time in Sweden is the same as Amsterdam, Paris and Rome and one hour ahead of London.

### Language
Swedish, but English is widely understood and spoken.

### Ferry crossings
You can reach Sweden via Copenhagen (Denmark) and Malmö (Southern Sweden) using the Øresundbron bridge and there are several popular ferry routes both from UK and mainland Europe ports.

## Border formalities
Many formalities and agreements about matters such as necessary travel documents, car papers, requirements relating to your means of transport and accommodation, medical expenses and taking pets with you do not only depend on the country you are travelling to but also on your departure point and nationality. The length of your stay can also play a role here. It is not possible within the confines of this guide to guarantee the correct and most up to date information with regard to these matters.

We advise you to consult the relevant authorities before your departure about:
- which travel documents you will need for yourself and your fellow passengers
- which documents you need for your car
- which regulations your caravan must meet;

- which goods you may import and export
- how medical treatment will be arranged and paid for in your holiday destination in cases of accident or illness
- whether you can take pets. Contact your vets well in advance. They can give you information about the necessary vaccinations, proof thereof and obligations on return. It would also make sense to enquire whether any special regulations apply to your pet in public places at your holiday destination. In some countries for example dogs must always be muzzled or transported in a cage.

You will find plenty of general information on ▶ www.europa.eu ◀ but make certain you select information that is relevant to your specific situation.

For the most recent customs regulations you should get in contact with the authorities of your holiday destination in your country of residence.

## Currency
The currency of Sweden is the Swedish kronor (SEK). Exchange rate September 2018 £1 = 11.81 SEK. You can pay in euros at post offices, railway stations and large shops, you will receive your change in Swedish kroner.

### Cash machines
Cash machines are thinly spread, especially outside the towns.

### Credit cards
You can pay by credit card in most places.

## Opening times

### Banks
Banks are open until 15:00, on Thursdays until 17.00 and closed on Saturdays.
In large towns banks may stay open till 18:00.
Banks close at 13:00 on the day preceding a public holiday.

### Shops
Shops in Sweden are open from 09:30 to 18:00 and on Saturdays till 16:00 or 17.00. Supermarkets are open between 08:00 and 21:00. You can only buy alcohol spirits in the state-run Systembolaget shops. These are open on weekdays until 18:00 and on Saturday until 13:00.

### Chemists
Chemists are open weekdays until 18:00 and on Saturdays until 14:00. In larger towns chemists are open on a rota basis during the evening and on Sundays (24 hour service).

## Communication

### (Mobile) phones
Southern Sweden has a full mobile network coverage. In northern Sweden there is coverage alongside main roads, on the coast and in towns, but not always in unpopulated areas or in the mountains. There is a 4G network for mobile internet.

### Wifi, internet
You will find internet cafes in cities, internet is free in public libraries. Wifi is becoming more common.

### Post
Post offices or agencies are now almost unknown in Sweden. Post is handled by grocers, filling stations or other shops.

## Roads and traffic

### Road network
Remember, all traffic in Sweden drives on the right and overtakes on the left! Headlight deflectors are advisable to prevent annoying oncoming drivers. Sweden uses the metric system, so distances are measured in kilometres (km) and speeds in kilometres per hour (km/h). When driving in Sweden take care to avoid wild animals crossing the road, especially at dawn and dusk. Driving in the dense forests of Central Sweden can lead to drowsiness due to the monotony and the silence. If you break down you can call Motormännen on 0046 20-211111.
E-mail address: service@motormannen.se.

### Traffic regulations
Traffic already on a roundabout usually has priority. This is shown by signs. Where there are no signs the driver wishing to enter the roundabout has priority.

*Maximum speed*

The maximum alcohol percentage is 0.2‰. Children under 7 must sit in a special child seat (this also applies to tourists). Cars must use dipped headlights during the day. Phones must be used hands-free. The use of winter tyres for cars and caravans is compulsory from 1 December to 31 March and in the rest of the year when weather conditions require it.

## Caravans, motorhomes

Service stations are becoming more common. In addition quick-stops are becoming popular: for a reduced rate you can use your pitch after 20:00 and you need to be on your way again before 10:00. It is prohibited to place a bucket under your caravan for waste water. You must have a self contained waste tank or waste container.

## Maximum allowed measurements of combined length

Height 4.5 metres, width 2.6 metres and maximum length 24 metres.

## Fuel

Lead free petrol is widely available. LPG is difficult to obtain.

## Filling stations

Filling stations which are staffed are open until 21:00. Most filling stations on major roads are open all night. Filling stations are few and far between in Northern Sweden. You can pay by credit card at most service stations.

## Tolls

You will have to pay on the Øresundbron bridge that connects Denmark with Sweden. Return tickets are not available.

## Emergency number

112: the national emergency number for police, fire or ambulance.

# Camping

Sweden has the so-called 'allemansrätten' (public rights). However you need to have permission from the owner and you need

to honour the principal agreement of allemansrätten which is 'do not disturb and do no damage'. There are more than enough campsites in the south of Sweden but the number reduces the further north you go. Northern Sweden has mostly small campsites.

Toilet facilities on campsites are usually adequate.

## Practical

If you are going camping in Sweden, there is a chance that you will need a special card that you must show at reception. You can purchase this card at the relevant campsite.

- Take note: there are only limited opportunities for refilling gas bottles. It is better to take sufficient gas with you. Butane gas is not available at all.
- Make sure you have a world adaptor for electrical equipment.
- Tap water is safe to drink.

## Älmhult, S-34394 / Jönköping

♀♂ ♿ 🛜

**19**

🔺 Sjöstugans Camping✱✱✱
📧 Badvägen
☎ +46 47 67 16 00
🕐 1/1 - 31/12
@ info@sjostugan.com

1,6ha 75T(50-80m²) 10A

**1** BCGIJKLMOPQ
**2** ADIKLRTWXY
**3** AFGUWZ
**4** KN
(Q+R+U+W+X+Z 1/5-30/9)
**5** ABDEFGIJKLMNOPTUWZ
**6** CEK(N 2km)RTV

💬 The campsite is beautifully located on a headland in the large lake Möckeln, in the beautiful countryside of Småland. Opportunities for water sports (sailing, fishing, swimming), hiking, cycling and golf. Boats and canoes for hire. A short distance from shops and department stores.

🚗 The campsite is signposted on route 23. On the E4 near Traryd take route 120 towards Älmhult.

Diö
Bråthult
CC
120  Älmhult
23
Killeberg  121

CC € **18**  1/1-20/6  1/9-31/12  7=6

▨ N 56°34'07" E 14°07'55"

---

## Årjäng, S-67295 / Värmland-Örebro

♀♂ ♿ 🛜 **iD**

**20**

🔺 Camp Grinsby
📧 Grinsbyn 100
☎ +46 57 34 20 22
🕐 30/4 - 1/9
@ campgrinsby@telia.com

3ha 105T(100-150m²) 10A

**1** ACDGIJKLMOPRS
**2** ABDIKLMRSUWXY
**3** AFHJKNQUWZ
**4** (Q 1/7-15/8) (R 25/6-15/8)
**5** ABDFGIJKLMNOPRUWZ
**6** CDEJ(N 9,9km)T

💬 2 km from the E18 (Stockholm-Karlstad-Oslo). You can ride your own bike or a rented one through the beautiful countryside along the Stora Bör lake. Maybe you will see moose, deer or beavers. In the Glaskogen nature reserve there are more than 300 km of marked footpaths, you can navigate the lake by boat or canoe and swim or fish in the crystal clear waters of the lake.

🚗 Take the exit on the E18 between Årjäng and Nysäter. Campsite signposted about 20 km van Årjäng.

Tenvik
Sillerud
E18  CC  Ed
Sillingsfors

CC € **18**  30/4-12/7

▨ N 59°18'11" E 12°26'42"

---

## Asarum/Karlshamn, S-37491 / Blekinge-Kalmar län

♀♂ ♿ 🛜 ✿ **iD**

**21**

🔺 Långasjönäs Camping & Stugby
📧 Långasjönäsvägen 49
☎ +46 4 54 32 06 91
🕐 1/4 - 1/12
@ info@langasjonas.com

11ha 92T(80-120m²) 16A CEE

**1** ACDGIJKLMOPQ
**2** ABDFIKLMQRSVWXY
**3** AFHJKLQUWZ
**4** N(Q+R 1/6-1/9)
(T+U+X+Z 24/6-21/8)
**5** ABFGIJKLMNOPQRUWZ
**6** BCDEGJLM(N 5km)V

💬 A beautifully located campsite in the middle of the Långasjönäs reserve. A campsite with beautiful views of the lake, located in an oasis of peace. Family friendly and with a lovely beach. It has the warmest beach in the whole of Blekinge.

🚗 From E22 exit 52 Karlshamn centre and follow camping signs from there. From route 29 exit Asarum then follow camping signs.

126  29
CC
Mörrum  E22
15  **Karlshamn**
E22

CC € **20**  1/4-20/6  25/8-1/12  7=6, 14=11

▨ N 56°13'55" E 14°51'11"

## Ed, S-66832 / Halland-Bohuslän 👫 🧍 ♿ 📶 **22**

🔺 Gröne Backe Camping & Stugor\*\*\*
📧 Södra Moränvägen 64
☎ +46 53 41 01 44
📅 1/1 - 31/12
@ info@gbcamp.nu

5ha 100T(100-120m²) 10A CEE

**1** CDGIJKLMOPRS
**2** ABDGILRSVWXY
**3** ABHJKNQUWZ
**4** N(Q+R 15/6-15/8) (V+X+Z ⊡)
**5** ABDFGIJKLMNOPUWZ
**6** CEGIJ(N 2km)OTV

💬 You will find fantastic countryside here, typical of this area. You can hire rowing boats and bicycles at the campsite. Opposite the site there is a moose farm within walking distance, highly recommended! Free internet and wifi. There is a floating sauna on a raft in Lake Lila, but it must be reserved in advance at the reception.

🚗 West of Ed there are signs to the campsite on route 164.

Håbol
Södra Hökedalen — CC 164 166
Bäckefors

**CC** €20 *1/1-3/6  1/9-9/10  14/10-31/12*  🗺 **N 58°53'58'' E 11°56'06''**

---

## Ellös (Orust), S-47492 / Halland-Bohuslän 👫 🧍 ♿ 📶 **23**

🔺 Stocken Camping\*\*\*\*
📧 Stockens Camping 101
☎ +46 30 45 11 00
📅 13/4 - 29/9
@ info@stockencamping.se

3ha 166T(100-125m²) 10-16A CEE

**1** CDGIJKLMOPQ
**2** AEGIOQRSTVW
**3** BFGHKNQUWY
**4** N(Q ⊡) (S 1/5-31/8) (T+Y+Z 24/6-14/8)
**5** ABDEFGIJKLMNOPRUW
**6** CEGHJM(N 6km)OPTV

💬 Located in natural surroundings. On the Skagerrak/Kattegat bay. A quiet family campsite on the west coast of the island of Orust, connected to the mainland by bridges (E6). Well stocked shop, good restaurant (24/6-14/8), fresh bread daily, excellent toilet facilities. Mini golf, football, crab fishing in the sea. Bike rentals on site and golf at Orust Golf Club. Welcome!
🚗 From Stenungssund to Orust on route 160. Then left on route 178 to Varekil, follow signs.

Grundsund
CC 178
Mollösund

**CC** €20 *23/4-4/6  1/9-28/9*  🗺 **N 58°08'52'' E 11°25'17''**

---

## Gäddede, S-83361 / Jämtland 👫 🎿 ♿ 📶 **iD** **24**

🔺 Gäddede Camping och Stugby\*\*\*
📧 Sagavägen 9
☎ +46 67 21 00 35
📅 1/1 - 31/12
@ info@gaddedecamping.com

3ha 70T(100m²) 10-16A CEE

NEW

**1** ACDGIJKLMOPQ
**2** DGKLORSTVWX
**3** AGHJQUWZ
**4** (C+H 25/6-15/8) N (U 1/2-30/9) (X+Y 19/6-15/9)
**5** ABDFGIJKLMNPRUW
**6** CEGJ(N 0,5km)V

💬 This campsite connects the Vildmarksvägen with Norway. There are many places of interest in the immediate vicinity of the campsite. You can fish, walk and enjoy the beautiful countryside.

🚗 In Strömsund from E45 take 342 direction Gäddede. Gäddede is just before the Norwegian border. Campsite is well signposted in Gäddede.

Gäddede CC
342
Spännviken

**CC** €20 *1/1-5/6  1/9-31/12*  🗺 **N 64°30'17'' E 14°08'58''**

## Gällö, S-84395 / Jämtland

👬 🎿 🏄 ♿ 📶 **iD** **25**

🏕 Camp Viking
✉ Hannåsen 107
☎ +46 7 27 00 40 03
📅 1/1 - 31/12
@ info@campviking.se

7ha 40T(100m²) 10A

**1** ACDGIJKLM**PQ**
**2** ABDGKLMRSWX
**3** HJK**WZ**
**4** (**A** 🔑) **N**(Q 15/6-31/8)
 (T+U 🔑) (X+Z 15/6-19/8)
**5** **AB**DEFGHIJKLMNOPRUW
**6** CDEGJ(N 0,5km)

💬 Viking Camp is centrally located in Sweden. Accessible from Sundsvall by car, bus and train. From the campsite you have a view of the Revsundssjön. You can go hiking, biking, fishing, canoeing in the area or just sit in front of your motorhome, caravan or tent. In short, a must do in Sweden.

🚗 On the E14, coming from Sundsvall towards Östersund, just before Gällö, after the petrol station on the right, you will find the entrance to the campsite.

Pilgrimstad
E14
Gällö CC
Stavre 323

CC € **20** 1/1-15/6 1/9-31/12

📐 N 62°55'03'' E 15°15'14''

---

## Gummarp/Eksjö, S-57593 / Jönköping

👬 📶 **iD** **26**

🏕 Mycklaflons Camping
✉ Norrsånna 2
☎ +46 38 14 30 00
📅 1/5 - 1/10
@ info@mycklaflonscamping.com

6ha 40T(90-110m²) 10A

**1** ACDGIJKLMOPQ
**2** ABDKMRTWXY
**3** AHIJQRU**WZ**
**4** (Q+T+U+X 🔑)
**5** **AB**CDGHIJKLMNO**P**UWYZ
**6** ACEGHJTV

💬 A small, intimate family campsite on the Mycklaflons lake. The campsite is located in lovely, relaxing surroundings with rolling hills scattered with boulders. The ideal spot for campers who want to stay in natural surroundings.

🚗 On route 40 Eksjö-Vimmerby, take exit Havik. Left on the end and then follow campsite signs.

Bruzaholm    Ingatorp
40
CC
Värne

CC € **18** 1/5-16/6 23/8-1/10

📐 N 57°35'23'' E 15°14'46''

---

## Gusum, S-61040 / Östergötland - Stockholms Län

👬 ♿ 📶 **iD** **27**

🏕 Yxningens Camping
✉ Yxningen
☎ +46 12 32 02 58
📅 18/4 - 15/9
@ info@yxningenscamping.se

2ha 42T(85-125m²) 6-16A CEE

**1** ABCDGIJKLMOPRS
**2** ABDFLMRTUVWXY
**3** AHIRU**WZ**
**4** M**N**(Q+R+U+V 🔑)
**5** **AB**CDFGHIJKLMNO**PR**UW
 XZ
**6** ACDEGKL(N 3km)

💬 Discover our small paradise and relax! Beautifully located at the imposing Lake Yxningen. Most suitable for nature, water and fishing enthusiasts. Also an ideal stop between Öland and Stockholm. Our qualities are personal contact, good service and clean toilet facilities. Plenty of elk and other game in the area. (Motor)boat and canoe hire. Free internet.

🚗 Take the E22 Ringarum or Gusum exit (follow camping signs).

Ringarum
CC Gusum
E22
Valdemarsvik

CC € **18** 18/4-20/6 23/6-1/7 18/8-15/9

📐 N 58°16'55'' E 16°27'48''

## Haverdal, S-30571 / Halland-Bohuslän  🛇🛇 🛇 📶  ②⑧

🔺 Haverdals Camping****
📧 Haverdalsvägen 62
☎ +46 3 55 23 10
🚗 17/4 - 15/9
@ info@haverdalscamping.se

5ha 230T(100-140m²) 10-16A CEE

**1** BCGIJKLMOQ
**2** AFGRVWX
**3** ABFHJKNQRU
**4** (Q+R 🅾)
**5** ABDFGJKLMNOPUWXYZ
**6** CEGIK(N 0,3km)OTV

💬 Anna-Lenna and Stefan guarantee a relaxing stay on their child-friendly campsite. The wide sandy beach and dunes which stretch for miles just 600m from the campsite, border a nature reserve with plenty of walking and cycling opportunities. The campsite has spacious pitches and modern toilet facilities. You have the use of a large communal kitchen next to the dining room.

🚗 E6, exit 46 Haverdal. Continue towards Haverdal.

🅲🅲 €⑳  17/4-20/6  23/6-1/7  18/8-15/9      📷 N 56°43'39'' E 12°40'25''

---

## Högsäter, S-45897 / Halland-Bohuslän  🛇🛇 🛇 📶  ②⑨

🔺 Ragnerudssjöns Camping & Stugby****
📧 Jolsäter 15
☎ +46 52 84 00 64
🚗 26/4 - 13/10
@ info@ragnerud.com

3ha 105T(80-120m²) 10A

**1** CDGIJKLMOPRS
**2** ABDJKLRTUVWX
**3** ABCFHJKQUWZ
**4** (Q 1/5-31/8) (R 1/6-31/8) (T+U+X+Z 1/7-1/8)
**5** ABDFGIJKLMNOPRSUW
**6** CEGIK(N 4km)TV

💬 This idyllic campsite is located on the edge of Kroppefjäll nature reserve (well-known for its many islands) and borders on Lake Ragnerudssjön. Almost all pitches have a view of the lake. Fishing and watersports options, swimming, cycling and marked-out walking routes. All ingredients for a wonderful holiday.

🚗 From route 172, 2 km north of Högsäter there are signs to the campsite (approx. 3 km).

🅲🅲 €⑳  26/4-19/6  18/8-13/10      📷 N 58°39'02'' E 12°06'10''

---

## Höör, S-24335 / Skåne  🛇🛇 🛇 📶  ③⓪

🔺 Jägersbo Camping***
📧 Sätofta
☎ +46 4 13 55 44 90
🚗 1/1 - 31/12
@ camping@jagersbo.se

5ha 150T(80-140m²) 10-16A CEE

**1** BCGIJKLMOPQ
**2** BDGKLMPRSTVWXY
**3** BFKQRUWZ
**4** NQ(1/5-15/9) (R 🅾) (S 13/6-16/8) (Z 🅾)
**5** ABDEFGHIJKLMNOPRUWZ
**6** CEGIK(N 3km)OT

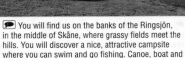

💬 You will find us on the banks of the Ringsjön, in the middle of Skåne, where grassy fields meet the hills. You will discover a nice, attractive campsite where you can swim and go fishing. Canoe, boat and bike rental.

🚗 On route 23 south of Höör, exit Sätofta; then 3 km. Or route 13, exit Sätofta. Located on Ringsjön lake.

🅲🅲 €⑳  1/1-20/6  23/6-1/7  18/8-31/12  7=6      📷 N 55°54'12'' E 13°33'54''

## Hova/Otterberget, S-54891 / Värmland-Örebro 👫 ♿ 📶 ⑶¹

🔺 Otterbergets Bad & Camping
🏕 Otterberget
☎ +46 50 63 31 27
🔓 14/4 - 1/11
@ info@otterbergetscamping.se

0,1ha 100T(100-120m²) 10A

**1** BCDGIJKLMOPQ
**2** ABDFLRSVWXY
**3** ABGHJNQRUWZ
**4** N(Q+R ⊙)
**5** ABCDFGHIJKLMNOPQRU
WZ
**6** ACEGHK(N 8km)V

💬 A very peaceful campsite on Lake Skagern with a kilometre-long beautiful sandy beach. Walking and cycling possible in the countryside of Tiveden.

🚗 On the E20 between Mariestad and Laxå, 5 km north of Hova. Turn off towards Otterberget. Campsite signposted here. Follow signs (3 km).

Gullspång
Finnerödja
CC E20
200
Hova

CC €⑱ *15/4-15/5  19/5-10/6  19/8-11/9  15/9-30/10*    📍 N 58°54'33'' E 14°17'26''

---

## Hultsfred, S-57736 / Blekinge-Kalmar län 👫 ♿ iD ³²

🔺 Camping Hultsfred
🏕 Folkparksvägen 10
☎ +46 7 02 17 31 16
🔓 1/5 - 16/9
@ info@camping-hultsfred.eu

7ha 176T(100-150m²) 8-16A

**1** ACDGIJKLMOPQ
**2** ABDLMRWX
**3** AJRUWZ
**4** (Q+R 1/6-31/8)
**5** ABCDFGIJKLMNOPRUWZ
**6** CDEG(N 1km)T

💬 The peaceful Hultsfred family campsite is located on the beautiful Hulingen lake with good opportunities for walking and cycling. The lake is ideal for swimming, canoeing and pedal boating. Ideal location for visiting the Astrid Lindgren Park at Vimmerby and the Virum or Målilla Elk Parks.

🚗 Take Hultsfred exit on route 34 from Målilla to Vimmerby. Campsite signposted.

Silverdalen
Vena
129
Hultsfred
CC
34
23
Järnforsen

CC €⑱ *1/5-16/6  18/8-16/9*    📍 N 57°29'31'' E 15°51'48''

---

## Kapellskär/Riddersholm, S-76015 / Östergötland - Stockholms Län 👫 ♿ 📶 iD ³³

🔺 Kapellskär Camping***
🏕 Fiskarängsvägen 8
☎ +46 17 64 42 33
🔓 1/5 - 30/9
@ campkapell@fritidsbyn.se

3,5ha 102T(70-100m²) 10A CEE

**1** ABCDGIJKLMOPQ
**2** ABFJMRSTWXY
**3** AGHJKQUW
**4** (A 1/5-25/9) N(Q ⊙)
(R+T 1/5-25/9)
**5** ABDFGHIJKLMNOPQUWXZ
**6** CDEGHJ(N 6km)TU

NEW

💬 This campsite with good facilities is located near the port of Kapellskär in the Riddarholm nature reserve, where there are marked hiking trails to a marina and a viewpoint. The campsite has a fairly large separate field for tents.

🚗 At the end of road E18, at Kapellskär harbour, turn right into a dirt road. Follow signs for 600 metres.

Västanvik
Södra
CC
E18

CC €⑳ *1/5-14/6  18/8-30/9*    📍 N 59°43'13'' E 19°03'02''

## Karlstad, S-65346 / Värmland-Örebro  👬 ♿ 🛜 34

🔺 Karlstad Swecamp Bomstad
Baden****
📧 Bomstadsvägen 640
☎ +46 54 53 50 68
🗓 1/1 - 31/12
@ info@bomstadbaden.se

9ha 160T(80-130m²) 10A CEE

1 CGIJKLMO**P**RS
2 ABDFGLRSVXY
3 B**F**GK**Q**UWZ
4 **KN**(Q+R 🈯)
  (T+U+X+Y+Z 1/5-31/8)
5 **AB**DEFGIJKLMNO**P**RUWX
6 CDEG**I**KM(N 5km)TV

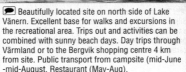

💬 Beautifully located site on north side of Lake Vänern. Excellent base for walks and excursions in the recreational area. Trips out and activities can be combined with sunny beach days. Day trips through Värmland or to the Bergvik shopping centre 4 km from site. Public transport from campsite (mid-June -mid-August. Restaurant (May-Aug).

🚐 Campsite signposted from the E18, west of Karlstad (Skutberget/Bomstad exit).

(CC) € 20  1/1-16/6  18/8-31/12     📷 N 59°21'44'' E 13°21'33''

## Kil, S-66591 / Värmland-Örebro  👬 ♿ 🛜 35

🔺 Frykenbadens Camping****
📧 Stubberud
☎ +46 55 44 09 40
🗓 1/1 - 31/12
@ info@frykenbaden.se

8ha 180T(100-120m²) 10A CEE

1 BCDGIJKLMOPRS
2 ABDIJKLORVWXY
3 BC**F**GHJKN**PQ**RU**W**Z
4 M**N**(Q 1/6-31/8)
  (R+T 15/6-15/8)
  (U+X+Z 15/6-30/8)
5 **AB**DEFGIJ**K**LMNO**PQ**UWZ
6 CDEGHIKM(N 7,5km)OTV

💬 A spaciously appointed and well equipped campsite on the shores of the Fryken lake. The site is divided by an access road and has one part on the steep shore of the lake with plenty of shade, and one part on a grassy field. A good base for cycling and walking, with fishing from the campsite.

🚐 On the east side of the Nedre Fryken Lake. There are signs to the campsite from route 61 near Kil.

(CC) € 18  1/1-19/6  19/8-31/12  7=6     📷 N 59°32'47'' E 13°20'29''

## Kungshamn, S-45691 / Halland-Bohuslän  👬 ♿ 🛜 36

🔺 Johannesvik Camping & Stugby****
☎ +46 52 33 23 87
🗓 1/1 - 31/12
@ info@johannesvik.se

25ha 370T(80-120m²) 10A CEE

1 CDGIJKLMO**P**RS
2 EGIKLMOQRVWX
3 B**F**HJKN**Q**U**V**WY
4 **KN**(Q+R 🈯)
  (S+T+V+X+Z 15/6-10/8)
5 **AB**DEFGIJKLMNO**PQ**RUWX
6 CEGH**J**L(N 2km)OTV

💬 Beautifully located among the Bohuslän cliffs. Having passed reception there is an opening in the cliff that takes you to the second part of the campsite. High quality toilet facilities. Many options for activities on as well as off the campsite. Kungshamn and the picturesque peninsula of Smögen are nearby and are definitely worth a visit.

🚐 From E6 route 171 to Askum. Dir. Kungshamn. Through Hovenäset, over bridge. After ± 1 km entrance of campsite on right.

(CC) € 18  1/4-10/6  18/8-31/12     📷 N 58°22'01'' E 11°16'51''

## Leksand, S-79327 / Dalarnas-Uppsala län

👫 ♿ 📶 **37**

🔺 Leksand Strand Camping & Resort\*\*\*\*
📧 Siljansvägen 61
☎ +46 24 71 38 00
📅 1/5 - 30/9
@ info@leksandresort.se

12ha 520T(100-120m²) 10-16A

1️⃣ CDGIJKLMO**PQ**
2️⃣ ADGIJKLRSTVWX
3️⃣ ABFHIJKLNP**QUW**Z
4️⃣ (C 24/6-20/8) **N** (Q+R+U+V+W+Y+Z 24/6-20/8)
5️⃣ **AB**DEFGIJKLMNOPQRUWZ
6️⃣ CDEGHK(N 2km)TUVX

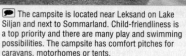

💬 The campsite is located near Leksand on Lake Siljan and next to Sommarland. Child-friendliness is a top priority and there are many play and swimming possibilities. The campsite has comfort pitches for caravans, motorhomes or tents.

🚗 From road 70 Borlänge-Rattvik in centre of Leksand follow exit Tällberg for 2 km, site is before Sommarland.

Siljansnäs

CC Leksand

70

©€ **18** 1/5-18/6 18/8-29/9

🗺 N 60°45'00'' E 14°58'23''

---

## Leksand, S-79392 / Dalarnas-Uppsala län

👫 📶 **iD** **38**

🔺 Västanviksbadets Camping Leksand\*\*\*\*
📧 Siljansnäsvägen 130
☎ +46 7 68 12 85 10
📅 26/4 - 18/9
@ info@vbcl.se

4ha 100T(100m²) 10A

1️⃣ ACDGIJKLMO**PQ**
2️⃣ ADGIJKLRSWX
3️⃣ A**F**HJKU**WZ**
4️⃣ (Q 19/6-15/8)
5️⃣ **AB**DFGIJNPUW
6️⃣ CEG**K**(N 4km)V

💬 A charming friendly campsite on the Siljan lake run by an enthusiastic young couple. The service is an added bonus. A natural experience in a lovely area with plenty of walking and cycling opportunities. Tourist attractions in Siljan are within easy reach.

🚗 From route 70 Borlänge-Mora, south of Leksand turn left towards Siljansnäs. Campsite is 4 km west of Leksand directly on the lake.

Siljansnäs

CC Leksand

70

©€ **20** 26/4-14/6 18/8-18/9

🗺 N 60°43'49'' E 14°57'05''

---

## Ljusdal, S-82730 / Gävleborg-Västernorrland

👫 🎿 ♿ 📶 **iD** **39**

🔺 Ljusdals Camping\*\*\*
📧 Ramsjövägen 56
☎ +46 65 11 29 58
📅 1/1 - 31/12
@ info@ljusdalscamping.se

4,5ha 75T(100-120m²) 10A

1️⃣ ACDGIJKLMO**PQ**
2️⃣ ACDGKLRSTWX
3️⃣ A**F**GHJK**QW**Z
4️⃣ **N**(Q 15/6-15/8) (U 15/6-31/8)
5️⃣ **AB**DFGHIJKLMNOPUW
6️⃣ CFGHKM(N 3km)

💬 Campsite is at the Växnan Lake in the beautiful Hälsingerland countryside. Large beach with diving board. Plenty of opportunities for fishing, canoeing etc. The lake flows out into the River Ljusnan which is abundant with fish. The friendly management ensures a lovely ambiance and a pleasant stay

🚗 From Ljusdal take route 83 and drive 3 km in the direction of Ånge. Next to route 83.

83 Tallåsen

CC Ljusdal

Färila 84

©€ **18** 1/1-14/6 20/8-31/12 7=6

🗺 N 61°50'20'' E 16°02'26''

## Marstrand, S-44030 / Halland-Bohuslän

👫 ♿ 📶 **40**

🔺 Marstrands Familje Camping
📧 Långedalsvägen 16
☎ +46 30 36 05 84
📅 26/4 - 29/9
@ info@marstrandscamping.se

2,5ha 85T(100-200m²) 10A CEE

**1** CDGIJKLMO**PQ**
**2** AEIMOQRSTVWX
**3** A**F**HK**Q**RUWY
**4** (Q+R 18/6-19/8)
  (T+U+V 1/5-14/8)
**5** **AB**DFGIJKLMNO**P**UW
**6** CDEGJ(N 1,5km)TV

💬 Ever dreamed of exploring the beautiful Swedish archipelago close to Gothenburg? This is your chance! You can enjoy a delightful stay at Marstrands Familjecamping. There is a small beach by the sea. Lovely walks can be taken from the site, 2.5 or 5 km with beautiful sights on the way. You can take the ferry to the car-free island Marstrand.

🚗 North of Kungälv (E6). Take route 168 towards Marstrand. Campsite is on the right at the end of the road (28 km). Signposted.

Skärhamn
169
Marstrand
CC

🇨🇨€⑳ 26/4-29/5 3/6-30/6 19/8-29/9   📍 N 57°53'39" E 11°36'17"

---

## Mellerud, S-46421 / Halland-Bohuslän

👫 ♿ 📶 **41**

🔺 Mellerud Swe-Camp Vita Sandar****
☎ +46 53 01 22 60
📅 1/1 - 31/12
@ mail@vitasandarscamping.se

14ha 210T(100-120m²) 10A CEE

**1** CDGIJKLMOPRS
**2** ADLRVWX
**3** ABC**F**GHJK**M**N**Q**UWZ
**4** (**C** 1/6-31/8) **N**
  (Q+S+T+U+W+X+Z 1/6-31/8)
**5** **AB**DFGIJKLMNO**P**QRUWZ
**6** CDFGH**K**(N 4km)OV

💬 Situated on the so-called Dalsland Riviera. Associations with summer, sunshine and swimming. Kilometres of long sandy beaches, rowing boats, canoes, outdoor pool, tennis, mini golf and football are all options for relaxation. There's even a shop and a restaurant (01/06-31/08).

🚗 On Lake Vänern. From route 45 near Mellerud there are signs to the campsite.

Dalskog
166
Mellerud
CC
Dals Rostock
E45

🇨🇨€⑳ 1/1-9/6 19/8-31/12   📍 N 58°41'22" E 12°31'01"

---

## Oxelösund, S-61351 / Östergötland - Stockholms Län

👫 🚣 📶 iD **42**

🔺 Jogersö Camping
📧 Jogersövägen
☎ +46 15 53 04 66
📅 1/1 - 31/12
@ info@jogerso.se

3ha 132T(80-120m²) 10-16A CEE

**1** ABCDGIJKLMOPQ
**2** ABEFLMQRUVWXY
**3** A**F**GHK**Q**UWY
**4** **N**(Q+R 18/6-13/8)
  (U+X+Y+Z 1/6-20/8)
**5** **AB**CDFGIJKLMNOPUWYZ
**6** ACDEGK(N 3km)TV

💬 Beautifully located campsite on an inlet of the Baltic Sea. 200m from a lovely large sandy beach, accessible from the campsite via a footpath. Excellent opportunity for swimming and other water sports. This is also the place to be if you enjoy fishing. The surroundings (nature reserve) are ideally suited for walking and cycling. Good stopover site when on the way to Stockholm.

🚗 E4, exit Oxelösund (road 53). Take the Frösang/ SSAB exit. Then follow camping signs.

E4 **Nyköping** 219
53
Oxelösund
CC

🇨🇨€⑳ 1/5-10/6 26/8-22/9   📍 N 58°40'00" E 17°03'25"

## Skummeslövsstrand, S-31272 / Halland-Bohuslän

♨ ⚲ 🎫 **43**

🔺 Skummeslövs Ekocamping****
🏠 Stora Strandvägen 35
☎ +46 43 02 10 30
🕐 15/4 - 15/9
@ info@ekocamping.nu

NEW

9ha 350T(100-150m²) 10A CEE

**1** BCGIJKLMOQ
**2** ABFGLRSTUVWX
**3** BFGMQUW
**4** (Q+R+T 19/6-1/9)
**5** ABDFGIJKLMNPUWXZ
**6** CEGII(N 0,5km)TUV

💬 Medium-sized campsite with good toilet facilities. Near to the sea with a beautiful sandy beach, car allowed on beach. Quick-stop possible (between 22.00 - 08.00).

🚐 E6 dir. Halmstad, exit 40 dir. Skottorp/ Skummeslövsstrand. The campsite is located on the right of the road. Do not follow sign for Skummelövscamping.

Laholm · E6
Skummeslövsstrand
CC
Båstad
115 · E20 · 24
105

(( € 18  15/4-20/6  18/8-15/9  🏔 N 56°27'34'' E 12°55'59''

---

## Sollerön, S-79290 / Dalarnas-Uppsala län

♨ 🎿 ⚲ 🛶 📶 iD **44**

🔺 Sollerö Camping***
🏠 Levsnäs
☎ +46 25 02 22 30
🕐 1/1 - 31/12
@ info@sollerocamping.se

0,7ha 93T(90-135m²) 16A CEE

**1** ACDGIJKLMOPQ
**2** ADGIJKLMRSTUVW
**3** ABCFGHJKMQUWZ
**4** N(Q+V+X+Y 🚐)
**5** ABDFGHIJKLMNOPUWZ
**6** CDEGHK(N 3km)OV

💬 A large, charming campsite. Beautifully located on Sollerön island in the Siljan lake. A good base for visiting the sights around the Siljan lake. Plenty of walking and cycling opportunities. Golf course next to the campsite.

🚐 From Mora route 45, left at Sollerön exit. Left in Gesunda and follow signs.

Mora
70
E45
Garsås
26
CC
Gesunda

(( € 20  1/1-30/5  3/6-20/6  18/8-31/12  🏔 N 60°54'05'' E 14°34'56''

---

## Stöllet, S-68051 / Värmland-Örebro

♨ ⚲ 📶 iD **45**

🔺 Alevi Camping
🏠 Fastnäs 53
☎ +46 56 38 60 50
🕐 27/4 - 13/9
@ info@alevi-camping.com

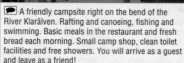

4,1ha 60T(120-180m²) 4-10A CEE

**1** ABCDGIJKLMOPRS
**2** CGLMRSVWX
**3** AGHJRUWX
**4** (A 7/7-24/8)
(Q+R+T+U+X 1/6-31/8)
**5** ABDFGIJKLMNOPRUWZ
**6** ACEGJLTV

💬 A friendly campsite right on the bend of the River Klarälven. Rafting and canoeing, fishing and swimming. Basic meals in the restaurant and fresh bread each morning. Small camp shop, clean toilet facilities and free showers. You will arrive as a guest and leave as a friend!

🚐 On route 62, 18 km south of the intersection with the 45 (Stöllet). Turn left immediately after the bridge over the Klarälven as signposted. Coming from Karlstad 14 km north of Ekshärad.

E45
Åstrandssätern
62
CC
Hara
239 · Hallen · Byn

(( € 20  27/4-5/7  24/8-13/9  🏔 N 60°17'07'' E 13°24'25''

## Strömstad, S-45297 / Halland-Bohuslän ♿ 📶 **46**

▲ Camping Daftö Resort*****
🏠 Dafter 1
☎ +46 52 62 60 40
📅 1/1 - 31/12
@ info@dafto.se

11,8ha 336T(100-120m²) 10A CEE

**1** CDGIJKLMO**P**RS
**2** AEFGJLQRVW
**3** BC**F**HKN**Q**RU**W**Y
**4** (C+H 1/6-31/8) I**K**N
   (Q+S 1/4-31/10)
   (T+U 15/6-15/8)
   (V+X 1/6-31/8) (Z 1/6-30/6)
**5** **AB**DEFGJKLMNOPRUWXY
**6** CDEGHKLM(N 5km)OSTV

💬 A luxury 5-star campsite directly on the reefs of Bohuslän. Little shade but excellent amenities such as a heated swimming pool, the famous outdoor play centre Daftöland, excellent toilet facilities, kayaks, pedalos, bikes, 100% (free) wifi, walking routes and 18 hole golf course close by.

🚗 Coming from the south follow the E6 as far as exit Sandfjord/Strömstad (route 176) near the Hydro-service station. After 6.5 km the campsite is located on the left of the road.

Strömstad
Skee
CC E6 164
176
Lur

CC €**20** 1/1-2/6 1/9-31/12     🗺 N 58°54'15'' E 11°12'05''

---

## Strömstad, S-45290 / Halland-Bohuslän 👫 ♿ **47**

▲ Seläter Camping***
🏠 Seläter
☎ +46 52 61 22 90
📅 1/1 - 31/12
@ info@selater.se

7ha 342T(100-120m²) 10A

**1** CDGIJKLMO**P**RS
**2** FGIRVWX
**3** A**F**HJK**Q**W
**4** (Q+R+U 1/5-30/9)
**5** **AB**DFGIJKLMNO**PQ**UW
**6** EGH(N 4km)TV

💬 Campsite Seläter is located in a rural area north-west of Strömstad, near the Capri beach. Free wifi at reception. It is possible to go to the centre of Strömstad and to use the ferry (special pass at reception). Bicycles for hire. Bus stop at campsite. Walking route 1.5 km around the campsite.

🚗 Take E6 from south dir. exit Strömstad N. Right on 1st roundabout. Campsite is on the road to Seläter.

Hvaler
CC E6 164
Strömstad
176

CC €**18** 1/4-19/6 18/8-30/9     🗺 N 58°57'23'' E 11°09'27''

---

## Tranås, S-57393 / Jönköping ⛵ ♿ 📶 🌸 **48**

▲ Hätte Camping****
🏠 Badvägen 2
☎ +46 14 01 74 82
📅 1/1 - 31/12
@ info@hattecamping.se

4ha 129T(80-100m²) 10A CEE

**1** BCDGIJKLMOPQ
**2** ABCDLMRUVWXY
**3** A**F**HJKN**Q**RU**W**Z
**4** M(Q 20/6-15/8) (R 📅)
   (U 1/5-31/8) (V 📅)
   (X+Y 1/5-31/8)
**5** **AB**DFGIJKLMNOPUWZ
**6** ACEGH**K**(N 4km)V

💬 Peaceful family campsite. Opportunities for swimming, watersport and fishing in the beautiful Lake Sommen. Centrally located for great trips out, such as Gränna and Eksjö. Good walking and cycling possibilities in the area. Good stopover location for trips to Stockholm and the Arctic Circle.

🚗 Campsite located 3 km east of Tranås and signposted from route 131 (in the direction of Hätte). On route 32 take Tranås Sud exit, dir centre and the campsite is signposted.

Sommen
32
Tranås CC
Gripenberg
131

CC €**18** 1/1-14/6 19/8-31/12     🗺 N 58°02'10'' E 15°01'44''

## Uddevalla/Hafsten, S-45196 / Halland-Bohuslän

👪 ♿ 🛜  **49**

🔺 Camping Hafsten Resort*****
📧 Hafsten 120
☎ +46 5 22 64 41 17
📅 1/1 - 31/12
@ info@hafsten.se

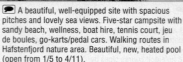

17ha 210T(80-100m²) 10A CEE

**1** CDGIJKLMO**P**RS
**2** AEIJKLQRSVWX
**3** BC**F**GHL**M**N**PQ**U**V**WY
**4** (A 1/7-15/8) (**C**+**H** 1/5-4/11)
 **JKL**MN**P**(Q+R 📅)
 (S 1/6-31/8) (T+U 📅)
 (V 1/6-31/8) (X+Y+Z 📅)
**5** **AB**DFGIJKLMNO**P**UWXYZ
**6** CDFGHIK(N 6km)OPSTV

💬 A beautiful, well-equipped site with spacious pitches and lovely sea views. Five-star campsite with sandy beach, wellness, boat hire, tennis court, jeu de boules, go-karts/pedal cars. Walking routes in Hafstenfjord nature area. Beautiful, new, heated pool (open from 1/5 to 4/11).

🚗 From E6 take 161 to Lysekil as far as 160. Left to Orust. Left after 2 km then another 4 km (follow signs). Site clearly marked, is in Hafstensfjord (nature reserve).

**Uddevalla**
Herrestad
Hafsten CC  E6
161
160
Orust

CC €**20** 1/1-17/4 23/4-28/5 9/6-18/6 18/8-30/10 3/11-31/12  📍 N 58°18'53'' E 11°43'24''

---

## Valdemarsvik, S-61533 / Östergötland - Stockholms Län

👪 ♿ 🛜 **iD** **50**

🔺 Grännäs Camping och Stugby****
📧 Festplatsvägen 1
☎ +46 12 35 14 44
📅 26/4 - 15/9
@ info@grannascamping.se

10ha 60T(80-120m²) 10A CEE

**1** ABCDGIJKLOPQ
**2** ABEFJKLMRVWXY
**3** A**M**N**Q**UWY
**4** (Q+T+U+W 📅) (X 1/6-18/8)
 (Z 📅)
**5** **AB**CDFGHIJKLMNOPUWZ
**6** CEGJ**K**(N 3km)TV

💬 Beautiful campsite in park-like surroundings, located directly on the only fjord of the Swedish eastern coast. The welcoming harbour town of Valdemarsvik is 1 km away. This campsite is on your way if you are driving to Stockholm from mainland Europe. You are very welcome.

🚗 From south take E22 exit Kårtorp/Gållósa and from here follow signs to Grännäs. From the north exit Valdemarsvik, then follow Grännäs.

Gusum
Snäckevarp
E22 CC Lövudden

CC €**20** 26/4-20/6 23/6-1/7 18/8-15/9  📍 N 58°11'39'' E 16°37'01''

---

## Vänersborg, S-46260 / Halland-Bohuslän

👪 ♿ 🛜 **51**

🔺 Ursands Resort & Camping****
☎ +46 52 11 86 66
📅 1/1 - 31/12
@ info@ursand.se

25ha 400T(80-100m²) 10-16A CEE

**1** BCDGIJKLMOPQ
**2** ABDIKLMRSTUVWXY
**3** ABDGHJN**Q**RUWZ
**4** (**C**+**H** 20/6-20/8) **JK**MN
 (Q+R 1/5-11/9) (T 20/4-16/9)
 (U 1/6-31/8)
 (X+Y+Z 15/6-15/8)
**5** **AB**DFGIJKLMNO**PQR**UWX
 YZ
**6** CDEGHKLM(N 6km)TV

💬 Beautiful location on Lake Vänern, the biggest lake in Sweden. Enjoy the large sandy beach. There are countless activities for children. The beautiful surrounding countryside is perfect for jogging, cycling and walking. Restaurant is open from 15/6 to 15/8. Beautiful new outdoor pool (2016). Special hardened pitches for motorhomes.

🚗 From Vänersborg take route 45 dir. Karlstad. After approx. 3 km follow signs, campsite is clearly indicated.

173
E45
Vänersborg
Vargön

CC €**20** 1/1-6/6 18/8-31/12  📍 N 58°24'50'' E 12°19'23''

## Varberg, S-43253 / Halland-Bohuslän

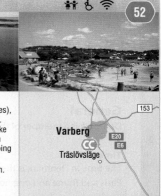

**52**

🏔 Camping Apelviken.se\*\*\*\*\*
🏖 Sanatorievägen 4
☎ +46 3 40 64 13 00
📅 1/1 - 31/12
@ info@apelviken.se

6ha 500T(80-120m²) 16A CEE

1. BCGIJKLMNOQ
2. AEGKORVW
3. BFGKQUWY
4. (B+H 1/5-31/8) **N**
   (Q+R 1/4-30/9) (X 15/6-15/8)
   (Y 23/3-27/10)
5. **AB**DFGHIJKLMN**P**RUWXY
6. CFGHIK(N 1,5km)PSTV

💬 Stunningly located on headland on Sweden's west coast. Swimming, surfing, SUP, golf (18 holes), walking, cycling (over the promenade to Varberg). estaurant open at weekends March-November. Take the train to Göteborg, Halmstad or beyond. 30 km from the site you will find Sweden's largest shopping centre: Gekås in Ullared.

🚗 E6, exit 53 to 55, depending on your direction. Keep on towards Varberg Centre, then follow the 'Apelviken' signs and the signs to the campsite.

**Varberg**
Träslövsläge
153
E20
E6
CC

**CC** € **20** 1/1-18/4 22/4-29/5 2/6-5/6 9/6-20/6 23/6-1/7 18/8-31/12 | 📷 **N 57°05'17'' E 12°14'52''**

---

## Värnamo, S-33131 / Jönköping

**53**

🏔 Värnamo Camping\*\*\*
🏖 Prostgårdsvägen
☎ +46 37 01 66 60
📅 1/5 - 16/9
@ info@varnamocamping.se

3ha 75T(100m²) 10A CEE

1. BCGIJKLMOPQ
2. BCDGLMRY
3. BFGKMN**QUW**Z
4. (Q+R 9/6-13/8)
5. **AB**DEFGIJKLMNOPUW
6. EGK(N 0,5km)TV

💬 A shaded campsite within walking distance of a lake and the town centre. 15 km from a large National Park.

🚗 E4, exit 85 Värnamo S, then follow camping signs. Also signposted on road 27.

**Värnamo**
Forsheda
151
127
E4
CC
27

**CC** € **20** 1/5-16/6 18/8-16/9 | 📷 **N 57°11'27'' E 14°02'45''**

---

# Denmark

## General
Denmark is a member of the EU.

### Time
The time in Denmark is the same as Amsterdam, Paris and Rome and one hour ahead of London.

### Language
Danish, but English and German are well understood and widely spoken.

### Ferry crossings
There are several ferry services which are heavily used in the summer months. It is advisable to book your crossing early.

## Border formalities
Many formalities and agreements about matters such as necessary travel documents, car papers, requirements relating to your means of transport and accommodation, medical expenses and taking pets with you do not only depend on the country you are travelling to but also on your departure point and nationality. The length of your stay can also play a role here. It is not possible within the confines of this guide to guarantee the correct and most up to date information with regard to these matters.

We advise you to consult the relevant authorities before your departure about:
- which travel documents you will need for yourself and your fellow passengers
- which documents you need for your car
- which regulations your caravan must meet
- which goods you may import and export
- how medical treatment will be arranged and

paid for in your holiday destination in cases of accident or illness
- whether you can take pets. Contact your vets well in advance. They can give you information about the necessary vaccinations, proof thereof and obligations on return. It would also make sense to enquire whether any special regulations apply to your pet in public places at your holiday destination. In some countries for example dogs must always be muzzled or transported in a cage.

You will find plenty of general information on ▸ www.europa.eu ◂ but make certain you select information that is relevant to your specific situation.

For the most recent customs regulations you should get in contact with the authorities of your holiday destination in your country of residence.

## Currency
The currency in Denmark is the krone (DKK). Approximate exchange rates September 2017: £1 = 8.37 DKK.

### Credit cards
You can pay by credit card in many places.

## Opening times
### Banks
Banks are open Monday to Friday until 16:00. On Thursdays until 17:30.

### Shops
Most shops are open from Monday to Thursday

until 18:00, on Fridays until 19.00 or 20:00. Shops open on Saturdays till 14:00. In tourist areas the shops are often open all day Sunday.

### Chemists
Chemists are normally open from 09:30 to 17:30 from Monday to Thursday. They stay open longer on Fridays. You can visit the chemist on Saturdays between 10:00 and 13:00.

## Communication
### (Mobile) phones
The mobile network works well in all of Denmark. There is a 4G network for mobile internet.

### Wifi, internet
Wifi is usually available in restaurants and bars.

### Post
Open Monday to Friday until 18:00, and on Saturdays until 13:00.

## Roads and traffic
### Road network
Remember, all traffic in Denmark drives on the right and overtakes on the left! Headlight

deflectors are advisable to prevent annoying oncoming drivers. Denmark uses the metric system, so distances are measured in kilometres (km) and speeds in kilometres per hour (km/h). In the event of a breakdown or accident use the emergency phones to contact Falck on 70102030 or FDM on 70133040.

### Traffic regulations
Traffic on roundabouts always has priority. You must let cyclists go first. On mountain roads and other steep roads ascending traffic has priority over descending traffic.

*Maximum speed*

| | |
|---|---|
| | 80-90 |
| | 70 |
| < 3,5 т | 80-90 |
| > 3,5 т | 70 |
| | 110-130 |
| | 80 |
| < 3,5 т | 110-130 |
| > 3,5 т | 80 |

The maximum alcohol percentage is 0.5‰. You must use dipped headlights during the day in Denmark. You must use a phone hands-free. The use of winter tyres is not compulsory.

### Caravans, motorhomes
For campers arriving late, the quick-stop service is gaining popularity: stay overnight after 20:00 and leave before 10:00, often outside the grounds. Camping overnight in a motorhome is not permitted on public roads, car parks or close to a beach.

### Maximum allowed measurements of combined length
Height 4 metres, width 2.55 metres and maximum length 18.75 metres (of which the trailer maximum 12 metres).

### Fuel
Lead-free and diesel is widely available. LPG is difficult to obtain.

### Filling stations
Filling stations are mostly open until 23:00. You can usually pay by credit card.

### Tolls
There are no tolls on Danish roads. You will have to pay on the Øresundbron and Storebælt bridges. For more information see ▶ www.storebaelt.dk ◀ and ▶ www.oresundsbron.com ◀

### Emergency number
112: the national emergency number for fire, police and ambulance.

## Camping
Free camping is not generally permitted in Denmark! It is only possible with the landowner's permission.
Peace and privacy are high on the list in Denmark. Camping grounds are often located further away from the outside world than in other countries. Danish campsites are predominantly family sites. The number of comfort pitches is increasing.

### Practical
At more and more campsites in Denmark, the Camping Key Europe (CKE) is no longer necessary, and you can also use your ACSI Club ID. However, the CKE card can still be required at a few Danish campsites. You can purchase this card at the campsite if necessary.

- Take note: facilities for filling propane gas bottles are extremely limited. You are advised to take a good supply with you.
- Make sure you have a world adaptor for electrical equipment.
- It is safe to drink tap water.

### Fishing
A fishing licence is required in Denmark for everyone between the ages of 18 and 65. This is available at post offices, tourist offices, hotels and campsites (valid for one year, one week or one day). For the many privately owned lakes and rivers you will also need local permission.

## Allingåbro, DK-8961

🛖 Dalgård Camping\*\*\*
📫 Nordkystvejen 65
☎ +45 86 31 70 13
🗓 30/3 - 15/9
@ info@dalgaardcamping.dk

5ha  125T(80-100m²)  10-16A

**1** ABCDFIJLMOPQ
**2** AEGJRSVX
**3** BFGHJNQRU**W**Y
**4** N(Q+S 🖳)
**5** **AB**DEFGHJL**P**RUZ
**6** CEG**K**M(N 3km)OV

💬 Pleasant campsite with warm welcome by Arne and Diana. Spacious pitches, good, modern toilet facilities. The fine sandy beach is a short walk away over a path framed by wild roses. Good options for anglers. Lovely wooded area. Cycling or walking possible from campsite.

🚗 Situated on route 547. About 4 km to the west of Fjellerup. Campsite located on the right of the road.

CC €20  30/3-6/6  10/6-29/6  18/8-14/9  📍 N 56°30'33'' E 10°32'45''

---

## Arrild/Toftlund, DK-6520

🛖 Arrild-Ferieby-Camping\*\*\*
📫 Arrild Ferieby 5
☎ +45 20 48 37 34
🗓 1/1 - 31/12
@ info@arrildcamping.dk

8ha  250T(100-140m²)  16A CEE

**1** ACDGIJKLMOPRS
**2** BDGRWXY
**3** BFGH**M**NOQRUW
**4** (F+H 🖳) J
  (S+T+U+W+Y 🖳)
**5** **AB**DEFGIJKLMNO**PQ**RUWX Z
**6** CEGHM(N 0,1km)

💬 A peaceful family campsite in wooded surroundings. Pitches sheltered from the wind. Heated indoor swimming pool with Denmark's longest water slide. Extensive hiking and cycling area. 18 hole golf course in close vicinity. The old towns of Ribe and Tønder are about 30 km away. Rømø island with beautiful beaches is 20 min away.

🚗 From the A7/E45 exit 73 route 175 towards Rømø. Follow the road at Toftlünd, campsite is indicated at the Arrild turning.

CC €16  1/1-22/6  20/8-31/12  📍 N 55°09'12'' E 08°57'24''

---

## Assens, DK-5610

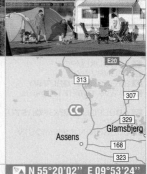

🛖 Camping Sandager Næs\*\*\*
📫 Strandgårdsvej 12, Sandager
☎ +45 64 79 11 56
🗓 12/4 - 15/9
@ info@sandagernaes.dk

3,7ha  135T(80-140m²)  10A CEE

**1** CD**G**IJKLMOPQ
**2** AEKLRVWX
**3** BF**J**KN**P**RU**W**Y
**4** (C 18/5-31/8) (H 15/5-31/8) J
  **N**(Q+S 🖳)
  (T+U+X 30/6-12/8)
**5** **AB**DEFGIJKLMNO**P**RUWZ
**6** ACEGHIK(N 3km)OTV

💬 Beautifully located campsite on the west coast of Fünen. The site has excellent heated toilet facilities in early and late seasons. The surroundings invite you for walking and cycling trips. Interesting trips out also possible, for example to Odense, Hans Christian Andersen's birthplace, the Danish Railway Museum and Egeskov, a medieval castle with museum.

🚗 Motorway E20, exit 57 direction Assens. Right at Sandager, follow the signs.

CC €20  12/4-29/5  10/6-1/7  1/9-15/9  📍 N 55°20'02'' E 09°53'24''

## Augustenborg, DK-6440

 ♿ 📶 iD **57**

🏕 Hertugbyens Camping**
📧 Ny Stavensbøl 1
☎ +45 74 47 16 39
📅 1/1 - 31/12
@ hertugbyenscamping@mail.dk

2,6ha 200T(100-150m²) 16A CEE

**1** AGIJKLMOPQ
**2** AEFIKORTWX
**3** AFHJKWY
**4** (Q 1/7-1/8)
**5** ABDEFGIJKLMNO**PQR**UWZ
**6** ACEGK(N 1km)

💬 Quiet peaceful campsite close to woods and water behind the Augustenborg castle park. Excellent opportunities for families with children, anglers, hikers and anyone who enjoys countryside and peace, but still close to Sønderborg. Fresh fish in farm shop every day.

🚗 Main route 8, beyond Sønderborg take Augustenborg exit on the right. Turn left in centre. Follow signs. Turn first right before the hospital, then left and follow the road to the beach.

CC € **18** 1/1-14/7 31/8-31/12     N 54°56'49'' E 09°51'15''

---

## Ballum/Bredebro, DK-6261

📶 iD **58**

🏕 Ballum Camping***
📧 Kystvej 37
☎ +45 74 71 62 63
📅 1/1 - 31/12
@ info@ballumcamping.eu

5,2ha 145T(100-240m²) 10A CEE

**1** ACDGIJKLMPQ
**2** GRWXY
**3** BHJKLNU
**4** (Q+R+U 🅿)
**5** ABDEFGHIJKLMNO**PQR**UWZ
**6** ACDEGK(N 1,5km)TV

💬 A peaceful family campsite with excellent heated toilet facilities in the low season. Natural surroundings rich in bird life where in spring and autumn enormous flocks of starlings form a natural phenomenon. Campsite suitable for winter activities. Fresh bread daily. Special motorhome pitches. Dutch owners.

🚗 Coast road 419 from Tønder to Ballum. Campsite signposted just before Ballum.

CC € **20** 1/1-20/6 30/8-31/12     N 55°04'08'' E 08°39'38''

---

## Bogense, DK-5400

♿ 📶 iD **59**

🏕 Bogense Strand Camping*****
📧 Vestre Engvej 11
☎ +45 64 81 35 08
📅 29/3 - 20/10
@ info@bogensecamping.dk

11ha 425T(80-200m²) 13A CEE

**1** ACDGIJKLMPQ
**2** AEGNRVWX
**3** BFGHJKM**N**PQRU**VW**Y
**4** (C 23/6-12/8) (F+H 🅿) JLN
**5** ABDEFGIJKLMNO**PQR**STUWXYZ
**6** CDEGHK(N 0,25km)OSTV

💬 Bogense Beach Campsite with outdoor and indoor pools, is just 5 minutes from the centre of Bogense, the port and the beach. The campsite is ideally located for a walk in the woods, a journey through the beautiful landscapes, or swimming in the sea. Suitable for both nature lovers and city people, as Odense is also nearby.

🚗 From Odense direction Havn, follow signs.

CC € **20** 12/4-29/5 10/6-29/6 11/8-25/8 1/9-20/10     N 55°33'41'' E 10°05'07''

## Bøjden/Faaborg, DK-5600

♿ 📶 iD **60**

▲ CampOne Bøjden Strand *****
🏠 Bøjden Landevej 12
☎ +45 63 60 63 60
🗓 13/4 - 20/10
@ bojden@campone.dk

6,5ha 308T(80-140m²) 10A CEE

**1** ACD**G**IJKLMOPQ
**2** AEGJKLRVWXY
**3** BCF**JKNQ**RU**WY**
**4** (**C** 1/6-15/9) (**F**+H 🖐) IJKN
  P(Q+S+T+U+V+X+Y+Z 🖐)
**5** **AB**DEFGIJKLMNO**PRST**U
  WXYZ
**6** CDEGH**K**(N 3km)O**P**TV

NEW

💬 Beautiful campsite with excellent toilet facilities. Located directly on the sea, sea view from all pitches. The sunset is very special. Very child friendly with many activities inside and outside.

🛣 Highway 323 and 329 Assens-Hårby-Faaborg. Before Faaborg take road 8 towards Bøjden or the Ferry Fynshav (South-Jutland)-Bøjden. Campsite signposted in Bøjden.

Håstrup
329 | 43
CC 8 | Faaborg
44

CC €**20** *13/4-30/6  18/8-20/10* ⛰ N 55°06'20'' E 10°06'28''

---

## Bork Havn/Hemmet, DK-6893

♿ 📶 iD **61**

▲ Bork Havn Camping ***
🏠 Kirkehøjvej 9A
☎ +45 75 28 00 37
🗓 12/4 - 19/10
@ mail@borkhavncamping.dk

4,5ha 115T(100-120m²) 6-10A CEE

**1** ACD**G**IJKLMPQ
**2** ADRUVWXY
**3** BGHJKN**Q**UW
**4** **N**(S+T+U 🖐)
**5** **AB**DEFGIJKLMNO**P**RUWZ
**6** CEGHK(N 0,05km)OTV

💬 A very well maintained campsite with heated sanitary facilities and all amenities. There is a supermarket next to the site. The attractive fishing harbour with its restaurant, shops and snack bar is just 100m away. The enclosed fjord lends itself to wind or kite surfing and to fishing. Walking and cycling in the area is sheer delight.

🛣 On the 423 Nørre Nebel-Tarn; north of the village of Nørr Bork follow the signs to Bork Havn on the left.

Tarm
Bjerregård
181 | CC | 423
Nørre Nebel

CC €**20** *12/4-28/5  10/6-29/6  18/8-19/10* ⛰ N 55°50'54'' E 08°17'00''

---

## Bramming, DK-6740

📶 iD **62**

▲ Darum Camping ***
🏠 Alsædvej 24
☎ +45 75 17 91 16
🗓 13/4 - 29/9
@ info@darumcamping.dk

4,4ha 50T(100-140m²) 10-16A CEE

**1** ACD**G**HIJKLMOPQ
**2** BCF**G**RSWXY
**3** A**F**GUW
**4** (Q+R+T+U+X+Z 🖐)
**5** **AB**DFGJMNO**P**QUW
**6** ACEGH**J**(N 7km)OV

💬 An idyllic and scenic campsite halfway between Ribe and Esbjerg, good shelter, large units and new service building. A peaceful place for adults who love nature, cycling along the Wadden Sea National Park. Discover Sneum sluice and a rich bird life. Dinner can be enjoyed in the café.

🚗 From the south follow route 11-24 exit St. Darum. Follow campsite signs. From the north route 24.

E20
191
12 | Bramming
**Esbjerg**
24 | CC
11
32

CC €**18** *13/4-29/6  19/8-29/9* ⛰ N 55°26'03'' E 08°38'28''

## Broager/Skelde, DK-6310

♚♛ ⚡ 🛜 iD **63**

⛺ Broager Strand Camping***
🏠 Skeldebro 32
☎ +45 74 44 14 18
🗓 1/1 - 31/12
@ post@broagerstrandcamping.dk

5,8ha 140T(80-125m²) 13-16A CEE

**1** ABCD**G**IJKLMOPQ
**2** AEFKLNRSTVWXY
**3** A**F**GHJLU**W**Y
**4** (Q 🖳)
**5** **AB**CDFGHIJKLMNOP**QRT**U
WXYZ
**6** ABCDEGHK(N 7km)OV

💬 Friendly beach campsite, located in a quiet and historically important area. Various cycling and hiking trails. Fishing and canoeing possible.

🚗 From E45 motorway exit 73 dir. Sønderborg. Follow route 8 to Nybol then towards Broager to 1st traffic lights left. After traffic lights in Broager 1st right dir. Skelde. After 3.5 km straight ahead in Dynt. From there signposted.

481　41　**Sønderborg**
8
Glücksburg　CC
(Ostsee)

CC €⑱ 1/1-30/6　16/8-27/8　29/8-31/12 　📐 N 54°52'04'' E 09°44'39''

---

## Ebeltoft, DK-8400

🛜 **64**

⛺ Blushøj Camping - Ebeltoft***
🏠 Elsegårdevej 55
☎ +45 86 34 12 38
🗓 29/3 - 15/9
@ info@blushoj.com

6,5ha 270T 10A CEE

**1** BCD**G**IJLPQ
**2** EJKORSWXY
**3** B**F**GHJK**Q**RU**W**Y
**4** (C+H 1/6-15/8) J(Q+S 🖳)
**5** **AB**DEFGJLNP**R**UWZ
**6** CEG**I**K(N 5km)OV

💬 You are warmly welcome at this lovely family campsite close to the charming and attractive village of Ebeltoft with views over the Kattegat. Peace, countryside, fresh sea air. Spacious pitches with plenty of privacy. The reception can give you information (also in English and German) about the many walking and cycling routes. Opportunity for golf in the neighbourhood.

🚗 Drive from Ebeltoft to Elsegårde (4 m). Left towards the site at the junction by the pond.

21
Syddjurs　Ebeltoft
CC

CC €⑳ 29/3-29/5　10/6-30/6　18/8-14/9 　📐 N 56°10'04'' E 10°43'49''

---

## Ebeltoft/Krakær, DK-8400

🛜 iD **65**

⛺ Krakær Camping***
🏠 Gl. Kærvej 18
☎ +45 86 36 21 18
🗓 1/4 - 20/10
@ info@krakaer.dk

8ha 227T(70-130m²) 10-16A CEE

**1** ACD**G**IJKLMOPQ
**2** BJRSVWX
**3** B**F**GHJN**OPQ**RU
**4** (C 1/6-31/8) (H 1/6-30/9)
(Q+S 🖳) (T+X 25/6-4/8)
**5** **AB**DEFGIJKLMNOP**QR**UWZ
**6** CEG**IK**M(N 8km)ORV

💬 Krakær is a pearl in one of Denmark's loveliest areas of natural beauty. The terraced campsite with its marked out pitches is located in a hilly wooded area with natural protection from the wind. Restaurant open at weekends in low season. Lovely walking and cycling trips from the campsite.

🚗 Via road 15 and 21 direction Ebeltoft. About 8 km before you reach Ebeltoft turn right direction Krakær. The campsite is signposted. For SatNav, use address: Gammell Kærvej 18.

Rønde　15
CC
21
Syddjurs　Ebeltoft

CC €⑳ 1/4-29/6　18/8-19/10 　📐 N 56°15'08'' E 10°36'09''

## Ejstrup Strand/Brovst, DK-9460 ♟♟ ♿ 🛜 iD 66

🔼 Tranum Klit Camping***
🏠 Sandmosevej 525
☎ +45 98 23 52 82
🔄 30/3 - 5/10
@ info@tranumklitcamping.dk

32ha 230T(100-200m²) 10A CEE

**1** ACDGIJKLMOPQ
**2** ABKRVWXY
**3** ABFHJKNQU
**4** (A+Q+S+V 🅾)
**5** ABCDEFGIJKLMNOPQRU
WZ
**6** CDEGJ(N 5km)OTU

💬 Picturesque campsite in the countryside with beautiful pitches. A real forest campsite yet still close to the sea.

🚗 From route 11, by Brovst via Tranum to Tranum Klit or from Fjerritslev via Slettestrand and Fosdalen.

Pandrup
Fjerritslev — 11

CC €18  30/3-30/6  1/8-15/8  1/9-5/10  7=6, 14=11   🧭 N 57°10'15'' E 09°27'48''

---

## Esbjerg V., DK-6710 ♟♟ ♿ 🛜 iD 67

🔼 EsbjergCamping.dk***
🏠 Gudenåvej 20
☎ +45 75 15 88 22
🔄 1/1 - 31/12
@ info@esbjergcamping.dk

7ha 240T(100m²) 13-16A CEE

**1** ACGIJKLPQ
**2** ACEGRVWXY
**3** BDJNRUY
**4** (C+H 1/6-1/9) JK
(Q 15/3-1/10) (R 1/4-1/10)
(T 1/7-13/8)
**5** ABDEFGIJKLMNOPRSUW
**6** CDEGHK(N 3km)OTV

💬 A friendly family campsite with spacious pitches and modern toilet facilities. A ten minute drive from the beach and the centre of Esbjerg. A fine location for walking and cycling enthusiasts. Golf course close by. Esbjerg offers lively shopping streets and an art and fishing museum. Esbjerg is certainly worth a visit!

🚗 Follow coast road 447 Esbjerg-Hjerting. Signs to the site appear at the end of Saedding village.

463
12  11
Sønderris
CC  E20  191
447
Esbjerg
24
Fanø

CC €20  1/1-30/6  19/8-31/12   🧭 N 55°30'47'' E 08°23'22''

---

## Farsø, DK-9640 ♿ 🛜 iD 68

🔼 Ertebølle Strand Camping***
🏠 Ertebøllevej 42
☎ +45 98 63 63 75
🔄 30/3 - 20/10
@ escamp@escamp.dk

3,5ha 100T(80-150m²) 10A

**1** ACDGIJKLMPQ
**2** AENRSTVWX
**3** BDGHJNRUY
**4** (C+H 25/5-1/9) (Q+S+X 🅾)
**5** ABDEFGIJKLOPQRUWXZ
**6** CEGHK(N 3km)OUV

💬 Lovely family campsite with natural, sheltered pitches in the nearby nature reserve and beautiful Lim Fjord. Walking and cycling opportunities. Free solar heated swimming pool. Ideal base for trips out. Separate field for tents. Catering facilities for groups up to 150 people. Welcoming restaurant.

🚗 The campsite in Ertebølle is signposted on route 533, 46 km north of Viborg.

Trend
Eskov  CC  187
533  Farsø
Durup

CC €18  30/3-18/4  22/4-8/6  18/8-20/10   🧭 N 56°48'44'' E 09°10'54''

## Farsø, DK-9640

👫 ♿ 🚻 📶 **iD** (69)

🏕 Farsø Fjord Camping***
📧 Gl. Viborgvej 13
☎ +45 98 63 61 76
🔓 15/3 - 1/10
@ info@farso-fjordcamping.dk

5ha 200T(80-120m²) 16A

**1** ACDGIJKLMOPQ
**2** ACEGKNRSVWX
**3** BFIJNQUWY
**4** (C 1/6-31/8) (H 🔓) IJ
(Q+S+T+U+Z 10/7-31/7)
**5** ABCDFGIJKLMNOPRUWZ
**6** CEGHK(N 8km)OV

NEW

💬 A quiet family campsite in a natural area 100 metres from the Limfjord. Solar heated swimming pool, fishing, minigolf and dog exercise area (2 hectares) on the campsite. Cycling and walking opportunities. Free wifi.

🚐 Campsite located on route 533 Viborg-Løgstør, 40 km north of Viborg in Stistrup. Campsite signposted.

Trend
Eskov · 187 · Farsø
CC
591 · 561
Jebjerg · 533

CC € 18  15/3-30/6  12/8-25/8  1/9-1/10        🗺 N 56°45'28''  E 09°14'36''

---

## Fredericia, DK-7000

♿ 📶 **iD** (70)

🏕 Dancamps Trelde Næs***
📧 Trelde Næsvej 297
☎ +45 75 95 71 83
🔓 12/4 - 20/10
@ info@dancamps.dk

10ha 480T 10A CEE

**1** ACDFIJKLMOPQ
**2** ABEGRVX
**3** BHKNQRUWY
**4** (B+G 14/5-27/9) IJKLN
(Q+S 🔓) (T+U 1/7-31/8)
(W 🔓) (X 1/7-31/8) (Z 🔓)
**5** ABFGIJKLMNOPQRUWXY
**6** ACEGHK(N 4km)OSTV

💬 Large campsite, no shade, beautifully located on the coast.

🚐 Route 28 (Vejle-Fredericia). From Vejle take Egeskov exit, then Trelde and Trelde-Næs. From Fredericia to Trelde, then Trelde Næs.

23
28 · CC
**Fredericia**
Strib

CC € 20  12/4-28/5  2/6-5/6  10/6-5/7  23/8-20/10  7=6, 14=11    🗺 N 55°37'30''  E 09°50'00''

---

## Frederikshavn, DK-9900

♿ 📶 **iD** (71)

🏕 Nordstrand Camping A/S****
📧 Apholmenvej 40
☎ +45 98 42 93 50
🔓 12/4 - 20/10
@ info@nordstrand-camping.dk

10ha 400T(100-150m²) 10-16A CEE

**1** ACDGIJKLMOPQ
**2** AEGLRSVWXY
**3** ABCFHJNQRUWY
**4** (F+H 🔓) (Q 1/7-5/8) (R 🔓)
**5** ABCDEFGHIJKLMNOPQRU
WXYZ
**6** CDEGJK(N 0,4km)OTUV

NEW

💬 A beautiful large campsite with many amenities and an indoor swimming pool. In the city of Frederikshavn, near the ferry to Norway and Sweden.

🚐 The campsite is on the northern edge of the town Frederikshavn, and is signposted from route 40 direction Skagen.

40
35 · CC
**Frederikshavn**
585 · E45
E45

CC € 20  12/4-27/5  1/6-5/6  9/6-29/6  18/8-20/10        🗺 N 57°27'51''  E 10°31'40''

**Frørup**, DK-5871

🏕 Kongshøj Strandcamping\*\*\*
✉ Kongshøjvej 5
☎ +45 65 37 12 88
📅 1/1 - 31/12
@ info@kongshojcamping.dk

6ha 120T(80-150m²) 16A CEE

**1** ACD**G**IJKLMOPQ
**2** AELORVWXY
**3** BD**F**GNQRU**W**Y
**4** (Q+R 1/4-1/10)
**5** **AB**DEFGIJKLMNO**PQR**UW
**6** CDEGHK(N 9km)OTUV

🔲 🛜 📱 **72**

💬 A peaceful family campsite, child-friendly, close to the beach with clean water (blue flag). Also suitable for taking walks along the pebble and sandy beach and in the woods. Please call the campsite in advance in low season.

🚗 Route 163 Nyborg-Svendborg, take second exit to Tårup after about 11 km and follow Kongshøj-Strand camping signs.

315 — Nyborg
8
301
Gislev 163 ℂℂ
Lohals

ℂℂ € **18**  1/1-30/6  1/9-31/12     🧭 N 55°13'18'' E 10°48'22''

---

**Grenå**, DK-8500

🏕 Grenå Strand Camping\*\*\*\*
✉ Fuglsangvej 58
☎ +45 86 32 17 18
📅 29/3 - 8/9
@ info@722.dk

22ha 579T(140-280m²) 10A

**1** CD**G**IJL**P**Q
**2** ABEGRSVX
**3** B**F**GHJNQRU**W**Y
**4** (C+H 15/5-15/8) J**KN**
   (Q+V 23/6-26/8)
**5** **AB**DEFGJLN**P**RUWXYZ
**6** CEG**IK**(N 4km)OTUV

📱 🛜 **73**

 NEW

💬 Spacious campsite with sunny and shady pitches with lots of play areas for children. Possible to go sea fishing. Many attractions nearby, on the beach and sea. A lovely heated swimming pool.

🚗 In Grenå direction harbour. The campsite is signposted south of the harbour.

547
16
**Grenaa**
ℂℂ
15

ℂℂ € **20**  29/3-30/6  18/8-8/9     🧭 N 56°23'22'' E 10°54'44''

---

**Hampen**, DK-7362

🏕 Dancamps Hampen\*\*\*
✉ Hovedgaden 31B
☎ +45 75 77 52 55
📅 1/5 - 1/9
@ info@dancamps.dk

10ha 180T(100-150m²) 10A CEE

**1** ACD**G**IJKLMOPQ
**2** GRSWX
**3** AGHJNU
**4** (Q+S+X 📅)
**5** **AB**DEFGIJKLMNOPRUW
**6** CEG**K**OV

👨‍👧 🔲 🛜 📱 **74**

💬 A peaceful campsite among woods and lakes. Walking and cycling routes on ancient roads pass by the grounds. Large pitches and a relaxing ambiance. Supermarket on the site. Enjoy natural activities such as a fishing trip or explore the heathland. Good base for visiting Legoland, Givskud Zoo safari park and the Aqua centrum in Silkeborg.

🚗 From Vejle route 13 till 7 km north of Nørre Snede, then left to Hampen St. Another 2 km to campsite.

52
13
439 — Ejstrupholm — 453
411
176    Nørre Snede
185

ℂℂ € **14**  1/5-1/7  18/8-1/9  7=5, 14=9     🧭 N 56°00'53'' E 09°21'53''

## Hesselager, DK-5874

⌂ Bøsøre Strand Feriepark★★★★★
✉ Bøsørevej 16
☎ +45 62 25 11 45
🕐 12/4 - 20/10
@ info@bosore.dk

♿ 📶 iD  **75**

23,6ha 275T(100-150m²) 10A CEE

**1** ACD**G**IJKLMOPQ
**2** AEGLORVWXY
**3** BCD**FG**JKN**OPQ**RU**W**Y
**4** (F+H 🕐) I**K**M**NP**
(Q+S+T+U+Y+Z 🕐)
**5** **AB**CDEFGIJKLMNO**PQ**R**ST**
UWXYZ
**6** CDEGH**K**(N 7km)OSTV

💬 Bøsøre Strand Feriepark is located between the woods and the sea in the fairytale countryside of Fyn. The site is set around a beautiful Manor House and accompanying farm buildings which are 200 years old.

🚗 E20, exit 45 to route 163 Nyborg-Svendborg. Take Vormark/Bøsøre exit at Langå and follow Bøsøre campsite signs.

301
8
163 CC
Lundeborg    Lohals

CC € ⑱  1/5-29/5  3/6-7/6  11/6-30/6  18/8-20/10    🏔 N 55°11'36'' E 10°48'23''

---

## Hjørring, DK-9800

⌂ City Camping Hjørring
✉ Idræts Alle 45
☎ +45 60 18 02 60
🕐 31/3 - 28/9
@ info@citycamping-hjoerring.dk

👫 📶 iD  **76**

NEW

4ha 135T(60-100m²) 10-16A

**1** ACD**G**IJKLMOPQ
**2** FGLRSVWXY
**3** BC**EF**GJKN**Q**RU
**4** (B 🕐) (G 1/6-28/9)
(Q+R 15/6-12/8)
**5** **AB**CFGIJKLMNO**PQ**RUWZ
**6** BCEG**K**(N 1km)OTV

💬 A quiet campsite near the town of Hjørring located in the woods. The campsite has a beautiful swimming pool and is suitable for use as a stopover campsite en route to the ferry to Norway and Iceland.

🚗 Coming from south, take E39 exit 3. Follow Hjørring campsite signs.

Harrerenden E39
Sindal
CC 35
Hjørring
55
190   553

CC € ⑳  31/3-29/6  18/8-28/9    🏔 N 57°27'59'' E 10°00'06''

---

## Holbæk, DK-4300

⌂ CampOne Holbaek Fjord★★★
✉ Sofiesminde Allé 1
☎ +45 63 60 63 63
🕐 13/4 - 20/10
@ holbaek@campone.dk

♿ 📶 ✿ iD  **77**

5ha 225T(80-120m²) 10-16A CEE

**1** AC**G**IJKLMQ
**2** EFGIKLRWX
**3** B**F**HJKNRUVWY
**4** (E+H 1/5-1/10) KN(Q+R 🕐)
**5** **AB**DFGIJKLMNOPQRUWZ
**6** CEGH**K**(N 1km)OV

💬 Sunny family campsite on the sea with sloping grounds. Among other things it has a playground, wellness centre and indoor pool. Fresh bread every day, free wifi, and walking and cycling routes. Near to Copenhagen.

🚗 Route 21 exit 15 coming from Copenhagen, direction Holbæk at the roundabout (10 km). Turn right as you enter Holbæk. Follow signs.

21    Skibby
53
155  **Holbæk** CC  Åhuse
23   57

CC € ⑳  13/4-30/6  18/8-20/10    🏔 N 55°43'05'' E 11°45'40''

## Hvide Sande, DK-6960

🔼 Dancamps Holmsland***
✉ Tingodden 141
☎ +45 75 52 14 82
🔓 17/4 - 15/9
@ info@dancamps.dk

♿ 🛜 ✿ iD 78

2,5ha 92T(15-105m²) 8A

**1** ACDG**IJKLMP**Q
**2** AEGKRSVW
**3** BJRU**W**Y
**4** (Q+R 🔲)
**5** **AB**DFGIJKLOP**R**UW
**6** CDEGK(N 4km)OV

💬 A small but friendly campsite right among a beautiful dune landscape on the west coast of Jutland. Surrounded by dunes you will find peace and quiet here. An ideal area for a relaxing holiday. Stroll along the wide white beaches together or go for a bike ride. The national cycle route, Nr. 1, the West coast route, passes the campsite.

🚗 Via the 181 coast road, about 3 km south of Hvide Sande, left onto 'Søholmvej'. Campsite at the end of this road.

Hvide Sande

ⒸⒸ

181

Bjerregård

ⒸⒸ €⑱ 17/4-28/5 2/6-6/6 10/6-5/7 23/8-15/9 7=6, 14=11   📍 N 55°57'45'' E 08°08'31''

---

## Hvide Sande, DK-6960

🔼 Dancamps Nordsø***
✉ Tingodden 3, Årgab
☎ +45 96 59 17 22
🔓 12/4 - 27/10
@ info@nordsoe-camping.dk

♿ 🛜 iD 79

12,5ha 299T(40-100m²) 10A CEE

**1** ACD**G**IJKLMPQ
**2** AEGRSTVW
**3** BF**H**JNQRU**W**Y
**4** (F+H 🔲) J**KLN**
   (Q+R+T+U 🔲)
   (W+Y 1/7-1/9)
**5** **AB**DEFGIJKOPR**S**UWXYZ
**6** ACDEGHKL(N 6km)OSV

💬 Dancamps Nordsø is located in the middle of the rugged countryside on the west coast of Jutland. It is a couple of kilometres from the Hvide Sande harbour town. The site is separated from the sea by a line of dunes. Lovely views from the dunes across the Ringkøbing Fjord and the North Sea. Indoor pool with slide, sauna and Turkish bath.

🚗 From Kolding to Esbjerg and then via Varde and coast road 181, north towards Hvide Sande. Look out for swimming pool with green slide on the left at Hourvig.

Hvide Sande

ⒸⒸ

181

Bjerregård

ⒸⒸ €⑳ 12/4-28/5 2/6-5/6 10/6-5/7 23/8-27/10 7=6, 14=11   📍 N 55°56'58'' E 08°09'01''

---

## Kalundborg/Saltbæk, DK-4400

🔼 Kalundborg Camping**
✉ Saltbækvej 88
☎ +45 93 88 79 00
🔓 1/1 - 31/12
@ info@kalundborg-camping.dk

🛜 iD 80

3,5ha 100T(120-180m²) 10-16A CEE

**1** ACDGIJKLMPQ
**2** BLORSTWXY
**3** BGHJNQR
**4** (Q+R 1/4-1/10)
**5** **AB**DFGIJKLMN**P**UW
**6** EGH**K**(N 6km)OT

💬 An attractive campsite with spacious pitches spread over fields, a lovely playground with a bouncy castle for the children. The site is about 1500m from the sea and a blue flag beach. Be sure to call in winter to see if anyone is there.

🚗 At Kalundborg first roundabout, follow campsite sing posts to Saltæk, circa 5 km.

**Kalundborg**

ⒸⒸ

155
23
22

ⒸⒸ €⑳ 1/1-7/7 25/8-31/12   📍 N 55°43'43'' E 11°06'42''

## Kolding, DK-6000 ♿ 📶 ⑧①

🏕 Dancamps Kolding***
📧 Vonsildvej 19
☎ +45 75 52 13 88
📅 1/1 - 31/12
@ info@dancamps.dk

11ha 125T(80-100m²) 10A

**1** CD**F**IJKLMOPQ
**2** FGLRX
**3** B**F**HIJM**T**U
**5** **AB**DEFGIJKLMNO**PRS**UW
**6** CFG**K**M(N 0,5km)OQRTV

💬 Stopover campsite. Good starting point for trips to the beautiful city of Kolding and to Legoland. Location in the suburbs with companies and industries.

🚗 Located on road 170, 3 km south of Kolding. Via E45 motorway, exit 65 Kolding-Syd.

CC €⑱ 1/1-6/6  10/6-5/7  23/8-31/12  7=6    🗺 N 55°27'48'' E 09°28'24''

---

## Lisbjerg/Århus-N, DK-8200 📶 iD ⑧②

🏕 Aarhus Camping***
📧 Randersvej 400
☎ +45 86 23 11 33
📅 1/1 - 31/12
@ info@aarhuscamping.dk

6,9ha 200T(80-150m²) 16A CEE

**1** ACD**G**IJLMNOPQ
**2** BFGRSWXY
**3** **A**FQRU
**4** (C+H 15/6-15/8) K
   (Q+S+T+U+X+Z 📅)
**5** **AB**EFGJLP**R**UZ
**6** CDEG**IK**(N 4km)OV

💬 The site has all the information for visiting Århus, Denmark's second city with its museums and parks. You can relax in the jacuzzi near the refurbished pool from mid-June to mid-August. Plenty of greenery at the well-equipped site with spacious level pitches. English spoken at reception. Daily menu with Danish specialities in the new restaurant.

🚗 From north: E45, exit 46 Århus N. Blue sign Lisbjerg, follow road 180 another 2.8 km. From south: E45, exit 44. Road 180.

CC €⑳ 1/1-6/6  11/6-29/6  19/8-31/12    🗺 N 56°13'36'' E 10°09'49''

---

## Løgstrup, DK-8831 ♿ 📶 iD ⑧③

🏕 Hjarbæk Fjord Camping***
📧 Hulager 2
☎ +45 22 13 15 00
📅 1/1 - 31/12
@ info@hjarbaek.dk

10ha 150T(100-120m²) 10-13A CEE

**1** ACD**G**IJKLMOPQ
**2** AEGJKLNRSVWX
**3** BCDGHJN**Q**RU**W**Y
**4** (B+G 15/6-15/8)
   (Q 31/3-24/9) (R 📅)
   (U 31/3-24/9)
**5** **AB**DFGIJKLMNOPRUWZ
**6** ACEGH**K**(N 4km)OUV

💬 A peaceful, well maintained campsite in a beautiful, varied landscape with views of the Limfjord. Partly terraced site. Large pitches. Dog exercise area. Lovely playground, open air swimming pool. Good cycling opportunities. Winter camping from 24 September to 4 April (reserve in advance).

🚗 From Viborg take route 26 in the direction of Skive. Take exit Løgstrup/Hjarbæk and then follow the signs to the campsite.

CC €⑱ 1/1-29/5  10/6-7/7  25/8-31/12    🗺 N 56°32'03'' E 09°19'53''

## Løkken, DK-9480 — 84

▲ Camping Rolighed\*\*\*
✉ Grønhøj Strandvej 35
☎ +45 98 88 30 36
🗓 1/1 - 31/12
@ info@camping-rolighed.dk

♿ 🛜 iD

2,8ha 310T(100-250m²) 13-16A CEE

**1** ACD**G**IJKLMOPQ
**2** AIKLRSVWXY
**3** ABCD**F**HIJNRU**W**
**4** (C+H 31/5-31/8)
(Q+S 1/4-20/10)
(U+Y 29/6-15/8)
**5** **AB**DEFGIJKLMNO**PQ**RUWX
**6** CDEGHKL(N 6km)OTUV

💬 This well-serviced family site is located within walking distance of Grønhøj beach, close to main route 55 and about 6 km south of Løkken. There are open and sheltered pitches. There is also a lovely heated swimming pool, a covered terrace and a minigolf court. Good opportunities for cycling and walking. Place for your horse by pitch possible on special part of campsite.

🚗 From the main route 55, 6 km south of Løkken to Grønhøj beach. Campsite 800 metres on the left.

55 · Saltum Strand CC · Pandrup · 559 · 585

CC €18 1/1-7/7 24/8-31/12 7=6, 14=11    🧭 N 57°19'04'' E 09°41'44''

---

## Løkken, DK-9480 — 85

▲ Løkken By Camping
✉ Søndergade 69
☎ +45 98 99 17 67
🗓 1/1 - 31/12
@ info@loekkenbycamping.dk

♿ 🛜 iD

4,2ha 150T(80-100m²) 13A

**1** ACD**G**IJKLMPQ
**2** AEGKRWXY
**3** ABF**H**JK**Q**U**W**Y
**4** (Q+R+T 21/4-20/10)
**5** **AB**CDEFGIJKLMNOP**Q**RU WZ
**6** CEGJ**K**(N 0,1km)OTV

💬 Small campsite near the centre of Løkken (400m) and the beach (400m). Lots of fixed pitches. Løkken, with it's beach, shops and restaurants, is a great place to be.

🚗 Take road 55 from Aalborg to Løkken. Campsite is signposted.

Løkken · CC · 55 · Saltum Strand

CC €20 1/1-29/6 18/8-31/12 7=6, 14=11    🧭 N 57°21'52'' E 09°42'34''

---

## Løkken/Ingstrup, DK-9480 — 86

▲ Grønhøj Strand Camping\*\*\*
✉ Kettrupvej 125
☎ +45 98 88 44 33
🗓 12/4 - 22/9
@ info@gronhoj-strand-camping.dk

♿ 🛜 iD

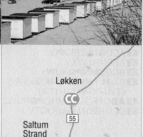

14ha 500T(100-150m²) 13A

**1** ACDGIJKLMOPQ
**2** ABLRSVWXY
**3** ABD**FGM**NP**Q**RTU
**4** **N**(Q+R+S 🗓)
**5** **AB**CDEFGHIJKLMNO**PQ**RU WXYZ
**6** ACDEGHK(N 1km)OTV

💬 Large campsite, surrounded by forest and 700 metres from the beach. Good sheltered pitches. Beautiful, wide, child-friendly sandy beach. Free wifi. Motorcyclists are welcome. Pony riding is free. There is a large fenced playground for children with a very large bouncy castle. Also ideal for guests with tents.

🚗 From the main road 55, 6 km south of Løkken to Grønhøjstrand. 2nd campsite on the left after about 2 km.

55 · Saltum CC Strand · Pandrup · 559

CC €18 12/4-29/6 18/8-21/9 7=6    🧭 N 57°19'15'' E 09°40'38''

## Malling, DK-8340

▲ CampOne Ajstrup Strand camping\*\*\*
🏠 Ajstrup Strandvej 81
☎ +45 63 60 63 64
🔑 13/4 - 20/10
@ ajstrup@campone.dk

9,2ha 380T(60-150m²) 6A CEE

**1** CDG**G**IJKLMO**P**Q
**2** AEGORSVWXY
**3** BFHJQUW**Y**
**4** (Q+R 🔑)
**5** **AB**DEFGIJLMN**P**QRUZ
**6** ACEG**K**M(N 4km)OTV

💬 Luxury campsite directly on clean sea (blue flag) with sandy beach. Attractive and extensive toilet facilities. In 2018 large new children's playground. Good cycle paths from the campsite. Visit Aarhuus, Denmark's second city with a lot of culture.

🚗 Leave route 451 between Odder and Århus at the exit to Malling. In Malling follow the signs in the direction of Ajstrup (beach) and campsite.

CC €**20**  13/4-29/6  18/8-20/10        N 56°02'29'' E 10°15'52''

---

## Middelfart, DK-5500

▲ Vejlby Fed Strand Camping\*\*\*\*
🏠 Rigelvej 1
☎ +45 64 40 24 20
🔑 5/4 - 7/9
@ mail@vejlbyfed.dk

55,7ha 259T(100-140m²) 10A CEE

**1** ACD**G**IJKLMO**P**Q
**2** AEFMRSWXY
**3** BCGK**MN**PQRUW**Y**
**4** (C+**H** 13/5-31/8) **N**(Q+S 🔑)
   (T+U+V+W 5/4-17/8)
**5** **AB**DEFGIJKLMNO**PQ**RUWZ
**6** DEGH**I**K(N 5km)OQTV

💬 On the island of Funen. A quiet, friendly campsite with extensive amenities close to the beach and the 'Lillebæltsbroen'(Little Belt Bridge) with opportunities for fishing.

🚗 E20 exit 58 towards route 317 Bogense (Drive 3/4 around the 1st roundabout, at 2nd roundabout go straight ahead). Campsite signposted from Bogensevej.

CC €**18**  5/4-29/5  1/6-7/6  10/6-1/7  20/8-7/9        N 55°31'11'' E 09°51'00''

---

## Nordborg/Augustenhof, DK-6430

▲ Augustenhof Strand Camping\*\*\*
🏠 Augustenhofvej 30
☎ +45 74 45 03 04
🔑 1/1 - 31/12
@ mail@augustenhof-camping.dk

4ha 252T(100-120m²) 16A CEE

**1** ACD**G**IJKLMO**P**Q
**2** AEGKLORTVWX
**3** BFHJNQUW**Y**
**4** (Q+S+T+U+Z 🔑)
**5** **AB**DEFGIJKLMNO**PQR**UWZ
**6** ACEGHKM(N 4km)O

💬 Quiet (sandy) beach campsite with private access from the site to the sea. Panoramic views of the Little Belt fjord. Very child friendly with clean, well-maintained toilet facilities. Beautiful marked-out hiking and cycling routes. Campsite received blue flag in 2014.

🚗 Left on road Sønderborg-Fynshav, direction Nordborg. Then continue in direction Købingsmark and Augustenhof.

CC €**18**  1/1-30/6  1/9-31/12        N 55°04'38'' E 09°42'53''

## Nymindegab/Nørre Nebel, DK-6830

♿ 📶 **iD** **90**

🏔 Nymindegab Familie Camping\*\*\*
✉ Lyngtoften 12
☎ +45 75 28 91 83
🗓 28/3 - 20/10
@ info@nycamp.dk

11,5ha 325T(100-150m²) 16A CEE

**1** ACG**H**IJKLMOPQ
**2** ABGIJKLRSVWXY
**3** BD**F**GHJKN**O**Q**RUW**
**4** (A 🗓) (C+H 4/5-6/9) IJKN
　(Q+S+T+U+W 🗓)
**5** **AB**DEFGIJKLMNOP**Q**RUWX
　Y
**6** ACEGH**K**LM(N 0,1km)OTV

💬 Peaceful family campsite, sloping grounds with terraces and shaded pitches. The new swimming pool, heated to 25°C has a 22 metre slide and whirlpool. The campsite is located on the Ringkøbing fjord and the North Sea. Amber can be found on the beach. Lovely fishing, surfing, cycling and walking area.
🚗 Direction Varde from the south. Follow the 181 as far as Nørre Nebel, then direction Nymindegab. Campsite signposted.

Bjerregård
Nymindegab 423
CC
Henne
Strand 181

CC € 20 28/3-28/5 2/6-6/6 10/6-27/6 25/8-20/10 16=14 　　📡 N 55°49'00'' E 08°12'02''

---

## Ortved/Ringsted, DK-4100

♿ 📶 **iD** **91**

🏔 Skovly Camping\*\*\*
✉ Nebs Møllevej 65
☎ +45 57 52 82 61
🗓 1/1 - 31/12
@ info@skovlycamping.dk

5,7ha 174T(80-120m²) 13A CEE

**1** ABC**G**IJKLPQ
**2** BCDFGIRVWXY
**3** ABF**G**J**Q**UW
**4** (**B+G** 15/6-1/9)
　(Q 1/4-30/9) (R 🗓)
**5** **AB**DEFGIJKLMNO**P**QUW
**6** CEGH**K**(N 7km)OTV

💬 A well maintained family campsite with a swimming pool and playground, located in an extensive wood. An ideal place to relax.

🚗 6 km from motorway E20 to Copenhagen. Route 14 Ringsted-Roskilde. In Ortved follow campsite sign posts to the left.

Hvalsø
255　　Viby
14
215　CC　Bjæverskov
Ringsted E20
150　269

CC € 20 1/4-29/5 2/6-7/6 10/6-7/7 24/8-30/9 　　📡 N 55°29'48'' E 11°51'28''

---

## Østbirk, DK-8752

♿ 📶 **92**

🏔 Elite Camp Vestbirk\*\*\*
✉ Møllehøjvej 4
☎ +45 75 78 12 92
🗓 1/1 - 31/12
@ vestbirk@vestbirk.dk

15ha 170T(90-130m²) 10-16A

**1** BCD**G**IJKLMOPQ
**2** CDRVWXY
**3** BCDGKN**Q**RU**W**Z
**4** (C+H 30/5-1/9) J**K**N
　(Q 29/6-11/8) (S 🗓)
　(T+U 29/6-18/8)
**5** **AB**DEFGIJKLMNOP**Q**RUW
**6** CDEGH**K**(N 5km)OTUV

💬 Elite Camp Vestbirk offers a family holiday with opportunities for everyone. The location right between the Vestbirk Lakes offers the possibility of beautiful walks and relaxation by the water. Good opportunities for fishing and canoeing. CampingCard ACSI holders: for stays before 13/4 and after 29/9 contact site first.

🚗 Exit 59 on the E45 at Vejle, route 13 towards Nørre Snede. After ±10 km route 409 direction Skanderborg. Site signposted 1 km before Vestbirk.

461　**Skanderborg**
453
170
52　CC　E45
409
185　433
**Horsens**

CC € 20 1/1-27/6 18/8-31/12 　　📡 N 55°57'50'' E 09°41'59''

## Otterup, DK-5450 ♿ 📶 iD 93

🔺 Hasmark Strand Camping***
📧 Strandvejen 205
☎ +45 64 82 62 06
🔁 29/3 - 22/9
@ info@hasmark.dk

12ha 500T(100-150m²) 10A CEE

**1** ACD**G**IJKLMOPQ
**2** AERVWX
**3** BGHJKN**Q**RUV**W**Y
**4** (**C** 29/6-11/8) (**F** 🔁) **IKLNP**
(Q+S 🔁) (T 29/6-11/8)
(Y+Z 🔁)
**5** **AB**DEFGIJKLMNOPQ**RST**U
WXYZ
**6** CDEGH**K**M(N 7km)OSTV

💬 Next to the most beautiful beach in Funen.
The site has a lovely leisure pool and an exclusive
wellness area with spa, sauna and solarium. There is
a varied activity programme for young and old and an
authentic Viking playground for the children. The site
also has a restaurant, pizzeria and supermarket.

🚗 Take direction Hasmark at the traffic lights in
Otterup; continue to end of the road 300 metres
before the beach. Campsite on the right side of the
road.

Hasmark
Strand CC

327
162    Munkebo

CC €18 12/4-29/5  10/6-29/6  11/8-25/8  1/9-22/9    📐 N 55°33'45'' E 10°27'16''

## Rebild/Skørping, DK-9520 📶 iD 94

🔺 Rebild Camping Safari***
📧 Rebildvej 17
☎ +45 29 13 11 72
🔁 1/1 - 31/12
@ info@safari-camping.dk

6ha 235T(80-120m²) 10-16A CEE

**1** ACDGIJKLMOPQ
**2** BFGRVWX
**3** AB**F**HJN**Q**U
**4** (Q 1/6-31/8) (S 🔁)
**5** **AB**DFGIJKLMNO**PR**UWZ
**6** ACDEGK(N 2,5km)OV

💬 Large and quiet campsite in the centre of the
magnificent scenic area 'Rebild-Bakker'. Lots of
opportunity for hiking and biking. Open all season,
winter sports possible in winter.

🚗 E45, exit 33 via route 535 dir. Rold to route
180 direction Aalborg or E45, exit 31 via route 519
towards Skørping, then via route 180 towards Hobro.
On the 180 take the Skørping/Rebild exit. Campsite
signposted.

507
Rebild   Skørping
E45     CC
13
Arden
180    535    519

CC €20 1/1-14/6  18/8-31/12    📐 N 56°49'57'' E 09°50'46''

## Ribe, DK-6760 ♿ 📶 iD 95

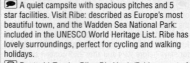

🔺 Ribe Camping***
📧 Farupvej 2
☎ +45 75 41 07 77
🔁 1/1 - 31/12
@ info@ribecamping.dk

9ha 485T(100-200m²) 10-16A

**1** ACD**G**IJKLMOPQ
**2** BRSUVWXY
**3** BD**F**HIJNRU
**4** (C+H 1/6-31/8) J(Q+R 🔁)
(T 1/7-15/8)
**5** **AB**DEFGIJKLMNO**PQRS**U
WXYZ
**6** ACDEGH**K**(N 1km)OSTUV

💬 A quiet campsite with spacious pitches and 5
star facilities. Visit Ribe: described as Europe's most
beautiful town, and the Wadden Sea National Park:
included in the UNESCO World Heritage List. Ribe has
lovely surroundings, perfect for cycling and walking
holidays.

🚗 Route 11 Tønder-Ribe. Dir. Varde/Esbjerg west of
the town Ribe, until campsite is signposted. Turn right
from the north of the town. From the south stay on
route 11 Ribe Nord. Left at 1st traffic light.

425
32
437
Ribe
Vester        24
Vedsted    179
11

CC €20 1/1-11/4  22/4-15/5  19/5-28/5  10/6-30/6  2/9-20/12  7=6, 14=12    📐 N 55°20'27'' E 08°46'00''

## Ringkøbing, DK-6950

🏕 Ringkøbing Camping***
✉ Herningvej 105
☎ +45 97 32 04 20
🔓 29/3 - 29/9
@ info@ringkobingcamping.dk

♿ 📶 [iD] **96**

7,5ha 110T(36-140m²) 10A CEE

**1** **AG**HIJKLMOPQ
**2** BRSTVWXY
**3** ABF**G**HJN**QRUW**
**4** (Q 1/7-31/8) (R 🔓)
**5** **AB**DFGIJK**L**MNO**P**RUWZ
**6** CEGHJ(N 5km)ORUV

💬 This quiet campsite has large sunny pitches with shade. With excellent shelter from the wind. Many walking, cycling and walking possibilities from the campsite. Danish / German / English and Dutch spoken. Upon arrival between 11.00 - 15.00 hours please call number: +45-97320420.

🚗 You will find the campsite on route 15, 4 km from Ringkøbing, direction Herning, on the left hand side of the road.

**Ringkøbing-Skjern** CC

16
15
181
28  11

CC €**18**  29/3-23/6  18/8-28/9

🧭 N 56°05'18'' E 08°19'00''

---

## Rømø, DK-6792

🏕 Kommandørgårdens Camping & Feriepark***
✉ Havnebyvej 201
☎ +45 74 75 51 22
🔓 1/1 - 31/12
@ sale@kommandoergaarden.dk

♿ 📶 **97**

8ha 500T(100m²) 10A

**1** CGIJLPQ
**2** AGKRSVWXY
**3** BF**H**JKN**OPQ**RUV
**4** (**A** 🔓) (C 1/7-31/8)
(**F**+H 🔓) J**KLN**(Q 🔓)
(S+T+U+V 1/7-31/8)
(Y+Z 🔓)
**5** **AB**DFGIJKLMNO**PQ**RUWX
**6** CEGHKOV

💬 Large campsite with good toilet facilities, level pitches and views of the Wadden Sea. Free admission to swimming leisure park and opportunities for cycling, horse riding, adventure programmes, internet cafe, restaurant and brasserie.

🚗 Enter Rømø via the dam (175). Left at first crossroads. Continue to hotel Kommandørgården. Campsite is located on left of road.

11
Lakolk  175
Kongsmark
CC
419
List

CC €**20**  1/1-7/7  24/8-31/12

🧭 N 55°05'55'' E 08°32'35''

---

## Rømø, DK-6792

🏕 Rømø Familiecamping***
✉ Vestervej 13
☎ +45 74 75 51 54
🔓 12/4 - 13/10
@ romo@romocamping.dk

📶 [iD] **98**

10ha 345T(100-120m²) 10A CEE

**1** AC**G**IJLMOPQ
**2** RSVWX
**3** BHNQU**W**
**4** (Q+R 🔓)
**5** **AB**EFGIJKLMNOPRUW
**6** CEGJ(N 4,5km)ORSV

💬 A quiet family campsite. The island of Rømø with its many sights lends itself perfectly to walking and cycle trips. The island is abundant with birds, making it ideal for the enthusiast. There is an unusual 'safari' minigolf on the campsite. Denmark's widest beach is just 3 km (5 mins. by road) and can be reached with your own car or motorhome.

🚗 At Skaerbaek follow the 175 to Rømø. Turn right at first traffic lights in Rømø. Campsite signposted 2.5 km further on.

11
Brøns
CC
175
Sønderstrand
419

CC €**20**  12/4-6/6  11/6-30/6  19/8-13/10  14=11

🧭 N 55°09'46'' E 08°32'51''

## Rønne, DK-3700    ♿ 📶 iD   99

🏔 Galløkken Strand Camping***
🏕 Strandvejen 4
☎ +45 40 13 33 44
🔑 1/5 - 2/9
@ info@gallokken.dk

2,6ha 125T(< 130m²) 13A CEE

**1** ACDGIJKLMOPQ
**2** ABEGLRSTUWXY
**3** ABFHJKRUWY
**4** (Q+R 🅿)
**5** ABDEFGIJKLMNOPQRUW
**6** CFGK(N 1km)QSTV

💬 A spaciously laid out family campsite a short distance from the beach and the town. Wooded surroundings.

🚗 From Rønne harbour turn right and follow coast road for 1 km towards Nexø. Campsite signposted on the road.

Klemensker °
159
Rønne
CC
38

CC €20 1/5-1/7 17/8-31/8    📡 N 55°05'21'' E 14°42'16''

---

## Sakskøbing, DK-4990    ♿ 📶 iD   100

🏔 Sakskøbing Camping***
🏕 Saxes Allé 15
☎ +45 54 70 45 66
🔑 23/3 - 30/9
@ camping@saxsport.dk

2,5ha 71T(80-144m²) 10A CEE

**1** ACDGIJKLMOPQ
**2** FGRVWXY
**3** BFGKMNQUVW
**4** (F 🅿) N(Q+X 🅿)
**5** ABDFGIJKLMNOPQRUW
**6** ACDEGK(N 0,3km)TV

💬 A warm welcome to this small, peaceful campsite, located close to the centre of Sakskøbing and a forest. A short footpath beside the campsite leads to the fjord. A fine stop-over campsite on the route from or to the Puttgarden-Rødby ferry.

🚗 Exit 46 from E47, approx. 25 km from Rødby. Campsite is located near the centre of Sakskøbing and is signposted.

289
E47
9
153
Sundby (Nykøbing Falster)
CC
283
297

CC €20 23/3-14/7 1/9-30/9    📡 N 54°47'54'' E 11°38'28''

---

## Silkeborg, DK-8600    👫 📶 iD   101

🏔 Sejs Bakker Camping***
🏕 Borgdalsvej 15-17
☎ +45 86 84 63 83
🔑 6/4 - 15/9
@ mail@sejs-bakker-camping.dk

4ha 170T(80-100m²) 10A

**1** ACDGIJKLMPQ
**2** GRSXY
**3** ABFGKMNQRU
**4** (Q+R 🅿)
**5** ABFGIJKLMNPRUW
**6** CEGIK(N 1km)OV

💬 A peaceful family campsite surrounded by woods and heathland, 5 km from Silkeborg and 800m from the lakes where the famous 'Hjejlen' river boat sails. It has a lovely playground, is 200m from a tennis court and 2 km from a child-friendly beach.

🚗 At Skanderborg via exit 52, over route 445 to Ry. Follow Silkeborg. Campsite is indicated in Sejs.

46
Silkeborg
Låsby
195
15
52
CC
455
Ry
445
461

CC €18 6/4-30/5 10/6-28/6 18/8-15/9 7=6    📡 N 56°08'25'' E 09°37'14''

## Sindal, DK-9870

♿ 📶 iD **102**

🏕 A35 Sindal Camping
Danmark & Kanoudlejning***
✉ Hjørringvej 125
☎ +45 98 93 65 30
🗓 1/1 - 31/12
@ info@sindal-camping.dk

4,6ha 175T(100-150m²) 13-16A CEE

**1** ACD**G**IJKLMOPQ
**2** BCFGLMRSVWXY
**3** BF**G**HIJK**MN**QRU**W**
**4** (A 1/7-15/8) (C+H 1/6-15/8)
(Q+R 1/4-20/9)
**5** **AB**DEFGHIJKLMNO**PQ**RU
WYZ
**6** ACDEGH**K**(N 0,5km)OTU

💬 This well equipped family campsite is located in the heart of the top part of northern Denmark. Perfect starting point for exploring the countryside and surrounding towns. Campsite offers excellent facilities including a heated swimming pool. Camping before 1 April and after 15 September is possible on request.

🚗 Approaching from the south via E39 exit 3 direction Sindal, route 35. Campsite located on the right after ± 6 km and ± 1 km before Sindal.

597
Sindal 40
Hjørring ℂℂ 35
55 Frederikshavn
E39 553 E45
190 585 541

CC € 20 1/1-29/6 18/8-31/12

📐 N 57°28'02" E 10°10'43"

---

## Sjølund/Grønninghoved, DK-6093

♿ 📶 iD **103**

🏕 Grønninghoved Strand
Camping****
✉ Mosvigvej 21
☎ +45 75 57 40 45
🗓 12/4 - 15/9
@ info@gronninghoved.dk

6ha 225T(80-120m²) 10A CEE

**1** ACDFHIJKLMOQ
**2** AEFIRX
**3** BHJ**MN**QRUWY
**4** (C+H 14/5-31/8) IJ**N**
(Q+S+U 🗓)
**5** **AB**DEFGIJKLMN**P**RUWXYZ
**6** ACDFGH**K**(N 4km)OTV

💬 Large and friendly campsite with plenty of recreational opportunities. Close to the sea, plenty of greenery. Excellent toilet facilities.

🚗 E45, take exit 65 Kolding S. and go in the direction of Kolding till route 170. Then go in the direction of Haderslev; after 5 km turn left towards Sjølund. After that via Grønninghoved there are signs to the campsite.

Middelfart E20
Kolding
25
ℂℂ
E45
170

CC € 20 12/4-28/5 3/6-6/6 11/6-30/6 18/8-14/9

📐 N 55°24'40" E 09°35'31"

---

## Skagen, DK-9990

♿ 📶 iD **104**

🏕 CampOne Grenen Strand***
✉ Fyrvej 16
☎ +45 63 60 63 61
🗓 13/4 - 20/10
@ grenen@campone.dk

5,5ha 270T(80-110m²) 10A CEE

**1** AC**G**IJKL**P**
**2** AELSX
**3** BU
**4** (Q+R 🗓)
**5** **AB**DEFIJMNO**PQRS**W
**6** CDEFI**JK**(N 1,5km)TUV

NEW

💬 The only campsite in Skagen directly on a (private) beach. Within walking distance of the city and of Grenen.

🚗 Campsite is located approximately 400 metres north of Skagen. From Skagen direction Grenen. After 400 metres campsite is on right.

Skagen ℂℂ
40

CC € 20 13/4-30/6 18/8-20/10

📐 N 57°43'53" E 10°36'52"

## Skagen, DK-9990

🚾 🛜 **iD** **105**

🔺 Råbjerg Mile Camping***
📧 Kandestedvej 55
☎ +45 98 48 75 00
📅 12/4 - 30/9
@ info@raabjergmilecamping.dk

20ha 446T(80-150m²) 10A CEE

**1** ACD**G**IJKLMOPQ
**2** AG**RS**TVWX
**3** ABF**G**HIJKM**N**QRU**W**
**4** (C 1/6-26/8) (F 📅)
(H 1/6-26/8) **KN**(Q+S 📅)
(T+U+V 1/7-15/8)
**5** **AB**CDEFGHIJKLMNO**PQ**RU
WZ
**6** CEGHK(N 8km)OTV

💬 Close to idyllic Skagen between two lovely beaches and outstanding countryside. Unique circular pitches provide peace, privacy and natural surroundings, and never far from the facilities. Great excursions and cycle trips to Skagen, Råbjerg Mile, Kattegat and the North Sea. Several playgrounds, outdoor and indoor pool, family-friendly.

🚗 Site is about 8 km north of Ålbæk. From route 40 direction Råbjerg Mile. Site 400m on the left.

Skagen
Højen

597
40

CC € 20  12/4-29/6  18/8-29/9    📍 N 57°39'19'' E 10°27'01''

---

## Skiveren/Aalbæk, DK-9982

🚾 🛜 **iD** **106**

🔺 Skiveren Camping****
📧 Niels Skiverens Vej 5-7
☎ +45 98 93 22 00
📅 19/3 - 30/9
@ info@skiveren.dk

18,4ha 595T(60-140m²) 10-16A CEE

**1** ACD**G**IJKLMOPQ
**2** AEGK**RS**VWX
**3** ABC**F**HJKM**N**QRTU**V**WY
**4** (C+H 1/6-1/9) **KLN**(Q+S 📅)
(T+U+W+X+Z 1/7-31/8)
**5** **AB**DEFGIJKLMNOPQR**S**U
WXYZ
**6** ACDEGHKOTV

💬 A luxurious campsite with extensive and well-maintained amenities (supermarket, fitness centre, minigolf, indoor play equipment etc.) The site is a stone's throw from the North Sea in the middle of a protected natural area.

🚗 From Frederikshaven route 40 Skagen, about 1 km after Aalbæk turn left at the roundabout towards Tversted. After 8 km right dir. Skiveren and follow camping signs.

Tversted  Ålbæk

597  40

CC € 20  19/3-29/6  18/8-29/9    📍 N 57°36'58'' E 10°16'50''

---

## Smidstrup, DK-3230

🚾 🛜 **iD** **107**

🔺 Kongernes Feriepark -
Gilleleje***
📧 Helsingevej 44
☎ +45 48 31 84 48
📅 1/1 - 31/12
@ kim.lundshoej@gmail.com

**NEW**

6,5ha 113T(110-150m²) 10-13A CEE

**1** ABCD**G**HIJKLMOPQ
**2** G**R**VWX
**3** B**F**GHJKN**Q**RU
**4** (**C**+H 1/5-30/9) **K**
(Q 1/4-1/10)
(S+T+U+W+X+Z 📅)
**5** **AB**DEFGI**J**KLMNO**P**RSTU
WZ
**6** CDEG**K**(N 1km)OTV

💬 Slightly sloping campsite, with reception in the centre. Well-equipped shop and beautiful pool.

🚗 Highway 237 Gilleleje-Rågeleje, take exit in Smidstrup, 2 km dir. Blistrup. Clearly indicated from then on.

Smidstrup
Strand

251
237  223  227
267  Gribskov

CC € 20  23/4-21/6  26/8-10/10    📍 N 56°05'55'' E 12°13'17''

## Stouby, DK-7140

🏕 Rosenvold Strand Camping***
✉ Rosenvoldvej 19
☎ +45 75 69 14 15
📅 29/3 - 29/9
@ info@rosenvoldcamping.dk

♿ 🛜 **iD** 108

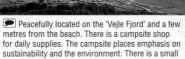
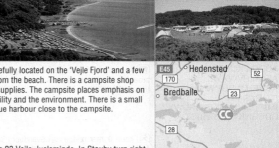

11,5ha 265T(100-150m²) 10A CEE

**1** ACD**G**IJKLMOPQ
**2** ABEKLRVWXY
**3** ABGHJNRU**W**Y
**4** (Q+R+T+U 🅿)
**5** **AB**DEFGIJKLMNO**PQR**UWX
**6** CEGHJ(N 3,2km)OUV

💬 Peacefully located on the 'Vejle Fjord' and a few metres from the beach. There is a campsite shop for daily supplies. The campsite places emphasis on sustainability and the environment. There is a small picturesque harbour close to the campsite.

🚗 Route 23 Vejle-Juelsminde. In Stouby turn right, follow camping sign.

E45 Hedensted 52
170
Bredballe 23
CC
28
**Fredericia**

CC €**20**  29/3-28/5  2/6-6/6  10/6-28/6  18/8-29/9   📍 N 55°40'36'' E 09°48'48''

---

## Strøby, DK-4671

🏕 Stevns Camping***
✉ Strandvejen 29
☎ +45 60 14 41 54
📅 1/1 - 31/12
@ info@stevnscamping.dk

♿ 🛜 **iD** 109

10ha 206T(110-140m²) 13-16A CEE

**1** ACD**G**IJKLMNOPQ
**2** GLRVWXY
**3** BF**G**HJKLNQRU
**4** (**A** 🅿) (C+H 1/6-15/8) (Q+R+U 1/5-31/8)
**5** **AB**DEFGIJ**KL**MNO**PRS**UW XYZ
**6** CEG**K**(N 1km)OTUV

💬 10 km from Køge, 50 km from Copenhagen, 40 km from BonBonland, 700 metres from Køge Beach. The region is suitable for walking, cycling and bird watching. For anglers there's Tryggevaelde River and Køge Bay. Enjoy walking on Stevns Klint and through the old city Køge, which has a warm atmosphere. The streets are filled with music in summertime and plenty of good restaurants.

🚗 In Køge take route 261 direction Stevns Klint. In Strøby turn left towards Strøby Ladeplads.

150 **Køge**
Herfølge
E47 209 CC
E55
151 261
Stevns

CC €**20**  1/1-7/6  11/6-30/6  18/8-31/12   📍 N 55°23'50'' E 12°17'25''

---

## Struer, DK-7600

🏕 Toftum Bjerge Camping***
✉ Gl. Landevej 4
☎ +45 97 86 13 30
📅 1/1 - 31/12
@ info@toftum-bjerge.dk

♿ 🛜 **iD** 110

5ha 205T(90-150m²) 10-13A CEE

**1** ACD**G**IJKLMPQ
**2** AEGILORSTUVWXY
**3** BD**F**GHJKNU**W**Y
**4** (Q+R+U+X+Z 30/3-30/9)
**5** **AB**DEFGIJKLMNO**PQR**UWZ
**6** CEGHK(N 1km)OUV

💬 The campsite is in a hilly area, near the Toftum Bjerge, with the Rømmer beach at the foot of the campsite. Since 2017, there's been an expansion in the number of pitches, and there's a new toilet block. The centrally located bar and restaurant are great fun. Make sure you visit the hamlet of Humlum and the Rømmer beach.

🚗 You reach the campsite via route 11, 5 km north of Struer, exit Humlum. Just outside Humlum along route 565 the campsite is located on the right.

Nørhede Mark

Lemvig 565
CC
Struer
521 509 11 513

CC €**20**  1/1-30/6  15/7-28/7  1/9-31/12   📍 N 56°32'28'' E 08°31'50''

## Svendborg, DK-5700

🔼 Svendborg Sund Camping***
✉ Vindebyørevej 52, Tåsinge
☎ +45 21 72 09 13
🗓 12/4 - 29/9
@ maria@
svendborgsund-camping.dk

♿ 📶 iD  **111**

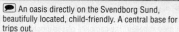

5ha 170T(80-120m²) 10A CEE

**1** ACDGIJKLMOPQ
**2** AEJKLRVWXY
**3** ABDFHJNRUVWY
**4** (Q+R+S 🅾)
**5** ABFGIJKLMNOPQRUWXZ
**6** CDEGHK(N 2,5km)OTV

💬 An oasis directly on the Svendborg Sund, beautifully located, child-friendly. A central base for trips out.

🚗 Route 9, then bridge over Svendborg Sund. At the traffic lights turn left twice then follow campsite signs.

CC €20  12/4-29/5  3/6-7/6  11/6-30/6  18/8-29/9      N 55°03'15" E 10°37'49"

## Tårup/Frørup, DK-5871

🔼 Tårup Strand Camping***
✉ Lersey Alle 25
☎ +45 65 37 11 99
🗓 5/4 - 22/9
@ mail@taarupstrandcamping.dk

♿ 📶 iD  **112**

11ha 140T(80-120m²) 10A CEE

**1** ACDGIJKLMOPQ
**2** AEIJKLMORVWXY
**3** BDFGNRUWY
**4** (Q+S 🅾)
**5** ABDEFGIJKLMNOPRUWZ
**6** CEGHK(N 9km)O

💬 Lovely, peaceful campsite in natural surroundings, 10 km from Nyborg and the motorway. Lovely views of the Great Belt and the magnificent Great Belt Bridge. Ideal base for visiting Odense, Svendborg and even Legoland and Copenhagen. Plenty of opportunities for swimming, fishing, sailing and cycling.

🚗 From route Nyborg- Svendborg, after 10 km take the first left to Tårup, follow Tårup beach camping signs.

CC €18  5/4-30/6  19/8-22/9      N 55°14'14" E 10°48'28"

## Tønder, DK-6270

🔼 Møgeltønder Camping
✉ Sønderstrengvej 2
☎ +45 74 73 84 60
🗓 1/1 - 31/12
@ info@mogeltondercamping.dk

👫 📶 iD  **113**

NEW

5ha 204T(80-120m²) 10A CEE

**1** ACDGIJKLMOPQ
**2** DGRSWXY
**3** BFHJNQRUW
**4** (C+H 1/6-31/8) J
(Q 15/6-31/8) (R 1/4-1/10)
(U 🅾)
**5** ABDFGIJKLMNOPQRUWZ
**6** BCEGHK(N 1km)OTV

💬 Beautiful campsite in a quiet area with excellent facilities. Swimming pool and large playground. There are plenty of cycling and walking possibilities. Town of Tønder is 3 km away, a nice bike ride. Village has old-English atmosphere with boutiques, restaurants and cafes. Castle Schackenborg plus park are worth a visit.

🚗 From road 11 exit to 419 dir. Højer. Second exit to Møgeltønder. Site is well signposted from then on.

CC €20  1/1-1/7  1/9-31/12  7=6      N 54°56'17" E 08°47'57"

## Tønder, DK-6270

♿ 👨‍👩‍👧 👨‍🦽 📶 iD **114**

🔺 Tønder Camping***
📧 Sønderport 4
☎ +45 74 92 80 00
🗓 1/1 - 31/12
@ booking@danhostel-tonder.dk

2ha 81T(80-130m²) 10-16A

**1** ACGIJKLMPQ
**2** CRVWXY
**3** BFGJKM**N**RS**UVW**X
**4** (F+H 🔒) J**LN**(Q 🔒)
**5** **AB**DEFGIJKLMNOPRUWX
**6** ACEGIK(N 1km)QTV

💬 A peaceful campsite in one of Denmark's oldest towns. The lively centre of Tønder is a 10 minute walk away. The pitches are well sheltered. Large sports field. An indoor swimming pool with fitness centre is right next to the campsite. Surroundings are excellent for walking and cycling trips. 40 newly constructed motorhome pitches with complete service.

🚐 Road 11 from the south. From the east take road 8 direction Tønder. Campsite located on east side of the village.

CC €20 1/1-30/6 1/9-31/12    📍 N 54°56'04'' E 08°52'36''

## Tversted, DK-9881

👨‍🦽 📶 iD **115**

🔺 Aabo Camping***
📧 Aabovej 18
☎ +45 98 93 12 34
🗓 15/3 - 8/9
@ info@aabo-camping.dk

14ha 500T(100-120m²) 13A CEE

**1** ACDGIJKLMOPQ
**2** ACFGRSVWX
**3** BF GHJKN**Q**RUW
**4** (C+H 10/6-1/9) JK
(Q 20/6-15/8) (S 30/6-15/8)
(T 23/6-15/8) (U 1/7-15/8)
(V+W 30/6-15/8) (Z 22/6-15/8)
**5** **AB**CDEFGHIJKLMNO**PQ**RU
WXYZ
**6** CEGHK(N 0,3km)OTV

💬 Beautifully located on hilly ground and has access to the north to a large protected area where you can walk through the dunes to the beach. The campsite has all you could wish for. Centrally located for excursions to the whole of Jutland. Great campsite to continue by ferry from Hirtshals, to Iceland and Norway.

🚐 Route 597 Hirtshals-Skagen. Turn right at the Tversted/Bindslev exit towards beach/Tversted. Turn left after 450m.

CC €20 15/3-29/6 18/8-7/9    📍 N 57°35'06'' E 10°11'06''

## Ulbjerg/Skals, DK-8832

👨‍👩‍👧 👨‍🦽 📶 iD **116**

🔺 Camping Ulbjerg***
📧 Skråhedevej 6
☎ +45 29 28 00 50
🗓 1/1 - 31/12
@ camping@ulbjerg.dk

23ha 80T(80-120m²) 10-16A CEE

**1** ACD**G**IJKLMOPQ
**2** BKMRSVWXY
**3** BDGJKM**N**RU**W**
**4** (B+G 1/6-1/9) (Q+S 🔒)
**5** **AB**DFGIJKLMNO**PR**UWZ
**6** ACEGJ**K**(N 2km)OV

💬 A beautifully located campsite in the middle of a nature reserve on the Limfjord with spacious pitches surrounded by natural vegetation. Suitable for the disabled. Solar heated swimming pool (20 x 7 metres). For winter camping please book ahead. Walking and cycling possible. CampingCard ACSI also accepted before and after the acceptance period if agreed by phone.

🚐 The campsite is just north of Ulbjerg on route 533 Viborg-Løgstør. Motorway exit 35 Hobro V.

CC €18 1/4-5/7 23/8-31/10    📍 N 56°38'42'' E 09°20'19''

## Ulvshale/Stege, DK-4780    117

🏕 Møn Strandcamping - Ulvshale**
📧 Ulvshalevej 236
☎ +45 55 81 53 25
📅 13/4 - 8/9
@ info@ulvscamp.dk

2,4ha 130T(80-120m²) 10A

**1** ACD**G**IJKLMPQ
**2** AEIKRSWXY
**3** A**F**KWY
**4** (Q+R 📅)
**5** **AB**FGIJKLMNO**PQR**UW
**6** CE**J**(N 6km)O

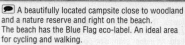

💬 A beautifully located campsite close to woodland and a nature reserve and right on the beach. The beach has the Blue Flag eco-label. An ideal area for cycling and walking.

🚗 From Stege direction Ulvshale. Follow campsite signs.

Bønsvig Strand

265   CC   59   Stege   287

CC € 20   13/4-7/7   24/8-8/9    📡 N 55°02'17'' E 12°16'55''

---

## Vejers Strand, DK-6853    118

🏕 Vejers Familie Camping***
📧 Vejers Havvej 15
☎ +45 75 27 70 36
📅 1/1 - 31/12
@ info@vejersfamiliecamping.dk

4,2ha 156T(80-100m²) 16A CEE

**1** ACG**I**JKLPQ
**2** AGRWXY
**3** B**FQ**RUW
**4** (**C** 25/5-25/8) (H 30/5-25/8) (Q+R 23/3-9/9)
**5** **AB**DEFGIJKLMNO**PQ**RUW
**6** AEG**K**(N 0,2km)OTV

💬 A quiet campsite by the North Sea. Beach accessible by car. Deer sometimes visit the site. Fishing is possible in Graerup lake and the North Sea. A lovely area for cycling, walking and relaxing. There are several boutiques in the village including an art gallery. Free admission to the 'Sportspark Blåvandshuk' water park in Oksbøl.

🚗 Via Oksbol 431 follow direction Vejers. Campsite at entrance to village. Signposted.

Vejers Strand

CC

463

Blåvand

CC € 18   1/1-29/5   10/6-4/7   21/8-31/12 7=6    📡 N 55°37'09'' E 08°08'11''

---

## Vejers Strand, DK-6853    119

🏕 Vejers Strand Camping***
📧 Vejers Sydstrand 3
☎ +45 75 27 70 50
📅 13/4 - 15/9
@ info@vejersstrandcamping.dk

21ha 450T 10A CEE

**1** **G**HIJKLMOPRS
**2** AEIKRSW
**3** AB**F**HJ**O**PRUW**Y**
**4** (R 📅) (T+U 1/7-10/8)
**5** **AB**DEFGIJKLMNO**P**RUW
**6** CDEGI**J**M(N 0,01km)OTV

💬 A quiet dune campsite directly on the sea. Unnumbered pitches. No reservations; there's always room. The beautiful countryside is perfect for walking or cycling. There's an art gallery and a few boutiques in the village. It's possible to drive the car onto the beach, leaving time 22:00.

🚗 Direction Vejers via Oksbøl 431. 500 metres after petrol station first road on left. Campsite is indicated (Vejers Strand).

Oksbøl

CC

Oksby

CC € 20   13/4-29/5   3/6-7/6   11/6-28/6   26/8-15/9    📡 N 55°37'09'' E 08°07'55''

# The Netherlands

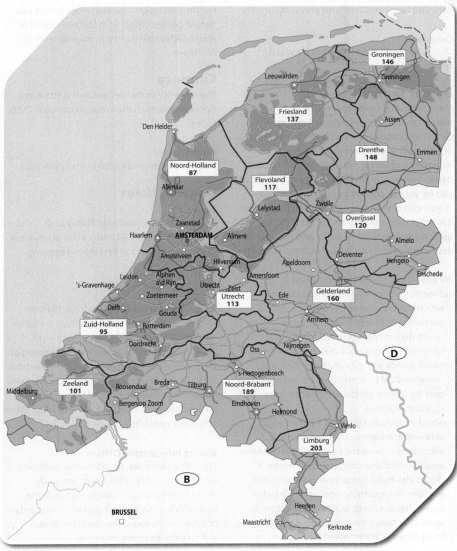

Groningen
**146**
Groningen

Leeuwarden

Friesland
**137**

Assen

Den Helder

Drenthe
**148**

Emmen

Noord-Holland
**87**

Alkmaar

Flevoland
**117**

Zwolle

Overijssel
**120**

Almelo

Zaanstad

Lelystad

Haarlem

AMSTERDAM

Almere

Deventer

Hengelo

Amstelveen

Hilversum

Apeldoorn

Enschede

Leiden

Alphen
a/d Rijn

Amersfoort

's-Gravenhage

Zoetermeer

Utrecht

Zeist

Utrecht
**113**

Ede

Gelderland
**160**

Delft

Gouda

Zuid-Holland
**95**

Rotterdam

Arnhem

Dordrecht

Oss

Nijmegen

**D**

's-Hertogenbosch

Zeeland
**101**

Roosendaal

Breda

Tilburg

Noord-Brabant
**189**

Middelburg

Bergen op Zoom

Eindhoven

Helmond

Venlo

Limburg
**203**

**B**

BRUSSEL
□

Heerlen

Maastricht

Kerkrade

83

## General
The Netherlands is a member of the EU.

### Time
The time in the Netherlands is the same as Berlin, Paris and Rome and one hour ahead of London.

### Language
Dutch, but English and German are widely spoken and understood.

## Border formalities
Many formalities and agreements about matters such as necessary travel documents, car papers, requirements relating to your means of transport and accommodation, medical expenses and taking pets with you do not only depend on the country you are travelling to but also on your departure point and nationality. The length of your stay can also play a role here. It is not possible within the confines of this guide to guarantee the correct and most up to date information with regard to these matters.

We advise you to consult the relevant authorities before your departure about:
- which travel documents you will need for yourself and your fellow passengers
- which documents you need for your car
- which regulations your caravan must meet
- which goods you may import and export
- - how medical treatment will be arranged and paid for in your holiday destination in cases of accident or illness
- whether you can take pets. Contact your vets well in advance. They can give you information about the necessary vaccinations, proof thereof and obligations on return. It would also make sense to enquire whether any special regulations apply to your pet in public places at your holiday destination. In some countries for example dogs must always be muzzled or transported in a cage.

You will find plenty of general information on ▸ *www.europa.eu* ◂ but make certain you select information that is relevant to your specific situation.

For the most recent customs regulations you should get in contact with the authorities of your holiday destination in your country of residence.

## Currency
The currency in the Netherlands is the euro. Approximate exchange rates September 2018: £1 = € 1.12.

### Credit cards
You can pay by credit card in many places.

## Opening times
### Banks
Banks are open Monday to Friday until 17:00. You can PIN money 24 hours a day at any bank and at most supermarkets during opening hours.

### Shops
Shops are open on Mondays from 13:00 to 18:00. From Tuesday to Friday shops are open until 18:00 and on Saturdays usually until 17:00. Most towns have late night shopping on Thursday or Friday when shops stay open until 21:00. Shops in larger cities such as Rotterdam, Amsterdam, Utrecht and The Hague are open on Sundays from 12:00 to 17:00 and some shops stay open even longer.

### Tourist Information Offices
The offices are open from 09:00 to 18:00 and on Saturdays until 17:00. These are easily recognised by a blue triangle sign with the letters VVV in white. Here you will find plenty of information about the town, the area, sightseeing, opening times etc.

### Chemists
Most chemists are open Monday to Friday until 18:00.

## Communication

### (Mobile) phones
The mobile network works well throughout the Netherlands. There is a 4G network for mobile internet.

### Wifi, internet
Many cafés and restaurants have free wifi for guests.

### Post
Post offices in the Netherlands have been replaced by postal agencies in supermarkets and other shops. These agencies are generally open Monday to Friday until 17:00 and on Saturday mornings. You can buy postage stamps in almost every supermarket.

## Roads and traffic

### Road network
Remember, all traffic in The Netherlands drives on the right and overtakes on the left! Headlight deflectors are advisable to prevent annoying oncoming drivers. The Netherlands uses the metric system, so distances are measured in

kilometres (km) and speeds in kilometres per hour (km/h). On the outskirts of large cities you will find the so-called 'transferiums' from where you can reach the city centre quickly and easily using public transport. You can contact the ANWB for breakdown assistance. A good alternative to the ANWB is Route Mobiel. More information tel. 088-2692888 (ANWB), tel. 020-6515115 (Route Mobiel).

*Maximum speed*

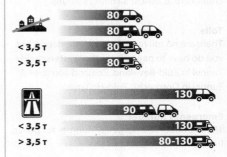

### Traffic regulations
On an increasing number of motorways you can drive at 130 km/h. Look carefully at the road signs. Maximum permitted alcohol level is 0.5‰. Traffic already on a roundabout usually

has priority. This is shown by signs. Where there are no signs the driver wishing to enter the roundabout has priority.

You are advised to use dipped headlights during the daytime. Phones must be used hands-free.

### Caravans, motorhomes

You may not stay overnight in a motorhome on the public highway.

### Maximum allowed measurements of combined length

Height 4 metres, width 2.55 metres and maximum length 18 metres (of which the trailer maximum 12m).

### Fuel

Lead-free petrol, diesel and LPG are widely available.

### Filling stations

Filling stations are open until 22:00. In larger cities and on motorways they are open 24 hours a day. You can pay by debit card and credit card at almost all filling stations.

### Tolls

There are no toll roads in the Netherlands, but you do have to pay tolls for the Westerschelde Tunnel in Zuid-Beveland, Zeeland and the Kil Tunnel in Dordrecht, Zuid-Holland.

### Emergency number

112: the national emergency number for police, fire and ambulance.

## Camping

Dutch campsites are among the best in Europe: there is extensive entertainment for children and the amenities (such as indoor playgrounds and football pitches) are innovative. Campsites are well organised and there is plenty of greenery. Cars often have to be parked outside the campsite, bringing more peace and quiet to the site.

Camping outside recognised sites is only allowed in a few communities. Many Dutch campsites have a so-called family rate for 4, 5 or more people including electricity. This means that 2 people often pay the same rate as an entire family.

### Practical

- Additional charges for items such as tourist taxes and environmental charges are sometimes quite high.
- Make sure you have a world adaptor for electrical appliances.
- Tap water is safe to drink.

### Classification of campsites

ACSI has chosen not to include any star ratings in information about campsites in the Netherlands. Any stars you may see in advertisements are awarded by the campsites themselves, but ACSI cannot accept any liability for the accuracy of these star ratings.

## Akersloot/Alkmaar, NL-1921 CE / Noord-Holland ♿ 🛜 🆔 120

🏕 Camping De Boekel
✉ Boekel 22
☎ +31 7 25 33 01 09
📅 1/1 - 31/12
@ info@deboekel.nl

2ha 40T(125-200m²) 16A CEE

**1** AG**IJ**KLMN**PQ**
**2** FGKRUVWX
**3** ADF**GH**JKLNRU**W**
**4** (Q+R 📅)
**5** **AB**CDFGHIJKLMNO**PR**UW Z
**6** ABCDEGH**K**(N 2km)TV

💬 Small, car-free, child friendly campsite with spacious camping pitches and a recreation area. Situated on the Noordhollands Canal. Good fishing opportunities. Starting point for lovely cycle trips. You can take a sightseeing boat from the campsite to the cheese market. Campsite open all year.

🚗 A9 Amstelveen-Alkmaar, exit 11 direction Akersloot. In Akersloot straight on to ferry. From ferry another 1.5 km direction Alkmaar.

Alkmaar — N245, N243, N246, A9, Purmerend

CC €**18**  1/1-26/4  5/5-28/5  11/6-13/6  23/6-11/7  1/9-31/12   🧭 N 52°35'10'' E 04°45'09''

---

## Alkmaar, NL-1817 ML / Noord-Holland ⊗ ♿ 🛜 🆔 121

🏕 Camping Alkmaar/Camperpark Alkmaar
✉ Bergerweg 201
☎ +31 7 25 11 69 24
📅 1/3 - 30/9
@ info@campingalkmaar.nl

6ha 290T(80-100m²) 6-10A CEE

**1** ABCDE**IJ**LMRS
**2** AFGRSUVWXY
**3** A**F**JKR
**4** (Q 📅)
**5** **AB**CDFGIJ**KL**MN**PQ**UWXY Z
**6** ABCDEG**K**(N 1km)T

💬 Natural campsite located on the Bergerweg between Alkmaar and Bergen. A base for trips out to Alkmaar (cheese market), the artists' village of Bergen, dunes, woods, not to mention the BEACH. The site has an artificial own sandy beach on the North Sea. Everything is within cycling distance.

🚗 Alkmaar ring west, exit Bergen. Follow campsite signs.

Heerhugowaard, Alkmaar, Heiloo — N9, N242, N244, N243, A9

CC €**20**  5/5-28/5  11/6-14/6  24/6-30/6  1/9-30/9   🧭 N 52°38'32'' E 04°43'24''

---

## Amstelveen, NL-1187 NZ / Noord-Holland ♿ 🛜 🆔 122

🏕 Camping Het Amsterdamse Bos
✉ Kleine Noorddijk 1
☎ +31 2 06 41 68 68
📅 18/3 - 3/11
@ info@campingamsterdam.com

6,8ha 430T(45-100m²) 6A CEE

**1** ABCF**IJ**KL**P**Q
**2** BDFGRUX
**3** BH**J**K**W**
**4** (Q+S 📅)
**5** **AB**DEFG**IJ**KLMN**P**U
**6** CDEGHJ(N 1km)R

💬 Campsite south of the lovely Amsterdam woods. A beautiful spot in the middle of nature and still very close to the city centre. A perfect operating base for a visit to Amsterdam, Keukenhof, Volendam, and so on.

🚗 A9 exit 6 Aalsmeer, then follow the N231 towards Aalsmeer. After 500 metres at traffic lights cross the water in direction Amstelveen. The campsite is another 2 km on the left.

Haarlem, Amsterdam — N205, A9, A4, N521, A2, N231, N201

CC €**20**  1/4-17/4  29/4-28/5  10/6-27/6  1/9-3/11   🧭 N 52°17'39'' E 04°49'23''

## Amsterdam, NL-1026 CP / Noord-Holland

🛖 Camping de Badhoeve
📧 Uitdammerdijk 10
☎ +31 2 04 90 42 94
📅 29/3 - 30/9
@ info@campingdebadhoeve.com

📶 📱 **123**

5ha 100T(15-50m²) 8A CEE

1 ABCD**G**IJLN**PRS**
2 DFGKLMRWX
3 B**F**HJKNRU**WZ**
4 (Q+R+T+U+X+Y+Z 🔑)
5 DGIJKLM**P**UWZ
6 CDEGHK(N 2km)TV

💬 Campsite located in the Waterland meadow and nature area on Lake Kinsel between Amsterdam (10 minutes) and picturesque Marken. Ideal starting point for cycling, hiking and fishing. The site has hardened pitches for motorhomes, well maintained toilet facilities and free wifi.

🚗 A10 north, exit S115. Direction Durgerdam at traffic lights. Direction Durgerdam at roundabout. Straight on past Durgerdam. Campsite 500m. Follow signs.

CC € 20  29/3-11/7  30/8-29/9

📍 N 52°23'04'' E 05°00'47''

## Amsterdam, NL-1108 AZ / Noord-Holland

🛖 Gaasper Camping Amsterdam
📧 Loosdrechtdreef 7
☎ +31 2 06 96 73 26
📅 15/3 - 1/11, 28/12 - 4/1
@ info@gaaspercamping.nl

📶 📱 **124**

5,5ha 350T(20-100m²) 10A CEE

1 ABCD**F**IJKL**PQ**
2 FGRUVWX
3 A**F**HJK**ORW**
4 (Q+S 🔑)
   (T+U+V+X+Z 1/4-1/11)
5 **AB**DFGIJKL**MOP**UWXYZ
6 ABCDEGHK(N 2,5km)OTV

💬 The campsite is quickly and easily accessible and is located on the edge of town, partly surrounded by a park and within walking distance of the metro station. The metro will take you to the centre of Amsterdam in 15 minutes. In addition to a relaxing stay the campsite offers many extras such as free wifi, a restaurant with ambiance and a well-stocked supermarket.

🚗 Section of A9 between the A1 and A2. Turn off at exit 1, Weesp (S113). Then follow camping signs.

CC € 20  18/3-14/4  6/5-23/5  11/6-30/6  2/9-6/10

📍 N 52°18'45'' E 04°59'25''

## Callantsoog, NL-1759 JD / Noord-Holland

🛖 Camping De Nollen
📧 Westerweg 8
☎ +31 2 24 58 12 81
📅 6/4 - 26/10
@ info@denollen.nl

♿ 📶 📱 **125**

9ha 227T(70-120m²) 10A CEE

1 ACD**G**IJKLMOPQ
2 ARSVWX
3 B**F**GJKNRU**W**
4 (Q+S+T+U 🔑)
5 **AB**CDEFGHIJKLMNOPUW
   XYZ
6 ACEGHKM(N 1,5km)OQSTV

💬 A quiet campsite on the edge of Callantsoog, with well sheltered fields and new toilet facilities. Located in the immediate vicinity of the nearby nature reserves of Kooijbosch and Zwanenwater. A perfect starting place for cycling or walking tours through the bulbfields.

🚗 From N9, take exit Callantsoog and follow signs to campsite 'De Nollen'.

CC € 18  6/4-28/5  3/6-6/6  11/6-8/7  25/8-26/10

📍 N 52°50'29'' E 04°43'08''

## Callantsoog, NL-1759 JD / Noord-Holland

 ♿ 📶 **iD** 126

🏕 Camping Tempelhof
📧 Westerweg 2
☎ +31 2 24 58 15 22
📅 1/1 - 31/12
@ info@tempelhof.nl

14ha 210T(80-135m²) 16A CEE

**1** ACD**F**IJKLMNOPQ
**2** ARSVWX
**3** AB**F**JKMNRUV**W**
**4** (F+H 29/3-27/10) JM**N**
(Q+S+T+U+Y+Z 29/3-27/10)
**5** **AB**DEFGIJK**L**MNOPQ**ST**U
WXY
**6** ABCEGH**K**M(N 1km)ORSTV

💬 A campsite with excellent, environmentally friendly toilet facilities. Small fields bordered by hedges ensure tranquillity. Relaxing in the indoor swimming pool or in the fitness room completes the holiday feeling at this attractive campsite which, in spring is located in the middle of the Dutch bulbfields.

🚗 Leave N9 at the exit for 't Zand and continue in the direction of Groote Keeten. Follow the camping signs Tempelhof.

**CC** € **18** 1/1-18/4 23/4-28/5 11/6-6/7 24/8-31/12   📍 N 52°50'48'' E 04°42'56''

---

## Callantsoog, NL-1759 NX / Noord-Holland

 ♿ 📶 **iD** 127

🏕 Vakantiepark Callassande
📧 Voorweg 5a
☎ +31 2 24 58 16 63
📅 29/3 - 3/11
@ receptie.callassande@roompot.nl

12,5ha 383T(60-120m²) 10A CEE

**1** ACD**G**IJKLMOPRT
**2** AGRSVWX
**3** BF**G**HJKLMNRU**W**
**4** (F+H ⊙) IJ
(Q+S+T+U+X+Y+Z ⊙)
**5** **AB**CDEFGHIJKLMNOP**S**U
WXYZ
**6** ACEGHKL(N 3km)STV

💬 A quiet campsite, just behind the dunes, right in the middle of the bulbfields. Plenty of shelter offered by bushes around the fields. An indoor swimming pool with a lively terrace. Many attractive restaurants in the area. The catering facilities at the campsite are open at weekends in the early and late seasons. There are no pitches for motorhomes available on this campsite.

🚗 N9 exit 't Zand, direction Groote Keeten. Follow the camping signs.

**CC** € **16** 29/3-12/4 12/5-29/5 11/6-19/6 24/6-9/7 26/8-3/11   📍 N 52°51'23'' E 04°43'03''

---

## Castricum, NL-1901 NH / Noord-Holland

 ♿ 📶 ✿ **iD** 128

🏕 Kennemer Duincamping Geversduin
📧 Beverwijkerstraatweg 205
☎ +31 2 51 66 10 95
📅 29/3 - 27/10
@ info@campinggeversduin.nl

23ha 295T(80-100m²) 16A CEE

**1** ABCD**G**IJKLPST
**2** BF**G**RSVWXY
**3** ABCGHJKNRU
**4** (**A** 19/4-5/5,12/7-1/9) M
(Q+R ⊙)
(T 19/4-5/5,12/7-1/9) (V ⊙)
(X 19/4-5/5,12/7-1/9) (Z ⊙)
**5** **AB**DEFGHIJKLMNOPQRU
WZ
**6** ABCEGHIJLM(N 3km)RT

💬 A wooded campsite in the dunes. Wonderful cycling through dunes and polder. Experience adventures on trips out with the forester. 4 km from the quiet beach at Heemskerk. Good amenities make it comfortable outside the summer season.

🚗 A9 exit 9. Right at roundabout towards Heemskerk. Straight on at traffic lights into Baandert. Left at the end into Mozartstraat. At roundabout turn right into Marquettelaan. At the end at Rijksstraatweg right. After 1.5 km left.

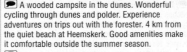

**CC** € **20** 29/3-18/4 5/5-28/5 3/6-6/6 11/6-19/6 23/6-30/6 1/9-27/10   📍 N 52°31'49'' E 04°38'55''

## Castricum aan Zee, NL-1901 NZ / Noord-Holland

⊗ & 🛜 ✿ **iD** **129**

🔺 Kennemer Duincamping Bakkum
✉ Zeeweg 31
☎ +31 2 51 66 10 91
🔑 29/3 - 27/10
@ info@campingbakkum.nl

60ha 337T(80-130m²) 16A CEE

**1** ABCDEIJKLPST
**2** BFRSUVWXY
**3** ABDFGHJKLMNRUV
**4** (A 19/4-5/5,12/7-1/9) M
(Q+S+T+U+V+X 🔑)
**5** ABCDEFGIJKLMNOPQRU
WZ
**6** ABCDEGHJKLM(N 4km)
ORT

💬 A pure camping experience awaits you in the North Holland dunes, close to the sea. Experience nostalgia at this dune campsite with good amenities: walking, cycling and living culture. Spacious pitches in natural surroundings.

🚗 A9 Beverwijk-Alkmaar exit 10 Castricum. Right at traffic lights N203 direction Castricum. At Castricum direction Castricum aan Zee. Over railway bridge, straight ahead at roundabout. Campsite 1.5 km further on right of the road.

**Alkmaar**

N244

CC  A9

Heemskerk  N246

CC € 20  29/3-18/4  5/5-28/5  3/6-6/6  11/6-19/6  23/6-4/7  1/9-27/10   📶 N 52°33'44'' E 04°38'00''

---

## De Cocksdorp (Texel), NL-1795 LN / Noord-Holland

& 🛜 **iD** **130**

🔺 Duinpark & Camping De Robbenjager Texel
✉ Vuurtorenweg 148
☎ +31 2 22 31 62 58
🔑 12/4 - 25/10
@ info@duinparkderobbenjager.nl

3,7ha 131T(80-160m²) 16A CEE

**1** ADFIJKLMOPQ
**2** AERSWX
**3** ABFHJKLNWY
**4** (Q+T+U+Y 🔑)
**5** ABCDFGHIJKLMNOPQUW
XY
**6** ABCDEGHKL(N 2,5km)OS

💬 Situated in the middle of the dune landscape on the foot of a lighthouse and directly behind the dykes with a wide sandy beach. Directly next to the landing stage for the ferry to Vlieland. Excellent starting point for sport fishing on the sea. In 2015 equipped with modern heated toilet facilities.

🚗 From the ferry follow the N501. At exit 10 direction De Cocksdorp. At exit 35 straight on to the lighthouse. Campsite is on the right. Attention, sharp turn.

CC

De Cocksdorp

De Koog

CC € 20  4/5-29/5  3/6-7/6  11/6-19/6  24/6-11/7  30/8-25/10   📶 N 53°10'38'' E 04°51'37''

---

## De Cocksdorp (Texel), NL-1795 JV / Noord-Holland

⛺ & 🛜 **iD** **131**

🔺 Vakantiepark De Krim Texel
✉ Roggeslootweg 6
☎ +31 2 22 39 01 12
🔑 1/1 - 31/12
@ reserveringen@krim.nl

31ha 413T(80-100m²) 10A CEE

**1** ACDGIJKLMNOPQ
**2** AGLRSVWXY
**3** ABCEGHJKLNOPQRTUV
W
**4** (A+C+F 🔑) IJKM
(Q+S+T+U+V+Y+Z 🔑)
**5** ABDEFGIJKLMNOPQSTU
WXYZ
**6** ACDEGHKLM(N 0,5km)OR
STUV

💬 Campsite located in wooded dunes with spacious pitches on well-sheltered fields. Direct connection to cycling and hiking trails. Many indoor and outdoor facilities concentrated around the attractive central square. New swimming pool with three slides, wild water rapids and indoor spray park.

🚗 Take the N501 from the ferry. At exit 10 direction De Cocksdorp. Left at exit 33 to Vakantiepark De Krim.

CC

De Koog

CC € 20  7/1-18/4  11/5-29/5  11/6-28/6  2/9-20/12   📶 N 53°09'06'' E 04°51'32''

### Den Helder, NL-1783 BW / Noord-Holland 📶 iD **132**

🏕 Camping De Donkere Duinen
📧 Jan Verfailleweg 616
☎ +31 2 23 61 47 31
📅 11/4 - 10/9
@ info@donkereduinen.nl

5,5ha 177**T**(100-140m²) 6-16A CEE

**1** ACD**G**IJKLMOPQ
**2** ABGLRSVWXY
**3** **FKLNW**
**5** **AB**CFGIJKLMNOPUWXYZ
**6** ACEG**K**(N 0,5km)

💬 Campsite on the edge of Den Helder, next to woods, dunes, and near the beach. Opposite the site is the Helderse valley with a treetop adventure park. Pitches with hedges provide excellent shelter from the wind. An excellent location to explore Texel by bike or walk through woods, dunes and along the beach.

🚗 Campsite on the Den Helder to Callantsoog road just out of town.

*N501*
Den Helder
CC
Julianadorp *N99*
*N249*
*N9*

CC € **18** 11/4-28/5 2/6-6/6 10/6-7/7 25/8-10/9 ⛱ N 52°56'12'' E 04°44'01''

---

### Den Hoorn, NL-1797 RN / Noord-Holland 👫 🚫 📶 iD **133**

🏕 Camping Loodsmansduin
📧 Rommelpot 19
☎ +31 2 22 39 01 12
📅 28/3 - 27/10
@ receptie.loodsmansduin@krim.nl

38ha 234**T**(60-120m²) 16A CEE

**1** ACD**G**IJKLMOPST
**2** ARSVWXY
**3** ABJKLRU**W**
**4** (C+H 1/5-1/10)
    (Q+T+Y+Z 📅)
**5** **AB**CDFGHIJKLMNOPQUW
    XYZ
**6** ABCDEGHK(N 0,5km)SUV

💬 This campsite is part of the Texel Dunes National Park in which a number of camping pitches have been created. Surrounded by rolling dunes, heath and pine trees with direct connection to beautiful cycling and walking routes. Close to the picturesque and culturally rich village of Den Hoorn and the vast North Sea beach.

🚗 From the ferry follow the N501. Take Exit 3. Now follow the green or white campsite signs 'Loodsmansduin'.

CC *N501*
Den Helder

CC € **18** 28/3-18/4 11/5-29/5 11/6-28/6 2/9-27/10 ⛱ N 53°01'17'' E 04°44'28''

---

### Edam, NL-1135 PZ / Noord-Holland 🚫 ♿ 📶 iD **134**

🏕 Camping Strandbad Edam
📧 Zeevangszeedijk 7A
☎ +31 2 99 37 19 94
📅 29/3 - 6/10
@ info@campingstrandbad.nl

4,5ha 150**T**(60-80m²) 10A CEE

**1** ABCDEIJKLOPQ
**2** DKLMRUWX
**3** ABFHJKNRU**WZ**
**4** (G 15/4-15/9)
    (Q+T+U+X+Y+Z 📅)
**5** **AB**CDEFGHIJKLMNO**PQR**
    UWZ
**6** ABCDEGH**K**M(N 1,2km)
    ORV

💬 Discover North Holland from Edam! The leading campsite at Edam, world famous for its cheese, has extensive views over the former Markermeer. A good base for visiting Marken and Volendam. Amsterdam is only 20 minutes away by regular public transport. Marked out cycle routes through the centuries old polders and meadows of North Holland.

🚗 N247 Amsterdam-Volendam-Hoorn. Exit Edam-Noord and follow camping signs. Switch off SatNav.

*N243*
*A7*
Purmerend CC
Monnickendam
*N235*
*N247*
*N701*

CC € **18** 29/3-28/5 11/6-4/7 1/9-6/10 ⛱ N 52°31'07'' E 05°04'26''

## Egmond aan Zee, NL-1931 AV / Noord-Holland

135

🏕 Kustcamping Egmond aan Zee
📧 Nollenweg 1
☎ +31 7 25 06 17 02
📅 1/1 - 31/12
@ receptie.egmond@roompot.nl

11ha 73T(100-120m²) 10A CEE

**1** ABCD**G**IJKOPQ
**2** GJRSVWX
**3** B**F**GHJKLNRU
**4** (C+H 19/4-23/9)
  (Q+S+T+U+V+X+Y+Z ⌧)
**5** **AB**DFGIJKLMNOPUWXY
**6** BEGHKM(N 0,6km)OST

💬 A sheltered campsite in various hollows in the dunes. Set around a central swimming pool and recreation building. Centre and beach at walking distance. Starting point for cycle and walking tours. No pitches for motorhomes at this campsite.

🚗 Alkmaar ring road west. Exit Egmond. Drive as far as the traffic lights near Egmond, turn right to Egmond aan Zee. At the second traffic lights keep right. After 150 metres turn right into narrow road leading to the site.

CC Alkmaar
N245
N244
A9
Uitgeest
N246

CC €20 15/2-12/4 12/5-29/5 11/6-19/6 24/6-9/7 26/8-3/11 20/12-31/12 🏔 N 52°37'19'' E 04°38'17''

---

## Hoorn/Berkhout, NL-1647 DR / Noord-Holland

136

🏕 Camping 't Venhop
📧 De Hulk 6a
☎ +31 2 29 55 13 71
📅 1/1 - 31/12
@ info@venhop.nl

8,5ha 80T(80-100m²) 10A CEE

**1** ABCD**F**IJKLN**P**RS
**2** FRVWXY
**3** A**F**HJKLR**U**W
**4** (Q+R+U+X+Y+Z ⌧)
**5** **AB**DG**IJKL**MNO**P**UXYZ
**6** ABCDG**K**(N 3km)OSVX

💬 Situated on good fishing and sailing water with a cosy terrace. The fields with touring pitches are surrounded by trees and shrubs. Starting point for canoe trips. Canoes and sups for rent at the campsite. Centrally located for trips to Amsterdam and places like Hoorn/Medemblik/Enkhuizen and Marken/Edam/Volendam.

🚗 A7 Purmerend-Hoorn exit 7 Berkhout. Or A7 Hoorn-Purmerend, exit 7 Avenhorn. At the traffic lights turn left to Hoorn-West. Then follow signs.

Noord-Scharwoude
N241
A7
N506
Hoorn
CC
N243
N247

CC €20 1/1-26/4 6/5-6/6 11/6-7/7 25/8-31/12 🏔 N 52°37'55'' E 05°00'42''

---

## Julianadorp aan Zee, NL-1787 CX / Noord-Holland

137

🏕 Ardoer camping 't Noorder Sandt
📧 Noorder Sandt 2
☎ +31 2 23 64 12 66
📅 30/3 - 27/10
@ noordersandt@ardoer.com

11ha 180T(100m²) 10A CEE

**1** ACD**G**IJKLMOPQ
**2** AELRSVWXY
**3** ABF**G**JKLN**O**PRUWY
**4** (F+H ⌧) IJ**N**
  (Q+R+T+U+V+Y+Z ⌧)
**5** **AB**DEFGIJKLMNOPQUWX YZ
**6** ABCDEGH**K**(N 2km)ORSV

💬 A campsite right behind the dunes in the middle of the bulbfields region. A field with unrestricted views of the bulbfields right on the canoe route, but also shaded fields. Separate pitches for motorhomes. The campsite is located directly on the cycle route network. The sauna and library ensure hours of relaxation.

🚗 From N9 exit Julianadorp. In the village continue straight to Julianadorp aan Zee. At the coast road turn right and follow signs to the campsite.

Den Helder
CC
N99
N249
N9

CC €18 30/3-12/4 5/5-28/5 11/6-18/6 23/6-6/7 24/8-26/10 🏔 N 52°54'22'' E 04°43'29''

## Julianadorp aan Zee, NL-1787 PP / Noord-Holland

📶 iD **138**

🔺 Camping De Zwaluw
📧 Zanddijk 259
☎ +31 2 23 64 14 92
🔄 27/3 - 15/10
@ campingdezwaluw@quicknet.nl

2ha 68T(50-100m²) 10-16A CEE

**1** ADGIJKLMOPQ
**2** AERSVW
**3** BFJNRTWY
**4** (Q+R+T+X+Z 🔑)
**5** ABCDFGHIJKLMNOPQU WZ
**6** ACDEGHK(N 2km)OR

💬 The campsite is sandwiched between the dunes and the bulbfields just 200 metres from the beach and 500 metres from a water paradise. Excellent places to eat in the campsite and close by.

🚗 From Alkmaar (N9) 1st exit Julianadorp (Zuid). From Den Helder (N9) 2nd exit Julianadorp (Zuid). Follow signs to Kustrecreatie. Turn right at the dunes. 1st campsite by the sea to your right in Julianadorp aan Zee.

Den Helder
CC
N99
Anna Paulowna

CC € **18** 27/3-28/5 11/6-7/7 26/8-14/10

📍 N 52°53'43'' E 04°43'04''

---

## Noord-Scharwoude, NL-1723 PX / Noord-Holland

♿ 📶 iD **139**

🔺 DroomPark Molengroet
📧 Molengroet 1
☎ +31 8 80 55 15 00
🔄 1/4 - 31/10
@ molengroet@droomparken.nl

11ha 150T(80-100m²) 10A CEE

**1** ACDFIJKLMOPQ
**2** ADLMRVX
**3** ABDFGHJKLNRUWZ
**4** (C 27/4-16/9) (Q+R+T+U+X+Y+Z 🔑)
**5** ABCDEFGHIJKLMNOPUW XYZ
**6** CDEGHKLM(N 1km)OSTUV

💬 A friendly family campsite centrally located in the top part of Noord-Holland in a nature reserve with a recreational lake. Modern heated toilet facilities. Many attractions in the vicinity.

🚗 N245 Alkmaar-Schagen. Exit Geestmerambacht/ camping sign Molengroet.

Schagen
N245
N241
Bergen
CC
N9
N507
**Alkmaar**
N243

CC € **16** 1/4-19/4 23/4-29/5 11/6-5/7 23/8-31/10

📍 N 52°41'41'' E 04°46'15''

---

## Petten, NL-1755 LA / Noord-Holland

🚫 ♿ 📶 iD **140**

🔺 Camping Corfwater
📧 Strandweg 3
☎ +31 2 26 38 19 81
🔄 15/3 - 27/10
@ camping@corfwater.nl

5,5ha 240T(80-120m²) 6A CEE

**1** ACDEIJKLNPS
**2** AEGJKRSVW
**3** BHJKLRUWY
**4** (Q+R 🔑)
**5** ABDEFGIJKLMNOPQSUW Z
**6** ABCDEGHKM(N 0,3km)OTV

💬 A peaceful campsite located in the dunes right by the beach and the sea and on the edge of the village of Petten. You will find all types of shops and places to eat in Petten.

🚗 N9 Alkmaar-Den Helder. At the roundabout in Burgervlotbrug, direction Petten. As far as the roundabout at the dunes. Drive straight ahead following the campsite signs.

Anna Paulowna
CC
N9
N245

CC € **20** 15/3-29/5 11/6-19/6 23/6-6/7 24/8-27/10

📍 N 52°46'14'' E 04°39'33''

## Schoorl, NL-1871 CD / Noord-Holland ⊗ 📶 iD (141)

🏕 Kampeerterrein Buitenduin
✉ Molenweg 15
☎ +31 7 25 09 18 20
📅 29/3 - 28/10
@ info@
    kampeerterreinbuitenduin.nl

1,2ha 33T(70-90m²) 10A CEE

1 ADEIJLN**P**ST
2 GRSVWX
3 A**F**HJNR
4 (A 7/7-25/8)
5 **AB**DGIJKLMOPUWXYZ
6 ABCDEH**K**(N 0,6km)

💬 A rural campsite in wooded surroundings within walking distance of the village centre and the dunes. Good base for walking and cycling tours. Site suitable for young children. The main feature of the site is the monumental 'Kijkduin' corn mill, still in working order and which can be visited weekly.

🚗 N9 Alkmaar-Den Helder, exit Schoorl, direction Schoorl. Turn right just before the traffic lights at the pedestrian crossing. Before the mill to the right.

CC €20  29/3-19/4  6/5-26/5  16/6-29/6  2/9-28/10          📍 N 52°42'24'' E 04°41'49''

---

## St. Maartenszee, NL-1753 BA / Noord-Holland ♿ 📶 iD (142)

🏕 Ardoer Camping St. Maartenszee
✉ Westerduinweg 30
☎ +31 2 24 56 14 01
📅 29/3 - 29/9
@ sintmaartenszee@ardoer.com

5ha 300T(60-90m²) 6-10A CEE

1 AD**G**IJKLMPRS
2 GRSVWXY
3 ABHJKN**Q**RU
4 (Q+S+U+V+X+Y+Z 📅)
5 **AB**CDEFGIJKLMNPQR**S**U
   WXYZ
6 ABCDEGHKM(N 0km)OST

💬 A friendly family campsite with luxurious heated toilets. Located right among the dunes. Intimate pitches for a restful stay and within walking distance of the beach.

🚗 N9 Alkmaar-Den Helder. In St. Maartensvlotbrug drive towards St. Maartenszee. On to the roundabout near the dunes. Turn right, first campsite on the right.

CC €18  29/3-12/4  5/5-28/5  11/6-18/6  23/6-5/7  24/8-29/9          📍 N 52°47'39'' E 04°41'22''

---

## Tuitjenhorn, NL-1747 CA / Noord-Holland 📶 iD (143)

🏕 Campingpark de Bongerd
✉ Bongerdlaan 3
☎ +31 2 26 39 14 81
📅 5/4 - 1/10
@ info@bongerd.nl

18ha 156T(100-120m²) 10A CEE

1 ABCD**G**IJKLNOPQ
2 RVWX
3 ABC**D**F**G**JKLNRU**W**
4 (C 26/4-2/9) (**F**+**H** 📅) JM
   (Q+S+T+X+Y 📅)
5 **AB**DEFGIJKLMNPUWXY
6 ABEGHKM(N 1km)OSTU

💬 A five star campsite in a parkland setting for children up to 11 years and their (grand)parents. Top class toilet facilities and an extensive children's programme. Spacious splash pool for toddlers. The park also has the 'Holle Bolle Boom' play park. Neither of these are included in the CampingCard ACSI rate. The attractive à la carte restaurant is open each weekend.

🚗 N245 Alkmaar-Schagen. Exit Tuitjenhorn/De Banne industrial area, then follow camping signs.

CC €20  5/4-17/4  5/5-29/5  3/6-6/6  11/6-9/7  26/8-1/10          📍 N 52°44'06'' E 04°46'33''

## Vogelenzang, NL-2114 AP / Noord-Holland

⊗ ♿ 🛜 **iD** **144**

🔺 Camping Vogelenzang
🏠 Tweede Doodweg 17
☎ +31 2 35 84 70 14
🔓 28/3 - 30/9
@ info@vogelenzang.nl

22ha 254T(80-120m²) 16A CEE

**1** ACDEIJKLPQ
**2** BLRVWXY
**3** BFJKLNRU
**4** (C+G 15/5-15/9)
　　(Q+S+T+U+X+Z 🔓)
**5** **AB**DFGIJKLMNOP**S**U
**6** ACEGH**K**(N 2km)OT

💬 Very quietly located campsite just outside the village of Vogelenzang. Intimate hikers' fields separated by high trees.

🚗 N206 Haarlem-Leiden. Camping sign at Vogelenzang. From Haarlem turn right. From Leiden turn left.

Haarlem

CC(( Noordwijk

**CC((** € **18** 28/3-11/4 15/4-28/5 11/6-4/7 25/8-30/9 　🧭 **N 52°18'55'' E 04°33'46''**

---

## Warmenhuizen, NL-1749 VW / Noord-Holland

♿ 🛜 **iD** **145**

🔺 Landschapscamping de Kolibrie
🏠 De Groet 2
☎ +31 2 26 39 45 39
🔓 29/3 - 12/10
@ info@dekolibrie.eu

4ha 100T(150-280m²) 6-10A CEE

**1** ABD**F**IJKLN**P**S
**2** KRVWX
**3** AD**F**JKLN**OP**RU
**4** (Q 🔓)
**5** **AB**DFGHIJMNOP**U**WXYZ
**6** ABCDEGK(N 2km)V

💬 Landscaped campsite with a central location in the rural part of Noord-Holland, 5 km from the lovely Schoorl wood and dunes area. Only 1500m from the Geestmerambacht recreation area. Spacious pitches, relaxed ambiance, peaceful surroundings. Lovely cycle and walking routes for the active holidaymaker.

🚗 N245 Alkmaar-Schagen, exit N504 Schoorl/Koedijk. Drive up to canal, then right. 1st road right. Right at fork in road (Diepsmeerweg). Follow road to campsite.

Schagen
N245
CC((
N9
Alkmaar
N507

**CC((** € **18** 29/3-25/4 5/5-28/5 11/6-4/7 1/9-12/10 　🧭 **N 52°41'58'' E 04°44'46''**

---

## Brielle, NL-3231 AA / Zuid-Holland

👫 ♿ 🛜 **iD** **146**

🔺 Camp. Jachthaven de Meeuw
🏠 Batterijweg 1
☎ +31 1 81 41 27 77
🔓 29/3 - 28/10
@ info@demeeuw.nl

13ha 165T(80-130m²) 10A CEE

**1** ACDGIJKLOPQ
**2** ADLRVWX
**3** BFJKNRU**W**Z
**4** (R+T+U+X 🔓)
**5** **AB**DFGIJKMOPRUWXYZ
**6** CEGHJ**K**L(N 0,5km)OV

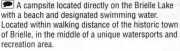

💬 A campsite located directly on the Brielle Lake with a beach and designated swimming water. Located within walking distance of the historic town of Brielle, in the middle of a unique watersports and recreation area.

🚗 A15, keep following Europoort. Follow Brielle. Signposted in Brielle.

A4
N15
Vlaardingen
CC((
A15
N57
Spijkenisse

**CC((** € **16** 2/4-18/4 23/4-25/4 6/5-28/5 11/6-4/7 31/8-27/10 　🧭 **N 51°54'24'' E 04°10'31''**

## Delft, NL-2616 LJ / Zuid-Holland     👨‍🦽 📶 ⚙ **iD** **147**

🔺 Vakantiepark Delftse Hout
📧 Korftlaan 5
☎ +31 1 52 13 00 40
📅 22/3 - 3/11
@ info@delftsehout.nl

6ha 170T(80-120m²) 6-16A CEE

**1** ACD**F**IJLMPQ
**2** DFGLRVWX
**3** B**F**HJKNRUWZ
**4** (A 1/4-31/10) (C+H 1/5-15/9)
   (Q 1/4-1/10) (S 1/4-31/10)
   (T+U+Y+Z 1/4-1/10)
**5** **AB**DEFGIJKLMNPQUW
   XYZ
**6** BCDEGH**IK**(N 2km)OSTV

💬 A modern campsite located in a nature reserve within walking distance of the picturesque centre. Countless opportunities for day trips in the 'randstad' urban area. This campsite has marked out pitches in secluded grounds.

🚗 Motorway A13. Exit 9 Delft, and from here on the campsite is signposted.

Den Haag — N206 — Zoetermeer — N211 — CC — N470 — **Delft** — A4 — A13 — N209 — N471 — **Rotterdam** — A16

**CC** € **20**   22/3-11/4   6/5-28/5   10/6-5/7   26/8-3/11     📡🔺 N 52°01'05'' E 04°22'45''

---

## Den Haag, NL-2555 NW / Zuid-Holland     👨‍🦽 📶 **iD** **148**

🔺 Kampeerresort Kijkduin
📧 Machiel Vrijenhoeklaan 450
☎ +31 7 04 48 21 00
📅 1/1 - 31/12
@ info@kijkduinpark.nl

29ha 350T(80-120m²) 10A CEE

**1** ACG**I**JKPQ
**2** AEGRSVX
**3** B**F**HJK**MNQ**RUWY
**4** (F+H 📅) K
   (Q+S+T+U+V+X+Y+Z 📅)
**5** **AB**DEFGIJKLMNOPQR**S**U
   XYZ
**6** FGHKLM(N 1,5km)STUV

💬 A modern 4-star campsite south-west of The Hague. Located in the dunes with its own access to the beach. Shaded pitches available and also walking and cycling opportunities. Kijkduin is 1 km away for a night out. There are no pitches for motorhomes available at this campsite. Free wifi on entire campsite.

🚗 Located at Kijkduin (SW-point of The Hague). Enter The Hague (Den Haag) via the A12 motorway. Then head towards Kijkduin. Then follow campsite signs.

N44 — CC **Den Haag** — Delft

**CC** € **20**   15/2-12/4   12/5-29/5   11/6-19/6   24/6-9/7   26/8-3/11   20/12-31/12    📡🔺 N 52°03'36'' E 04°12'43''

---

## Hellevoetsluis, NL-3221 LJ / Zuid-Holland     📶 ⚙ **iD** **149**

🔺 Camping 't Weergors
📧 Zuiddijk 2
☎ +31 1 81 31 24 30
📅 29/3 - 1/11
@ info@weergors.nl

7ha 100T(90m²) 6A CEE

**1** ACD**G**IJKLMO**P**Q
**2** ARX
**3** BK**M**NRUW
**4** (G 15/5-15/9) (S 1/5-1/9)
   (T 1/4-15/9) (Y 📅)
**5** **AB**DEFGIJ**K**LMNO**PQ**UWZ
**6** CDEGH**K**(N 2km)OQRSUV

NEW

💬 't Weergors combines the atmosphere of a former farm with the appearance of a modern campsite without exaggerated luxury but mindful of the environment and the natural surroundings.

🚗 N57, exit Hellevoetsluis. Follow signs.

Maassluis — A15 — N57 — CC — Hellevoetsluis — N215

**CC** € **18**   29/3-29/5   3/6-7/6   11/6-12/7   29/8-1/11     📡🔺 N 51°49'47'' E 04°06'57''

## Melissant, NL-3248 LH / Zuid-Holland  👫 📶 iD  150

🏕 Camping Elizabeth Hoeve
📧 Noorddijk 8a
☎ +31 1 87 60 15 48
📅 15/3 - 31/10
@ info@campingelizabethhoeve.nl

8ha 18T(250m²) 16A CEE

**1** ADGIJKLMOPQ
**2** RVWX
**3** ABFGJRW
**5** ABGIJKMNOPUWXYZ
**6** ACEGK(N 0,5km)T

💬 Very peaceful campsite located in the South Holland polder landscape with large pitches. Perfect for those who seek rest. All water sports are available close by.

🚗 N215 from Hellevoetsluis or Ouddorp, turn right at the km-marker 13.4. From Middelharnis, turn left at the km-marker 13.4.

Hellevoetsluis
N57
Sommelsdijk
N215
N59

CC € **16** 15/3-4/7 2/9-31/10 14=12, 21=18, 28=24  🧭 N 51°45'47'' E 04°04'10''

---

## Nieuwe-Tonge, NL-3244 LK / Zuid-Holland  👫 📶 iD  151

🏕 Camping de Grevelingen
📧 Havenweg 1
☎ +31 1 87 65 12 59
📅 15/3 - 1/11
@ info@degrevelingen.nl

NEW

6ha 80T(100-125m²) 10A CEE

**1** ADGIJKLMNPQ
**2** CDRVW
**3** BGNRUW
**4** (T 30/6-31/8)
**5** ABFGIJMNOPRUWXYZ
**6** CDEGHKL(N 2km)O

💬 Besides a large number of pitches for mobile homes, campsite de Grevelingen has various fields with spacious touring pitches. The campsite is located directly on the Grevelingenmeer. The area is very suitable for cycling, fishing and water sports.

🚗 N215, from Oude-Tonge towards Nieuwe-Tonge, signposted from there.

N215
Oude-Tonge
Nieuwerkerk
N257

CC € **16** 16/3-25/4 6/5-28/5 11/6-30/6 1/9-31/10  🧭 N 51°42'20'' E 04°08'10''

---

## Noorden, NL-2431 AA / Zuid-Holland  📶 iD  152

🏕 Koole Kampeerhoeve
📧 Hogedijk 6
☎ +31 1 72 40 82 06
📅 1/4 - 30/9
@ info@kampeerhoevekoole.nl

1ha 30T(40-100m²) 6A CEE

**1** AGIJLNPQ
**2** GRX
**3** BJKNW
**5** DGIJKLMNOPUZ
**6** EGK(N 0,4km)

💬 A campsite located in rural settings with countryside, peace and space. The site is located close to the Nieuwkoopse Plassen lakes where you can go canoeing and sailing on a 'whisper boat'. There are plenty of lovely cycle routes.
🚗 A2 exit 5 direction Kockengen (N401). Turn right at roundabout beyond Kockengen (N212), stay on first road to the left dir. Woerdens Verlaat/Noorden. The campsite is signposted past the church in Noorden with its own bill-board.

N231 N201
Mijdrecht
N207
A2
Alphen aan den Rijn
N212
Nieuwkoop
N11
N458

CC € **18** 1/4-25/5 14/6-30/6 2/9-30/9  🧭 N 52°09'53'' E 04°49'08''

## Noordwijk, NL-2204 AN / Zuid-Holland

    ♿ 🛜 iD **153**

🏕 Camping De Carlton
📧 Kraaierslaan 13
☎ +31 2 52 37 27 83
🗓 1/4 - 15/10
@ info@campingcarlton.nl

2,1ha 55T(100-150m²) 10-16A CEE

**1** AGIJKLNQ
**2** FRTVW
**3** B**FK**O**P**R
**5** **AB**DGIJMN**P**U
**6** ACEGK(N 2km)T

💬 Nice friendly campsite where peace, quiet and privacy have priority. Spacious pitches, greenery and good toilet facilities: the ultimate holiday in the heart of the bulbfields. Beach, dunes and woods within walking or cycling distance. The campsite is an ideal base for day trips.

🚗 A44 exit 3 Sassenheim/Noordwijkerhout, direction Nwh. At roundabout Congrescentrum turn right (Gooweg). At the next roundabout turn left (Schulpweg). Turn right after 'Bakker' stables.

CC € ⑱   1/5-17/5   15/6-30/6   1/9-1/10     📡 N 52°16'17'' E 04°28'35''

---

## Noordwijk, NL-2204 AS / Zuid-Holland

    🛜 iD **154**

🏕 Camping De Duinpan
📧 Duindamseweg 6
☎ +31 2 52 37 17 26
🗓 1/1 - 31/12
@ contact@campingdeduinpan.com

3,5ha 81T(100-140m²) 16A CEE

**1** ACDGIJKLNPQ
**2** FRTVWX
**3** A**F**KL
**4** (Q 🍴)
**5** **AB**GIJMNOPUXYZ
**6** BCEGHK(N 3km)OST

💬 De Duinpan campsite is a friendly, well equipped site with attractive grounds and clean toilets. Rurally located near woods and dunes. 1 km from a beautiful beach with the international Blue Flag classification. Good base for cycling and walking tours.

🚗 A44 exit 3 Sassenheim/Noordwijkerhout, direction Noordwijkerhout. At roundabout (Congrescentrum) turn right (Gooweg). Next roundabout turn left (Schulpweg) turns into Duindamseweg.

CC € ⑱   1/1-9/4   6/5-29/5   11/6-5/7   25/8-31/12     📡 N 52°16'06'' E 04°28'11''

---

## Noordwijk, NL-2204 BC / Zuid-Holland

    🛜 iD **155**

🏕 Camping Le Parage
📧 Langevelderlaan 43
☎ +31 2 52 37 56 71
🗓 15/3 - 1/10
@ info@leparage.nl

4ha 45T(85-100m²) 6A CEE

**1** ACD**G**IJLNPRS
**2** FRSVWX
**3** B**F**HJKLNRU
**4** (T+U+X+Z 1/4-1/10)
**5** **AB**DFGIJKLMNOPUZ
**6** CEG**K**(N 3km)TV

💬 A quiet campsite with nice small fields for touring pitches. Woods, sea, recreational lake and stables all within a radius of 2 km.

🚗 On the N206 take Langevelderslag exit towards Langevelderslag. Second left. Right at the end. Campsite signposted.

CC € ⑳   17/5-28/5   11/6-1/7   31/8-1/10     📡 N 52°16'57'' E 04°29'12''

## Noordwijkerhout, NL-2211 XR / Zuid-Holland    ♿ 🛜 iD   **156**

🏕 Camping Op Hoop van Zegen
🏠 Westeinde 76
☎ +31 2 52 37 54 91
📅 15/3 - 31/10
@ info@
   campingophoopvanzegen.nl

1,8ha 140T(80-100m²) 6-12A CEE

**1** ACD**G**IJKLPRS
**2** FRWX
**3** ABCDHJKNR
**4** (Q 15/3-15/10)
**5** **AB**CDEFGIJ**MPQ**UWZ
**6** ABCDEGHK(N 2km)O

💬 'Op Hoop van Zegen' campsite is a friendly family campsite located between Noordwijk and Noordwijkerhout. Surrounded by bulbfields and woods, yet only 2.5 km from the Noordwijk beaches. Lovely cycling and walking routes. 'Op Hoop van Zegen' campsite is located in a hundred year old farm where they used to make cheese.

🚗 A44 direction Sassenheim/Noordwijkerhout, direction Noordwijkerhout. Continue straight at roundabout 'congrescentrum'. Turn left at T-junction.

CC € **16**   1/4-11/4   22/4-29/5   10/6-5/7   25/8-31/10    📍 N 52°14'56'' E 04°27'49''

---

## Ouddorp, NL-3253 MG / Zuid-Holland    ♿ 🛜 iD   **157**

🏕 Camping Port Zélande
🏠 Port Zélande 2
☎ +31 1 11 67 40 20
📅 1/1 - 31/12
@ camping.portzelande@
   groupepvcp.com

6ha 220T(100m²) 6-10A CEE

**1** ACD**F**IJKLMOPQ
**2** ADEMSWX
**3** ADGHJKL**MNOPQR**T**UWY**Z
**4** (**C**+F+H 📅) IJ**KLN**
   (Q+S+T+U+V+W+Y+Z 📅)
**5** **AB**EFGIJKLMNOPRUWZ
**6** CDEGHK**P**RTU

💬 The campsite is located in a unique natural area on the Brouwersdam. The site is encircled by several different beaches and 0.5 km from the North Sea beach.

🚗 From Zierikzee N59 Renesse - Burgh-Haamstede. Then N57 Ouddorp-Rotterdam, follow signs Port Zélande/Kabbelaarsbank.

CC € **20**   8/1-15/2   5/3-17/4   6/5-29/5   11/6-19/6   24/6-27/6   1/9-10/10    📍 N 51°45'22'' E 03°51'53''

---

## Ouddorp, NL-3253 LR / Zuid-Holland    ♿ 🛜 iD   **158**

🏕 RCN Vakantiepark Toppershoedje
🏠 Strandweg 2-4
☎ +31 8 50 40 07 00
📅 29/3 - 4/11
@ reserveringen@rcn.nl

13ha 138T(100m²) 10-16A CEE

**1** ACD**G**IJKLNOPQ
**2** AEGRSX
**3** AKNRUWY
**4** (S+T+U+X+Y 📅)
**5** **AB**GJLNPUW
**6** EGHK(N 3km)

💬 The campsite is within walking distance of the North Sea beach. Many water sports opportunities close by. There is a restaurant, snack bar and croissant bakery on the campsite. Excellent walking and cycling area and near the seaside resort of Ouddorp.

🚗 Motorway Hellegatsplein-Oude Tonge-Ouddorp. Campsite signposted in Ouddorp.

CC € **18**   29/3-29/5   3/6-7/6   11/6-27/6   1/7-12/7   30/8-4/11    📍 N 51°49'24'' E 03°55'00''

## Rijnsburg, NL-2231 NW / Zuid-Holland

⛰ Vakantiepark Koningshof
✉ Elsgeesterweg 8
☎ +31 7 14 02 60 51
🕐 22/3 - 2/11
@ info@koningshofholland.nl

**NEW**

8,7ha 200T(80-100m²) 10A CEE

**1** ACD**F**IJKLMOPQ
**2** FLRTUVX
**3** B**F**JKL**M**NRUW
**4** (C 15/5-15/9) (F+H 🅿) JM (Q+S+T+U+Y+Z 1/4-1/11)
**5** **AB**DEFGIJKLMNOPUW XYZ
**6** CDEGHKL(N 2km)OSTV

💬 Large campsite with spacious, partly paved pitches separated by hedges. Sheltered location among the many flower nurseries of Rijnsburg.

🚗 A44, exit 7 Oegstgeest/Rijnsburg, towards Rijnsburg. In Rijnsburg follow the signs to the campsite.

N205 N207 A44 A44 A445 N441 A4 N44 Leiden Alphen aan den Rijn

CC € 20  22/3-13/4  5/5-29/5  10/6-6/7  24/8-2/11    N 52°11'58'' E 04°27'16''

---

## Rockanje, NL-3235 LL / Zuid-Holland

⛰ Midicamping Van der Burgh
✉ Voet- of Kraagweg 9
☎ +31 1 81 40 41 79
🕐 1/1 - 31/12
@ info@midicamping.nl

5ha 85T(150m²) 10A CEE

**1** ADG**I**JKLMNOPQ
**2** RWX
**3** BDJKPR
**4** (Q 1/7-31/8)
**5** **AB**CDGI**J**MNO**PQ**UWXYZ
**6** ACDEGH**K**LO

💬 The campsite is located on the islands of South-Holland, close to the beach, dunes and fishing water. A medium-sized campsite with a new toilet pavilion and large pitches.

🚗 Rotterdam-Europoort A15, exit 12 direction Brielle. N57 Rockanje then N496, signposted in Rockanje.

Maassluis A15 Hellevoetsluis N57 N215

CC € 16  1/1-18/4  6/5-28/5  11/6-11/7  2/9-31/12    N 51°51'23'' E 04°05'36''

---

## Rockanje, NL-3235 LA / Zuid-Holland

⛰ Molecaten Park Rondeweibos
✉ Schapengorsedijk 19
☎ +31 1 81 40 19 44
🕐 29/3 - 31/10
@ rondeweibos@molecaten.nl

**NEW**

32ha 100T(80m²) 10A CEE

**1** ACD**G**IJLPQ
**2** AEGRSVWX
**3** BGHJK**M**NRUW
**4** (C+G 1/5-31/8) (Q+S+T+U+Y 30/3-15/9)
**5** **AB**FGIJKLMNOP**S**UWXYZ
**6** CDEGH**K**(N 2,5km)OSTV

💬 The campsite is a 10-minute walk from the beach. There is a very large playground. Beautiful, historic fortified towns in the area.

🚗 A15/N57. Exit Rockanje. Follow the Rondeweibos signs.

N15 Hellevoetsluis N57 Middelharnis

CC € 18  29/3-18/4  5/5-28/5  11/6-19/6  23/6-9/7  26/8-31/10    N 51°51'25'' E 04°05'04''

## Rockanje, NL-3235 CC / Zuid-Holland

⊗ ♿ 🛜 **iD** 162

🔺 Molecaten Park Waterbos
📧 Duinrand 11
☎ +31 1 81 40 19 00
📅 29/3 - 31/10
@ waterbos@molecaten.nl

7,5ha 118T(100m²) 6-10A CEE

**1** ACDEIJLPQ
**2** RSVWXY
**3** BGJKNRUW
**4** (C+H 30/4-1/9) (Q+R 🔲)
  (T+X 15/6-15/9)
**5** **AB**DFGJLMNO**PST**UWZ
**6** CDEGH**K**(N 1km)SV

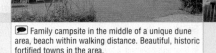

💬 Family campsite in the middle of a unique dune area, beach within walking distance. Beautiful, historic fortified towns in the area.

🚗 A15, exit Europoort drive towards Hellevoetsluis, exit Rockanje, and then follow the signs.

N15
Brielle
CC
Hellevoetsluis
N57

CC € 18 5/5-28/5 11/6-19/6 23/6-9/7 26/8-31/10 📍 N 51°52'48'' E 04°03'15''

## Zevenhuizen, NL-2761 ED / Zuid-Holland

♿ 🛜 **iD** 163

🔺 Recreatiepark De Koornmolen
📧 Tweemanspolder 6A
☎ +31 1 80 63 16 54
📅 1/4 - 29/9
@ info@koornmolen.nl

6ha 88T(90-140m²) 6A CEE

**1** ACD**G**IJKLMNO**P**Q
**2** CDFLRUWXY
**3** BD**F**GHJK**Q**RU**VW**Z
**4** (F 🔲) (Q+T+U 20/7-31/8)
  (X+Y 🔲)
**5** **AB**DFIJKLMNP**S**Z
**6** DEGH**K**(N 2km)OTV

💬 A friendly family campsite, part of 'De Koornmolen' recreation park on the edge of the Rottemeren lakes. Touring fields surrounded by greenery and separated from the permanent pitches.

🚗 A12 exit 9 Zevenhuizen-Waddinxveen; on the A20 exit 17 Nieuwerkerk a/d IJssel-Zevenhuizen. Then direction Zevenhuizen. Left at fire station to Tweemans Polder. Entrance to De Koornmolen about 1 km on the right.

A4
Zoetermeer N207
N470
CC
A13
N471 A20
Rotterdam

CC € 16 1/4-20/4 5/5-29/5 10/6-7/7 26/8-28/9 📍 N 52°00'32'' E 04°33'54''

## Aagtekerke, NL-4363 RJ / Zeeland

♿ 🛜 ✿ **iD** 164

🔺 Ardoer camping Westhove
📧 Zuiverseweg 2
☎ +31 1 18 58 18 09
📅 29/3 - 27/10
@ westhove@ardoer.com

8,4ha 261T(81-100m²) 6-10A CEE

**1** AD**FI**JLNPQ
**2** RVWX
**3** BC**F**GJKNRU**V**
**4** (F+H 🔲) **N**(Q+S+T+X 🔲)
**5** **AB**DFGIJLMNPR**S**UWXYZ
**6** ACDEGHKM(N 1,5km)OSTV

💬 Westhove campsite is located just 1500 metres from the resort of Domburg. Lovely spacious pitches, indoor swimming pool on the site, indoor playground and a bathhouse in Ancient Greek style.

🚗 Follow signs to Domburg from Middelburg. Signposted before Domburg.

CC N287
N288 N57
Middelburg
Oost-
Souburg

CC € 18 29/3-19/4 5/5-29/5 3/6-7/6 11/6-6/7 24/8-27/10 📍 N 51°33'21'' E 03°30'52''

## Baarland, NL-4435 NR / Zeeland

📶 ✿

165

🏕 Ardoer comfortcamping Scheldeoord
✉ Landingsweg 1
☎ +31 1 13 63 99 00
🕐 29/3 - 27/10
@ scheldeoord@ardoer.com

17ha 200T(120m²) 16A CEE

1 CDGIJKLMNOPQ
2 AEGKLRVX
3 BCGJKMNRUWY
4 (A 9/7-26/7) (C 19/4-15/9)
  (F+H 🕐) JN
  (Q+S+T+U+X+Z 🕐)
5 ABDEFGIJKLMNOPRSTUX
  YZ
6 CDEGHK(N 2km)OPRSTV

💬 An active family campsite providing all amenities. Quietly located near the Westerschelde sea defences in Southern Beveland, a lovely area classified as a National Landscape. Plenty of space for being active but still having some peace. Walking, cycling, fishing? It's up to you!

🚗 A58 exit 's-Gravenpolder (35). Via 's-Gravenpolder to Hoedekenskerke. Follow 'Scheldeoord' signs.

CC € 18  29/3-29/5  3/6-7/6  11/6-5/7  27/8-27/10

🧭 N 51°23'47'' E 03°53'53''

---

## Brouwershaven, NL-4318 TV / Zeeland

📶 iD

166

🏕 Camping Den Osse
✉ Blankersweg 4
☎ +31 1 11 69 15 13
🕐 5/4 - 27/10
@ info@campingdenosse.nl

8,5ha 80T(80-120m²) 6-16A CEE

1 ACDGIJKLMNOPQ
2 GRVX
3 BJMNRUW
4 (C+H 8/5-31/8)
  (Q+R+T+X 🕐)
5 ABFGIJKLMNOPUWXY
6 CDEGHKL(N 2km)STV

💬 A lively family campsite a stone's throw from the Grevelingenmeer and the Brouwersdam. Ideal for diving or if you enjoy rest, space, watersports, sun, sea and the beach. Heated swimming pool and entertainment in the summer.

🚗 N59 towards Zierikzee. In Zierikzee drive in the direction of Brouwershaven. In Brouwershaven the campsite is signposted.

CC € 18  5/4-18/4  23/4-29/5  11/6-19/6  26/8-27/10  7=6

🧭 N 51°44'18'' E 03°53'21''

---

## Burgh-Haamstede, NL-4328 GR / Zeeland

⊗ ♿ 📶 iD

167

🏕 Ardoer camping Ginsterveld
✉ Maireweg 10
☎ +31 1 11 65 15 90
🕐 29/3 - 27/10
@ ginsterveld@ardoer.com

14ha 310T(80-100m²) 16A CEE

1 ADEIJKLOPQ
2 GRSVX
3 BJKNRUW
4 (F+H+Q+S+T+U+V+X+Y 🕐)
5 ABDEFGIJKNOPRSUWXY
6 CEGHKL(N 2km)OST

💬 A campsite 2 km from the beach and a stone's throw from some charming villages. Plenty of opportunities for walking and cycling. The site features an indoor swimming pool with waterslide. Free wifi.

🚗 Signposted from Burgh-Haamstede. Follow R107.

CC € 16  29/3-19/4  5/5-29/5  11/6-6/7  31/8-11/10

🧭 N 51°42'59'' E 03°43'46''

## Burgh-Haamstede, NL-4328 GR / Zeeland

👫 ♿ 📶 iD **168**

🏕 Camping De Duinhoeve B.V.
✉ Maireweg 7
☎ +31 1 11 65 15 62
🔑 28/3 - 27/10
@ info@deduinhoeve.nl

47,5ha 820T(100-110m²) 10A CEE

**1** ACD**G**IJKLMNO**PQ**
**2** GRSVX
**3** AJK**M**N**Q**RUW
**4** **K**M**N**(S+T+U+Y 🔑)
**5** **AB**EF**G**IJMNOP**QS**UWZ
**6** CDEGHKL(N 2,5km)ORTV

💬 Luxury, or simply basic, young or not so young, you will always feel at home here! Camping De Duinhoeve is located in the middle of a lovely nature reserve on the Kop van Schouwen. The campsite is close to the beach and the woods. There are sheltered pitches with or without facilities.

🚗 A29 Dinteloord-Rotterdam. From Hellegatsplein towards Zierikzee. Then direction Renesse/Haamstede. Follow Route 107.

Brouwershaven
N59
N57    Zierikzee

CC € 18 28/3-29/5  11/6-27/6  1/9-27/10    📍 N 51°43'07'' E 03°43'44''

---

## Burgh-Haamstede, NL-4328 GV / Zeeland

✈ 📶 iD **169**

🏕 Camping Groenewoud
✉ Groenewoudswegje 11
☎ +31 1 11 65 14 10
🔑 30/3 - 27/10
@ info@campinggroenewoud.nl

17ha 62T(100-125m²) 10A CEE

**1** AEIJKLOPQ
**2** DLRSVWX
**3** BHJKNRUVWZ
**4** (C+H 1/5-1/10)
   (Q+T+U+X+Y 🔑)
**5** **AB**DFGIJKLMNO**PQ**UWY
**6** ACDEGH**K**(N 0,2km)OSV

💬 Located in a beautiful 17 hect. natural area, this site is recommended for rest and nature. Lovely outdoor pool with cafe serving bar meals, 2 ponds, luxurious new toilets with underfloor heating make your holiday complete. Pitches 100-125 m². Cable TV (free) and wireless internet available.

🚗 From Burgh-Haamstede drive towards 'vuurtoren' (lighthouse). After the traffic lights turn left down the fourth road and then after 200 metres the campsite is located on the left.

Brouwershaven
CC
N59
N57    Zierikzee
N256

CC € 18 30/3-27/4  12/5-29/5  2/6-7/6  10/6-6/7  1/9-27/10    📍 N 51°42'29'' E 03°43'18''

---

## Cadzand, NL-4506 HK / Zeeland

📶 iD **170**

🏕 Camping Wulpen
✉ Vierhonderdpolderdijk 1
☎ +31 1 17 39 12 26
🔑 1/4 - 14/10
@ info@campingwulpen.nl

4,7ha 135T(100-130m²) 6-10A CEE

**1** AD**F**IJKLNOPQ
**2** AGRVWX
**3** AB**F**GJKLNRU**W**
**4** (Q+R 🔑)
   (Z 6/7-1/9,30/5-10/6)
**5** **AB**DFGHIJKLMNOPUWXYZ
**6** ABCDEGHK(N 0,5km)OV

💬 A very well maintained family campsite with lots of privacy, sheltered pitches and a cozy living room with TV. The campsite is located directly on the cycle route junction system.

🚗 When entering Cadzand turn right at the mill and then take the first road to the right.

Vlissingen

Knokke-Heist  CC    N676
N49         N253      N61
N300
N374    E34

CC € 18 1/4-12/4  26/4-29/5  2/6-6/6  11/6-19/6  23/6-6/7  25/8-14/10    📍 N 51°22'12'' E 03°25'00''

## Dishoek/Koudekerke, NL-4371 NT / Zeeland

171

🏕 Camping Dishoek
📧 Dishoek 2
☎ +31 1 18 55 13 48
🗓 29/3 - 3/11
@ info@roompot.nl

4,6ha 270T(< 80m²) 6A CEE

**1** ACD**G**IJKLNOPQ
**2** AEFRSVWX
**3** ABKNRUWY
**4** (S+T+U+V+X+Z ⊙)
**5** **AB**DFGIJKLMNOPUWXY
**6** DEG**K**M(N 4km)OSTV

💬 For camping 'right by the beach and the sea' this intimate four star family campsite is the ultimate holiday destination. You will be camping at the foot of the dunes. Beyond the dunes is the sunniest and the only truly south-facing beach in the Netherlands. There are lovely walking and cycling routes in the nearby wooded nature reserve. There are no motorhome pitches available at this campsite.
🚗 A58 as far as Vlissingen, exit Dishoek. Follow signs.

🅲🅲 € ⑯ *29/3-12/4  12/5-29/5  11/6-19/6  24/6-9/7  26/8-3/11*    📍 N 51°28'08'' E 03°31'25''

---

## Domburg, NL-4357 RD / Zeeland

172

🏕 Camping Hof Domburg
📧 Schelpweg 7
☎ +31 1 18 58 82 00
🗓 1/1 - 31/12
@ info@roompot.nl

20ha 473T(80m²) 6A CEE

**1** ACDGIJKNOPQ
**2** EGRSVX
**3** ABC**E**JK**M**N**QRST**UVW
**4** (C 1/4-31/10) (F ⊙) J**LNP** (S+T+U+X+Y ⊙)
**5** **AB**FGJLMNP**S**UWXYZ
**6** EGHKL(N 0,5km)OSTX

💬 A friendly family campsite located 100m from the town of Domburg and 400m from the North Sea beaches. Subtropical leisure pool on the site. There are no motorhome pitches available at this campsite.

🚗 Motorway A58 Bergen op Zoom-Vlissingen, Exit Middelburg. Follow the signs to Domburg. In Domburg the campsite is signposted.

🅲🅲 € ⑳ *1/1-12/4  12/5-29/5  11/6-19/6  24/6-9/7  26/8-31/12*    📍 N 51°33'33'' E 03°29'12''

---

## Ellemeet, NL-4323 LC / Zeeland

173

🏕 Camping Klaverweide
📧 Kuijerdamseweg 56
☎ +31 1 11 67 18 59
🗓 15/3 - 27/10
@ info@klaverweide.com

4ha 76T(100-120m²) 10A CEE

**1** ACD**G**IJKLMNOPQ
**2** GRW
**3** BJKNRU
**4** (Q+S+T+X 1/4-25/10)
**5** **AB**EFGIJKLMNO**P**UWXY
**6** CDEGIK(N 0,2km)S

💬 Friendly campsite by the North Sea and Grevelingenmeer. Many watersports opportunities. Spacious pitches with 10A power, TV connection, water and drainage. Fresh bread in the supermarket each morning. Clean modern toilets. Close by: lovely villages, walking and cycling paths through the countryside.

🚗 Located on the N57 Brouwersdam-Serooskerke, exit Ellemeet.

🅲🅲 € ⑱ *15/3-28/5  11/6-27/6  23/8-27/10*    📍 N 51°43'55'' E 03°49'13''

## Groede, NL-4503 PA / Zeeland

♿ 🛜 **iD** (174)

🏕️ Strandcamping Groede
📧 Zeeweg 1
☎ +31 1 17 37 13 84
📅 28/3 - 27/10
@ receptie@
strandcampinggroede.nl

28ha 706T(80-200m²) 6-16A CEE

**1** ADGIJKLMOPQ
**2** AERVWX
**3** ABFGHJKNRUWY
**4** (Q+S+T+U+Y+Z ⊙)
**5** ABCDEFGHIJKLMNOPQU
WXYZ
**6** ABCDEGHKLM(N 6km)OST
UV

💬 Family campsite directly on one of the cleanest beaches in the Netherlands, located in a beautiful natural area. Camping pitches of 80 to 200 m². Excellent toilet facilities offering every amenity. Positioned on marked-out cycle and walking routes. Motorhomes longer than 6 metres need to book comfort pitches. With CampingCard ACSI a surcharge applies for this.

🚗 Just before the town of Groede take the direction to the beach (strand) and follow the signs.

CC € 20 28/3-12/4 26/4-29/5 2/6-6/6 11/6-19/6 23/6-6/7 25/8-27/10 　 N 51°23'48'' E 03°29'21''

---

## Groot Valkenisse/Biggekerke, NL-4373 RR / Zeeland

⊗ 🛜 ♿ **iD** (175)

🏕️ Strandcamping Valkenisse bv
📧 Valkenisseweg 64
☎ +31 1 18 56 13 14
📅 1/4 - 26/10
@ info@campingvalkenisse.nl

10,2ha 150T(100m²) 10-16A CEE

**1** ADEIJLOPQ
**2** AEFRVWX
**3** ACKNRUWY
**4** (Q+S+T+U+X+Y ⊙)
**5** ABDEFGIJKLMNOPSTUXY
**6** ACEGHKM(N 2km)OSV

💬 Ideal holiday destination. Sunbathing on the beach, swimming and fishing; watching the sun go down, getting a breath of fresh air and enjoying the wild waves as they break on the shore; walking over the highest dunes in the Netherlands with lovely panoramic views of the passing ships; an ideally situated starting point for walking and cycling trips.

🚗 Vlissingen-Koudekerke, take the direction of Zoutelande, exit Groot Valkenisse.

CC € 18 1/4-18/4 23/4-28/5 3/6-6/6 11/6-4/7 1/9-26/10 　 N 51°29'32'' E 03°30'24''

---

## Hengstdijk, NL-4585 PL / Zeeland

♿ 🛜 (176)

🏕️ Camping Recreatiecentrum
De Vogel
📧 Vogelweg 4
☎ +31 1 14 68 16 25
📅 29/3 - 3/11
@ info@de-vogel.nl

54ha 215T(100-110m²) 6A CEE

**1** DGIJLMOPQ
**2** ADGLRVXY
**3** BGKMNOPQRUVWZ
**4** (F+H ⊙) JN(S 30/3-27/10)
(T+U+V+X+Y+Z ⊙)
**5** ABDEFGIJKLMNOPQUW
**6** CDEGHKM(N 0,5km)OPS
TUV

NEW

💬 A spacious family campsite with refurbished toilet facilities, a large swimming pool with water slide, various playgrounds and indoor playground, indoor plaza with restaurant, cafeteria and terrace. Ideally located as a starting point for walking and cycling.

🚗 N61 Terneuzen-Zaamslag-Hulst, exit Vogelwaarde direction Hengstdijk, and then follow the signs.

CC € 18 6/5-29/5 11/6-5/7 26/8-29/9 　 N 51°20'31'' E 03°59'25''

## Hoek, NL-4542 PN / Zeeland

👫 ♿ **177**

🏕 Oostappen Vakantiepark Marina Beach
📧 Middenweg 1
☎ +31 1 15 48 17 30
🗓 6/4 - 28/10
@ info@
vakantieparkmarinabeach.nl

212ha 475T(100-110m²) 4-6A CEE

**1** DGIJKLMOPQ
**2** ADGKLRSVWXY
**3** BCGJKNQRUWZ
**4** (A 1/7-31/8)
(Q+S+T+U+X+Y+Z
18/4-26/10)
**5** ABDEFGIJKLMNOPQUW
XYZ
**6** CDEG(N 3,5km)STUV

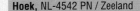

💬 A park with plenty of facilities located right by the water. Various indoor and outdoor sports activities. It has all the ingredients of a wonderful (family) holiday. Includes use Aquadome Scheldorado in Terneuzen.

🚗 On route N61, 4 km west of Hoek.

Breskens
Terneuzen
N61 CC
Axel
N62
N456

CC € 12  27/4-29/5  10/6-5/7  2/9-28/10   🧭 N 51°18'52'' E 03°43'34''

---

## Kamperland, NL-4493 PH / Zeeland

📶 iD **178**

🏕 Camping Roompot Beach Resort
📧 Mariapolderseweg 1
☎ +31 1 13 37 40 00
🗓 1/1 - 31/12
@ info@roompot.nl

72ha 584T(90-115m²) 6-16A CEE

**1** ACDGIJKNPQ
**2** AEGLRVWX
**3** ABCGJKMNQRSTUWY
**4** (F+H 🅿) IJKLN
(Q+S+T+U+V+W+Y+Z 🅿)
**5** ABDEFGIJKLMNOPSUW
XYZ
**6** AEGHJKLM(N 3km)OSTV

💬 Camping Roompot is located close to the Oosterschelde. Numerous children's activities are organised on the campsite. The campsite has a subtropical leisure pool. There are no motorhome pitches available at this campsite.

🚗 Motorway A58 Bergen op Zoom-Vlissingen, exit Zierikzee. Before the Zeeland bridge drive towards Kamperland. In Kamperland there are signs to the campsite.

Zierikzee
N57
N256
CC
N287
Middelburg  A58  Goes

CC € 16  1/1-12/4  12/5-29/5  11/6-19/6  24/6-9/7  26/8-31/12   🧭 N 51°35'23'' E 03°43'17''

---

## Kamperland, NL-4493 CX / Zeeland

📶 iD **179**

🏕 RCN vakantiepark de Schotsman
📧 Schotsmanweg 1
☎ +31 8 50 40 07 00
🗓 29/3 - 28/10
@ reserveringen@rcn.nl

30ha 668T(100m²) 10-16A CEE

**1** ACDFIJKLNPQ
**2** DLRSX
**3** BJKMNQRUWZ
**4** (C+H 1/5-14/9) J
(S+T+U+X+Y 🅿)
**5** ABFGIJKLMNOPUWXYZ
**6** ACDEGHK(N 2km)ORS

💬 RCN de Schotsman campsite is positioned right by the water on the Veerse Meer lake and next to an extensive wood for walking. The North Sea beaches are about 2 km away.

🚗 A58 Bergen op Zoom-Vlissingen, exit Zierikzee. Before the Zeeland Bridge direction Kamperland. Signposted in Kamperland.

Oostkapelle
CC
N57
Middelburg
A58
N254

CC € 18  29/3-29/5  3/6-7/6  11/6-12/7  30/8-28/10   🧭 N 51°34'06'' E 03°39'48''

## Kortgene, NL-4484 NT / Zeeland

🏕 Ardoer vakantiepark de Paardekreek
📧 Havenweg 1
☎ +31 1 13 30 20 51
📅 29/3 - 3/11
@ paardekreek@ardoer.com

180

10ha 120T(80-120m²) 10A CEE

**1** ADGIJKLMOPQ
**2** DGLRVX
**3** BCJKNRUWZ
**4** (C 🔧) (D 1/5-30/9) KLMN (Q+S+T+Y 🔧)
**5** ABDEFGIJMNOPUWXY
**6** CDEGHKLM(N 0,5km)STUV

💬 Campsite de Paardekreek is located directly on the Veere Lake, so ideal for a wonderful water sports holiday. There is a large recreation hall and an indoor children's pool on the campsite. There is also a new outdoor pool.

🚗 Motorway A58 Bergen op Zoom-Vlissingen take exit Zierikzee. In the direction of Zierikzee, take exit Kortgene. Signposted from here.

[map: Zierikzee, N57, N256, CC, Middelburg, Goes, A58, N254, N62]

CC € **18** 29/3-26/4 5/5-29/5 3/6-7/6 11/6-6/7 24/8-3/11    📡 N 51°33'04'' E 03°48'28''

---

## Nieuwvliet, NL-4504 AA / Zeeland

🏕 Ardoer camping International
📧 St. Bavodijk 2D
☎ +31 1 17 37 12 33
📅 29/3 - 3/11
@ international@ardoer.com

181

8ha 112T(80-140m²) 6A CEE

**1** ACDGIJKLMOPRS
**2** ARVWX
**3** ABCDFGJKMNRUW
**4** (G 30/5-15/9) M (Q+R+T+U 🔧)
**5** ABDFGIJKLMNOPSUWXYZ
**6** BCDEGHKM(N 0,5km)ORSTV

💬 Peaceful campsite with views of rustic windmills, located directly on the cross-border cycle route network. Comfort pitches with CampingCard ACSI have every convenience.

🚗 Via Terneuzen (Toll) direction Breskens. Before Breskens, direction Goede and drive to Nieuwvliet. At roundabout R102 turn right. Campsite situated 700 metres further on.

[map: Vlissingen, N662, Knokke-Heist, CC, N676, N253, N49, N61, E34]

CC € **16** 29/3-18/4 23/4-26/4 5/5-28/5 11/6-19/6 24/6-6/7 24/8-2/11    📡 N 51°22'28'' E 03°28'10''

---

## Nieuwvliet-Bad, NL-4504 PT / Zeeland

🏕 Camping Schippers
📧 Baanstpoldersedijk 6
☎ +31 1 17 37 12 50
📅 1/4 - 26/10
@ info@campingschippers.nl

182

4ha 51T(80m²) 10A CEE

**1** ADFIJKLNPRS
**2** AERVWX
**3** AFJNOPRWY
**5** ABDFGIJMNOPUWZ
**6** ABDEGHJ(N 2,5km)

💬 A small family campsite with very well shaded pitches on small fields, recommended for those seeking relaxation as it is only 300m from the beach. Cycle track intersection right by the site. Good base for visits to Knokke, Bruges, Ghent and Sluis.

🚗 Via Terneuzen (toll) towards Breskens. Before Breskens drive via Groede to Nieuwvliet. At roundabout take R102 towards Nieuwvliet-Bad. Follow the signs to the campsite.

[map: Vlissingen, Knokke-Heist, CC, N676, N253, N49, N61, E34]

CC € **18** 1/4-18/4 2/5-29/5 24/6-5/7 2/9-26/10    📡 N 51°23'23'' E 03°27'23''

## Nieuwvliet-Bad, NL-4504 PS / Zeeland 📶 iD 183

🏕 Camping Zonneweelde
✉ Baanstpoldersedijk 1
☎ +31 1 17 37 19 10
📅 1/1 - 31/12
@ info@campingzonneweelde.nl

7,5ha 75T(130m²) 10A CEE

**1** ACD**G**IJKLMNOPQ
**2** ARVWX
**3** ABC**F**GJKLNRU**W**
**4** (C+H 15/5-15/9) M
(Q+S+T+U+V+Y+Z 19/4-3/11)
**5** **ABC**DEFGI**JKL**MNO**PQ**U
WXY
**6** ABCDEGH**K**M(N 5km)OSV

💬 Quietly located family campsite 600 metres from a beautiful sandy beach. The site has unique 250 m² large heated water playground and heated swimming pool. Campsite shop, snack bar and restaurant. Located directly on the cycle route junction system. Good base for trips to Sluis, Bruges and Ghent.

🚗 Via Terneuzen (toll) take the direction of Breskens. Just before the town of Breskens via Groede to Nieuwvliet. At roundabout turn right (R102) and follow the signs.

Vlissingen

Knokke-Heist

N676

N49

N61

N374 E34

N456

CC €20 1/1-29/5 2/6-7/6 11/6-19/6 24/6-6/7 26/8-2/11 ▲ N 51°22'56'' E 03°27'28''

---

## Oostkapelle, NL-4356 RE / Zeeland ♿ 📶 ✿ iD 184

🏕 Ardoer camping De Pekelinge
✉ Landmetersweg 1
☎ +31 1 18 58 28 20
📅 29/3 - 27/10
@ pekelinge@ardoer.com

10ha 323T(80-120m²) 10A CEE

**1** ACD**G**IJKLMNOPQ
**2** LRVX
**3** BCD**F**J**KM**NRU
**4** (F+H 📅) J(S+T+X 📅)
**5** **AB**DEFGIJKLMNPR**S**UWX
YZ
**6** CDEGHIKLM(N 1km)OSTV

💬 The Pekelinge is a spacious family campsite 3 km from the North Sea coast. The campsite has a heated indoor swimming pool and a separate toddlers' pool.

🚗 Motorway A58 Bergen op Zoom-Vlissingen, exit Middelburg. Follow signs 'Domburg/Oostkapelle'. Signposted in Oostkapelle.

N288

N57

Middelburg

Oost-Souburg

A58

CC €18 29/3-12/4 5/5-29/5 3/6-7/6 11/6-19/6 24/6-29/6 24/8-27/10 ▲ N 51°33'25'' E 03°33'03''

---

## Oostkapelle, NL-4356 RJ / Zeeland ⊗ ♿ 📶 ✿ iD 185

🏕 Ardoer campingpark Ons Buiten
✉ Aagtekerkseweg 2A
☎ +31 1 18 58 18 13
📅 29/3 - 4/11
@ onsbuiten@ardoer.com

7,6ha 308T(110-150m²) 8-16A CEE

**1** ADEIJKLNOPQ
**2** GRVX
**3** BC**F**GJKNRU
**4** (C+D+F+H 📅) KLN
(Q+S+T+U+X+Y 📅)
**5** **AB**DEFGIJKLMNOPQR**S**U
WXYZ
**6** CDEGHKL(N 0,3km)STV

💬 A lovely child-friendly campsite. The site has a heated pool with a sliding roof and an indoor water playground. There is a sauna and wellness and a grand café. It is 2 km from the sea, beach and woods on the outskirts of Oostkapelle and close to Domburg. Pitches up to 125 m² are available for CampingCard ACSI holders.

🚗 Motorway A58 Bergen op Zoom-Vlissingen, exit Middelburg. Follow signs 'Domburg-Oostkapelle'. Directions in Oostkapelle.

N288

N57

Middelburg

Oost-Souburg

A58

N254

CC €20 29/3-12/4 5/5-29/5 11/6-19/6 24/6-12/7 29/8-4/11 ▲ N 51°33'47'' E 03°32'47''

## Renesse, NL-4325 DM / Zeeland

⊗ ♿ 🛜 ✿ **iD** 186

🏕 Ardoer Camping Julianahoeve
📧 Hoogenboomlaan 42
☎ +31 1 11 46 14 14
🔑 29/3 - 3/11
@ info@julianahoeve.nl

39ha 314T(85-110m²) 16A CEE

**1** ACDEIJKLMOPQ
**2** AERSVX
**3** BC**MNOP**RUW
**4** (F+H 🔑) JKLM
(Q+S+T+U+X+Y+Z 🔑)
**5** **AB**DEFGIJKLMNO**PS**UW
XYZ
**6** CDFGHK(N 1,5km)OST

💬 A lovely campsite situated in the dunes at Renesse. You could not spend a holiday closer to the beach at Renesse. CampingCard ACSI is only valid on the comfort pitches at park Reiger.

🚗 A29 Dinteloord-Rotterdam. From Hellegatsplein direction Zierikzee.Afterwards, direction Renesse. Renesse-West R104.

CC
Burgh-Haamstede   N59
N57   Zierikzee

CC € 20  5/4-11/4  6/5-28/5  3/6-6/6  12/6-18/6  24/6-27/6  2/9-3/11    N 51°43'50'' E 03°45'19''

---

## Renesse, NL-4325 EP / Zeeland

♿ 🛜 **iD** 187

🏕 Camping Duinhoeve
📧 Scholderlaan 8
☎ +31 1 11 46 13 09
🔑 15/3 - 1/11
@ receptie@campingduinhoeve.nl

4,5ha 200T(90-120m²) 16A CEE

**1** A**F**IJKLMOPQ
**2** EGRSVWX
**3** BJK**N**O**P**RUW
**4** (E+S+T+U+X+Y 13/4-28/10)
**5** **AB**DEFGIJ**M**NPUWXYZ
**6** ACEG**K**(N 1km)OS

💬 Located in a quiet corner of Renesse, in the middle of a nature reserve, within walking distance (5 mins.) of the sea and dunes; a cycling and walking area for sure. A wealth of facilities on campsite; modern toilet facilities, a central building containing a fully stocked Spar minimarket, launderette, reception, snack bar and restaurant.

🚗 A29 Dinteloord-Rotterdam, from Hellegatsplein towards Zierikzee. Direction Renesse. Follow route 101 and 102. Follow signs to campsite.

CC
Burgh-Haamstede   N59
N57   Zierikzee

CC € 18  15/3-12/4  6/5-27/5  14/6-18/6  23/6-7/7  1/9-31/10    N 51°44'21'' E 03°46'39''

---

## Renesse, NL-4325 LD / Zeeland

♿ 🛜 **iD** 188

🏕 Camping International
📧 Scharendijkseweg 8
☎ +31 1 11 46 13 91
🔑 17/3 - 3/11
@ info@camping-international.net

3,1ha 320T(80-100m²) 16A CEE

**1** AD**G**IJLM**P**Q
**2** EGRSX
**3** BJKLRUW
**4** (Q+S+Z 🔑)
**5** **AB**DEFGIJK**L**MNOPUWXY
**6** CDEGHKL(N 1,5km)OSTV

💬 An attractive family camp located 300m from the North Sea beach. All the camping fields are surrounded by rows of trees and bushes, and you will camp on well maintained grassland.

🚗 A29 Dinteloord-Rotterdam, from Hellegatsplein intersection direction Zierikzee. Then direction Renesse. Follow route 101 at first roundabout.

Ouddorp

CC
N59
N57   Zierikzee

CC € 18  17/3-17/4  24/4-28/5  3/6-6/6  12/6-18/6  1/7-8/7  25/8-3/11    N 51°44'20'' E 03°47'19''

## Renesse, NL-4325 CP / Zeeland ♿ 🛜 ✿ iD **189**

⬛ Camping Molecaten Park
　Wijde Blick
✉ Lagezoom 23
☎ +31 1 11 46 88 88
⌚ 1/1 - 31/12
@ wijdeblick@molecaten.nl

8ha 218T(90-120m²) 6-16A CEE

**1** ACD**G**IJKLMNOPQ
**2** GRSX
**3** BGJKN**OP**RU
**4** (F+H+Q ⌚)
　(S+T+U+X 1/3-30/10)
**5** **AB**EFGIJKLMNOP**S**UW
　XYZ
**6** ACDEGH**I**KL(N 1,5km)OR
　STV

💬 Peacefully located campsite with plenty of cycling and walking opportunities. 1.5 km from one of the loveliest and widest beaches in the Netherlands.

🚗 From before Renesse continue on route R106. Signposted from here.

Burgh-Haamstede  N59
N57  Zierikzee
N256

CC €**20** 1/1-18/4  5/5-28/5  11/6-19/6  23/6-9/7  26/8-31/12  📐 N 51°43'07'' E 03°46'05''

---

## Renesse, NL-4325 DJ / Zeeland ⊗ 🛜 ♿ 🛜 iD **190**

⬛ Vakantiepark Schouwen
✉ Hoogenboomlaan 28
☎ +31 1 11 46 12 31
⌚ 15/3 - 27/10
@ info@vakantieparkschouwen.nl

9ha 80T(80-125m²) 10A CEE

**1** ACDEIJL**P**RS
**2** GHSVXY
**3** BKN**OP**RUW
**4** (S+T+X ⌚)
**5** **AB**FGIJKLMNO**P**UXY
**6** CDEGHJ**K**(N 0,5km)OST

💬 A fun family campsite on one of the widest beaches in the Netherlands, and close to the vibrant seaside resort of Renesse. There are cycling and walking paths everywhere, and plenty to see and do, although you can also come here for a more quiet holiday. Camping pitches from 80 to 125 m2 (with surcharge) and spacious paved motorhome pitches (100 m2).
🚗 Take the A29 Dinteloord-Rotterdam. At the Hellegatsplein head toward Zierikzee and then Renesse. Renesse-West R104.

Ouddorp

N59
N57  Zierikzee

CC €**16** 15/3-29/5  11/6-19/6  24/6-27/6  30/8-27/10  📐 N 51°43'43'' E 03°45'48''

---

## Retranchement/Cadzand, NL-4525 LX / Zeeland ♿ 🛜 iD **191**

⬛ Ardoer camping De Zwinhoeve
✉ Duinweg 1
☎ +31 1 17 39 21 20
⌚ 29/3 - 3/11
@ zwinhoeve@ardoer.com

9ha 116T(80-125m²) 10A CEE

**1** ACD**G**IJKLMOPQ
**2** AERVWX
**3** AB**F**GJR**W**Y
**4** **KN**(Q+R+T+U+Y+Z ⌚)
**5** **AB**DFGIJKLMNOP**S**UW
　XYZ
**6** ABCDEGH**K**(N 2km)S

💬 Campsite located directly behind the sea wall of 'Het Zwin' nature reserve and the dunes. Cycle tracks right by the campsite forming part of a route network crossing over the border into Belgium. Very good base for visiting the towns of Ghent, Sluis and Bruges. Storks nest in the campsite surroundings in June and July.
🚗 Via Cadzand to Cadzand-Bad. Follow signs to 'Het Zwin'. Via Antwerpen to Sluis, direction Retranchement.

Vlissingen

Knokke-Heist  CC  N676
N300
N374
N376  E34

CC €**18** 5/4-11/4  6/5-28/5  4/6-6/6  11/6-18/6  24/6-27/6  2/9-3/11  📐 N 51°21'57'' E 03°22'26''

## Retranchement/Cadzand, NL-4525 LW / Zeeland

📶 iD **192**

🔺 Camping Cassandria-Bad
📧 Strengweg 4
☎ +31 1 17 39 23 00
📅 29/3 - 31/10
@ info@cassandriabad.nl

5,5ha 110T(80-100m²) 10A CEE

**1** A**F**IJKLMNOPQ
**2** ARVWX
**3** AB**F**JKNRU**W**
**4** (Q+T+U+Z 📅)
**5** **AB**CDFGHIJMNOPUWXY
**6** ABEGH**K**(N 1,7km)OSV

💬 Rural area. Sheltered pitches and good toilet facilities (renovated 2018). On cycle route network near sea. Trips to Sluis, Damme, Bruges and Gent. Personal attention. Large TV in cafe. Cable internet on all pitches and 100% wifi.

🚗 Via Terneuzen (toll) as far as Schoondijke, then dir. Oostburg to Cadzand and Retranchement. Turn right and follow signs. Or N49 Antwerpen-Knokke exit Sluis. Left after 1 km (Retranchement). Through village then turn left and follow signs.

Vlissingen
Knokke-Heist CC
N676
N61
N300
A11 E34
N376

CC € **18** 29/3-7/7 25/8-31/10

📍 N 51°21'57'' E 03°23'11''

---

## Retranchement/Cadzand, NL-4525 LW / Zeeland

📶 iD **193**

🔺 Camping Den Molinshoeve
📧 Strengweg 2
☎ +31 1 17 39 16 74
📅 1/4 - 12/10
@ info@molinshoeve.nl

5,2ha 39T(160-190m²) 10A CEE

**1** AD**G**IJKLPQ
**2** AKRVWX
**3** AB**F**GJRU**W**
**4** (Q 7/7-24/8)
**5** **AB**CDFGHIJKLMNOPR**S** UWXYZ
**6** ABCDEGHK(N 1,5km)

💬 Charming site at a Zeeland farm. Heated, luxury toilet facilities. Spacious pitches, free wifi. Pitches with wide views over typical Dutch landscape for extra fee. Bicycles can be stored indoors. Close to beach. Many cycling/walking options. Good base to visit Belgium.

🚗 Via Terneuzen (toll) up to Schoondijke. Then to Cadzand. Then to Retranchement, turn right. Follow signs. Or N49 Antwerpen-Knokke, Sluis. Left after 1 km to Retranchement. Through village, turn left.

Vlissingen
Knokke-Heist CC
N676
N300
N374
N376 E34

CC € **18** 1/4-19/4 22/4-29/5 2/6-7/6 10/6-6/7 25/8-12/10

📍 N 51°21'42'' E 03°23'01''

---

## Scharendijke, NL-4322 NM / Zeeland

♿ 📶 iD **194**

🔺 Camping Duin en Strand
📧 Kuyerdamseweg 39
☎ +31 1 11 67 12 16
📅 1/1 - 31/12
@ info@duinenstrand.nl

8ha 300T(60-100m²) 4-10A CEE

**1** AD**G**IJKLMNOPRS
**2** GRWX
**3** JNRU
**4** (Q+S+T 15/3-15/11)
**5** **AB**DGIJMNO**P**UWXYZ
**6** ACDEGKLORV

💬 Campsite located at walking distance to North Sea beach, on the foot of the Brouwersdam with its many water sports options. Many cycle routes in the area. The lively resort Renesse is 4 km from the campsite. Most pitches have free wifi. CampingCard ACSI is valid on certain pitches.

🚗 Follow N59 Zierikzee-Renesse, Rotterdam-Ouddorp. Take Ellemeet-Scharendijke exit, turn left below.

Nieuwerkerk
CC
N57 Zierikzee

CC € **16** 1/1-28/5 2/6-6/6 10/6-26/6 30/6-4/7 25/8-31/12

📍 N 51°44'06'' E 03°49'40''

## Scharendijke, NL-4326 LK / Zeeland  🛜 iD  (195)

🏕 Camping Resort Land & Zee
✉ Rampweg 28
☎ +31 1 11 67 17 85
⌚ 1/1-6/1,22/2-17/11,20/12-24/12
@ info@landenzee.nl

7ha 57T(80-200m²) 4-16A CEE

**1** ACD**G**IJKLMNO**P**Q
**2** ERVX
**3** BKR
**4** (R 14/3-1/11) (Y 🔑)
**5** **AB**DEFGIJMNO**P**QUWXYZ
**6** CDEGKS

💬 The campsite is close to North Sea beach and Grevelingen lake. The pitches are car-free, plenty of water on the site where swimming and fishing is not allowed. Possibility to camp in a tent on one of the islands.

🚗 N59 Zierikzee-Renesse, follow Rotterdam Ouddorp, exit Ellemeet, Scharendijke, left at end of exit road. Follow 'Resort Land en Zee' signs at roundabout.

Burgh-Haamstede   N59
N57   Zierikzee

CC€18 22/2-19/4 23/4-29/5 2/6-7/6 11/6-19/6 1/7-8/7 25/8-17/11   📶 N 51°44'17'' E 03°49'03''

---

## St. Kruis/Oostburg, NL-4528 KG / Zeeland  🛜 iD  (196)

🏕 Camping Bonte Hoeve
✉ Eiland 4
☎ +31 1 17 45 22 70
⌚ 30/3 - 3/11
@ info@bontehoeve.nl

9ha 50T(100-130m²) 10A CEE

**1** A**F**IJKLMOPQ
**2** GRVXY
**3** BC**F**GJNRUW
**4** (Q 🔑) (R+T+Z 1/7-31/8)
**5** **AB**FGI**J**K**L**MN**P**UWXYZ
**6** ADEGH**K**(N 3km)OSTV

💬 Enjoy peace, space and freedom. A lively family campsite with bar and snack bar with playground on terrace. Spacious pitches, separated by hedges, with 10A, water and TV connection, wireless internet, modern toilet facilities (2019), private bathroom possible. Golf course and beach close by. Great cycling. Near Bruges and Ghent, plenty of opportunities for trips. Ideal base for a varied holiday in Zeelandic Flanders.

💬 Located on the road Oostburg-St.Margriete (B).

Breskens
N676
Oostburg   N61
N49
E34
Maldegem   N456
N434

CC€18 30/3-14/7 1/9-3/11 7=6   📶 N 51°18'05'' E 03°30'36''

---

## Vrouwenpolder, NL-4354 NN / Zeeland  🛜 iD  (197)

🏕 Camping De Zandput
✉ Vroondijk 9
☎ +31 1 18 59 72 10
⌚ 29/3 - 3/11
@ info.zandput@roompot.nl

12ha 246T(70-110m²) 6-10A CEE

**1** ACD**G**IJKPQ
**2** AERVWX
**3** BJKNRUW
**4** (Q+S+T+Y 🔑)
**5** **AB**DFGIJMNPUWXYZ
**6** EGKM(N 2km)STV

💬 Enjoy the peace, space and freedom to the full. A friendly family campsite with a bar and chip shop. Playground on the terrace. Modern toilet facilities. The ideal base for a holiday with variety at Walcheren. There are no motorhome pitches available at this campsite.

🚗 Motorway A58 Bergen op Zoom-Vlissingen, take exit Middelburg, Oostkapelle-Vrouwenpolder. In the village there are signs to the campsite.

Domburg
N287
N288   N57
Middelburg   A58

CC€14 29/3-12/4 12/5-29/5 11/6-19/6 24/6-9/7 26/8-3/11   📶 N 51°35'11'' E 03°36'19''

## Baarn, NL-3744 BC / Utrecht

 ♿ 🛜 ✿ **iD** **198**

🏕 Allurepark De Zeven Linden
📧 Zevenlindenweg 4
☎ +31 3 56 66 83 30
📅 28/3 - 27/10
@ info@dezevenlinden.nl

11,5ha 326T(110m²) 6-10A CEE

**1** AD**G**IJKLMNPRS
**2** BFGRVWXY
**3** A**F**GHJKLNRU
**4** (Q+R+S+T 🔲)
**5** **ABC**DEFGHI**J**KLMNO**PQ**R
UWXYZ
**6** ABCDEGH**K**L(N 3km)OU

💬 Camping grounds for natural, simple yet comfortable camping. The six camping fields each have their own playground. For older children there are jungle huts. Drakensteyn Castle, Soestdijk Palace and the small village of Lage Vuursche are all within walking distance.

🚗 The campsite is well signposted on the N415 Hilversum-Baarn about 2 km from Baarn.

Bussum
A1
A27 CC
**Amersfoort**
N227

CC € **20** 28/3-18/4 23/4-26/4 6/5-24/5 11/6-15/7 1/9-27/10    🧭 **N 52°11'48'' E 05°14'49''**

---

## Bilthoven, NL-3722 GZ / Utrecht

🛜 **iD** **199**

🏕 Camping Bos Park Bilthoven
📧 Burg.van de Borchlaan 7
☎ +31 3 02 28 67 77
📅 30/3 - 26/10
@ info@bosparkbilthoven.nl

20ha 130T(< 175m²) 16A CEE

**1** ACDGIJKLOPST
**2** BFGLRSVWXY
**3** B**E**GHJ**MN**O**PQ**RU
**4** (C+H 1/5-15/9)
(T+X+Y+Z 🔲)
**5** **AB**CEFGHIJKLMNO**PQ**U
WXYZ
**6** ABCEGHKL(N 1km)OSTV

💬 Bos Park Bilthoven is a lovely wooded site in the middle of dunes with spacious seasonal (comfort) pitches up to 175 m² encircled by beautiful trees. Heated outdoor pool (also toddlers' pool) and various play equipment. You can walk or cycle to the woods from your pitch. Within walking distance of the station for trips out including Utrecht and Amersfoort. You will love Bos Park Bilthoven.

🚗 The campsite is well-signposted from the Den Dolder-Bilthoven road.

A1
A27 **Amersfoort**
CC
N227
**Utrecht**
A12

CC € **18** 30/3-24/5 11/6-5/7 24/8-26/10    🧭 **N 52°07'52'' E 05°13'14''**

---

## Bunnik, NL-3981 HG / Utrecht

🛜 **iD** **200**

🏕 Buitengoed de Boomgaard
📧 Parallelweg 9
☎ +31 3 06 56 38 96
📅 30/3 - 13/10
@ info@buitengoeddeboomgaard.nl

11ha 200T(150m²) 6-10A CEE

**1** ACD**G**IJKLMNO**P**RS
**2** DFGRTWXY
**3** ABD**F**GHJKN**OP**RUWZ
**4** M(Q+R 🔲)
**5** **AB**CDFGHIJKLMNOPQ
UWZ
**6** ACDEG**K**LM(N 1,5km)OTV

💬 Caravans and tents are pitched among gently swaying fruit trees in a former orchard. Varying grounds with wooded banks, small lake, barn and children's farm. Lovely cycling in spring along the many orchards in blossom. Lovely walks in the meadows in early and late seasons. Cycling distance from Utrecht (7 km).

🚗 A12, exit 19 Bunnik/Odijk/Wijk bij Duurstede. Turn right immediately after exit onto Parallelweg.

N402   **Amersfoort**
A28
**Utrecht**
N224
CC A12
A27 N225
A2 N227

CC € **18** 30/3-29/5 10/6-5/7 25/8-13/10    🧭 **N 52°03'35'' E 05°11'56''**

## Doorn, NL-3941 ZK / Utrecht ⚓ ♿ 📶 iD **201**

🏔 RCN Vakantiepark Het Grote Bos
📧 Hydeparklaan 24
☎ +31 8 50 40 07 00
🔑 29/3 - 28/10
@ reserveringen@rcn.nl

80ha 350T(75-150m²) 10A CEE

**1** ACDG**I**JKLNOPQ
**2** BFGLRSTVWXY
**3** BFGHJKLM**N**OPQRTU
**4** (**A**+C+H 🔒) J
(Q+S+T+U+X+Y+Z 🔒)
**5** **AB**CDEFGHIJKLMNOPQR
UWXYZ
**6** ABCDEGH**K**LM(N 1,5km)O
STUV

💬 A complete holiday resort, with attractive fields or real woodland pitches, in a beautiful nature reserve on the southern edge of the Utrechtse Heuvelrug (Utrecht Hill Ridge).

🚐 A12 Utrecht-Arnhem, exit Driebergen. Enter village and follow signs. Campsite located in the Doorn-Driebergen-Maarn triangle.

N234 — Leusden — Utrecht — Zeist — A28 — N224 — CC — A27 — N229 — N227 — A12 — N226

CC € ⑱ 29/3-19/4  10/5-29/5  11/6-12/7  30/8-28/10 — 📐 N 52°03'22'' E 05°18'49''

---

## Doorn, NL-3941 XR / Utrecht ⊗ ♿ 📶 iD **202**

🏔 Recr. Centr. De Maarnse Berg
📧 Maarnse Bergweg 1
☎ +31 3 43 44 12 84
🔑 29/3 - 27/10
@ info@maarnseberg.nl

20ha 75T(100-225m²) 10A CEE

**1** ADEIJKLMNOPQ
**2** BFRVWXY
**3** ABF**G**HJN**Q**RTU
**4** (G 1/5-31/8)
(T+U+X+Y+Z 🔒)
**5** **AB**CDGHIJK**L**MN**PQ**UXYZ
**6** ABEGH**K**(N 2,5km)O

💬 A campsite in a wonderful location among the woods of the 'Utrechtse Heuvelrug' National Park. Enjoy this peaceful campsite to the full, especially in the spring and autumn, in natural surroundings with extensive cycling and walking opportunities.

🚐 Campsite sign on the A12 from Utrecht at Maarn/ Doorn exit, twice to the right under the exit. A12 from Arnhem, exit Maarsbergen. Through centre of Maarn. Follow the signs on the N227.

A27 — **Amersfoort** — Zeist — N802 — CC — A12 — Houten — N227 — N226

CC € ⑯ 29/3-29/5  11/6-30/6  18/8-27/10 — 📐 N 52°03'48'' E 05°21'06''

---

## Leersum, NL-3956 KD / Utrecht ⊗ ♿ 📶 iD **203**

🏔 Molecaten Park Landgoed Ginkelduin
📧 Scherpenzeelseweg 53
☎ +31 3 43 48 99 99
🔑 29/3 - 31/10
@ info@landgoedginkelduin.nl

95ha 220T(80-110m²) 10A CEE

**1** ACDEIJKLMNOPQ
**2** BFLRSVWXY
**3** ABCD**FG**HIJKLMN**OPQ**RTU
**4** (A 1/5-31/5, 1/7-31/8)
(C 15/5-15/9) (F+H 🔒) **KLN**
(Q+S+T+U+X+Y+Z 🔒)
**5** **AB**CDEFGHIJKLMNOPQRS
UWXYZ
**6** BCDEGH**K**M(N 3km)OSTV

💬 Situated in the middle of the Utrechtse Heuvelrug National Park; close to 'the quietest spot in the Netherlands'. Spacious camping fields with comfort (plus) pitches are encircled by beautiful trees.
The campsite offers an indoor swimming pool, outdoor pool, tennis courts, restaurant, shop and bike hire. There are several lovely walking and cycle routes to be enjoyed close by.

🚐 N225. In the centre of the town of Leersum signs are posted near the church.

N226 — N802 — A30 — A12 — Ede — N227 — CC — Veenendaal — Wageningen — N835

CC € ⑱ 29/3-18/4  5/5-28/5  11/6-9/7  26/8-31/10 — 📐 N 52°01'46'' E 05°27'31''

## Maarn, NL-3951 KD / Utrecht

👫 ⊗ ♿ 📶 ❀ iD **204**

🏕 Allurepark Laag Kanje
✉ Laan van Laagkanje 1
☎ +31 3 43 44 13 48
🔑 30/3 - 29/9
@ allurepark@laagkanje.nl

30ha 241T(100m²) 6-10A CEE

1 ADEIJKLMNPQ
2 ABDGLRTVWXY
3 ABDFGHIJKLMNOPRUWZ
4 (Q+S+T+U+Y+Z 🔑)
5 ABCDEFGHIJLMNOPQRU WXYZ
6 ACDEGHKM(N 2km)OSTV

💬 Beautiful grounds with car free camping in a wooded area by the Henschotermeer lake; this undulating and varying landscape (with woods, heath and sand drifts) offers good camping also in spring and autumn.

🚗 On the N227 Amersfoort-Doorn the campsite is clearly signposted, both near Maarn and at the crossing 'Quatre Bras'.

Amersfoort · A1 · N226 · N802 · A12 · CC · Veenendaal · N227

CC €20 30/3-28/5 11/6-12/7 1/9-28/9 · N 52°04'39'' E 05°22'46''

---

## Renswoude, NL-3927 CJ / Utrecht

📶 iD **205**

🏕 Camping de Grebbelinie
✉ Ubbeschoterweg 12
☎ +31 3 18 59 10 73
🔑 1/4 - 12/10
@ info@campingdegrebbelinie.nl

4,5ha 125T(105-140m²) 6-10A CEE

1 ADGIJKLMPRS
2 DFKLRWX
3 ABDGHIJKLUZ
4 (Q 🔑)
5 ABCDEFGIJMNOPQRUWX Y
6 ACDEGHK(N 2km)ST

💬 De Grebbelinie is a unique campsite centrally located in the Netherlands between the Utrechtse Heuvelrug and the Veluwe. On the Grebbelinie (defence line) with Fort Daatselaar. Various walking and cycling routes start from the camp site through varied countryside.

🚗 From the A30 Scherpenzeel exit. Straight ahead at roundabout dir. Renswoude (follow camping signs). From the A12 exit 23 Renswoude/Veenendaal. Follow signs to Renswoude. Then follow camping signs.

Amersfoort · A1 · N805 · N802 · A30 · CC · N304 · N226 · N224 · Veenendaal · N225 · A12

CC €18 1/4-28/5 12/6-11/7 29/8-11/10 · N 52°05'05'' E 05°33'04''

---

## Woerden, NL-3443 AP / Utrecht

📶 iD **206**

🏕 Camping Batenstein
✉ van Helvoortlaan 36
☎ +31 3 48 42 13 20
🔑 29/3 - 27/10
@ campingbatenstein@planet.nl

1,6ha 40T(60-100m²) 6A CEE

1 ACGIJLNPRS
2 FRUVWX
3 BHJKRVW
4 (F+H 🔑) IJN
5 ABEFGIJKLMNOPUWYZ
6 ACDEGIJ(N 1,5km)O

💬 A pleasant campsite in green surroundings on the edge of Woerden. Excellent, well maintained sanitary facilities. The whole site is surrounded by water. There is a new leisure pool and fitness centre right next to the site.

🚗 On the A2 you follow exit 5 towards Kockengen. Then, the N212 to Woerden. In Woerden, the campsite is signposted. Or A12, exit 14, then follow signposts.

N212 · N402 · A2 · N11 · De Meern · CC · A12 · Nieuwegein · Gouda · N228 · N204

CC €18 29/3-19/4 5/5-29/5 11/6-5/7 1/9-27/10 · N 52°05'34'' E 04°53'06''

## Woudenberg, NL-3931 MK / Utrecht

🏕 Camping 't Boerenerf
📧 De Heygraeff 15
☎ +31 3 32 86 14 24
📅 29/3 - 28/9
@ info@campingboerenerf.nl

4,5ha 50T(80-100m²) 6-16A CEE

**1** ADGIJKLM**P**Q
**2** ADFGRTVWXY
**3** ABD**F**GHJKLNPRU**W**Z
**5** **AB**CDEFGIJ**KL**MNO**P**UW XYZ
**6** AEGH**K**(N 3km)OT

💬 An environment, child and animal friendly site and camping farm near extensive woods and the Henschotermeer lake. Plenty of cycling and walking in the area. Rucksack route on Tuesdays past open farmhouses is very popular. No arrival/departure on Sunday.

🚐 A28 exit 5, Maarn-Amersfoort Zuid; A12, exit Maarn-Doorn towards Amersfoort. N224 in the direction of Woudenberg; turn right at the 1st road, Henschotermeer. Turn left after 50 metres and then turn right immediately.

CC € **16** 29/3-24/5 11/6-14/7 31/8-28/9

📡 N 52°04'51'' E 05°23'12''

---

## Woudenberg, NL-3931 ML / Utrecht

🏕 Vakantiepark De Heigraaf
📧 De Heygraeff 9
☎ +31 3 32 86 50 66
📅 28/3 - 26/10
@ info@heigraaf.nl

16ha 250T(100-250m²) 4-16A CEE

**1** ADEIJKLM**P**Q
**2** ADFGMRVWXY
**3** ABCD**F**GHJKN**O**P**R**UWZ
**4** (Q+S+T 📅) (Y 27/4-30/8)
**5** **AB**CDEFGHIJ**KL**MNO**PQR**S**UWXYZ
**6** ABCDEGH**K**M(N 2,5km)OST

💬 Beautiful holiday park on the Utrechtse Heuvelrug/Gelderse Valley. Perfect for cycling, woods, heathland, meadows. 150m from the Henschoten (swimming) lake. Spacious touring pitches and (early and late) seasonal pitches. English double-decker bus serving snacks, 'Eeterij' (Eatery), supermarket. Entertainment programme, play equipment, bouncy castles. Plenty of atmosphere. No arrival on Sunday.

🚐 Via the A12 or A28, exit Maarn, then indicated.

CC € **18** 28/3-24/5 11/6-15/7 1/9-26/10

📡 N 52°04'47'' E 05°22'54''

---

## Zeist, NL-3707 HW / Utrecht

🏕 Allurepark De Krakeling
📧 Woudenbergseweg 17
☎ +31 3 06 91 53 74
📅 29/3 - 29/9
@ allurepark@dekrakeling.nl

22ha 347T(120m²) 10A CEE

**1** ACDGIJKLMOPQ
**2** BDFGRSVWXY
**3** BD**F**GHJKLN**O**P**R**UWZ
**4** (Q+R+T+U+X+Y+Z 📅)
**5** **AB**CDFGHIJ**KL**MNO**PQ**R**U**W
**6** ABCEGH**K**M(N 2,5km)OS

💬 A friendly, quiet family campsite in the extensive woods and rural parks in the 'Utrechtse Heuvelrug' area.

🚐 A28 Utrecht-Amersfoort, exit Zeist-Oost, A28 from Amersfoort exit Zeist. Easy to find from Zeist via Woudenbergseweg.

CC € **20** 29/3-26/4 6/5-24/5 11/6-14/7 1/9-29/9

📡 N 52°05'35'' E 05°16'58''

## Almere, NL-1324 ZZ / Flevoland

🏕 Camping Waterhout
📧 Trekvogelweg 10, Noorderplassen
☎ +31 3 65 47 06 32
📅 5/4 - 27/10
@ info@waterhout.nl

1ha 311T(100m²) 10-16A CEE

**1** ADG**I**JKLMOPRS
**2** ADFGLMRTVWXY
**3** BD**F**GHJK**MNOP**R**TU**VWZ
**4** (A 1/7-31/8) **KLMNP**
    (Q+R+T+U+X+Z 🔒)
**5** **AB**CDEFGHIJKLMNOPQRU
    WXYZ
**6** ACDEGH**J**L(N 2km)TV

💬 Camping Waterhout is the ideal place to stay. Close to the town but in the middle of the countryside. Close to the Noorderplassen lakes, Amsterdam, Walibi, Aviodrome and the Gooi. Cycling, sailing, fishing, walking and enjoying the peace of the countryside. Entertainment for young and old during the holidays.

🚗 A6, exit 6. N702 turn right Noorderplassen. Follow signs. From Amsterdam: junction Gooimeer, N705.

CC € **18** 5/4-29/5 3/6-7/6 11/6-5/7 26/8-13/9 15/9-27/10    N 52°24'07'' E 05°13'32''

---

## Biddinghuizen, NL-8256 RZ / Flevoland

🏕 Molecaten Park Flevostrand
📧 Strandweg 1
☎ +31 3 20 28 84 80
📅 29/3 - 31/10
@ flevostrand@molecaten.nl

25ha 330T(80-120m²) 10-20A CEE

**1** ABCD**G**IJKLMNOPQ
**2** ADFGKLRSVWX
**3** ABC**F**GHJK**M**N**Q**R**U**W**Z**
**4** (A 1/4-31/8) (C 27/4-1/9)
    (**F**+H 🔒) IJ
    (Q+S+T 1/4-31/10) (Y+Z 🔒)
**5** **AB**DEFGIJK**L**MNOPQUW
    XYZ
**6** ABCEGH**K**(N 3,5km)OSTV

💬 Located on the shores of lake Veluwemeer. An excellent location for watersports enthusiasts. Many cycling and walking opportunities in the surrounding area. Camping Flevostrand has spacious camping pitches by the water or behind the dikes. Activity complex including a restaurant and bar, indoor swimming pool, supermarket and boat and bike hire.

🚗 A28 exit 13, direction Lelystad. Follow Walibi signs. Located between the N306 and the Veluwemeer. Signposted.

CC € **18** 29/3-18/4 5/5-28/5 11/6-19/6 23/6-9/7 26/8-31/10    N 52°23'07'' E 05°37'45''

---

## Dronten, NL-8251 ST / Flevoland

🏕 Camping 't Wisentbos
📧 De West 1
☎ +31 3 21 31 66 06
📅 1/4 - 30/9
@ info@wisentbos.nl

9ha 50T(80-110m²) 10A CEE

**1** ACD**G**IJKLMO**P**Q
**2** BCGLRWX
**3** BFJRU**W**X
**4** (U 🔒)
**5** **AB**CDFGHIJ**K**LMN**P**UWZ
**6** ACDEGH**K**M(N 1km)V

💬 Large campsite with many permanent pitches, located in wooded surroundings on a fishing lake. Fishing competitions are held regularly. The campsite has a lovely big playing field, around which are positioned the sunny touring pitches. Good amenities. Dronten is centrally located for for many attractions: Lelystad, Harderwijk/Veluwe, Zwolle, Kampen, Urk.

🚗 Turn left at the roundabout on the N309 Lelystad-Dronten. Campsite on the left after about 500 metres.

CC € **16** 1/5-1/7 19/8-30/9    N 52°31'16'' E 05°41'31''

## Dronten, NL-8251 PX / Flevoland ♿ 🛜 **iD** 213

△ Camping De Ruimte
🏕 Stobbenweg 23
☎ +31 3 21 31 64 42
🔑 29/3 - 29/9
@ info@campingderuimte.nl

6ha 97T(80-120m²) 6A CEE

**1** AD**G**IJKLMNOPQ
**2** BRSVWXY
**3** A**F**HJKNRU
**4** (H 29/5-1/9) M
  (Q+R+T+U+V+Y+Z 🔑)
**5** **AB**CDFGHIJKLMNOPQRU
  WXYZ
**6** ACDEGK(N 7km)OPV

💬 De Ruimte is a natural campsite with atmosphere in the middle of a wood. There are quiet pitches hidden away in the trees but also pitches on fields with playground equipment. Excellent amenities, also for disabled people. The site is located close to the Veluwe lake with its fine beaches. The lovely towns of Kampen and Elburg are within cycling distance.

🚗 A28 exit 16, past Elburg to Dronten. Bridge over Veluwemeer at the traffic lights towards Kampen. Campsite signposted.

CC € **18** 29/3-29/5 3/6-7/6 11/6-7/7 24/8-29/9 14=12, 21=18, 28=24 | 🏔 N 52°29'48'' E 05°50'15''

---

## Kraggenburg, NL-8317 RD / Flevoland ⊗ ♿ 🛜 **iD** 214

△ Camping Netl de Wildste Tuin
🏕 Leemringweg 19
☎ +31 5 27 20 30 43
🔑 5/4 - 27/10
@ info@netl.nl

10ha 66T(100-150m²) 4-10A CEE

**1** ACDEJKLMNPQ
**2** ADGLRUVWX
**3** BDEHJNRUWZ
**4** (Q+V+X+Z 🔑)
**5** **AB**FGIJKLMNO**P**UWZ
**6** ACDEGHK(N 3,5km)RV

💬 Netl de Wildste Tuin recreation park (48 hectares) with campsite, natural camping pitches and motorhome pitches (camp fires allowed). Beaches for swimming, natural playground, bamboo jungle, 9 hole pitch & putt, obstacle training course and beach pavilion.

🚗 Noordoostpolder main road Marknesse-Kraggenburg. NW Overijssel Vollenhoven direction Marknesse.

CC € **16** 5/4-18/4 22/5-29/6 31/8-27/10 | 🏔 N 52°40'55'' E 05°52'28''

---

## Lelystad, NL-8245 AB / Flevoland ♿ 🛜 **iD** 215

△ Camping 't Oppertje
🏕 Uilenweg 11
☎ +31 3 20 25 36 93
🔑 29/3 - 1/10
@ info@oppertje.nl

3ha 85T(120-150m²) 6A CEE

**1** AD**G**IJKLMNO**P**RS
**2** ADLMRSVWXY
**3** A**F**HJK**Q**R**WZ**
**5** **AB**CDFGHI**J**KMNO**PQ**RU
  WXYZ
**6** ABCDEGHK(N 2km)T

💬 Quiet, natural campsite next to Oostvaardersplassen lakes. On a lake with sailing and surfing. Close to fishing park and canoe rental etc. Separate field for tents. Hardened motor home pitches. Dogs not allowed on some fields.

🚗 From A6 exit 10 take the Larserdreef direction Lelystad. Four roundabouts straight ahead. After fifth roundabout turn left into Buizerdweg. Follow the signs to the campsite.

CC € **18** 29/3-24/5 13/6-5/7 24/8-1/10 | 🏔 N 52°29'09'' E 05°25'01''

## Urk, NL-8321 NC / Flevoland 〈📶 iD〉 **216**

🏕 Vakantiepark 't Urkerbos
📧 Vormtweg 9
☎ +31 5 27 68 77 75
🗓 1/4 - 30/9
@ info@urkerbos.nl

14ha 180T(120-150m²) 10A CEE

**1** ADG**I**JKLMOP**Q**
**2** BLRSVWX
**3** BDHJKLN**OP**RU
**4** (B 10/5-31/8) (G 13/5-31/8)
  (Q 1/7-3/9)
  (T+U+X+Z 13/7-25/8)
**5** **AB**CDFGIJMNOPQUWXYZ
**6** CDEGH**K**M(N 2km)OSV

💬 The campsite has spacious fields, mostly ringed by tall trees. Urk, with its many sights, harbour and beach is just 2 km from the campsite. Good walking opportunities (Urkerbos woods) and cycling (Schokland, Emmeloord). The lovely towns of Kampen, Zwolle and Hasselt are all within 40 km.

🚗 A6 exit 13 to Urk. Follow road right through Urk, turn left at 3rd roundabout (signposted). Campsite 1.5 km on the right.

Emmeloord
N351
N50
Urk
N352
A6
N302

CC € **16**  1/4-29/5  11/6-6/7  26/8-30/9    📷▲ N 52°40'45'' E 05°36'35''

---

## Zeewolde, NL-3896 LB / Flevoland 〈📶 iD〉 **217**

🏕 Camping Erkemederstrand
📧 Erkemederweg 79
☎ +31 3 65 22 84 21
🗓 22/3 - 28/10
@ info@erkemederstrand.nl

35ha 229T(120-180m²) 10-16A CEE

**1** ADG**I**JKLMNOPQ
**2** ABDFKLMRSVWX
**3** ABD**F**GJKN**Q**R**U**W**Z**
**4** (Q+R+T+U+V+X+Z 🅾)
**5** **AB**DFGIJMNO**P**QUWXYZ
**6** ACDEGHK(N 7km)TUV

💬 Located between the Horsterwold and the Nuldernauw. Own yacht harbour. Good restaurant, many sports opportunities. Special facilities for dogs, including a separate beach. Tourist spots such as Nijkerk, Harderwijk and Bunschoten are within cycling distance. CampingCard ACSI valid on pitches within the dike. NKC members welcome with CampingCard ACSI.

🚗 A28 exit 9 towards Zeewolde. Cross the bridge and turn right, then left (Erkemederweg). There are signs to the campsite.

N305
A27
Harderwijk
N705
A28
CC
Putten
N798
N303
N301
Soest
A1

CC € **18**  22/3-19/4  22/4-29/5  10/6-6/7  1/9-28/10    📷▲ N 52°16'12'' E 05°29'19''

---

## Zeewolde, NL-3896 LS / Flevoland 〈♿ 📶 ❀ iD〉 **218**

🏕 Camping het Groene Bos
📧 Groenewoudse Weg 98
☎ +31 3 65 23 63 66
🗓 1/4 - 11/10
@ info@hetgroenebos.nl

4ha 50T(85-225m²) 6-10A CEE

**1** ACD**G**IJKLOP**Q**
**2** BRSVWX
**3** BD**F**GJKLRU
**4** (Q+Z 🅾)
**5** **AB**CDFGHIJKLMNPUWXYZ
**6** EGH**K**(N 4km)V

💬 A park-like campsite located in the Horsterwold in the heart of the province of Flevoland with excellent toilet facilities. The spacious pitches are shaded by high bushes. A good place for those seeking relaxation.

🚗 A28 exit 9 direction Zeewolde. Campsite is located west of Zeewolde and is signposted.

N305
A6
N306
A27
Harderwijk
CC
A28
N302
Ermelo
N301
N705
N303
N798

CC € **16**  1/4-25/5  11/6-8/7  26/8-11/10    📷▲ N 52°20'24'' E 05°30'20''

## Zeewolde, NL-3896 LT / Flevoland  ♿ 📶 ✿ iD  **219**

▲ RCN Vakantiepark Zeewolde
✉ Dasselaarweg 1
☎ +31 8 50 40 07 00
🕐 29/3 - 28/10
@ reserveringen@rcn.nl

43ha 350T(100-120m²) 10A CEE

**1** ACD**G**IJKLMNOPQ
**2** ADKLMRSVWX
**3** ABD**F**GHIJKL**M**NRU**WZ**
**4** (F+H 🕐) M
  (Q+S+T+U+Y+Z 🕐)
**5** **AB**DEFGIJKLMNPUWXYZ
**6** CDEGH**I**KM(N 1,5km)OSV

💬 A large campsite with separate spacious grounds surrounded by two meters high bushes, located on the Wolderwijd lake area with many leisure activities. Part of the site is beyond the dike on the waterfront. Good toilet facilities.

🚗 A28 exit 9, direction Zeewolde. Campsite is on the south side, 1 km outside Zeewolde and is signposted.

CC € **16**  29/3-29/5  3/6-7/6  11/6-12/7  30/8-28/10  📍 N 52°18'42'' E 05°32'37''

---

## Balkbrug, NL-7707 PK / Overijssel  ♿ 📶 ✿ iD  **220**

▲ Camping 't Reestdal
✉ De Haar 5
☎ +31 5 23 65 62 32
🕐 1/4 - 28/10
@ info@reestdal.nl

8,5ha 76T(100-120m²) 6-16A CEE

**1** AD**F**IJKLMNOPRS
**2** LRSVWXY
**3** ABF**H**JKN**P**RU**W**
**4** (A 1/7-31/8) (C+H 1/5-15/9)
  (Q+R+T+U+X+Y+Z 🕐)
**5** **AB**EFGIJKLMNOPQR**ST**U
  WXYZ
**6** ACDEGK(N 2km)OTV

💬 Camping including private toilet facilities for CampingCard ACSI holders. Experience the comfort of your own heated bathroom on your pitch. TV connection optional. Uniquely located in the lovely Reestdal valley with various cycle and walking routes from the campsite via the route.nl app. Enjoy the silence. Special pitches for motorhomes. Restaurant in authentic farm style.

🚗 In Balkbrug direction De Wijk. Then follow the brown signs (avoiding the dirt track).

CC € **20**  1/4-27/5  11/6-15/7  2/9-28/10  📍 N 52°36'37'' E 06°22'17''

---

## Balkbrug, NL-7707 PK / Overijssel  📶 iD  **221**

▲ Camping Si Es An
✉ De Haar 7
☎ +31 5 23 65 65 34
🕐 15/3 - 1/11
@ info@si-es-an.nl

9,5ha 60T(100-120m²) 10-16A CEE

**1** ADG**I**JKLMOPQ
**2** RSWXY
**3** ABF**H**IJKLNRU
**4** (Q+T+U+V+X+Y 🕐)
**5** **AB**DFGIJK**L**MN**PQ**UWXY
**6** ABCDEGK**K**(N 2km)OTV

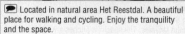

💬 Located in natural area Het Reestdal. A beautiful place for walking and cycling. Enjoy the tranquility and the space.

🚗 In Balkbrug head in direction De Wijk. Then follow the brown campsite signs. Avoid the sandy road!

CC € **16**  15/3-29/5  11/6-14/7  1/9-1/11  📍 N 52°36'35'' E 06°22'19''

## Bathmen, NL-7437 RZ / Overijssel

  &#9855; &#128246; **iD** (222)

▲ Camping de Flierweide
🏠 Traasterdijk 16
☎ +31 5 70 54 14 78
🔒 15/3 - 1/11
@ info@flierweide.nl

2ha 60T(120-140m²) 4-16A CEE

**1** AG IJKLMNPQ
**2** FGRUVWXY
**3** AFGHJU
**5** ABDEFGIJKLMNPQUWXY
**6** ACDEGK(N 1km)SUV

💬 Very spacious and comfortable pitches, with TV and wireless internet connections if desired. Peacefully located on the edge of a village next to the woods. The modern heated toilet facilities with luxurious amenities transform this from a modest campsite into a comfortable one. Bathmen is a pleasant and agreeable village in the Salland countryside, located between Deventer and the Holterberg.

🚗 A1 exit 25 Bathmen. Follow camping signs (dir. Flierweide).

CC €16   15/3-29/5   11/6-5/7   23/8-1/11    N 52°15'22'' E 06°17'31''

---

## Beerze/Ommen, NL-7736 PK / Overijssel

  &#9855; &#128246; &#10052; **iD** (223)

▲ Camping Beerze Bulten
🏠 Kampweg 1
☎ +31 5 23 25 13 98
🔒 30/3 - 28/10
@ info@beerzebulten.nl

26ha 540T(100-120m²) 8-16A CEE

**1** ADFIJKLNPQ
**2** ACDLRSVWXY
**3** ABCFGHJKLMNQRTUVWXZ
**4** (A 1/7-31/8) (B 20/4-10/9) (F+H 🔒) JKLMN (Q+S+T+U+V+X+Y+Z 🔒)
**5** ABDEFGIJKLMNOPQRST UWXYZ
**6** ACEGHKLM(N 2km)OSTV

💬 Beautiful, child friendly five star campsite. Every comfort within reach in truly natural surroundings.

🚗 Take the Beerze exit from the N36. Signposted from here.

CC €20   30/3-15/4   6/5-29/5   11/6-19/6   24/6-6/7   31/8-12/10    N 52°30'41'' E 06°32'43''

---

## Belt-Schutsloot, NL-8066 PT / Overijssel

  &#128246; **iD** (224)

▲ Camping Kleine Belterwijde
🏠 Vaste Belterweg 3
☎ +31 3 83 86 67 95
🔒 29/3 - 1/11
@ camping@kleinebelterwijde.nl

3,5ha 40T(70-100m²) 6A CEE

**1** ADGIJKLMNOPQ
**2** ADKLMRSVWXY
**3** ABGHJKMNRUWZ
**4** (G 🔒) M(Z 27/4-31/10)
**5** ABDEFGIJKLMNOPQUXYZ
**6** ADEGJL(N 0,2km)OT

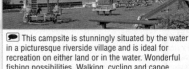

💬 This campsite is stunningly situated by the water in a picturesque riverside village and is ideal for recreation on either land or in the water. Wonderful fishing possibilities. Walking, cycling and canoe routes from the site. Excellent toilet facilities.

🚗 N334 direction Giethoorn exit Belt-Schutsloot. Campsite signposted in village.

CC €18   1/4-27/5   11/6-8/7   26/8-1/11    N 52°40'15'' E 06°03'38''

## Beuningen, NL-7588 RK / Overijssel

🚫 📶 iD **225**

🏕 Natuurkampeerterrein
  Olde Kottink
📧 Kampbrugweg 3
☎ +31 5 41 35 18 26
🅾 5/4 - 29/9
@ info@campingoldekottink.nl

6ha 90T(120-200m²) 6A CEE

**1** ADEIJKLMNOPQ
**2** ABCDFIRSWXY
**3** AHIJKLRUWZ
**4** (Q 30/5-11/6,8/7-26/8)
**5** **AB**DFGHIJKLMNOP**U**WXZ
**6** AEHK(N 3km)

💬 Enjoy authenticity and simplicity. Olde Kottink has an ideal location, surrounded by woods, meadows and on a river. Very spacious pitches, on grass. Countryside, culture, picturesque towns and villages, it's all here for you. Twente is a region where you could spend the rest of your life.

🚗 A1 Hengelo-Oldenzaal. The campsite is well signposted from the Oldenzaal-Denekamp road.

**Nordhorn**

N349  N342
N343
CC
A30
Bad Bentheim
A1  L39
L42  B403
A31

CC € **18** 5/4-28/5  11/6-7/7  24/8-29/9  🧭 N 52°21'14'' E 07°00'45''

---

## Blokzijl, NL-8356 VZ / Overijssel

♿ 📶 iD **226**

🏕 Watersportcamping
  'Tussen de Diepen'
📧 Duinigermeerweg 1A
☎ +31 5 27 29 15 65
🅾 30/3 - 31/10
@ camping@tussendediepen.nl

5,2ha 60T(60-80m²) 10A CEE

**1** AD**G**IJKLMNOP**Q**
**2** CKLRVWX
**3** AHJKNRUW
**4** (C+H 1/5-15/9)
  (Q+R+T+U+V+X+Y+Z 🅾)
**5** **AB**CFGIJKLMOP**U**WZ
**6** ACDEGHKLM(N 1km)OPV

💬 Plenty of water sports opportunities. Ideally situated for cycling and walking in the Weerribben (National Park). Camping in well maintained meadows, excellent toilets, free use of the heated swimming pool.

🚗 From Zwolle direction Hasselt-Zwartsluis-Vollenhove. Right along the sea wall at the roundabout to Blokzijl. Follow the camping signs.

**Steenwijk**

N351
CC  N334
Vollenhove  N762
N50  N352  Zwartsluis

CC € **16** 30/3-24/5  11/6-4/7  21/8-31/10  🧭 N 52°43'43'' E 05°58'13''

---

## Dalfsen, NL-7722 KG / Overijssel

👨‍👩‍👧 ♿ 📶 iD **227**

🏕 Camping Starnbosch
📧 Sterrebosweg 4
☎ +31 5 29 43 15 71
🅾 1/1 - 31/12
@ info@starnbosch.nl

8ha 248T(100-140m²) 10A CEE

**1** AD**G**IJKLMNOPQ
**2** BLRVWXY
**3** ABJKLNRU
**4** (C+E+F+H 1/4-1/11) **N**
  (Q+R+S+T+U+Y+Z 🅾)
**5** **AB**CDEFGHI**J**KLMNOP**Q**R
  **ST**UWXYZ
**6** ACDEGHJ**K**M(N 4,5km)OTV

💬 Starnbosch campsite is set among villas, country estates and castles and is the greenest campsite in the Vecht valley. A really hospitable site, noted for its relaxed and peaceful atmosphere, where people of all ages can enjoy their holiday.

🚗 A28 Zwolle-Meppel-Hoogeveen, exit 21 Dalfsen (N340). Follow the signs.

N48
A28
Zwolle  N340
CC  N348
Heino
N337  N35
Raalte

CC € **16** 1/1-29/5  11/6-10/7  27/8-31/12  7=6, 14=10, 21=15  🧭 N 52°28'31'' E 06°15'47''

## Dalfsen, NL-7722 HV / Overijssel

228

Vechtdalcamping Het Tolhuis
Het Lageveld 8
+31 5 29 45 83 83
30/3 - 28/9
info@tolhuis.com

5ha 54**T**(120-150m²) 10A CEE

1 ADEIJKLNOPST
2 LRTVWXY
3 ABGHIJKMN**Q**RU**W**
4 (C+H 27/4-15/9) (Q )
(T+U+V+X+Y+Z 20/4-15/9)
5 **AB**DEFGIJKLMNO**PQ**UW
XYZ
6 ACDEG**K**M(N 5km)OSTV

Excellent base for cycling and walking enthusiasts. Free routes are available for you to enjoy the delightful Vechtdal valley. A 4 star site with 5 star toilet facilities. The atmosphere is worth sampling.

A28, exit 21, N340 direction Dalfsen. In Dalfsen direction Vilsteren. Follow the signs.

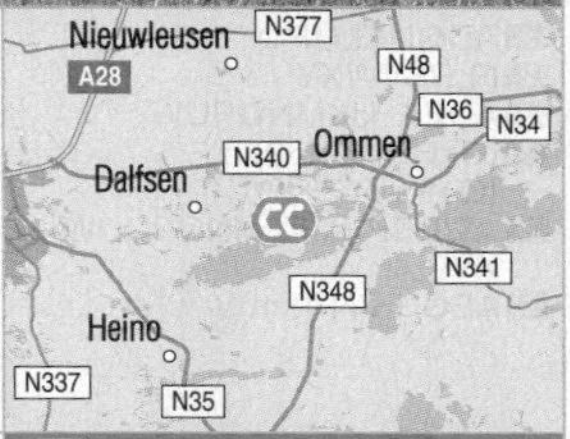

Nieuwleusen
N377
A28
N48
N36
N34
Ommen
N340
Dalfsen
N341
N348
Heino
N337
N35


€18 *30/3-28/5 11/6-10/7 27/8-28/9*

N 52°30'07'' E 06°19'18''

## De Bult/Steenwijk, NL-8346 KB / Overijssel

229

Camping Residence De Eese
Bultweg 25
+31 5 21 51 37 36
1/1 - 31/12
info@residencedeeese.nl

12,5ha 83**T**(80-100m²) 8-10A CEE

1 ABD**G**IJKLMNOPQ
2 BFLRSVWXY
3 ABDGHJKL**M**NR**T**U
4 (C+H 1/4-30/9)
(Q+T+U+V+X+Y+Z )
5 **AB**CDEFGHI**J**MNPQSUWX
YZ
6 ACDEGHK(N 3,5km)STV

A luxurious family campsite in wooded surroundings. Unique cycling and walking routes. You can take a boat trip in Giethoorn and De Weerribben National Park. The campsite includes a heated outdoor pool, trampoline. Entertainment for all ages. Free 'poffertjes' (pancakes) on Sundays!

A32, exit 6: Steenwijk/Vledder and follow the road signs.

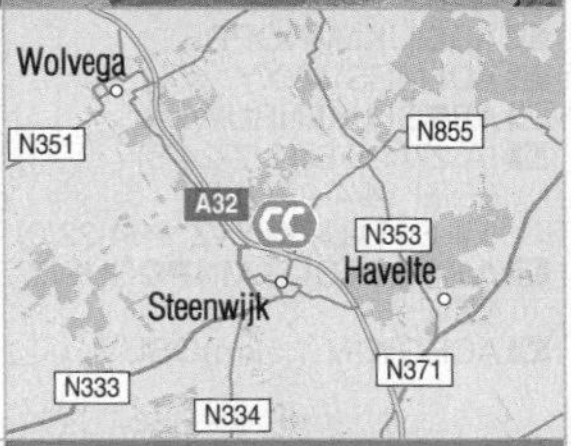

Wolvega
N351
N855
A32
N353
Havelte
Steenwijk
N333
N371
N334


€18 *1/1-18/4 24/4-27/5 12/6-14/7 2/9-31/12*

N 52°48'52'' E 06°07'12''

## De Lutte, NL-7587 LH / Overijssel

230

Landgoedcamping Het Meuleman
Lutterzandweg 16
+31 5 41 55 12 89
1/4 - 30/9
info@camping-meuleman.nl

7ha 111**T**(100-300m²) 6A

1 AD**G**IJKLMNOPQ
2 ABDFIRSXY
3 A**F**GHIJK**Q**RWZ
4 (Q+U+Y )
5 **AB**DEFGIJKLMNPQRUWZ
6 AEGHIJ(N 3km)O

This campsite with a recreational lake is located where the River Dinkel meanders through the countryside. It is in the 'Meuleman' country estate. Set in woods with beautiful scenery all around: the Lutterzand. The campsite is also a good base for cyclists and walkers who want to visit the surprisingly beautiful region of Twente.

A1 Hengelo-Oldenzaal exit De Lutte. Drive through De Lutte towards Beuningen, and follow the signs to the campsite.

N349
N342
B403
A30
L68
Oldenzaal
L39
Bad
Bentheim
A1
A31
N733
L42
L582


€20 *1/4-29/5 11/6-30/6 1/9-30/9*

N 52°20'01'' E 07°01'46''

## Delden, NL-7491 DZ / Overijssel ♿ 🛜 iD **231**

▲ Park Camping Mooi Delden
🏠 De Mors 6
☎ +31 7 43 76 19 22
📅 31/3 - 1/11
@ info@mooidelden.nl

3ha 45T(100-130m²) 10A CEE

**1** AD**G**IJKLMPQ
**2** FLRSVWXY
**3** AD**EF**HJKMN**Q**RUW
**4** (C+H 1/5-15/9) J
   (Q+R+T+Z 📅)
**5** **AB**DEFGIJKLMNOPQUW
   XYZ
**6** AEGHK(N 1km)V

💬 The campsite is located in parkland surroundings right next to an extensive sports complex with swimming pool, golf course and a canal for fishing; partly under trees with spacious pitches. This really is a lovely site.

🚘 The campsite is clearly signposted in and around Delden.

Almelo   Enschede

CC € **18** 31/3-28/5  10/6-6/7  23/8-31/10   📍 N 52°15'16'' E 06°43'37''

---

## Denekamp, NL-7591 NH / Overijssel ♿ 🛜 iD **232**

▲ Camping De Papillon
🏠 Kanaalweg 30
☎ +31 5 41 35 16 70
📅 30/3 - 29/9
@ info@depapillon.nl

16ha 265T(130-160m²) 4-16A CEE

**1** AD**G**IJKLMNOPRS
**2** ADLMRSVWXY
**3** ABF**G**HJKLNRUWZ
**4** (A 27/4-5/5,13/7-24/8)
   (E+H 14/4-22/9) M
   (Q+S+T+U+X+Y+Z 14/4-22/9)
**5** **AB**CDEFGI**JL**MN**PQ**RUWX
   YZ
**6** ACEG**K**(N 1,5km)OSUV

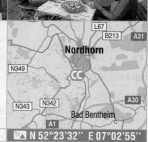

💬 Family campsite where nothing is missing for you and your family. The five-star campsite is also adapted for the disabled. Spacious pitches, a theatre with entertainment for young and old and indoor swimming facilities. An excellent starting point for cyclists and walkers wishing to explore the region of Twente and the County of Bentheim (Germany).

🚘 Follow the signs on the road N342 Denekamp-Nordhorn.

Nordhorn   Bad Bentheim

CC € **16** 30/3-26/4  6/5-26/5  11/6-7/7  31/8-29/9   📍 N 52°23'32'' E 07°02'55''

---

## Diffelen/Hardenberg, NL-7795 DA / Overijssel 👫 ♿ 🛜 iD **233**

▲ Camping de Vechtvallei
🏠 Rheezerweg 76
☎ +31 5 23 25 18 00
📅 1/4 - 30/10
@ info@devechtvallei.nl

7,6ha 50T(100-120m²) 16A CEE

**1** AD**G**IJKL**PQ**
**2** GLRSVWXY
**3** AIJKLNRUW
**4** (E 📅) (G 1/5-30/8)
   (Q+T+U+X+Z 📅)
**5** **AB**DEFGI**JK**LMN**P**UWX
**6** ACEGH**K**(N 4,5km)OV

💬 The campsite is located in wooded surroundings and is set peacefully in the countryside. Amenities are more than adequate and you can go on lovely bike trips from the campsite. Electric bikes are available for rent on request. Swimming at campsite.

🚘 Hardenberg-Rheeze. Through Rheeze, direction Diffelen. On left of road after about 2 km.

Gramsbergen  Laar
Ommen

124

CC € **12** 1/4-19/4  3/5-29/5  10/6-6/7  30/8-30/10   📍 N 52°32'08'' E 06°34'10''

## Enschede, NL-7534 PA / Overijssel  ⛺ 📶 ✿ iD  **234**

🏕 Euregio-Cp 'De Twentse Es'
📧 Keppelerdijk 200
☎ +31 5 34 61 13 72
🗓 1/1 - 31/12
@ info@twentse-es.nl

10ha 80T(100-130m²) 10A CEE

**1** ACDGIJKLMOPQ
**2** DFLRSVWXY
**3** AHJKNRUW
**4** (C+H 4/5-7/9)
(Q+S+T 1/4-1/10)
(U+V+X+Y+Z 🔒)
**5** **AB**DFGIJKLMNOPQUWXY
Z
**6** ACDEGHK(N 1km)ORSTV

💬 An ideal campsite for visiting Enschede amongst other places. Yet this site is located in the middle of the countryside next to a beautiful (fishing) lake. Lovely grassy fields, well maintained toilet facilities. A campsite for young and old. Also an excellent stating point for cyclists and walkers.

🚗 A35/N35 to Enschede, exit Glanerbrug. Keep in dir. Glanerbrug. Campsite is well signposted.

Hengelo — Enschede
A1, L42, L39, N732, CC, N18, B54, A31, B474, L574

CC €**20** 1/1-29/5 4/6-8/6 11/6-7/7 26/8-30/12  🧭 N 52°12'37'' E 06°57'05''

---

## Haaksbergen (Twente), NL-7481 VP / Overijssel  ♿ 📶 ✿ iD  **235**

🏕 Camping & Bungalowpark
't Stien'n Boer
📧 Scholtenhagenweg 42
☎ +31 5 35 72 26 10
🗓 30/3 - 1/10
@ info@stien-nboer.nl

10,5ha 110T(80-100m²) 6-10A CEE

**1** AD**G**IJKLMNPRS
**2** BFRSVWXY
**3** ABCD**E**GHJKM**N**QRUW
**4** (A 30/5-10/6,13/7-25/8)
(C 1/5-1/9)
(F+H+Q+R+T+U+X+Y+Z 🔒)
**5** **AB**CDEFGI**J**KLMNO**PQ**UW
XYZ
**6** CDEGHIJ**K**M(N 1,5km)OS
TUV

💬 Family campsite in natural surroundings and with excellent facilities. Perfect base for cyclists and walkers who can benefit fully from the beautiful landscape and the typical Twente friendliness. Perfect for children; among other things an indoor playground, indoor swimming pool with pools for kids and toddlers and play equipment on the camping fields. Wifi throughout the grounds.

🚗 From N18 exit Haaksbergen-Zuid, campsite signposted from there.

Enschede
N739, Haaksbergen, CC, N315, N18, L608

CC €**18** 30/3-29/5 11/6-13/7 30/8-1/10  🧭 N 52°08'24'' E 06°43'28''

---

## Haaksbergen (Twente), NL-7481 VP / Overijssel  ♿ 📶 iD  **236**

🏕 Camping Scholtenhagen B.V.
📧 Scholtenhagenweg 30
☎ +31 5 35 72 23 84
🗓 1/1 - 31/12
@ campingscholtenhagen@
planet.nl

9,3ha 80T(100-110m²) 10A CEE

**1** AD**G**IJKLMOPQ
**2** FRSVWX
**3** AB**F**GHJKLNRU**W**
**4** (F+H 🔒) IJ(Q 16/7-26/8)
(T+U+X 1/7-31/8) (Z 🔒)
**5** **AB**CDFGI**J**KLMNO**PQ**UW
XYZ
**6** ACDEGHK(N 1,5km)OSUV

💬 Relax in welcoming surroundings. There is a leisure pool next to the campsite equipped with a sauna and a Turkish bath. Free swimming with a ticket from the campsite.

🚗 From north: N18 exit Haaksbergen. From south: N18 exit Haaksbergen-Zuid. Then follow campsite signs.

Enschede
N739, Haaksbergen, CC, N315, N18

CC €**18** 1/1-29/5 2/6-7/6 11/6-7/7 26/8-31/12  🧭 N 52°08'53'' E 06°43'23''

## Hardenberg, NL-7771 TD / Overijssel
&#9855; &#128246; **iD** (237)

🏕 Camping De Kleine Belties
✉ Rheezerweg 79
☎ +31 5 23 26 13 03
📅 5/4 - 26/10
@ info@kleinebelties.nl

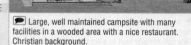
NEW

16ha 100T(80-120m²) 6-10A CEE

**1** ADG**I**JKLPQ
**2** ABDGLRSVWX
**3** ABCGHJKNRUWZ
**4** (C 1/6-15/9) (F+H 📅) JK
　(Q+S+T+U+V+Y 📅)
**5** **AB**DEFG**I**JLMNOP**S**UW
**6** CDEGHKM(N 1km)OTV

💬 Large, well maintained campsite with many facilities in a wooded area with a nice restaurant. Christian background.

🚗 Take the main Ommen-Hardenberg road. Turn right at the traffic lights in Hardenberg. Follow signs to Rheeze. Campsite on your right 2 km beyond Hardenberg.

CC € **16** 5/4-26/4 3/5-29/5 1/6-7/6 11/6-5/7 30/8-26/10
N 52°33'47'' E 06°35'32''

---

## Hardenberg/Heemserveen, NL-7796 HT / Overijssel
&#9855; &#128246; ✿ **iD** (238)

🏕 Ardoer vakantiepark 't Rheezerwold
✉ Larixweg 7
☎ +31 5 23 26 45 95
📅 1/4 - 26/10
@ rheezerwold@ardoer.com

11ha 128T(100-150m²) 6-10A CEE

**1** ACD**G**IJKLPRS
**2** BLRSVWX
**3** ABGHJKMNRUW
**4** (C 1/5-1/9) (F+H 📅) J**N**
　(Q+R+T+X+Y+Z 📅)
**5** **AB**DFG**I**JKLMNOP**RS**UW
　XYZ
**6** ACEGHK(N 4km)OSV

💬 The campsite is located in a natural area and is peacefully situated amid the greenery. The toilet facilities are modern. There is a lovely indoor swimming pool with a Finnish sauna, infrared sauna, sunbathing lawns, an outdoor pool, play equipment on all fields, etc. The ambiance on the site is excellent. There are interactive games.

🚗 N343 exit Hardenberg/Slagharen, follow Slagharen and campsite signs, then turn left.

CC € **18** 1/4-26/4 6/5-28/5 3/6-7/6 11/6-6/7 23/8-26/10
N 52°34'28'' E 06°33'56''

---

## Heino, NL-8141 PX / Overijssel
&#128246; **iD** (239)

🏕 Camping Heino
✉ Schoolbosweg 10
☎ +31 5 72 39 15 64
📅 29/3 - 30/9
@ info@campingheino.nl

13ha 220T(100-120m²) 10A CEE

**1** ACD**G**IJKLMNOPQ
**2** ADFGLRSTVWXY
**3** ABCDGHJKN**OP**RUZ
**4** (A 12/6-14/7,28/8-30/9)
　(F+H 📅) J
　(Q+R+T+U+X+Y+Z 📅)
**5** **AB**CDEFGH**I**J KMNP**QR**U
　WXYZ
**6** CDEGHJ**K**M(N 2,5km)ORS
　TUV

💬 Family campsite, an oasis for pensioners. Recreational programme also in early and late seasons.

🚗 Motorway Amersfoort-Zwolle-Meppel, exit 20 Zwolle-Noord, N35 direction Raalte. From Almelo N35 direction Zwolle, exit Heino-Noord, from Deventer direction Raalte-Zwolle.

CC € **18** 29/3-29/5 11/6-14/7 1/9-30/9
N 52°26'21'' E 06°16'48''

## Holten, NL-7451 HL / Overijssel  ♿ 📶 iD (240)

🏕 Ardoer camping De Holterberg
📧 Reebokkenweg 8
☎ +31 5 48 36 15 24
📅 1/1 - 31/12
@ holterberg@ardoer.com

6,5ha  120T(80-100m²)  6A  CEE

**1** ADGIJKLMPQ
**2** BFLRVWXY
**3** ABCDGHJKLRUV
**4** (C+H 29/5-8/9) (Q 19/4-8/9)
(R 📷) (T+U+Y+Z 19/4-8/9)
**5** ABDEFGIJKLMNOPQUW
XYZ
**6** ACEGHK(N 1km)OV

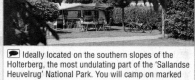

💬 Ideally located on the southern slopes of the Holterberg, the most undulating part of the 'Sallandse Heuvelrug' National Park. You will camp on marked out spacious pitches in fields with play and sports facilities. Excellent toilet facilities and a first rate restaurant guarantee you will want to stay longer.

🚗 A1 Deventer-Hengelo, exit Holten. Just before Holten take the direction of Rijssen (Rd 350). Camping signs before you reach the roundabout.

CC €18  1/1-28/5  11/6-12/7  29/8-31/12  14=12    🧭 N 52°17'31'' E 06°26'06''

---

## Holten, NL-7451 RG / Overijssel  ♿ 📶 iD (241)

🏕 Camping Ideaal
📧 Schreursweg 5
☎ +31 5 48 36 17 25
📅 1/4 - 30/9
@ info@campingideaal.nl

2ha  50T(100-150m²)  6A

**1** ADFIJLPQ
**2** FGKRTUVWXY
**3** AGHJRU
**5** ABEFGIJKLMNOPQUZ
**6** CDEGK(N 0,3km)T

💬 This small-scale campsite is in an undulating stage-like landscape within walking distance of the village of Holten. The spacious, bordered pitches are available in sunnier or shadier spots. Every evening a game of jeu de boules is played here. Plenty of rest and relaxation then.

🚗 On the A1 take exit 27 towards Holten then the 2nd exit on the right. The campsite is signposted.

CC €14  1/4-26/4  6/5-29/5  11/6-13/7  31/8-30/9  7=6, 14=12, 21=18, 28=21    🧭 N 52°16'43'' E 06°26'52''

---

## Lemele, NL-8148 PC / Overijssel  ⊗ ♿ 📶 ✿ iD (242)

🏕 de Lemeler Esch Natuurcamping
📧 Lemelerweg 16
☎ +31 5 72 33 12 41
📅 17/4 - 26/10
@ info@lemeleresch.nl

12ha  189T(100-150m²)  6-10A  CEE

**1** ACDEIJKLMNPRS
**2** LRSVWXY
**3** ABFGHIJKLNRU
**4** (A 1/5-1/10) (C+H 22/4-15/9)
N(Q+R+T+U+X+Z 📷)
**5** ABDEFGIJKLMNPRSUW
XYZ
**6** ACDEGHKM(N 1,5km)O
STV

💬 Perfect for those looking for space, peace and the countryside. Located right on the Lemelerberg, a perfect starting point for walking and cycling pleasure. Ommen, Hellendoorn and Den Ham are close by. Good toilet facilities. Special 55+ rates all year. Also good for grandparents with grandchildren. Comfort pitches available (2 Euros surcharge)

🚗 N347 between Ommen and Hellendoorn. Take exit Lemele and immediately right onto parallel road. Campsite 200 metres on your left.

CC €18  17/4-25/4  6/5-25/5  11/6-5/7  24/8-25/10    🧭 N 52°28'03'' E 06°25'39''

## Lemelerveld, NL-8151 PP / Overijssel  🛜 iD 243

🏔 Charmecamping Heidepark
✉ Verbindingsweg 2a
☎ +31 5 72 37 15 25
⊙ 30/3 - 30/9
@ info@campingheidepark.nl

5,5ha 100T(100-200m²) 6-10A CEE

**1** ACD**G**IJKLMNOPRS
**2** ADF**G**LRSWXY
**3** ABCD**F**GHJK**M**NRU**W**Z
**4** (C+H 15/4-30/9)
(Q+R+T+U+X+Z ⊙)
**5** **AB**CDEFGHIJKLMNOP**PQS**
UWXYZ
**6** ACEGH**K**(N 0,5km)OSTV

💬 Friendly family parkland campsite in wooded surroundings located in the Vecht valley on the border between the regions Salland and Twente. Play equipment in all fields. Child-friendly and traffic free.

🚗 A28 Amersfoort-Zwolle, exit 18 Zwolle-Zuid. Then N35 towards Almelo/Heino. At Raalte go towards Ommen. Exit Lemelerveld. Coming from the north, the campsite is located along the Hoogeveen-Raalte Road. Exit Lemelerveld.

CC € 18  30/3-29/5  11/6-6/7  1/9-30/9    🗺 N 52°26'26'' E 06°20'51''

## Luttenberg, NL-8105 SZ / Overijssel  ♿ 🛜 iD 244

🏔 Vakantiepark De Luttenberg
✉ Heuvelweg 9
☎ +31 5 72 30 14 05
⊙ 30/3 - 30/9
@ receptie@luttenberg.nl

8,6ha 190T(80-200m²) 10A CEE

**1** ADF**I**JKLMOPRS
**2** RSVWXY
**3** BD**F**GHJKLMN**P**QU**W**
**4** (**A** ⊙) (B 29/5-1/9)
(E+G ⊙) JK**LN**
(Q+R+T+U+V+X+Y+Z ⊙)
**5** **AB**CDEFGHIJKLMNOPQR
**S**UWXYZ
**6** CFGHKM(N 1km)OSTV

💬 Welcoming family campsite with hospitable, relaxing atmosphere and good amenities. The woods and beautiful countryside are lovely for cycling and walking.

🚗 Via Deventer: A1 exit Deventer direction Raalte N348. After Raalte, at the T-junction N348 follow direction Ommen. Signposts, exit Luttenberg.

CC € 16  30/3-29/5  3/6-7/6  11/6-5/7  24/8-30/9    🗺 N 52°23'41'' E 06°21'42''

## Mander/Tubbergen, NL-7663 TD / Overijssel  ♿ 🛜 iD 245

🏔 Camping Dal van de Mosbeek
✉ Uelserweg 153
☎ +31 5 41 68 06 44
⊙ 29/3 - 31/10
@ receptie@dalvandemosbeek.nl

6ha 132T(160-200m²) 10-16A CEE

**1** ADG**G**IJKLMNOPQ
**2** RSVWX
**3** ADGHJNOPRU
**4** (Q+Z ⊙)
**5** **AB**CDEFGHIJKLMNOP**PQ**R
UWXYZ
**6** ACEGK(N 1km)SV

💬 Cosy site near the historic artists' town of Ootmarsum. Spacious pitches. Almost all fields are traffic-free. Lovely toilet building with underfloor heating, spacious showers, baby changing room and toilet and washing facilities for the disabled. Peaceful wooded surroundings. Plenty of opportunities for cycling and walking.

🚗 A1 exit Almelo. Towards Tubbergen. Direction Uelsen. On Uelserweg 153, entrance Plasdijk to get to campsite.

CC € 18  29/3-29/5  11/6-7/7  24/8-31/10  14=12, 21=18    🗺 N 52°26'40'' E 06°49'25''

## Mariënberg/Hardenberg, NL-7692 PC / Overijssel

♿ 🛜 ✿ iD **246**

🏕 Camping de Pallegarste
🏠 Pallegarsteweg 4
☎ +31 5 23 25 14 17
📅 30/3 - 26/10
@ info@depallegarste.nl

14ha 85T(120m²) 16A CEE

**1** ADG**I**JKLMPQ
**2** ADFGLRSVWX
**3** ABCD**F**GKL**M**NRUWZ
**4** (C+H 1/5-1/9) IM
  (Q+S+T+U+V+X 🔌)
**5** **AB**FGIJMNO**P**UWXY
**6** EGH**K**M(N 0,5km)OSV

💬 The campsite is located on the edge of the attractive village of Mariënberg. The site is perfectly maintained and it has a friendly ambiance. Wonderful recreation in and next to the lovely water playground. This campsite is certainly worth a visit.

🚗 In Mariënberg with village church on the left, direction Sibculo. Campsite signposted.

[Map showing Ommen, Westerhaar-Vriezenveensewijk, N48, N36, N34, L43, N341, N343, CC]

CC € **16** 30/3-28/5 3/6-6/6 14/6-12/7 29/8-26/10  📷 N 52°30'24'' E 06°34'57''

---

## Markelo, NL-7475 ST / Overijssel

👫 ♿ 🛜 iD **247**

🏕 Camping De Bovenberg
🏠 Bovenbergweg 14
☎ +31 5 47 36 17 81
📅 30/3 - 16/10
@ info@debovenberg.nl

4,5ha 63T(100-200m²) 10A CEE

**1** ADG**I**JKLMNPRS
**2** ADFLRTVWXY
**3** ABGHJNRUZ
**4** (Q+R+T 🔌)
**5** **AB**FGIJKLMNO**PQ**UW
  XYZ
**6** ACDEGHK(N 4km)TV

💬 De Bovenberg is located at the foot of the Friezenberg in rolling countryside, surrounded by fields, woods, heathland and historic burial mounds. You will camp on spacious, marked out pitches on a grassy field. The young landscaping means there are many sunny pitches. The new toilet building offers all modern comfort.

🚗 A1 Apeldoorn-Hengelo, exit 27. In Markelo take direction Rijssen, campsite signposted on the left before the roundabout about 3 km outside Markelo.

[Map showing Nijverdal, Almelo, Goor, N347, N350, N344, A1, N332, N346, CC]

CC € **18** 30/3-27/4 6/5-29/5 11/6-12/7 30/8-16/10 21=18  📷 N 52°15'56'' E 06°31'13''

---

## Nieuw-Heeten, NL-8112 AE / Overijssel

🛜 iD **248**

🏕 Vakantiepark Sallandshoeve
🏠 Holterweg 85
☎ +31 5 72 32 13 42
📅 29/3 - 30/9
@ info@sallandshoeve.nl

3ha 67T(100-150m²) 10A CEE

**1** ACD**F**IJLPQ
**2** FRVWX
**3** AHJKLN**Q**R**T**U
**4** (F+H 🔌) M
  (Q+R+T+U+V+X+Y+Z 🔌)
**5** **AB**DFGHIJMNOPUWXYZ
**6** DEGK(N 6km)ST

💬 You will camp around a lake on spacious, bordered pitches. Most are sunny pitches, but there's shade towards the edge of the site. The campsite is located in an area a bit like a stage setting, bordering on the Sallandse Heuvelrug. Extensive walking and cycling options.

🚗 A1 motorway exit Holten, N332 direction Raalte. Turn right after 7 km (signposted).

[Map showing Raalte, Rijssen, Deventer, N35, N332, N347, N348, N344, A1, CC]

CC € **18** 29/3-27/4 6/5-29/5 11/6-14/7 31/8-30/9  📷 N 52°19'15'' E 06°20'35''

## Nijverdal, NL-7441 DK / Overijssel  ♿ 📶 iD  **249**

🏔 Ardoer camping De Noetselerberg
📧 Holterweg 116
☎ +31 5 48 61 26 65
🔑 5/4 - 27/10
@ noetselerberg@ardoer.com

12ha 210T(90-110m²) 8-16A CEE

**1** ACD**F**IJKLNPRS
**2** RSVWXY
**3** ABC**F**HJKLNRU
**4** (B 2/5-1/9) (F+H 🔑) JM (Q+R+S+T+U+V+Y 🔑)
**5** **AB**DEFGIJKLMNOPQRUWXYZ
**6** ABCEGH**K**M(N 1,5km)ORSTV

💬 Pleasant family campsite, located at the foot of the hills of the 'Sallandse Heuvelrug'. Divided into several fields. Each field has its own play equipment. An attractive site for making the most of your discount card in early and late season.

🚗 In Nijverdal follow the road to Rijssen. Follow the signs to campsite.

N348   N36
Raalte
N35   **Almelo**
CC   Wierden
N332
N350
N344   A1

CC €**18**  5/4-18/4  6/5-28/5  3/6-7/6  12/6-6/7  24/8-27/10   📍 N 52°21'00'' E 06°27'21''

---

## Oldemarkt/Paasloo, NL-8378 JB / Overijssel  ♿ 📶 iD  **250**

🏔 Camping De Eikenhof
📧 Paasloërweg 12
☎ +31 5 61 45 14 30
🔑 1/1 - 31/12
@ info@eikenhof.nl

11ha 101T(90-115m²) 6-10A CEE

**1** AD**G**IJKLMOPQ
**2** FGLRSVWXY
**3** BCDHJKLNRU
**4** (C+H 1/5-31/8) (Q 🔑) (T+U+X+Y 1/5-15/9) (Z 🔑)
**5** **AB**DEFGIJMNOPQUWXYZ
**6** ACDEGH**K**M(N 1km)ORSUV

💬 Well-maintained family campsite with a heated outdoor pool. Camping fields surrounded by trees. The toilet facilities are top class. A perfect area for cycling. The campsite is located close to De Weerribben nature reserve. Tree top adventure park next to campsite.

🚗 Via N351 Emmeloord-Wolvega. In Kuinre direction Oldemarkt. Or via A32 Steenwijk-Wolvega; exit 7 and follow signs to Oldemarkt.

N353
Wolvega
N924
N351   A32   N855
CC   Steenwijk
De Weerribben
Giethoorn
N334

CC €**18**  1/4-28/5  12/6-14/7  1/9-31/10   📍 N 52°48'57'' E 05°59'48''

---

## Olst, NL-8121 SK / Overijssel  👨‍👧 ♿ 📶 iD  **251**

🏔 Camping 't Haasje
📧 Fortmonderweg 17
☎ +31 5 70 56 12 26
🔑 15/4 - 30/9
@ info@kampeeridee.eu

15ha 100T(80-120m²) 4A CEE

**1** ACD**G**IJKLMOPRS
**2** ACKLRSTVWXY
**3** BHJKNRUWX
**4** (C+H 15/5-9/9) (Q+R+T+U+V+X+Y+Z 🔑)
**5** **AB**DFGIJKLMN**P**RUZ
**6** CEGH**K**M(N 5km)ORTV

💬 A family campsite, beautifully located by the IJssel river.

🚗 Along the Zwolle-Deventer Road (N337), road east of the IJssel. Campsite is located north of Olst. Exit near Den Nul.

Wezep
A28
Heerde   N35
   Raalte
Epe   A50   CC   N348
N337

CC €**16**  15/4-29/5  11/6-7/7  24/8-30/9  7=6   📍 N 52°21'47'' E 06°05'14''

## Ommen, NL-7731 PB / Overijssel

👫 ♿ 📶 **iD** **252**

🏕 Camping & Bungalowpark Besthmenerberg
✉ Besthemerberg 1
☎ +31 5 29 45 13 62
📅 29/3 - 30/9
@ info@besthmenerberg.nl

25ha 477**T**(100-120m²) 4-10A CEE

**1** ADG**I**JKLMOPQ
**2** BLRSXY
**3** ABD**F**GHJKLN**OP**RU
**4** (A 1/4-1/10) (C 1/5-1/9) (**F**+H+Q+S+T+U+V+X+Y +Z 🔑)
**5** **AB**DEFGHIJKLMNOPQRU WXYZ
**6** AEGHJ**K**L(N 2km)OSTV

💬 A campsite located in the woods close to the charming village of Ommen. It has modern toilet facilities and an indoor swimming pool and restaurant. The surroundings are beautiful and perfect for walking and cycling.

🚐 Located beside the R103 Ommen-Beerze. Cross the railway line at the camping sign.

CC € **14** 29/3-18/4 23/4-25/4 6/5-28/5 11/6-4/7 31/8-29/9 | 📡 N 52°30'30'' E 06°26'37''

---

## Ommen, NL-7731 RC / Overijssel

📶 **iD** **253**

🏕 Resort de Arendshorst
✉ Arendshorsterweg 3a
☎ +31 5 29 45 32 48
📅 30/3 - 12/10
@ info@resort-de-arendshorst.nl

12ha 125**T**(150-250m²) 6-10A CEE

**1** ADG**I**JKLMOP**S**
**2** ABCFLRSVWXY
**3** BD**F**GHJKLN**OQ**RUWX
**4** (A 1/7-1/9) (G 15/6-15/9) (Q+R+T+U+V+Y+Z 🔑)
**5** **AB**DFGIJKLMNO**PQRS**U WXYZ
**6** ADEGJ**K**(N 3km)OTV

💬 Situated on the river Vecht, close to the lively town of Ommen. Spacious pitches on beautifully undulating grounds. Your discount card offers you value-for-money relaxation. CampingCard ACSI holders have a comfort pitch. When reserving (recommended) mention that you will be coming with CampingCard ACSI!

🚐 Camping signs are posted on the road N340 Ommen-Zwolle.

CC € **18** 30/3-29/5 11/6-8/7 25/8-12/10 | 📡 N 52°31'10'' E 06°21'52''

---

## Ootmarsum, NL-7638 PP / Overijssel

♿ 📶 **iD** **254**

🏕 Camping Bij de Bronnen
✉ Wittebergweg 16-18
☎ +31 5 41 29 15 70
📅 1/1 - 31/12
@ info@campingbijdebronnen.nl

8ha 43**T**(70-120m²) 6A CEE

**1** ADFIJKLMOPRS
**2** BRSWXY
**3** BGHJKMNU
**4** (T+U 1/4-1/10) (X+Z 🔑)
**5** **AB**CDEFGHI**JKL**MNOPU XYZ
**6** ACDEGHIK(N 2,5km)OV

💬 A campsite located in a wood with attractive grounds and sunny pitches. There is excellent cycling and walking from here through surroundings that are so varied that you will be surprised time after time. Excellent 5 star toilet facilities with underfloor heating and every imaginable comfort make camping here a true delight.

🚐 The campsite is clearly indicated in Ootmarsum (with the SatNav in Nutter).

CC € **16** 1/1-29/5 11/6-6/7 23/8-31/12 | 📡 N 52°25'29'' E 06°53'23''

## Ootmarsum, NL-7631 CJ / Overijssel ♿ 📶 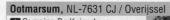 **255**

🏕 Camping De Kuiperberg
✉ Tichelwerk 4
☎ +31 5 41 29 16 24
🔑 1/4 - 14/10
@ info@kuiperberg.nl

4ha 80T(100m²) 10-16A CEE

**1** A**G**IJKLMOPRS
**2** GIKRSUVWXY
**3** GHJKLU
**4** (Q+T+U+X+Z 🔑)
**5** **AB**DFGHIJKLMNO**PQ**UW XYZ
**6** ACDEGJ**K**(N 1km)SV

💬 Rural campsite within walking distance of the picturesque Ootmarsum. Starting point for various hiking, cycling and mountain biking routes.

🚗 On route N349 from Ootmarsum to Almelo the campsite is clearly signposted.

CC € ⑱ *1/4-29/5  11/6-15/7  1/9-14/10*  📐 N 52°24'29''  E 06°53'04''

---

## Ootmarsum, NL-7637 PM / Overijssel ♿ 📶 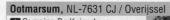 **256**

🏕 Camping De Witte Berg
✉ Wittebergweg 9
☎ +31 5 41 29 16 05
🔑 29/3 - 7/10
@ info@dewitteberg.nl

6,5ha 136T(100-140m²) 6-10A CEE

**1** AD**G**IJKLM**P**ST
**2** ABDLMRSUVWXY
**3** ABCGHJKL**M**NPQRUWZ
**4** M(Q+T+U+X+Y+Z 🔑)
**5** **AB**CDEFGIJKL**O**PQR**ST**U WXYZ
**6** ACEGHK(N 2,5km)OVX

💬 This welcoming family campsite is situated on the edge of a beautiful nature reserve. You can enjoy the most delicious dishes in the restaurant, and the luxurious toilet facilities and the free wifi will make your stay a real pleasure.

🚗 Campsite clearly signposted in Ootmarsum.

CC € ⑯ *29/3-29/5  11/6-6/7  23/8-7/10*  📐 N 52°25'25''  E 06°53'35''

---

## Ootmarsum/Agelo, NL-7636 PL / Overijssel ♿ 📶 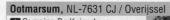 **257**

🏕 Camping De Haer
✉ Rossummerstraat 22
☎ +31 5 41 29 18 47
🔑 1/4 - 1/11
@ info@dehaer.nl

5,5ha 130T(100-140m²) 6-10A CEE

**1** AD**G**IJKLMNOPQ
**2** BFGRSUVWXY
**3** ABGHJKLNRU
**4** (B 9/5-1/9) (Q+T+U+X+Z 🔑)
**5** **AB**CDEFGIJK**L**MNOP**U** WXY
**6** ACDEGK(N 1,5km)OVX

💬 The campsite is close to the attractive little town of Ootmarsum. Modern toilets with sepkey. Not for young single people. The surroundings are beautiful and suitable for walking and cycling. Television with digitenne (for rent). The campsite has existed for over 30 years and the young generation is enthusiastically working to make it even better for campers.

🚗 The campsite is located on the Ootmarsum to Oldenzaal road and is well signposted.

CC € ⑱ *1/4-29/5  11/6-13/7  30/8-1/11*  📐 N 52°23'25''  E 06°54'06''

## Ootmarsum/Hezingen, NL-7662 PH / Overijssel

👫 ♿ 📶 iD  **258**

🔺 Camping Hoeve Springendal
✉ Brunninkhuisweg 3
☎ +31 5 41 29 15 30
📅 1/1 - 31/12
@ info@hoevespringendal.nl

3ha 58T(120-200m²) 10A CEE

1 ADGIJKLMNOPQ
2 BCKRSUVWXY
3 ADGHJKLUW
4 (A+Q 📅)
5 ABDFGIJMNOPQRUW XYZ
6 ABEGHK(N 4,5km)SV

💬 A wonderfully quiet campsite located in the pretty Twente countryside. Close to a lovely stream, far away from the outside world. The site is run by an enthusiastic family who are there to help the camping guests with anything they need. Excellent walking and cycling options and also riding on horseback or with a wagon. Guided horse-drawn-carriage ride on Sundays.

🚗 Campsite well signposted in Ootmarsum.

Uelsen  Neuenhaus
N343
CC  **Nordhorn**
N349
**Almelo**
N342

CC €18  31/3-19/4  23/4-26/4  6/5-29/5  3/6-6/6  11/6-16/6  18/8-31/10   📍 N 52°26'30'' E 06°53'38''

---

## Raalte, NL-8102 SV / Overijssel

⊗ ♿ 📶 iD  **259**

🔺 Camping Krieghuusbelten
✉ Krieghuisweg 19
☎ +31 5 72 37 15 75
📅 1/4 - 30/9
@ info@krieghuusbelten.nl

26ha 200T(100-120m²) 10A CEE

1 ADEIJKLMOPQ
2 DLRSVWXY
3 ABCGHJKMNOPQRUWZ
4 (E+H 📅) J (Q+R+S+T+U+X+Y 📅)
5 ABDFGHIJKLMNOPQU WXY
6 CEGHK(N 4km)OSTV

💬 Very child-friendly campsite in a woody area, close to a fishing and surfing lake. Also perfect for older people due to the many cycling and walking routes, but also because of the peace and quiet at the campsite.

🚗 At junction N35 Zwolle-Almelo and N348 towards Deventer head north. Follow signs. From Ommen turn right at the 'De Lantaren' restaurant.

Ommen
**Zwolle**
N341
N337
N35  CC
Raalte
Nijverdal
N348

CC €18  1/4-26/4  6/5-29/5  11/6-5/7  26/8-30/9   📍 N 52°25'37'' E 06°18'36''

---

## Reutum, NL-7667 RR / Overijssel

♿ 📶 iD  **260**

🔺 Camping De Weuste
✉ Oldenzaalseweg 163
☎ +31 5 41 66 21 59
📅 1/4 - 30/9
@ info@deweuste.nl

9,5ha 68T(100-165m²) 10A CEE

1 ADGIJKLMOPRS
2 CGRSVWXY
3 ABDGHIJKNOPRTUW
4 (C+H 25/4-15/9) (Q+R+T+U+X+Z 📅)
5 ABCDEFGIJKLMNOPQRU WXYZ
6 ACEGHK(N 1,5km)SV

💬 Spacious comfort pitches with 10A electricity, luxury (children's) toilets, heated outdoor pool with free sun loungers, beautiful surroundings with various walking and cycle routes. Pure enjoyment for young and old at this friendly family campsite in the beautiful region of Twente. The restaurant is open at weekends in early and late season.

🚗 Campsite located on the N343 Oldenzaal-Tubbergen. Well signposted.

N343
Denekamp
**Almelo**  CC
N342
Oldenzaal
A1

CC €16  1/4-8/7  25/8-30/9   📍 N 52°21'59'' E 06°50'02''

**133**

## Reutum/Weerselo, NL-7667 RS / Overijssel    261

▲ Camping De Molenhof
🏠 Kleijsenweg 7
☎ +31 5 41 66 11 65
🗓 13/4 - 29/9
@ info@demolenhof.nl

16ha 500T(100-130m²) 10A CEE

**1** ADG IJKLMNOPQ
**2** GLRSVWXY
**3** ABCGHJKNQRUW
**4** (C 26/4-1/9) (F+H ⌨) IJM (Q+S+T+U+V+W+Z ⌨)
**5** ABDEFGIJKLMNOPQRUW XYZ
**6** ACEGHKM(N 1km)ORSV

💬 Large campsite run by a family. The site is well-designed and very spaciously appointed. It stands out for its excellent, very modern toilet facilities. Beautiful water plaza with swimming pools with water slide, separate toddler's pool, outdoor pool and play equipment. New PlonsPlas pond is a place for children to play with water and sand; they'll love it!

🚗 The site is signposted in Weerselo. It is on the road Weerselo-Tubbergen.

CC € 18   6/5-29/5   11/6-10/7   27/8-29/9    N 52°21'57'' E 06°50'37''

---

## Rheeze, NL-7794 RA / Overijssel    262

▲ Camping 't Veld
🏠 Grote Beltenweg 15
☎ +31 5 23 26 22 86
🗓 5/4 - 28/9
@ info@campingtveld.nl

8ha 105T(80-100m²) 6-10A CEE

**1** ADGIJKLNOPQ
**2** ADMRSVWX
**3** ACGHIJKNRUW
**4** (E+H ⌨) J (Q+R+T+U+V+X ⌨)
**5** ABDFGIJKLNOPSTUW XYZ
**6** ACEGHKM(N 3,5km)OQ STV

💬 A friendly five-star campsite in the Vechtdal valley. Plenty of hiking, cycling and night life. Pitches, both standard and comfort, are car-free. And: unique indoor swimming pool, restaurants, catering with bread service, modern heated toilets, laundry, bike rental, fishing and boating lake with play beach, entertainment.

🚗 Ommen-Hardenberg main road, turn right at service station. Follow Hardenberg-Rheeze. Turn right about 1 km outside Hardenberg. Follow signs.

CC € 16   5/4-26/4   5/5-28/5   11/6-5/7   31/8-27/9    N 52°32'48'' E 06°34'19''

---

## Rheeze/Hardenberg, NL-7794 RA / Overijssel    263

▲ Kampeerdorp de Zandstuve
🏠 Grote Beltenweg 3
☎ +31 5 23 26 20 27
🗓 29/3 - 27/10
@ info@zandstuve.nl

10ha 286T(100-125m²) 8-16A CEE

**1** ADFIJKLMOPQ
**2** BRSVWXY
**3** ABCHIJKNRU
**4** (C 26/4-16/9) (F+H ⌨) IJ (Q+S+T+U+V+W+X+Y+Z ⌨)
**5** ABDEFGIJKLMNOPQRSU WXYZ
**6** ACDEGHJK(N 2km)ORSV

💬 This quiet family campsite for families and senior citizens is located in the beautiful Vechtdal in Overijssel, where you can enjoy the beautiful countryside. The campsite has spacious pitches. Relax and enjoy! There is a splendid theatre auditorium... People meet each other on the square.

🚗 Ommen-Hardenberg main road, turn right at traffic lights in Hardenberg. Follow signs to Rheeze. About 2 km past Hardenberg on the right.

CC € 20   29/3-19/4   6/5-29/5   3/6-7/6   11/6-6/7   31/8-27/10    N 52°33'30'' E 06°35'16''

## St. Jansklooster, NL-8326 BG / Overijssel 📶 iD (264)

🏕 Kampeer- & Chaletpark Heetveld
🏠 Heetveld 1
☎ +31 5 27 24 62 43
🔑 29/3 - 14/10
@ info@campingheetveld.nl

5ha 51T(140-150m²) 6A CEE

**1** ADGIJKLMNOPRS
**2** GRTVVWXY
**3** HJKLU
**4** (Q+U 🔑) (X 1/4-30/9) (Z 🔑)
**5** **AB**CDGHI**J**LMNOPUWXYZ
**6** AEGK(N 1,5km)OTV

💬 At the top of Overijssel, in the Weerribben-Wieden National Park, close to St. Jansklooster and the village of Heetveld. You can relax here in natural surroundings. All facilities are here to make your stay as enjoyable as possible. New toilet facilities since 2015.

🚗 On N331 Zwartsluis-Vollenhove direction St. Jansklooster when in Barsbeek. Campsite in Heetveld indicated with blue signs.

CC € **14** 1/4-27/5 12/6-10/7 28/8-30/9 📍 N 52°40'05'' E 06°00'48''

---

## Steenwijk/Baars, NL-8336 MC / Overijssel ✈ 📶 iD (265)

🏕 Camping 't Kappie
🏠 Bergweg 76
☎ +31 5 21 58 85 75
🔑 30/3 - 30/9
@ info@campingkappie.nl

4ha 52T(120-200m²) 6-10A CEE

**1** ADEHIJKLMNOPRS
**2** BFMRVVWXY
**3** AHJ
**4** (A 1/5-1/9) (G 🔑) M(R 🔑)
**5** **AB**CDEFGHI**JKL**MNO**PQR**UWYZ
**6** AEGK(N 3,5km)OST

💬 Camping 't Kappie is noted for its tranquillity and beautiful countryside. Located in the middle of 3 National Parks: the Drents-Friese Wold, Weerribben and Dwingelderveld. A child friendly campsite with top class toilet facilities.

🚗 A32 Zwolle-Leeuwarden, exit 7. 1st exit at roundabout. Right 500m at Witte Paarden. Follow signs.

CC € **14** 30/3-29/5 12/6-14/7 1/9-30/9 📍 N 52°48'49'' E 06°06'18''

---

## Stegeren/Ommen, NL-7737 PE / Overijssel ♿ 📶 iD (266)

🏕 Camping De Kleine Wolf
🏠 Coevorderweg 25
☎ +31 5 29 45 72 03
🔑 29/3 - 16/9, 27/9 - 27/10
@ info@kleinewolf.nl

24ha 475T(100-160m²) 8-10A CEE

**1** ADG**I**JKLNOPQ
**2** ADLRSVWXY
**3** ABCD**F**GHJKL**M**N**Q**RUWZ
**4** (C 26/4-10/9) (F+H 🔑) IJM (Q+S+T+U+V+X+Y+Z 🔑)
**5** **AB**DEFGIJKLMNOP**Q**RUWXYZ
**6** ACEGH**I**K(N 5km)OSTUV

💬 Very child friendly 5 star campsite with a unique outdoor swimming pool and a new themed indoor pool. Set in beautiful surroundings not far from the 'Overijsselse Vecht'. Your discount card offers luxurious facilities at bargain prices in the low season. When reserving you should mention that you travel with CampingCard ACSI. You must show your card on arrival.

🚗 From the N36 via roundabout between Ommen and Hardenberg, exit Stegeren. Follow camping signs.

CC € **20** 29/3-19/4 4/5-29/5 11/6-20/6 23/6-6/7 24/8-16/9 27/9-27/10 📍 N 52°32'40'' E 06°29'41''

## Tubbergen, NL-7651 KP / Overijssel

👨‍👧 ♿ 📶 **iD** **267**

🏕 Ardoer recreatiepark 'n Kaps
✉ Tibsweg 2
☎ +31 5 46 62 13 78
🔓 29/3 - 7/10
@ kaps@ardoer.com

10ha 113T(100-120m²) 6A CEE

**1** ACD**F**IJKLMNOPQ
**2** RSVWXY
**3** ABC**E**HJKLNR**T**UW
**4** (C+H 19/4-15/9)
   (Q+R+T+U+X+Y+Z 🔓)
**5** **AB**DFGI**J**K**L**MNPQRUWXY
   Z
**6** ACEGHK(N 1,5km)OSV

💬 This well-run campsite is located in the beautiful region of Twente. It offers a personal touch, well-maintained amenities, peace and quiet. There is excellent walking and cycling; free routes are available at reception.

🚗 Signposted from the Tubbergen ring road (N343). Follow campsite signs.

Neuenhaus
N341
N36  N343
N349
**Almelo**
N342
Oldenzaal

CC €**16** *29/3-29/5   11/6-8/7   25/8-7/10*   📍 N 52°24'36" E 06°48'19"

---

## Vollenhove, NL-8325 PP / Overijssel

♿ 📶 **iD** **268**

🏕 Ardoer vakantiepark 't Akkertien
✉ Noordwal 3
☎ +31 5 27 24 13 78
🔓 1/1 - 31/12
@ akkertien@ardoer.com

11ha 150T(100-140m²) 10A CEE

**1** AD**G**IJKLMOPRS
**2** CGKLRUVWX
**3** ABDGHJKLNQRUWX
**4** (E+H 1/4-30/9) J**N**(Q+R 🔓)
   (T 1/4-30/9) (Z 🔓)
**5** **AB**CDEFGIJKLMNOPQRU
   WXYZ
**6** CDEGHK(N 0,8km)OSV

💬 A friendly family campsite located near the Wieden and Weerribben nature reserves. Perfect for cyclists and walkers. Fishing and swimming opportunities. Spacious pitches and excellent toilet facilities. Within walking distance of the historic town of Vollenhove.

🚗 N331 direction Vollenhove then follow the signs. Do not go through the centre of Vollenhove.

A6
N333
Emmeloord
N334
N762
CC
N352
Genemuiden
N50   N331

CC €**14** *1/4-28/5   11/6-7/7   26/8-30/9*   📍 N 52°40'32" E 05°56'22"

---

## IJhorst, NL-7955 PT / Overijssel

♿ 📶 **iD** **269**

🏕 Camping De Vossenburcht
✉ Bezoensweg 5
☎ +31 5 22 44 16 26
🔓 1/1 - 31/12
@ info@devossenburcht.nl

20ha 94T(90-100m²) 16A CEE

**1** AD**G**IJKLMOPRS
**2** FLRSTVWXY
**3** BDHJNRUW
**4** (C+H 1/5-15/9)
   (T+U+X+Z 1/4-1/11)
**5** **AB**DEFGHI**J**K**L**MNO**PQ**U
   WZ
**6** ACDEGHK(N 3km)OSTV

💬 Campsite in the beautiful Reestdal valley. Plenty of opportunities for cycling and walking tours.

🚗 A28 exit 23 Staphorst or A28 exit 24 De Wijk direction IJhorst. Follow the signs in IJhorst.

A32
Hoogeveen
N375
Meppel
CC
N48
A28
Nieuwleusen  N377

CC €**18** *1/1-29/5   11/6-12/7   1/9-31/12  7=6*   📍 N 52°39'16" E 06°18'07"

## Zuna/Nijverdal, NL-7466 PD / Overijssel

👫 ♿ 📶 ✿ **iD** **270**

🏕 Vakantiepark Mölke
✉ Molendijk 107
☎ +31 5 48 51 27 43
📅 29/3 - 1/11
@ info@molke.nl

9,5ha 75T(90-125m²) 4-10A CEE

**1** ADF**IJ**KLMOPQ
**2** ACFLRSVWXY
**3** ABCD**F**IJKLNR**T**U**W**X
**4** (F+H 🔓) N(Q 🔓)
  (R 1/5-1/10)
  (T+U+X+Y+Z 🔓)
**5** **AB**DEFGIJKLMNOPQ**ST**U
  WXYZ
**6** ACEGH**IJK**(N 2km)OSTUV

💬 A campsite with atmosphere on the picturesque River Regge. Easy going, child friendly and in a parkland setting.

Nijverdal · N35 **Almelo**
N332 CC
Rijssen
N344 A1

🚗 The campsite is clearly signposted on road N347 between Rijssen and Nijverdal.

**CC** € **16** 29/3-27/4 6/5-29/5 3/6-7/6 10/6-7/7 24/8-1/11 | 📡 **N 52°19'35'' E 06°31'07''**

---

## Zwolle, NL-8034 PJ / Overijssel

📶 **iD** **271**

🏕 Camping Molecaten Park
  De Agnietenberg
✉ Haersterveerweg 27
☎ +31 3 84 53 15 30
📅 29/3 - 31/10
@ deagnietenberg@molecaten.nl

14ha 64T(80-100m²) 10A CEE

**1** ACD**F**IJKLNOPQ
**2** ABCDFLMRVWXY
**3** AB**F**HJKNRU**W**XZ
**4** (Q+R+T+U+V+X+Z 🔓)
**5** **AB**FGI**J**KLMNO**P**UWXYZ
**6** ACDEGH**K**(N 3km)OSV

💬 Family campsite located in a natural area on the outskirts of Zwolle. Plenty of opportunities for walking, cycling and water recreation.

N331
IJsselmuiden A28
N50 CC N340
**Zwolle**
N308 N35
A50 N337

🚗 A28 direction Leeuwarden/Groningen, below Zwolle-Noord exit turn right, then directly left. After 400 metres turn left at the traffic lights, and follow the road.

**CC** € **18** 29/3-18/4 5/5-28/5 11/6-9/7 26/8-31/10 | 📡 **N 52°32'13'' E 06°07'47''**

---

## Akkrum, NL-8491 CJ / Friesland

♿ 📶 **iD** **272**

🏕 Camping Drijfveer &
  Tusken de Marren
✉ Ulbe Twijnstrawei 31
☎ +31 5 66 65 27 89
📅 1/4 - 1/11
@ info@drijfveer.nl

2,5ha 80T(72-100m²) 10A CEE

**1** ADGIJKLMNO**P**RS
**2** CDFMRUWX
**3** ABD**JM**RUWXZ
**4** (A 🔓) (Q 15/5-15/9)
  (Z 1/5-30/9)
**5** **AB**DFGHIJKLMNOPUWYZ
**6** CDEGHIK(N 0,5km)T

💬 Atmospheric campsite located in the Frisian lake district. It has its own marina and special, hardened motorhome pitches. View of the water from all over the site. Free wifi, boat hire, catering. Enjoy peace, space and water on this easy-going campsite. Within walking distance of the lively centre of Akkrum.

N384
Sneek N392
CC
N354 A32
Heerenveen A7

🚗 Exit Akkrum from A32. Dir. Akkrum Oost. Follow signs 'Jachthaven Tusken de Marren'.

**CC** € **18** 1/4-28/5 24/6-30/6 1/9-30/10 | 📡 **N 53°02'54'' E 05°49'33''**

## Anjum, NL-9133 DV / Friesland

🏕 Camping Landal Esonstad
📧 Skanserwei 28
☎ +31 5 19 32 95 55
🕐 5/4 - 28/10
@ esonstad@landal.nl

5ha  129T(100-120m²)  16A  CEE

**1** CD**G**IJKLMOPQ
**2** ACDGKLMRUV
**3** ABC**E**GHIJKLMNRU**WZ**
**4** (**A** 2/7-1/9) (F+H 🔲) KLMN
(Q+S+T+U+V+X+Y+Z 🔲)
**5** **A**BCDEFGHIJKLMNOPUW
XYZ
**6** CDEGHK(N 0,3km)

💬 On the edge of Het Lauwersmeer National Park
you will be camping right by the water. You can make
use of the facilities of the bungalow park. Day trips
out to Dokkum, Pieterburen and Schiermonnikoog.

🚗 From Leeuwarden N355 Dokkum direction
Lauwersoog N361.

CC € **14**  5/4-11/7  13/9-27/10      🧭 N 53°22'30'' E 06°09'32''

---

## Appelscha, NL-8426 EP / Friesland

🏕 Camping Alkenhaer
📧 Alkenhaer 1
☎ +31 5 16 43 26 00
🕐 31/3 - 31/10
@ info@campingalkenhaer.nl

11ha  100T(80-120m²)  10A  CEE

**1** ACDFIJKLMOPRS
**2** FGLRTVWXY
**3** A**F**HJKN**OP**RUW
**4** (**A** 1/5-30/9) (G 1/5-1/9)
(Q+R 🔲) (T+U+X 1/4-30/9)
(Z 🔲)
**5** **AB**CDEFGHI**JKL**MNOP**S**U
WXYZ
**6** ACDEGHKM(N 1,5km)OV

💬 Peaceful campsite set in the countryside on
the border of the Drenthe and Friesland provinces.
Spacious pitches in small, marked out fields. Perfect
for walkers and cyclists. Centrally located between
the Drenthe-Friesland Forest and the Fochteloërveen.
Swimming pool and village within walking distance.

🚗 N381 Drachten-Appelscha, exit Appelscha. N371
Meppel-Assen, exit Appelscha. Campsite signposted
with brown signs.

CC € **16**  31/3-29/5  11/6-10/7  27/8-31/10      🧭 N 52°56'45'' E 06°21'44''

---

## Appelscha, NL-8426 GK / Friesland

🏕 RCN Vakantiepark De Roggeberg
📧 De Roggeberg 1
☎ +31 8 50 40 07 00
🕐 23/3 - 28/10
@ reserveringen@rcn.nl

69ha  375T(100-120m²)  10A  CEE

**1** AC**G**IJKLMNOPQ
**2** BFLRSVWXY
**3** AB**F**GHJKL**M**N**Q**RU
**4** (A 🔲) (C+G 1/5-1/9) J
(Q+S+T+U+X+Y+Z 🔲)
**5** **AB**DEFGIJKLMNOPQR**ST**U
WXYZ
**6** CEGHKM(N 2,5km)OSTUV

💬 A well laid out campsite with spacious pitches in
very attractive natural surroundings. Plenty of walking
and cycling opportunities in the extensive Drents-
Friese Wold national park.

🚗 This campsite is clearly signposted from the
N381 near Appelscha.

CC € **16**  29/3-29/5  3/6-7/6  11/6-12/7  30/8-28/10      🧭 N 52°56'18'' E 06°20'30''

## Bakhuizen, NL-8574 VC / Friesland

♿ 📶 iD **276**

🔼 Camping De Wite Burch
✉ Wite Burch 7
☎ +31 5 14 58 13 82
🔄 15/3 - 31/10
@ info@witeburch.nl

10ha 60T(80-100m²) 10A CEE

**1** ADGHIJKLMOPRS
**2** RSVWXY
**3** ABCDFJKLNPRU
**4** (Q+R+T+X+Z ⊙)
**5** ABDEFGHIJMNOPUWXYZ
**6** AEGK(N 0,6km)OSV

💬 The campsite is peacefully located in the wooded Gaasterland. An excellent departure point for cycle and car trips along the IJsselmeer or Frisian lakes. Comfort pitches with RTV connection. New indoor games pavilion and a luxurious new toilet block.

🚗 From Lemmer N359 direction Koudum. Exit Rijs to the left. Towards Bakhuizen at crossroads, follow camping signs. Campsite outside the village on the north side.

N359

Tjerkgaast

CC

CC € **18** 15/3-29/5 31/5-8/6 11/6-12/7 29/8-31/10 | 📡 N 52°52'18'' E 05°28'08''

---

## Bakkeveen, NL-9243 KA / Friesland

📶 iD **277**

🔼 Camping De Ikeleane
✉ Duerswâldmerwei 19
☎ +31 5 16 54 12 83
🔄 30/3 - 30/9
@ info@ikeleane.nl

9ha 86T(90-100m²) 10A CEE

**1** ADFIJKLMNPST
**2** FGKRSVWX
**3** ABCDGHJKLNRU
**4** (Q ⊙) (T 1/4-30/9) (U+V+X ⊙) (Z 1/4-30/9)
**5** ABCDFGHIJKLMNOPQRS UWXYZ
**6** ACDEGK(N 1,5km)OSV

💬 A peaceful campsite in Southeast Friesland with spacious natural grounds and comfort pitches. Complete and modern luxury toilet facilities. Excellent cycling possibilities in the vicinity.

🚗 From Heerenveen A7 to Drachten. At exit 31 direction Frieschepalen. In Frieschepalen direction Bakkeveen. In Bakkeveen direction Wijnjewoude. Campsite about 1.5 km on the left.

N369 N358 Leek
Drachten A7
N917
N381 CC
N919
Gorredijk

CC € **16** 30/3-29/5 11/6-6/7 25/8-30/9 | 📡 N 53°04'16'' E 06°14'34''

---

## Bakkeveen, NL-9243 JZ / Friesland

📶 iD **278**

🔼 Camping De Wâldsang
✉ Foarwurkerwei 2
☎ +31 5 16 54 12 55
🔄 1/4 - 28/10
@ info@waldsang.nl

13ha 142T(100-120m²) 16A CEE

**1** ADGIJKLMNOPQ
**2** BFGRSVWX
**3** ABCDGHJKNRUVW
**4** (Q+T+U+V+X+Z ⊙)
**5** ABDFGHIJKLMNOPQRSTU WXYZ
**6** ACDEGK(N 0,5km)OSTV

💬 Quiet campsite with comfort pitches only, good amenities and attention for the guests. It is located in a wooded area and surrounded by De Slotplaats estate (run by the Dutch Society for preservation of nature monuments). Plenty of options for walking and cycling! Supermarket at walking distance is open every day. Site has free wifi.

🚗 A7 exit 31 (Frieschepalen). In Frieschepalen take direction Bakkeveen. Before Bakkeveen follow De Wâldsang campsite signs.

N369 N358 N980 Leek
Roden
Drachten A7
N917
N381 CC
N919
Gorredijk

CC € **18** 1/4-26/4 6/5-28/5 12/6-1/7 23/8-28/10 | 📡 N 53°05'08'' E 06°13'00''

## Bakkeveen, NL-9243 KA / Friesland ♿ 📶 iD **279**

🏕 Molecaten Park 't Hout
✉ Duerswâldmerwei 11
☎ +31 5 16 54 12 87
🕐 29/3 - 30/9
@ thout@molecaten.nl

21,4ha 210T(100-120m²) 10A CEE

**1** ADG**I**JKLMNPQ
**2** BFGLRSVWXY
**3** ABCDHJKNRU
**4** (C+H 27/4-1/9) JM
   (Q+T 27/4-12/5,13/7-1/9)
   (U 27/4-12/5,8/7-1/9)
   (V+X 27/4-12/5,13/7-1/9)
**5** **AB**DEFG**I**J**KL**MNOPQUW
   XYZ
**6** ACDEGH**K**(N 0,3km)OSTV

💬 Peaceful campsite in the wooded surroundings. Outdoor pool, indoor playground and large sea of balls. Ideal camp for young families and, in the early and late seasons, for senior citizens. Extensive walking and cycling opportunities. Free cycle routes. Spacious pitches on various grassy fields, surrounded by trees and shrubbery.

🚗 A7 junction Oosterwolde, direction Oosterwolde. Exit Wijnjewoude/Bakkeveen. Or A7 Heerenveen-Groningen, exit 31 direction Bakkeveen. Follow signs.

Leek
N369 N358 N980
Drachten A7
N917
N381 CC
Gorredijk N919

CC € **18** 29/3-18/4 5/5-28/5 11/6-9/7 26/8-30/9 ⛺ N 53°04'44'' E 06°15'11''

---

## Dokkum, NL-9101 XA / Friesland 📶 iD **280**

🏕 Camping Harddraverspark
✉ Harddraversdijk 1a
☎ +31 5 19 29 44 45
🕐 1/4 - 1/11
@ info@campingdokkum.nl

2,5ha 80T(100-120m²) 4-16A CEE

**1** ABDG**I**JKLMO**P**Q
**2** CGRSTUVWXY
**3** ABGHJ**M**W
**4** (Q 🕐)
**5** **AB**CG**I**J**KL**MNO**P**UWXYZ
**6** ACDEGHK(N 0,4km)OT

💬 A campsite set in parkland just a stone's throw from the historical town centre of Dokkum, with its ramparts, alleyways and small harbours.

🚗 From Leeuwarden direction Dokkum-Oost, follow signs. From Drachten direction Dokkum-Oost. Follow ring road (Lauwersseewei). From Groningen-Zoutkamp via N361 direction Dokkum. Follow the signs.

N357
Dokkum
CC
Kollum
Buitenpost ○
N361 Bûtenpost
N355 N358

CC € **16** 1/4-26/5 12/6-14/7 9/9-31/10 ⛺ N 53°19'36'' E 06°00'17''

---

## Franeker, NL-8801 PG / Friesland ♿ 📶 iD **281**

🏕 Recreatiepark
   Bloemketerp bv
✉ Burg. J. Dijkstraweg 3
☎ +31 5 17 39 50 99
🕐 1/1 - 31/12
@ info@bloemketerp.nl

5ha 85T(100m²) 10A CEE

**1** ACDG**I**JKLMO**P**Q
**2** CFGLRUVWX
**3** ABC**H**JKLN**ST**UVW
**4** (A+F+G 🕐) I**JN**
   (S+T+U+Y+Z 🕐)
**5** **AB**DFG**I**JKLMNO**P**UXYZ
**6** ACDEGH**KL**(N 0km)SV

💬 A 4 star campsite and recreation park bordering the Franeker ramparts. Luxurious pitches with connections for water, electricity, waste water, cable TV and internet. Neat toilet facilities. Franeker is centrally located in Friesland and is a good base for visiting other Frysian towns and villages. Supermarket 50 metres from the campsite.

🚗 A31 exit Franeker, direction Franeker. Follow signs.

N393 N383 N398
N384
Harlingen/ A31
Harns ○ CC
Franeker N359
N31

CC € **18** 1/1-8/7 26/8-31/12 ⛺ N 53°11'22'' E 05°33'09''

## Harlingen, NL-8862 PK / Friesland

🛖 Camping De Zeehoeve
📧 Westerzeedijk 45
☎ +31 5 17 41 34 65
🔑 29/3 - 28/10
@ info@zeehoeve.nl

10ha 125T 16A CEE

**1** ACD**G**IJKLMOPQ
**2** AEFLRWX
**3** ABJKNRUWY
**4** (Q 🔲) (T+U+Y+Z 30/5-9/9)
**5** **AB**DFGIJK**L**MNO**PQ**RUW
XYZ
**6** CDEGH**K**(N 1km)OV

💬 The campsite is right on the Wadden Sea, a World Heritage Site since 2009. Day trips to Terschelling and Vlieland. Sightseeing boat trips to the seal colony. The campsite is just outside the historic (Eleven Towns) town of Harlingen. Fishing on site and excellent catering facilities.

🚗 On the N31 Zurich-Harlingen, take Kimswerd exit. 3rd exit on roundabout and follow camping signs. Campsite located about 1 km on the right.

**282**

CC €**20** 29/3-18/4 25/4-24/5 17/6-8/7 7/9-28/10

N 53°09'44" E 05°25'01"

---

## Leeuwarden, NL-8926 XE / Friesland

🛖 Camping De Kleine Wielen
📧 De Groene Ster 14
☎ +31 5 11 43 16 60
🔑 29/3 - 1/10
@ info@dekleinewielen.nl

15ha 180T(80-120m²) 4-16A CEE

**1** ABCD**G**IJKLMOPRS
**2** ADFGLRSVWXY
**3** ABE**H**JKLN**Q**RUWZ
**4** (Q 🔲) (R 1/6-1/9) (X+Z 🔲)
**5** **AB**DFGIJKLMNOPUWZ
**6** ACDEGHK(N 2km)OTV

💬 Pleasant campsite in Friesland in the middle of nature reserve De Groene Staer, 5 km from the centre of Leeuwarden. The area has many hours' worth of walking and cycling routes. Visit theatre De Harmonie or De Oldehove, the leaning tower of Leeuwarden. A wonderful holiday destination for nature lovers, sports enthusiasts, peace seekers and culture spotters.

🚗 Along the N355 between Hardegarijp and Leeuwarden. It is sign posted.

**283**

CC €**18** 29/3-24/5 11/6-5/7 24/8-1/10

N 53°12'59" E 05°53'18"

---

## Noordwolde, NL-8391 KB / Friesland

🛖 Recreatiecentrum Hanestede
📧 Elsweg 11
☎ +31 5 61 43 19 01
🔑 1/4 - 30/9
@ info@hanestede.nl

10ha 60T(100m²) 6A CEE

**1** AD**G**IJKLMOPQ
**2** ADGLRSVX
**3** ABDGHJ**M**NRUZ
**4** (**C**+G 1/5-1/9)
(T 30/5-10/6,13/7-17/8)
(Z 🔲)
**5** **AB**DEFGIJKLMNO**P**UW
XYZ
**6** CEGK(N 0,5km)OTV

💬 De Hanestede campsite is located in a beautiful landscape on the point where three provinces meet in Friesland, close to Noordwolde. Spacious comfort pitches, free wifi. Clear forest lake fed by springs with a white sandy beach. Beautiful area for walking and cycling. Good base for nice trips such as Weerribben, Giethoorn, hunebeds, museum etc.

🚗 A32 towards Heerenveen, exit 6 in the direction of Noordwolde and then follow the signs.

**284**

CC €**16** 1/4-29/5 11/6-14/7 1/9-30/9

N 52°52'58" E 06°08'16"

## Offingawier, NL-8626 GG / Friesland

🛜 285

⛺ RCN Vakantiepark De Potten
🏠 De Potten 2-38
☎ +31 08 50 40 07 00
🗓 29/3 - 28/10
@ reserveringen@rcn.nl

3ha  222T(100m²)  10A  CEE

**1** CD**G**IJKLMNOPQ
**2** ADFLRVWX
**3** ABHJKL**MNQ**RUWZ
**4** (Q+R+T+U+Y+Z 🗓)
**5** **AB**DEFGIJKLMNOPRUWZ
**6** ADEGHKLM(N 5km)OTV

💬 A lively watersports campsite. The site has two private marinas on the Sneekermeer lake and on the Grote Potten. The restaurant has a terrace by the waterside.

🚗 From the A7 direction Sneek, then follow the N7. Direction Sneekermeer. Follow campsite signs.

N384 · A7 · Sneek · CC · A32 · Heerenveen · N354

CC € **14**  29/3-29/5  3/6-7/6  11/6-12/7  30/8-28/10   📷 N 53°01'47'' E 05°43'28''

---

## Oudega, NL-8614 JD / Friesland

♿ 🛜 iD 286

⛺ Camping De Bearshoeke
🏠 Tsjerkewei 2a
☎ +31 5 15 46 98 05
🗓 29/3 - 1/11
@ info@bearshoeke.nl

2ha  45T(100m²)  6A  CEE

**1** AD**G**IJKLNO**P**Q
**2** ADGKLRVWXY
**3** ABHJKLRU**WZ**
**5** **AB**DFGIJKLMNO**P**UZ
**6** ADEGHK(N 0,5km)UV

💬 Attractively landscaped and well maintained campsite by the water. The site is centrally located in Southwest Friesland. There are wonderful cycling trips to the various Eleven Towns. The village of Oudega is a 5 minute walk from the campsite.

🚗 Exit 18 from the A6. Follow N354 towards Sneek. Left in Hommerts towards Osingahuizen, follow road to Oudega. Follow camping signs.

Bolsward · Sneek · CC · N354 · A7 · N359 · N928

CC € **18**  29/3-29/5  11/6-8/7  1/9-1/11   📷 N 52°59'30'' E 05°32'40''

---

## Oudemirdum, NL-8567 HB / Friesland

🛜 iD 287

⛺ Camping De Wigwam
🏠 Sminkewei 7
☎ +31 5 14 57 12 23
🗓 1/4 - 31/10
@ camping@dewigwam.nl

4,5ha  70T(80-100m²)  16A  CEE

**1** ACDGIJKLO**P**Q
**2** BFRTVWX
**3** ABD**F**KLNRU
**4** (A 22/7-19/8) (G 15/6-15/8) (Q 🗓) (T+Z 23/7-19/8)
**5** **AB**FGHIJ**K**LMNO**PQ**UXY
**6** ACEGH**K**M(N 2km)OV

💬 The campsite is located in a woodland setting close to the IJsselmeer. There are several lovely fields surrounded by trees and bushes. Good sanitation facilities. A good base from which to explore Friesland on foot or by bike.

🚗 A6, exit Lemmer N359 direction Balk/Koudum. Exit Oudemirdum.

N359 · N928 · N354 · CC · Lemmer · A6

CC € **18**  1/4-29/5  11/6-8/7  25/8-31/10   📷 N 52°51'37'' E 05°32'42''

## Reahûs, NL-8736 JB / Friesland

 ♿ 🛜 **iD** **288**

🏕 Camping De Finne
✉ Sànleansterdyk 6
☎ +31 5 15 33 12 19
📅 16/3 - 13/10
@ info@campingdefinne.nl

2ha 50T(< 140m²) 6A CEE

**1** ADGIJKLMOPQ
**2** CFKLRSUVWX
**3** ADKNRU**WX**
**4** (Q 1/7-28/8) (R 1/5-1/10)
**5** **AB**FGIJKLMNOPUWZ
**6** ABCDEGK(N 3km)OV

💬 Camping De Finne is located 6 km east of Bolsward and about 4 km north of Sneek. The site has a large fishing pier and you can enjoy lovely sailing and cycling. The campsite has modern toilet facilities, a recreation room with basic catering facilities and a terrace. An ideal place for peace and quiet.

🚗 From the Sneek roundabout direction Leeuwarden. Roundabout direction Scharnegoutum. Turn right to Wommels/Oosterend, direction Roodhuis. Follow camping signs.

CC € **16**  16/3-19/4  23/4-25/5  11/6-15/7  1/9-13/10

📐 N 53°04'35'' E 05°37'58''

---

## Rijs, NL-8572 WG / Friesland

🛜 **iD** **289**

🏕 Camping Rijsterbos
✉ Marderleane 4
☎ +31 5 14 58 12 11
📅 15/3 - 1/11
@ info@rijsterbos.nl

5ha 50T(100m²) 6-10A CEE

**1** ADG**IJ**KLMOPQ
**2** BFGLRSXY
**3** BDFKLNRU
**4** (C 17/5-30/9) Q
 (T+U+V+X+Y+Z 1/5-30/9)
**5** **AB**DFGIJ**K**LMNO**PQS**
 UWX
**6** ACEGH**K**(N 2km)OSV

💬 Friendly family campsite, centrally located in Gaasterland between the IJsselmeer and the Fluessen: plenty of woodland and water. Ideal base for exploring Friesland on foot, by bike or by car. Camping pitches surrounded by trees and bushes. Heated outdoor pool from mid May. Campsite has a restaurant with a snack menu.

🚗 From Lemmer N359 direction Koudum, exit Rijs. At the junction in Rijs turn left. The campsite is 100m on the right.

CC € **18**  15/3-29/5  11/6-8/7  25/8-1/11

📐 N 52°51'44'' E 05°29'58''

---

## Sloten, NL-8556 XC / Friesland

 ♿ 🛜 **iD** **290**

🏕 Recreatiepark De Jerden
✉ Lytse Jerden 1
☎ +31 5 14 53 13 89
📅 15/3 - 31/10
@ info@campingdejerden.nl

3,5ha 65T(120-150m²) 10-16A CEE

**1** ACD**G**IJKLMO**P**RS
**2** CDFGRVWXY
**3** AB**F**JKNWZ
**4** (Q+R 📅)
**5** **AB**CDFGHIJ**K**LMNO**PQ**U
 WZ
**6** ACDEG**K**(N 0,45km)O

💬 A beautifully located campsite close to Sloten. Peace and privacy are the most important features. The campsite is located next to a waterway and is an excellent starting point for cycling and walking trips. Also an excellent spot for fishing.

🚗 From Emmeloord take A6 exit Oosterzee. N354 direction Sneek. At Spannenburg take direction Sloten.

CC € **18**  15/3-25/5  11/6-6/7  1/9-31/10

📐 N 52°53'58'' E 05°38'32''

## Sneek, NL-8605 CP / Friesland ♿ 🛜 [iD] (291)

🏕 Camping de Domp
📧 Jachthaven de Domp 4
☎ +31 5 15 75 56 40
🗓 1/1 - 31/12
@ camping@dedomp.nl

1ha 117T(80-100m²) 6-16A

**1** ADFIJKLMNOPQ
**2** LMSTWX
**3** AJKLW
**4** (X 🔌)
**5** ABDFGHIJKMNOPQUW XYZ
**6** ACDEGHK(N 0,5km)OU

💬 A uniquely situated campsite in the sailing town of Sneek in the middle of Friesland. Includes hardened motorhome pitches and beautiful views of the yacht harbour. Modern toilet facilities. Supermarket, swimming pool and lively city centre within walking distance.

🚗 Follow A7 as far as Sneek. Then follow N7 direction Sneekermeer. Follow camping signs.

(CC) € ⑱ 1/1-26/5 11/6-29/6 1/9-31/12 📡 N 53°02'08'' E 05°40'38''

---

## St. Nicolaasga, NL-8521 NE / Friesland 🛜 (292)

🏕 Camping Blaauw
📧 Langwarderdijk 4
☎ +31 5 13 43 13 61
🗓 1/4 - 31/10
@ info@campingblaauw.nl

6ha 150T(80m²) 10A CEE

**1** DGIJKLNOPQ
**2** ADLRSWX
**3** ABDFHJKLNRUWZ
**4** (Q+X+Z 15/7-18/8)
**5** ABFGIJKLMNOPUXYZ
**6** ACEGHK(N 1,5km)T

💬 Atmospheric campsite in a green oasis, in the midst of woods, meadows and the Frisian lakes. There's walking, cycling and water sports in the surroundings and you can play golf in St. Nicolaasga. Own harbour with slipway.

🚗 From A6 direction St. Nicolaasga. Through this village direction Joure. Exit direction Langweer. Campsite is located on the right of the road.

(CC) € ⑯ 1/4-25/5 11/6-6/7 26/8-31/10 📡 N 52°56'18'' E 05°45'00''

---

## Suameer/Sumar, NL-9262 ND / Friesland ♿ 🛜 [iD] (293)

🏕 Vakantiepark Bergumermeer
📧 Solcamastraat 30
☎ +31 5 11 46 13 85
🗓 30/3 - 27/10
@ info@bergumermeer.nl

28ha 260T(90-120m²) 10-16A CEE

**1** ACDGIJKLMNOPQ
**2** ACDFKLMRSUVWXY
**3** ABCDHJKMNQRUWZ
**4** (F+H 🔌) IJM (Q+S+T 16/4-30/9) (U 24/4-31/10) (V 25/5-30/6,1/7-27/8) (W+X+Y+Z 1/4-31/10)
**5** ABCDEFGHIJKLMNOPQU WXYZ
**6** CDEGHJKM(N 5km)OSV

💬 A large family campsite with plenty of facilities, comfort pitches, water points etc. and options for relaxing. Campsite is located on the Bergumermeer lake and the Prinses Margriet canal.

🚗 Coming from A7 exit Drachten to Burgum (N356). At Sumar follow the signs. Coming from N31 Leeuwarden-Drachten exit Nijega (N356) take the direction of Burgum.

(CC) € ⑱ 30/3-27/4 4/5-29/5 2/6-7/6 10/6-6/7 31/8-27/10 📡 N 53°11'29'' E 06°01'27''

## Witmarsum, NL-8748 DT / Friesland

♿ 📶 **iD** **294**

⛺ Camping Mounewetter
🏠 Mouneplein 1
☎ +31 5 17 53 19 67
📅 1/4 - 13/10
@ info@rcmounewetter.nl

4ha 33T(100m²) 10A CEE

**1** ADG IJKLMOPQ
**2** CFGLRTVWX
**3** ABE JKLM NRUW
**4** (C+G 27/4-7/9) IJ
 (T+Z 1/6-1/9)
**5** **AB** DEFGI **JKL** MN **PQ** RUW
 XYZ
**6** ACDEG **KL** (N 1km)OSV

💬 A peaceful, excellently maintained campsite with large pitches sheltered by hedges. The site is situated on the Eleven Towns waterway for use by small boats. The toilet facilities are excellent and the welcome is very warm. Centrally located for discovering Friesland.

🚗 From the A7 direction Witmarsum. Follow the signs in the village through the residential area.

CC € **18** 1/4-29/5 11/6-12/7 2/9-13/10 📡 N 53°05'56'' E 05°28'14''

---

## Workum, NL-8711 GX / Friesland

♿ 📶 **iD** **295**

⛺ Camping It Soal
🏠 Suderséleane 29
☎ +31 5 15 54 14 43
📅 29/3 - 3/11
@ camping@itsoal.com

20ha 235T(60-100m²) 6-10A CEE

**1** ACD **G** IJKLMNOPQ
**2** ADEFKLMRSVWXY
**3** ABKL **M** NRUWZ
**4** M(Q+S+T+U+X+Y+Z 📅)
**5** **AB** DFGIJKLMN **PQ** UWXYZ
**6** ACDEGHIKL(N 2km)ORS
 TUV

💬 An attractive 4 star campsite located right on the clear waters of the IJsselmeer, just beyond the historic town of Workum. A unique setting for sailing and surfers. Spacious pitches and good sanitary facilities. A superb base for exploring the province of Friesland. Your dog is only allowed to be at the touristic campsite field.

🚗 From A6 at Lemmer route N359 direction Balk/Bolsward, exit Workum, follow signs in the area.

CC € **18** 29/3-18/4 23/4-29/5 11/6-19/6 24/6-6/7 31/8-3/11 📡 N 52°58'08'' E 05°24'52''

---

## Woudsend, NL-8551 NW / Friesland

♿ 📶 **iD** **296**

⛺ Aquacamping De Rakken
🏠 Lynbaen 10
☎ +31 5 14 59 15 25
📅 1/1 - 31/12
@ info@derakken.nl

4ha 40T(80m²) 6-16A CEE

**1** ACD **F** IJKLMNOPQ
**2** CDFGKLRVWXY
**3** BD **F** GJKL **M** NRWZ
**4** ( **A** 16/7-25/8)
**5** **AB** DFGIJKL **M** NOPUZ
**6** ACDEGHKLM(N 0,3km)TUW

💬 The campsite is located on the navigation course between the Heegermeer and the Slotermeer lakes and has its own marina with slipway. Woudsend is centrally located amid Friesland's most beautiful countryside. There are spacious pitches in sheltered fields and modern toilet facilities. A good base for exploring Friesland.

🚗 A6 Lemmer-Joure, exit Oosterzee, direction Sneek. Exit N354 direction Woudsend. Campsite located at edge of village, signposted.

CC € **18** 1/1-27/4 6/5-29/5 11/6-20/6 24/6-1/7 26/8-31/12 📡 N 52°56'46'' E 05°37'40''

## Bourtange, NL-9545 VJ / Groningen

🛇 🛜 **iD** 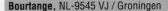 ❽❾❼

▲ Camping 't Plathuis
🏕 Bourtangerkanaal Noord 1
☎ +31 5 99 35 43 83
🔑 1/4 - 31/10
@ info@plathuis.nl

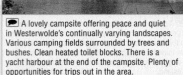

4ha 100T(100-150m²) 6-10A CEE

**1** ADGIJKLMOPQ
**2** ACDFGLRVWXY
**3** AFHJKLNRUWZ
**4** (Q+T 🔑) (Z 31/10-31/10)
**5** ABDFGIJKLMNOPRUW XYZ
**6** ACDEGJ(N 0,5km)O

💬 A lovely campsite offering peace and quiet in Westerwolde's continually varying landscapes. Various camping fields surrounded by trees and bushes. Clean heated toilet blocks. There is a yacht harbour at the end of the campsite. Plenty of opportunities for trips out in the area.

🚗 Route Zwolle-Hoogeveen-Emmen-Ter Apel-Sellingen-Jipsinghuizen exit Bourtange. Follow the signs. Or autobahn 31 (Germany) exit 17, dir. Bourtange (7 km). Signposted in Bourtange.

N969
N368
CC A31 B70
Dörpen
N366 Dersum
N976 Sustrum

CC € ⓲ 1/4-28/5  11/6-7/7  25/8-31/10  7=6    📐 N 53°00'34'' E 07°11'05''

---

## Lauwersoog, NL-9976 VS / Groningen

🛇 🛜 ✿ **iD** ❷❾❽

▲ Camping recreatiecentrum Lauwersoog
🏕 Strandweg 1
☎ +31 5 19 34 91 33
🔑 1/1 - 31/12
@ info@lauwersoog.nl

25ha 177T(120-250m²) 10A CEE

**1** ACDGIJKLMNOPQ
**2** ABDEFGLMRSTUVWXY
**3** ABCDFGHIJKLMNOPRU WYZ
**4** (A 🔑) M(Q+S 🔑)(T 1/4-1/11) (U+V+X+Y+Z 🔑)
**5** ABCDEFGHIJKLMNOPQRU WXYZ
**6** CDEGHIJKLM(N 0,5km)OPR STUV

💬 Parkland grounds on the Lauwersmeer lake with natural landscaping and various types of camping pitches. All amenities are available. The campsite is located in the Lauwersmeer National Park. It is also a museum for nostalgic ships. Extensive children's play equipment, indoors and outdoors. Also own boat trips including seal trips.

🚗 The campsite is on road N361 Groningen-Dokkum in the Lauwersmeer National Park (ferry to Schiermonnikoog).

Schiermonnikoog
Skiermûntseach

CC
N358
N361 N388

CC € ⓲ 1/1-27/4  4/5-29/5  10/6-6/7  2/9-31/12  7=6, 14=11, 28=21    📐 N 53°24'07'' E 06°12'56''

---

## Leek, NL-9351 PG / Groningen

🛜 **iD** ❷❾❾

▲ Landgoedcamping Nienoord
🏕 Midwolderweg 19
☎ +31 5 94 58 08 98
🔑 30/3 - 31/10
@ info@campingnienoord.nl

5,5ha 122T(120-140m²) 10A CEE

**1** ADGIJKLMOPQ
**2** BFGRSUWXY
**3** ABHJNRU
**4** I(Q 1/4-31/10) (X+Y 🔑)
**5** ABCDEFGIJKLMNOPQRUW XYZ
**6** CDEGJM(N 1km)OS

💬 Family campsite in Nienoord Park. Delicious pancakes in the pancake castle next to the campsite. The site is being modernised.

🚗 A7 exit 34 Leek. Then follow sign posts immediately. Entrance to the campsite is along the slip road.

Zuidhorn N983 N361
Groningen
N388
N980 A7 CC N372
Leek
N386

CC € ⓰ 30/3-29/5  2/6-7/6  11/6-12/7  31/8-27/10    📐 N 53°10'17'' E 06°22'57''

## Midwolda, NL-9681 AH / Groningen

300

**Camping De Bouwte**
Hoofdweg 20A
+31 5 97 59 17 06
29/3 - 21/10
info@campingdebouwte.nl

14,5ha 100T(100-120m²) 10A CEE

**1** ACD**G**IJKLMOPQ
**2** ADFGLRVWXY
**3** AJNRUWZ
**4** IJM**N**(Q+U+X+Z 1/4-30/9)
**5** **AB**D**G**IJ**KL**MNPQUWXYZ
**6** ACDEGKM(N 2,0km)OSV

De Bouwte is a large natural campsite in a surprising region. Characteristic farmhouses, varying landscapes with distant views of the polders. Close to the Oldambtmeer lake and the Dollard. This is Enjoyment with a capital E. Had its 25 year anniversary in 2018. There is a FLOTI obstacle course in the recreational lake.

Via A7 Groningen-Nieuweschans. Exit 45 Scheemda-Midwolda, direction Midwolda. Follow camping signs.

CC € **20**   29/3-28/5   3/6-7/6   11/6-9/7   26/8-21/10

N 53°11'24''  E 06°59'26''

---

## Opende, NL-9865 XE / Groningen

301

**Camping De Watermolen**
Openderweg 26
+31 5 94 65 91 44
13/4 - 15/9
info@campingdewatermolen.nl

12,5ha 68T(100-125m²) 10-16A CEE

**1** AD**G**IJKLMNPQ
**2** ABDFKLMRSUVWXY
**3** ABHJKLRU**W**Z
**4** M(Q+R )
   (T+V 30/5-2/6,8/7-23/8)
   (X+Z )
**5** **AB**DFGIJKLMNOPQUWXYZ
**6** ABCDEG**K**(N 2,5km)OV

Enjoy peace, space, nature and water in a beautiful green, sheltered landscape. Fishing and swimming lake and plenty of cycling and walking. Wifi, terrace and heated toilet facilities. For over 50s and young families not interested in mass tourism. Limited space during Ascension and Whitsun: booking ahead is compulsory.

From the A7 exit 32 Marum/Kornhorn dir Kornhorn. Turn left at the church in Noordwijk. After about 2 km turn into the Openderweg then turn right.

CC € **16**   13/4-5/7   25/8-15/9

N 53°09'52''  E 06°13'22''

---

## Sellingen, NL-9551 VT / Groningen

302

**Camping De Bronzen Eik**
Zevenmeersveenweg 1
+31 5 99 32 20 06
1/4 - 1/11
info@debronzeneik.nl

4ha 65T(100-130m²) 6A CEE

**1** ACD**G**IJKLMOPRS
**2** BCLRVWX
**3** A**F**HIJKLNW
**4** (U+X+Y+Z )
**5** **AB**DEFGIJKLMNPUWXYZ
**6** ACEGKM(N 1km)O

Small-scale site in the wooded Sellingen nature reserve. Sellingen is within walking distance, only 2 km from Germany. Free entry to the heated municipal pool. The excellent De Ruiten Aa restaurant is next to the campsite. Starting point for cycle, mountainbike and walking routes. Footgolf course near the site.

Campsite clearly indicated in Sellingen. Turn left on the Ter Apel-Sellingen road just beyond the village. From Vlagtwedde turn right before the village.

CC € **18**   1/4-29/5   10/6-6/7   1/9-1/11

N 52°57'16''  E 07°08'17''

## Termunterzijl (Gem. Delfzijl), NL-9948 PP / Groningen 🦽 📶 iD 303

▲ Camping Zeestrand Eems-Dollard
✉ Schepperbuurt 4A
☎ +31 5 96 60 14 43
🕒 29/3 - 1/11
@ info@campingzeestrand.nl

6,5ha 85T(100-120m²) 6-10A CEE

**1** ABCD**G**HIJKLMO**P**Q
**2** ACDEGLMPRVWXY
**3** ABHJNRU**W**YZ
**4** (Q+T+U+Z 1/5-28/9)
**5** **AB**GIJKMNO**P**UWZ
**6** ACDEGHI**K**MOTV

💬 The campsite is located close to a marina by the mudflats. Peace and space (lots of space for your dog), swimming, sailing, fishing, cycling and walking. Temporary Eemsdelta seal sanctuary on the campsite.

🚗 From A7 Groningen-Oldenburg exit 45. Direction Delfzijl then follow the 'Zeestrand Eems-Dollard' signs. Set SatNav to 'main roads'.

CC € 16 29/3-29/5 3/6-6/6 11/6-8/7 27/8-1/11

📡▲ N 53°18'06'' E 07°01'48''

---

## Vierhuizen, NL-9975 VR / Groningen 📶 iD 304

▲ Camping Lauwerszee
✉ Hoofdstraat 49
☎ +31 5 95 40 16 57
🕒 1/4 - 1/11
@ info@camping-lauwerszee.nl

4ha 110T(120-225m²) 6A CEE

**1** AD**F**IJKLOP**S**
**2** GRTVWXY
**3** ABHJKL
**4** (Y 24/4-30/9)
**5** **AB**DEFGIJKL**M**NO**P**UWX
**6** ACDEGHJK(N 2,5km)OT

💬 A friendly, natural campsite with a restaurant bordering the Lauwerszee nature reserve where peace, space, nature and geniality are the key points.

🚗 Via the N361 Groningen-Dokkum, after the Ulrum exit onto the N388. Follow camping signs from Vierhuizen.

CC € 18 1/4-28/5 11/6-4/7 30/8-31/10

📡▲ N 53°21'36'' E 06°17'42''

---

## Amen, NL-9446 TE / Drenthe 🦽 📶 iD 305

▲ Ardoer Vakantiepark Diana Heide
✉ Amen 53
☎ +31 5 92 38 92 97
🕒 1/4 - 1/10
@ dianaheide@ardoer.com

30ha 300T(100-200m²) 10A CEE

**1** AD**G**IJKLMOPRS
**2** BDLRSVWXY
**3** ABF**H**JKNRUWZ
**4** (Q+R+T+X+Z 🕒)
**5** **AB**DEFGIJKLMNOPQ**S**U WXY
**6** ACEGH**K**(N 4km)ST

💬 A family campsite in wooded surroundings where you will find an oasis of rest. Restaurant. The camping pitches are surrounded by trees and bushes.

🚗 A28 Zwolle-Groningen exit 31, direction Hooghalen. Exit Grolloo/Amen, follow sign posts.

CC € 16 1/4-27/4 6/5-29/5 11/6-6/7 23/8-1/10

📡▲ N 52°55'57'' E 06°35'12''

## Assen, NL-9405 VE / Drenthe

▲ Vakantiepark Witterzomer
✉ Witterzomer 7
☎ +31 5 92 39 35 35
⌖ 1/1 - 31/12
@ info@witterzomer.nl

**306**

75ha 510T(100-120m²) 6-10A CEE

**1** ACD**G**IJKLMOPQ
**2** ABDFLRSVWXY
**3** ABC**F**GHIJKL**MN**PQR**T**
  UWZ
**4** (C+H 1/5-2/9) J(Q ⊙)
  (S+T+U+X+Y 1/4-1/10)
**5** **AB**CDEFGHIJKLMNOPQR**S**
  UWXYZ
**6** ACDEGH**K**M(N 3km)ORSTV

💬 A multi-purpose and natural holiday park. The amenities are endless and neither you nor the (grand)children will be bored for a moment. It has a wide choice of pitches including plus-pitches (CampingCard rates) and comfort pitches. Witterzomer is located in the heart of the province of Drenthe and within cycling distance of the lively town of Assen.

🚗 A28 Hoogeveen-Groningen exit Assen/Smilde (second exit), then follow the signs.

N858 · N919 · N373 · Annen · **Assen** CC · N33 · A28 · Grolloo · N371 · N381 · N374

CC € **18**  1/1-29/5  11/6-24/6  2/9-31/12  7=6, 14=12

N 52°58'44'' E 06°30'20''

---

## Borger, NL-9531 TC / Drenthe

▲ Bospark Lunsbergen
✉ Rolderstraat 11A
☎ +31 5 99 23 65 65
⌖ 29/3 - 27/10
@ info@bosparklunsbergen.nl

**307**

20ha 194T(100m²) 10A CEE

**1** ACD**G**IJKLMNOPQ
**2** BFRSVWX
**3** A**F**GHIJKLMN**QRUW**
**4** (F+H+Q+S+T+U+X+Y+Z ⊙)
**5** **AB**DFGIJKLMNOPQUWXY
**6** ACEGHKM(N 3km)OSTUV

💬 Well-equipped family campsite, surrounded by a forest. With a heated indoor swimming pool and a recreation room. Very suitable for bicycle and/or hiking holidays. There are no motorhome pitches available at this campsite.

🚗 A28, exit Assen-Zuid, take the N33 direction Veendam. Then exit Borger. About 2 km before you reach Borger, road signs leading to the campsite 'Euroase Borger' are posted.

**Assen** · N33 · Stadskanaal · N379 · N376 · CC · N34 · N374 · Westerbork

CC € **12**  29/3-9/7  26/8-27/10

N 52°55'55'' E 06°44'52''

---

## Borger, NL-9531 TK / Drenthe

▲ Camping Hunzedal
✉ De Drift 3
☎ +31 5 99 23 46 98
⌖ 29/3 - 27/10
@ receptie.hunzedal@roompot.nl

**308**

30ha 346T(100m²) 6-16A CEE

**1** ACD**G**IJKLMNOPQ
**2** ADFGLRSVWXY
**3** AB**F**GHIJKL**MN**QR**T**U**WZ
**4** (C+F+H ⊙) IJ**LN**
  (Q+S+T+U+X+Y+Z ⊙)
**5** **AB**DEFGIJKLMNOPRUW
  XYZ
**6** ACDEGH**K**(N 0,5km)OSTUV

💬 This luxurious, all-round recreation park is located just outside Borger on the borders of the wooded Drentse Hondsrug. Excellent amenities for all weather conditions. The park is suitable as a family park and for people who appreciate the Drenthe countryside. There are no motorhome pitches available at this campsite.

🚗 From the N34 Groningen-Emmen direction Borger/Stadskanaal, follow the signposts.

N33 · Stadskanaal · Nieuw-Buinen · N857 · CC · N34 · N379 · N374 · N376

CC € **14**  29/3-19/4  12/5-29/5  11/6-9/7  26/8-27/10

N 52°55'22'' E 06°48'14''

## Diever, NL-7981 LW / Drenthe  🛜 ✿ iD **309**

🏕 Camping Diever
🏠 Haarweg 2
☎ +31 5 21 59 16 44
🔑 1/4 - 1/11
@ info@campingdiever.nl

8,5ha 150T(80-160m²) 10A CEE

**1** ADGIJKLMNOPRS
**2** BGSVX
**3** ABDGHJKNRU
**4** (A+Q+R+V 🖐)
**5** ABCDFGHIJKLMNOPQST
UWXYZ
**6** ACEGIK(N 1km)OTV

💬 Diever campsite is a unique woodland site, located right in the woods and within walking distance of the rustic village of Diever. Plenty of privacy. The ideal starting point for a full day's cycling and walking in the Drenthe-Friesland Forest national park or the Dwingelderveld. Something not to be missed: the annual Shakespeare performances.

🚐 From Diever direction Zorgvlied. After 1 km the campsite is signposted.

CC € ⑱ 1/4-28/5  11/6-10/7  28/8-1/11  📐 N 52°52'00'' E 06°19'13''

---

## Diever/Wittelte, NL-7986 PL / Drenthe  🛜 ✿ iD **310**

🏕 Camping Wittelterbrug
🏠 Wittelterweg 31
☎ +31 5 21 59 82 88
🔑 1/4 - 26/10
@ info@wittelterbrug.nl

4,6ha 90T(80-115m²) 10A CEE

**1** ADGIJKLPQ
**2** CGLRSVX
**3** ABFGJKNRUWX
**4** (F+H 1/5-9/9)
(Q+R+T+U+X+Z 🖐)
**5** ABDFGIJKLMNOPUWXY
**6** ADGKM(N 4km)OV

💬 A campsite with a swimming pool and children's play equipment. Welcoming, complete and child friendly. Luxurious toilet facilities and an attractive cafeteria. Interesting trips out.

🚐 Beside the Drentse Hoofdvaart canal Dieverbrug-Wittelte. Campsite indicated after 3 km. From Meppel exit A32 Havelte, then continue by the canal, campsite signposted beyond Uffelte.

CC € ⑫ 1/4-22/5  11/6-14/7  1/9-26/10  📐 N 52°49'30'' E 06°19'06''

---

## Dwingeloo, NL-7991 PM / Drenthe  ♿ 🛜 iD **311**

🏕 Camping Meistershof
🏠 Lheebroek 33
☎ +31 5 21 59 72 78
🔑 5/4 - 28/9
@ info@meistershof.nl

6ha 120T(100-160m²) 10A CEE

**1** ACDGHIJKLNOPQ
**2** FKLMRSVWX
**3** ABCDFGHJKNQRUW
**4** (A 1/5-1/9) M(Q+R 🖐)
(T 1/5-1/9)
**5** ABCDEFGHIJKLMNOPQR
STUWXYZ
**6** ACEGK(N 5km)ORSTUV

💬 Quiet and beautiful rural parkland campsite with very spacious pitches, equipped with optical fibre internet. Located on the edge of the Dwingelderveld National Park. Discounts in spring and autumn low seasons. First rate toilet facilities. Open all year for motorhomes.

🚐 From Dieverbrug direction Dwingeloo. Campsite is signposted by the road junction just before Dwingeloo.

CC € ⑱ 5/4-26/4  6/5-26/5  12/6-5/7  23/8-28/9  📐 N 52°50'43'' E 06°25'40''

## Dwingeloo, NL-7991 SE / Drenthe

▲ Camping Torentjeshoek
✉ Leeuweriksveldweg 1
☎ +31 5 21 59 17 06
🗓 30/3 - 27/10
@ info@torentjeshoek.nl

**312**

10ha 223T(100-140m²) 10A CEE

**1** ADGIJKLMNOPQ
**2** BFLRSVWXY
**3** ABDFGHJKNOPRUW
**4** (A 1/7-23/10) (C+H 1/5-1/9) J
(Q 1/4-27/9) (R+T+Z 🖸)
**5** ABCEFGIJKLMNOPQUW
XYZ
**6** ACEGHIKM(N 1,5km)OSV

💬 A friendly family campsite with large comfort pitches in the beautiful natural surroundings of the National Park Dwingelderveld. Excellent base for cycling and walking trips.

🚗 From Dieverbrug in the direction of Dwingeloo. Cross through Dwingeloo until the crossing on the edge of the woods. Follow the campsite signs along the forest road and turn right past Planetron.

CC € 18   30/3-28/5   11/6-10/7   28/8-26/10    🧭 N 52°49'09'' E 06°21'39''

---

## Dwingeloo, NL-7991 PB / Drenthe

▲ RCN Vakantiepark De Noordster
✉ Noordster 105
☎ +31 8 50 40 07 00
🗓 29/3 - 28/10
@ reserveringen@rcn.nl

**313**

42ha 220T(90-100m²) 10A CEE

**1** ADGIJKLMNOPQ
**2** BFRSWX
**3** ABDFGHJKLMNQRU
**4** (A 🖸) (C+H 1/5-1/9) J
(Q+R+T+U+X+Y+Z 🖸)
**5** ABCDFGHIJKLMNOPQ
UWZ
**6** ACEHIKM(N 2km)OSV

💬 A campsite with plenty of facilities and good catering in the middle of the woods of Dwingelderveld National Park. The Park covers an area of more than 3700 hectares. The heathlands are the most beautiful and best preserved wetlands in Europe. A large flock of sheep contributes to nature conservation.

🚗 From Dieverbrug towards the centre of Dwingeloo. Through Dwingeloo to the five road junction by the woods. Follow signs on the woodland road.

CC € 16   29/3-29/5   3/6-7/6   11/6-12/7   30/8-28/10    🧭 N 52°48'48'' E 06°22'42''

---

## Echten, NL-7932 PX / Drenthe

▲ Vakantiepark Westerbergen
✉ Oshaarseweg 24
☎ +31 5 28 25 12 24
🗓 30/3 - 27/10
@ info@westerbergen.nl

**314**

55ha 334T(110m²) 6-16A CEE

**1** ACDGIJKLMNOPQ
**2** BFLRSWXY
**3** ABCGHIJKLMNQRUW
**4** (A 1/7-31/8) (F 🖸) HM
(Q+S+T+U+V+X+Y+Z 🖸)
**5** ABDEFGIJKLMNOPQRSUW
XYZ
**6** ACDEGHJKM(N 5km)OSTV

💬 Spacious recreation park in the woods. Plenty of high quality facilities. A real family campsite in the middle of beautiful scenery.

🚗 Coming from A28 exit Zuidwolde/Echten, continue towards Echten and follow signs to the campsite.

CC € 16   30/3-29/5   11/6-7/7   25/8-27/10    🧭 N 52°42'01'' E 06°22'40''

## Een (Gem. Noordenveld), NL-9342 TC / Drenthe

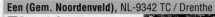

♿ 🛜 ✿ **iD** **315**

🔺 Recreatie Centrum 'Ronostrand'
🚏 Amerika 16
☎ +31 5 92 65 62 06
🔓 1/4 - 30/9
@ info@ronostrand.nl

35ha 190T(80-120m²) 10-16A CEE

**1** ADG**I**JKLMNPST
**2** ADFKLMRSVWXY
**3** ABF**GH**JKN**OP**RUZ
**4** (Q+R 🔓)
  (S+T+U+V+W+Y 1/4-15/9)
**5** **ABC**DEFG**IJ**K**L**MO**PQR**UW
  XYZ
**6** ACEGH**K**LM(N 4km)OSTV

💬 Sheltered campsite on the lake with fresh water from a well. Large beach and meadow. Many cycling and walking possibilities.

🚗 Road Roden-Norg. Beyond the cemetery and sport facilities turn right. Follow the signs.

CC € ⑱ 1/4-28/5 3/6-6/6 11/6-7/7 25/8-30/9 · 📐 N 53°06'01'' E 06°22'19''

---

## Een-West/Noordenveld, NL-9343 TB / Drenthe

🛜 **iD** **316**

🔺 Camping De Drie Provinciën
🚏 Bakkeveenseweg 15
☎ +31 5 16 54 12 01
🔓 30/3 - 29/9
@ info@dedrieprovincien.nl

6ha 139T(110-130m²) 10A CEE

**1** ADF**I**JKLPQ
**2** FGKRSVWX
**3** HJKLW
**4** (X+Y 🔓)
**5** **ABD**G**HJL**MNO**P**UWXYZ
**6** ADEGH**JK**(N 4km)

💬 This well serviced and rurally located campsite is right on the border of Groningen, Friesland and Drenthe. Park-like grounds, partly arranged around three fishing lakes with spacious, sheltered pitches and provided with various landscaping. Plenty of walking and cycling opportunities. Excellent à la carte restaurant with garden terrace.

🚗 A32 direction Wolvega, exit Wolvega, N351 direction Oosterwolde. Then Haulerwijk/Een-West. Follow signs to De Drie Provinciën.

CC € ⑱ 30/3-29/5 11/6-8/7 25/8-29/9 · 📐 N 53°05'19'' E 06°18'41''

---

## Ees, NL-9536 TA / Drenthe

♿ 🛜 **iD** **317**

🔺 Camping De Zeven Heuveltjes
🚏 Odoornerstraat 25
☎ +31 5 91 54 92 56
🔓 1/4 - 10/10
@ info@dezevenheuveltjes.nl

6ha 135T(80-100m²) 6A CEE

**1** ADG**I**JKLOPRS
**2** BFGRSVXY
**3** ABF**GH**JKNR
**4** (C+H 1/5-1/9)
  (Q 27/4-5/5,13/7-25/8)
**5** **AB**CDEFGHIJKLMNOPQRU
  WXY
**6** ABCDEGHK(N 4km)OST

💬 Located in a lovely wooded walking and cycling area of the Hondsrug. A well run, peaceful campsite with comfort pitches and excellent toilet facilities. The campsite also has a heated outdoor swimming pool, including toddlers' pool which is filled with salt water. Nature, relaxation and ambiance. Discover it for yourself! Free wifi (with codes).

🚗 N34 Groningen-Emmen, exit Exloo. Take secondary road back to Ees, direction Groningen (about 500 metres).

CC € ⑯ 1/4-29/5 11/6-6/7 23/8-6/10 7=6, 14=12, 21=18 · 📐 N 52°53'39'' E 06°49'05''

## Exloo, NL-7875 TA / Drenthe

♿ 🛜 **iD** **318**

🏕 Camping Exloo
📧 Valtherweg 37
☎ +31 5 91 54 91 47
🕐 1/1 - 31/12
@ info@campingexloo.nl

3ha 60T(100-120m²) 6-10A CEE

**1** A**G**IJKLMNOP**Q**U
**2** KRVWXY
**3** FGHJU**W**
**5** **AB**DGIJKLMNPUXZ
**6** ABCEGHK(N 2,5km)UV

💬 A peaceful and hospitable campsite. The site is located in the Hondsrug Geopark and close to delightful Exloo. Cycling and walking routes from the campsite.

🚗 N34 direction Groningen, exit Exloo. Turn right at end of village towards Valthe. After 2 km campsite on the left.

Buinerveen · N857 · N379
Borger · N366
N34 CC
N376
Emmen · N391

**CC** €**16** 1/1-29/5 11/6-6/7 24/8-31/12  📍 N 52°51'54" E 06°53'11"

---

## Gasselte, NL-9462 TB / Drenthe

♿ 🛜 **iD** **319**

🏕 Camping De Lente van Drenthe
📧 Houtvester Jansenweg 2
☎ +31 5 99 56 43 33
🕐 6/4 - 29/9
@ info@delentevandrenthe.nl

15ha 140T(100m²) 6A CEE

**1** AD**G**IJKLMOPRS
**2** ABDFRSVWXY
**3** ABD**F**GHJKLMNRU**W**Z
**4** (C+G 1/5-14/9)
(Q+R+T+U 27/4-1/9)
**5** **AB**DEFGIJKLMNO**PQ**UW XYZ
**6** ACDEGH**K**(N 3km)OST

💬 Located in the Hondsrug area on the edge of the Gieten-Borger forest. 250 metres from 2 lakes with sandy beaches and huge open water park DX Adventurepark. Spacious pitches on small fields. Modern toilet facilities. Base for exploring area by bike. Beautiful countryside, including De Drentsche Aa National Park and 'Hunebedden' stone megaliths.

🚗 Coming from N34 Groningen-Emmen right at Gasselte junction into woods. Follow signs 'De Lente van Drenthe'.

A28 · N34
Assen · N33 · Stadskanaal
CC · N379
N376 · N857 · Buinerveen
N374

**CC** €**18** 6/4-30/5 11/6-6/7 25/8-29/9  📍 N 52°58'35" E 06°45'23"

---

## Gasselte, NL-9462 TT / Drenthe

♿ 🛜 ✿ **iD** **320**

🏕 Camping Het Horstmannsbos
📧 Hoogte der Heide 8
☎ +31 5 99 56 42 70
🕐 19/4 - 30/9
@ info@horstmannsbos.nl

6,5ha 100T(100-130m²) 10A CEE

**1** AD**G**IJKLMNOPRS
**2** BFGRSVWXY
**3** AB**F**GHJKL**M**NRU
**4** M(Q+T+U+X+Z 🔌)
**5** **AB**CDFGHIJKLMNOPQRU WZ
**6** ABCDEGJ**K**(N 3km)OSTV

💬 A quiet spacious natural campsite located in woodland. It has a unique location right by Het Drouwenerzand nature area and has several grassy fields with spacious camping pitches as well as a woodland strip especially for nature lovers.

🚗 From the N34 Groningen-Emmen follow the road signs to the Gasselte exit.

Annen
N366
N33 · Stadskanaal
CC
N376 · Borger
N34 · N379
N374

**CC** €**18** 19/4-29/5 10/6-6/7 24/8-30/9  📍 N 52°58'15" E 06°48'26"

## Gieten, NL-9461 AP / Drenthe 🛜 iD 321

🏕 Camping Zwanemeer
📫 Voorste Land 1
☎ +31 5 92 26 13 17
📅 1/4 - 30/9
@ info@zwanemeer.nl

6ha 160T(80-120m²) 6-10A CEE

**1** ADGIJKLMNO**PRS**
**2** ABFGLRSVWXY
**3** AD**F**GHIJKLNRU**W**
**4** (A 📅) (C+H 28/4-1/9) JM
   (Q 📅)
**5** **AB**CDEFGHIJKLMNOPQRU
   WXYZ
**6** AEGH**K**(N 0,8km)OST

💬 A friendly family campsite on the edge of the Drentsche Aa and the Zwanemeerbos areas of natural beauty with brooks and traditional villages.

🚗 Via the N33 Assen-Gieten, follow the campsite signs through the village.

CC € 18  1/4-6/7  24/8-30/9    📍 N 53°00'56'' E 06°46'00''

---

## Havelte, NL-7971 CT / Drenthe 🛜 iD 322

🏕 Camping Jelly's Hoeve
📫 Raadhuislaan 2
☎ +31 5 21 34 28 08
📅 1/4 - 31/10
@ info@jellyshoeve.nl

2ha 42T(< 130m²) 10A CEE

**1** ACD**G**IJKLMO**P**QU
**2** BFGRSTVWXY
**3** **F**HJ
**4** (Q 📅)
**5** **AB**CDGHIJKLMNO**P**UWYZ
**6** ABEGH**K**(N 1km)

💬 This site is situated between National Parks Dwingelderveld, De Weerribben and the Drents Friese Wold. Unique base for a ramble through forests, heath, along fens and Drenthe villages. Within walking distance of Havelte. Only for adults.

🚗 Take exit 4 on the A32. Then the N371 direction Havelt/Diever. After about 4 km cross the bridge and take the N371 towards Uffelte/Diever/Assen. Left from the N371 at the bridge after 1 km (60 km zone), keep right then first right.

CC € 18  1/4-28/5  11/6-30/6  1/9-30/10    📍 N 52°46'07'' E 06°14'57''

---

## Hoogersmilde, NL-9423 TA / Drenthe 👫 ♿ 🛜 iD 323

🏕 Ardoer Camping De Reeënwissel
📫 Bosweg 23
☎ +31 5 92 45 93 56
📅 5/4 - 29/9
@ info@reeenwissel.nl

18ha 180T(90-110m²) 10A CEE

**1** ADGLMRS
**2** U
**3** DHJKLU
**4** (A 📅) (B+G 1/5-1/9)
   (Q+X 📅)
**5** **AB**DEFGIKL**M**NOPQUW
   XYZ
**6** AEGH**IK**(N 1km)OSTUV

💬 Camping De Reeënwissel is a luxurious family campsite located directly on the Drents-Friese Wold National Park. Perfect for campers who love walking and cycling.

🚗 Past the 'Drentse Hoofdvaart' (west side) drive from Dieverbrug direction Hoogersmilde. The campsite is signposted along this road.

CC € 16  5/4-26/4  6/5-28/5  11/6-11/7  28/8-29/9    📍 N 52°54'14'' E 06°22'50''

## Hooghalen, NL-9414 TG / Drenthe

▲ Camping Tikvah
✉ Oosthalen 5
☎ +31 5 93 59 20 97
⌁ 1/4 - 15/10
@ info@campingtikvah.nl

1,3ha 53T(120-250m²) 6-16A CEE

**1** ADG**I**JKLMNO**PQ**
**2** RSVWX
**3** AHJKLNRU
**5** **AB**CDFGHIJ**M**NOPUWXYZ
**6** ACDEGKM(N 0,5km)OUV

324

💬 Camping Tikvah is surrounded by pine and deciduous trees, heathland, ponds and sand dunes. You can walk into the woods directly from the campsite. It is about 2 km from Hooghalen village and 500m from 'Kamp Westerbork'.

🚗 From A28 take exit Beilen-Noord/Emmen/Hooghalen. Then follow signs to Hooghalen for ± 10 km. Just before Hooghalen follow the brown sign 'voormalig Kamp Westerbork'.Just before roundabout turn right across railroad, then 1.5 km.

CC € 16   1/4-27/4   6/5-29/5   11/6-27/6   1/7-15/7   1/9-15/10

N 52°55'13'' E 06°33'33''

---

## Klijndijk/Odoorn, NL-7871 PE / Drenthe

▲ Camping De Fruithof
✉ Melkweg 2
☎ +31 5 91 51 24 27
⌁ 5/4 - 23/9
@ info@fruithof.nl

17ha 250T(100m²) 6-16A CEE

**1** ADG**I**JKLOPQ
**2** ADGLMRVWX
**3** ABC**F**GHJKL**MNQ**RUZ
**4** (E+H 19/4-23/9) J
   (Q+S+T+U+X+Y+Z 19/4-15/9)
**5** **AB**DFGIJKLMNOPQUW
   XYZ
**6** ACFGH**K**(N 3km)OSTV

325

💬 This perfectly equipped campsite is located in the Hondsrug area in the province of Drenthe, nearby Klijndijk and Odoorn villages. There is a zoo (Wildlands Adventure) situated about 5 km away, in Emmen. Plenty of sights (nature and culture) in direct surroundings.

🚗 N34 Emmen-Groningen exit Klijndijk. Then follow the signs. Campsite next to the roundabout.

CC € 18   5/4-27/4   5/5-29/5   2/6-7/6   10/6-7/7   24/8-23/9

N 52°49'44'' E 06°51'27''

---

## Meppen, NL-7855 TA / Drenthe

▲ Camping De Bronzen Emmer
✉ Mepperstraat 41
☎ +31 5 91 37 15 43
⌁ 30/3 - 27/10
@ info@bronzenemmer.nl

20ha 230T(100-140m²) 4-10A CEE

**1** AD**F**IJKLMNOPQ
**2** BFLRSVWXY
**3** ABD**F**GHJK**M**NOPRU
**4** (F+G 26/4-27/10) **N**(Q ⌁)
   (R 26/4-10/6,13/7-24/8)
   (T+U+X+Z 26/4-15/9)
**5** **AB**DEFGIJKLMNOPUWXYZ
**6** ACEGHK(N 2km)OSV

326

💬 This lovely campsite is located in the wooded surroundings of the flatlands of Drenthe. Run by an enthusiastic family. Plenty of touring pitches with caravans and tents. Also car-free pitches. You will immediately feel at home here.

🚗 A37 Hoogeveen-Emmen, exit Oosterhesselen (N854) direction Meppen. Campsite signposted in Meppen in direction Meppen/Mantinge.

CC € 18   30/3-29/5   3/6-7/6   11/6-9/7   26/8-27/10   7=6, 14=12, 21=18, 28=24

N 52°46'44'' E 06°41'11''

## Meppen, NL-7855 PV / Drenthe 📶 iD

**327**

🏕 Camping Erfgoed de Boemerang
📧 Nijmaten 2
☎ +31 5 91 37 21 18
📅 12/4 - 1/10
@ info@erfgoeddeboemerang.nl

1,7ha 47T(100-200m²) 6-10A CEE

**1** **AG**IJKLMNO**P**Q
**2** DFRSUVWXY
**3** DFHJKU
**5** **AB**CDGHIJMNOPUWXYZ
**6** ABDEGK(N 2km)S

💬 This idyllic campground is set in the historic village of Meppen in wooded, peaceful surroundings and is run by an enthusiastic couple who maintain an eye for detail on the site.

🚗 A37 Hoogeveen-Emmen. Oosterhesselen exit (N854) towards Meppen. Then direction Mantinge. Follow the signs.

Beilen · N381 · N376 · Emmen
N374 · ℂℂ · N34
Hoogeveen · A37

ℂℂ € **16** 12/4-24/5  12/6-5/7  26/8-1/10

🧭 N 52°46'49'' E 06°41'30''

---

## Norg, NL-9331 AC / Drenthe 📶 iD

**328**

🏕 Boscamping Langeloërduinen
📧 Kerkpad 12
☎ +31 5 92 61 27 70
📅 5/4 - 29/9
@ info@boscamping.nl

7,5ha 120T(100-120m²) 10-12A CEE

**1** ACD**G**IJKLMNOPQ
**2** BGRSWXY
**3** ABHJNR
**5** **AB**CDFGHIJKLMNOPQUW
XYZ
**6** EG**JK**(N 0,7km)OS

💬 A lovely natural woodland campsite where you can camp undisturbed. Shops and restaurants are a 10 minute walk from the site. You can walk or cycle from your pitch further into the woods. Every pitch can have electricity, TV and internet if required. On arrival you will be given various walking and cycling routes to explore the multi-faceted surroundings. You will be pleasantly surprised!

🚗 From N371 direction Norg, follow directions in the village.

Leek · N372 · Eelde
N386
N34
ℂℂ
N919 · N373 · A28
Oosterwolde Easterwâlde · Assen

ℂℂ € **18** 5/4-26/4  5/5-29/5  2/6-7/6  10/6-12/7  30/8-29/9

🧭 N 53°04'21'' E 06°27'25''

---

## Norg, NL-9331 VA / Drenthe ♿ 📶 ✿ iD

**329**

🏕 Camping De Norgerberg
📧 Langeloërweg 63
☎ +31 5 92 61 22 81
📅 29/3 - 27/10
@ info@norgerberg.nl

20ha 150T(100-150m²) 10A CEE

**1** AD**F**IJKLPQ
**2** BFGRTUVWXY
**3** ABF**H**IJKLMNRU
**4** (A 30/4-16/5,9/7-28/8)
(C+F+H 📅) **KN**
(Q+R+T+U+X+Y 📅)
**5** **AB**CDEFGHIJKLMNOPQR**S**
**T**UWXYZ
**6** ACDEGHK(N 1km)OSTV

💬 Pleasant family campsite, quietly located, surrounded by woods and within walking distance of the village of Norg. An excellent base for visiting Groningen and Friesland. At the centre of an extensive network of cycle paths and opportunities for walking. All pitches are spacious and of comfort plus standard. Modern new toilet facilities and wellness. Leisure pool.

🚗 The campsite is located on the N373, 2 km north of Norg on the road Norg-Roden.

Leek · N372 · Eelde
N386
N34
ℂℂ
N919 · N373 · A28
Oosterwolde Easterwâlde · Assen

ℂℂ € **20** 29/3-26/4  6/5-29/5  4/6-6/6  11/6-7/7  24/8-13/10

🧭 N 53°04'40'' E 06°26'55''

## Oude Willem, NL-8439 SN / Drenthe    ♿ 🛜 **iD** 330

🔺 Camping Hoeve aan den Weg
🏠 Bosweg 12
☎ +31 5 21 38 72 69
🔓 29/3 - 13/10
@ camping@hoeveaandenweg.nl

9ha 110T(100-200m²) 10A CEE

**1** ADG**I**JKLMOPQ
**2** LRVXY
**3** ABDHJKLNRU
**4** (C+H 1/5-15/9)
(Q+R+T+U+V+X+Y+Z 🔑)
**5** **AB**CDFGHI**J**KLMNO**PQ**
UWZ
**6** AEGIKM(N 4km)OTV

💬 This family campsite is located in the centre of the Drents-Friese Wold National Park. Spacious pitches in various fields. A good base for cycling and walking. Enjoy the countryside and the unexpected recreational opportunities.

🚗 From Diever drive towards Zorgvlied. The campsite is located on the right of the road in the little village Oude Willem.

Oosterwolde
N351
CC
N381
Beilen
A28
N855
N353   N371

**CC** € **16**   29/3-28/5   11/6-7/7   30/8-12/10    N 52°53'25'' E 06°18'48''

---

## Rolde, NL-9451 AK / Drenthe    🛜 **iD** 331

🔺 Camping De Weyert
🏠 Balloërstraat 2
☎ +31 5 92 24 15 20
🔓 1/4 - 28/10
@ info@deweyert.nl

6,5ha 80T(100-120m²) 4-6A CEE

**1** ADG**I**JKLMOPS
**2** FGRSVWX
**3** ABCD**F**GHJKNRUV
**4** (Q 1/4-26/9)
**5** **AB**CDEFG**I**J**K**LMNO**P**U
WXY
**6** ACDEGH**K**(N 0,5km)OST

💬 You will camp on spacious comfortable pitches in the five star surroundings of the Drentsche Aa close to the village square of Rolde (500 metres), with plenty of opportunities for cycling and walking. The Drentsche Aa cycle route is the second most beautiful cycle route in the Netherlands.

🚗 Route Assen-Gieten N33, exit Rolde. Direction centre, continue through the centre, direction Ballo, turn right and follow signs.

Norg   Annen
N373   N34
N33
Assen CC   Gasselte
N371   N376
A28   N857
N374

**CC** € **18**   1/4-29/5   3/6-7/6   11/6-6/7   23/8-28/10    N 52°59'27'' E 06°38'31''

---

## Ruinen, NL-7963 RB / Drenthe    ♿ 🛜 **iD** 332

🔺 Camping De Wiltzangh
🏠 Witteveen 2
☎ +31 5 22 47 12 27
🔓 29/3 - 28/10
@ info@dewiltzangh-ruinen.nl

13ha 86T(80-145m²) 6A CEE

**1** ADG**I**JKLMN**P**Q
**2** BRSVXY
**3** BDGHJKLN**Q**RU
**4** (C+H+Q+R+T+Y 🔑)
**5** **AB**DEFGIJKLNPUWZ
**6** ACDEGKM(N 2,5km)OSV

💬 A spaciously appointed campsite with good amenities located in the woods between the Drente villages of Ruinen and Dwingeloo. Located in the Dwingelderveld National Park.

🚗 From Ruinen in the direction of Ansen/Havelte. Follow 1st road to the right after about 1 km. Campsite signposted.

Beilen
N855   A28
N353   N371
CC
A32   Hoogeveen
N375
Meppel

**CC** € **20**   29/3-28/5   12/6-7/7   25/8-28/10    N 52°47'00'' E 06°21'59''

## Ruinen, NL-7963 PX / Drenthe

♿ 🛜 iD **333**

🏕 Camping Landclub Ruinen
📧 Oude Benderseweg 11
☎ +31 5 22 47 17 70
🔆 5/4 - 22/9
@ info@landclubruinen.nl

25ha 202T(110-150m²) 6-10A CEE

**1** ACD**G**IJKLMNOPQ
**2** BFGLRSVWXY
**3** ABC**D**F**G**HJK**P**QRU
**4** (A 1/7-31/8) (**B** 1/5-1/9)
(F+H+Q+R+T+U+X 🔆)
**5** **AB**DEFGIJKLMNOPQR**S**U
WXYZ
**6** CEGK(N 1,5km)OSTV

💬 Landclub camping Ruinen is adjacent to the Dwingelderveld nature reserve. A naturally landscaped family campsite with lovely big pitches, suitable for the over 50s and families with children. Indoor pool, restaurant and a children's zoo. The campsite is right on beautiful cycling routes.

🚗 Ruinen direction Pesse. After 600 metres, the fourth street on the left. Campsite is signposted, also from Ruinen via Engeland.

CC € 18 5/4-26/4  10/5-28/5  3/6-7/6  11/6-5/7  23/8-22/9  ⛶ N 52°46'31'' E 06°22'14''

---

## Schipborg, NL-9469 PL / Drenthe

♿ 🛜 iD **334**

🏕 Camping De Vledders
📧 Zeegserweg 2a
☎ +31 5 04 09 14 89
🔆 5/4 - 20/10
@ info@devledders.nl

13ha 220T(80-100m²) 6A CEE

**1** AD**G**IJKLMPRS
**2** ABDFLRSVWXY
**3** ABF**H**IJKN**OP**RUWZ
**4** (Q+R+S+T+U+Y 🔆)
**5** **AB**CDEFGHIJKLNPQRUWZ
**6** ACEG**K**(N 3km)OTV

💬 Attractively laid out grounds in the 'Drentsche Aa' National Park. Equally suitable for both active campers and those seeking relaxation, and ideal for children (including (pony) activities and recreational lake). Lovely cycling and walking opportunities in the area.

🚗 From the A28 Zwolle-Groningen and the N34 Groningen-Emmen, exit Zuidlaren. Just before this place turn right, direction Schipborg and follow the campsite signs.

CC € 18 5/4-24/5  11/6-8/7  26/8-20/10  ⛶ N 53°04'46'' E 06°39'56''

---

## Schoonebeek, NL-7761 PJ / Drenthe

♿ 🛜 iD **335**

🏕 Camping Emmen
📧 Bultweg 7
☎ +31 5 24 53 21 94
🔆 1/1 - 31/12
@ info@campingemmen.nl

4,6ha 50T(120m²) 8-16A CEE

**1** AD**G**IJKLMNOPQ
**2** DFGRVWXY
**3** ABD**F**HIJKRUWZ
**4** (C+G 🔆) M(Q+T+U+X+Z 🔆)
**5** **AB**DFGIJMNOPUWXZ
**6** ABCEGHJ**K**M(N 1km)OUV

💬 A convenient campsite suitable for young and old. Suitable for a visit to the Wildlands Adventure Zoo in Emmen. The camping pitches are spacious. Heated swimming pool near reception. There are various fields with picnic tables. Many cycling routes from the campsite.

🚗 A37 exit 5 direction Schoonebeek. Campsite signposted from there, turn left just before Schoonebeek.

CC € 18 1/1-1/7  31/8-31/12  ⛶ N 52°40'11'' E 06°52'43''

## Uffelte/Havelte, NL-7975 PZ / Drenthe    ♿ 🛜 **iD** | 336

🏕 Camping De Blauwe Haan
📧 Weg achter de es 11
☎ +31 5 21 35 12 69
🗓 29/3 - 27/10
@ info@blauwehaan.nl

5,5ha 120T(120m²) 6-10A CEE

**1** ADGIJKLMNPQ
**2** BRSVWX
**3** ABC**F**GHJKLNRU
**4** (G 1/5-1/9) M(Q+R+T+Z 🖢)
**5** **AB**DFGIJKLMNOPQRU
    WYZ
**6** CDEGH**K**M(N 5km)OV

📋 A peaceful family campsite located in a scenic area with good amenities. A nice friendly atmosphere prevails. Lovely walks can be made from the campsite.

🚗 The campsite is located about 2 km north of Uffelte. Follow the signs to the left on the N371 Meppel-Assen road. Then along a dirt road.

N381 · Dwingeloo · N855 · N371 · Steenwijk · N353 · **CC** · Havelte · A28 · A32 · N375

CC €**18** 29/3-26/4 5/5-29/5 11/6-9/7 26/8-27/10 7=6, 14=11    📍 N 52°48'12'' E 06°16'22''

---

## Wateren, NL-8438 SC / Drenthe    🛜 **iD** | 337

🏕 Molecaten Park Het Landschap
📧 Schurerslaan 4
☎ +31 5 21 38 72 44
🗓 29/3 - 30/9
@ hetlandschap@molecaten.nl

16ha 205T(100-150m²) 6-10A CEE

**1** ACD**G**IJKLM**PQ**
**2** ADLRSWXY
**3** ABGHJKLN**OPQ**RUWZ
**4** (A 5/7-17/8) (F+H 1/5-30/9)
    (Q+S+T+U+X+Z 🖢)
**5** **AB**FGIJKLMNOPUWXYZ
**6** EGH**IK**(N 6km)OSTV

📋 The campsite is located in the Drents Friese Wold (6000 hectare) national park by an idyllic lake which is suitable for swimming. Plenty of walking and cycling opportunities in the area. Spacious camping pitches.

🚗 From Diever drive towards Zorgvlied. The campsite is located just before Zorgvlied on the right side.

N919 · N381 · Gorredijk · N351 · N371 · **CC** · N353 · N855

CC €**14** 29/3-18/4 5/5-28/5 11/6-9/7 26/8-30/9    📍 N 52°55'19'' E 06°16'04''

---

## Wezuperbrug, NL-7853 TA / Drenthe    ♿ 🛜 **iD** | 338

🏕 Molecaten Park Kuierpad
📧 Oranjekanaal NZ 10
☎ +31 5 91 38 14 15
🗓 29/3 - 31/10
@ kuierpad@molecaten.nl

53,5ha 635T(95-200m²) 6-10A CEE

**1** ADG**I**JKLMOPRS
**2** ADFLRSVWX
**3** AB**F**GHIJKN**Q**RUWZ
**4** (C 10/5-1/9) (F+H 🖢) J**L**
    (Q 🖢) (S 9/4-5/9) (T 🖢)
    (U 1/5-5/9) (X+Y 1/4-1/11)
    (Z 1/5-5/9)
**5** **AB**DEFGIJKLMNOPQRUW
    XYZ
**6** ACEGH**K**M(N 2km)OSTV

📋 Located in remarkably beautiful countryside, ideal for cyclists, hikers and families with children.

🚗 N31 Beilen-Emmen exit Westerbork. Via Orvelte in the direction of Schoonoord.

Buinerveen · **CC** · N34 · N381 · N376 · Emmen · N374 · Sleen

CC €**16** 29/3-18/4 5/5-28/5 11/6-9/7 26/8-31/10    📍 N 52°50'26'' E 06°43'28''

## Zorgvlied, NL-8437 PE / Drenthe
♿ 📶 iD **339**

🏠 Park Drentheland
✉ De Gavere 1
☎ +31 5 21 38 81 36
🕒 1/4 - 31/10
@ info@parkdrentheland.nl

8ha 130T(100m²) 16A CEE

**1** ADG|JKLMPQ
**2** FLMRSVWXY
**3** ABHJKL**MNOPQ**RU
**4** (A 1/7-1/9) (C+H 1/5-1/9) J (Q+R+T 1/5-1/9)
**5** **AB**DEFGI**JKL**MNOPUW XYZ
**6** AEGHIK(N 7km)STV

💬 The campsite is a perfect base for those seeking relaxation, for nature lovers, walkers, cyclists, horse riders and amusement. Close to the attractive villages of Diever, Vledder and Dwingeloo with their lively street cafes, restaurants and markets. Relaxation, space and comfort are the main features of Park Drentheland. Here you will find the right ambiance close to nature to unwind.

🔲 In Zorgvlied turn down the street opposite the church.

CC € **14** 1/4-30/6 19/8-31/10     🧭 N 52°55'25'' E 06°15'02''

---

## Zweeloo, NL-7851 AA / Drenthe
♿ 📶 iD **340**

🏠 Camping De Knieplanden
✉ Hoofdstraat 2
☎ +31 5 91 37 15 99
🕒 1/4 - 30/9
@ info@campingknieplanden.nl

2,5ha 64T(90-110m²) 4-8A CEE

**1** ADG|JKLMNO**PQ**
**2** FGLRSVWXY
**3** A**F**GHJNRU**W**
**4** (C+G 1/5-31/8) J (T+U 18/7-28/8)
**5** **AB**DEFGIJMNOPQRUWZ
**6** EGK(N 0,3km)

NEW

💬 Quiet campsite situated on the edge of the picturesque and atmospheric village of Zweeloo, known for its village greens. Beautiful walking and cycling area. A paradise for everyone who loves peace, nature or an active holiday.

🚗 A37 Hoogeveen-Emmen, exit Oosterhesselen N854. Campsite clearly indicated in Zweeloo.

CC € **16** 1/4-29/5 3/6-7/6 11/6-9/7 26/8-30/9     🧭 N 52°47'41'' E 06°43'27''

---

## Aalten, NL-7121 LJ / Gelderland
♿ 📶 iD **341**

🏠 Camping 't Walfort
✉ Walfortlaan 4
☎ +31 5 43 45 14 07
🕒 1/4 - 1/10
@ info@campingwalfort.nl

5,5ha 48T(80-100m²) 6-10A CEE

**1** ADG**H**IJKLMOPQ
**2** BCRVWX
**3** ABJNR**W**
**4** (G 30/5-25/8) (Q 30/5-10/6,13/7-25/8)
**5** **AB**CDFGI**J**KLMNO**PQ**R UWY
**6** G**K**(N 2km)

💬 Located close to Germany in beautiful countryside, just 2 km from the literary town of Bredevoort. Neat, clean toilet block. There is an indoor pool next to the campsite.

🚗 A18, then towards Varsseveld-Aalten-Winterswijk. Follow signs before you get to Bredevoort.

CC € **16** 1/4-28/5 11/6-6/7 23/8-1/10 7=6, 14=12     🧭 N 51°56'04'' E 06°36'20''

## Aalten, NL-7122 PC / Gelderland ♀♂ 📶 iD **342**

🏕 Camping Goorzicht
📧 Boterdijk 3
☎ +31 5 43 46 13 39
📅 29/3 - 30/9
@ info@goorzicht.nl

6,5ha 60T(70-100m²) 6A CEE

**1** ACD**G**IJKLMO**P**Q
**2** BFRSWXY
**3** ABGHJKNRU
**4** (**C**+G 27/4-31/8)
   (Q+T+Z 27/4-5/5,6/7-1/9)
**5** **AB**DEFI**J**K**L**MNO**P**UXZ
**6** BDEGH**K**(N 3km)V

💬 On the edge of the beautiful nature reserve 'Het Goor'. Plenty of cycling and walking opportunities. Enjoy peace, space and rural life. The site stands out for its spacious comfort pitches with a choice of sunny pitches or more shade. Modern and heated toilet block.

🚗 A18, N318 direction Varsseveld-Aalten-Winterswijk, before Aalten follow the brown-white ANWB signs.

CC € **16** 29/3-28/5 11/6-9/7 28/8-29/9 7=6, 14=12, 21=18, 28=24  ▨ N 51°56'40'' E 06°32'37''

---

## Aalten, NL-7121 LZ / Gelderland 📶 iD **343**

🏕 Camping Lansbulten
📧 Eskesweg 1
☎ +31 5 43 47 25 88
📅 1/4 - 15/10
@ info@lansbulten.nl

10ha 65T(110-120m²) 6A CEE

**1** ADG**I**JKLMOPQ
**2** BCLRSWXY
**3** BJNR**W**X
**4** (**C**+G 27/4-14/9)
   (Q 27/4-5/5,12/7-24/8)
**5** **AB**DEFGI**J**MNO**P**UXYZ
**6** ADEGHI**K**L(N 1,5km)

💬 Peaceful family campsite with plenty of greenery on the edge of Aalten. Very spacious pitches with water, electricity and drainage. Fishing possible in the adjacent stream (Keizersbeek). Wireless internet available. Good walking and cycling opportunities. Plenty of sports opportunities and a heated swimming pool for children.

🚗 N318 Varsseveld-Winterswijk. Follow brown and white signs at Bredevoort.

CC € **16** 1/4-25/4 6/5-28/5 11/6-14/7 1/9-15/10 14=12, 21=18  ▨ N 51°55'34'' E 06°36'15''

---

## Aerdt, NL-6913 KH / Gelderland ⊗ ♿ 📶 iD **344**

🏕 Camping De Rijnstrangen V.O.F.
📧 Beuningsestraat 4
☎ +31 3 16 37 19 41
📅 1/1 - 31/12
@ info@derijnstrangen.nl

0,6ha 30T(100m²) 6A CEE

**1** AEIJLMNPRS
**2** FLRVWXY
**3** HJKU
**4** N
**5** **A**CIJKLMNOPQRUW
**6** ABDEHK(N 3km)O

💬 A well maintained campsite in Aerdt (close to Lobith) with underfloor heating in the toilet buildings, and located in 'de Gelderse Poort' nature reserve on the old course of the Rhine. Conveniently located for cycle trips through the polders and meadows but also for Montferland. Bed and breakfast available.

🚗 A12 exit 29, direction Lobith as far as Aerdt exit. Turn right onto the dike. Continue 1.5 km to church. Down to the left after 100 metres.

CC € **14** 1/1-25/4 6/5-28/5 11/6-4/7 26/8-31/12 14=13  ▨ N 51°53'47'' E 06°04'13''

## Apeldoorn, NL-7345 AP / Gelderland ⟨📶⟩ iD (345)

🏕 Camping De Parelhoeve
✉ Zwolseweg 540
☎ +31 5 53 12 13 32
🔑 1/4 - 31/10
@ camping@deparelhoeve.nl

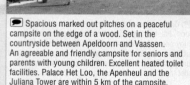

2,5ha 70T(100m²) 6-10A CEE

**1** ADG IJKLMPQ
**2** BFGKRVWXY
**3** AHJKLRW
**4** (Q 🔑)
**5** ABDGIJKLMOPUXZ
**6** DEGHK(N 3km)OT

💬 Spacious marked out pitches on a peaceful campsite on the edge of a wood. Set in the countryside between Apeldoorn and Vaassen. An agreeable and friendly campsite for seniors and parents with young children. Excellent heated toilet facilities. Palace Het Loo, the Apenheul and the Juliana Tower are within 5 km of the campsite.

🚗 A50 Zwolle-Arnhem, exit 25 Apeldoorn-Noord towards Paleis Het Loo. Then direction Vaassen. Campsite 3 km on the right.

N337 A50 N310 CC Deventer Apeldoorn A1 N789

CC € 16 1/4-29/5 11/6-5/7 22/8-31/10 📍 N 52°15'32'' E 05°57'12''

---

## Arnhem, NL-6816 RW / Gelderland 👫🚻 ⟨📶⟩ ✿ iD (346)

🏕 Oostappen Vakantiepark Arnhem
✉ Kemperbergerweg 771
☎ +31 2 64 43 16 00
🔑 6/4 - 28/10
@ info@vakantieparkarnhem.nl

36ha 450T(80-150m²) 10A CEE

**1** ACDG IJKLMOPST
**2** BFLRSWXY
**3** ABFGHJKMNOPQRU
**4** (D+H 🔑) KLN
(Q+S+T+U+X+Y+Z 🔑)
**5** ABDEFGIJKLMNOPUWXY
**6** CDGHIJ(N 8km)OSTV

💬 The perfect family campsite located in woodland close to the Hooge Veluwe National Park and Arnhem. Many facilities including an indoor swimming pool.

🚗 A12 (in both directions) and A50 from the south take exit Arnhem North. Then follow the signs. From Apeldoorn (A50), take exit Schaarsbergen.

N304 N310 Ede N224 N311 A12 CC Wageningen Arnhem A50

CC € 12 27/4-29/5 10/6-5/7 2/9-28/10 📍 N 52°01'27'' E 05°51'36''

---

## Barchem, NL-7244 NA / Gelderland 👫🚻 ♿ ⟨📶⟩ iD (347)

🏕 Camping De Heksenlaak B.V.
✉ Zwiepseweg 32
☎ +31 5 73 44 13 06
🔑 1/4 - 31/10
@ heksenlaak@planet.nl

NEW

7,5ha 120T(100-110m²) 6-10A CEE

**1** ADF IJKLMPRS
**2** RVWXY
**3** BDFGHJNOPRU
**4** (B+G 15/5-1/9)
(T+U+X+Z 🔑)
**5** ABDEFGIJKLMNOPQUZ
**6** FGHKM(N 2km)OV

💬 Charming family campsite at the foot of the Lochemse Berg hill with swimming pool and riding stables. You can also stable your horse(s) here.

🚗 From Lochem to Barchem direction Zwiep 1.5 km. Signposted.

N346 Goor N339 N332 Lochem CC N825 Neede N312 N18 N319 N316 N315 Groenlo

CC € 16 1/4-24/5 11/6-7/7 25/8-31/10 📍 N 52°08'20'' E 06°26'50''

## Barchem, NL-7244 RC / Gelderland

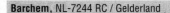

🔼 Camping Reusterman
📧 Looweg 3
☎ +31 5 73 44 13 85
📅 1/4 - 1/10
@ info@reusterman.nl

⟨iD⟩ 348

6ha 100T(80-100m²) 6A CEE

1 ADGIJKLPRS
2 BGRSVWXY
3 ABFHJRU
4 (B 15/5-1/9) (Z ⊙)
5 ABCDGIJKLMNOPQUWZ
6 EGK(N 0,5km)OV

💬 Peaceful family campsite for families with young children, and those seeking peace and quiet. Extensive cycling and walking opportunities.

N339 N332 N346
Lochem
N825 Neede
⟨CC⟩
N319
N316
N315 Groenlo
N312

🚗 From Barchem towards Lochem 500m. Campsite signposted.

⟨CC⟩ € 16  1/4-24/5  11/6-5/7  24/8-1/10    📍 N 52°07'38'' E 06°26'09''

---

## Beek (gem. Montferland), NL-7037 CN / Gelderland

🔼 Vakantiepark De Byvanck BV
📧 Melkweg 2
☎ +31 3 16 53 14 13
📅 1/1 - 31/12
@ info@byvanck.nl

⟨iD⟩ 349

7,2ha 30T(80-120m²) 6A CEE

1 ACDGIJKLMPQ
2 FRSWVXY
3 FJRU
4 (F ⊙) N
5 ABDFGIJNOPTUWZ
6 EGKM(N 4km)SV

💬 Campsite with partially shaded level pitches, located just outside the village of Beek at the foot of the Montferland hills in the heart of the Gelderland Achterhoek. Heated toilet facilities with indoor swimming pool. Water temperature minimum 28°C. Excellent base for walking and cycling tours.

🚗 A12 Arnhem-Oberhausen (after German border) exit 2 Beek/Elten on A3 in Germany. Turn right towards Beek. After the Dutch border turn left at the first road.

N315
N336 Doetinchem
Zevenaar N336 A18
N317
⟨CC⟩ N335
B8
Emmerich am A3
Rhein
L8

⟨CC⟩ € 16  1/1-5/7  23/8-31/12  7=6, 14=12, 21=18    📍 N 51°53'59'' E 06°10'44''

---

## Beekbergen, NL-7361 TM / Gelderland

🔼 Camping Het Lierderholt
📧 Spoekweg 49
☎ +31 5 55 06 14 58
📅 1/1 - 31/12
@ info@lierderholt.nl

⟨iD⟩ 350

25ha 210T(100-150m²) 6-10A CEE

1 ACDGIJKLMNPQ
2 BFLRSVWXY
3 ABGHIJKLMNPQRU
4 (A 28/4-21/5,9/7-28/8)
  (C+G 25/4-16/9) IQ ⊙)
  (R 1/4-31/10) (T+U+Y+Z ⊙)
5 ABDEFGIJKLMNOPQRU
  WXY
6 ACDEGHKM(N 3,2km)OSTV

💬 A lovely, friendly family campsite set in the woods, with endless possibilities. Also open spaces, a site built on different levels.

Apeldoorn
A1
N789
N304 Eerbeek
A50
N310

🚗 A50 from Arnhem, exit 22 Beekbergen or A50 from Zwolle, exit 22 Hoenderloo. Follow signs.

⟨CC⟩ € 16  1/1-29/5  11/6-12/7  30/8-31/12  14=12, 21=18    📍 N 52°07'59'' E 05°56'44''

## Beekbergen, NL-7361 TG / Gelderland

 🛜 ✿ iD **351**

🔺 Vak.centrum De Hertenhorst
📧 Kaapbergweg 45
☎ +31 5 55 06 13 43
📅 29/3 - 27/10
@ info@hertenhorst.nl

22ha 55T(80-100m²) 4-6A CEE

**1** ACD**G**IJKL**PQ**
**2** BFIRSVWXY
**3** ABGHIJK**M**N**Q**RU
**4** (C+H 26/4-15/9) J
    (Q+R+T+X+Z 📅)
**5** **AB**DFG**IJ**MNO**PS**UWXY
**6** ACDEGH**K**(N 2km)OSTV

💬 Beautiful location in the Veluwe woods. Close to Hoge Veluwe park and Het Loo Palace. Friendly campsite with spacious comfort and motorhome pitches. Dogs allowed. Facilities: heated pool with slide (Easter - August), playground with trampoline, tennis courts, snack bar, wifi, cafe, supermarket, motorhome service and entertainment team. Experience the Veluwe with us at Hertenhorst!

🚗 A50 exit 22, right at end of exit then 1st right. Then second road on the left.

CC € **16** 29/3-26/4 6/5-28/5 11/6-12/7 30/8-26/10 7=6, 14=12, 21=18 | 📍 N 52°08'06'' E 05°57'51''

---

## Beesd, NL-4153 XC / Gelderland

🚫 ♿ 🛜 iD **352**

🔺 Camping Betuwestrand
📧 A. Kraalweg 40
☎ +31 3 45 68 15 03
📅 30/3 - 29/9
@ info@betuwestrand.nl

27ha 160T(80-100m²) 10A CEE

**1** ADEIJKLPQ
**2** ADFLRVWX
**3** BGHJ**M**NRUWZ
**4** J(Q+S+T+U+Y+Z 📅)
**5** **AB**DFGHI**JKL**MNO**PQ**RUW
    XYZ
**6** ABCDEGHJ**K**M(N 2km)OTV

💬 For many years one of the loveliest and most hospitable campsites in the Netherlands, with excellent amenities. Spaciously appointed, located on its own recreational lake with a sandy beach. In the fascinating Betuwe countryside with plenty of cycling and walking opportunities. Centrally positioned in the Netherlands between Utrecht (25 km) and 's-Hertogenbosch.

🚗 A2 's-Hertogenbosch-Utrecht, exit 14 Beesd, thereafter signposted.

CC € **16** 30/3-26/4 6/5-30/5 10/6-5/7 25/8-28/9 | 📍 N 51°53'56'' E 05°11'18''

---

## Berg en Dal, NL-6571 CH / Gelderland

👫🧒 ♿ 🛜 iD **353**

🔺 Camping Nederrijkswald
📧 Zevenheuvelenweg 47
☎ +31 2 46 84 17 82
📅 15/3 - 30/10
@ info@nederrijkswald.nl

1,5ha 52T(80-130m²) 6A CEE

**1** AD**G**IJKLO**PRS**
**2** BGLRSVWXY
**3** AD**EF**GHIJKLNU
**4** (A 📅)
**5** **AB**CDFGHI**JKL**MNOP**QT**U
    WXZ
**6** ABCDEGH**K**M(N 3km)OTV

💬 Located near the Nederrijk estate on the edge of Berg en Dal en Groesbeek, and is surrounded on three sides by woods. You can enjoy to the full the beautiful nature, peace, space, places of interest, hospitality and the rural lifestyle. Spacious pitches and good toilet facilities.

🚗 A73, exit 3 Malden. N271 direction Groesbeek. Direction Berg en Dal at roundabout; left at T junction, 2nd road to the right N841 (at service station). After 750 metres on the left.

CC € **18** 15/3-25/4 6/5-28/5 11/6-4/7 25/8-30/10 | 📍 N 51°48'08'' E 05°55'25''

## Braamt, NL-7047 AP / Gelderland

▲ Camping Recreatie Te
Boomsgoed
▤ Langestraat 24
☎ +31 3 14 65 18 90
◔ 1/1 - 31/12
@ info@teboomsgoed.nl

6ha 35T(100m²) 10-16A CEE

**1** ADGIJKLMNOPQ
**2** BDFGLRSVXY
**3** ABGHJN**O**PQ**R**U
**4** (Q 27/4-6/5,9/7-3/9) (T+V ▣)
**5** **AB**DFGHIJKLMN**P**UWXZ
**6** BCDEGHJOTV

💬 Located on the Pieterpad route in the Montferland. Camping pitches marked out by beech hedges. Meal delivery is possible. The site offers stables, a minigolf course and a recreation hall.

🚗 A18 exit 3 to Doetinchem/Zelhem/Zeddam. Turn left after the exit, left at second roundabout towards Braamt. Campsite 250 metres further on.

**354**

Zevenaar A18
N336 N316 N330 N315
N317 N818
N335
Emmerich am Rhein A3

CC € **12** 1/1-25/4 6/5-28/5 11/6-6/7 23/8-31/12 ⛅ N 51°55'31'' E 06°15'42''

## Doesburg, NL-6984 AG / Gelderland

▲ Camping & Jachthaven Het
Zwarte Schaar
▤ Eekstraat 17
☎ +31 3 13 47 31 28
◔ 1/1 - 31/12
@ info@zwarteschaar.nl

17ha 77T(90-120m²) 10-16A CEE

**1** ADG|JKLMO**P**RS
**2** ACFKLMSTVWX
**3** ACHJKLNR**T**U**W**X
**4** (**E** 30/3-31/10) (G 1/5-15/9) I JM(T+X+Y+Z ▣)
**5** **AB**DEFGIJ**K**LMN**PS**UW XYZ
**6** BCDEGH**K**(N 5km)OTV

💬 Het Zwarte Schaar campsite and yacht harbour is a friendly family campsite for young and old, located on a tributary of the IJssel river on the border with the agreeable Achterhoek region and the extensive Veluwe woods. Watersports, cycling, walking, anything is possible.

🚗 From the A348 right direction Doetinchem (N317). After 3.9 km take 3rd exit on the roundabout and follow the camping signs.

**355**

Eerbeek N319
N314 N316
N348
A348
CC
Duiven N336 Doetinchem N315

CC € **16** 1/1-12/4 6/5-29/5 23/6-12/7 30/8-31/12 7=6, 14=12, 21=18 ⛅ N 52°02'10'' E 06°09'43''

## Doesburg, NL-6984 AG / Gelderland

▲ Camping IJsselstrand
▤ Eekstraat 18
☎ +31 3 13 47 27 97
◔ 1/1 - 31/12
@ info@ijsselstrand.nl

50ha 200T(80-120m²) 6-10A CEE

**1** ACD**G**IJKLMO**P**Q
**2** ACFLRUWXY
**3** ABCHIJKLMN**O**P**R**T**U**WX
**4** (E+H 29/3-31/10) IJ**K** (Q+S 29/3-31/10) (T+X+Y+Z ▣)
**5** **AB**DEFGIJK**L**MN**PST**UW XYZ
**6** CDEGH**K**(N 3km)OSTV

💬 The site is ideal for relaxing in early or late seasons. Children can have fun in the large indoor playground or the new covered outdoor pool, in the morning you can lie on the IJssel beach. Special hardened motorhome pitches, spacious pitches and private toilet facilities.

🚗 Coming from Arnhem on the A348 turn right towards Doetinchem (N317). After 3.9km take 3rd exit on roundabout (camping sign shown). Take 3rd exit on next roundabout after 1.2 km. Left after 1.4 km.

**356**

Eerbeek
N314 N316
N348
A348
CC
N336 Doetinchem N315
Zevenaar A18

CC € **18** 1/1-12/4 6/5-28/5 22/6-12/7 30/8-31/12 7=6, 14=12, 21=18 ⛅ N 52°01'44'' E 06°09'43''

## Doetinchem, NL-7004 HD / Gelderland
👫 📶 iD **357**

- 🏕 Camping De Wrange
- ✉ Rekhemseweg 144
- ☎ +31 3 14 32 48 52
- 🔑 29/3 - 29/9
- @ info@dewrange.nl

10ha 75T(90-110m²) 10A CEE

1 ACD**G**IJKLMNO**P**Q
2 BFLRSVWXY
3 B**F**GIJKLN**Q**RU
4 (C+H 27/4-2/9)
  (Q+S+T+U+X+Y+Z 1/4-31/8)
5 **AB**DFGI**J**KLMNOPUWXYZ
6 AEGH**K**(N 3km)OUV

💬 Peaceful campsite in wooded surroundings, but not isolated. Spacious non fenced off pitches in grassy clearings in the woods.

🚗 From the A18, exit 4 Doetinchem-Oost. Turn left under the main road. Continue to the next traffic lights, then turn right and follow the signs (partially a residential area).

Doesburg · N315 N312 · N316 · Doetinchem · N330 · A18 CC N317 N818 · Ulft · B8 A3

CC €**18** 29/3-25/4 6/5-28/5 11/6-7/7 26/8-28/9 7=6, 14=12, 21=18 📡 N 51°56'47'' E 06°20'01''

## Doornenburg, NL-6686 MC / Gelderland
♿ 📶 ❁ iD **358**

- 🏕 Camping De Waay
- ✉ Rijndijk 67a
- ☎ +31 4 81 42 12 56
- 🔑 1/4 - 30/9
- @ info@de-waay.nl

19ha 140T(100-120m²) 10A CEE

1 ACDGIJKLMPQ
2 ADFLRWX
3 ABCD**F**GJKM**N**RUWZ
4 (C+**E**+H 27/4-15/9) **N**
  (Q+R+T+U+X+Y
  27/4-5/5,6/7-24/8) (Z 🔑)
5 **AB**DEFGIJKLMNOPQRU
  WYZ
6 CEGHK(N 2km)OSTUV

💬 Pleasant campsite with modern sanitary facilities. Orchards all around. Separate fields for touring campers, and another for permanent pitches. Indoor swimming pool.

🚗 From A15 exit Bemmel/Gendt. Turn left in Gendt and follow the signs. Follow signs from Arnhem.

**Arnhem** N336 · CC · B8 · **Nijmegen**

CC €**18** 1/4-27/5 11/6-4/7 27/8-29/9 7=6, 14=12, 21=18 📡 N 51°54'16'' E 05°59'08''

## Eck en Wiel, NL-4024 BM / Gelderland
👫 📶 iD **359**

- 🏕 Camping Verkrema
- ✉ Rijnbandijk 10a
- ☎ +31 3 44 69 16 55
- 🔑 1/4 - 30/9
- @ info@verkrema.nl

6,5ha 50T(100-150m²) 10-16A CEE

1 ADFHIJKLN**P**Q
2 ACFKLRWX
3 A**F**GHJNUWX
4 (B 28/4-15/9) (G 15/5-15/9)
5 **AB**DFGHIJKLMOPUWXY
6 AEGH**K**(N 1km)OT

💬 A quiet family campsite located on the River Nederrijn. Grassy field with unmarked pitches and sufficient shade. Views of the Amerongen hill. Suitable for walking and cycling, watersports and fishing. Located on the edge of the Betuwe with views of the Utrechtse Heuvelrug.

🚗 A15 exit 33 at Tiel. Campsite is signposted from Eck en Wiel. Or exit Culemborg on A2, N230 towards Kesteren, exit Eck en Wiel. See campsite signs.

Driebergen-Rijsenburg · N224 A30 · A12 · N226 · N227 · Veenendaal · N416 · CC · N320 N225 · N835 · A15 · Tiel

CC €**16** 1/4-24/5 14/6-12/7 1/9-30/9 📡 N 51°58'56'' E 05°27'03''

## Ede, NL-6718 SM / Gelderland 🛜 iD 360

🏕 Bos- en Heidecamping
   Zuid-Ginkel
✉ Verlengde Arnhemseweg 97
☎ +31 3 18 61 17 40
🗓 29/3 - 29/9
@ info@zuidginkel.nl

4,7ha 75T(100-130m²) 6A CEE

**1** ADFIJKLMNPQ
**2** BFRSVWXY
**3** ABFHJKLR
**4** (Q+R ⬚)
**5** ABCDFGIJKLMNOPRU
   WXY
**6** AEGHK(N 4,5km)OS

💬 A unique, attractive and hospitable campsite in the middle of countryside full of woods and heath. Ideally suited to cycling and walking. Plenty of opportunities for trips out in the immediate surroundings. Very clean, heated toilet facilities. Camping in large or small fields, or if you prefer, on your own spot. Quality and personal service are guaranteed and privacy respected.

🚗 A12, exit Ede-Oost. See sign.

CC € 18  29/3-28/5  11/6-4/7  22/8-19/9  23/9-28/9  7=6, 14=12, 21=18   📍 N 52°02'18'' E 05°44'08''

---

## Eerbeek, NL-6961 LD / Gelderland 🛜 ✿ 361

🏕 Camping Landal Coldenhove
✉ Boshoffweg 6
☎ +31 3 13 65 91 01
🗓 15/3 - 11/11
@ coldenhove@landal.nl

20ha 180T(100-120m²) 10A CEE

**1** CDGIJLPQ
**2** BFILRSVX
**3** ABCDFGHJKLNQRTU
**4** (A+F+H+Q+S+T+U+X+Y
   +Z ⬚)
**5** ABDEFGIJKLMNOPRU
   WXZ
**6** AEGHJLM(N 3km)OSTV

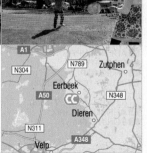

💬 A very spacious campsite set in the woods. Every possible amenity and excellent facilities.

🚗 A50 exit Loenen/Eerbeek direction Loenen/ Eerbeek. Then at the roundabout direction Dieren. Follow signs to Coldenhove.

CC € 18  15/3-18/4  3/5-23/5  14/6-4/7  30/8-10/11   📍 N 52°05'31'' E 06°02'05''

---

## Eerbeek, NL-6961 LK / Gelderland 👫 🛜 iD 362

🏕 Camping Robertsoord
✉ Doonweg 4
☎ +31 3 13 65 13 46
🗓 1/4 - 27/10
@ info@campingrobertsoord.com

2,5ha 25T(80-100m²) 6-10A CEE

**1** ADFIJKLPST
**2** BFGRSWXY
**3** ABHJKLNRU
**4** (Q 1/7-31/8) (T 1/7-1/9)
**5** ABDFGIJKLMNOPQU
   WXZ
**6** CEGK(N 1km)STV

💬 The campsite is located on the border of the Veluwezoom National Park and the IJssel Valley and is therefore suitable for cyclists and walkers. Some camping pitches are in the shade and some in the sun. Modern heated toilet facilities and there is a playground for the children.

🚗 Towards Eerbeek, then follow signs.

CC € 16  1/4-29/5  11/6-12/7  30/8-26/10   📍 N 52°06'05'' E 06°04'50''

## Eibergen, NL-7152 DB / Gelderland

&#9855; &#128246; **iD** **363**

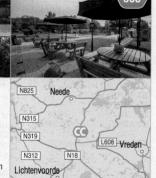

- ▲ Camping Het Eibernest
- ✉ Kerkdijk 1
- ☎ +31 5 45 47 12 68
- ⊙ 1/1 - 31/12
- @ recreatie@eibernest.nl

17ha 100T(100m²) 10A CEE

- **1** ACD**G**IJKLMOPQ
- **2** GLRSVWXY
- **3** ABF**G**HJHKLN**OPQ**RU
- **4** (C+H 1/4-31/10) (Q ⊙)
  (T+U+X+Y 1/4-31/10) (Z ⊙)
- **5** **AB**DEFGIJKLMNPUWXYZ
- **6** ACDFGH**K**M(N 3km)OTUV

💬 A friendly family campsite located in the Gelderland Achterhoek region. Lovely undulating countryside, perfect for walking, cycling or for taking a car trip. Provided with spacious pitches, heated toilet block. Friendly bar/restaurant, billiards, playground, swimming pools launderette and bike hire.

🚗 Take the exit for Vrede or the exit for Eibergen on the N18, then follow the brown signs for Eibergen campsite.

CC € **16** 1/1-7/7 25/8-31/12      📷 N 52°04'18'' E 06°38'25''

---

## Elburg, NL-8081 LB / Gelderland

&#10680; &#128246; **iD** **364**

- ▲ Natuurcamping Landgoed Old Putten
- ✉ Zuiderzeestraatweg Oost 65
- ☎ +31 5 25 68 19 38
- ⊙ 15/4 - 15/9
- @ info@oldputten.nl

5ha 70T(100-120m²) 4A CEE

- **1** ADEHIJLNPRS
- **2** CFGLRTWXY
- **3** AHJK**MOP**UW
- **4** (A 30/5-10/6,22/7-16/8)
  (G ⊙)
  (Q 30/5-10/6,22/7-16/8)
- **5** **A**EFGIJMNPUWZ
- **6** EGK(N 0,5km)T

💬 A peaceful family campsite, perfect for small children. Spacious pitches. Beautiful countryside and cycling area close to the fortified town of Elburg.

🚗 A28, exit 16 't Harde. N309 direction Elburg. Right opposite Elburg-Vesting exit on roundabout N309 entrance on left.

CC € **14** 15/4-29/5 10/6-12/7 29/8-15/9 8=7, 16=13, 24=28      📷 N 52°26'31'' E 05°50'40''

---

## Emst, NL-8166 GT / Gelderland

&#128107;&#128107; &#128246; **iD** **365**

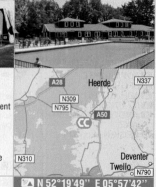

- ▲ Ardoer Camping De Zandhegge
- ✉ Langeweg 14
- ☎ +31 5 78 61 39 36
- ⊙ 29/3 - 1/10
- @ info@zandhegge.nl

5,9ha 100T(80-120m²) 16A CEE

- **1** AD**G**IJKLMPQ
- **2** FRVWXY
- **3** ABCDGHJKLNRU
- **4** (C+H 27/4-2/9) (Q+T+U ⊙)
- **5** **AB**DEFGIJKLMNOPUW XYZ
- **6** ABCEGHJ**K**(N 2km)OSTV

💬 A friendly family campsite with excellent toilet facilities. You will be camping on spacious marked out pitches. A lovely campsite for young and old where you can enjoy the swimming pool and excellent cycling and walking. The rural surroundings are an oasis of peace.

🚗 A50 Apeldoorn-Zwolle, exit 27 Epe. Turn left at the traffic lights, direction Emst, then take the first road to the right. The campsite is signposted before the traffic lights.

CC € **18** 29/3-26/4 6/5-29/5 12/6-7/7 25/8-30/9 7=6, ·14=12, 21=17      📷 N 52°19'49'' E 05°57'42''

## Emst, NL-8166 JA / Gelderland

🛜 iD **366**

🔺 Camping De Veluwse Wagen
✉ Oranjeweg 67
☎ +31 5 78 66 16 28
🚐 1/4 - 31/10
@ info@veluwse-wagen.nl

2ha 58T(100-120m²) 6-10A CEE

**1** ADGIJKLNPQ
**2** CFRUVWXY
**3** ADHJ
**4** (Q+U+Y 7/7-1/9)
**5** ABDGIJMNOPUWXZ
**6** DEGKL(N 1,5km)O

💬 On the edge of the Crown Domein, the Vierhouterbos and the Gortelse Heathland. Sheltered spacious pitches where your caravan will stand on a hard base surrounded by grass.

🚘 On the A50 Apeldoorn-Zwolle take exit Epe towards Emst then follow the signs. On the A28 Amersfoort-Zwolle take exit Epe towards Emst then follow the signs.

Nunspeet — N309 — Heerde
A28
N310 — CC — A50 — N337
**Apeldoorn** — Deventer
N344

CC € **14** 1/4-1/7 18/8-31/10 14=12

📐 N 52°19'21'' E 05°57'29''

---

## Emst, NL-8166 JJ / Gelderland

⊗ ♿ 🛜 ✿ iD **367**

🔺 Camping De Wildhoeve
✉ Hanendorperweg 102
☎ +31 5 78 66 13 24
🚐 29/3 - 30/9
@ info@wildhoeve.nl

12ha 310T(80-120m²) 6-10A CEE

**1** ACDEIJKLMNOPQ
**2** BFRVWXY
**3** ABGHKLMNRU
**4** (A 26/4-5/5,6/7-1/9)
(C 1/5-31/8) (F+H 🚐) IJM
(Q+S+T+Y 🚐)
**5** ABDEFGIJKLMNOPQRUW
XYZ
**6** CDEGHJK(N 3km)OSTV

💬 Camping de Wildhoeve is a lovely campsite located in the Veluwe and on the edge of Het Loo Royal Estate. It makes a perfect base for walking, cycling and game spotting.

🚘 A50 Arnhem-Zwolle, exit 26 Vaassen and then towards Emst. Follow the signs.

Nunspeet — N309
A28 — Epe
N310 — CC — A50 — N337
N302 — **Apeldoorn** — Twello
N344

CC € **18** 29/3-25/4 6/5-28/5 11/6-4/7 24/8-30/9

📐 N 52°18'50'' E 05°55'36''

---

## Enspijk, NL-4157 PB / Gelderland

♿ 🛜 iD **368**

🔺 Ardoer Camping De Rotonde
✉ Panweg 1
☎ +31 3 45 65 13 15
🚐 30/3 - 28/9
@ rotonde@ardoer.com

32ha 150T(100m²) 6-10A CEE

**1** ADFIJLNPQ
**2** ADFGLMRWX
**3** ABDGJMNRUWZ
**4** (G 3/4-26/9) JM
(Q+R+S+T 1/4-15/9)
(U+Y 🚐) (Z 1/7-31/8)
**5** ABCDEFGHIJKLMNOPQRU
WXYZ
**6** ACDEGHKM(N 3km)OSTUV

💬 A family campsite with small touring camping fields, surrounded by overgrowth and with a small sandy beach by a natural swimming lake. Spacious pitches. Swimming, brand new playground, fishing lake. The location is unique: in the centre of the Netherlands, close to everything, in the middle of the region Betuwe, at walking distance to the river Linge.

🚘 Motorway A2 Den Bosch-Utrecht, exit Geldermalsen. Right after the exit, then right again.

Culemborg
A27
N833
A2
N327 — CC
N848
A15
N830 — Zaltbommel
N322

CC € **18** 30/3-26/4 5/5-20/5 11/6-6/7 25/8-28/9

📐 N 51°52'42'' E 05°12'50''

## Epe, NL-8162 PV / Gelderland

**369**

🔺 Camping De Veldkamp
📧 Veldkampweg 2
☎ +31 5 78 61 43 48
🔓 1/4 - 31/10
@ info@develdkamp.nl

1,5ha 35T(90-100m²) 10A CEE

**1** **AG**JKLOPST
**2** BFRVWXY
**3** ABGHJKLRU
**4** (C+G 15/5-1/9) (U+V+X 🔓)
**5** **AB**DGIJKLMNOPUWXZ
**6** ADEGJ**K**(N 5km)

💬 Hospitable, child-friendly family campsite in wooded surroundings where everyone will feel at home.

🚗 A50 motorway Zwolle/Apeldoorn, take exit Epe/Nunspeet (27). Drive towards Nunspeet until the exit Wissel. A28 Amersfoort-Zwolle take exit Epe (15), N309.

CC € **14** 1/4-10/7 27/8-31/10 21=18 N 52°20'26'' E 05°56'25''

---

## Epe, NL-8162 PT / Gelderland

**370**

🔺 Camping De Vossenberg
📧 Centrumweg 17
☎ +31 5 78 61 38 00
🔓 1/4 - 27/10
@ info@campingvossenberg.nl

6ha 50T(80-100m²) 10A CEE

**1** ADGIJKLMNOPRS
**2** BFRSTVWXY
**3** AB**F**GHJN**Q**RU
**4** (C+H 27/4-1/9) (Q 🔓)
   (T+U 1/4-31/8)
   (X+Y 27/4-5/5,13/7-23/8)
   (Z 🔓)
**5** **AB**DFGHIJKLMNOPRUWX
**6** BEGHK(N 3km)OSV

💬 A beautiful campsite located between various natural areas and close to the Veluwe woods where you can go cycling. The campsite has very spacious pitches, a lovely heated outdoor pool, WiFi network, modern toilet buildings and every facility.

🚗 A50 Zwolle-Apeldoorn, exit 27 Nunspeet as far as Wissel exit. A28 Amersfoort-Zwolle, exit 15 Epe (N309) as far as Wissel exit. Then follow signs.

CC € **16** 1/4-26/4 6/5-29/5 11/6-10/7 27/8-27/10 N 52°20'28'' E 05°56'17''

---

## Epe, NL-8162 PP / Gelderland

**371**

🔺 Campingpark de Koekamp
📧 Tongerenseweg 126
☎ +31 5 78 61 41 17
🔓 1/4 - 31/10
@ info@dekoekamp.nl

8ha 95T(100-120m²) 16A CEE

**1** **A**G**I**JKLMOPQ
**2** FRSWXYZ
**3** ABD**F**GHJR
**4** (B+T+X+Z 🔓)
**5** **AB**DEGHI**J**K**L**MOPUZ
**6** DEGK(N 0,7km)OT

💬 A peacefully located farmhouse campsite close to woods, heathland, peat fields and the village centre.

🚗 A28 exit 15 - N795 after 7.6 km N309 - A50 exit 27 N309 after 4 km right on roundabout, left after 175 metres.

CC € **16** 1/4-30/5 11/6-1/7 18/8-31/10 N 52°21'02'' E 05°57'42''

## Epe, NL-8162 NR / Gelderland    ♿ 🛜 iD   372

🏕 RCN Vakantiepark de Jagerstee
✉ Officiersweg 86
☎ +31 8 50 40 07 00
🔓 29/3 - 28/10
@ reserveringen@rcn.nl

33ha 350T(100m²) 10A CEE

**1** ACD**G**IJKLNPRS
**2** BFLRSWXY
**3** ABCD**F**GHJKLNQRU
**4** (A 🔲) (C+H 27/4-15/9) M
(Q+S+T+U+X+Y+Z 🔲)
**5** **AB**DFGIJKLMNPQUWZ
**6** CDEGHJKM(N 3km)OSTV

💬 Located in a wooded area with plenty of space, tranquillity and atmosphere and in the heart of De Hoge Veluwe National Park. An ideal area for walking and cycling. The campsite has an open-air theatre and a supermarket. Many attractive towns close by such as Apeldoorn and Zwolle.

🚗 A50 Apeldoorn-Zwolle, exit 27, follow the N309 towards Nunspeet, after the roundabout follow the 'Jagerstee' camping signs.

CC € **16**   29/3-29/5   3/6-7/6   11/6-12/7   30/8-28/10     📐 N 52°21'51" E 05°57'32"

---

## Ermelo, NL-3852 AM / Gelderland    ✈ 🛜 iD   373

🏕 Ardoer cp. &
bungalowpark De Haeghehorst
✉ Fazantlaan 4
☎ +31 3 41 55 31 85
🔓 1/1 - 31/12
@ haeghehorst@ardoer.com

7ha 245T(75-120m²) 6-10A CEE

**1** ADEIJKLMOPQ
**2** BFGLRSVWXY
**3** ABF**G**HIJKL**M**N**OP**RU
**4** (A 14/4-31/8) (C 27/4-28/10)
(F+H 1/4-30/10) IJK**LM**N
(Q 1/4-30/10) (R 🔲)
(T+U+V+Y 1/4-30/10) (Z 🔲)
**5** **AB**CDEFGHIJKLMNOPQU
WXY
**6** ACEGKL(N 1,5km)OSV

💬 The campsite is family-oriented and very well equipped, ideally located on the edge of Ermelo, close to the Veluwe woods in the direction of Harderwijk. Excellent toilet facilities. The campsite has an indoor and outdoor swimming pool.

🚗 A28, exit 12 direction Ermelo, then follow camping signs. Campsite is located on the north side of Ermelo.

CC € **18**   1/1-19/4   6/5-29/5   11/6-5/7   31/8-31/12     📐 N 52°18'47" E 05°37'48"

---

## Ermelo, NL-3852 MC / Gelderland    ♿ 🛜 iD   374

🏕 Camping De Kriemelberg
✉ Drieërweg 104
☎ +31 3 41 55 21 42
🔓 29/3 - 19/10
@ info@kriemelberg.nl

7ha 80T(80-140m²) 6-10A CEE

**1** AD**F**IJKLMNOPQ
**2** ABFGRSVWXY
**3** ABHIJKNRU
**4** (A 🔲) M(Q+R 🔲)
(T 1/4-14/9) (Y 🔲)
(Z 1/4-14/9)
**5** **AB**CDEFGHI**J**MNO**PQS**UW
XYZ
**6** CEH**K**(N 3km)OS

💬 A campsite in parkland setting with spacious pitches, imaginatively laid out between hedges and large bushes. Large modern toilet block with family showers. The site has extensive woods and the Ermelo Heath is slightly further away. Many tourist places (Ermelo, Putten, Garderen, Harderwijk) within easy reach.

🚗 A28 exit 12 (Ermelo) direction Ermelo. Left at 5th roundabout towards Drie. Campsite signposted.

CC € **16**   29/3-18/4   6/5-28/5   11/6-7/7   25/8-18/10     📐 N 52°17'12" E 05°38'48"

## Ermelo, NL-3852 ZD / Gelderland ⚡ 🛜 iD 375

🏔 Camping In de Rimboe
🚩 Schoolweg 125
☎ +31 3 41 55 27 53
📅 1/1 - 31/12
@ info@inderimboe.nl

10,1ha 40T(80-110m²) 6A CEE

**1** ADGIJKLMOPST
**2** BFGRSVWXY
**3** BGHJKLNRU
**4** (C+H 29/4-30/9)
(Q 14/7-31/8)
(T+U+X+Y+Z 15/2-31/12)
**5** ABCDFGHIJKMNOPUW
XYZ
**6** AEGK(N 3km)OSTV

💬 Campsite with pitches in the wood and around a playing field. Plenty of cycling and walking opportunities from the campsite. It also has an excellent restaurant with affordable prices. Outdoor pool (free)

🚗 A28, exit 12 direction Ermelo. Left at 5th roundabout towards Drie (south side of Ermelo). Signposted from here.

CC €18 1/1-29/5 11/6-14/7 1/9-31/12 📍 N 52°17'29'' E 05°38'59''

---

## Ermelo, NL-3852 MA / Gelderland ♿ 🛜 ❀ iD 376

🏔 Recreatiecentrum De Paalberg
🚩 Drieërweg 125
☎ +31 3 41 55 23 73
📅 1/1 - 31/12
@ info@paalberg.nl

30ha 186T(100-120m²) 6-10A CEE

**1** ADGIJKLMNPRS
**2** BFGLRSVWXY
**3** ABGHIJKLMNQRU
**4** (C 1/5-31/8) (F+H 📅) IJKLM
N(Q+S 29/3-27/10)
(T+U+Y+Z 📅)
**5** ABDFGHIJKLMNOPQUW
XYZ
**6** ABCDEGHK(N 3km)OSTV

💬 Wonderful woodland campsite bordering the Ermelo Heath. Plenty of options for walking and cycling. Close to the inner lakes. Attractively designed leisure pool and toilet facilities. Campsite open all year, advance reservation is possible within three weeks of arrival. During CCA acceptance period one pet is allowed at most. Free wifi.

🚗 A28 exit 12 direction Ermelo. Turn left at the 6th roundabout (on the south side of Ermelo) direction Drie. Campsite signposted.

CC €18 1/1-27/4 12/5-29/5 11/6-7/7 25/8-31/12 📍 N 52°17'16'' E 05°39'25''

---

## Garderen (Veluwe), NL-3886 PG / Gelderland ✈ ♿ 🛜 ❀ iD 377

🏔 Ardoer camping De Hertshoorn
🚩 Putterweg 68-70
☎ +31 5 77 46 15 29
📅 29/3 - 27/10
@ hertshoorn@ardoer.com

10ha 306T(80-150m²) 4-10A CEE

**1** ACDEHIJKLMNOPQ
**2** BFGLRSVWXY
**3** ABCDFGHJKLMNRU
**4** (C 27/4-30/9) (E+H 📅) JM
(Q+S+T+U+Y 📅)
**5** ABCDEFGHIJKLMNOPQU
WXY
**6** BCDEGHIKM(N 1,5km)O
STV

💬 The campsite has very good amenities and is centrally located on the Veluwe, close to Garderen. The spacious yet still intimate fields are surrounded by trees and high bushes. Various cycling and walking routes start right from the campsite. Many tourist attractions are within a short distance. The site runs its own restaurant.

🚗 A1 exit 17. Through the town of Garderen direction Putten. The campsite is located directly after Garderen on the right.

CC €18 29/3-20/4 6/5-29/5 11/6-7/7 26/8-27/10 📍 N 52°14'12'' E 05°41'21''

## Groenlo, NL-7141 DH / Gelderland ⬡ 🌀 iD 378

🔺 Marveld Recreatie B.V.
✉ Elshofweg 6
☎ +31 5 44 46 60 00
📅 1/1 - 31/12
@ info@marveld.nl

37ha 287T(100-110m²) 6-16A CEE

**1** ACD**F**IJKLMN**P**RS
**2** CGLRSVWXY
**3** ABCD**EF**GHJKL**MN**OPQR**T**
UW
**4** (C 1/5-15/9) (**F**+**H** 📅) IJK**L**
M**N**(Q+S+T+V+X+Y+Z 📅)
**5** **AB**CDEFGIJKLMNOPQ**S**UW
XYZ
**6** ACDEGH**I**KLM(N 1km)ORS
TVX

💬 Reasonably luxurious holiday resort, located on the edge of a fortified city, with all possible amenities. Entertainment for all ages, inside as well as outside. There's an underground disco for teenagers.

🚗 Via N18 Enschede-Doetinchem or N319 Zutphen-Winterswijk. From here don't use SatNav. Clearly indicated with signs.

Neede
N315
N18
L608 Vreden
N312
CC
Winterswijk
N313 N318 N319

CC €**20** 1/1-29/5 11/6-7/7 24/8-31/12 📡 N 52°02'10'' E 06°37'58''

## Groesbeek, NL-6561 KR / Gelderland 👪 ♿ ⬡ iD 379

🔺 Vakantiepark De Oude Molen
✉ Wylerbaan 2a
☎ +31 2 43 97 17 15
📅 1/4 - 31/10
@ vakantiepark@oudemolen.nl

6,5ha 150T(80-120m²) 4-16A CEE

**1** AD**G**IJLPQ
**2** FGIRSVWX
**3** ABD**F**GJNRU
**4** (C 28/4-26/8) (H 22/4-31/8) J
N(Q 27/4-5/5,6/7-28/8)
(R+T+U+Y+Z 📅)
**5** **AB**DEFGIJKLMNOPQRU
WXY
**6** CEGHK(N 0km)OTV

💬 The campsite has very luxurious and extensive toilet facilities with special facilities for children with jungle decoration. Very varied plant life. Located in the village.

🚗 On A73 exit Groesbeek. In Groesbeek continue through centre, follow signs. Campsite is on the right. On A50 or A15 exit Kleve. Continue towards Kleve. Right after the border then second turning right.

N325
**Nijmegen**
**Kleve**
CC
N321 A73 B504 L484
N264

CC €**14** 1/4-18/4 23/4-23/5 11/6-5/7 24/8-30/10 14=12, 21=18 📡 N 51°47'04'' E 05°56'06''

## Harfsen, NL-7217 MD / Gelderland ⬡ iD 380

🔺 Camping De Huurne
✉ Harfsensesteeg 15
☎ +31 5 73 45 90 26
📅 30/3 - 1/10
@ campingdehuurne@hotmail.com

1,5ha 65T(80-180m²) 16A

**1** AD**G**IJKLMOPQ
**2** RTVWXY
**3** BDJR
**4** M
**5** **A**BGHIJMNO**PS**UWZ
**6** CH**K**(N 3km)

💬 Campsite on edge of Gorssel heath in wooded surroundings. You will be camping on a large field around play equipment, or on a small field among the plants. Gorssel is 5 km away. Located in typical Dutch farming countryside. A few pitches have private bathrooms.

🚗 A1 exit 23 Deventer direction Eefde. Keep left around the church. After 2 km Harfsense Steeg. After 4 km campsite on the left. Some GPS navigation systems don't work here. If so enter coordinates.

Deventer N348 N344
A1
N790 N339 N332
N345 CC Lochem
Zutphen N346
N314 N319 N312

CC €**12** 30/3-29/5 10/6-14/7 1/9-1/10 📡 N 52°10'50'' E 06°16'28''

## Harfsen, NL-7217 PG / Gelderland

🗐 Camping De Waterjuffer
📧 Jufferdijk 4
☎ +31 5 73 43 13 59
📅 29/3 - 29/9
@ info@campingdewaterjuffer.nl

📶 iD 381

11,9ha 85T(120-150m²) 10-16A CEE

**1** ADGIJKLMPQ
**2** ADFGLRVWXY
**3** ABDGHJKLNRUZ
**4** (T+X+Y 🖰)
**5** ABDFGIJMNPUWXYZ
**6** ACDEGHK(N 0,8km)OT

💬 Unique, lush campsite situated on the border of Gelderland and Overijssel in the attractive Achterhoek bocage landscape, near the Hanseatic cities of Zutphen and Deventer. An oasis of peace and space on small-scale fields in a green park-like environment. Clean toilet facilities. The perfect base for cycling or hiking. Excellent restaurant.

🚗 A1 exit 23 Zutphen (N348). In the town of Epse go to Laren-Lochem (N339). Just before reaching Harfsen signposted.

CC € 18  29/3-29/5  11/6-5/7  23/8-29/9  14=12    🧭 N 52°12'34'' E 06°17'13''

---

## Hattem, NL-8051 PW / Gelderland

🗐 Molecaten Park De Leemkule
📧 Leemkuilen 6
☎ +31 3 84 44 19 45
📅 29/3 - 31/10
@ deleemkule@molecaten.nl

NEW

🛇 📶 iD 382

24ha 150T(100m²) 10A CEE

**1** ACDEIJKLMNOPQ
**2** BFLRSTVWXY
**3** ABDFHJKLMNQRU
**4** (A 10/7-20/8) (B 27/4-1/9) (F+H 🖰) KLN (Q+S+T+U+X+Y+Z 🖰)
**5** ABDFGIJKLMNOPQUW XYZ
**6** EGHKM(N 4km)OSTV

💬 Attractive holiday park in the Veluwe woods close to Hattem and the Molecaten Country Estate. Comfort pitches, indoor swimming pool, tennis courts, restaurant, shop and bike hire. Walking and cycling routes. Close to Apenheul, Het Loo Palace and the Dolfinarium.

🚗 A28 exit 17 Wezep, straight ahead at roundabout then at the next junction direction Heerde. Over the railway line after 3.5 km as far as Hattem Wapenveld exit. Turn left. Entrance to the park about 3 km on the left.

CC € 18  29/3-18/4  5/5-28/5  11/6-9/7  26/8-31/10    🧭 N 52°27'22'' E 06°02'11''

---

## Hattem, NL-8051 PM / Gelderland

🗐 Molecaten Park Landgoed Molecaten
📧 Koeweg 1
☎ +31 3 84 44 70 44
📅 29/3 - 31/10
@ landgoedmolecaten@ molecaten.nl

📶 iD 383

10ha 41T(100m²) 10A CEE

**1** ADFIJKLMNOPQ
**2** BFGRVWXY
**3** AFIJKR
**4** (A+Q+T+X 🖰)
**5** ABCDGIJKLMNOPQUXZ
**6** EGK(N 1km)OTV

💬 The campsite is situated in wooded surroundings but is also close to the lovely village of Hattem. You will find both sunny and shaded pitches in a number of small fields.

🚗 A50 exit Hattem. Via Hessenweg and Gelderse Dijk. Turn right at the end. Turn right on Nieuweweg into Stationsstraat. Left into Stadslaan. Then right into Eliselaan and left into Koeweg.

CC € 16  29/3-18/4  5/5-28/5  11/6-9/7  26/8-30/9    🧭 N 52°27'59'' E 06°03'26''

## Heerde, NL-8181 LP / Gelderland

👬 📶 iD **384**

🏕 Camping De Zandkuil
📧 Veldweg 25
☎ +31 5 78 69 19 52
🔓 1/4 - 31/10
@ info@dezandkuil.nl

11,5ha 160T(90-100m²) 10A CEE

**1** AD**G**IJKLMOPST
**2** BFRSVWXY
**3** AB**F**GHJKNRU
**4** (C+H 1/5-1/9)
  (Q+R+T+U+X+Y 🔓)
**5** **AB**DFG**IJKL**MNOP**Q**RUW
**6** BCDEGH**K**(N 2,5km)OST

NEW

💬 A comfortable family campsite in the Noord Veluwe woods.

🚗 A50 Apeldoorn-Zwolle, exit 29, Heerde. At 1st roundabout second exit (Molenweg), at second roundabout, first turn. At third roundabout second turn towards Wapenveld. Left to the Koerbergseweg. Follow signs.

CC € **18** 1/4-29/5 11/6-30/6 1/9-31/10 14=13

🚩 N 52°24'38'' E 06°02'37''

---

## Heerde, NL-8181 LL / Gelderland

♿ 📶 iD **385**

🏕 Molecaten Park De Koerberg
📧 Koerbergseweg 4/1
☎ +31 5 78 69 98 10
🔓 29/3 - 31/10
@ dekoerberg@molecaten.nl

22ha 130T(80-100m²) 10A CEE

**1** ACD**F**IJKLMOPQ
**2** BFILRSVWXY
**3** AB**F**HJK**M**NR**T**U
**4** (C+H 25/4-1/9)
  (Q+R+T+U+X+Y+Z 🔓)
**5** **AB**DEFGHIJKLMNOP**QR**U WXY
**6** ACDEGHJ**K**(N 3km)OSTV

💬 The location of the Koerberg is fantastic. The Zwolsche Bos (woodland) and the beautiful heaths of the Veluwe are the greatest attractions.

🚗 A50 Apeldoorn/Zwolle, exit 29 Heerde/Wapenveld. Direction Heerde. 2nd exit at roundabout (Molenweg), next roundabout 3rd exit (Veldweg). At end of Veldweg left into Koerbergseweg, then immediately right.

CC € **16** 29/3-18/4 5/5-28/5 11/6-9/7 26/8-31/10

🚩 N 52°24'34'' E 06°03'05''

---

## Heteren, NL-6666 LA / Gelderland

📶 iD **386**

🏕 Camping Overbetuwe
📧 Uilenburgsestraat 3
☎ +31 2 64 74 22 33
🔓 1/1 - 31/12
@ info@campingoverbetuwe.nl

4,2ha 39T(100-200m²) 10A CEE

**1** A**G**IJKLMN**P**Q
**2** FGLRSX
**3** ABD**F**GHJN**O**RUW
**5** **AB**DFG**IJ**MNO**P**UZ
**6** ADEGJ(N 3km)T

💬 More than just a campsite. Centrally and quietly located and easily accessible from the A50. Pitches are marked out by bushes and there is adequate shade. Ideally located for trips out (by bike) to the Veluwe and the Betuwe. There are various play options for the little ones. In wet weather guests can read a book or play a game in the recreation room.

🚗 A50, exit 18 Heteren. Then follow camping signs.

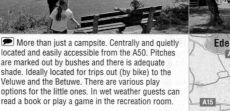

CC € **16** 1/1-29/6 18/8-31/12

🚩 N 51°56'55'' E 05°46'21''

## Hoenderloo, NL-7351 TN / Gelderland

⊗ 🛜 ✿ **iD** **387**

🏕 Camping De Pampel
📧 Woeste Hoefweg 35
☎ +31 5 53 78 17 60
📅 1/1 - 31/12
@ info@pampel.nl

14,5ha 278T(100-200m²) 6-16A CEE

**1** ACDEIJLMPQ
**2** BFGILRSVWXY
**3** ABCGHIJKL**M**NO**P**RU
**4** (D 30/3-30/9,13/10-28/10) IJ
(Q+S 16/4-30/9)
(T+U+V+Y 1/4-30/9)
**5** **AB**CDEFGIJKLMNOPQR**ST**
UWXYZ
**6** ACDEGH**K**(N 1km)OSTV

💬 Beautiful 5 star campsite in wooded surroundings. Spacious pitches on a grassy field, or private pitches surrounded by trees and bushes. Underfloor heating and climate control in the toilet blocks make this an ideal winter location. Heated indoor swimming pool. Arrival after 13:00 and departure before 12:00.

🚗 A1 exit 19 Apeldoorn/Hoenderloo. In Hoenderloo continue in the direction of Loenen. Or take A50 Arnhem-Apeldoorn, exit 22 Hoenderloo. Follow the Hoenderloo signs.

Apeldoorn

CC € 🔞 1/1-19/4 6/5-28/5 11/6-12/7 29/8-31/12 7=6, 14=12, 21=18 📐 N 52°07'10'' E 05°54'19''

---

## Hoenderloo, NL-7351 TM / Gelderland

🛜 **iD** **388**

🏕 Recreatiepark 't Veluws Hof
📧 Krimweg 152-154
☎ +31 5 53 78 17 77
📅 23/3 - 27/10
@ info@veluwshof.nl

32ha 70T(100-130m²) 6A CEE

**1** AD**G**IJLPQ
**2** BFLRSVWXY
**3** ABGHJKL**M**N**Q**R**T**U
**4** (A 1/7-1/9) (C+H 26/4-14/9) I
J(Q+S+T+U+Y+Z ⊙)
**5** **AB**CDFGIJMNOPQRUWXY
**6** AEGH**K**M(N 0km)OSTV

💬 Recreatiepark 't Veluws Hof is located close to the Hoge Veluwe National Park among woods where you can enjoy cycling and walking. All the pitches are spacious comfort pitches with every amenity. Maximum two pets allowed (first pet is free). There is a recreation team in high season.

🚗 A1, exit 19 Apeldoorn-Hoenderloo, in Hoenderloo follow camping signs or A50 Arnhem-Hoenderloo, exit 22 Hoenderloo, follow signs to Hoenderloo.

Apeldoorn

CC € 🔞 23/3-28/5 11/6-12/7 30/8-26/10 7=6, 14=12, 21=18 📐 N 52°07'21'' E 05°55'17''

---

## Hoenderloo, NL-7351 BP / Gelderland

🛜 ✿ **iD** **389**

🏕 Veluwe camping 't Schinkel
📧 Miggelenbergweg 60
☎ +31 5 53 78 13 67
📅 5/4 - 27/10
@ info@hetschinkel.nl

7,5ha 200T(80-100m²) 6-16A CEE

**1** AD**G**IJLMNPQ
**2** FILRSVWX
**3** BCGHJKLNRU
**4** (C+H 22/4-15/9) IJ
(Q+R+T+U+X+Y ⊙)
**5** **AB**DEFGIJKLMNOPQRUW
XYZ
**6** ACDEG**K**(N 1km)OST

💬 Campsite is an oasis of peace and tranquillity in both early and late seasons. The site is located on the edge of a wood in a sunny and spacious setting. Its central position in the heart of the Veluwe makes the campsite the perfect base for cycling or walking in the endless Veluwe and for discovering the rich culture.

🚗 From Arnhem/Apeldoorn/Ede maintain direction Hoenderloo. Then follow the sign Beekbergen/Loenen direction Beekbergen and follow the camping signs.

Apeldoorn

CC € 🔟 5/4-19/4 6/5-28/5 11/6-5/7 22/8-27/10 7=6, 14=12, 21=18 📐 N 52°07'42'' E 05°54'15''

## Hulshorst, NL-8077 RP / Gelderland

🛜 iD **390**

🏔 Campingpark De Vuurkuil
✉ Vuurkuilweg 15
☎ +31 3 41 45 13 80
🔓 1/1 - 31/12
@ info@vuurkuil.nl

2ha 35T(200m²) 10-16A CEE

**1** ABD**F**IJKLPRS
**2** FGLRTVWX
**3** AD**F**HJKLR
**4** (**A**+Q+X+Z 🔓)
**5** **A**CDGHIJKLMNOPUXY
**6** CEGK(N 1,5km)ST

💬 Campsite with big pitches on the edge of the forest. Owner keeps bees. Beautiful and spacious toilet block.

🚗 N310 between Hierden and Hulshorst. Exit at Chinese restaurant. Follow the road to the 1st sign. Turn SatNav off!

CC € **16** 1/1-29/5 3/6-6/6 11/6-10/7 27/8-31/12 　　📍 N 52°20'58'' E 05°42'23''

---

## Hummelo, NL-6999 DW / Gelderland

♿ 🛜 iD **391**

🏔 Camping Jena
✉ Rozegaarderweg 7
☎ +31 3 14 38 14 57
🔓 6/4 - 27/10
@ info@camping-jena.nl

6ha 120T(100-150m²) 6-10A CEE

**1** ADGIJKLMPRS
**2** BFGRSVWXY
**3** A**F**HIJKLNRU
**4** M(Q+R+T 🔓)
**5** **AB**CFGHIJKLMOPRUWZ
**6** CDEHJ(N 2km)TV

💬 A campsite near the farmhouse of an estate (castle). The campsite is particularly suitable for seniors and families with small children. There is a GPS fairy hike and a cross-country bike track for children.

🚗 A18 exit 2 Wehl and on to Zutphen. Straight ahead at roundabout beyond Hummelo. From Doetinchem take N317 dir. Doesburg. Turn right at roundabout beyond Langerak and follow signs.

CC € **18** 6/4-28/5 12/6-5/7 26/8-27/10 14=12, 21=18 　　📍 N 51°59'35'' E 06°15'23''

---

## Kootwijk, NL-3775 KB / Gelderland

🛜 ✿ iD **392**

🏔 Camping Harskamperdennen
✉ H. van 't Hoffweg 25
☎ +31 3 18 45 62 72
🔓 29/3 - 26/10
@ info@harskampedennen.nl

16ha 302T(100-200m²) 6-10A CEE

**1** ACDFHIJLNPQ
**2** BFGRSWXY
**3** ABGHIJKNRU
**4** M(Q 🔓)
**5** **AB**DEFGIJKMN**P**RUWYZ
**6** ACEGHJL(N 2,5km)OTV

💬 Perfectly located in a Dutch Forestry Commission (Staatsbosbeheer) nature reserve. Within walking distance of Kootwijker Zand and Radio Kootwijk in the heart of the Amersfoort-Apeldoorn-Arnhem triangle. An attractive, characteristic woodland campsite with a large variety of pitches; only touring pitches and no permanent pitches.

🚗 A1, exit 17 towards Harskamp, and then follow the signs.

CC € **18** 29/3-28/5 12/6-8/7 26/8-25/10 　　📍 N 52°09'01'' E 05°44'28''

## Laag-Soeren, NL-6957 DP / Gelderland

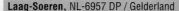

📶 ✿ **iD** ⟨**393**⟩

🏔 Ardoer Vakantiedorp De Jutberg
📧 Jutberg 78
☎ +31 3 13 61 92 20
📅 1/1 - 31/12
@ info@jutberg.nl

18ha 153T(80-120m²) 6-10A CEE

**1** ACD**G**IJKLPQ
**2** BFILRSVWXY
**3** ABGHIJKLNRU
**4** (A 8/7-26/8) (D+H 1/4-31/10)
J(Q+R 1/4-31/10)
(T+U+X+Y 1/4-30/10)
(Z 1/4-31/10)
**5** **AB**DFGIJKLMNOPQRUW
XYZ
**6** ACEGHIKL(N 3km)OSTVX

💬 A top class campsite which lives up to the expectations of all its campers.

🚗 A1 exit Apeldoorn-Zuid direction Dieren, follow the signs. From the A12 direction Zutphen-Dieren, Laag-Soeren then follow the signs.

N789 · Zutphen
N786
A50 · N787
CC · N348
N311 · Dieren · N314
A348
**Arnhem**
N336

CC € ⑱ 1/1-28/5 12/6-12/7 30/8-31/12 7=6, 14=12, 21=18 ⛰ N 52°04'05'' E 06°04'48''

---

## Lieren/Beekbergen, NL-7364 CB / Gelderland

⊗ ✕ 📶 **iD** ⟨**394**⟩

🏔 Ardoer comfortcamping De
Bosgraaf
📧 Kanaal Zuid 444
☎ +31 5 55 05 13 59
📅 29/3 - 27/10
@ bosgraaf@ardoer.com

22ha 237T(100-144m²) 6A CEE

**1** ACDEIJKLPQ
**2** BFRSWXY
**3** AB**F**GHJKL**M**NRU**W**
**4** (C+H 26/4-15/9) JM**N**
(Q+S+T 🔲) (X 3/4-15/9)
(Z 🔲)
**5** **AB**DFGIJKLMNOPQR**ST**U
WXZ
**6** EGH**K**(N 2,5km)OSTV

💬 A large but peaceful campsite outside the village next to a canal. Lovely pitches in open fields and in the woods.

🚗 A1 exit 20 Apeldoorn-Zuid/Beekbergen turn left after the exit and then follow the signs. Or A50 exit 23 Loenen, towards Loenen and then turn left towards Klarenbeek. Follow the signs.

**Apeldoorn** · A1 · N790
N789 · N348
N304 · Zutphen
N788 · CC
A50 · N787

CC € ⑱ 29/3-28/5 11/6-11/7 29/8-26/10 ⛰ N 52°08'39'' E 06°02'09''

---

## Lunteren, NL-6741 KG / Gelderland

📶 **iD** ⟨**395**⟩

🏔 Camping De Rimboe
📧 Boslaan 129
☎ +31 3 18 48 23 71
📅 1/3 - 28/10
@ info@campingderimboe.com

10,5ha 140T(80-120m²) 6-10A CEE

**1** ACD**FI**JKLMOPQ
**2** BFIRSVWXY
**3** ABGHJKNRU
**4** (A 1/7-1/9)
**5** **AB**CDFGI**J**K**L**MNO**P**RUW
XYZ
**6** ACEGH**K**(N 2,5km)OTV

💬 A friendly and hospitable campsite for relaxing and cycling. Beautiful pitches in various fields (both sunny and shaded), or free camping in the wood. The campsite has excellent toilet facilities. Many cycling and walking opportunities. Lively tourist towns such as Lunteren, Ede and Barneveld. A short distance from an open air swimming pool.

🚗 A30, exit Lunteren. Follow ring road (so not into the centre) after which the campsite is signposted.

N301 · A1
Barneveld · N310
N802 · N304
A30 · CC
Veenendaal · **Ede** · N224
A12

CC € ⑯ 1/3-28/5 12/6-8/7 26/8-27/10 14=12, 21=18 ⛰ N 52°05'31'' E 05°39'47''

## Maurik, NL-4021 GH / Gelderland

♿ 📶 **iD** **396**

🏕 Camp. Jachthaven de Loswal
📧 Rijnbandijk 36
☎ +31 3 44 69 28 92
📅 1/4 - 1/10
@ info@loswal.com

5,5ha 50T(100m²) 6A CEE

**1** ADFIJKLNPQ
**2** ACDFLRSTWX
**3** BFNRUWX
**4** (T+U+X 📅)
**5** ABDFGIJKLMNOPUW
**6** EGHK(N 1km)OTV

💬 Beautiful harbour campsite in the Betuwe on the Lower Rhine. Camping pitches are marked out and have adequate shade. Close to the historic towns of Wijk bij Duurstede, Buren and Culemborg.

🚗 A15 Gorinchem-Nijmegen, exit Tiel/Maurik, continue towards Maurik. Signposted in Maurik. A2 exit 13 Culemborg/Kesteren N320. Follow camping signs.

CC € **16** 1/4-29/5  11/6-7/7  24/8-1/10

🧭 N 51°57'47'' E 05°24'25''

---

## Maurik, NL-4021 GG / Gelderland

♿ 📶 **iD** **397**

🏕 Vakantiepark Eiland van Maurik
📧 Eiland van Maurik 7
☎ +31 3 44 69 15 02
📅 29/3 - 1/11
@ receptie@eilandvanmaurik.nl

14ha 250T(110-120m²) 10A

**1** ACDGIJKLMNP
**2** ADLRVVWX
**3** BCFHJKLNOPQRUWZ
**4** (E 1/4-31/10) M
   (Q+S+T+U+V+X+Z 📅)
**5** ABDEFGIJKLMNOPQRUW
   XYZ
**6** CDEGHK(N 2km)OSTV

💬 In the heart of the Betuwe region with meandering dikes and orchards in bloom. Hospitable, spacious and comfortable camping pitches near the beach or fishing lake and luxurious clean facilities. Wonderful relaxation and enjoyment for families as well as for those seeking rest.

🚗 Via A15 exit 33 Tiel/Maurik, via A2 exit 13 onto N320 Culemborg/Kesteren. Towards Maurik, follow 'Eiland van Maurik'.

CC € **16** 29/3-26/4  13/5-29/5  3/6-7/6  11/6-5/7  26/8-11/10  28/10-31/10

🧭 N 51°58'34'' E 05°25'49''

---

## Neede, NL-7161 LW / Gelderland

👫 ♿ 📶 **iD** **398**

🏕 Camping Den Blanken
📧 Diepenheimseweg 44
☎ +31 5 47 35 13 53
📅 29/3 - 29/9
@ info@campingdenblanken.nl

7,2ha 184T(100-150m²) 6-10A CEE

**1** ADGIJKLMOPRS
**2** CLRVWXY
**3** ABCEFGHJMNRUWX
**4** (C+H 1/5-15/9)
   (Q+R+T+U+V+X+Y 📅)
**5** ABCDEFGIJKLMNOPQUW
   XYZ
**6** ABCDEGHKM(N 3km)OTV

💬 Wonderful campsite (Zoover 9+), suitable for seniors and families with children up to 11 years old. Nice, spacious pitches, very clean toilet facilities with disabled facilities. 100% wifi coverage (1 code free). Good base for cycling and walking through the Achterhoek and Twente. Good facilities including food and drinks, tennis, and jeu-de-boules court. Fishing possible in adjacent Schipbeek.

🚗 On the Diepenheim-Neede road. Campsite signposted.

CC € **18** 29/3-28/5  11/6-5/7  24/8-28/9  7=6, 14=12, 21=18

🧭 N 52°10'49'' E 06°35'13''

## Nieuw-Milligen, NL-3888 NR / Gelderland ⊗ 🛜 **iD** **399**

🏕 Camping Landal Rabbit Hill
✉ Grevenhout 21
☎ +31 5 77 45 64 31
📅 1/1 - 31/12
@ rabbithill@landal.nl

6ha 130T(100-120m²) 10-16A CEE

**1** ACDEIJKLMOPQ
**2** BFGLRSVXY
**3** ABCD**F**HIJKL**MNQR**T**U
**4** (**A** 📅) (C 1/5-1/9) (F+H 📅) I (Q+S+T+U+Y+Z 📅)
**5** **AB**DEFGIJKLMNOPQR**S**UW XYZ
**6** ACEGHJ**K**LM(N 5km)OSV

💬 Lovely campsite with large pitches, both sunny and sheltered (woodland) pitches. Plenty of (indoor) recreation including swimming, tennis, bowling and a playground. Booking conditions will be determined by the campsite. Reservations max. 2 weeks before arrival. In May, June and September booking only possible on day of arrival.

🚗 A1 exit 18 direction Harderwijk. Turn right just before the N344. Campsite clearly signposted.

Ermelo
N302
N303
CC **Apeldoorn**
A1
N310
Barneveld N304
A50

CC €**16** 1/1-18/4 3/5-23/5 11/6-11/7 29/8-31/12     🏔 N 52°13'06'' E 05°47'07''

---

## Nunspeet, NL-8072 PK / Gelderland 🛜 **iD** **400**

🏕 Camping De Witte Wieven
✉ Wiltsangh 41
☎ +31 3 41 25 26 42
📅 29/3 - 31/10
@ info@wittewieven.nl

18,8ha 70T(100m²) 6-10A CEE

**1** AD**G**IJKLMNO**P**RS
**2** BFRWX
**3** AFJKL**OP**RU
**4** (**A** 📅) (B+G 1/6-1/9) (T+U+X+Z 📅)
**5** **AB**DFGIJMNO**P**UWZ
**6** CEG**K**(N 1km)OVX

💬 Beautiful campsite in the Nunspeet woods. There is new play equipment for youngsters and pony riding is among the possibilities. You can also take your own horse/pony.

🚗 On A28 take exit 15 towards Nunspeet, 1st right after level crossing.

N308
N305
A28
N306
Nunspeet N309
Harderwijk CC
Epe
N302 N310

CC €**14** 29/3-28/5 11/6-5/7 26/8-31/10     🏔 N 52°22'50'' E 05°49'01''

---

## Otterlo, NL-6731 SN / Gelderland 🛜 **iD** **401**

🏕 Camping Beek en Hei
✉ Heideweg 4
☎ +31 3 18 59 14 83
📅 1/1 - 31/12
@ info@beekenhei.nl

5ha 120T(60-100m²) 4-6A CEE

**1** ACD**G**IJKLN**P**ST
**2** BFGRSVWXY
**3** ABHJKL**O**RU
**4** (Q 28/4-1/10)
**5** **AB**DFGIJKLMNO**P**RUWXY
**6** ACDEGH**K**(N 1km)TV

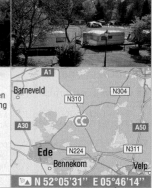

💬 Friendly campsite just outside Otterlo. Set in a beautiful area close to the Hoge Veluwe national park, the Kröller-Müller modern art museum, Planken Wambuis and Ginkelse Heide. A good base for cycling and walking.

🚗 A12 exit 23 Arnhem-Oosterbeek direction Arnhem. Then direction Otterlo and follow the campsite signs.

A1
Barneveld
N310 N304
CC
A30 A50
Ede N224 N311
Bennekom Velp

CC €**18** 1/1-28/5 12/6-12/7 30/8-31/12 7=6, 14=12, 21=18     🏔 N 52°05'31'' E 05°46'14''

## Otterlo, NL-6731 CK / Gelderland

▲ Camping DroomPark De Zanding
✉ Vijverlaan 1
☎ +31 8 80 55 15 00
🔓 1/4 - 31/10
@ dezanding@droomparken.nl

402

40ha 225T(60-120m²) 4-10A CEE

**1** CD**G**IJKLMOPQ
**2** ABDGLRSVWXY
**3** ABHJKLNRU**V**WZ
**4** (F+H 🔓) M**N**
   (Q+R+S+T+U+X+Y+Z 🔓)
**5** **AB**DEFGIJKLMNOPRUW
   XYZ
**6** ABCEGHKLM(N 0,5km)STV

💬 A very attractive, peaceful campsite situated in the woods with its own natural lake and sandy beach. Equipped with every comfort. The park is located just outside the small village of Otterlo in the Veluwe natural area. New indoor pool with wellness facilities.

🚗 A1 exit 17 Stroe direction Otterlo and follow signs. A12 exit 25 Oosterbeek direction Arnhem and follow Otterlo signs.

CC € 18 1/4-19/4 23/4-29/5 11/6-5/7 23/8-31/10 | N 52°05'34'' E 05°46'38''

## Otterlo, NL-6731 BV / Gelderland

▲ Europarcs Resort De Wije Werelt
✉ Arnhemseweg 100-102
☎ +31 8 80 70 80 90
🔓 1/1 - 31/12
@ info.resortdewijewerelt@
   europarcs.nl

403

12ha 190T(100-150m²) 6-16A CEE

**1** ACD**F**IJKLMPQ
**2** BFGLRSVWXY
**3** ABCDHIJKLNRU
**4** (A 7/7-25/8) (C+H 25/4-15/9)
   M(Q+S+T+U+X+Y+Z 🔓)
**5** **AB**DEFGIJKLMNOPQ**S**U
   WXY
**6** ACDEGHJKLM(N 2km)OSTV

💬 A beautifully located campsite near the Hoge Veluwe National Park, adjoining the Wambuis Ginkel and Ginkel Heath nature reserves. The campsite has spacious pitches and excellent facilities. The beautiful Veluwe woods and fields make this campsite an ideal base for cyclists and walkers.

🚗 A12 exit 23 or 25. A1 exit 17 or 19. All exits signposted to Park Hoge Veluwe. In Otterlo follow signs.

CC € 20 1/1-26/4 6/5-29/5 11/6-12/7 29/8-31/12 14=12, 21=18, 28=24 | N 52°05'12'' E 05°46'10''

## Putten, NL-3882 RN / Gelderland

▲ Strandparc Nulde
✉ Strandboulevard 27
☎ +31 3 41 36 13 04
🔓 1/4 - 1/10
@ strandparcnulde@vdbrecreatie.nl

404

8ha 50T(90-110m²) 6-12A CEE

**1** ACD**G**IJKLMNOPQ
**2** ADFKLMRSVWX
**3** B**F**HJ**M**NRU**W**Z
**4** M(Q+T+U+X+Y+Z 🔓)
**5** **AB**DEFGIJKLMNO**PQ**UW
   XYZ
**6** ABCGHKL(N 0,2km)SV

💬 A campsite with spacious sunny and shaded pitches located on the Nuldernauw. Own beach, lovely views of the water from every pitch, plenty of watersports opportunities and good toilet facilities.

🚗 A28, exit 10 Strand Nulde. Campsite located near the water, signposted from exit.

CC € 18 1/4-29/5 11/6-7/7 26/8-30/9 | N 52°16'17'' E 05°32'14''

## Ruurlo, NL-7261 MR / Gelderland

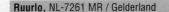

♿ 📶 🆔 **405**

🔺 Camping Tamaring
📧 Wildpad 3
☎ +31 5 73 45 14 86
🔓 1/4 - 6/10
@ info@camping-tamaring.nl

3,5ha 108T(100-150m²) 10A CEE

**1** ADG IJKLMPQ
**2** BRSVWXY
**3** ABFGHIJKLRU
**4** (G 15/5-31/8) (Q+R 🔓)
**5** ABCDEFGIJKLMNOPQUW XYZ
**6** ACDEGHJK(N 2km)OS

💬 A wonderfully hospitable and friendly campsite, located right in the middle of the Achterhoek region. The site is suitable for those wanting to relax and for families with young children. Surrounded by various nature reserves. Ideal for cycling and walking.

🚗 Motorway A1, exit 26 when coming from the north. N332 direction Lochem-Barchem-Ruurlo. Follow signs.

CC € ⑱ 1/4-29/5 12/6-6/7 24/8-6/10    🧭 N 52°06'10'' E 06°26'29''

---

## Stokkum, NL-7039 CW / Gelderland

👫 📶 🆔 **406**

🔺 Camping De Slangenbult
📧 St. Isidorusstraat 12
☎ +31 3 14 66 27 98
🔓 1/1 - 31/12
@ info@deslangenbult.nl

10ha 60T(100-140m²) 10-16A CEE

**1** ADG IJKLMOPQ
**2** BFGILRSWX
**3** ABDFGHJKLNR
**5** ABCDFGIJKLMNOPUZ
**6** ACEGK(N 3km)S

💬 Peacefully located in the heart of the Montferland woods on the Dutch-German border, close to 's-Heerenberg (Huis Bergh Castle). Spacious pitches with cable television. Modern clean toilet facilities. Excellent base for cycling, mountain biking, walking or Nordic Walking.

🚗 A12 exit 30 to Beek, continue towards Beek. Turn right at 1st roundabout in Beek then immediately left, follow road for 3 km. 1st street on the right in Stokkum (long hedge). Follow camping signs.

CC € ⑯ 18/1-23/5 13/6-7/7 24/8-13/12    🧭 N 51°52'43'' E 06°12'53''

---

## Stokkum, NL-7039 CV / Gelderland

♿ 📶 🆔 **407**

🔺 Camping Landgoed Brockhausen
📧 Eltenseweg 20
☎ +31 3 14 66 12 12
🔓 1/3 - 31/10
@ campingbrockhausen@ gmail.com

NEW

4ha 76T(100-140m²) 4-10A CEE

**1** ADG IJKLMOPS
**2** BFRSWXY
**3** AFGHIJ
**4** (A+Q 🔓)
**5** ABDEFGHIJKLMNOPQRU WXYZ
**6** BCDEGKT

💬 Quality, peace and nature. Peaceful family campsite set in rural woodland. Spacious pitches in several grassy fields, surrounded by trees and shrubbery. Excellent toilet block with many facilities.

🚗 A12/A3 exit 's-Heerenberg, then direction Stokkum, then follow campsite signs.

CC € ⑱ 1/3-18/4 6/5-23/5 11/6-30/6 18/7-31/7 1/9-30/10    🧭 N 51°52'40'' E 06°12'39''

## Stroe, NL-3776 PV / Gelderland

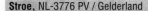 📶 iD **408**

🔺 Camping Jacobus Hoeve
📧 Tolnegenweg 53
☎ +31 3 42 44 13 19
📅 1/2 - 30/11
@ info@jacobus-hoeve.nl

5ha 60T(100-150m²) 10-16A CEE

1️⃣ ACDC**G**IJKLMNO**P**Q
2️⃣ FRSTUVWX
3️⃣ ABDF**G**HJKL**M**R
4️⃣ (**A** 30/4-30/8)
  (Q 30/5-11/6,13/7-14/8)
  (T+X+Y+Z 📅)
5️⃣ **AB**CDFGIJMNO**P**UWXY
6️⃣ ABDEGKM(N 1km)OSV

💬 Friendly family campsite surrounded by woods and sandy areas. Beautifully located on the edge of the Veluwe. The campsite has its own sports hall.

🚗 A1 exit 17 direction Stroe. Left at 1st roundabout, right before level crossing. Campsite 800m on the left of the road.

(CC) € **16** 1/2-29/5  11/6-5/7  24/8-30/11  🏕 N 52°11'38'' E 05°40'42''

## Ugchelen, NL-7339 GG / Gelderland

🚹🚺 ⚲ 📶 iD **409**

🔺 Camping De Wapenberg
📧 Hoenderloseweg 187
☎ +31 5 55 33 45 39
📅 29/3 - 1/11
@ info@dewapenberg.nl

4ha 59T(80-140m²) 6-16A CEE

1️⃣ AD**G**IJKLPQ
2️⃣ BFIRSTVWXY
3️⃣ AHJKRU
4️⃣ M
5️⃣ **AB**DEFGIJKLMNO**P**UW
  XYZ
6️⃣ ACEG**K**(N 2km)T

💬 This attractive campsite is located in an extensive area of woodland, heathland, hills and by the source of several springs. You will be camping on the edge of a wood with unusually laid out individual pitches. Rest, nature, walking and cycling with the sights of Apeldoorn close by.

🚗 A1 exit 19 Hoenderloo dir. Ede/Hoenderloo. Follow camping signs. Via A50 exit 22. In Beekbergen left at first traffic lights. Follow road till campsite is signposted.

(CC) € **16** 29/3-26/4  5/5-29/5  11/6-5/7  22/8-1/11  21=18  🏕 N 52°10'19'' E 05°54'45''

## Vaassen, NL-8171 RA / Gelderland

⚲ 📶 ✿ iD **410**

🔺 Camping De Helfterkamp
📧 Gortelseweg 24
☎ +31 5 78 57 18 39
📅 1/3 - 31/10
@ info@helfterkamp.nl

4ha 180T(100-120m²) 6-16A CEE

1️⃣ ACD**G**IJKLNPQ
2️⃣ FRVWXY
3️⃣ ABDGHJKLNRU
4️⃣ M(Q 31/3-28/10) (S 📅)
5️⃣ **AB**DEFGI**J**KLMNO**P**QRUW
  XYZ
6️⃣ ABCEGHK(N 2,5km)OV

💬 The site is located on the edge of the Veluwe crown estate. You will camp in various fields surrounding a Gelderland farmhouse. Plenty of cycling and walking opportunities right by the site. New heated toilet block.

🚗 A50 Apeldoorn-Zwolle, exit 26 Vaassen, then follow signs.

(CC) € **18** 1/3-26/4  13/5-29/5  11/6-2/7  19/8-31/10  🏕 N 52°17'27'' E 05°56'42''

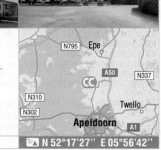

## Vierhouten, NL-8076 PM / Gelderland

👬 ♿ 📶 📱 **411**

🏕 Recreatiepark Samoza
📧 Plaggeweg 90
☎ +31 5 77 41 12 83
🕐 29/3 - 28/10
@ info@samoza.nl

70ha  310T(100m²)  10A CEE

**1** ACDGIJKLMOPQ
**2** BFLRSTVWXY
**3** ABDFGHJKLMNOPRU
**4** (C+F+H 📱) J
   (Q+S+T+X+Y+Z 📱)
**5** ABDEFGHIJKLMNOPQUXY
   Z
**6** CFGHJKL(N 2km)OSTV

💬 A family campsite, hidden in the woods. Extensive amenities such as a swimming pool, restaurant, riding stables and modern toilet facilities. The beautiful surroundings are an invitation to take endless walks and cycle trips.

�car Motorway A28 Amersfoort-Zwolle, exit 14 Nunspeet/Elspeet. Then direction Vierhouten. Follow the signs.

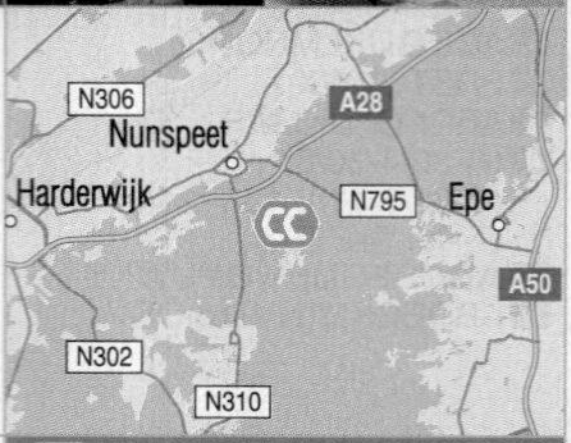

N306  A28
Nunspeet
Harderwijk        N795   Epe
                              CC
                                   A50
N302
     N310

CC € 16  29/3-18/4  23/4-25/4  6/5-28/5  11/6-4/7  31/8-27/10  📐 N 52°20'54''  E 05°49'27''

## Voorst, NL-7383 AL / Gelderland

📶 📱 **412**

🏕 Camping De Adelaar
📧 Rijksstraatweg 49
☎ +31 5 75 50 19 72
🕐 29/3 - 31/10
@ info@campingdeadelaar.nl

1ha  55T(120-150m²)  6-10A CEE

**1** ADFIJKLMNPQ
**2** CFKRSTVWXY
**3** ACFHJRU
**4** M
**5** ABDEGIJMNOPQUVWXZ
**6** CDEGK

💬 Beautiful country estate site between Apeldoorn, Deventer and Zutphen, which invites you to explore the area. The IJssel Valley and Bussloo lake nearby. The MORE Museum in Gorssel is well worth a visit.

🚗 The A1 exit towards Zutphen (N345) runs beside the campsite. The campsite is located before the residential part of Voorst on the left. From the A50 take exit 24 towards Zutphen (N345) the campsite is located before the residential part of Voorst on the left.

N344
                   A1
Apeldoorn
      N790  N348  N339
A50              CC
        N345    Zutphen
N786
              N314

CC € 16  29/3-19/4  10/5-26/5  13/6-30/6  1/9-31/10  📐 N 52°10'37''  E 06°08'26''

## Voorthuizen, NL-3781 NJ / Gelderland

♿ 📶 ✿ 📱 **413**

🏕 Ardoer Vakantiepark Ackersate
📧 Harremaatweg 26
☎ +31 3 42 47 12 74
🕐 29/3 - 26/10
@ ackersate@ardoer.com

15ha  194T(100-120m²)  6-10A CEE

**1** ACDFIJKLMNOPQ
**2** FGRSVWX
**3** ABDFGIJKLMNQRU
**4** (C 1/5-15/9) (F+H 📱) IJKM
   (Q+S+T+U+Y+Z 📱)
**5** ABDEFGIJKLMNOPQRSU
   WXY
**6** CEGHKL(N 1,5km)OSV

💬 A large campsite with spacious fields. The amenities are excellent, the swimming pool includes a 20 metre indoor pool and, since 2018, a heated outdoor pool. Voorthuizen has many tourist amenities. It is located between the woods of the Veluwe and the agricultural Gelderse Valley.

🚗 A1 exit 16. In Voorthuizen turn right onto N344 direction Garderen. Turn right just past Voorthuizen. Campsite signposted.

Putten
          N302
A28
Nijkerk   N303
N301
       CC  A1
Barneveld
              N310
N802  A30

CC € 18  29/3-26/4  6/5-29/5  11/6-5/7  26/8-11/10  📐 N 52°11'11''  E 05°37'30''

## Voorthuizen, NL-3781 NJ / Gelderland ♿ 📶 iD ④④④

🏕 Recreatiepark De Boshoek
📧 Harremaatweg 34
☎ +31 3 42 47 12 97
📅 23/3 - 25/10
@ info@deboshoek.nl

4,5ha 116T(110-120m²) 10A CEE

**1** ACDFIJKLMNOPQ
**2** FGLRSVW
**3** ABDFGIJKLMNOPQRTU
**4** (C 1/5-30/9) (F+H 📅) LN (Q+R+S+T+U+Y+Z 📅)
**5** ABDEFGIJKLMNPQSUWXY
**6** ADEGHK(N 1,5km)OSX

💬 A new, modern campsite with spacious pitches, separated by hedges. Partly car-free. Swimming pool and catering at the bungalow park opposite the campsite. Supplement for private toilet facilities 8 Euros per night. 1.50 Euros per night supplement for the 10A connection.

🚗 A1 exit 16 direction Voorthuizen, towards Garderen at the roundabout on the N344. Turn right just after Voorthuizen. Campsite signposted. Reception opposite the site entrance!

CC € ⑱ 23/3-19/4 23/4-26/4 3/5-29/5 11/6-5/7 30/8-25/10 7=6, 14=11 ⛰ N 52°11'15'' E 05°37'51''

---

## Vorden, NL-7251 KT / Gelderland 📶 iD ④④⑤

🏕 Camping 't Meulenbrugge
📧 Mosselseweg 4
☎ +31 5 75 55 66 12
📅 1/4 - 31/10
@ info@meulenbrugge-vorden.nl

4ha 109T(100-150m²) 10-16A CEE

**1** ADGIJKLMNPQU
**2** CRSUWXY
**3** GHJKL
**4** (Q 15/4-15/9)
**5** ABDGIJKLMNPUWXYZ
**6** ACDEGIK(N 2,5km)O

💬 Located in a beautiful nature area on the edge of a wood and beside a stream. Only peace and space. No playground equipment or entertainment, so less suitable for children.

🚗 From Vorden roundabout dir. Ruurlo. Left at double bend after 2.5 km (Mosselseweg), stay on road for 400m then turn right to campsite. From N319 Ruurlo dir. Vorden. Through Kranenburg, right at double bend, follow this road for 400m to campsite.

CC € ⑱ 1/4-28/5 11/6-5/7 24/8-31/10 ⛰ N 52°06'28'' E 06°21'16''

---

## Vorden, NL-7251 JL / Gelderland 👫 📶 iD ④④⑥

🏕 Camping De Goldberg
📧 Larenseweg 1
☎ +31 5 75 55 16 79
📅 1/4 - 26/10
@ info@degoldberg.nl

4,5ha 45T(100-120m²) 6-10A CEE

**1** ADGIJKLMNOPRS
**2** RSVWXY
**3** BDFHJKLOPU
**4** (Q+R+T+U+X+Z 📅)
**5** ABDEFGHIJKLMNOPQUW XYZ
**6** CDEGHKM(N 2km)OV

💬 Modern, well-designed campsite among woods and vast estates. Perfect starting point for cycling, walking and horseback routes. Stabling for your own horse or pony is possible. Riding lessons possible for horse or pony (for a fee). Plenty of fishing options. Modern, heated toilet facilities.

🚗 From Vorden N319 direction Ruurlo. Turn left past the level crossing, signposted.

CC € ⑯ 1/4-28/5 12/6-5/7 30/8-26/10 14=12, 21=18 ⛰ N 52°07'04'' E 06°19'26''

## Vorden, NL-7251 KA / Gelderland 🛜 iD **417**

🏕 Camping De Reehorst
📧 Enzerinckweg 12
☎ +31 5 75 55 15 82
📅 1/4 - 31/10
@ info@dereehorst.nl

7,5ha 49T(100-140m²) 6-10A CEE

**1** ADG**IJKL**P**S**
**2** BSVWXY
**3** AB**F**HJNRU
**4** (G 1/5-1/9)
(Q+T+U+X+Y+Z 📅)
**5** **AB**DFG**IJJL**MNO**PQ**UXY
**6** ADEG**K**(N 2km)OSV

💬 A lovely campsite located in woodland for those seeking relaxation and for families with children. The campsite is located on a beautiful castle route for cyclists and walkers. There is a heated outdoor swimming pool in the immediate vicinity.

🚌 From Vorden N319 direction Ruurlo. Past the level crossing, 40 metres on the left. Signposted.

CC € **18** 1/4-8/7 25/8-3/10 📍 N 52°06'58'' E 06°20'12''

---

## Wilp, NL-7384 CT / Gelderland ♿ 🛜 iD **418**

🏕 Kampeerhoeve Bussloo
📧 Grotenhuisweg 20
☎ +31 6 20 98 16 59
📅 29/3 - 31/10
@ piethulscher@
kampeerhoevebussloo.nl

1ha 35T(144m²) 10A CEE

**1** ADG**HIJKLMNP**Q
**2** FKRVWX
**3** AD**F**JKLU
**5** **AB**DFGIJMNOPQUWXY
**6** ACDEG**K**(N 3km)T

💬 The campsite is located at an equal distance to the three towns Apeldoorn, Deventer and Zutphen. You will be camping on marked out pitches around an old farm. Bussloo, a recreational area, is only 300 metres away. Sauna complex "Thermen Bussloo" is a 2 km cycle trip away. The campsite is open all year round for motorhomes.

🚌 A1 exit 22 Twello direction Wilp. After 200m turn right (Molenallee). Follow road until campsite (Grotenhuisweg).

CC € **18** 29/3-29/5 11/6-6/7 23/8-31/10 📍 N 52°12'33'' E 06°06'33''

---

## Winterswijk, NL-7115 AG / Gelderland 🛜 iD **419**

🏕 Camping Het Winkel
📧 De Slingeweg 20
☎ +31 5 43 51 30 25
📅 1/1 - 31/12
@ info@hetwinkel.nl

20ha 350T(90-200m²) 10-16A CEE

**1** AD**F**IJKLMOPQ
**2** BLRSVWX
**3** ABCD**F**HIJKL**M**NR**T**U
**4** (C+H 27/4-1/9) J**N**
(Q+R+T+U+V+X+Y+Z
1/3-3/11)
**5** **AB**CDFGIJKLMNOPQ**S**UW
XZ
**6** BDEGH**K**(N 3km)V

💬 A campsite with spacious pitches, a luxury swimming pool with water slide and a children's pool. Private toilet facilities are available. It is a good base for cycling and walking trips.

🚌 Winterswijk direction Borken. Campsite is signposted.

CC € **18** 1/1-4/4 6/5-28/5 11/6-18/6 24/6-6/7 2/9-10/10 28/10-19/12 📍 N 51°57'08'' E 06°44'13''

## Winterswijk, NL-7103 EA / Gelderland  ♿ 📶 iD **420**

🏕 Camping Klompenmakerij
ten Hagen
🏠 Waliënsestraat 139A
☎ +31 5 43 53 15 03
📅 1/1 - 31/12
@ info@hagencampklomp.nl

2ha 46T(100-150m²) 10-16A CEE

**1** ACD**F**IJKLMOP**Q**
**2** DRSVWXY
**3** ABF**H**JNR**U**W**Z**
**5** **AB**CDFGIJ**K**LMNO**P**U**W**
XYZ
**6** CDEGH**K**(N 1km)T

💬 Located on the shore of 't Hilgelo recreational lake. Various watersports such as surfing, swimming and diving. Cycling and walking routes. Also suitable for the disabled.

🚗 N319 Groenlo-Winterswijk. At roundabout on the Groenloseweg continue to of Winterswijk.'t Hilgelo recreational lake. Follow signs. Located about 1 km north

CC €**16** 1/1-18/4 23/4-28/5 3/6-7/6 12/6-19/6 24/6-9/7 26/8-31/12   📍 N 51°59'28'' E 06°43'09''

---

## Winterswijk, NL-7104 AA / Gelderland  📶 **421**

🏕 Camping Sevink Molen
🏠 Meddoseweg 40
☎ +31 5 43 51 32 29
📅 1/1 - 31/12
@ camping@sevinkmolen.nl

7,5ha 60T(140m²) 10A CEE

NEW

**1** CD**G**IJKLMOP**Q**
**2** ADLRSWXY
**3** B**CD**F**H**JW**Z**
**4** (Q 27/4-5/5,13/7-23/8)
(T+U+W+X+Y 📅)
**5** **AB**DEFGIJKLMNOP**ST**UW
XYZ
**6** CDEGH**KS**

💬 Campsite holiday park Sevink Molen, located directly on the lake 't Hilgelo. Many amenities, including a very extensive restaurant, a brand new heated toilet block, themed indoor play hall and a historic mill that can be visited.

🚗 Coming from Aalten or Groenlo continue straight on. At the second roundabout follow signposts.

CC €**18** 1/1-18/4 23/4-24/4 6/5-28/5 11/6-23/6 1/7-7/7 1/9-31/12   📍 N 51°59'47'' E 06°43'16''

---

## Winterswijk, NL-7109 AH / Gelderland  📶 iD **422**

🏕 Camping Vakantiepark De
Twee Bruggen
🏠 Meenkmolenweg 13
☎ +31 5 43 56 53 66
📅 1/1 - 31/12
@ info@detweebruggen.nl

30ha 390T(80-100m²) 10-16A CEE

**1** ACD**G**IJKLMOP**Q**
**2** CDLRSWXY
**3** ABD**F**GHJKL**MN**QR**TU**W**Z**
**4** (C 15/5-15/9) (**F**+H 📅) J**N**
(Q+R+S+T+X+Y+Z 📅)
**5** **AB**DFGIJKLMNOP**ST**UW
XYZ
**6** BCDEGHI**K**M(N 6km)SV

💬 Spaciously laid out, friendly campsite. Various large and very large fields with camping pitches. Modern comforts including private toilet facilities. Brand new indoor swimming pool on the site.

🚗 From A18 (Doetinchem) to N18 Varsseveld: over N318 to Aalten. Just before Winterswijk turn left. Clearly signposted.

CC €**20** 7/1-18/4 23/4-28/5 3/6-6/6 11/6-7/7 26/8-31/12   📍 N 51°56'58'' E 06°38'47''

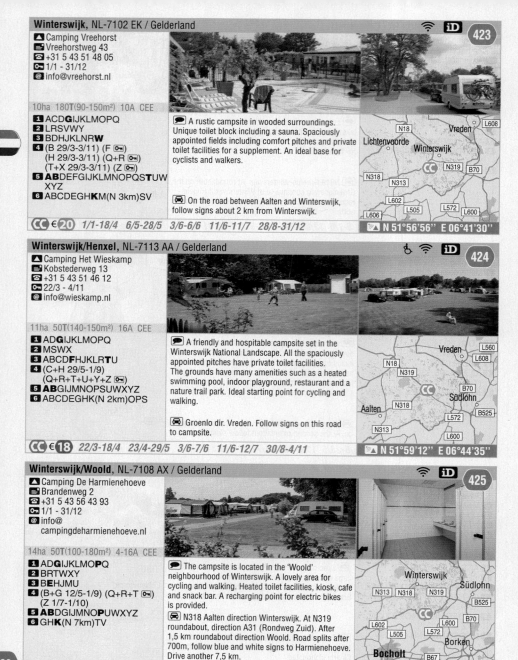

## Winterswijk, NL-7102 EK / Gelderland

🏕 Camping Vreehorst
✉ Vreehorstweg 43
☎ +31 5 43 51 48 05
📅 1/1 - 31/12
@ info@vreehorst.nl

**423**

10ha 180T(90-150m²) 10A CEE

**1** ACDGIJKLMOPQ
**2** LRSVWY
**3** BDHJKLNRW
**4** (B 29/3-3/11) (F 🔒)
(H 29/3-3/11) (Q+R 🔒)
(T+X 29/3-3/11) (Z 🔒)
**5** ABDEFGIJKLMNOPQSTUW
XYZ
**6** ABCDEGHKM(N 3km)SV

💬 A rustic campsite in wooded surroundings. Unique toilet block including a sauna. Spaciously appointed fields including comfort pitches and private toilet facilities for a supplement. An ideal base for cyclists and walkers.

🚗 On the road between Aalten and Winterswijk, follow signs about 2 km from Winterswijk.

CC €20  1/1-18/4  6/5-28/5  3/6-6/6  11/6-11/7  28/8-31/12   📍 N 51°56'56'' E 06°41'30''

## Winterswijk/Henxel, NL-7113 AA / Gelderland

🏕 Camping Het Wieskamp
✉ Kobstederweg 13
☎ +31 5 43 51 46 12
📅 22/3 - 4/11
@ info@wieskamp.nl

**424**

11ha 50T(140-150m²) 16A CEE

**1** ADGIJKLMOPQ
**2** MSWX
**3** ABCDFHJKLRTU
**4** (C+H 29/5-1/9)
(Q+R+T+U+Y+Z 🔒)
**5** ABGIJMNOPSUWXYZ
**6** ABCDEGHK(N 2km)OPS

💬 A friendly and hospitable campsite set in the Winterswijk National Landscape. All the spaciously appointed pitches have private toilet facilities. The grounds have many amenities such as a heated swimming pool, indoor playground, restaurant and a nature trail park. Ideal starting point for cycling and walking.

🚗 Groenlo dir. Vreden. Follow signs on this road to campsite.

CC €18  22/3-18/4  23/4-29/5  3/6-7/6  11/6-12/7  30/8-4/11   📍 N 51°59'12'' E 06°44'35''

## Winterswijk/Woold, NL-7108 AX / Gelderland

🏕 Camping De Harmienehoeve
✉ Brandenweg 2
☎ +31 5 43 56 43 93
📅 1/1 - 31/12
@ info@
campingdeharmienehoeve.nl

**425**

14ha 50T(100-180m²) 4-16A CEE

**1** ADGIJKLMOPQ
**2** BRTWXY
**3** BEHJMU
**4** (B+G 12/5-1/9) (Q+R+T 🔒)
(Z 1/7-1/10)
**5** ABDGIJMNOPUWXYZ
**6** GHK(N 7km)TV

💬 The campsite is located in the 'Woold' neighbourhood of Winterswijk. A lovely area for cycling and walking. Heated toilet facilities, kiosk, cafe and snack bar. A recharging point for electric bikes is provided.

🚗 N318 Aalten direction Winterswijk. At N319 roundabout, direction A31 (Rondweg Zuid). After 1,5 km roundabout direction Woold. Road splits after 700m, follow blue and white signs to Harmienehoeve. Drive another 7,5 km.

CC €14  1/3-5/6  12/6-30/6  29/7-11/8  1/9-31/10   📍 N 51°54'30'' E 06°43'31''

## Zennewijnen, NL-4062 PP / Gelderland ♿ 📶 ✿ iD 426

🏕 Campingpark Zennewijnen
📧 Hermoesestraat 13
☎ +31 3 44 65 14 98
📅 15/3 - 31/10
@ info@campingzennewijnen.nl

5ha 50T(100-120m²) 10A CEE

**1** ACD**F**IJKLMPST
**2** ACFGLRSVWX
**3** BFGHJNRUW
**4** (B+G 15/5-15/9)
(Q+R+T+U+X+Z 🔅)
**5** **AB**CDFGHI**J**KLMNO**PQ**RU
WXYZ
**6** ACDEGH**K**M(N 2km)OTV

💬 Located in the heart of the Betuwe region, the friendly Zennewijnen family campsite is situated between Tiel and Ophemert. Excellent base for cycling, walking and strolling beside the River Waal.

🚗 A15 from Rotterdam exit 31. From Nijmegen exit 32. Campsite signposted from the exit.

Culemborg  N835
N833  Tiel  Beneden-
A15  Leeuwen
N830
N322  N329
A2
Oss

CC €**18** 15/3-28/5  11/6-13/7  1/9-31/10  🧭 N 51°51'17'' E 05°24'26''

---

## Alphen (N.Br.), NL-5131 NZ / Noord-Brabant ♿ 📶 iD 427

🏕 Camping 't Zand
📧 Maastrichtsebaan 1
☎ +31 1 35 08 17 46
📅 29/3 - 29/9
@ info@tzand.nl

20ha 75T(100-120m²) 10A CEE

**1** AD**F**IJKLMNOPQ
**2** ABDFLMRSVWXY
**3** ABF**G**HIJKMNRUZ
**4** (A+Q+R 27/4-5/5,8/7-3/9)
(T 🔅) (U 27/4-5/5,1/7-31/8)
(V 26/4-5/5,1/7-5/9) (X 🔅)
(Z 27/4-5/5,8/7-3/9)
**5** **AB**DEFGI**J**KLMNO**PQ**R**ST**
UWXYZ
**6** ACDEGH**K**(N 1,5km)OSUV

💬 Campsite located by a lake in the middle of a recreational area. Forms part of the green triangle Baarle-Tilburg-Turnhout. Woodland cycling area. Lovely towns such as Baarle-Nassau nearby.

🚗 A58 exit Gilze/Rijen, direction Baarle-Nassau. Follow signs in Alphen. Be sure to follow campsite signs, not the sign 'recreatiegebied'.

**Breda**  **Tilburg**
A58  Goirle
N269
N630
N639  N12
N14
N260

CC €**16** 29/3-19/4  5/5-29/5  3/6-7/6  11/6-6/7  24/8-29/9  🧭 N 51°29'34'' E 04°56'59''

---

## Alphen (N.Br.), NL-5131 NH / Noord-Brabant ♿ 📶 iD 428

🏕 Camping Buitenlust
📧 Huisdreef 1
☎ +31 1 35 08 14 80
📅 1/2 - 1/10
@ actie@campingbuitenlust.nl

7ha 30T(90-120m²) 6A CEE

**1** ACD**G**IJKLOPRS
**2** BFRSVWXY
**3** ABF**H**JKNRU
**4** (C+H 1/4-1/9) (Q 25/9-30/9)
(R 🔅) (T+U+X+Z 1/4-31/10)
**5** **AB**DEFGIJKLMNO**P**UWYZ
**6** ABCDEGHKL(N 2km)SUV

💬 An agreeable family campsite in the Chaam woods. Enjoy the peace and local Brabant hospitality. Ideal surroundings for walking and cycling in the varying countryside with woods and fields.

🚗 A58 from Breda exit 14 Chaam, then follow signs. From Tilburg exit 12 Gilze-Alphen.

**Breda**  N631  N282  **Tilburg**
A58
A27
A16  N630
E19  N639
N14
Minderhout  N12
N260

CC €**14** 1/2-18/4  22/4-29/5  2/6-7/6  10/6-9/7  26/8-1/10  🧭 N 51°30'02'' E 04°54'43''

## Andel, NL-4281 NE / Noord-Brabant

🏕 Camping De Hoge Waard
Hoge Maasdijk 57 t/m 61
☎ +31 4 16 69 37 76
🔓 1/4 - 30/9
@ camping@dehogewaard.nl

8ha 42T(80-90m²) 6A CEE

**1** ADGIJKLNPQ
**2** ACDFLMRSVWXY
**3** BFGHJNRUWXZ
**4** (Q 1/6-1/9) (T+U+Y+Z 🔓)
**5** ABDFGIJKLMNOPQRUWXY Z
**6** ABCDEGHJ(N 3km)SV

💬 This welcoming, child-friendly family campsite is located between the distinctive fortified towns of Woudrichem and Heusden. The grounds border on water on two sides. The beautiful surroundings invite you to go on walks, cycle tours and days out. Whatever you are looking for, you will find it here: a private beach, a spot for your boat or a relaxing bite to eat.

🚗 A27 Gorinchem-Breda exit Nieuwendijk, then dir. Almkerk via N267 exit Andel. Follow (ANWB) signs.

CC €18  1/4-8/7  25/9-29/9       🌄 N 51°46'40'' E 05°04'48''

---

## Asten/Heusden, NL-5725 TG / Noord-Brabant

🏕 Camping De Peel
Behelp 13
☎ +31 4 93 69 32 22
🔓 15/3 - 31/10
@ info@campingdepeel.nl

2,2ha 75T(100m²) 6A CEE

**1** ADFIJKLMNOPQ
**2** FLRVWXY
**3** ABDFGHJKLNRU
**4** (B 1/7-31/8) (Q 8/7-16/8)
**5** ABCDFGIJMNOPUWXYZ
**6** ACDEGK(N 1km)

💬 Small friendly site where over-50s seeking peace and quiet will feel at home. Near De Groote Peel with excellent cycling and walking options. Ride in the Peel Express. Playground and covered bike storage. Comfort and motorhome pitches. Good new toilet facilities. Free wifi.

🚗 From A67 exit 36 towards Asten, then N279 towards Someren. Turn right after 2 km and left after 1 km towards Heusden. Follow signs in Heusden. From Someren direction Asten then follow signs.

CC €18  15/3-29/5  11/6-5/7  22/8-31/10       🌄 N 51°22'23'' E 05°45'09''

---

## Asten/Heusden, NL-5725 TM / Noord-Brabant

🏕 Camping De Peelpoort
Gezandebaan 29a
☎ +31 4 93 56 05 19
🔓 1/1 - 31/12
@ info@campingdepeelpoort.nl

2,5ha 100T(80-140m²) 6-16A CEE

**1** ACDGIJLMNPRS
**2** FRVW
**3** ABEGHJKLOPRW
**4** (Q+T+X+Y+Z 🔓)
**5** ABCDFGIJKLMNPUWXYZ
**6** ACDEGJK(N 3km)

💬 Newly laid out in 2015, a spaciously appointed campsite in a natural setting on the edge of a wood. Convenient toilet facilities. Lovely fishing lake and golf course next to the campsite. Brasserie with long opening hours also in low season. Ride in the Peel Express possible.

🚗 A67 exit 35 Someren, N256 drection Nederweert. At Someren-Eind bridge over water direction Asten. Campsite on the left of the road after 4 km.

CC €18  1/1-15/7  1/9-31/12       🌄 N 51°21'44'' E 05°46'10''

## Asten/Ommel, NL-5724 PL / Noord-Brabant  👫 📶 🆔 **432**

🏕 Oostappen Vakantiepark
   Prinsenmeer
✉ Beekstraat 31
☎ +31 4 93 68 11 11
🔓 6/4 - 28/10
@ info@vakantieparkprinsenmeer.nl

**NEW**

50ha 480T(80-100m²) 10A CEE

**1** ACD**G**IJKLMOPQ
**2** ADFLMRVWX
**3** ABC**F**GHJKLMNQR**T**UZ
**4** (F+H 🔲) IJKLN
   (S+T+V+Y+Z 🔲)
**5** **AB**DEFGIJKLMNOPQU
   WXY
**6** CFGHJM(N 3km)OSTUV

💬 The camping grounds are situated on a Plaza with countless amenities. There is a large recreational lake with slides and a sandy beach containing plenty of playground equipment. Fun in the water not only outside but also in the subtropical leisure pool.

🚗 A67 Eindhoven-Venlo, exit 36 Asten. Direction Ommel. Follow the signs.

Helmond  N270  N277
Geldrop  A67
Heeze  N266
A2  N279

CC € **16** 27/4-29/5 10/6-5/7 2/9-28/10  📍 N 51°25'21'' E 05°44'09''

---

## Bergen op Zoom, NL-4625 DD / Noord-Brabant  ♿ 📶 🆔 **433**

🏕 Camping Uit en Thuis
✉ Heimolen 56
☎ +31 1 64 23 33 91
🔓 1/4 - 30/9
@ info@campinguitenthuis.nl

8ha 80T(80-100m²) 6-10A CEE

**1** AD**F**IJKLMOPQ
**2** BFRSVX
**3** BDGHJKL**M**NQRU
**4** (C+H 27/4-15/9)
   (R+T+U+X+Z 🔲)
**5** **AB**FGIJMNO**P**RUXYZ
**6** CDEGH**K**(N 5km)OSTV

💬 Located in the Brabantse Wal countryside, this natural campsite is an oasis of peace. You will be surrounded by nature but the site offers all the comfort you would expect from a modern campsite. A trip out to the culinary town of Bergen op Zoom is recommended. There are dozens of historical sights such as the Markiezenhof.

🚗 A58 exit Bergen op Zoom-Zuid/Huijbergen. Follow the signs.

A17  A4  A58
Bergen op Zoom  N659  CC
N289  N117
N111

CC € **18** 1/4-29/5 11/6-5/7 26/8-30/9  📍 N 51°28'09'' E 04°19'20''

---

## Bladel, NL-5531 NA / Noord-Brabant  ♿ 📶 🆔 **434**

🏕 Recreatiepark De Achterste Hoef
✉ Troprijt 10
☎ +31 4 97 38 15 79
🔓 5/4 - 29/9
@ info@achterstehoef.nl

23ha 385T(100-160m²) 6-10A CEE

**1** ACD**G**IJKLMOPRS
**2** ABDFLMRVWXY
**3** ABCD**E**GHJKN**Q**RUZ
**4** (C 19/4-1/9) (F+H 🔲) J
   (S+T+X+Z 🔲)
**5** **AB**CDEFGHIJKLMNOPQR**S**
   UWXY
**6** ACEGH**K**(N 3km)OSU

💬 On the edge of an extensive wooded natural landscape, this campsite has lots of amenities. In particular, the restaurant with long opening hours, the covered pool, and the golf course spring to mind. Cycling area unparalleled for its beauty, with Eersel and the Abbey of Postel less than 10 km away.

🚗 A67 Eindhoven-Antwerpen exit 29 Hapert/Bladel. Follow signs to Bladel. In Bladel follow signs to the campsite.

Veldhoven  N269
Bladel  A67
N118  CC
E34  A21
Retie  N69
N18  N746

CC € **20** 5/4-18/4 6/5-28/5 11/6-5/7 23/8-28/9  📍 N 51°20'36'' E 05°13'40''

## Breda, NL-4838 GV / Noord-Brabant 🛜 iD 435

🏕 Camping Liesbos
✉ Liesdreef 40
☎ +31 7 65 14 35 14
📅 1/4 - 1/10
@ info@camping-liesbos.nl

5ha 50T(100m²) 10A CEE

**1** ACD**F**IJKLMPQ
**2** FLRSVX
**3** B**F**HJK**M**NRU
**4** (C+H 30/4-30/9)
(Q+R+T+U 1/4-30/9)
(Y+Z 🚗)
**5** **AB**CFGIJMNO**P**UW
**6** ACDEGHK(N 3km)OSTV

💬 Liesbos campsite is a charming family campsite located in a wooded area 5 km from the centre of the royal town of Breda. Its central location 'just outside Breda' makes Liesbos campsite easy to reach. Ideal for a cycling and walking holiday, a city break or a weekend away. The historic city of Breda is worth visiting.

🚗 Motorway A58 Breda-Roosendaal exit 18 Etten-Leur. Then follow camping signs.

CC €18 1/4-9/4 23/4-28/5 3/6-6/6 11/6-6/7 26/8-30/9 | N 51°33'54'' E 04°41'47''

---

## Chaam, NL-4861 RC / Noord-Brabant ♿ 🛜 iD 436

🏕 RCN vakantiepark De Flaasbloem
✉ Flaasdijk 1
☎ +31 8 50 40 07 00
📅 29/3 - 4/11
@ reserveringen@rcn.nl

100ha 440T(80-150m²) 10-16A CEE

**1** ACD**G**IJKLMNOPQ
**2** ABDFLMRSWXY
**3** ABDFGHJKLMNRUWZ
**4** (F 🚗) (H 1/5-1/9) JM**N**
(Q+S+T+U+V+X+Y 🚗)
**5** **AB**CDEFGIJKLMNOPQR**S**UWZ
**6** CDEGH**K**M(N 2km)OS

💬 A large campsite with plenty of recreational opportunities. There is a fantastic water play park for the youngest ones. Indoor pool for family swimming. New in 2017: a 'smugglers beach' and a frisbee field.

🚗 A58 exit 14 Ulvenhout direction Chaam. From Chaam direction Alphen. Then follow the signs to campsite.

CC €16 29/3-29/5 3/6-7/6 11/6-12/7 30/8-4/11 | N 51°29'28'' E 04°53'47''

---

## Cromvoirt/Vught, NL-5266 AJ / Noord-Brabant ♿ 🛜 iD 437

🏕 Vakantiepark Fortduinen
✉ Pepereind 13b
☎ +31 4 11 64 14 31
📅 1/1 - 31/12
@ info@fortduinen.nl

8,5ha 84T(60-120m²) 6A CEE

**1** ABCD**G**IJKLO**P**Q
**2** ABDFRSVWXY
**3** ABGHJKMNQRUZ
**4** (B+G 1/6-15/9) (R 15/5-1/10)
**5** **AB**DEFGIJMNOPQUWZ
**6** ACDEGJ(N 2,5km)

💬 A holiday resort for all ages. Beautiful pitches, many amenities. Natural areas, towns and amusement parks nearby. Because of the excellent location you will not be bored for a minute.

🚗 N65 Den Bosch-Tilburg exit Cromvoirt. Follow main road (Boslaan and Pepereind) for 2.2 km to get to campsite.

CC €14 1/1-7/7 24/8-31/12 7=6, 14=11 | N 51°39'24'' E 05°14'33''

## De Heen, NL-4655 AH / Noord-Brabant ♿ 📶 **iD** 438

🏕 Camping De Uitwijk
✉ Dorpsweg 136
☎ +31 1 67 56 00 00
🗓 29/3 - 29/9
@ info@de-uitwijk.nl

2,5ha 56T(100-150m²) 4-10A CEE

**1** ACD**G**IJKLMNO**P**RS
**2** CFGRVX
**3** ABD**F**GHJKN**Q**RU**W**X
**4** (C+H 21/4-29/9) **N**
(Q+U+Y+Z 🖭)
**5** **AB**CDEFGHIJKLMNOPRUW
XYZ
**6** ACDEGH**K**(N 0km)OSTUV

💬 Peaceful sheltered site with a beautiful authentic farmhouse with restaurant and close to a nature reserve and yacht harbour. Excellent toilet facilities. New: heated swimming pool, toddlers' pool and sauna. Starting point for cycling and boat trips. Friendly and welcoming owner.

🚗 A4 exit 25 to Steenbergen. Then follow signs to 'De Heen'.

CC € **18** 29/3-19/4 22/4-26/4 12/5-29/5 10/6-5/7 25/8-29/9   🗺 N 51°36'37'' E 04°16'22''

---

## Eerde, NL-5466 PZ / Noord-Brabant 📶 439

🏕 Camping Het Goeie Leven
✉ Vlagheide 8b
☎ +31 4 13 31 01 71
🗓 1/4 - 6/10
@ info@hetgoeieleven.nl

3ha 60T(120-200m²) 6-16A CEE

**1** D**F**IJKLMN**P**Q
**2** FGLRWXY
**3** B**F**GHJKLNRUW
**4** (**A** 6/7-31/8) (C 🖭)
(Q 27/4-4/5,6/7-31/8)
(T+U+Y+Z 🖭)
**5** **AB**CDEFGHIJKLMNPQU
WXY
**6** ACEGHKL(N 1km)OV

💬 A naturally laid out campsite on the outskirts of the attractive village of Eerde. Partly surrounded by woods. Suitable for both families with children and those seeking relaxation though its diversity of camping pitches. Attractive bistro with woodland patio and extended opening times. Village shop in the windmill within walking distance. Very suitable for a visit to the city of 's-Hertogenbosch.

🚗 A50 exit 10 Veghel-Eerde. Continue towards Eerde and follow signs.

CC € **18** 1/4-20/4 11/5-29/5 11/6-6/7 24/8-6/10   🗺 N 51°36'24'' E 05°29'13''

---

## Eersel, NL-5521 RD / Noord-Brabant 👫 ⊗ ♿ 📶 **iD** 440

🏕 Camping Recreatiepark
TerSpegelt
✉ Postelseweg 88
☎ +31 4 97 51 20 16
🗓 5/4 - 28/10
@ info@terspegelt.nl

65ha 490T(80-130m²) 6-16A CEE

**1** ACDEIJKLMNPQ
**2** ADFLMRVWXY
**3** ABCD**F**GHJKLMN**Q**RUWZ
**4** (F+H 🖭) JKM
(S+T+U+V+X+Y+Z 🖭)
**5** **AB**DEFGIJKLMNOPQ**S**UW
XYZ
**6** ACFGHJ**K**LM(N 3km)ORST

💬 Five-star park in wooded Brabantse Kempen with three recreational lakes and unique amenities such as Sterrenstrand leisure pool and playground. Special activities for the over-55s in spring and autumn. Information about the many cycling and walking options in the natural surroundings opposite the campsite. Camp quietly by the water or in a more lively ambiance on the fields. Comfort pitches at a supplement.

🚗 Via A67 Eindhoven-Antwerpen, exit 30 Eersel. Follow signs.

CC € **20** 5/4-19/4 13/5-29/5 3/6-7/6 11/6-19/6 24/6-6/7 24/8-28/10   🗺 N 51°20'16'' E 05°17'37''

## Esbeek, NL-5085 NN / Noord-Brabant    ♿ 🛜 iD   **441**

🔺 Camping De Spaendershorst
📧 Spaaneindsestraat 12
☎ +31 1 35 16 93 61
🔓 29/3 - 27/10
@ info@spaendershorst.nl

11ha 90T(80-130m²) 10A CEE

**1** ABD**G**IJKLNOPQ
**2** GLRSVWXY
**3** ABFHJNRU
**4** (C+H 🔓) (T+Z 1/4-1/10)
**5** **AB**DFG**IJK**L**M**NO**P**UWXY
**6** BEGH**K**(N 1,5km)O

💬 A friendly and peaceful family campsite on the edge of extensive woodlands that continue into Belgium. Good, heated toilet facilities.

🚗 A58 exit 10 to N269 direction Reusel. Follow camping signs beyond Hilvarenbeek at Esbeek.

CC € **16** *29/3-29/5   11/6-13/7   30/8-27/10*    📐 **N 51°28'00'' E 05°07'37''**

---

## Hilvarenbeek, NL-5081 NJ / Noord-Brabant    ♿ 🛜 iD   **442**

🔺 Vakantiepark Beekse Bergen
📧 Beekse Bergen 1
☎ +31 1 35 49 11 00
🔓 29/3 - 3/11
@ info@beeksebergen.nl

75ha 413T(100m²) 6-10A CEE

**1** ACD**F**IJKLPQ
**2** ACDFLRSVWXY
**3** ABF**F**HJKNQRUWZ
**4** (**A** 1/5-1/8) (F+H 🔓) J
   (Q+S+T+U+V+X+Y+Z 🔓)
**5** **AB**DEFGIJKLMNOPUWXYZ
**6** ABCEGHJM(N 4km)OSTUV

💬 A camping holiday at Beekse Bergen Holiday Park will feel like a holiday with a touch of Africa. The fields are named after African animals, which can be seen in the Beekse Bergen Safari Park next door, and countries. The site has modern toilet facilities which are partially heated.

🚗 N65 Den Bosch-Tilburg. A65 exit Beekse Bergen. A58 Breda-Eindhoven. Follow 'Beekse Bergen' signs.

CC € **14** *29/3-18/4   5/5-23/5   11/6-5/7   2/9-11/10*    📐 **N 51°31'42'' E 05°07'29''**

---

## Hoeven, NL-4741 SG / Noord-Brabant    ⊗ ♿ 🛜 iD   **443**

🔺 Molecaten Park Bosbad Hoeven
📧 Oude Antwerpsepostbaan 81b
☎ +31 1 65 50 25 70
🔓 29/3 - 31/10
@ bosbadhoeven@molecaten.nl

56ha 220T(110-160m²) 10A CEE

**1** ACDEIJKLMOPRS
**2** BDFGLRSVWXY
**3** ABCDGHJK**M**QRUW
**4** (C 27/4-1/9) (F+H 🔓) IJM
   (Q+R+T 🔓)
   (Y+Z 1/4-1/9,12/10-27/10)
**5** **AB**DFGIJKLMNO**PQ**UWXY
**6** ACEGH**K**(N 2,5km)OSTV

💬 Wonderfully wooded campsite for the whole family! As campsite guest you have free entry to the 'Splesj' (Splash) water park (May to early September). Cycling and walking close by. The camping fields with comfort pitches are beautifully laid out and surrounded by trees. The site also has an indoor swimming pool, tennis court, large playground and a restaurant.

🚗 A58 Roosendaal-Breda, exit 20 St. Willebrord (take note, SatNav may differ). Direction Hoeven. Follow signs.

CC € **18** *29/3-18/4   5/5-28/5   11/6-9/7   26/8-31/10*    📐 **N 51°34'11'' E 04°33'42''**

### Lierop/Someren, NL-5715 RE / Noord-Brabant

⛺ Camping De Somerense Vennen
🏠 Philipsbosweg 7
☎ +31 4 92 33 12 16
📅 29/3 - 27/10
@ info@somerensevennen.nl

10ha 139T(100-150m²) 6-16A CEE

**1** ACDGIJKLMPQ
**2** BFRVWXY
**3** ABCFGHJNRU
**4** (F+H+T+U+X+Y+Z 19/4-29/9)
**5** ABCDEFGHIJMNPUWXYZ
**6** ACEGKM(N 2km)S

💬 Attractive quality site for families and lovers of the quiet, with spacious pitches on the edge of a forest. Beautiful, heated indoor pool with separate toddlers' pool, indoor playground and attractive restaurant and snack bar. Located in a delightful natural area with walking, mountain biking, riding and cycling, in a cycle-route network. Comfort pitch 16A and cable TV for extra charge.

🚗 A67 Eindhoven-Venlo, exit 35 Someren. In Someren dir Lierop. Follow signs.

CC € 18 29/3-26/4 6/5-29/5 11/6-5/7 22/8-27/10 | N 51°24'00'' E 05°40'35''

---

### Luyksgestel, NL-5575 XP / Noord-Brabant

⛺ Vakantiecentrum De Zwarte Bergen
🏠 Zwartebergendreef 1
☎ +31 4 97 54 13 73
📅 30/3 - 28/9
@ info@zwartebergen.nl

25,5ha 227T(100-120m²) 6A CEE

**1** ADGIJKLMNOPRS
**2** BFLRVWXY
**3** ABFGHJKMNQRU
**4** (C+H 29/5-25/8) (Q 🔲)
  (R 6/7-25/8) (T 27/4-29/9)
  (X+Y+Z 27/4-28/9)
**5** ABDEFGIJKLMNOPQUWX
**6** ACEGHKM(N 3km)OS

💬 The spacious open camping pitches are located in the middle of the pinewoods in Brabant. A cycle track runs past the campsite. Close to the Belgian border. There is a holiday atmosphere here even outside the high season.

🚗 A67 exit Eersel. At roundabout exit Bergeijk. Follow signs.

CC € 20 30/3-29/5 11/6-6/7 24/8-28/9 | N 51°17'29'' E 05°17'42''

---

### Mierlo, NL-5731 XN / Noord-Brabant

⛺ Boscamping 't Wolfsven
🏠 Patrijslaan 4
☎ +31 4 92 66 16 61
📅 29/3 - 27/10
@ receptie.wolfsven@roompot.nl

67ha 120T(100-120m²) 6A CEE

**1** ACDFIJKLMOPQ
**2** ABDFGLMRVWXY
**3** BCFGHJKLMNQRUWZ
**4** (F+H 🔲) K
  (S+T+U+X+Y+Z 🔲)
**5** ABDFGIJMNPQUWXY
**6** ADEGHKLM(N 2km)OSUV

💬 Family campsite with comfortable pitches in the woods. Have fun in the natural pool and indoor swimming pool. Amenities open all season.

🚗 A2 to Eindhoven. Then A67 to Venlo. Exit 34 Geldrop, direction Geldrop, then Mierlo. In Mierlo signs Wolfsven are posted.

CC € 14 29/3-19/4 12/5-29/5 11/6-9/7 26/8-27/10 | N 51°26'20'' E 05°35'25''

## Netersel, NL-5534 AP / Noord-Brabant 📶 🆔

🔺 Camping De Couwenberg
📧 De Ruttestraat 9A
☎ +31 4 97 68 22 33
📅 1/1 - 31/12
@ info@decouwenberg.nl

8ha 97T(80-100m²) 4-6A CEE

**1** ADGIJKLMOPRS
**2** FLRVWXY
**3** BFHJRUW
**4** (C+H 1/5-15/9) (Q 🔑)
  (T+X 19/4-5/5,6/7-18/8)
  (Z 19/4-29/9)
**5** ABDEFGIJKLMNPUWXZ
**6** AEGJKM(N 5km)OV

💬 Welcoming family campsite with heated outdoor pool. Surrounded by forests. Heath and fens in direct vicinity. (De The Utrecht estate). Excellent for cycling. 20 minutes (by car) from Safari and recreation park Beekse Bergen.

🚗 A58 exit 10 Hilvarenbeek, take the direction of Reusel. Reaching Lage Mierde, go to Netersel. Coming from A67 to Antwerpen, Belgium: exit 29 Hapert/Bladel, direction of Bladel. Then exit Bladel-Netersel. Follow the signs.

CC € 18 1/1-5/7 22/8-31/12 7=6

🛰 N 51°24'47'' E 05°11'59''

---

## Nijnsel/St. Oedenrode, NL-5492 TL / Noord-Brabant 📶 🆔

🔺 Landschapscamping De Graspol
📧 Bakkerpad 17
☎ +31 4 99 33 82 29
📅 1/3 - 1/10
@ info@campingdegraspol.nl

2,5ha 50T(100-200m²) 6-16A CEE

**1** ADFIJKLPST
**2** CFRVWXY
**3** FGHIJKUVW
**4** (Q+Z 🔑)
**5** ABDGHIJKLMNOPUWXY
**6** ABCDEGKL(N 2km)OSV

💬 A beautiful, spacious, rural campsite for the active nature lover. Bordering a nature reserve and the River Dommel. Luxurious toilet facilities and a warm welcome. Covered bicycle storage available. CampingCard ACSI pitches are car-free. Supplement for comfort pitch. Pets are only allowed on some of the comfort pitches.

🚗 A50 exit St. Oedenrode/Nijnsel, direction Nijnsel. Then follow signs.

CC € 20 1/3-29/5 10/6-15/7 1/9-1/10

🛰 N 51°32'52'' E 05°29'12''

---

## Nispen/Roosendaal, NL-4709 PB / Noord-Brabant 🚫 📶 🆔

🔺 Camping Zonneland
📧 Turfvaartsestraat 4-6
☎ +31 1 65 36 54 29
📅 16/3 - 27/10
@ info@zonneland.nl

15ha 54T(100-130m²) 10A CEE

**1** ACDEIJKLMOPQ
**2** BFRSVXY
**3** BJNRUVW
**4** (C 1/5-1/9) (R 1/5-27/10)
**5** ABDEGIJMPRUXYZ
**6** CDEGHK(N 3,5km)STV

💬 This campsite is close to the Dutch-Belgian border and has spacious pitches in the woods or in the fields. You can take enjoyable trips out on foot or by bike in the woods or heaths close by.

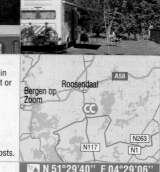

🚗 A58 exit 24 Nispen. Follow N262 until sign posts.

CC € 18 16/3-30/6 19/8-27/10

🛰 N 51°29'40'' E 04°29'06''

## Oirschot, NL-5688 MB / Noord-Brabant

📶 🆔 **450**

🔺 Camping de Bocht
🏠 Oude Grintweg 69
☎ +31 4 99 55 08 55
📅 1/1 - 31/12
@ info@campingdebocht.nl

1,8ha 31T(100m²) 6-10A CEE

**1** ADF**IJ**LPQ
**2** FRVWXY
**3** ABF**H**JK**OR**T**U**
**4** (B+G 1/7-31/8)
  (T+U+X+Z 📅)
**5** **AB**DFGIJKLMNO**PQ**UW
  XYZ
**6** ACDEGHKM(N 1km)OSV

💬 Enjoy old-fashioned relaxation in Brabant. Heathland, woods, fens, country estates. Near historical Oirschot. Wonderful area with extensive walking and cycling. Spacious comfort pitches. Convenient toilet facilities. A good restaurant with patio and skittle alley.

🚗 A58 exit 8 Oirschot direction Oirschot, turn right at 4th roundabout. On the left after 800m. Or A2 exit 26 direction Boxtel, over roundabout, left towards Oirschot. After 8 km on the right.

CC € 20  1/1-29/5  11/6-5/7  22/8-31/12    📍 N 51°31'01'' E 05°18'28''

---

## Oirschot, NL-5688 GP / Noord-Brabant

🚹🚺 ♿ 📶 🆔 **451**

🔺 Vakantiepark Latour
🏠 Bloemendaal 7
☎ +31 4 99 57 56 25
📅 29/3 - 1/10
@ latour@kempenrecreatie.nl

7,3ha 60T(100-120m²) 6-10A CEE

**1** ACD**G**IJKLMPQ
**2** FGLRVWXY
**3** ABF**G**HJ**M**NR**VW**
**4** (C 1/5-31/8) (F+H 📅) JKLN
  (T 20/4-11/5,6/7-17/8)
  (Z 7/7-31/8)
**5** **AB**CDEFGHIJKLMNOPQU
  WXYZ
**6** ACEGHK(N 1,5km)OSV

💬 Nicely landscaped, quiet family campsite, partially car-free, with mostly tourist pitches. Located in a cycling and walking area near the historic village of Oirschot. Large indoor and outdoor swimming pools next to the campsite, free for guests. Full HD television connection. Comfort pitches for 2 Euros extra.

🚗 On A58, take exit Oirschot. Follow the Latour camping sign.

CC € 20  29/3-5/7  22/8-1/10  7=6, 14=11    📍 N 51°29'47'' E 05°19'12''

---

## Oisterwijk, NL-5062 TP / Noord-Brabant

📶 ✿ 🆔 **452**

🔺 Cambiance Vakantiepark
  De Reebok
🏠 Duinenweg 4
☎ +31 1 35 28 23 09
📅 1/1 - 31/12
@ info@dereebok.nl

8ha 90T(80-100m²) 16A CEE

**1** ABCD**F**IJKLOPRS
**2** BFRSX
**3** BD**F**GHIJKNR**T**U
**4** (Q+R+T+U 1/4-31/10) (Y 📅)
**5** **AB**DFGIJKLMNPRUWXYZ
**6** ACDEGHJKM(N 2,7km)OS

💬 A friendly holiday park in a top location in a green oasis of woods, fens and heathland. Situated within the Den Bosch, Tilburg, Eindhoven triangle, with Oisterwijk as its lively heart. This is a stylish town with about 50 outdoor cafes and many exclusive boutiques and shops.

🚗 In Oisterwijk follow signs to the recreation centre. Watch out for the street named Duinenweg.

CC € 18  1/1-26/4  4/5-29/5  11/6-5/7  26/8-31/12    📍 N 51°34'24'' E 05°13'56''

## Oisterwijk, NL-5062 TE / Noord-Brabant

♿ 🛜 ✿ iD **453**

🏕 Camping Cambiance
   Streekpark Klein Oisterwijk
✉ Oirschotsebaan 6
☎ +31 1 35 28 20 59
🔓 1/1 - 31/12
@ info@kleinoisterwijk.nl

13ha 198T(100-120m²) 10A CEE

**1** ACD**F**IJKLPRS
**2** ABDFLMRSVWXY
**3** ABCD**FGH**IJN**Q**RU**WZ**
**4** (C+H 29/5-28/8) M
   (Q+R+U+X 1/4-26/9) (Y 🔌)
   (Z 1/4-26/9)
**5** **AB**DFGIJKLMNOPQRUW
   XYZ
**6** AEGH**K**M(N 3km)OSUV

💬 A friendly family campsite in a woodland setting.
Restaurant with indoor play area. Lovely area for
walking and cycling.

🚗 A58 exit Oirschot direction Oisterwijk.
A58 Eindhoven-Tilburg and N65 's-Hertogenbosch-
Tilburg, exit Oirschot direction Oisterwijk. Follow
signs to the other leisure facilities. Stay on the
'Oirschotsebaan'. Using SatNav: from N65 take
Oisterwijk exit.

CC € **18** 1/1-26/4 4/5-29/5 11/6-5/7 26/8-31/12   📐 N 51°33'13'' E 05°13'32''

## Oisterwijk, NL-5062 TM / Noord-Brabant

♿ 🛜 iD **454**

🏕 Natuurkampeerterrein
   Morgenrood
✉ Scheibaan 15
☎ +31 8 80 99 09 67
🔓 1/1 - 31/12
@ prmorgenrood@gmail.com

3ha 75T(100-150m²) 4-6A CEE

**1** AD**G**IJKLNPQ
**2** BFLRSWXY
**3** AB**F**GHJKNR
**5** **AB**DFGIJMNOPUWZ
**6** ADEHIK(N 4km)

💬 Camping in the countryside. Peaceful, spacious
grounds in open woodland. Ideal for walking and
cycling. Free access to the Kampina nature reserve.
Part of the campsite includes the Nivon natural
camping grounds. Dogs permitted only on one part of
the campsite. New toilet facilities since 2015.

🚗 In Oisterwijk follow signs to the recreational
amenities as far as the Scheibaan. Morgenrood is
located on this road, no. 15.

CC € **18** 1/5-29/5 11/6-29/6 2/9-31/12   📐 N 51°34'05'' E 05°14'07''

## Oosterhout, NL-4904 SG / Noord-Brabant

🛜 iD **455**

🏕 Camping De Katjeskelder
✉ Katjeskelder 1
☎ +31 1 62 45 35 39
🔓 29/3 - 27/10
@ receptie.katjeskelder@
   roompot.nl

28ha 102T(80m²) 4A CEE

**1** ACD**F**IJNPRS
**2** BFRSVXY
**3** AB**F**HIJKLN**Q**R**T**U
**4** (C 26/4-26/10) (F+H 🔌) J
   (Q+S+T+U+X+Y+Z 🔌)
**5** **AB**DEFGIJKLMNOPRUWZ
**6** AFGHJKLM(N 3km)OSTV

💬 A friendly camping ground surrounded by
woods. Own large recreation park, large playground
and tropical leisure pool. Lovely surroundings for
walking and cycling trips. There are no motorhome
pitches available at this campsite.

🚗 A27 exit 17 Oosterhout-Zuid. Follow signs to
Katjeskelder.

CC € **16** 29/3-19/4 12/5-29/5 11/6-9/7 26/8-27/10   📐 N 51°37'44'' E 04°49'57''

## Sint Anthonis, NL-5845 EB / Noord-Brabant

🏕 Ardoer vak.centrum De Ullingse Bergen
🏠 Bosweg 36
☎ +31 4 85 38 85 66
📅 1/4 - 29/9
@ ullingsebergen@ardoer.com

**456**

11ha 113T(100-150m²) 10-16A CEE

1 ACDEIJKLMPST
2 BFLRSVWXY
3 ABCGHIJKMRU
4 (C+H 27/4-10/9) J(Q+T 🔑) (U 28/4-23/9) (Y 🔑)
5 **AB**DFGIJKLMNPUWXYZ
6 ABCEGH**K**(N 1,5km)OST

💬 Take advantage of the peace and quiet of the countryside. There is extensive walking and cycling right from the campsite, over heathland and sand drifts. The perfect site for young families (with children up to about 10 years), senior citizens and nature lovers. Camp in a small field or in one of the quiet avenues. All pitches are separated by greenery.

🚗 A73 exit St. Anthonis. Follow the signs in St. Anthonis.

Genneр
N264
A77
A73
N271
N272
N277
Gemert
Venray

CC € 18 1/4-29/5 3/6-7/6 11/6-7/7 24/8-29/9 | N 51°37'39'' E 05°51'42''

## Sint Hubert, NL-5454 NA / Noord-Brabant

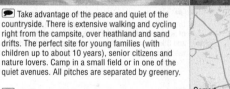

🏕 Camping Van Rossum's Troost
🏠 Oude Wanroijseweg 24
☎ +31 4 85 47 01 93
📅 30/3 - 29/9
@ info@rossumstroost.nl

**457**

5,5ha 45T(90-120m²) 6A CEE

1 ABD**G**IJKLNPRS
2 BFGRVX
3 BGHIJK**M**NOPQRUV
4 (A 27/4-5/5,27/7-18/8) (G 27/4-5/5,20/7-18/8) (Q 🔑) (T+Z 20/7-18/8)
5 **AB**CEFGIJMOP**Q**UXYZ
6 ACEGH**K**(N 0,8km)OST

💬 A welcoming family campsite located on the edge of the Molenheide nature reserve. 260 hectares with plenty of cycling and walking (free routes at the campsite). Spaciously laid out grounds with lovely touring and comfort pitches, clean toilet facilities with large showers and wireless internet.

🚗 A73 exit Haps direction Mill. After St. Hubert direction Wanroij. Follow signs.

Schaijk
N271
N321
Genneр
A73
Uden
N277
CC
Boxmeer
N272

CC € 16 30/3-29/5 16/6-7/7 24/8-29/9 14=12 | N 51°40'09'' E 05°47'48''

## Soerendonk, NL-6027 RD / Noord-Brabant

🏕 Recreatiepark Slot Cranendonck
🏠 Strijperdijk 9
☎ +31 4 95 59 16 52
📅 30/3 - 29/9
@ info@slotcranendonck.nl

**458**

17,8ha 208T(100m²) 6A CEE

1 ACD**G**IJKLMPRS
2 FGRWXY
3 ABC**F**GHIJKLMN**Q**RUW
4 (B 15/5-1/9) (F+H 🔑) J (S+T+U+Y+Z 🔑)
5 **AB**DEFGIJKLMNOPUWXY
6 ADFGHJ**K**M(N 5km)OSUV

💬 A friendly Brabant family campsite in natural surroundings on the edge of the Kempen and De Peel. Grassy camping pitches surrounded by woodland and with playground equipment in each field. Lovely indoor and outdoor swimming pool. Good restaurant with an attractive patio and extended opening times, also out of season.

🚗 Motorway A2 Eindhoven-Weert, exit Soerendonk. Direction Soerendonk. Follow signs.

Veldhoven
N69
Valkenswaard
N266
CC
A2
N71
N76
N564
N292

CC € 18 30/3-26/4 5/5-30/5 11/6-6/7 23/8-29/9 | N 51°19'11'' E 05°34'29''

## Someren, NL-5712 PD / Noord-Brabant ⚥ 📶 iD ④⑤⑨

🏕 Camping De Kuilen
📧 Kuilvenweg 15
☎ +31 4 93 49 45 82
⏱ 1/3 - 31/10
@ info@campingdekuilen.nl

3ha 45T(120m²) 6-10A CEE

**1** ADG IJKLM**PQ**
**2** FRVWX
**3** A EHJNU
**4** (Z 🔒)
**5** **AB**DGIJMNO**P**X
**6** ACEGHK(N 3km)V

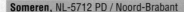

💬 A small-scale and friendly family campsite. Unusually attractive and quiet location on the edge of an extensive nature reserve. Next to a golf course and 3 km from Someren with its shops. Pleasant cafe with terrace.

🚗 A67 exit 34 towards Heeze, then towards Someren. Take a right before Someren, signposted.

Helmond
Eindhoven  N612  A67
Geldrop
CC  N279
A2  N266
N275

CC € ⑯ 1/3-1/7 18/8-31/10    📡 N 51°22'39'' E 05°40'19''

---

## St. Oedenrode, NL-5491 TE / Noord-Brabant 📶 iD ④⑥⓪

🏕 Camping De Kienehoef
📧 Zwembadweg 35-37
☎ +31 4 13 47 28 77
⏱ 1/4 - 29/9
@ info@kienehoef.nl

15ha 160T(80-100m²) 10A CEE

**1** ACD**G**IJLPQ
**2** ADFLMRVWXY
**3** AB**F**GHJMNRUWZ
**4** (C+H 20/4-1/9) (Q+R 🔒)
    (T+U+X+Z 20/4-1/9)
**5** **AB**DFGIJKLMNPQUWXZ
**6** ACDEGJKM(N 1km)

💬 Atmospheric and beautifully landscaped campsite, bordering an attractive recreational park with a restaurant and petting farm. Close to the characterful village of St. Oedenrode. Ample opening hours in the catering facilities, also outside of school holidays.

🚗 The campsite is accessible from the A2 (exit 27) and A50 (exit 9) St. Oedenrode. Towards Schijndel after the built-up area 1st left, then 2nd left. Campsite is signposted.

Uden
Vught
Schijndel  Veghel
A2  N279  A50
CC
N615
A58

CC € ⑳ 1/4-29/5 11/6-5/7 24/8-29/9 7=6, 14=11, 21=15    📡 N 51°34'39'' E 05°26'46''

---

## Udenhout, NL-5071 RR / Noord-Brabant ⚥ 📶 iD ④⑥①

🏕 Recreatiepark Duinhoeve
📧 Oude Bossche Baan 4
☎ +31 1 35 11 13 63
⏱ 30/3 - 30/9
@ info@duinhoeve.nl

9ha 80T(100-120m²) 6A CEE

**1** ACD**G**IJLPRS
**2** FRSVWX
**3** ABJKNRU**V**
**4** (C+H 25/4-31/8)
    (Q 27/4-5/5,1/7-1/9)
    (R 1/4-25/9)
    (T+U+X 27/4-5/5,15/7-15/8)
**5** **AB**EFGHIJLMNO**P**QUW
    XYZ
**6** ADEGH**IK**(N 4km)SV

💬 Recreatiepark Duinhoeve is a quiet and welcoming family campsite on the edge of the nature area Loonse en Drunense Duinen. Ideal starting point for cycling and walking tours. Efteling (amusement park) 7 km, Beekse Bergen (safari park) 20 km.

🚗 A58 Breda-Tilburg-Den Bosch, exit Udenhout (N65). From Waalwijk N261 direction Efteling. Pass Efteling and take exit Loon op Zand. Follow first the major road, then the camping signs.

's-Hertogenbosch
A59
CC  N261  N65
N260
Tilburg

CC € ⑱ 6/5-10/5 13/5-21/5 11/6-5/7 26/8-30/9    📡 N 51°38'11'' E 05°07'05''

## Ulicoten/Baarle Nassau, NL-5113 BD / Noord-Brabant

🛰 iD **462**

🔺 Camping De Ponderosa BV
✉ Maaijkant 23-26
☎ +31 1 35 19 93 91
🗓 1/4 - 3/11
@ info@ponderosa.nl

22ha 71T(100-120m²) 10A CEE

**1** ABD**G**IJKLMOPRS
**2** RSVWXY
**3** ABD**F**GHJKNRU
**4** (F+H 🅿) J
(Q+R+T+U+V+X+Y 🅿)
(Z 1/7-1/9)
**5** **AB**FGI**J**MNOPQUWXYZ
**6** ABFGHK(N 5km)ORSUV

💬 A lovely, luxuriously appointed and friendly family campsite. Swimming pool. Touring pitches clearly separated from the permanent pitches.

🚗 A16 Breda, exit towards Ulvenhout/Baarle Nassau, then follow signs. Follow camping signs in Ulicoten or Chaam. Do not drive via the Fransebaan!

(CC) € **20**  1/4-18/4  6/5-29/5  11/6-14/7  1/9-3/11  7=6

🛰 **N 51°28'13'' E 04°52'45''**

Bavel
A58
A16 · N639 · N260 · N630
E19
Meer
A1 · N14
Hoogstraten · N260 · N12
N118

---

## Valkenswaard, NL-5556 VB / Noord-Brabant

🛰 iD **463**

🔺 Oostappen Vakantiepark
Brugse Heide
✉ Maastrichterweg 183
☎ +31 4 02 01 83 04
🗓 6/4 - 28/10
@ info@vakantieparkbrugseheide.nl

7ha 75T(81-100m²) 6A CEE

**1** AD**G**IJKLMPQ
**2** FLRVWXY
**3** ABC**F**GHJKNQRU
**4** (B+G 27/4-1/9)
(Q+T+X+Z 5/7-1/9)
**5** **AB**DEFGIJKLMNPQUWXY
**6** ACEGHJM(N 1,5km)S

💬 Well equipped campsite in woody surroundings with a big hiking and cycling area. Plenty of sights within cycling distance.

🚗 Via A2 exit Valkenswaard to Achel. Follow the signs.

(CC) € **12**  27/4-29/5  10/6-5/7  2/9-28/10

🛰 **N 51°19'44'' E 05°27'45''**

Veldhoven
A67 · N69
Valkenswaard
A2
Lommel · N71

---

## Veldhoven, NL-5504 PZ / Noord-Brabant

🛰 iD **464**

🔺 Vakantiepark Witven
✉ Witvenseweg 6
☎ +31 4 02 30 00 43
🗓 1/4 - 29/9
@ info@witven.nl

13,3ha 117T(80-120m²) 6-10A CEE

**1** ACD**F**IJKLMNPRS
**2** ADFLRVWXY
**3** ABD**F**GHJK**M**N**Q**RUWZ
**4** (Q+R+T+U+X+Y+Z 🅿)
**5** **AB**DFGIJKLMNPQ**S**UW
XYZ
**6** ACDEGHJK(N 2km)OV

💬 A campsite situated near a recreational lake and restaurant just outside Veldhoven, surrounded by countryside. Private toilet facilities can be rented. Use of the indoor pool in Veldhoven (3 km) is included. Wifi is not included.

🚗 Randweg (Ring) Eindhoven N2 exit 32 direction Veldhoven. Then follow signs.

(CC) € **20**  1/4-29/5  3/6-7/6  11/6-14/6  16/6-5/7  22/8-29/9

🛰 **N 51°23'42'' E 05°24'43''**

N395
Eindhoven
A67 · N69
N284 · Valkenswaard
A2

## Veldhoven/Zandoerle, NL-5506 LA / Noord-Brabant 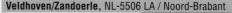 **465**

▲ Vakantiepark Molenvelden
✉ Banstraat 25
☎ +31 4 02 05 23 84
📅 29/3 - 1/10
@ molenvelden@
  kempenrecreatie.nl

14ha 61T(80-100m²) 10A CEE

**1** ACDG IJKLPQ
**2** FRVWXY
**3** ABFGHJNQRUW
**4** (C+H 1/5-30/9) M
  (T+U+X+Y+Z 🔒)
**5** ABDEFGHIJKLMNOPQU
  WXY
**6** ACEGHJ(N 3km)S

💬 A family campsite with nice, open pitches, located in woodland. Rural area with many walking and cycling opportunities. The restaurant and cafe with its lovely patio have extended opening hours.

🚗 N2 ring road Eindhoven, exit number 31 Veldhoven. Follow signs.

CC € 20  29/3-5/7  22/8-1/10  7=6, 14=11  ▲ N 51°24'30'' E 05°21'27''

---

## Vessem, NL-5512 NW / Noord-Brabant  **466**

▲ Eurocamping Vessem
✉ Zwembadweg 1
☎ +31 4 97 59 12 14
📅 23/3 - 1/10
@ info@eurocampingvessem.com

50ha 450T(120-200m²) 6A CEE

**1** ACDG IJKLMOPQ
**2** BFGLRWXY
**3** ABDFHJKLMNQRUW
**4** (B+G 15/5-1/9)
  (R+T+X+Z 1/7-31/8)
**5** ABCFGIJMNOPUWXYZ
**6** ACDEGKM(N 1,5km)

💬 A unique campsite located in the heart of Brabant. Large wooded grounds with plenty of space and attractively laid out fields. Many cycling and walking opportunities. Large fishing lake surrounded by woods. Special motorhome pitches in front of the campsite.

🚗 A58 exit 8 Oirschot direction Middelbeers, then Vessem. Campsite signposted on Vessem-Hoogeloon road.

CC € 18  23/3-29/5  2/6-7/6  11/6-12/7  29/8-1/10  ▲ N 51°24'38'' E 05°16'35''

---

## Vinkel, NL-5382 JX / Noord-Brabant  **467**

▲ Vakantiepark Dierenbos
✉ Vinkeloord 1
☎ +31 7 35 34 35 36
📅 29/3 - 3/11
@ info@dierenbos.nl

55ha 390T(115-125m²) 16A CEE

**1** ABCDFIJKLOPQ
**2** ABDFLRSWXY
**3** ABDFGHIJKLNQRTUWZ
**4** (F+H 🔒) J
  (Q+S+T+U+Y+Z 🔒)
**5** ABDEFGIJKLMNOPQUW
  XYZ
**6** ACEGHK(N 3km)OSU

💬 At Dierenbos Holiday Park you can have a wonderful holiday among the abundant woodland wildlife on large camping fields. There is plenty to see and do for young and old! You can enjoy fun in the water, fantastic nature walks and exciting bowling evenings.

🚗 A59, exit 51. From there sign posted.

CC € 12  29/3-18/4  5/5-23/5  11/6-5/7  2/9-11/10  ▲ N 51°42'17'' E 05°25'48''

## Wanroij, NL-5446 PW / Noord-Brabant ♿ 🛜 iD **468**

🏔 Camping Vakantiepark De Bergen
📧 Campinglaan 1
☎ +31 4 85 33 54 50
🗓 29/3 - 27/10
@ info@debergen.nl

92ha 300T(80-125m²) 10-16A CEE

**1** ADF IJKLMPQ
**2** ADFLMRVWXY
**3** ABCDGHJKLMNPQRUWZ
**4** J(S 🔒)
  (T+U+V+X+Y+Z 6/7-1/9)
**5** ABDEFGIJMNPQUWXYZ
**6** ACDEGHJKM(N 2km)OSU

💬 Great camping in the countryside. A beautiful family park with extensive and well-maintained campsite amenities. Various places for food and drink where you can enjoy the warm and hospitable atmosphere. A large swimming lake which is great for all ages, including the little ones, and an indoor playground for lots of grand adventures.

🚗 A73 take exit Boxmeer towards St. Anthonis and then turn right to Wanroij. The campsite is clearly signposted.

(CC) € 16 29/3-29/5 11/6-13/7 30/8-27/10 🧭 N 51°38'26'' E 05°48'40''

---

## Afferden, NL-5851 AG / Limburg ♿ 🛜 iD **469**

🏔 Camping Klein Canada
📧 Dorpsstraat 1
☎ +31 4 85 53 12 23
🗓 29/3 - 28/10
@ info@kleincanada.nl

12ha 135T(100-120m²) 6-10A CEE

**1** ADF IJKLMNPRS
**2** FGLRSUWX
**3** ABDEFGJKLMNRUW
**4** (A 26/4-19/5,5/7-25/8)
  (B 26/4-31/8)(F+G 22/3-27/10)
  JN (Q+R+T+X+Y+Z
  26/4-19/5,5/7-25/8)
**5** ABDEFGIJLMNOPQRSTU
  WXYZ
**6** BCDFGHK(N 0,5km)OSTUV

💬 Spaciously laid out family campsite with many amenities on the edge of the National Park 'De Maasduinen'. Each of the various fields has its own character. A number of pitches have their own toilet facilities. Some are close to the fishing lake. Catering available in the grounds.

🚗 From Nijmegen A73 exit A77 (Köln), then N271 turn left before Afferden. From Venlo turn right beyond Afferden.

(CC) € 16 29/3-29/5 11/6-13/7 30/8-27/10 🧭 N 51°38'20'' E 06°00'15''

---

## Afferden, NL-5851 EK / Limburg 🛜 iD **470**

🏔 Camping Roland
📧 Rimpelt 33
☎ +31 4 85 53 14 31
🗓 1/1 - 31/12
@ info@campingroland.nl

11ha 89T(80-120m²) 6A CEE

**1** ADGIJKLMNOPQ
**2** FLRVX
**3** BCFGHJKNQRUW
**4** (C+H 27/4-20/9) J
  (Q+R+S+T+U+Y 1/4-20/9)
  (Z 27/4-5/5,7/7-26/8)
**5** ABDFGJLMNOPRUWXYZ
**6** BCDEGHK(N 1km)OSTUV

💬 A luxurious family campsite with a delightful location in the heart of the Maasduinen national park. You can walk or cycle to your heart's content around these beautiful woods, pastures and lakes which are located between the River Maas and the German border.

🚗 A73 (Nijmegen-Venlo), at the junction Rijkevoort drive via the A77 to exit 2, route N271 (Nieuw-Bergen/Afferden). After approximately 5 km, direction Venlo. Follow the signs.

(CC) € 16 1/1-28/5 11/6-4/7 26/8-31/12 🧭 N 51°38'04'' E 06°02'03''

## Arcen, NL-5944 EX / Limburg

♿ 📶 **iD** (471)

🏕 Klein Vink
🏠 Klein Vink 4
☎ +31 7 74 73 25 25
📅 1/1 - 31/12
@ receptie.kleinvink@roompot.nl

17ha 310T(80-90m²) 10A CEE

**1** ABCDGIJKLMOPQ
**2** ADFLMRSVWXY
**3** ABCGHJKLMNQRU**V**WZ
**4** (F+H 🅗) **KLNOP**
(Q+S+T+X+Y+Z 🅗)
**5** **AB**CDFGHIJKLMNOPUW
XYZ
**6** ACDEGHKLM(N 0,1km)OST
UVX

💬 A lovely campsite with a nice atmosphere. Very well taken care of. There are excellent thermal baths on the grounds. The recreational lake is wonderful for swimming. The entertainment team is out in force during the school holidays. Separate grassy spots for motorhomes.

🚐 N271 Nijmegen-Venlo. Well signposted.

CC € **14** 1/1-19/4 12/5-29/5 11/6-9/7 29/8-31/12

📍 N 51°29'46'' E 06°11'04''

---

## Baarlo, NL-5991 NV / Limburg

🚻 📶 **iD** (472)

🏕 Oostappen Vakantiepark
De Berckt
🏠 Napoleonsbaan Noord 4
☎ +31 7 74 77 72 22
📅 6/4 - 28/10
@ info@vakantieparkdeberckt.nl

40ha 281T(80-120m²) 10A CEE

**1** ACD**G**IJKLMOPQ
**2** BFGLRSWXY
**3** ABD**E**GHJKNQRU
**4** (F+H 🅗) IJKLN
(Q+S+T+U+X+Y+Z 🅗)
**5** **AB**DEFGIJKLMNOPQUW
XYZ
**6** CEGHJ**K**M(N 2km)STV

💬 A cheerful family campsite set in woodland with a beautiful leisure pool in a fairytale setting. There is also a lovely play castle outside for your enjoyment!

🚐 A73 exit Baarlo (N273). The campsite is located on the west side of the N273 (Napoleonsbaan) between Blerick and Baarlo
💬 A quiet, small-scale natural campsite, traffic-free

CC € **14** 27/4-29/5 10/6-5/7 2/9-28/10

📍 N 51°20'46'' E 06°06'20''

---

## Beesel, NL-5954 PB / Limburg

🚫 📶 **iD** (473)

🏕 Camping Petrushoeve
🏠 Heidenheimseweg 3
☎ +31 7 74 74 19 84
📅 15/3 - 15/10
@ info@campingpetrushoeve.nl

6ha 107T(120-140m²) 6-10A CEE

**1** ADEIJKLMNPQ
**2** BFRSVWXY
**3** AD**F**GHIJKLNRU
**4** (**A**+Q+V 🅗)
**5** **AB**DFGIJKLMNOPUWZ
**6** AEG**K**(N 4,5km)T

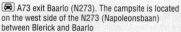

and pet-free, located in flat central Limburg between Roermond and Venlo. Very spacious with marked out pitches. Adjacent to the Meerlebroek nature protection area, the extensive Brachter Wald and Pieterpad. Varied surroundings for walking and cycling. Nearby Drakenrijk recreational lake.

🚐 From A73 exit 18 Reuver/Beesel. Then follow signs.

CC € **16** 15/3-29/5 3/6-7/6 10/6-5/7 22/8-15/10

📍 N 51°15'08'' E 06°04'22''

## Blitterswijck, NL-5863 AR / Limburg

**474**

⌂ Camping 't Veerhuys
✉ Veerweg 7
☎ +31 4 78 53 12 83
☷ 30/3 - 31/10
@ info@campingveerhuys.nl

2,8ha 75T(72-150m²) 10A CEE

**1** ACD**F**IJKLPQ
**2** CFJKLRSW
**3** ABF**G**HJKN**OP**RUWX
**4** (G 1/5-31/10)
　(Q+T+U+X+Y+Z ☷)
**5** **AB**CDFGIJLMN**P**UWXZ
**6** CDEGH**J**M(N 1km)QSTV

💬 Lovely campsite with heated toilet facilities on the River Maas, with a foot and cycle ferry that will take you across the river to the Maas Dunes National Park. The campsite cafe 'De Proeverij' with its adjoining 'Tante Jet' restaurant is recommended.

🚗 A73, exit 9 towards Wanssum. Turn right and keep left immediately at the roundabout in Wansssum. Follow the signs in direction Blitterswijck.

CC €**18** 30/3-28/5 11/6-5/7 23/8-30/10 7=6, 14=12, 21=18 📍 N 51°31'52'' E 06°07'05''

---

## Echt, NL-6102 RD / Limburg

**475**

⌂ Camping Marisheem
✉ Brugweg 89
☎ +31 4 75 48 14 58
☷ 1/4 - 30/9
@ info@marisheem.nl

12ha 95T(80-100m²) 4-10A CEE

**1** AD**G**IJKLPQ
**2** FGLRVWXY
**3** ABF**G**HJR
**4** (B+G 17/5-1/9) J
　(Q+T+Z 21/7-17/8)
**5** **AB**FGIJKLMNOPQUWZ
**6** ACGIK(N 2km)OSTV

💬 CampingCard ACSI is also valid during the early May, the Ascension and Pentecost (Whitsun) holidays. Rate includes one dog, max. 3 children up to 5 years, free showers and warm water, a pitch of ± 80-100 m² with free wifi! Marisheem is located in Echt, in central Limburg, 'the narrowest part of the Netherlands'. Lovely woodland cycling and walking routes.

🚗 A2 direction Maastricht. Exit 45 Echt. Follow Camping Marisheem signs.

CC €**18** 1/4-30/6 18/8-30/9 14=13, 21=19 📍 N 51°05'33'' E 05°54'40''

---

## Geijsteren/Maashees, NL-5823 CB / Limburg

**476**

⌂ Natuurkampeerterrein
　Landgoed Geijsteren
✉ Op den Berg 5a
☎ +31 4 78 53 26 01
☷ 5/4 - 28/10
@ info@
　campinglandgoedgeijsteren.nl

3ha 60T(80-100m²) 6A CEE

**1** AD**F**IJKLN**P**RS
**2** BCFKLMORSTVXY
**3** AEF**H**IJWX
**4** (Q 15/7-15/8)
**5** **AB**CDFGIJKLMNPQUW
**6** AEGK(N 2,5km)

💬 A small-scale country estate campsite, beautifully located on the River Maas close to the Pieterpad. Ideally suited to cycle and walking tours through the woods and wetlands and past places of interest such as the Rosmolen and the St. Willibrordus Chapel (1680).

🚗 A73, exit 8 Venray-Noord in direction Maashees. After 4 km exit at Geijsteren. 800m further turn left at the place name sign.

CC €**16** 5/4-26/4 6/5-28/5 11/6-5/7 2/9-27/10 📍 N 51°33'36'' E 06°02'30''

## Grubbenvorst, NL-5971 ND / Limburg ♀♂ 🛜 iD ④⑦⑦

🏕 Camping Californië
🏠 Horsterweg 23
☎ +31 7 73 66 20 49
🗓 15/3 - 15/10
@ info@limburgsecamping.nl

2ha 80T(100-200m²) 10-16A CEE

**1** ADGIJKLMNOPQ
**2** FRSUWXY
**3** AHJKU
**5** **AB**DGIJKLMNOPUWXYZ
**6** ACDFGJ(N 2km)

💬 Friendly family campsite with pitches around attractive ponds. The campsite is run by enthusiastic people. Behind the farmhouse it is surprisingly beautiful.

🚗 From A73, exit Grubbenvorst. Continue towards Grubbenvorst then follow camping signs. Well indicated.

CC € ⑭ 15/3-5/7 2/9-15/10     📍 N 51°25'13'' E 06°06'24''

---

## Gulpen, NL-6271 NP / Limburg 🛜 iD ④⑦⑧

🏕 Panorama Camping Gulperberg
🏠 Berghem 1
☎ +31 4 34 50 23 30
🗓 16/3 - 2/11
@ info@gulperberg.nl

7,9ha 266T(100-120m²) 10A CEE

**1** ADGIJKLMPQ
**2** FJKLRVWX
**3** BFGHIJKLNOPRU
**4** (A 28/4-6/5,2/7-30/8)
   (C+H 1/5-1/10) I
   (Q+R+S+T+U+V+Y+Z 🗓)
**5** **AB**DFGIJKLMNOPRUW
   XYZ
**6** ACDEGHK(N 2km)OSTVX

💬 A warm welcome to the Gulperberg for a high level of recreation with panoramic views. Centrally located for trips out to Maastricht, Valkenburg, Aachen and Liège. Free entry to the Mosaqua leisure pool in Gulpen.

🚗 Heerlen-Vaals, exit Gulpen. Left at last traffic lights in Gulpen, then follow signs. With SatNav: select post code then follow Landsraderweg to T junction, turn left. Campsite 200m on the right.

CC € ⑳ 1/4-19/4 12/5-29/5 2/6-7/6 10/6-14/6 17/6-6/7 1/9-1/11   📍 N 50°48'25'' E 05°53'39''

---

## Gulpen, NL-6271 PP / Limburg 🛜 iD ④⑦⑨

🏕 Terrassencamping Osebos
🏠 Euverem 1
☎ +31 4 34 50 16 11
🗓 30/3 - 3/11
@ info@osebos.nl

7ha 210T(100-120m²) 6-10A CEE

**1** ABDGIJKLPRS
**2** FGJKLRTVWX
**3** ABFHIJNRU
**4** (B+G 15/5-30/9)
   (Q+S+T+U+Y+Z 🗓)
**5** **AB**DEFGIJKLMNPQUW
   XYZ
**6** ABCEGK(N 1,5km)OS

💬 A campsite consisting of a series of terraces with a fantastic view over the hilly surroundings. The region has a unique micro-climate: more sun and warmth than on average in the rest of Holland. Comfort of high quality.

🚗 N278 Maastricht-Vaals. Just before Gulpen take the direction of Euverem/Beutenaken, first road on the right.

CC € ⑱ 30/3-27/4 5/5-28/5 2/6-5/7 22/8-3/11   📍 N 50°48'27'' E 05°52'15''

## Heel, NL-6097 NL / Limburg

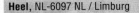

▲ Narvik HomeParc
Heelderpeel B.V.
🏠 De Peel 13
☎ +31 4 75 45 22 11
📅 29/3 - 4/11
@ info@heelderpeel.nl

**480**

55ha 160**T**(100m²) 10A CEE

**1** ACD**G**IJKLMNOPQ
**2** ADFLRSVX
**3** BGHJKMNQRUWZ
**4** (C 15/5-15/9) (Q+U 1/7-31/8)
(X+Z 🔲)
**5** **AB**DFGIJKLMNOPUWZ
**6** AEGHJ**K**(N 3km)STU

💬 A family campsite in Central Limburg. Plenty of cycling and walking opportunities in the vicinity. There are also plenty of watersports possibilities close by.

🚗 From Eindhoven A2, exit 41. On the N273 take direction Venlo. The campsite is signposted after ± 3 km on the left.

Weert · N562 · N279 · N273 · N280 · A73 · N292 · A2 CC Roermond · N292 · N762 · Maasbracht · N271 · N757 · N78 · N276 · N274

CC €**14** 29/3-5/7 23/8-4/11 📍 N 51°11'49'' E 05°52'31''

---

## Heerlen, NL-6413 TC / Limburg

▲ Camping Hitjesvijver
🏠 Willem Barentszweg 101
☎ +31 4 55 21 13 53
📅 1/1 - 31/12
@ info@hitjesvijver.nl

**481**

4,5ha 84**T**(90-100m²) 6-10A CEE

**1** AD**G**IJKLMNO**P**Q
**2** FGJLRUWXY
**3** ABF**G**HIJNRU
**4** (C+H 15/5-1/9) (Y 🔲)
(Z 12/7-12/8)
**5** **AB**DFGIJ**K**LMNO**P**UWZ
**6** ACDEGJ**K**(N 0,6km)OT

💬 Downtown campsite. Heated toilet facilities. Brasserie open all year Fr to Mo. Numerous opportunities to enjoy the beautiful South Limburg countryside. Visit many sights such as the historic cities of Maastricht, Aachen and Liège.

🚗 From Eindhoven follow signs A76 direction Heerlen, after Nuth take N281 to Heerlen exit Heerlen-Nrd. Left after exit, left at roundabout after McDonald's, then right at 1st roundabout. William Barentszweg. Site 800m on the left.

A2 · B221 · L410 · B56 · N276 · Geilenkirchen · A76 · Brunssum · L364 · Hoensbroek · CC · **Heerlen** · L47 · A79 · Herzogenrath · N595

CC €**18** 1/1-19/4 22/4-27/5 17/6-5/7 2/9-31/12 7=6, 14=11 📍 N 50°55'16'' E 05°57'26''

---

## Helden, NL-5988 NH / Limburg

▲ Ardoer Camping De
Heldense Bossen
🏠 De Heldense Bossen 6
☎ +31 7 73 07 24 76
📅 29/3 - 27/10
@ heldensebossen@ardoer.com

**482**

30ha 399**T**(80-120m²) 10A CEE

**1** AD**G**IJKLMOPQ
**2** BFLRVWXY
**3** BD**F**GHJKNRU
**4** (C 27/4-1/9) (F+H 🔲) JM
(Q+S+T+U+Y+Z 🔲)
**5** **AB**CDEFGHIJKLMNOPQU
WXYZ
**6** CEGHKM(N 2km)OSV

💬 A site with plenty of atmosphere and spacious pitches. A unique location in wooded surroundings with plenty of walking and cycling routes. The site has a heated indoor and outdoor pool. There is also a special playground, children's farm, boating lake, sports fields and an open air theatre.

🚗 From N277, Midden Peelweg, take exit Helden. From Helden direction Kessel. Turn left after 1 km. Campsite about 1 km further on.

A67 · Blerick · **Venlo** · N279 · CC · N562 · N273 · Brüggen · L373

CC €**16** 30/3-29/5 3/6-6/6 11/6-5/7 26/8-27/10 📍 N 51°19'05'' E 06°01'25''

## Hulsberg, NL-6336 AV / Limburg ♿ 🛜 iD **483**

🏕 Camping 't Hemelke
📧 Klimmenerweg 10
☎ +31 4 54 05 13 86
📅 1/4 - 30/9
@ info@hemelke.nl

7ha 330T(110-120m²) 6-10A CEE

**1** ADG IJLPQ
**2** FGIJLRVWXY
**3** ABDFGHIJNQRUV
**4** (B+G 20/4-15/9) J
(Q+R+T+Y 30/5-10/6,
6/7-25/8) (Z 📅)
**5** ABEFGIJKLMNOPUWZ
**6** ACDEGK(N 0,2km)OSTUV

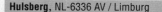

💬 A campsite with spacious pitches, where a long tourist tradition reflects itself in ambiance and hospitality.

🚗 From A2 exit A76 direction Heerlen. Exit Nuth. In Nuth direction Hulsberg. Campsite signposted in Hulsberg.

CC € **18** 1/4-27/4 5/5-29/5 3/6-7/6 11/6-6/7 26/8-30/9 ⛺ N 50°53'16'' E 05°51'46''

---

## Kelpen-Oler, NL-6037 NR / Limburg 🛜 iD **484**

🏕 Camping Geelenhoof
📧 Grathemerweg 16
☎ +31 4 95 65 18 58
📅 15/3 - 31/10
@ info@geelenhoof.nl

5ha 57T(120-150m²) 6-10A CEE

**1** ADFIJKLMNPRS
**2** FGRSVWX
**3** ABCFGHJKLNQRUW
**4** (Q+R 📅)
**5** ABCDFGHIJMNOPUWXYZ
**6** ACDEGHIJ(N 3km)ST

💬 Quiet campsite with large comfort pitches with wifi and TV connections. Minigolf, 'farmers golf', skittles, jeu de boules and fishing lake. Indoor bike shed and recharging point for e-bikes. Local sights include the white village Thorn, the town of Roermond and De Groote Peel National Park.

🚗 From Eindhoven: A2, exit 40 dir. Kelpen/Oler. Take Kelpen/Oler exit on the N280 and follow the main road. From Maastricht: A2, exit 41 dir. Grathem. Follow camping signs from the N273.

CC € **16** 15/3-29/5 11/6-15/7 1/9-31/10 7=6, 14=12, 21=18 ⛺ N 51°12'35'' E 05°49'47''

---

## Kessel, NL-5995 RP / Limburg ♿ 🛜 iD **485**

🏕 Camping Oda Hoeve
📧 Heldenseweg 10
☎ +31 7 74 62 13 58
📅 1/4 - 1/11
@ info@odahoeve.nl

2,5ha 99T(180-200m²) 6A CEE

**1** ADGIJKLMNOPQ
**2** FKRUVWX
**3** FGHJU
**5** ABCDGHJLNPUWXY
**6** EGHK(N 1km)TV

NEW

💬 Small, easy-going campsite for senior citizens and the over 50s, situated on beautifully landscaped grounds with low vegetation and paved camping pitches. Located in an area with many cycling routes, 1 km from the Meuse. Owner organizes covered wagon trips and excursions. Free wifi.

🚗 Via Napoleonsweg N273, drive to Kessel. At the traffic lights in Kessel, turn right in dir. Helden. After 800 metres, the campsite is on right.

CC € **14** 1/4-24/5 3/6-7/6 10/6-6/7 24/8-30/10 ⛺ N 51°17'54'' E 06°02'14''

## Landgraaf, NL-6374 LE / Limburg ♿ 🛜 **iD** (486)

🏕 Camping De Watertoren
📧 Kerkveldweg 1
☎ +31 4 55 32 17 47
📅 1/4 - 11/10
@ info@campingdewatertoren.nl

5,3ha 120T(100-150m²) 6-10A CEE

**1** ADGIJKLMPRS
**2** BFRTWXY
**3** ABFGHIJKNRU
**4** (A 13/7-22/8) (C+H 15/5-1/9) (Q+R+U+Y+Z 📧)
**5** ABDEFGIJKLMNOPQR UWZ
**6** ACDEGHJKM(N 1km)OSV

💬 Ideal for young families and nature lovers. Close to a large woodland area. Restaurant. Heated outdoor swimming pool and heated toilet block with facilities for the disabled. Spacious pitches. Walking and cycling routes from campsite.

🚗 A2 exit 47 Born/Brunssum. Follow Brunssum. From Maastricht/Heerlen: exit Kerkrade-West (Beitel) or Park Gravenrode signs. Follow Hofstr., Einsteinstr., Dr.Calsstr., Torenstr. Left at Europaweg-Zuid roundabout.

L227 L42 L240 L164 Hoensbroek **Heerlen** A76 Würselen N595 CC

CC €**18** 1/4-28/5 3/6-6/6 12/6-6/7 24/8-11/10 📷 N 50°54'38'' E 06°04'23''

## Meerssen, NL-6231 RV / Limburg ♿ 🛜 **iD** (487)

🏕 Camping 't Geuldal
📧 Gemeentebroek 13
☎ +31 4 36 04 04 37
📅 1/4 - 1/11
@ info@camping-geuldal.nl

8ha 154T(100-150m²) 6-10A CEE

**1** ACDGIJKLMPRS
**2** BCFRVWXY
**3** BDFGHJRU
**4** (Q+T+V 13/7-26/8)
**5** ABDFIJKLMNOPRUWZ
**6** ABCDEGK(N 3km)OV

💬 Attractive site located in beautiful natural area between steep white cliffs and River Geul. Wonderful for cycling or walking. Excellent toilet facilities and very spacious pitches. Centrally located between Maastricht and Valkenburg.

🚗 A2 exit 51. 1st roundab. left 2nd roundab. right 3rd roundab. left. Over track directly left. Right before left bend or via A79 to Heerlen exit 2 to Meerssen, left on roundab., left after train track. Motorhomes higher than 2.8m: see website.

E314 Brunssum A76 N77 A2 **Heerlen** N2 A79 Valkenburg CC N595 N671 N278 N598

CC €**16** 1/4-19/4 12/5-29/5 10/6-5/7 1/9-31/10 7=6, 14=11 📷 N 50°52'21'' E 05°46'17''

## Meijel, NL-5768 PK / Limburg ♿ 🛜 **iD** (488)

🏕 Camping Kampeerbos De Simonshoek
📧 Steenoven 10
☎ +31 7 74 66 17 97
📅 1/1 - 31/12
@ info@simonshoek.nl

8,5ha 75T(120-130m²) 6A CEE

**1** ADGIJKLMOPQ
**2** BFLRSVWX
**3** AGHJKNRU
**4** (C+D+H 📧) (Q 31/3-31/10) (T+X 1/4-31/8) (Z 📧)
**5** ABDFGIJKLMNOPUWZ
**6** CEGHJ(N 1km)STVX

💬 Kampeerbos De Simonshoek is centrally located in the 'Land van Peel en Maas' in Dutch Limburg, in large wooded surroundings close to the Groote Peel National Park. Quietly located with large camping pitches, good toilet facilities, and Simon's Swimming Arena offering fun every day for young and old. Lovely cycling and walking routes in the area.

🚗 From A67 Eindhoven-Venlo, take Asten/Meijel exit, direction Meijel. Right after about 12 km. Campsite 700m on the right.

Someren N279 A67 Maasbree N266 N277 CC N275 N562 A2 N273 Weert

CC €**16** 1/1-7/7 24/8-31/12 📷 N 51°20'23'' E 05°52'16''

## Noorbeek, NL-6255 PB / Limburg  ⚡ 📶 iD 489

🏕 Camping Grensheuvel
Natuurlijk Limburg
✉ Voerenstraat 11
☎ +31 6 28 83 41 23
📅 1/1 - 31/12
@ grensheuvelnatuurlijklimburg@
gmail.com

2,5ha 80T(75-100m²) 6A CEE

**1** A**G**IJKLMOPRS
**2** GJKWX
**3** AHJ
**4** (X+Z 1/3-31/12)
**5** DGIJM**P**UWX
**6** ACDEGK(N 1km)

💬 A terraced campsite located in undulating countryside. Ideal for walking and cycling. Enjoy the lovely views and the countryside. Quiet surroundings. Heated toilet facilities and free wifi. Unmanned reception.

🚗 A2 direction Maastricht, via Maastricht towards Liège, exit Gronsveld junction 56. Via St. Geertruid and Mheer to Noorbeek. Grensheuvel campsite before Noorbeek on the right.

CC €16  1/1-28/5  11/6-4/7  26/8-31/12   N 50°46'22" E 05°48'07"

*Map: Maastricht, Valkenburg, N595, N278, A2, N598, N671, CC, Oupeye, N608, N648, N627*

---

## Panningen, NL-5981 NX / Limburg  ♿ 📶 iD 490

🏕 Camping Beringerzand
✉ Heide 5
☎ +31 7 73 07 20 95
📅 1/1 - 31/12
@ info@beringerzand.nl

20ha 370T(80-100m²) 10A CEE

**1** ADGIJKLMOPQ
**2** FLRSVWXY
**3** ABC**F**GHIJKNQRUW
**4** (C 1/5-1/10) (F+H 📅) JM
(Q+S+T+U+X+Z 📅)
**5** **AB**CDEFGHIJKLMNPQRU
WXY
**6** ACEGHJK(N 3km)OSTV

💬 A superb four star campsite with five star comfort! Heated toilet block with special bathrooms for children, toilets for older guests and facilities adapted for the disabled. Spotlessly clean! Winter camping is also possible.

🚗 From A67 exit 38, then take direction Koningslust. Follow the signs to campsite Beringerzand.

CC €16  1/1-19/4  13/5-29/5  3/6-7/6  11/6-8/7  26/8-31/12   N 51°20'56" E 05°57'40"

*Map: N277, N556, A73, A67, Maasbree, Blerick, CC, N279, N275, N562, Reuver, N273*

---

## Plasmolen, NL-6586 AL / Limburg  📶 iD 491

🏕 Camping De Geuldert
✉ Schildersweg 6
☎ +31 2 46 96 27 67
📅 1/4 - 3/11
@ info@degeuldert.nl

**NEW**

4,7ha 102T(100m²) 6-10A CEE

**1** ADG IJLPQ
**2** FGRSVWXY
**3** BD**F**GHIJRU
**4** (**A** 8/7-31/8) (Q+R 📅)
(T 8/7-31/8) (Z 📅)
**5** **AB**DFGIJKLMNO**P**UWXYZ
**6** CDEGH**K**(N 1km)OSTV

💬 This family campsite with beautiful, spacious marked out pitches and a cosy cafeteria is located at the foot of the Sint Jansberg. Many facilities for kids, such as a playground with air trampoline, a petting zoo, a volleyball field, a table tennis table, a youth club with TV and a table football game. Great starting point for cyclists and hikers.

🚗 A73, exit 3 Malden. N271 to Plasmolen/Mook. At Plasmolen, follow campsite sign.

CC €16  1/4-28/5  11/6-30/6  1/9-2/11   N 51°44'08" E 05°55'28"

*Map: Nijmegen, Wijchen, Kranenburg, Kleve, N271, L484, N321, A73, CC, B504, A57, Boxmeer*

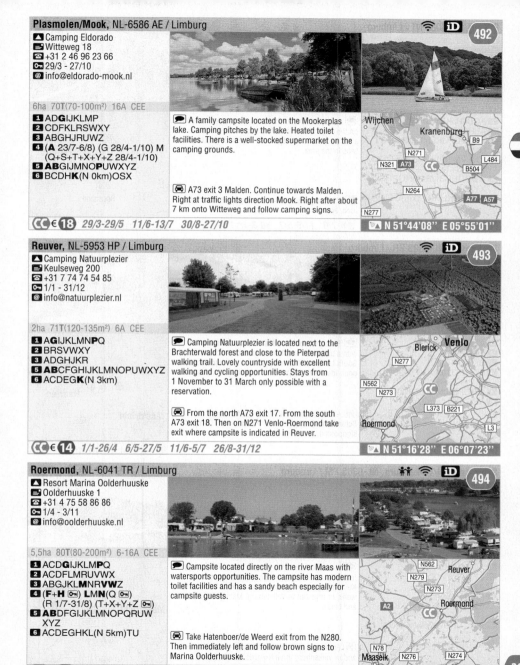

## Plasmolen/Mook, NL-6586 AE / Limburg

🏕 Camping Eldorado
🏠 Witteweg 18
☎ +31 2 46 96 23 66
🗓 29/3 - 27/10
@ info@eldorado-mook.nl

492

6ha 70T(70-100m²) 16A CEE

**1** ADG IJKLMP
**2** CDFKLRSWXY
**3** ABGHJRUWZ
**4** (A 23/7-6/8) (G 28/4-1/10) M (Q+S+T+X+Y+Z 28/4-1/10)
**5** ABGIJMNOPUWXYZ
**6** BCDHK(N 0km)OSX

💬 A family campsite located on the Mookerplas lake. Camping pitches by the lake. Heated toilet facilities. There is a well-stocked supermarket on the camping grounds.

🚗 A73 exit 3 Malden. Continue towards Malden. Right at traffic lights direction Mook. Right after about 7 km onto Witteweg and follow camping signs.

CC € 18  29/3-29/5  11/6-13/7  30/8-27/10

N 51°44'08'' E 05°55'01''

## Reuver, NL-5953 HP / Limburg

🏕 Camping Natuurplezier
🏠 Keulseweg 200
☎ +31 7 74 74 54 85
🗓 1/1 - 31/12
@ info@natuurplezier.nl

493

2ha 71T(120-135m²) 6A CEE

**1** AG IJKLMN PQ
**2** BRSVWXY
**3** ADGHJKR
**5** ABCFGHIJKLMNOPUWXYZ
**6** ACDEGK(N 3km)

💬 Camping Natuurplezier is located next to the Brachterwald forest and close to the Pieterpad walking trail. Lovely countryside with excellent walking and cycling opportunities. Stays from 1 November to 31 March only possible with a reservation.

🚗 From the north A73 exit 17. From the south A73 exit 18. Then on N271 Venlo-Roermond take exit where campsite is indicated in Reuver.

CC € 14  1/1-26/4  6/5-27/5  11/6-5/7  26/8-31/12

N 51°16'28'' E 06°07'23''

## Roermond, NL-6041 TR / Limburg

🏕 Resort Marina Oolderhuuske
🏠 Oolderhuuske 1
☎ +31 4 75 58 86 86
🗓 1/4 - 3/11
@ info@oolderhuuske.nl

494

5,5ha 80T(80-200m²) 6-16A CEE

**1** ACDG IJKLM PQ
**2** ACDFLMRUVWX
**3** ABGJKLM NRVWZ
**4** (F+H 🅾) LMN(Q 🅾) (R 1/7-31/8) (T+X+Y+Z 🅾)
**5** ABDFGIJKLMNOPQRUWXYZ
**6** ACDEGHKL(N 5km)TU

💬 Campsite located directly on the river Maas with watersports opportunities. The campsite has modern toilet facilities and has a sandy beach especially for campsite guests.

🚗 Take Hatenboer/de Weerd exit from the N280. Then immediately left and follow brown signs to Marina Oolderhuuske.

CC € 18  1/4-18/4  5/5-29/5  11/6-19/6  24/6-5/7  26/8-3/11

N 51°11'32'' E 05°56'58''

## Roggel, NL-6088 NT / Limburg 👫 ♿ 📶 iD **495**

🏕 Recreatiepark De Leistert
📧 Heldensedijk 5
☎ +31 4 75 49 30 30
📅 29/3 - 4/11
@ info@leistert.nl

90ha 750T(90-130m²) 10-16A CEE

**1** ACD**G**IJKLMOPQ
**2** ALRSVWXY
**3** ABC**F**GHJKLMN**OPQ**R**ST** U**V**W
**4** (C 15/5-1/9) (F+H 📅) IJK**L**M **N**(Q+S+T+U+V+X+Y+Z 📅)
**5** **AB**CDEFGIJKLMNOPRSUW XYZ
**6** ACFGHKLM(N 1km)OSUV

💬 Lovely campsite with spacious pitches, located on the edge of the beautiful Leudal valley. There is a leisure pool on the campsite. Plenty of good cycle trips in the area.

🚗 The campsite is located along the Helden-Roggel road, approx. 1 km from Roggel.

Maasbree — N275 — N277
N562 — Reuver
CC — N273
N279
A2 — Roermond — A52

CC € **18** 29/3-19/4 3/5-29/5 3/6-7/6 11/6-5/7 30/8-4/11 📍 N 51°16'27'' E 05°55'55''

---

## Schimmert, NL-6333 BR / Limburg 📶 iD **496**

🏕 Camping Mareveld
📧 Mareweg 23
☎ +31 4 54 04 12 69
📅 1/1 - 31/12
@ info@mareveld.nl

3,5ha 43T(80m²) 6A CEE

**1** ACD**G**IJKLN**P**RS
**2** FGKRWXY
**3** BDHIJN
**4** (C 1/6-31/8) (Q 7/7-19/8) (X+Y+Z 📅)
**5** **AB**DFGIJMNOPUWXYZ
**6** AEG**K**(N 1km)UV

💬 Rustic campsite with a very special brasserie with a unique atmosphere. Beautifully located in South Limburg. The campsite has a heated outdoor pool. Ideal starting point for cyclists and walkers.

🚗 A76 exit Spaubeek, turn right towards Schimmert. 2nd on the left in Schimmert. Campsite signposted.

E314 — N276
A2 — CC — Heerlen
Maastricht — A76
N595
N278

CC € **16** 1/4-6/7 26/8-28/10 📍 N 50°54'26'' E 05°49'54''

---

## Schin op Geul/Valkenburg, NL-6305 PM / Limburg ♿ 📶 iD **497**

🏕 Camping Vinkenhof/Keutenberg
📧 Engwegen 2a
☎ +31 4 34 59 13 89
📅 1/1 - 2/1, 8/3 - 31/12
@ info@campingvinkenhof.nl

2,5ha 109T(80-100m²) 6-10A CEE

**1** ACD**G**IJKLMOPQ
**2** CFGRTVWXY
**3** A**F**GHJN**OP**RU
**4** (C 1/5-15/9) (Q 27/4-12/5,6/7-17/8) (T+U+V+Y+Z 1/4-1/10)
**5** **AB**CDFGIJKLMNO**P**UW XYZ
**6** ACDEG**K**(N 2km)TV

💬 Vinkenhof campsite is located in a unique spot in the South Limburg landscape at the foot of the Keutenberg and Sousberg hills. An ideal location for walks or trips out to Valkenburg, Maastricht, Aachen and Liége.

🚗 From A76 exit Nuth, via Hulsberg to Valkenburg and in Valkenburg drive towards Schin op Geul.

Heerlen
Maastricht — A76
CC — N595
N278 — N598
A2
N648

CC € **18** 8/3-16/4 22/4-26/4 4/5-28/5 2/6-6/6 10/6-4/7 21/8-31/12 📍 N 50°51'00'' E 05°52'23''

## Sevenum, NL-5975 MZ / Limburg

♿ 📶 **iD** (498)

🏕 Camping De Schatberg
🛏 Middenpeelweg 5
☎ +31 7 74 67 77 77
🔓 1/1 - 31/12
@ info@schatberg.nl

96ha 500T(100-150m²) 10-16A CEE

**1** ACD**G**IJKLMOPST
**2** ABD**F**LMRVWXY
**3** B**E**FGHJKLNR**ST**U**WZ**
**4** (B 1/5-1/9) (F 🔓) (H 1/5-1/9)
IJKM
(Q+S+T+U+V+X+Y+Z 🔓)
**5** **AB**DEFGIJKLMNOPQR**S**U
WXYZ
**6** ACEGHKM(N 6km)OSTUV

💬 A large family campsite in a unique location in the North Limburg Peel. Open all year. Plenty of indoor and outdoor amenities. Lovely cycling and walking routes. Reservation recommended for Ascension Day and Whitsun holidays.

🚗 From A67 Eindhoven-Venlo, take exit 38 Helden and then follow the signs. Campsite is located along the N277, the Midden Peelweg.

CC € 18  1/1-26/4  4/5-29/5  11/6-6/7  24/8-31/12  14=11

🧭 N 51°22'58'' E 05°58'34''

---

## Vaals, NL-6291 NM / Limburg

📶 **iD** (499)

🏕 Camping Hoeve de Gastmolen
🛏 Lemierserberg 23
☎ +31 4 33 06 57 55
🔓 1/4 - 31/10
@ info@gastmolen.nl

6ha 100T(100-140m²) 6A CEE

**1** A**DG**IJKLN**PQ**
**2** CGIJKRTVWXY
**3** **A**CF**GH**IJ**MN**O**PQR**STU
**4** (Q 🔓) (T 6/7-17/8)
**5** **AB**DFGIJKLMNO**PQ**UW
XYZ
**6** ADEJ(N 1,5km)OV

💬 Hoeve de Gastmolen used to be a Limburg courtyard farm. The meadows which now form part of the natural camping grounds border onto the babbling Selzer brook. Completely new bathhouse in 2015.

🚗 From A76 intersection Bocholtz dir. N281. At Nijswiller N278 dir. Vaals. Campsite signposted just before Vaals. Take note: GPS takes you not to main entrance but to the crossroads you need to take to the site.

CC € 18  1/4-27/4  5/5-29/5  10/6-6/7  24/8-31/10

🧭 N 50°46'44'' E 06°00'17''

---

## Valkenburg aan de Geul, NL-6301 WP / Limburg

♿ 📶 **iD** (500)

🏕 Camping De Bron BV
🛏 Stoepertweg 5
☎ +31 4 54 05 92 92
🔓 1/4 - 20/12
@ info@camping-debron.nl

8ha 365T(100-120m²) 4-6A CEE

**1** AD**G**IJKLPRS
**2** FLRVWXY
**3** B**F**GHJKNRU
**4** (B+G 1/6-31/8) (Q 1/4-1/11)
(R+T+U+X+Y 1/4-1/9) (Z 🔓)
**5** **AB**DEFGIJKLMNPUW
**6** ACDEGHJ**K**(N 2km)OSTVX

💬 Parklike appearance thanks to the many trees spread all over the campsite. Perfectly maintained toilet facilities, lively cafe/restaurant on the site.

🚗 A2 from the north: A76 dir. Heerlen, exit Nuth, at end of exit towards Valkenburg. Follow camping signs beyond Hulsberg. From south: A79 dir. Heerlen, exit 4 then follow camping signs.

CC € 18  1/4-18/4  23/4-29/5  11/6-5/7  23/8-31/10

🧭 N 50°52'50'' E 05°50'00''

## Valkenburg aan de Geul, NL-6325 AD / Limburg 📶 iD 501

🏕 Camping De Cauberg
✉ Rijksweg 171
☎ +31 4 36 01 23 44
📅 22/3 - 27/10, 16/11 - 23/12
@ info@campingdecauberg.nl

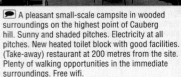

1ha 60T(70-110m²) 10-16A CEE

**1** ADGIJKLPQ
**2** FGIJKRUWXY
**3** AFHIJ
**4** (A 22/3-27/10)
(Q+R+U+Z 🔒)
**5** ABDFGIJMNPUWXZ
**6** ACDEGK(N 1,5km)S

💬 A pleasant small-scale campsite in wooded surroundings on the highest point of Cauberg hill. Sunny and shaded pitches. Electricity at all pitches. New heated toilet block with good facilities. (Take-away) restaurant at 200 metres from the site. Plenty of walking opportunities in the immediate surroundings. Free wifi.

🚗 A2 exit 53 direction Berg en Terblijt/Valkenburg. Campsite is signposted after 5 km on the left of the road.

Heerlen · Maastricht · N276 · A76 · N595 · N278 · A2 · N598 · N648

CC €18 22/3-18/4 23/4-29/5 3/6-7/6 11/6-6/7 25/8-26/10 📍 N 50°51'24" E 05°49'08"

---

## Valkenburg aan de Geul, NL-6301 AN / Limburg 📶 iD 502

🏕 Camping De Linde
✉ Klein Linde 2
☎ +31 4 36 01 28 66
📅 12/4 - 27/10
@ info@campingdelinde.nl

1,5ha 170T(80-100m²) 4-10A CEE

**1** ADGIJKLMPRS
**2** FGLRWXY
**3** BFGHJU
**4** (B+G 29/5-1/9)
(Q+T 12/4-30/9) (X 🔒)
(Z 12/4-30/9)
**5** ABGIJKLMNOPUW
**6** ACDEJ(N 2km)OV

💬 This campsite with spacious pitches and plenty of flowers has a traditional farm at its centre. Ideal base for people who like to be active while also enjoying some peace and quiet. Lovely cycling and walking in the hills of south Limburg.

🚗 From the A2 near Maastricht continue in the direction of Berg and Terblijt. Drive past Berg and Terblijt and turn right near Vilt in the direction of Sibbe. Signposted in the centre of Sibbe.

Heerlen · Maastricht · A76 · A79 · N595 · N278 · A2 · N598 · N671

CC €18 12/4-17/4 23/4-26/5 11/6-1/7 26/8-27/10 📍 N 50°50'39" E 05°49'41"

---

## Valkenburg/Berg en Terblijt, NL-6325 PE / Limburg ♿ 📶 iD 503

🏕 Camping Oriëntal
✉ Rijksweg 6
☎ +31 4 36 04 00 75
📅 10/4 - 27/10
@ info@campingoriental.nl

6,5ha 290T(100m²) 6-10A CEE

**1** ACDGIJKLPRS
**2** FGLRUVWXY
**3** ABFGHJNRU
**4** (A 6/7-25/8)
(C+E+H 18/4-1/10) (Q+S 🔒)
(T 6/7-25/8) (X+Z 🔒)
**5** ABDEFGIJKLMNOPQRUW
XYZ
**6** ACDEGHK(N 0,5km)OSTUV

💬 Family campsite, an ideal location for trips out. New indoor pool (29 °C). Pitches have 6A connections. 10A, TV and a water tap are available upon payment. Lovely walking and cycling routes from the campsite. Brand new toilet facilities. Bus stop Maastricht-Valkenburg in front of the entrance. Free wifi.

🚗 From A2 near Maastricht exit 53 towards Berg en Terblijt. The campsite is 3 km along this road on the right just before the roundabout.

Lanaken · Maastricht · E314 · N276 · A76 · N595 · N278 · N671 · A2 · N598

CC €18 10/4-18/4 23/4-25/4 6/5-28/5 11/6-2/7 19/8-27/10 7=6, 14=12, 21=18 📍 N 50°51'36" E 05°46'21"

## Venray/Oostrum, NL-5807 EK / Limburg

♿ 📶 **iD** （504）

🏕 ParcCamping de Witte Vennen
🏘 Sparrendreef 12
☎ +31 4 78 51 13 22
🔑 13/4 - 28/9
@ info@wittevennen.nl

17ha 150T(120-150m²) 6-10A CEE

**1** ADGIJKLMNOPQ
**2** ADFGLMRWXY
**3** ABDFGHJKMNQRUWZ
**4** (A 8/7-24/8) (G 1/5-30/9) JL
N(Q+R 8/7-24/8)
(T 7/7-25/8)
(Z 29/4-4/5,8/7-24/8)
**5** ABDEFGIJKLMNPUWXYZ
**6** ABCDEGJK(N 3km)STV

💬 Parkland family site on lake. Large pitches in spacious fields. Good toilet facilities. Friendly lounge-cafe and terrace. Tennis, jeu de boules. Good fishing location. Own cycle- and walking routes through Maasdal valley and the Dutch-German border region. Lido for the children, large playground and (free) pedalos. Wellness.

🚗 A73 exit 9 Venray/Oostrum. N270 towards Oostrum, straight on at first roundabout, right at the 2nd roundabout and then turn left immediately.

CC € ⑱ 13/4-18/4 23/4-26/4 13/5-28/5 3/6-6/6 11/6-5/7 31/8-27/9  ⛺ N 51°31'25'' E 06°02'08''

---

## Vijlen, NL-6294 NE / Limburg

📶 **iD** （505）

🏕 Camping Cottesserhoeve
🏘 Cottessen 6
☎ +31 4 34 55 13 52
🔑 1/4 - 1/10
@ info@cottesserhoeve.nl

5,5ha 180T(90-100m²) 6-10A CEE

**1** ADGIJKLPRS
**2** CJKLRTUVWXY
**3** BFHJNRU
**4** (C+H 27/4-9/9) (Q+R 1/4-9/9)
(T+V+X+Z
27/4-10/6,6/7-25/8)
**5** ABDFGIJKLMNOPUWXZ
**6** ACDEGHK(N 5km)OSV

💬 Situated in a picturesque part of the Geul valley. Terraced campsite next to a 17th century farmhouse. All modern comforts and many activities. 10A available for a surcharge.

🚗 From A76 intersection Bochholz direction N281. At Nijswiller N278 direction Vaals. Exit Vijlen. In Vijlen direction Epen. Signposted from here.

CC € ⑱ 1/4-26/4 6/5-29/5 11/6-6/7 26/8-1/10  ⛺ N 50°45'34'' E 05°56'26''

---

## Vijlen/Vaals, NL-6294 NB / Limburg

♿ 📶 **iD** （506）

🏕 Camping Rozenhof
🏘 Camerig 12
☎ +31 4 34 55 16 11
🔑 1/1 - 31/12
@ info@campingrozenhof.nl

2ha 69T(< 110m²) 10A CEE

**1** ACDGIJKLNOPQ
**2** JKLRTWXY
**3** BFHJNRU
**4** (A 15/7-16/8) (C+H 1/5-30/9)
(Q+S+T+Y+Z 🔑)
**5** ABDFGIJKLMNOPUWXY
**6** ACDFGK(N 2km)OSV

💬 A warm welcome to this beautifully appointed terraced campsite, with exclusively comfort pitches, so 10 Amp connection and panoramic views of Epen (1.5 km) and Vijlen (5 km). A delight for walkers and cyclists. Maastricht, Valkenburg, Aachen and Liège are all within a reasonable distance.

🚗 From A75 intersection Bochholz direction N281. At Nijswiller 278 direction Vaals. Exit Vijlen. From Vijlen direction Epen. Left at fork in road. Signposted from here.

CC € ⑱ 1/1-26/4 6/5-29/5 11/6-6/7 26/8-31/12  ⛺ N 50°46'12'' E 05°55'45''

## Voerendaal, NL-6367 HE / Limburg 📶 iD **507**

🏔 Camping Colmont
📧 Colmont 2
☎ +31 4 55 62 00 57
🔑 29/3 - 29/9
@ info@colmont.nl

4ha 160T(80-120m²) 6-16A CEE

**1** ADGIJKLOPQ
**2** FGJKRTVWXY
**3** ABFGHIJKLNRU
**4** (C+H 27/4-15/9) (Q 🔲)
(T 27/4-10/6,6/7-25/8)
(U+V 🔲)
(X+Z 27/4-10/6,6/7-25/8)
**5** ABDEFGIJKLMNOPUWZ
**6** ACDEGK(N 3km)OTV

💬 Our panoramic campsite (180m above ground level) is located between Heerlen and Maastricht in the hills of south Limburg. We offer sunny and shaded pitches with 6A and well-maintained toilet facilities. Ideal base for cycling and walking and for day trips to Maastricht, Valkenburg, Aachen and Liege. Free wifi.

🚗 From A79 on junction Voerendaal direction Kunrade. In Kunrade direction Ubachsberg. Indicated from Ubachsberg centre.

A76   L225   A2   A79   N595 CC   **Heerlen**   N278   A4   N598   **Aachen**

CC € 16   29/3-7/7   24/8-29/9   N 50°51'08" E 05°56'03"

---

## Well, NL-5855 EG / Limburg ♿ 📶 iD **508**

🏔 Camping Leukermeer
📧 De Kamp 5
☎ +31 4 78 50 24 44
🔑 29/3 - 28/10
@ vakantie@leukermeer.nl

14ha 259T(100m²) 10A CEE

**1** ACDFIJKLMNOPQ
**2** ABDGKLRSTVWXY
**3** BFGHIJKLMNOPQRUVWZ
**4** (C 26/4-15/9) (F+H 🔲) KMN
(Q+S+T+U+X+Y+Z 🔲)
**5** ABDEFGJKLMNPQRUW
XYZ
**6** BCDEGHKM(N 3km)OSTVX

💬 This campsite is located close to water. Ideal camping place for fans of water sport. Nature lovers can enjoy De Maasduinen national park on foot, or by bike.

🚗 Coming from Venlo, on reaching Well follow the signs 't Leukermeer. Coming from Nijmegen via Bergen en Aijen follow the signs 't Leukermeer. Or take the A73 exit 9 via the N270 direction Wanssum.

Boxmeer   L361   A57   L486   Kevelaer   A73 CC   **Venray**   N271   N270   N277

CC € 18   29/3-17/4   6/5-28/5   11/6-18/6   24/6-5/7   26/8-27/10   N 51°34'03" E 06°03'37"

---

## Wijlre, NL-6321 PK / Limburg ♿ 📶 iD **509**

🏔 Camping De Gele Anemoon
📧 Haasstad 4
☎ +31 8 80 99 09 57
🔑 30/3 - 28/9
@ degeleanemoon@nivon.nl

1,1ha 58T(90-100m²) 6A CEE

**1** ABCDFIJLNPQ
**2** CRWXY
**3** AFHIJRU
**4** (G 🔲)
**5** ABCDEFGHIJKLMNOP
UWZ
**6** ADEGJ(N 1,4km)OV

💬 A superbly located campsite in an old orchard next to the River Geul at the foot of the Keutenberg hill. Perfect departure point for cycling and walking tours and for trips out, for example to Maastricht, Valkenburg, Aachen and Liége.

🚗 A2 as far as Maastricht, then direction Vaals. In Gulpen continue towards Wijlre. Signposted in Wijlre.

**Heerlen**   **Maastricht**   A76   CC   N278   A2   N598   N648

CC € 18   30/3-29/5   11/6-6/7   23/8-28/9   N 50°50'26" E 05°52'46"

**Wijlre**, NL-6321 PK / Limburg 📶 ✿ iD (510)

🏕 Camping De Gronselenput
✉ Haasstad 3
☎ +31 4 34 59 16 45
🚐 30/3 - 29/9
@ gronselenput@
paasheuvelgroep.nl

2ha 60T(60-120m²) 10A CEE
**1** ACD**G**IJLNPQ
**2** CRUVWX
**3** AB**F**HIJNRU
**4** M(Q+R+V+Z 🔳)
**5** **AB**DFGIJKLMNOPUWXY
**6** ADEG**K**(N 3km)OV

💬 A natural campsite with a location quite different from what you would expect in the Netherlands right by the Keutenberg. A small site with accessible pitches, ideal for families with small children.

🚐 A2 as far as Maastricht, then direction Vaals. In Gulpen direction Wijlre. Signposted in Wijlre.

Heerlen
Maastricht CC
N278 A76
A2 N598
N648

CC € 18 30/3-27/4 6/5-29/5 11/6-6/7 25/8-29/9 📷 N 50°50'31'' E 05°52'38''

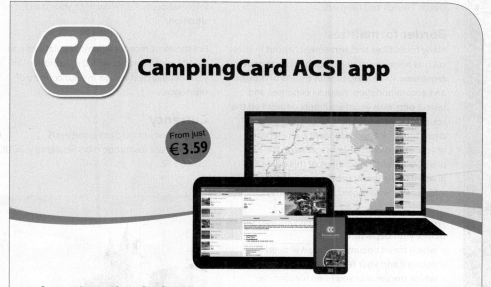
217

# Belgium

## General
Belgium is a member of the EU.

### Time
The time in Belgium is the same as Amsterdam, Paris and Rome and one hour ahead of London.

### Languages
Dutch, French and German.

## Border formalities
Many formalities and agreements about matters such as necessary travel documents, car papers, requirements relating to your means of transport and accommodation, medical expenses and taking pets with you do not only depend on the country you are travelling to but also on your departure point and nationality. The length of your stay can also play a role here. It is not possible within the confines of this guide to guarantee the correct and most up to date information with regard to these matters.

We advise you to consult the relevant authorities before your departure about:
- which travel documents you will need for yourself and your fellow passengers
- which documents you need for your car
- which regulations your caravan must meet
- which goods you may import and export
- how medical treatment will be arranged and paid for in your holiday destination in cases of accident or illness
- whether you can take pets. Contact your vets well in advance. They can give you information about the necessary vaccinations, proof thereof and obligations on return. It would also make sense to enquire whether any special regulations apply to your pet in public places at your holiday destination. In some countries for example dogs must always be muzzled or transported in a cage.

You will find plenty of general information on ▶ *www.europa.eu* ◀ but make certain you select information that is relevant to your specific situation.

For the most recent customs regulations you should get in contact with the authorities of your holiday destination in your country of residence.

## Currency
The currency in Belgium is the euro. Approximate exchange rates September 2018: £1 = € 1.12.

**Credit cards**
You can pay by credit card in many places.

## Opening times
### Banks
Banks in Belgium are open from Monday to Friday until 16:00 with a break between 12:00 and 14:00.

### Shops
Generally, shops are open from Monday to Saturday until 18:00. In a few large towns the shops are open until 21:00 on Friday.

### Chemists
Most chemists are open from Monday to Friday until 18:00/19:00. Some are also open on Saturdays.

## Communication
### (Mobile) phones
The mobile network works well throughout Belgium. There is a 4G network for mobile internet.

### Wifi, internet
You can make use of a wifi network at more and more public locations, often for free.

### Post
Open from Monday to Friday until 17:00, Saturday until 12:00. Postal agencies in supermarkets and other shops have often replaced smaller post offices.

## Roads and traffic
### Road network
Secondary roads in French speaking Wallonia can be of inferior quality. On motorways you can get help with a breakdown by using the emergency phones. Ask for Touring on 070-344777.

## Traffic regulations

Remember, all traffic in Belgium drives on the right and overtakes on the left! Headlight deflectors are advisable to prevent annoying oncoming drivers. Belgium uses the metric system, so distances are measured in kilometres (km) and speeds in kilometres per hour (km/h). All drivers coming from the right, including slow vehicles, have priority. When you are on a roundabout you have priority over someone entering the roundabout. Trams always have priority.

*Maximum speed*

| | | |
|---|---|---|
| | 70-90 | |
| | 70-90 | |
| < 3,5 т | 70-90 | |
| > 3,5 т | 70-90 | |
| | 120 | |
| | 120 | |
| < 3,5 т | 120 | |
| > 3,5 т | 90 | |

Maximum permitted alcohol level is 0.5‰. Phones must be used hands-free. It is not compulsory to drive with dipped headlights during the day. Driving through an amber light is an offence. You are not permitted to leave the engine running when the car is not moving. The use of winter tyres is not compulsory.

## Caravans, motorhomes

If travelling with a caravan in Belgium be aware that the road surface can sometimes be damaged. If you have a motorhome weighing more than 7.5 tonnes you may not overtake on motorways or main roads. Overnight stops by the roadside in a caravan or motorhome are permitted provided you are not camping.

## Maximum allowed measurements of combined length

Height 4 metres, width 2.55 metres and length 18.75 metres (of which the trailer maximum 12 metres).

## Fuel

Lead-free petrol, diesel and LPG are widely available.

## Filling stations

Filling stations on motorways are usually open day and night. Other service stations are generally open on Monday to Saturday between 08:00 and 20:00 and on Sunday until 19:00.

## Tolls

There are no toll roads in Belgium. You do however have to pay a toll for the Liefkenshoek Tunnel in the vicinity of Antwerp.

## Emergency number

112: national emergency number for fire, police and ambulance.

# Camping

If you are planning to camp on the Belgian coast in high season, you are advised to reserve well in advance. Belgian campsites are very child-friendly: there is plenty of entertainment and amenities such as playgrounds and sports fields are provided.

## Practical

- Make sure you always have a world adaptor for electrical equipment.
- It is safe to drink tap water.

## Adinkerke/De Panne, B-8660 / West-Vlaanderen

🏕 Camping Kindervreugde**
📧 Langgeleedstraat 1a
☎ +32 50 81 14 40
📅 8/4 - 30/9
@ info@kindervreugde.be

3ha 40T(95-130m²) 6A CEE

**1** AFIJKLMOPRS
**2** FGRVWXY
**3** AFHJW
**4** (Q 🔌)
**5** ABDFGJLNPQUYZ
**6** AEGJ(N 0,8km)T

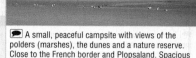

💬 A small, peaceful campsite with views of the polders (marshes), the dunes and a nature reserve. Close to the French border and Plopsaland. Spacious pitches and well maintained toilet facilities.

🚗 E40 (A18) exit 1 direction Plopsaland. After ± 800 metres after railway and tram overpass, turn left at third roundabout towards Bray Dune. After ± 800 metres turn left. Then another 200 metres.

**511**

CC €18 8/4-30/6 1/9-30/9 7=6, 14=11

N 51°04'35'' E 02°35'11''

---

## Amel/Deidenberg, B-4770 / Liège

🏕 Camping Oos Heem BVBA***
📧 Zum Schwarzenvenn 6
☎ +32 80 34 97 41
📅 1/1 - 31/12
@ info@campingoosheem.be

3,5ha 40T(100m²) 16A CEE

**1** ADGIJKLMOPQ
**2** CFJKLRVWX
**3** BDGHJKLNPRU
**4** (B+G 1/7-31/8) (Q+R+T+U+X+Z 1/4-1/10)
**5** ABDFGIJKMNPSUWZ
**6** DEGHJ(N 3,5km)OTV

NEW

💬 Campsite with a family atmosphere, located in the Belgian Ardennes, in the German-speaking East Cantons, near the High Fens Nature Park. Many walking and cycling possibilities on the RAVel Vennbahn. Bicycle rent possible. Comfortable living room with free wifi. Pets welcome.

🚗 E42 Verviers-St. Vith exit 13. E42 St. Vith-Verviers, exit 13A. Follow signs Camping Oos Heem from there.

**512**

CC €18 1/1-1/7 1/9-31/12

N 50°20'54'' E 06°07'12''

---

## Arlon, B-6700 / Luxembourg

🏕 Camping Officiel Arlon**
📧 373 route de Bastogne
☎ +32 63 22 65 82
📅 1/4 - 1/11
@ campingofficiel@skynet.be

1,4ha 78T(80-100m²) 6A CEE

**1** AGIJKLMOPRS
**2** FIKLRTWXY
**3** J
**4** (B 15/6-15/9) (Q+R 🔌) (X+Z 1/4-31/10)
**5** ABGIJMNOPUWZ
**6** ACDEGK(N 0,1km)SU

💬 Ideal stopover campsite with a restaurant, a pleasant terrace and a lovely swimming pool. Partly undulating, partly level grounds. Free wifi.

🚗 From E411 exit 31 direction Arlon. Follow 'autres directions' and Bastogne signs. Continue on N82 (do not turn off at the 2 roundabouts). This road ends in a bend to the left onto the N4 after about 4 km. Campsite past the bend 200 metres on right.

**513**

CC €20 1/4-1/6 1/9-31/10

N 49°42'08'' E 05°48'24''

## Aywaille, B-4920 / Liège   👪 ♿ 📶 🆔 **514**

🔺 Camping Domaine Château
   de Dieupart*
✉ 37 route de Dieupart
☎ +32 42 63 12 38
📅 1/3 - 15/11, 20/12 - 6/1
@ jeroen@dieupart.be

5ha 100T(80-120m²) 10A CEE

**1** ACD**F**IJKLOPRS
**2** BCFGRTVWXY
**3** AGHJR**W**
**4** (Q+S+Z 📅)
**5** **AB**DEFGIJKLMOP**U**WXYZ
**6** CDEGK(N 0,1km)SV

💬 Touring pitches by the side of the Amblève,
sheltered by the valley with a mild climate all year
round. Shops, pavement cafes, a public indoor pool
and tennis courts are all within 500 metres.

🚗 Leave E25 at exit 46 Remouchamps/Aywaille.
Turn right at traffic lights direction Aywaille, and
right by the church. Immediate left and then right
at Delhaize car park, take avenue up to the castle.
Signposted.

(( €**18** 1/1-6/1 1/3-29/5 11/6-30/6 1/9-14/11 20/12-31/12 ▨ N 50°28'35'' E 05°41'21''

## Bertrix, B-6880 / Luxembourg   📶 🆔 **515**

🔺 Ardennen Camping Bertrix****
✉ route de Mortehan
☎ +32 61 41 22 81
📅 29/3 - 11/11
@ info@campingbertrix.be

16ha 299T(80-120m²) 10A CEE

**1** ACD**G**IJKLM**PQ**
**2** BFIJRTVWXY
**3** BCGHJ**M**NRU
**4** (A 1/7-31/8) (C+H 30/4-15/9)
   (Q+R+T+U+Y+Z 📅)
**5** **AB**DEFGIJKLMNOPRUWXY
   Z
**6** CDEGHJM(N 3km)OTUV

💬 A wonderful terraced campsite with a high
level of service and first class amenities. Bordering
immense forests with streams and game. Luxury
camping in an oasis of peace and unspoiled
countryside, ideal for a complete holiday or as a
stopover campsite.

🚗 From E411 exit 25 Bertrix. Follow N89 as far as
Bertrix exit. Take the N884 to the centre. Then follow
camping signs.

(( €**18** 29/3-7/7 25/8-11/11 7=6, 14=11 ▨ N 49°50'18'' E 05°15'07''

## Blankenberge, B-8370 / West-Vlaanderen   ♿ 📶 🆔 **516**

🔺 Camping Bonanza 1***
✉ Zeebruggelaan 137
☎ +32 50 41 66 58
📅 29/3 - 29/9
@ info@bonanza1.be

5ha 65T(80-100m²) 10A CEE

**1** ACD**F**HIJKLM**PQ**
**2** RTWX
**3** BGHJKRU
**4** (Q+T+U+Y 1/7-31/8) (Z 📅)
**5** **AB**DFGIJKLMOP**U**X
**6** ACDEG**K**(N 0,5km)OSV

💬 Bonanza 1 is a modern family campsite located
within walking distance of the beach and the lively
centre of Blankenberge town. An ideal base for
visiting Ghent, Bruges, Ostend, Knokke, Damme and
Sluis (NL). CampingCard ACSI users pay cash.

🚗 E40 direction Oostende, exit Brugge/Zeebrugge
drive towards Blankenberge. In Blankenberge
turn right at the 2nd traffic lights. The campsite is
signposted.

(( €**20** 29/3-28/5 2/6-6/6 11/6-4/7 22/8-29/9 ▨ N 51°18'41'' E 03°09'12''

## Blier-Erezée, B-6997 / Luxembourg

👫 🚣 🤽 📶 **iD** **517**

🏕 Camping Le Val de l'Aisne★★★★
🏠 rue du T.T.A. 1a
☎ +32 86 47 00 67
📅 1/1 - 31/12
@ info@levaldelaisne.be

NEW

25ha 110T(100-140m²) 16A

**1** ACD**G**IJKLMOPQ
**2** CDKLRTVWXY
**3** B**F**GHJKLMNRU**W**
**4** (A 1/4-11/11)
(Q+T+U+V+Y+Z 📅)
**5** **AB**DFG**IJKL**MNO**P**UWXZ
**6** CDEGHKL(N 2km)OPRSTU
V

💬 Large campsite located around a constructed lake (fishing). Extensive options for sports and recreation. Excellent restaurant (open all year). Free WiFi! If you prefer a campsite with touring pitches only, you can go to Camping Eau Zone in Hotton, 8 km away.

🚗 Coming from NL: E25/A26 exit 49 Manhay, direction Erezée. Coming from Flanders: N4 - as far as Marche direction Hotton/Erezée. Follow the signs to the campsite.

[map: Durbuy, Tohogne, N66, N983, N30, N929, N807, A26, CC, E25, N86, N833, Samrée, N89, N4, N888]

CC €**18** 1/1-29/5  3/6-6/6  11/6-15/7  1/9-31/12  7=6, 14=12  🧭 N 50°16'45'' E 05°32'52''

---

## Bocholt, B-3950 / Limburg

♿ 📶 **iD** **518**

🏕 Camping Goolderheide★★★★
🏠 Bosstraat 1
☎ +32 89 46 96 40
📅 19/4 - 30/9
@ info@goolderheide.be

45ha 350T(100-150m²) 6-16A CEE

**1** ACD**G**IJKLMPQ
**2** ABDGLRSUVXY
**3** BGHJK**M**N**Q**RUWZ
**4** (C+H 10/5-31/8) IJM(Q 📅)
(S+T+U+V+Y 1/7-31/8)
(Z 📅)
**5** **AB**DEFG**IJ**KLMNOPQR**ST**
UWXYZ
**6** ACDEGJ(N 3km)OSTV

💬 Large family campsite with children's farm in a wooded park close to the Dutch-Belgian border and just three kilometres from the centre of Bocholt. There is a swimming pool complex with water slide. The fishing lake is beautifully integrated into the surroundings and freely available for campers. There is also a self-service restaurant.

🚗 Route Weert-Bocholt. In Kaulille drive towards Bocholt. Half way between Kaulille and Bocholt (3 km) the campsite is clearly signposted.

[map: Weert, Neerpelt, N71, N564, N748, N747, N74, CC, Kinrooi, Peer, N73, N721, N76, N719, N730]

CC €**18** 19/4-7/7  26/8-30/9  🧭 N 51°10'24'' E 05°32'21''

---

## Bohan, B-5550 / Namur

👫 ♿ 📶 **iD** **519**

🏕 Camping Confort★★★
🏠 rue Mont les Champs 214
☎ +32 61 50 02 01
📅 1/1 - 31/12
@ info@camping-confort.be

NEW

5ha 50T(100m²) 10A

**1** ACDGIJKLMOPQ
**2** CLRTVW
**3** BGHJNRU**W**X
**4** (Q+Z 1/7-31/8)
**5** **AB**DFGIJKLMN**P**UWX
**6** CDEG**K**(N 1km)OTV

💬 Holiday park with touring pitches on the banks of the Semois. Village centre within walking distance. La Table des Fées', the bar, is open July and August and in other months during weekends and holidays.

🚗 On the N95 (Dinant-Bouillon) direction Vresse-sur-Semois. Follow the town name and campsite signs. At the church follow the water. After the half bridge, continue for about 1.5 km. The campsite is on the left.

[map: N935, N95, D1, D31, N914, CC, N945, D989, Bogny-sur-Meuse, N819, Nouzonville, D979]

CC €**16** 1/1-20/4  6/5-24/5  3/6-7/6  11/6-5/7  22/8-31/12  🧭 N 49°52'24'' E 04°52'00''

## Bomal-sur-Ourthe, B-6941 / Luxembourg
👫 📶 iD **520**

🏕 Camping International**
📧 2 rue Pré-Cawiaï
☎ +32 4 98 62 90 79
🔓 23/2 - 12/11
@ info@campinginternational.be

2,5ha 40T(80-150m²) 4-10A

**1** ACDGIJKLMOPRS
**2** BCGRTWX
**3** AFGHJRUWX
**4** (T+U+X+Z 🔓)
**5** ABDGIJMPUW
**6** AEIK(N 1km)OV

💬 Small friendly site on river Ourthe with plenty of greenery in picturesque area. Small town, weekly Sunday market. Enjoy the countryside or take part in something active like kayaking, fishing and hiking. Tavern open every day from 9-21.

🚗 On the E25 Liège-Bastogne-Luxembourg exit 46. Then towards Aywaille. Follow the N86 towards Durbuy as far as Bomal. In Bomal take the N806 towards Tohogne. After ± 300 metres just over the bridge take the small road downhill on your left.

CC € **14** 23/2-29/5  11/6-7/7  24/8-12/11       N 50°22'30'' E 05°31'10''

---

## Bredene, B-8450 / West-Vlaanderen
📶 iD **521**

🏕 Camping 17 Duinzicht
📧 Rozenlaan 23
☎ +32 59 32 38 71
🔓 15/3 - 3/11
@ info@campingduinzicht.be

10ha 92T(80-120m²) 10A CEE

**1** ACDGHIJKLOPQ
**2** AEFGLRUWX
**3** BDFGHJMNRY
**4** (T+X+Z 🔓)
**5** ABDFGIJKLMNPQRUXYZ
**6** ACDEGK(N 0,5km)ORS

💬 Camping 17 Duinzicht is a pleasant, carefully tended family campsite where young and old will feel at home. The De Coster family will make your holiday into a special event. Stunningly located 300m from the beach and near the unique range of dunes of Bredene. There are many walking and cycling opportunities. Open 09:00-12:00 and 14:00-19:00.

🚗 E40 at end of motorway direction Bredene/De Haan. On the Driftweg follow 'campingzone' sign, then 'camping 17' sign.

CC € **18** 15/3-11/4  23/4-28/5  3/6-6/6  11/6-30/6  2/9-3/11    N 51°14'55'' E 02°58'01''

---

## Bredene, B-8450 / West-Vlaanderen
📶 iD **522**

🏕 Camping Veld en Duin***
📧 Koningin Astridlaan 87
☎ +32 59 32 24 79
🔓 1/3 - 15/11, 15/12 - 31/12
@ info@veldenduin.be

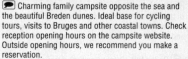

5ha 20T(80-100m²) 10A CEE

**1** ABDGHIJKLOPQ
**2** AEFGRUW
**3** BFGHIJW
**4** N
**5** ABDGIJKLMOPUWXZ
**6** DEGK(N 0,3km)S

💬 Charming family campsite opposite the sea and the beautiful Breden dunes. Ideal base for cycling tours, visits to Bruges and other coastal towns. Check reception opening hours on the campsite website. Outside opening hours, we recommend you make a reservation.

🚗 E40 dir. Bredene-Blankenberge, follow coastline as far as Bredene. Turn off at 'Bredene' sign, follow 'campingzone Astrid' sign. Turn off at Alaska chip shop and drive to end of street.

CC € **20** 1/3-16/4  22/4-29/5  3/6-6/6  10/6-7/7  25/8-15/11  15/12-31/12    N 51°15'08'' E 02°58'41''

## Bree, B-3960 / Limburg

&#9837; &#128506; &#128246; iD **523**

- 🔺 Recreatieoord Kempenheuvel
- ✉ Heuvelstraat 8
- ☎ +32 89 46 21 35
- 📅 1/3 - 4/11
- @ info@campingkempenheuvel.be

7,5ha 80T(80-140m²) 6A CEE

1. ACD**F**IJKLMPRS
2. GLRSUVWXY
3. BGHJNRUW
4. (C+H 15/5-15/9)
   (T+U+Y 1/7-31/8) (Z 🔑)
5. **AB**DFGIJKLMNOPUWYZ
6. ACDEGH**K**(N 1km)OTUV

💬 A family campsite 2 km from the centre of Bree with a playground and heated open air swimming pool, toddlers' pool, fish pond and lawns. There is a completely new area with touring pitches with modern toilet facilities. There is a restaurant with a varied menu. The campsite is connected to the Limburg cycle route network.

🚗 Route Eindhoven-Hasselt. In Hechtel drive via Peer to Bree. The campsite is located 1 km before Bree at the left of the road and is signposted.

CC € **16**  1/3-6/7  23/8-4/11  14=12

📍 N 51°08'14'' E 05°34'07''

---

## Bure/Tellin, B-6927 / Luxembourg

&#9837; &#128246; iD **524**

- 🔺 Camping Parc La Clusure****
- ✉ Chemin de la Clusure 30
- ☎ +32 84 36 00 50
- 📅 1/1 - 31/12
- @ info@parclaclusure.be

15ha 314T(100-120m²) 10-16A CEE

1. ACD**F**IJKLMO**PQ**
2. BCFLRTWXY
3. BGHJKL**M**NRU**WX**
4. (A 1/4-31/10)
   (C+H 22/4-16/9) (Q 🔑)
   (S+T+U+V+Y+Z 5/4-3/11)
5. **AB**CDEFGIJKLMNOPUWYZ
6. ACDFGHKLM(N 4km)ORST
   UVW

💬 A charming campsite under Dutch management in the heart of the Ardennes, in a sheltered valley and on the banks of a river well stocked with fish. The lovely countryside offers unique walking opportunities. Clean toilet facilities and quality amenities guarantee a comfortable stay.

🚗 From Brussels A4/E411, exit 23a via Bure/Tellin or from Liége N63 Marche, Rochefort direction St. Hubert. From Luxembourg A4/E411, exit 24 past Bure/Tellin.

CC € **18**  1/1-28/5  3/6-5/6  10/6-7/7  25/8-31/12  7=6

📍 N 50°05'46'' E 05°17'09''

---

## Burg-Reuland, B-4790 / Liège

👫 &#9837; &#128246; iD **525**

- 🔺 Camping Hohenbusch*****
- ✉ Hohenbusch, Grüfflingen 31
- ☎ +32 80 22 75 23
- 📅 29/3 - 3/11
- @ info@hohenbusch.be

5ha 74T(100-175m²) 5-10A CEE

1. ACD**G**HIJKLMOPRS
2. FGJKRVWX
3. BDGHJLRU
4. (C+H 29/5-31/8) **K**
   (Q+T+U+X+Z 🔑)
5. **AB**CDFGJLN**PQRS**UWXYZ
6. ACEG**K**(N 5km)STUV

💬 A spacious family campsite with very good toilet facilities. Close to Luxembourg and Germany. 6 km to the VENNbahn cycle route. Heated swimming pool with terrace and lawn. All pitches have electricity, water and drainage. 3km from the E42, exit 15.

🚗 E42/A27 exit 15 Sankt Vith. On road N62 Sankt Vith direction Luxembourg. Campsite after 3 km at the right. Use GPS coordinates.

CC € **18**  29/3-29/5  2/6-7/6  10/6-8/7  26/8-3/11  14=11

📍 N 50°14'30'' E 06°05'35''

## Bütgenbach, B-4750 / Liège

▲ Camping Worriken*
🏠 Worriken 9
☎ +32 80 44 69 61
🔓 1/1 - 31/12
@ info@worriken.be

🧑‍🧒 ⛷ ⛵ ♿ 🛜 **iD** 526

16ha 45T(80-100m²) 10A CEE

**1** ABC**G**HIJKLO**PRS**
**2** A**D**IJKLMORTV**WX**
**3** AGHJL**M**N**RS**U**WZ**
**4** (F 1/1-22/11,20/12-31/12) **N**
 (Q+T 🔓)
 (U 2/1-20/11,23/12-31/12)
 (X 🔓)
 (Y 2/1-20/11,23/12-31/12)
**5** **AB**DGIJKMNPUXYZ
**6** ACEGHJ(N 0,5km)V

💬 The campsite is located by a large lake next to a sports centre with entertainment. Marked out pitches. The toilet blocks are heated. Opportunities for skiing close by in the winter months. Carnaval is celebrated with exuberance. CampingCard ACSI not accepted during Francorchamps F1.

🚗 E40/A3 exit 38 Eupen, direction Malmedy, follow the signs Worriken.

B258
N669
N68    B265
Malmedy
N62    N632
N676  N658
E42
Meyerode    Manderfeld

**CC** € **16** 1/1-30/6  1/9-30/12   📐 N 50°25'29'' E 06°13'19''

---

## De Haan, B-8421 / West-Vlaanderen

▲ Camping Strooiendorp
🏠 Wenduinesteenweg 125
☎ +32 59 23 42 18
🔓 1/1 - 31/12
@ info@strooiendorp.be

🛜 **iD** 527

3,5ha 28T(80-100m²) 10A CEE

**1** A**G**IJKLO**PRS**
**2** ABG**RU**WX
**3** B**F**GHJQRU
**5** **AB**DGIJKLMNO**P**UXYZ
**6** CDEG**IJ**(N 0,6km)SUV

💬 A small family campsite on the coast. Well-maintained camping pitches and neat toilet facilities. Wifi.

🚗 Stay on E40 exit Jabbeke direction De Haan. Left after about 10 km at T junction. Campsite 200m on the left.

N34    N31
N371
N348
N307
CC
**Oostende**
N9
N377    **Brugge**
N33    A10

**CC** € **20** 1/1-5/3  23/4-29/5  3/6-7/6  11/6-7/7  24/8-31/12   📐 N 51°16'39'' E 03°03'00''

---

## De Haan, B-8421 / West-Vlaanderen

▲ Camping Ter Duinen
🏠 Wenduinesteenweg 143
☎ +32 50 41 35 93
🔓 15/3 - 15/10
@ info@campingterduinen.be

♿ 🛜 **iD** 528

12,5ha 214T(90-100m²) 16A CEE

**1** AD**G**HIJKLOPQ
**2** AEG**RW**X
**3** A**F**GHJUY
**5** **AB**CDEFG**IJKL**MNOPUZ
**6** EG**K**(N 0,3km)SV

💬 Campsite situated in the wooded dunes of De Haan, Belle Epoque town on the coast. Nice, well-maintained pitches. Cafeteria with a terrace.

🚗 E40 towards Ostend exit Jabbeke, towards De Haan, follow signs 'Ter Duinen'.

N34    N31
N34E    N307
CC
Oostende
N9
N377
N33    A10    **Brugge**

**CC** € **18** 15/3-7/7  25/8-29/9   📐 N 51°17'00'' E 03°03'23''

## De Klinge, B-9170 / Oost-Vlaanderen

🛆 Camping Fort Bedmar**
📧 Fort Bedmarstr. 42
☎ +32 37 70 56 47
📅 1/1 - 31/12
@ camping@fortbedmar.be

90ha 50T(100-110m²) 10A CEE

**1** ACD**G**HIJKLMO**P**Q
**2** BFGRSVWXY
**3** BGHJNRUW
**4** (C+H 27/5-15/9) (Q 1/7-31/8)
 (T+V+Z 6/4-22/4,1/7-31/8)
**5** **AB**CDGIJ**KL**MNO**P**UZ
**6** ACEG**K**(N 2,5km)OTV

💬 Rurally located. Numerous walking and cycling routes. Discover the history of Fort Bedmar and the 'Staats-Spaanse Linies'. Close to Zeeland-Flanders, Antwerp, Ghent and Bruges. Attractive poolside terrace. Own fishing lake. Ideal for those seeking rest and nature.

🚗 From E34 exit 11 or Sint-Niklaas: N403 dir. Hulst. From Zeeland-Flanders: N290 dir. Sint-Niklaas. To De Klinge roundabout. Signposted from the centre.

**529**

**Antwerpen**
A4 / A12 / N290 / N451 / E34 / Beveren / A11 / N70 / E17 / **Sint-Niklaas**

CC € **16** 1/1-15/7 1/9-31/12

📐 N 51°16'01'' E 04°06'41''

---

## Dochamps, B-6960 / Luxembourg

🛆 Camping Petite Suisse****
📧 Al Bounire 27
☎ +32 84 44 40 30
📅 6/4 - 3/11
@ info@petitesuisse.be

**NEW**

7ha 200T(80-125m²) 10A CEE

**1** ACD**G**IJKLMO**P**Q
**2** BGJKLRTUVWXY
**3** BGHJ**M**NRU
**4** (C+H 1/5-1/9) (Q 1/4-2/11) S
 (T+Y 1/4-2/11) (Z 📅)
**5** **AB**DEFGIJKLMNPUWXYZ
**6** CDEGHJM(N 8km)OSTV

💬 Terraced campsite in a wooded area with swimming pool and a varied recreational programme. Beautiful views of the surroundings, numerous hiking possibilities and mountain bike trails.

🚗 From Baraque Fraiture, exit 50 on the E25, via N89 direction La Roche. Right at Samree direction Dochamps via D841. Campsite at entrance to Dochamps. Signposted.

**530**

Bra / N86 / Soy / N807 / Lierneux / Bihain / N833 / E25 / A26 / N888 / N30 / N4 / N89 / N834 / N860

CC € **16** 6/4-26/4 6/5-29/5 3/6-7/6 11/6-29/6 31/8-2/11 7=6, 14=11

📐 N 50°13'53'' E 05°37'54''

---

## Grand-Halleux, B-6698 / Luxembourg

🛆 Camping Les Neufs Prés***
📧 8 av. de la Resistance
☎ +32 80 21 68 82
📅 1/4 - 30/9
@ camping.les9pres@gmail.com

5ha 151T(80-100m²) 10A CEE

**1** ACD**G**IJKLOPQ
**2** CGLRWXY
**3** BGHJ**MN**Q**R**U**W**
**4** (**C**+G+Z 1/7-31/8)
**5** **AB**DGIJKLMNOPU
**6** DEGH**K**(N 0,5km)TV

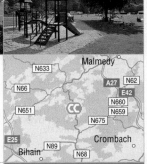

💬 A lovely, well maintained campsite by a small river in natural surroundings. Attractive playground, many sports and play facilities. Large swimming pool.

🚗 The campsite is located on the N68 Vielsalm-Trois Ponts, 1 km from the centre.

**531**

Malmedy / N633 / A27 / N62 / E42 / N66 / N660 / N651 / N659 / N675 / Crombach / E25 / N89 / Bihain / N68

CC € **16** 1/4-30/6 1/9-30/9

📐 N 50°19'50'' E 05°54'05''

## Hechtel/Eksel, B-3941 / Limburg ♿ 📶 iD **532**

🏕 Vakantiecentrum De Lage
Kempen*****
📧 Kiefhoekstraat 189
☎ +32 11 40 22 43
📅 19/4 - 3/11
@ gonnie.appel@delagekempen.be

3,5ha 70T(100-140m²) 6A CEE

**1** ACD**F**IJKLMOPQ
**2** LRVWX
**3** BGHIJK**Q**RU
**4** (C 23/5-1/9) (H 23/5-2/9) IJ
(Q+T+X+Z 📅)
**5** **AB**CDFGHIJKLMNPQUWZ
**6** ACDEGHJ**KL**(N 4km)OTV

💬 This small, welcoming family campsite is located
in the middle of the countryside. Close to the Dutch
cycling route network. The beautiful woods are also
ideal for lovely walks. Or visit one of the many lovely
spots in the area. Great place to read a book, swim,
do nothing for a bit or surf the internet.

🚗 Route 74 Eindhoven-Hasselt, turn right 12
kilometres after the border, direction Kerkhoven,
follow for 4 kilometres. Turn left in the woods, clearly
signposted.

CC € **14** 23/4-28/5   10/6-5/7   26/8-2/11      📡 N 51°09'40'' E 05°18'53''

---

## Houthalen, B-3530 / Limburg ♿ 📶 iD **533**

🏕 Camping De Binnenvaart****
📧 Binnenvaartstraat 49
☎ +32 11 52 67 20
📅 1/1 - 31/12
@ debinnenvaart@
limburgcampings.be

6ha 200T(100-150m²) 6-16A CEE

**1** A**G**IJKLMOPRS
**2** ABDFKLRSVWXY
**3** B**F**GHJMNRU**W**Z
**4** **K**(Q+T+U+V+Y+Z 📅)
**5** **AB**DEFGI**J**KLMNO**PQR**UW
XYZ
**6** ACDEGK(N 2,5km)STV

💬 Reasonably large campsite. Very large pitches for
touring campers in the middle of the grounds. There
is a lake next to the campsite. The site borders a large
recreation park with a restaurant and fishing pond.
There is also a snack bar on the site itself.

🚗 Follow Eindhoven-Hasselt as far as Houthalen.
Then turn left towards 'Park Midden-Limburg'. At the
second roundabout, near the furniture store, turn left
towards the campsite and follow the signs.

CC € **18** 1/1-1/6   6/6-4/7   26/8-31/12 7=6      📡 N 51°01'55'' E 05°24'58''

---

## Houthalen/Helchteren, B-3530 / Limburg 👫 ♿ 📶 iD **534**

🏕 Oostappen Vakantiepark
Hengelhoef
📧 Tulpenstraat 141
☎ +32 89 38 25 00
📅 1/1 - 31/12
@ info@vakantieparkhengelhoef.be

15ha 290T(80-120m²) 10A CEE

**1** ACD**G**IJKLMPQ
**2** ABDFGKLRSVWXY
**3** BC**F**GHJKMNQRUW
**4** (C+F+H 1/7-31/8) IJKLMN
(Q+S 📅) (T+U 1/7-31/8)
(V 7/7-31/8) (Y+Z 1/7-31/8)
**5** **AB**DFGIJKLMNOPUWXYZ
**6** CEGHJ(N 2km)STV

💬 Campsite in a recreation park that belongs to
the 'Oostappen' group. It has excellent swimming
facilities including a wave pool. The pool is only open
on Friday, Saturday and Sunday outside the holiday
period.

🚗 From Eindhoven in Houthalen keep following
road as far as the E314. Cross bridge, take E314 and
drive in the direction of Aachen (Aken). After approx.
5 km exit 30 'Park Midden Limburg'. Follow signs to
Hengelhoef and campsite.

CC € **16** 27/4-29/5   10/6-5/7   2/9-31/12      📡 N 51°00'52'' E 05°28'00''

## Jabbeke/Brugge, B-8490 / West-Vlaanderen ⚙ 📶 ✿ iD 535

⛺ Camping Klein Strand
✉ Varsenareweg 29
☎ +32 50 81 14 40
🗓 1/1 - 31/12
@ info@kleinstrand.be

28ha 92T(100m²) 10A CEE

**1** ACD**F**HIJKLMOPQ
**2** ADFGRVWXY
**3** B**F**GHJKRU**WZ**
**4** (G 1/6-30/9) JM
   (Q+R 1/7-31/8)
   (T+U+X+Z 🗓)
**5** **AB**DEFGIJKLMNO**P**UWYZ
**6** CGK(N 1km)ORSV

📷 A child friendly campsite located by a lake with its own sandy beach. Plenty of amenities and a good location between Bruges and the coast make this campsite unique.

🚗 Take exit 6 from the E40 Brussel-Oostende. Campsite signposted in the city centre of Jabbeke.

CC € ⑳ 1/1-30/6  1/9-31/12  7=6, 14=12, 21=18   📡 N 51°11'04'' E 03°06'18''

---

## Kasterlee, B-2460 / Antwerpen 🚻 ♿ 📶 iD 536

⛺ Camping Houtum★★★★
✉ Houtum 39
☎ +32 14 85 92 16
🗓 1/1 - 31/12
@ info@campinghoutum.be

9ha 70T(100-130m²) 10A CEE

**1** ACD**G**IJKLM**P**Q
**2** CFGRVWX
**3** ABC**D**GHIJ**Q**RU**W**
**4** (**A** 🗓) (Q 1/4-30/9)
   (T+U 1/7-31/8) (W 1/4-30/9)
   (Y 🗓) (Z 1/4-30/9)
**5** **AB**CDFGHI**J**KLMNO**PQR**U
   WXYZ
**6** ACEGK(N 1km)V

📷 Campsite with an excellent restaurant close by. You will find more than 250 km of footpaths in the surroundings.

🚗 E34 exit 24 Kasterlee. Campsite signposted 500m past the village centre, near the windmill. Or E313, exit 23 Kasterlee/Turnhout. Follow N19 (not N19-g). Turn right 1 km before village centre.

CC € ⑱ 1/5-26/6  18/8-30/9   📡 N 51°13'59'' E 04°58'40''

---

## La Roche-en-Ardenne, B-6980 / Luxembourg 🚻 📶 iD 537

⛺ Camping Benelux★★
✉ 26 rue de Harzé
☎ +32 84 41 15 59
🗓 29/3 - 3/11
@ info@campingbenelux.be

7ha 250T(100m²) 6-10A

**1** ADG**I**JKLMO**P**RS
**2** CGKLRWXY
**3** BGHJNRU**W**X
**4** (A 12/7-18/8) (C 1/5-30/9)
   (Q+S+T+Y+Z 🗓)
**5** **AB**GIJLMNPU
**6** AEGJ(N 0,5km)OV

📷 Family campsite located on the bank of the Ourthe, at walking distance from the lovely town of La Roche. Own restaurant with charming pavement café. New heated outdoor pool (2018). Many options for walking.

🚗 From centre direction Marche. Follow camping signs at bridge over River Ourthe. Campsite located 500m from the centre.

CC € ⑱ 29/3-29/5  10/6-30/6  25/8-3/11   📡 N 50°11'28'' E 05°34'24''

## Lommel, B-3920 / Limburg

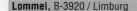

👪 🚹 ♿ 📶 **iD** **538**

⛺ Oostappen Vakantiepark
Blauwe Meer★★★★★
✉ Kattenbos 169
☎ +32 11 54 45 23
🔁 6/4 - 28/10
@ receptie@
vakantieparkblauwemeer.be

27ha 240T(80-100m²) 10A CEE

**1** ACD**G**IJKLMOPQ
**2** ABDGLRSVWXY
**3** BGHJKNQRWZ
**4** (Q+S 🔁)
(T+U+Y+Z 1/7-31/8)
**5** **AB**DFGIJKLMNOPUWYZ
**6** ACFGHJ**K**M(N 5km)STUV

💬 A large pond dominates this woodland setting.
Lots of water sports and plenty of other things to do.

🚗 On the road from Leopoldsburg to Lommel, route
746, close to the German cemetery located to the
right of the road.

[Map showing: N69, Lommel, Neerpelt, N71, Mol, N748, N18, N746, N74, Peer, N141, N73]

CC € **12** 27/4-29/5 10/6-5/7 2/9-28/10     📍 N 51°11'39'' E 05°18'13''

---

## Lommel-Kolonie, B-3920 / Limburg

👪 🚹 ♿ 📶 **iD** **539**

⛺ Oostappen Vakantiepark
Parelstrand
✉ Luikersteenweg 313A
☎ +32 11 64 93 49
🔁 6/4 - 28/10
@ info@vakantieparkparelstrand.be

40ha 130T(100m²) 10A CEE

**1** ACD**G**IJKLMOPQ
**2** ADLMRVWX
**3** BGHJKMNQRUW
**4** (Q+S+T+U+X+Z 1/7-31/8)
**5** **AB**DEFGHIJKLMNOPUWXY
**6** CEGHJM(N 1,5km)STV

💬 A campsite with spacious pitches and fishing
lake. Located close to the Dutch border.

🚗 On route 715 Hasselt-Eindhoven, in the Lommel
district 2.5 km from the Dutch-Belgian border, turn
left 100 metres after the Kempisch Canal.

[Map showing: N69, Lommel, N71, Overpelt, N76, N746, N74, Bocholt, N748]

CC € **12** 27/4-29/5 10/6-5/7 2/9-28/10     📍 N 51°14'36'' E 05°22'43''

---

## Malempré/Manhay, B-6960 / Luxembourg

👪 🚹 ♿ 📶 **iD** **540**

⛺ Camping Domaine Moulin
de Malempré★★★★
✉ rue Moulin de Malempré 1
☎ +32 4 76 30 38 49
🔁 1/1 - 31/12
@ info@camping-malempre.be

12ha 192T(100-200m²) 10-16A CEE

**1** ACD**G**IJKLMOPQ
**2** BCFIJRTVWXY
**3** BGHJNRUV
**4** (C 20/5-17/9) (H 28/5-14/9)
(Q+S 🔁) (Y+Z 1/7-31/8)
**5** **AB**DFGIJKLMNO**PRS**UWX
Y
**6** ACDEGJ(N 6km)TV

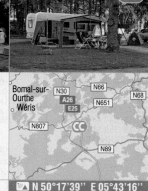

💬 Centrally located four-star campsite bordering
on woodland. Modern heated toilet blocks with
provisions for the disabled, private bathrooms with
bath. New outdoor pool (2016), motorhome service
station and pitches for stopover guests. Restaurant
at weekends and school holidays. All pitches have
electricity, water and drainage.

🚗 From E25 exit 49 Manhay. Then follow N822
direction Lierneux (500m). First exit to Malempré.
Follow camping signs, 4 km from exit E25.

[Map showing: Bomal-sur-Ourthe, N30, N66, N68, A26, N651, Wéris, E25, N807, N89]

CC € **18** 1/1-5/7 26/8-31/12 7=6, 14=11     📍 N 50°17'39'' E 05°43'16''

## Malmedy/Arimont, B-4960 / Liège

👫 📶 **iD** **541**

🔺 Camping Familial
📧 19 rue des Bruyères
☎ +32 80 33 08 62
🗓 1/1 - 31/12
@ info@campingfamilial.be

2,2ha 60T(80-100m²) 6A CEE

1 ADGIJKLOPQ
2 FIJKRTWX
3 BGHJRU
4 (B+Q 1/7-31/8) (R 1/4-1/11)
(T+U+X+Z 1/7-31/8)
5 **AB**DFGIJ**MNOP**UZ
6 DEG**K**(N 1,5km)O

💬 Peacefully located in a wooded area on a south-facing slope with a beautiful views. Close to the lively village of Malmedy and the Hoge Venen. Ideal for walking, cycling and mountain biking. 500m from the RAVeL cycle path.

🚗 A27/E42 exit 11 dir. Malmedy. Then dir. Weismes. 900m past Carrefour second exit left dir. Arimont. From St. Vith right at roundabout in Baugnez dir. Weismes. 3rd exit at roundabout, first left, then first right.

**CC** € **16** 1/1-5/7 26/8-31/12 7=6

📍 N 50°25'13" E 06°04'15"

---

## Mol, B-2400 / Antwerpen

👫 ♿ 📶 🌼 **542**

🔺 Provinciaal
Recreatiedomein Zilvermeer★★★★
📧 Zilvermeerlaan 2
☎ +32 14 82 95 00
🗓 1/1 - 18/11, 13/12 - 31/12
@ info@zilvermeer.be

150ha 282T(98-184m²) 16A CEE

1 BCD**G**IJKLMNOPQ
2 ABDGLSVXY
3 BD**F**GHJK**MN**QRUVWZ
4 (A 1/7-31/8) JM
(Q+S+T+U+W 1/4-30/9)
(X 1/1-18/11) (Y 🗓)
(Z 1/1-18/11)
5 **AB**DEFGHIJKLMNOPUWZ
6 CDEGHIJK(N 5km)OTU

💬 A well-maintained campsite located on a large lake with a water playground and climbing course. Three restaurants with differing opening dates. Extensive playground.

🚗 E34 Antwerpen-Eindhoven, exit 26 Retie/Arendonk and then follow the signs 'Molse Meren' or E313 Hasselt/Antwerpen exit 23 Geel-West then via N19, R14, N71, N712, N136 to the campsite.

**CC** € **16** 1/4-28/5 4/6-6/6 12/6-4/7 30/8-29/9

📍 N 51°13'10" E 05°10'52"

---

## Mouzaive, B-5550 / Namur

👫 📶 **iD** **543**

NEW

🔺 Camping Le Héron★★★
📧 rue de Lingue 50
☎ +32 61 50 04 17
🗓 1/1 - 31/12
@ info@camping-le-heron.be

8ha 76T(100-140m²) 10A

1 ACDGIJKLMOPQ
2 CILVWX
3 BGHJRX
4 (Q 1/7-31/7) (Z 1/7-31/8)
5 **AB**DFGIJK**P**UWZ
6 CDEG**K**V

💬 Holiday park on the banks of the Semois with touring pitches by the water. New playground, indoor jeu-de-boules court.

🚗 E411 exit 25 Bertrix, N89 direction Bouillon. N819 direction Alle and Mouzaive. Follow signs 'camping' from here.

**CC** € **16** 1/1-20/4 6/5-24/5 3/6-7/6 11/6-5/7 22/8-31/12

📍 N 49°51'14" E 04°57'12"

## Neufchâteau, B-6840 / Luxembourg ⏚ 📶 🆔 **544**

🏕 Camping Spineuse
Neufchâteau\*\*\*
✉ Malome 7
☎ +32 61 27 73 20
☷ 8/1 - 19/12
@ info@camping-spineuse.be

6,5ha 76T(100-120m²) 6-16A CEE

**1** ACD**G**IJKLMO**PQ**
**2** CDFLRVWXY
**3** BDHMNRUW
**4** (C 15/5-15/9) (Q ☷)
(T+U+Y+Z 1/4-4/11)
**5** **AB**CDFGHIJKLMNPUWZ
**6** ACDEGHKL(N 2,5km)UV

💬 Parkland 3-star site, homely atmosphere, located in heart of Ardennes. Dogs welcome. Clean toilet facilities, cosy bistro (open from 1 apr to 4 nov, rest of year only weekend). Spacious pitches, fishing lake, well-stocked fishing river, swimming and playing pool, campfire, free wifi.

🚗 E25/E411 from Brussels exit 26, from Liége 27, from Luxembourg 28 to Neufchâteau. From centre take N85 dir. Florenville. About 2 km further on left.

CC € 18 8/1-5/7 25/8-19/12 7=6, 14=12 ⛺ N 49°49'54'' E 05°24'55''

---

## Nieuwpoort, B-8620 / West-Vlaanderen ♿ 📶 ✿ 🆔 **545**

🏕 Kompas Camping
Nieuwpoort\*\*\*\*
✉ Brugsesteenweg 49
☎ +32 58 23 60 37
☷ 29/3 - 11/11
@ nieuwpoort@kompascamping.be

23ha 372T(8-150m²) 10A CEE

**1** ACD**G**IJKLMOPRS
**2** DFRUVWXY
**3** BCD**F**GHJKNRU**W**
**4** (C+H 9/5-16/9) J(Q+S ☷)
(T+U+Y+Z 30/3-15/4,1/7-31/8)
**5** **AB**DEFGJLNPQRUWXYZ
**6** ABCDEGH**K**(N 2km)OTUV

💬 A spacious family campsite with renovated toilet facilities, a large swimming pool with slides, large playgrounds, bar, shop and restaurant. Located beside a reservoir suitable for all types of water recreation. 4 km from the sea.

🚗 E40 exit 3 Diksmuide/Nieuwpoort. Direction Westende on roundabout. Continue to T junction. Turn right here. Campsite immediately on the left.

CC € 18 29/3-4/4 22/4-28/5 2/6-6/6 10/6-28/6 31/8-24/10 3/11-10/11 ⛺ N 51°07'48'' E 02°46'20''

---

## Opglabbeek, B-3660 / Limburg ♿ 📶 🆔 **546**

🏕 Recreatieoord Wilhelm Tell\*\*\*\*\*
✉ Hoeverweg 87
☎ +32 89 81 00 13
☷ 1/1 - 31/12
@ wilhelmtell@limburgcampings.be

6ha 75T(80-100m²) 16-20A CEE

**1** AB**G**IJKLMPQ
**2** FLRVWX
**3** BC**F**GHJKRU
**4** (C 1/7-31/8) (F ☷)
(H 1/7-31/8) IJK
(Q+R+T+U+V+Y+Z ☷)
**5** **AB**DEFGIJ**KL**MN**PR**UWXY
Z
**6** CDEGHK(N 2km)STV

💬 A campsite 2 km from the centre of Opglabbeek. Peaceful location among greenery. It has a large open-air swimming pool with water slide. Swimming in the indoor pool is possible all year, including in the winter. Modern toilet facilities with excellent amenities!

🚗 E314 Aachen-Brussels; exit 32. Continue on the A2 in the direction of As and then to Opglabbeek. The campsite is signposted to the right, before the centre.

CC € 20 1/1-5/7 26/8-31/12 7=6 ⛺ N 51°01'42'' E 05°35'52''

## Opgrimbie/Maasmechelen, B-3630 / Limburg

⛺ Recreatieoord Kikmolen
✉ Kikmolenstraat 3
☎ +32 89 77 09 00
🗓 1/4 - 31/10
@ info@kikmolen.be

547

20ha 126T(80-100m²) 6A CEE

**1** ABEHIJKLMO**P**RS
**2** BDFLMRTVWX
**3** BGHJ**M**NU**WZ**
**4** (A 1/7-30/9) J(Q 1/4-15/9)
  (S 1/6-30/9) (T 1/4-15/9)
  (U 1/7-15/9) (X+Y 1/7-30/9)
  (Z 🗓)
**5** **AB**CDFGHIJ**K**L**M**N**P**RUZ
**6** CD**K**(N 1,5km)TV

💬 Located in the natural richness of the Limburg Maasland on the edge of the Hoge Kempen national park. On attractive grassy plots, some of them shaded. Large swimming lake with 2 slides. Trout stream within walking distance. Large retail centre Maasmechelen-Village 6 km away.
🚗 Leave the A2/E314 at exit 33 in the direction of Lanaken. At the roundabout go straight ahead and after 1 km turn right towards Zutendaal. Then follow the signs to the campsite.

CC € **18** 1/4-5/7 26/8-31/10 | N 50°57'14'' E 05°39'45''

---

## Opoeteren, B-3680 / Limburg

⛺ Camping Zavelbos****
✉ Kattebeekstraat 1
☎ +32 89 75 81 46
🗓 1/1 - 31/12
@ zavelbos@limburgcampings.be

548

6ha 50T(100-120m²) 16-20A CEE

**1** AB**G**HIJKLMPQ
**2** BGRTVWY
**3** B**F**GHJKRUW
**4** **KP**(Q+T+U+Y+Z 🗓)
**5** **AB**DEFG**IJKL**MN**PQR**UWX Y
**6** ACDEGK(N 1km)SV

💬 Campsite with a fish pond in wooded surroundings. Excellent toilet facilities. Located on marked out footpaths, cycle paths and bridleways just 6 km from the 6000 hectare Hoge Kempen National Park.

🚗 A2 Eindhoven-Maastricht, exit Maaseik. Then via Neeroeteren to Opoeteren. The campsite is located on the right of the Opoeteren-Opglabbeek road.

CC € **20** 1/1-4/7 26/8-31/12 7=6 | N 51°03'29'' E 05°37'45''

---

## Oteppe, B-4210 / Liège

⛺ Camping L'Hirondelle
  Holiday Resort
✉ 76a rue de la Burdinale
☎ +32 85 71 11 31
🗓 1/4 - 31/10
@ hirondelle@capfun.com

549

45ha 106T(80-120m²) 10A

**1** ACD**F**IJKL**PQ**
**2** GIJLRTVW
**3** BGHJ**M**NRU
**4** (A 9/7-20/8) (B 1/6-10/9)
  (E 1/4-30/9) (G 1/6-10/9) J
  (Q+S+T+U+W+X+Y+Z 1/4-21/9)
**5** **AB**EFGIJKLMN**P**UZ
**6** CGHK(N 0,2km)OTV

💬 Campsite on a country estate with a castle on the edge of the Ardennes. Many fixed pitches, but also enough touring pitches. Water theme park with 8 slides. Supermarket on site. Many opportunities for sports and cultural activities in the area.

🚗 Route 80 St. Truiden-Namur. Turn left in Burdinne, follow the signs to Oteppe. Clearly signposted.

CC € **16** 1/4-30/6 1/9-30/10 | N 50°34'56'' E 05°07'34''

## Overijse, B-3090 / Vlaams Brabant ♿ 🛜 iD **550**

🏕 Camping Druivenland★★★
📧 Nijvelsebaan 80
☎ +32 26 87 93 68
📅 1/4 - 1/10
@ info@campingdruivenland.be

5ha 34T(150-200m²) 16A CEE

**1** **A**G**I**JKLMO**P**ST
**2** FGKRVWX
**3** GHJR
**5** **AB**DEGIJKLMO**P**UWXYZ
**6** BCEG**K**OT

💬 Overijse, home of the Belgian table grape, renowned for its grape festivals. From here you can visit the art cities of Brussels and Leuven. Waterloo, Walibi and the Afrikamuseum in Tervuren are nearby. The boat lifts are a Unesco heritage site and definitely worth a day's visit.

🚗 On the A4/E411, take exit 3 direction Overijse, then first right on the N218 (Nijvelsebaan) as far as the campsite.

**Brussel** N227 N3 E40
N4 N25
A4 CC
N4B
N253 E411 **Wavre**
N5 N275 N243

**CC** €**20** 1/4-7/7 26/8-30/9 📷 N 50°45'43'' E 04°32'50''

---

## Polleur, B-4910 / Liège 🛜 iD **551**

🏕 Camping Polleur
📧 53 route du Congrès
☎ +32 87 54 10 33
📅 1/4 - 1/11
@ info@campingpolleur.be

3,7ha 102T(80-100m²) 10A

**1** ACD**G**IJKLNO**P**Q
**2** CFLRVWX
**3** BGINRU**W**X
**4** (A 1/7-31/8) (C 30/4-30/9)
(G 30/4-10/9) J(Q 📅)
(S+T+U 1/7-30/8)
(V 15/7-15/8) (X+Z 📅)
**5** **AB**FGIJKLMNOPUWXY
**6** CDEGH**K**M(N 1km)OSTUV

💬 Family campsite in a valley on the banks of a stream in the woods of Spa. Swimming pool with water slide. Plenty of entertainment for young people. The shop is also open at weekends and holidays in early and late season. CampingCard ACSI not accepted during the Francorchamps F1 period.

🚗 E42/A27 take exit Polleur. Follow signs campsite Polleur. In Polleur Route du Congrès direction Theux. The campsite is signposted. Enter house number 90 in SatNav instead of 53.

N621
N604 **Verviers**
N61 N672
N673 N657 N68
Theux N629
E25 E42
N697 Spa
A26 N62 A27
N633
N622

**CC** €**12** 1/4-28/5 3/6-7/6 12/6-9/7 26/8-1/11 📷 N 50°31'54'' E 05°51'46''

---

## Poupehan, B-6830 / Luxembourg ♿ 🛜 iD **552**

🏕 Camping Ile de Faigneul★★★
📧 54 rue de la Chérizelle
☎ +32 61 46 68 94
📅 1/4 - 30/9
@ info@iledefaigneul.com

3ha 130T(100m²) 6A CEE

**1** ACD**G**IJLPQ
**2** BCLRTVWXY
**3** BGHJNRU**W**X
**4** (Q+R+T+U+Z 📅)
**5** **AB**DFGIJKLMNPRUWZ
**6** EGHK(N 5km)V

💬 In the middle of unspoilt nature. Dozens of marked out walking routes in wooded surroundings. Opportunities for mountain biking, fishing and canoeing. Lovely playground equipment for the children.

🚗 E411 exit 25, N89 towards Bouillon. N819 towards Rochehaut, in village N893 towards Poupehan. Campsite is signposted in village.

N853
D13 N914 N95
D31 N89
N935 N945
N810 N816
D777 N865
**Vrigne-aux-Bois** N83
Vivier-au-Court N58

**CC** €**18** 1/4-28/5 3/6-6/6 11/6-30/6 2/9-29/9 📷 N 49°48'59'' E 05°00'57''

## Poupehan, B-6830 / Luxembourg ♙♙ 📶 iD **553**

🏕 Camping Le Prahay*
📧 Rue de la Chérizelle 48
☎ +32 4 76 83 84 00
📅 1/4 - 3/11
@ info@camping-leprahay.com

5ha 60T(100-130m²) 6-16A

1 ACDGIJKLP
2 BCLTVWXY
3 BGHJRWX
4 (Q+R 🔌) (T 1/7-31/8) (Z 🔌)
5 ABGIJMPUZ
6 ABCDEGJ(N 5km)V

NEW

💬 Camping on a lawn on the banks of the Semois, without luxury or entertainment, amidst the Belgian Ardennes countryside. The new owners (March 2018) are working hard to preserve the calming character.

🚗 E411 exit 25, N89 in direction Bertrix/Bouillon. After Plainevaux direction Rochehaut via N819. Before Rochehaut, N893 dir. Poupehan, then follow campsite signs.

CC € 16 1/4-7/7 26/8-3/11          🧭 N 49°48'49'' E 05°00'53''

---

## Remersdaal/Voeren, B-3791 / Limburg ♙♙ 📶 iD **554**

🏕 Camping Natuurlijk
   Limburg BVBA
📧 Roodbos 3
☎ +32 4 79 93 79 84
📅 1/1 - 31/12
@ campingnatuurlijklimburg@
   gmail.com

6ha 70T(80-100m²) 6A CEE

1 ABGIJKLMNOPRS
2 GIRTXY
3 BHJKLNRU
4 (A 1/7-30/9) (C 1/6-1/10)
  (Q 🔌) (T+X+Z 1/3-1/12)
5 ABDGIJKLMNOPQUWZ
6 ACDEGK(N 2km)V

💬 A quiet campsite with every amenity located in the lovely countryside of Voeren with beautiful views of the hilly landscape. Walking and cycling routes are available at the reception. Fresh bread delivered daily if ordered in advance. Lively terrace and bar.

🚗 Leave the A2/E25 in Maastricht direction Aachen/ Vaals. Right just before Margraten direction De Planck. Cross Belgian border (± 5 km) towards Aubel.

CC € 16 1/1-29/5 11/6-5/7 2/9-31/12          🧭 N 50°43'46'' E 05°51'53''

---

## Retie, B-2470 / Antwerpen ♿ 📶 iD **555**

🏕 Camping Berkenstrand****
📧 Brand 78
☎ +32 14 37 90 41
📅 31/3 - 15/10
@ info@berkenstrand.be

10ha 33T(120-150m²) 10A CEE

1 ADGIJKLNOPST
2 ACDFLRSVWXY
3 BDGHJNUWZ
4 (A 1/7-31/8)
  (Q+R+T+U+X+Z 🔌)
5 ABDFGIJKLMNOPUXY
6 ACDEGHJK(N 3,5km)TUV

💬 Quiet family campsite. 3 ponds with swimming and fishing, several playgrounds, located on the 'Antwerp Kempen' cycle network and a starting point for several walking trails. You are welcome in the tavern with small or big appetite.

🚗 E34 exit 26 direction Retie, left at traffic lights then 1st right towards Postel. Campsite signposted (SatNav: Postelsebaan 3).

CC € 16 1/5-30/6 18/8-30/9          🧭 N 51°16'32'' E 05°07'44''

## Rochefort, B-5580 / Namur ♿ 📶 iD **556**

🏕 Camping Les Roches★★★★
📧 26 rue du Hableau
☎ +32 84 21 19 00
📅 29/3 - 11/11
@ lesroches@rochefort.be

74T(50-80m²) 16A CEE

**1** ACDGIJKLMO**PQ**
**2** GILSTWX
**3** AGHJRU
**4** (Q 💬) (T+U+X+Z 1/7-31/8)
**5** **AB**DFGIJKLMNPQRUWXY
**6** ACDGIK(N 0,5km)V

💬 Beautiful, recently renovated campsite near the city centre. The heated outdoor swimming pool is open from June to September. There are a variety of tourist activities in the area, including visiting various caves, castles and fortresses, and walking through cities or forests.

🚗 From E411 exit 23 (Rochefort/Han-sur-Lesse). Via N86 to centre. Campsite signposted just before the village.

CC € **18** 1/4-1/7 1/9-11/11

🛰 N 50°09'34'' E 05°13'35''

---

## Sart-lez-Spa, B-4845 / Liège ♿ 📶 iD **557**

🏕 Corsendonk Camping Spa d'Or★★★★
📧 Stockay 17
☎ +32 87 47 44 00
📅 26/4 - 12/11
@ info@campingspador.be

6,5ha 200T(80-100m²) 10A CEE

**1** ACD**G**IJKLO**PQ**
**2** CF**G**ILRTVWX
**3** AB**F**GHNRUW
**4** (A 1/7-31/8) (C+H 27/4-15/9)
(Q+S 💬) (T 7/7-15/8)
(U+V+X+Y+Z 💬)
**5** **AB**DEFGIJKLMNOPUWYZ
**6** EGHJM(N 4km)TV

💬 Camping Spa d'Or is located on the edge of 'Hautes Fagnes-Eiffel' nature area 4 km from Spa. Grounds slope down to the river Wayai. Heated swimming pool and children's pool. Snacks and takeaway meals available in the bar.

🚗 From the south, take A27/E42, exit 10 Francorchamps. Follow signs. From the north take exit 8 and follow the Spa d'Or cp signs. Coming from Luxembourg E25 exit Remouchamps direction Spa/Francorchamps. Follow signs on the left just outside Spa.

CC € **16** 6/5-29/5 11/6-7/7 27/8-24/10 7=6, 14=11

🛰 N 50°30'29'' E 05°55'10''

---

## Stavelot, B-4970 / Liège ♿ 📶 iD **558**

🏕 Camping l'Eau Rouge★★
📧 Cheneux 25
☎ +32 80 86 30 75
📅 15/3 - 11/11
@ info@eaurouge.nl

4ha 100T(100-120m²) 6-10A

**1** A**G**IJKLMO**PRS**
**2** CFRTWXY
**3** BGHJNRU**W**
**4** (C 1/5-30/9)
(Q+T+Z 29/5-10/6,6/7/7-26/8)
**5** **AB**DEFGIJKLMN**P**RUZ
**6** CEG**K**(N 1,5km)V

💬 A charming natural family campsite 2 km from the centre. Modern toilet facilities. Separate field for tents. Located by a small river in the valley of l'Eau Rouge. Heated outdoor pool.

🚗 From the E42 take exit 11, roundabout dir. Stavelot (switch off SatNav), continue for ± 5 km as far as T-junction on right. Then 1st road on right, small road downhill. The site can easily be reached, also when the Francorchamps race circuit is closed.

CC € **18** 15/3-29/5 10/6-6/7 26/8-10/11

🛰 N 50°24'43'' E 05°57'03''

## Tenneville, B-6970 / Luxembourg

🏕 Camping Pont de Berguème***
✉ Berguème 9
☎ +32 84 45 54 43
📅 1/1 - 31/12
@ info@pontbergueme.be

**559**

3ha 100T(80-100m²) 6A CEE

1 ACD**G**IJKLMPQ
2 CLRVVWXY
3 BGHJN**O**RU**W**X
4 (A 15/7-15/8) (Q+R+T+Z 🔲)
5 **AB**DFGIJKLMNOPUZ
6 CEGJ(N 4km)OV

💬 Well maintained peaceful campsite located in the middle of the countryside on the banks of the River Ourthe. Modern toilet facilities. Lovely playground. Plenty of opportunities for walking.

🚗 Via the N4, exit Berguème. Then follow the Berguème and campsite signs.

CC €18 1/1-29/5 10/6-1/7 18/8-31/12 🅿 N 50°04'33'' E 05°33'19''

## Tintigny, B-6730 / Luxembourg

🏕 Camping de Chênefleur***
✉ rue Norulle 16
☎ +32 63 44 40 78
📅 1/4 - 1/10
@ info@chenefleur.be

**560**

7,2ha 210T(100-125m²) 6A CEE

1 ACD**G**IJKLMO**P**RS
2 CFGLRVVWXY
3 BGHIJRU**W**X
4 (C+H 15/5-15/9)
   (Q+R 1/4-30/9)
   (T+U+V+Y+Z 1/7-31/8)
5 **AB**DEFGIJKLMNOPUWXZ
6 ADEGJ**K**(N 2km)OUV

💬 Located on the river Semois, well stocked with fish, this is a friendly campsite. There is a swimming pool. Restaurant, snacks and take-away meals every day in high season (1/7-1/9) and school holidays, only at weekends in other periods (1/4-30/6 and 3/9-30/9). Many options for hiking and cycling. Various cultural outings.

🚗 From E411 exit 29 direction Etalle (N87). In Etalle go towards Florenville (N83). Follow camping signs in Tintigny village. Clearly signposted.

CC €18 1/4-5/7 24/8-30/9 7=6, 14=12 🅿 N 49°41'06'' E 05°31'14''

## Turnhout, B-2300 / Antwerpen

🏕 Camping Baalse Hei****
✉ Roodhuisstraat 10
☎ +32 14 44 84 70
📅 1/1 - 31/12
@ info@baalsehei.be

**561**

30ha 74T(55-250m²) 16A CEE

1 ACD**G**IJKLMNOPQ
2 ACDFLRSWXY
3 ABGHJKMNRU**W**Z
4 (Q+R+T+U+X+Y+Z 1/4-30/9)
5 **AB**DGI**JKL**MN**P**UWXYZ
6 CDEGHK(N 4km)OSV

💬 Baalse Hei is hidden away in the beautiful countryside of the Antwerp Kempen. Relaxation, space, comfort and in particular plenty of privacy are the trump cards of this site. Marked out walks and direct access to the cycle route network. Spacious comfortable pitches for tents, caravans or motorhomes. 3 km from Turnhout, 20 mins. from Bobbejaanland theme park. Free wifi.

🚗 From the Netherlands: follow the Breda/Baarle-Nassau/Turnhout road. Campsite signposted after 10 km.

CC €18 1/5-30/5 2/6-8/7 26/8-30/9 7=6, 14=11 🅿 N 51°21'27'' E 04°57'32''

## Vogenée, B-5650 / Namur

🛜 📱iD (562)

▲ Camping Le Cheslé
✉ 1 rue d'Yves
☎ +32 71 61 26 32
📅 15/2 - 15/12
@ info.camping.chesle@gmail.com

6ha 78T(100m²) 10-16A CEE

**1** ACD**G**IJKLM**P**Q
**2** KLRVWXY
**3** A**F**GHJ
**4** (Q+R+T+U+X+Z 🔑)
**5** **AB**GIJKLMOPUWXYZ
**6** ACEGK(N 3km)TV

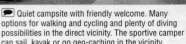

💬 Quiet campsite with friendly welcome. Many options for walking and cycling and plenty of diving possibilities in the direct vicinity. The sportive camper can sail, kayak or go geo-caching in the vicinity.

🚗 N5 Charleroi-Philippeville, exit Yves Gomezee. After the railroad turn right to Vogenee (4 km).

CC €18 15/2-30/6 1/9-15/12  📍 N 50°14'24'' E 04°27'34''

---

## Westende, B-8434 / West-Vlaanderen

♿ 🛜 ✿ 📱iD (563)

▲ Kompas Camping Westende***
✉ Bassevillestraat 141
☎ +32 58 22 30 25
📅 29/3 - 11/11
@ westende@kompascamping.be

12ha 168T(100-150m²) 10A CEE

**1** ACD**G**IJKLMOPRS
**2** EFGLRVWX
**3** BC**F**GHJKNUY
**4** M(Q+S 🔑)
   (T+U+Y+Z 30/3-15/4, 1/7-31/8)
**5** **AB**DEFGJKLNPQRUWXZ
**6** ABCDEGH**IK**(N 0,3km)OTV

💬 A fully equipped and environmentally friendly campsite with bar, shop and restaurant within walking distance of the dunes and the sea. Suitable for cycling or taking trips out along the coast or to attractive villages. Separate grounds for motorhomes (open all year).

🚗 E40 exit 4 direction Middelkerke. Over canal after about 2 km towards Middelkerke. Left at church towards Westende. 4th road on the right (Hovenierstraat) past Westende church and drive to the end.

CC €18 29/3-4/4 22/4-28/5 2/6-6/6 10/6-28/6 31/8-24/10 3/11-10/11  📍 N 51°09'27'' E 02°45'40''

---

## Westerlo/Heultje, B-2260 / Antwerpen

🚻 👫 ♿ 🛜 📱iD (564)

▲ Camping Hof van Eeden***
✉ Kempische Ardennen 8
☎ +32 16 69 83 72
📅 1/1 - 31/12
@ info@hofvaneeden.be

120ha 125T(100-150m²) 10A CEE

**1** ACD**G**IJKLMPQ
**2** ABDFGLMRSVWXY
**3** BGHJNRUWZ
**4** (B+G 21/6-31/8)
   (Q 1/6-31/8, 6/4-22/4)
   (R 6/4-22/4, 1/6-31/8)
   (T 15/3-31/10) (U 1/5-31/10)
   (X+Y 15/3-31/10) (Z 🔑)
**5** **AB**CDGIJKLMNO**P**UXYZ
**6** CDEGHK(N 2km)OSTV

💬 A quiet, hospitable campsite. Lovely walking and cycling around the Merode Castle and Merode woods. New toilet facilities and spacious comfort pitches, hardened motorhome pitches.

🚗 On E313 Herentals-oost, Olen, take exit 22, follow N152 until Zoerle-Parwijs, then towards Heultje. At the church there is a campsite sign to Hulshout-Heultje industrial area. Campsite sign along the industrial road.

CC €18 1/1-8/7 25/8-31/12  📍 N 51°05'17'' E 04°49'20''

## Zele, B-9240 / Oost-Vlaanderen

👫 👨‍👩‍👧 📶 ✿ **iD** **565**

🔺 Camping Groenpark***
📧 Gentsesteenweg 337
☎ +32 93 67 90 71
📅 20/4 - 1/10
@ groenpark@scarlet.be

50ha 70T(105-160m²) 16A CEE

**1** AGIJKLMPQ
**2** BDFGRSVWXY
**3** AGHJRU
**4** (Q 1/7-31/8) (Z 🔑)
**5** **AB**DGHIJKLMNOPRUXY
**6** ACDEG**IK**(N 0,3km)TV

💬 Campsite located between Ghent, Antwerp and Dendermonde. Plenty of opportunities for walking and cycling in the immediate surroundings.

🚗 From NL: E17 exit 12, follow N47 left. Take 1st exit N445 on 3rd roundabout. Take 2nd exit on 1st and 2nd roundabouts. Left after 2 km to campsite. From France: E17 exit 11, follow N449 left. Take the N445 left at T-junction. 2nd exit on roundabout after 7 km. Campsite 500 metres on the right.

**CC** € **18** *20/4-1/7  1/9-1/10*

📍 N 51°03'10''  E 03°58'48''

---

## Zonhoven, B-3520 / Limburg

♿ 📶 **iD** **566**

🔺 Camping Holsteenbron
📧 Hengelhoefseweg 9
☎ +32 11 81 71 40
📅 1/4 - 11/11
@ camping.holsteenbron@
   telenet.be

4ha 57T(80-100m²) 6A

**1** A**G**IJKLPRS
**2** FRSVXY
**3** A**F**GHJKRUW
**4** (Q+T+X+Z 🔑)
**5** **AB**DGIJKLMNO**P**UWZ
**6** CEGHK(N 3km)TV

💬 Yvo and Hilda ensure a varied range of entertainment at this campsite. Trips out and bike rides in the surroundings are offered regularly. The site has a fishing lake and spacious, marked out pitches.

🚗 E314 exit 29 direction Hasselt; after 800 metres turn left at traffic lights and follow the signs. Or road Eindhoven-Hasselt; cross the bridge over the E314. After 800 metres left; at traffic lights left and follow the signs.

**CC** € **18** *1/4-30/6  1/9-11/11*

📍 N 50°59'42''  E 05°24'59''

# Luxembourg

## General
Luxembourg is a member of the EU.

### Time
The time in Luxembourg is the same as Amsterdam, Paris and Rome and one hour ahead of London.

### Languages
Luxembourgish, French and German. English is also widely understood.

### Border formalities
Many formalities and agreements about matters such as necessary travel documents, car papers, requirements relating to your means of transport and accommodation, medical expenses and taking pets with you do not only depend on the country you are travelling to but also on your departure point and nationality. The length of your stay can also play a role here. It is not possible within the confines of this guide to guarantee the correct and most up to date information with regard to these matters.

We advise you to consult the relevant authorities before your departure about:
- which travel documents you will need for yourself and your fellow passengers
- which documents you need for your car
- which regulations your caravan must meet
- which goods you may import and export
- how medical treatment will be arranged and paid for in your holiday destination in cases of accident or illness
- whether you can take pets. Contact your vets well in advance. They can give you

information about the necessary vaccinations, proof thereof and obligations on return. It would also make sense to enquire whether any special regulations apply to your pet in public places at your holiday destination. In some countries for example dogs must always be muzzled or transported in a cage.

You will find plenty of general information on ▶ *www.europa.eu* ◀ but make certain you select information that is relevant to your specific situation.

For the most recent customs regulations you should get in contact with the authorities of your holiday destination in your country of residence.

## Currency
The currency in Luxembourg is the euro. Approximate exchange rates September 2018: £1 = € 1.12.

### Credit cards
You can pay by credit card in many places.

## Opening times
### Banks
Most banks are open from Monday to Friday from 9:00 to 16:30.

### Shops
In general, the shops are open from Tuesday to Saturday from 9:00 to 18:00. On Mondays the shops don't open until 14:00.

# Communication

### (Mobile) phones
The mobile network works well throughout Luxembourg, There is a 4G network for mobile internet.

### Wifi, internet
You can make use of a wifi network at more and more public locations, often for free.

### Post
Open Monday to Friday from 08:00 to 12:00 and from 14:00 to 17:00.

## Roads and traffic

### Road network
The Luxembourg automobile association ACL has a breakdown service 'Service Routier' that operates day and night: tel. 26000.

### Traffic regulations
Remember, all traffic in Luxembourg drives on the right and overtakes on the left! Headlight deflectors are advisable to prevent annoying oncoming drivers. Luxembourg uses the metric system, so distances are measured in kilometres (km) and speeds in kilometres per hour (km/h). Traffic coming from the right has priority. Trams always have priority. Buses and school transport have priority when moving away from a bus stop.

*Maximum speed*

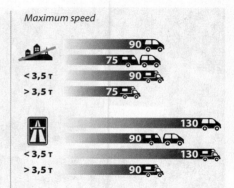

Maximum permitted alcohol level is 0.5‰. You must drive with dipped headlights during the day. Drivers may only use telephones hands-free. You can also overtake on the right in one-way streets. Cars must be fitted with winter tyres in winter conditions during the winter months.

### Caravans, motorhomes
If driving with a caravan longer than 7m and following another caravan, you must leave a space of 50m. There are plenty of service stations for motorhomes in Luxembourg.

### Maximum allowed measurements of combined length
Height 4 metres, width 2.55 metres and maximum length 18.75 metres (of which the trailer maximum 12 metres).

### Fuel
Fuel in Luxembourg is cheaper than in most other countries. Lead-free petrol and diesel are widely available. LPG is available in a limited number of places.

### Filling stations
Filling stations on the borders are usually open 24 hours, as fuel prices are less expensive. Other

service stations are usually open until 20:00. You can usually pay by credit card at service stations.

**Tolls**
Roads in Luxembourg are free of tolls.

**Emergency number**
- 112: national emergency number for fire and ambulance
- 113: emergency number for police

## Camping
Toilet facilities in Luxembourg are of above average quality. More than half of the campsites are classified using a star rating from 1 to 5 stars. The categories apply only to campsites that voluntarily cooperate in the scheme.
There are still some campsites that have chosen to remain with the 'old' classification, based on categories. Take note: there are high quality campsites that have chosen not to be included in any classification system.
Overnight camping on the roadside and free camping in cars, caravans or motorhomes is prohibited. Camping on farms is permitted with permission of the farmer and provided no more than 3 tents each with 2 adults are pitched on the same property.

**Practical**
- You will need a world adaptor for electrical equipment.
- It is safe to drink tap water in Luxembourg.

## Alzingen, L-5815 / Centre

&#9855; &#128246; **iD** **567**

&#9650; Camping Bon Accueil Kat.I
&#128231; 2 rue du Camping
&#9742; +352 36 70 69
&#128336; 1/4 - 15/10
@ syndicat.dinitiative@internet.lu

2,5ha 70T(100-120m²) 16A

**1** A**F**HIJKLMOPST
**2** FGRUVWXY
**3** BGJNU
**4** (T+Z &#128273;)
**5** **AB**DFGIJKLMNOPUWX
**6** CDEGHKM(N 0,20km)V

&#128488; A well maintained campsite in the heart of the city, located directly next to a public park. Suitable as a resting place on a journey down south but also as a base with a direct bus connection for visiting Luxembourg City and its lovely surroundings. Reception closed 12.00-14.00.

&#128739; A3/E25 direction Luxembourg City. Exit 1 Hesperange/Howald. 1st right on roundabout towards Hesperange. Follow camping signs at 3rd roundabout. Campsite on your right, before the church.

**CC** €**18** 1/4-30/6  1/9-14/10  7=6

&#128506; N 49°34'09'' E 06°09'36''

---

## Beaufort, L-6310 / Mullerthal

&#9855; &#128246; **iD** **568**

&#9650; Camping Plage Beaufort Kat.I
&#128231; 87 Grand Rue
&#9742; +352 8 36 09 93 00
&#128336; 1/1 - 31/12
@ camplage@pt.lu

4ha 190T(70-100m²) 10A CEE

**1** ACD**G**IJKLMOP**Q**
**2** BGIJLRSVWXY
**3** ABHJKL**M**NRU
**4** (C+H 18/5-1/9) J
   (T+U+X+Z &#128273;)
**5** **AB**DFGIJKLMNOPUZ
**6** AEGHIJ(N 0,1km)

&#128488; A campsite in the middle of the countryside close to the village centre of Beaufort. An ideal starting point for walking and mountain bike trips. Outdoor swimming pool in the summer, ice rink in winter, tennis courts, barbecue facilities, playground, bike hire, free wifi point. Pitches for caravans and tents. Open all year.

&#128739; Follow the N10 Diekirch-Echternach as far as Reisdorf. Turn right towards Beaufort. In Beaufort the campsite is located on the right of the road.

**CC** €**18** 1/1-30/6  2/9-31/12

&#128506; N 49°50'22'' E 06°17'17''

---

## Berdorf, L-6552 / Mullerthal

&#9855; &#128246; **iD** **569**

&#9650; Camping Martbusch Kat.I/***
&#128231; 3 beim Martbusch
&#9742; +352 79 05 45
&#128336; 1/1 - 31/12
@ info@camping-martbusch.lu

3ha 104T(80-100m²) 16A CEE

**1** ACD**G**IJKLMOPQ
**2** BRSVWXY
**3** BGHJKLN**Q**U
**4** (A 1/4-20/10) (Q &#128273;)
   (T+U+X 4/4-31/10)
**5** **AB**DEFGIJKLMNOPQRU
   WXZ
**6** CDEGK(N 1km)OV

&#128488; A shaded campsite, located in a pine forest on the edge of the rocky 'Little Switzerland' hiking area. The camping pitches are marked out by shoulder-high hedges. New toilet facilities with showers for families and children.

&#128739; N17/N19/N10 Diekirch-Echternach as far as Grundhof and then drive towards Berdorf. In Berdorf take the 2nd street on the left and then follow the signs.

**CC** €**18** 1/1-18/4  5/5-29/5  10/6-30/6  1/9-20/10  4/11-31/12

&#128506; N 49°49'34'' E 06°20'37''

## Consdorf, L-6211 / Mullerthal  ♿ 🛜 iD  (570)

🏕 Camping La Pinède
 Burgkapp Kat.I/***
📧 33 rue Burgkapp
☎ +352 79 02 71
📅 15/3 - 14/11
@ info@campconsdorf.lu

3ha  117T(100-140m²) 10A CEE

**1** ABCD**G**IJKLMOPQ
**2** BGIJRVWXY
**3** BGHJKL**MNQ**RU
**4** (A 1/7-15/8)
 (Q+T+U+X+Z ⌂)
**5** **AB**DFGIJKLMNOPUWZ
**6** CDEGK(N 0,5km)O

NEW

💬 Beautiful and well maintained quiet terraced
campsite with marked out pitches. Located along
the forest with beautiful rocks in the heart of
'Little Switzerland'. Tennis and mini golf course.
New restaurant with bar and terrace.

🚗 Follow the N14 Diekirch-Larochette. In Larochette
turn left towards Christnach/Consdorf. Follow the
signs in Consdorf.

CC € **18**  6/5-26/5  17/6-30/6  1/9-1/11   🧭 N 49°46'51'' E 06°19'54''

---

## Diekirch, L-9234 / Ardennes  ♿ 🛜 iD  (571)

🏕 Camping De la Sûre***
📧 route de Gilsdorf
☎ +352 80 94 25
📅 1/4 - 30/9
@ tourisme@diekirch.lu

5ha  196T(50-100m²) 10A CEE

**1** ACD**F**IJKLM**P**Q
**2** CFGRSVWXY
**3** BGJKLNRU**W**
**4** (Q+T+Z ⌂)
**5** **AB**DFGIJKLMN**P**UWXZ
**6** ACDEGJ(N 0,5km)V

💬 A lovely level campsite situated on the banks
of the River Sûre with sufficient shaded pitches, 5
minutes' walk from the centre of Diekirch. Indoor
swimming pool close by.

🚗 In Diekirch drive towards Larochette. After the
bridge over the Sûre turn left towards Gilsdorf. After
100 metres, 1st campsite.

CC € **20**  1/4-12/6  18/6-30/6  1/9-29/9   🧭 N 49°51'57'' E 06°09'54''

---

## Diekirch, L-9234 / Ardennes  👫 🛜 ✿ iD  (572)

🏕 Camping Op der Sauer Kat.I
📧 route de Gilsdorf
☎ +352 80 85 90
📅 29/3 - 27/10
@ info@campsauer.lu

5ha  270T(100m²) 10A CEE

**1** ACD**G**IJKLMOPRS
**2** CFGLRSVWXY
**3** BFGHJQR**W**X
**4** (Q+X+Y+Z ⌂)
**5** **A**DGIMNOPUYZ
**6** AEGJ(N 1km)V

💬 A level campsite with shaded pitches, located
on the Sûre (fishing opportunities) within walking
distance of the village of Diekirch. Sports facilities
in and around the site: minigolf, cycling, walking,
canoeing, possibility to swim in the indoor municipal
pool. Informal restaurant with bar and terrace.
16 Euros including tourist tax.

🚗 In Diekirch drive towards Larochette. After
the bridge over the Sûre turn left towards Gilsdorf:
second campsite. Entrance at roundabout.

CC € **16**  29/3-11/6  17/6-14/7  1/9-27/10  7=6, 14=12   🧭 N 49°51'55'' E 06°10'12''

## Dillingen, L-6350 / Mullerthal 🛜 iD **573**

🏕 Camping Wies-Neu Kat.I
🏠 12 rue de la Sûre
☎ +352 83 61 10
📅 22/3 - 3/11
@ info@camping-wies-neu.lu

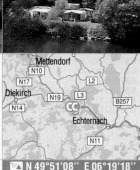

4,8ha 190T(100-120m²) 6A CEE

**1** AGIJKLMOPRS
**2** CGJRVWXY
**3** ABDHJKLRUWX
**4** (A 1/7-15/8) (Q 15/5-15/9)
   (R 14/4-3/11) (T 15/5-10/9)
**5** ABDFGIJKLMNOPU
**6** EGJ(N 4km)OV

💬 A well maintained family campsite positioned on the banks of the Sûre with spacious, marked out level pitches, and with plenty of shade. Opportunities for canoeing. The campsite is situated on the cycle route between Diekirch and Echternach. Ideal starting point for walks in 'Little Switzerland'.

🚗 Follow the N19/N10 Diekirch-Echternach as far as Dillingen. In Dillingen turn left at the crossroads then keep to the right.

CC €18 22/3-30/6  1/9-2/11        📷 N 49°51'08'' E 06°19'18''

---

## Echternach, L-6430 / Mullerthal ♿ 🛜 iD **574**

🏕 Camping Officiel
🏠 17 route de Diekirch
☎ +352 72 02 72
📅 1/4 - 31/10
@ info@camping-echternach.lu

4ha 298T(80-120m²) 6-10A

**1** ADGIJKLMOPQ
**2** GJLRTVWXY
**3** BGHJKMNRU
**4** (A 15/7-15/8)
**5** ABGIJMNOPUWZ
**6** BCDEGJ(N 0,3km)TV

💬 A spacious terraced campsite in three sections with grounds for long stays, a stopover area in an orchard and a youth area. Large playground and sports ground. A 10 minute walk from the centre, bordering on the cliff and hiking area of 'Little Switzerland'.

🚗 Follow N10-N19 Diekirch-Echternach. Campsite on the right before Echternach.

CC €18 1/4-29/6  18/8-30/10        📷 N 49°49'01'' E 06°24'38''

---

## Eisenbach, L-9838 / Ardennes ♿ 🛜 iD **575**

🏕 Camping Kohnenhof Kat.I/****
🏠 7 Kounenhaff
☎ +352 92 94 64
📅 1/4 - 31/10
@ info@campingkohnenhof.lu

6ha 125T(100-130m²) 6-16A CEE

**1** ACDGIJKLMPQ
**2** CGIJLRVWXY
**3** BFGHIJLNORUWX
**4** (A 15/7-19/8)
   (Q+R+T+U+X+Y+Z 📷)
**5** ABDEFGHIJKLMNPQRSU
   WXYZ
**6** ACDEGHKL(N 4km)OV

💬 A peaceful, family friendly campsite in wooded countryside on the banks of the Our. A good starting point for exploring the Eifel and the Ardennes and for visiting towns such as Vianden and Clervaux. Places to play in the river. Special arrangements for golfers. 6A is included as standard, 16A available for a 3 Euros fee.

🚗 On N7 near Hosingen take exit Rodershausen or Eisenbach. In the valley follow the signs to 'Kohnenhof' campsite.

CC €18 1/4-26/4  5/5-28/5  10/6-5/7  1/9-30/10 7=6    📷 N 50°00'59'' E 06°08'12''

## Enscherange, L-9747 / Ardennes

📶 ✿ **iD** **576**

🏕 Camping Val d'Or Kat.1/****
🏠 Um Gaertchen 2
☎ +352 92 06 91
📅 1/1 - 31/12
@ info@charmecamping.lu

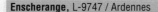

NEW

4ha 70T(80-120m²) 6A CEE

**1** ABCD**G**IJKLMNOPRS
**2** CKLRUWXY
**3** AB**F**GHJLNRUX
**4** M(Q+T+U+X+Y+Z 📅)
**5** **AB**CDF**G**IJK**L**MNOPUW
**6** ACDEGJK(N 9,9km)ORT

💬 Peaceful family campsite located by the river, walks possible in the lovely nature park. Car free campsite. Plenty of play activities for children.

🚗 E25 exit 15 St Vith, direction Luxembourg, exit Marnach/Munshaüsen/ Drauffelt/Encherange, campsite on your left.

Wincrange  Clervaux
N874      N7
N12    N10
N84
Wiltz
N15

**CC** € **14** 1/1-7/7 25/8-31/12 📡▲ N 50°00'01'' E 05°59'27''

---

## Ermsdorf, L-9366 / Mullerthal

📶 **iD** **577**

🏕 Camping Neumuhle Kat.I/****
🏠 27 Reisduerferstrooss
☎ +352 87 93 91
📅 1/4 - 20/10
@ info@camping-neumuhle.lu

3ha 105T(80-100m²) 6A CEE

**1** AD**G**IJKL**P**RS
**2** CGJRVWXY
**3** BGHJNRU
**4** (A 15/7-15/8) (B 1/5-30/8) (Q+R 📅) (T 7/7-24/8) (X+Z 📅)
**5** **AB**DFG**IJ**K**L**MNPUWZ
**6** ACEGK(N 4km)OV

💬 A well maintained terraced campsite on a hill with marked out pitches of maximum 100 m². Lovely views. A small swimming pool provides cool refreshment on hot days. A good base for countless trips out and walks. Free wifi. Dutch owners.

🚗 Follow the N14 Diekirch-Larochette as far as Medernach and then turn left towards Ermsdorf. In Ermsdorf continue driving for approx. 1 km towards Reisdorf as far as Hostellerie and campsite Neumühle.

N17    L2
Diekirch    N19   L3
Ettelbrück   N14
N10
Echternach
N7    N11

**CC** € **18** 1/4-7/7 25/8-19/10 📡▲ N 49°50'21'' E 06°13'31''

---

## Esch-sur-Sûre, L-9650 / Ardennes

♿ 📶 **iD** **578**

🏕 Camping Im Aal ***
🏠 1 Am Aal
☎ +352 83 95 14
📅 1/3 - 15/12
@ info@campingaal.lu

2,5ha 150T(100m²) 10A CEE

**1** A**G**IJKLMOPQ
**2** CGLRVWXY
**3** BGHINRU**W**X
**4** (A 15/7-15/8) (Q+R+Z 1/4-30/9)
**5** **AB**DFGIJMNOPUWZ
**6** ACEGJ(N 7km)TV

💬 Located in wooded surroundings on the banks of the Sûre. Quiet, calm and laid out with respect for the countryside. Walking and various leisure opportunities close by.

🚗 Take Bastogne-Diekirch N15, exit Esch-sur-Sûre. Through the tunnel, campsite 150 further on by the river.

N84    Wiltz
N15
N7
N12
Rambrouch    Ettelbrück

**CC** € **18** 1/3-18/4 22/4-28/5 2/6-6/6 10/6-4/7 25/8-14/12 📡▲ N 49°54'24'' E 05°56'34''

## Ettelbruck, L-9022 / Ardennes

♿ 📶 ✿ **iD** **579**

▲ Camping Ettelbrück
🏠 88 chemin du Camping
☎ +352 81 21 85
📅 1/4 - 1/10
@ camping@ettelbruck.lu

3ha 100T(80-120m²) 16A CEE

**1** ACDGIJKLMO**P**Q
**2** FGJKRVWXY
**3** BGHIJKLRU
**4** (A+Q+T+U+X+Z 🔌)
**5** **A**BDFGIJKLMNOPUWZ
**6** ACDEHJ(N 1km)UV

💬 Peacefully located terraced campsite on a hillside in the countryside and close to the town of Ettelbrück. Campsite Ettelbrück is a municipal campsite with reliable and well-maintained amenities. There is also a bistro, where you can get a bite to eat, fresh food every day.

🚗 In Ettelbrück town centre take the N15 to Wiltz/Bastogne. Follow the camping signs 300m on the left. Coming from Wiltz turn right before the centre.

**CC** € **18** 1/4-7/7 26/8-30/9

📷 N 49°50'46'' E 06°04'56''

---

## Goebelsmühle, L-9153 / Ardennes

📶 ✿ **iD** **580**

▲ Camping du Nord Kat.1
🏠 1 route de Dirbach
☎ +352 99 04 13
📅 1/4 - 1/11
@ info@campingdunord.lu

2ha 70T(100-150m²) 6A

**1** ACD**G**IJKLMOPRS
**2** CLRVWX
**3** BGHJNRU**W**X
**4** (Q+U+X+Z 🔌)
**5** **AB**DFGIJKMNOPUWZ
**6** AEGKOUV

💬 This lush campsite is on the banks of the River Sûre. It is a simple welcoming campsite with plenty of fishing. Peace and quiet really mean something here.

🚗 Goebelsmühle is next to the N27 on the banks of the Sûre. A campsite sign at this spot points the way downhill. About 700m from Goebelsmühle station.

**CC** € **18** 1/4-25/4 5/5-29/5 2/6-6/6 10/6-7/7 25/8-31/10

📷 N 49°55'32'' E 06°02'44''

---

## Ingeldorf/Diekirch, L-9161 / Ardennes

♿ 📶 **iD** **581**

NEW

▲ Camping Gritt Kat.I/***
🏠 2 rue Gritt
☎ +352 80 20 18
📅 17/4 - 27/10
@ info@camping-gritt.lu

3,5ha 130T(75-100m²) 10-16A CEE

**1** ACD**G**HIJKLMOPRS
**2** CFGRVWXY
**3** BHJ**W**
**4** (T+U+X+Z 🔌)
**5** **AB**DEFGHIJMNOPQUWZ
**6** BCDEGJ(N 0,8km)V

💬 Quiet, completely renovated campsite set in picturesque surroundings on the bank of the river Sûre. Shady, spacious pitches. A friendly bar with a terrace. The campsite is located within walking distance of the shopping centre and the town of Diekirch and Ettelbrück. Ideal for cycling tours.

🚗 Take the N7 Ettelbrück-Diekirch. After about 2 km take the direction of Ingeldorf. Then follow the signs.

**CC** € **20** 17/4-13/7 1/9-26/10

📷 N 49°51'02'' E 06°08'04''

## Larochette, L-7633 / Mullerthal
👨‍👧‍👦 ♿ 📶 iD **582**

▲ Iris Parc Camping
Birkelt Kat.I/*****
✉ 1 Um Birkelt
☎ +352 87 90 40
🕐 12/4 - 29/9
@ info@birkelt.com

12ha 184T(100-200m²) 10-16A CEE

**1** ACD**G**IJKLMOPRS
**2** BGILRVWXY
**3** BCF**G**HJLM**Q**RU
**4** (C+E+Q+S+T+U+V+X+Y+Z 🕐)
**5** **AB**DEFGIJKLMNOPQRUW
XYZ
**6** CEGHK(N 2,5km)OSV

💬 A modern, well maintained family campsite with spacious pitches with man-sized hedges. The campsite offers every comfort. Camp shop. Plenty of recreational opportunities including an all-weather swimming pool, horse riding, mini-golf, tennis on request. Children's entertainment in the early season.

🚗 Follow the N14 Diekirch-Larochette. Turn right in the centre of Larochette and then follow the signs to the campsite.

CC € **18** 12/4-7/6 2/9-29/9
🏕 N 49°47'05'' E 06°12'40''

---

## Lieler, L-9972 / Ardennes
⛷ ♿ 📶 iD **583**

▲ Camping Trois Frontières
Kat.I/****
✉ Hauptstrooss 12
☎ +352 99 86 08
🕐 1/1 - 31/12
@ info@troisfrontieres.lu

2ha 90T(120-130m²) 6-10A CEE

**1** ABCD**G**IJKLMO**P**Q
**2** GKLRSWXY
**3** B**F**GHJNRU
**4** (A 1/7-31/8) (E 1/4-15/9)
(H 1/7-31/8)
(Q+T+U 1/4-31/10)
(X 1/4-15/10) (Z 1/4-31/10)
**5** **AB**DEFGHIJKLMNPQRU
WYZ
**6** ACEGHK(N 3km)OTV

💬 Pleasant hospitality for families with children. The campsite is up in the hills with lovely views. There is a semi-covered swimming pool. Lovely area for walking.

🚗 N7 Weiswampach towards Diekirch, turn left about 3 km beyond Weiswampach direction Lieler. Campsite signposted.

CC € **18** 1/1-5/7 23/8-31/12
🏕 N 50°07'26'' E 06°06'18''

---

## Mamer/Luxemburg, L-8251 / Centre
♿ 📶 iD **584**

▲ Camping Mamer Kat.I
✉ 4 route de Mersch
☎ +352 31 23 49
🕐 1/4 - 16/10
@ campingmamer@gmail.com

1,5ha 60T(80m²) 6-16A CEE

**1** A**G**IJKLMO**P**RS
**2** BCFLRSWXY
**3** AHJ
**4** (Q 1/7-30/8)
(U+X+Z 1/4-30/9)
**5** DGIJMNOPUZ
**6** DGJL(N 2km)U

💬 A campsite for stopover campers. Busy in the mornings and evenings, exceptionally quiet during the day. A real stopover campsite, with a restaurant that is open from 1/4-30/9.

🚗 A6/E25 dir. France, exit 2. Follow Mamer, left at 3rd roundabout (do not enter tunnel!). Look out for signs. A6/E25 dir. Netherlands, exit 4. Follow Strassen/Capellen, Right at 2nd roundabout. Look out for signs.

CC € **16** 1/4-30/6 26/8-15/10
🏕 N 49°37'45'' E 06°02'48''

## Maulusmühle, L-9974 / Ardennes

🗘 🛜 ✿ **iD** `585`

🏕 Camping Woltzdal Kat.I/***
🏨 Maison 12 / Om camping 12
☎ +352 99 89 38
🔆 20/4 - 26/10
@ info@woltzdal-camping.lu

2ha 20T(70-140m²) 4A CEE

1 ABCD**G**IJKL**P**RS
2 BCGRTUVXY
3 B**F**GHIJNRUX
4 (Q+S+T+U+V+X+Z 🔆)
5 **AB**CDEFGIJKLMN**PQ**RUXZ
6 ADEGK(N 7km)OTV

💬 The campsite is located in a beautiful valley. It is very quiet despite the trains. Close to the historic village of Clervaux.

🚗 Road CR355 Clervaux-Troisvierges. Maulusmühle is located on the road 6 km north of Clervaux. The campsite is located on this road in the vally.

CC €**16** 20/4-5/7 23/8-26/10 7=6, 14=12    📧 N 50°05'31'' E 06°01'40''

## Mersch, L-7572 / Centre

🗘 🛜 **iD** `586`

🏕 Camping Krounebierg*****
🏨 2 rue du Camping, BP 35
☎ +352 32 97 56
🔆 30/3 - 31/10
@ contact@campingkrounebierg.lu

3ha 140T(60-200m²) 6-10A CEE

1 ACD**G**IJKLMPQ
2 FJLRTVWXY
3 BGHJNRU**V**
4 (A 6/7-17/8) (**F** 🔆)
   (G 1/6-30/9) **IJKLN**
   (Q+S+T+U+Y+Z 🔆)
5 **AB**DFGIJKLMNOPQUWZ
6 ACDEGHK(N 1,5km)OUV

💬 At 1.5 km from Mersch, marked-out pitches. Near N7 and A7, suitable for people who are passing through. Next to a water recreation centre (free for 2 hours a day for stays longer than 3 nights). Restaurant open in afternoon and evening.
🚗 From the north A7, exit Kopstal; dir. Mersch. Follow camping signs. Follow signs from the N7 in Mersch town centre. From the south A6 dir. Bruxelles; then exit 3 Bridel/Kopstal. Dir. Mersch, then follow camping signs.

CC €**18** 30/3-7/7 24/8-30/10    📧 N 49°44'37'' E 06°05'23''

## Nommern, L-7465 / Centre

🗘 🛜 ✿ **iD** `587`

🏕 Europacamping
   Nommerlayen Kat.I/*****
🏨 rue Nommerlayen
☎ +352 87 80 78
🔆 5/4 - 3/11
@ info@nommerlayen-ec.lu

15ha 388T(70-130m²) 10-16A CEE

1 ABCD**G**IJKLMO**PQ**
2 FJKRVWXY
3 AB**F**GHIJKLNR**T**U
4 (A 27/4-4/5/5,6/7-1/9)
   (B+E+F+H 1/5-15/9) **KMN**
   (Q+S+T+U+X+Y+Z 🔆)
5 **AB**CDEFGHIJKLMNOP**RS**U
   WXYZ
6 ACDEGHIK(N 8km)OTV

💬 Luxury terraced campsite in walking area with spacious, marked out level pitches with water and drainage. Modern toilets including private bathrooms. Two open air pools, one with sliding roof. More expensive pitches (better location) also possible with CampingCard ACSI for extra fee.
🚗 N7 as far as Ettelbrück/Schieren and then exit 7, Cruchten, Colmarberg. At end of exit, after petrolstation, turn left towards Cruchten/Nommern. In Cruchten turn left and then follow signs.

CC €**18** 6/5-28/5 10/6-5/7 24/8-2/11    📧 N 49°47'06'' E 06°09'55''

## Rosport, L-6484 / Mullerthal ♿ 📶 iD **588**

🔺 Camping Du Barrage
  Rosport Kat.I
🚐 1, rue du camping
☎ +352 73 01 60
🗓 1/3 - 31/10
@ campingrosport@pt.lu

4,2ha 128T(100m²) 12-16A CEE

**1** ACD**G**IJKLPQ
**2** CGLRSVWX
**3** BGHJKLNRU**W**
**4** (C+H 15/5-15/9) (Q 🔑)
  (T 15/6-15/9) (Z 🔑)
**5** **AB**DEFGIJKMNOPQUWZ
**6** CFGHK(N 0,5km)

💬 A level family campsite located on the banks of the Sûre with spacious pitches, a paradise for cyclists and anglers (fishing season 15/6 - 28/2). New toilet facilities and an outdoor swimming pool. A good starting point for making trips out in the region.

🚗 Follow route N10 Echternach-Wasserbillig as far as Rosport. Then follow the signs.

CC € **16** 1/3-30/6 1/9-30/10 7=6, 14=12 | N 49°48'33'' E 06°30'12''

---

## Troisvierges, L-9912 / Ardennes ♿ 📶 iD **589**

🔺 Camping Troisvierges Kat.I
🚐 rue de Binsfeld
☎ +352 99 71 41
🗓 1/4 - 30/9
@ info@camping-troisvierges.lu

5ha 140T(80-120m²) 10A

**1** ABCD**G**IJKLN PQ
**2** CGJLRVXY
**3** BF GHJMNR**S**U
**4** (A 10/7-17/8) (C+G 1/6-31/8)
  J(Q+T+U+X+Z 🔑)
**5** **AB**DFGJLMNPUWXYZ
**6** ACDEGHK(N 0,2km)TV

💬 Relaxation for all ages in a nature park. Lovely walking and cycling country, including the Venbahn. Located on the edge of a small town. Various sports facilities.

🚗 The campsite is located 300 metres from the centre of the small town Troisvierges, on the road to Binsfeld. In Troisvierges: follow the camping signs.

CC € **18** 1/4-30/6 1/9-30/9 | N 50°07'07'' E 06°00'05''

---

## Vianden, L-9415 / Ardennes ♟ 📶 iD **590**

🔺 Camping de l'Our
🚐 3 route de Bettel
☎ +352 83 45 05
🗓 1/4 - 20/10
@ campingour@pt.lu

1,5ha 120T(70-150m²) 10A

**1** ACD**G**IJKL**P**Q
**2** CGIRVWXY
**3** AGHJRU**W**X
**4** (Q+R+T+U+X+Y+Z 🔑)
**5** **AB**FGIKMOP**U**Z
**6** EGK(N 4km)OV

💬 Campsite is located at walking distance from Vianden centre. Quiet location with spacious pitches. Lightly undulating grounds. Fishing possible in river.

🚗 N17 Diekirch-Vianden. Turn right in Fouhren, N17B, 2 km past Bettel. 2nd campsite on right.

CC € **18** 1/4-28/5 17/6-5/7 2/9-19/10 7=6, 14=11 | N 49°55'40'' E 06°13'15''

## Walsdorf, L-9465 / Ardennes

♿ 🛜 📱 **591**

🏕 Camping Vakantiepark Walsdorf****
📧 Tandlerbaach
☎ +352 83 44 64
📅 13/4 - 26/10
@ info@campingwalsdorf.com

6ha 100T(100-160m²) 4-6A CEE

**1** ABCD**G**IJKLOPRS
**2** BCJLRSUVWXY
**3** AHJKLNRU
**4** (Q+R+T+Z 🔒)
**5** **AB**DEFGHIJKLMNOPUWZ
**6** DEGJ**K**(N 9km)

💬 Beautifully situated campsite in peaceful natural surroundings. Plenty of amenities including modern sanitary facilities. Spacious pitches including some on the 'Tandelerbach' brook. The site is operated by 'Beter-uit'. Close to the historic towns of Vianden and Diekirch.

🚗 Take the N17 Diekirch-Vianden. Beyond Tandel turn left. Follow the signs. The campsite access road is very narrow.

CC € **14** 13/4-25/4  4/5-4/7  31/8-25/10

N 49°55'02'' E 06°10'43''

---

## Wiltz, L-9554 / Ardennes

♿ 🛜 📱 **592**

🏕 Camping-Park KAUL Kat.I
📧 60 Campingstrooss
☎ +352 9 50 35 91
📅 1/4 - 4/11
@ info@kaul.lu

6ha 77T(100m²) 10A CEE

**1** ACD**G**IJKLMOPQ
**2** GILRTVWX
**3** BGHJLM**N**RU
**4** (A 10/7-15/8)
(C+H 15/6-31/8) J
(T 1/7-15/8) (U+X+Y+Z 🔒)
**5** **AB**DFGIJKLMNOP**QRS**U WXY
**6** ACDEGHK(N 0,2km)V

💬 A town campsite with every comfort, situated next to the Wiltz sports park and within walking distance of the centre. A peaceful, attractive location surrounded by greenery. Situated on the edge of the Ardennes woods and a starting point for lovely long walks.

🚗 The campsite is located 300 metres from the centre of the lower town of Wiltz. Camping signs are posted on the road Troisvierges-Clervaux.

CC € **18** 1/4-6/7  24/8-4/11

N 49°58'23'' E 05°56'01''

# Germany

Kiel

Schleswig-Holstein
**273**

Rostock

Lübeck

Mecklenburg-Vorpommern
**282**

Hamburg

Bremen

NL

Niedersachsen
**256**

PL

BERLIN

Braunschweig

Hannover

Magdeburg

Brandenburg
**295**

Münster

Bielefeld

Nordrhein-Westfalen
**305**

Sachsen-Anhalt
**293**

Gelsenkirchen

Oberhausen
Dortmund
Duisburg
Essen
Bochum

Halle

Leipzig

Sachsen
**299**

Dresden

Düsseldorf

Kassel

Mönchengladbach

Erfurt

Chemnitz

Köln

Aachen

Bonn

Thüringen
**303**

B

Koblenz

Hessen
**313**

PRAHA

Frankfurt am Main

L

Wiesbaden

Rheinland-Pfalz
**318**

CZ

LUXEMBURG

Nürnberg

Saarland
**337**

Mannheim

Regensburg

Karlsruhe

Bayern
**354**

Stuttgart

FR

Baden-Württemberg
**337**

Augsburg

München

Freiburg

# General

Germany is a member of the EU.

## Time

The time in Germany is the same as Amsterdam, Paris and Rome and one hour ahead of London.

## Language

German, but you can usually get by in English.

# Border formalities

Many formalities and agreements about matters such as necessary travel documents, car papers, requirements relating to your means of transport and accommodation, medical expenses and taking pets with you do not only depend on the country you are travelling to but also on your departure point and nationality. The length of your stay can also play a role here. It is not possible within the confines of this guide to guarantee the correct and most up to date information with regard to these matters.

We advise you to consult the relevant authorities before your departure about:
- which travel documents you will need for yourself and your fellow passengers
- which documents you need for your car
- which regulations your caravan must meet
- which goods you may import and export
- how medical treatment will be arranged and paid for in your holiday destination in cases of accident or illness
- whether you can take pets. Contact your vets well in advance. They can give you information about the necessary vaccinations, proof thereof and obligations on return. It would also make sense to enquire whether any special regulations apply to your pet in public places at your holiday destination. In some countries for example dogs must always be muzzled or transported in a cage.

You will find plenty of general information on ▶ www.europa.eu ◀ but make certain you select information that is relevant to your specific situation.

For the most recent customs regulations you should get in contact with the authorities of your holiday destination in your country of residence.

# Currency

The currency in Germany is the euro. Approximate exchange rates September 2018: £1 = € 1.12.

## Credit cards

You can pay by credit card in most places.

# Opening times

## Banks

There are no standard opening times for banks. Most of them close at 16:00.

## Shops

Opening times are Monday to Friday from 09:30 to 18:00. On Saturdays shops in larger cities are open till 18:00.

## Chemists

Chemists are open Monday to Friday until 18:00; and on Saturdays until 12:00.

# Communication

## (Mobile) phones

The mobile network works well throughout Germany. There is a 4G network for mobile internet.

## Wifi, internet

You can make use of a wifi network at more and more public locations, often for free.

### Post

Generally open from Monday to Friday until
18:00. On Saturday till 12:00.

# Roads and traffic

### Road network

Remember, all traffic in Germany drives on
the right and overtakes on the left! Headlight
deflectors are advisable to prevent annoying
oncoming drivers. Germany uses the metric
system, so distances are measured in kilometres
(km) and speeds in kilometres per hour (km/h).
You can use emergency phones on motorways
to call the 'Straßenwachthilfe'. If you don't do
this the 'Straßendienst' will come and you will
have to pay for assistance. Elsewhere you should
call the ADAC: tel. 01802-222222 or the ACE:
tel. 01802-343536.

### Traffic regulations

All traffic from the right has priority, except on
roundabouts. If you are driving on a roundabout
you have priority over drivers wishing to enter
the roundabout. The rule on narrow mountain
roads is that the vehicle that can move over
more easily gives priority.
Take note! You may not indicate a direction
when approaching or joining a roundabout.
It is compulsory to indicate when exiting a
roundabout.
An alcohol level above 0.5‰ is an offence. Use
of dipped headlights is not compulsory, except
in tunnels. Drivers may only phone hands-free.
You may not repair your vehicle by the side of
the motorway. You must be towed away in all
circumstances. At tailbacks on main roads you
should wherever possible move to the right or
left to leave room in the middle for emergency
services. Cars in Germany (including tourists'
cars) are required to take extra precautions in
winter conditions. This means they need to
be fitted with winter tyres and have sufficient
antifreeze in the windscreen washers.

*Maximum speed*

### Caravans, motorhomes

Take note! In Germany you need to have one
green card for your car and another one for
your caravan, if it weighs more than 750 kg.
The environmental badge is required if driving
a motorhome. You will find more information
under 'Environmental Badge'. An overtaking
ban for lorries also applies to motorhomes
heavier than 3500 kg.

### Tempo 100 exemption

To tow a trailer or caravan at maximum
100 km/h you need a so-called 'Tempo 100'
exemption. Your car and caravan must meet a
number of test requirements. You can get more
information about this from TÜV:
▸ www.tuev-nord.de/en/private ◂

### Maximum allowed measurements of
### combined length

Height 4 metres, width 2.55 metres and length
18 metres (of which the trailer maximum
12 metres).

### Environmental Badge

More and more German cities require you
to display an environmental badge on your
car windscreen. Cost: € 13.95. The badge
may be yellow or green depending on the

environmental requirements. This rule applies also to non-German registered cars. You will see traffic signs in these specific towns with the word 'Umweltzone'. You may only enter this zone if you are displaying a sticker.

If you enter this zone without a badge you risk a € 80 fine. Older diesel vehicles and cars without a catalytic converter are not allowed in the centre of these cities. The badge can be ordered (also online) from TÜV Nord.
More information: ▶ *www.umwelt-plakette.de* ◀

**Fuel**
Lead-free petrol and diesel are widely available and LPG is becoming more available. Since 2011 German filling stations are changing over to the new E10 fuel.

**Filling stations**
Filling stations are generally open between 08:00 and 20:00. Service stations on motorways are generally open day and night.

**Tolls**
German roads are free of toll for private cars.

**Emergency number**
- 110: the emergency number for police
- 112: the emergency number for fire and ambulance

# Camping
German campsites are among the better in Europe. Campsites specialise increasingly to target groups such as families with children, hikers and cyclists or wellness enthusiasts.
The number of comfort pitches and motorhome pitches with service stations has been sustained.
Nearly all campsites operate a lunch break (usually between 13:00 and 15:00) which is strictly enforced.

**Practical**
- Tourist Offices in Germany are open from 10:00 to 16:00.
- Make sure you have a world adaptor for electrical equipment.
- It is safe to drink tap water.

**Fishing**
A recreational fishing licence is mandatory in Germany. You will also need a fishing permit for specific fishing areas. You can get this permit and additional information from the local tourist office.

## Bad Bederkesa, D-27624 / Niedersachsen

&#9855; &#128246; **iD** **593**

&#9650; Ferienanlage Bad Bederkesa**
&#9993; Ankeloherstraße 14
&#9742; +49 47 45 64 87
&#8986; 1/4 - 31/10
@ badbederkesa@regenbogen.ag

12ha 100T(80-120m²) 16A CEE

**1** ACD**G**HIJKLMOPQ
**2** CFRVWXY
**3** AB**F**HJNR**W**
**4** (Q 1/4-30/9) (U+X+Y+Z &#9000;)
**5** **AB**DEFGIJKLMNOP**QR**UW XYZ
**6** CEGK(N 1km)OTU

&#128488; A large campsite in an attractive village. Many watersports opportunities close by. Frequently used as a stopover campsite. Large, spacious camping pitches. Restaurant closed on Mondays and Tuesdays from 1 October to the end of March. The restaurant is open for the rest of the year.

&#128663; Motorway A27 Bremerhaven-Cuxhaven, exit Debstedt. Direction Bederkesa. Turn off in Bederkesa by the white 'Ferienpark' sign.

L118 L119 L117 L144 L116 A27 L120 CC Spaden Kührstedt L128 Schiffdorf

**CC** € **18** 1/4-15/4  23/4-28/5  12/6-29/6  25/8-31/10  &#9650; N 53°37'15'' E 08°50'57''

---

## Bad Bentheim, D-48455 / Niedersachsen

&#128246; **iD** **594**

&#9650; Camping Am Berg
&#9993; Suddendorferstraße 37
&#9742; +49 59 22 99 04 61
&#8986; 4/3 - 1/12
@ info@campingplatzamberg.de

3ha 81T(100-120m²) 16A CEE

**1** A**G**IJKLMOPRS
**2** GRWXY
**3** FHJ
**4** (Q 18/4-30/9) (X &#9000;)
**5** **AB**DGHIJLMNOP**S**U
**6** EG**K**(N 4km)

&#128488; You can camp at this site just outside the historic village in a meadow surrounded by trees or in a lovely 'avenue'. The surrounding area is excellent for walks and bike rides. You will be welcomed by the Dutch owners.

&#128663; A1 Hengelo border direction Osnabrück (A30). Exit 3 direction Bad Bentheim. Follow road 403. Campsite signposted.

L40 B403 A30 Schüttorf A1 L39 CC A31 L42 Gronau (Westfalen) L582 L567 B70

**CC** € **18** 4/3-28/5  11/6-15/7  1/9-30/11  &#9650; N 52°17'52'' E 07°11'30''

---

## Bad Gandersheim, D-37581 / Niedersachsen

&#9855; &#128246; **iD** **595**

&#9650; Kur Campingpark
&#9993; Braunschweiger Straße 12
&#9742; +49 53 82 15 95
&#8986; 1/1 - 31/12
@ info@ camping-bad-gandersheim.de

9ha 250T(100m²) 6-16A CEE

**1** ACD**G**HIJKLMOPQ
**2** CDFRTVX
**3** BHJN**OP**QRXZ
**4** (Q 1/4-31/10,20/12-31/12)
(R 1/4-31/10) (U 1/5-31/10)
(Y 1/5-31/10,20/12-31/12)
(Z 1/5-31/10)
**5** **AB**CDEFGIJKLMNOPUWZ
**6** CDGJ**K**(N 2km)O

&#128488; Well-maintained, even grounds with marked-out pitches for 4 to 8 units. A romantic brook separates the site into two parts. Via the bordering spa you will be in the idyllic centre of Bad Gandersheim in 5 minutes.

&#128663; BAB 7 Kassel-Hannover, exit 67 Seesen. Follow the signs to Bad Gandersheim for 9 km, turn right on B64 before the town.

L466 B82 B243 B248 L489 Seesen L487 B242 B64 CC Münchehof Einbeck A7 B445 B3 L572 L525

**CC** € **18** 1/1-30/6  18/8-31/12  7=6  &#9650; N 51°52'02'' E 10°03'00''

## Bad Rothenfelde, D-49214 / Niedersachsen

♿ 📶 **iD** **596**

🏕 Camping Campotel\*\*\*\*\*
📧 Heidland 65
☎ +49 54 24 21 06 00
🕐 1/1 - 31/12
@ info@campotel.de

13ha 140T(75-180m²) 16A CEE

**1** ACGHIJKLMOPQ
**2** AFLMNRTUVWXY
**3** ACDFGHIJKMNOPQRSU VW
**4** KLN(Q+R 🔌)
(T 8/7-24/8,3/10-26/10)
(U 24/8-24/8,3/10-26/10)
(X 🔌)
**5** ABDFGJKLNPQRUWXYZ
**6** CDEGHK(N 0,5km)OT

💬 Campotel, a campsite with unusual features and with excellent toilet facilities. A great area for cycling, walking and inhaling the healthy air by the salt walls. The new thermal bath is recommended.

🚗 A30 Enschede as far as Lotte Kreuz. Then drive towards Hannover. At Autobahnkreuz Osnabrück-Süd take the A33 towards Bielefeld/Bad Rothenfelde. Then exit 13 direction Bad Rothenfelde. Straight ahead at roundabout, then follow signs.

Hagen am Teutoburger Wald

**CC** € **18** 14/1-18/4 29/4-24/5 11/6-12/7 29/8-27/12

🏕 N 52°05'53'' E 08°10'22''

## Bleckede, D-21354 / Niedersachsen

♿ 📶 **iD** **597**

🏕 Knaus Campingpark Bleckede/Elbtalaue\*\*\*\*
📧 Am Waldbad 23
☎ +49 5 85 43 11
🕐 1/1 - 31/12
@ elbtalaue@knauscamp.de

6,5ha 142T(80-100m²) 16A CEE

**1** ACDGHIJKLMOPQ
**2** BCGLRVWXY
**3** BGHJKLMRUW
**4** (C+H 1/5-15/9) JN(Q+R 🔌)
**5** ABDEFGHJLNPQUWZ
**6** CDEGK(N 6km)OU

NEW

💬 A beautifully laid out campsite in the 'Niedersächsische Elbtalaue' bio-reserve, a paradise for cyclists, watersports, walkers and anglers. Comfortable, easily accessible, modern, spacious toilet facilities. Located next to extensive woodland with unlimited entry.

🚗 A7 Hannover-Hamburg exit Soltau-Ost direction Lüneberg/Dahlenburg. Left to Bleckede, then Hitzacker.

Bleckede
Amt Neuhaus

**CC** € **18** 1/1-29/5 3/6-7/6 24/6-15/7 1/9-31/12

🏕 N 53°15'34'' E 10°48'20''

## Bleckede (OT Radegast), D-21354 / Niedersachsen

👫 ♿ 📶 **iD** **598**

🏕 Camping Elbeling
📧 Hinter den Höfen 9a
☎ +49 5 85 75 55
🕐 15/3 - 1/10
@ info@elbeling.de

3,8ha 100T(100-360m²) 16A CEE

**1** AGIJKLPQ
**2** ACGKLMRWXY
**3** BFGHJRUWX
**4** (G 1/5-1/10)
(Q+T+U+V+X+Z 1/4-1/10)
**5** ABEFGHIJLMNOPUWXZ
**6** ACDEGHK(N 5km)OTV

💬 A beautiful, well-kept and comfortable campsite with spacious pitches. Level and situated on the Elbe and recognized by UNESCO as a 'biosphären reservat' nature reserve. Unique surroundings for nature lovers with plenty of cycling and walking opportunities. The campsite was renovated in 2012 and is Dutch-owned.

🚗 From Luneburg direction Bleckede, then towards Radegast. Campsite signposted in Radegast. Take side road at covered wagon. Entrance: Hinter den Höfen 9a.

Lauenburg/ Elbe
Bleckede

**CC** € **20** 15/3-4/7 22/8-30/9

🏕 N 53°20'27'' E 10°43'46''

## Burhave, D-26969 / Niedersachsen

**iD** 599

▲ Knaus Camp.park
  Fedderwardersiel/Nordsee
🏠 Lagunenweg
☎ +49 47 33 16 83
📅 15/4 - 15/10
@ burhave@knauscamp.de

1ha 76T(80-100m²) 16A CEE

**1** ACD**G**IJKLMOPQ
**2** EKLMPRVW
**3** ABGHJNWY
**5** **AB**DGIJMNOPUWXZ
**6** CDEG(N 0,2km)OU

💬 On the Butjadingen headland, near the Wadden Sea, with small harbour. Even campsite situated next to the dyke. Designed for guests with dogs. Here you and your dog can enjoy the nature, endless mudflats, the fresh air and the beautiful beaches. The first pet is free.

🚗 Through Burhave direction Tossens. Exit Fedderwardersiel. Turn left on the dike. Campsite signposted as 'Knaus Campingpark'. Report to the Knaus campsite in Butjadingen/Burhave.

**Nordenham**

CC € 16 15/4-29/5  3/6-7/6  24/6-15/7  1/9-15/10    N 53°35'00'' E 08°22'13''

---

## Butjadingen/Burhave, D-26969 / Niedersachsen

🏊 🛜 **iD** 600

▲ Knaus Campingpark
  Burhave / Nordsee****
🏠 An der Nordseelagune 1
☎ +49 47 33 16 83
📅 15/4 - 15/10
@ burhave@knauscamp.de

2,5ha 100T(90m²) 16A CEE

**1** ACD**G**HIJKLMOPQ
**2** ADEGKLMPRSTUVW
**3** BGIJKLN**OPQ**UWYZ
**4** (**A** 1/6-31/8)
  (Q+R+T+U+Y 🚗)
**5** **AB**DEFGIJKLMNOPUWXYZ
**6** CDEG**K**(N 2km)OUVX

💬 A quiet beach campsite by the World Heritage List Waddenzee with good amenities, next to the Nordseelagune leisure pool complex. Plenty of good restaurants and small shops in the village. Pitches right by the sea. Mud-walking. Close to a large indoor children's playground.

🚗 A7 Groningen-Leer. Dir. A28 Oldenburg. Exit 14 direction Wilhelmshaven. Exit 8 Varel. Exit Schweiburg direction Nordenham/Butjadingen. Exit Tossens direction Langwarden. Campsite signposted.

**Bremerhaven**

CC € 20 15/4-29/5  3/6-7/6  24/6-15/7  1/9-15/10    N 53°35'01'' E 08°22'12''

---

## Clausthal-Zellerfeld, D-38678 / Niedersachsen

🎿 🛜 **iD** 601

▲ Camping Prahljust****
🏠 An den langen Brüchen 4
☎ +49 53 23 13 00
📅 1/1 - 31/12
@ camping@prahljust.de

13ha 450T(80-110m²) 16A CEE

**1** ABCD**G**IJKLMOPQ
**2** BDILNRTUX
**3** BHJRU**W**Z
**4** (F 🚗) **N**(Q+T+U+Y 🚗)
**5** **AB**DFGIJKLMNOPUWZ
**6** CDEGK(N 4km)OU

💬 A peaceful family campsite with plenty of trees and lakes in the immediate vicinity. Excellent walking and cycling in the summer. Opportunities for wintersports in the winter. The site has heated toilet facilities. Lovely villages such as Clausthal-Zellerfeld and Goslar nearby.

🚗 A7, exit 67 Seesen. To Bad Grund and Clausthal-Zellerfeld. Then on B242 direction Braunlage.

**Osterode am Harz**

CC € 18 14/1-31/3  1/5-29/5  24/6-27/6  29/8-15/12    N 51°47'05'' E 10°21'01''

## Dorum/Neufeld, D-27632 / Niedersachsen 🛜 iD 602

▲ Knaus Campingpark Dorum
✉ Am Kutterhafen
☎ +49 47 41 50 20
📅 1/4 - 30/9
@ dorum@knauscamp.de

8,5ha 120T(80-140m²) 16A CEE

**1** ACD**G**HIJKLO**P**Q
**2** EGKLMRVW
**3** ABHJY
**4** (C 20/4-30/9) (Q 📅)
   (T 20/4-30/9) (X+Y+Z 📅)
**5** A**B**GIJKLMNOPUWZ
**6** ACDEG**K**(N 7km)O

💬 The campsite is located on level grounds beyond the dike. Plenty of options for eating and drinking within 50m of the site. Lovely small harbour. The campsite is constructed in the early season and dismantled again in late season.

🚗 Motorway A27 Bremerhaven-Cuxhaven. Exit Neuenwalde. Head in the direction of Dorum, subsequently in the direction of Dorum/Neufeld-Kutterhafen. Drive for about 7 km up to the harbour. Turn to the right and follow the signs to the campsite.

Nordholz

CC

Dorum    A27
   L118
   L129
   L135

CC €18  1/4-29/5  3/6-7/6  24/6-15/7  1/9-30/9    N 53°44'19'' E 08°31'03''

---

## Dorum/Neufeld, D-27639 / Niedersachsen    iD 603

▲ Knaus Campingpark
   Spieka/Wattenmeer
✉ Am Kutterhafen
☎ +49 47 41 50 20
📅 1/4 - 30/9
@ spieka@knauscamp.de

1ha 80T(30-100m²) 16A CEE

**1** ACD**G**HIJKLMOQ
**2** EKLRUVW
**3** HJ**WY**
**4** (T+U+Z 📅)
**5** A**D**GIJKLMNOPUWXZ
**6** BCDEG(N 8km)O

NEW

💬 A small campsite outside the dykes with a small marina. The marina accommodates sailboats from the sailing club, which is just in front of the campsite. Please note: registration is at Knaus Camping Park, Dorum-Neufeld.

🚗 Via the A27 until exit 3. Then direction Nordholz, airport and Wannhöden. Then take K14 towards Spieka-Neufeld. Use coordinates rather than address in SatNav.

Altenwalde

CC    A27
   L135
Dorum  L118
   L129   L119

CC €18  1/4-29/5  3/6-7/6  24/6-15/7  1/9-30/9    N 53°44'23'' E 08°31'00''

---

## Eckwarderhörne, D-26969 / Niedersachsen ♿ 🛜 iD 604

▲ Knaus Campingpark
   Eckwarderhörne★★★★
✉ Zum Leuchtfeuer  116
☎ +49 47 36 13 00
📅 1/1 - 31/12
@ eckwarderhoerne@
   knauscamp.de

6ha 25T(80-130m²) 16A CEE

**1** AD**G**HIJKLM**P**Q
**2** AEMPRSUVWX
**3** BGHIJKLNRUWY
**4** (**A** 1/6-30/9)
   (Q+R+T+U+Y 📅)
**5** A**B**DEFGIJKLMNOPUWXYZ
**6** CDEG**K**(N 3km)OUV

💬 A rural camp site on the Wadden Sea (UNESCO). Your pets are also welcome in specially designated areas. The cycle ferry will take you directly from Eckwarderhörne to the Helgoland Quay in Wilhelmshaven several times a week.

🚗 A7 Groningen-Leer. A28 at Oldenburg, exit 14 dir. Wilhelmshaven. A29 exit 8 Varel. Exit Schweiburg B437 dir. Norderham/Butjadingen/Eckwarden then dir. Burhave. Campsite signposted.

   L858
A29   L859
CC   L860
**Wilhelmshaven**
   L855

CC €20  1/1-29/5  3/6-7/6  24/6-15/7  1/9-31/12    N 53°31'17'' E 08°14'06''

## Egestorf, D-21272 / Niedersachsen　♿ 📶 iD　605

🏕 Regenbogen Ferienanlage Egestorf
🏠 Hundornweg 1
☎ +49 4 17 56 61
📅 29/3 - 27/10
@ urlaub@regenbogen.ag

22ha 240T(100-120m²) 10A CEE

1 ACD**G**IJKLMOPST
2 BFG**I**JLRSTVWX
3 BHJK
4 (B 15/5-15/9) **N**(Q+R+Y 🔑)
5 **AB**DEFGJLNPUWZ
6 ACEGJ(N 3,5km)OTU

💬 A campsite located in the Lüneburger Heath. The area is perfect for long walks on the heathland or for trips to Hamburg and Lüneburg. The campsite has an outdoor swimming pool.

🚗 Motorway A7 Hamburg-Hannover exit Evendorf, and then drive towards Egestorf.

Hanstedt　Kirchgellersen
L213　L216
L234
A7
L212　B209
L211

CC € **18** 29/3-29/6　1/9-27/10　　📍 N 53°10'27'' E 10°03'36''

---

## Essel/Engehausen, D-29690 / Niedersachsen　👫 📶 iD　606

🏕 Camping Aller-Leine-Tal
🏠 Marschweg 1
☎ +49 50 71 51 15 49
📅 1/3 - 31/10
@ camping@camping-allerleinetal.de

5ha 80T(100-120m²) 10A

1 ACD**G**IJKLMPQ
2 BCDFRWXY
3 BHJK**Q**RU**W**XZ
4 (Q 15/3-15/10) (U+X+Z 🔑)
5 **AB**DFGIJKLMNPUWZ
6 AEGJ(N 7km)OV

💬 The campsite is located in woodland 100m from the Aller. Its location on the southern edge of the Lüneburger Heath makes it suitable for longer stays. The campsite is 800m from the A7 and is ideal as a stopover campsite. Friendly Dutch owners.

🚗 A7 Hannover-Bremen, exit 'Rasthof Allertal', direction Celle. Follow camping signs.

L159
L157
Essel　A7
Schwarmstedt　CC　L180
B214　Wietze
L190
L191
L383

CC € **18** 1/3-30/6　18/8-31/10　　📍 N 52°41'22'' E 09°41'53''

---

## Ganderkesee/Steinkimmen, D-27777 / Niedersachsen　♿ 📶 iD　607

🏕 Camping & Ferienpark Falkensteinsee★★★★
🏠 Falkensteinsee 1
☎ +49 4 22 29 47 00 77
📅 1/1 - 31/12
@ camping@falkensteinsee.de

24ha 120T(100-150m²) 16A CEE

1 ACD**G**HIJKLMOPQ
2 ABDFLMRVWXY
3 ABF**G**HJN**Q**RU**W**Z
4 (Q+R+T+U+Y+Z 1/4-31/10)
5 **AB**DEFGJLMN**PQRS**UWXYZ
6 CDEGH**K**(N 6km)OUV

💬 Camping and pure nature by the Falkensteinsee lake! Water, beach, fields, woods: the campsite has everything! It offers one of the loveliest spots in North Germany, surrounded by the Hasbruch nature reserve and the Wildeshauser Geest, between Oldenburg and Bremen. Simply relax as a couple, as a family, as cyclists, relaxation-seekers, adventurists...

🚗 Motorway Groningen-Leer-Oldenburg. Direction Bremen, exit 18 Hude direction Falkenburg. The campsite is signposted.

L866　L875
L867 B212
L868
A28　Delmenhorst
L871　CC
Ganderkesee
B213　L776
L872　L890　A1

CC € **20** 1/4-17/4　1/5-27/5　4/6-6/6　11/6-18/6　1/9-27/9　7/10-30/10　　📍 N 53°02'50'' E 08°27'52''

## Garlstorf, D-21376 / Niedersachsen

🏕 👫 ♿ 🛜 iD **608**

🔺 Freizeit-Camp-Nordheide e.V.
✉ Egestorfer Landstraße 50
☎ +49 1 52 28 49 13 77
🗓 1/1 - 31/12
@ camping-garlstorf@t-online.de

6ha 250T(80-140m²) 16A

**1** ACD**G**HIJKLMOPQ
**2** BFRTWXY
**3** ABHJNRU
**5** **AB**DEFGJKLMNOPUWYZ
**6** CEGK(N 2km)OV

💬 A campsite in the middle of the Nordheide, just 2 km from the autobahn. Ideal as stopover campsite. Just 40 km from Hamburg. 4 km from the Wildpark Nindorf. Heideblütenfest. Luxurious toilet facilities.

🚗 A7 exit 40 Garlstorf. Then Hansteder-Landstrasse direction Garlstorf. Campsite signposted towards Egerstorf.

Jesteburg   Vierhöfen
Hanstedt
L215
L213 CC   L216
A7   L234
L212
B209

CC €**18** 1/1-15/7  1/9-31/12   📍 N 53°13'30'' E 10°05'16''

## Hameln, D-31787 / Niedersachsen

♿ 🛜 iD **609**

🔺 Campingplatz Hameln an der Weser
✉ Uferstraße 80
☎ +49 5 15 16 74 89
🗓 11/3 - 17/11
@ info@campingplatz-hameln.de

1,2ha 120T(80-100m²) 16A CEE

**1** A**G**HIJKLMOPQ
**2** CGKLRUWXY
**3** BF**HJKW**X
**4** (Q+R 🅿)
**5** **AB**DEFIJKLMNOPUWZ
**6** ACDEG**K**(N 1km)

💬 The campsite is located on the River Weser, 10 minutes' walk from the centre. There are woodlands nearby with opportunities for walking. New toilet facilities (2016).

🚗 A2 Dortmund-Hannover exit 35. B83 to Hameln, follow signs.

Hachmühlen
L433   B83   L423   B442
CC
**Hameln**
L432
B1   L431   L424

CC €**20** 6/5-10/5  13/5-17/5  20/5-23/5  1/6-5/6  13/6-30/6  1/9-30/9   📍 N 52°06'33'' E 09°20'52''

## Hann. Münden, D-34346 / Niedersachsen

🛜 iD **610**

🔺 Spiegelburg Camping und Gasthaus
✉ Zella 1-2
☎ +49 55 41 90 47 11
🗓 31/3 - 1/11
@ info@gasthausspiegelburg.de

20ha 80T(100m²) 16A CEE

**1** A**G**IJKLMOPQ
**2** BCFGIKMRTVWX
**3** HJRU**WX**
**4** (Q+Y+Z 🅿)
**5** GI**J**MNOPUWZ
**6** EGJ(N 5km)V

💬 Campsite located on the River Werra in wooded surroundings 5 kilometres from the half-timbered village of Hann. Münden. The cafe/restaurant and the recreation room are open for the whole camping period. The surroundings are perfect for walking, cycling and watersports. River is perfect for canoeing.

🚗 A7 Kassel-Göttingen, 2nd exit at roundabout B80 Hann. Münden then left at bridge over the Werra. Follow camping signs.

L561
B80   L559   L564
Friedland
**Hann. Münden**   L3468
B3   A7   CC
L562
L3235  L533   L3401   B27
L3237   L563   B451

CC €**18** 1/4-1/7  18/8-1/11  7=6   📍 N 51°23'43'' E 09°43'31''

## Hattorf, D-37197 / Niedersachsen

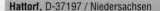 📶 iD **611**

🏕 Camping Oderbrücke***
🛬 B27
☎ +49 55 21 43 59
🕐 1/1 - 31/12
@ info@campingimharz.de

2,5ha 70T(100m²) 16A CEE

**1** ADGIJKLOPQ
**2** CRTWXY
**3** BFGHIJKRWX
**4** (Q+T+U+Y 🕐)
**5** ABDGIJKLMNOPUWZ
**6** CDFGJ(N 2km)OUV

💬 Well-maintained family campsite with excellent restaurant on the B27.

🚗 Along the B27 between Göttingen and Braunlage. 6 km beyond Gieboldshausen and 5 km before Herzberg.

Osterode am Harz

CC € **16** 1/1-30/6 1/9-31/12

📍 N 51°37'41'' E 10°16'15''

---

## Heidenau, D-21258 / Niedersachsen

🪂 ♿ 📶 iD **612**

🏕 Camping Ferienzentrum Heidenau****
🛬 Zum Ferienzentrum
☎ +49 41 82 42 72
🕐 1/1 - 31/12
@ info@ferienzentrum-heidenau.de

70ha 87T(100-120m²) 16A CEE

**1** ADEHIJKLMOPQ
**2** BDFLRWXY
**3** ABCGHIJKMNPRUVW
**4** (C+H 1/5-15/9) NP(Q+R 🕐) (U+Y 1/1-31/10,1/12-31/12) (Z 🕐)
**5** ABDFGIJKLMNOPUWXYZ
**6** ACDEGJ(N 5km)V

💬 The campsite is suitable both as a stopover site or for longer stays. The tourist section is separate and comprises a series of fields and several small lakes. Modern toilet facilities, lovely swimming pool, restaurant and wifi. A good starting point for cycling and walking tours and for visiting Hamburg, Bremen, Stade and Lüneburg.

🚗 Motorway A1 Bremen-Hamburg, exit 46 direction Heidenau. In Heidenau follow signs.

Ahlerstedt

Sittensen

Tostedt

CC € **20** 1/3-19/4 23/4-29/5 31/5-4/6 1/9-31/10

📍 N 53°18'31'' E 09°37'14''

---

## Heinsen, D-37649 / Niedersachsen

👫 📶 ⚙ iD **613**

🏕 Weserbergland Camping
🛬 Weserstraße 66
☎ +49 55 35 87 33
🕐 15/4 - 15/10
@ info@ weserbergland-camping.com

2,5ha 128T(120m²) 10A CEE

**1** ADGIJKLMPRS
**2** CGLMRUWX
**3** ABFGHJNRWX
**4** (B 1/5-15/10) (Q+Z 🕐)
**5** ABCDGIJKLMNOPQUWX
**6** ACEGHK(N 2km)OTV

💬 A real family campsite in beautiful countryside and peacefully located on the Weser. Own slipway and an ideal base for walking and cycling trips. Fishing and canoeing possible. Swimming pool provided.

🚗 Via Hameln and Bodenwerder to Heinsen, B83. Follow signs.

Bad Pyrmont

Holzminden

CC € **20** 15/4-6/7 25/8-15/10

📍 N 51°53'06'' E 09°26'33''

## Hohegeiß (Harz), D-38700 / Niedersachsen

🎿 🛜 **iD** **614**

▲ Camping Am Bärenbache****
🏠 Bärenbachweg 10
☎ +49 55 83 13 06
📅 1/1 - 31/12
@ info@campingplatz-hohegeiss.de

3ha 150T(80-100m²) 10A CEE

**1** AGIJKLMOPQ
**2** BJKLRTUVX
**3** BHIJR
**4** (A 🅾) (C+G 1/6-30/8)
(Q 🅾)
(T 1/6-31/8,20/12-31/12)
(U 1/6-31/8)
(X 1/6-31/8,20/12-31/12)
**5** ABDEFGIJKLMNOPUWZ
**6** CDEGK(N 0km)OU

💬 Centrally located in the Harz. Conveniently situated for all the sights in the area. Plenty of walking and skiing opportunities. Close to a woodland swimming pool. Excellent restaurant on the campsite. Various activities are organised during the holidays. Camping equipment available.

🚗 A7 Kassel-Hannover, exit 72 Göttingen. Via Herzberg and Walkenried (or Braunlage) to Hohegeiß.

Braunlage
L519 — L98
L520 — B27 — B4 — L97 — B81
Bad Lauterberg
im Harz — L601
CC
L1037

CC €16 1/1-30/6 18/8-31/12 🗺 N 51°39'25'' E 10°40'04''

## Holle, D-31188 / Niedersachsen

🦽 🛜 **iD** **615**

▲ Seecamp Derneburg
🏠 Seecamp 1
☎ +49 5 06 25 65
📅 1/4 - 31/10
@ info@seecamp-derneburg.de

7,8ha 60T(80-100m²) 16A CEE

**1** AGHIJKLMOPQ
**2** DFGKLMRTUX
**3** BFHJQRVWZ
**4** (Q+R+U+Y+Z 🅾)
**5** ABDFGIJKMNOPUWZ
**6** CEGK(N 4km)OU

💬 A family campsite situated by a lake. Well maintained grassy field planted with trees. Lovely trips out possible from here to the nearby region. CampingCard ACSI campers receive one free hour of internet per day.

🚗 A7 Derneburg exit 63, then follow signs.

Hildesheim — Salzgitter
A7 — B444
CC
L670
B243
A7 — L498
B248

CC €20 24/4-26/5 17/6-30/6 1/9-31/10 7=6, 14=12 🗺 N 52°06'11'' E 10°08'18''

## Hösseringen/Suderburg, D-29556 / Niedersachsen

🦽 🛜 **iD** **616**

▲ Camping Am Hardausee*****
🏠 Campingplatz 1
☎ +49 58 26 76 76
📅 1/4 - 31/10
@ info@camping-hardausee.de

10ha 100T(90-100m²) 16A CEE

**1** ADGHIJKLMOPQ
**2** ADGLMRVWXY
**3** ABGHIJKRWZ
**4** (A 1/6-15/9)
(Q+R+T+U+X 🅾)
**5** ABDEFGJLNPUWXYZ
**6** ACDEGK(N 1,5km)OSU

💬 The perfect base for a holiday in the countryside with healthy air, clean water and a unique landscape. The campsite has open grounds but also pitches separated by hedges (with connections for power, water and in some cases drainage). Opportunities for all types of activities and trips out to historic towns, water parks, and so on.

🚗 Route 191 from Celle to Uelzen, exit Suderburg. In Suderburg turn right towards Hösseringen/Räber to Hardausee.

B71
Suderburg — Stadensen
CC — B4
Unterlüss
L280 — L265
B191

CC €20 1/4-14/4 28/4-26/5 16/6-15/7 1/9-31/10 🗺 N 52°52'11'' E 10°25'22''

## Jade, D-26349 / Niedersachsen

👫 📶 **iD** **617**

🏠 Höpken's Hof & Campingplatz
🏡 Molkereistraße 64
☎ +49 4 73 49 10 68 33
📅 1/1 - 31/12
@ hi@moinurlaub.de

3ha 63**T**(70-110m²) 16A CEE

**1** ACD**G**IJKLMOPQ
**2** EMNRUVWX
**3** BHJKLY
**4** (Q 1/3-30/10) (R 🔑)
**5** **AB**DFGIJKLMNOPUWX
**6** DEK(N 6km)OU

NEW

💬 Quietly situated campsite around an old East Frisian farm and directly behind a dike. This family campsite focuses on cyclists and dog owners. Special fenced pitches for campers with dogs. Enjoy the water at the Jadeboezem or a treat in Tante Emma's Hofladen.

🚗 From Groningen the A28, exit 6 Westerstede, direction Varel. Follow signs direction Jade, left into 437 then right. Drive along dike on Baderstrasse to campsite signs.

Wilhelmshaven

L860
B212
L855
B437
A29
L862

**CC** € **14** 1/5-25/5 17/6-11/7 1/9-30/9

📍 N 53°25'35'' E 08°17'55''

---

## Laatzen/Hannover, D-30880 / Niedersachsen

♿ 📶 **iD** **618**

🏠 Campingplatz Birkensee
🏡 Campingplatz Birkensee
☎ +49 5 11 52 99 62
📅 1/1 - 31/12
@ info@camping-birkensee.de

8,5ha 100**T**(80-120m²) 16A CEE

**1** ABD**G**HIJKLMOPQ
**2** ABDFKLMRWXY
**3** B**F**HJKRZ
**4** (Q+T+U+X+Z 🔑)
**5** **AB**DFGIJMNOPQUWXZ
**6** ACDEGJ(N 3km)OTV

💬 The idyllic Birkensee, surrounded by woods is located in the protected Bockmerholz nature reserve. Ideal for rest and relaxation and to take lovely walks. Child friendly, open all year and with its own lake and beach. Ideal location (5 minutes from the A7 or 5 minutes to Hannover Messe) for trips out to Hannover.

🚗 A7, Hamburg-Kassel, exit 59, N443 direction Laatzen. After a few kilometres turn left into a small road that leads to the campsite.

Hannover
Ronnenberg

A2
A7
A2
B3
A7
L411

**CC** € **20** 1/1-14/4 29/4-1/6 1/9-31/12

📍 N 52°18'13'' E 09°51'44''

---

## Löwenhagen, D-37127 / Niedersachsen

📶 **iD** **619**

🏠 Campingplatz Am Niemetal
🏡 Mühlenstraße 4
☎ +49 55 02 99 84 61
📅 1/4 - 31/10
@ info@am-niemetal.com

2,5ha 75**T**(100-125m²) 16A CEE

**1** A**G**IJKLPQ
**2** BCFGRVWXY
**3** BDHIJRUX
**4** (Q+U+X+Z 🔑)
**5** **AB**CDFGHIJKLMNOPQUW XYZ
**6** ACEGK(N 5km)OV

💬 Campingplatz Am Niemetal is positioned in an idyllic spot in the middle of the countryside in the valley of the River Nieme. A campsite where peace and space play a leading role and hospitality is central. Plenty of cycling and walking opportunities in the direct vicinity of the campsite.

🚗 A7 Hannover-Kassel, exit 73 dir. Dransfeld, then on to Imbsen. Then dir. Bursfelde, Löwenhagen. Campsite signposted.

Adelebsen
B80
L561
Rosdorf
Dransfeld
L3229
L559
A7
L3232
B3

**CC** € **16** 1/4-6/7 25/8-31/10

📍 N 51°31'12'' E 09°41'41''

## Müden/Örtze (Gem. Faßberg), D-29328 / Niedersachsen

620

- Camping Sonnenberg
- Sonnenberg 3
- +49 50 53 98 71 74
- 15/4 - 15/10
- info@campingsonnenberg.com

5ha 100**T**(150-350m²) 16A

1 A**G**IJKLMOPQ
2 BJRVWXY
3 ABHJKLU
4 (Q 1/5-1/10) (T+U+X)
5 **AB**DGIJKLMNOP**S**UWZ
6 ACEGHJ(N 1,5km)OTV

Peaceful campsite located in the middle of the Lüneburgerheide. An ideal base for walking and cycling trips and for enjoying the beautiful countryside.

A7 Hannover-Hamburg exit Soltau-Ost, then on route B71 to Munster. After Munster exit Celle. In Müden follow camping signs.

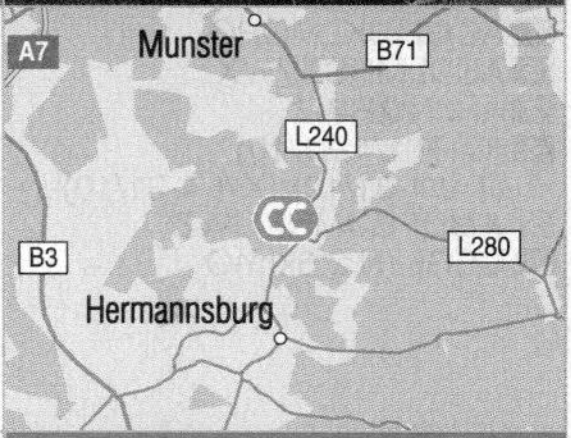


CC € 18 *15/4-7/7 1/9-15/10*

N 52°53'16'' E 10°05'58''

## Neustadt/Mardorf, D-31535 / Niedersachsen

621

- Campingplatz Mardorf GmbH
- Uferweg 68
- +49 5 03 65 29
- 1/1 - 31/12
- info@camping-steinhuder-meer.de

4,2ha 80**T**(70-110m²) 16A CEE

1 ABCD**G**HIJKLMOPQ
2 BDGKLRUVWXY
3 B**F**HJKL**W**Z
4 (Q 1/4-31/10) (T+U+X)
5 **AB**DEFGIJMNO**P**UWXZ
6 CDEGJ(N 1,5km)O

Water sports campsite on the Steinhuder lake. Good cycling and walking possibilities. Excellent toilet facilities.

B6 Nienburg-Neustadt. In Neustadt dir Steinhuder Meer. In Mardorf follow campsite signs. SatNav: Entrance is on Weidebruchsweg.

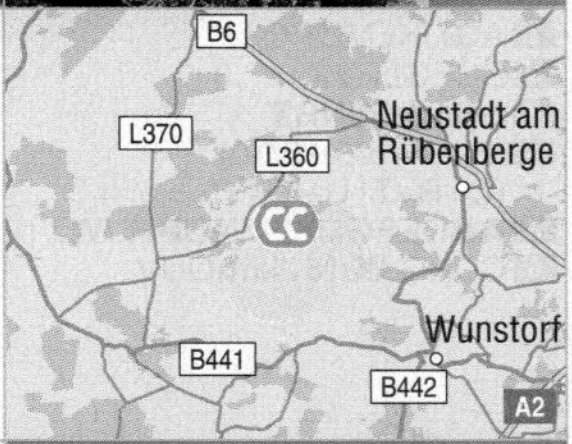


CC € 18 *1/1-24/5 13/6-19/6 24/6-28/6 1/9-31/12*

N 52°29'30'' E 09°19'29''

## Osnabrück, D-49076 / Niedersachsen

622

- Campingplatz Bullerby
- Zum Attersee 50
- +49 5 41 12 41 47
- 1/1 - 31/12
- info@campbullerby.de

26ha 36**T** 16A CEE

1 AGIJKLMOP
2 ADFLMRSVW
3 A**F**R**W**Z
4 (Q+R)
5 **AB**DFG**J**N**P**UX
6 O

The owner of this campsite is busy putting new life into this outdated site, with many perennial and annual plants. There is a new field for tourist campers with a view of the lake. The toilet facilities have been excellently renovated. It's also ideally situated next to the motorway for onward travel.

A1 exit 71 Osnabrück-Hafen. Signs to Attersee, then signs Bullerby. Becomes one way street.

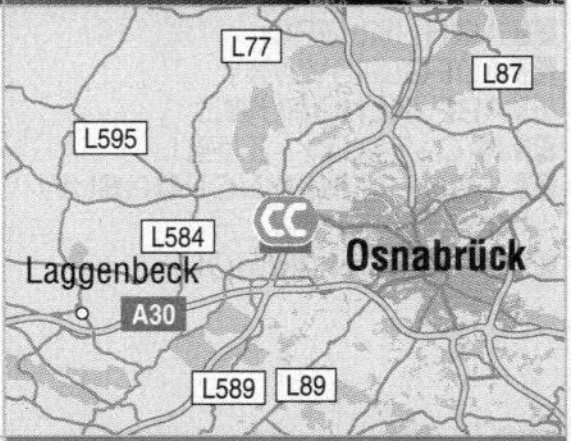


CC € 18 *1/1-18/4 24/4-29/5 12/6-7/7 1/9-31/12*

N 52°18'00'' E 07°56'28''

## Ostercappeln/Schwagstorf, D-49179 / Niedersachsen ♿ iD 623

🏕 Freizeitpark Kronensee
✉ Zum Kronensee 9
☎ +49 54 73 22 82
📅 1/1 - 31/12
@ info@kronensee.de

30ha 90T(70-100m²) 16A CEE

**1** ACG**H**IJKLMOPQ
**2** ACDLMRSTVWX
**3** AHJNQ**R**W**Z**
**4** (Q+R 1/4-31/10)
   (T 6/4-31/10) (X 1/4-31/10)
**5** **AB**DFGJ**M**N**P**UWZ
**6** CEGH(N 2,5km)O

💬 A friendly campsite in a natural recreation area located by a beautiful lake with swimming, sailing and fishing. Attractive lakeside pitches for tents. A lovely area for cycling.

🚗 A30 Oldenzaal-Osnabrück. At the Lotte crossroads, drive towards Bremen. Take exit 68 Bramsche, towards Bramsche B218 in the direction of Minden. After approx. 15 km towards Schwagstorf-Ostercappeln. The campsite is located approx. 10 km further on. Follow signposts Mitteland Kanal.

CC € 18  1/1-29/5  24/6-7/7  26/8-31/12      N 52°22'18'' E 08°13'46''

---

## Osterode (Harz), D-37520 / Niedersachsen 🎿 ♿ 📶 iD 624

🏕 Campingplatz Eulenburg***
✉ Scheerenberger Straße 100
☎ +49 55 22 66 11
📅 1/1 - 31/12
@ ferien@eulenburg-camping.de

4,1ha 65T(80-200m²) 16A CEE

**1** A**G**IJKLMOPQ
**2** BCFGLRVX
**3** BGHJK**M**NR**T**
**4** (B+G 15/5-15/10)
   (Q+R+T+U+X ⊠)
**5** **AB**DEFGIJKLMNO**P**RUWZ
**6** CDEGJ**K**(N 2km)OUV

💬 The campsite is located on the edge of a wood and has marked out and unmarked pitches. The site is surrounded by streams and has wooded surroundings and romantic footpaths. Also suitable for large groups.

🚗 Motorway A7 Kassel-Hannover, exit 67 Seesen. Drive towards Osterode (Sösestausee). Exit Osterode-Süd. Follow the signs to Sösestausee.

CC € 20  7/1-24/6  19/8-31/12      N 51°43'38'' E 10°16'59''

---

## Ostrhauderfehn, D-26842 / Niedersachsen ♿ 📶 iD 625

🏕 Camping-u.
   Freizeitanlage Idasee
✉ Idafehn-Nord 77B
☎ +49 49 52 99 42 97
📅 1/1 - 31/12
@ info@campingidasee.de

7,4ha 90T(100m²) 6A CEE

**1** A**G**HIJKLMPQ
**2** ADFGLRSVWXY
**3** AB**F**JKLNORU**W**Z
**4** **N**(Q+T+U+Y+Z ⊠)
**5** **AB**DFGIJKLMNOP**Q**R**S**UW
   XYZ
**6** CDEG**K**(N 2km)OU

NEW

💬 Located on the Idasee with many recreational possibilities: fishing, swimming and water skiing. One of the most beautiful cycling routes in Germany begins close to the campsite: the German Fehn route through the typical East Frisian landscape with its peat marshes, canals and rivers. Adventure playground for children.

🚗 Groningen-Leer, then B70 direction Lingen. In Folmhusen turn left B438 direction Ostrhauderfehn, then left B72. Follow signs.

CC € 16  1/1-28/5  11/6-30/6  1/9-31/12      N 53°09'14'' E 07°38'33''

## Oyten, D-28876 / Niedersachsen

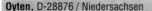

▲ Knaus Campingpark Oyten
🏠 Oyter See 1
☎ +49 42 07 28 78
📅 1/3 - 3/11
@ oyten@knauscamp.de

3ha 114T(70-100m²) 16A CEE

**1** ACD**G**HIJKLMOPQ
**2** ADFGLMRVWXY
**3** ABD**FJQRW**Z
**4** (T 1/5-1/10)
**5** **AB**DEFGIJKLMNOPUWZ
**6** ACDEG**K**(N 2km)O

💬 A lovely family campsite next to a lake. Being located on the A1 it is perfect as a stopover campsite en route to Scandinavia.

🚗 A1 Bremen-Hamburg, exit 52 direction Oyten. Left at Lidl, through Oyten then direction Oyter See and follow camping signs.

CC € **18** 1/3-29/5 3/6-7/6 24/6-15/7 1/9-3/11 🧭 N 53°02'47'' E 09°00'24''

---

## Rieste, D-49597 / Niedersachsen

▲ Alfsee Ferien- und Erholungspark*****
🏠 Am Campingpark 10
☎ +49 5 46 49 21 20
📅 1/1 - 31/12
@ info@alfsee.com

16ha 350T(110m²) 16A CEE

**1** ACD**F**HIJKLMOPQ
**2** ADFLMRTUVWXY
**3** ABC**F**HJKL**M**NOPQRU**VW**Z
**4** **LN**(Q+S+T 6/4-27/10) (U+Y+Z 📵)
**5** **AB**DEFGJKLNP**S**UWXYZ
**6** CDEGHK(N 2km)OSTUV

💬 The campsite is part of a large holiday park with plenty of amenities. The wonderful wellness park in Roman style is highly recommended. There is also good cycling in the vicinity.

🚗 A1 Osnabrück-Bremen, exit Neuenkirchen/ Vörden, towards Alfsee. Campsite is signposted.

CC € **20** 3/1-5/4 28/4-29/5 24/6-3/7 27/8-2/10 28/10-20/12 🧭 N 52°29'07'' E 07°59'23''

---

## Rinteln, D-31737 / Niedersachsen

▲ Erholungsgebiet DoktorSee****
🏠 Am Doktorsee 8
☎ +49 57 51 96 48 60
📅 1/1 - 31/12
@ info@doktorsee.de

90ha 400T(80-140m²) 16A CEE

**1** ACD**G**HIJKLMOPQ
**2** ADFKLMRUVWX
**3** BF**G**HJK**M**N**Q**R**T**U**W**Z
**4** (A 1/4-30/9) J**LN**(Q+S 📵) (T 1/4-30/9) (U+V+X+Y+Z 📵)
**5** **AB**DEFGHIJKLMNO**P**UWXYZ
**6** ACDEGH(N 1,5km)OTV

💬 A large campsite around a lake, intended for longer stays. Plenty of recreational opportunities and wellness, extensive catering facilities. The spacious touring pitches are in several areas spread over the campsite. The area invites you to go cycling or visit Hameln, Lemgo, Detmold and Hannover.

🚗 A2 Dortmund-Hannover, take exit 35 towards Rinteln, follow B238 around Rinteln. Follow signs to DoktorSee.

CC € **20** 1/1-12/4 28/4-29/5 12/6-30/6 1/9-31/12 🧭 N 52°11'12'' E 09°03'35''

## Schiffdorf/Spaden, D-27619 / Niedersachsen ⠀⠀⠀ 🛜 iD 629

🔺 Camping-und Ferienpark
⠀⠀Spadener See★★★★
✉ Seeweg 2
☎ +49 4 71 30 83 64 56
🕐 15/3 - 31/10
@ info@
⠀⠀campingplatz-spadener-see.de

1,6ha 120T(100-150m²) 16A CEE

NEW

**1** ADG**HI**JKLPQ
**2** ADFLMRUWXY
**3** ABHJRU**WZ**
**4** (Q+R+T+U+X+Y+Z 🔲)
**5** **AB**DEGIJKLMNOPUWXYZ
**6** CEGJ(N 2km)O

💬 Campsite located on a large lake, with the option of waterskiing. The port city of Bremerhaven, with various museums and a large shopping centre, is about 6 km away.

🚗 A27 Bremerhaven-Cuxhaven, exit Spaden, Follow campsite signs, well signposted.

Bremerhaven
Nordenham

CC € 18 ⠀ 15/3-14/4 ⠀ 24/4-6/6 ⠀ 1/9-15/10 ⠀⠀⠀⠀ 🔲 N 53°34'30'' E 08°38'48''

---

## Schüttorf, D-48465 / Niedersachsen ⠀⠀⠀ ♿ 🛜 iD 630

🔺 Camping Quendorfer See
✉ Weiße Riete 3
☎ +49 59 23 90 29 39
🕐 1/4 - 3/11
@ info@camping-schuettorf.de

1,5ha 53T(100-120m²) 16A CEE

**1** ACG**HI**JKLMOPRS
**2** ADFGLRUVWX
**3** AHJNRZ
**4** (Q+R 🔲)
**5** **AB**DEFGHJLNPUWXY
**6** CDEG**K**(N 2km)O

💬 This rustic campsite is situated behind a row of old trees. Spacious pitches, open views, very well maintained toilet facilities. Within walking distance of a lovely lake for swimming, surfing and fishing.

🚗 A1/A30 exit 4 Schüttorf-Nord or A31 exit 28 Schüttorf-Ost towards town centre, follow camping signs.

Nordhorn
Schüttorf

CC € 18 ⠀ 1/4-12/4 ⠀ 5/5-29/5 ⠀ 12/6-19/6 ⠀ 1/9-1/10 ⠀⠀⠀ 🔲 N 52°20'19'' E 07°13'36''

---

## Seeburg, D-37136 / Niedersachsen ⠀⠀⠀ 🧑‍🧑‍🧒 ♿ 🛜 iD 631

🔺 Comfort-Camping
⠀⠀Seeburger See
✉ Seestraße 20
☎ +49 55 07 13 19
🕐 1/4 - 31/10
@ info@campingseeburgersee.com

3ha 95T(100-140m²) 16A CEE

**1** ADG**I**JKLMPQ
**2** ADLMPRUVX
**3** BDF**GHI**JKL**MNOPQR**T**W**Z
**4** (A 1/7-31/8) (**G** 15/5-15/9)
⠀⠀(Q+R+T+U+Y+Z 🔲)
**5** **AB**DFGIJKLOPQUWZ
**6** ACEGKL(N 4km)OUV

💬 Hospitable family campsite on the Seeburger Lake. Modern toilet facilities. Swimming in lake. Many options for walking and cycling. Various restaurants at walking distance.

🚗 Motorway A7, exit 72 Göttingen-Nord. Via the B27/B446 direction Duderstadt.

Gieboldehausen
Göttingen
Duderstadt

CC € 18 ⠀ 1/4-7/6 ⠀ 25/8-31/10 ⠀ 14=12, 21=17 ⠀⠀⠀ 🔲 N 51°33'49'' E 10°09'13''

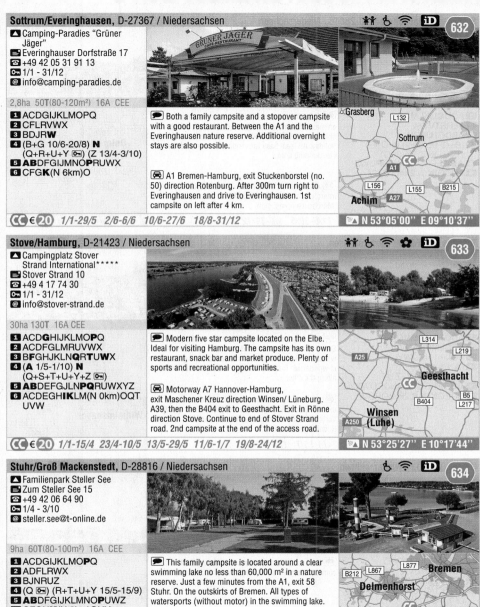

## Sottrum/Everinghausen, D-27367 / Niedersachsen

👪 👨‍🦽 📶 iD **632**

🏕 Camping-Paradies "Grüner Jäger"
✉ Everinghauser Dorfstraße 17
☎ +49 42 05 31 91 13
📅 1/1 - 31/12
@ info@camping-paradies.de

2,8ha 50T(80-120m²) 16A CEE

**1** ACDGIJKLMOPQ
**2** CFLRVWX
**3** BDJRW
**4** (B+G 10/6-20/8) N
(Q+R+U+Y 📷) (Z 13/4-3/10)
**5** ABDFGIJMNOPRUWX
**6** CFGK(N 6km)O

💬 Both a family campsite and a stopover campsite with a good restaurant. Between the A1 and the Everinghausen nature reserve. Additional overnight stays are also possible.

🚗 A1 Bremen-Hamburg, exit Stuckenborstel (no. 50) direction Rotenburg. After 300m turn right to Everinghausen and drive to Everinghausen. 1st campsite on left after 4 km.

CC €20  1/1-29/5  2/6-6/6  10/6-27/6  18/8-31/12

N 53°05'00'' E 09°10'37''

## Stove/Hamburg, D-21423 / Niedersachsen

👪 👨‍🦽 📶 ✿ iD **633**

🏕 Campingplatz Stover Strand International*****
✉ Stover Strand 10
☎ +49 4 17 74 30
📅 1/1 - 31/12
@ info@stover-strand.de

30ha 130T 16A CEE

**1** ACDGHIJKLMOPQ
**2** ACDFGLMRUVWX
**3** BFGHJKLNQRTUWX
**4** (A 1/5-1/10) N
(Q+S+T+U+Y+Z 📷)
**5** ABDEFGJLNPQRUWXYZ
**6** ACDEGHIKLM(N 0km)OQT UVW

💬 Modern five star campsite located on the Elbe. Ideal for visiting Hamburg. The campsite has its own restaurant, snack bar and market produce. Plenty of sports and recreational opportunities.

🚗 Motorway A7 Hannover-Hamburg, exit Maschener Kreuz direction Winsen/ Lüneburg. A39, then the B404 exit to Geesthacht. Exit in Rönne direction Stove. Continue to end of Stover Strand road. 2nd campsite at the end of the access road.

CC €20  1/1-15/4  23/4-10/5  13/5-29/5  11/6-1/7  19/8-24/12

N 53°25'27'' E 10°17'44''

## Stuhr/Groß Mackenstedt, D-28816 / Niedersachsen

👨‍🦽 📶 iD **634**

🏕 Familienpark Steller See
✉ Zum Steller See 15
☎ +49 42 06 64 90
📅 1/4 - 3/10
@ steller.see@t-online.de

9ha 60T(80-100m²) 16A CEE

**1** ACDGIJKLMOPQ
**2** ADFLRWX
**3** BJNRUZ
**4** (Q 📷) (R+T+U+Y 15/5-15/9)
**5** ABDFGIJKLMNOPUWZ
**6** CFGHK(N 2km)OUV

💬 This family campsite is located around a clear swimming lake no less than 60,000 m² in a nature reserve. Just a few minutes from the A1, exit 58 Stuhr. On the outskirts of Bremen. All types of watersports (without motor) in the swimming lake.

🚗 From the A1 take the Stuhr intersection (from Hamburg or Osnabrück), first exit 58, right at exit dir. Groß Mackenstedt. Enter village, right at petrol station. Follow 'Steller See' signs.

CC €18  1/4-6/6  11/6-30/6  1/9-2/10

N 53°00'25'' E 08°41'33''

## Stuhr/Groß Mackenstedt, D-28816 / Niedersachsen   ♿ 🛜 iD   635

🔺 Märchencamping
📧 Zum Steller See 83
☎ +49 42 06 91 91
🗓 1/1 - 31/12
@ info@maerchencamping.de

10ha 100T(120m²) 16A CEE

**1** ACD**G**IJKLMOPQ
**2** FLRSTVWX
**3** ABDGHJKRU
**4** (B+G 1/5-30/9) **N**(Q 🔑)
   (T+U+X+Z 1/4-30/9)
**5** **AB**DEFGHIJLMNO**P**UWZ
**6** ACDGI**K**(N 2km)OTUV

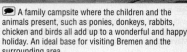

💬 A family campsite where the children and the animals present, such as ponies, donkeys, rabbits, chicken and birds all add up to a wonderful and happy holiday. An ideal base for visiting Bremen and the surrounding area.

🚗 A1 Osnabrück-Bremen to exit 58 (Stuhr interchange) direction Groß Mackenstedt and follow 'Märchencamping' sign.

CC € **18**   1/1-19/4   23/4-28/5   11/6-30/6   1/9-31/12   7=6    🏖 N 53°00'37'' E 08°41'23''

---

## Tossens, D-26969 / Niedersachsen   ♿ 🛜 iD   636

🔺 Knaus Campingpark Tossens****
📧 Zum Friesenstrand 1
☎ +49 4 73 62 19
🗓 15/4 - 15/10
@ tossens@knauscamp.de

6ha 130T(80-100m²) 16A CEE

**1** AD**G**HIJKLM**P**Q
**2** AEGLMPRSUVW
**3** BGIJKLNRUWY
**4** (**A** 1/6-31/8)
   (Q+R+T+U+Y+Z 🔑)
**5** **AB**DEFGIJKLMNOPUWXYZ
**6** CDEG**K**(N 0,2km)OPUV

💬 A rurally located beach campsite on the Wadden Sea. The healthy sea air and the mild climate do wonders. Also cycling in this breathtaking landscape is wonderful. Tossens is suitable for extended walks along the dike.

🚗 A7 Groningen-Leer, direction A28 Oldenburg, exit 14 direction Wilhelmshaven (A29). Then exit 8 Varel. Exit Schweiburg direction Norderham/Butjadingen/Tossens.

CC € **20**   15/4-29/5   3/6-7/6   24/6-15/7   1/9-15/10    🏖 N 53°34'44'' E 08°14'37''

---

## Uetze, D-31311 / Niedersachsen   ♿ 🛜 iD   637

🔺 Camping Irenensee****
📧 Fritz-Meinecke-Weg 2
☎ +49 5 17 39 81 20
🗓 1/1 - 31/12
@ info@irenensee.de

45ha 110T(80-125m²) 6-10A CEE

**1** ACD**G**HIJKLMOPQ
**2** ADFGKLRUVX
**3** B**F**GHJKNR**W**Z
**4** (Q+R 1/4-15/10) (T 4/7-14/8)
   (Y 1/4-30/11)
**5** **AB**DEFGIJKLMNO**PQRST**
   UWXYZ
**6** CDEG**K**(N 1km)OPU

💬 Campsite with excellent amenities, lots of comfort. Located on a lake between two natural areas.

🚗 Motorway A2 direction Celle, exit 49 Burgdorf. Then on to the B188 direction Gifhorn/Uetze.

CC € **18**   1/1-17/4   29/4-27/5   12/6-1/7   15/9-23/12    🏖 N 52°27'56'' E 10°09'36''

## Walkenried, D-37445 / Niedersachsen

🎿 ♿ 🛜 **iD** **638**

🏕 Knaus Campingpark
Walkenried****
✉ Ellricherstraße 7
☎ +49 5 52 57 78
📅 1/1 - 31/12
@ walkenried@knauscamp.de

5,5ha 98T(70-100m²) 16A CEE

**1** ACD**G**IJKLMO**P**Q
**2** DIRTUVVY
**3** BHIJKLNQRU
**4** (A+**F** 📅) **N**(Q+R 1/1-4/11)
(U+Y 📅)
**5** **AB**DEFGIJKLMNOPUWXYZ
**6** CDEGH**K**(N 1km)OV

💬 A lovely campsite with a fantastic and friendly couple running it. Extremely clean toilets and excellent service. CampingCard ACSI rate does not include entrance to indoor pool.

🚗 Motorway A7, exit 67 Seesen and via Herzberg and Bad Sachsa to Walkenried.

L520 B27 L97
Bad Lauterberg
im Harz L601 B4
CC
L1037
**Nordhausen**

CC €**18** 7/1-29/5 3/6-7/6 24/6-15/7 1/9-20/12 📶 N 51°35'21'' E 10°37'28''

---

## Werlte, D-49757 / Niedersachsen

♿ 🛜 **iD** **639**

🏕 Camping Hümmlinger Land****
✉ Rastdorfer Straße 80
☎ +49 59 51 53 53
📅 1/1 - 31/12
@ info@huemmlingerland.de

1,8ha 41T(100-110m²) 16A CEE

**1** ACD**G**HIJKLMPQ
**2** RSVWX
**3** BHIJNRU
**4** (Q+R 📅)
**5** **AB**DFGJLNPUW
**6** CEGK(N 3km)OSV

💬 A well maintained campsite with excellent toilet facilities just outside the village of Werlte. The municipality has an active tourism policy. Good area for cycling.

🚗 B233 Emmen-Meppen-Cloppenburg direction Werlte. Campsite signposted (direction Rastdorf).

Börgerwald L63
Börger L30
L51 L62 Vrees L831
CC L836
L837
L65 L55 L839

CC €**18** 2/1-14/4 23/4-28/5 11/6-15/7 1/9-22/12 📶 N 52°52'12'' E 07°41'17''

---

## Wiesmoor, D-26639 / Niedersachsen

👫 ♿ 🛜 ✿ **iD** **640**

🏕 Cp. & Bungalowpark
Ottermeer*****
✉ Am Ottermeer 52
☎ +49 49 44 94 98 93
📅 1/1 - 31/12
@ camping@wiesmoor.de

80ha 205T(90-120m²) 16A CEE

**1** ACD**G**IJKLMO**P**Q
**2** ADLMRSVWXY
**3** B**F**HJKLNRU**W**Z
**4** J(Q+R+T+U+X+Z 1/4-31/10)
**5** **AB**DEFGIJKLMNOPR**S**UW
XY
**6** CDEGH**K**(N 2km)OTUV

💬 Comfortable campsite located on a beautiful natural lake. There are lovely cycle routes along the Fehn wetlands where peat is still collected. The floral town of Wiesmoor is 1.5 km from the campsite.

🚗 Motorway A31 Groningen-Leer. Exit 2 Leer-Ost towards Aurich B72/B436. Then take exit B436 Bagband towards Wiesmoor. In Wiesmoor the campsite is clearly signposted 'Ottermeer'.

B210 L11
L34
Friedeburg
L12
Grossefehn B437
CC
L14 B72 L18
Neukamperfehn
B436

CC €**20** 1/1-18/4 23/4-29/5 31/5-6/6 11/6-7/7 26/8-31/12 📶 N 53°24'56'' E 07°42'38''

## Wilsum, D-49849 / Niedersachsen ⚏ 📶 **iD** `641`

⚑ Campingplatz Wilsumer Berge Ost
🚏 Zum Feriengebiet 4
☎ +49 59 45 99 55 80
🔓 2/1 - 21/12
@ info@wilsumerberge.nl

36,8ha 424T(100-150m²) 6-16A CEE

**1** ACD**G**IJKLMOPQ
**2** ABDGIJLMRSTVWXY
**3** AGHJKLNRUZ
**4** (G 27/4-2/11) (Q 🔓)
(R+T+U+X 16/3-2/11)
**5** **AB**DEFGHJLNPQUXYZ
**6** CEGHK(N 3km)STVX

💬 In the middle of the lovely natural beauty of the Wilsumer Berge with forests, heathland, sand drifts and recreational lake, this campsite offers a variety of pitches. Peace, relaxation, fun and convenience, for all ages: you can find it here.

🚐 On the B403 Coevorden-Nordhorn, the campsite is located between Wilsum and Uelsen. Campsite is signposted.

Emlichheim
B403
L44
**CC** Uelsen
L45
N343
**Nordhorn**

**CC** € **18** 16/3-28/5  2/6-6/6  10/6-29/6  30/8-3/11      🧭 N 52°30'46'' E 06°51'49''

---

## Wingst/Land Hadeln, D-21789 / Niedersachsen ♿ 📶 **iD** `642`

⛰ Knaus Campingpark Wingst****
🚏 Schwimmbadallee 13
☎ +49 47 78 76 04
🔓 1/1 - 31/12
@ wingst@knauscamp.de

9ha 265T(100m²) 16A CEE

**1** ACD**G**HIJKLMOPQ
**2** ABDIJLPRTUVWXY
**3** ABDHJKLN**Q**R**U**W
**4** (**A** 15/5-10/6,1/7-31/8)
(B 1/5-15/9) (F+H 🔓) IJ
(Q+S+U+X+Y+Z 🔓)
**5** **AB**DFGIJKLMNOP**R**UWXZ
**6** ACDEGH**K**(N 3km)OTUV

💬 Large natural campsite in a wooded area. Well maintained terrain. Friendly welcome. Ideal as a touring campsite. Plenty of activities with 50 metres of the site.

🚐 Road B73 Cuxhaven-Stade exit Wingst Schwimmbad.

Otterndorf
L111
L117
**CC**
L113
L144
Hemmoor  Osten
B495  B73

**CC** € **18** 1/1-29/5  3/6-7/6  24/6-15/7  1/9-31/12      🧭 N 53°45'09'' E 09°05'00''

---

## Winsen (Aller), D-29308 / Niedersachsen ⚏ 📶 **iD** `643`

⚑ Campingplatz Winsen (Aller)
🚏 Auf der Hude 1
☎ +49 5 14 39 31 99
🔓 1/1 - 31/12
@ info@campingplatz-winsen.de

13ha 220T 16A

**1** ACD**G**HIJKLMOPQ
**2** ACGKLRWXY
**3** ABD**F**GHJ**OP**R**W**X
**4** (Q+R+U 🔓) (X 1/10-31/12)
**5** **AB**DFGIJKLMNOPUWZ
**6** CDEG**K**(N 0,5km)OUV

💬 A pleasantly landscaped campsite. Some of the pitches are in a big field next to the Aller, some in a park-like grounds. The centre of Winsen is within walking distance.

🚐 A7 Hannover-Bremen, exit Allertal (petrol station) direction Celle. Signposted to the campsite in Winsen (turn right). Campsite near centre of Winsen.

Winsen
(Aller)
L180
L240
Wietze
**CC**
L298
A7
B214
**Celle**
L310

272

**CC** € **18** 1/1-7/7  25/8-31/12      🧭 N 52°40'36'' E 09°54'05''

## Winsen/Aller-Meißendorf, D-29308 / Niedersachsen ♿ 🛜 iD 644

🏕 Campingpark Hüttensee
✉ Hüttenseepark 1
☎ +49 50 56 94 18 80
📅 1/1 - 31/12
@ info@
campingpark-huettensee.de

18ha 200T(100-120m²) 16A CEE

**1** ACD**G**HIJKLMOP**Q**
**2** ADRW
**3** BD**F**HJN**QR**W**Z**
**4** (Q+R+U 1/4-30/10) (Y 📅)
**5** **AB**DEFGIJMNOPUWZ
**6** CDEG**K**(N 8km)OTUV

💬 Lovely family campsite with many recreational opportunities, located by a swimming lake with beach, behind which are a number of lakes for sailing. The camping field is close to the entrance, near the beach. Environmental tax is not included in the CampingCard ACSI rate.

🚗 A7 Hamburg-Hannover, exit 49 (Westenholz) direction Winsen. Campsite is in Meißendorf 7 km before Winsen. Follow the 'Hüttenseepark' signs in Meißendorf.

Bergen

CC

A7   L180   Winsen
B214   Wietze   L298
L190   Hambühren

CC € **18** 1/1-28/5   11/6-3/7   1/9-31/12    📍 N 52°43'12'' E 09°49'31''

---

## Zetel/Astederfeld, D-26340 / Niedersachsen 👫 🛜 iD 645

🏕 Campingplatz am Königssee
✉ Tarbarger Landstr. 30
☎ +49 44 52 17 06
📅 1/3 - 31/10
@ info@
campingplatz-am-koenigssee.de

2,5ha 40T(100-150m²) 10-16A CEE

**1** AD**G**IJKLMNPQ
**2** ADLMRSW
**3** ABFJNRU**WZ**
**4** (Q+R 📅)
**5** **AB**DGIJKLMN**P**UWXY
**6** DEGI**K**(N 4km)OU

💬 Located directly on a swimming lake with a sandy beach and located in the Wadden Sea World Heritage Site. The campsite invites you to relax. You will find peace and relaxation at this well maintained site. There is a small kiosk and fresh bread is available daily.

🚗 A28 exit 6 Westerstede, L815 direction Zetel. After 14 km turn left towards Astederfeld. Campsite signposted.

B436   L816
   A29
B437   **Varel**
L12   L815   L818
  L819
L18
L24   A28   L820   L824
**Westerstede**

CC

CC € **18** 1/5-28/5   11/6-14/7   1/9-31/10    📍 N 53°21'19'' E 07°55'46''

---

## Altenteil (Fehmarn), D-23769 / Schleswig-Holstein ♿ 🛜 iD 646

🏕 Belt-Camping-Fehmarn★★★★
✉ Altenteil 24
☎ +49 4 37 23 91
📅 1/4 - 6/10
@ info@belt-camping-fehmarn.de

9ha 160T(70-100m²) 16A CEE

**1** AD**G**IJKLMOPQ
**2** EKMNORUVWX
**3** ABJNRUWY
**4** (Q+R+U+V 📅)
**5** **AB**CDEFGHIJKLMNOP**QR**
**S**UWX
**6** ACDEGH**K**(N 5km)OPT

💬 A quiet campsite with spacious pitches by the Baltic Sea. All pitches have their own water and electricity supply. The campsite is in a quiet location and is very dog friendly. There is a restaurant/pizzeria for an excellent meal. Luxury new toilet blocks since 2018.

🚗 E47 exit Puttgarden direction Gammendorf. Then past Dänschendorf to Altenteil. Campsite signposted.

Burg auf Fehmarn   B207

CC

CC € **18** 1/4-29/5   12/6-29/6   1/9-6/10    📍 N 54°31'43'' E 11°05'40''

## Augstfelde/Plön, D-24306 / Schleswig-Holstein ♿ 📶 ⚙ **iD** 647

🔺 Camping Augstfelde-
Vierer See****
✉ Augstfelde 1
☎ +49 45 22 81 28
🗓 30/3 - 20/10
@ info@augstfelde.de

2,6ha 200T(90-110m²) 16A CEE

**1** A**G**HIJKLMO**PQ**
**2** ADILMRUVWX
**3** B**D**FGKN**Q**RV**W**Z
**4** **N**(S+T+U+Y+Z 🅿)
**5** **AB**DEFGIJKLMNO**PQ**RUW
XY
**6** CDEG**JK**(N 3km)OPRSTU

💬 A lovely family campsite on the Vierermeer lake with a 1 km long private sandy beach. Clear swimming water. Close to the Plöner lake plateau.

🚗 From the A1 to Eutin, then towards Plön via the B76. Clearly indicated after Bösdorf exit.

€ **18** 30/3-13/4 23/4-29/5 11/6-28/6 25/8-19/10 📷 **N 54°07'43'' E 10°27'18''**

---

## Basedow, D-21483 / Schleswig-Holstein 👫 📶 **iD** 648

🔺 Camping Lanzer See
✉ Am Lanzer See 1
☎ +49 41 53 59 91 71
🗓 29/3 - 6/10
@ info@camping-lanzer-see.de

5ha 60T(50-150m²) 16A CEE

**1** AD**G**HIJKLMOPQ
**2** CDKLMRTUVWXY
**3** AHJKNR**W**Z
**4** J(Q+R+T+Y 🅿)
**5** **AB**DFGIJKMNOPUWXYZ
**6** CEGJ(N 7km)O

💬 Idyllically located on the Elbe-Lübeck canal and Lake Lanzer. Spacious pitches on a headland right by the water. Restaurant with a terrace. Cycle route along the Elbe and the Alte Salzstraße, two nature parks and the Hanseatic towns of Hamburg, Lübeck and Lüneburg nearby.

🚗 From Hamburg A24 exit Hornbek dir. Lauenburg. Indicated from Basedow. From Lüneburg on the B5 turn off right towards Boizenburg. After 1 km left to Lanze. 5 km to campsite.

€ **16** 29/3-28/5 3/6-6/6 11/6-28/6 19/8-5/10 📷 **N 53°24'36'' E 10°35'50''**

---

## Bliesdorf, D-23730 / Schleswig-Holstein ♿ 📶 **iD** 649

🔺 Camping Walkyrien*****
✉ Strandweg
☎ +49 45 62 67 87
🗓 29/3 - 19/10
@ info@camping-walkyrien.de

6ha 130T(80-100m²) 16A CEE

**1** AC**G**HIJKLMO**PQ**
**2** AEFILRTVW
**3** B**D**F**K**N**P**RUWY
**4** **N**(Q+R+T+U+X+Y+Z 🅿)
**5** **AB**DEFGHIJKLMNOPRS**TU**
WXYZ
**6** CDEG**K**(N 5km)OTV

💬 A five star holiday park right on the Baltic Sea. Motorhome park, campsite. Walkyrien Spas 'Sauna & Wellness über dem Meer', restaurant, supermarket, playground and sports ground, entertainment for young and old, natural sandy beach.

🚗 Leave the E47/E22 Hamburg-Puttgarden at Neustadt-Nord exit, direction Grömitz. Right after 5 km in Bliesdorf. Signposted.

**Neustadt in Holstein**

€ **20** 29/3-11/4 28/4-28/5 11/6-19/6 2/9-1/10 7/10-19/10 📷 **N 54°07'23'' E 10°55'17''**

## Dahme, D-23747 / Schleswig-Holstein

650

🔺 Camping Stieglitz
✉ Reinhold-Reshöft-Damm
☎ +49 43 64 14 35
🕐 29/3 - 27/10, 20/12 - 31/12
@ info@camping-stieglitz.de

14ha 200T(90-160m²) 16A CEE

**1** ACD**G**IJKLMOPQ
**2** ACELORVWXY
**3** BDJRUWY
**4** (Q+S 🅿) (T 1/5-15/9)
　 (U+Y 🅿)
**5** **ABC**DEFGHIJKLMNO**PQR**
　 UWXYZ
**6** ABCDEG**K**(N 2km)OPTV

💬 Located on Baltic Sea north of the spa resort of Dahme. Surrounded by meadows, dunes and a long sandy beach. There are standard, comfort and premium pitches. All have 16A connections. Comfort and premium pitches also have water connections. CampingCard ACSI provides you with a standard pitch for 14 Euros, a comfort pitch for 16 Euros and a pitch closer to the dike for 18 Euros. Rates are excl. tourist tax.

🚗 Campsite located on the north side of Dahme (last campsite).

CC € **14** 29/3-7/7 25/8-27/10 20/12-31/12

📍 N 54°14'33'' E 11°04'49''

---

## Fehmarnsund (Fehmarn), D-23769 / Schleswig-Holstein

651

🔺 Camping Miramar*****
✉ Fehmarnsund 70
☎ +49 43 71 32 20
🕐 1/1 - 31/12
@ campingmiramar@t-online.de

13ha 212T(80-135m²) 16A CEE

**1** ACD**E**IJKLMOPQ
**2** AEGKMORVWXY
**3** BF**J**LN**Q**UWY
**4** **N**(Q+S+T+U+Y 1/4-31/10)
**5** **ABC**DEFGHIJKLMNOP**QR**
　 UWXY
**6** ACDEG**K**(N 5km)OPTUVX

💬 Lovely beach campsite on the south beach of Fehmarn. Plenty of opportunities for sport, games and wellness for the whole family. The restaurant offers a good dish of the day. Ideal as a stopover to and from Scandinavia. CampingCard ACSI is valid for pitches up to 90m², there is a supplement of 1 or 2 Euros for larger pitches. The campsite has a bicycle service point.

🚗 E47 from northerly direction exit Landkirchen. From south exit Avendorf. Signposted from Avendorf.

CC € **18** 1/1-29/5 2/6-7/6 11/6-28/6 27/8-31/12

📍 N 54°24'16'' E 11°08'25''

---

## Gammendorf (Fehmarn), D-23769 / Schleswig-Holstein

652

🔺 Camping Am Niobe****
☎ +49 43 71 32 86
🕐 1/4 - 10/10
@ info@camping-am-niobe.de

7,5ha 134T(80-120m²) 16A CEE

**1** AD**F**HIJKLMOPRS
**2** AEFMNORVWX
**3** ABDHJKN**P**RUWY
**4** (Q+R 🅿) (T 1/7-31/8) (Y 🅿)
**5** **AB**DFGIJKLMNO**P**RUWXY
　 Z
**6** CDEG**K**(N 9,9km)OT

💬 A campsite located directly on the Baltic Sea with views of the ships and the sea. Informal campsite with plenty of space for rest and relaxation. Large pitches and playing fields. Walking and cycling are allowed in the adjoining protected nature reserve. Good restaurant and shop. There is a supplement of 2 Euros for a comfort pitch.

🚗 E47 to just before ferry port, left here to Puttgarden. Right after village dir. Gammendorf. Follow signs on right.

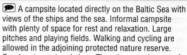

CC € **18** 1/4-29/5 17/6-23/6 2/9-10/10

📍 N 54°31'19'' E 11°09'09''

## Glücksburg, D-24960 / Schleswig-Holstein

♿ 🛜 **iD** **653**

🏕 Ostseecamp Glücksburg-Holnis****
🏠 An der Promenade 1
☎ +49 46 31 62 20 71
🗓 29/3 - 3/11
@ info@ostseecamp-holnis.de

6ha 125T(100m²) 16A CEE

**1** ABCD**F**IJKLMOP**Q**
**2** AEGLRSWX
**3** AB**F**HJKN**OPQ**RU**W**Y
**4** (T+U+X+Z 🅿)
**5** **AB**DEFGIJKLMNOPUWXYZ
**6** CDEGI**K**(N 4km)UV

💬 Campsite with a newly opened bistro beach cafe beautifully located on the Holnis peninsula. Walking, cycling, playing golf, horseback riding. One of the most appealing sandy beaches of the Baltic sea. Food and drink. Castle Glücksburg, harbour town Flensburg.

🚗 From Glücksburg drive towards Holnis. Camp site well signposted.

CC € **20** *29/3-24/5 10/6-18/6 1/9-3/11*

📶 N 54°51'26'' E 09°35'29''

---

## Grömitz, D-23743 / Schleswig-Holstein

👪 ♿ 🛜 **iD** **654**

🏕 Ahoi Camping Resort
🏠 Mittelweg 129
☎ +49 45 62 85 86
🗓 1/4 - 31/10
@ moin@ahoi-camping.de

8ha 70T(80-120m²) 10A CEE

**1** AC**G**HIJKLMNOP**Q**
**2** AEFGLORU
**3** AB**F**RY
**4** **N**(Q+R+T+U+X+Z 🅿)
**5** **AB**DEFGI**J**KLMNO**P**RUWZ
**6** CDEG**J**(N 0,2km)OT

💬 Very well-maintained campsite with spacious pitches, both sunny and shady pitches are available. Excellent washing facilities in all respects. Location of the campsite is on a beach road, and opposite a climbing park. Close to Lensterstrand and Grömitz, a luxurious seaside resort with nice shops and terraces. Directly on the Baltic Sea. Great for cycling.

🚗 E47/E22 Hamburg-Puttgarden, take Neustadt exit. Take B501 to Grömitz. Take Mittelweg in Grömitz centre.

CC € **20** *1/4-7/6 11/6-30/6 1/9-15/10*

📶 N 54°09'38'' E 10°59'32''

---

## Großenbrode, D-23775 / Schleswig-Holstein

🛜 **iD** **655**

🏕 Camping Großenbrode****
🏠 Südstrand 3
☎ +49 43 67 86 97
🗓 1/4 - 31/10
@ info@camping-grossenbrode.de

8ha 90T(80-95m²) 6-16A

**1** AD**G**IJKLMOP**Q**
**2** AEGORUVW
**3** BGJRUWY
**5** **AB**CDEFGHIJK**L**MNO**PQR** UWXY
**6** ABCDEGH**K**(N 0,3km)OPT U

💬 A perfectly run campsite with very clean toilet facilities. Großenbrode Boulevard with restaurants and retailers is within walking distance. Sports opportunities for all ages between the campsite and boulevard including fitness apparatus and playground. Ideal for relaxing in early and late season. The wardens do their very best to satisfy all the campers.

🚗 A1 Hamburg-Lübeck as far as Heiligenhafen. Then the E47 as far as Großenbrode. The campsite is clearly signposted.

CC € **16** *1/4-26/5 14/6-30/6 28/8-27/10*

📶 N 54°21'37'' E 11°05'15''

## Husum, D-25813 / Schleswig-Holstein    ♿ 🛜 iD   656

🏕 Husumer Campingplatz
📧 Dockkoog Strasze 17
☎ +49 4 84 19 39 79 60
📅 1/4 - 31/10
@ husum@regenbogen.ag

2,5ha 65T(90-110m²) 16A CEE

**1** ACD**G**HIJKLMOP**Q**
**2** EKLMRVWX
**3** CFHJRUY
**4** (Q+R 📅)
**5** **AB**FGIJKLMNOP**Q**UW
**6** CDEGJ(N 2,5km)OT

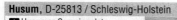

NEW

💬 Well maintained (transit) campsite just behind a dike with little vegetation and fairly spacious pitches.

🚗 From road B5 follow Husum-centrum. Under the railway, left, and then left over the railway. The campsite is signposted there.

Behrendorf
L273 B200
L30 B201
CC **Husum**
L37
B5 L38

CC € **16**   1/4-15/4   23/4-28/5   12/6-29/6   25/8-31/10    🏔 N 54°28'46'' E 09°00'39''

---

## Kappeln, D-24376 / Schleswig-Holstein    🛜 iD   657

🏕 Camping Schleimünde
📧 Olpenitzer Dorfstrasse 29
☎ +49 4 64 28 16 47
📅 1/4 - 15/10
@ info@
   campingplatz-schleimuende.de

1,8ha 70T(80-100m²) 4-16A

**1** ACD**G**IJKLMOP**Q**
**2** ELORSWX
**3** B**F**N
**4** (Q+T+U+Y 📅)
**5** GHIJKLMNO**P**W
**6** **K**(N 1km)

NEW

💬 Campsite Schleimunde means sand, sea and good food. Kilometres of sandy beaches, beautiful cycling and hiking trails. The charming town of "Kappeln" is definitely worth a visit. Also suitable for large motorhomes.

🚗 At Rendsburg exit, take B203 in direction Eckernförde and just before Kappeln turn right in direction Olpenitz. Follow Ostseeresort Olpenitz and the signs 'Campingplatz' in the direction of Olpenitz village.

B199
L21   Kappeln   CC
B201
B203
Vogelsang-
Grünholz

CC € **16**   1/4-18/4   24/4-29/5   3/6-8/6   10/6-30/6   1/9-15/10    🏔 N 54°39'47'' E 10°00'24''

---

## Katharinenhof (Fehmarn), D-23769 / Schleswig-Holstein    ♿ 🛜 iD   658

🏕 Campingplatz Ostsee
   Katharinenhof*****
☎ +49 43 71 90 32
📅 1/4 - 15/10
@ info@camping-katharinenhof.de

14ha 230T(80-110m²) 10-16A CEE

**1** AD**G**HIJKLMOPRS
**2** AEFGNORUVWXY
**3** ABDJKN**P**RUWY
**4** M(Q+S+T+U+Y 📅)
**5** **AB**DEFGIJKLMNOPQUWX
   Y
**6** ACDEG**K**(N 6km)OTVX

💬 Family friendly campsite on the island of Fehmarn. A good location for diving. Attractive playgrounds. Long beach. Pony riding possible and a lovely base for cycle trips. CampingCard ACSI entitles you to a comfort pitch with at least a 10 Amp connection. The campsite is dog-friendly and has a beach for dogs.

🚗 E47 exit Burg. Then to Katharinenhof, campsite signposted from here.

Fehmarn   CC
B207
Grossenbrode

CC € **18**   1/4-29/5   12/6-29/6   1/9-15/10    🏔 N 54°26'42'' E 11°16'43''

## Klausdorf (Fehmarn), D-23769 / Schleswig-Holstein ♙♙♙ ♿ 🛜 ❀ iD 659

- ⛺ Camping Klausdorfer Strand****
- 🏠 Klausdorfer Strandweg 100
- ☎ +49 43 71 25 49
- 📅 1/4 - 13/10
- @ info@
  camping-klausdorferstrand.de

17ha 200T(80-170m²) 16A CEE

1 ACD**G**IJKLMO**P**Q
2 AEGKLORUVWX
3 ABCGJLNRUWY
4 **KLN**(Q+S 🔑) (T 1/7-31/8)
(U+Y 🔑)
5 **AB**CDFGHIJKLMNOP**QRS**
UWXY
6 ACDEGH**K**(N 6km)OPSTU

💬 A campsite quietly located beside the beach with good facilities for swimming, walking or cycling. Sauna with views of the sea. Attractive restaurant with a covered terrace. Wonderful views. CampingCard ACSI is valid for pitches up to 90m², for larger pitches there is a supplement of 2 Euros and for pitches with a sea view, 4 Euros.

🚗 E47, exit Burg. Direction Burg. From Burg to Niendorf, then on to Klausdorf. Signposted.

Burg auf Fehmarn
B207

CC € 18  1/4-27/5  21/6-29/6  1/9-13/10   📍 N 54°27'27'' E 11°16'20''

## Klein Rönnau/Bad Segeberg, D-23795 / Schleswig-Holstein ♿ 🛜 iD 660

- ⛺ KlüthseeCamp & Seeblick
- 🏠 Stipsdorferweg/Klüthseehof 2
- ☎ +49 4 55 18 23 68
- 📅 1/1 - 31/1, 1/3 - 31/12
- @ info@kluethseecamp.de

25ha 200T(100-140m²) 16A CEE

1 ACD**G**HIJKLMOQ
2 ADFKLMNRWX
3 B**F**HJKNRU**VW**Z
4 (**C** 1/5-31/8) **LN**
(Q+R+T 1/4-31/10) (U+Y 🔑)
5 **AB**DEFGHIJMNOP**S**UWXY
Z
6 ACDEG**I**K(N 2,5km)OTUV

💬 A lovely child-friendly campsite with good amenities next to a lake. Friendly atmosphere. Lovely cycling and walking paths. Good restaurant and snack bar. Extensive wellness possibilities.

🚗 From the town of Bad Segeberg take the B432 towards Scharbeutz Ostsee. Campsite clearly signposted in Klein Rönnau.

Trappenkamp   L69
B205
A21   B432
**Bad**   CC
**Segeberg**   A20
B206
L167   L84   L71

CC € 20  1/1-31/1  1/3-30/6  1/9-31/12  7=6, 14=12   📍 N 53°57'41'' E 10°20'15''

## Kleinwaabs, D-24369 / Schleswig-Holstein ♿ 🛜 iD 661

- ⛺ Ostsee-Campingplatz Heide
- 🏠 Strandweg 31
- ☎ +49 43 52 25 30
- 📅 1/4 - 27/10
- @ info@waabs.de

22ha 280T(95-160m²) 16A CEE

1 ABCD**F**HIJKLMOPRS
2 ELNRUVWXY
3 ABCHK**MN**O**PQ**RUV**W**Y
4 (A 1/7-31/8) (**F** 🔑) **LN**P
(Q+S+T+U+V 🔑)
(Y 1/4-31/8) (Z 🔑)
5 **AB**DEFGJKLMNOP**QRS**UW
XYZ
6 CDEGH**IK**M(N 0km)OPRST
UV

💬 A large family campsite with plenty of atmosphere. The well-run site is by the sea and has everything a camper could need.

🚗 B203 Eckernförde-Kappeln, exit Loose. Then towards Waabs at crossroads. Continue to Kleinwaabs. Campsite well signposted in the village.

B203
L27   L26
CC
**Eckernförde**   L285   Strande
B76

CC € 20  27/4-25/5  22/6-6/7  24/8-29/9   📍 N 54°31'52'' E 10°00'03''

## Medelby, D-24994 / Schleswig-Holstein  ♿ 📶 **iD** (662)

🏕 Camping Mitte
✉ Sonnenhügel 1
☎ +49 46 05 18 93 91
📅 1/1 - 31/12
@ info@camping-mitte.de

5,2ha 200T(< 120m²) 10-16A CEE

**1** ACDFIJKLMOPQ
**2** LRTVWX
**3** ABCJRU
**4** (C+**F**+G 📅) **N**(Q+R+V 📅)
(Z 1/1-1/3,1/9-31/12)
**5** **AB**DEFGIJKLMNOPQRUW
XYZ
**6** CEK(N 1km)OTU

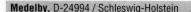

💬 A modern, quiet, open campsite in the middle of a nature reserve. Indoor and outdoor pool. Plenty of flexibility in the way you choose to spend your time. Good stopover site for people driving to or from Scandinavia.

🚗 A7 exit 2, road 199 direction Niebüll. Follow signs from Wallsbüll.

**401** L192 L1 L245 Padborg **E45** L246 L212 Handewitt **Leck** B199 L14 L96 **CC**

**CC** €**20** 1/1-8/7 26/8-31/12    🧭 N 54°48'54'' E 09°09'49''

---

## Rabenkirchen-Faulück, D-24407 / Schleswig-Holstein  ♿ 📶 **iD** (663)

🏕 Campingpark Schlei-Karschau
✉ Karschau 56
☎ +49 46 42 92 08 20
📅 1/1 - 31/12
@ info@campingpark-schlei.de

4,8ha 112T(100m²) 10A CEE

**1** ABCD**F**HIJKLMOPQ
**2** ADEILRSVWX
**3** B**F**KNRU**W**YZ
**4** (Q+R+T+U+X+Y 25/3-31/10)
(Z 📅)
**5** **AB**DEFGIJKLNOPRUWXZ
**6** ACDEG**K**(N 7km)OTUV

💬 Clean campsite, ideal for watersports enthusiasts. Friendly family campsite. Loved by anglers. Lovely cycling routes along the Schlei Fjord.

🚗 A7 Hamburg-Flensburg, exit Schleswig/Schuby direction Kappeln (B201). Exit Faulück/Arnis, then direction Karschau.

L21 Hasselberg Mohrkirch Kappeln L28 B201 **CC** B203 L27 L26

**CC** €**20** 7/1-14/4 6/5-30/5 24/6-1/7 1/9-1/10 7/10-22/12    🧭 N 54°37'11'' E 09°53'02''

---

## Rosenfelde/Grube, D-23749 / Schleswig-Holstein  👫 ♿ 📶 ✿ **iD** (664)

🏕 Rosenfelder Strand
Ostsee Camping*****
✉ Rosenfelder Strand 1
☎ +49 43 65 97 97 22
📅 29/3 - 13/10
@ info@rosenfelder-strand.de

24ha 350T(100-150m²) 16A CEE

**1** ADG IJKLMOPQ
**2** AEKLMORUVWX
**3** ABDJLN**Q**RUWY
**4** M**N**(Q+S 📅) (T 10/5-25/8)
(U+Y+Z 📅)
**5** **AB**CDEFGHIJKLMNOP**QR**
**ST**UWXYZ
**6** ABCDEGH**K**(N 4km)OPTUV

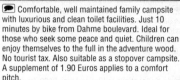

💬 Comfortable, well maintained family campsite with luxurious and clean toilet facilities. Just 10 minutes by bike from Dahme boulevard. Ideal for those who seek some peace and quiet. Children can enjoy themselves to the full in the adventure wood. No tourist tax. Also suitable as a stopover campsite. A supplement of 1.90 Euros applies to a comfort pitch.

🚗 Route B501 between Grube and Fargemiel. Direction Rosenfelde.

A1 Oldenburg in Holstein L59 **CC** B501 L58 L231

**CC** €**18** 29/3-29/5 11/6-29/6 26/8-13/10    🧭 N 54°15'54'' E 11°04'39''

## Scharbeutz, D-23683 / Schleswig-Holstein

&#9855; &#128246; **iD** **665**

⛺ Ostseecamp Lübecker Bucht
🏠 Bormwiese 1
☎ +49 45 63 52 03
🕐 1/4 - 31/10
@ info@
ostseecamp-luebecker-bucht.de

5,5ha 75T(65-150m²) 16A CEE

**1** ACD**G**HIJKLMNOPS
**2** FGJRVWXY
**3** ABHIJKLU
**4** (Q+T+U+X+Z 🔑)
**5** **AB**EFGHIJKLMNOPQRSTU
WXY
**6** BCDE**GJ**(N 1km)O

💬 Beautifully situated on the edge of a nature reserve. Within walking distance of the Autobahn.

🚗 A1 HH-Puttgarden/Fehmarn. Exit Haffkrug/ Scharbeutz, B76 direction Eutin, near the motorway.

CC € **16** 1/5-1/6 1/9-31/10    🏔 N 54°03'18'' E 10°43'49''

---

## Schobüll, D-25875 / Schleswig-Holstein

&#128246; **iD** **666**

⛺ Camping Seeblick
🏠 Nordseestraße 39
☎ +49 48 41 33 21
🕐 22/3 - 20/10
@ info@camping-seeblick.de

3,4ha 140T(80-85m²) 10A CEE

**1** ACD**F**HIJKLMOPQ
**2** AEKMNRTVWX
**3** AB**F**JRUY
**4** (Q+T+U 🔑)
**5** ABDEFGIJKLMNOPQUWZ
**6** CEG**K**(N 0,3km)OTUV

💬 A campsite on the mud flats with open views of the North Sea. Slightly sloping grounds. Adjoining a (municipal) swimming pool. An ideal area for surfing or mudflat hiking. Located directly on the 'Wattenmeer' National Park. Boat trips to watch the seals.

🚗 From the A7 south, through the Elbe Tunnel, A23 direction Itzehoe-Husum as far as Heide exit. Towards Husum. Then follow signs as far as Schobüll. Then follow camping signs.

CC € **18** 22/3-18/4 23/4-6/6 11/6-30/6 16/9-20/10    🏔 N 54°30'35'' E 09°00'11''

---

## Schönberg (Ostseebad), D-24217 / Schleswig-Holstein

&#9855; &#128246; &#10057; **iD** **667**

⛺ California Ferienpark GmbH****
🏠 Große Heide 26
☎ +49 43 44 95 91
🕐 1/4 - 30/9
@ info@camping-california.de

8ha 174T(80-120m²) 10A CEE

**1** ACD**G**HIJKLMO**PQ**
**2** AEGLRVWX
**3** BGHJKLN**OPQR**TU**W**Y
**4** (Q+S+T+U+Y 🔑)
**5** **AB**DEFGJKLMNO**P**UWXY
**6** ACDEGH**K**(N 1km)OSTV

💬 A beautiful and restful beach campsite on the Baltic coast, directly behind the sea defences. Spacious pitches marked by hedges. Good walking and cycling opportunities. Excellent beach facilities. A good base for a great holiday.

🚗 In Kiel continue to 'Ostufer' then B502 direction Schönberg. At first roundabout in Schönberg direction Kalifornien. Campsite signposted.

CC € **18** 1/4-25/5 17/6-30/6 24/8-30/9    🏔 N 54°25'42'' E 10°21'50''

## Strukkamphuk (Fehmarn), D-23769 / Schleswig-Holstein ♿ 🛜 iD (668)

🏕 Strukkamphuk-Fehmarn*****
☎ +49 43 71 21 94
🗓 29/3 - 3/11
@ info@strukkamphuk.de

20ha 308T(100-160m²) 16A CEE

1️⃣ ACD**G**IJKLMOPQ
2️⃣ AEGMNORUVWX
3️⃣ AB**F**GJLNRUWY
4️⃣ **N**(Q+S+U+Y 🅾)
5️⃣ **AB**CDEFGHIJKLMNOPQ**R**
UWXYZ
6️⃣ ACDEGH**K**(N 7km)OPTU

💬 A beautiful beach campsite secluded behind a dike. Close to the bridge that connects the island of Fehmarn with the mainland. Good surfing here. Plenty of opportunities for sport and games.

🚌 E47 coming from the north, exit Landkirchen. From the south take Avendorf exit. Signposted from Avendorf.

Fehmarn
Heiligenhafen
CC
B207
A1
B501

CC €18 29/3-12/4 26/4-24/5 16/6-28/6 2/9-3/11 📶 N 54°24'42'' E 11°05'54''

---

## Wallnau (Fehmarn), D-23769 / Schleswig-Holstein ♿ 🛜 iD (669)

🏕 Strandcamping Wallnau****
🏠 Wallnau 1
☎ +49 4 37 24 56
🗓 29/3 - 27/10
@ wallnau@strandcamping.de

22ha 370T(90-130m²) 6-16A CEE

1️⃣ AD**G**IJKLMOPQ
2️⃣ AEFNORVWXY
3️⃣ BJLN**OP**RUWY
4️⃣ **NP**(Q+S 🅾) (T 1/7-31/8)
(U+Y 🅾)
5️⃣ **AB**CDFGHIJKLMNOP**QR**U
WXYZ
6️⃣ ACEGHJ**K**(N 3km)OPT

💬 A very 'lively' campsite with so much to do. There is a large bird park close by. Good walking and cycling opportunities. Protected natural area. Watersports opportunities. Own riding school. Plenty of emphasis on wellness and fitness. Dog friendly. Supplement for comfort pitches.

🚌 From the E47 continue via Landkirchen, Petersdorf and Bojendorf. Look out for signs.

Fehmarn
Burg auf
Fehmarn
CC
B207

CC €18 29/3-29/5 2/6-7/6 31/8-27/10 📶 N 54°29'15'' E 11°01'07''

---

## Wulfen (Fehmarn), D-23769 / Schleswig-Holstein ♿ 🛜 ✿ iD (670)

🏕 Camping Wulfener Hals*****
🏠 Wulfener Hals Weg 100
☎ +49 4 37 18 62 80
🗓 1/1 - 31/12
@ info@wulfenerhals.de

34ha 393T(80-260m²) 16A CEE

1️⃣ ACD**G**IJKLMOPQ
2️⃣ AEGKLORUVWXY
3️⃣ AB**EF**GHJLN**OPQ**RUVWY
4️⃣ (A 1/4-31/10) (**C** 15/4-15/10)
**K N** (Q+S 1/4-31/10,25/12-31/12)
(T+U+W 1/4-31/10) (X
19/3-3/10) (Y 1/4-4/11,25/
12-31/12) (Z 1/4-31/10)
5️⃣ **AB**CDEFGHIJKLMNOP**QRST**U
WXY
6️⃣ ABCDEGH**K**M(N 4km)OPSTUVW

💬 Campsite with an relaxed atmosphere with everything you could possibly want. Natural beaches on the Baltic Sea and Burger Lake, heated pool (supplement) with jacuzzi, own small golf course. Next to Fehmarn Golf Course (18 holes). Activities and events for all ages with shows and live music. Archery, horse riding, surfing, kite flying, sailing, diving, bike hire.

🚌 E47 from northerly direction exit Landkirchen. From south exit Avendorf. Signposted from Avendorf.

Fehmarn
Heiligenhafen
B207 CC
L60

CC €20 1/1-18/4 23/4-29/5 12/6-29/6 31/8-23/12 📶 N 54°24'22'' E 11°10'38''

## Ahrensberg, D-17255 / Mecklenburg-Vorpommern

&#9650; Campingplatz Am
   Drewensee****
&#9742; +49 3 98 12 47 90
&#9055; 30/3 - 3/11
@ info@haveltourist.de

**671**

4,6ha 130T(80-125m²) 16A CEE

**1** ACD**G**HIJKLM**P**Q
**2** ABDLRVWY
**3** BKNW**Z**
**4** (Q+R &#9055;) (T 1/5-14/9)
**5** **AB**FGIJKLMNO**P**RUW
**6** CEG**K**OT

💬 Camping at Drewensee lake is something special.
The campsite is located on grassland directly by
the lake and surrounded by forests. Facilities for
motorhomes, volleyball, facilities for the disabled,
bike hire, jetty. This is an ideal starting point for your
tours by canoe or by motor boat.

🚗 From A19 exit 18, B198 to Wesenberg/
Neustrelitz. Between Wesenberg and Neustrelitz
exit Ahrensberg. In Ahrensberg immediately turn left
and keep left.

Neustrelitz

L25

B198

B122

B96

L15

Fürstenberg/
Havel

**CC** € **18** 30/3-18/4 22/4-30/5 3/6-7/6 11/6-29/6 18/8-3/11 7=6, 14=11    N 53°15'46'' E 13°03'03''

---

## Alt Schwerin, D-17214 / Mecklenburg-Vorpommern

&#9650; Camping am See
&#9993; An den Schaftannen 1
&#9742; +49 39 93 24 20 73
&#9055; 1/4 - 31/10
@ info@camping-alt-schwerin.de

**672**

3,6ha 138T(80-120m²) 10A CEE

**1** ACD**G**HIJKLMOPQ
**2** ADFKLRVWX
**3** B**F**HIJNRU**WZ**
**4** (A 1/6-30/6, 1/9-30/9)
  (Q+R &#9055;) (X+Z 1/5-31/10)
**5** **AB**DEFGJMNOPRUWXYZ
**6** ACFG**J**(N 4km)OV

💬 Located right by a lake. A well maintained
campsite with many pitches by the water. All pitches
are maximum 40m from the shore. Large playground.
Various sports opportunities. Beach with gently
sloping shores. Right on the Plauer See cycle route.
Just 70 km to Schwerin Castle.

🚗 A19 exit Malchow. The campsite is located on the
B192, between Alt Schwerin and Karow.

L20

L205

A19

B103   Malchow

Göhren-
Lebbin

Plau am See

**CC** € **20** 1/4-28/6 2/9-31/10    N 53°31'23'' E 12°19'07''

---

## Altenkirchen, D-18556 / Mecklenburg-Vorpommern

&#9650; Camping Drewoldke****
&#9993; Zittkower Weg 27
&#9742; +49 38 39 11 29 65
&#9055; 1/1 - 31/12
@ info@camping-auf-ruegen.de

**673**

9ha 340T(80m²) 16A CEE

**1** ACD**G**HIJKLMO**P**ST
**2** ABEKNORSWXY
**3** ABHJKRWY
**4** (Q &#9055;) (R+T+U 1/5-30/9)
  (X 1/5-31/8) (Z 1/3-1/10)
**5** **AB**DEFGHIJKLMNO**PQRS**
  **T**UWZ
**6** ACDEGI**K**(N 3km)OQSTV

💬 The campsite is located 10 metres from the Baltic
Sea coast. Excellent base for cycle trips to sights
such as: cape Arkena with chalk cliffs, historic fishing
village Vitt, the historical town of Altenkirchen with
the oldest church in Rügen and Breege harbour for
boat trips. National Park Jasmund with King's Chair
is 20 km away.

🚗 B96 Stralsund-Bergen dir. Sassnitz then dir.
Altenkirchen. Campsite signposted.

Dranske

L30

Sagard

**CC** € **18** 1/5-28/5 11/6-20/6 28/8-30/9 14=12, 21=18    N 54°38'04'' E 13°22'24''

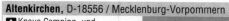

## Altenkirchen, D-18556 / Mecklenburg-Vorpommern 📶 🆔 674

🔺 Knaus Camping- und Ferienhauspark Rügen
📧 Zittkower Weg 30
☎ +49 3 83 91 43 46 48
🔑 1/1 - 31/12
@ ruegen@knauscamp.de

3,7ha 108T(80m²) 16A

**1** ACD**G**HIJKLMOPQ
**2** EKNORWX
**3** BGHJKLWY
**4** **N**(Q 1/4-31/10)
  (R+U+Y+Z 🔑)
**5** **AB**DFGIJKLMNO**PRS**UWX YZ
**6** ACDEG**K**(N 2km)O

💬 A campsite on Rügen directly by the sea with beautiful views of the peaceful, calm Baltic Sea. Ideal for surfers. 3 family baths, a sauna and even a whirlpool. A cycle and footpath goes from the campsite right along the beach to the famous chalk cliffs and the fishing village of Vitt which is a protected monument.
🚗 Coming from Sagard B96 to Altenkirchen, past Juliusruh. Turn right after 300m and the campsite is about 1200m beyond the woodland campsite.

Dranske  CC  L30
Glowe
Vaschvitz

CC €20 7/1-29/5 3/6-7/6 24/6-15/7 1/9-20/12  N 54°38'11" E 13°22'31"

## Born, D-18375 / Mecklenburg-Vorpommern ♿ 📶 ✿ 🆔 675

🔺 Regenbogen Ferienanlage Born
📧 Nordstraße 86
☎ +49 38 23 42 44
🔑 1/4 - 31/10
@ born@regenbogen.ag

10ha 470T 16A CEE

**1** ACD**G**HIJKLMO**P**Q
**2** BDLMRWXY
**3** AJKR**WZ**
**4** (Q+R 🔑) (T 15/5-1/10)
**5** **AB**DFGIJKLMNOP**QRS**UW Z
**6** CEGJ(N 3km)OT

💬 A large campsite with a private beach, many shaded pitches and plenty of water sports opportunities.

🚗 From Rostock take route B105 direction Ribnitz, left at Darß/Prerow headland. Follow signs before Born.

Zingst
Bresewitz
L21
CC Fuhlendorf
B105

CC €16 1/4-15/4 23/4-28/5 12/6-29/6 1/9-31/10  N 54°23'02" E 12°30'16"

## Dierhagen-Strand, D-18347 / Mecklenburg-Vorpommern 👫 ♿ 📶 🆔 676

🔺 OstseeCamp Dierhagen GbR
📧 Ernst-Moritz-Arndt Str. 1
☎ +49 38 22 68 07 78
🔑 15/3 - 31/10
@ info@ostseecamp-dierhagen.de

6ha 300T(80-120m²) 16A CEE

**1** ACD**G**HIJKLMO**P**Q
**2** BGLRTUVWXY
**3** BHJKR**W**
**4** (Q+R+T 1/4-15/9)
**5** **AB**DFGIJKLMNO**P**UWZ
**6** CDEGK(N 0,7km)O

💬 Camp in the Baltic seaside resort of Dierhagen between the Baltic sea and Bodden in the heart of the Fischland-Darß-Zingst peninsula. Far from the noise and traffic you will be camping on a sunny field or in the light shade of deciduous and coniferous trees.

🚗 On B105 at Altheide take exit dir. Prerow, Ahrenshoop, then left at traffic lights dir. Dierhagen-Strand.

L21
CC
Ribnitz-Damgarten
B105  L191

CC €18 15/3-5/6 13/6-30/6 1/9-30/10  N 54°17'29" E 12°20'37"

## Dobbertin, D-19399 / Mecklenburg-Vorpommern ♀♂ ✦ 🛜 [iD] 677

⛺ Campingplatz am
   Dobbertiner See
📧 Am Zeltplatz 1
☎ +49 17 47 37 89 37
🗓 1/4 - 15/10
@ dobbertincamping@aol.com

4ha 90T(100m²) 16A CEE

1 A**G**IJKLMOPQ
2 BDGILMRWXY
3 BHJKLRU**W**Z
4 (Q 1/5-30/9)
5 **AB**DFGIJMNO**P**UWXZ
6 ACEGJ(N 0,5km)S

💬 Located directly on the Dobbertiner See lake, an idyllic unmarked campsite with free choice of pitches. With the Mecklenburger Seenplatte lakes and the woods so close you can relax wonderfully or be active on foot, by bike or in a boat. Plenty of birds for bird spotters. The 'Nossentiner Schwinzer Heide' and 'Sternberger Seenland' Nature reserves are close by.

🚗 A19 exit Malchow / A24 exit Parchim / A20 exit Bützow, continue towards Dobbertin. Follow camping signs.

Ⓒ € ⑯  1/4-30/6  1/9-14/10     ▲ N 53°37'09'' E 12°03'54''

## Dranske, D-18556 / Mecklenburg-Vorpommern ✦ 🛜 ✿ [iD] 678

⛺ Regenbogen Ferienanlage
   Nonnevitz
📧 Nonnevitz 13
☎ +49 38 39 18 90 32
🗓 1/4 - 31/10
@ nonnevitz@regenbogen-camp.de

20ha 550T(< 120m²) 16A CEE

1 ACD**G**HIJKLNO**P**Q
2 ABEGKRSVWXY
3 AB**F**HJKRW**Y**
4 (A 1/5-31/8) N(Q 🔑)
   (S 1/5-31/10) (T+U 🔑)
   (V 1/5-30/9) (X 🔑)
5 **AB**DEFGJMNOP**QR**UWZ
6 CDEGJ(N 8km)OQTV

💬 A large forest/beach campsite with a beautiful clean beach in the quiet, extreme north of Rügen. Lots of privacy on lovely and large pitches in the forest. New clean toilet facilities in existing buildings relatively close by. Plenty of opportunity for cycling amongst poppies and cornflowers.

🚗 Via Bergen B96 towards Dranske, right in Kuhle towards Gramtitz, then follow Nonnevitz. Campsite signposted.

Ⓒ € ⑱  1/4-15/4  23/4-28/5  12/6-29/6  1/9-31/10     ▲ N 54°40'01'' E 13°17'47''

## Flessenow, D-19067 / Mecklenburg-Vorpommern ✦ 🛜 ✿ [iD] 679

⛺ Seecamping Flessenow****
📧 Am Schweriner See 1A
☎ +49 3 86 68 14 91
🗓 29/3 - 13/10
@ info@seecamping.de

8ha 170T(80-110m²) 10A CEE

1 ACD**G**IJKLMOPQ
2 ADFGLMRSVWXY
3 BGHJK**O**RW**Z**
4 (**A** 1/7-31/8)
   (Q+R+T+U+X+Z 🔑)
5 **AB**DFGIJKLMNOPRUWXY
   Z
6 ACEGJOTV

💬 Well run campsite under Dutch management. The site is in a sheltered position on the Schwerin lake. Plenty of watersports activities or trips by bike to Schwerin.

🚗 From the north: A14 exit Jesendorf dir. Schwerin. From the south: A14 exit 5 dir. Cambs-Güstrow. Turn right at traffic lights towards Retgendorf-Flessenow.

Ⓒ € ⑳  29/3-6/6  11/6-28/6  1/9-13/10     ▲ N 53°45'07'' E 11°29'47''

## Freest, D-17440 / Mecklenburg-Vorpommern

🏕 Camping Waldcamp Freest
✉ Dorfstrasse 74
☎ +49 38 37 02 05 38
🗓 1/4 - 15/10
@ info@campingplatz-freest.de

**3,5ha 80T(100-150m²)**

**1** ABG**H**IJKLMOP
**2** EKRVWX
**3** ABE**J**KL**Q**RWY
**4** (Q 🗓)
**5** **AB**DEFGHIJKMNO**P**UWZ
**6** CEGJ(N 0,5km)

💬 Space and tranquility characterise this small campsite. On the edge of reedlands and with a view of the sea, 200 metres from the beach. Even, spacious pitches in the grass. Good area for cycling.

🚗 Freest is on the L262. From Lubmin turn left 100 metres before Freest sign. This is at the beginning of the built-up area. Site is signposted. Coming from the other direction the campsite is on right at end of built-up area.

**680**

Zinnowitz
L262
**Wolgast** B111
L26

CC € **18**  1/4-20/6  28/8-15/10   🏔 N 54°08'22'' E 13°43'02''

---

## Groß Quassow/Userin, D-17237 / Mecklenburg-Vorpommern

🏕 Camping- und Ferienpark Havelberge*****
✉ An den Havelbergen 1
☎ +49 3 98 12 47 90
🗓 1/1 - 31/12
@ info@haveltourist.de

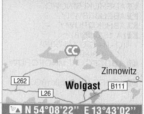

**24ha 320T(90-287m²) 16A CEE**

**1** ACD**G**HIJLM**P**Q
**2** ADIJLMRSVWY
**3** ABJKN**O**RU**W**Z
**4** **(A** 1/7-31/8) **N**(Q 🗓) (R+T+U+Y 1/4-31/10) (Z 🗓)
**5** **AB**DEFGIJKLMNO**P**UWXY Z
**6** CDE**I**K(N 7km)OTUV

💬 Camping and more in the attractive Camping and Holiday Resort in the Mecklenburg Lake District: here 'more' really means more... Restaurant, shop, canoe and boating centre, play- sport grounds, teepee tent camp, trampoline, sauna, outdoor swimming area with beach, Waldhochseilgarten.

🚗 B198 from Mirow or Neustrelitz as far as Wesenberg. Then via Klein Quassow as far as Groß Quassow. Then drive towards the lake. The site is signposted from Wesenberg.

**681**

B193
**Neustrelitz**

L25 Wesenberg
B198    CC
B122
B96

CC € **20**  1/1-18/4  22/4-30/5  3/6-7/6  11/6-29/6  18/8-31/12   🏔 N 53°18'32'' E 13°00'08''

---

## Hohenkirchen, D-23968 / Mecklenburg-Vorpommern

🏕 Campingplatz 'Liebeslaube'
✉ Wohlenberger Wiek 1
☎ +49 38 42 86 02 19
🗓 1/1 - 31/12
@ info@ campingplatz-liebeslaube.de

NEW

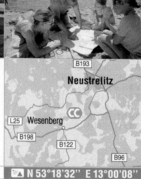

**9ha 150T(70-150m²) 16A CEE**

**1** AD**G**IJKLMOPQ
**2** AEGKRTVWXY
**3** BF**H**JKLRWY
**4** (Q+R 🗓) (T+U+X 1/5-30/9) (Z 🗓)
**5** **A**DEFGIJMNO**PR**UW
**6** CEG**J**(N 6km)OQTU

💬 A pleasant family campsite with panoramic views of the sea. Located right on a lovely beach with no road between. Surfing school and restaurant with kiosk. A good base for going on cycle trips.

🚗 A20, exit 8 Wismar Mitte dir. Wismar. Take the B106 dir. Lübeck at roundabout. In Gägelow take L1 exit dir. Boltenhagen. Continue 6 km to the Baltic Sea. Campsite on the Wohlenberger Wiek beach.

**682**

L01
CC
L03    **Wismar**
B105  A20
**Grevesmühlen**  B208

CC € **20**  13/4-28/5  11/6-20/6  26/8-8/12   🏔 N 53°55'50'' E 11°17'17''

## Karlshagen, D-17449 / Mecklenburg-Vorpommern

👬 ♿ 🛜 **iD** **683**

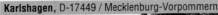

🏕 Dünencamp Karlshagen*****
📧 Zeltplatzstraße 11
☎ +49 38 37 12 02 91
🗓 1/1 - 31/12
@ camping@karlshagen.de

5ha 265**T**(80-90m²) 16A CEE

**1** AD**F**HIJKLMNO**P**Q
**2** ABEGJRSWXY
**3** ABHJK**Q**RU**W**Y
**4** (A 15/6-15/8)
   (Q+R+T+U 1/5-30/9)
   (X 1/4-30/9)
**5** **AB**DEFGIJKLMNOPQRUW
   Z
**6** ACDEGJ(N 0,05km)OSTV

💬 Family campsite right on the Baltic Sea with its own large sandy beach. Suitable for cycle trips.

🚗 B111 Wolgast-Ahlbeck. In Bannemin turn left towards Karlshagen. Campsite signposted.

Zinnowitz
Wolgast
B111

ⓒⓒ € 20 1/1-16/6 1/9-31/12

📍 N 54°07'04" E 13°50'42"

---

## Klein Pankow, D-19376 / Mecklenburg-Vorpommern

👬 🛜 ✿ **iD** **684**

🏕 Camping am Blanksee
📧 Am Blanksee 1
☎ +49 38 72 42 25 90
🗓 1/4 - 13/10
@ info@campingamblanksee.de

12ha 80**T**(100-150m²) 10-16A CEE

**1** A**G**IJKLMO**P**Q
**2** ABDKLMRSUWXY
**3** BJKNRU**WZ**
**4** (Q+R+S 🅿)
   (T+U+X+Z 1/5-13/10)
**5** **AB**FGIJLMNO**P**UWZ
**6** ADEG**K**(N 7km)O

💬 An idyllic campsite situated by a beautiful lake with its own beach between two protected nature reserves. Lovely cycling and walking area and a place to enjoy real relaxation. Ideal for bird spotters and game spotters. Small 'Gaststätte' and shop.

🚗 A24 Hamburg-Berlin. Exit 16 Suckow. Suckow-Siggelkow-Groß Pankow dir. Klein Pankow. Then follow camping signs.

Lübz
L16
B191
Parchim
L17
L09 ⓒⓒ
B321
Marnitz
L14
L08 A24 L13

ⓒⓒ € 18 1/4-30/6 1/9-12/10

📍 N 53°23'13" E 12°01'14"

---

## Koserow, D-17459 / Mecklenburg-Vorpommern

♿ 🛜 **iD** **685**

🏕 Camping Am Sandfeld
📧 Am Sandfeld 5
☎ +49 38 37 52 07 59
🗓 15/4 - 13/10
@ camping@amsandfeld.de

4ha 150**T**(80-100m²) 16A CEE

**1** A**G**HIJKLMO**P**Q
**2** AGIRSWXY
**3** ABHJKRU
**4** (Q+R 🅿)
**5** **AB**DFGIJKLMNOP**S**UW
**6** CDEG**K**(N 0,5km)OSTV

💬 The campsite is located in quiet surroundings at the edge of a nice village, at 700 metres from the beach. The campsite is easy-going and has a natural lay-out with spacious pitches in the grass.

🚗 B111 Wolgast dir. Swinoujscie. Take 2nd exit Koserow, campsite indicated from here.

B111
ⓒⓒ
Heringsdorf

ⓒⓒ € 18 15/4-7/6 10/6-23/6 1/9-13/10

📍 N 54°02'48" E 14°00'40"

D-18551 / Mecklenburg-Vorpommern  686

**Lohme/Nipmerow**
- Krüger Natur... 5
- Jasmunder... 4
- +49 3 8... naturcamping.de
- 13/4...
- inf...

(...00m²) 16A CEE

**1** ...MOPQ
**2** ...QRSTUWXY
**3** ...ANQRU
**4** ...) (U 17/4-20/10)
**5** ...)
**6** ...GIJKLMNO**PQ**TUWZ
...**GJ**(N 8km)OST

A campsite in the countryside on the island of Rügen, 8 km north of Sassnitz. Ideal base for walks in the Jasmund National Park. Dogs welcome. The ideal stopover for holidaymakers en route to Northern Europe. 1.5 km from the Baltic Sea. Excursions to the cliffs with a forester are possible.

B96 Bergen-Altenkirchen, turn right after Bobbin towards Sassnitz. Campsite signposted.

CC € 20  13/4-27/6  2/9-4/11     N 54°34'10'' E 13°36'36''

---

**Lütow**, D-17440 / Mecklenburg-Vorpommern     👫 ♿ 🛜 ✿ iD 687

- Natur Camping Usedom
- Zeltplatzstraße 20
- +49 38 37 74 05 81
- 1/4 - 31/10
- @ info@natur-camping-usedom.de

18ha 450**T**(30-250m²) 16A CEE

**1** AD**G**IJKLMOPQ
**2** ABEJRVWXY
**3** ABJKLNRU**W**Y
**4** (A 10/7-20/8) (Q 🔲)
(S 1/5-1/9) (U 🔲)
(Y 1/5-30/9) (Z 🔲)
**5** **AB**DEFGIJLMNOPUWXY
**6** ACEGJ(N 8km)OTV

Quiet family campsite with pitches right by the lagoon. 18 hectare grounds with tent, caravan and motorhome pitches partly marked out. The campsite has a restaurant, shop, and a surfing and sailing school. Canoes and bicycles for rent.

B111 from Wolgast to Ahlbeck. Turn right before Zinnowitz. Campsite signposted.

Karlshagen

Wolgast

Klein Bünzow     L26     B111

CC € 20  1/4-19/4  22/4-30/5  2/6-7/6  10/6-30/6  1/9-31/10     N 54°00'41'' E 13°51'29''

---

**Markgrafenheide/Rostock**, D-18146 / Mecklenburg-Vorpommern     ♿ 🛜 iD 688

- Camp. & Ferienpark Markgrafenheide
- Budentannenweg 2
- +49 38 16 61 15 10
- 1/1 - 31/12
- @ info@baltic-freizeit.de

28ha 1114**T**(100-140m²) 16A CEE

**1** AD**G**IJKLMOPQ
**2** ABEGRSVWXY
**3** BHJKL**MOQ**R**SW**Y
**4** (**B** 1/5-30/9) (**F** 🔲) **KLN**
(Q 🔲) (S 15/5-15/10)
(T 1/7-31/8) (U 🔲)
(V 1/7-31/8) (W 1/3-31/10)
(Y+Z 🔲)
**5** **AB**DFGJNPUWZ
**6** ACDEG**J**M(N 0,6km)OUV

A large campsite on the Baltic beaches close to Warnemünde. Large pitches under tall pine trees on a hard sandy base. Good facilities, well maintained toilets, cinema, good food, sauna, wellness, 2 indoor squash courts. Plenty of places to see in the nearby cultural region and in Hanseatic Rostock. CampingCard ACSI valid only in the 'Randlage' sectors A, B, C, M, pitches of 100 m².

B105 Rostock-Stralsund exit Rövershagen-Hinrichshagen-Markgrafenheide.

Graal-Müritz

Markgrafenheide

Elmenhorst/ Lichtenhagen     L22  B105
B103     L182

CC € 18  15/4-30/5  10/6-30/6  30/8-27/10     N 54°11'39'' E 12°09'20''

## Ostseebad Rerik, D-18230 / Mecklenburg-Vorpommern

🏕 Campingpark 'Ostseebad Rerik'*****
🏠 Straße am Zeltplatz 8
☎ +49 38 29 67 57 20
🔑 1/1 - 31/12
@ info@campingpark-rerik.de

5,2ha 240T(80-100m²) 16A CEE

**1** ACD**G**IJKLMOPQ
**2** AEGLORTUVWXY
**3** ABHJKN**P**RU**W**Y
**4** **N**(Q+R 🔑) (S 1/4-31/10) (T+U 🔑) (Y 1/4-31/10) (Z 🔑)
**5** **AB**CDEFGIJKLMN**PQRS**U WXYZ
**6** ACDEGIK(N 0,8km)OQSTV

💬 A friendly campsite with a new and very modern toilet block, in peaceful surroundings, 300 metres from the Baltic Sea. A perfect area for walking, cycling, swimming and fishing. 2 minutes by car to the centre.

🚗 A20 exit 12 Kröpelin (L11). A20 Autobahnkreuz/Wismar 105 as far as Neubukow. Then direction Rerik. Follow the camping signs in Rerik.

**689**

Kühlungsborn
CC  L11
B105
Neubukow
L12

CC € **18**  1/1-29/5  10/6-24/6  18/8-31/12  21=20, 28=25    🏖 N 54°06'47'' E 11°37'51''

---

## Ostseebad Zinnowitz, D-17454 / Mecklenburg-Vorpommern

🏕 Familien-Campingplatz Pommernland GmbH*****
🏠 Dr. Wachsmannstr. 40
☎ +49 38 37 74 03 48
🔑 1/1 - 5/1, 1/3 - 31/12
@ camping-pommernland@m-vp.de

7,5ha 360T(80-100m²) 6A CEE

**1** ACD**G**HIJKLMO**P**Q
**2** ABEIRSTXY
**3** ABHKQRU**W**Y
**4** (A 15/6-31/8) (**F+H** 🔑) (Q 1/3-31/12) (R+S 1/4-31/10) (T 1/6-31/8) (U+Y 1/4-30/11) (Z 🔑)
**5** **AB**DEFGIJKLMNO**PQRS**U WXYZ
**6** ACDEG**IJ**(N 1km)ORSTV

💬 Woodland campsite with many shaded pitches. Spacious unmarked pitches. Perfect for walking and cycling tours. Restaurant with excellent cooking on the campsite. Plenty to do for children. A short walk from the lively centre of Zinnowitz.

🚗 B111 Wolgast-Ahlbeck, left at the traffic lights in Zinnowitz, turn right at 1st roundabout. Left at the chemist, then continue to the end of the road.

**690**

Wolgast
CC  B111
Ückeritz
L26

CC € **20**  1/3-25/6  1/9-31/12    🏖 N 54°04'56'' E 13°53'57''

---

## Plau am See/Plötzenhöhe, D-19395 / Mecklenburg-Vorpommern

🏕 Campingpark Zuruf
🏠 Seestraße 38D
☎ +49 38 73 54 58 78
🔑 1/1 - 31/12
@ campingpark-zuruf@t-online.de

8ha 126T(70-100m²) 10-16A CEE

**1** ACD**G**HIJKLMOPQ
**2** ADLMRUVWXY
**3** BJKLRU**W**Z
**4** (Q+R 🔑) (T 27/4-6/10) (U 15/4-15/10) (V+Z 27/4-6/10)
**5** **AB**DEFGIJKLMNO**PQST**U WXYZ
**6** ACDEG**J**(N 2,5km)OTV

💬 Campsite attractively located on the Plauer See. Spacious marked out pitches. Close to the pleasant town of Plau. Combined cycle and boat trips possible. Special section and beach for dog owners.

🚗 A24/E26 Hamburg-Berlin take Meyenburg exit. Then B103 towards Plau. In Plau, at traffic lights turn right towards Plötzenhöhe. Campsite (on the lake) is signposted.

**691**

B103  B192  L20
Malchow
Plau am See  A19
CC  Fünfseen
L17  L206

CC € **20**  1/3-25/4  6/5-24/5  17/6-30/6  1/9-30/10    🏖 N 53°26'17'' E 12°17'13''

## Prerow, D-18375 / Mecklenburg-Vorpommern

(symbols) 🦯 📶 ✿ **iD** (692)

🏕 Regenbogen Ferienanlage
Prerow
☎ +49 38 23 33 31
🗓 1/4 - 31/10
@ prerow@regenbogen-camp.de

35ha 850T(12-100m²) 16A CEE

**1** ACD**G**IJKLMNOP**Q**
**2** ABEGKRSVWXY
**3** ABHJKN**Q**R**W**Y
**4** **N**(Q+R+T+U+V+Y+Z 🔟)
**5** **AB**DEFGIJKLMNOP**QS**UWZ
**6** CDEG**J**M(N 0,6km)OQTVW

💬 Large campsite on the sea with a private beach, lots of shade and many water sports options on offer.

🚗 In Prerow head to centre, campsite is clearly signposted there.

CC Zingst
L21
**Barth**

**CC** € **20**  1/4-15/4  23/4-28/5  12/6-29/6  1/9-31/10    N 54°27'16'' E 12°32'51''

---

## Pruchten, D-18356 / Mecklenburg-Vorpommern

(symbols) 🦯 📶 **iD** (693)

🏕 NATURCAMP Pruchten****
📧 Am Campingplatz 1
☎ +49 3 82 31 20 45
🗓 1/4 - 31/10
@ info@naturcamp.de

6ha 250T(80-100m²) 16A

**1** ACD**G**HIJKLMOP**Q**
**2** BEGLMRVWXY
**3** ABDJKLN**OP**R**W**Y
**4** (Q+S+U+Y+Z 1/5-31/10)
**5** **AB**DEFGJLNPQR**S**UWXYZ
**6** ACDEGH**IK**(N 3,5km)OQRT U

💬 A peaceful campsite suitable for discovering the Darss/Zingst peninsula. An interesting natural phenomenon can be observed from September. Thousands of cranes settle in the area. Large unmarked pitches.

🚗 B105 Ribnitz-Darmgarten towards Stralsund. In Löbnitz drive in the direction of Barth, and then towards Pruchten. The campsite is signposted.

Zingst
Prüchten
Fuhlendorf   CC   Barth
L21
L23
B105

**CC** € **18**  1/4-6/6  12/6-30/6  1/9-30/10    N 54°22'46'' E 12°39'43''

---

## Rerik/Meschendorf, D-18230 / Mecklenburg-Vorpommern

(symbols) 🦯 📶 **iD** (694)

🏕 Camping Ostseecamp Seeblick
📧 Meschendorfer Weg 3b
☎ +49 3 82 96 71 10
🗓 29/3 - 3/11
@ info@ostseecamp.de

9ha 400T(80-130m²) 16A CEE

**1** ACD**G**HIJKLOP**Q**
**2** AEKLORTVWX
**3** BHJKNRU**W**Y
**4** (A 1/6-28/10) **N**(Q+S 🔟) (T 1/7-1/9) (U 1/5-30/9) (Y 🔟)
**5** **AB**DEFGJKLMNO**PR**UWXY Z
**6** CEGIK(N 4km)OTUV

💬 A beautiful, large campsite directly on the sea with a lovely beach. Spacious, sunny pitches. Campsite offers all comforts. The area is perfect for cycling and fishing. There is a diving school on the campsite called 'Ostseebasis Rerik'.

🚗 A20, exit 9, then B105 direction Neubukow. Then left towards Rerik. Follow Rerik-Meschendorf, then 2nd campsite.

**Kühlungsborn**

CC
B105
L11
L12

**CC** € **18**  29/3-20/4  23/4-29/5  11/6-23/6  7/9-3/11    N 54°07'40'' E 11°38'44''

## Sternberg, D-19406 / Mecklenburg-Vorpommern ♿ 📶 iD **695**

🏕 Camping Sternberger Seenland
📧 Maikamp 11
☎ +49 38 47 25 34
🗓 1/4 - 31/10
@ info@camping-sternberg.de

7,5ha 120T(80-100m²) 16A CEE

**1** A**G**IJKLMOPQ
**2** ADGJKLRSTVWXY
**3** BHJKLRUWZ
**4** (**A** 1/5-1/7) (Q+R+T+Y ⌨)
**5** **AB**DFGJLNPUW
**6** CDEGIK(N 0,5km)OQTV

💬 The campsite is next to a small lake and on the edge of a wood. Lovely spacious marked out pitches on grass. Kayaking and canoeing possible. Natural locations close to a small village with a historic centre and many beautiful restored houses.

🚗 Route 192 Wismar-Malchow. Follow camping signs at Sternberg.

CC €20  1/4-28/5  12/6-30/6  1/9-31/10    📷 N 53°42'48'' E 11°48'46''

---

## Trassenheide, D-17449 / Mecklenburg-Vorpommern ♿ ✿ iD **696**

🏕 Camping Ostseeblick****
📧 Zeltplatzstraße 20
☎ +49 38 37 12 09 49
🗓 29/3 - 3/11
@ campingplatz@trassenheide.de

4,1ha 250T(65-100m²) 16A CEE

**1** ACD**G**IJKLMOPQ
**2** ABCEJRSVXY
**3** ABGHJKR**W**Y
**4** (Q ⌨) (R+T 15/5-15/9)
    (U 1/4-31/10) (X 15/5-15/9)
    (Z 29/5-15/9)
**5** **AB**DFG**IJ**KLMNO**P**UWXZ
**6** CDEGI(N 1,5km)QT

💬 Family campsite directly on the Baltic Sea with its own large sandy beach. Suitable for making cycle trips.

🚗 B111 Wolgast-Ahlbeck. Turn left in Bannemim to Trassenheide. Campsite well signposted.

CC €20  29/3-29/5  3/6-7/6  1/9-3/11    📷 N 54°05'25'' E 13°53'08''

---

## Ückeritz, D-17459 / Mecklenburg-Vorpommern ♿ 📶 iD **697**

🏕 Naturcamping Hafen Stagnieß
📧 Stagnieß Hafenstrasse 10A
☎ +49 38 37 52 04 23
🗓 1/4 - 31/10
@ info@
   camping-surfen-usedom.de

4ha 180T(80-100m²) 16A CEE

**1** A**G**IJKLMO**P**Q
**2** DKRSTWXY
**3** K
**4** (Q+T ⌨)
**5** **AB**DEFGIJMNO**P**UW
**6** EG**J**(N 2km)O

💬 Quiet and centrally-located campsite on the island of Usedom. Pitches are not marked out and are on grass. Situated on the lake, forest edge, and harbour. Good cycle and walking routes nearby, and within cycling distance of the lovely Baltic Sea, bathing resorts and Swinemünde in Poland.

🚗 From Anklam via B110 and B111. From Wolgast on B111. Campsite clearly signposted around the village of Ückeritz.

CC €18  1/4-28/5  3/6-7/6  11/6-30/6  1/9-30/9    📷 N 54°00'02'' E 14°02'56''

## Ummanz, D-18569 / Mecklenburg-Vorpommern

🚶 📶 ⚙ **iD** **698**

🏕 Ostseecamp. Suhrendorf GmbH****
✉ Suhrendorf 4
☎ +49 38 30 58 22 34
📅 18/4 - 31/10
@ ostseecamp.suhrendorf@t-online.de

9ha 250T(100-150m²) 16A CEE

**1** ADGIJKLMPQ
**2** AEGLMRSVWXY
**3** ABCHKN**OPQ**RUW Y
**4** (A 1/7-31/8) (R 1/5-30/9) (T+U+W+X+Y+Z ⊝)
**5** **AB**DEFGIJKLMNO**P**RUWXYZ
**6** EG**K**(N 2km)OSTV

💬 Spacious campsite on the beautiful Baltic coast on the quiet island of Ummanz, 20 km² in size. Campsite is located in Boddenlandschaft National Park. Good roads and paths for cycling and walking between poppies and cornflowers. Spacious pitches in the grass. Good toilet facilities including children's toilets.

🚗 From Stralsund B96 drive towards Bergen; at Samtens turn left towards Gingst. In Gingst turn left towards Insel Ummans. After bridge left. Campsite signposted.

Schaprode

Klausdorf

CC L30

€ **20** 18/4-30/4 3/5-6/6 11/6-20/6 1/9-31/10 | 🧭 N 54°27'51'' E 13°08'19''

---

## Waren (Müritz), D-17192 / Mecklenburg-Vorpommern

🚶 📶 **iD** **699**

🏕 CampingPlatz Ecktannen
✉ Fontanestraße 66
☎ +49 39 91 66 85 13
📅 1/1 - 31/12
@ info@camping-ecktannen.de

17ha 400T 16A CEE

**1** ACD**G**HIJKLMO**P**Q
**2** DILMRSX
**3** ABDHIJKN**Q**R**W**Z
**4** (Q ⊝) (R+T+X 1/4-30/10)
**5** **AB**DEFGIJKLMNPUW
**6** CDEGIK(N 4km)OTU

💬 A large campsite without marked pitches on the southern outskirts of the spa town of Waren (Müritz). The site is right on Germany's largest inland sea, the Müritzsee, bordering the national park with about 400 km of cycle and hiking trails. Ideal for families (beach with lifeguards) and for dogs (dog walking area and dog beach) and more.

🚗 A19 exit Waren (Müritz), B192 as far as Heilbad Waren (Müritz). Then follow CampingPlatz Ecktannen signs.

B108 L202 B194
L205
CC Waren (Müritz)
B192
L24

€ **18** 1/1-26/5 13/6-20/6 1/9-31/12 | 🧭 N 53°29'58'' E 12°39'48''

---

## Wesenberg, D-17255 / Mecklenburg-Vorpommern

🚶 📶 ⚙ **iD** **700**

🏕 Camping Am Weissen See****
✉ Am Weissen see 1
☎ +49 3 98 12 47 90
📅 30/3 - 13/10
@ info@haveltourist.de

3,5ha 100T(90-112m²) 16A

**1** ACD**G**HIJLMO**P**Q
**2** ADGIJLSVWX
**3** AHJKR**W**Z
**4** (Q+R+T+U+X+Z ⊝)
**5** **AB**GIJKLMNO**P**UW
**6** EG**K**(N 1km)OT

💬 A campsite set under tall pine trees with a variety of levels. The site is spaciously appointed and is located on a lake which allows for swimming. There is a restaurant and a campsite shop. Plenty of amenities.

🚗 Campsite well signposted from the centre of Wesenberg. Follow the C63.

Neustrelitz
L25
Granzow B96
B198 CC Wesenberg
B122

€ **16** 30/3-18/4 22/4-30/5 3/6-7/6 11/6-29/6 18/8-13/10 7=6, 14=11 | 🧭 N 53°17'02'' E 12°56'54''

## Wooster Teerofen, D-19399 / Mecklenburg-Vorpommern  🛜 iD  **701**

▲ Camping Oase Waldsee
✉ Köhlerweg 9
☎ +49 17 49 37 04 69
🔓 1/4 - 31/10
@ info@campingoase-waldsee.de

7ha 160T(50-110m²) 16A CEE

**1** ADGHIJKLMNOPQ
**2** ABDLMNRSXY
**3** ABCHJKLRUVWZ
**4** (A 🔓) N(Q+R+T 🔓)
**5** ABDEGIJKLMNOPUWXZ
**6** ACDEGK(N 9,5km)ORSTUV X

💬 Campsite located in a forest and on a lake. Spacious shady pitches. Lots of lovely cycle rides nearby.

🚗 On the B192 Goldberg-Karow take exit Wooster Teerofen. Then follow signs.

CC € **12**  1/4-6/6  12/6-30/6  1/9-30/10   ◩ N 53°35'19'' E 12°12'56''

---

## Zislow, D-17209 / Mecklenburg-Vorpommern  👫 ♿ 🛜 iD  **702**

▲ Wald- u. Seeblick Camp GmbH
✉ Waldchaussee 1
☎ +49 3 99 24 20 02
🔓 1/1 - 31/12
@ info@camp-zislow.de

11ha 220T(80-100m²) 16A CEE

**1** ACDGHIJKLMOPQ
**2** BDFLMRSTVWXY
**3** BHIJKNRUWZ
**4** (Q 🔓) (R+T 15/4-15/9) (X 1/4-30/9)
**5** ABFGIJKLMNOPUWXYZ
**6** CEGJ(N 9,8km)OS

💬 Whether you're on holiday with your family or a group, in a tent, with a caravan or motorhome, you'll be sure to enjoy a nice relaxing holiday at Wald-und-Seeblick Camp, directly on Lake Plauer.

🚗 From A19 (B192) at exit Waren/Petersdorf head towards Adamshoffnung/Zislow. Then follow signs.

CC € **18**  1/1-28/5  12/6-30/6  1/9-31/12   ◩ N 53°26'32'' E 12°18'50''

---

## Zwenzow, D-17237 / Mecklenburg-Vorpommern  🛜 ✿ iD  **703**

▲ Camping Zwenzower Ufer★★★★
✉ Am Großen Labussee (C56)
☎ +49 3 98 12 47 90
🔓 30/3 - 3/11
@ info@haveltourist.de

5ha 65T(80-132m²) 16A CEE

**1** ACDGHIJLMOPQ
**2** DGLMRSVWX
**3** AHJKWZ
**4** N(S+T+U 🔓)
**5** ABDEFGIJKLMNOPUW
**6** CEGK(N 0km)OT

💬 Located on the Großen Labussee lake and directly borders the Müritz National Park. Numerous lakes in the forests can easily be reached. The level terrain is lush with grass, shrubs, leafy trees and conifers. The toilet facilities offer all the comforts and some facilities for the disabled. Children's playground, waterslide, naturist beach, bike hire, canoe point, restaurant near by.

🚗 B96 From Berlin via Neustrelitz direction Userin and Useriner Mühle to Zwenzow.

CC € **16**  30/3-18/4  22/4-30/5  3/6-7/6  11/6-29/6  18/8-3/11  7=6, 14=11   ◩ N 53°19'08'' E 12°56'42''

## Zwenzow, D-17237 / Mecklenburg-Vorpommern

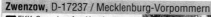

**704** NEW

⌂ FKK-Camping Am Useriner See****
☎ +49 3 98 12 47 90
⊙ 30/3 - 13/10
@ info@haveltourist.de

8ha 120T(80-162m²) 10A CEE

**1** ACF HIJLMOP Q
**2** ABDILRSVX
**3** ABHJKN W Z
**4** (Q+S ⊡)
**5** AB DEGIJKLMNO P UWZ
**6** EK(N 0km)OT

💬 Situated in between the Userin lake and the one-of-a-kind woods of the Müritz National Park, this camping is a central stopover for boat tours. Nudist section. Shop, restaurant at short distance, facilities for the disabled, playground, sports field, boat landings, boat and bike hire.

🚗 B198 to Mirow. On the L25 turn off towards Userin. Continue via Granzow and Roggentin to Zwenzow.

Neustrelitz — B193 — L34 — CC — L25 Wesenberg — B198 — B122 — B96

CC €18 30/3-18/4 22/4-30/5 3/6-7/6 11/6-29/6 18/8-13/10 7=6, 14=11 🧭 N 53°19'49'' E 12°57'19''

## Bergwitz/Kemberg, D-06901 / Sachsen-Anhalt

**705**

⌂ Bergwitzsee Resort
🏠 Strandweg 1
☎ +49 34 92 12 82 28
⊙ 1/1 - 31/12
@ reception@bergwitzsee.de

11ha 100T(70-150m²) 16A CEE

**1** ACG HIJLOPQ
**2** ADLMRY
**3** BHJKNR W Z
**4** M(Q+R ⊡) (T+U+Y 1/5-2/10) (Z 1/5-30/10)
**5** AB DFGIJKLMN P UWXYZ
**6** CEGK(N 1,3km)ORT

💬 A site by a large lake. Suitable for water sports. Own boats allowed. It has upper and lower levels. The lower level is right by the lake. Close to the Lutheran city of Wittenberg, Oranienbaum 16 km away and the beautiful Wörlitzerpark 16 km. Good for longer stays.

🚗 A9 Berlin-Leipzig exit 8. B187 via Wittenberg, B2 Leipzig. In Eutzsch take B100 direction Gr-Hainchen, 2nd exit behind Service Station-Bergwitz. Campsite sign at 5-way interchange in village.

Wittenberg, Lutherstadt — B187 — L131 — CC — B107 — L132 — L129 — B2 — B100

CC €18 1/1-28/5 12/6-3/7 10/9-31/12 🧭 N 51°47'28'' E 12°34'15''

## Harzgerode/OT Neudorf, D-06493 / Sachsen-Anhalt

**706**

⌂ Ferienpark Birnbaumteich***
🏠 Am Birnbaumteich 1
☎ +49 3 94 84 62 43
⊙ 1/1 - 31/12
@ info@ ferienpark-birnbaumteich.de

11,5ha 150T(50-100m²) 16A CEE

**1** AG HIJKLOPQ
**2** ABDLRSTWX
**3** ABNRUV W Z
**4** N(Q+R ⊡) (T+U+X+Z 1/4-30/9)
**5** AB DEFGIJKL NO P Q UWXZ
**6** CEGK(N 5km)OV

💬 A very peacefully located campsite in the Harz Mountains, by a lake with a beach for swimming. Restaurant with a lovely terrace. Beautiful walking and cycling in the area. Lovely villages close by such as Stolberg, and a trip by steam train to the Brocken is a must.

🚗 B81 Magdeburg-Nordhausen, exit Hasselfelde B242 direction Halle. 1 km past Harzgerode towards Stolberg. Turn right 4.3 km further on. Left at campsite signs near bus stop.

Friedrichsbrunn — B185 — L95 — B242 — Harzgerode — L230 — CC — L236 — L232 — L1037 — L234 — L231

CC €18 1/1-6/7 23/8-21/12 🧭 N 51°36'30'' E 11°05'05''

293

## Havelberg, D-39539 / Sachsen-Anhalt ‡‡ ᚶ 📶 iD 707

△ Campinginsel Havelberg*****
✉ Spülinsel 6
☎ +49 39 38 72 06 55
📅 1/3 - 31/10
@ info@campinginsel-havelberg.de

2,7ha 80T(80-120m²) 16A CEE

**1** ACDGIJKLMOPQ
**2** ACGKLMRSUVWXY
**3** ABCGJNQRUWX
**4** (Q 🔒) (T+X+Z 1/4-30/9)
**5** ABEFGIJKLMNOPUWXYZ
**6** ACDEGJ(N 1km)ORTUV

💬 This campsite is situated on an island surrounded by the River Havel with lovely views of the Dom (cathedral). The historic centre is linked to the island by a bridge, 200 metres away. Ideal for cycling and walking in the beautiful countryside.

🚗 A24 exit 18 Meyenburg, follow the B107 50 km to Havelberg. In Havelberg follow the signs.

L10  Breddin  L141
L3
L16  Havelberg  L4
CC
Iden
B107  L18  L2

CC €20  1/3-28/5  12/6-30/6  4/9-30/10    N 52°49'36'' E 12°04'14''

## Naumburg, D-06618 / Sachsen-Anhalt ‡‡ ᚶ 📶 iD 708

△ Campingplatz Blütengrund
✉ Blütengrund 6
☎ +49 34 45 26 11 44
📅 1/3 - 31/10
@ info@campingplatz-naumburg.de

14ha 250T(100m²) 16A CEE

**1** ACDGHIJKLMOPQ
**2** CLRWXY
**3** BHJKNRW
**4** (Q 🔒) (R+U+X+Z 1/4-31/10)
**5** ABDFGIJKLMNOPUWZ
**6** CEGJ(N 3km)OU

NEW

💬 Campsite located on Saale and Unstrut rivers with possibility of canoeing. Cycling and walking routes nearby. Close to the cathedral city of Naumburg.

🚗 Signposted from B180 and B87. Campsite is situated on the river Saale (Naumburg direction Freyburg).

B91
B176  L206
B180  L205
CC
Naumburg  L199
(Saale)  A9
B87
L203  B88

CC €20  1/5-15/5  12/6-14/7  1/9-31/10  7=6, 14=12, 21=18    N 51°10'31'' E 11°48'15''

## Plötzky/Schönebeck, D-39217 / Sachsen-Anhalt ᚶ 📶 iD 709

△ Camping Ferienpark Plötzky
✉ Kleiner Waldsee 1
☎ +49 39 20 05 01 55
📅 1/1 - 31/12
@ info@ferienpark-ploetzky.de

12ha 170T(100m²) 16A CEE

**1** ACGIJKLOPQ
**2** ABDLRVWX
**3** ABCDJKNOPQRTUVWZ
**4** (A 🔒) JKMN
   (Q+R 1/4-31/10)
   (T+U+V+Y+Z 🔒)
**5** ABDEFGIJKLMNOPRSTU
   WXYZ
**6** DEGK(N 2km)OTV

💬 A peaceful campsite located on the edge of a wood. Lovely walking and cycling opportunities. Various excursions possible, including the city of Magdeburg. Water sports possible nearby. The River Elbe is close by. It has a lovely wellness centre and bowling centre.

🚗 Via A2 to A14 (Kreuz Magdeburg), exit 7 dir. Schönebeck/Gommern. Campsite signposted on route B246a past Plötzky. Or A2 exit Möser dir. Möser B1/ Biederitz B184/B246A,Gommern/Plötzky.

B1
Magdeburg
B246A
B184  L56
CC
A14  Schönebeck
(Elbe)
B71  L65  L51

CC €20  1/1-17/4  23/4-28/5  11/6-3/7  1/9-30/12    N 52°03'46'' E 11°48'01''

## Schlaitz (Muldestausee), D-06774 / Sachsen-Anhalt ♋ ⅜ iD **710**

🏕 Heide-Camp Schlaitz GbR
📍 Am Muldestausee
☎ +49 34 95 52 05 71
📅 1/1 - 31/12
@ info@heide-camp-schlaitz.de

12ha 130T(110-170m²) 16A

**1** A**F**HIJLO**PQ**
**2** ADGLRSTX
**3** AHJRU**VWZ**
**4** (**A** 1/5-30/9) (Q+R 1/3-3/10) (T+U+Y 🐕)
**5** **AB**DFGIJKLMNOPUW
**6** DEG(N 4km)OV

💬 A campsite situated by a lake. Cities such as Leipzig, Halle and Oranienbaum are close by. Located in the Dübener Heide nature park.

🚗 Campsite signposted on the B100 between Bitterfeld and Gossa.

B2
B100
CC
Bitterfeld-Wolfen
B183
B183A
B107

CC €**20** 1/1-28/5 11/6-28/6 1/9-30/12 📍 N 51°38'55'' E 12°25'23''

---

## Süplingen/Haldensleben, D-39343 / Sachsen-Anhalt ♋ **711**

🏕 Campingplatz Alte Schmiede***
📍 Steinerberg 5
☎ +49 39 05 32 04
📅 15/4 - 15/10
@ alteschmiedesueplingen@ t-online.de

43ha 55T(80-100m²) 16A CEE

**1** CD**G**HIJKLMNOPQ
**2** ABDLMRSUWXY
**3** ABHLRWZ
**4** M(Q+R+U+Y 🐕)
**5** **A**CDFGHIJKLMNO**P**UW
**6** EG(N 3km)O

💬 A campsite for those seeking relaxation. Located in a wood around a small lake where you can go fishing. Sandy beach. Lovely areas for cycling. The town of Magdeburg, the aquaduct over the Elbe and the boat lift (Schiffshebewerk) at Rothensee are 20 km away. Also suitable as a stopover campsite.

🚗 Via the A2 exit Haldensleben drive via Bregenstedt and Altenhausen to Süplingen. Campsite is signposted.

L25
L43
B71
Haldensleben
CC
Niedere Börde
B1
A2

CC €**18** 15/4-30/6 1/9-14/10 📍 N 52°16'47'' E 11°19'15''

---

## Altglobsow, D-16775 / Brandenburg 📶 iD **712**

🏕 Ferienhof Altglobsow
📍 Seestraße 11
☎ +49 33 08 25 02 50
📅 1/1 - 31/12
@ info@ferienhof-altglobsow.de

4,5ha 40T(60-80m²) 16A CEE

**1** A**G**IJKLO**PQ**
**2** BDGILRWX
**3** AJRU**WZ**
**4** (A 1/6-30/9) **N**(Q+X+Y 🐕)
**5** **A**DGJMN**P**UWZ
**6** CEG**K**(N 7km)OT

💬 An extremely peaceful campsite on the edge of a small, quiet village, bordering the woods and a lake. A good base for making cycling and walking trips.

🚗 From Berlin take the B96 as far as Fürstenberg, direction Neuglobsow. Follow signs to Ferienhof Altglobsow.

L15
Fürstenberg/ Havel
CC
B96
Grosswoltersdorf
B122
L223

CC €**14** 2/1-18/4 23/4-29/5 11/6-20/6 1/9-20/12 📍 N 53°07'53'' E 13°07'01''

## Beetzseeheide/Gortz, D-14778 / Brandenburg ♀♂ iD 713

🏕 Camping Flachsberg
✉ Flachsberg 1
☎ +49 17 13 64 47 42
🔑 1/4 - 31/10
@ info@camping-flachsberg.de

12ha 40T(80-120m²) 16A CEE

**1** ADGHIJKLOPQ
**2** ABDGIKLRWXY
**3** ABHJRWZ
**5** AGHIJKLMNOPUW
**6** EG(N 9,9km)OU

💬 A quiet campsite in the hills of the Havelland region with beautiful views over the lake. Beautiful area for cycling. Really a campsite for those looking for peace and quiet.

🚗 From Brandenburg direction Nauen, at Päwesin take direction Bagow/Gortz. Left before Gortz towards campsite.

CC € 16 1/4-28/6 18/8-30/10  🗺 N 52°30'18'' E 12°39'36''

---

## Berlin-Schmöckwitz, D-12527 / Berlin/Brandenburg ♀♂ ♿ 🛜 iD 714

🏕 Campingplatz Krossinsee 1930 GmbH***
✉ Wernsdorfer Straße 38
☎ +49 3 06 75 86 87
🔑 1/1 - 31/12
@ anfrage@campingplatz-berlin.de

8ha 180T(20-100m²) 10A CEE

**1** ACDGIJKLMOPST
**2** ABDGLMRTXY
**3** BJKRWZ
**4** (Q+R 1/4-31/10) (Y+Z 🔑)
**5** ABDFGIJKLMNOPUWZ
**6** CFGIJ(N 3km)OV

💬 In the green heart of Berlin, right on the Krossinsee lake nature area. Natural grounds between tall pine trees, semi shaded pitches. Modern toilet facilities, bakery with fresh bread daily and an attractive restaurant. Direct connections to Berlin-Mitte. The three lakeside pitches are not available at CampingCard ACSI rates.

🚗 A10 southeast, exit 9 Niederlehme, direction Wernsdorf. Then follow Schmöckwitz camping signs.

CC € 20 1/1-14/4 29/4-28/5 12/6-29/6 5/9-31/12  🗺 N 52°22'12'' E 13°41'04''

---

## Ferchesar, D-14715 / Brandenburg ♿ 🛜 iD 715

🏕 Campingpark Buntspecht****
✉ Weg zum Zeltplatz 1
☎ +49 33 87 49 00 72
🔑 1/4 - 15/10
@ campingpark-buntspecht@web.de

6ha 155T(90-120m²) 16A CEE

**1** ADGHIJKLMOPQ
**2** ABDJLMRVWXY
**3** BDFGHJKLNRWZ
**4** (Q+R+U+V+Y+Z 🔑)
**5** ABDEFGIJKLMNOPQRSU WXY
**6** ACDEGIKOQTUV

💬 This (4-star) environmentally friendly campsite is located in the middle of Westhavelland nature reserve, right on the lake. Spacious comfort pitches and luxurious toilet facilities. Opportunities for sport and play. Suitable for city visits to Berlin/Potsdam, also by train from Rathenow. Visit the observatory and see special birds.

🚗 From A10 take B188 after 5 km, east of Rathenow exit Stechow, then right towards Ferchesar. Campsite signposted with yellow signs.

CC € 20 1/4-28/5 11/6-30/6 1/9-14/10  🗺 N 52°39'15'' E 12°25'47''

## Grünheide, D-15537 / Brandenburg

🛜 iD **716**

🏕 Grünheider Camping am Peetzsee GmbH
✉ Am Schlangenluch 27
☎ +49 33 62 61 20
🗓 5/4 - 30/9
@ campingplatz-gruenheide@t-online.de

6,5ha 50T(20-120m²) 16A CEE

**1** AGHIJKL**P**Q
**2** ABDFGKLMNRTWX
**3** W**Z**
**4** AB**DG**IJMN**P**UZ
**5** EJ(N 1km)OS

💬 Site with large pitches, friendly staff and good toilet facilities in densely wooded area, with idyllic sandy beach along lake on other side of road. Located on the R1, the Euro Route cycle path from London to St. Petersburg. Also many other cycling and walking possibilities.

🚗 A10 exit 6 Erkner/Grünheide direction Fangschleuse, then through the village and turn left at cross roads. 'Am Schlangenluch' after 200 metres and the campsite is 500 metres on the right.

**Hoppegarten**
**Rüdersdorf bei Berlin**
B1
B5
L30
CC
A10  L38
L23  L36
A12

CC €20 5/4-7/7  30/8-30/9

📍 N 52°25'18'' E 13°50'11''

## Ketzin, D-14669 / Brandenburg

🛜 iD **717**

🏕 Campingplatz An der Havel
✉ Friedrich-Ludwig-Jahn Weg 33
☎ +49 33 23 32 11 50
🗓 6/4 - 31/10
@ havelcamping@arcor.de

2,5ha 55T(70-100m²) 16A CEE

**1** A**F**HIJKLOPQ
**2** CDFGLRVWX
**3** BFJKRU**W**X
**4** (Q 🗓)
**5** AB**D**FGIJKLMNO**P**UWXZ
**6** ACEGJ(N 1km)O

💬 A lovely, peaceful campsite located on the Havel Radweg (cycle route), so perfect for cycling. For visiting Berlin you first drive 13 km to Wustermark, then within half an hour by train you are in the centre of Berlin. Perfect!

🚗 From A2 to A10 direction Potsdam. Beyond Potsdam take Ketzin exit. Follow camping signs.

B5
**Ketzin**
L92
CC
L91  L86
B1
A10  B273
L90
**Werder (Havel)**

CC €20 6/4-28/5  11/6-28/6  1/9-30/10

📍 N 52°28'14'' E 12°50'54''

## Lauchhammer, D-01979 / Brandenburg

♿ 🛜 iD **718**

🏕 Themencamping Grünewalder Lauch****
✉ Lauchstrasse 101
☎ +49 35 74 38 26
🗓 29/3 - 27/10
@ gruenewalder-lauch@themencamping.de

8,5ha 126T(100-120m²) 16A CEE

**1** ACDGIJKLMPQ
**2** ADFLMORSTUVWXY
**3** AKQ**R**UZ
**4** (Q+R+T+U+X 🗓)
**5** AB**D**EFGIJKL**M**NOPUXY
**6** CDEG**K**(N 3km)OTW

💬 Family campsite in a quiet nature reserve on a large lake with a sandy beach, naturist beach and beach for dogs. Cafe restaurant with patio. Many walls bear fun quotes from the owner and anyone can add their contribution. Cycling and walking round the lake.

🚗 A13 exit Ruhland no. 17. Then B169 direction Lauchhammer. In Lauchhammer towards Grünewalde and follow camping signs.

L60
L62
CC
**Lauchhammer**
**Elsterwerda**  B169
B101  L63  A13

CC €20 29/3-3/6  1/9-27/10

📍 N 51°30'25'' E 13°40'01''

## Lübbenau/Hindenberg, D-03222 / Brandenburg ♿ 🛜 iD (719)

▲ Spreewald-Natur Camping
"Am See"★★★★
✉ Seestraße 1
☎ +49 35 45 66 75 39
📅 1/1 - 31/12
@ am-see@spreewaldcamping.de

15ha  85T(40-120m²)  16A  CEE

**1** ACG**I**JKLMO**P**Q
**2** ABDFGJLMNRUVWXY
**3** BDJKLMN**O**RTUWZ
**4** (A 1/7-31/8) **N**
(Q+R+U+X+Y+Z 🔌)
**5** **AB**DEFGIJKLMNOP**U**WXY
**6** CEGJ(N 7km)OQSV

NEW

💬 Natural campsite with marked-out comfort pitches directly on a beautiful recreational lake, far from the hustle and bustle of the Spreewald and yet in the middle of it. Luxury toilet facilities and sauna. Attractive restaurant with good cuisine, nice bar and sunny terrace, all pleasantly staffed. In addition to a meadow with animals and a playground, there is also a bowling alley.

🚗 On A13, AS9 Spreewalddreieck, direction Luckau. After 4 km campsite is on left.

**Lübben (Spreewald)**
**Lübbenau (Spreewald)**
**Luckau**
B115  L71  B87  L49  CC  A15  B96  L52  A13  L55

CC €20  1/1-25/5  10/6-15/7  1/9-31/12   🏕 N 51°51'28'' E 13°51'23''

---

## Märkische Heide/Groß Leuthen, D-15913 / Brandenburg ♿ 🛜 ✿ iD (720)

▲ EuroCamp Spreewaldtor★★★★★
✉ Neue Straße 1
☎ +49 35 47 13 03
📅 1/1 - 31/12
@ info@eurocamp-spreewaldtor.de

9ha  130T(80-100m²)  16A  CEE

**1** ACD**G**IJKLMOPQ
**2** ADLMRTVWX
**3** BHJKLNRU**W**Z
**4** (A 1/7-31/8) N(Q+R 🔌)
(U 1/4-30/10) (X 1/4-31/10)
**5** **AB**DFGIJKLMNOP**R**UWX
**6** CDEG**K**OU

💬 Young, easy-going owner offers a campsite with spacious pitches on solid ground. Excellent toilet facilities; no shower tokens. Reception is on a nice little square together with the facilities and a restaurant, the square is used for activities. Shuttle services for visits to nearby locations.

🚗 A13 Dresden-Berlin, exit Lübben, B87 dir. Beeskow, left at intersection Birkenhainchen onto B179 dir. Königs Wusterhausen. In Gross Leuthen turn right; follow the campsite signs.

L443  B179  CC  B87  L42  B320  Mochow  L44  Hartmannsdorf

CC €20  1/1-28/5  10/6-30/6  18/8-31/12   🏕 N 52°02'53'' E 14°02'08''

---

## Ortrand, D-01990 / Brandenburg ♿ 🛜 iD (721)

▲ ErlebnisCamping Lausitz
✉ Am Bad 1
☎ +49 3 57 55 55 35 09
📅 1/1 - 31/12
@ erlebniscamping@t-online.de

5ha  80T(100-120m²)  16A  CEE

**1** ABD**G**HIJKLMO**P**Q
**2** CFRVWXY
**3** BHJKR**W**
**4** (Q+R 🔌)
**5** **AB**DFGIJKLMNOPUWXY
**6** AEGJ(N 2km)O

NEW

💬 Located 35 km from Dresden. Very suitable for children. The rock playground with sandstone-like climbing elements will make every child's heart beat faster. There is plenty of space to play, walk or fish in peace. Located directly on the Brandenburg cycle path.

🚗 A13, exit 18 Ortrand, L59, then follow the L55, turn right into Waldteichstrasse, then turn left into Heinersdorferstrasse. At Am Bad, turn right where the campsite is located.

Plessa  B169  Ruhland  L63  L55  L57  A13  L59  CC  Schwepnitz  B97  B98

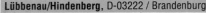

CC €20  1/1-7/7  26/8-31/12   🏕 N 51°22'20'' E 13°46'45''

## Warnitz (Oberuckersee), D-17291 / Brandenburg 📶 iD (722)

🏕 Camping am Oberuckersee
📧 Lindenallee 2
☎ +49 39 86 34 59
🔑 1/4 - 5/10
@ info@camping-oberuckersee.de

5ha 160T(80m²) 6A

**1** AD**G**IJKLO**PQ**
**2** BDFGIJLMNRSXY
**3** BJKNR**WZ**
**4** (Q 🔲) (R 3/7-1/9)
**5** **AB**EGIJMNO**P**UWZ
**6** CEG**K**(N 0,6km)OT

💬 Idyllically located rural campsite in the middle of the Schorfheide-Chorin nature reserve where you can not only enjoy wonderful views, but can also go fishing, swimming, sailing in a boat and much more. Easily accessible by bike, train, car or boat.

🚗 Campsite can be reached via the A11/E28 exit 7 Warnitz. Follow signs to Warnitz and in Warnitz cross the railway and immediately turn left. Follow this road. The campsite is located 6 km from exit 7.

| B109 | Gramzow |
| Oberuckersee | B166 |
| Gerswalde | A11 |
| | B198 |
| | L24 | L285 |
| L241 | L28 |

CC €**18** 1/4-28/5 2/6-6/6 10/6-27/6 1/9-4/10 12=10, 21=18 🧭 N 53°10'38'' E 13°52'25''

---

## Wusterhausen/Dosse, D-16868 / Brandenburg 👫 ♿ 📶 iD (723)

🏕 Camping Wusterhausen****
📧 Seestraße 42
☎ +49 33 97 91 42 74
🔑 1/4 - 31/10
@ koellner@
  camping-wusterhausen.de

12ha 80T(80-120m²) 16A CEE

**1** ACD**G**HIJKLMO**PQ**
**2** BDLMRVWXY
**3** BDHJKNR**TVW**Z
**4** (B 15/5-31/8) (F 🔲) J**LN**
  (Q+R+T+U+X+Z 🔲)
**5** **AB**DFGIJKLMNO**PR**UWXYZ
**6** CEG**K**(N 2,5km)OS

💬 A 4 star campsite, open all year, in a rural setting, right on the Kyritzer Seenkette. Marked out comfort pitches with cable, water and drainage connections available. Fitness studio with saunas, solarium, heated indoor swimming pool, bowling alley, ice cream, restaurant, fresh bread.

🚗 A24/E26 Hamburg-Berlin, exit 22 Neuruppin. Turn left via route B167 to Bückwitz. Turn right to Kyritz. In Wusterhausen centre follow signs beyond the bridge. Campsite on the left.

| B103 | |
| | A24 |
| Kyritz | |
| L14 | |
| | CC | B167 | L166 |
| Wusterhausen/ | |
| Dosse | B5 |
| B102 | |

CC €**20** 1/4-28/5 11/6-30/6 1/9-31/10 5=4 🧭 N 52°54'26'' E 12°27'39''

---

## Bautzen, D-02625 / Sachsen ♿ 📶 iD (724)

🏕 Natur- und Abenteuercamping
📧 Nimschützer Straße 41
☎ +49 35 91 27 12 67
🔑 1/4 - 31/10
@ camping-bautzen@web.de

5ha 100T(90-150m²) 16A CEE

**1** AD**G**IJKLMOPQ
**2** ADFGIJKLRSTUVX
**3** ABCJKRU**WZ**
**4** (Q+R 🔲)
**5** **AB**DFGHIJLMNOPRUWXYZ
**6** ACEK(N 1,5km)OV

💬 A well maintained, quiet campsite with views of the Bautzen reservoir. Modern, heated toilet facilities. Cycling, hiking and water sports are possible. Cultural Dresden is 20 minutes by car.

🚗 On A4 motorway coming from Görlitz and Dresden, exit at Bautzen east. Then towards Weißwasser, then direction B156.

| B96 | |
| | B156 |
| | CC |
| | **Bautzen** |
| Demitz- | B6 |
| Thumitz | |

CC €**20** 1/4-18/4 23/4-29/5 11/6-30/6 1/9-31/10 🧭 N 51°12'08'' E 14°27'38''

## Boxberg, D-02943 / Sachsen

⚐ Campingplatz Sternencamp
Bärwalder See****
🚏 Zur Strandpromenade 2
☎ +49 3 57 74 55 21 73
📅 12/4 - 31/10
@ info@sternencamp-boxberg.de

4ha 94T(100m²) 16A CEE

**1** ACD**G**IJKLMOPQ
**2** ABDGJKLMUVWX
**3** BHJKL**WZ**
**4** (Q+R+T+U+X+Z 📅)
**5** **AB**DEFGIJMNP**R**UWXYZ
**6** DEGKL(N 0,5km)OU

💬 A comfortable campsite next to Saxony's largest lake. Spacious pitches with water, drainage and electrical supply. Modern toilet facilities. Mooring for your boat close by. (Kite)surfing possible. Cycle and skate paths along the shore of the lake.

🚗 From B156 from Bautzen-Ost to Weißwasser exit Kringelsdorf. Follow campsite signs.

CC € 20  12/4-26/5  24/6-7/7  31/8-31/10

📡 N 51°23'45'' E 14°34'28''

## Dresden, D-01217 / Sachsen

⚐ Camping Dresden-Mockritz
🚏 Boderitzerstr. 30
☎ +49 35 14 71 52 50
📅 1/1 - 7/2, 1/3 - 31/12
@ camping-dresden@t-online.de

0,5ha 158T 6A CEE

**1** ACD**G**IJKLMOPQ
**2** DFGLRTWXY
**3** BKLNRZ
**4** (C 1/5-31/8) (Q+R 📅)
(U 1/4-31/10) (X 📅)
**5** **AB**CDEFGHIJKLMNO**P**UWZ
**6** CEGIKL(N 0,5km)OQUX

💬 Campsite is located in a beautiful, quiet suburb of Dresden, 4 km from the town centre. Bus stop is right by the campsite and a cycle path goes from the campsite. There is an outdoor pool, wifi, playground, volleyball field, bicycle hire and shop on the site.

🚗 A4 intersection Dresden-W direction Prag on A17. Then exit 3 Dresden-Sud, B170 direction Dresden. Turn right after about 1 km. Right again after 800m. After 1 km the campsite is on left.

CC € 18  2/1-7/2  1/3-1/7  1/9-31/12

📡 N 51°00'52'' E 13°44'49''

## Großschönau, D-02779 / Sachsen

⚐ Camping Trixi Park
🚏 Jonsdorferstraße 40
☎ +49 3 58 41 63 10
📅 1/1 - 31/12
@ info@trixi-park.de

15ha 70T(72-100m²) 16A CEE

**1** AC**G**HIJKLMOPQ
**2** ADGLMNRTVW
**3** ABGKLNQRU**V**
**4** (A 📅) (B 1/5-30/9)
(F+H 📅) J**KLNP**
(Q+R+T+U+W+Y+Z 📅)
**5** **AB**DEFGHIJLMNOPRUWXYZ
**6** CEGHIKL(N 1km)OUVW

💬 Located in Zittauer Gebirge, a luxurious campsite with comprehensive and good toilet facilities.

🚗 From Bautzen take the B6 to Löbau-Zittau. Turn right in Herrnhut towards Oberoderwitz. Then direction Großschönau and follow camping signs.

CC € 20  1/1-29/5  2/6-7/6  10/6-29/6  18/8-31/12

📡 N 50°52'44'' E 14°40'25''

## Leipzig, D-04159 / Sachsen

⛏ ♿ **iD** 728

🔺 Knaus Campingpark
 Leipzig Auensee
📧 Gustav-Esche-Straße 5
☎ +49 34 14 65 16 00
🔓 1/1 - 31/12
@ leipzig@knauscamp.de

9,5ha 159T(100m²) 16A CEE

**1** ABCD**G**HIJKLMO**P**
**2** BFGRTUVWXY
**3** AB**F**HJ**M**NRW
**4** (Q 🅿)
**5** **AB**DEFGIJKLMNOPUWZ
**6** CDEG(N 1km)OQT

💬 Large campsite in the city of Leipzig with good washing facilities. Good base for exploring the city by public transport.

🚗 A9 exit Großkugel, exit Leipzig West, B6 to Leipzig. At sign 'Leipzig', keep on B6 for ± 10 km. At traffic lights head to centre. At next traffic lights, turn right. Site is 1 km further on right.

CC € **20**  1/1-29/5  3/6-7/6  24/6-15/7  1/9-31/12

🧭 N 51°22'12'' E 12°18'49''

---

## Leupoldishain/Königstein, D-01824 / Sachsen

📶 **iD** 729

🔺 Camping Nikolsdorfer Berg
📧 Nikolsdorfer Berg 7
☎ +49 35 02 19 91 44
🔓 1/4 - 31/10
@ info@
 camping-nikolsdorferberg.de

1,2ha 50T 10-16A CEE

**1** AD**G**HIJKLMOPQ
**2** BGRTVWX
**3** AHRU
**4** (Q+R 🅿)
**5** **AB**DGIJKLMNOPUW
**6** CEGK(N 4km)T

NEW

💬 Small family campsite idyllically situated in a beautiful mountain landscape. The campsite has excellent toilet facilities.

🚗 Via Dresden B172 direction Pirna/Badschandau. 10 km after Pirna turn right to Leupoldishain. Follow signs.

CC € **18**  1/4-30/6  1/9-31/10

🧭 N 50°54'16'' E 14°02'19''

---

## Olbersdorf, D-02785 / Sachsen

👪 ♿ 📶 **iD** 730

🔺 SeeCamping Zittauer Gebirge
📧 Zur Landesgartenschau 2
☎ +49 35 83 69 62 92
🔓 1/1 - 31/12
@ info@seecamping-zittau.com

5,7ha 185T(100m²) 10A CEE

**1** AC**G**HIJKLMOPQ
**2** ADGLRTWX
**3** AHKRU**W**Z
**4** (Q+R 1/5-31/10) (X 🅿)
**5** **AB**DEFGHIJKLMNOP**U**W
**6** CDEG**K**(N 1km)OUV

NEW

💬 Green campsite located near a recreational lake with modern toilet facilities. Good cycling and walking options. There is a narrow gauge railway in the vicinity, a steam train, and Kelchstein is a paradise for climbers. Zittauer with its historic town centre is 3.5 km away.

🚗 A4, exit 90 Bautzen-Ost. Then via B6 to Löbau and B178 to Zittau. In Zittau follow ring road to B96. Then follow signs to Olbersdorfer See campsite. Left on roundabout.

CC € **18**  1/4-20/4  1/5-29/5  11/6-5/7  1/9-31/10

🧭 N 50°53'39'' E 14°46'14''

## Pirna, D-01796 / Sachsen ♿ 📶 iD 731

🏕 Waldcamping Pirna-Copitz
📧 Äußere Pillnitzer Straße 19
☎ +49 35 01 52 37 73
🗓 10/4 - 7/10
@ waldcamping@
stadtwerke-pirna.de

6ha 151T(90-100m²) 16A CEE

**1** A**G**HIJKLMOPQ
**2** ABDGLMRTUVWX
**3** ARZ
**5** **AB**DEFGHIJKLMNOPUWXY
Z
**6** CEGHK(N 0,3km)QT

💬 The Pirna-Copitz, a parkland and wooded campsite on a natural lake is located on the outskirts of the historic town of Pirna between Sächsische Schweiz and Dresden. The pitches are marked out, about 100 m² and some of them offer lovely views of the lake. Modern clean toilet facilities.

🚗 Motorway A4 exit Prague. A17 towards Pirna via B172. In Pirna cross the Elbe bridge in the direction of Pirna/Copitz, and then take exit Graupa.

Neustadt B6
**Dresden**
Prohlis
CC **Pirna**
A17
B172

CC €**20** 10/4-29/5 11/6-30/6 2/9-7/10 　N 50°58'54'' E 13°55'30''

---

## Pöhl, D-08543 / Sachsen 👪 ♿ 📶 iD 732

🏕 Talsperre Pöhl,
Campingplatz Gunzenberg****
📧 Möschwitz, Hauptstraße 38
☎ +49 37 43 94 50 50
🗓 29/3 - 1/11
@ tourist-info@talsperre-poehl.de

11ha 126T(80-120m²) 16A CEE

**1** AC**G**HIJKLMOPQ
**2** DFGILORTVWX
**3** AB**F**HJKLNR**W**Z
**4** (A 🔌) (Q+R 1/5-30/9)
(T+U+X+Y 🔌)
**5** **AB**CDFGHIJKLMNOPUVW
**6** CDEGHK(N 1,5km)OQT

💬 A large campsite on the Talsperre Pöhl with good toilet facilities and watersports opportunities. Located in picturesque hillsides. Visit the dam or the Elstertalbrücke, the second largest brick-built bridge in the world. The campsite has the 'Strandhaus' restaurant.

🚗 A72 exit 7 Plauen-Ost/Thalsperre Pöhl. Drive towards the city centre and then towards Talsperre Pöhl. The campsite is located on the left side of the Stausee, beyond the car park.

Reichenbach im Vogtland
B94
B92 A72
**Plauen** CC
B169
B173

CC €**20** 29/3-28/5 24/6-30/6 1/9-30/9 　N 50°32'19'' E 12°11'06''

---

## Seiffen, D-09548 / Sachsen 👪 ⛷ ♿ 📶 iD 733

🏕 Ferienpark Seiffen****
📧 Deutschneudorferstr. 57
☎ +49 37 36 21 50
🗓 1/1 - 31/12
@ info@ferienpark-seiffen.de

5ha 100T 10-16A CEE

**1** ACDGIJKLMOPQ
**2** IJKLRTVWX
**3** ACGIJKLNOQRUV
**4** **NP**(Q+R+U+X+Y+Z 🔌)
**5** **AB**FGIJKLMNOPUWXZ
**6** CDEGK(N 3km)OV

NEW

💬 Terraced campsite in Kurort Seiffen at an altitude of about 700 metres and with fine panoramas of the highlands. Excellent toilet facilities. Lovely trips out to Dresden and Prague.

🚗 A4 exit 69 Chemnitz-Nord. Then the B174 to Marienberg. Stay on the B171 towards Olbernhau then to Seiffen. Signposted from there.

B171
Olbernhau
CC **Litvínov**
**Most**

CC €**18** 1/1-8/7 1/9-13/10 21/10-24/11 　N 50°37'36'' E 13°27'26''

## Catterfeld, D-99894 / Thüringen

△ Camping Paulfeld*****
🏠 Straße am Steinbühl 3
☎ +49 36 25 32 51 71
📅 1/1 - 31/12
@ info@paulfeld-camping.de

**734**

7ha 80T(80-100m²) 16A CEE

1 ADGIJKLMOPQ
2 BDLRSVWXY
3 ABDHJLRWZ
4 N(Q+R 📷) (U+X+Z
   1/1-31/10,1/12-31/12)
5 ABDFGIJKLMNOPUWZ
6 CDEGK(N 3km)OT

💬 A friendly family campsite at an altitude of 450 metres in the Thüringerwald forest. A natural swimming lake and excellent toilet facilities. An ideal base for walks in the woods and city trips, including Eisenach, Weimar and Erfurt.

🚗 A4 towards Dresden, exit Waltershausen and then drive towards Friedrichroda, then take the B88 towards Ohrdruf. In Catterfeld turn right and continue for 3 km.

Waltershausen
A4
L1027
L1024    Ohrdruf
L1026    CC
         B88
L1028    L3247
         L1046

CC €20  1/1-12/4  29/4-26/5  17/6-7/7  26/8-16/12    📍 N 50°49'27'' E 10°36'41''

---

## Drognitz, D-07338 / Thüringen

△ Camping Thüringer Wald
🏠 Mutschwiese 1
☎ +49 17 36 46 60 39
📅 30/3 - 30/10
@ info@camping-t-w.de

**735**

13ha 250T 16A CEE

1 AGIJKLMOPQ
2 BIJLRSTWXY
3 HJNRW
4 (Q+R+X+Z 📷)
5 ABDFGIJKLMNOPUWZ
6 AEGJOT

💬 Campsite located in a natural area in Thüringen. Surrounded by woods. Hohenwarte reservoir at about 900 metres.

🚗 B281 from Saalfeld to Pößneck, exit Kamsdorf direction Hohenwarte. Across reservoir to Drognitz. Follow signs from Drognitz.

L1107    Ranis
Gorndorf        L2365
         L1105
Kamsdorf    CC    L1103
              L1102
B85    B90

CC €18  30/3-28/5  12/6-21/6  1/9-30/10    📍 N 50°35'45'' E 11°33'44''

---

## Ettersburg, D-99439 / Thüringen

△ Bad-Camp Ettersburg
🏠 Badteichweg 1
☎ +49 1 76 22 84 14 64
📅 1/4 - 31/10
@ info@camping-weimar.de

**736**

32ha 38T(30-120m²) 10-16A CEE

1 AGIJKLMOPQ
2 BGLRWXY
3 HJ
4 (Q+R 📷)
5 AFGIJKLMNOPUWZ
6 EGJ(N 3km)

💬 Small, green campsite near Weimar. The campsite is located near the memorial site of Buchenwald and Schloss Ettersburg.

🚗 A4 exit 49 Weimar. North of Weimar direction Buchenwald. Straight ahead at Buchenwald exit and follow campsite signs.

L1058
Grossrudestedt
A71   L1054       L1057
              B85
L1056  L1055   CC
               B87
         B7    Weimar
         A4

CC €18  1/4-31/5  11/6-30/6  1/9-31/10 7=6    📍 N 51°02'08'' E 11°17'14''

## Frankenhain, D-99330 / Thüringen
🎿♿ 📶 iD **737**

🔺 Oberhof Camping
✉ Am Stausee 9
☎ +49 36 20 57 65 18
🗓 1/1 - 31/12
@ info@oberhofcamping.de

10ha 150T(80-100m²) 16A CEE

**1** ACD**G**IJKLMOPQ
**2** BDFIJLNORTUWXY
**3** ABHJR**WZ**
**4** (Q+R ✋)
(U+X 1/4-31/10,1/12-31/12)
**5** **AB**DFGIJKLMNOPR**ST**UWZ
**6** CEGK(N 5km)OT

💬 Idyllic campsite in the Thüringer Forest by the Lütsche Reservoir. Restaurant and take-away meals also open in December.

🚗 A71, exit 17 Gräfenroda. Then take B88 direction Frankenhain. Follow 'Lütsche Stausee/Campingpark' sign. Or via A4 exit Gotha direction Oberhof. In Ohrdruf direction Grawinkel/Frankenhain. Follow signs. Don't use SatNav.

CC €**20** 14/1-7/4 6/5-26/5 17/6-30/6 1/9-30/9 1/11-15/12

N 50°44'01'' E 10°45'24''

---

## Hohenfelden, D-99448 / Thüringen
♿ 📶 iD **738**

🔺 Camping Stausee
Hohenfelden★★★★
☎ +49 36 45 04 20 81
🗓 1/1 - 31/12
@ info@stausee-hohenfelden.de

22,5ha 194T(100-140m²) 16A CEE

**1** ACD**G**HIJKLMO**P**Q
**2** ABDFG**J**LRTVWXY
**3** ABHJKNR**WZ**
**4** (Q+R 1/5-30/9) (X 1/4-31/8)
**5** **AB**DEFGIJMNO**P**RUWXYZ
**6** CDE**K**(N 3km)OT

💬 A large campsite located by a reservoir. Watersports opportunities. There is an (indoor) swimming pool with wellness facilities 700 metres from the site. The perfect base for making city trips (Erfurt, Weimar, Gera etc.). Within walking distance of the campsite is a large outdoor centre with climbing, mini golf and organized hiking tours.

🚗 A4 exit Erfurt-Ost, then direction Kranichfeld (about 6 km). Campsite on the right side.

CC €**18** 1/1-29/5 11/6-30/6 1/9-31/12

N 50°52'20'' E 11°10'42''

---

## Jena, D-07749 / Thüringen
📶 iD **739**

🔺 Campingplatz Jena unter dem Jenzig
✉ Am Erlkönig 3
☎ +49 36 41 66 66 88
🗓 1/3 - 31/10
@ post@camping-jena.com

1ha 42T(100m²) 6-16A CEE

**1** ACD**G**IJKLOPQ
**2** CFGRTWXY
**3** ABHJU
**4** (**B**+**G** 15/5-15/9) J(Q ✋)
(T 1/5-30/9)
**5** **AB**FGIJKLMNOPQUW
**6** CEGJ(N 0,4km)OT

💬 Modest but authentic campsite at the foot of the Jenzig hills, close to a lovely swimming pool. Breakfast available on the site. Also a good base for city trips to Jena and Weimar. Countless cycling and walking opportunities. Open in winter on request.

🚗 On the B7 from Jena direction Gera, bridge over the Saale, turn left at traffic lights after 200 metres. Campsite clearly signposted.

CC €**18** 1/3-28/5 23/6-30/6 1/9-31/10

N 50°56'09'' E 11°36'30''

## Pahna, D-04617 / Thüringen    ♿ 🛜 **iD** 740

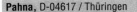

- 🏕 See-Camping Altenburg-Pahna****
- ☎ +49 34 34 35 19 14
- 🗓 1/1 - 31/12
- @ camping-pahna@t-online.de

10ha 100T(80-120m²) 16A CEE

1 ACD**G**IJKLMOP**Q**
2 ABDGLMRTWXY
3 ABHJKLNRU**WZ**
4 (Q+S+T+U+X 1/4-31/10)
5 **AB**DEFGIJKLMNO**PQRST**U WXYZ
6 CDEG**IK**(N 5km)OTUV

💬 A campsite located by a recreational lake with walking and cycling opportunities. Centrally situated for city trips to Leipzig, Chemnitz and Gera.

🚗 A4 exit 60 (Ronneburg), then B7 to Altenburg. B93 direction Leipzig, right B7 direction Frohburg, follow signs at Eschefeld.

**Borna**

L1355   CC

B7

**Altenburg**    B95

**CC** € **20**   1/1-26/5   13/6-30/6   1/9-31/12     🗺 N 51°02'37'' E 12°29'49''

---

## Weberstedt, D-99947 / Thüringen    👫 ♿ 🛜 **iD** 741

- 🏕 Camping Am Tor zum Hainich****
- 📧 Hainichstraße 22
- ☎ +49 36 02 29 86 90
- 🗓 1/1 - 31/12
- @ info@camping-hainich.de

3,5ha 161T(80-100m²) 16A CEE

1 ADGIJKLMOPQ
2 BJKLRWX
3 ABHJKRU
4 (G+Q+R 🅿)
5 **AB**DFGIJKMNOPUWXYZ
6 CEGIK(N 2km)OTV

💬 Located on the border of the Hainich National Park, this quiet campsite has lovely views towards the Süd-Harz. A UNESCO heritage site since 2011 with the largest protected deciduous woods.

🚗 Leave the A4 at Eisenach, follow B84 as far as Bad Langensalza. Follow signs to Weberstedt.

L1031

L1042   **Bad Langensalza**
CC

L1016

B84    B247

L1029

**CC** € **18**   1/1-29/5   11/6-30/6   1/9-31/12   7=6, 14=11    🗺 N 51°06'10'' E 10°30'32''

---

## Attendorn/Biggen, D-57439 / Nordrhein-Westfalen    ♿ 🛜 **iD** 742

- 🏕 Camping Hof Biggen
- 📧 Finnentroper Straße 131
- ☎ +49 2 72 29 55 30
- 🗓 1/1 - 31/12
- @ info@biggen.de

18ha 100T(80-100m²) 6-16A CEE

1 ACD**G**IJKLMOP**Q**
2 BGJKRTWX
3 ANR**T**UW
4 (Q+S+T+U+Y+Z 🅿)
5 **AB**DFGIJKLMNOPUVWZ
6 ACDEG**J**(N 4km)OUV

💬 A peaceful family friendly campsite just 5 minutes by car from Bigge lake and the village of Attendorn with its medieval centre and famous stalactite caves. Free loan of car for motorhome campers.

🚗 A45 Dortmund-Frankfurt, exit 16 Meinerzhagen. After about 20 km you come to Attendorn, then take direction Finnentrop. The campsite is beyond the village opposite restaurant 'Haus am See'.

Plettenberg   L687    L880

Herscheid
L696
L697    CC   Lennestadt
B236
L707    B55   B517
L728

**CC** € **18**   1/1-29/6   1/7-14/7   1/9-30/12    🗺 N 51°08'12'' E 07°56'23''

## Barntrup, D-32683 / Nordrhein-Westfalen

♿ 📶 **iD** 743

🔺 Ferienpark
Teutoburgerwald Barntrup****
✉ Badeanstaltsweg 4
☎ +49 52 63 22 21
⌚ 1/4 - 6/10
@ info@
ferienparkteutoburgerwald.de

3ha 110T(90-250m²) 16A CEE

**1** ACD**G**IJKLMPQ
**2** BG**I**JLRUVWXY
**3** ABE**F**GHJK**M**NRU
**4** (A 14/7-23/8) (C+H 1/5-15/9)
(Q 🔲)
**5** **AB**CDEFGHIJKLMNOPQR**S**
**T**UWXZ
**6** ABCDEGHIK(N 0,5km)OSV
WX

💬 Holiday park in woodland surroundings, 5 minute walk to the centre of Barntrup. Good starting point for several trips of cultural interest. Excellent toilet facilities. Beautiful swimming pool next to the site. Camping guests can make free use of it.

🚗 B66 towards Lage, Lemgo, Barntrup. In Barntrup direction swimming pool. Or A2 exit 35 Bad Eilsen, N328 direction Rinteln/Barntrup. From Paderborn B1 direction Hameln via Blomberg to Barntrup. Follow camping signs in Barntrup.

Aerzen
B66 · L758
B66N
CC
**Bad Pyrmont**

**CC** €**18** 1/4-28/5 2/6-6/6 11/6-8/7 25/8-6/10

📐 N 51°59'12'' E 09°06'30''

## Bielefeld, D-33649 / Nordrhein-Westfalen

👫 ♿ 📶 **iD** 744

🔺 CampingPark Bielefeld
✉ Vogelweide 9
☎ +49 52 14 59 22 33
⌚ 1/1 - 31/12
@ bielefeld@meyer-zu-bentrup.de

10ha 110T(< 120m²) 16A CEE

**1** AD**G**HIJKLMO**P**Q
**2** BFGRWXY
**3** BD**F**GHJ**M**RUW
**4** (Q+S 1/4-30/9)
(V 15/4-31/10)
(Z 15/4-15/10)
**5** **AB**DGIJMNO**P**UWXY
**6** CEG**I**J(N 3km)OQUV

💬 Located on the outskirts of Bielefeld. Situated partly in a wood and partly in an open field. The town of Bielefeld is worth a visit. The Teutoburgerwald is wonderful for walking and cycling.

🚗 Kreuz Bielefeld signs A33 direction Paderborn, keep right. Exit towards B61, then B68 dir. Osnabrück Halle-West, right into Osnabrückerstraße, left into Fortunastraße. Follow camping signs.

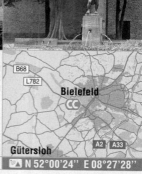

B68
L782
**Bielefeld**
CC
**Gütersloh**
A2 A33

**CC** €**20** 1/3-30/6 1/9-31/10

📐 N 52°00'24'' E 08°27'28''

## Brilon, D-59929 / Nordrhein-Westfalen

⛷ 📶 **iD** 745

🔺 Camping & Ferienpark Brilon
✉ Hoppecker-Straße 75
☎ +49 29 61 97 74 23
⌚ 1/1 - 20/10, 20/12 - 31/12
@ info@campingbrilon.de

19ha 100T(120-160m²) 10-16A CEE

**1** AD**G**IJKLMO**P**Q
**2** BG**I**JKRTUVW
**3** BEH**I**JOR
**4** (A+Q+X+Y+Z 🔲)
**5** **AB**DEFGIJKLMNOPUWXYZ
**6** ACDEG**K**(N 2,5km)S

💬 Summer and winter campsite in the Sauerland with spectacular views. Spacious pitches right next to a wood. Its unique location makes it an ideal base for (winter) sports activities. Dutch/German management. Restaurant in 400 metres.

🚗 B251 dir. Willingen; turn right towards Brilon. Follow signs.

L776 B516 L637 L956
**Brilon**
B7
Bestwig B480 CC
L743 B251
Willingen L3393
(Upland)

**306**

**CC** €**18** 7/1-27/5 2/6-6/6 12/6-11/7 1/9-19/10

📐 N 51°22'45'' E 08°35'08''

## Essen-Werden, D-45239 / Nordrhein-Westfalen　♿ 📶 iD 746

▲ Knaus Campingpark Essen-Werden
🏠 Im Löwental 67
☎ +49 2 01 49 29 78
🔑 1/1 - 31/12
@ essen@knauscamp.de

6ha 140T(80-100m²) 16A CEE

**1** ADGHIJKLMOPQ
**2** CFGILRSTUVWXY
**3** BHJRW
**4** (Q+R 🔑)
(T+U+X+Z 1/2-31/12)
**5** ABDEGIJKLMNOPQRUW
**6** ABCDEGK(N 1km)OTUV

💬 Campsite in a quiet area. Level camping pitches situated on a river. Campsite has a small shop for necessities. Campsite is in the town of Essen.

🚘 On A52, exit 26 Essen/Kettwig/airport. Follow signs Werden (x2). Site is then signposted.

**Essen**
**Mülheim an der Ruhr**
A3　A52　CC
B224　L925　L427
A44　L107

CC €20 1/1-29/5 3/6-7/6 24/6-15/7 1/9-31/12　📍 N 51°22'56'' E 06°59'46''

---

## Extertal, D-32699 / Nordrhein-Westfalen　⛷♿ 📶 iD 747

▲ Campingpark Extertal****
🏠 Eimke 4
☎ +49 52 62 33 07
🔑 1/1 - 31/12
@ info@campingpark-extertal.de

10ha 80T(100-120m²) 16A CEE

**1** ADGHIJKLMOPQ
**2** CDGKLMRVWX
**3** ABDFGHJNRUWZ
**4** (Q+R+T+U+X+Z 1/4-31/10)
**5** ABDEFGIJKLMNOPUWXYZ
**6** ACEGK(N 2km)TUV

💬 A campsite on the edge of woodland with views of undulating hills. The touring pitches are located on a field by the spacious toilet facilities. The site is located on a main road that causes hardly any disturbance and a museum railway line. Close to the towns of Lemgo, Blomberg, Lügde and Rinteln.

🚘 A2 Dortmund-Hannover, exit 35, direction Rinteln-Barntrup. The campsite is located about 1 km south of Bösingfeld close to the village of Asmissen. Clearly signposted.

L435　L434
L957　L861　L432
L963　CC
**Lemgo**　B66　B1
L712　L758　**Bad Pyrmont**

CC €16 1/1-30/6 1/9-31/12　📍 N 52°03'04'' E 09°06'08''

---

## Extertal/Bösingfeld, D-32699 / Nordrhein-Westfalen　👫 📶 iD 748

▲ Camping Bambi****
🏠 Hölmkeweg 1
☎ +49 52 62 43 43
🔑 1/1 - 31/12
@ info@camping-bambi.de

1,7ha 30T(80-120m²) 10A CEE

**1** AGHIJKLMOPQ
**2** JRUVWX
**3** AFHJRUW
**4** (Q 🔑)
**5** ABDGIJMNOPUWZ
**6** ACDEGK(N 4km)OU

💬 Small-scale campsite between Rinteln and Hameln in a rural and idyllic setting. Many towns worth visiting are within 50 km and there are plenty of possibilities for cycling and walking.

🚘 From Bösingfeld drive towards Hameln. Left towards Egge after 2 km past roundabout in Bösingfeld. From there 2 km to campsite.

L435　B83
L961　L434　**Hameln**
L758
**Bösingfeld** CC　L432
L963
B66　B1

CC €16 1/1-14/7 1/9-31/12 7=6, 14=12, 21=18　📍 N 52°04'59'' E 09°09'31''

## Extertal/Meierberg, D-32699 / Nordrhein-Westfalen 📶 🆔 749

▲ Ferienpark Buschhof
📧 Meierbergstraße 15
☎ +49 52 62 25 75
📅 1/1 - 31/12
@ ferienpark-buschhof@t-online.de

4,4ha 55T(100-120m²) 16A CEE

**1** AGHIJKLMOPQ
**2** BRUVWX
**3** BGHJNPR
**4** (B+G 1/5-15/9) N
   (Q 1/5-30/9) (U+Y+Z 💧)
**5** ABDFIJKLMNOPWXZ
**6** CDEGJ(N 5km)OUV

💬 Campsite with spacious pitches near a former farm. Large field with new playground equipment and sports facilities. Swimming pool with organic purification. Horse lovers will certainly find what they are looking for. Also very suitable for groups.

🚗 A2, exit 35 direction Rinteln (B238). Then direction Barntrup. Campsite is signposted about 8.5 km after exit. Turn left in direction Meierberg.

CC € **14** 1/1-15/6 15/9-31/12   📍 N 52°06'17'' E 09°07'06''

---

## Höxter, D-37671 / Nordrhein-Westfalen 📶 🆔 750

▲ Wesercamping Höxter***
📧 Sportzentrum 4
☎ +49 52 71 25 89
📅 1/1 - 31/12
@ info@campingplatz-hoexter.de

30ha 80T(80-120m²) 6-10A CEE

**1** AGHIJKLMOPQ
**2** CGKLRVX
**3** BGHJKLMNOUWX
**4** (Q+R+T+U+X 15/4-15/10)
   (Z 1/4-15/10)
**5** ABDGIJKMNOPRUWZ
**6** CDEGK(N 1km)OV

💬 A pleasant, child and youth friendly campsite on the Weser, you can bring your own boat. Friendly couple. Pretty village. A good base for cycling, walking, Nordic walking, mountain biking and fishing. Good opportunities for cultural trips out. The new swimming pool will be opened in 2019.

🚗 A44 direction Kassel, exit Bühren direction Paderborn. B64 direction Höxter. In Höxter direction Boffzen/Fürstenberg and follow signs to campsite and Brückfeld.

CC € **18** 1/1-26/4 3/5-26/5 23/6-15/7 1/9-31/12   📍 N 51°46'00'' E 09°23'00''

---

## Ladbergen, D-49549 / Nordrhein-Westfalen ♿ 📶 🆔 751

▲ Regenbogen Ferienanlage Ladbergen
📧 Buddenkuhle 1
☎ +49 5 48 59 63 53
📅 1/4 - 31/10
@ ladbergen@regenbogen.ag

6ha 80T(90-110m²) 16A CEE

**1** ACDGHIJKLMOPQ
**2** ADFLMRSWXY
**3** AFGOPRWZ
**4** (Q+R+T+U+X 💧)
**5** ABGJNPSUWXZ
**6** GJ(N 5km)OTU

💬 This centrally located campsite between Münster and Osnabrück is positioned by a beautiful lake where you can go swimming, fishing or sailing. The lake is also popular with day trippers.

🚗 From Hengelo A30 as far as Lottekruis, then direction A1 Münster/Dortmund, exit 74 Ladbergen. Campsite signposted from the roundabout.

CC € **18** 1/4-15/4 23/4-28/5 12/6-29/6 25/8-31/10   📍 N 52°09'56'' E 07°45'37''

## **Lemgo**, D-32657 / Nordrhein-Westfalen

**752**

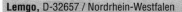

- Campingpark Lemgo
- Regenstorstraße 10
- +49 5 26 11 48 58
- 1/3 - 30/11
- lemgo@meyer-zu-bentrup.de

2,6ha 60T(90-100m²) 16A CEE

1. A**G**IJKLMO**P**Q
2. CGRTUWXY
3. ABHJRU**W**
4. (**C**+**F**+**H** ) J**KLN** (Q 1/4-30/9)
5. **AB**DEFGIJMNO**P**UWXY
6. ACDEGJ(N 0,5km)OV

This campsite is located within walking distance of the beautiful old town of Lemgo with its restored facades. Swimming pool and sauna at reduced rates. The area is an invitation for walking, cycling and making cultural trips out. Well-maintained toilet block.

Follow the camping signs in Lemgo.

Bad Salzuflen
Lemgo
B66
CC
Detmold


CC € 20 *1/3-26/5 11/6-30/6 1/9-31/10*

N 52°01'30'' E 08°54'31''

## **Lienen**, D-49536 / Nordrhein-Westfalen

**753**

- Camping Eurocamp
- Holperdorp 44
- +49 5 48 32 90
- 1/1 - 31/12
- info@camping-lienen.de

7,8ha 60T(80-100m²) 16A CEE

1. ACD**G**IJKLMO**PQ**
2. JKRSTWX
3. BGHR
4. M(X )
5. **AB**DEGJN**P**UWZ
6. EK(N 5km)O

Tranquil (dog-friendly) campsite with well-maintained toilet facilities. You can also leave or enter the campsite between 1 and 3 pm. Many walking routes signposted in the area. Visits to Bad Iburg and Osnabrück are recommended.

B51 Osnabrück/Nahne direction Bad Iburg then direction Holperdorp. The campsite is signposted.

A30
A1
L89
Georgsmarienhütte
L95
A33
CC
L555
L834
B51
L98
B475
L94


CC € 18 *1/1-12/7 1/9-31/12*

N 52°10'00'' E 07°58'52''

## **Meinerzhagen**, D-58540 / Nordrhein-Westfalen

**754**

- Camping Seeblick
- Seeuferstr. 2
- +49 2 35 83 81
- 22/3 - 9/10
- info@campingplatz-seeblick.com

2ha 25T(80-100m²) 16A CEE

1. A**G**IJKLMO**P**Q
2. DFIJLMORTW
3. BRU**WZ**
4. (Q+R ) (T+U 5/4-9/10)
5. **AB**DFGIJKLMNOPU
6. DEGJ(N 2km)OV

Small campsite with pitches overlooking the lake. You have to cross the road to get to the lake. New pitches with panoramic views.

On the A45 Dortmund-Siegen take exit 16 Meinerzhagen towards Attendorn. After 4km turn right towards Listertalsperre. Campsite is 10km further on the left.

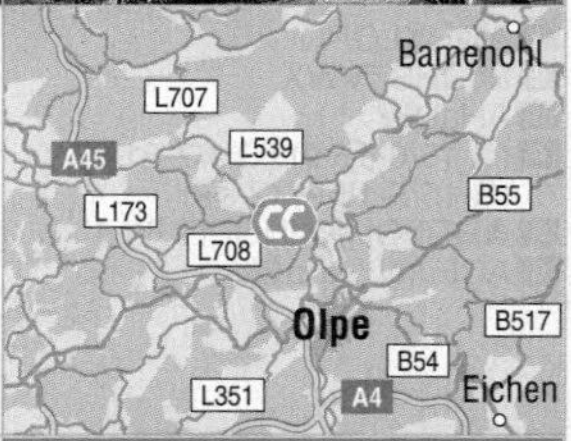

Bamenohl
L707
L539
A45
B55
L173
CC
L708
Olpe
B517
B54
L351
A4
Eichen


CC € 16 *22/3-28/5 24/6-14/7 1/9-9/10*

N 51°04'41'' E 07°48'57''

## Meschede (Hennesee), D-59872 / Nordrhein-Westfalen

▲ Knaus Campingpark
Hennesee*****
✉ Mielinghausen 7
☎ +49 2 91 95 27 20
🕐 1/1 - 31/12
@ hennesee@knauscamp.de

12,5ha 182T(80-130m²) 6-16A CEE

**1** ACD**G**HIJKLMOP**Q**
**2** DFGJLMORTVWXY
**3** ABGHJKLNRU**W**Z
**4** (F 1/1-15/11,19/12-31/12) **N**
(Q+R+T+U+Y+Z 🕐)
**5** **AB**DEFGIJKLMNOPR**ST**UW
XYZ
**6** ACDEG**K**(N 3km)OSUV

💬 A terraced campsite separated by rows of trees. Peacefully located at a reservoir. CampingCard ACSI rate does not include entrance to indoor pool.

🚗 B55 from Meschede to Olpe. After 7 km, at the end of the reservoir, cross the bridge and turn left towards the campsite.

Meschede

CC €20 7/1-29/5 3/6-7/6 24/6-15/7 1/9-20/12 N 51°17'54'' E 08°15'51''

755

---

## Monschau/Imgenbroich, D-52156 / Nordrhein-Westfalen

▲ Camping Zum Jone-Bur****
✉ Grünentalstraße 36
☎ +49 24 72 39 31
🕐 1/1 - 31/12
@ camping@zum-jone-bur.de

8ha 60T(60-80m²) 6A CEE

**1** AD**F**HIJKLO**PR**S
**2** GRTUVWX
**3** AHJLRU
**4** (**A** 🕐) (G 15/6-15/9) (U 🕐)
(X+Z 1/4-31/12)
**5** **AB**DFGIJKLMNO**P**UWXYZ
**6** ACDEGJ**K**(N 1km)OV

💬 Well maintained campsite close to Monschau. Pitches marked out by trees and hedges. Good restaurant. A good starting point for walks in the Nord Eifel Nature Park, Eifel National Park and the Hoge Venen. 500 metres from a large retail outlet.

🚗 The campsite is marked on the B258 Aachen-Monschau or the B399 Düren-Monschau. In Imgenbroich turn to the left. Well marked.

Monschau

Hellenthal

CC €20 1/1-18/4 23/4-29/5 3/6-7/6 11/6-11/7 28/8-29/11 2/12-23/12 N 50°34'01'' E 06°16'02''

756

---

## Monschau/Perlenau, D-52156 / Nordrhein-Westfalen

▲ Camping Perlenau****
☎ +49 24 72 41 36
🕐 15/4 - 3/10
@ familie.rasch@
monschau-perlenau.de

3ha 70T(50-80m²) 16A CEE

**1** A**G**IJKLOPQ
**2** BCJRSTVWX
**3** AHJU**W**
**4** (G 15/6-15/9) (Q 1/7-31/8)
(R 15/5-15/9) (Z 🕐)
**5** **AB**DFGIJKMNOPRUWZ
**6** ACEJ(N 1km)OV

💬 A campsite set in a valley in the middle of woodland. A lovely 1.5 km walk to the town of Monschau. Be sure not to miss a visit to the glass works.

🚗 Campsite can be reached via B258 Monschau-Trier. Well signposted along the road.

Roetgen
Simmerath

CC €20 5/5-29/5 23/6-7/7 24/8-3/10 N 50°32'38'' E 06°14'15''

757

## Sassenberg, D-48336 / Nordrhein-Westfalen

♿ 🛜 **iD** `758`

🔺 Camping Münsterland
    Eichenhof✶✶✶✶✶
📧 Feldmark 3
☎ +49 25 83 15 85
📅 1/1 - 31/12
@ info@campmuensterland.de

18ha 80T(100-120m²) 16A CEE

1 **ACDGHIJKLMOPQ**
2 **ADGLRSUWXY**
3 **BFJKLRUWZ**
4 (Q 📅) (R 30/3-20/10)
   (T+U+Y 1/1-20/1,19/2-31/12)
5 **ABDEFGHJLNPSUWXY**
6 **ACDEGHK**(N 2km)OSU

💬 This beautiful campsite is located directly on the Felmarksee and there is also a private swimming lake available for guests. Private toilet facilities are available and there is a restaurant with a beer garden. Bicycle routes directly from the campsite. City tours of Münster, Osnabrück and Bielefeld are highly recommended.

🚗 A30 dir. Osnabrück. Exit 18, N475 dir. Warendorf, then Sassenberg. In Sassenberg dir. Versmold. Signs to campsite outside the built-up area.

**CC** € **18** 1/1-17/4  23/4-26/5  11/6-12/7  1/9-31/12

📍 N 52°00'16''  E 08°03'51''

---

## Sassenberg, D-48336 / Nordrhein-Westfalen

♿ 🛜 **iD** `759`

🔺 Campingpark Heidewald✶✶✶✶✶
📧 Versmolder Straße 44
☎ +49 25 83 13 94
📅 1/2 - 30/11
@ campheidewald@web.de

8,5ha 90T(100-130m²) 16A CEE

1 **ADGHIJKLMOPQ**
2 **GRVWX**
3 **BFHJKLNR**
4 (Q 1/4-31/10)
5 **ABDEFGJLNPUWXYZ**
6 **ACDEGK**(N 1,5km)OSUV

💬 A five star campsite for those who seek rest close to a lake. Ideal for cyclists directly on the 100 castles route. Lovely towns in the area include Warendorf, Münster and Osnabrück. Bakery service. Excellent modern toilet facilities.

🚗 A30 direction Osnabrück. Exit 18, N475 direction Warendorf, then direction Sassenberg. Follow camping signs.

**CC** € **20** 1/2-26/5  24/6-14/7  1/9-30/11

📍 N 52°00'00''  E 08°03'55''

---

## Tecklenburg/Leeden, D-49545 / Nordrhein-Westfalen

♿ ♿ 🛜 ✿ **iD** `760`

🔺 Regenbogen Ferienanlage
    Tecklenburg
📧 Grafenstraße 31
☎ +49 54 05 10 07
📅 1/4 - 31/10
@ tecklenburg@regenbogen.ag

30ha 500T(90-100m²) 16A CEE

1 **ACGHIJKLOPQ**
2 **FGLRVWXY**
3 **BGJMNQRU**
4 (B 1/6-31/8) (F+G 📅) **KL**N
   (Q 15/4-31/10)
   (R 14/5-31/10)
   (T+U+X 15/4-31/10)
5 **ABDEGJLNPSUWYZ**
6 **CDFGIJ**(N 4km)OTV

💬 The campsite is located in the Teutoburgerwald Forest. The holiday park offers many amenities with an indoor and outdoor pool and many sports facilities. Good starting point for walking and cycling.

🚗 A1 Hengelo-Osnabrück exit Ibbenbüren-Laggenbeck direction Tecklenburg-Lengerich. Signposted thereafter.

**CC** € **20** 1/4-15/4  23/4-28/5  12/6-29/6  1/9-31/10

📍 N 52°13'47''  E 07°53'25''

## Wesel/Flüren, D-46487 / Nordrhein-Westfalen ♿ 🛜 **iD** ⑦⑥①

▲ Campingplatz Grav-Insel
🏠 Gravinsel 1
☎ +49 2 81 97 28 30
🕐 1/1 - 31/12
@ info@grav-insel.com

250ha 500T(90-200m²) 16A CEE

**1** ADGIJKLMOPRS
**2** ACDFGLRUVWX
**3** ABCDFGHIJNPRUWXZ
**4** (A 26/6-10/8) (Q 🕐)
(S 1/1-15/1,15/3-31/12)
(T+U+V+Y 🕐) (Z 5/2-31/12)
**5** ABDEFGIJLMNOPQRUWXZ
**6** CDEGHKLM(N 0km)OTUV

💬 A large campsite with the touring pitches positioned by the water where you can go boating and swimming. Central building housing shops, bars, cafes and toilet facilities.

🚗 On the A3 exit 5, follow the B473. Direction Rees B8, exit Flüren. In Flüren over the dike towards Rees. Campsite on the left.

Rees  L8  L602  B8  B473  A3  L1  B70  L6  CC Wesel B58  L77 L480  Friedrichsfeld  L463  B57  L396  A57  L137  L4

CC € ⑱  1/1-8/7  25/8-31/12     📍 N 51°40'05'' E 06°33'22''

## Wettringen, D-48493 / Nordrhein-Westfalen ♿ 🛜 **iD** ⑦⑥②

▲ Campingpark Haddorfer
Seen****
🏠 Haddorf 59
☎ +49 59 73 27 42
🕐 1/1 - 31/12
@ info@campingpark-haddorf.de

14,6ha 135T(80-200m²) 16A CEE

**1** ADGHIJKLMOPQ
**2** ADLMRSWX
**3** AJQRWZ
**4** M(Q+R+T+U+X+Z 1/4-31/10)
**5** ABDEFGJLNPQWXYZ
**6** ACFGHIJK(N 7km)OS

💬 This campsite with many seasonal pitches is located in unusual surroundings where you can go cycling, sailing, fishing and swimming. For tourist campers there are pitches under the trees, at the entrance or on a large field next to the natural swimming pool.

🚗 A31 exit Schüttorf-Ost direction Wettringen. Campsite signposted north of this town.

Bad Bentheim  A30  L39  L593  L501  A31  CC  Rheine  B403  L582  L567  L70  B499

CC € ⑳  1/1-12/4  29/4-26/5  24/6-1/7  2/9-31/12     📍 N 52°16'25'' E 07°19'12''

## Winterberg/Niedersfeld, D-59955 / Nordrhein-Westfalen 👫 🎿 ♿ 🛜 **iD** ⑦⑥③

▲ Camping Vossmecke
🏠 Am Eschenberg 1a
☎ +49 29 85 84 18
🕐 1/1 - 31/12
@ info@camping-vossmecke.de

4ha 20T(80-100m²) 16A CEE

**1** AGHIJKLOPQ
**2** BCJRTVWX
**3** ABFGHJNRU
**4** (A+Q+R+T+U+X+Y+Z 🕐)
**5** ABDFGIJKLMNOPUW
**6** EGK(N 3km)O

💬 Very quiet campsite for people who like walking, cycling and skiing, lift on the campsite.

🚗 A44 Dortmund-Kassel, exit to A46 Arnsberg. Follow this road to Bestwig. Then direction Winterberg. The campsite is signposted about 800 metres after Niedersfeld.

L3393  B480  B251  Niedersfeld  L854  L742  CC  L872  Winterberg  L740  B236  L617  L640

CC € ⑱  8/1-13/7  1/9-19/12     📍 N 51°14'23'' E 08°31'33''

## Alheim/Licherode, D-36211 / Hessen  📶 iD  764

🏕 Camping Alte Mühle
✉ Zur Alten Mühle 4
☎ +49 17 35 90 47 17
📅 1/4 - 1/10
@ info@camping-altemuehle.de

4,5ha 100T(100m²) 16A CEE

**1** ACD**G**IJKLMOPQ
**2** BCDFRTUWXY
**3** ABHJKLUW
**4** (Q+U+X+Z 🔌)
**5** **AB**DGIJKLMNOPUWX
**6** DEGK(N 6km)OV

💬 An ideal campsite for lovers of peace, quiet and the beauty of nature. Very good and welcoming restaurant. Walking and cycling routes.

🚗 From Kassel: exit 83 Malsfeld. Then dir. Rotenburg. To Morschen then follow Licherode. In Licherode turn right. From Bad-Hersfeld: exit 84 Homberg. Then follow Rotenburg. To Sterkelhausen, turn left. Then follow Licherode, turn right in Licherode.

CC € **16** 1/4-15/7  1/9-1/10

🧭 N 51°02'10'' E 09°34'51''

---

## Eschwege, D-37269 / Hessen  ♿ 📶 iD  765

🏕 Knaus Campingpark Eschwege*****
✉ Am Werratalsee 2
☎ +49 56 51 33 88 83
📅 1/3 - 3/11
@ eschwege@knauscamp.de

6,8ha 123T(100m²) 16A CEE

**1** ACD**G**HIJKLMOPQ
**2** ACDGKLMNPRTUVWX
**3** BCGHJKL**MNOP**RU**WZ**
**4** (Q 1/3-30/10) (T+U+X+Z 🔌)
**5** **AB**DEFGIJKLMNOPQR**S**UW XYZ
**6** CDEG**K**(N 1km)OUV

💬 A campsite next to a lake. Excellent toilet facilities. Good cycling opportunities, close to the lovely village of Eschwege.

🚗 A4 Kassel-Hannover, exit 74. B27 direction Bebra, exit Eschwege. Or A4 Frankfurt-Dresden, exit 32. Then B27 direction Eschwege.

CC € **20** 1/3-29/5  3/6-7/6  24/6-15/7  1/9-3/11

🧭 N 51°11'29'' E 10°04'07''

---

## Eschwege/Meinhard, D-37276 / Hessen  👥 🚫 📶 iD  766

🏕 Campingplatz Meinhardsee
✉ Freizeitzentrum 2
☎ +49 56 51 62 00
📅 1/1 - 31/12
@ info@ werra-meissner-camping.de

18ha 200T(80-100m²) 6A CEE

**1** A**G**HIJKLMOPQ
**2** ADKLMNRSTUVWXY
**3** BGHJNQRU**WZ**
**4** (B 🔌) JM(Q 1/4-31/8) (R 1/4-31/10) (T+U 1/6-31/8) (Y 1/2-31/12)
**5** **AB**DFGIJKLMNOPUW
**6** CDEGHK(N 2km)OV

💬 Located in the hills of North Hessen. The lake with a beach is ideal for a swim, pedal boating and wind surfing. Activities include water sliding, minigolf, fishing and cycling and walking routes.

🚗 A7 Kassel-Göttingen, exit Friedland. B524 dir. Eschwege. Then in Meinhard dir. Grebendorf. Campsite signposted. Or: Meinhard, Ziegelweg. Tunnel not for motorhomes higher than 3m. Alternative route: dir. Grebendorf, and follow signs.

CC € **18** 1/1-1/6  24/8-31/12

🧭 N 51°12'13'' E 10°02'53''

## Fischbachtal, D-64405 / Hessen  🧍👫 ♿ [iD] (767)

🏕 Camping Odenwaldidyll
📧 Campingplatz 1
☎ +49 61 66 85 77
📅 30/3 - 27/10
@ kontakt@
   camping-odenwaldidyll.de

4,7ha 49T(70-110m²) 10A CEE

**1** A**G**IJKLMN**PQ**
**2** DGLMRVWXY
**3** ABHJRU**W**
**4** (B 12/5-27/10)
   (Q+R+T+U+X 🔑)
**5** **AB**DEFGIJKLMNO**P**UWXYZ
**6** CDEG(N 3km)OTUV

💬 On about 4.7 hectares the guests are offered not only spaciously appointed caravan and tent pitches but also very modern toilet facilities. This extremely family and child friendly site is also appealing to those who are looking for a pastime locally because of its natural swimming pool. Campsite, natural pool, playground, kiosk.

🚗 A5 exit Ober-Ramstadt to Fischbachthal. Then follow camping signs.

**Darmstadt**
L3104
B45
L3106  L3065
B3  L3099 ⓒⓒ  L3318
L3102  B38
L3399
**Bensheim**  B47

(CC) € **18**  30/3-30/6  1/9-27/10  7=6, 14=12  |  📐 N 49°46'35'' E 08°48'33''

---

## Fuldatal/Knickhagen, D-34233 / Hessen  ♿ 📶 [iD] (768)

🏕 Fulda-Freizeitzentrum
📧 Fulda-Freizeitzentrum 1
☎ +49 5 60 73 40
📅 1/1 - 31/12
@ patzke.michael@t-online.de

3,2ha 40T(80-120m²) 10A CEE

**1** AD**G**HIJKLMOPQ
**2** RTUVWX
**3** AHJR
**4** (Q+R+U+Y+Z 🔑)
**5** **AB**CDFGIJKLMNOPUW
**6** EGJ(N 9,9km)O

💬 Idyllically located campsite on the edge of a wood. Casual atmosphere. Pleasant restaurant with a lovely 'Biergarten'. Here you will find the peace to enable you to relax.

🚗 Exit A7 Kassel-Nord direction Kassel Calden airport. B3 Hann.Münden towards Knickhagen. Or A7 exit Hedemünden direction Hann.Münden. B3 direction Kassel/Knickhagen. Follow campsite signs in Knickhagen. Don't use SatNav.

L3229  B80
L3233  L3232  L561
   B83  **Hann.**
   **Münden**
ⓒⓒ
B7  B3
A7
**Kassel**  L563

(CC) € **18**  1/1-7/7  25/8-31/12  |  📐 N 51°23'21'' E 09°33'49''

---

## Fürth (Odenwald), D-64658 / Hessen  ❌ ♿ 📶 ✿ [iD] (769)

🏕 Nibelungen-Camping am
   Schwimmbad
📧 Tiefertswinkel 20
☎ +49 62 53 58 04
📅 30/3 - 20/10
@ info@camping-fuerth.de

5ha 45T(80-120m²) 16A CEE

**1** AEHIJKLMOP**Q**
**2** GKLRUVWXY
**3** BHJ**M**RU
**4** (**C**+**H** 15/5-15/9) J
   (Q+R+Z 🔑)
**5** **AB**DFGIJKLMNO**P**RUWXYZ
**6** CDEG**IKL**(N 0,1km)O

💬 A quietly located campsite close to a heated municipal swimming pool and large supermarket. It makes an excellent stopover campsite.

🚗 From north A5 Darmstadt-Heidelberg, exit 31 Heppenheim B460. Campsite on left past Fürth. From south exit 33 Weinheim B38a. Campsite on left past Fürth. Follow signs from Fürth.

L3399
B47  B38
L3099  L3260
ⓒⓒ
**Heppenheim**
**(Bergstraße)**  L3346  B460
A5  L3105
B3  L3120

(CC) € **20**  3/5-28/5  23/6-30/6  1/9-30/9  |  📐 N 49°39'35'' E 08°47'01''

## Gedern, D-63688 / Hessen

🏕 Campingplatz Am Gederner See
📭 Am Gederner See 19
☎ +49 60 45 95 26 43
🔑 1/1 - 31/12
@ info@campingpark-gedern.de

👫 👤 📶 **iD** 770

**NEW**

15ha 157T(80-120m²) 16A CEE

**1** ABCD**G**HIJKLM**PQ**
**2** ADLMNRTVWXY
**3** BFHJ**Q**RU**WZ**
**4** (**A** 1/3-31/10) M
(Q+R+T+U+Y 🔑)
**5** **AB**DFGIJKMNOPUWZ
**6** CDEGJ(N 2km)OQTV

💬 Very spacious family site located on a lake with sandy beach. Ideal for swimming, cycling, mountain biking, hiking, fishing and paddle-boating. Near several cycling routes, for example the Vulkan Cycling Trail and the Bahn Cycling Trail Hesse. Close to the 'Hoherodskopf', which includes a treetop adventure park.

🚗 A45 Frankfurt-Giessen, exit 38 Florstadt. B275 direction Lauterbach, then exit Gedern. From Gedern, follow signs (approx. 1.5 km in north-westerly dir.).

*Ilbeshausen* L3338
B455 B276
L3183 B275
CC L3010
*Wenings*
*Ranstadt*

CC € **20** 1/1-29/5 31/5-7/6 10/6-19/6 23/6-1/7 1/9-31/12
📷 N 50°25'44'' E 09°10'50''

---

## Greifenstein/Beilstein, D-35753 / Hessen

🏕 Camping Ulmbachtalsperre
📭 Ulmbachtalsperre 1
☎ +49 2 77 93 49
🔑 1/4 - 15/10
@ ulmbach-camping@t-online.de

👤 📶 **iD** 771

17ha 80T(80-100m²) 10-16A CEE

**1** AD**G**HIJKLMOPRS
**2** DGIJKLORTWXY
**3** ABHJKLNRUZ
**4** (A+Q+R+T+U+Z 🔑)
**5** **AB**DGIJKLMNOP**U**WZ
**6** CEG**IK**(N 2km)OV

💬 Camping grounds surrounded by rows of trees, spacious pitches partly located on the reservoir. Campsite close to the A45.

🚗 A45, exit 27 Herborn-Süd dir. Greifenstein, Mengerskirchen, via Beilstein dir. Biskirchen. Site located between Beilstein and Holzhausen. A45 exit 28 Ehringshausen, via Katzenfurt, Holzhausen. In Holzh. and Beilst. follow signs.

**Herborn**
B255 L3461 L3052
A45
*Westernohe* CC L3282 B277
L3046 L3044
L3324 B49
*Laufdorf*

CC € **18** 2/5-29/5 1/6-6/6 25/6-5/7 21/8-31/8 6/9-30/9
📷 N 50°36'10'' E 08°16'00''

---

## Hirschhorn/Neckar, D-69434 / Hessen

🏕 Odenwald Camping Park
📭 Langenthalerstraße 80
☎ +49 6 27 28 09
🔑 1/4 - 6/10 **N**
@ odenwald-camping-park@
t-online.de

👤 📶 **iD** 772

8ha 200T(80-120m²) 6A CEE

**1** AF**H**IJKLMOPQ
**2** CGLRTVWXY
**3** BF**G**HJK**MOP**QRU**W**X
**4** (C 2/6-10/9) **N**
(Q+S+U+Y+Z 🔑)
**5** **AB**DFGHIJKLMNOPUW
**6** CFG**K**(N 1,5km)OSTV

💬 Set in peaceful woodland on the outskirts of Hirschhorn, with a friendly warden. A good starting point for cycling and walking trips along the Neckar or for car trips in the beautiful Odenwald forest. The campsite has a swimming pool with a bar and new toilet facilities. Good train connections to Heidelberg.

🚗 A5, exit 37 Heidelberg. On the B37 direction Eberbach/Mosbach. Exit Hirschhorn. In Hirschhorn follow signs, dir. Langenthal at the end of Hirschhorn.

B45
L2311
L3119
L3105
L524
L596 L595
L535
CC
**Heidelberg** B37
*Neckargemünd*

CC € **20** 1/4-26/5 23/6-30/6 18/8-6/10
📷 N 49°27'09'' E 08°52'40''

## Hünfeld, D-36088 / Hessen ♿ 📶 iD **773**

🔺 Knaus Campingpark
Hünfeld Praforst*****
✉ Dr.-Detlev-Rudelsdorff-Allee 6
☎ +49 66 52 74 90 90
🔌 1/1 - 31/12
@ huenfeld@knauscamp.de

4,7ha 136T(100m²) 16A

1 **ACDGHIJKLMOPQ**
2 **BFGJRTUVWX**
3 **AEFHJKLNQRUW**
4 (A 1/6-31/10) (Q 1/4-30/9)
(R 🔌) (T 1/1-31/10,
1/12-31/12) (U 1/1-31/10)
(V 1/3-30/11) (X 🔌)
(Y 1/1-30/10,1/11-31/12)
5 **ABDEFGIJKLMNOPUWXZ**
6 **CDEGJK**(N 5km)OTV

💬 A short distance from the main road and located on the edge of extensive woods. Shaded and sunny pitches next to a newly laid out golf course. Easily accessible for stopover campers. Beautiful countryside, 20% discount at the golf course next door.

🚗 A7 Kassel-Frankfurt, exit 90 Hünfeld/Schlitz. Campsite then signposted. Can also be reached via B27, exit Hünfeld/Schlitz.

L3140 L3169 Hünfeld L3176 A7 CC L3143 L3378 Hofbieber L3174 B254 Petersberg

CC €20 1/3-29/5 3/6-7/6 24/6-15/7 1/9-3/11 N 50°39'12'' E 09°43'26''

---

## Kirchheim/Waldhessen, D-36275 / Hessen ⛷ ♿ 📶 iD **774**

🔺 Camping Seepark*****
✉ Brunnenstraße 20-25
☎ +49 66 28 15 25
🔌 1/1 - 31/12
@ info@campseepark.de

10ha 300T 16A CEE

1 **ACDGHIJKLMOPQ**
2 **ADFGJKLRTUVWX**
3 **AEFHJKLMQRSTUWZ**
4 (A 1/7-31/8) (F+H 🔌) J
(Q+R+T+U+X+Y+Z 🔌)
5 **ABDEFGIJKLMNOPUWXYZ**
6 **CDEGK**(N 5km)OTUV

💬 Large campsite with all imaginable amenities. Toilet blocks in three places. Both sunny and less sunny pitches in this woodland area of Germany. Outdoor pool 5 km away.

🚗 A7 Kassel-Würzburg, exit 87 Kirchheim. Campsite immediately indicated.

L3158 A7 **Bad Hersfeld** L3156 L3157 B454 A4 Ottrau L3431 L3160 A5 B62 L3144 L3140 A7

CC €20 1/1-25/5 1/6-7/6 23/6-30/6 1/9-31/12 N 50°48'52'' E 09°31'05''

---

## Lindenfels/Schlierbach, D-64678 / Hessen ♿ 📶 ✿ iD **775**

🔺 Terrassen Camping Schlierbach
✉ Am Zentbuckel 11
☎ +49 6 25 56 30
🔌 1/4 - 27/10
@ info@
terrassencamping-schlierbach.de

4,5ha 35T(80-100m²) 10A CEE

NEW

1 **ACDGHIJKLMOPQ**
2 **CGIJKLRSUVWXY**
3 **ABHJR**
4 M(Q+R 🔌)
5 **AB**CDEFGHIJKLMNOPQUW XY
6 DEGJ(N 2km)OU

💬 Terraced campsite in UNESCO Geopark/Berg-strasse, near the Felsenmeer lake with comfortable toilet facilities. Ideal start for active holidaymakers and those looking for peace and quiet. Mountain biking, racing, climbing, bouldering and hiking. Heated swimming pool at 700 metres. All pitches have water, electricity and sewage. Free wifi.

🚗 A5 Frankfurt-Basel, exit 30 Bensheim, B47 direction Michelstadt, signs for Fürth. In Schlierbach left, follow campsite signs.

B3 L3103 A5 B47 B38 CC **Heppenheim (Bergstraße)** B460 L3398 L3120 L3409

CC €18 23/4-28/5 24/6-5/7 1/9-27/10 N 49°40'55'' E 08°46'12''

## Naumburg (Edersee), D-34311 / Hessen

🎿 ⚒ 📶 **iD** 776

🏕 Camping in Naumburg****
📧 Am Schwimmbad 12
☎ +49 5 62 59 23 96 70
📅 1/1 - 31/12
@ camping@naumburg.eu

6,5ha 120T(80-160m²) 16A CEE

**1** ACG**H**IJKLMPQ
**2** CGJLRUVWXY
**3** AB**F**GHJKRUV
**4** (**C** 1/5-30/9) (H 1/6-30/9) JN
(Q+T+U 📅) (Z 1/6-31/8)
**5** **AB**DEFGIJKLMNO**P**UWXYZ
**6** CEGIK(N 0,3km)O

💬 Spacious terraced campsite designed by architect. Adjacent municipal swimming pool can be used all day at a reduced rate. Tickets for the swimming pool are available at the campsite reception.

🚗 A44 Dortmund-Kassel, exit Zierenberg, B251 towards Edersee as far as Ippinghausen; turn left towards Naumburg. Campsite signposted.

Wolfhagen
A44
Schauenburg
B251
L3083 CC
L3200 L3215
L3086 L3214
A49

CC € **18** 1/1-30/6 1/9-31/12 📍 **N 51°15'02'' E 09°09'37''**

---

## Oberweser/Gieselwerder, D-34399 / Hessen

⚒ 📶 **iD** 777

🏕 Camping Gieselwerder
📧 In der Klappe 21
☎ +49 55 72 76 11
📅 1/4 - 31/10
@ info@camping-gieselwerder.de

2,5ha 80T(80-100m²) 16A CEE

**1** ACD**G**HIJKLMOPQ
**2** CGKRVWX
**3** BHJKLN**OP**RUW X
**4** (**A** 1/7-15/9) (C+H 15/5-2/9)
(Q+T+U+V+Y+Z 📅)
**5** **AB**DFGIJKLMNOPR**S**UWZ
**6** CEGJ(N 0,2km)O

💬 The campsite is located on the Weser, on an elongated piece of land, next to a (free) heated pool. The Weser cycle route is next to the campsite, the wooded hills stretch to just 1 km from the campsite. A few attractive towns are within 40 km.

🚗 A21 exit 35, B83 to Bad Karlshafen. B80, in Gieselwerder turn left at Aral, before the bridge turn right. A7: exit 75 or 76 to Hann.Münden, then via B80 direction Bad Karlshafen. In Gieselwerder to the right.

B241
Beverungen L551 Uslar
B83 B80
L554
CC
L763 Gottsbüren
L561

CC € **18** 1/4-26/5 24/6-30/6 1/9-31/10 7=6, 14=12 📍 **N 51°35'55'' E 09°33'18''**

---

## Oberweser/Oedelsheim, D-34399 / Hessen

⚒ 📶 **iD** 778

🏕 Campen am Fluss****
📧 Am Hallenbad 3
☎ +49 55 74 94 57 80
📅 1/4 - 31/10
@ info@campen-am-fluss.de

2,3ha 46T(95-110m²) 16A CEE

**1** ACD**G**HIJKLMOPQ
**2** CGKRVWX
**3** BHJKLNRU**W**X
**4** (F+H+Q+T+U+X 📅)
**5** **AB**DEFGIJKLMNOPUWXZ
**6** ACEGH**K**(N 0,3km)OTUV

💬 Quiet campsite on the edge of Oedelsheim between the Weser and an indoor pool. A large number of sights in the vicinity. A joy for cyclists and watersports enthusiasts. Weser cycle route passes by the campsite.

🚗 Via A7 (north): exit 71, Harste/Adelebsen/ Offensen/Oedelsheim. Via A7 (south): exit 76, Hann. Münden/Gimte/Hemeln. Via A44: exit 66, Breuna/ Oberlistingen/Hofgeismar/Gottsbüren/Gieselwerder/ Oedelsh.

B241 L551 Uslar
Bodenfelde
Adelebsen
CC
B80
L561
L560

CC € **18** 26/4-28/5 22/6-30/6 1/9-27/9 7/10-31/10 📍 **N 51°35'34'' E 09°35'24''**

## Schlüchtern/Hutten, D-36381 / Hessen 📶 iD **779**

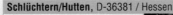

🏕 Camping Hutten-Heiligenborn
📧 Am Heiligenborn 6
☎ +49 66 61 24 24
🔓 1/1 - 31/12
@ helga.herzog-gericke@online.de

5ha 50T(80-100m²) 10A CEE

**1** AGHIJKLMOPQ
**2** FJLRTWX
**3** AHU
**4** (**B**+**G** 1/6-15/9) (Q+R+Y 🔓)
**5** A**D**GIJMNOP**U**WZ
**6** CEG**K**(N 1km)O

💬 Terraced campsite with modern toilet facilities. Idyllically situated between Röhn, Spessart and Vogelsberg, next to a heated outdoor pool. Numerous day trips possible in the hilly surroundings.

🚗 From the A66 take exit 48, 49 or 50 direction Schlüchtern/Hutten. Campsite 7 km further on. In Hutten follow the 'Sportplatz-Freibad' signs.

CC € **16** 30/3-7/7 25/8-30/10 📍 N 50°22'06'' E 09°36'30''

---

## Witzenhausen, D-37213 / Hessen 🎿 📶 iD **780**

🏕 Campingplatz Werratal
📧 Am Sande 11
☎ +49 55 42 14 65
🔓 1/1 - 31/12
@ info@campingplatz-werratal.de

3ha 70T(120m²) 6-16A

**1** AD**G**HIJKLMOPQ
**2** CFGLNORSTUWXY
**3** ABHIJ**MNOPQRSTUWX**
**4** (A 🔓) (**C**+**H** 15/5-15/9) J (Q+R+Z 🔓)
**5** **AB**DFGIJKLMNOP**U**W
**6** CDEGJ(N 0,6km)OTV

💬 Located on the River Werra. Spacious pitches for visitors, plenty of sports possibilities on, and in the vicinity of, the campsite. Large pool.

🚗 A44 Dortmund-Kassel, then A7 Kassel-Hannover. Exit 75 Hedemünden/Werratal/Witzenhausen. B80 towards Witzenhausen. There are signs to the campsite there.

CC € **18** 1/1-30/6 1/9-31/12 📍 N 51°20'49'' E 09°52'09''

---

## Ahrbrück, D-53506 / Rheinland-Pfalz 📶 iD **781**

🏕 Camping Denntal★★★★
📧 Denntalstraße 49
☎ +49 26 43 69 05
🔓 1/4 - 3/11
@ urlaub@camping-denntal.de

8,2ha 70T(100-120m²) 16A CEE

**1** AD**G**IJKLMOPQ
**2** BCKRUVWX
**3** BHJKLRV
**4** **LN**(Q+R+U+Y 🔓)
**5** **AB**DFGIJLMNOP**U**WXY
**6** ABCDEGK(N 1,5km)OTU

💬 A peaceful and well-equipped campsite located by the Dennbach, a stream in a beautiful valley. Good base for walking, cycling and trips out into the Ahr Valley and Eiffel (also by train). The site has excellent toilets, sauna and fitness.

🚗 A61 Meckenheimer Kreuz exit Altenahr. B257 direction Nürburgring/Adenau. Nearly through Ahrbrück. On Hauptstrasse turn left to Kesseling (L85). After about 800 metres turn right (Dentalstrasse) and follow camping signs.

CC € **20** 1/4-17/4 23/4-27/5 11/6-18/6 24/6-14/7 1/9-1/10 7/10-3/11 📍 N 50°28'55'' E 06°59'22''

## Alf, D-56859 / Rheinland-Pfalz

🏕 Moselcampingplatz Alf
✉ Am Mühlenteich
☎ +49 6 54 29 69 17 28
📅 19/4 - 3/11
@ info@moselcampingplatz.de

2ha 40T(80-100m²) 6-16A CEE

**1** ABDGIJKLMO
**2** BCGLMNRUVX
**3** ABHJRUWX
**4** (A+Q+R+T+U+X+Z 🔒)
**5** **AB**DGIJKLMNPUWZ
**6** ABCDGK(N 1,50km)OTV

🏔 **782**

💬 Surrounded by mountains and countryside and blessed with vineyards, this campsite has been newly opened this year (2018). On the outskirts of the town of Alf on the Moselle.

🚗 A1, exit 125 Wittlich. Via B49 to Alf. On roundabout take first exit. Then follow signs.

Cochem
L98
L106
B421 | L103
A1 | B49 | B53 | L199 | L194
Wengerohr

CC € **16** 22/4-28/5 2/6-6/6 10/6-18/6 23/6-12/7 15/9-3/11 🏔 N 50°03'10'' E 07°06'51''

---

## Bacharach, D-55422 / Rheinland-Pfalz

🏕 Camping Sonnenstrand
✉ Strandbadweg 9
☎ +49 67 43 17 52
📅 29/3 - 31/10
@ info@camping-sonnenstrand.de

1,2ha 45T(100m²) 6A CEE

**1** AD**G**IJKLMO**PQ**
**2** ACFGLRSTWX
**3** BNRU**W**X
**4** (Q+R+U+X+Z 🔒)
**5** **AB**FGIJMNOP**U**W
**6** CDG**K**(N 0,5km)OV

🏔 **783**

💬 Campsite with a sandy beach located directly on the Rhine near the town of Bacharach. Good restaurant. Excellent cycling and walking opportunities. Cycle route along the Rhine. Pitches on the Rhine 2 euros extra. Dutch owner.

🚗 Via the A61. Exit 44 Laudert via Oberwesel to Bacharach (B9). Turn SatNav off after Laudert. Follow signs Oberwesel-Bacharach.

L337
L206 | L338 | L3031
L220 | B9 | L339 | L3033
| | L3272
A61 | L224 | B42 | L3454
L223
L239 | L214 | **Bingen am**
L242 | **Rhein**

CC € **18** 29/3-30/5 10/6-15/7 1/9-31/10 🏔 N 50°03'13'' E 07°46'22''

---

## Bad Dürkheim, D-67098 / Rheinland-Pfalz

🏕 Knaus Campingpark Bad Dürkheim****
✉ In den Almen 1
☎ +49 6 32 26 13 56
📅 1/1 - 31/12
@ badduerkheim@knauscamp.de

16ha 280T(80-160m²) 16A CEE

**1** ACD**G**HIJKLMO**PQ**
**2** ADFGLRSVWX
**3** BD**F**GHJK**MN**O**P**RUW**Z**
**4** **N**(Q+R+T+U 15/3-30/11)
    (V 1/2-31/12)
    (Y+Z 15/3-30/11)
**5** **AB**DFGIJKLMNOP**S**TUWZ
**6** ABCEGH**K**(N 1km)OTV

🏔 **784**

💬 A very attractive campsite in the middle of the wine area with vineyards on the campsite. Located next to a small airfield but with little disturbance, and a site suitable for longer stays.

🚗 A61, exit 60 Autobahnkreuz (motorway intersection) Ludwigshafen. Then route 650 to Bad Dürkheim. At the second traffic lights turn right and then immediately turn right again at the second road.

**Frankenthal (Pfalz)**
L520
A6 | L454 | A61
B37
B271
B39 | A65

CC € **20** 1/1-29/5 3/6-7/6 16/6-12/7 2/9-31/12 🏔 N 49°28'23'' E 08°11'29''

## Bockenau, D-55595 / Rheinland-Pfalz 📶 iD 785

🏕 Camping Bockenauer Schweiz
✉ Daubacher Brücke 3
☎ +49 6 75 62 98
🕐 23/3 - 20/9
@ campingbockenauerschweiz@
  gmail.com

20ha 60T(< 100m²) 16A CEE

**1** **A**GIJKLMOPQ
**2** BCGLRTUX
**3** BHJ
**4** (Q+R+U+V+Y+Z 🔑)
**5** **AB**DGIJKLMNOPU
**6** ACEG**JK**(N 8km)V

💬 A lovely campsite but with few shaded pitches. The campsite has a speciality restaurant featuring German cuisine. Plenty of walking and cycling opportunities.

🚗 A61 exit 51 Bad Kreuznach. Follow B41 to Wald Bockelheim, then towards Bockenau/Winterburg.

CC € 16  23/3-30/6  31/8-20/9  🧭 N 49°51'05'' E 07°39'34''

---

## Bollendorf, D-54669 / Rheinland-Pfalz ♿ 📶 iD 786

🏕 Camping Altschmiede****
☎ +49 6 52 63 75
🕐 1/4 - 31/10
@ info@camping-altschmiede.de

5,5ha 250T 6A CEE

**1** **A**GIJKLOPQ
**2** CKLRSVWX
**3** AHJNRU**WX**
**4** (A 1/7-21/8) (C 1/6-31/8) IJ
  (Q 1/5-21/8) (R 1/6-21/8)
  (T 6/7-18/8) (U 1/6-21/8)
  (Z 🔑)
**5** **AB**DEFGIJKLMNO**P**UZ
**6** AEGJ(N 2km)V

💬 Everyone is a guest on this campsite; you'll feel really at home. Set on the grassy banks of a river. Excellent toilet facilities. It even has its own cows and own distillery! Really unique! Free heated pool during the summer months with 3 slides.

🚗 B257 from Bitburg, exit Echternacherbrück. Right direction Bollendorf before the border bridge. In village direction Körperich. It is the 2nd campsite and is signposted.

CC € 18  1/4-29/5  24/6-5/7  28/8-31/10  🧭 N 49°50'28'' E 06°20'13''

---

## Bullay (Mosel), D-56859 / Rheinland-Pfalz 📶 iD 787

🏕 Bären-Camp****
✉ Am Moselufer 1 + 3
☎ +49 65 42 90 00 97
🕐 18/4 - 10/11
@ info@baeren-camp.de

1,9ha 150T(70-105m²) 16A CEE

**1** ACD**G**HIJKLM**P**Q
**2** CGRVWXY
**3** AHJN**WX**
**4** (A 1/7-1/9) (Q+R+U+X 🔑)
  (Y 18/4-31/10)
**5** **AB**DFGIJKLMNO**P**UWZ
**6** ACEG**K**(N 0,2km)OT

💬 'Bären-Camp' is surrounded by the Marienburg, Arras Castle and steep vineyards. There are very sunny pitches on the campsite, but also shaded pitches. The site has a very attractive restaurant. The campsite is located beside the Moselle on the Moselle cycle route.

🚗 A1 exit 125 Wittlich, via B49 to Alf. Then cross the bridge to Bullay.

CC € 18  18/4-7/7  25/8-9/11  🧭 N 50°03'14'' E 07°07'49''

## Bürder, D-56589 / Rheinland-Pfalz ♿ 📶 iD 788

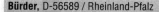

▲ Camping
  Zum stillen Winkel*****
✉ Brunnenweg 1c
☎ +49 1 57 77 72 22 16
🗓 29/3 - 3/11
@ info@
  camping-zumstillenwinkel.de
5ha 90T(100-150m²) 16A CEE

1 ACDGIJKLMOPQ
2 BCGLRUWXY
3 ABHJNRUWX
4 (Q+R+U 🗓)
5 ABCDEFGHIJKLMNOPQRS
  UWXYZ
6 AEGK(N 4km)OTV

💬 A friendly, attractive campsite situated by a river with all the camping pitches on the river bank. New and luxurious toilet facilities. Fresh bread available daily and a restaurant-delivery service. Beautiful hilly surroundings where peace and relaxation play an important role. Dutch warden.

🚗 A3, exit 36 Neuwied towards Neuwied, and then drive towards Kurtscheid. Continue to Niederbreitbach then turn left towards Neuwied as far as Bürder exit. Campsite sign number 2.

CC € 18  29/3-28/5  12/6-18/6  24/6-12/7  1/9-3/11

📍 N 50°30'56'' E 07°25'46''

---

## Burgen, D-56332 / Rheinland-Pfalz ♿ 📶 iD 789

▲ Camping Burgen****
✉ Am Moselufer
☎ +49 26 05 23 96
🗓 10/4 - 13/10
@ info@camping-burgen.de

4ha 120T(60-100m²) 16A

1 ADGHIJKLMOPQ
2 CGKORVWXY
3 BHJNRUWX
4 (B 31/5-15/9) (Q+R 🗓)
5 ABDFGIJKLMNOPSUWZ
6 ACDFGHK(N 9km)OTUV

💬 Burgen campsite is just 300m from the village of Burgen, right by the Moselle, with wonderful views of the Bischofstein castle. An ideal starting point for walks, bike rides and trips out along the Moselle. Excellent amenities complete the picture. Arrival is not possible between 13:00 and 15:00 due to the afternoon break.

🚗 Follow the A61 and take exit 39 Dieblich. Then follow the B49 towards Cochem/Trier as far as the edge of the village Burgen.

CC € 18  10/4-26/5  24/6-7/7  26/8-13/10

📍 N 50°12'53'' E 07°23'24''

---

## Burgen, D-56332 / Rheinland-Pfalz ♿ 📶 iD 790

▲ Knaus Campingpark
  Burgen/Mosel
✉ Am Bootshafen(B49)
☎ +49 26 05 95 21 76
🗓 1/4 - 20/10
@ mosel@knauscamp.de

4ha 120T(80-120m²) 16A CEE

1 ACDGHIJKLMOPQ
2 CGKLRSWX
3 AHJRWX
4 (C 15/5-15/9)
  (Q+R+T+U+X+Y+Z 🗓)
5 ABDFGIJKLMNOPUWZ
6 ACDFK(N 6km)OTU

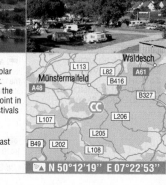

💬 A beautiful campsite located directly on the Moselle overlooking a romantic castle. Small, solar heated, swimming pool, restaurant and harbour. You can go canoeing, water skiing or fishing on the Moselle. This site is of course a good starting point in low season for visiting one of the lively wine festivals in the area.

🚗 A61 exit 39 Dieblich. Follow the B49 until past Burgen.

CC € 20  1/4-29/5  3/6-7/6  24/6-15/7  1/9-20/10

📍 N 50°12'19'' E 07°22'53''

## Dausenau, D-56132 / Rheinland-Pfalz ♿ 🛜 iD 791

🏕 Camping Lahn Beach
📧 Hallgarten 16
☎ +49 2 60 31 39 64
📅 1/4 - 31/10
@ info@canutours.de

3ha 80T(80m²) 6-16A CEE

**1** AGIJKLMO**P**Q
**2** CGLRTWX
**3** BGNR**W**X
**4** (Q+V+Z ⌂)
**5** **AB**GIJKLMNO**P**UW
**6** CFG**K**(N 4km)OT

💬 A campsite located in the Nassau national park between 'Lahnbergen' directly on the river and on the R36 walking and cycle route. Cycle and canoe rental at the campsite. Spacious pitches, well maintained toilet facilities, informal atmosphere.

🚗 Campsite located on the B260 and the Lahn between Nassau (4 km) and Bad Ems (4 km).
In Dausenau cross the bridge over the Lahn then turn right.

CC €18 1/4-25/5 23/6-30/6 18/8-30/10    N 50°19'39'' E 07°45'19''

## Diez an der Lahn, D-65582 / Rheinland-Pfalz 🛜 iD 792

🏕 Camping Oranienstein
📧 Strandbadweg 1a
☎ +49 64 32 21 22
📅 1/4 - 27/10
@ info@camping-diez.de

7ha 150T(100m²) 10A CEE

**1** ADGHIJKLMO**P**Q
**2** CFGLRTUWX
**3** AGJKRU**W**X
**4** (Q+Q+R+T+U+X+Z ⌂)
**5** **AB**DFGI**J**K**L**MNO**P**UWZ
**6** CDEG**K**(N 2km)OT

💬 Well-maintained campsite on the left bank of the river Lahn. The campsite is suitable for anglers and canoeists. Walking and cycling routes are also popular. Also very good stopover campsite.

🚗 A3 Köln-Frankfurt am Main, exit 41 Diez. Follow the signs to the campsite.

CC €18 1/5-29/5 24/6-30/6 1/9-27/10    N 50°22'53'' E 08°00'02''

## Dockweiler, D-54552 / Rheinland-Pfalz ♿ 🛜 iD 793

🏕 Campingpark Dockweiler Mühle
📧 Mühlenweg 1
☎ +49 65 95 96 11 30
📅 1/1 - 31/12
@ info@
campingpark-dockweiler-muehle.de

10ha 100T(80-90m²) 16A

**1** ACD**G**HIJKLMOPQ
**2** CDFGJLRUVWX
**3** BGHJRW
**5** **AB**DFGIJKLMNO**P**UWZ
**6** ACDEG**K**(N 8km)OTU

💬 A large campsite located in a protected area with its own fishing lake. There are pitches for tourists on the terrace next to the permanent pitches, but there is also a separate field surrounded by a hedge.

🚗 A61 and A1 direction Daun. Via Hillesheim and B410 follow campsite signs.

CC €18 1/1-26/5 11/6-30/6 26/8-31/12    N 50°15'20'' E 06°46'47''

## Echternacherbrück, D-54668 / Rheinland-Pfalz

&♿ 🛜 iD **794**

🏕 Campingpark Freibad
Echternacherbrück
✉ Mindenerstraße 18
☎ +49 6 52 53 40
🗓 1/4 - 15/10
@ info@echternacherbrueck.de

8ha 400T 12A CEE

1 ADGIJKLMOPRS
2 CGLRVXY
3 BGHJKNQRUWX
4 (A 1/7-31/8) (C+G 1/5-15/9) J
(Q+S+T+U+V 🔒) (X 1/5-1/9)
(Z 1/5-30/9)
5 ABDEFGIJKLMNOPUWZ
6 CFIK(N 0,3km)OV

💬 Plenty of trees and grass on marked out pitches.
From the campsite you can walk across the bridge
into Echternach in Luxembourg! (Really nice). Extra
charge for pitches on the river.

🚗 From Maastricht-Verviers direction
St. Vith/Bitburg. Then to Echternach direction
Echternacherbrück. Campsite signposted.

CC € **18** 1/4-29/5 24/6-5/7 28/8-15/10

🧭 N 49°48'44'' E 06°25'53''

---

## Ediger/Eller, D-56814 / Rheinland-Pfalz

🛜 iD **795**

🏕 Camping Zum Feuerberg
✉ Moselweinstraße
☎ +49 2 67 57 01
🗓 15/3 - 31/10
@ info@zum-feuerberg.de

1,8ha 165T(100-150m²) 16A CEE

1 ACDGIJKLMOPQ
2 CGLMRVWXY
3 EFHJKLRWX
4 (A 🔒) (B 19/5-30/9) (Z 🔒)
5 ABDFGIJKLMNOPUWZ
6 CEGK(N 0,3km)OTU

💬 This residential campsite on the Moselle is
located close to the picturesque wine village of
Ediger/Eller at the foot of the 'Calmont', Europe's
steepest vineyard hill. The campsite has a friendly
restaurant. Campsite is on the "Moselle cycling
route".

🚗 A48 exit 3 Laubach dir. Cochem then towards
Senheim and another 4 km along the Moselle. Don't
use SatNav but follow the Moselle to Cochem.

CC € **18** 15/3-29/5 3/6-7/6 11/6-19/6 24/6-30/6 1/9-5/9 9/9-31/10

🧭 N 50°05'30'' E 07°09'48''

---

## Erden, D-54492 / Rheinland-Pfalz

&♿ 🛜 iD **796**

🏕 Camping Erden
✉ Am Moselufer 1
☎ +49 65 32 40 60
🗓 6/4 - 3/11
@ camping-erden@gmx.de

2ha 70T(80-120m²) 16A CEE

1 AGIJKLMOPQ
2 CFKLRSWXY
3 BDHJKRUWX
4 (Q+R+T+U+X+Z 🔒)
5 ABFGIJKLMNOPWZ
6 CDFGK(N 4,5km)OTUV

💬 The campsite for top wines! Situated directly on
the Moselle and the Moselradweg cycle path. Peace,
space and enjoyment.

🚗 A1 exit Wittlich direction Bernkastel Kues.
In Zeltingen cross bridge towards Traben-Trarbach.

CC € **20** 6/4-5/7 4/9-27/9 8/10-2/11

🧭 N 49°58'48'' E 07°01'13''

## Gerbach, D-67813 / Rheinland-Pfalz 📶 iD 797

🏕 Camping Donnersberg
✉ Kahlenbergweiher 1
☎ +49 63 61 82 87
📅 30/3 - 15/9
@ info@campingdonnersberg.com

10ha 130T(80-140m²) 10A CEE

**1** ADG IJKLPQ
**2** BCIJLRTVWXY
**3** BFHIJKLMNR
**4** (A 1/7-31/8) (B 1/7-30/9) N
   (Q+R+T+U+Y 🛁)
**5** ABCDEFGIJKLMNOPQUWX
**6** AEGK(N 9,9km)OTV

💬 A beautifully situated campsite in the woods with plenty of walking opportunities. The camping pitches are spread over several fields around a small lake. The campsite has a Biotop swimming pool. Opportunities for outdoor activities.

🚗 From the A61 exit 54 (A63 Kirscheim-Bolanden). From the A63 exit 11 at the L401 dir. Rockenhausen. Turn right at the intersection with the 404, then follow camping signs at the 385 towards Gerbach. Don't use SatNav.

L404
L405
B420
**Kirchheimbolanden**
CC
A63

CC €20 30/3-18/4 22/4-29/5 2/6-6/6 10/6-19/6 23/6-7/7 1/9-15/9 📍 N 49°40'14'' E 07°53'11''

---

## Gerolstein, D-54568 / Rheinland-Pfalz 📶 iD 798

🏕 Camping Eifelblick /
   Waldferienpark Gerolstein****
✉ Hillenseifen 200
☎ +49 6 59 16 78
📅 10/2 - 17/11
@ waldferienpark-gerolstein@
   t-online.de

2ha 50T(100-120m²) 16A CEE

**1** ADG IJKLMPQ
**2** JKRTUVW
**3** BDFGHJNQRU
**4** (F 🛁) N(Q+T+U+X+Y+Z 🛁)
**5** ABCDFGHIJMNOPUWXYZ
**6** ACDEGHK(N 5km)OTV

💬 You will have panoramic views of the hills from this terraced campsite. The site forms part of an established holiday park whose many facilities can also be used by camping guests. Free entry to indoor swimming pool.

🚗 Coming from Prüm (B410) Waldferienpark Gerolstein is indicated 4 km before Gerolstein exit Hinterhausen.

Hillesheim
B51
Prüm
CC
Gerolstein
L24
L30    L29
L16    B257
L32
A60    L46

CC €18 10/2-7/7 1/9-17/11 📍 N 50°13'02'' E 06°36'28''

---

## Gillenfeld, D-54558 / Rheinland-Pfalz 📶 iD 799

🏕 Feriendorf Pulvermaar
✉ Vulkanstraße
☎ +49 65 73 99 65 00
📅 1/1 - 31/12
@ info@feriendorf-pulvermaar.de

4ha 50T(60-120m²) 16A CEE

**1** AGHIJKLOPQ
**2** DFKLRTUWXY
**3** ABHJLNRWZ
**4** (A 1/4-30/11) (Q 1/3-1/12)
   (R 🛁) (T+U 21/4-1/12)
   (Z 1/3-1/12)
**5** ABDFGIJKLMNOPUWZ
**6** ACDEGJ(N 2km)OTU

💬 Campsite on the Pulvermaar, a volcanic lake (the deepest lake in the Eifel). Volcano themed excursions. You can go hunting for minerals with a guide. A perfect base for walks, bike rides and mountain bike tours. You can swim in the volcanic lake for a fee.

🚗 A1 exit 121 Mehren. Turn right to B421 towards Zell. Sign to campsite after 6.7 km 'Feriendorf'.

Ulmen
**Daun**    A48    B259
Neroth    L102
CC
L46    L52    L106
Bettenfeld    L103
A1

CC €16 1/1-29/5 3/6-7/6 12/6-19/6 24/6-5/7 26/8-31/12 📍 N 50°07'52'' E 06°56'00''

**Girod**, D-3412 / Rheinland-Pfalz    ♿ **iD** **800**

▲ Camping Eisenbachtal
☎ +49 6 49 38
FAX +49 6 2
⌚ 1/1

(80m²) 6A CEE

KLMOPQ
TUVWX
U
-15/9) M(Q 8/6-31/8)
⌚
GIJKLMNO**P**UWXYZ
G(N 1km)OTV

💬 In natural countryside at the foot of an old volcano in the Nassau Nature Park. Interesting biotopes have been laid out including a natural lake. Visitors are informed and children challenged to an adventure in nature and technology. Well marked out walking and cycling paths. Also suitable as a stopover campsite, being a short distance from the A3 motorway.

🚗 A3 Köln-Frankfurt exit 41 Wallmerod/Diez. Then dir. Montabaur. Campsite 5 km further (see sign).

L303   L300   L3364
B255   L316
  B54
L314
A3   CC   B8
  L3462
L309   L313   **Limburg an**
L329   L326   **der Lahn**
L327   B417   L318

CC € **18**   1/4-15/7   1/9-30/9     N 50°26'16'' E 07°54'16''

---

**Guldental**, D-55452 / Rheinland-Pfalz    ♿ 📶 ✿ **iD** **801**

▲ Campingpark Lindelgrund
🏠 Im Lindelgrund 1
☎ +49 6 70 76 33
⌚ 15/3 - 30/11
@ info@lindelgrund.de

8ha 48T(80m²) 10A CEE

**1** ACD**G**HIJKLOPQ
**2** FJRTUX
**3** BGHJKRU
**4** (Q+Y 15/4-15/10)
**5** **AB**DGHIJKLMNOPQRUWXYZ
**6** ACDEG**K**(N 1,5km)OTV

💬 Terraced campsite with grass cover, some shaded pitches. Narrow gauge railway museum and sandpit on the site. Suitable as a stopover campsite. At 8 pitches, caravans do not have to be uncoupled.

🚗 A61 exit 47 Waldlaubersheim, through Windesheim/Guldental. Follow the camping signs beyond Guldental.

A61   **Bingen am**   **Ingelheim**
  **Rhein**   **am Rhein**

**Bad Kreuznach**   CC

B41   B48

CC € **20**   15/3-25/5   12/6-30/6   2/9-25/10     N 49°53'03'' E 07°51'25''

---

**Hausbay/Pfalzfeld**, D-56291 / Rheinland-Pfalz    📶 **iD** **802**

▲ Country Camping
   Schinderhannes****
🏠 Campingplatz 1
☎ +49 6 74 68 00 54 40
⌚ 1/1 - 31/12
@ info@countrycamping.de

30ha 350T(100-120m²) 16A CEE

**1** ACD**G**IJKLMOPQ
**2** DFJLRTWXY
**3** BHJ**M**NR**TUW**Z
**4** (Q+R+U ⌚) (Y 16/2-19/10)
**5** **AB**DFGIJKLMNOP**R**UWXYZ
**6** ABCDEG**J**(N 1km)OTV

💬 A large campsite with shaded pitches around a swimming lake. There is a restaurant and a small shop in the grounds. You can enjoy peace, healthy air and panoramic views of the Hunsrück from here. Excellent cycling and walking opportunities from the campsite. Suitable both for longer stays and as a stopover campsite.

🚗 A61 exit 43 Pfalzfeld, then follow the camping signs (3 km). Enter: Hausbayerstraße/Pfalzfeld into your SatNav.

B9
A61   Oberwesel
CC   B42
Kastellaun
L214
B327   L219
Rheinböllen

CC € **18**   1/1-1/7   18/8-31/12     N 50°06'21'' E 07°34'04''

## Heidenburg, D-54426 / Rheinland-Pfalz

&#9650; Camping Moselhöhe★★★★
&#9993; Bucherweg 1
&#9742; +49 6 50 99 90 16
&#8986; 1/4 - 1/11
@ vandijk1968@hotmail.com

&#9855; &#128246; **iD** 803

3ha 65T(100-120m²) 16A CEE

**1** A**G**HIJKLMO**P**Q
**2** FGJKRVWX
**3** ABDHNRU
**4** (B 1/5-1/9) (Q &#8986;)
   (X+Z 1/4-1/10)
**5** **AB**CDFGIJKLMNOPUWXY
**6** ACDEGJ**K**LOT

&#128172; You have wonderful views of the hilltops around the Moselle valley from this hilltop terraced campsite. Enjoy the clean air and the peace. A good base for sports activities and for trips out to Trier, Bernkastel-Kues and Idar-Oberstein, for example.

&#128663; A1, take exit 131 Mehring towards Thalfang. 7 km till the sign to the campsite, turn left towards Heidenburg at the Talling crossing.

Hetzerath · L50 · B53 · L157 · L155 · Morbac · **CC** · Mertesdorf · A1 · L150 · B327 · B52 · L148 · L164 · L152

**CC** € **18** 1/4-30/6 1/9-31/10     &#9650; N 49°47'58'' E 06°55'37''

---

## Irrel, D-54666 / Rheinland-Pfalz

&#9650; Camping Nimseck★★★
&#9742; +49 6 52 53 14
&#8986; 16/3 - 3/11
@ info@camping-nimseck.de

&#9855; &#128246; **iD** 804

7ha 150T(100-120m²) 16A CEE

**1** A**G**IJKLOPRS
**2** CFIJKLRTVWXY
**3** AHJRUX
**4** (C 15/6-31/8) (Q 15/6-15/8)
   (T+U 1/6-15/8) (Y+Z &#8986;)
**5** **AB**DFGIJKLMNOPUWYZ
**6** ACEGK(N 0,5km)OV

&#128172; Well maintained campsite with its own heated pool, nestling peacefully in undulating grassland close to the border with Luxembourg. Plenty of shaded pitches.

&#128663; B257 from Bitburg direction Echternach. Take exit Irrel, campsite on your left. Signposted.

L2 · B257 · B51 · N19 · L3 · B422 · Echternach · N10 · N11 · Trierweiler · **Trier**

**CC** € **16** 16/3-6/7 24/8-3/11 7=6, 14=12     &#9650; N 49°51'13'' E 06°27'45''

---

## Irrel, D-54666 / Rheinland-Pfalz

&#9650; Camping Südeifel
&#9993; Hofstraße 19
&#9742; +49 6 52 55 10
&#8986; 1/4 - 31/10
@ info@camping-suedeifel.de

&#9855; &#128246; **iD** 805

3ha 60T 6A CEE

**1** AD**G**IJKLOPRS
**2** CFGLRWX
**3** BDHJRU**W**X
**4** (A 1/7-31/8)
   (Q+T+X+Z 1/5-30/9)
**5** **AB**FGIJKLMNOPUWXZ
**6** AEG**K**(N 0,5km)OV

&#128172; Relax on grasslands next to a river just a few kilometres from the Luxembourg border. Friendly bar on the site, supermarket close by. Wifi at every pitch. Luxurious toilet facilities. Quiet campsite with central location and level pitches.

&#128663; B257 Bitburg-Echternach. Take exit Irrel towards the village (Ortsmitte). There are signs to the campsite.

L2 · B257 · B51 · N19 · L3 · Kordel · Echternach · N10 · N11 · B418 · **Trier**

**CC** € **16** 1/4-6/7 24/8-31/10 7=6, 14=12     &#9650; N 49°50'31'' E 06°27'26''

## Lahnstein, D-56112 / Rheinland-Pfalz

📶 **iD** **806**

🏕 Camping Wolfsmühle
✉ Hohenrhein 79
☎ +49 26 21 25 89
🗓 15/3 - 1/11
@ info@camping-wolfsmuehle.de

3ha 150T(70-150m²) 6A CEE

**1** ADG**I**JKLMOP**Q**
**2** CLRTVWX
**3** BRU**W**X
**4** (Q 🗓) (R+T+X+Z 1/4-1/11)
**5** **AB**DG**I**JLMNPUW
**6** ACDFGHJ(N 2km)OTV

💬 Popular with guests for years, located directly on Lahn in romantic Lahntal valley. Many cycling and walking options. Beautiful, even grounds with heated toilet facilities and restaurant. Very centrally located, Koblenz easily accessible by bike and bus (7 km). Dutch owner.

🚗 A61 or A3 to Koblenz A48 exit Vallendar B42 to Koblenz then Rüdesheim exit Oberlahnstein. First right at roundabout. Follow signs. Put Ostallee in your SatNav. Then follow camping signs.

Koblenz — A48 — L329 — B261 — B416 — B49 — **Bad Ems** — A61 — B9 — L335 — L334

CC € **18** 15/3-7/7 24/8-1/11

🏔 N 50°18'52'' E 07°37'40''

---

## Langsur/Metzdorf, D-54308 / Rheinland-Pfalz

♿ 📶 **iD** **807**

🏕 Camping Alter Bahnhof***
✉ Uferstraße 42
☎ +49 6 50 11 26 26
🗓 1/3 - 31/12
@ info@camping-metzdorf.de

2,2ha 53T(50-120m²) 16A CEE

**1** ACDG**I**JKLMOP**Q**
**2** BCFGRUWXY
**3** ABGHJRT**W**X
**4** (Q 1/5-1/10) (U+Y+Z 🗓)
**5** **AB**DFG**I**JMNOP**QR**UZ
**6** ACDFG**K**(N 5km)OTV

💬 The campsite is situated on the border between Germany and Luxembourg on the banks of the River Sauer. This river offers opportunities for fishing and canoeing. Excellent cycle paths in area. Relaxed atmosphere.

🚗 E44 towards Luxembourg exit Mertert (Luxembourg). On the N1 towards Wasserbillig. In Wasserbillig turn left on B418 after the bridge over the River Sauer. Approx. 6 km further.

N10 — L1 — B418 — B51 — B52 — N11 — A64 **Trier** — Boudler — N14 — **Konz** — B268 — N1 — L136

CC € **16** 1/3-1/7 1/9-31/12

🏔 N 49°45'11'' E 06°30'08''

---

## Leiwen, D-54340 / Rheinland-Pfalz

♿ 📶 **iD** **808**

🏕 Camping Landal Sonnenberg*****
✉ Sonnenberg 1
☎ +49 6 50 79 36 90
🗓 29/3 - 4/11
@ sonnenberg@landal.com

2,5ha 125T(65-120m²) 10A CEE

**1** ACDG**I**JKLMOP**Q**
**2** BJRTUVWXY
**3** ABCD**F**HJKN**Q**R**T**
**4** (A+F+H 🗓) K
 (Q+S+T+U+X+Y 🗓)
**5** **AB**DFG**I**JMNOPQRUWZ
**6** ABCEGHJ**K**L(N 4km)OST

💬 A family campsite on a wooded plateau above the Moselle vineyards. Many indoor and outdoor activities (including an indoor pool with whirlpool, indoor playground with climbing wall, 'vinotheque', bowling alley, climbing wood, large playground, animal park with deer). These good facilities make it very suitable for camping holidays outside the high season.

🚗 A1 Koblenz-Trier, exit 128 Föhren-Leiwen. Follow signs Sonnenberg.

Zemmer — L49 — A1 — B53 — L155 — Mehring — B52 — L150 — Osburg — A1

CC € **18** 29/3-14/4 3/5-29/5 3/6-7/6 24/6-7/7 30/8-27/9

🏔 N 49°48'12'' E 06°53'30''

**Lingerhahn,** D-56291 / Rheinland-Pfalz  📶 ✿ iD **809**

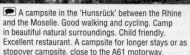

🔺 Camping und Mobilheimpark
    Am Mühlenteich★★★★
☎ +49 6 74 65 33
🔓 1/1 - 31/12
@ info@muehlenteich.de

15ha 150T 6-16A CEE

**1** AD**G**HIJKLMOPQ
**2** BCFILRTWXY
**3** BCHJNRU
**4** (A 1/7-15/8)
    (B+Q+R+T+U+Y+Z 🔓)
**5** **AB**DFGIJKLMNO**P**UWZ
**6** CDEG**K**(N 1km)OTV

💬 A campsite in the 'Hunsrück' between the Rhine and the Moselle. Good walking and cycling. Camp in beautiful natural surroundings. Child friendly. Excellent restaurant. A campsite for longer stays or as stopover campsite, close to the A61 motorway.

🚗 A61 exit 44 Laudert, direction Laudert. In Laudert direction Lingerhahn. Follow the camping signs (4 km). Your navigation system may show another route; but still follow the signs.

CC € **20**  1/1-24/6  9/9-31/12    🏔 N 50°05'57'' E 07°34'25''

---

**Mendig,** D-56743 / Rheinland-Pfalz  ♿ 📶 iD **810**

🔺 Camping Siesta
📧 Laacherseestrasse 6a
☎ +49 26 52 14 32
🔓 1/4 - 31/10
@ walter.boehler@t-online.de

3ha 100T 16A CEE

**1** A**G**HIJKLMOP
**2** FIRWXY
**3** BR
**4** (Q+R+Z 🔓)
**5** **AB**GIJKMNOPU
**6** DFGJ(N 2km)OT

💬 A small campsite 200m from the A61, primarily suitable as a stopover campsite. Hunt for stones from volcanoes and quarries in the area.

🚗 A61 exit Mendig. Turn right at the end of the exit and then drive towards Maria Laach. After approx. 100 metres turn right and drive through the car park to the campsite.

CC € **18**  1/4-30/6  1/9-31/10    🏔 N 50°23'14'' E 07°16'09''

---

**Monzingen,** D-55569 / Rheinland-Pfalz  👫 ♿ 📶 iD **811**

🔺 Camping Nahemühle
📧 Nahemühle 1
☎ +49 67 51 74 75
🔓 1/3 - 31/10
@ info@camping-nahemuehle.de

7,5ha 150T(80-100m²) 16A CEE

**1** AD**G**HIJKLMOPQ
**2** CLNORTWX
**3** BGHJKNR**W**X
**4** (A 1/6-1/10)
    (Q+R+T+U+Y+Z 🔓)
**5** **AB**DEFGIJMNOP**S**UWZ
**6** ACDEGJ(N 2km)OT

💬 Large grounds with both marked out and open pitches. Plenty of walking and cycling opportunities. 20 km from Idar-Oberstein jewellery town. Situated on the Naheweinstrasse tourist route.

🚗 On the B41 between Bad Kreuznach and Idar-Oberstein. Turn off at campsite sign in Monzingen, over level crossing then immediately right.

CC € **20**  15/3-15/4  2/5-29/5  10/6-19/6  1/9-30/9    🏔 N 49°47'45'' E 07°34'42''

## Neuerburg, D-54673 / Rheinland-Pfalz

 ♿ 📶 **iD** **812**

🏕 Camping in der Enz****
🏠 In der Enz 25
☎ +49 65 64 26 60
🗓 16/3 - 31/10
@ info@camping-inderenz.com

6ha 77T(80-100m²) 16A CEE

**1** ACD**G**IJKLOP**Q**
**2** CRTV**WX**
**3** BHJ**MOR**U**W**
**4** (C+H 15/5-1/9) J(Q 🚿)
  (T+U 1/6-31/8)
**5** **AB**DEFGIJKLMNO**P**UWXY
**6** ACDEGK(N 1,5km)O

💬 Campsite on grassland in the woods with excellent toilet facilities. Good cycling and walking opportunities close to the historic town of Neuerburg. Campsite run by an enthusiastic Dutch couple.

🚗 From E42, in Germany A60 exit 3 direction Neuerburg. Via Arzfeld to Emmelbaum and Zweifelscheid. After 3 km turn left at Camping In der Enz. Signposted.

**CC** € **18** 16/3-6/7 24/8-31/10

🗺 N 50°01'40'' E 06°16'37''

---

## Obernhof/Lahn, D-56379 / Rheinland-Pfalz

 📶 **iD** **813**

🏕 Camping Schloß Langenau
🏠 An der B417
☎ 📠 +49 26 04 46 66
🗓 1/4 - 31/10

6,1ha 140T 16A CEE

**1** A**G**IJKLMOP**Q**
**2** CLRUW**X**Y
**3** BU**W**X
**4** (Q+R+U+X 🚿)
**5** **AB**DGIJMNOPU
**6** CEGJ(N 5km)OT

💬 Quiet campsite with lovely location on the Lahn river. Beautiful, even grounds with well-maintained toilet facilities. Cycling, walking, fishing and canoeing are options here.

🚗 Campsite located on B417. Closest exit on A3 is exit 40 Montabaur, about 5 km from Nassau, dir. Obernhof.

**CC** € **16** 1/4-15/7 1/9-31/10

🗺 N 50°18'33'' E 07°50'33''

---

## Oberweis, D-54636 / Rheinland-Pfalz

 ♿ 📶 ✿ **iD** **814**

🏕 Prümtal-Camping Oberweis*****
🏠 In der Klaus 17
☎ +49 6 52 79 29 20
🗓 1/1 - 31/12
@ info@pruemtal.de

3,8ha 240T(65-100m²) 16A CEE

**1** AD**G**IJKLOP**Q**
**2** C**G**LRUVW**X**Y
**3** BHJN**R**U**W**X
**4** (A 15/5-30/8) (C+H 1/5-1/9) J
  (Q+R 🚿) (T 1/6-21/8)
  (U+V+X+Y+Z 🚿)
**5** **AB**DEFGIJKLMNOP**R**UWXY
  Z
**6** ACDEGIK(N 9km)OSTUV

💬 Ideal campsite in the Eifel with plenty of amenities. Lovely swimming pool. Marked out pitches on grass. Excellent restaurant. Very friendly and enthusiastic owner. Winner of the golden medal Germany 2006 and Warden of the Year 2011. Free wifi on the campsite. You can occupy any pitches with CCA, including those with water, power and drainage!

🚗 B50 from Bitburg direction Vianden. Turn left in the centre of the village. Follow the signs campsite and swimming pool.

**CC** € **20** 1/1-6/7 25/8-31/12

🗺 N 49°57'32'' E 06°25'28''

## Oberwesel, D-55430 / Rheinland-Pfalz  🛜 iD 815

🏕 Camping Schönburgblick
🏠 Aussiedlung B9
☎ +49 67 44 71 45 01
📅 15/3 - 3/11
@ camping-oberwesel@t-online.de

0,8ha 40T(80m²) 6-10A CEE

**1** **AG**HIJKLMOQ
**2** CFGKNRUVWX
**3** AJ**W**
**4** (Q) (T+U 18/4-3/10)
**5** **AB**GIJMNOPUW
**6** ABCDFG**K**(N 0,25km)O

💬 A small campsite directly on the banks of the Rhine near Oberwesel. Wonderful views of the Rhine. Watch the boats sail upstream and downstream. Supermarket 200m, city centre 1 km. Rhine cycle route goes past the campsite. Closed lunchtimes from 13:00 to 14:00.

🚗 A61, exit 44 Laudert. Located directly on the B9 in Oberwesel.

CC € **18** 15/3-30/5 10/6-14/7 1/9-8/9 22/9-3/11 📍 N 50°06'08'' E 07°44'11''

---

## Otterberg, D-67697 / Rheinland-Pfalz  🛜 ✿ iD 816

🏕 Camping Gänsedell
🏠 In der Gänsedell 1
☎ +49 63 01 55 37
📅 1/1 - 31/12
@ info@camping-otterberg.de

2,6ha 30T(80m²) 16A CEE

**1** **AG**HIJKLMOPQ
**2** BFJRTVWXY
**3** A**M**N
**4** (V) 
**5** **AB**GIJKLMNOPUW
**6** DEGJ(N 1km)OT

NEW

💬 The campsite is located in a wide strip on the edge of the forest, in a quiet, south facing slope just a few metres from the beautiful natural swimming pool Otterberg, and about 10 minutes from the village.

🚗 B40 exit Otterberg. In Otterberg go in the direction of Rockenhausen. The campsite is located on the left after 1 km.

CC € **16** 1/1-19/4 2/5-30/5 11/6-1/7 15/9-31/12 📍 N 49°30'44'' E 07°46'58''

---

## Pommern, D-56829 / Rheinland-Pfalz  🧑‍🧒 ♿ 🛜 iD 817

🏕 Camping Pommern
🏠 Moselweinstraße 12
☎ +49 26 72 24 61
📅 1/4 - 31/10
@ campingpommern@netscape.net

4,5ha 250T(60-100m²) 16A

**1** AD**G**IJKLMO**P**Q
**2** CGLRUVWXY
**3** ABGHJRU**W**X
**4** (B+G 1/5-15/9)
      (Q+R+T+U)
      (V+Y 15/4-15/10) (Z)
**5** **AB**DEFGIJKLMNOPUWZ
**6** ACFGJK(N 4km)OTUV

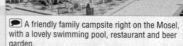

💬 A friendly family campsite right on the Mosel, with a lovely swimming pool, restaurant and beer garden.

🚗 A61 Koblenz, exit B416 Cochem/Trier.

CC € **18** 1/4-7/7 25/8-31/10 10=9 📍 N 50°10'08'' E 07°15'56''

## Pünderich, D-56862 / Rheinland-Pfalz

**818**

🏕 Camping Moselland
📧 Im Planters
☎ +49 65 42 26 18
🔓 1/4 - 26/10
@ campingplatz.moselland@
   googlemail.com

3,1ha 150T 16A CEE

**1** AG**I**JKLMOPQ
**2** CKLRVWXY
**3** ABHJNRU**W**X
**4** (Q+R+T+U+Z 🔓)
**5** **AB**DGIJMNO**P**UWXZ
**6** CDEGIJ(N 1,5km)OV

💬 Relaxed camping on large sunny or shaded pitches on the banks of the Moselle at Moselland Campsite. The starting point for many wonderful cycle trips along the Moselle, and on your return to enjoy the views of the hillside vineyards.

🚗 A48 exit 125 Wittlich. Via Kinderbeuern, Bengel, Reil and Pünderich.

**CC** € **18** *1/4-1/7   1/9-26/10*

📍 N 50°02'16'' E 07°07'19''

---

## Saarburg, D-54439 / Rheinland-Pfalz

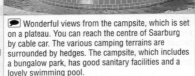 

**819**

🏕 Camping Landal Warsberg****
📧 In den Urlaub
☎ +49 65 81 91 46 10
🔓 29/3 - 4/11
@ warsberg@landal.de

11ha 460T(80-100m²) 16A CEE

**1** ACD**G**IJKLMOPQ
**2** IKRVWXY
**3** BDGHIJKLN**Q**RU
**4** (A 1/7-31/8) (F+H 🔓) **KL**M**N**
   (Q+S 🔓) (T 1/7-31/8)
   (U+X+Y 🔓)
**5** **AB**DFGIJLMNOPQRUWZ
**6** ACFGHJ**K**(N 3,5km)OTUV

💬 Wonderful views from the campsite, which is set on a plateau. You can reach the centre of Saarburg by cable car. The various camping terrains are surrounded by hedges. The campsite, which includes a bungalow park, has good sanitary facilities and a lovely swimming pool.

🚗 A60, exit Bitburg, follow B51. In Konz direction Saarburg. In Saarburg follow the Warsberg camping signs.

**CC** € **18** *29/3-11/4   3/5-23/5   14/6-11/7   30/8-4/11*

📍 N 49°37'14'' E 06°32'33''

---

## Saarburg, D-54439 / Rheinland-Pfalz

**820**

🏕 Camping Leukbachtal***
📧 Auf der Lay 1
☎ +49 65 81 22 28
🔓 13/4 - 13/10
@ info@camping-leukbachtal.de

2,5ha 75T(80-130m²) 6A CEE

**1** AD**G**IJKLMO**P**Q
**2** CRUVWXY
**3** AGHJRU
**5** **AB**DFGIJKLMNOPUWZ
**6** ACDEGJ(N 0,2km)OTU

💬 This agreeable campsite is located by the river at Saarburg, within walking distance of the lively centre. The parklike grounds make a good starting point for walking and cycling trips. The toilet building was fully modernised in 2017.

🚗 From Trier take the B51 towards Saarburg. Follow the signs to the hospital and then the signs to the campsite.

**CC** € **18** *28/4-29/5   23/6-7/7   25/8-13/10*

📍 N 49°35'58'' E 06°32'29''

## Saarburg, D-54439 / Rheinland-Pfalz

🛖 Camping Waldfrieden****
📧 Im Fichtenhain 4
☎ +49 65 81 22 55
📅 1/3 - 3/11
@ info@campingwaldfrieden.de

6,5ha 62T(85-120m²) 16A CEE

**1** ADG IJKLMOPQ
**2** BGILRUVWXY
**3** BHJK OPRU
**4** (A 15/7-15/8) (Q+R 🅿)
   (T+U+X 1/4-15/10)
**5** AB DFGIJKLMNOPUWZ
**6** ACDEGK(N 1,5km)OTU

💬 Lovely peaceful campsite located between woods and a town. Interesting possibilities with horses (such as therapy with Icelandic horses). Comfort pitches for a supplement.

🚗 From Trier take the B51 direction Saarburg, follow the signposts of the hospital, through the tunnel, after that follow the signposts to the campsite.

CC € 18  1/3-3/7  21/8-3/11

📍 N 49°36'03'' E 06°31'40''

**821**

---

## Schönenberg-Kübelberg, D-66901 / Rheinland-Pfalz

🛖 Camping Ohmbachsee****
📧 Campingpark Ohmbachsee 1
☎ +49 63 73 40 01
📅 1/1 - 31/12
@ jungfleisch@
   campingpark-ohmbachsee.de

7ha 68T(100m²) 16A CEE

**1** ACDG IJKLMOPQ
**2** DFGJKLRTUVWXY
**3** BFHJM QRTUW Z
**4** (B+G 1/6-31/8)
   (Q+R+T+U+Y+Z 🅿)
**5** AB DEFGIJKLMNOPQRS U
   WZ
**6** ACDEGK(N 0,7km)OTU

💬 The campsite is located on a wooded hillside and has a number of camping fields surrounded by hedges, right by the lake. There is a hotel/restaurant on the grounds with very good cuisine. New toilet facilities with private bathrooms for hire.

🚗 A6 exit 11 Bruchmühlbach-Miesau. Then follow signs to Schönenberg-Kübelberg. Turn right before village.

CC € 20  1/1-28/5  11/6-18/6  23/6-6/7  24/8-31/12  7=6, 14=11

📍 N 49°24'43'' E 07°24'14''

**822**

---

## Schweich, D-54338 / Rheinland-Pfalz

🛖 Camping Zum Fährturm
📧 Am Yachthafen
☎ +49 6 50 29 13 00
📅 13/4 - 20/10
@ camping@kreusch.de

3,5ha 115T(100m²) 16A CEE

**1** AG IJKLMO PQ
**2** CFGLRUVWXY
**3** ABFHJM NW
**4** (C+H 1/5-30/9) J
   (Q+T+U+Y+Z 🅿)
**5** AB CFGHIJKLMNOPUWZ
**6** ACDG K(N 0,1km)OTU

💬 Large open campsite on the Moselle river on the edge of Schweich. Loved by watersports enthusiasts because of its yacht harbour and sports facilities. Trier can be visited easily from the site using the nearby Moselradweg cycle path. Dreieck Moseltal is close by and easily accessible.

🚗 Follow the A1 take exit Schweich. In Schweich directly before the bridge over the Moselle turn left. After 100m turn right under the bridge to the campsite.

CC € 18  13/4-30/6  1/9-20/10

📍 N 49°48'52'' E 06°45'01''

**823**

## Schweppenhausen, D-55444 / Rheinland-Pfalz

⌂ Camping Aumühle
✉ Naheweinstraße 65
☎ +49 67 24 60 23 92
📅 1/4 - 31/10
@ info@camping-aumuehle.de

2,5ha 61T(< 100m²) 10A CEE

**1** ADGIJKLMO**PQ**
**2** BCFLRTWXY
**3** B**F**GJLR
**4** (Q+T+U+X+Z 🔒)
**5** **AB**DGIJMNOPUW
**6** AEGIKUV

💬 Peacefully located campsite by the river in the Guldenbachtal valley. Lovely shaded pitches on level ground. Plenty of walking opportunities.

🚗 A61 exit 47 Waldlaubersheim. Direction Schweppenhausen. Then follow signs.

A61 · B42 · B50 · L214 · **Bingen am Rhein** · L239 · CC · L108 · **Bad Kreuznach** · B41

CC €⑱ 1/4-30/6  1/9-30/10

📍 N 49°56'02'' E 07°47'30''

---

## Seck, D-56479 / Rheinland-Pfalz

⌂ Camping Park Weiherhof*****
✉ Campingplatz Weiherhof
☎ +49 26 64 85 55
📅 15/3 - 27/10, 15/12 - 6/1
@ info@camping-park-weiherhof.de

10ha 120T(100m²) 16A CEE

**1** ADG**H**IJKLMOPQ
**2** ADIJKLMRTUVWXY
**3** ABC**F**HJKNRU**W**Z
**4** (A 1/7-31/8) M
 (Q+S 1/4-31/10,20/12-31/12)
 (T+U+Y 🔒)
 (Z 1/4-31/10,20/12-31/12)
**5** **AB**DEFGHIJKLMNO**PQ**RU
 WXYZ
**6** ACDEGIJ**K**(N 5km)OUV

💬 A tranquil campsite with spacious pitches on a sloping meadow, partly with views of the lake. Afternoon break from 14:00 to 15:00. Plenty of walking opportunities. Comfortable toilet facilities.

🚗 From north A3 Köln-Frankfurt, exit 40 Montabaur, then the B255 to Rennerod as far as Hellenhahn, at roundabout to Seck and immediately left again. From south: exit 42 Limburg an der Lahn N, then B49/54 to Siegen. Signposted.

B54 · L281 · B255 · CC Mengerskirchen · Merenberg

CC €⑳ 1/4-17/4 28/4-28/5 24/6-29/6 18/8-30/9 6/10-26/10

📍 N 50°35'12'' E 08°02'07''

---

## Senheim am Mosel, D-56820 / Rheinland-Pfalz

⌂ Camping Holländischer Hof****
✉ Am Campingplatz 1
☎ +49 26 73 46 60
📅 12/4 - 27/10
@ holl.hof@t-online.de

4ha 207T(60-200m²) 10A CEE

**1** ABCDEIJKLMPQ
**2** CGKLMRUVWXY
**3** A**F**GHJK**M**NRU**W**X
**4** (A+Q+S+T+U+V+X+Y+Z 🔒)
**5** **AB**DEFGIJKLMNO**P**UWZ
**6** ABCDEGHI**K**M(N 5km)OTV

💬 Walking, cycling, good food and drink, rest and above all hospitality are the keywords for a stay on Holländischer Hof campsite.

🚗 A1/A48, exit 4 Kaisersesch towards Cochem. Cross the bridge in Cochem and then drive towards Senheim. Continue alongside the Mosel.

L98 · L108 · **Cochem** · B49 · L204 · L106 · L202 · CC · Zell (Mosel) · B421 · B53 · L194

CC €⑱ 12/4-7/7  15/9-27/10

📍 N 50°04'56'' E 07°12'29''

## Sippersfeld, D-67729 / Rheinland-Pfalz

👫 ⛷ ♿ 📶 ❀ **iD** ⑧②⑦

🏕 Naturcampingplatz
Pfrimmtal★★★★
✉ Pfrimmerhof 2a
☎ +49 63 57 97 53 80
🗓 1/3 - 30/11
@ info@campingplatz-pfrimmtal.de

8,2ha 260T(100m²) 16A CEE

**1** AGHIJKLMOPQ
**2** BCDIJLRTWXY
**3** BHNRUWZ
**4** (A 1/7-15/8) (Q+R+X+Y) 🔑
**5** ABDFGIJKMNOPUW
**6** DEGJ(N 2km)OQRT

💬 A beautiful campsite in the Pfälzer Forest, an ideal destination for a comfortable holiday in the countryside. Perfect for guests seeking rest and relaxation. Walking options from the campsite.

🚗 A61, at Alzey junction take A63 direction Kaiserslautern as far as Göllheim exit, then direction Dreissen. Via Standenbühl, then left towards Sippersfeld. Turn left after 4 km towards Pfrimmerhof.

CC €20 1/4-18/4 2/5-29/5 3/6-7/6 11/6-19/6 1/9-30/9 14/10-31/10    N 49°33'07'' E 07°57'38''

---

## Stadtkyll, D-8004 DE / Rheinland-Pfalz

📶 ❀ **iD** ⑧②⑧

🏕 Camping Landal Wirfttal★★★★
✉ Wirftstraße 81
☎ +49 65 97 92 92 10
🗓 1/1 - 31/12
@ wirfttal@landal.de

5ha 150T(75-80m²) 16A CEE

**1** ACDGIJKLMPQ
**2** BCDLRTVWXY
**3** ABCHJKLMNQRSW
**4** (A+F+H 🔑) KN
  (Q+S+U+X+Y+Z 🔑)
**5** ABDFGIJKLMNOPQUW
**6** ABCEGHJK(N 1km)OSTU

💬 Large woodland campsite with a large variety of pitches, some of them with views over the small lake, suitable for boating. The campsite, which includes a bungalow park, has much to offer and is perfect for a stay out of high season!

🚗 Leave A1 at Blankenheim, follow the B51 direction Trier. In Stadtkyll follow signs Ferienzentrum Wirfttal.

CC €16 1/1-18/4 3/5-23/5 14/6-4/7 30/8-10/10 25/10-31/12    N 50°20'18'' E 06°32'21''

---

## Traben-Trarbach, D-56841 / Rheinland-Pfalz

👫 ♿ 📶 **iD** ⑧②⑨

🏕 Moselcamping Rissbach★★★★★
✉ Rissbacherstraße 155
☎ +49 65 41 31 11
🗓 29/3 - 31/12
@ info@moselcampingplatz.de

1,8ha 80T(80-100m²) 6-16A CEE

**1** ACDGIJKLMOPQ
**2** CGLRUVVWXY
**3** BHJKNRUWX
**4** (C+G 15/5-15/9)
  (Q+R+T+U+X+Z 🔑)
**5** ABDFGIJKLMNOPUWZ
**6** CDEGIK(N 1,5km)OUV

💬 Camp directly on the Moselle in a unique natural area, surrounded by the Eifel and Hunsrück. Well maintained pitches under walnut trees. A fantastic choice of cycling and walking routes.

🚗 A48 as far as exit 125 Wittlich, and then the B50 towards Mosel. Turn left along the Mosel towards Traben-Trarbach. There are signs to the campsite from there on.

CC €20 29/3-19/4 22/4-28/5 2/6-6/6 10/6-18/6 23/6-5/7 15/9-21/11    N 49°57'55'' E 07°06'19''

## Treis-Karden, D-56253 / Rheinland-Pfalz ♿ 🛜 iD ⑧③⓪

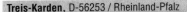

🏔 Mosel-Islands Camping*****
📧 Am Laach
☎ +49 26 72 72 26 13
📅 1/4 - 27/10
@ campingplatz@mosel-islands.de

6ha 130T(80-120m²) 16A CEE

**1** ADFHIJKLMOPQ
**2** CGLRVWXY
**3** BHJMNQRWX
**4** (Q+X+Y 📅)
**5** ABDEFGIJKLMNOPUWXY
**6** CDEGK(N 0,5km)OQTU

💬 Lovely, large family campsite, directly on the river Moselle. The pitches are on grass and there are sufficient shady pitches. There is a marina by the site.

🚗 A48, exit 5 Kaifenheim towards Treis-Karden and then follow the signs.

Münstermaifeld
A48 L109
B416
L107
Cochem CC
L205
B49 L202 L108
L98 L204

CC €⓴ 6/5-28/5 3/6-7/6 24/6-3/7 30/8-30/9    📍 N 50°10'15'' E 07°17'33''

---

## Trippstadt, D-67705 / Rheinland-Pfalz ♿ 🛜 ✿ iD ⑧③①

🏔 Camping Freizeitzentrum
  Sägmühle*****
📧 Sägmühle
☎ +49 6 30 69 21 90
📅 1/1 - 3/11, 20/12 - 31/12
@ info@saegmuehle.de

10ha 200T(100-120m²) 16A CEE

**1** AGHIJKLMOPQ
**2** BDGJLMRVWXY
**3** BGHJMNQRWZ
**4** (Q 1/3-31/10,20/12-31/12)
  (R+U+X+Y+Z 1/3-31/10)
**5** ABDEFGIJKLMNOPUWXYZ
**6** BCEGK(N 3km)OT

💬 Sägmühle campsite and leisure centre is located in the Pfälzer Forest natural park, south of Trippstadt spa town. The campsite is located on an idyllic and natural lake. The restaurant is famed for its regional Pfälzer specialities.

🚗 A6 until exit Kaiserslautern-West. Stay on B270 direction Pirmasens. After 9 km turn left, direction Karlstal/Trippstadt. Follow the camping signs.

Kaiserslautern B37
Einsiedlerhof L504
L503
L363 L500 B48
B270 CC
L474 L499
L498

CC €⑱ 1/1-29/5 2/6-7/6 23/6-13/7 31/8-3/11 20/12-24/12    📍 N 49°21'06'' E 07°46'51''

---

## Waldfischbach, D-67714 / Rheinland-Pfalz ♿ 🛜 iD ⑧③②

🏔 Camping Clausensee****
📧 Schwarzbachstraße
☎ +49 63 33 57 44
📅 1/1 - 31/12
@ info@campingclausensee.de

13ha 100T(100-125m²) 6-16A CEE

**1** ADFHIJKLPQ
**2** ABCDLRSVX
**3** ABFGHJRUWZ
**4** (Q+S+T+U+X+Z 1/4-31/10)
**5** ABDEFGJLNPRSTUWXYZ
**6** CDEGK(N 3km)OTV

💬 This lovely campsite is situated by a lake where all sorts of fun can be had in the water. A small trout stream flows round the campsite, ensuring a pleasant atmosphere.

🚗 A6 exit 15. Route 270 direction Pirmasens. Take Waldfischbach exit on the 270 and follow camping signs. Site located 7 km beyond Waldfischbach.

L499
A62 L496
B48
Münchweiler an
der Rodalb B10
Pirmasens CC

CC €⓴ 2/1-12/4 28/4-29/5 23/6-28/6 1/9-30/11    📍 N 49°16'31'' E 07°43'15''

## Wassenach/Maria Laach, D-56653 / Rheinland-Pfalz

♿ 🛜 ✿  **833**

🔺 Camping Laacher See****
📧 Am Laacher See/ L113/ Vulkaneifel
☎ +49 26 36 24 85
🔒 3/4 - 29/9
@ info@camping-laacher-see.de

7ha 95T(80-120m²) 16A CEE

**1** BFIJKLMOPQ
**2** BDFGIJKLMPRUVWXY
**3** ABHJQRU**VW**Z
**4** (A+Q 🔒) (R 1/5-1/9) (T+U+X+Y 🔒)
**5** **AB**DEFGIJKLMNO**P**UWXYZ
**6** ABCEG**K**(N 2km)OTV

💬 An idyllically situated campsite with 'Blockhausgastronomie' on the north west shores of the Laacher See. The Laacher See is the Eifel's largest volcanic lake. Suitable for cycling and walking tours, for example to the Maria Laach Benedictine Monastery. Arrivals check in from 15:00, depart before 11:00. Only cash payment possible, no debit or credit cards.

🚗 A61 exit Mendig/Maria Laach. Then approx. 5 km to the north.

CC € **20** 3/4-17/4  1/5-29/5  2/6-7/6  1/9-29/9

L83  L86  L255
L88  L87
**Andernach**
**Neuwied**
CC
A61
L10
A48

N 50°25'19''  E 07°15'54''

---

## Waxweiler, D-54649 / Rheinland-Pfalz

🛜 **iD**  **834**

🔺 Campingpark Eifel*****
📧 Schwimmbadstraße 7
☎ +49 6 55 49 20 00
🔒 30/3 - 31/10
@ info@ferienpark-waxweiler.de

2ha 95T(80-120m²) 16A CEE

**1** AD**FI**JKLO**PRS**
**2** CFLRVWX
**3** BHJKRU
**4** (C 15/5-15/9) (Q 🔒) (R 15/5-15/9) (T+U+X 🔒)
**5** **AB**DEFGIJKLMNOPUWZ
**6** CEG**J**(N 1km)V

💬 Well organised campsite situated on grassland on level grounds. Sunny pitches are marked out with hedges. Award winning toilet facilities. Lovely area for walking and cycling along the River Prüm in Bitburger Land. Close to Belgium and Luxembourg. Large pool directly on the campsite. CampingCard ACSI pitches 80m².

🚗 On the Prüm-Bitburg road take exit Waxweiler. In the village follow the signs to 'Ferienpark Camping'.

CC € **18** 30/3-6/7  26/8-30/10

Watzerath  A60
B410
Neidenbach
CC
L12  L5
L13
L10  L9  Fließem

N 50°05'32''  E 06°21'32''

---

## Waxweiler/Heilhausen, D-54649 / Rheinland-Pfalz

🛜 **iD**  **835**

🔺 Camping Heilhauser Mühle
📧 Heilhauser Mühle 1
☎ +49 6 55 48 05
🔒 1/4 - 31/10
@ walter.tautges@t-online.de

6ha 70T 10A CEE

**1** A**G**IJKLMOPQ
**2** CFGRTUXY
**3** BHJNRU**W**X
**4** (A 1/7-15/8) (Q 1/7-31/8) (U+Y+Z 🔒)
**5** **AB**DFGI**J**KLMNO**P**UW
**6** EGJ(N 2km)OU

💬 Quiet campsite on grassland positioned between the hills. This small, well maintained campsite is ideal for cyclists and walkers. Good restaurant housed in an old mill-house with a terrace is open all year.

🚗 E42 Luik (Liège)-St. Vith-Prüm to exit 3 direction Habscheid/Pronsveld. In Pronsveld direction Lünebach-Waxweiler.

CC € **16** 1/4-30/6  18/8-31/10

Prüm
Habscheid  L16  Wallersheim
A60
L1
L32
B410  CC  L5
L14  L33
L13  L9  L12
L10  L8

N 50°06'29''  E 06°20'58''

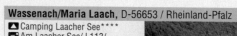

## Wolfstein, D-67752 / Rheinland-Pfalz

♿ 📶 ✿ **iD** **836**

🏕 Camping am Königsberg****
📧 Am Schwimmbad 1
☎ +49 63 04 41 43
📅 1/3 - 31/10
@ info@campingwolfstein.de

3,8ha 90T(100-150m²) 16A CEE

**1** ADGIJKLMOPQ
**2** CLRTVWXY
**3** ABGHJKLNQRUVW
**4** (A 💻) (C 15/5-15/9) N (Q+R+U+V+Y+Z 💻)
**5** ABDEFGIJKLMNOPQRUWXYZ
**6** ABEGIK(N 1km)OQTVW

📷 At the foot of the Köningsberg, located on the edge of the rustic town of Wolfstein and in the middle of the beautiful nature area of the Lautertal. Pleasant atmosphere, peace and quiet, relaxation, cycling, walking, history and culture are some of the key words. You can enjoy excellent food and drink in the friendly Gaststätte.

📍 On the B270 between Kaiserslautern and Idar Oberstein. Just south of Wolfstein. When coming from the south turn right, from the north turn left.

Rockenhausen
B420
L169
L368
CC
L388
L382
Weilerbach

CC € **20** 1/3-30/6 1/9-31/10

📡 N 49°34'49'' E 07°37'06''

---

## Rehlingen/Siersburg, D-66780 / Saarland

♿ 📶 **iD** **837**

🏕 Camping Siersburg****
📧 Zum Niedwehr 1
☎ +49 68 35 21 00
📅 1/4 - 31/10
@ info@campingplatz-siersburg.de

3ha 115T(100m²) 6-16A CEE

**1** ADGIJKLMOPQ
**2** CFKLRVWXY
**3** BFGHJW
**4** (Q+R+U+X+Z 💻)
**5** ABDEFGIJMNOPUWZ
**6** CEGK(N 0,7km)OTUV

📷 A level campsite with greenery right next to River Nied. Peaceful surroundings where you can go walking and cycling. The restaurant's patio looks out over the Nied and the campsite. New shower rooms in the main building.

📍 A8 or B51 direction Saarlouis. Follow Rehlingen, turn off to Siersburg. In Siersburg at roundabout take 1st exit Niedstrasse. After Niedbrucke turn left after about 100 metres and follow campsite signs.

Merzig
L170
L156
D855
L381
L172
A8
D956
CC
L142
D65
L341
D19
Saarlouis
D918
B269
L167
L140
D23

CC € **18** 1/4-15/7 1/9-30/10

📡 N 49°22'02'' E 06°39'39''

---

## Aichelberg, D-73101 / Baden-Württemberg

♿ 📶 **iD** **838**

🏕 Camping Aichelberg***
📧 Bunzenberg 1
☎ +49 71 64 27 00
📅 5/4 - 6/10
@ info@camping-aichelberg.de

2,6ha 50T(80-100m²) 10A CEE

**1** ACDGHIJKLMPST
**2** FRTUVWX
**3** FHJN
**4** (Q+R 💻) (T 1/6-30/9) (U+Y 30/5-30/9) (Z 💻)
**5** ABDEGIJKLMNOPUWZ
**6** CGK(N 1km)OU

📷 Quiet campsite close to motorway. Also suitable as a base for walks and days out to the Swabian Alps low mountain range.

📍 A8 München-Stuttgart, exit 58, then turn right. Left after 50m. A8 Stuttgart-München, exit 58 at roundabout 3rd on right, right after 200m.

Göppingen
L1225
L1201
B297
L1214
L1218
Kirchheim
unter Teck
CC
A8
L1217
B466
B465
L1200

CC € **16** 5/4-14/6 9/9-6/10

📡 N 48°38'22'' E 09°33'18''

## Allensbach/Markelfingen, D-78315 / Baden-Württemberg

🏕 Camping Willam★★★★
📧 Schlafbach 10
☎ +49 75 33 62 11
🔓 1/4 - 3/10
@ info@campingplatz-willam.de

4,5ha  180T(70-100m²)  16A CEE

**1** ABDEHIJKLMNO**P**ST
**2** DLMNORSUWX
**3** ABHJNR**WZ**
**4** (Q+R+U+X+Y+Z 🔓)
**5** **AB**FGIJKLMNOP**U**W
**6** ABCEJM(N 3km)ORT

💬 Campsite located between Allensbach and Markelfingen in the wonderfully relaxing Bodensee landscape. Lovely beach with a gently sloping shore and excellent water quality. Ideal for the camper seeking relaxation. In addition to recreation on the site you can explore the versatility of the region at your leisure from Bodensee cycle path.

🚗 From Radolfzell direction Konstanz. Take Allensbach exit on the B33, follow 'Willam' signs. Campsite between Markelfingen and Allensbach.

🆔 **839**

CC €20  1/4-29/5  23/6-14/7  1/9-3/10

📍 N 47°43'45'' E 09°01'31''

## Bad Bellingen/Bamlach, D-79415 / Baden-Württemberg

🏕 Camping Lug ins Land-Erlebnis★★★★
📧 Römerstraße 3
☎ +49 76 35 18 20
🔓 1/1 - 31/12
@ info@camping-luginsland.de

9ha  220T(80-120m²)  16A CEE

**1** ADG**I**JKLMOPQ
**2** FGJKLRVWXY
**3** BD**EF**GHJK**M**NOPRU**VW**
**4** (A 12/7-6/9) (C+G 7/4-31/10) **P**(Q 15/3-15/11) (S 15/3-30/11) (T+U 1/3-1/11) (V 1/3-30/11) (Y 15/3-15/11)
**5** **AB**FGIJKLMNOP**S**UWXYZ
**6** CDEGH**IK**(N 2km)OTVWX

💬 A campsite in terrace form. Views of the Rhine and the Vogues. The site has a small pool and multifunctional playing field with artificial grass. Special trips by inflatable boats are organised on the Rhine tributary. Excellent golf centre within walking distance. The campsite has a health centre with massage and a good restaurant. Public transport in the area is free.

🚗 A5 exit 67 Efringen-Kirchen/Bad Bellingen, drive towards Bad Bellingen, and then follow the signs.

🆔 **840**

CC €20  1/1-12/4  6/5-26/5  3/6-6/6  23/6-4/7  1/9-31/12

📍 N 47°42'44'' E 07°32'49''

## Bad Liebenzell, D-75378 / Baden-Württemberg

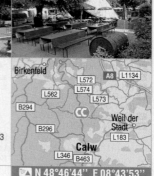

🏕 Campingpark Bad Liebenzell
📧 Pforzheimerstr. 34
☎ +49 70 52 93 40 60
🔓 1/1 - 31/12
@ info@campingpark-bad-liebenzell.com

3ha  150T(80-100m²)  16A CEE

**1** ACD**F**IJKLMPQ
**2** CGLRVWX
**3** BF**G**HJ**M**NRU**W**
**4** (C+G 15/5-15/9) J (T+U+X 🔓)
**5** **AB**DGJLNP**R**SU
**6** ACEG**K**(N 0,5km)OQTV

💬 The site is situated in the northern part of the Black Forest in parkland on the outskirts of Bad Liebenzell. You can take the waters in the many Thermal Baths. It offers relaxation, but also activity. You can go fishing and canoeing in the nearby stream. The municipality has made tourist tax mandatory.

🚗 Take the A8, exit 43 Pforzheim-W, then the B463 direction Bad Liebenzell. Campsite on edge of town next to public swimming pool.

🆔 **841**

CC €20  1/1-1/7  1/9-31/12

📍 N 48°46'44'' E 08°43'53''

## Bad Rippoldsau-Schapbach, D-77776 / Baden-Württemberg

🎿 ♿ 🛜 **iD** (842)

△ Schwarzwaldcamping Alisehof
🏠 Rippoldsauer Straße 2-8
☎ +49 7 83 92 03
📅 1/1 - 3/11, 13/12 - 31/12
@ camping@alisehof.de

4ha 110T(90-120m²) 16A

**1** ADGHIJKLMOPQ
**2** CGJRTVWXY
**3** AHJRUWX
**4** (A 1/5-30/10)
(Q+R+T+U+V+Z 📅)
**5** ABDEFGIJKLMNOPQSUWX
Y
**6** ACDFGJ(N 2km)OV

💬 A family campsite in the lovely village of Schapbach. A place to unwind. Wellness department. A quiet campsite, centrally located in the Black Forest nature park. Plenty of walking and mountain bike opportunities.

🚗 A5 exit Offenburg, B33 Villingen-Schwenningen, which becomes B294 direction Freudenstadt after Haslach. After the tunnel at Wolfach, follow Bad Rippoldsau-Schapbach.

Oppenau · Freudenstadt
B28 · L404 · L93 · CC · B462 · L94 · L405 · L96 · L422 · B294

ⓒⓒ €20 7/1-11/4 29/4-26/5 24/6-1/7 2/9-3/11

🧭 N 48°23'00'' E 08°17'59''

---

## Bad Urach, D-72574 / Baden-Württemberg

🛜 (843)

△ Camping Pfählhof***
🏠 Pfählhof 2
☎ +49 71 25 80 98
📅 1/1 - 31/12
@ camping@pfaehlhof.de

4,5ha 50T(80-120m²) 16A CEE

**1** DFHIJKLMOPQ
**2** CRUVWX
**3** BHJR
**4** (Q+R+T+U+Y 📅)
**5** ABDFGJLNPUW
**6** CDEGJ(N 2km)OQ

💬 A peaceful and well-maintained campsite located in wooded surroundings near a former farm. Ideal base for walks around Bad Urach and on Germany's highest footpath in 2016, the Bad Uracher Wasserfallsteig. Suitable for trips into the Schwäbische Alb, relaxing in the Urach thermal baths or shopping in Metzingen Outlet City (12 km).

🚗 A8 exit 56 Nürtingen. Follow the B297. In Nürtingen follow the B313 as far as Metzingen. After this follow the B28 as far as Bad Urach.

L1210 · L1212 · L1250 · L211 · Eningen unter Achalm · CC · B28 · L380 · B465 · L245 · L249 · B313

ⓒⓒ €20 1/3-1/6 1/9-31/12 7=6

🧭 N 48°30'14'' E 09°25'28''

---

## Bodman-Ludwigshafen, D-78351 / Baden-Württemberg

👤 🛜 ✿ **iD** (844)

△ Campingplatz Schachenhorn
🏠 Radolfzeller Straße 23
☎ +49 7 77 39 37 68 51
📅 15/3 - 15/10
@ info@camping-schachenhorn.de

2,6ha 180T(50-70m²) 16A CEE

**1** AFHIJKLMOPQ
**2** DFKLMNRWXY
**3** AHJNRUWZ
**4** (Q+R+Y 20/3-10/10)
**5** ABCDEFGIJKLMNOPUWZ
**6** CFGK(N 2km)OQRTV

💬 Even, partly sloping field between Boden Lake cycle route and nature reserve on the banks of the lake. Pitches aren't marked-out. Field for tents, diving bottle filling service. Cafe and bistro with home-made cake, fine foods and a nice garden with view of the lake. Quiet, relaxed atmosphere, 2 km from the town Überlingen.

🚗 From Stuttgart A81 Singen-Stockach West. Via Espasingen dir. Ludwigshafen. Site on the right on B31. From München A96 Lindau-Friedrichshaven.

B313 · L440 · L194 · B31 · A98 · B31N · L205 · L223 · B34 · CC · L220 · **Radolfzell am Bodensee**

ⓒⓒ €20 15/3-29/5 23/6-30/6 4/9-14/10

🧭 N 47°49'04'' E 09°02'20''

### Creglingen/Münster, D-97993 / Baden-Württemberg

♿ 📶 **iD** **845**

🔺 Cp. Romantische Strasse
📧 Münstersee Strasse 24-26
☎ +49 7 93 32 02 89
📅 15/3 - 15/11
@ camping.hausotter@web.de

6ha 100T(80-120m²) 6A CEE

**1** ABCD**G**HIJKLMOPQ
**2** CDJLNRUWXY
**3** BHIN**Q**RU**W**XZ
**4** (F 25/3-4/11) **N**
　(Q+R 25/3-1/11)
　(U+V 27/3-4/11)
**5** **AB**DFGIJKLMNOPUWXYZ
**6** CEGK(N 4km)S

💬 Your arrival at the campsite is unusually hospitable. There is time enough for a chat and somebody will go with you to find a suitable pitch. The campsite is in a 'luftkurort', a health spa. Spaciously landscaped and with luxurious amenities. A campsite that is sympathetic to dogs.

🚗 A7 exit Rothenburg. Drive in the direction of Bad-Mergentheim. In Creglingen signposted, direction Münster. The campsite is located just after Münster on the right side of the road.

L1003　A7
CC
Rothenburg ob
der Tauber
L1001

**CC** € **18**　15/3-6/6　10/6-6/7　1/9-14/11　14=13, 21=19

📍 N 49°26'21'' E 10°02'32''

---

### Eberbach, D-69412 / Baden-Württemberg

**iD** **846**

🔺 Camping Eberbach
📧 Alte Pleutersbacherstraße 8
☎ +49 62 71 10 71
📅 1/4 - 3/11
@ info@campingpark-eberbach.de

2ha 100T(60-80m²) 16A CEE

**1** A**F**HIJKLMOPQ
**2** CGLRVWX
**3** ABF**HJ**M**NOP**W**X
**4** (**C** 15/6-30/9)
　(**F**+**G**+Q+R+U+Y+Z 📅)
**5** **AB**DFGJLMNOPUW
**6** FG(N 0,8km)OTV

💬 Well run campsite in the town, right on the river Neckar with an extensive restaurant. Good train and bus connections with Heidelberg. Level marked out pitches by the water. Friendly and helpful owner.

🚗 Take the A5, exit 37 Heidelberg. Follow B37 direction Eberbach. Cross over bridge.

L3120　L3108
B45　L2311
L3119
L3105　L595　L589
L535　B37　L527
Neckargemünd
**Mosbach**

**CC** € **18**　1/4-28/5　11/6-18/6　24/6-30/6　1/9-3/11

📍 N 49°27'38'' E 08°58'57''

---

### Ellwangen, D-73479 / Baden-Württemberg

♿ 📶 **iD** **847**

🔺 AZUR Cp. Ellwangen a.d. Jagst
📧 Rotenbacher Str. 37-45
☎ +49 79 61 79 21
📅 6/4 - 20/10
@ ellwangen@azur-camping.de

3,5ha 80T(80-120m²) 16A CEE

**1** ACD**G**HIJKLM**P**Q
**2** CFGRUWXY
**3** HJ**W**
**4** (**F** 6/4-15/7,11/8-21/10)
　(Q+T+U+X+Z 📅)
**5** **AB**DFGIJKLMNOPUWZ
**6** CEGK(N 1km)OT

💬 For a municipal campsite this one has a lovely setting on the Jagst, next to an indoor swimming pool. Perfect for an overnight stop but also suitable for a longer stay to see what the local area has to offer. Starting point for various cycle paths for young and old.

🚗 Take the A7, exit 113 Ellwangen. Through the tunnel in Ellwangen. Turn right at T junction after tunnel. Over the bridge (railway and river) and first left. Follow the signs to the campsite.

L1060
B290
Ellwangen
(Jagst)
CC
L1072
Westhausen
A7

**CC** € **20**　6/4-29/6　26/8-19/10

📍 N 48°57'35'' E 10°07'15''

## Engen im Hegau, D-78234 / Baden-Württemberg

🎿 🛜 **iD** 848

🏕 Campingplatz Sonnental
✉ Im Doggenhardt 1
☎ +49 77 33 75 29
🗓 1/1 - 31/12
@ info@camping-sonnental.de

3ha 90T(10-80m²) 10A CEE

**1** AGIJKLMOP**Q**
**2** FGIJRUVWXY
**3** ABHJNR
**4** (**B** 1/5-1/10) (Q 🔌)
 (T+U+X+Y+Z 1/3-31/12)
**5** **AB**DFGIJKLMNOPUWXYZ
**6** ACDEGJ(N 1km)OT

💬 Beautiful campsite with a quiet location on a hill with a lovely view. Large pitches. Engen, with its historic centre is within walking distance from the site. 5km from the main road to Switzerland. Cycling and walking routes.

🚗 Take the A81 towards Singen, exit 39 Engen and then follow the signs to the campsite.

**CC** € **16** 8/3-14/7 1/9-11/11

📍 N 47°51'43'' E 08°45'39''

## Essingen/Lauterburg, D-73457 / Baden-Württemberg

🎿 ♿ 🛜 **iD** 849

🏕 Camping Hirtenteich
✉ Hasenweide 2
☎ +49 7 36 52 96
🗓 1/1 - 31/12
@ info@
 campingplatz-hirtenteich.de

3,5ha 60T(70-100m²) 16A CEE

**1** ADGIJKLMPST
**2** GKLRTUVWXY
**3** BHJNR
**4** (B 15/5-15/9) **N**
 (Q+R+U+Y+Z 🔌)
**5** **AB**DFGIJKLMNOPQUWZ
**6** ACEGHJK(N 3km)OTU

💬 A peaceful and idyllic campsite on the Schwäbische Alb on the edge of woods. Ideal for walking, cycling and mountain biking. Open air pool, sauna or just relaxing. Activities: football, barbecue area, large outdoor area, Legoland, Schwaben Park, Playmobilland, Märklin Museum Göppingen, etc.

🚗 A7 exit Aalen/Westhausen, direction Schwäbisch Gmünd. Take the B29 Aalen-Schwäbisch Gmünd, approx. 6 km west of Aalen in the direction Essingen/Skizentrum Hirtenteich.

**CC** € **18** 1/1-15/7 1/9-31/12 14=12

📍 N 48°47'12'' E 09°58'54''

## Freiburg, D-79104 / Baden-Württemberg

🎿 🛜 ✿ **iD** 850

🏕 Freiburg Camping Hirzberg
✉ Kartäuserstraße 99
☎ +49 76 13 50 54
🗓 1/1 - 31/12
@ hirzberg@freiburg-camping.de

1,2ha 85T(60-100m²) 10A

**1** ACD**G**HIJLMOST
**2** FGJKRWXY
**3** AFHJKU
**4** (Q 1/4-31/10) (R+U+Y 🔌)
**5** **AB**DGIJKLMNOPU
**6** CFGK(N 1,2km)OST

💬 The campsite is located on a hillside under trees. Almost in the middle of the town, 15 to 20 minutes walk to centre, but still quiet. You can even get breakfast from the shop. Plenty of opportunities for walks from the campsite.

🚗 A5 exit Freiburg-Mitte, towards Titisee. Follow the signs, keep to the left before the tunnel and turn left towards the (Ebnet) Sporthaus Kiefer stadium.

**CC** € **20** 7/1-12/4 5/5-23/5 1/6-7/6 23/6-30/6 1/9-1/10 4/11-20/12

📍 N 47°59'34'' E 07°52'26''

## Freiburg/Hochdorf, D-79108 / Baden-Württemberg

♿ 📶 **iD** **851**

🏕 Tunisee Camping
✉ Seestraße 30
☎ +49 76 65 22 49
📅 1/4 - 31/10
@ info@tunisee.de

30ha 150T(80-119m²) 16A CEE

1 ACD**G**HIJKLMOPQ
2 DFLORTVWXY
3 BJKNRU**WZ**
4 (Q+R+T+U 📅) (Y 1/4-16/10)
5 **AB**DGIJKLMNOPUWXYZ
6 ACFG**K**L(N 2km)OT

💬 A large campsite on a swimming lake with a cable water-ski and iceberg raft, not far from the motorway. Pleasant ambiance. Good meals available in the restaurant. Spacious grassy pitches. Freiburg is a beautiful old university town with a historical centre.

🚗 A5 Karlsruhe-Basel, exit 61 Freiburg-Nord. Turn right at the traffic lights, then 4 times to the left. Campsite signposted.

**CC** € **20** 1/4-30/6 1/9-30/10

N 48°03'51'' E 07°48'52''

---

## Gaienhofen/Horn, D-78343 / Baden-Württemberg

♿ 📶 **iD** **852**

🏕 Campingplatz Horn GmbH &Co. Kg
✉ Strandweg 3-18
☎ +49 7 73 56 85
📅 12/4 - 3/10
@ info@campingplatz-horn.de

6ha 175T(60-150m²) 16A CEE

1 ACD**G**HIJKLMNOPQ
2 ADLRWXY
3 ABHJKLNQR**WZ**
4 (Q+R+U+V+Y+Z 📅)
5 **AB**DFGIJKLMNO**P**UWZ
6 ABCEGHK(N 1km)OT

💬 A very pleasant, lively campsite on Lake Constance with spacious pitches. Cars may not be parked on the site. There is a restaurant by the lake and on the campsite. Many facilities are powered by solar energy.

🚗 From Radolfzell direction Stein am Rhein-Moos-Gaienhofen-Horn. Then follow signs.

**CC** € **20** 12/4-26/5 23/6-30/6 1/9-3/10

N 47°41'18'' E 08°59'41''

---

## Grafenhausen/Rothaus, D-79865 / Baden-Württemberg

⛷ ♿ 📶 **iD** **853**

🏕 Rothaus Camping
✉ Mettmatalstraße 2
☎ +49 7 74 88 00
📅 1/1 - 31/12
@ info@rothaus-camping.de

2,5ha 40T(80-100m²) 16A CEE

1 A**G**HIJKLMOPQ
2 BGJRVWXY
3 AFGHJR
4 (Q+U+Y+Z 📅)
5 **AB**DGIJKLMNO**P**UW
6 CEGH**K**(N 2km)OT

💬 A terraced campsite with both sunny and shaded pitches. Good restaurant. The campsite has a friendly atmosphere. Plenty of walking opportunities in the vicinity, including the Heimatmuseum. About 3 km from the Schluchsee and Schlüchtsee lakes. Free public transport.

🚗 Titisee to Schluchsee, and then towards Rothaus/ Grafenhausen, turn right after approx. 4 km.

**CC** € **18** 1/1-30/6 1/9-31/12

N 47°47'42'' E 08°14'06''

## Hemsbach (Bergstraße), D-69502 / Baden-Württemberg

854

△ Camping Wiesensee****
🏠 Ulmenweg 7
☎ +49 6 20 17 26 19
🗓 1/1 - 31/12
@ info@camping-wiesensee.de

3,5ha 60T(70-80m²) 16A CEE

**1** ABD**G**IJKLMOPQ
**2** ADFGLMRTUVWX
**3** ABF**J**M**O**R**W**Z
**4** (A 🅾) (C 1/5-15/9)
 (Q 15/3-15/10)
 (T+U+V+X+Y+Z 🅾)
**5** **AB**DEFGIJKLMNO**P**UWXYZ
**6** CDEG**K**(N 0,5km)OTV

💬 A friendly campsite with a beach on the Wiesensee lake. The touring pitches are spacious and marked out. Close to several supermarkets. Hemsbach is on the Badische (wein)Bergstrasse. Free swimming pool and lake. Archery and golf in the immediate surroundings. Suitable as a stopover campsite (3 km from the A5).

🚗 From the north take the A5 at Darmstädter Kreuz direction Heidelberg. Until exit 32 to Hemsbach. Follow campsite signs.

Heppenheim (Bergstraße)
Weinheim
L3111 B38
A67
L3110 CC L3409
A5 L3120
A6 L3408
L3257

CC € **18** 1/1-12/4 6/5-27/5 2/6-7/6 23/6-28/6 30/6-1/7 1/9-31/12

📍 N 49°35'52'' E 08°38'25''

---

## Herbolzheim, D-79336 / Baden-Württemberg

855

△ Terrassencamping
 Herbolzheim****
🏠 Laue-Dietweg 1
☎ +49 76 43 14 60
🗓 18/4 - 3/10
@ s.hugoschmidt@t-online.de

2,2ha 80T(80-120m²) 10A CEE

**1** ACD**F**HIJKLMOPQ
**2** JLRVWXY
**3** ABHJK**M**NRU
**4** (**C** 15/5-15/9) (**G** 🅾) **J**
 (Q+R+Y 🅾)
**5** **AB**FGIJKLMNOPUW
**6** ACDEG**J**(N 2km)OT

💬 A modern, beautiful and peaceful campsite with excellent toilet facilities. Located next to the swimming pool 1 km from the centre of the village. A starting point for trips to the Black Forest, Kaiserstuhl and the Europapark Rust. There is an amiable atmosphere on the campsite.

🚗 Take the A5, exit 58 Herbolzheim, just before the village turn right towards the swimming pool. Campsite is clearly signposted.

Ettenheim
Emmendingen
D468
D20 L102
L103
CC L106 L110
A5

CC € **20** 18/4-7/7 1/9-3/10

📍 N 48°12'59'' E 07°47'18''

---

## Hohenstadt, D-73345 / Baden-Württemberg

856

△ Camping Waldpark Hohenstadt
🏠 Waldpark 1
☎ +49 73 35 67 54
🗓 1/3 - 31/10
@ camping@
 waldpark-hohenstadt.de

7,5ha 60T(100-150m²) 16A CEE

**1** ACD**G**IJKLMPQ
**2** FGIJKLRTUVWXY
**3** AHJLNR
**4** (Q 1/5-30/9) (U+V+Y+Z 🅾)
**5** **AB**DGIJKLMNO**P**UWXYZ
**6** ACEG**K**(N 7km)OU

💬 Peacefully located at 800m. The campsite offers 50 spacious pitches with water, drainage and electrical connections on a 7.5 hectare terrain. The pitches are either shaded or in the full sun. The area is ideal for walking, cycling and climbing. Restaurant and playground. Family business, very friendly management.

🚗 A8/E52 Stuttgart-Ulm, take exit 60 Behelfsausfahrt. Follow signs to Hohenstadt.

Geislingen an der Steige
A8
L1200
CC
L252 L1234
L1236
B28 L1230

CC € **20** 1/3-29/6 1/9-31/10

📍 N 48°32'51'' E 09°40'02''

## Horb am Neckar, D-72160 / Baden-Württemberg

🐿 ♿ 📶 **iD** **857**

🏕 Camping Schüttehof
📧 Schütteberg 7
☎ +49 74 51 39 51
🗓 1/1 - 31/12
@ info@camping-schuettehof.de

8ha 64T(60-100m²) 16A

**1** ACD**G**HIJKLMOPQ
**2** FLRWX
**3** ABGHIJ**M**NPRU
**4** (B+G 1/6-15/9) (Q+R 🔒) (U+Y 1/3-31/10)
**5** **AB**DFGIJLMNO**P**QRUW
**6** ABCDG**K**M(N 3km)OSV

💬 A campsite in a peaceful location overlooking the medieval town of Horb am Neckar, on the edge of the Black Forest, and with its own swimming pool. Restaurant with good traditional cooking at a reasonable price.

🚗 A81 Stuttgart-Singen. Exit 30 direction Horb. In Horb left towards B14. Left to Altheimerstraße. Campsite on the left. From Freudenstadt: B14, then turn right immediately.

(CC) € **18** 1/3-30/6 1/9-30/10

📍 N 48°26'43'' E 08°40'25''

---

## Isny im Allgäu, D-88316 / Baden-Württemberg

📶 **iD** **858**

🏕 Waldbad Camping Isny GmbH****
📧 Lohbauerstraße 61-69
☎ +49 75 62 23 89
🗓 15/3 - 15/10
@ info@camping-isny.de

4,5ha 50T(100m²) 16A CEE

**1** A**G**HIJKLMOPQ
**2** ABDKLRUVXY
**3** AGK**M**NRUZ
**4** (Q+T+U+X+Y+Z 🔒)
**5** **AB**DGJLN**P**UWXYZ
**6** ACEG**K**(N 2km)ST

💬 An extremely quiet campsite located by a natural lake in wooded surroundings. Nice toilet facilities and a restaurant with an extensive menu. Within walking distance of the town of Isny for shopping and various restaurants; definitely worth a visit.

🚗 A7 Ulm then A96 Memmingen-Lindau. Exit 8 Leutkirch-Sud towards Isny. Follow signs from here.

(CC) € **20** 15/3-12/4 5/5-7/6 23/6-28/6 7/9-15/10

📍 N 47°40'39'' E 10°01'49''

---

## Kirchberg (Iller), D-88486 / Baden-Württemberg

👫 ♿ 📶 **iD** **859**

🏕 Camping Christophorus****
📧 Werte 6
☎ +49 7 35 46 63
🗓 1/1 - 31/12
@ info@camping-christophorus.de

8ha 150T(80-100m²) 16A CEE

**1** AD**F**HIJKLMOPQ
**2** DFKLRVWX
**3** ABGJL**M**N**Q**R**TW**Z
**4** (**F** 🔒) **N**(Q 1/1-31/10) (R 1/1-15/10) (T+U 1/4-15/10) (Y 🔒) (Z 1/4-15/10)
**5** **AB**DFGJLNPUW
**6** CDEG**K**(N 3km)OT

💬 A beautifully situated campsite with three lovely lakes. Ideal for families. New playground with badminton/volleyball field, barbecue, located directly on the Iller cycle path, excellent, new and modern restaurant, quiet location.

🚗 Leave the A7 Ulm-Memmingen at exit 125. In Altenstadt drive towards Kirchberg. Follow the signs before Kirchberg.

(CC) € **20** 1/1-30/6 1/9-31/12

📍 N 48°08'21'' E 10°06'11''

## Leibertingen/Thalheim, D-88637 / Baden-Württemberg

🔺 Campinggarten Leibertingen
📧 Beim Freibad 1 - Vogelsang
☎ +49 75 75 20 91 71
📅 1/4 - 25/10
@ info@
   campinggarten-leibertingen.de

2ha 44T(100m²) 16A CEE

**1** AFIJKLMOPRS
**2** GJKLRUVW
**3** ABCDHRU
**4** (B+G 🔑) JM
   (Q+R+T+U+X+Z 🔑)
**5** **AB**DFGJLNPWXYZ
**6** CEGJ(N 6km)OV

💬 Beautiful new campsite with a panoramic view of the Alps. Aimed at children, with a real farm in action and a natural swimming pool. Nature, peace, hospitality, and excellent soup from grandmother's kitchen.

🚗 B311 Freiburg-Ulm, exit Leibertingen.
In Thalheim turn left into 'Schwimmbadstraße'. Follow signs. The campsite is located on the right, at the top, next to the road.

**Sigmaringen**

Nendingen

CC €**18** 1/4-29/5 24/6-7/7 26/8-25/10

🧭 N 48°00'37'' E 09°01'42''

---

## Machtolsheim, D-89150 / Baden-Württemberg

**NEW**

🔺 Camping Heidehof****
📧 Heidehofstraße 50
☎ +49 73 33 64 08
📅 1/1 - 31/12
@ info@camping-heidehof.de

25ha 150T(60-100m²) 16A CEE

**1** ACD**G**HIJKLMOPQ
**2** FILRVWX
**3** BHJN**PQ**RU
**4** (C+H 15/5-15/9)
   (Q+R+T+U+V+Y 🔑)
**5** **A**DEFGIJKLMNOP**ST**UW
**6** CDE**K**(N 2km)OUV

💬 Good transit campsite with lots of comfort, also suitable for longer stays. There is an outdoor pool with children's pool, sauna, sports, mini-golf and several playgrounds. The campsite offers a wide choice of holiday and relaxation options in all seasons.

🚗 Take the A8 Stuttgart-Ulm, exit 61 Merklingen, then drive towards Blaubeuren. The campsite is located 2 km outside Machtolsheim. Campsite is well-signposted from motorway.

Neidlingen

Ennabeuren

Blaustein

CC €**20** 1/3-11/6 10/9-31/10

🧭 N 48°28'39'' E 09°44'41''

---

## Münsingen, D-72525 / Baden-Württemberg

🔺 Camping Ferienanlage
   Hofgut Hopfenburg
📧 Hopfenburg 12
☎ +49 73 81 93 11 93 11
📅 1/1 - 31/12
@ veranstaltungen@
   hofgut-hopfenburg.de

10ha 80T(100-120m²) 16A CEE

**1** ACD**G**HIJKLMNOPRS
**2** BJKLRVW
**3** BCK**OP**R
**4** (Q+R 🔑)
**5** **A**CDFGJLNPQRWXYZ
**6** BCDFGIJ(N 1km)O

💬 A completely different holiday. Here, you will find pitches for the night that have been designed in detail. New toilet facilities (2012) with family showers. Paved pitches for mobile homes and caravans available.

🚗 A8 Stuttgart-München. Exit 55 dir. Nürtingen-Metzingen-Bad Urach. In Münsingen follow signs. Campsite is just outside the town. Or exit Merklingen and then follow Munsingen.

Zainingen
Bad Urach

CC €**20** 1/1-2/6 1/9-31/12

🧭 N 48°24'12'' E 09°30'31''

## Neckargemünd, D-69151 / Baden-Württemberg

♿ 🛜 **iD** **863**

🏕 Camping Friedensbrücke
✉ Falltorstraße 4
☎ +49 62 23 21 78
📅 1/4 - 13/10
@ info@camping-bei-heidelberg.de

3ha  150T(60-80m²)  16A  CEE

**1** **A**F**H**IJKLMO**PQ**
**2** **C**G**L**R**W**X
**3** **A**F**H**J**U**W
**4** (Q+R+T+U+W+X ⊡)
**5** **AB**DFG**I**J**K**L**M**N**O**P**U**W
**6** **C**G**K**(N 0,3km)O**T**V

💬 Attractive, well maintained campsite on the Neckar river. Visit Heidelberg by train, boat, bus or car. Cycling and walking routes along the 'Romantische Straße'. Friendly owners. Pitches by the water cost 4 Euros extra. Lunch break from 13.00 - 15.00.

🚗 Take the A5, exit 37 at Heidelberg. Then follow the B37 towards Eberbach. In Neckargemünd, turn left at the Poststraße or turn right before the bridge. Follow the signs.

**CC** € **20**  1/4-1/7  1/9-13/10

📍 N 49°23'47'' E 08°47'40''

---

## Neckarzimmern, D-74865 / Baden-Württemberg

🛜 **iD** **864**

🏕 Camping Cimbria
✉ Wiesenweg 1
☎ +49 62 61 25 62
📅 1/4 - 26/10
@ info@camping-cimbria.de

3ha  150T(80-110m²)  16A  CEE

**1** **A**CD**F**IJKL**M**PQ
**2** **C**G**L**R**T**U**V**W**X**Y
**3** **B**G**HJ**M**N**R**U**W
**4** (C 15/5-30/9)
   (Q+T+U+X+Y+Z ⊡)
**5** **AB**GJL**M**NO**PQ**U**W
**6** **C**EG**K**(N 1km)O**T**

💬 A well run campsite located right on the River Neckar. Within walking distance of the village. The site is run by an enthusiastic owner. Comfort pitches Euro3 extra. Good eating and drinking at reasonable prices.

🚗 Take the A6, exit 33 Sinsheim. B292 direction Mosbach. On Mosbachkreuz take direction Heilbronn. Exit Neckarzimmern. Campsite located before the town of Neckarzimmern.

**CC** € **20**  1/4-29/5  3/6-8/6  24/6-7/7  1/9-26/10

📍 N 49°19'10'' E 09°07'32''

---

## Neubulach, D-75387 / Baden-Württemberg

🎿 🛜 **iD** **865**

🏕 Camping Erbenwald
✉ Miss Gasse
☎ +49 70 53 73 82
📅 1/1 - 31/12
@ info@camping-erbenwald.de

7,9ha  75T(80-130m²)  16A  CEE

**1** **A**G**H**IJKLMO**PQ**
**2** **L**R**V**W**X**
**3** **A**B**HJ**N**O**P**R**T**U**W**
**4** (A 1/7-31/8) (C 1/6-31/8)
   (H 1/5-30/9)
   (Q+R+T+U+Y ⊡)
**5** **AB**DFGH**I**JKLMNO**P**UXYZ
**6** EG**K**(N 2,5km)O**P**QR**T**V

💬 A campsite located on the edge of the village with a new toilet block. The site is ideal for making trips out to the beautiful 'Schwarzwald' (Black Forest). Plenty of pitches with shade. Wifi.

🚗 Take the A8, exit 43 Pforzheim-West. Then the B463 to Calw. In Calw. turn right direction Neubulach/Liebelsberg and then follow the signs to the campsite.

**CC** € **20**  1/1-1/7  1/9-31/12

📍 N 48°40'39'' E 08°41'23''

## Oberried, D-79254 / Baden-Württemberg

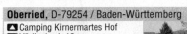

🏕 Camping Kirnermartes Hof
🏠 Vörlinsbach 19a
☎ +49 76 61 47 27
🔑 1/1 - 31/12
@ info@kirnermartes.de

2,5ha 55T(75-100m²) 16A CEE

**1** A**G**HIJKLMOPQ
**2** CGJKRTUWXY
**3** ADFHJRU
**4** **N**(Q 🔑) (X 1/4-30/10)
　(Z 1/4-31/10)
**5** **AB**DFGIJ**K**LMNPUWZ
**6** CDEG**K**(N 0,2km)OTV

💬 Campsite is located opposite a farm where children can enjoy rural life. Cosy atmosphere. Many hiking trails in and near the woods. Only 2 km to modern swimming pool.

🚗 In Freiburg centre take B31 direction Donaueschingen. At Kirchzarten L126 direction Totnau. Exit Oberried. Well signposted.

Freiburg im Breisgau L133
B500
L122
L124 CC B31
L126
L123
B317

**CC** € **20**　1/1-12/4　6/5-29/5　3/6-7/6　24/6-7/7　26/8-31/12　🏔 N 47°55'50" E 07°57'33"

---

## Oedheim, D-74229 / Baden-Württemberg

🏕 Sperrfechter Freizeit-Park
🏠 Hirschfeld 3
☎ +49 7 13 62 26 53
🔑 1/1 - 31/12
@ info@sperrfechter-freizeitpark.de

30ha 200T(100m²) 16A CEE

**1** ACD**G**HIJKLMOPST
**2** CDFLRUVWXY
**3** ABGHJKLNR**W**XZ
**4** J(Q+R 🔑)
**5** **AB**DFGHIJKLMNOPQUWZ
**6** CEGH**K**(N 2km)OT

💬 Large family campsite in natural area. Many water recreation options, such as fishing, rowing, swimming and healing sulfur baths. Renovated toilet blocks.

🚗 From A81, exit Neuenstadt to Bad Friedrichshall to Oedheim. From A6: exit Heilbronn/Neckarsulm to Bad Friedrichshall/Oedheim, then follow signs.

B27
L1096
L1097
A81
Bad Rappenau CC L1088
L549 Bad Friedrichshall
B39 A6
**Heilbronn**

**CC** € **18**　15/3-15/4　2/5-28/5　23/6-30/6　1/9-1/10　7/10-30/11　7=6, 14=12　🏔 N 49°14'29" E 09°13'56"

---

## Orsingen, D-78359 / Baden-Württemberg

🏕 Camping und Ferienpark Orsingen****
🏠 Am Alten Sportplatz 8
☎ +49 7 77 49 23 78 70
🔑 15/3 - 10/11
@ info@camping-orsingen.de

11,5ha 175T(77-136m²) 16A CEE

**1** ACD**GI**JKLMOPST
**2** FGJKLRVW
**3** AB**E**FGHJKN**OPQ**RW
**4** (**C**+**H** 1/4-8/9) (Q+S 1/4-8/9)
　(T 1/4-8/9) (U+Y+Z 1/4-3/11)
**5** **AB**DEFGIJKLMNOPRUWXZ
**6** ABCDEG**K**M(N 0,05km)O**P**T
　V

💬 A large, newly established campsite with large pitches on a sandy field. 10 km from the Bodensee lake with its walking and cycle paths. Restaurant with sun terrace and heated swimming pool with children's pool. Near Langenstein Castle and the Fastnachtmuseum.

🚗 Stockach dir. Nenzingen, from Nenzingen on to Orsingen. Then follow signs.

B14
B491 B313
L440
L194
B31 B31N
A81 A98 CC
B34
L190
**Radolfzell am Bodensee** L220
B33

**CC** € **20**　15/3-11/4　29/4-6/6　2/9-10/11　🏔 N 47°50'31" E 08°56'12"

## Salem/Neufrach, D-88682 / Baden-Württemberg

🛆 Gern-Campinghof Salem★★★★
✉ Weildorferstraße 46
☎ +49 75 53 82 96 95
🕒 1/4 - 31/10
@ info@campinghof-salem.de

2ha 94T(80-100m²) 10-16A CEE

**1** ADG**HIJ**KLMOPQ
**2** BCGLRVWX
**3** ABCD**F**HIJK**M**N**OP**RUW
**4** **N**(Q+R+T+U+X+Z 🛇)
**5** **AB**DEFGIJKLMNOPUWXYZ
**6** ABEGK(N 1km)OQSTV

💬 Wonderful location in Salem valley near the Bodensee. Marked walking and cycling paths at the camping. 10 minute walk to the Schloßsee, a very nice swimming lake in the region. Salem Castle close by. A small restaurant, bakery service and entertainment in the holiday period.

🚐 A81 Stuttgart-Singen, towards Lindau. Then B31 towards Überlingen-Salem. From Ulm: B30 Ulm-Ravensburg. Then B33 towards Markdorf. Then direction Salem/Neufrach.

CC € 18   1/4-6/6   24/6-13/7   8/9-30/10      ⛰ N 47°46'12'' E 09°18'27''

---

## Schömberg/Langenbrand, D-75328 / Baden-Württemberg

🛆 Höhencamping-Langenbrand★★★★
✉ Schömbergerstraße 32
☎ +49 70 84 61 31
🕒 1/1 - 31/12
@ info@hoehencamping.de

1,6ha 39T(100-120m²) 16A CEE

**1** A**F**HIJKLPQ
**2** GRVWX
**3** AHJRU
**4** (S+T 🛇)
**5** **AB**FG**J**LMNPU
**6** CDEG**K**(N 0km)OT

💬 The campsite is located in the middle of the town with plenty of shaded pitches and excellent toilet facilities.

🚐 Take the A8, exit 43 Pforzheim-West. Left on B10 as far as the 'Bauhaus' on the right. Turn right dir. Brötzingen. Right at 4th traffic lights in Bad Büchenbronn/Schömberg. Dir. Schömberg as far as Langenbrand.

CC € 18   1/1-1/7   1/9-31/12      ⛰ N 48°47'55'' E 08°38'08''

---

## Schurrenhof/Donzdorf, D-73072 / Baden-Württemberg

🛆 Camping Schurrenhof
✉ Schurrenhof 4
☎ +49 71 65 92 85 85
🕒 15/3 - 15/10
@ info@schurrenhof.de

2,8ha 125T(80-120m²) 10A CEE

**1** ADG**HIJ**KLPQ
**2** KRUVWX
**3** AB**F**HJK**OP**QRU
**4** (B 1/6-30/9)
   (Q+R+T+U+Y+Z 🛇)
**5** **AB**DGIJKLMNO**P**UWXY
**6** CDEG(N 3km)O

💬 Campsite at an altitude of 550 metres. Lovely panorama. Walking, cycling, mountain biking, swimming, horse riding, museums including the 'Märklin' in Göppingen, Schwäbisch Gmünd. Legoland Günzburg.

🚐 A8, exit 56, dir. Göppingen. B10 dir. Donzdorf, follow 'Heidenheim' signs at 1st roundabout. After 1 km le. to Reichenbach/Schurrenhof. From B29, dir. Schwäbisch Gmünd. In Schwäbisch Gmünd dir. Donzdorf. Turn ri. in Rechburg towards Schurrenhof.

CC € 18   15/3-15/7   1/9-15/10      ⛰ N 48°43'40'' E 09°46'12''

## Simonswald, D-79263 / Baden-Württemberg 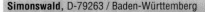 872

🏕 Camping Schwarzwaldhorn****
📧 Ettersbach 4b
☎ +49 7 68 34 77
🔓 1/4 - 20/10
@ info@schwarzwald-camping.de

1,5ha 36T(60-120m²) 16A CEE

**1** ADG**IJK**LMNO**P**Q
**2** CG**IJK**RTWXY
**3** AB**HIJ**K**Q**RU**WX**
**4** (A 🔓) (C+H 15/5-15/9)
(Q+R 🔓) (T 1/6-20/10)
(Z 1/5-20/10)
**5** **AB**DFG**IJK**LMNOPUWXYZ
**6** ADEGK(N 2km)OV

💬 Small friendly campsite in a little village with plenty of walking opportunities. Beautiful views of the Simonswald valley. Swimming pool within walking distance. One free hour of wifi a day.

🚗 Take the A5 Karlsruhe-Basel, exit Freiburg-Nord. Then take the B294 direction Waldkirch. Through the tunnel and take the 2nd exit direction Simonswald. Straight over the roundabout from Ortseingang Simonswald. The campsite on your right after about 4 km.

L110   L101
L109
Waldkirch   CC   B500
Denzlingen   L173
Gundelfingen
L112
L127

CC €20  1/4-1/7  1/9-20/10    📍 N 48°06'03'' E 08°03'05''

---

## Sonnenbühl/Erpfingen, D-72820 / Baden-Württemberg 873

🏕 AZUR Rosencp.
   Schwäbische Alb
📧 Hardtweg 80
☎ +49 7 12 84 66
🔓 1/1 - 31/12
@ erpfingen@azur-camping.de

9ha 150T(100m²) 16A CEE

**1** ABCDG**HIJK**LMNOPQ
**2** **IJK**LRTVWXY
**3** ABG**HJ**N**Q**R
**4** (C 15/5-15/9) (Q 1/5-1/10)
(R+U 1/4-31/10) (Y 🔓)
**5** **AB**DFG**IJK**LMNPUW
**6** ACDEG(N 3km)O

💬 Very large quiet campsite with many permanent pitches in the middle of a natural area. Campsite has its own swimming pool.

🚗 From Stuttgart Reutlingen take the B312/311. Follow the signs to Bärenhöhle-Sonnenbühl-Erpfingen, well signposted.

Mössingen   L382
L230
B312
CC
B32   L385   B313
Trochtelfingen
Burladingen

CC €20  1/1-29/6  26/8-30/12    📍 N 48°21'47'' E 09°11'00''

---

## St. Peter, D-79271 / Baden-Württemberg 874

🏕 Camping Steingrubenhof
📧 Haldenweg 3
☎ +49 7 66 02 10
🔓 20/3 - 20/10, 20/12 - 10/1
@ info@camping-steingrubenhof.de

2ha 70T(70-100m²) 16A CEE

**1** ADG**HIJK**LMOPQ
**2** G**IJK**RTWX
**3** AB**HJ**R**W**
**4** (A 1/7-31/8) (Q+Y+Z 🔓)
**5** **AB**DG**IJK**LMNPUW
**6** ACDEGH**K**(N 0,8km)O

💬 Steingrubenhof is located close to the health resort of Luftkurort St. Peter with its famous monastery. The terraced campsite is at an altitude of 760 metres and offers panoramic views of the Kandel mountain. Ideal starting point for hiking and for mountainbike tours.

🚗 A5 as far as Freiburg-Nord, then the B294 to Denzlingen. Turn off to St. Peter on the Glottertalstraße. Up the hill. Campsite located just before St. Peter on the left.

L112   L173
Freiburg im CC   B500
Breisgau   L127   L128
B31
L124   L126

CC €18  20/3-8/7  25/8-20/10    📍 N 48°01'25'' E 08°02'05''

## Staufen, D-79219 / Baden-Württemberg

🚴 ♿ 🛜 ✿ **iD** ⑧75

🏕 Camping Belchenblick★★★★
✉ Münstertäler Straße 43
☎ +49 76 33 70 45
🗓 1/1 - 31/12
@ info@camping-belchenblick.de

2,2ha 180T(80-110m²) 16A

**1** ADG**H**IJKLMOPQ
**2** CGLRTVWXY
**3** BF**H**JK**M**NRU**W**
**4** (B 1/5-15/9)
  (F 1/1-10/11,15/12-31/12)
  (G 1/5-15/9) **N**P(Q 👓)
  (S 1/1-10/11,15/12-31/12)
  (T 15/1-10/11)
**5** **AB**DFGIJKLMNOPRSUWYZ
**6** CFG**K**M(N 2km)ORST

💬 Campsite equipped with many amenities, next to village and pool. Has a welcoming, homely atmosphere and offers many unique trips into the surrounding area. Public transport with Konus card in Black Forest. It's a 10-minute walk along the stream to the lovely centre.

🚗 A5 exit Bad Krözingen towards Staufen/Münstertal. In Staufen drive in the direction of Münstertal. The campsite is located approx. 500 metres outside the village.

CC €**20** 1/1-17/4 27/4-1/7 1/9-31/12    📷 N 47°52'20'' E 07°44'09''

---

## Stockach (Bodensee), D-78333 / Baden-Württemberg

🛜 **iD** ⑧76

🏕 Campingpark Papiermühle
✉ Johann-Glatt-Straße 3
☎ +49 7 77 19 19 04 90
🗓 1/3 - 30/11
@ campingpark-stockach@web.de

4ha 40T(72-120m²) 6A CEE

**1** ABD**G**IJKLMOPQ
**2** BCFGJLRVWXY
**3** **F**HJR
**4** (Q+R 👓)
**5** **AB**DGIJKLMNOPUWZ
**6** ACDFGK(N 1km)OU

💬 A lovely campsite with ancient trees situated on the edge of Stockach. Perfect starting point for exploring the Bodensee region. Directly connected to the Bodensee-Radweg cycling network. 10 minutes to Stockach train station. Good shopping options and a shop with camping supplies next to the campsite.

🚗 Follow the A81 as far as the Hegau intersection, direction Stockach. Exit Stockach-West.

CC €**18** 1/3-30/6 1/9-30/11    📷 N 47°50'31'' E 08°59'42''

---

## Sulzburg, D-79295 / Baden-Württemberg

🚴 ♿ 🛜 ✿ **iD** ⑧77

🏕 Camping Sulzbachtal★★★★★
✉ Sonnmatt 4
☎ +49 76 34 59 25 68
🗓 1/1 - 31/12
@ a-z@camping-sulzbachtal.de

2,4ha 100T(100-120m²) 16A CEE

**1** ACD**G**HIJKLMOPQ
**2** BFGJKUWXY
**3** AHJK**M**O**R**U
**4** (A 1/7-31/8) (B 1/5-30/9)
  (Q+R+T+U+X 👓)
**5** **AB**DFGIJKLMNOPRWXYZ
**6** ACDEG**K**(N 1km)OT

💬 The campsite is located at the foot of a hill and within walking distance of the village with a beautiful natural swimming pool. Attractive cafeteria and bar. Walking and cycling possibilities among the vineyards. Health resort in the vicinity. Wellness, massage and pedicure at the campsite. Free public transport throughout Black Forest.

🚗 A5 exit Heitersheim. B3 exit Sulzburg, turn right before the village.

CC €**20** 1/1-17/4 28/4-6/7 1/9-31/12    📷 N 47°50'52'' E 07°41'53''

## Tengen, D-78250 / Baden-Württemberg ♿ 📶 iD 878

🏕 Hegi Familien Camping*****
📫 An der Sonnenhalde 1
☎ +49 7 73 69 24 70
📅 6/4 - 4/11
@ info@hegi-camping.de

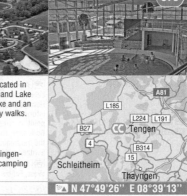

12ha 250T(< 146m²) 16A CEE

**1** ABCD**G**IJKLMOPQ
**2** DJLMRTVWX
**3** ABCGHJ**MPQ**RUVZ
**4** (F+H 🔌) **KLN**(Q+R+Y+Z 🔌)
**5** **AB**DFGIJKLMNOP**RST**UW XYZ
**6** ABCDEGHIK(N 0,7km)OTU W

💬 Peaceful, very luxurious campsite located in a volcanic area between the Black Forest and Lake Constance. The site has both a private lake and an indoor swimming pool with sauna. Lovely walks.

🚗 Northwest of Engen. Then the A81 Singen-Stuttgart, take exit 39 Engen. Follow the camping signs.

CC €20  5/5-26/5  2/6-7/6  24/6-14/7  1/9-30/9  7/10-25/10    N 47°49'26'' E 08°39'13''

---

## Titisee, D-79822 / Baden-Württemberg ♿ 📶 iD 879

🏕 Camping Sandbank****
📫 Seerundweg 9
☎ +49 7 65 19 72 48 48
📅 6/4 - 3/11
@ info@camping-sandbank.de

 NEW

2ha 220T(80-115m²) 16A CEE

**1** ACD**G**IJKLMOPQ
**2** ABDJKLRSTVWX
**3** B**F**HJKR**W**Z
**4** (Q+R+U+X+Z 🔌)
**5** **AB**DFGIJKLMNOP**U**W
**6** CEGH**J**(N 4km)OT

💬 Terraced campsite located in a quiet nature reserve on the south side of the romantic Titisee lake. From each pitch there is a beautiful view over the lake and the mountains. Directly next to the campsite there is a private beach for campsite guests with a kiosk and restaurant with terrace.

🚗 A5 exit Freiburg-Mitte, follow signs till Titisee village, then direction Bruderhalde, 4th campsite from Titisee.

CC €18  6/4-26/5  2/6-7/6  24/6-14/7  2/9-29/9  7/10-25/10    N 47°53'15'' E 08°08'18''

---

## Todtnau/Muggenbrunn, D-79674 / Baden-Württemberg 🎿 ♿ 📶 iD 880

🏕 Camping Hochschwarzwald****
📫 Oberhäuserstraße 6
☎ +49 76 71 12 88
📅 1/1 - 31/12
@ info@ camping-hochschwarzwald.de

2,2ha 53T(75-80m²) 10A CEE

**1** AD**G**IJKLPQ
**2** GJKRSTVWX
**3** ABHNR
**4** (Q+R+U+Y 🔌)
**5** **AB**DFGIJKLMNOPRUW
**6** ACEG**K**(N 5km)O

💬 Located right on the edge of a natural area among the Black Forest's highest peaks (1050m). Fantastic for walking, relaxing, swimming and playing tennis nearby. In the winter there are ski lifts, beautiful pistes and hiking routes. The campsite has a lovely personal feel. Free public transport with the Konus card.

🚗 A5 Karlsruhe-Basel exit Freiburg-Mitte, and then via Kirchzarten and Oberried towards Todtnau.

CC €18  4/3-7/7  2/9-8/12    N 47°51'55'' E 07°54'58''

## Wahlwies/Stockach, D-78333 / Baden-Württemberg

&#9856; Campinggarten Wahlwies
&#9993; Stahringer Straße 50
&#9742; +49 77 71 35 11
&#9200; 1/1 - 14/11, 15/12 - 31/12
@ info@camping-wahlwies.de

881

1,2ha 55T(70-120m²) 16A CEE

**1** ACD**G**IJKLMOP**Q**
**2** FGRTXY
**3** AHIJRU
**4** (Q+R+Z &#128275;)
**5** **AB**DFGIJKLMNOPUWXZ
**6** ABCEGK(N 1,5km)OTU

&#128488; A friendly, small campsite idyllically located between orchards in a typical Bodensee landscape. Here you can enjoy a peaceful, relaxed stay in an informal atmosphere. Wahlwies is the ideal starting point for trips out, bike and walking tours to the Bodensee, the volcanic landscape of the Hegau or to the mountain areas of the Danube and neighbouring Switzerland.
&#128663; From Stuttgart take the A81/98, exit 12 Stockach-West. Follow 'Wahlwies' camping sign.

**Radolfzell am Bodensee**

CC € **18**   1/1-5/7   1/9-14/11   15/12-31/12

&#9993; N 47°48'31'' E 08°58'11''

---

## Weikersheim/Laudenbach, D-97990 / Baden-Württemberg

&#9856; Camping Schwabenmühle****
&#9993; Weikersheimer Straße 21
&#9742; +49 79 34 99 22 23
&#9200; 13/4 - 6/10
@ info@
   camping-schwabenmuehle.de

882

2,3ha 70T(80-100m²) 16A CEE

**1** ABD**G**HIJKLMOP**Q**
**2** CGKLRTUVWXY
**3** ABHIJRU
**4** (A 1/5-30/9) (Q+Z &#128275;)
**5** **AB**CDEFGIJMNOPQRUWX YZ
**6** ABCDEG**K**(N 3km)OV

&#128488; On a river and centrally located in the Lieblichen Taubertal on the Romantische Straße. 70 comfort pitches, excellent toilets, friendly owners. Cyclists' paradise, lovely footpaths and many sights. Shops close by. Good train connections, bikes go free.
&#128663; A81 Stuttgart-Würzburg. Exit 3 Tauberbischofsheim. B290 as far as Bad Mergentheim, B19 dir. Würzburg. In Jagerheim dir. Weikersheim, then dir. Laudenbach (3 km). Campsite on the right.

CC € **18**   13/4-12/7   31/8-6/10

&#9993; N 49°27'28'' E 09°55'34''

---

## Wertheim, D-97877 / Baden-Württemberg

&#9856; Camping Wertheim-Bettingen
&#9993; Geiselbrunnweg 31
&#9742; +49 93 42 70 77
&#9200; 1/4 - 3/11
@ info@
   campingpark-wertheim-bettingen.de

883

7,5ha 100T(80-100m²) 10A CEE

**1** AD**G**HIJKLMOP**Q**
**2** CFRTWXY
**3** AJNR**W**X
**4** (Q+R+U+Y &#128275;)
**5** **AB**DFGIJKLMNO**P**UWZ
**6** CG**K**(N 6km)O

&#128488; A campsite with a hospitable atmosphere, on the banks of the river Main in the Frankish vineyards. Perfect for water sports (harbour and boat ramp). Level terrain. Campers on the move have their own facilities; a special area where you can leave at any time day or night. New sanitary facilities.

&#128663; A3 Aschaffenburg-Würzburg, exit 66 Wertheim. Follow the signs to the campsite.

CC € **18**   1/4-11/4   5/5-28/5   2/6-6/6   16/6-30/6   1/9-2/11

&#9993; N 49°46'51'' E 09°34'00''

## Wertheim/Bestenheid, D-97877 / Baden-Württemberg

884

▲ AZUR Cp-park Wertheim am Main
🏠 An den Christwiesen 35
☎ +49 9 34 28 31 11
📅 6/4 - 20/10
@ wertheim@azur-camping.de

7ha 220T(80-95m²) 6-16A CEE

**1** ACD**G**HIJKLM**P**Q
**2** CRTWX
**3** GJNQRUV**W**
**4** (C+H 15/5-15/9) J (Q+U+Y 📅)
**5** **AB**DEFGIJKLMNOPUWZ
**6** CEGJ(N 1km)O

💬 Campsite amongst tall trees, on the Main and cycle route. Close to the lovely village of Wertheim. Free access to the outdoor pool next door.

🚗 A3 Frankfurt-Würzburg. From the north: take exit 65 Wertheim/Marktheidenfeld as far as Wertheim and then drive in the direction of Miltenberg as far as Bestenheid. Then follow the signs to the campsite.

Marktheidenfeld

A3  B8

L2310  CC  Wertheim

L508

L506

**CC** € **20**  6/4-1/6  26/8-19/10    🏞 N 49°46'40'' E 09°30'33''

---

## Wildberg, D-72218 / Baden-Württemberg

885

▲ Camping Carpe Diem***
🏠 Martinsholzle 6-8
☎ +49 70 54 93 18 51
📅 1/4 - 1/10
@ campingcarpediem@live.de

3ha 130T(80-110m²) 16A CEE

**1** ADG**I**JKLMOPQ
**2** CRVWX
**3** ABHIJLRU
**4** (B 1/7-31/8) (Q+U 📅) (X+Y+Z 1/5-8/9)
**5** **AB**DFGJMN**P**UWXZ
**6** ADFG**K**(N 2km)OTV

💬 A campsite in wooded surroundings beside the River Nagold. Many walking and cycling opportunities. Campingstüble with German and Dutch specialities.

🚗 Take the A8, exit 43 Pforzheim-West direction Calw. In Calw follow the B463 direction Nagold. Follow the road in Wildberg. Follow the camping signs.

B463

CC  Herrenberg

Nagold  A81

**CC** € **18**  1/4-4/7  1/9-30/9  7=6    🏞 N 48°36'41'' E 08°44'06''

---

## Willstätt/Sand, D-77731 / Baden-Württemberg

886

▲ Europa Camping Sand
🏠 Waldstraße 32
☎ +49 78 52 23 11
📅 22/3 - 3/11
@ europacamping.sand@gmail.com

1,2ha 40T(90-120m²) 16A CEE

**1** ACD**G**HIJKLMOPST
**2** FLRTVWX
**3** R
**4** (Q+U+Y 📅)
**5** **AB**DGIJMOPUW
**6** DEJ(N 3km)O

💬 Ideal stopover campsite to and from the south at only 5 minutes from exit 54 on the A5. This is the right place for a holiday on the Rhine plain. Trips to Straßburg and the Black Forest are possible. Fresh bread service. Restaurant with excellent German-Mediterranean cuisine. Peace and quiet at this campsite!

🚗 A5 exit 54 Appenweier/Straßburg. Then direction Straßburg. Follow cp signs through Sand. Campsite 150 metres outside village. Keep your eyes peeled.

Schiltigheim

L95  B3  L86A

CC

A5

Offenburg

**CC** € **18**  22/3-16/6  15/9-3/11    🏞 N 48°32'36'' E 07°56'07''

## Arlaching/Chieming, D-83339 / Bayern

👫 ♿ 📶 **iD** 887

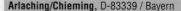

🔺 Camping Kupferschmiede
📧 Trostbergerstraße 4
☎ +49 8 66 74 46
📅 1/4 - 3/10
@ info@campingkupferschmiede.de

2,5ha 80T(80-100m²) 16A CEE

**1** ACDGIJKLMOPQ
**2** DGLMNRVWXY
**3** ABFHJRUWZ
**4** (Q+R+T 📅) (V 1/4-30/9) (X+Y 📅) (Z 1/4-30/9)
**5** ABFGIJKLMNOPUWZ
**6** ACFJ(N 1km)OU

💬 A campsite with grassy pitches 2 minute's walk from the Chiemsee, with a private beach on the lake. Most suitable for water sports. There are good walking and cycling routes around the Chiemsee from the campsite. Restaurants next to the campsite and restaurants and shops 6 km away in Chieming. Day trips to Kufstein, Salzburg, Passau and Munich.

🚗 A8 Salzburg-München, exit Grabenstätt. Direction Seebruck. Campsite located 1 km on the right before Seebruck.

CC €18 1/5-8/6 8/9-3/10

📍 N 47°55'47'' E 12°29'33''

---

## Augsburg-Ost, D-86169 / Bayern

📶 **iD** 888

🔺 Camping Bella Augusta***
📧 Mühlhauser Straße 54b
☎ +49 8 21 70 75 75
📅 1/1 - 31/12
@ info@bella-augusta.de

6,6ha 60T(< 120m²) 16A CEE

**1** ADGIJKLMOPQ
**2** DFLMNRTUVWXY
**3** BFGKRWZ
**4** (Q+R+T 1/4-31/10) (U+V+Y 📅)
**5** ABDFGIJKLMNOPRUW
**6** CEGIK(N 3km)OT

💬 Campsite located by a lovely large lake. Most suitable for visits to Augsburg. Large wood with climbing trail a few minutes from the campsite. Very convenient for a stopover on the way south (A8).

🚗 A8, exit 73 Augsburg-Ost, towards Neuburg on the Donau (Danube), towards the airport. Turn right at the first traffic lights, and after 200 metres the campsite is located on the right on the Mühlhauser Straße.

CC €20 7/1-9/7 26/8-20/12

📍 N 48°24'44'' E 10°55'24''

---

## Bad Abbach, D-93077 / Bayern

♿ 📶 **iD** 889

🔺 Camping Freizeitinsel
📧 Inselstr. 1a
☎ +49 9 40 59 57 04 01
📅 5/4 - 3/11
@ info@
campingplatz-freizeitinsel.de

2ha 78T(60-120m²) 6-16A CEE

**1** AGHIJLMPQ
**2** CFJKLRVW
**3** ADFHJW
**4** (Q+R+Z 📅)
**5** ABDFGIJKLMNOPUXYZ
**6** CDEGHK(N 3km)O

💬 An idyllic and quietly located new campsite on the Danube, plenty of sports such as cycling, canoeing and visiting Regensburg (15 km) and Kelheim. ±500m from a beautiful natural swimming pool. Stay on a comfort pitch (with 16A) for a Euro3 supplement. Reception open 08:00-12:00 and 15:00-19:00.

🚗 From the north: A93 exit Pentling (B16) dir. Kelheim. Then exit Poikam dir.Inselbad. From the south: A93 exit Bad Abbach (B16) dir. Kelheim. Then exit Poikam dir. Inselbad.

CC €20 5/4-15/7 1/9-2/11

📍 N 48°56'12'' E 12°01'15''

## Bad Füssing/Egglfing, D-94072 / Bayern

🚶 📶 **iD** **890**

🔺 Fuchs Kur-Camping****
🏠 Falkenstraße 14
☎ +49 8 53 73 56
🗓 1/1 - 31/12
@ info@kurcamping-fuchs.de

1,5ha 90T(65-100m²) 16A CEE

**1** ACGHIJKLMOPQ
**2** GRTUVWXY
**3** AB**EF**HJRU
**4** (A 1/5-30/9) (C 15/4-15/10)
(Q 🅿) (R 1/3-1/11)
(U+Y+Z 1/1-31/1, 1/3-31/12)
**5** **AB**DGHIJKLMNOPUWXYZ
**6** ACDEGIK(N 0,5km)OSV

💬 A peaceful campsite with various amenities and a restaurant with heated terrace. Bad Füssing with its many spas, restaurants and shops is 2 km away. Beautiful cycling and walking trails in this level area. The three-river city of Passau with its many attractions is 34 km away. Free internet.

🚗 A3 Nürnberg-Passau, exit 118 Poching/Bad Füssing direction Egglfing. Follow signs.

*Pocking* — B388 A3
Bad Füssing
CC A8
B12 A94
B143
B148

**CC** € **18** *1/1-14/7 1/9-30/12*

🗺 N 48°20'00'' E 13°18'58''

---

## Bad Füssing/Kirchham, D-94148 / Bayern

🚶 📶 **iD** **891**

🔺 Camping Preishof
🏠 Angloh 1
☎ +49 85 37 91 92 00
🗓 1/1 - 31/12
@ info@preishof.de

6,5ha 230T(100m²) 16A CEE

**1** ACD**G**HIJKLMOPQ
**2** RSTVWX
**3** AB**EF**HJKUV
**4** **LNP**(Q 🅿) (Y 1/2-30/11)
**5** **AB**DFGIJKLMNO**P**UWXY
**6** ACEGIK(N 1,5km)OUVW

💬 Campsite with quiet location in a rural area with more than 400 km of level cycle routes. Massages, bathing options and a good restaurant on the campsite. Golf course with 18 holes next door (30% discount). Passau, Salzburg and Regensburg are great for a day out and are at driving distance. Free bus to Bad Füssing.

🚗 A3/E56, exit 118 to the B12 direction Simbach. Exit Tutting/Kirchham, through the centre of Kirchham, direction golf course.

*Pocking* — B388 A3
B12 Bad Füssing
CC A8
A94 B148
B143
Altheim

**CC** € **18** *1/1-14/7 1/9-30/12*

🗺 N 48°20'17'' E 13°16'56''

---

## Bad Kissingen, D-97688 / Bayern

🚶 **iD** **892**

🔺 Knaus Campingpark Bad Kissingen
🏠 Euerdorfer Str. 1
☎ +49 9 71 78 51 39 66
🗓 1/1 - 31/12
@ badkissingen@knauscamp.de

2ha 80T(80-110m²) 16A CEE

**1** A**G**HIJKLMO**P**Q
**2** CGRTUWXY
**3** AH**W**
**4** (Q+R 🅿)
**5** **AB**DGIJMNOPUWXYZ
**6** BCEGL(N 0,8km)O

NEW

💬 Open grounds near the town's ring road and the Saale river. Adjacent to a health resort with a large park, which is accessible via its own entrance. Free use of the special spa bus line through the area.

🚗 A7 Würzburg-Fulda, exit Bad Kissingen. Via B286 Bad Kissingen on the southern Saalebridge follow the signs.

B286 B287
**Bad Kissingen**
CC A71
A7
Hammelburg
B19

**CC** € **18** *7/1-29/5 3/6-7/6 24/6-15/7 1/9-20/12*

🗺 N 50°11'22'' E 10°04'20''

## Bayerbach, D-94137 / Bayern

👫 ⛷ ♿ 📶 ❀ **iD** 893

🏕 Vital Camping Bayerbach*****
✉ Huckenham 11
☎ +49 8 53 29 27 80 70
📅 1/1 - 31/12
@ info@vitalcamping-bayerbach.de

12ha 330T(70-130m²) 16A CEE

**1** ACD**G**IJKLMOQ
**2** GJKLMRTUVW
**3** AB**F**HIJRU
**4** (A 1/5-30/9) (**F** 🔒) **LNO**
   (Q+R+T+U+V+W+X+Y+Z 🔒)
**5** **AB**DEFGIJKLMNOP**QRST**U
   WXYZ
**6** ABCEGK(N 0,5km)OUV

💬 Modern and very well-equipped terraced campsite with splendid views. Three swimming pools and an indoor thermal bath. The campsite has a very good restaurant, in Bavarian style, which hosts many themed evenings.

🚐 A3 Regensburg-Linz. Exit 118 direction Pocking/Pfarrkirchen (388). Then exit Bayerbach. Follow camping signs.

Bad Birnbach — B388 — CC — **Pocking** — B12

CC € **18** 1/1-14/7  1/9-30/12     📍 N 48°24'55'' E 13°07'48''

---

## Bischofsheim an der Rhön, D-97653 / Bayern

👫👫 ⛷ 📶 **iD** 894

🏕 Camping Rhöncamping****
✉ Kissingerstraße 53
☎ +49 97 72 13 50
📅 1/1 - 31/12
@ info@rhoencamping.de

3,8ha 80T(80-100m²) 16A CEE

**1** A**G**HIJKLMOPQ
**2** GJLRTVWX
**3** AHJ**Q**RU
**4** (C+H 15/5-1/9) (Q+R 🔒)
**5** **AB**CDGHIJKMNO**P**RUWZ
**6** CDEGK(N 0,5km)O

💬 A level campsite on the foot of the Kreuzberg mountain. Ideal base for walks. Free entrance to heated pool next door. Excellent toilet facilities and many options for relaxing in nature. The area is characterised by the 'Hochrhön' nature reserve with heights up to 800-900 metres.

🚐 A7 Würzburg-Fulda, exit 95 Bad Brückenau/Wildflecken direction Bischofsheim. In Bischofsheim follow the signs to the campsite.

L3395 — B278 — B279 — Bischofsheim A.D. Rhön — CC

CC € **18** 1/1-24/5  23/6-1/7  1/9-31/12     📍 N 50°23'44'' E 10°01'14''

---

## Bischofswiesen, D-83483 / Bayern

⛷ 📶 **iD** 895

🏕 Camping Winkl-Landthal****
✉ Klaushäuslweg 7
☎ +49 86 52 81 64
📅 1/4 - 13/10, 18/12 - 7/1
@ camping-winkl@t-online.de

2,5ha 50T(80-100m²) 10A

**1** A**G**IJKLMOPQ
**2** CGJKRTVWXY
**3** A**F**HJRU**WX**
**4** (Q+R+Z 🔒)
**5** **AB**DFGIJ**KL**MNOPUWXYZ
**6** ABCDEGHK(N 0,5km)OSW

💬 A peaceful campsite, excellent walking opportunities from the site. A good starting point for day trips to Salzburg, Berchtesgaden or Großglockner among other places. Bus stop 100 metres from the campsite. It is recommended to reserve via the contact form on campsite website.

🚐 On the A8 München-Salzburg, take exit Bad Reichenhall. Then, the B20 towards Berchtesgaden. 11 km before Berchtesgaden (Winkl).

**Bad Reichenhall** — A10 — B21 — CC — B319 — B305

CC € **20** 1/4-15/7  1/9-11/10     📍 N 47°40'36'' E 12°56'10''

## Breitenthal, D-86488 / Bayern

**896**

△ See Camping Günztal
✉ Oberrieder Weiherstraße 5
☎ +49 82 82 88 18 70
🚐 13/4 - 27/10
@ info@see-camping-guenztal.de

2,5ha 90T(80-100m²) 10A CEE

**1** ADF HIJKLMOPQ
**2** CDKLMTUVW
**3** AGJRWZ
**4** (Q+R+T+U+Z 🚐)
**5** AB DEFGIJKLMNOPUWXYZ
**6** CDEGIK(N 1km)OQV

💬 A quietly situated campsite on the shores of a 40 hectare lake. Plenty of comfort and modern toilet facilities. You can go surfing and sailing, but no motor boats are allowed.

🚗 A8 Stuttgart-München, exit 67 Günzburg direction Krumbach. Straight on to Breitenthal and follow Oberrieder Weiherstraße. Look out for camping signs.

CC € 18  13/4-7/6  23/6-12/7  1/9-26/10

N 48°13'39'' E 10°17'32''

---

## Chieming, D-83339 / Bayern

**897**

△ Camping Möwenplatz
✉ Grabenstätterstraße 18
☎ +49 8 66 43 61
🚐 12/4 - 30/9
@ h.lintz@t-online.de

0,8ha 80T(80-100m²) 16A

**1** ACDEIJKLMOPST
**2** DFLNORSTVWXY
**3** ABFHJRWZ
**4** (Q+R 🚐)
**5** AB DGIJKLMNOPUWZ
**6** ACGK(N 0,8km)OW

💬 A small extended campsite on the shores of the Chiemsee lake. It is a 10 minute walk to Chieming. There are three restaurants in the vicinity. The site is situated right next to a cycle path. This cycle path goes all round the Chiemsee lake. 800m from a landing stage. Free wifi on your pitch.

🚗 A8 Salzburg-München, exit Grabenstätt/Chieming.

CC € 18  12/4-15/7  1/9-30/9

N 47°52'50'' E 12°32'00''

---

## Chieming, D-83339 / Bayern

**898**

△ Chiemsee Strandcamping
✉ Grabenstätter Straße
☎ +49 8 66 45 00
🚐 1/4 - 3/10
@ info@
chiemsee-strandcamping.de

1,5ha 90T(80-90m²) 16A CEE

**1** ABCD GIJKLMOPST
**2** DFKNRTVWXY
**3** ABFHJRWZ
**4** (Q+R+U+Z 🚐)
**5** AB DGIJKLMNOPUWZ
**6** ACFGK(N 1km)OW

💬 Chiemsee Strandcamping is a well-kept site right on Lake Chiemsee. Attractive pitches for tents. Maintenance and upkeep of motorhomes. Table tennis, billiards, basketball, children's playground, kiosk. Three restaurants within 1 km. Landing stage and boat rental 1200m away. Minigolf, surfing school, bike hire and beach volleyball within 600m.

🚗 A8 München-Salzburg. Junction 109 direction Chieming. First campsite on the left about 5 km from the exit.

CC € 18  1/4-7/6  23/6-1/7  8/9-3/10

N 47°52'35'' E 12°31'44''

357

## Chieming/Stöttham, D-83339 / Bayern    👫 📶 iD  **899**

🏕 Camping Seehäusl★★★★
✉ Beim Seehäusl 1
☎ +49 8 66 43 03
🔓 1/4 - 1/10
@ info@camping-seehaeusl.de

1,5ha 44T(50-110m²) 16A CEE

**1** **AG**IJKLMOPST
**2** DFKLMNRUVWXY
**3** **A**FGHJ**W**Z
**4** (Q+R+U+V+X+Y+Z 🔓)
**5** **AB**DEFGIJKLMNOPUWZ
**6** ABCEG**K**(N 2km)UW

💬 A friendly family campsite on the Chiemsee lake with views of the mountains. Comfortable toilet facilities. Beach, boat and sailing activities. Excellent restaurant. Located on cycle routes. Access road is narrow. Campsite owner will assist with entering and exiting the campsite and will park your caravan.

🚌 A8 München-Salzburg, exit 109 Grabenstätt/Chieming/Stöttham follow signs to Seehäusl. Special attention for long and/or wide vehicles on narrow access roads.

CC € **18**  1/4-1/6  1/9-1/10    N 47°54'08'' E 12°31'10''

Traunreut
B304
CC Traunstein
B306
A8

---

## Ebrach, D-96157 / Bayern    📶 iD  **900**

🏕 Camping Weihersee
✉ Schwimmbadweg 21
☎ +49 9 55 39 89 05 79
🔓 5/4 - 13/10
@ weihersee@t-online.de

3ha 105T(90-100m²) 16A

**1** AGIJKLMPQ
**2** BCDGJRVWX
**3** BHJ
**4** (Q 🔓)
**5** **AB**DGIJKLMNOPUWX
**6** EG**K**(N 4km)

NEW

💬 A well-kept terraced campsite located in the Steigerwald Nature Park. With leisure facilities for all ages, including a garden for experiencing nature, playground equipment, hiking and biking trails.

🚌 A3 exit Geiselwind, direction Ebrach for about 15 min. Then follow campsite signs.

CC € **20**  5/4-1/6  1/9-13/10    N 49°50'44'' E 10°28'57''

Gerolzhofen
B286
CC B22
Aschbach
A3

---

## Eggelstetten/Donauwörth, D-86698 / Bayern    👫 📶 iD  **901**

🏕 Donau-Lech Camping
✉ Campingweg 1
☎ +49 90 90 40 46
🔓 1/1 - 31/12
@ kontakt@donau-lech-camping.de

5ha 127T(100m²) 16A CEE

**1** AC**F**HIJKLMOPST
**2** DLNRTVWXY
**3** **A**FRZ
**4** (Z 🔓)
**5** **AB**DGIJKMNOPUWZ
**6** CDEGJ(N 5km)OT

💬 A wonderfully peaceful campsite on the Romantische Straße. Close to the picturesque village of Donauwörth. The site has its own lake with lawns. Ideal base for walking and cycling trips. Also suitable as a stopover en route to the south.

🚌 Site south of Donauwörth, 1 km from the Asbach-Bäumenheim exit towards Eggelstetten on the B2.

B25
Donauwörth
B16
Tapfheim
CC
B2

CC € **18**  1/1-28/5  11/6-13/7  1/9-31/12    N 48°40'32'' E 10°50'28''

## Eging am See, D-94535 / Bayern

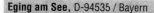

902

🏕 Bavaria Kur- und Sport
    Camping****
📧 Grafenauer Str. 31
☎ +49 85 44 80 89
🕐 1/1 - 31/12
@ info@bavaria-camping.de

6ha 120T(120m²) 16A CEE

**1** ACD**G**HIJKLMPQ
**2** CFJLRSUVXY
**3** ABF**H**JK**M**NQRUV
**4** (Q 1/4-30/10) (R 🕐)
    (U+Y+Z 1/4-31/10)
**5** **AB**DFGJLMNOPUWZ
**6** CDEG**IK**(N 0,7km)ORTV

💬 A lovely terraced campsite with adequate shade. All comforts, modern and well maintained toilet facilities. Health spa, swimming pool and lake all within walking distance.

🚗 A3 Motorway exit 113. Direction Eging am See. Campsite signposted before Eging am See.

Vilshofen an
der Donau

CC € **18** 1/1-15/7 1/9-31/12    🏔 N 48°43'16'' E 13°15'55''

---

## Fichtelberg, D-95686 / Bayern

903

🏕 Camping Fichtelsee*****
📧 Fichtelseestraße 30
☎ +49 9 27 28 01
🕐 1/1 - 31/10, 6/12 - 31/12
@ info@camping-fichtelsee.de

2,6ha 100T(90-140m²) 16A CEE

**1** AD**G**HIJKLMOPQ
**2** DGLRTVWXY
**3** ABF**H**JQ**Q**RUZ
**4** (A+Q+R 🕐)
**5** **AB**DFGIJKLMNOPUVWXYZ
**6** ACEG**J**(N 2km)OSV

💬 A lovely campsite in the Fichtel hills. Good toilet facilities. Excellent starting point for walks, Nordic walking and mountain bike trips.

🚗 Take the B303 direction Fichtelberg/Marktredwitz. Follow the white 'Fichtelsee' and camping signs from here.

Gefrees
Wunsiedel

CC € **20** 7/1-11/4 29/4-28/5 24/6-14/7 1/9-31/10    🏔 N 50°00'59'' E 11°51'20''

---

## Frickenhausen/Ochsenfurt, D-97252 / Bayern

904

🏕 Knaus Campingpark
    Frickenhausen
📧 Ochsenfurterstraße 49
☎ +49 93 31 31 71
🕐 1/1 - 31/12
@ info@knauscamp.de

3,4ha 77T(80-100m²) 16A CEE

**1** ACD**G**HIJKLMO**P**Q
**2** CLRTVWXY
**3** BHJKRU**W**
**4** (B 1/5-1/10) (Q 1/4-16/10)
    (Y 🕐)
**5** **AB**DFGIJKLMNOPUWZ
**6** ABCEGH**K**(N 0,5km)OV

💬 This campsite with bushy vegetation and swimming pool is located on the River Main, in the middle of the idyllic Mainfranken countryside. The villages in the area, famous for their wine, are worth a visit. Prime and comfort pitches available for a supplement.

🚗 A3 Würzburg-Nürnberg, exit 71 Randersacker. B13 as far as Frickenhausen. Do not cross the Main in Ochsenfurt but keep left before the bridge. Campsite on the right past the sign.

Reichenberg
Kitzingen
Iphofen

CC € **20** 1/1-29/5 3/6-7/6 24/6-15/7 1/9-31/12    🏔 N 49°40'09'' E 10°04'28''

## Geslau, D-91608 / Bayern

👫 ♿ 📶 ✿ **iD** **905**

🏕 Camping Mohrenhof
🏠 Lauterbach 3
☎ +49 98 67 97 86 09
🔄 1/1 - 31/12
@ info@mohrenhof-franken.de

4ha 128T(80-100m²) 16A CEE

**1** ACD**G**IJKLMOPQ
**2** ADFJKLMRUVWX
**3** BCD**F**HJLN**OP**QRU**W**Z
**4** (Q+R 🔄) (U 25/3-4/11)
(Y+Z 25/3-4/11,27/12-31/12)
**5** **AB**DEFGIJKLMNO**P**QUWXY
Z
**6** ACDEGI**K**(N 2km)OQUV

💬 A family campsite with comfort pitches and heated indoor playground on the Romantische Strasse near Rothenburg. Walking, cycling and culture. Schillingsfürst with its castle and water mill and birds of prey show. The campsite has an excellent restaurant and a lovely swimming lake with lawns.

🚗 A7 exit 108 Rothenburg ob der Tauber. Direction Geslau. Turn left after Geslau towards Lauterbach. Then turn right towards the campsite.

Rothenburg ob
der Tauber

**CC** € **18** 7/1-12/4 5/5-1/6 23/6-15/7 4/9-2/10 6/10-25/10 3/11-23/12 7=6, 14=12 🏔 N 49°20'42'' E 10°19'26''

---

## Grainau, D-82491 / Bayern

👫 🚣 📶 **iD** **906**

🏕 Camping Erlebnis
Zugspitze GmbH***
🏠 Griesener Straße 2
☎ +49 8 82 19 43 91 11
🔄 1/1 - 31/12
@ office@pure-camping.de

3ha 120T(60-100m²) 16A CEE

**1** ACD**G**HIJKLMO**PQ**
**2** CGKRSTWX
**3** ABF**H**J**V**X
**4** (A 🔄) **N**(Q 🔄)
**5** **AB**DGIJKLMNOPUWXY
**6** CDFG**K**(N 0,1km)O

💬 The campsite between a through road and a small river, surrounded by deciduous and fir trees with views of the high mountain (Zugspitze).

🚗 From Munich dir. Garmisch-Partenkirchen to A95 Eschenlohe. Via B2 and B23 dir. Garmisch-P. On B23 Fernpass/Ehrwald. Site is on the river. Or: via A7 Ulm, Kempten and Füssen, past Reutte. Then dir. Garmisch-P. via B23.

Garmisch-
Partenkirchen

**CC** € **20** 7/1-28/2 11/3-11/4 29/4-7/6 24/6-27/6 9/9-24/10 4/11-19/12 🏔 N 47°28'49'' E 11°03'13''

---

## Gunzenhausen, D-91710 / Bayern

♿ 📶 **iD** **907**

🏕 Campingplatz Fischer-Michl
🏠 Wald Seezentrum 4
☎ +49 98 31 27 84
🔄 1/4 - 31/10
@ fischer-michl@t-online.de

4,5ha 120T(120m²) 16A CEE

**1** AD**G**HJLMO**PQ**
**2** ADGLMRTVW
**3** BGKOPR**W**Z
**4** M(Q+R+T+U+X+Z 🔄)
**5** **AB**DEFGJMNOPUWZ
**6** ACDEGHK(N 3km)OST

💬 Spacious campsite in rustic surroundings. Ideal operating base for cycling tours. Plenty of watersport activities.

🚗 Take the A6 Heilbronn/Nürnberg, exit 52 direction Gunzenhausen. Then direction Nördlingen/Altmühlsee Südufer-Wald.

Bechhofen

Gunzenhausen

**CC** € **18** 1/4-6/6 24/6-15/7 1/9-31/10 🏔 N 49°07'32'' E 10°43'00''

## Hirschau, D-92242 / Bayern

👫 ♿ 📶 iD 908

🏕 Freizeitpark Monte Kaolino
🏠 Wolfgang Drossbachstraße 114
☎ +49 9 62 28 15 02
🔓 1/1 - 31/12
@ info@montekaolino.eu

3,3ha 210T(60-100m²) 16A CEE

**1** ACD**G**HIJKLMOPQ
**2** AGLRTVWXY
**3** ABHJ**Q**RU
**4** (C+H 1/5-30/9) IJM
(Q 1/5-30/9) (R+T 15/5-15/9)
(U+X+Y 1/5-30/9)
**5** **AB**DFGIJKLMNO**P**UWXZ
**6** ACDEGHK(N 2km)OTV

💬 A friendly campsite with clearly marked out pitches. Lovely swimming pool, ideal for families. There is a challenging sandy hill next to the campsite where you can go skiing. The Hochseilgarten and Summer Toboggan Run (roller coaster) are new features. Table tennis in a sort of control tower.

🚗 Signposted on B14 in centre of Hirschau. Then follow signs. Site ± 2 km south west of Hirschau.

A93
Wernberg-Köblitz
B299
B14 CC
A6
**Amberg**

CC €20 1/1-12/4 29/4-6/6 24/6-15/7 10/9-31/12

📷 N 49°31'52'' E 11°57'58''

---

## Illertissen, D-89257 / Bayern

👫 ♿ 📶 iD 909

🏕 Camping Illertissen****
🏠 Dietenheimerstraße 91
☎ +49 73 03 78 88
🔓 1/4 - 31/10
@ info@camping-illertissen.de

3ha 50T(70-80m²) 16A

**1** AC**G**HIJKLMOPQ
**2** CFGLRWX
**3** A
**4** (B 31/5-15/9)
(Q+R 1/4-30/10)
**5** **A**BCDFGJLMNOPUW
**6** AEG**K**(N 1,5km)O

💬 An ideal long-stay or stopover campsite in peaceful surroundings. Excellent toilet facilities and electrical connections. Hot showers, free use of the swimming pool and a limited stock of provisions. Legoland can be reached in just under one hour.

🚗 Take the A7 Ulm-Memmingen. At exit 124 Illertissen, direction Dietenheim. From there on the campsite is clearly signposted.

**Weissenhorn**
L260
**Illertissen**
CC
A7
B300

CC €20 1/4-30/6 1/9-31/10

📷 N 48°12'44'' E 10°05'17''

---

## Inzell, D-83334 / Bayern

🎿 ♿ 📶 iD 910

🏕 Camping Lindlbauer
🏠 Kreuzfeldstraße 44
☎ +49 8 66 59 28 99 88
🔓 1/1 - 10/11, 20/12 - 31/12
@ info@camping-inzell.de

3ha 91T(80-130m²) 16A CEE

**1** ACD**G**HIJKLMOPQ
**2** DGIJKLTUVWX
**3** ABFHJ
**4** (Q+R 🔓)
**5** **AB**DFGIJKLMNOPQR**S**UWX
YZ
**6** ACEG**K**(N 0,5km)O

💬 The campsite is located at walking distance from the new ice-stadium (world class). The campsite is still new, without shade and with very spacious pitches. Luxury toilet facilities with private units for rent. Good restaurant at walking distance. Inzell is a town with a touristic liveliness.

🚗 A8 München-Salzburg. Exit 112 Siegsdorf dir. Bad Reichenhall/Inzell. Then follow signs.

B304
B306
A8
CC
B305 **Bad Reichenhall**
B21

CC €20 31/1-8/6 1/9-10/11

📷 N 47°46'02'' E 12°45'12''

## Kinding/Pfraundorf, D-85125 / Bayern

♿ 📶 ✿ **iD** **911**

▲ Camping Kratzmühle\*\*\*\*
🏠 Mühlweg 2
☎ +49 8 46 16 41 70
🔓 1/1 - 31/12
@ info@kratzmuehle.de

15ha  375T(80-130m²)  16A CEE

**1** ACGHIJKLMOPQ
**2** CDFGJLMORTUVWX
**3** BFJKNPQRUWZ
**4** (A 1/4-31/10) N
 (Q+R 1/4-31/10)
 (T+U 1/4-30/9) (Y 🔓)
**5** ABDEFGIJKLMNOPSUWX
 Y
**6** ACDEGHIK(N 5km)OQTV

💬 A friendly natural campsite with excellent opportunities for cycling and walking. There is a lovely lake next to the site where you can go swimming. Also very suitable as an overnight campsite.

🚗 A9 Nürnberg-München, exit 58 Altmühltal direction Kinding. Campsite is signposted.

CC €20  1/1-29/5  2/6-7/6  23/6-7/7  1/9-31/12

🏕 N 49°00'12'' E 11°27'07''

---

## Lackenhäuser, D-94089 / Bayern

⛷ ♿ 📶 **iD** **912**

▲ Knaus Campingpark
 Lackenhäuser\*\*\*\*
🏠 Lackenhäuser 127
☎ +49 8 58 33 11
🔓 1/1 - 31/12
@ lackenhaeuser@knauscamp.de

19ha  322T(80-100m²)  16A CEE

**1** ACGHIJKLMPQ
**2** BCJKLMRTUVWXY
**3** BHJKLNQRTUW
**4** (A 1/7-15/8) (C 15/5-15/9)
 (F+H 1/1-31/10,1/12-31/12)
 N(Q+S 🔓)
 (U+Y 1/1-31/10,1/12-31/12)
**5** ABDEFGIJKLMNOPUWXYZ
**6** CEGHIK(N 5km)OSV

💬 Lovely terraced campsite situated in woodland. Very child friendly; the various swimming pools, children's farm, entertainment clubhouse, adventure village, small lake and playgrounds are an added attraction. A relaxing or sportive holiday for young and old. CampingCard ACSI rate does not include entrance to indoor pool.

🚗 Take exit Waldkirchen on B12 between Freyung and Passau. Continue to Waldkirchen-Ost. Campsite signposted from here. Follow signs for about another 28 km.

CC €18  7/1-29/5  3/6-7/6  24/6-15/7  1/9-20/12

🏕 N 48°44'56'' E 13°49'00''

---

## Lechbruck am See (Allgäu), D-86983 / Bayern

👫 ⛷ ♿ 📶 ✿ **iD** **913**

▲ Via Claudia Camping\*\*\*\*
🏠 Via Claudia 6
☎ +49 88 62 84 26
🔓 1/1 - 31/12
@ info@camping-lechbruck.de

18ha  418T(100-200m²)  16A CEE

**1** ACDGHIJKLMOPQ
**2** DGJKLMRUVWXY
**3** ABCFGHIJNRUWZ
**4** (A 7/7-1/9) (Q+R 🔓)
 (T+U+X 13/4-3/11)
**5** ABDEFGIJKLMNOPRSTU
 WXYZ
**6** ACDEGHIK(N 3km)ORTUV

💬 A large campsite located on the Lechsee lake which has been greatly improved and modernised. Various outdoor sports possibilities. Swimming in the Baderwäldlesee lake with its warm 'Moorwasser'. Ideal base for walking and cycling trips. Motorhomes can pitch on the nearby camper park.

🚗 A7 exit 138 Nesselwang, then over the Seeg to Roßhaupten. Then B16 direction Markt-Oberdorf. First exit to Lechbruck. In Lechbruck continue to the campsite.

CC €20  1/1-7/6  24/6-30/6  9/9-31/12

🏕 N 47°42'42'' E 10°49'07''

## Mittenwald, D-82481 / Bayern

🚠 🚶 ♿ 📶 ✿ **iD** 914

🏕 Naturcampingpark Isarhorn
📧 Am Horn 4
☎ +49 88 23 52 16
🔓 1/1 - 4/11
@ info@camping-isarhorn.de

7,5ha 200T(60-120m²) 16A CEE

**1** ADGIJKLMOPQ
**2** BCGIKNRTUWXY
**3** BHJ
**4** (Q+R+T+U+X 🔓)
**5** ABDGIJKLMNOPUWZ
**6** CFGHK(N 3km)O

💬 A natural campsite in the middle of woods with the mountains as a backdrop. Very suitable for cyclists and motorcyclists. Pitches partly in recesses on the plateaus. Opportunities for walking and cycling trips. Use of the climbing tower and abseiling over the Isar are possible.

🚗 From the Munich ring road follow signs to Garmisch-Partenkirchen as far as the end of the A95 Eschenlohe. Then continue on the B2/B23 to Garmisch. Then continue on the B2 to Mittenwald.

**CC** €**20** 1/1-28/5 2/6-7/6 1/7-14/7 1/9-3/11

🏕 N 47°28'21'' E 11°16'39''

## Mitterteich, D-95666 / Bayern

👫 🚠 🚶 ♿ 📶 **iD** 915

🏕 Panorama und Wellness Cp.
　 Großbüchlberg*****
📧 Großbüchlberg 32
☎ +49 96 33 40 06 73
🔓 1/1 - 31/12
@ camping@freizeithugl.de

1,6ha 60T(80-110m²) 16A CEE

**1** ACDGHIJKLMOPQ
**2** FIJKTUVWX
**3** HJQU
**4** KLN(Q+R+U+X+Y 🔓)
**5** ABDFGIJKLMNOPRUWXYZ
**6** CDEGK(N 3km)O

💬 Site with two terraces, 600 metres high. 5 km from A93 and 15 km from Czech Republic. 300 m² spa oasis with pool, relaxation room, sauna, steam bath, toilet facilities easily accessible. Every pitch: electricity, water, drainage and wifi. 3 children up to and including 5 years free.

🚗 A93 exit 17 or 16, then to Mitterteich. At crossroads with traffic lights in town centre follow 'freizeithugl'. Left after 200m to Großbüchlberg. There, after town sign, right and follow signs.

**CC** €**20** 1/1-15/7 1/9-31/12

🏕 N 49°58'23'' E 12°13'30''

## Motten/Kothen, D-97786 / Bayern

📶 **iD** 916

🏕 Camping Rhönperle
📧 Zum Schmelzhof 36
☎ +49 9 74 84 50
🔓 1/4 - 30/10
@ info@camping-rhoenperle.de

3ha 80T(80-90m²) 16A

**1** ACDGHIJKLMOPQ
**2** DFGJRTUWXY
**3** HJRUZ
**4** (Q+R+Y 🔓)
**5** ABCDFGIJKLMNOPUWZ
**6** CDEGK(N 4km)O

💬 Campsite in idyllic surroundings with a swimming lake, trees and large tent lawn. New toilet facilities. Walking and cycling paths. Bakery and restaurant nearby.

🚗 A7, exit 94 Bad Brückenau/Volkers/Motten. B27 direction Fulda/Motten. Campsite 6 km further on in Kothen, municipality of Motten.

**CC** €**20** 1/4-17/4 23/4-28/4 6/5-28/5 11/6-20/6 1/9-29/10

🏕 N 50°22'25'' E 09°46'11''

## **Neualbenreuth**, D-95698 / Bayern

917

- Campingplatz Platzermühle
- Platzermühle 2
- +49 96 38 91 22 00
- 1/1 - 31/12
- info@camping-sibyllenbad.de

1ha 44T(100-120m²) 16A CEE

1 A**G**IJKLMOPQ
2 JRTUVWX
3 B**F**HJRU
4 (Q ) (Y 1/4-31/10)
5 **AB**DGIJKLMNOPUWXY
6 CEG(N 1km)O

A terraced campsite, excellent toilet facilities. Warm welcome, 2 km from the Sibyllenbad wellness centre. Wintersports opportunities 14 km away.

A93 exit Mitterteich-Süd, then continue towards Neualbenreuth.

Cheb
B299
CC
B15
Tirschenreuth


N 49°58'15'' E 12°26'41''

CC € 16 *1/1-14/7 1/9-31/12*

## **Neubäu**, D-93426 / Bayern

918

- See-Campingpark Neubäu****
- Seestraße 4
- +49 9 46 93 31
- 1/1 - 31/10
- info@see-campingpark.de

4ha 70T(70-140m²) 10-16A CEE

1 ACD**G**HIJKLMOPQ
2 ABDGKLNRTVWXY
3 BRU**W**Z
4 (A 1/5-31/10) **N**(U+V+Y )
5 **AB**CDEFGIJKLMNOPQ**S**U WXYZ
6 CEGH**K**(N 0,1km)OV

Idyllically situated family campsite directly on the lake with excellent restaurant and new toilet facilities.

The campsite is located in Neubäu on the lake on the Schwandof-Bodenwöhr-Roding-Cham road.

Neukirchen-
Balbini
B85
CC
Nittenau
Roding
B16N
B16


N 49°14'09'' E 12°25'28''

CC € 20 *1/3-19/4 28/4-29/5 3/6-7/6 1/9-30/10*

## **Oberammergau**, D-82487 / Bayern

919

- Campingpark Oberammergau
- Ettalerstraße 56b
- +49 8 82 29 41 05
- 1/1 - 11/11, 10/12 - 31/12
- info@camping-oberammergau.de

2ha 85T(60-150m²) 16A CEE

1 A**G**IJKLMOPQ
2 CGKLRTUVWX
3 CHJ**MN**Q**RS**U**W**
4 (Q+X )
5 **AB**DEFGIJKLMNOPR**ST**U WXY
6 BCDEGK(N 0,5km)ORSTU

A campsite with smallish trees, but also some pitches without shade. The pitches have pebbles. Lovely views of the mountains, a site well positioned for trips out (walking, cycling). Close to the village.

A7 to exit 128 Memmingen, follow the A96 towards München. Take exit 25, Landsberg. Follow the B17 to Schongau. Then the B23 direction Garmisch-Partenkirchen.

A95
CC
B2
B23
Garmisch-
Partenkirchen


N 47°35'25'' E 11°04'07''

CC € 18 *14/1-28/6 16/9-9/11*

## Oberwössen, D-83246 / Bayern

🚣 ♿ 📶 **iD** **920**

▲ Camping Litzelau★★★★
✉ Litzelau 4
☎ +49 86 40 87 04
⌚ 1/1 - 31/12
@ camping-litzelau@t-online.de

4ha 62T(80-120m²) 16A CEE

1 A**G**IJLMOP**Q**
2 BCGJKRSVWXY
3 BDFHJNPUX
4 **KN**(Q+R+Y ⌂)
5 **AB**DFGIJKLMNO**P**UWXY
6 CEGK(N 1km)OTV

💬 The campsite is located in a valley next to a mountain stream and is completely surrounded by woods. Many walking and cycling routes from the campsite. Plenty of sports facilities in the immediate vicinity (such as gliding and paragliding, natural toboggan run, ski lifts, ski school, inline skating, tennis and golf).

🚗 Take the A8 München-Salzburg, exit 106 Bernau and via B305 direction Reit im Winkl to Oberwössen (20 km).

Bernau A. Chiemsee
B307 **CC**
B305
Kössen
B172

**CC** €**18** 1/1-7/6 1/9-15/12

📍 N 47°43'03'' E 12°28'45''

---

## Pleinfeld, D-91785 / Bayern

♿ 📶 **iD** **921**

▲ Waldcamping Brombach e.K.
✉ Sportpark 13
☎ +49 91 44 60 80 90
⌚ 1/1 - 31/12
@ anfrage@
    waldcamping-brombach.de

14ha 421T(100m²) 8-10A CEE

1 ACD**G**HIJKLMO**P**ST
2 ABDGMRTUVVWXY
3 AB**F**JKL**MN**P**Q**R**U**WZ
4 **N**(Q ⌂) (S 1/4-30/9)
    (T 1/5-15/9) (U+Y+Z ⌂)
5 **AB**DEFGIJKLMNPR**S**UWX
    YZ
6 CEG**J**(N 1,5km)OQTV

💬 A family campsite with water sports opportunities within 800m on the large Brombachsee lake and in a wooded area with lovely cycling.

🚗 A6 Heilbronn towards Nürnburg, exit 52 in the direction of Gunzenhausen/ Pleinfeld. See 'Waldcamping Brombach' campsite signs by the large Brombach lake.

B466
**CC**
B13
B2
**Weißenburg in Bayern**

**CC** €**18** 1/1-30/6 1/9-31/12

📍 N 49°06'46'' E 10°58'14''

---

## Prien am Chiemsee, D-83209 / Bayern

♿ 📶 **iD** **922**

▲ Camping Hofbauer
✉ Bernauerstraße 110
☎ +49 80 51 41 36
⌚ 1/4 - 30/10
@ ferienhaus-campingpl.hofbauer@
    t-online.de

NEW

1,5ha 90T(75-100m²) 16A CEE

1 AD**G**IJKLMOPQ
2 FGIRUVWX
3 B**F**IJKRU
4 (C+D+H 1/5-30/9) (Q+R ⌂)
    (U+X 30/4-3/10) (Z ⌂)
5 **AB**DFGIJKLMNOPUWXYZ
6 CFGK(N 0,6km)OSTV

💬 This friendly, family-run campsite is nestled in the beautiful Chiemgau countryside. Very suitable for walks and cycling tours. Also a good base to visit Salzburg.

🚗 Take the A8 München-Salzburg, exit 106 Bernau. Then approximately 3 km towards Prien. 100 metres after the roundabout, the campsite is located on the left of the road.

Prien am Chiemsee
**CC**
A8
B305
Unterwössen

**CC** €**20** 1/4-8/6 7/9-30/10

📍 N 47°50'20'' E 12°21'04''

## Roth/Wallesau, D-91154 / Bayern

♿ 🛜 ✿ **iD** `923`

🏕 Camping Waldsee★★★★
✉ Badstraße 37
☎ +49 91 71 55 70
🗓 1/1 - 31/12
@ info@camping-waldsee.de

4ha 100T(80-120m²) 16A CEE

**1** ABCD**G**HIJKLMO**P**Q
**2** BDLMRTVWXY
**3** BJRU**W**Z
**4** (A+Q+R+U+X 🔌)
**5** **AB**DFGIJKLMNOPUWXYZ
**6** ACDEG**K**(N 4km)OST

💬 An idyllic comfort campsite with its own lake in the woods. Ideal as a starting point for walking or cycling. Located in the Frankish lake area.

🚗 A9 Nürnberg-München, exit Allersberg towards Hilpoltstein. Turn right in Hilpoltstein towards Roth/Eckersmühlen, continue to Wallesau. On the left when entering the village.

**B2**
Roth

**CC** Hilpoltstein

**A9**

**CC** € **18** 1/1-8/6  24/6-1/7  1/9-31/12  7=6, 14=12    🧭 N 49°11'21''  E 11°07'28''

---

## Rottenbuch/Ammer, D-82401 / Bayern

🚹🚺 🎿 🛜 ✿ **iD** `924`

🏕 Terrassen-Camping am Richterbichl★★★★
✉ Solder 1
☎ +49 88 67 15 00
🗓 1/1 - 31/12
@ info@camping-rottenbuch.de

1,2ha 50T(80-100m²) 16A CEE

**1** ACD**G**HIJKLMOPQ
**2** DGJLRVX
**3** BHJL**M**NRUZ
**4** (A 1/7-31/8) (Q+R+T 🔌)
    (X 1/5-30/9) (Z 🔌)
**5** **AB**DFGIJKLMNOPUWZ
**6** ACDEG**K**(N 0,5km)OTV

💬 A slightly sloping terraced campsite with a rural character surrounded by trees and meadows. Centrally placed for trips out (Linderhof, Oberammergau, Neuschwanstein). Lovely cycle routes safe from the traffic.

🚗 In Ulm take the A7 direction Kempten. Exit 134, then the B12 until Marktoberdorf. Follow the B472 direction Schongau. Then the B23 direction Garmisch-Partenkirchen. Campsite directly at the Romantische Straße.

Schongau  **Peissenberg**
**B472**
**B17**
**CC**

**B23**

**CC** € **18** 10/1-15/7  1/9-20/12    🧭 N 47°43'39''  E 10°58'01''

---

## Schillingsfürst, D-91583 / Bayern

♿ 🛜 **iD** `925`

🏕 Camping Frankenhöhe
✉ Fischhaus 2
☎ +49 98 68 51 11
🗓 1/1 - 31/12
@ info@
    campingplatz-frankenhoehe.de

2ha 160T(100m²) 16A CEE

**1** ACD**G**HIJKLMOPQ
**2** DFILRUWXY
**3** BFGHJKRU**W**Z
**4** (Q+R+T+U+X+Z 1/4-31/10)
**5** **AB**DFGHIJKLMNOPUWZ
**6** ACDEG**K**(N 1,5km)OV

💬 Campsite located at an altitude of 500 metres in the 'Frankenhöhe' nature area, 20 km from the medieval town of Rothenburg, Dinkelsbühl and the rococo town of Ansbach. Modern toilet facilities and sauna. Plenty of opportunities for walking in the woods or making cycle trips. Modest swimming lake and restaurant.

🚗 A7 exit 109 Wörnitz, direction Schillingsfurst. In Schillingsfurst direction Dombuhl, campsite signposted. Turn right 100 metres after Fischhaus.

Neusitz

Leutershausen

**CC**          Aurach
**A7**    **A6**

**CC** € **18** 1/1-15/7  1/9-31/12  7=6, 14=12    🧭 N 49°16'25''  E 10°15'57''

## Seefeld am Pilsensee, D-82229 / Bayern   ♿ 🛜 📱 926

🏕 Camping Pilsensee
✉ Am Pilsensee 2
☎ +49 81 52 72 32
📅 1/1 - 31/12
@ info@camping-pilsensee.de

10ha 140T(100m²) 16A CEE

**1** ACD**G**HIJKLMO**P**Q
**2** DGLMRUVWXY
**3** B**F**NR**W**Z
**4** (Q 1/5-30/9)
   (S+T+U 1/4-31/10)
   (Y 1/5-30/9)
**5** **AB**EFGIJKLMNOP**R**UWX
**6** ABDEGH**K**M(N 1km)OTU

💬 A woodland campsite right by the lovely Pilsensee lake with plenty of watersports opportunities (paddle boarding, boat hire, fishing, surfing). Newly built jetties and a large children's playground. Restaurant with beer garden by the water. Close to Munich with tram connections.

🚗 From the 2068 main road Oberpfaffenhofen-Hersching exit south of Seefeld.

CC € 20   1/1-12/4   28/4-30/4   3/5-29/5   2/6-7/6   1/9-31/12    📡 N 48°01'49'' E 11°11'57''

---

## Selb, D-95100 / Bayern   ⛹ 🛜 📱 927

🏕 Camping Halali-Park
✉ Heidelheim 37
☎ +49 92 87 23 66
📅 1/4 - 31/10
@ info@halali-park.de

5,2ha 80T 16A CEE

**1** ACD**G**HIJKLMO**P**Q
**2** D**F**IJLRTWXY
**3** BHJUZ
**5** **AB**GIJKLMNO**P**UW
**6** ACEG**J**(N 8km)OV

💬 Peaceful campsite in an old orchard. Small lake for swimming and recreation. Excellent starting point for lovely walks, trips to the Czech Republic (15 km) and the pottery town of Selb.

🚗 Take the A93, exit 9 Selb-West/Marktleuthen. At 5.5 km marker turn left towards Heidelheim. Follow the signs to the campsite. A9 exit 37 Gefrees direction Selb. Follow the signs from Marktleuthen.

CC € 16   1/4-15/7   1/9-31/10    📡 N 50°08'39'' E 12°03'04''

---

## Simmershofen/Walkershofen, D-97215 / Bayern   ♿ 🛜 📱 928

🏕 Camping-Paradies-Franken****
✉ Walkershofen 40
☎ +49 98 48 96 96 33
📅 1/1 - 31/12
@ camping-paradies-franken@
   web.de

1,5ha 68T(80-140m²) 16A CEE

**1** AB**G**HIJKLM**P**Q
**2** FGKLRTVW
**3** BHJKR**W**
**4** (Q+R 📅) (U+Y+Z 1/4-31/10)
**5** **AB**DFGIJKLMNOPUWXYZ
**6** CEGK(N 5km)O

💬 Ideal for trips out to Rothenburg, Würzburg, Bad Mergentheim, Bad Windsheim and other cultural destinations. Very peaceful location. Suitable as a stopover campsite on the A7 between junctions 105 and 106. The restaurant serves local dishes and homemade cakes at a reasonable price.

🚗 From the north (A7) exit 105 dir. Aub, from Gollachostheim follow camping signs. From the south exit 106 dir. Bad Mergentheim, from Langensteinach follow camping signs.

CC € 18   1/1-6/7   23/8-31/12    📡 N 49°31'21'' E 10°07'28''

## Spatzenhausen/Hofheim, D-82447 / Bayern ♿ 📶 ✿ iD **929**

🏕 Camping Brugger am Riegsee
📧 Seestraße 2
☎ +49 8 84 77 28
📅 26/4 - 13/10
@ office@camping-brugger.de

6ha 100T(60-120m²) 16A CEE

1 AD**F**HIJKLOPQ
2 DJKLMNRUVWXY
3 BHJK**Q**RU**W**Z
4 (Q+R+T+U+Y 🔌)
5 **AB**DEFGIJKLMN**PQ**RUWX YZ
6 ABCDEGHK(N 3km)OQTUV

💬 A campsite located right by a swimming lake with panoramic views of the foothills of the Bavarian Alps, the Garmisch-Partenkirchen region and Murnau am Staffelsee. Terraced campsite in a protected natural area. Large swimming beach and lawns.

🚗 Follow the A95 direction Garmisch-Partenkirchen. Take exit 9, Sindelsdorf. Left to the B472 dir. Habach then dir. Murnau, then follow the signs Hofheim.

**Peissenberg**

B472

CC
**Murnau A. Staffelsee** A95
B2
B11

CC €**20** 26/4-6/6 6/9-13/10 📍 N 47°42'23'' E 11°13'05''

---

## Stadtsteinach, D-95346 / Bayern 👫 ♿ 📶 iD **930**

🏕 Camping Stadtsteinach
📧 Badstraße 5
☎ +49 92 25 80 03 94
📅 1/3 - 1/11
@ info@camping-stadtsteinach.de

3,5ha 100T(90-110m²) 16A CEE

1 ACD**G**HIJKLMOPQ
2 GIJLRSTVWXY
3 BHJ**MRT**
4 (**C**+H 15/5-15/9) (Q+U+X+Y+Z 🔌)
5 **AB**CDEGIJKLMNOPUWZ
6 CEG**K**(N 0,5km)OV

💬 Quietly situated campsite on the south side of the beautiful forest Frankenwald. The stunning countryside invites you to hike and cycle. Guests can use the lovely municipal swimming pool opposite the campsite for 0.50 euro per person. Arrival/departure not possible between 13h-15h.

🚗 A9 München-Berlin exit Himmelkron/ Stadtsteinach. B303 direction Untersteinach/ Kulmbach. Just before Untersteinach turn right at the roundabout towards Stadtsteinach. Follow cp signs.

**Kronach**
B303

B289

CC

**Kulmbach**

CC €**18** 30/4-1/7 1/9-30/9 📍 N 50°09'37'' E 11°30'57''

---

## Taching am See, D-83373 / Bayern 👫 ♿ 📶 iD **931**

🏕 Seecamping Taching am See
📧 Am Strandbad 1
☎ +49 86 81 95 48
📅 1/4 - 15/10
@ info@seecamping-taching.de

1,6ha 100T(80-100m²) 16A CEE

1 ACD**F**HIJKLMOPQ
2 ADGLMNRUVWXY
3 B**F**GHJKNR**W**Z
4 (Q+U+V+X+Y 1/5-15/9)
5 **AB**DFGIJKLMNOPUWZ
6 ACEGHK(N 0,5km)

💬 A family friendly campsite. Lovely location right on the Tachinger See, one of Bavaria's warmest lakes and suitable for watersports. Good restaurant with terrace on the lake and lovely views of the mountains. Many cycling and walking opportunities into the mountains from the site. Trips to Salzburg, Passau and Munich. Free wifi on all pitches.

🚗 A8 München-Salzburg, exit Traunstein/Siegsdorf. From Waging/Tittmoning road at Taching to the lake, then another 300m.

Trostberg
B20

**Traunreut** CC

B304

CC €**18** 1/4-14/6 1/9-14/10 📍 N 47°57'42'' E 12°43'54''

## Triefenstein/Lengfurt, D-97855 / Bayern ♿ 🛜 **iD** `932`

🏕 Camping Main-Spessart-Park★★★★★
📧 Spessartstraße 30
☎ +49 93 95 10 79
🔑 1/1 - 31/12
@ info@camping-main-spessart.de

9,5ha 180T(90-110m²) 6-10A CEE

**1** ACD**F**HIJKLMPRS
**2** FJRTUVWXY
**3** ADF**G**JNRU
**4** (Q+R 1/4-31/10)
(U+V+Y+Z 🔑)
**5** **AB**DEFGIJKLMNOPUWXYZ
**6** ABCDEG**K**(N 2km)OV

💬 Well maintained campsite. Modern toilet facilities. 300 metres from swimming pool and 500 metres from River Main. Park-like landscaping between the terraces. Walking and cycling in beautiful Main Valley and Spessart Nature Park. Comfort pitches available for a supplement.

🚗 A3 exit 65 Marktheidenfeld. Over bridge in Triefenstein/Lengfurt and follow camping signs. Total 6 km. Or A3 exit 66 Wertheim. Along the Main dir. Lengfurt. Follow camping signs. Total 8 km.

Marktheidenfeld
CC
Wertheim  A3
L506

**CC** € **20**  28/4-26/5  23/6-30/6  1/9-31/10   📷 N 49°49'06" E 09°35'18"

---

## Viechtach, D-94234 / Bayern 👫 🎿 ⛷ ♿ 🛜 **iD** `933`

🏕 Adventurecamp 'Schnitzmühle'
📧 Schnitzmühle 1
☎ +49 9 94 29 48 10
🔑 1/1 - 31/12
@ info@schnitzmuehle.de

2ha 80T(120m²) 10A CEE

**1** ACD**G**IJKLMOPQ
**2** CDLNRSUX
**3** BGHIJN**OP**RUWXZ
**4** (A 1/7-31/8) **KLN**(Q+R 🔑)
(T 1/7-1/9) (U 🔑)
(Y 1/1-30/10,1/12-31/12)
(Z 🔑)
**5** **AB**DFGIJKLMNOP**QR**SUW
Z
**6** CDEG**IJ**L(N 3km)OQRUV

💬 Idyllic location on a river and (swimming) lake for adventure and fun. Excellent wellness and a Thai and Bavarian restaurant. The Waldbahn stops at the campsite. Every hour there is a free train to various towns in the vicinity.

🚗 A3 Regensburg-Passau exit 110 direction Deggendorf. Take B11/E53 to Patersdorf. Left on B85 to Viechtach. Follow campsite signs. Attention: the access road has an incline of 12% and a bridge which is 3.20 m high.

Böbrach
CC
B85
Ruhmannsfelden  B11

**CC** € **20**  1/1-30/5  17/6-23/6  2/9-31/12   📷 N 49°04'10" E 12°54'49"

---

## Viechtach, D-94234 / Bayern ⛷ ♿ 🛜 ✿ **iD** `934`

🏕 Knaus Campingpark Viechtach★★★★
📧 Waldfrieden 22
☎ +49 99 42 10 95
🔑 1/1 - 31/12
@ viechtach@knauscamp.de

5,7ha 183T(80-100m²) 16A CEE

**1** ACD**G**HIJKLMOPQ
**2** BIJLRTUVWXY
**3** ABGHIJLNRU
**4** (F 🔑) **N**(Q+R+T 🔑)
**5** **AB**DEFGIJKLMNPUW
**6** CDEG**IK**(N 2km)OSTUV

💬 The new owners have launched a new concept of 'dog friendly campsite' with separate marked out pitches, agility training field and a dog toilet in the woods. The many footpaths and attractions in the area promise an enjoyable and active holiday. CampingCard ACSI rate does not include entrance to indoor pool.

🚗 A3 Regensburg-Passau, exit 110 direction Deggendorf. Take the B11/ E53 as far as Patersdorf. Then left onto the B85 as far as Viechtach. Follow the Knaus camping signs.

Bad Kötzting
B85
CC
Viechtach
Ruhmannsfelden

**CC** € **18**  7/1-29/5  3/6-7/6  24/6-15/7  1/9-20/12   📷 N 49°04'57" E 12°51'12"

## Viechtach/Pirka, D-94234 / Bayern

▲ Camping Höllensteinsee
✉ Leitenweg 12
☎ +49 99 42 85 01
🛏 26/4 - 5/10
@ info@
  camping-hoellensteinsee.de

3,5ha 100T 12A CEE

**1** **A**G**IJKLMOPQ**
**2** CDGKLRWXY
**3** HWXZ
**4** (Q+R+Z 🔧)
**5** **AB**GIMNOPU
**6** EK(N 3km)Q

💬 Quietly located natural campsite with many unnumbered and spacious pitches, surrounded by countryside and a side branch of the Höllenstein Lake. Options for swimming, canoeing and fishing. Good amenities. Days out to Bavaria natural park and all its other attractions. Free on-demand shuttle bus from campsite.

🚗 B85 to Viechtach. Follow Bad Kötzting direction Pirka (ST2139). Follow camping signs in Pirka.

Bad Kötzting
Viechtach B85
B11

CC € **18** 26/4-7/6  24/6-30/6  26/8-5/10

📷 N 49°06'03'' E 12°52'34''

---

## Wackersdorf, D-92442 / Bayern

▲ Camping Murner See****
✉ Sonnenriederstraße 1
☎ +49 94 31 38 57 97
🛏 1/4 - 31/10
@ info@see-camping.de

14ha 100T(120-150m²) 16A CEE

**1** AD**G**HIJKLMOPQ
**2** ADFLRVWX
**3** BF**N**Q**RZ
**4** (Q+R+Y+Z 🔧)
**5** **AB**DEFGIJKLMNOPRUWXZ
**6** CEGJ(N 5km)O

💬 A campsite with luxurious facilities. A beautiful location on the Murner See lake with good cycling and walking opportunities.

🚗 A93 Regensburg-Weiden-Hof, exit 33 Schwandorf, then B85 direction Wackersdorf. Signposted.

A6
A93
Neunburg vorm Wald
Schwandorf
B85
B15

CC € **16** 1/4-7/6  1/9-30/10

📷 N 49°20'44'' E 12°12'31''

---

## Wertach, D-87497 / Bayern

▲ Camping Waldesruh****
✉ Bahnhofstr. 19
☎ +49 83 65 10 04
🛏 1/1 - 10/11
@ info@camping-wertach.de

1,7ha 30T(60-80m²) 16A CEE

**1** **A**F**HIJKLNPQ**
**2** FGKRTVWX
**3** ABRU
**5** **AB**CDGJLMNOPUW
**6** CDEG**IK**(N 0,5km)OQV

💬 A small, peaceful campsite located on the edge of the village. This family oriented site with well-maintained pitches is ideal for families, cyclists and walkers. Lovely surroundings with plenty of excursion possibilities.

🚗 A7 Stuttgart-Ulm-Kempten, exit 137 Oy. B310 towards Wertach. 2 km before Wertach to the Alte Staatsstraße to Wertach (signposted).

Buchenberg
Waltenhofen
A7
B19
B309
B310
B308
B199

CC € **18** 30/3-13/7  1/9-3/11

📷 N 47°36'31'' E 10°25'04''

# Switzerland

## General
Switzerland is not a member of the EU.

### Time
The time in Switzerland is the same as Amsterdam, Paris and Rome and one hour ahead of London.

### Languages
German, French and Italian, but you will also get by in English.

## Border formalities
Many formalities and agreements about matters such as necessary travel documents, car papers, requirements relating to your means of transport and accommodation, medical expenses and taking pets with you do not only depend on the country you are travelling to but also on your departure point and nationality. The length of your stay can also play a role here. It is not possible within the confines of this guide to guarantee the correct and most up to date information with regard to these matters.

We advise you to consult the relevant authorities before your departure about:
- which travel documents you will need for yourself and your fellow passengers
- which documents you need for your car
- which regulations your caravan must meet
- which goods you may import and export
- how medical treatment will be arranged and paid for in your holiday destination in cases of accident or illness
- whether you can take pets. Contact your vets well in advance. They can give you information about the necessary vaccinations, proof thereof and obligations on return. It would also make sense to enquire whether any special regulations apply to your pet in public places at your holiday destination. In some countries for example dogs must always be muzzled or transported in a cage.

Make certain you assemble the information that is relevant to your specific situation.

For the most recent customs regulations you should get in contact with the authorities of your holiday destination in your country of residence.

## Currency
The currency in Switzerland is the Swiss franc (CHF). Approximate exchange rates September 2018: £1 = CHF 1.27. Euros are widely accepted, but change will be given in Swiss Francs.

### Credit cards
You can pay almost everywhere by credit card.

## Opening times
### Banks
Banks in towns are open Monday to Friday until 16:30. In country areas the banks often close between 12:00 and 13:30.

### Shops
Shops are open on weekdays from 08:00 to 18:30. Many shops are closed on Monday mornings. Shops close at 17:00 on Saturdays.

in mountain passes. Help can be summoned in an emergency by calling 0800-140140, ▶ *www.tcs.ch* ◀

## Traffic regulations

Remember, all traffic in Switzerland drives on the right and overtakes on the left! Headlight deflectors are advisable to prevent annoying oncoming drivers. Switzerland uses the metric system, so distances are measured in kilometres (km) and speeds in kilometres per hour (km/h). Traffic from the right has priority. Traffic on roundabouts has priority. On mountain roads give way to traffic driving uphill.
On narrow roads a heavy vehicle has priority over a lighter vehicle. Switzerland also has 'Bergpoststrassen' where postal vehicles always have priority.

### Chemists, doctors

Chemists are open until 18:30 except on Sundays. You can find out which chemists and doctors are open by phoning 1811.

## Communication

### (Mobile) phones

The mobile network works well throughout Switzerland, except in some uninhabited areas of the Alps. There is a 4G network for mobile internet.

### Wifi, internet

You can make use of a wifi network at more and more public locations, often for free.

### Post

Post offices are generally open until 18:30. Also open on Saturday mornings.

## Roads and traffic

### Road network

The Swiss breakdown service is the TCS. There are emergency phones on major roads and

*Maximum speed*

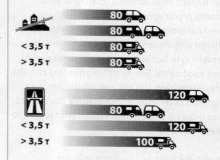

The maximum permitted alcohol level is 0.5‰. Dipped headlights are mandatory during daytime. Phones must be used hands-free. Winter tyres are not compulsory, but strongly recommended. Snow chains are compulsory on certain mountain routes when weather conditions require them.

## Caravans, motorhomes

Driving in the Swiss mountains requires considerable experience when travelling with a caravan. On three lane motorways you may not drive a caravan in the left hand lane. Overnight stays in cars, motorhomes or caravans are permitted in some cantons (sometimes on payment) in car parks alongside motorways. Two 'Autobahnvignetten' are required for a car and caravan! One for the car and one for the caravan. See ´Tolls´ for more details.

## Maximum allowed measurements of combined length

Height 4 metres, width 2.55 metres and length 18.75 metres (of which the trailer maximum 12 metres).

## Fuel

Petrol and diesel are easily available everywhere. LPG is reasonably well available.

## Filling stations

Filling stations are usually open till 20:00. Most filling stations also have card terminals at night.

## Tolls

All Swiss and foreign vehicles using the motorway network in Switzerland must buy an 'Autobahnvignet' (sticker). This vignette is valid for all cars vehicles and motorhomes up to a combined weight of 3.5 tonnes and is valid for one year. Failure to display a vignette can lead to a CHF 200 (about £160) fine.

Take note: You cannot pass the Basel-Weil border without a vignette.

Vehicles above 3.5 tonnes must pay the Schwerverkehrsabgabe. More information on
▶ *www.ezv.admin.ch* ◀

It is advisable to order the vignette online, for example on ▶ *www.tolltickets.com* ◀
This will save a lot of waiting at the border.

## Mountain passes

The following passes are prohibited for caravans: Klausenpass between Altdorf and Linthal, Umbrailpass from Santa Maria to Bormio and Furkapass between Gletsch and Realp. The following passes are not recommended if you are towing a caravan: Albulapass between Tiefencastel and La Punt, Grimselpass between Meiringen and Gletsch.

## Road tunnels

Swiss road tunnels are open all year round. Most of them are toll-free as they are included in the 'Autobahnvignet'. There are however 2 tunnels where you have to pay: the Grand St. Bernard and Munt la Schera. Munt la Schera has a single carriageway, you may only pass through the tunnel at specified times. You can also take your car on the train through the tunnels.

## Emergency numbers

- 112: national emergency number for police, fire and ambulance
- 117: police
- 118: fire
- 144: ambulance (in larger cities)
- 1414: rescue helicopter

## Camping

Tent campers dominate mountainous areas. Campsites in the west of Switzerland often have many permanent pitches. Free camping is only permitted with advance permission from the land owner or the local police.

## Practical

- Additional charges for items such as tourist taxes and environmental charges are sometimes quite high.
- Tourist information offices are open from Monday to Friday from 09:00 to 18:00.
- Make sure you have a world adaptor for electrical appliances.
- Drinking water is safe.

## Acquarossa, CH-6716 / Tessin

🛜 iD **938**

🏕 Camping Acquarossa**
📧 Via Lucomagnio 163
☎ +41 9 18 71 16 03
📅 1/1 - 31/12
@ madlen.burri@bluewin.ch

9ha 50T(50-80m²) 10A

1 AFHIJKLMPQ
2 CGKRWX
3 AHJRUW
4 (B 15/6-1/9) (Q 15/6-15/9) (R 1/5-15/10) (Z 15/6-15/9)
5 ABDGIJKLMNOPUWZ
6 EJ(N 1,5km)OT

💬 Situated in a meadow by the Brenno river and virtually circled by trees. Views of the partly cultivated mountain slopes. Perfect location for trips out by car to St.Gotthard and Oberalp among other places.

🚗 1 km north of Acquarossa on the route through Lukmanier pass. Access from the north is difficult. Then turn in Acquarossa and drive in without a problem.

CC € 20  15/4-30/6  1/9-30/9

N 46°27'35''  E 08°56'31''

---

## Aeschi/Spiez, CH-3703 / Bern

🛜 iD **939**

🏕 Camping Panorama-Rossern***
📧 Rossern Scheidgasse 26
☎ +41 3 36 54 43 77
📅 15/5 - 15/10
@ postmaster@camping-aeschi.ch

1ha 45T(80m²) 10A CEE

1 ABFIJLMPST
2 GJRWXY
3 AHR
4 (Q 18/7-31/8)
5 ABFGIJKLMOPUW
6 AEIJ(N 1km)

💬 A terraced campsite with shaded pitches situated just outside the town. Basic but well maintained grounds.

🚗 Motorway Bern-Spiez, exit Spiez direction Aeschi.

CC € 18  15/5-1/7  1/9-15/10

N 46°39'13''  E 07°41'59''

---

## Andeer, CH-7440 / Graubünden

🛜 iD **940**

🏕 Camping Andeer****
📧 Sut Baselgia 120c
☎ +41 8 16 61 14 53
📅 1/1 - 31/12
@ camping.andeer@bluewin.ch

1,2ha 40T(40-80m²) 10A

1 AGHIJKLMNPQ
2 FGKRSWX
3 AHJMUW
4 (C 1/6-31/8) (F 🔒) (H 1/6-31/8) (Q 🔒) (T+X+Z 1/1-30/10,1/12-31/12)
5 ABDGIJKLMNOPUWZ
6 CEGK(N 0,1km)O

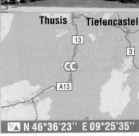

💬 Quiet family campsite, beautiful location in the valley of the Hinterrhein river. Many options for walking to the rustic villages on the hillsides. There is an indoor medicinal mineral spa just next to the campsite with wellness facilities. There is a heated outdoor pool next to the campsite. Free wifi.

🚗 A13, exit Zillis or Andeer. The campsite is on the north side of the village by the mineral bath.

CC € 20  1/2-30/6  15/9-15/12

N 46°36'23''  E 09°25'35''

## Brig, CH-3900 / Wallis

⛺ Camping Geschina★★★★
📧 Geschinaweg 41
☎ +41 2 79 23 06 88
🕐 28/4 - 19/10
@ geschina@bluewin.ch

2ha 100T 10A

**1** A**G**IJKLM**PQ**
**2** CFGKRWX
**3** ARU
**4** (**C**+**H** 1/5-30/9) **J**(Q+R 🖭)
**5** **AB**FGIJKLMNO**P**UW
**6** CEJ(N 0,5km)OTV

941

💬 A lovely, well maintained campsite on the banks of a fast-flowing stream. Shaded pitches. Outdoor pool close to the site. Within walking distance of the historic village of Brig.

🚗 Drive to Brig, then follow Brig-Glis and 'Altstadt' (P) signs. Then follow camping signs.

Ernen
Brig
Visp

CC € 20   28/4-6/7   25/8-19/10     N 46°18'34''  E 07°59'36''

---

## Chur (GR), CH-7000 / Graubünden

⛺ CampAu Chur★★★
📧 Felsenaustraße 61
☎ +41 8 12 84 22 83
🕐 1/1 - 31/12
@ info@camping-chur.ch

2,7ha 80T(30-110m²) 10A CEE

**1** ACD**G**HIJKLMO**PQ**
**2** CFGLRSTUVWXY
**3** B**F**JM**N**OPQR**SW**
**4** (**C** 1/5-1/9) (**F**+**H** 🖭) **J** (Q+R+T+U+X+Y+Z 🖭)
**5** **AB**DFGIJKLMNOPRUWZ
**6** ACDFGH**K**(N 0,5km)O

942

💬 The campsite is a grassy field surrounded by trees located between the Rhine and a large sports centre with a swimming pool, tennis court etc. It is 2.5 km from the town centre and there is a direct bus service. Good base for a trip with the Bernina or Glacier Express.

🚗 A13, exit Chur-Süd (also Arosa/Lenzerheide) then follow main road and signs.

13
E43
A13
Chur
Domat/Ems
19
A13
3

CC € 20   11/3-23/6   2/9-8/12     N 46°51'43''  E 09°30'27''

---

## Cinuos-chel/Chapella, CH-7526 / Graubünden

⛺ Camping Chapella★★
☎ +41 8 18 54 12 06
🕐 1/5 - 31/10
@ info@campingchapella.ch

2ha 100T(40-100m²) 16A CEE

**1** A**G**IJKLM**PQ**
**2** CIJKLRSTWX
**3** A**F**HJRW
**4** (Q 5/6-15/9) (R 15/6-15/9)
**5** **AB**DGIJKLMNOPUWZ
**6** AE**I**K(N 3km)O

943

💬 A romantic grassy campsite with unreserved pitches and circled by trees. Perfect for canoeists. Modern heated toilet block. Close to the entrance to the National Park.

🚗 Located on route 27, a few kilometres south of Cinuos-chel. Beware sharp bend and bridge!

28
27
Trepalle
Livigno

CC € 18   1/5-30/6   26/8-30/10     N 46°37'57''  E 10°00'49''

## Cugnasco, CH-6516 / Tessin

♿ 🛜 **iD** 944

🏕 Camping Riarena★★★★
✉ Via Campeggio 1
☎ +41 9 18 59 16 88
🔓 15/3 - 20/10
@ info@campingriarena.ch

3,2ha 100T(70-100m²) 10A

1 ACD**G**IJKLMO**P**Q
2 BCFGLRSVWX
3 ABHJNRU**W**X
4 (B+G 15/5-30/9)
  (Q+R+T+U+V+X+Y 🔓)
5 **AB**EFGIJKLMNOPRUW
6 ACEGK(N 2km)OTV

💬 Well-maintained, peacefully located family campsite with a swimming pool. Lovely playground. Excellent base for cycling and walking. Good facilities for the disabled. Credit cards accepted.

🚗 A2, exit Bellinzona-Süd/Locarno. After 8 km turn right to airfield. Continue towards Gordola-Gudo. Direction Gudo. In Cugnasco follow camping signs.

**CC** € 20 15/3-30/6 1/9-20/10

📐 **N 46°10'11'' E 08°54'51''**

---

## Davos Glaris, CH-7277 / Graubünden

⛷ 🛜 **iD** 945

🏕 Camping RinerLodge
✉ Landwasserstraße 64
☎ +41 8 14 17 00 33
🔓 1/1 - 31/12
@ rinerlodge@davosklosters.ch

1ha 84T(40-80m²) 10-16A CEE

1 ACD**F**HIJKLMPQ
2 CGTUVW
3 BFHJU**W**
4 (Q+R+T+X 🔓) (Z 1/5-30/10)
5 **AB**DFGIJMNOPUWZ
6 CFGI**J**(N 8km)OV

💬 The campsite has hardened level grounds and is a short distance from Davos and the base of the Rinerhornlift. Camping guests can make free use in the summer of six mountain lifts and public transport.

🚗 Campsite located 10 minutes by car west of Davos. Access road from Klosters not a problem.

**CC** € 20 1/5-16/6 15/9-30/10 14=13

📐 **N 46°44'39'' E 09°46'46''**

---

## Egnach, CH-9322 / Ostschweiz

♿ 🛜 **iD** 946

🏕 Camping Seehorn★★★★
✉ Wiedehorn
☎ +41 7 14 77 10 06
🔓 1/3 - 31/10
@ info@seehorn.ch

2,5ha 80T(100-120m²) 13A CEE

1 ACD**F**HIJKLMOPQ
2 DFGKLMORVWX
3 ABCKRUZ
4 (G 1/5-1/9)
  (Q+R+T+U+X+Y 🔓)
5 **AB**DEFGIJKLMNOPQR**STU**
  WXYZ
6 ABCDEG**K**(N 2km)OUV

💬 Campsite on a transit route, separated from the Bodensee lake by lawns. Good cycling and walking opportunities, cooking facilities available. The sanitary facilities are good and there is a good restaurant.

🚗 The campsite is located on route 13 between Romanshorn and Arbon. Signposted from both the west and east approaches.

**CC** € 20 1/3-18/4 22/4-29/5 2/6-7/6 10/6-20/6 23/6-28/6 1/9-31/10

📐 **N 47°32'12'' E 09°23'52''**

## Engelberg, CH-6390 / Zentralschweiz

🏕 Camping Eienwäldli★★★★★
✉ Wasserfallstraße 108
☎ +41 4 16 37 19 49
🕐 1/1 - 31/12
@ info@eienwaeldli.ch

3,7ha 125T(60-120m²) 10A CEE

**1** ACD**F**IJKLMPQ
**2** CGKLRTUVWXY
**3** BC**EF**HIJKLNRU**V**W
**4** (A 1/7-30/10)
(**F+H** 1/1-5/5,25/5-31/12) **IJ**
**KLNP**(Q+S+T+U+V+X 🔲)
(Y 1/1-10/11,6/12-31/12)
(Z 🔲)
**5** **AB**DEFGJLN**P**UWXYZ
**6** ACDEGHKL(N 1,5km)OSTV

💬 An attractively located campsite in the mountains. Most suitable for mountain and winter sports. Good bus service. The main building has an extensive wellness area.

🚗 A2, exit Stans-Süd. At the monastery in Engelberg turn right towards Eienwäldli. After 1.5 km the campsite is located behind Hotel Eienwäldli.

947

Sarnen  Oberrickenbach

Meien

CC € 20   11/3-12/4  5/5-29/5  24/6-1/7  1/9-13/12

📍 N 46°48'34'' E 08°25'26''

---

## Filisur, CH-7477 / Graubünden

🏕 Camping Islas★★★★
☎ +41 8 14 04 16 47
🕐 1/4 - 31/10
@ info@campingislas.ch

4,4ha 120T(30-80m²) 13-16A

**1** ACDGHIJKLMNPQ
**2** BCKLRSTWXY
**3** ABF**H**JR**W**
**4** (**A** 1/7-30/8) (B 1/6-1/9)
(Q+R+U+V+Y+Z 🔲)
**5** **AB**DFGIJKLMNOPUWZ
**6** ADEGJ**K**(N 2km)OTV

💬 A sheltered and very tranquil location in a valley on a level grassy field. Modern amenities. There is a modern 18 hole Alpine golf course a few kilometres from Alvaneu-Bad and therapeutic sulphur baths with many facilities.

🚗 From Tiefencastel, first direction Davos/Albula, then Albula. Follow signs. The Albula bypass is difficult to drive in the other direction by caravan.

948

Vaz/Obervaz

**Tiefencastel** CC

CC € 18   1/4-30/6  1/9-31/10

📍 N 46°40'17'' E 09°40'27''

---

## Frutigen, CH-3714 / Bern

🏕 Camping Grassi★★★★
✉ Grassiweg 60
☎ +41 3 36 71 11 49
🕐 1/1 - 31/12
@ info@camping-grassi.ch

2,6ha 68T(20-120m²) 10A CEE

**1** ACDGIJKLPQ
**2** CGKRTWXY
**3** AGHKLRU**W**
**4** (Q 1/7-30/8)
**5** **AB**DGIJKLMNOPUW
**6** ACDEGHK(N 1km)OV

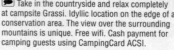

💬 Take in the countryside and relax completely at campsite Grassi. Idyllic location on the edge of a conservation area. The view over the surrounding mountains is unique. Free wifi. Cash payment for camping guests using CampingCard ACSI.

🚗 Follow the Spiez-Kandersteg road and take exit Frutigen-Dorf. Over the bridge and enter village. Turn left at Hotel Simplon. The campsite is clearly signposted.

949

Wimmis

Frutigen 223

CC

Adelboden

CC € 20   1/1-30/6  1/9-31/12

📍 N 46°34'55'' E 07°38'29''

## Gstaad, CH-3780 / Bern 🎿 📶 iD (950)

🏕 Camping Bellerive***
📧 Bellerivestraße 38
☎ +41 3 37 44 63 30
📅 1/1 - 31/12
@ bellerive.camping@bluewin.ch

0,8ha 35T(80-100m²) 12A CEE

1 **AG**IJKLOPQ
2 CGRTUVWX
3 AHJU**W**
4 (Q 📅)
5 **AB**DGIJKLMN**P**UW
6 CDFJ(N 1,5km)OV

💬 Small campsite on the edge of the village. Connected to the village by a footpath. Trains pass by occasionally.

🚗 From Saanen drive in the direction of Gstaad. Follow the signs. Campsite located on the right of the road, 1.3 km past the roundabout in Saanen.

Zweisimmen
Saanen
CC
Lenk
11

**CC** € 20  7/1-31/1  4/3-21/6  19/8-2/9  16/9-22/12     📷 N 46°28'52'' E 07°16'22''

---

## Gudo, CH-6515 / Tessin ♿ 📶 iD (951)

🏕 Camping Isola****
📧 Via al Gaggioletto 3
☎ +41 9 18 59 32 44
📅 1/1 - 31/12
@ isola2014@ticino.com

3ha 48T(40-100m²) 10A CEE

1 ACD**G**IJKLMOPQ
2 BCFGLRVXY
3 ABHJKNRU
4 (B 15/5-30/9) (G 1/5-30/9)
   (Q+R 15/4-30/10)
   (T+V+X+Y+Z 15/3-15/12)
5 **AB**DFGIJKLMNOPUWZ
6 E**IK**(N 3km)V

💬 A quietly located campsite with unheated swimming pool in the Ticino valley. Bar and cocktail bar. Ideally located for walking and cycling trips. Day trips to Valle Maggia, Como and Milan for example, or the fossil museum in Meride or the Monte Generoso.

🚗 A2 exit Bellinzona-Süd/Locarno direction Locarno. After ±8 km turn right towards airport. Then towards Gordola-Gudo, then direction Gudo. Campsite is signposted between Cugnasco and Gudo. Narrow access road.

A2    A13
Bellinzona
Locarno    CC
405
E35

**CC** € 18  1/1-7/7  25/8-31/12     📷 N 46°10'15'' E 08°55'53''

---

## Innertkirchen, CH-3862 / Bern 📶 iD (952)

🏕 Camping Aareschlucht***
📧 Hauptstraße 34
☎ +41 3 39 71 27 14
📅 1/5 - 31/10
@ campaareschlucht@bluewin.ch

0,5ha 45T(50-100m²) 10A

1 ACD**G**IJKLMOPQ
2 GKRWX
3 BRU**W**
4 (Q 15/6-15/9)
5 **AB**DGIJKLMNO**P**UW
6 CDFK(N 1km)OQ

💬 A friendly, pleasant campsite. Beautiful views of the mountain ranges. Excellent sanitation. Located by the 'Aareschlucht' in the direction of Susten and the Grimsel pass.

🚗 Coming from Meiringen the campsite is located between Meiringen and Innertkirchen, on the left of the road, just past the entrance to Aareschlucht near Innertkirchen.

4
A8
Meiringen
11
CC
6
Grindelwald

**CC** € 18  1/5-7/7  26/8-31/10     📷 N 46°42'34'' E 08°12'53''

## Interlaken/Unterseen, CH-3800 / Bern ♿ 🏊 📶 iD (953)

🏕 Camping Alpenblick****
🏠 Seestraße 130
☎ +41 3 38 22 77 57
🗓 1/1 - 31/12
@ info@camping-alpenblick.ch

2ha 130T(60-100m²) 16A

**1** ABCD**G**IJKLMOP**Q**
**2** CDFGKRUVWXY
**3** ABF**G**HJNRU**W**XZ
**4** (Q+R+T+U+Y+Z 🔧)
**5** **AB**DFGIJKLMNOPQRUWXZ
**6** CDFGKM(N 3km)OTV

💬 A well-run family campsite next to the Thunnersee lake, no marked out pitches, agreeable atmosphere. Level grounds comprising long avenues with grassy strips on each side. Quite a large number of tall trees. Restaurant with reasonable prices.

🚗 Take the A8 Thun-Interlaken-Brienz. Exit 24 Interlaken-West. Follow campsite symbol 2.

CC € 20  1/1-12/7  1/9-31/12

📍 N 46°40'47'' E 07°49'04''

---

## Krattigen, CH-3704 / Bern 👫 🏊 📶 iD (954)

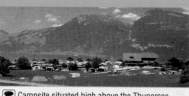

🏕 Camping Stuhlegg****
🏠 Stueleggstraße 7
☎ +41 3 36 54 27 23
🗓 1/1 - 31/12
@ info@camping-stuhlegg.ch

2,4ha 65T(80m²) 13A

**1** ACD**F**IJKLMNOPST
**2** FGJKRWX
**3** BGHJNRU
**4** (C+H 1/5-30/9) M
(Q+R+T+U+X 1/1-31/10,
1/12-31/12)
**5** **AB**DFGIJKLMNO**P**UW
**6** ACDEHK(N 0,3km)OTV

💬 Campsite situated high above the Thunersee, with lovely grassy fields, nice little shop and snack bar, all with a friendly feel.

🚗 Motorway Basel-Bern-Interlaken. Exit Leissigen, direction Krattigen.

CC € 20  1/1-30/6  1/9-31/12

📍 N 46°39'32'' E 07°43'01''

---

## La Fouly, CH-1944 / Wallis 👫 ♿ 📶 iD (955)

🏕 Camping Des Glaciers****
🏠 route de Tsamodet 36
☎ +41 2 77 83 18 26
🗓 11/5 - 6/10
@ info@camping-glaciers.ch

7ha 200T(50-120m²) 10A CEE

**1** ACD**G**IJKLMOPQ
**2** BCGJKLRTVWXY
**3** ABGHJ**M**RUW
**4** (Q 1/6-30/9) (R 🔧)
**5** **AB**DEFGIJKLMNPUWZ
**6** ACEIKM(N 0,5km)OV

💬 An idyllically located campsite with excellent sanitation at the foot of a glacier; a Mecca for hikers. Pitches partly on terraces, partly on large grassy fields.

🚗 Martigny towards St. Bernhard. In Orsières direction La Fouly/Val Ferret. Turn right at the end of the village. The no entry sign does not apply to campsite guests.

CC € 20  11/5-5/7  24/8-6/10

📍 N 45°56'00'' E 07°05'43''

## Le Landeron, CH-2525 / Neuchâtel

♿ 📶 iD **956**

🏕 Camping Des Pêches****
🏠 Route du Port
☎ +41 3 27 51 29 00
📅 1/4 - 15/10
@ info@camping-lelanderon.ch

4ha 170T(64-100m²) 16A CEE

**1** ABCDGIJKLMOP**Q**
**2** ACDFGLMRVX
**3** B**F**GHJKLMNR**WZ**
**4** (H 15/5-31/8) JM
  (Q+S+X+Z 📅)
**5** **AB**DFGIJKLMNOP**U**WX
**6** CDEGK(N 0,5km)OTV

💬 A campsite located in an oasis of greenery with wonderful views of the Chasseral. The touring pitches are separate from the permanent pitches. There is a Euro-Relais right next to the entrance. Very good restaurant. Free pool about 800 metres away.

🚗 From La Neuville drive towards Le Landeron. In the village there are signs to the campsite. Take care: very high humps on the tourist road to the campsite; drive at walking pace.

**Biel/Bienne**
30
**CC**
5
**Neuchâtel** 10 22
E25

CC € 20 1/4-30/6 19/8-15/10    📍 N 47°03'11'' E 07°04'12''

---

## Le Prese, CH-7746 / Graubünden

♿ 📶 iD **957**

🏕 Camping Cavresc***
🏠 Via del Canton 757a
☎ +41 8 18 44 02 59
📅 1/1 - 31/12
@ camping.cavresc@bluewin.ch

1ha 84T(30-75m²) 13A CEE

**1** ACD**G**IJKLMN**PQ**
**2** CGKRSVWX
**3** BHJKMRU**W**
**4** (Q+R 📅)
  (T+V+X+Z 1/4-31/10)
**5** **AB**DFGIJKLMNOP**U**WXYZ
**6** CEG**IK**(N 0,3km)OV

💬 Pitches on grassy meadows in the Valposchiavo valley with its southern climate. Newly built campsite, with ultramodern sanitation. Close to Italy and the Poschiavo Lake (water sport). A lot of touristic attractions / places of interest.

🚗 Reaching the village Le Prese, take the side-road of the main road (29) on the eastside. Follow the signs.

29
**Poschiavo**
**CC**
Tirano
SS38

CC € 20 1/1-1/7 22/8-31/12    📍 N 46°17'41'' E 10°04'49''

---

## Les Haudères, CH-1984 / Wallis

⛷ ♿ 📶 iD **958**

🏕 Camping Molignon****
🏠 route de Molignon 163
☎ +41 2 72 83 12 40
📅 1/1 - 31/12
@ info@molignon.ch

2,5ha 110T(75-100m²) 10A CEE

**1** ACD**G**IJKLMOP**Q**
**2** CGIJKRTVWXY
**3** AGHJRU
**4** (C+D+H 20/5-15/9)
  (Q+R 15/6-15/9) (U 1/6-20/9)
  (Y 1/5-31/10) (Z 1/6-30/9)
**5** **AB**DFGJKLMNOP**U**WZ
**6** AEGK(N 1km)O

💬 Beautifully situated campsite with mountains all around, but still with plenty of sun. Lovely indoor pool for all ages.

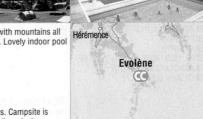

🚗 At Sion turn off to Val d'Hérens. Campsite is 3 km past Evolène on the right. Well marked.

Hérémence
**Evolène**
**CC**

CC € 20 1/5-30/6 24/8-15/10    📍 N 46°05'29'' E 07°30'29''

## Lignières, CH-2523 / Neuchâtel ♿ ⛷ 🏕 📶 **iD** 〔959〕

🏕 Camping Fraso Ranch★★★★
✉ ch. du Grand-Marais
☎ +41 3 27 51 46 16
📅 1/1 - 31/10
@ camping.fraso-ranch@
　 bluewin.ch

4ha 47T(50-100m²) 10A CEE

**1** ACD**G**HIJKLMOPQ
**2** FGLRVX
**3** BGJMNR
**4** (C+H 1/6-31/8) **K**N
　 (Q 1/1-30/10) (R 20/5-2/9)
　 (T 5/5-30/9) (X 🔲)
　 (Y 1/1-30/10)
**5** **AB**DFGIJ**K**LMNO**P**UW
**6** AEGHI**K**(N 1km)OV

💬 A sports campsite on the sunny slopes of the Chasseral with an extensive programme of sporting events. Really recommended for sports lovers. Sauna and jacuzzi.

🚗 In Le Landeron drive towards Lignières, past the Lignières village 1 km on the right side of the road.

Biel/Bienne
Neuchâtel

**CC** € **18** 1/1-30/6 1/9-30/10 🗺 N 47°05'10'' E 07°04'16''

---

## Lungern, CH-6078 / Zentralschweiz 👫 ⛷ 🏕 📶 **iD** 〔960〕

🏕 Camping Obsee★★★
✉ Campingstraße 1
☎ +41 4 16 78 14-63
📅 1/1 - 31/12
@ camping@obsee.ch

2,2ha 92T(40-80m²) 10A CEE

**1** AC**F**IJKLMN**P**Q
**2** DFGJLNRVWX
**3** AHJN**Q**RUZ
**4** (A 1/7-31/8) (Q 15/5-31/10)
　 (R+U+Y 🔲)
**5** **AB**DFGIJLMNO**P**UW
**6** CDEGK(N 0,5km)OTV

💬 A sunny and quiet location right by the lake. Own restaurant with specialities from a wood burning grill. A holiday paradise in summer and winter. Tourist tax is not included in the CampingCard ACSI rate.

🚗 From Brienz direction Luzern. In Lungern village turn left at the first traffc lights. Follow the signs.

Giswil
Brienz
Meiringen

**CC** € **20** 1/1-29/5 3/6-7/6 11/6-1/7 1/9-31/12 🗺 N 46°47'06'' E 08°09'06''

---

## Meierskappel, CH-6344 / Zentralschweiz 📶 **iD** 〔961〕

🏕 Campingplatz Gerbe
✉ Landiswilerstraße
☎ +41 4 17 90 45 34
📅 1/3 - 31/10
@ info@swiss-bauernhof.ch

1,6ha 60T(80m²) 10A CEE

**1** ACD**F**HIJLPQ
**2** FGIRWX
**3** AHJ**P**RU
**4** (B 15/5-30/9) (Q+R+T+X 🔲)
**5** **AB**GIJKLMNOPUW
**6** CEK(N 0,5km)OV

💬 Campsite on the farm, you choose your own pitch, without restrictions.

🚗 A4 Rotkreuz-Schwyz, exit Küssnacht. Then follow the signs 'Meierskappel'. Just before the junction turn left at the farmhouse.

Hochdorf Zug
Luzern

382

**CC** € **18** 1/3-30/6 18/8-31/10 🗺 N 47°07'16'' E 08°26'54''

## Meiringen, CH-3860 / Bern

▲ AlpenCamping****
🏠 Brünigstraße 47
☎ +41 3 39 71 36 76
🗓 1/1 - 31/12
@ info@alpencamping.ch

1,4ha 47T(80-110m²) 10A CEE

**1** ACGIJKLMPQ
**2** FGKLRTVW
**3** BHJU
**4** N(Q+R 1/1-31/10,1/12-31/12)
(T 1/5-30/9,1/12-31/12)
**5** ABDFGIJKLMNOPUWXZ
**6** ACDEGJK(N 0,4km)OV

💬 A campsite with lovely toilet facilities and enthusiastic wardens. In the heart of the Swiss Alps and the starting point for enjoyable excursions. All pitches have power and mains water. Camp shop. Tourist tax is not included in the CampingCard ACSI rate.

🚗 From Interlaken to Luzern, via A8 to Meiringen. Follow camping signs at Meiringen.

A8
Lungern
Brienz
CC
Meiringen
11
6

CC € 20 28/4-7/7 25/8-31/10

⛰ N 46°44'04'' E 08°10'18''

962

---

## Molinazzo di Monteggio, CH-6995 / Tessin

▲ Camping Tresiana****
🏠 Via Cantonale 21
☎ +41 9 16 08 33 42
🗓 6/4 - 20/10
@ info@camping-tresiana.ch

1,5ha 90T(56-80m²) 10A

**1** ACDGHIJKLMNPQ
**2** CGRTVWXY
**3** ABFHJNRUWX
**4** (B 1/5-30/9) (G 1/5-15/9)
(Q+R+T+U+X 🗓)
**5** ABFGIJKLMNOPQRUWZ
**6** ACEGK(N 5km)OV

💬 A peaceful and well maintained campsite with spacious pitches on the River Tresa. The pitches are well cared for and clean. Swimming pool in the grounds.

🚗 A2, exit Lugano-Nord/Ponte Tresa, towards Ponte Tresa. In Ponte Tresa drive in the direction of Luino until the border and then turn right. In Molinazzo di Monteggio there are signs to the campsite.

2
SS34
Luino
Lugano
E35
CC
A2
Cuveglio
SS394
SS344

CC € 18 23/4-30/6 1/9-20/10

⛰ N 45°59'28'' E 08°49'00''

963

---

## Müstair, CH-7537 / Graubünden

▲ Camping Muglin
🏠 Via Muglin 223
☎ +41 8 18 58 59 90
🗓 18/4 - 27/10
@ info@campingmuglin.ch

4,5ha 65T(100m²) 13A CEE

**1** ACDGIJKLMPQ
**2** BCGKLRWX
**3** ABMU
**4** MN(Q+R+T+X+Z 1/5-27/10)
**5** ABDFGIJKLMNOPWXYZ
**6** ACDEGIK(N 1km)OPV

💬 A campsite on a former farm with a large open grassy field. Large free sauna. New toilets. Little or no shade. Restaurant and communal area.

🚗 In the village on road 28, follow turning to campsite.

Malles
Venosta
SS41
SS40
Prato Allo
Stelvio
CC
28
SS38

CC € 18 18/4-30/6 20/8-27/10

⛰ N 46°37'26'' E 10°26'56''

964

## Ottenbach, CH-8913 / Zürich

🛜 iD 965

⛺ Camping Reussbrücke****
📧 Muristraße 34
☎ +41 4 47 61 20 22
🗓 13/4 - 12/10
@ info@camping-reussbruecke.ch

1,5ha 40T(80-120m²) 6A CEE

**1** AFHIJKLNOQ
**2** CFGRUX
**3** BHJRUX
**4** (B 1/6-15/9)
   (Q+R+T+X+Z 🚿)
**5** ABGIJKLMNOPU
**6** CDEGJ(N 0,5km)OTV

💬 The campsite is located on the river Reuss in a beautiful nature area where you can walk or cycle. Level grounds (partially) with trees.

🚗 On the A4 Zürich-Gotthard take exit 31 Affoltern am Albis. Then go via Obfelden to Ottenbach. In Ottenbach campsite is signposted. The campsite is right before the bridge and is accessible via the car park.

CC €20  27/4-7/6  17/6-30/6  1/9-12/10    📡 N 47°16'47'' E 08°23'43''

---

## Raron/Turtig, CH-3942 / Wallis

👫 🛜 iD 966

⛺ Camping Santa Monica****
📧 Kantonstraße 56
☎ +41 2 79 34 24 24
🗓 30/3 - 21/10
@ info@santa-monica.ch

4ha 124T(80-120m²) 16A CEE

**1** ACDGIJKLMOPRS
**2** CFGKLRTVWX
**3** AFHIJMNRU
**4** (A 1/6-30/9) (C 19/5-9/9)
   (H 20/5-10/9)
   (Q+R+T+U+X+Z 🚿)
**5** ABDFGIJKLMNOPRSTUW
   XYZ
**6** ACEGIK(N 0,3km)OV

💬 An appealing campsite with excellent toilet facilities and friendly management. Positioned next to 2 cable cars and centrally located for various walks in sunny Valais. Excellent base for day trips to Zermatt, Saas Fee, the Aletsch Glacier and the Simplon Pass. Only cash payment possible with CampingCard ACSI.

🚗 Campsite is located along the road Gampel-Visp. The entrance is next to the Renault Garage.

CC €20  20/4-30/6  19/8-19/10    📡 N 46°18'11'' E 07°48'08''

---

## Saas-Grund, CH-3910 / Wallis

🛜 iD 967

⛺ Camping Am Kapellenweg***
☎ +41 2 79 57 49 97
🗓 10/5 - 13/10
@ camping@kapellenweg.ch

0,7ha 100T(30-80m²) 10A CEE

**1** ACDGIJKLMPQ
**2** CGKRWX
**3** HJU
**4** (Q+R+Z 🚿)
**5** ABDGIJKLMNOPUW
**6** CEGIJ(N 1km)V

💬 Alpine campsite located in beautiful scenery near a village. Perfect for walking, also for inexperienced walkers. Mandatory use of a 'Bürgerpass'(excluded) gives you the right to use the cable cars in the Saas Valley.

🚗 In Visp direction Saas-Grund and Saas-Fee. In Saas-Grund centre direction Saas-Almagell. Campsite after 700m on the right.

CC €20  10/5-30/6  19/8-13/10    📡 N 46°07'00'' E 07°56'24''

## Splügen, CH-7435 / Graubünden  ⛷ 📶 iD  968

🏕 Camping Splügen****
🏠 Campingstrasse 18
☎ +41 8 16 64 14 76
📅 1/1 - 31/12
@ camping@spluegen.ch

0,8ha 30T(80-120m²) 10A CEE

**1** ACD**G**IJKLMQ
**2** CFGKRSTX
**3** BHIJ**M**RU**W**
**4** (**A**+Q+R+T+Z 📅)
**5** **AB**DEGIJKLMNOPUWZ
**6** CEGJ(N 0,5km)OU

💬 A quiet family campsite in the Hinter-Rhein valley. Plenty of comfort in both summer and winter seasons. Ideal base for trips out including the source of the Rhine. Free wifi.

🚗 A13, exit Splügen. Follow signs in Splügen. About 500 metres west of the village.

Vals — Andeer — Splügen — CC — A13 — 13 — SS36

CC € **20**  1/4-30/6  1/9-15/12    🏔 N 46°32'58'' E 09°18'51''

---

## Sta Maria, CH-7536 / Graubünden  iD  969

🏕 Camping Pè da Munt***
☎ +41 8 18 58 71 33
📅 30/5 - 7/10
@ campingstamaria@bluewin.ch

2ha 60T(30-85m²) 10A

**1** A**G**IJKLM**PQ**
**2** CGIJKRSTVWX
**3** AHJU
**4** (Q 📅)
**5** **AB**GIJKLMNOPUWZ
**6** CE(N 0,5km)V

💬 Very peacefully located and with good amenities. Grassy fields partly in terraces. Little shade but a sheltered location. It is 5 km from the Italian border and 15 km to the Umbrail pass. Each pitch has its own wooden bench and place for a log fire. One of the entrances to the National Park is located in the village.

🚗 Just outside the village, on the road to the Umbrail pass.

Malles Venosta — SS40 — SS41 — Prato Allo Stelvio — 28 — CC — SS38

CC € **18**  30/5-30/6  19/8-7/10    🏔 N 46°35'49'' E 10°25'33''

---

## Stechelberg, CH-3824 / Bern  👫 ⛷ 📶 iD  970

🏕 Camping Breithorn***
🏠 Sandbach
☎ +41 3 38 55 12 25
📅 1/1 - 30/10, 15/12 - 31/12
@ breithorn@stechelberg.ch

1ha 35T(80m²) 10A CEE

**1** A**F**IJLQ
**2** CGRUWX
**3** AHJ**W**
**4** (Q+R 📅)
**5** **AB**DGIJKLMNPUW
**6** EK(N 4km)O

💬 A friendly, well maintained campsite between Lauterbrunnen and Stechelberg. Many opportunities for walking. Fishing possible.

🚗 Take the Interlaken-Lauterbrunnen road. In Lauterbrunnen drive towards Stechelberg. After 3 km the campsite is located on the right.

Lauterbrunnen — CC

CC € **18**  1/5-30/6  18/8-30/9    🏔 N 46°34'05'' E 07°54'34''

## Stechelberg, CH-3824 / Bern

👥 📶 iD **971**

▲ Camping Rütti\*\*\*
☎ +41 3 38 55 28 85
📅 1/5 - 30/9
@ campingruetti@stechelberg.ch

1ha 100T(40-100m²) 10A

1️⃣ **A**F**IJ**KL**O**Q
2️⃣ CG**K**RTUWXY
3️⃣ A**HJ**RU
4️⃣ (Q+R+T 🖵)
5️⃣ **AB**GI**J**LMN**P**UW
6️⃣ ACEK(N 6km)OT

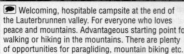

💬 Welcoming, hospitable campsite at the end of the Lauterbrunnen valley. For everyone who loves peace and mountains. Advantageous starting point for walking or hiking in the mountains. There are plenty of opportunities for paragliding, mountain biking etc.

Lauterbrunnen

CC

🚐 The campsite is located at the end of the Lauterbrunnen-Stechelberg road.

CC € **18** *1/5-29/6 18/8-29/9*    📍 N 46°32'47'' E 07°54'07''

---

## Sutz/Lattrigen, CH-2572 / Bern

👥 📶 iD **972**

▲ Camping Sutz am Bielersee\*\*\*\*
📧 Kirchrain 40
☎ +41 3 23 97 13 45
📅 30/3 - 31/10
@ mail@camping-sutz.ch

10ha 56T(60-80m²) 10-15A

1️⃣ AC**G**IJLMN**P**Q
2️⃣ DFGLMNRUVX
3️⃣ ABGHJKLNR**T**UWX
4️⃣ M(Q+S+U+X 🖵)
5️⃣ **AB**DEFGIJKLMNOPUWXYZ
6️⃣ CDEHJ(N 1km)OT

NEW

💬 Campsite directly on the lake. Modern new toilet block.

🚐 From Biel drive towards Nidau-Täuffelen. After 1 km past city centre of Ipsach turn right, just behind Wood Mill Spychiger A.G Holz + Imprägnierung.

30   6   **Grenchen**
A5
**Biel/Bienne**
CC   A6
5   E27 | A6
22

CC € **20** *1/5-29/6 1/9-29/9*    📍 N 47°06'33'' E 07°13'13''

---

## Thusis, CH-7430 / Graubünden

⛷ ♿ 📶 iD **973**

▲ Camping Thusis\*\*\*
📧 Pantunweg 3
☎ +41 8 16 51 24 72
📅 1/1 - 31/12
@ info@camping-thusis.ch

4,5ha 104T(50-100m²) 16A CEE

1️⃣ ABCD**G**HIJKLMN**P**Q
2️⃣ BCFGRSWXY
3️⃣ ABHJ**M**NR**W**
4️⃣ (Q+X 🖵)
5️⃣ **AB**DEFGIJKLMNOPUWXZ
6️⃣ ACDEGJ(N 0,5km)O

💬 An attractive, peaceful campsite. Excellent amenities. Ideal starting point for walking, cycling, motor or car tours and winter sports. Excellent base for a tour with the Bernina Express (World Heritage). Free wifi. Swimming pool nearby.

🚐 On A13 take exit Thusis-Süd and follow campsite signs.

A13   3
CC   417
**Thusis  Tiefencastel**
13

CC € **20** *1/1-30/6 26/8-31/12*    📍 N 46°41'56'' E 09°26'42''

## Unterägeri, CH-6314 / Zentralschweiz

⊗ 🎿 ⛷ ♿ 📶 **iD** **974**

🏕 Camping Unterägeri****
📧 Wilbrunnenstraße 81
☎ +41 4 17 50 39 28
🔓 1/1 - 31/12
@ info@campingunteraegeri.ch

4,8ha 150**T**(70-100m²) 10A CEE

**1** ACDEHIJKLMO**PQ**
**2** DKLNRVWXY
**3** BGHJRU**WZ**
**4** (A 1/6-30/9) (Q+R 1/4-31/10)
    (S 1/4-30/9)
    (T+U+W+X+Y+Z 1/4-31/10)
**5** **AB**DFGIJKLMNOPUW
**6** CDEGHK(N 2km)OV

💬 Lovely campsite in natural landscape with spacious marked out pitches. Located right on the lake, where you can swim. Also a nice area for walking and/or cycling.

🚗 A4 Luzern-Zürich, exit Baar towards Ägeri. Drive via Baar to Unterägeri. In the village follow the signs.

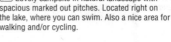

**CC** € **20** 1/1-19/4 22/4-30/5 2/6-7/6 10/6-20/6 23/6-30/6 1/9-31/12

🏔 N 47°07'40'' E 08°35'31''

---

## Visp, CH-3930 / Wallis

🎿 ♿ 📶 **iD** **975**

🏕 Camping/Schwimmbad
    Mühleye****
📧 Mühleye 7
☎ +41 2 79 46 20 84
🔓 1/4 - 31/10
@ info@camping-visp.ch

3,6ha 177**T**(50-150m²) 16A CEE

**1** ACD**G**IJKLM**PQ**
**2** CFGKLRVWX
**3** A**EF**HJN**O**RU
**4** (**A** 1/7-31/8)
    (**C+H** 26/4-8/9) J(Q 🔓)
    (T+U+X+Y 26/4-8/9)
**5** **AB**GIJKLMNOPUWXY
**6** ACFHK(N 2km)OQ

💬 Friendly centrally located campsite in Upper Valais which organises free walking trips. Splendid views of the mountains. Ideal base for trips to Zermatt, Saas Valley, the Aletsch Glacier, Simplon and Lower Valais.

🚗 Located on the Gampel to Visp road. Drive to the first set of traffic lights in Visp, turn left before the bridge at the BP station. Clearly signposted.

**CC** € **20** 1/4-1/7 20/8-31/10

🏔 N 46°17'53'' E 07°52'23''

---

## Winden, CH-9315 / Ostschweiz

♿ 📶 ✿ **iD** **976**

🏕 Camping Manser***
📧 Täschliberg
☎ +41 7 14 77 22 91
🔓 1/4 - 31/10
@ info@manserferien.ch

1ha 30**T** 16A CEE

**1** A**G**IJKLMNOPQ
**2** FKLRWX
**3** ABDJOPRU
**4** (Q+R 15/6-31/8)
**5** AFGIJMNOPQ**ST**UWZ
**6** CDEKL(N 2,5km)O

💬 Small camping grounds in the countryside between fruit trees. Lovely views. 4 km from the Bodenmeer lake. Farming experience with plenty of animals. Playground with trampoline and go-karts. Pleasant communal room with a kitchen. Lovely cycle paths, friendly atmosphere. Ideal for those who like nature and animals.

🚗 A1 exit 1 Arbon-west, left to Neukirch, 3rd exit left at roundabout to Wittenbach (camping sign). Left after 2.2 km to Täschliberg (camping sign).

**CC** € **20** 1/4-18/4 22/4-29/5 2/6-7/6 10/6-20/6 23/6-28/6 1/9-15/9

🏔 N 47°30'39'' E 09°21'43''

## Zweisimmen, CH-3770 / Bern

♿ 🚴 📶 iD  **977**

🏔 Camping Vermeille★★★★
📧 Ey Gässli 2
☎ +41 3 37 22 19 40
🗓 1/1 - 31/12
@ info@camping-vermeille.ch

1,3ha  20T(80-120m²)  10A  CEE

**1** ACD**G**IJKLMO**PQ**
**2** CGKRTWX
**3** A**F**HJKLRU**W**
**4** (**C**+G 1/6-31/8) (R 🔑)
**5** **AB**DFGIJKLMNOPQRUW
**6** ACDEGHKL(N 0,5km)ORUV

💬 Well-placed campsite with endless possibilities for summer and winter holidays: kayaking, mountain biking, mountain walks and winter sports.

🚗 Follow road 11 from Spiez to Zweisimmen. Campsite well signposted on road 11, located just before Zweisimmen. At exit to campsite drive 200 metres further. Second campsite after railroad crossing.

189  505

CC
Zweisimmen
11
Saanen
Adelboden

**CC** €**20**  7/1-10/2  18/3-26/5  11/6-6/7  26/8-15/12

🏔 N 46°33'45'' E 07°22'41''

# Austria

## General
Austria is a member of the EU.

### Time
The time in Austria is the same as Amsterdam, Paris and Rome and one hour ahead of London.

### Language
German.

## Border formalities
Many formalities and agreements about matters such as necessary travel documents, car papers, requirements relating to your means of transport and accommodation, medical expenses and taking pets with you do not only depend on the country you are travelling to but also on your departure point and nationality. The length of your stay can also play a role here. It is not possible within the confines of this guide to guarantee the correct and most up to date information with regard to these matters.

We advise you to consult the relevant authorities before your departure about:
- which travel documents you will need for yourself and your fellow passengers
- which documents you need for your car
- which regulations your caravan must meet
- which goods you may import and export
- how medical treatment will be arranged and paid for in your holiday destination in cases of accident or illness
- whether you can take pets. Contact your vets well in advance. They can give you information about the necessary vaccinations, proof thereof and obligations

on return. It would also make sense to enquire whether any special regulations apply to your pet in public places at your holiday destination. In some countries for example dogs must always be muzzled or transported in a cage.

You will find plenty of general information on ▶ *www.europa.eu* ◄ but make certain you select information that is relevant to your specific situation.

For the most recent customs regulations you should get in contact with the authorities of your holiday destination in your country of residence.

## Currency
The currency in Austria is the euro. Approximate exchange rates September 2018: £1 = € 1.12.

### Credit cards
You can pay by credit card at most restaurants, shops and petrol stations in towns and tourist areas.

## Opening times
### Banks
Banks are generally open from 09:00 to 12:00 and from 14:00 to 16:00.

### Shops
Most shops are open Monday to Friday until 18:00 and on Saturdays often until 17:00.

### Chemists, doctors
Information about duty doctors can be obtained from the local police. Chemists are

open on workdays between 09:00 and 17:00. When closed they display a sign with the name of the nearest chemist on duty.

## Communication

### (Mobile) phones
The mobile network works well throughout Austria, except in very remote areas. There is a 4G network for mobile internet.

### Wifi, internet
You can make use of a wifi network at more and more public locations, often for free.

### Post
Post offices are open Monday to Friday from 09:00 to 12:00 and from 14:00 to 16:00.

## Roads and traffic

### Road network
Remember, all traffic in Austria drives on the right and overtakes on the left! Headlight deflectors are advisable to prevent annoying oncoming drivers. Austria uses the metric system, so distances are measured in kilometres (km) and speeds in kilometres per hour (km/h). In the Alps, inclines of 6 to 15% and more are common. Most mountain roads have crash barriers on the valley side. The Austrian breakdown service ÖAMTC is available on tel. 120, ARBÖ on tel. 123. Take note: a light flashing on emergency phones on motorways indicates an incident or an accident.

### Traffic regulations
Traffic from the right has priority. If you are driving on a priority road and stop, you forfeit your priority. Traffic which can most easily move over must give priority on narrow mountain roads. You are not allowed to overtake on level crossings.
Maximum permitted alcohol level is 0.5‰. Phones must be used hands-free. It is not compulsory to use dipped headlights during the day. Children up to 12 years must wear a helmet when cycling. It is mandatory to make room on the centre lane for emergency services and the police when there is a tailback

on the motorway. They no longer use the hard shoulder for this. More information on
▶ *www.rettungsgasse.com* ◀
From 1 November until 15 April you are obliged to drive with winter tyres if conditions require them.

*Maximum speed*

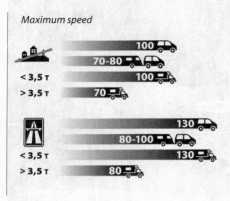

## Caravans, motorhomes

An 'Autobahnvignet' (sticker) is compulsory for motorhomes. No extra toll vignet is required for caravans. All vehicles over 3.5 tonnes pay a kilometre toll using the so-called GO boxes. This box is available at the border. You will find more information about these stickers in Austria under 'Autobahnvignet'. Overnight stays in caravans and motorhomes away from campsites are permitted for one night if travelling en route, except in Vienna, Tyrol and national parks.

## Maximum allowed measurements of combined length

Height 4 metres, width 2.55 metres and length 18.75 metres (of which the trailer maximum 12 metres).

## Fuel

All types of petrol are easily available in Austria, but LPG is hardly available.

## Filling stations

Filling stations on motorways are open 24 hours, other service stations are open between 08:00 and 20:00.

## Tolls

The main toll roads are: Arlbergstrassentunnel, Grossglockner-Hochalpenstrasse, Felbertauern-strasse, Brenner-, Tauern and Pyhrnautobahn.

## Autobahnvignet

To use motorways you need an 'Autobahnvignet'. Tourists can buy a special vignet for 10 days, 2 months or for one year. Vignets can be purchased at filling stations and post offices near the border. It is advisable to order the 'Autobahnvignet' online, for example on ▶ *www.tolltickets.com* ◀
In addition to this sticker, which must be stuck on the left-hand side of the windscreen, there is also a 'digital toll sticker' from 2018. This digital sticker is registered by license plate and can be ordered online at ▶ *www.asfinag.at* ◀
The price and validity of the online sticker is the same as the classic sticker. Please ensure that you order your vignette a minimum of 18 days before the desired start date.

## Korridorvignette

With the completion of the Pfänder tunnel the 'Korridorvignette' has been discontinued. On the 23 kilometre route on the A14 Rheintal/Walgau between the German border and the Hohenems interchange in Vorarlberg, you now need an Autobahnvignet or GO-box.

## Emergency numbers

- 112: national emergency number for fire, police and ambulance
- 133: police
- 122: fire
- 144: ambulance
- 140: mountain rescue service

## Camping

Austrian campsites are among the best in
Europe. Carinthia springs to mind for its
excellent location, stable climate and beautiful
lakes, Many campsites in the Tyrol specialise in
wellness and sportive camping. Campsites in
Vorarlberg, Tyrol and Salzburg are very busy in
winter.

### Practical

- Additional charges for things such as tourist
  taxes and environmental charges are
  sometimes quite high.
- Make sure you always have a world adaptor
  for electrical appliances.
- Tap water is safe to drink.

## Abersee/St. Gilgen, A-5342 / Salzburg

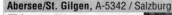

**▲ Camping Birkenstrand Wolfgangsee****

🏠 Schwand 17a
☎ +43 66 49 40 48 79
🔑 1/4 - 26/10
@ camp@birkenstrand.at

📶 📱 iD **978**

1,8ha 110T(80-100m²) 12A CEE

1. ACDFIJKLMOPST
2. DGKLRTVWXY
3. AHJKLRUWZ
4. N(Q+R+T+U+V+X 🔑)
5. ABDFGIJKLNOPUWXYZ
6. ACEGK(N 5km)OV

💬 Idyllic campsite with direct access to the lake and sunbathing area. The sheltered comfort pitches on the lake are also available for CampingCard ACSI. Kayak, SUP and bicycle rental. Modern toilet facilities and private Finnish sauna. Fresh bread in the mini-market. Typical Austrian restaurant on the campsite. Close to direct bus connection to Salzburg.

🚗 B158 from St. Gilgen to Strobl. 4 km past St. Gilgen in Schwand exit left. Follow signs.

Thalgau · B154 · B151 · B153
Sankt Gilgen
CC · B158

CC €20 1/4-29/6 1/9-26/10 7=6 · N 47°44'21'' E 13°24'02''

---

## Abersee/St. Gilgen, A-5342 / Salzburg

♿ 📶 iD **979**

**▲ Romantik Camp. Wolfgangsee Lindenstrand****

🏠 Schwand 19
☎ +43 62 27 32 05
🔑 1/4 - 15/10
@ camping@lindenstrand.at

3ha 150T(80-110m²) 12A CEE

1. ACDGIJKLMOPQ
2. DGKLNRTVWXY
3. ABCHJKNUWZ
4. (A 1/7-31/8) (Q+R 🔑) (S+V 1/5-30/9)
5. ABDFGIJKLMNOPRUW XYZ
6. ACEGK(N 4,5km)OPV

💬 A peaceful family campsite right by the Wolfgangsee lake with a 140m beach and large landing stage. Modern toilet facilities, free wifi, spacious comfort pitches (water, drainage and electricity). Fresh bread daily, newspapers, ice cream, snacks and much more on sale in the nostalgic mini-market. A lovely area with plenty of opportunities for sport and culture.

🚗 B158 from St. Gilgen to Strobl. The exit is signposted in Schwand. Go to the left 4 km from St. Gilgen.

Thalgau · B154 · B151 · B153
Sankt Gilgen
CC · B158

CC €20 1/4-29/6 1/9-15/10 7=6 · N 47°44'23'' E 13°24'08''

---

## Abersee/St. Gilgen, A-5342 / Salzburg

📶 iD **980**

**▲ Seecamping Primus**

🏠 Schwand 39
☎ +43 62 27 32 28
🔑 26/4 - 29/9
@ seecamping.primus@aon.at

2ha 75T 10A

1. AGIJKLMOPQ
2. DGKLORTVWXY
3. BHJWZ
4. (A 1/7-1/9) (Q 🔑)
5. ABGIJKLMNOPUWXYZ
6. ACEIK(N 0km)

💬 A peaceful campsite right on the crystal clear Wolfgangsee lake (the campsite with the second longest beach). A haven of peace in this beautiful region with plenty of opportunities for watersports (own landing stage), cycling and walking. 3 km from St. Gilgen and 40 km from Salzburg.

🚗 B158 from St. Gilgen to Strobl. The exit is signposted. Schwand 4 km after St. Gilgen. Take care: the campsite is the last but one!

Thalgau · B154 · B151 · B153
Sankt Gilgen
CC · B158

CC €20 27/4-29/6 1/9-29/9 7=6 · N 47°44'27'' E 13°24'21''

## Abersee/St. Gilgen, A-5342 / Salzburg 📶 iD 981

🏕 Seecamping Wolfgangblick
✉ Seestraße 115
☎ +43 65 05 93 42 97
🗓 26/4 - 29/9
@ camping@wolfgangblick.at

2,2ha 80T(70-95m²) 12A

**1** ACFIJKLMOPQ
**2** DGKLNORTVWXY
**3** AFHJQRUWZ
**4** (A 1/6-31/8) (Q+S 9/5-9/9)
(T+U+V 9/5-31/8) (Z 🖱)
**5** ABFGJLMNOPUW
**6** CDEGK(N 3km)OV

💬 Family campsite close to the lake, with level beach. With the neighbouring ferry, you'll be in St. Wolfgang in a few minutes, and at the station of the Schafberg Railway. Free wifi. Small shop with bread and pastries, newspapers and a snack bar. Ideal base for various nature reserves, and for walkers, cyclists and climbers.

🚗 Take B158 from St. Gilgen to Strobl. At the km-marker 34 exit Abersee. Signposted.

CC € 20  26/4-29/6  1/9-29/9  7=6    N 47°44'14'' E 13°25'58''

## Aigen (Ennstal), A-8943 / Steiermark 📶 iD 982

🏕 Camping Putterersee
✉ Hohenberg 2A
☎ +43 3 68 22 28 59
🗓 15/4 - 31/10
@ camping.putterersee@aon.at

2ha 70T(90-100m²) 13A CEE

**1** AGIJKLOPST
**2** ADJKLRWX
**3** AHJRUWZ
**4** (Q+R+T+V+X+Z 1/5-30/9)
**5** ABDGIJKLMNOPSUWZ
**6** ACDEK(N 1km)V

💬 A beautiful campsite right next to Styria's warmest lake, idyllically and peacefully located in a protected nature reserve. Lovely walks around the lake and cycle trips through the Ennstal valley. An informal camping cafe for light meals (snacks and pizza) and a camp shop for supplies for breakfast. Since 2011 new, modern toilet facilities, environmentally heated.

🚗 A10 Salzburg, exit Radstadt direction Graz. At Wörschach continue towards Aigen/Ketten and follow signs.

CC € 18  15/4-30/6  1/9-31/10  10=9    N 47°31'16'' E 14°07'56''

## Bad Waltersdorf, A-8271 / Steiermark 👫 ♿ 📶 iD 983

🏕 Thermenland Camping Rath & Pichler
✉ Campingweg 316
☎ +43 66 43 11 70 00
🗓 1/1 - 31/12
@ thermenland@
camping-bad-waltersdorf.at

1,6ha 73T(80-98m²) 16A CEE

**1** ACDGHIJKLMOPQ
**2** CFKRTUVWX
**3** AFHJKUW
**4** (Q+R 🖱)
**5** ABDFGIJKLMNOPQRUW XYZ
**6** ACEGJ(N 1km)OV

💬 An attractive and spacious family campsite. Very well-equipped toilet facilities. Suitable for visiting the thermal baths. Entry to the swimming pool in the village is free for campsite guests.

🚗 A2 exit 126 Sebersdorf/Bad Waltersdorf, direction Heil Therme and the resort of Bad Waltersdorf.

CC € 20  7/1-12/4  24/4-29/5  2/6-7/6  11/6-30/6  15/9-24/10  3/11-23/12    N 47°09'45'' E 16°01'23''

## Biberwier, A-6633 / Tirol

🏔 ♿ 📶 **iD** **984**

⛺ Feriencenter Camping Biberhof
📧 Schmitte 8
☎ +43 56 73 29 50
🗓 1/1 - 31/12
@ reception@biberhof.at

2,5ha 80T(80-100m²) 10A CEE

1 A**F**IJKLMOP**Q**
2 BCGKLRTVWXY
3 A**F**HJNR
4 (Q+Y+Z 🅿)
5 **AB**DFGIJKLMNOPR**S**UW XYZ
6 ACEGK(N 0,5km)OU

💬 A real family campsite. Beautifully located in the Tiroler Zugspitzen area. Spacious pitches. A super trampoline and various other sports for enthusiasts. Thanks to its location this is also a good campsite to visit during the winter.

🚗 Reutte in the direction Lermoos. In Lermoos centre take direction Biberwier. At the T-junction in Biberwier direction Ehrwald. Campsite 300 metres on the right.

CC € 20  21/4-29/6  1/9-15/12

📍 N 47°22'56'' E 10°54'07''

Untergrainau
B187
CC
B179
Nassereith    Telfs
B189    A12

---

## Bruck, A-5671 / Salzburg

🏔 ♿ 📶 **985**

⛺ Sportcamp Woferlgut****
📧 Krössenbach 40
☎ +43 6 54 57 30 30
🗓 1/1 - 31/12
@ info@sportcamp.at

18ha 270T(100-180m²) 16A CEE

1 D**G**IJKLMOPQ
2 DFGKLMRVWXY
3 BCD**F**GHJKLMNOP**Q**RU**V**Z
4 (A 🅿) (B 27/4-31/12) **IK**LM **NP**(Q+S+T+U+V+Y+Z 🅿)
5 **AB**DEFGIJKLMNOP**ST**UW XYZ
6 ACEGI**K**(N 0,5km)**O**PRSV

💬 One of the 'LeadingCampings of Europe', this campsite is located at the entrance to 'Nationalpark Hohe Tauern'. A park-like design, and many options for sports, leisure and relaxation. Indoor leisure pool (5 pools including 50-metres pool) with wellness and fitness. Open all year round. Excellent restaurant.

🚗 No vignette necessary via A8 (München-Salzburg), exit Siegsdorf, then dir. Inzell, Lofer, Zell am See, Bruck and follow campsite signs.

CC € 20  6/1-2/2  16/3-5/4  27/4-25/5  22/6-29/6  21/9-21/12

📍 N 47°17'01'' E 12°49'00''

Zell am See
B168    CC    B311

---

## Dellach im Drautal, A-9772 / Kärnten

♿ 📶 **iD** **986**

⛺ Camping Am Waldbad
📧 Rassnig 8
☎ +43 4 71 42 88
🗓 19/4 - 30/9
@ sigrid.goldberger@ktn.gde.at

3ha 195T(60-110m²) 10A

1 ACD**G**IJKLMOPQ
2 CGLRTVWXY
3 ABF GHJKLNRUV**W**X
4 (A 1/6-30/9) (C+H 🅿) IJ (Q+R+T+U+X+Z 🅿)
5 **AB**CEFGIJKLMNOPQR UWZ
6 CEGHK(N 0,5km)OTUV

💬 Campsite is located close to the Drauradweg cycle route, in the middle of the countryside. The swimming pool is free for campsite guests. Walking, cycling, climbing, rafting and canyoning all possible directly from campsite. Excellent restaurant and modern sanitary facilities.

🚗 2 routes: a) road B100 Spittal-Lienz; b) Mittersill-Felbertauerntunnel-Lienz-Dellach im Drautal. Site is signposted at a sharp bend in the village.

CC € 16  19/4-29/6  1/9-29/9

📍 N 46°43'54'' E 13°04'41''

B100    B87
CC
B110
Kötschach-Mauthen    B111    Kirchbach

## Döbriach, A-9873 / Kärnten

👪 ⛷ ♿ 📶 **iD**  **987**

🏕 Camping Brunner am See
📧 Glanzerstraße 108
☎ +43 42 46 71 89
🔓 1/1 - 31/12
@ office@camping-brunner.at

3,5ha 215T(60-107m²) 6A CEE

**1** ACD**G**IJKLMOPRS
**2** ACDGKLMRSTUVWX
**3** BC**F**HIJKL**M**N**Q**RU**W**Z
**4** (A 1/5-30/10) N(Q 🔓)
   (S+U+V+X+Y+Z 15/5-30/9)
**5** **AB**CDEFGHIJKLMNOPQ
   R**S**UVWXYZ
**6** ACFGHIK(N 0,2km)OTUV

💬 1st class comfort site on Millstätter See near the lake. Sunny grounds, excellent toilets. Shops, restaurants, watersports, golf, tennis, cycling, mountain biking. Guided mountain walks from Easter to autumn.

🚗 A10 Salzburg-Villach, exit 139 Millstätter See. At traffic lights left on the B98 direction Radenthein. After 12 km right towards Döbriach-See. After ca. 1.5 km right at 'ADEG-Markt'. From south: exit 178 Villach-Ossiacher See dir. Millstätter See.

Spittal an der Drau

CC € **20** 1/1-30/6 1/9-31/12

📐 N 46°46'04'' E 13°38'53''

---

## Döbriach, A-9873 / Kärnten

♿ 📶 **iD**  **988**

🏕 Happy Camping Golser GmbH
📧 Mauerweg 4
☎ +43 42 46 77 14
🔓 1/5 - 30/9
@ info@happycamping.at

1,5ha 120T(70-90m²) 6-10A

**1** A**G**IJKLMOPRS
**2** ADGKLRTVWX
**3** A**F**HJ**MN**O**QRW**Z
**4** **N**(Q+R 10/6-30/9)
**5** **AB**CDEFGIJKLMNOPR
   UWZ
**6** CEG**K**(N 1km)OTV

💬 A peacefully located family campsite right by the water. Spacious pitches, excellent toilet facilities. Take advantage of the mountains and the water. Experience it here.

🚗 A10 Salzburg-Villach, exit 139 Millstätter See (exit on the left!). Left at traffic lights on the B98 direction Radenthein. At the Spar supermarket turn round and drive back 600 metres. From the south exit 178 Villach-Ossiacher See direction Millstätter See.

Spittal an der Drau

CC € **18** 1/5-30/6 1/9-30/9

📐 N 46°46'33'' E 13°38'28''

---

## Döbriach, A-9873 / Kärnten

👪 ♿ 📶 ✿ **iD**  **989**

🏕 Seecamping Mössler
📧 Seefeldstraße 1
☎ +43 42 46 73 10
🔓 24/3 - 3/11
@ camping@moessler.at

1ha 72T(70-100m²) 6A

**1** ACD**G**IJKLMOPRS
**2** ACDKLMRTVWX
**3** AB**F**HJK**O**P**RW**Z
**4** (A 1/6-30/9) (C+H 13/5-30/9)
   (Q 15/5-30/9)
   (S+U+V+Y 6/5-30/9)
**5** **AB**CDEFGIJKLMNOPUW
   XYZ
**6** ABEGK(N 1,5km)OTV

💬 Small friendly site on the Millstätter See where the guests are looked after. Swimming in the heated pool or in the lake. Entertainment for all ages, including hiking. No environment surcharge.

🚗 A10 Salzburg-Villach. Exit 139 Millstätter See. Left at traffic lights on the B98 dir. Radenthein. After ± 12 km turn right towards Döbriach-See. The site is on the right about 1.5 km further on. From the south: exit 178 Villach-Ossiachersee dir. Millstätter See.

Spittal an der Drau

CC € **18** 24/3-30/6 1/9-2/11

📐 N 46°46'06'' E 13°38'56''

## Eberndorf, A-9141 / Kärnten

🏕 Naturisten Feriendorf Rutar Lido
📧 Lido 1
☎ +43 42 36 22 62
📅 1/1 - 31/12
@ fkkurlaub@rutarlido.at

**990**

15ha  228T(70-140m²)  16A CEE

1 ACD**G**HIJKLMOPQ
2 DKLMRVWXY
3 AF**G**HIJLRUV**WZ**
4 (A 1/5-30/9) (C 1/6-30/9)
(F 📅) (H 1/5-30/9) K**N**
(Q 📅) (S 1/5-30/9)
(T+U+Y 📅)
5 **AB**CDGHIJKLMNOPRS**U**W
XYZ
6 ACEG**K**(N 1km)OTUVW

💬 Naturist campsite. Spacious grounds with various outdoor pools, a small lake, indoor pool and a naturist meadow. Many pitches with privacy. Separate area for dogs, dog meadow and a separate swimming area for dogs in these large grounds. Free sauna when weather is rainy in period 1/5 - 30/9.

🚗 A2 from Klagenfurt, exit 298 Grafenstein turn left, B70 direction Graz. After 4 km turn right to Tainach, Eberndorf, Rutar Lido. From Graz A2, exit 278 Völkermarkt-Ost.

Völkermarkt  B80
A2
Eberndorf
CC
B81
B85    B82

CC €20  1/3-30/6  1/9-31/10      🏔 N 46°35'02'' E 14°37'34''

---

## Faak am See, A-9583 / Kärnten

🏕 Camping Arneitz
📧 Seeuferlandesstraße 53
☎ +43 42 54 21 37
📅 25/4 - 30/9
@ camping@arneitz.at

**991**

6,5ha  400T(90-120m²)  16A CEE

1 AD**F**HIJKLMPQ
2 DFGKLNORSUVWXY
3 ABC**F**HJ**M**NRU**WZ**
4 (A 5/7-22/8) J(Q 📅)
(S+U+V+W+Y+Z 1/5-20/9)
5 **AB**CDEFGIJKLMNOPQRU
WXYZ
6 CEGH**I**K(N 1km)RSTUV

💬 Pitches separated by hedges and trees with power supply, drainage and TV. (Lakeside pitches for a surcharge.) Modern toilet facilities, large supermarket and self service restaurant. Suitable as starting point for walking and cycling tours and Nordic Walking. Enjoy the hospitality of the Arneitz, Pressinger and Ramusch families!

🚗 A10 Salzburg-Villach, then A2 or A11, exit Villach/ Faaker See. Then first campsite on right in direction Egg.

A10          Velden am
Villach      Wörther See
CC     A11
A2                    B85
B109

CC €20  25/4-29/6  9/9-29/9      🏔 N 46°34'28'' E 13°56'08''

---

## Feistritz im Rosental, A-9181 / Kärnten

🏕 Camping Juritz
📧 Campingstraße
☎ +43 42 28 21 15
📅 15/4 - 30/9
@ office@camping-juritz.com

**992**

3ha  90T  10-16A

1 AD**G**IJKLMNOPQ
2 FGKLRTWX
3 AHJRU
4 (A 1/6-30/9)
(D+Q+U+Y+Z 📅)
5 **AB**DFGIJKLN**P**RUW
6 ACEK(N 0,5km)UV

💬 Car-free site. Sunny meadow with unreserved pitches. Several trees provide shade. Swimming pool with sliding roof which can be used from early on in the season. Excellent views of the Karawanken. Trips to Slovenia or city of Klagenfurt (15 minutes by car). A beautiful area for cycling or walking. New toilet facilities. Wifi in the low season 1 euro per day.

🚗 Villach, Karawankentunnel (SLO) exit St. Jakob im Rosental. Direction Feistritz (follow signs and not the SatNav).

Velden am
Wörther See

A11    B85   CC

B91

CC €18  15/4-30/6  1/9-29/9      🏔 N 46°31'31'' E 14°09'38''

## Fieberbrunn, A-6391 / Tirol

�️ 🛰 **iD** 993

🏕 Tirol Camp****
📧 Lindau 20
☎ +43 5 35 45 66 66
📅 28/5 - 3/11, 5/12 - 28/4
@ office@tirol-camp.at

4,7ha 250T(80-150m²) 10A

**1** ACD**G**HIJKLMOPQ
**2** GJLRTUVWX
**3** ABFHJKN**OP**RU**V**
**4** (A 28/5-3/11) (C 1/6-1/10)
(F+H 🕐) IJ**KLNP**
(Q+S+T+U+Y+Z 🕐)
**5** **AB**DFGIJKLMNOPR**STU**W
XYZ
**6** CEGH**I**K**L**(N 1km)OSV

💬 The comfortable 4 star terraced campsite is located in the centre of the Pillerseetal holiday region, right next to the gondola to the best concealed walking and skiing area in the Alps. It has a peaceful, sunny location.

🚗 B164 St. Johann in Tirol-Saalfelden. Signposted in Fieberbrunn.

Sankt Johann in Tirol · B311
CC B164
**Kitzbühel**
B161

CC €**20** 28/5-29/6 1/9-2/11

📍 N 47°28'06'' E 12°33'14''

---

## Fisching/Weißkirchen, A-8741 / Steiermark

🚫 🛰 **iD** 994

🏕 50plus Campingpark Fisching****
📧 Fisching 9
☎ +43 3 57 78 22 84
📅 15/4 - 15/10
@ campingpark@fisching.at

1,5ha 62T(100-130m²) 6A CEE

**1** AEHIJKLMOPQU
**2** DFGKLRUVWX
**3** F**HIJKLUZ
**4** (A+Q+T+U+Y+Z 🕐)
**5** **AB**DGIJKLMNOPUWXYZ
**6** ACDEGIK(N 0,6km)OQSTV
WX

💬 Resplendent valley with mountains in the background. A comfortable campsite for the over fifties. Parkland setting equipped with every amenity, all pitches with cable TV. Beautiful biological swimming pool with terrace. Smaller and larger towns and countryside. 7 km from the thermal baths. Extensive cycling network from campsite with itineraries. Free wifi on entire site.

🚗 S36, exit Zeltweg-West, B78 direction Weißkirchen, direction Fisching at roundabout. Follow signs.

S36
**Knittelfeld**
**Judenburg** CC B77
B78

CC €**20** 15/4-27/6 1/9-15/10

📍 N 47°09'47'' E 14°44'18''

---

## Gösselsdorf, A-9141 / Kärnten

🛰 **iD** 995

🏕 Sonnencamp am Gösselsdorfer See
📧 Seestraße 23
☎ +43 42 36 21 68
📅 1/5 - 30/9
@ office@goesselsdorfersee.com

7ha 230T(80-144m²) 10A CEE

**1** ACD**G**HIJKLMOPQ
**2** CDGLRVWXY
**3** AFHJNRU**W**XZ
**4** (A+Q 🕐)
(T+U+V+Y 1/7-30/8)
**5** **AB**CDFGHIJKLMNOPUW
XYZ
**6** ACEGI**K**(N 2km)OTV

💬 A spacious, tranquil campsite, set on level ground. Swimming pond, and a 15-minute walk from the lake that forms part of a large nature reserve. The area offers stalactite caves, a cable car to the 2114-metre-high Petzenberg, regional museum Völkermarkt and the Eberndorf abbey with open air performances. CampingCard ACSI users pay cash.

🚗 After Völkermarkt, follow the B82 2 km past Eberndorf direction Eisenkappel. Follow the camping signs in Gösselsdorf.

**Völkermarkt** B80
A2
Eberndorf
CC
B85 B82

CC €**20** 1/5-30/6 1/9-30/9

📍 N 46°34'29'' E 14°37'28''

## Grän, A-6673 / Tirol

🏔 🚶 📶 **iD** 996

🅰 Comfort-Camp Grän GmbH****
📧 Engetalstr. 13
☎ +43 56 75 65 70
🔑 10/5 - 1/11, 15/12 - 14/4
@ info@comfortcamp.at

3,3ha 150T(80-100m²) 16A CEE

**1** A**G**HIJKLMOPQ
**2** CGIJKRTUVWX
**3** ABCHIJKL**OP**RUW
**4** (A 15/7-15/10) (F 🔑) **LN**
  (Q+R+T+U+V+Y+Z 🔑)
**5** **AB**CDEFGHIJKLMNOPQR
  **S**UWXYZ
**6** ABCDEGK(N 0,8km)OSV

💬 Site with luxurious toilet facilities and indoor pool in Tannheim Valley with many cycling and walking opportunities. Many (water) sports opportunities at Lake Halden (2 km). The green pitches offer magnificent views of the mountains. The compulsory additional cost per night per pitch is 9.90 euros for the All Inclusive Package. With it, all lifts, indoor pool, wifi and outdoor pool in Haldensee are free.

🚗 A7 from Kempten, Oy exit, via Wertach, Oberjoch, Grän.

**CC** € **20** 10/5-30/6 1/9-11/9

📍 N 47°30'36'' E 10°33'22''

---

## Grein, A-4360 / Oberösterreich

🚶 📶 **iD** 997

🅰 Camping Grein
📧 Campingplatz 1
☎ +43 7 26 82 12 30
🔑 1/4 - 1/10
@ office@camping-grein.at

2ha 87T(100m²) 6A

**1** AD**G**IJKLPQ
**2** CGKRVWXY
**3** ABJK**W**
**4** (Q+R+T+U+X+Z 🔑)
**5** **AB**DFGJMNOPUW
**6** AGK(N 0,3km)OUV

💬 A friendly campsite with marked out partially shaded pitches on level grass. The site is situated right by the Danube with excellent cycle routes on both banks, and is just 200 metres from the idyllic centre of Grein, with its numerous pavement cafes.

🚗 A1 Linz-Wien, exit 123 Amstetten. Then follow Grein signs. Campsite signposted and located in Grein on the B3.

**CC** € **20** 1/4-30/6 1/9-1/10

📍 N 48°13'30'' E 14°51'11''

---

## Hall (Tirol), A-6060 / Tirol

🚶 📶 **iD** 998

🅰 Schwimmbad Camping Hall
  in Tirol***
📧 Scheidensteinstr. 26
☎ +43 5 22 35 85 55 50
🔑 1/5 - 30/9
@ info@camping-hall.at

0,9ha 85T(60-100m²) 10A CEE

**1** AD**G**IJKLPQ
**2** FGKLRVX
**3** A**F**HJ**MQ**
**4** (A 1/6-30/8) (C+H 15/5-15/9)
  J(Q+R+T+U+X 🔑)
**5** **AB**DFGIJKLMNOPQRUW
**6** CDEGHK(N 0,6km)V

💬 A small, friendly campsite with good toilet facilities, right next to the lovely free swimming pool (4000 m²). The trees on the site provide a number of shadier pitches. Plenty of leisure and sports opportunities in the immediate vicinity. Also free wifi on the campsite.

🚗 Inntal motorway, exit 68 Hall and follow signs (direction swimming pool, B171).

**CC** € **18** 1/5-29/6 1/9-29/9

📍 N 47°17'06'' E 11°29'45''

## Heiligenblut, A-9844 / Kärnten ⛷ 📶 iD **999**

- 🏕 Nationalpark Camping Grossglockner
- 🏠 Hadergasse 11
- ☎ +43 48 24 20 48
- 📅 1/1 - 31/12
- @ nationalpark-camping@heiligenblut.at

1,5ha 70T(80-120m²) 16A

1 ACD**G**IJKLMOPQ
2 CJKRTWX
3 AHJNR**W**
4 (A 15/6-15/9) (Q 🔑)
(R 1/5-15/10,20/12-20/12)
(T+U+X 1/5-20/9,20/12-22/4)
(Y 1/6-20/9,20/12-22/4)
(Z 🔑)
5 **AB**DIJKLMNOPUWZ
6 CEGJ(N 1km)OV

💬 Well located campsite where you will be welcomed as a friend. Stunning walking routes near the Großglockner. Typical Austrian ambiance in the restaurant. Wonderful panoramic views and ultimate relaxation. Motorcycle riders are welcome.

🚗 3 routes: a. Zell am See-Großglockner-Heiligenblut; b. Mittersill-Felbertauerntunnel-Lienz-Heiligenblut; c. Tauern-Spittal motorway/Drau-Großglocknerstraße-Heiligenblut. Follow camping signs from village.

CC €20 1/5-29/6 1/9-30/11    📍 N 47°02'13'' E 12°50'20''

---

## Hermagor-Pressegger See, A-9620 / Kärnten ♿ 📶 iD **1000**

- 🏕 Naturpark Schluga Seecamping*****
- ☎ +43 42 82 27 60
- 📅 10/5 - 20/9
- @ camping@schluga.com

8,8ha 350T(80-140m²) 16A

1 ACD**G**IJKLMOPQ
2 ABD**G**JKLRTUVWXY
3 BHJK**M**NP**Q**R**U**W**Z**
4 (A 🔑) (Q 15/5-20/9)
(S+T+U+V+W 20/5-20/9)
(Y 1/6-10/9) (Z 🔑)
5 **AB**DEFGIJKLMNOPR**S**UW
XYZ
6 CEG**IK**(N 6km)OPRTUV

💬 Campsite Schluga See is located mostly in the forest and is well-maintained. At only a few hundred metres from Lake Pressegger with an own field of 30,000 m². Special guided mountain-bike tours, mountain and walking tours for beginners and advanced.

🚗 A23 Villach-Italian border, exit 364 Hermagor/Gailtal. Then follow the B111 till 6 km before Hermagor. The campsite is located on the right. The route via 'Windische Höhe' is blocked for caravans.

CC €20 10/5-30/6 1/9-20/9    📍 N 46°37'55'' E 13°26'42''

---

## Hermagor-Pressegger See, A-9620 / Kärnten ⛷ ♿ 📶 iD **1001**

- 🏕 Schluga Camping Hermagor*****
- 🏠 Vellach 15
- ☎ +43 42 82 20 51
- 📅 1/1 - 31/12
- @ camping@schluga.com

5,6ha 297T(80-120m²) 16A

1 ACD**G**IJKLMOPQ
2 AGKLRTUVXY
3 BC**D**HJK**M**NP**RT**U**V**W
4 (A 1/6-30/9) (C+**F**+**H**
1/5-30/9) **LN**(Q 🔑)
(S 15/5-15/9) (U+W+Y+Z 🔑)
5 **AB**DEFGIJKLMNOPQR**ST**
UWXYZ
6 ACDEG**IK**(N 2km)OPQRST
UV

💬 Schluga campsite is one of the absolute top sites in Austria. Perfect starting point for all types of holiday, active or relaxed. During the winter (from 1/11 to 30/4) you will be charged extra for electricity above 4 kWh.

🚗 A23 Villach-Italian border, exit 364 Hermagor/Gailtal. Then B111 until 2 km before Hermagor. Right at camping sign. Campsite 50m on the left. Route via 'Windische Höhen' is closed for caravans.

CC €20 6/1-30/6 1/9-20/12    📍 N 46°37'53'' E 13°23'46''

## Hermagor-Pressegger See, A-9620 / Kärnten

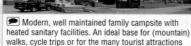

🏕 Sport-Camping-Flaschberger
📧 Obervellach 27
☎ +43 42 82 20 20
🗓 1/1 - 31/12
@ office@flaschberger.at

2ha 80T(90-120m²) 16A

1 AGIJKLMPQ
2 GKLRTVWXY
3 AHJKMNQRTUV
4 (A 1/6-30/9) (C 25/5-30/9) N (Q+T+U+X 🗓)
5 ABDGIJKLMNOPRSUW XYZ
6 ACDEGIK(N 2km)OSTUV

💬 Modern, well maintained family campsite with heated sanitary facilities. An ideal base for (mountain) walks, cycle trips or for the many tourist attractions in Carinthia.

🚗 A23 Villach-Italian border, exit 364 Hermagor/ Gailtal. Then B111 till ± 2 km before Hermagor and right at campsite sign. Site about 100m on right. Road via 'Windische Höhen' is closed for caravans.

1002

Hermagor-Pressegger See CC
B87

CC € 16 1/1-30/6 1/9-31/12

N 46°37'56" E 13°23'48"

---

## Hopfgarten, A-6361 / Tirol

🏕 Camping Reiterhof****
📧 Kelchsauer Straße 49
☎ +43 53 35 35 12
🗓 1/1 - 31/12
@ info@campingreiterhof.at

2,6ha 65T(80-100m²) 13-16A CEE

1 AGIJKLMOPQ
2 DGKMRTUX
3 BFHJLMNQRTUZ
4 (A 1/5-30/6,1/9-1/11) (Q+U+Y 🗓)
5 ABCDEFGHIJKLMNOPUW XYZ
6 CEGK(N 2km)OV

💬 Lightly sloping grounds with partially marked out pitches. There is a children's play park right next to the campsite with a small lake, playground and tennis courts for those a bit older. Plenty of walking and sports facilities in the vicinity. There is a heated outdoor pool and heated toddlers' pool close to the campsite.

🚗 A12, exit 17 Wörgl-Ost, direction Hopfgarten (Brixental).

1003

Kirchbichl
Wörgl
Kundl
B178
B170
CC

CC € 18 16/3-29/6 1/9-30/10

N 47°25'50" E 12°08'58"

---

## Imst, A-6460 / Tirol

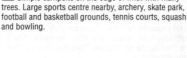

🏕 Aktivcamping Am Schwimmbad
📧 Schwimmbadweg 10
☎ +43 5 41 22 13 55
🗓 1/4 - 15/10
@ info@camping-imst.at

1,2ha 53T(60-100m²) 6A CEE

1 AGIJKLMOPQ
2 FGIKRVWXY
3 AHIJKMUV
4 (A 1/5-21/9) (C+H 15/6-7/9) J (Q 🗓)
5 ABGIJKMOPUWZ
6 EGK(N 0,3km)O

💬 Simple campsite on the edge of Imst with many trees. Large sports centre nearby, archery, skate park, football and basketball grounds, tennis courts, squash and bowling.

🚗 From roundabout Imst, exit 2. Follow signs.

1004

B189 Haiming
CC
A12 B186
Arzl im Pitztal
Zams

CC € 16 12/4-28/6 1/9-13/10

N 47°14'24" E 10°44'43"

## Irschen, A-9773 / Kärnten 🦽 📶 iD ⟨1005⟩

🏕 Rad-Wandercamping-
　Ponderosa***
🏠 Glanz 13
☎ +43 66 06 86 70 55
🚗 29/4 - 29/9
@ info@rad-wandercamping.at

0,9ha 33T(80-130m²) 6A

**1** AGIJKLMOPQ
**2** GJKLRTWXY
**3** FHIJRU
**4** (A+Q+R+T+U+V+X+Z 🔌)
**5** ABDFGIJKLMNOPRSTUW
　XYZ
**6** EGK(N 2km)T

💬 A small, charming campsite in the natural herb village of Irschen. Pitches with your own herb garden, water, electricity and drainage. Free heated individual washing cubicles. Restaurant with reasonable prices and specialty evenings from the charcoal grill. Fresh bread daily. Ideal starting point for hiking and cycling trips. Free wifi.

🚐 From Lienz or Spittal follow route B100/E66, exit Glanz (municipality of Irschen). Campsite turning clearly signposted.

CC € ⟨16⟩ 29/4-30/6 1/9-29/9　　　📐 N 46°44'39'' E 13°02'39''

---

## Itter/Hopfgarten, A-6305 / Tirol 🎿 🦽 📶 iD ⟨1006⟩

🏕 Terrassencamping
　Schlossberg Itter*****
🏠 Brixentalerstraße 11
☎ +43 53 35 21 81
🚗 1/1 - 4/11, 1/12 - 31/12
@ info@camping-itter.at

4ha 150T(80-110m²) 10A

**1** AGIJKLMOPQ
**2** CFGIJLRVX
**3** BFHJNRU
**4** (A 1/7-28/8) (C+H 1/5-15/9)
　LN(Q+R+T+U+Y 🔌)
**5** ABDEFGIJKLMNOPSUW
　XYZ
**6** ACDEGHIK(N 2km)OQSV

💬 A large, well planned terraced campsite surrounded by woods in the Brixental valley. The lovely large playground typifies its child-friendliness. Heated outdoor pool. Plenty of sports opportunities in the immediate surroundings. Well placed for trips out. Restaurant on the site.

🚐 Inntal motorway, exit 17 Wörgl-Ost, direction Brixental. After 5 km turn right onto the B170 direction Brixental. Turn left 2 km before Hopfgarten.

CC € ⟨20⟩ 1/5-29/6 1/9-30/10　　　📐 N 47°27'59'' E 12°08'22''

---

## Kals am Großglockner, A-9981 / Tirol 👫 🎿 🦽 📶 iD ⟨1007⟩

🏕 Nationalparkcamping Kals****
🏠 Burg 22
☎ +43 4 85 26 73 89
🚗 25/5 - 12/10, 15/12 - 22/4
@ info@
　nationalpark-camping-kals.at

2,5ha 108T(100-120m²) 13A CEE

**1** AGIJKLMOPQ
**2** BCGJKRVW
**3** AHJRUWX
**4** (Q+R 15/12-31/12,25/5-12/10)
**5** ABDEGIJKLMNOPUWZ
**6** EGJ(N 1km)O

💬 The campsite, which has excellent toilet facilities, is located in a stunning nature reserve. Ideal for mountain bikers, walkers and nature lovers. It is really peaceful and quiet. There are walks of varying difficulty from the campsite. Also a new walking path to the village along the river. Trails and ski runs from the campsite.

🚐 Kufstein-Kitzbühel-Mittersill-Felbertauern-Matrei-Huben, then turn left towards Kals. Campsite signposted from Kals.

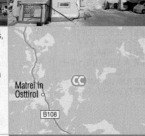

CC € ⟨20⟩ 7/1-3/3 25/3-22/4 25/5-29/6 2/9-12/10 15/12-23/12　　📐 N 47°01'18'' E 12°38'20''

## Kaumberg, A-2572 / Niederösterreich 　 ♿ 🛜 **iD** (1008)

🏕 Camping Paradise Garden
📧 Höfnergraben 2
☎ +43 67 64 74 19 66
🗓 1/4 - 30/9
@ grandl@camping-noe.at

1,5ha 65T(80-120m²) 16A CEE

**1** AGIJKLMO**P**Q
**2** CRWX
**3** HJU
**4** (R ⛽)
**5** **AB**DEG**IJ**K**L**MNPRUW
**6** EGJK(N 3km)ORS

💬 Pleasant comfort campsite on the edge of the Vienna Woods (Wienerwald) with luxurious toilet facilities. Well positioned for day trips (Vienna, the Danube, Baden and Voralpen). Well-marked walking and cycling routes in the direct vicinity. CCA also gives discounts outside the acceptance periods, ask reception.

🚗 A1, exit 59 Pölten-Süd and follow B20 to Traisen. Left at roundabout over B18 via Hainfeld to Kaumberg. Right 3 km beyond Kaumberg, 1 km to campsite.

Hainfeld — A21 — B11 — CC — B18 — **Berndorf**

CC € **18** 1/4-30/6 1/9-30/9 　 📷 N 48°01'28'' E 15°56'55''

---

## Keutschach am See, A-9074 / Kärnten 　 🛜 **iD** (1009)

🏕 Strandcamping Süd
📧 Dobeinitz 30
☎ +43 42 73 27 73
🗓 1/5 - 30/9
@ info@strandcampingsued.at

2ha 160T(80-100m²) 13-14A

**1** AG**I**JKLOPQ
**2** BDFKLNRTVWXY
**3** **B**FHJRUZ
**4** (Q+R+T+U+Y+Z ⛽)
**5** **AB**FG**IJ**KLMNOPUW
**6** ACEGHK(N 2km)TU

💬 Family campsite with lake and woods. Beautiful in low season, also for swimming. Tennis, cycling, horse riding, golf and minigolf, walking and fishing in the vicinity. Outings to observation tower and monkey park. CampingCard ACSI not valid for pitches directly on the lake.

🚗 A2 exit Klagenfurt West-Süduferstraße direction Reifnitz. At Gemeindeamt Reifnitz turn left towards Keutschach. Over the roundabout and straight ahead for 1 km to the campsite.

B95 — **Klagenfurt am Wörthersee** — A2 — CC — A11 — B85 — B91

CC € **20** 1/5-26/5 3/6-27/6 1/9-30/9 　 📷 N 46°35'07'' E 14°10'23''

---

## Klosterneuburg, A-3400 / Niederösterreich 　 ♿ 🛜 **iD** (1010)

🏕 Donaupark Camping Klosterneuburg
📧 In der Au 1
☎ +43 2 24 32 58 77
🗓 18/3 - 3/11
@ campklosterneuburg@oeamtc.at

2,3ha 193T(60-90m²) 6A CEE

**1** ACDGIJKLM**P**Q
**2** FGRTUVWX
**3** **B**C**F**HJKR
**4** (Q+R+U+X ⛽)
**5** **AB**DG**IJ**KLMNOPUWZ
**6** ABCDFGK(N 0,5km)OSTUV

💬 The campsite is within walking distance of Klosterneuburg with its famous monastery. The station for bus and train services to Vienna is close by. The site is next to the Donauradweg cycle route. Vienna centre is 14 km by bike.

🚗 When approaching from the west: A1, exit Sankt Christophen B19, via Tulln and B14 to Klosterneuburg. The campsite is signposted in Klosterneuburg.

A22 — **Korneuburg** — S1 — CC — **Klosterneuburg** — S2

CC € **20** 18/3-30/6 1/9-3/11 　 📷 N 48°18'38'' E 16°19'42''

## Kötschach/Mauthen, A-9640 / Kärnten

🏕 Alpencamp Kärnten****
📫 Kötschach 284
☎ +43 4 71 54 29
📅 1/1 - 4/11, 15/12 - 31/12
@ info@alpencamp.at

♦ 🖥 📶 **iD** **1011**

1,6ha 80T(80-135m²) 16A CEE

**1** ACD**G**IJKLMOPQ
**2** CGKRVWXY
**3** BHJKL**MOP**RUV**W**X
**4** (A 1/1-31/3,1/5-15/10) **LN**
(Q 🕐) (R 1/5-31/10)
(T+U+V+Y 🕐)
**5** **AB**DFGHIJKLMNOPUW
**6** CEGIK(N 0,3km)OTVW

💬 The impressive view of the mountains and the high-altitude spa resort (healing air), combined with excellent service in this four-star campsite and excellent offerings for all ages, means your holiday will be extra special. New: 350 m2 sauna and wellness centre. One free internet access per pitch.

🚗 B100 Lienz-Spittal an der Drau. In Oberdrauburg take Plöckenpass/Italy exit. Campsite well signposted in Kötschach direction Lesachtal.

**CC** € **20**  6/1-29/6  1/9-4/11

📍 N 46°40'11'' E 12°59'30''

---

## Kramsach (Krummsee), A-6233 / Tirol

🏕 Seencamping Stadlerhof****
📫 Seebühel 14
☎ +43 5 33 76 33 71
📅 1/1 - 31/12
@ office@camping-stadlerhof.at

♦ 🖥 📶 **iD** **1012**

3ha 100T(80-120m²) 6-13A

**1** AD**G**HIJKLMO**P**Q
**2** DFGJKLMNRTUVY
**3** BCHJLRU
**4** (A+C 🕐) (H 1/6-30/9) **KLN**
(Q+R+T+U+Y 🕐)
**5** **AB**CDEFGIJKLMNOPR**S**U
WXYZ
**6** ACDEGJ**K**(N 1,5km)OSUV

💬 A beautifully established campsite with partly level grounds and sections in terraces, located on the Krummsee lake with its own beach. Plenty of shaded and marked out pitches. Charges are made for using the swimming pool in low season.

🚗 Inntal motorway, exit 32 Kramsach. Then follow the signs 'Zu den Seen'.

**CC** € **20**  1/5-22/6  7/9-16/12

📍 N 47°27'24'' E 11°52'51''

---

## Kramsach (Reintalersee), A-6233 / Tirol

🏕 Camping Seeblick Toni*****
📫 Moosen 46
☎ +43 5 33 76 35 44
📅 1/1 - 31/12
@ info@camping-seeblick.at

♦ 🚷 📶 **iD** **1013**

4,5ha 230T(90-120m²) 16A

**1** ACD**G**IJKLMOPQ
**2** DFGIJKLMRTUVY
**3** BCDHJLN**OP**RU**W**Z
**4** (A 🕐) **LN**(Q+S 🕐)
(T 1/6-30/9) (U+Y 🕐)
**5** **AB**DEFGHIJKLMNOP**S**UW
XYZ
**6** ACDEG**IK**(N 3km)OPSVW

💬 Lovely level or sloping grounds, peacefully located in the woods around the Reintaler See lake. Spacious marked out pitches. Perfect for nature lovers and sports enthusiasts. Excellent restaurant and supermarket. Special feature: a 'wash land' for young children.

🚗 Take the A12, exit 32 Kramsach. Follow the green 'Zu den Seen' signs for about 5 km, then third campsite. Drive past campsites to the left and the right of the road until past the green Seeblick Toni sign.

**CC** € **20**  7/1-29/6  1/9-7/9  22/9-21/12

📍 N 47°27'39'' E 11°54'24''

## Kramsach (Reintalersee), A-6233 / Tirol

🏂 ⛷ ♿ 📶 **iD** (1014)

🔺 Camping und Appartements Seehof*****
📧 Moosen 42
☎ +43 5 33 76 35 41
📅 1/1 - 31/12
@ info@camping-seehof.com

4ha 130T(90-120m²) 13-16A CEE

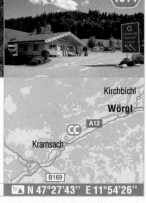

**1** ACD**G**IJKLMO**P**Q
**2** DFGJKLNRTUVX
**3** BDHJKL**OP**RUVW**Z**
**4** (A 1/7-31/8)
(Q+R+T+U+Y 📅)
**5** **AB**DEFGHIJKLMNOP**S**UW XYZ
**6** ABCDEGI**K**(N 3km)OQSUV

💬 Spacious, marked-out, sunny pitches, partly in terraces. Private lawn on Reintaler See. Direct access to lake. Petting zoo. Playground. Exclusive toilet facilities, rental bathrooms. Good restaurant. Free Alpbachtal Seenland Card!

🚗 A12 exit 32 Kramsach. Follow green 'Zu den Seen' or 'Campingplätze' signs for about 5 km. 2nd campsite on this road. Reception on left next to entrance. If you take mountain road (not permitted) site on right.

CC € **18** 7/1-29/6  1/9-14/12

📍 N 47°27'43'' E 11°54'26''

---

## Krems (Donau), A-3500 / Niederösterreich

♿ 📶 **iD** (1015)

🔺 Donaupark Camping Krems
📧 Yachthafenstraße 19
☎ +43 2 73 28 44 55
📅 1/4 - 27/10
@ donaucampingkrems@aon.at

0,8ha 60T 6A

**1** ACDGIJKLMOPST
**2** CFKRWX
**3** HJKLRUW**X**
**4** (Q+R+T 📅)
**5** **AB**GIJKLMNOPUW
**6** EGHI**K**(N 0,5km)V

💬 Campsite right by the Danube. The old town of Krems and sightseeing boats are within walking distance. Cycle paths both sides of the Danube. Around 21st of June 'Sonnewende Fest' with amongst others fire works.

🚗 From the eastern intersection St. Pölten S33. Then B37 direction Krems. 3rd exit at roundabout in Krems, then immediately left past Schifffahrtszentrum Krems/Stein to the campsite.

CC € **18** 1/4-30/6  1/9-27/10

📍 N 48°24'14'' E 15°35'33''

---

## Lienz, A-9900 / Tirol

♿ 📶 **iD** (1016)

🔺 Comfort & Wellness Camping Falken****
📧 Falkenweg 7
☎ +43 66 44 10 79 73
📅 19/4 - 14/10
@ camping.falken@tirol.com

2,5ha 132T(70-120m²) 6A

**1** ACD**G**HIJKLMO**P**Q
**2** GKRVWXY
**3** A**F**HJLM**R**U
**4** (Q+R+T+U+Z 📅)
**5** **AB**CDFGIJK**L**MNOPRUW XYZ
**6** CEGK(N 1km)ORSTVW

💬 Quiet site with very luxurious toilet facilities. 900m from centre of 'Sunny town' Lienz. New wellness centre with sauna (incl. bio sauna, infrared), herbal steam bath. Mini market, dog washing, free wifi. Ideal for shopping, kayaking, canoeing, walking, cycling. Restaurant 400m away.

🚗 Via Kufstein-Kitzbühel-Mittersil-Felbertauern tunnel towards Lienz. In Lienz direction Spittal at roundabout. Right at 2nd roundabout (ÖAMTC). Then follow signs.

CC € **20** 19/4-29/6  1/9-14/10

📍 N 46°49'22'' E 12°46'14''

## Lienz/Amlach, A-9908 / Tirol

🚶 ⛷ ♿ 🛜 **iD** (1017)

🏕 Dolomiten Camping
Amlacherhof★★★★
🏠 Seestrasse 20
☎ +43 6 99 17 62 31 71
🗓 1/4 - 31/10
@ info@amlacherhof.at

2,5ha 85T(80-120m²) 16A CEE

**1** AG IJKLMOPQ
**2** FGKLRVWX
**3** AFHJKLMOPQRU
**4** (B 1/6-15/9) (Q 1/5-31/10)
(R 1/5-15/9)
(T+U+Z 1/7-31/8)
**5** ABDEFGIJKLMNOPSTUW
XYZ
**6** CEGJK(N 2km)ORTVX

💬 A really lovely campsite with spacious pitches. Rural location with beautiful views of the mountains. Always something to see at the stables which border the site. A good base for walkers and cyclists. Lienz at 2 km.

🚗 Felbertauerntunnel-Lienz, at Lienz after the roundabout direction Spittal. At the second traffic lights direction Feriendorf/Amlach. Then another 2 km, follow signs.

B108
B106
Nussdorf-Debant
**Lienz**
CC
B100

CC € **14** 1/4-6/6 22/6-28/6 2/9-30/10 11=10, 22=20 📍 N 46°48'48'' E 12°45'47''

---

## Lienz/Tristach, A-9907 / Tirol

🛜 **iD** (1018)

🏕 Camping Seewiese★★★★
🏠 Tristachersee 2
☎ +43 4 85 26 97 67
🗓 4/5 - 16/9
@ seewiese@hotmail.com

2,3ha 95T(100-200m²) 6A

**1** AG IJKLMOPQ
**2** BDGIKLMNRTWX
**3** ABFHJNRUWZ
**4** (G 1/6-1/9) (Q 14/5-16/9)
(R+T+Z 10/6-31/8)
**5** ABDGIJKLMPUWZ
**6** CDEGK(N 3km)TV

💬 Charmingly located natural site in a 5.5 hectare volcanic lake. Free swimming in healing spring water. Absolute peace! Base for excellent walks at every level. The site is located at a height of 830m. The last 1500m is a steep incline of 10%. A walk to the culture and sunshine town of Lienz is 5 km.

🚗 From Kufstein-Kitzbühel-Felbertauerntunnel dir. Lienz. Follow Tristach-Tristachersee and Seewiese signs in Lienz.

B108
B106
Nussdorf-Debant
**Lienz**
CC
B100

CC € **20** 4/5-19/6 1/9-16/9 📍 N 46°48'23'' E 12°48'08''

---

## Maishofen, A-5751 / Salzburg

⛷ ♿ 🛜 **iD** (1019)

🏕 Camping Neunbrunnen am
Waldsee
🏠 Neunbrunnen 56
☎ +43 6 54 26 85 48
🗓 1/1 - 31/12
@ camping@neunbrunnen.at

3ha 100T(70-100m²) 16A CEE

**1** AG IJKLMOPQ
**2** BDKLRUWX
**3** BFQRWZ
**4** (Q+U+V+Y+Z 🛒)
**5** ABDGIJKLMNOPUWZ
**6** CEGK(N 2km)OU

💬 Beautiful lakeside family campsite. The views are spectacular and the site is a good base for cyclists and walkers. A paradise for fishers. Wonderful ski area. Excellent restaurant. The perfect holiday centre. Limited payment options, please pay with cash.

🚗 No toll via A8 Munich-Salzburg. Take exit Siegsdorf, then B306 dir. Inzell, Lofer and Zell am See. In Maishofen before the tunnel follow signs to the campsite.

**Saalfelden am Steinernen Meer**
B164
CC
**Zell am See**
B311

CC € **18** 1/5-29/6 1/9-29/9 📍 N 47°22'40'' E 12°47'43''

## Malta, A-9854 / Kärnten ♿ 📶 iD 1020

🏕 Terrassencamping Maltatal*****
📧 Malta 6
☎ +43 4 73 32 34
⌚ 20/4 - 20/10
@ info@maltacamp.at

3,9ha 238T(60-150m²) 6-13A CEE

**1** ACD**G**IJKLMOPRS
**2** CFGIJKLRTVXY
**3** BDHJKM**M**PRU
**4** (**A** 1/6-1/10)
    (**C+H** 1/6-15/9) **LN**
    (Q+S+T+U+V+Y+Z 27/4-7/10)
**5** **AB**CDEFGHIJKLMNOPQR**S**
    UWXYZ
**6** ACEGKM(N 6km)OUVW

💬 A beautiful campsite in the Malta valley in Carinthia. Especially loved by walkers and families with children. Heated swimming pool. Plenty of animals on the campsite; you can ride our ponies for free. Come and experience it. CampingCard ACSI holders can only pay in cash.

🚗 A10 Salzburg-Villach, exit 130 Gmünd. Follow the signs in Gmünd in the direction of Maltatal. The campsite is located on the right 2 km past Fischerstratten.

CC €20 20/4-30/6 1/9-19/10       🧭 N 46°56'58'' E 13°30'34''

---

## Marbach an der Donau, A-3671 / Niederösterreich 📶 iD 1021

🏕 Marbacher Freizeitzentrum
📧 Campingweg 2
☎ +43 7 41 32 07 33
⌚ 2/4 - 26/10
@ info@marbach-freizeit.at

0,4ha 50T(70-100m²) 20A CEE

**1** AD**G**IJKLMOPST
**2** CGRTVWX
**3** B**F**JKU**W**X
**4** (Q+R ⌚)
**5** **AB**DGJLNOPUWYZ
**6** FGIK(N 0,5km)O

💬 Lovely, small campsite on the left bank of the Danube with partly marked out pitches on grass. Next to a popular yacht harbour and right on the well-known Danube Cycle Route. There are many walking routes marked out in the vicinity and fishing is also possible.

🚗 A1 Linz-Wien, exit 100 Ybbs/Wieselburg. Follow road towards Ybbs/Persenbeug. Cross the Danube towards Krems. Campsite ± 7 km on the right.

CC €20 2/4-30/6 1/9-26/10       🧭 N 48°12'49'' E 15°08'26''

---

## Matrei in Osttirol, A-9971 / Tirol 📶 iD 1022

🏕 Camping Edengarten
📧 Edenweg 15A
☎ +43 48 75 51 11
⌚ 1/4 - 31/10
@ info@campingedengarten.at

1,5ha 75T(80-100m²) 16A CEE

**1** AG**J**KLMPQ
**2** GKLRWXY
**3** AHJRU**W**
**4** (T+X+Y+Z ⌚)
**5** **AB**DFGIJKLMNO**P**QUWZ
**6** FGJ(N 0,5km)OTV

💬 Lovely quiet campsite with good, clean toilets, just 200m from a delightful village. The site is in a valley with lovely views of the Großvenediger and Großglockner. Plenty of opportunities for walking, cycling and mountain climbing. 500m from a cable car, 300m from supermarkets. The campsite has an excellent restaurant.

🚗 When approaching from Felbertauerntunnel, take the second exit to Matrei/Goldriedbahn/Virgen. The campsite is on right after 500 metres.

CC €18 1/4-29/6 1/9-30/10       🧭 N 46°59'43'' E 12°32'20''

## Mauterndorf, A-5570 / Salzburg

👪 🎿 ⛷ ♿ 📶 iD **1023**

🏕 Camping Mauterndorf★★★★
✉ Hammer 145
☎ +43 6 47 27 20 23
📅 1/1 - 31/12
@ info@camping-mauterndorf.at

2,5ha 163T(65-100m²) 12A CEE

**1** ACD**G**IJKLMOPQ
**2** CFGJKLRTUVWXY
**3** ABF**H**JKLUV
**4** (C 1/7-31/8) L**N**(Q+R+U 📷)
(V+Y 1/12-30/4,1/7-10/9)
(Z 📷)
**5** **AB**DEFGIJMNOP**S**UWXYZ
**6** CFGIK(N 2km)OSV

💬 Lovely campsite open all year in the heart of the Salzburger Lungau. Right next to the Erlebnisberg Grosseck-Speiereck cable car. Wonderful walking throughout the year. On the site: sauna, solarium, steam bath, fitness room and massage.

🚗 A10, exit St. Michael im Lungau, direction Mauterndorf. Follow B99 Erlebnisberg Grosseck-Speiereck. On B99 after 1.5 km, campsite is on the left.

**A10** Mauterndorf — CC **Tamsweg** B96 B95 — B99

**CC** €**20** 1/5-30/6 11/9-15/11

🗺 N 47°08'35'' E 13°39'53''

---

## Mayrhofen, A-6290 / Tirol

🎿 ⛷ ♿ 📶 iD **1024**

🏕 Camping Alpenparadies Mayrhofen★★★★
✉ Laubichl 125
☎ +43 5 28 56 25 80 51
📅 1/1 - 20/10, 18/12 - 31/12
@ camping@alpenparadies.com

2,5ha 220T(60-100m²) 16A CEE

**1** ACD**G**IJKLMOPQ
**2** GKLRVX
**3** BHJRU**W**
**4** (C+F+H 📷) K**L**N
(Q+S+T+U+Y 📷)
**5** **AB**CDFGIJKLMNOPQ**S**T**U**
WXYZ
**6** CEGH**K**(N 1km)OV

💬 Campsite with lovely level grounds on the edge of the woods. The indoor and outdoor swimming pool offers swimming in all weather conditions. The restaurant will take care of your appetite. Infra-red cabins on the campsite. Many sports facilities in the immediate vicinity, such as cycling, walking and climbing.

🚗 Inntal motorway, exit 39 Zillertal, take the B169 to Mayrhofen.

Zell am Ziller B165 — CC Mayrhofen

**CC** €**18** 6/5-30/6 2/9-29/9 7/10-19/10

🗺 N 47°10'34'' E 11°52'11''

---

## Millstatt/Dellach, A-9872 / Kärnten

👪 ♿ 📶 iD **1025**

🏕 Camping Neubauer
✉ Dellach 3
☎ +43 47 66 25 32
📅 1/5 - 13/10
@ info@camping-neubauer.at

1,5ha 120T(80-90m²) 6A CEE

**1** ACD**G**IJKLMPRS
**2** DGIJKLMORTVWXY
**3** ABD**F**HJRW**Z**
**4** (Q 📷) (U 15/5-15/9)
(V 1/7-31/8) (X 15/5-15/9)
**5** **AB**DEFGIJKLMNOPRUW
**6** EGK(N 4km)OQV

💬 This terraced campsite with spacious pitches is located directly on the Millstätter See lake. An excellent base for walkers, cyclists and water lovers. There is an 18 hole golf course close by, but you can of course just relax in one of our sunny spots.

🚗 A10 Salzburg-Villach, exit 139 Millstätter See (exit located on the left!). At the traffic lights turn left on the B98 direction Radenthein. About 4 km after Millstatt turn right in Dellach. Follow the signs.

B99 — **Spittal an der Drau** B88 — CC B100 B98 — A10

**CC** €**18** 1/5-30/6 1/9-12/10

🗺 N 46°47'18'' E 13°36'49''

## Mondsee, A-5310 / Oberösterreich  ⚹ 📶 (1026)

🏕 AustriaCamp
✉ St. Lorenz 229
☎ +43 62 32 29 27
🗓 1/4 - 30/9
@ office@austriacamp.at

2ha 100T(50-70m²) 16A CEE

**1** CD**F**HIJKLMN**OP**ST
**2** DFKLMRVX
**3** ABFHJ**MO**RUWZ
**4** (A 1/7-31/8) **N**
(Q+R+T+U+V 🔌)
(X 1/5-29/9) (Y+Z 🔌)
**5** **AB**DEFGIJKLMNOPUW
**6** CEGH**K**(N 8km)OPRTUV

💬 This quiet, well maintained campsite with panoramic views over the lake and the mountains around is located directly on the Mondsee. Large toilet blocks are at your disposal. There is a restaurant with ample choice. Ideal as a base for trips to Salzburg, Bad Ischl and the Salzkammergut.

🚗 B154 from Mondsee to St. Gilgen. After 5 km at left side follow 'AustriaCamp' signs.

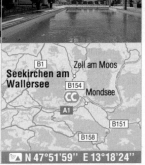

CC € 20  1/4-3/6  1/9-29/9          🏔 N 47°49'49'' E 13°21'53''

---

## Mondsee/Tiefgraben, A-5310 / Oberösterreich  ⚹ 📶 iD (1027)

🏕 Camp MondSeeLand*****
✉ Punzau 21
☎ +43 62 32 26 00
🗓 13/4 - 6/10
@ austria@campmondsee.at

4ha 100T(80-120m²) 16A CEE

**1** ACG**I**JKLM**OP**Q
**2** FKLRVWX
**3** BFHJN**OP**QRUW
**4** (**A** 1/7-31/8) (C 1/5-30/9)
(Q+S+U+V+Y+Z 🔌)
**5** **AB**DFGIJKLMNOPRS**U**W
XYZ
**6** CEGH**IK**(N 4km)OTUV

💬 A peaceful luxury campsite with new toilet facilities located between the Mondsee and Irrsee lakes. Lovely cycling and walking routes from the campsite. The fortified town of Salzburg is 27 km away and is easily reached. Ideal for a breath of fresh air on the way to Vienna or further east (Hungary/ Czech Republic).

🚗 A1 Salzburg-Vienna. Exit 264 Mondsee, 1st roundabout direction Straßwalchen, 3rd exit on 2nd roundabout then follow campsite signs.

CC € 20  13/4-29/6  1/9-6/10          🏔 N 47°51'59'' E 13°18'24''

---

## Nassereith, A-6465 / Tirol  ⛷ 📶 iD (1028)

🏕 Camping Rossbach****
✉ Rossbach 325
☎ +43 52 65 51 54
🗓 1/1 - 30/10, 15/12 - 31/12
@ rainer.ruepp@gmx.at

1ha 80T(70-80m²) 6A CEE

**1** AG**I**JKLOPQ
**2** CGKLRVWXY
**3** AFHJ**OP**RUW
**4** (A 1/5-30/10)
(C+H 15/5-15/9) (Q+R 🔌)
(T+U+X 1/7-31/8)
**5** **AB**DFGIJKLMNOPUWZ
**6** ACEG**J**(N 1,5km)OTUV

💬 A friendly family campsite in the Gurgeltal valley with plenty of fruit trees and a swimming pool by a babbling brook, located at the foot of the Fern Pass and surrounded by woods and meadows. Plenty of sports facilities in the vicinity. Guided mountain trips are also possible.

🚗 Follow the B179 from Reutte to Nassereith (through the Fern pass), exit Nassereith. Direction Domitz/Rossbach in the centre. Follow the signs.

CC € 16  1/3-29/6  1/9-30/10          🏔 N 47°18'37'' E 10°51'20''

## Natters, A-6161 / Tirol

**1029**

🔼 Camping Ferienparadies
Natterer See*****
✉ Natterer See 1
☎ +43 5 12 54 67 32
🕐 1/1 - 31/12
@ info@natterersee.com

11ha 176T(60-160m²) 6-16A

**1** ACD**G**IJKLMOPQ
**2** BDFG**J**KLRUVWXY
**3** BCF**G**HJKLN**PR**U**W**Z
**4** (A 1/6-15/10) IJ(Q+S+T 🕐)
(U 15/3-1/10)(V 15/5-1/10)
(W+Y 15/3-1/10)(Z 15/6-30/9)
**5** **AB**DEFGIJKLMNOPR**S**UW
XYZ
**6** ACDEG**K**(N 2,5km)OPRS
TUV

💬 This lovely campsite is positioned by two small lakes. By one of the lakes the pitches are terraced and by the other lake they are level. There is a very extensive entertainment programme for everyone, kids and adults, also sports activities. Exclusive toilet facilities. Just 7 km from Innsbruck.

🚗 A13 Brenner motorway, exit 3 Innsbruck-Süd/ Natters. Follow the signs direction Natterer See.

CC € **20** 10/1-13/4 5/5-8/6 23/6-30/6 1/9-30/11

📍 N 47°14'18'' E 11°20'21''

---

## Neustift, A-6167 / Tirol

**1030**

🔼 Camping Stubai****
✉ Stubaitalstraße 94
☎ +43 52 26 25 37
🕐 1/1 - 31/12
@ info@campingstubai.at

2ha 110T(60-100m²) 6A CEE

**1** ACD**G**IJKLMO**P**Q
**2** CFGIJKRTUWX
**3** ABCGHJKRU**W**
**4** (A 10/7-9/10) **KLN**
(Q+S+T+U+Y 🕐)
**5** **AB**DFGIJKLMNOP**ST**UWY
**6** ACEGK(N 0km)OQTV

💬 This campsite with level grounds and spacious pitches is positioned at the foot the mountains in the village of Neustift, right next to a supermarket. Wonderful views from the campsite of the surrounding hills. You can also go hunting with an instructor in the campsite's own hunting area.

🚗 A13 Brenner motorway, exit Europabrücke and on the B183 to Stubaital and then to Neustift.

CC € **18** 30/4-29/6 3/9-29/9

📍 N 47°06'36'' E 11°18'31''

---

## Oberdrauburg, A-9781 / Kärnten

**1031**

🔼 Natur- & Familiencamping
Oberdrauburg
✉ Gailbergstraße
☎ +43 47 10 22 49 22
🕐 1/5 - 30/9
@ tourismus@oberdrauburg.at

1,2ha 68T(80-110m²) 12A

**1** AD**G**IJKLMOPQ
**2** GIJKLRTVWXY
**3** A**F**HJK**M**NRU
**4** (**A** 🕐) (C+H 3/6-31/8) J
(Q+Y+Z 3/6-31/8)
**5** **AB**CEFGIJKLMNOPRUWZ
**6** CEGHK(N 0,5km)OV

💬 Pleasantly located family campsite on the edge of the woods. Good base for walkers, canoeists, motor cyclists (Plöckenpass), nature lovers and cyclists. Fine restaurant. New pavement café. Free wifi. Ideal stopover site on your way to Italy. Adjoining leisure pool with a 58 metre water slide. Lovely panoramic views of mountains.

🚗 Spittal dir. Lienz (B100) to Oberdrauburg, or Mittersill-Felbertauerntunnel-Lienz-Oberdrauburg. Exit Plöckenpass, site after 500 metres.

CC € **16** 1/5-29/6 1/9-29/9

📍 N 46°44'33'' E 12°58'11''

## Oggau (Burgenland), A-7063 / Burgenland  ♿ 🛜 iD (1032)

🏕 Camping Oggau
☎ +43 26 85 72 71
🗓 31/3 - 31/10
@ office@campingoggau.at

8ha 151T(50-80m²) 16A

**1** ABCD**G**HIJKLMOPQ
**2** RTVWXY
**3** B**F**HJK**M**N**W**
**4** (**B**+**G** 15/5-1/9) J
(Q+R+U+X+Y 🔑)
**5** **AB**DFGIJKLMNO**P**UWZ
**6** ACEGK(N 1,5km)OU

💬 A peaceful campsite in the wine producing area of Austria, 70 km from Vienna. Close to Oggau swimming pool. Lovely toilet facilities, restaurant and self-service shop. Boats for hire at the marina. The Neusiedlersee cycle route crosses over the campsite. The Neusiedlerseecard (1.28 p.p.) offers discounts on places of interest and transport.

🚗 Take the B50 from the A4 or A3 and turn off towards Oggau and Rust. Follow camping signs in Oggau.

ⓒⒸ €**20** 31/3-7/6 11/6-29/6 1/9-31/10   📡 N 47°50'39'' E 16°41'15''

---

## Ossiach, A-9570 / Kärnten  👫 🛜 iD (1033)

🏕 Camping Kalkgruber
🏠 Alt-Ossiach 4
☎ +43 4 24 35 27
🗓 26/4 - 30/9
@ office@camping-kalkgruber.at

0,9ha 30T(80-100m²) 10A CEE

**1** A**G**IJKLOPQ
**2** GJKRTVWX
**3** ADHJNRU
**4** (Q 🔑)
**5** **AB**DFGIJMNO**P**UW
**6** ACEGK(N 1km)U

💬 A small but very well kept campsite close to the Ossiacher See lake. Here you will find peace, space and countryside. Frau Schabus will greet you with open arms. Lively recreation room. Fresh trout on sale. Good local food 1km away. Suitable as stopover site, 12km from the Ossiacher See exit.

🚗 A10 Salzburg-Villach, exit Ossiacher See direction Feldkirchen. In Steindorf turn right towards Ossiach. Then first campsite on the right.

ⓒⒸ €**16** 26/4-30/6 1/9-29/9 10=9, 20=18, 30=27   📡 N 46°41'15'' E 14°01'10''

---

## Ossiach, A-9570 / Kärnten  ♿ 🛜 iD (1034)

🏕 Camping Kölbl
🏠 Süduferstraße 106
☎ +43 42 43 82 23
🗓 10/4 - 10/10
@ info@camping-koelbl.at

17ha 180T(80-100m²) 10A

**1** A**F**HIJKLMOPQ
**2** ADFGKLMRTVWX
**3** BHJK**M**NO**PQ**RUWZ
**4** (A 1/7-31/8) (Q+R 🔑)
(T+U+V 1/5-30/9)
(Y 1/6-30/9)
**5** **AB**DEFGIJKLMNOPR**S**UW
XYZ
**6** ACDEGHKL(N 1km)OPTV

💬 A well maintained campsite right next to the Ossiacher See. If you like sportive holidays this is the place for you. You can walk or cycle round the lake and you will find all types of sport in the area. You will also feel at home here in spring and autumn.

🚗 A10 Salzburg-Villach, exit Ossiacher See direction 'Süfufer'. First campsite on the left past 'Heiligen Gestade'.

ⓒⒸ €**18** 10/4-29/6 1/9-10/10   📡 N 46°39'44'' E 13°58'20''

## Ossiach, A-9570 / Kärnten

♿ 📶 **iD** (1035)

🔺 Ideal Camping Lampele****
🏠 Alt-Ossiach 57
☎ +43 4 24 35 29
📅 1/5 - 30/9
@ camping@lampele.at

4ha 172T(80-100m²) 8-16A

**1** A**G**IJKLOPQ
**2** ADGIJKLRTVWXY
**3** AHJKLNR**T**U**VW**Z
**4** (F 🔲) **N**
(Q+S+T+U+V+Y+Z 15/5-15/9)
**5** **AB**DFGIJKLMNOPUWXYZ
**6** ACEGK(N 1km)OTUV

💬 A lovely campsite with marked out pitches right by the Ossiacher See. In addition to swimming you can go mountain climbing, walking or take bike rides. There is an indoor pool next to the site and you can take part in various sports in the vicinity. Shop on site. Supplements for comfort pitches and pitches right by the water.

🚗 A10 Salzburg-Villach, exit Ossiacher See direction Südufer. Continue as far as Ossiach and the campsite is on the left.

**Feldkirchen in Kärnten**

B95 B93
CC
A10  A2
**Villach**
A11

**CC** € **18** 1/5-30/6 1/9-29/9

📍 N 46°40'58'' E 13°59'54''

---

## Ossiach, A-9570 / Kärnten

♿ 📶 **iD** (1036)

🔺 Terrassen Camping Ossiacher See
🏠 Ostriach 67
☎ +43 4 24 34 36
📅 1/5 - 30/9
@ martinz@camping.at

10ha 520T(80-100m²) 6-16A CEE

**1** ACD**G**HIJKLMOPQ
**2** ADFGJKLMNRVWXY
**3** BCHJKL**MN**QRUW**Z**
**4** (A 1/7-30/8) J(Q+S 🔲)
(U+V+W+Y+Z 15/5-15/9)
**5** **AB**DEFGIJKLMNOP**QRS**T UWYZ
**6** ACEGHJKM(N 1km)ORTUV

💬 The pitches separated by hedges and bushes offer privacy, are partially terraced and have lovely views of the lake. "Terrasse-/Seeplatz' costs extra.

🚗 A10 Salzburg-Villach, exit Ossiacher See direction Südufer. Left at traffic lights towards Ossiach, campsite ± 5 km on the left.

**Feldkirchen in Kärnten**

B94  B95
B98
CC
A10  B83
**Villach**  A2
B84  A11

**CC** € **18** 1/5-29/6 1/9-29/9

📍 N 46°39'49'' E 13°58'29''

---

## Pesenthein, A-9872 / Kärnten

👫 🐕 📶 **iD** (1037)

🔺 Terrassencamping Pesenthein
🏠 Pesenthein 19
☎ +43 47 66 26 65
📅 15/4 - 30/9
@ camping@pesenthein.at

5ha 218T(70-95m²) 6A CEE

**1** ACD**G**IJKLMOPRS
**2** ADGIJKLRTVWX
**3** B**F**HJKRUZ
**4** J(Q+Y+Z 🔲)
**5** **AB**CFGIJKLMNOPUW
**6** AFGK(N 2km)TV

💬 A terraced campsite with a private beach and stunning views of the Millstätter See lake. Both the campsite and the beach have a separate area reserved for naturists. Separate beach for dogs.

🚗 A10 Salzburg-Villach, exit 139 Millstätter See (exit on left!). Left at traffic lights B98 direction Radenthein. Campsite about 2 km past Millstatt, east of Pesenthein on the left.

**Spittal an der Drau**

B99
B98  B88
CC
A10

**CC** € **20** 15/4-30/6 1/9-30/9

📍 N 46°47'47'' E 13°35'57''

## Pettneu am Arlberg, A-6574 / Tirol

🏔 ❄ 📶 iD (1038)

🏕 Arlberglife Ferienresort
📧 Dorf 58 A-C
☎ +43 54 48 83 52
📅 1/1 - 1/11, 1/12 - 31/12
@ camping@arlberglife.com

1ha 30T(70-100m²) 10-13A

**1** AGIJKLMOPQ
**2** FGKRUVWXY
**3** F**H**JRU**W**
**4** (A 1/6-30/9)
(Q+R+T+V+X+Z 🔑)
**5** **AB**DGIJKLMNO**PQR**UW
XYZ
**6** ACEGK(N 0,5km)OUV

💬 A small four-star resort within walking distance of the lovely village of Pettneu. Beautiful views of the mountains. Very well equipped. Starting point for lovely walks. Free entrance into indoor pool. Free wifi. Tourist and environmental tax are not included in ACSI rate.

🚗 Via Bregenz-Innsbruck: from Bregenz exit St. Anton, then direction Pettneu; from Innsbruck exit Flirsch. Follow Arlberg Panoramacamping signs in Pettneu.

B198

Sankt Anton am Arlberg  CC S16

B188

CC €⑳ 7/1-8/2 18/3-30/6 1/9-1/11 1/12-31/12    🏔 N 47°08'53'' E 10°20'48''

---

## Prutz, A-6522 / Tirol

👫 ❄ ♿ 📶 iD (1039)

🏕 Aktiv Camping Prutz****
📧 Pontlatzstraße 22
☎ +43 54 72 26 48
📅 1/1 - 31/12
@ info@aktiv-camping.at

1,5ha 125T(60-120m²) 6-10A CEE

**1** ACD**G**IJKLMOPQ
**2** CFGKRTUVWX
**3** BHJKLN**O**RU**W**
**4** (A 1/5-1/10) (Q+R 🔑)
(T+U+X 15/5-15/10,
20/12-10/4)
**5** **AB**DEFGHIJKLMNOPU
WXZ
**6** ABCDEG**K**L(N 0,5km)OV

💬 A comfortably laid out site, right by a river and in the village centre. Centrally located in the Serfaus-Fiss-Ladis ski regions. The perfect spot for walks and trips out. An ideal stop on your journey down south. Can be reached toll-free from Germany via the Fernpass.

🚗 Via toll-free road: From Imst to Landeck, then on the B180 dir. Serfaus (Reschenpass)to Prutz. Or A12 direction Reschenpaß, through tunnel at Landeck, then on B180 (toll charges).

Landeck  Fliess

Prutz  CC

B180

CC €⑱ 1/4-12/4 26/4-29/6 1/9-20/12 7=6, 14=12, 21=18, 28=24    🏔 N 47°04'49'' E 10°39'34''

---

## Purbach, A-7083 / Burgenland

♿ 📶 iD (1040)

🏕 Campingplatz
Storchencamp Purbach
📧 Campingplatz 1
☎ +43 26 83 51 70
📅 1/4 - 26/10
@ office@gmeiner.co.at

NEW

10ha 50T(80-100m²) 6A CEE

**1** AG**H**IJKLM**P**Q
**2** GLRWX
**3** AB**F**JKM**R**W
**4** (**C**+**H** 1/5-30/8) **J**
(Q+R+T+U+Y+Z 🔑)
**5** **A**DFGIJKLMNOPUWZ
**6** EG**J**(N 1km)V

💬 The campsite is quietly located directly next to the adventure swimming pool and offers opportunities for football, tennis, volleyball and basketball. The restaurant offers dishes from the local cuisine on the campsite grounds. Wine tasting and other events from May to October.

🚗 B50 Eisenstadt-Neusiedl am See. In the village follow campsite sign or 'zum See'.

B60

Neusiedl am See  A4

B50  B51

B15  CC

Eisenstadt

CC €⑳ 1/5-30/6 1/9-30/9    🏔 N 47°54'34'' E 16°42'20''

## Reisach, A-9633 / Kärnten

📶 **iD** (1041)

🏕 Camping Alpenferienpark
Reisach
📧 Schönboden 1
☎ +43 4 28 43 01
🗓 1/5 - 15/9, 1/12 - 1/4
@ info@alpenferienpark.com

3ha 57T(40-100m²) 10A

**1** ADG**I**JKLPQ
**2** BJKLRTUVXY
**3** AB**F**HJNRU
**4** (B+G 1/6-15/9) M(Q 🔒)
(R 1/5-15/9) (V+X+Y+Z 🔒)
**5** **AB**DEFGIJKLMNOPUWZ
**6** AEGJ(N 2km)TV

💬 A peacefully located terraced campsite on the southern slopes of the Reißkofel. Modern toilet facilities. Pitches separated by trees and bushes. Naturally fed swimming pool. Loved by hikers and families. Enthusiastic Dutch warden's family.

🚗 Accessible via Kötschach or Hermagor. Follow B111 to Reisach. In Reisach take the 'Alpenferienpark' exit and follow the signs for about 1.5 km.

Dellach im Irschen Drautal
B87
B111
CC
SS52BIS

**CC** € **18**  1/5-30/6  1/9-15/9

🗺 N 46°39'17'' E 13°08'57''

## Rennweg am Katschberg, A-9863 / Kärnten

🎿 📶 **iD** (1042)

🏕 Camping Ramsbacher
📧 Gries 53
☎ +43 4 73 46 63
🗓 1/1 - 31/12
@ info@camp-ram.at

**NEW**

1,4ha 65T(80-100m²) 16A CEE

**1** ACDGIJKLMOPRS
**2** CFGKLRTVWXY
**3** A**F**HIJKLM**Q**R**W**
**4** (A 1/6-30/9) (C+G 15/6-1/9)
(Q+U+Y+Z 🔒)
**5** **AB**DGIJKLMNOPUW
**6** CEG**K**(N 2km)O

💬 Pleasant and sunny summer and winter campsite in the Pölltal valley on the southern slope of Katschberg mountain. Because of its location near the A10, it is also very suitable as a transit campsite. Excellent campsite restaurant.

🚗 A10 Salzburg-Villach, exit 112 Rennweg. B99 direction Rennweg, first road on the right. Turn right at the traffic control office. Follow this main road as far as Gries. Then follow the camping signs.

Sankt Michael im Lungau
B99
CC
A10

**CC** € **16**  15/4-30/6  1/9-14/12

🗺 N 47°01'56'' E 13°35'44''

## Ried, A-6531 / Tirol

🎿 📶 **iD** (1043)

🏕 Camping Dreiländereck****
📧 Gartenland 37
☎ +43 54 72 60 25
🗓 1/1 - 31/12
@ info@tirolcamping.at

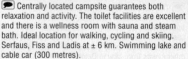

1ha 60T(70-100m²) 16A CEE

**1** A**G**IJKLMOQ
**2** FGRTUVWX
**3** ACGHJKLMNPQR**S**U
**4** (A 🔒) **LNP**
(Q+S+T+U+V+Y+Z 🔒)
**5** **AB**DEFGIJKLMNOPRUW
**6** ACDEG**K**M(N 0km)OTV

💬 Centrally located campsite guarantees both relaxation and activity. The toilet facilities are excellent and there is a wellness room with sauna and steam bath. Ideal location for walking, cycling and skiing. Serfaus, Fiss and Ladis at ± 6 km. Swimming lake and cable car (300 metres).

🚗 Toll-free road: via Imst on route 171 to Landeck, (direction Reschenpass) and on to Ried. Or A12 direction Meran (Reschenpaß), then on B180 towards Serfaus (toll charges).

Zams
**Landeck**
CC
B180

**CC** € **18**  6/1-2/2  26/4-29/6  1/9-20/12  14=13 21=19

🗺 N 47°03'21'' E 10°39'24''

## Salzburg-Nord, A-5023 / Salzburg

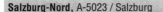 iD (1044)

🏕 Camping Nord-Sam★★★★
✉ Samstraße 22a
☎ +43 6 62 66 04 94
📅 18/4 - 6/10
@ office@camping-nord-sam.com

1,3ha 100T(80-120m²) 10A CEE

**1** ADG IJKLMO PQ
**2** FGILRSTVWXY
**3** AF HJKU
**4** (C 15/5-31/8) (Q+S+Z 🔲)
**5** AB DFGIJKLMNOPUW
**6** CG K(N 0,5km)

💬 Attractively laid out campsite with plenty of shrubs and trees, located on the outskirts of Salzburg. Bus stop, cycle and foot paths 100m from the site which lead to the city or to the beautifully undulating Salzkammergut.

🚗 A1 München-Wien (Vienna), exit 288 Salzburg-Nord. Filter to the left past 1st traffic lights and follow camping signs. 500 metres to the campsite.

CC € 20  24/4-1/6  1/9-6/10

N 47°49'37'' E 13°03'47''

---

## Salzburg-Nord, A-5020 / Salzburg

♿ 📶 iD (1045)

🏕 Panoramacamping Stadtblick
✉ Rauchenbichlerstraße 21
☎ +43 6 62 45 06 52
📅 1/1-6/1,20/3-5/11,5/12-15/12
@ info@panorama-camping.at

0,8ha 70T(40-70m²) 6A

**1** AFIJKLMO PQ
**2** BFJKRUVWX
**3** AF HJNU
**4** (Q+R 🔲) (T+X+Y 14/5-5/10)
**5** AB FGIJKLMNOPUWXYZ
**6** CFG K(N 1km)OV

💬 On the outskirts of the city, a hillside campsite with beautiful views over the city. Pitches with panoramic views not available for guests with CampingCard ACSI.

🚗 A1 Salzburg-Wien exit Salzburg-Nord. Immediately turn right and follow signs 'Camping Stadtblick' (right at first traffic light after exit).

CC € 20  20/3-12/4  1/5-7/6  7/9-1/10

N 47°49'44'' E 13°03'07''

---

## St. Georgen am Kreischberg, A-8861 / Steiermark

🎿 ♿ 📶 iD (1046)

🏕 Camping Olachgut★★★★★
✉ Kaindorf 90
☎ +43 35 32 21 62
📅 1/1 - 31/12
@ office@olachgut.at

10ha 140T(100-140m²) 16A CEE

**1** AG IJKLMO PQ
**2** CDGJKLRTVWXY
**3** AB FHJN OP RUWZ
**4** (A 1/7-31/8) N (Q+R+U+X+Z 🔲)
**5** AB CDEFGIJKLMNOPR S TU WXYZ
**6** ACEG K(N 2km)OUV

💬 Lovely 5 star site with own lake for fishing and swimming. Our farm with its many animals and recognized riding school is popular with children. Direct, safe cycle path to the popular Mur cycle route. Wheelchair friendly amenities on the site. Good family ski area close by.

🚗 A10/E55, exit 104 St. Michael. Route 96 as far as Tamsweg, then route 97 as far as St. Georgen. The campsite is located on the right after 2 km.

CC € 20  1/1-30/6  1/9-31/12

N 47°06'27'' E 14°08'22''

## St. Georgen am Längsee, A-9313 / Kärnten

🛜 iD (1047)

🏕 Camping Wieser Längsee
📧 Bernaich 8
☎ +43 65 06 00 36 80
📅 1/5 - 1/10
@ info@campingwieser.com

2ha 80T(120-160m²) 10A

**1** AGHIJKLMPQ
**2** FKLRVWXY
**3** AEFHJUW
**4** (Q ◒)
**5** ABGIJKLMNOPUW
**6** CFGJ(N 5km)

💬 Quiet, welcoming, natural campsite with pitches of 120 m² in the heart of Carinthia with a fresh-water lake and a sun meadow. Near the Längsee lake. Ideal base for cycling and walking and cultural days out, for example to Hochosterwitz castle, roman-celtic discoveries in Magdalensberg, Harrer museum, ducal town St. Veit, Klagenfurt - and for shopping and theatre.

🚗 B317 (also shown as B83) 5 km north of St. Veit exit 281, then another 500 metres.

Sankt Veit an der Glan

B93 | B92 | B94 | S37 | B82 | CC

CC € ⑱ 1/5-30/6  1/9-1/10    📍 N 46°48'08'' E 14°24'45''

---

## St. Johann im Pongau, A-5600 / Salzburg

⛷ ♿ 🛜 iD (1048)

🏕 Camping Kastenhof
📧 Kastenhofweg 6
☎ +43 64 12 54 90
📅 1/1 - 31/12
@ info@kastenhof.at

2ha 40T(80m²) 15A CEE

**1** ADGIJKLMPQ
**2** CGKLRTVWXY
**3** ABFGHJPRUVW
**4** LN(Q+R ◒)
**5** ABDFGIJKLMNOPUW
**6** CDEGIJ(N 0,5km)OSTV

💬 Hospitable, favourable and sunny location. Beautiful views of the mountains, within walking distance of the centre of St. Johann. Modern toilet facilities and extensive wellness programme. Ideal starting point for lovely walks and car and bike trips. Located on the 'Tauernradweg' cycle route.

🚗 A10, exit 46 Bischofshofen. Dir. Zell am See B311 as far as exit St. Johann im Pongau/Grossarl/Hüttschlag. Under viaduct; cross over bridge; first road on the left. Entrance after 150m.

Sankt Johann im Pongau

B99 | A10 | B163 | B311 | B167 | CC

CC € ⑳ 1/5-30/6  1/9-31/10    📍 N 47°20'29'' E 13°11'53''

---

## St. Martin bei Lofer, A-5092 / Salzburg

⛷ ♿ 🛜 ✿ iD (1049)

🏕 Camping Park Grubhof*****
📧 St. Martin 39
☎ +43 6 58 88 23 70
📅 12/4 - 3/11, 13/12 - 24/3
@ home@grubhof.com

10ha 225T(< 180m²) 10-16A CEE

**1** ADGIJKLMOPQ
**2** CGKLRUVWXY
**3** BFHIJKLNRUVWX
**4** (A 1/7-1/10) LNP
(Q+S+T+U+V+X+Y+Z ◒)
**5** ABDFGIJKLMNOPRSUW
XYZ
**6** ACDEGHIKL(N 1km)OT

💬 Idyllically situated in the grounds of an old park right by the river. Beautiful mountain views. Perfect for cyclists and walkers. Modern toilet buildings and mega-comfort pitches (up to 200 m²). Separate fields for families, campers without children and dog owners. Run with care and enthusiasm by the Stainer family. Sauna, wellness en winter camping.

🚗 Leave the B312 in Lofer in the direction of Zell am See (B311). Turn left after 1 km. The campsite is signposted.

Ramsau bei Berchtesgaden

B305 | Waidring | Lofer | B178 | CC | B311

CC € ⑳ 6/1-24/3  12/4-8/6  1/9-3/11    📍 N 47°34'27'' E 12°42'21''

## St. Michaël, A-9143 / Kärnten

👪 🏊 ⛷ ♿ 📶 **iD** (1050)

🔺 Petzencamping Pirkdorfer See
🏠 Pirkdorf 29
☎ +43 4 23 03 21
🗓 1/1 - 31/12
@ office@pirkdorfersee.at

10ha  27T(90m²)  12A CEE

**1** ACD**G**IJKLMPQ
**2** DGKLMRVW
**3** AHJN**O**R**U**W**Z**
**4** (A 1/5-30/9) (Q+R+U+Y 🔑)
**5** **AB**CDFGHIJKLMNOPUWX
**6** EGK(N 3km)OTV

💬 Campsite is located at the foot of the 2114-metres high Petzen, accessible by cable car. Situated directly on Austria's warmest swimming lake, the Pirkdorfersee. Summers up to 27 degrees, but also pleasant weather in spring and autumn. Skiing and ice skating possible in winter. Fine restaurant. Good, heated toilet facilities.

🚗 From Klagenfurt B70, exit Klopeiner See. Then B82 to Eberndorf, B81 to St. Michael. Follow signs.

**NEW**

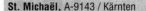

Völkermarkt  B80  B80A
B81  CC
B82  Crna na Koroskem

🆑🆑 € **16**  6/1-8/2  24/2-30/6  1/9-20/12        📶 N 46°33'30'' E 14°45'05''

---

## St. Peter am Kammersberg, A-8842 / Steiermark

♿ 📶 **iD** (1051)

🔺 Camping Bella Austria****
🏠 Peterdorf 100
☎ +43 3 53 67 39 02
🗓 19/4 - 29/9
@ info@camping-bellaustria.com

5,5ha  45T(110m²)  16A CEE

**1** A**G**IJKLMOPRS
**2** CKLRTVWX
**3** ABHJNRU**W**
**4** (B+G 15/6-10/9) **N** (Q+R 1/6-31/8) (U+Y+Z 🔑)
**5** **AB**CDEFGIJKLMNOPUW XYZ
**6** EGJ(N 2km)TV

💬 The campsite is located on the edge of the woods in the Katschtal valley in Styria, 1 km from the village of St. Peter am Kammersberg. The site has comfort pitches and a lovely swimming pool. It also has a good restaurant.

🚗 Via B99 direction Tamsweg. Take the Turracher Bundesstraße and via B95 to Ramingstein. Continue to Predlitz, then from Falkendorf to Murau. Through Murau to Frojach-Katsch, then to Peterdorf and Camping Bella Austria.

Sankt Peter am Kammersberg  CC  B75
B96
B97  **Murau**

🆑🆑 € **18**  19/4-30/6  1/9-29/9        📶 N 47°10'49'' E 14°12'55''

---

## St. Pölten, A-3100 / Niederösterreich

♿ 📶 (1052)

🔺 Camping am See
🏠 Bimbo Binder-Promenade 15
☎ +43 67 68 98 79 88 98
🗓 15/4 - 31/10
@ office@campingamsee.at

2ha  50T(100-200m²)  16A CEE

**1** BCD**G**HIJKLMOPQ
**2** DFGLMNORTVWXY
**3** ABF HJK**MQ**R**TVW**Z
**4** (Q 🔑)
**5** **AB**DGIJKLMNOPUWXYZ
**6** CEGJ(N 2km)TV

💬 Beautifully appointed campsite with new toilet facilities. Located next to a recreational lake with clear water and on the edge of the cultural town of St. Pölten. Very suitable for a visit to Vienna and for travelling on to Hungary. Large fitness centre. Walking and cycling in the surroundings.

🚗 From A1 at St. Pölten intersection S33 towards Krems. Then St. Pölten Nord exit. West at second intersection.

B1
**Sankt Pölten** CC Böheimkirchen
A1
B39 B20

🆑🆑 € **20**  15/4-20/5  29/5-30/6  1/9-31/10        📶 N 48°13'27'' E 15°39'33''

## St. Primus, A-9122 / Kärnten

🛆 Camping Breznik - Turnersee
☎ +43 42 39 23 50
🖸 13/4 - 29/9
@ info@breznik.at

(1053)

7,5ha 202T(80-110m²) 8-16A

1️⃣ ACD**G**HIJKLMOPQ
2️⃣ DLRVWXY
3️⃣ BFHJN**O**R**U**W**Z**
4️⃣ (A+Q+S 🖸)
　(T+U+V 24/5-10/9)
　(Y 1/6-10/9)
5️⃣ **AB**CDEFGHIJKLMNOPRU
　WXYZ
6️⃣ ACFGK(N 1km)OPRSTV

💬 Right on Turnersee Lake. Lawns, good swimming. First-rate amenities. Walking and cycling. Pretty villages, mountain landscapes and waterfalls. In low seasons campsite restaurant open during weekend. Restaurants in the locality. Not far from fashionable Klopeinersee.

🚐 From Klagenfurt A2, exit 298 Grafenstein, B70 direction Völkermarkt, direction Tainach/St. Kazian. Follow Turnersee campsite signs. From Graz A2, exit 278 Völkermarkt-Ost.

Völkermarkt  B80
A2
Sankt Kanzian am
Klopeiner See
CC
B85  B81
B82

CC €18  13/4-30/6  1/9-29/9

🔼 N 46°35'09'' E 14°33'59''

## St. Veit im Pongau, A-5621 / Salzburg

🛆 Sonnenterrassencamping
　St.Veit im Pongau****
📧 Bichlwirt 12
☎ +43 6 41 55 73 33
🖸 1/1 - 31/12
@ office@
sonnenterrassen-camping-stveit.at

(1054)

20ha 64T(80-100m²) 16A CEE

1️⃣ AGIJKLMPQ
2️⃣ GJKRTUVWX
3️⃣ ABD**F**HJRU
4️⃣ (A 15/6-15/9) (Q+R+T+U 🖸)
5️⃣ **AB**DEFGIJLMNOPUWXYZ
6️⃣ ACFG**K**(N 1,5km)OSUV

💬 Beautiful terraced campsite bathing in the sun with extremely modern toilet facilities. Centrally located for trips to Salzburg, the Großglockner, the Liechtensteinklamm, the Eisriesenwelt or for swimming in the many Thermal baths or cycling on the Tauern cycle route. All types of winter sport in the winter.

🚐 A10, exit 46 Bischofshofen. Then B311 direction Zell am See via St. Johann im Pongau, till exit St. Veit. Campsite is 500 metres on the right.

B164
Sankt Johann
im Pongau
CC  B163
B311
B167

CC €18  1/5-30/6  1/9-31/10

🔼 N 47°19'30'' E 13°10'02''

## Stams, A-6422 / Tirol

🛆 Camping Eichenwald
📧 Schiesstandweg 10
☎ +43 52 63 61 59
🖸 1/4 - 15/10, 1/12 - 6/1
@ info@tirol-camping.at

(1055)

5ha 100T(70-100m²) 13A CEE

1️⃣ A**G**IJKLMOPQ
2️⃣ BCFGJKLRTUVWXY
3️⃣ B**F**GHJLNRU**W**
4️⃣ (A 10/7-20/8) (C 1/5-30/9)
　(H 1/5-31/8) **N**(Q+R 🖸)
　(T+U+V+Y 1/5-30/9) (Z 🖸)
5️⃣ **AB**CDFGHIJKLMNOPRUW
　XYZ
6️⃣ CDEGK(N 0,5km)OTUV

💬 This terraced, centrally located campsite in the Inn valley offers shaded and spacious pitches. There are many opportunities around Stams, where kings and emperors took their holiday, for an active vacation: swimming, horse riding, (snow)hiking, golf, (cross country) skiing, mountain climbing (3000 routes). Eichenwald in the Oberinntal is the place for rest, relaxation and adventure.

🚐 Reutte, Fernpass, Nassereith, Mieming, direction Mötz/Stams. Campsite signposted.

B179
Telfs  B171
B189
Haiming  A12  CC
Oetz

CC €18  1/4-29/6  1/9-14/10  1/12-31/12

🔼 N 47°16'32'' E 10°59'10''

## Steindorf, A-9552 / Kärnten
♿ 🛜 **iD** (1056)

🔼 Seecamping Laggner****
✉ Strandweg 3
☎ +43 65 07 30 07 06
🔓 11/5 - 23/9
@ heidi.hinkel@gmail.com

1ha 40T(60-90m²) 10A

**1** AFIJKLOPQ
**2** DFGIKLMRVWXY
**3** BFGHJMRWZ
**4** (Q+T+U+X+Z 🔾)
**5** ADFGIJKLMNOPRSUW
**6** AEGK(N 0,2km)

💬 An attractive campsite with lawns. Plenty of sun and shade near the Ossiacher See lake. Wifi. Toilet facilities with access for the disabled, bakery. Opportunities for watersports, tennis, fitness, walking. Terrace, restaurant and nature reserve close by.

🚗 A10 Salzburg-Villach, exit Ossiacher See B94 dir. Nordufer and Feldkirchen. Turn right after 15 km towards Ossiach over railway line, then right and back towards Steindorf. About 900m on left past Gasthof dir. Strandweg 3.

CC € **18** 11/5-30/6 1/9-23/9 | 📡 N 46°41'40'' E 14°00'34''

---

## Steindorf/Stiegl, A-9552 / Kärnten
🛜 **iD** (1057)

🔼 Seecamping Hoffmann****
✉ Uferweg 65
☎ +43 42 43 87 04
🔓 1/5 - 30/9
@ info@seehotel-hoffmann.at

1ha 42T(70-90m²) 16A

**1** AFIJKLMOPQ
**2** DFGJKLMNRTVWXY
**3** BEFHIJKLMRWZ
**4** (A 🔾) N(Q+R 🔾)
   (T 1/7-7/9) (U+Y+Z 🔾)
**5** ABEFGJLNPUW
**6** AEGK(N 1km)V

💬 A small terraced campsite surrounded by old trees, right beside the Ossiacher Lake. Suitable as a base for trips out, free wifi. 100 metres from a restaurant. Pitches on lake ('Seeplätze') cost extra!

🚗 A10 Salzburg-Villach exit Villach/Ossiachersee, B94 direction Feldkirchen. Follow signs in Steindorf.

CC € **18** 1/5-29/6 1/9-29/9 | 📡 N 46°41'42'' E 13°59'48''

---

## Strassen, A-9918 / Tirol
👫 🛜 **iD** (1058)

🔼 Camping Lienzer Dolomiten***
✉ Tassenbach 23
☎ +43 48 42 52 28
🔓 1/4 - 31/10
@ camping-dolomiten@gmx.at

2ha 75T(80-120m²) 6-16A CEE

**1** AGIJKLMPQ
**2** GKRTUVWX
**3** AHJNW
**4** (B 1/6-31/8) (Q 🔾)
   (T+U+Z 15/6-31/8)
**5** ABDFGIJKLMNOPUWZ
**6** CEGK(N 2km)

💬 Quiet campsite with beautiful location in the Dolomites, close to Italy and at the confluence of four valleys. Spectacular views from all angles. Excellent toilet facilities and free wifi. Starting point for many walking and cycling trips.

🚗 München-Kufstein-Mittersill-Felbertauernstraße-Lienz direction Sillian, 3 km before Sillian Strassen/Tassenbach.

CC € **18** 1/4-29/6 1/9-31/10 14=12, 21=18 | 📡 N 46°44'47'' E 12°27'49''

## Techendorf (Weißensee), A-9762 / Kärnten

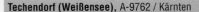

👫 🏊 ♿ 📶 **iD** **1059**

🏕 Camping Knaller
📧 Techendorf 16
☎ +43 47 13 22 34 50
📅 4/5 - 31/10, 20/12 - 28/2
@ info@knaller.at

**NEW**

1,4ha 140**T**(70-120m²) 16A CEE

**1** AC**G**IJKLM**P**Q
**2** DGIJKLNRWXY
**3** BHJNR**W**Z
**4** (T+U 15/6-10/9)
**5** **AB**DEFGIJKLMNOPR**S**UW
**6** CEGK(N 0,5km)

💬 Camping on Lake Weissensee means rest and relaxation in the midst of a unique nature reserve. Private beach with sunbathing area and self-service restaurant.

🚗 A10 Salzburg-Villach, exit 139 Spittal/Millstatter See, B100 as far as Greifenburg. Left on the B87 direction Hermagor. Follow the signs in the direction of Weißensee-Süd as far as Techendorf, turn left after the bridge.

B100

CC

B87

Kirchbach    Hermagor
B111

**CC** € **18**  10/5-23/6  7/9-19/10

📍 N 46°42'50'' E 13°17'45''

---

## Traisen, A-3160 / Niederösterreich

📶 **iD** **1060**

🏕 Terrassen-Camping Traisen
📧 Kulmhof 1
☎ +43 2 76 26 29 00
📅 1/3 - 30/9
@ info@camping-traisen.at

2,2ha 40**T**(60-80m²) 6A CEE

**1** A**G**IJKLMO**P**Q
**2** GJLRVWXY
**3** BHJKNRU
**4** (A 1/7-31/8) (C 15/5-30/9)
   (Q 1/6-30/9) (R 📅)
   (T 12/5-10/9) (Z 📅)
**5** **AB**DGJLN**P**RUW
**6** CEG**I**J(N 0,4km)OT

💬 Terraced campsite with spacious pitches in meadows with trees. Perfect starting point for trips out to Vienna, the Danube and Mariazell. The site has a shop for groceries and other necessities and a swimming pool heated by solar power. Lovely cycle routes close by.

🚗 A1 Linz-Vienna (Wien), exit 59 St. Pölten-Sud in the direction of Mariazell. After 15 km Traisen. Follow the signs, before the church you turn right.

Sankt Veit an der Gölsen

CC
**Lilienfeld**

B214

**CC** € **20**  1/3-30/6  1/9-30/9

📍 N 48°02'33'' E 15°36'11''

---

## Tulln an der Donau, A-3430 / Niederösterreich

♿ 📶 **iD** **1061**

🏕 Donaupark Camping Tulln
📧 Donaulände 76
☎ +43 2 27 26 52 00
📅 1/4 - 15/10
@ camptulln@oeamtc.at

10ha 90**T**(80-100m²) 6A CEE

**1** ACDGIJKLMO**P**Q
**2** CDGLRWXY
**3** BJK**LMNQRW**Z
**4** J(R+T+U+X+Y 15/4-14/10)
**5** **AB**DFGIJKLMNOPUW
**6** CDEG**I**J(N 1km)OSTV

💬 Lovely, well maintained campsite on the Danube with spacious, partially marked out pitches on a grassy base. There is a large playpark next to the campsite with swimming facilities which are free of charge to campsite guests.

🚗 A1 Linz-Vienna, exit St. Christophen exit 41 direction Tulln (B19). At Tulln follow the signs to Klosterneuburg. Under the railway viaduct, 1st on the right. Left after 650 metres, follow 'camping' signs.

B19  B4  **Stockerau**

**Tulln an der** S5
**Donau**
CC

**Wien**

**CC** € **20**  1/4-30/6  1/9-15/10

📍 N 48°19'59'' E 16°04'08''

## Waidring, A-6384 / Tirol

🏔 Camping Steinplatte GmbH
✉ Unterwasser 43
☎ +43 53 53 53 45
📅 1/1 - 31/12
@ info@camping-steinplatte.at

**1062**

4ha 220T 10A

**1** ACD**G**HIJKLMOPQ
**2** DGKLNRTVWX
**3** BFHJKL**MO**QRTUZ
**4** (A 1/7-31/8) **N**
(Q+R 1/1-1/11,1/12-31/12)
(T+U+V+X+Y 1/1-31/10,
1/12-31/12)(Z 📅)
**5** **AB**DFGIJKLMNOPUWZ
**6** ACEG**K**(N 0km)OSV

💬 Peaceful, by small lake, beautiful views of Loferer Steinberg. Ideal for walking and cycling. Countless possibilities for sporting activities and leisure. Good, friendly eating in the restaurant.

🚗 From the north toll-free: München - exit Oberaudorf, B172 via Walchsee and Kössen far as Erpfendorf. Then direction Lofer as far as Waidring. From the west: Inntal-Autobahn - Exit Wörgl Ost as far as St. Johann, then direction Waidring.

Kössen — B305
B178
B311
Sankt Johann in Tirol
B164

(CC) € 20  7/1-29/6  1/9-24/12

🏔 N 47°35'00'' E 12°34'59''

---

## Walchsee, A-6344 / Tirol

🏔 Ferienpark
Terrassencamping Süd-See****
✉ Seestraße 76
☎ +43 53 74 53 39
📅 1/1 - 31/12
@ info@terrassencamping.at

**NEW**

**1063**

11ha 150T(70-150m²) 16A CEE

**1** A**G**IJKLMO**PQ**
**2** DFJKLMRSTVWXY
**3** BFHJKL**OP**STW**Z**
**4** (A 1/6-1/10) (Q 📅)
(R 12/4-15/10)
(T+U 12/4-15/10,20/12-31/12)
(X+Y 1/1-31/10,1/12-31/12)
**5** **AB**DEFGIJLMNOPUWXYZ
**6** CDEGHK(N 2km)OU

💬 Perfect campsite in summer and winter in the 'Kaiserwinkl' walking, cycling and cross country paradise. All pitches have fantastic views of the lake. Modern toilet facilities, free hot water, private individual cabins. Restaurant, mini-market, lakeside lawns (24°C in summer). Peaceful location. Open all year round. Toll free motorway as far as Walchsee.

🚗 B172 from Niederndorf to Kössen. Campsite signposted before Walchsee village on the right.

B307
B305
Kössen
B175
Ebbs
Kufstein

(CC) € 20  28/4-5/6  23/6-30/6  12/9-13/10

🏔 N 47°38'26'' E 12°19'26''

---

## Weer, A-6116 / Tirol

🏔 Alpencamping Mark****
✉ Bundesstraße 12
☎ +43 5 22 46 81 46
📅 1/4 - 31/10
@ info@alpencampingmark.com

**1064**

2ha 95T(80-130m²) 10-16A

**1** ACD**G**IJKLMOPQ
**2** FGIKLRUVY
**3** BHJKL**M**N**O**PRU
**4** (**A** 1/7-31/8) (C+H 1/5-15/9)
(Q+R 📅) (T+U 20/5-15/9)
(Y 1/5-1/9)
**5** **AB**CDFGHIJKLMNOPR UWZ
**6** ACEGHK(N 0,1km)UVWX

💬 Nicely appointed family campsite on even or lightly inclined, well-maintained meadow with several trees. Many shady, spacious pitches. The campsite has an outdoor swimming pool and climbing wall. Own horse breeding (Haflinger). There is an 'Alpine and Leisure School' on the campsite.

🚗 From Innsbruck direction Kufstein, exit 61 Wattens. From Kufstein direction Innsbruck, exit 49 Schwaz or 53 Vomp, then to Weer.

A12
Schwaz
Hall in Tirol

(CC) € 18  1/4-29/6  1/9-30/10

🏔 N 47°18'23'' E 11°38'57''

## Wertschach bei Nötsch, A-9612 / Kärnten 🛜 iD 1065

🏕 Camping Alpenfreude
📧 Wertschach 27
☎ +43 42 56 27 08
📅 1/5 - 30/9
@ camping.alpenfreude@aon.at

5ha 150T(50-120m²) 16A CEE

**1** ACD**G**IJKLMOPQ
**2** FGJKLRTVWX
**3** AHN**Q**RU
**4** (A 1/7-25/8) (C+H 1/6-31/8) J
(S 🈁) (T+U+V+W+X+Y+Z
15/5-15/9)
**5** **AB**FGIJKLMNOP**S**UWZ
**6** ACDEGJ(N 3,5km)OTV

💬 Attractive campsite located on the south side of the Gailtaler Alps. Lovely, completely refurbished heated pool. Ideal for mountain walks or for taking trips out to Italy or Slovenia. Only 12 km from the autobahn.

🚗 A10 Salzburg-Villach-Italia, then A2 to Italy exit Hermagor B111. Follow signs beyond Nötsch.

CC € 18  1/5-30/6  1/9-29/9      📸 N 46°36'26'' E 13°35'26''

---

## Westendorf, A-6363 / Tirol 🎿 ♿ 🛜 iD 1066

🏕 Panoramacamping
📧 Mühltal 70
☎ +43 53 34 61 66
📅 1/1 - 19/10, 18/12 - 31/12
@ info@panoramacamping.at

2,2ha 90T(85-90m²) 12A

**1** AD**G**HIJKLMOPQ
**2** GJKRTVWXY
**3** B**F**HIJKLNRU
**4** (**A** 1/6-30/9)
(C+H 20/5-15/9) **JN**
(Q+R+U+Y+Z 🈁)
**5** **AB**DFGIJKLMNOPQ**S**UW
XYZ
**6** ACEG**K**(N 1km)OQSTV

💬 A beautifully laid-out family campsite with level, well maintained grounds. Plenty of opportunities for sports enthusiasts. A 10 minute walk to Westendorf. There is an outdoor pool 5 minutes walk from the site. Westendorf is the top address for paragliding.

🚗 Inntal-motorway, exit 17 Wörgl, to Westendorf (Brixental).

CC € 18  2/5-29/6  6/9-19/10      📸 N 47°25'58'' E 12°12'07''

---

## Zell am See, A-5700 / Salzburg 🎿 🛜 iD 1067

🏕 Panorama Camp Zell am See
📧 Seeuferstraße 196
☎ +43 6 54 25 62 28
📅 1/1 - 19/10, 20/12 - 31/12
@ info@panoramacamp.at

1ha 50T(70-90m²) 16A CEE

**1** AD**G**HIJKLMOPQ
**2** GKLMRTWXY
**3** BD**F**HIJKRU**W**
**4** (A 1/7-1/9) (Q 🈁)
(R+V 1/6-15/9)
**5** **AB**DFGIJKLMNOPUW
XYZ
**6** CEG**K**(N 2km)OSUV

💬 Your home in the mountains! Small family campsite on a sunny and quiet location on the south bank of Lake Zeller. Beautiful panoramic view of Kitzsteinhorn mountain. Ideal base for walking, cycling and mountain-biking. Only 500 metres from the beach.

🚗 No vignette. From Lofer direction Zell am See, do not enter tunnel. Take Thumersbach exit. Campsite on the southern bank 6 km on the right.

CC € 20  5/1-28/6  1/9-19/10      📸 N 47°18'07'' E 12°48'57''

## Zell im Zillertal, A-6280 / Tirol

🏔 Campingdorf Hofer
✉ Gerlosstraße 33
☎ +43 52 82 22 48
🔄 1/1 - 31/12
@ info@campingdorf.at

1,6ha 100**T**(80-100m²) 6-16A CEE

**1** ACD**G**IJKLMOPQ
**2** GKLRV**X**
**3** A**F**HJRU**W**
**4** (A 1/6-15/9) (E 1/5-15/10)
(Q+R 🔄)
(T+U+Y 30/5-15/10,
15/12-15/4)
**5** **AB**DFGIJKLMNOPRUWZ
**6** BCEGHKOV

💬 Friendly family campsite with about 100 spacious pitches. Centrally located within walking distance of the centre of Zell im Zillertal. Indoor and heated outdoor pools provide a chance to cool down. There is a 45,000 m² leisure park in Zell with countless sports and leisure facilities. Tourist and environmental taxes are not included in the CampingCard ACSI rates.

🚗 Inntal motorway, exit 39 Zillertal, take the B169 to Zell am Ziller (fourth campsite in the Zillertal).

Zell am Ziller
B165
Mayrhofen

**CC** € **18** 3/4-29/6  1/9-10/10

▲ N 47°13'44'' E 11°53'10''

You can easily find a campsite that meets your needs on the website. Search using the map, a place name, or amenities.

# www.CampingCard.com

# Poland

## General
Poland is a member of the EU.

### Time
The time in Poland is the same as in Amsterdam, Paris and Rome and one hour ahead of London.

### Language
Polish, but English is a good alternative.

## Border formalities
Many formalities and agreements about matters such as necessary travel documents, car papers, requirements relating to your means of transport and accommodation, medical expenses and taking pets with you do not only depend on the country you are travelling to but also on your departure point and nationality. The length of your stay can also play a role here. It is not possible within the confines of this guide to guarantee the correct and most up to date information with regard to these matters.

We advise you to consult the relevant authorities before your departure about:
- which travel documents you will need for yourself and your fellow passengers
- which documents you need for your car
- which regulations your caravan must meet
- which goods you may import and export
- how medical treatment will be arranged and paid for in your holiday destination in cases of accident or illness
- whether you can take pets. Contact your vets well in advance. They can give you information about the necessary vaccinations, proof thereof and obligations on return. It would also make sense to enquire whether any special regulations apply to your pet in public places at your holiday destination. In some countries for example dogs must always be muzzled or transported in a cage.

You will find plenty of general information on ▸ www.europa.eu ◂ but make certain you select information that is relevant to your specific situation.

For the most recent customs regulations you should get in contact with the authorities of your holiday destination in your country of residence.

## Currency
The currency in Poland is the zloty (PLN). Exchange rate September 2018: £1 = PLN 4.83. In Poland you can only exchange foreign currency at recognised bureau de changes, banks or post offices.

### Cash machines
There are plenty of cash machines where you can withdraw money.

### Credit cards
You can pay by credit card at many restaurants, large shops and tourist centres.

## Opening hours
### Banks
Banks are open on weekdays until 16:00 and on Saturdays until 13:00.

## Shops

Most shops are open Monday to Friday until
19:00 and on Saturday to 16:00

## Communication

### (Mobile) phones

The mobile network in Poland is very good.
There is a 4G network for mobile internet. You
can make international calls at tourist centres
and in large cities. In smaller towns or cities,
you can go to a post office for an international
telephone connection.

### Wifi, internet

You can make use of a wifi network at more and
more public locations, often for free.

### Post

On weekdays post offices are open until 06:00
and on Saturday to 14:00.

## Roads and traffic

### Road network

The motorways in Poland are good quality. You
will only find unpaved roads in the countryside.
It is not recommended to drive on secondary
roads after sunset. In Poland, you can call the
following roadside assistance: Starter tel: 00 48
600 222 222.

### Traffic regulations

Traffic from the right has priority. Trams always
have priority. If you are driving on a roundabout
then you have priority over drivers approaching
the roundabout. At cycle crossings, cyclists have
priority.
The maximum permitted alcohol limit is 0.2 %.
You should call hands-free. During the day, it
is compulsory to drive with dipped headlights.
In the event of an accident, you should call the
police. It is forbidden to transport someone in
an 'intoxicated state' in the front passenger seat
of your car.

*Maximum speed*

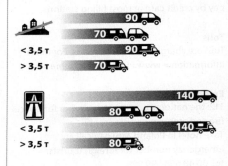

The so-called 'Mehrzweckstreifen' are a type of
hard shoulder along roads outside urban areas.
You can recognise them  by the broad, white
solid line separating them from the driving
lane. You should be mindful that this lane is
also intended for slow traffic such as  cyclists,
pedestrians, mothers with pushchairs etc.
Winter tyres are not compulsory in Poland, but
they are recommended.

### Caravans, motorhomes

Take note! In Poland, you should have  a green
card for your car and another for your caravan,
if it weighs over 750 kg.

### Maximum allowed measurements of combined length

Height 4 metres, width 2.55 metres and length
18.75 metres (of which, the maximum length of
the trailer is 12 metres).

### Fuel

Lead-free petrol, diesel and LPG are widely
available.

### Filling stations

Filling stations are generally open from 08:00
to 19:00. In big cities and on motorways many

filling stations are open day and night. You can pay by credit card at most filling stations.

## Tolls
Tolls are charged on various roads. For more information ▸ www.viatoll.pl/en/home ◂

### Emergency number
112: the national emergency number for police, fire and ambulance.
Take note! In Poland, you can call an emergency number for foreign tourists: tel. 00 48 608 599 999.

# Camping
The quality of Polish campsites varies from simple to modern grounds that compete at European level. Poland has very few demarcated pitches, but on the other hand, all campsites have electricity. Campsites by the Baltic Sea and in the Carpathians are highly popular. In these regions, in particular, a chemical toilet is by no means a luxury.

## Practical
- Make sure you always have an adapter plug (world plug) with you.
- You are recommended to drink bottled (mineral) water rather than tap water.

### Kolobrzeg, PL-78-100 / Zachodniopomorskie   ♯♯ ♿ 🛜 iD  (1069)

🔺 Camping Nr. 78 Baltic****
🏠 ul. 4 Dywizji-WP nr. 1
☎ +48 6 06 41 19 54
📅 15/4 - 15/10
@ baltic78@post.pl

4ha 220T 16A

1 ACDGIJKLMPQ
2 AEGRTUVWX
3 ABKNRUY
4 (Q+S 1/5-15/9) (T 1/7-31/8) (X 1/6-30/9) (Z 1/5-15/9)
5 ADGIJKLMNOPUWZ
6 CDFGK(N 0,1km)TV

💬 A lovely campsite with excellent toilet facilities. The lively town centre and the beach are within walking distance. Many health treatments available close to the site. A path from near the site leads along the beach.

🚗 Campsite on east side of Kolobrzeg. Route 11. From Gdansk turn right at 1st roundabout. Campsite after 100 metres. From Sczecin 3rd exit on second roundabout. After 500 metres to the right, campsite is located after 100 metres.

Kolobrzeg
Grzybowo
CC

CC € 14  15/4-20/6  1/9-14/10   📍 N 54°10'53'' E 15°35'45''

## Leba, PL-84-360 / Pomorskie

👫 🦽 📶 **iD** `1070`

🏕 Camping Lesny Nr. 51***
📧 Brzozowa 16A
☎ +48 5 98 66 28 11
🕒 15/4 - 30/10
@ camping_51_lesny@wp.pl

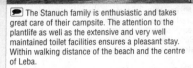

NEW

1,2ha 150T 16A

**1** AGIJKLO**PQ**
**2** AELRSTWX
**3** AKRUVWY
**4** **N**(Q+S 15/6-30/8)
**5** **AB**DFGIJKLMNOPUWZ
**6** CEGK(N 0,5km)TV

💬 The Stanuch family is enthusiastic and takes great care of their campsite. The attention to the plantlife as well as the extensive and very well maintained toilet facilities ensures a pleasant stay. Within walking distance of the beach and the centre of Leba.

🚗 Turn right at 1st roundabout, then follow road at 2nd roundabout. Turn right at tennis court, after 200 metres the campsite is on left of road.

Sasino
CC
Leba
Wicko

**CC** €**14** *15/4-29/6  1/9-30/10*

📍 N 54°45'44'' E 17°33'59''

---

## Miedzyzdroje, PL-72-500 / Zachodniopomorskie

👫 📶 **iD** `1071`

🏕 Camping no. 24
📧 Ul. Polna 36
☎ +48 9 13 28 02 75
🕒 1/4 - 15/10
@ info@camping24.info.pl

3ha 300T(60-120m²) 16A

**1** ACG**H**IJKLMPQ
**2** LRSTVWX
**3** AHJRU
**4** (T 1/6-15/9)
**5** **A**GIJKLMNOPUWXYZ
**6** CEGK(N 0,5km)TV

💬 Pleasant campsite with very friendly owner. Situated near the Wolinsky nature reserve (where you can spot bison). Close to the beach (600m) and within walking distance of the lively boulevard and large square (centre) with lots of shops and (fish) restaurants. Another recommendation is a walk to the lovely beach pier, which is 400m long.

🚗 Swinoujscie (Swinemünde) road 3, exit Miedzyzdroje road 102. Campsite 24 is signposted.

CC
**Swinoujscie**

**CC** €**16** *1/4-29/6  1/9-14/10*

📍 N 53°55'16'' E 14°26'09''

---

## Sciegny, PL-58-534 / Dolnoslaskie

🎿 🦽 📶 **iD** `1072`

🏕 Camp 66****
📧 Widokowa 9
☎ +48 7 92 56 65 69
🕒 1/1 - 30/11, 29/12 - 31/12
@ biuro@camp66.pl

NEW

3ha 72T(60-200m²) 16A

**1** ACD**G**IJKLMOPQ
**2** KRUVW
**3** BHJ
**4** (**A**+R+T+U+V+X+Z 🕒)
**5** **A**CDEGHIJKLMNOPQRUW XYZ
**6** EGIKTV

💬 Modern, environmentally friendly campsite close to the popular winter sports resort Karpacz with attractive restaurant and covered barbecue area. Suitable for winter sports activities, hiking and biking in the Giant Mountains.

🚗 Follow road 365 direction Karpacz. At roundabout (ignore SatNav) straight ahead. Follow signs. After 1 km turn left. Follow road with bridge ± 500 metres.

**Jelenia Góra**
Myslakowice
CC
Spindleruv Mlýn
252

**CC** €**12** *1/1-30/4  5/5-18/6  10/9-30/11*

📍 N 50°47'35'' E 15°46'12''

## Szczecin/Dabie, PL-70-800 / Zachodniopomorskie

**1073**

🔺 Camping Marina★★★★
🏠 ul. Przestrzenna 23
☎ +48 9 14 60 11 65
📅 1/1 - 31/12
@ campingmarina@
campingmarina.pl

4ha 120T 16A CEE

1 ACD**G**IJLM**PQ**
2 DFGLRTWXY
3 AKU
4 (Q+U+X 📧) (Z 1/3-31/10)
5 **AB**CDGHJLMNOPUWZ
6 CFGK(N 3km)RT

NEW

💬 Beautifully landscaped campsite with marina. Great care for the borders around the pitches. Helpful reception staff; many leaflets about the area available. Suitable as a base for visiting the city centre with bus stop 50 metres from the campsite.

🚗 On motorway A6 take exit Sczcecin-centre. After 4 km sharp turn to the right towards Dabie. Turn left just past the church and then drive another 2 km to the campsite.

Szczecin

Kolbaskowo

A6

CC € **16** 1/1-13/6 22/8-31/12

N 53°23'43'' E 14°38'12''

---

## Uciechów, PL-58-211 / Dolnoslaskie

**1074**

🔺 Camping Forteca
🏠 ul. Wroclawska 12
☎ +48 7 25 48 80 00
📅 1/4 - 30/9
@ info@campingforteca.nl

5,2ha 70T(70-150m²) 16A

1 A**G**IJKLMOPQ
2 DKMRTWXY
3 ABJRUZ
4 (Q+U+Y+Z 📧)
5 **A**GIJKLMNOPUW
6 DEIK(N 1km)TV

NEW

💬 Pleasant family campsite with its own swimming lake, beautifully situated at the foot of the Giant Mountains. Perfect for children.

🚗 From A4 take Udanin exit via Swidnica direction Dzierzoniów (road 382). Before Dzierzoniów, turn left at roundabout, road 384, and take second exit left towards Uciechów to parallel road.

Dzierzoniów

Bielawa

CC € **14** 1/5-30/6 1/9-30/9

N 50°45'21'' E 16°41'40''

---

## Zlocieniec, PL-78-520 / Zachodniopomorskie

**1075**

🔺 Inter Nos Island Camping
🏠 Ul. Bledno 1/Lubieszewo
☎ +48 9 43 63 11 90
📅 1/5 - 31/10
@ m.moser@inter-nos.pl

8,5ha 150T 6A

1 ACD**G**IJKLPQ
2 BDIKLMRSTWXY
3 AHJU**WZ**
4 (**A**+Q+R+T+X+Y+Z 📧)
5 **AB**GIJKLMNOPUWZ
6 CEK(N 1,5km)V

NEW

💬 Located on the island of Schulzewerder. The ideal place for those looking for peace and quiet and a true Mecca for anglers and water sports enthusiasts. The campsite on the 8.5 hectare island is accessible by private ferry. Foot and bicycle traffic to and from the mainland via a wooden footbridge.

🚗 From Drawsko Pomorskie centre head to Lubieszewo. After approx. 13 km follow large campsite signs to ferry. Free ferry transport to the island for car, caravan or motorhome every two hours.

Drawsko Pomorskie

Zlocieniec

CC

428

CC € **16** 1/5-19/6 1/9-30/10 7=6, 14=11

N 53°27'25'' E 15°55'12''

# Czech Republic

## General
The Czech Republic is a member of the EU.

### Time
The time in the Czech Republic is the same as Amsterdam, Paris and Rome and one hour ahead of London.

### Languages
Czech, but English and German are well understood.

## Border formalities
Many formalities and agreements about matters such as necessary travel documents, car papers, requirements relating to your means of transport and accommodation, medical expenses and taking pets with you do not only depend on the country you are travelling to but also on your departure point and nationality. The length of your stay can also play a role here. It is not possible within the confines of this guide to guarantee the correct and most up to date information with regard to these matters.

We advise you to consult the relevant authorities before your departure about:
- which travel documents you will need for yourself and your fellow passengers
- which documents you need for your car
- which regulations your caravan must meet
- which goods you may import and export
- how medical treatment will be arranged and paid for in your holiday destination in cases of accident or illness
- whether you can take pets. Contact your vets well in advance. They can give you

information about the necessary vaccinations, proof thereof and obligations on return. It would also make sense to enquire whether any special regulations apply to your pet in public places at your holiday destination. In some countries for example dogs must always be muzzled or transported in a cage.

You will find plenty of general information on ▶ *www.europa.eu* ◄ but make certain you select information that is relevant to your specific situation.

For the most recent customs regulations you should get in contact with the authorities of your holiday destination in your country of residence.

## Currency
The currency in the Czech Republic is the koruny (or crown) (CZK). Approximate exchange rates September 2018: £1 = CZK 28.59. You can exchange money at the border exchange offices and also at banks and travel agencies.

### Cash machines
There are sufficient cash machines in the Czech Republic.

### Credit cards
Many restaurants, shops and service stations accept credit cards.

## Opening times
### Banks
Banks are open weekdays from 09:00 to 12:00 and from 13:00 to 17:00.

### Shops
Open weekdays until 18:00, on Saturdays until 13:00.

### Chemists
There are plenty of chemists in the cities. Prague has 24 hour chemists.

## Communication
### (Mobile) phones
The mobile network works well throughout the Czech Republic. There is a 4G network for mobile internet.

### Wifi, internet
You can make use of a wifi network at more and more public locations, often for free.

### Post
Open on weekdays until 17:00 and on Saturday mornings.

## Roads and traffic
### Road network
Main roads are of good quality. Driving after dark has its risks, because of vehicles without lights on the road. In view of the congestion in the centre of Prague you are advised to use the Park and Ride car parks on the outskirts and travel to the centre by tram. You can contact the breakdown service (ÚAMK CR) day and night on tel. 1230.

### Traffic regulations
There is a total ban on alcohol when driving. Remember, all traffic in the Czech Republic drives on the right and overtakes on the left! Headlight deflectors are advisable to prevent annoying oncoming drivers.
The Czech Republic uses the metric system, so distances are measured in kilometres (km) and speeds in kilometres per hour (km/h). Traffic from the right has priority except on main roads. Traffic on a roundabout has priority over traffic wishing to enter it. Accidents involving injury or damage must be reported immediately to the police. The use of dipped headlights during the day and throughout the year is mandatory. You may only phone hands-free. Children under 18 years must wear a cycle helmet, helmets are also advised for older people. In the case of tailback you must move to the left or right of the road and leave space in the middle for the emergency services. Winter tyres are recommended between 1 November and 31 March.

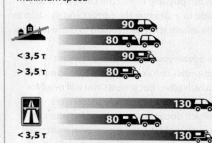

*Maximum speed*

| | |
|---|---|
| | 90 |
| | 80 |
| < 3,5 т | 90 |
| > 3,5 т | 80 |
| | 130 |
| | 80 |
| < 3,5 т | 130 |
| > 3,5 т | 80 |

### Caravans, motorhomes
It is not allowed to stay overnight in a caravan

...notorhome on public roads. Motorhomes weighing more than 3.5 tonnes must pay a toll per kilometre by means of an electronic box. See ▶ *www.premid.cz* ◀ for more information.

### Maximum allowed measurements of combined length
Height 4 metres, width 2.55 metres and maximum length 18.75 metres (of which the trailer maximum 12 metres).

### Tolls
You must have a special vignette (toll sticker) on motorways and major roads. Nearly all the roads leading to Prague fall into this category. Vignettes are on sale for varying periods. They are available at border crossings, post offices and larger service stations. More information: ▶ *www.mytocz.eu* ◀

### Fuel
All types of fuel are available in the Czech Republic. LPG is also available in many places.

### Filling stations
Filling stations on motorways and in larger towns are open permanently; elsewhere they are usually open until 19:00. At filling stations with internationally recognised brands in larger towns you can pay by credit card.

### Emergency number
112: national emergency number for fire, police and ambulance.

## Camping
Camping has a nostalgic character in the Czech Republic as many Czechs still go camping with a tent. But campsites are developing: more marked out pitches are being created, electricity is nearly always available, the number of service stations for motorhomes is increasing and more and more campsites offer their guests WiFi.

### Practical
- Make sure you have a world adaptor for electrical appliances.
- You are advised to drink bottled (mineral) water in preference to mains water.

## Bozanov, CZ-54974 / Kralovehradecky kraj 📶 iD 1076

🔺 Camping Bozanov
📧 Bozanov 307
☎ +420 6 02 36 13 50
🔑 27/4 - 16/9
@ info@bozanov.nl

1ha 50T(90-130m²) 16A CEE

**1** ABGIJKLMNOPQ
**2** BDGJKLRTUVWXY
**3** ABDHJMNOPRUWZ
**4** (A+C+Q+Z 🔑)
**5** ABDGIJKLMNPQUWZ
**6** DEGIK(N 1km)

💬 Easy-going, atmospheric campsite. Tranquil location, in a nature reserve with unique rock formations. Spacious, level pitches with a breathtaking view over the estates and mountains. Modern, clean toilet facilities. Small swimming lake and heated pool. Ideal for hikers/ cyclists. Info folder upon arrival. Free wifi on entire campsite.

🚗 Prague E67 to Náchod and 303 to Broumov-Janovicky. At T-junction towards Božanov. Right in Božanov, follow signs Camping Bozanov.

Nowa Ruda
302
303
Police nad Metuji
CC

CC € 18 27/4-6/7  26/8-16/9      N 50°31'28'' E 16°21'06''

---

## Cerná v Pošumaví, CZ-38223 / Jihocesky kraj ♿ 📶 iD 1077

🔺 Camping Olšina***
☎ +420 6 08 02 99 82
🔑 20/4 - 10/10
@ info@campingolsina.cz

5,5ha 300T 10A CEE

**1** ABGIJKLMOPQ
**2** ABDJKLORXY
**3** AKRWZ
**4** (R 1/7-30/8) (T+X 🔑)
**5** ABGIJKLMNPUW
**6** EGIK(N 1,5km)TV

💬 A friendly campsite full of character situated partly in the woods, terraced, and leading down to a quiet part of Lake Lipno. Within walking distance of Cerná v Pošumaví and 20 km from the historic town of Ceský Krumlov. The campsite has wifi.

🚗 From Cerná v Pošumaví direction Ceský Krumlov. After about 1 km to the left. Campsite is signposted.

Ceský Krumlov
39
CC
162
163

CC € 18 20/4-30/6  24/8-10/10  7=6, 14=12      N 48°44'46'' E 14°07'00''

---

## Chvalsiny, CZ-38208 / Jihocesky kraj 📶 iD 1078

🔺 Camping Chvalsiny
📧 Chvalsiny 321
☎ +420 3 80 73 91 23
🔑 19/4 - 15/9
@ info@campingchvalsiny.nl

7,5ha 140T(120-150m²) 6A CEE

**1** ABGIJKLMOPQ
**2** ACDGJKLMRSVWX
**3** BDFHJNRUWZ
**4** (A 19/4-5/7,24/8-14/9)
　　(B 1/6-31/8)
　　(Q+T+X+Z 1/6-30/8)
**5** ABDEFGIJKLMNOPQUWZ
**6** ACEGK(N 0,4km)TV

💬 A well run terraced campsite with magnificent views, located between Chvalsiny with its unique Czech atmosphere. Fishing lake, swimming pool, free wifi. Marked out walks. 10 km from Cesky Krumlov with castles and historic lanes.

🚗 From Ceské Budejovice to Ceský Krumlov. Past Ceský Krumlov after about 3 km direction Chvalsiny. Follow camping signs with 'NL'. Route 39 Ceské Budejovice dir. Lipno. ±3 km past Ceský Krumlov follow NL camping signs.

143
122
CC
Ceský Krumlov
39
162

CC € 18 19/4-5/7  24/8-15/9      N 48°51'36'' E 14°12'53''

## Decín 3, CZ-40502 / Ustecky kraj 🛈 1079

🏕 Camping Kemp Decín
📮 Polabí
☎ +420 7 74 26 21 11
🔓 15/4 - 31/10
@ info@campingdecin.cz

12ha 55T 16A CEE

1. AGIJKLMOPQ
2. CFGKLRTWX
3. ABHIJKLMRSTWX
4. (A 🔓) M(Q+T+U+Z 🔓)
5. ABCEFGHIJKLMNOPQTUWZ
6. FGIKM(N 0,4km)OTUWX

💬 Campsite close to the old town, next to the river Elbe. Very suitable for cyclists. Many facilities at 500 metres. Also suitable as a stopover site. 5 minutes from national park Bohemian Switzerland and 1 minute from aquapark. Canoeing, kayaking and rafting possible on the Elbe.

🚗 Follow route 13 from Jilové. In Decin cross River Elbe, direction E442. Campsite right next to the river and is signposted.

Ludvíkovice · Decín · Tisá · 13 · 262 Zandov · 261 · 62 · 240

CC €14 15/4-30/6 1/9-31/10 · N 50°46'24'' E 14°12'38''

## Dvur Králové n. L., CZ-54401 / Kralovehradecky kraj 🛈 1080

🏕 Safari Kemp Resort
📮 Stefanikova 1029
☎ +420 4 99 31 12 15
🔓 1/1 - 31/12
@ safarikemp@zoodvurkralove.cz

2ha 70T(100-150m²) 6A CEE

1. ABCGIJKLMOPQ
2. GKLRTWXY
3. ABMORT
4. (C+H 1/6-30/9) K (Q 1/6-30/8) (R 🔓) (T+V 1/6-30/9) (W+Y 🔓)
5. ABDHIJMNOPUWXYZ
6. EGIKM(N 1,5km)OT

💬 The campsite has a swimming pool and jacuzzi, a shop, bike rental, laundry room and children's play areas. You have access to a viewing platform where you can watch the animals in the nearby zoo. You can also visit the safari park for free during your stay.

🚗 Route 33 Hradec Králové-Jaromer. Route 37 direction Trutnov as far as Dvur Králové exit. Then route 300 to centre and Safari park. Entrance next to Zoo car park.

Horní Olesnice 16 · 300 · Dvur Králové nad Labem · 299 · 325 · 307 · 284 300 · 37 · 33 · Horice · 285 Josefov

CC €20 1/1-1/6 1/9-31/12 · N 50°26'02'' E 15°47'48''

## Horní Planá, CZ-38226 / Jihocesky kraj ♿ 🛈 1081

🏕 Autocamp Jenišov***
📮 Jenišov
☎ +420 3 80 73 81 56
🔓 25/4 - 5/10
@ hajny.pa@seznam.cz

2,5ha 246T 6-10A CEE

1. ABGIJKLMOPQ
2. ADGIKLNRWX
3. AMRWZ
4. (R+Y 1/5-5/10)
5. ABGIJLMNPU
6. EGK(N 1,5km)V

💬 Pretty, quiet and welcoming family campsite directly on Lipno Lake. Terraced, lightly sloping to lake. You can rent bicycles and go fishing. Come and enjoy the excellent restaurant. A visit to the historic town of Ceský Krumlov is recommended.

🚗 Campsite is on the Lipnolake between Horní Planá and Cerná v Posumaví. Campsite is signposted.

39 · Cerná V Posumaví · 162 · 163 · Frymburk

CC €18 25/4-29/6 25/8-29/9 7=6, 14=12 · N 48°45'04'' E 14°02'36''

## Opatov (Okr. Trebíc), CZ-67528 / Kraj Vysocina

&#9855; &#128246; **iD** `1082`

- ⛺ Camping Vídlák
- 🚏 Opatov 322
- ☎ +420 7 36 67 86 87
- 🕐 15/4 - 15/10
- @ info@campingvidlak.cz

2ha  50T(150-250m²)  10A  CEE

1 ABG**IJ**KLMO**PQ**
2 BCDKRWX
3 AHJRUZ
4 (Q 1/6-20/8)
5 **A**DGIJKLMNOPUWZ
6 AEGJ(N 2km)V

💬 Well-located, peaceful family campsite with 50 pitches on Lake Vidlák, under Dutch management, situated in the Telc-Jihlava-Trebic triangle. Spacious pitches, modern toilet facilities, club room with internet, tourist information and small library. Ideal for children, walking and making camp fires.

🚐 Take E59/38 from Jihlava dir. Znojmo. After approx. 20 km in Dlouhá Brtnice towards Opatov. Follow signs to the campsite.

**CC** € **18**  15/4-9/7  26/8-14/10  14=11

🧭 N 49°12'32'' E 15°39'22''

---

## Planá u Mariánských Lázní, CZ-34815 / Plzensky kraj

&#9855; &#128246; **iD** `1083`

- ⛺ Camp Karolina****
- 🚏 Brod nad Tichou
- ☎ +420 7 77 29 69 90
- 🕐 20/4 - 13/10
- @ office@camp-k.cz

3ha  60T(70-100m²)  10A

1 A**G**IJKLM**PQ**
2 BCFKLRTUXY
3 ABHJNRU
4 (B 1/7-31/8)
   (Q+T+U+V+Z 🚐)
5 **A**DGIJKLMNOPUWZ
6 AEGJ(N 6km)

💬 Campsite with idyllic location in wooded area, with modern heated toilet facilities. Perfect location for visits to Prague, Plzen, Karlovy Vary, Marianske Lazne and Cheb. Free wifi. Bistro on the campsite. Senior citizens and child friendly. 9.5 km from the motorway.

🚐 From Planá take road 21 towards Bor. Clearly marked with campsite signs. 10km from the Nürnberg-Praha (Prague) motorway. From Bor you will pass 1800 metres of pretty countryside to the campsite, water and forest.

**CC** € **16**  20/4-30/6  1/9-13/10

🧭 N 49°49'13'' E 12°45'12''

---

## Praag 6, CZ-16000 / Praha

&#128246; **iD** `1084`

- ⛺ Prague camping Dzban
- 🚏 Nad Lávkou 5
- ☎ +420 7 25 95 64 57
- 🕐 1/5 - 30/9
- @ info@campdzban.eu

2ha  100T(80-85m²)  10A

1 ABC**G**IJLMPQ
2 DFGRWX
3 BHJ**M**NZ
4 (Q+U+Y 🚐)
5 **A**GIJMNOPUW
6 EGJ(N 0,5km)T

💬 Situated on the edge of the Divoká Šárká nature reserve, a 10 minute walk from the subway station (15 minute ride to the city centre). Just perfect to discover the magic of Prague and Bohemia.

🚐 Route 7 from Slany to airport to centre Vokovice district. Campsite is signposted on Europsko road.

**CC** € **18**  1/5-2/7  20/8-29/9  7=6, 14=12

🧭 N 50°05'56'' E 14°20'11''

## Praag 8/Dolní Chabry, CZ-18400 / Praha

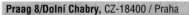

△ Camping Triocamp***
✉ Obsluzná 1148/35
☎ +420 2 83 85 07 93
⌖ 1/1 - 31/12
@ triocamp.praha@telecom.cz

1085

1ha 65T(80-100m²) 6-10A

1 ABC**G**IJKLM**PQ**
2 FGIRTX
3 MNR
4 (B 15/5-1/9) (Q+R ⌖)
   (T+X 1/4-31/10)
5 **A**GIJKLMNOPUW
6 EG**K**(N 1km)OR

💬 A basic campsite, a good place to stay for visiting Prague.

🚗 From centre D8/E55 direction Teplice, exit Zdiby, via 608 Dolní Chabry. Right 3 km further on.

Kralupy nad Vltavou
D8
CC
610
R10
R7    240
R6    7
12    R1
Praha

CC € 18  1/1-19/6  18/8-31/12     N 50°09'09'' E 14°27'01''

---

## Praag 9/Dolní Pocernice, CZ-19012 / Praha

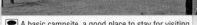

△ Camping Sokol Praha****
✉ Národních hrdinù 290
☎ +420 7 77 55 35 43
⌖ 29/3 - 31/10, 27/12 - 6/1
@ info@campingsokol.cz

1086

2,5ha 37T(80-100m²) 16A CEE

1 ABCD**G**IJKL**P**Q
2 FGRVWX
3 A**F**JKNQRU
4 (B 1/5-30/9)
   (G+Q+R+T+U+X+Y+Z ⌖)
5 **AB**DEFGIJKLMNOPQRUW
6 ACEG**I**K(N 3km)OQRTVW

💬 Very complete campsite, with swimming pool and excellent toilet facilities and renewed restaurant. Various possibilities to visit Prague and upon arrival you will immediately receive a comprehensive information folder about the campsite, bus, tram, metro and train where you can be taken with a van for free.

🚗 Campsite in the eastern part of Prague. E65/67 to Hradec Králové/Kolin exit Dolní Pocernice. Follow the signs from then on.

E55
Celákovice
8    610    R10    E67
608
611   D11
601   CC   12
Praha
101
E50
Ricany   2

CC € 18  29/3-30/6  24/8-31/10  7=6, 14=11     N 50°05'18'' E 14°35'00''

---

## Praag 9/Klánovice, CZ-19014 / Praha

△ Camping Praha Klánovice
✉ V Jehlicine 391
☎ +420 7 74 55 35 42
⌖ 20/4 - 14/9
@ info@campingpraha.cz

NEW

1087

2ha 61T(70-100m²) 16A CEE

1 ABCGIJKLM**PQ**
2 FGLMRVW
3 BC**F**HJKNQRU
4 (B+G 1/5-14/9)
   (Q+R+S+T+U+Y+Z ⌖)
5 **AB**DEFGIJKLMNOPRUWXY
   Z
6 CEGH**K**(N 1,5km)OTV

💬 This brand new campsite with large swimming pools is located in the beautiful surroundings of Prague. Just 1 minute from the lovely woods in the village of Klánovice. The campsite offers quality and service.

🚗 Prague ring road, exit Bechovice direction Kolin route 12 to Ujezd nad Lesy. Turn left at cross roads towards Klánovice, about 3 km and take the last street on the right towards Slechtitelska.

244
Stará Boleslav
610    611
D10    D11
E67    Sestajovice    272
E65    CC    12
Praha
101
333

CC € 20  21/4-29/6  31/8-14/9     N 50°05'55'' E 14°41'06''

## Roznov pod Radhostem, CZ-75661 / Zlinsky kraj ♿ 🛜 iD **1088**

🏕 Camping Roznov
🏤 Radhoštská 940
☎ +420 7 31 50 40 73
📅 1/5 - 31/10
@ info@camproznov.cz

4ha 150T(50-100m²) 16A

**1** ABCD**G**IJKLMOPQ
**2** GRVX
**3** ABHJKMNRU
**4** (**B** 1/6-30/9) (Q+R 1/7-31/8)
   (X 1/6-30/9) (Z 1/7-31/8)
**5** **AB**GIJKLMNOPUW
**6** EGK(N 2km)QRTV

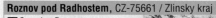

💬 A campsite located on the edge of the town of Roznov. Site has a beautiful swimming pool. Ideal area for hiking; near the Valasské open air museum.

🚗 Located close to Roznov on the E442 dir Zilina. The campsite is located on the left of the road.

CC € **16** 1/5-30/6 1/9-15/10    📡 N 49°28'00'' E 18°09'50''

---

## Strázov, CZ-34021 / Plzensky kraj 🛜 iD **1089**

🏕 Camping u Dvou Orechu
🏤 Splz 13 Stràzov
☎ +420 6 02 39 44 96
📅 27/4 - 29/9
@ info@camping-tsjechie.nl

2ha 30T(80-100m²) 10A CEE

**1** A**G**IJKLM**P**QU
**2** GIJKLRX
**3** AHJU
**4** (Q 🚿) (T 15/6-16/8)
   (X+Z 🚿)
**5** **A**IJLMNOPU
**6** EIK(N 3km)V

💬 A small, adults only site set in the hills of the Sumava. You can explore the countryside, hidden villages and rugged castles of the Bohemian Forest on foot, by bike or in your car using our free routes. A site with spacious pitches, clean toilets, free wifi, lively bar, personal attention and Dutch managers.

🚗 From Klatovy route 191 direction Nýrsko, then route 171 towards Strázov. In Strázov turn right and drive towards R. Depoltice/Divisovice on the left. After 2 km Splíz/Hajek.

CC € **18** 27/4-6/7 26/8-29/9    📡 N 49°16'53'' E 13°14'24''

---

## Týn nad Vltavou, CZ-37501 / Jihocesky kraj 👫 🛜 iD **1090**

🏕 Camping Prima
🏤 Kolodeje nad Luznici 6
☎ +420 7 25 02 50 75
📅 27/4 - 30/9
@ info@campingprima.cz

1,5ha 50T(90-130m²) 10A

**1** BCDFIJKLMOPQ
**2** CGKLMRTVWY
**3** AGHJKRU**W**X
**4** (Q 🚿) T(X+Z 🚿)
**5** **AB**FGIJMNOPQUWZ
**6** AEGKTV

💬 Campsite located on a small river where you can swim and canoe, with a jetty. Slightly sloping grounds. Castle within walking distance.

🚗 Route 105 from Ceské Budejovice to Milevsko. Past Tyn nad Vltavou signposted.

CC € **14** 27/4-6/7 24/8-30/9 7=6, 14=11    📡 N 49°15'15'' E 14°25'12''

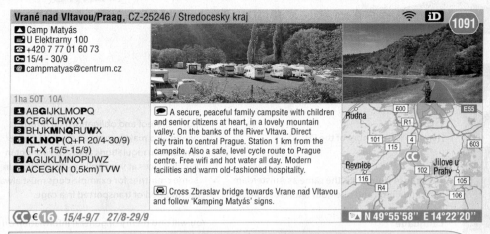

**Vrané nad Vltavou/Praag,** CZ-25246 / Stredocesky kraj

1091

- Camp Matyás
- U Elektrarny 100
- ☎ +420 7 77 01 60 73
- ⌚ 15/4 - 30/9
- @ campmatyas@centrum.cz

1ha 50T 10A

**1** ABGIJKLMOPQ
**2** CFGKLRWXY
**3** BHJKMNQRUWX
**4** KLNOP(Q+R 20/4-30/9)
   (T+X 15/5-15/9)
**5** AGIJKLMNOPUWZ
**6** ACEGK(N 0,5km)TVW

💬 A secure, peaceful family campsite with children and senior citizens at heart, in a lovely mountain valley. On the banks of the River Vltava. Direct city train to central Prague. Station 1 km from the campsite. Also a safe, level cycle route to Prague centre. Free wifi and hot water all day. Modern facilities and warm old-fashioned hospitality.

🚗 Cross Zbraslav bridge towards Vrane nad Vltavou and follow 'Kamping Matyás' signs.

CC € 16  15/4-9/7  27/8-29/9

📍 N 49°55'58'' E 14°22'20''

# Hungary

## General

Hungary is a member of the EU.

### Time

The time in Hungary is the same as Amsterdam, Paris and Rome and one hour ahead of London.

### Language

Hungarian, but many Hungarians also speak English or German.

## Border formalities

Many formalities and agreements about matters such as necessary travel documents, car papers, requirements relating to your means of transport and accommodation, medical expenses and taking pets with you do not only depend on the country you are travelling to but also on your departure point and nationality. The length of your stay can also play a role here. It is not possible within the confines of this guide to guarantee the correct and most up to date information with regard to these matters.

We advise you to consult the relevant authorities before your departure about:
- which travel documents you will need for yourself and your fellow passengers
- which documents you need for your car
- which regulations your caravan must meet
- which goods you may import and export
- how medical treatment will be arranged and paid for in your holiday destination in cases of accident or illness
- whether you can take pets. Contact your vets well in advance. They can give you information about the necessary vaccinations,

proof thereof and obligations on return. It would also make sense to enquire whether any special regulations apply to your pet in public places at your holiday destination. In some countries for example dogs must always be muzzled or transported in a cage.

You will find plenty of general information on ► *www.europa.eu* ◄ but make certain you select information that is relevant to your specific situation.

For the most recent customs regulations you should get in contact with the authorities of your holiday destination in your country of residence.

## Currency

The currency in Hungary is the forint (HUF). The approximate rate September 2018 is: £ 1 = 362.66 HUF. You can pay with euros in many places. You cannot pay by debit card in most shops. Money can be exchanged at border offices and banks.

### Credit cards

You can pay by credit card in most restaurants, filling stations, car rental companies and large supermarkets.

## Opening times

### Banks

Banks are open Monday to Thursday until 16:00.

### Shops

Shops are open on weekdays until 18:00 and on Saturdays until 13:00.

### Chemists

Chemists in Hungary are open between
08:00 and 18:00.

## Communication

### (Mobile) phones

The mobile network works well throughout
Hungary. There is a 4G network for mobile
internet.

### Wifi, internet

You can make use of a wifi network at more and
more public locations, often for free.

### Post

Generally open on weekdays until 18:00 and on
Saturday until 14:00.

## Roads and traffic

### Road network

If you need urgent assistance call the Hungarian
breakdown service (MAK), tel. 188.

### Traffic regulations

Remember, all traffic in Hungary drives on the
right and overtakes on the left! Headlight

*Maximum speed*

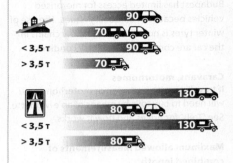

deflectors are advisable to prevent annoying
oncoming drivers. Hungary uses the metric
system, so distances are measured in kilometres
(km) and speeds in kilometres per hour (km/h).
Traffic coming from the right has priority, except
on main roads. Buses and trams always have
priority. There is a total ban on alcohol when
driving. Take note: if a green traffic light starts to
flash, you must prepare to stop. Dipped
headlights are compulsory during the day
outside built-up areas. You must use phones
hands-free. You must inform the police of any

traffic accident. Attention: the centre of Budapest has limited access for motorised vehicles because of air quality issues. The use of winter tyres is not mandatory. Snow chains in the car are compulsory in wintry conditions.

### Caravans, motorhomes
If travelling with a caravan or motorhome you will need to pay tolls by means of an e-vignette. See 'Tolls' for prices and how it works.

### Maximum allowed measurements of combined length
Height 4 metres, width 2.55 metres and length 18.75 metres (of which the trailer maximum 12 metres).

### Tolls
In Hungary tolls are levied by means of a so-called e-vignette. When you buy an e-vignette the vehicle's licence number is registered, and checks are made using the licence number. It is therefore essential to purchase a toll vignette before joining a toll road! All motorways in Hungary are toll roads.
For more information about the e-vignette and prices, see ▶ *www.motorway.hu* ◀

You will need to keep the e-vignette for 12 months after it expires in case of any incorrect fines. The e-vignette is available at the borders and at most Hungarian service stations.

### Fuel
Petrol and diesel are freely available. Lead free petrol is shown as 'Bleifrei' or 'Ólommentes'. LPG is easily available.

### Filling stations
Filling stations are generally open between 06:00 and 20:00. You can usually pay by credit card.

### Emergency number
112: national emergency number for fire, police and ambulance.

# Camping
The biggest concentration of campsites is around Lake Balaton. Toilet facilities in Hungary are of a reasonable standard. The advantage is that Hungarian campsites are among the cheapest in Europe.

### Practical
- Gas is available but you should make sure you have the right connectors.
- Make sure you have a world adaptor for electrical appliances.
- Tap water is safe, but if you don't trust it drink (bottled) mineral water.

## Badacsonytomaj, H-8258 / Veszprém

👫 🛉 🛜 **iD** **1092**

🏕 Tomaj Camping\*\*\*
✉ Balaton u. 28
☎ +36 87 47 13 21
🗓 1/5 - 30/9
@ tomajcamping@t-online.hu

3,5ha 174T(80-100m²) 10A

1 ACD**E**IJKLMOP**R**S
2 DGMRVWXY
3 AJRZ
4 (T 🔌)
5 **A**GIJKLMNOPUW
6 EGK(N 0,7km)T

💬 Friendly Hungarian campsite for those people who love some peace and quiet. Swimming and pedalo-boating possible from the campsite. Site is close to cycle route around Lake Balaton. Small meals available.

🚗 Turn off the 71 between km-marker 77 and 76.

Tapolca
7301
84
CC Balatonboglár
71
Fonyód
7 E71
M7

© € **14** 2/5-1/7 2/9-29/9

🧭 N 46°48'16'' E 17°31'09''

---

## Balatonberény, H-8649 / Somogy

🤸 🛜 **iD** **1093**

🏕 Balatontourist Camping
Naturist Berény
✉ Hetvezer u.2
☎ +36 85 37 72 99
🗓 10/5 - 15/9
@ bereny@balatontourist.hu

6ha 119T(80-110m²) 10A

1 ABC**G**HIJKLPRS
2 DFGLMRVWXY
3 AJRU**W**Z
4 (Q+R 1/7-15/8) (T+U+W 🔌)
5 AGIJKLNPUWZ
6 CEGIK(N 0,3km)TV

NEW

💬 Lovely, spacious naturist campsite just outside the village and beautifully situated on the lake in a very quiet nature reserve. The huge sunbathing lawn and the artificial island are remarkable. Restaurant, bar and a small shop.

🚗 Coming from Keszthely drive via route 71 and 76 and turn left after 7 km and then follow the signs.

Badacsony
Keszthely 71
75 71345
76
CC
E71
M7 E661
68
7

© € **14** 10/5-27/6 20/8-14/9

🧭 N 46°42'48'' E 17°18'39''

---

## Balatonfüred, H-8230 / Veszprém

🛉 ♿ 🛜 **iD** **1094**

🏕 Balatontourist Camping &
Bungalows Füred\*\*\*
✉ Széchenyi u.24
☎ +36 87 58 02 41
🗓 26/4 - 29/9
@ fured@balatontourist.hu

21ha 648T(60-120m²) 6-16A CEE

1 ACD**E**IJKLMOP**R**S
2 ADGKLMRVWXY
3 AB**F**JKN**Q**RUZ
4 (B+G 11/6-28/8) J**N**(Q 🔌)
   (S 14/5-18/9)
   (T+U+V+X+Y+Z 🔌)
5 **AB**EFGIJKLNPUW
6 CFG**IJK**(N 0,1km)QRTV

💬 Large campsite on the edge of Balatonfüred town centre with shaded pitches. Beautiful heated pool and a lovely beach on the lake. For a fee you can make use of the cable skiing. Recreation for the whole family. The Balaton cycle path runs right by the campsite.

🚗 Route 71 (north side of Lake Balaton), exit between km-marker 40 and 41. Directly alongside the lake. Signposted.

Balatonalmádi
7301 73
Balatonfüred
CC Siófok
7117
71
7 E71
M7

© € **12** 26/4-27/6 20/8-28/9

🧭 N 46°56'45'' E 17°52'36''

## Budapest, H-1106 / Pest

🛖 Arena Camping &
   Guesthouse Budapest
📧 Pilisi utca 7
☎ +36 3 02 96 91 29
🗓 1/1 - 31/12
@ info@budapestcamping.hu

3ha 200T(80-120m²) 16A

**1** AGIJKLMOPQ
**2** CFGRTWXY
**3** AR
**4** (Y 🚿)
**5** ADGIJKLMNOPUWX
**6** CEGIK(N 0,5km)TV

🛈 Located in Budapest centre. Well maintained, natural, hospitable. Camping in the city on grass between the trees (plenty of shade). Free wifi. Renovated facilities. Customer-friendly staff. Comprehensive information pack about Budapest. Walking distance from shops, bank and university cafeteria. Possible inconvenience from railway line.

🚗 M1/M7 to centre, Elisabeth Bridge (white bridge) over Danube, then straight for 8 km. Right 500m past camping sign, right after 100m.

CC € 18   15/1-14/4   29/4-20/5   16/6-28/6   28/8-31/10       📍 N 47°30'15'' E 19°09'30''

---

## Budapest, H-1096 / Pest

🛖 Haller Camping**
📧 Haller utca 27
☎ +36 3 02 31 09 23
🗓 1/1 - 31/12
@ info@hallercamping.com

1,5ha 89T 16A

**1** AGIJKLMOPQ
**2** FGRSX
**3** A
**4** (Q+U+V+Y+Z 🚿)
**5** ABGIJKLMNOPUW
**6** CEGK(N 0,5km)T

🛈 In the city centre, ideally located for visiting Budapest. Friendly staff. Free use of hot showers, wifi and information pack. Clean showers. Small restaurant. Safe and patrolled. Metro 700m. Tram, supermarkets and shopping centre all close by.

🚗 From the south via M5 dir. centre. At first ring road direction Lagymanyosi hid (bridge). Turn right before the bridge next to the large (Lurdy-Ház) shopping centre. Campsite signposted.

CC € 18   1/1-30/6   1/9-31/12   7=6       📍 N 47°28'33'' E 19°04'59''

---

## Budapest, H-1121 / Pest

🛖 Zugligeti 'Niche' Camping***
📧 Zugligeti ut 101
☎ +36 12 00 83 46
🗓 1/1 - 31/12
@ info@campingniche.hu

2ha 90T(20-45m²) 4-10A CEE

**1** ACDGIJKLMOPQ
**2** BGHIJRTVY
**3** U
**4** (R 1/7-31/8) (T+X+Y+Z 🚿)
**5** ADGIJKLMNOPUW
**6** CEGIJ(N 0,5km)OQRV

🛈 Idyllically situated three star campsite, good toilet facilities. Bus to the centre every 20 minutes. An ideal base for visiting the city. CampingCard ACSI holders can buy an excellent breakfast for only 3 Euros each.

🚗 From Austria via the M1 or M7 from Balaton, exit 14 Budakeszi. From the M0, follow this road to the end then Route 1 direction Budakeszi. From Budakeszi follow camping signs. From the city; to Moszkva Ter then follow the camping signs.

CC € 18   1/1-15/4   25/4-15/7   1/9-25/12       📍 N 47°30'58'' E 18°58'27''

## Bükfürdö, H-9740 / Vas ♿ 🛜 iD (1098)

▲ Romantik Camping***
🏠 Thermal krt. 12
☎ +36 94 35 83 62
📅 1/1 - 31/12
@ info@romantikcamping.com

4ha 400T 10-12A

1 ACD**G**IJKLMO**P**Q
2 GLRXY
3 AB**FKM**
4 (B 1/5-1/10) (U+Y 🔑)
5 ADGJLMNOPUW
6 EGJ(N 3km)OQRV

💬 The campsite is open all year and offers large shaded or unshaded pitches which you can choose yourself. The site has its own swimming pool, restaurant, disabled toilet and free wifi. The thermal baths at Bük are just 400 metres from the campsite. Reservation not necessary.

🚗 Route 87 or 84 direction Bük. In Bük follow signs direction Bükfürdö, follow signs 'Romantik Panzio és camping' to campsite.

CC €16 1/1-30/6 18/8-31/12 7=6        📷 N 47°23'02'' E 16°47'26''

---

## Cserszegtomaj, H-8372 / Zala 🛜 iD (1099)

▲ Camping Panoráma***
🏠 Barát Utca 43
☎ +36 83 33 02 15
📅 1/4 - 31/10
@ matuska78@freemail.hu

1,4ha 50T(80-120m²) 10A

1 ABG**IJ**KLMPRS
2 JKLRVWXY
3 AR
4 (B+Q 🔑)
5 ADGJLMNOPUWZ
6 CEGK(N 3,5km)OT

💬 Close to the city but far away from the stress. From the campsite, comprising six terraces and level grounds you have wonderful views of the Hévíz thermal resort. The transfer service will take you to the thermal baths or to Lake Balaton. There is a swimming pool and plenty of space for games and sport. Local wine is on sale at the reception.

🚗 The campsite is located on the road from Keszthely to Hévíz.

CC €14 1/4-15/7 1/9-31/10        📷 N 46°48'29'' E 17°12'44''

---

## Galambok, H-8754 / Zala ♿ 🛜 iD (1100)

▲ Camping Castrum Zalakaros****
🏠 Ady E. út 113
☎ +36 93 35 86 10
📅 30/5 - 30/9
@ zalakaros@castrum.eu

NEW

2,5ha 144T(40-100m²) 6-10A

1 ACD**G**IJKLMOPRS
2 FGLRVWXY
3 JUV
4 (F 🔑) I**N**O(U+X 🔑)
5 **A**DGIJKLMNOPUWXYZ
6 ACEGK(N 1km)TV

💬 The campsite is located in the village of Galambok, only 2 km away from the beautiful thermal resort Zalakaros. The campsite has an indoor thermal bath. Entrance of 2,- euro per person is included in the overnight rate.

🚗 In Zalakaros drive towards Galambok. campsite is signposted after approx. 2 km.

CC €20 30/5-7/7 25/8-30/9        📷 N 46°31'54'' E 17°07'27''

## Gyenesdiás, H-8315 / Zala ♿ 🛜 iD 1101

▲ Wellness Park Camping
✉ Napfény utca 6
☎ +36 3 05 48 72 03
🗓 1/3 - 31/10
@ info@wellness-park.hu

2ha 80T(80-100m²) 16A

**1** ACGIJKLMPQ
**2** GRVWX
**3** BFGJKMR
**4** (B 15/5-15/9) KN
    (Q+U+Y+Z 15/5-31/8)
**5** AGIJMNOPUW
**6** CEGJ(N 1km)R

💬 A small, peaceful campsite situated between Lake Balaton and a hilly region. 1 km from the beach. The campsite has modern toilet facilities and an excellent restaurant.

🚐 Turn off towards the lake between 100 and 99 marker signs on road 71.

(CC) € **14** 1/3-6/7 27/8-31/10    🧭 N 46°45'51'' E 17°18'09''

---

## Keszthely, H-8360 / Zala ♿ 🛜 iD 1102

▲ Camping Castrum****
✉ Mora F.U.48
☎ +36 83 31 21 20
🗓 1/5 - 31/10
@ info@castrum.eu

2,2ha 126T(40-100m²) 6A

**1** ABCGIJKLPRS
**2** GLRUVWXY
**3** ABJRU
**4** (B 1/6-30/9) (G 1/7-30/9)
    (U+Y 1/6-31/8)
**5** AGIJKLNPUWXY
**6** EGK(N 0,5km)TV

💬 Campsite with lovely location on the edge of Keszthely. Renovated pool, clean toilet facilities, good restaurant, free wifi.

🚐 Indicated on route 71 between km-marker 103 and 104.

(CC) € **14** 1/5-4/7 22/8-30/10    🧭 N 46°46'05'' E 17°15'34''

---

## Mátrafüred/Sástó, H-3232 / Heves ♿ 🛜 iD 1103

▲ Mátra Kemping Sástó****
✉ Farkas utca 4
☎ +36 37 37 40 25
🗓 1/1 - 31/12
@ info@matrakemping.hu

NEW

2,7ha 27T(70-140m²) 16A CEE

**1** ABCDGIJKLMOPQ
**2** BDGRTUVWXY
**3** ABHJNRU
**4** (A+F+H 🗓) **KLNP**
    (T+U+W+X 🗓) (Y 1/6-31/8)
    (Z 🗓)
**5** ABFGIJKLMNOPUWXYZ
**6** CDEGHK(N 9,8km)RSTV

💬 Beautifully renovated, quiet, ecological site on reed lake (Sástó) in a wooded walking and cycling area. Spacious marked-out pitches, some with shade. Modern toilet facilities and magnificent wellness centre. Guests also receive discount on entrance price to the adventure park for all ages which is within 10 minutes walking distance or by cable car.

🚐 Coming from Gyöngyös follow route 24, 2 km beyond Mátrafüred cross over large car park on the left to campsite.

(CC) € **16** 1/5-9/6 1/9-30/9    🧭 N 47°50'39'' E 19°57'26''

## Nagyatád, H-7500 / Somogy ♿ 🛜 **iD** (1104)

🔺 Thermalcamping Castrum****
✉ Zrínyi ut 75
☎ +36 82 45 21 36
🗓 1/5 - 30/9
@ nagyatad@castrum.eu

2,8ha 150T(40-100m²) 10A

**1** ACGIJKLMOPQ
**2** GLRVWXY
**3** ABJKMNORUV
**4** (C 15/5-30/9)
　(F 1/5-15/5,1/10-15/10)
　(H 🔌) IJKNO
　(Q+R+T+U+X 🔌)
**5** ABGIJKLMNOPUWXYZ
**6** EGHJ(N 1km)T

💬 Beautiful campsite with very good toilet facilities. Discount on (continuous) access to adjacent spacious leisure pool with large sunbathing lawns. Quiet atmosphere. Thermal bath next to the campsite.

🚗 Follow route 68 as far as the town centre, follow Castrum camping signs.

CC € **14** 1/5-2/6 1/9-30/9 　　 📷 N 46°14'21'' E 17°21'50''

---

## Révfülöp, H-8253 / Veszprém ♿ 🛜 **iD** (1105)

🔺 Balatontourist Camping Napfény***
✉ Halász Útca 5
☎ +36 87 56 30 31
🗓 26/4 - 29/9
@ napfeny@balatontourist.hu

7,2ha 350T(60-110m²) 10A

**1** ACGHIJKLMOPRS
**2** DGMRVWXY
**3** ABJKNQRUWZ
**4** (G 1/6-27/9) (Q+R 🔌)
　(T 1/6-31/8) (U+V+X+Y 🔌)
**5** ABEFGHIJKLMNOPSTUW
**6** CEGIJK(N 0,6km)RTV

💬 Beautiful campsite with everything you need. Long beach. Motorboats are prohibited on Lake Balaton.

🚗 On route 71 (northside of Lake Balaton). Between km-marker 65 and 66, directly alongside the lake. Campsite is signposted.

CC € **14** 26/4-27/6 20/8-28/9 　　 📷 N 46°49'46'' E 17°38'24''

---

## Siófok/Sóstó, H-8604 / Somogy 👫 🛜 **iD** (1106)

🔺 Siocamping Kft.
✉ Pusztatorony Tér
☎ +36 7 05 97 53 13
🗓 15/4 - 30/9
@ siocampingkft@gmail.com

8,2ha 560T(50-100m²) 16A

**1** ACDGIJKLMPRS
**2** DFGRVWXY
**3** JQRUWZ
**4** (Q+S+T+Y 🔌)
**5** ABGIJKLMNOPUW
**6** ACEGIJ(N 0,1km)QRTV

💬 Quiet campsite with shady pitches, situated directly on a 7-hectare fishpond. Several restaurants right next to the campsite.

🚗 From road M7 on south side of Lake Balaton the campsite is indicated between mile marker 105 and 106.

CC € **12** 1/5-3/7 21/8-29/9 7=6, 14=11 　　 📷 N 46°56'19'' E 18°07'49''

# Slovenia

## General
Slovenia is a member of the EU.

### Time
The time in Slovenia is the same as Amsterdam, Paris and Rome and one hour ahead of London.

### Language
Slovenian, but English is also spoken in many places.

## Border formalities
Many formalities and agreements about matters such as necessary travel documents, car papers, requirements relating to your means of transport and accommodation, medical expenses and taking pets with you do not only depend on the country you are travelling to but also on your departure point and nationality. The length of your stay can also play a role here. It is not possible within the confines of this guide to guarantee the correct and most up to date information with regard to these matters.

We advise you to consult the relevant authorities before your departure about:
- which travel documents you will need for yourself and your fellow passengers
- which documents you need for your car
- which regulations your caravan must meet
- which goods you may import and export
- how medical treatment will be arranged and paid for in your holiday destination in cases of accident or illness
- whether you can take pets. Contact your vets well in advance. They can give you information about the necessary vaccinations, proof thereof and obligations on return.
It would also make sense to enquire whether any special regulations apply to your pet in public places at your holiday destination. In some countries for example dogs must always be muzzled or transported in a cage.

You will find plenty of general information on ▸ *www.europa.eu* ◂ but make certain you select information that is relevant to your specific situation.

For the most recent customs regulations you should get in contact with the authorities of your holiday destination in your country of residence.

## Currency
The currency in Slovenia is the euro. Approximate exchange rates September 2018: £1 = € 1.12.

### Credit cards
Credit cards are accepted at nearly all hotels, restaurants, shops and filling stations.

## Opening times
### Banks
Banks are open weekdays until 17:00 with a lunch break from 12:00 to 14:00.

### Shops
Mostly open until 19:00. Saturdays until 13:00.

### Chemists

Chemists in Slovenia are open from 07:00 to 19:00, on Saturdays from 07:00 to 13:00.

## Communication

### (Mobile) phones

The mobile network works well throughout Slovenia, except in remote areas. There is a 4G network for mobile internet.

### Wifi, internet

You can make use of a wifi network at more and more public locations, often for free.

### Post

Open weekdays until 18:00 and on Saturdays until 12:00.

## Roads and traffic

### Road network

Primary and secondary roads are of reasonably good quality. You are advised not to drive on roads other than motorways after dark. You can contact the Slovenian breakdown service AMZS on 1987.

### Traffic regulations

Remember, all traffic in Slovenia drives on the right and overtakes on the left! Headlight deflectors are advisable to prevent annoying oncoming drivers. Slovenia uses the metric system, so distances are measured in kilometres (km) and speeds in kilometres per hour (km/h). Traffic from the right has priority. You have priority on roundabouts over vehicles entering the roundabout. Army vehicles and military convoys always have priority.

*Maximum speed*

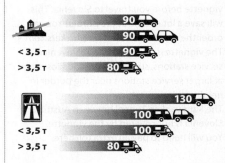

Maximum permitted alcohol level is 0.5‰. Dipped headlights must be used during the day. Phones can only be used hands-free. When overtaking another vehicle you must keep your indicator lights on until you have passed the vehicle. When reversing you must use your hazard lights. In wintry conditions you must drive with winter tyres or snow chains.

**Caravans, motorhomes**
If you are towing a caravan you must carry two emergency triangles, one for the car and one for the caravan. It is also advisable to take with you registration documents or receipts for expensive equipment in your caravan or motorhome. Vehicles less than 3.5 tonnes must have a toll vignette. See ´Tolls´ for an explanation. For vehicles above 3,5 tonnes different rules apply. More information on ▸ *www.darsgo.si* ◂

**Maximum allowed measurements of combined length**
Height 4 metres, width 2.55 metres and maximum length 18.75 metres (of which the trailer maximum 12 metres).

**Tolls**
A toll vignette (sticker) is required on motorways for all vehicles under 3.5 tonnes. Order your vignette before you travel to Slovenia. This will save a lot of time at the border! You can order the vignette on ▸*www.tolltickets.com* ◂ The vignette is also available at Slovenian service stations, supermarkets and kiosks and at larger service stations near the border in neighbouring countries.
The Karawanken Tunnel between Austria and Slovenia is not covered by the vignette. You will need to pay an extra toll here.

**Fuel**
Lead free petrol and diesel are available everywhere. LPG is available reasonably well.

**Filling stations**
Filling stations on motorways are open

24 hours, elsewhere between 07:00 and 20:00. You can usually pay by credit card.

**Emergency numbers**
- 112: fire and ambulance
- 113: police

# Camping
A number of Slovenian campsites specialise in wellness and spas. These campsites are above average standard. The lovely situated campsites in the Julian Alps bordering on Austria and Italy are more basic, and gear themselves to sportive camping guests such as hikers, mountain bikers and climbers. Many campsites have playgrounds and entertainment for young children.

Slovenian campsites are classified by 1 to 5 stars. The higher the star rating, the better the amenities. Free camping is not permitted. For camping outside official campsites you must have permission from the local authorities or the police.

**Practical**
- Make sure you have a world adaptor for electrical appliances.
- Tap water is drinkable but it can be a bit hard.

## Ankaran, SLO-6280

▲ Camping Adria★★★★
☎ +386 56 63 73 50
🗓 7/4 - 15/10
@ camp@adria-ankaran.si

♿ 🛜 iD **1107**

7ha 308T(60-90m²) 10A

1 ABCD**G**IJKLMOPST
2 EGLMNRVXY
3 AGK**LMNOPQR**TU**VW**Y
4 (B 1/6-30/9) (**F** ⌂) (**G** 1/6-30/9) **KLMNP** (Q 1/5-14/10) (R+V 1/5-30/9) (W+X 20/6-15/9) (Y+Z ⌂)
5 **AB**EFGIJKLMNOP**S**UVW
6 ACFGHIJ**K**(N 0km)QRTUV

💬 Campsite by the sea in a Mediterranean setting. Open in winter for motorhomes that wish to use the wellness centre. Ideal for nature lovers, also a base for visiting attractions in Slovenia. Supermarket, various bars, small restaurants and a free wifi point. Registration: 0.80 Euro p.p. Warm water and pool: 1 Euro p.p. per stay.

🚗 On the motorway coming from Italy or Ljubljana take the Ankaran exit. Then to Ankaran. Campsite 5 km on the left.

**Trieste**

CC

**Koper**

CC € 20 7/4-1/7 1/9-15/10

🗺 N 45°34'40'' E 13°44'09''

---

## Banovci/Verzej, SLO-9241

▲ Camping Terme Banovci★★★
📧 Banovci 1a
☎ +386 25 13 14 40
🗓 29/3 - 3/11
@ terme@terme-banovci.si

🚫 🛜 iD **1108**

0,3ha 240T(80-100m²) 16A

1 ABCD**G**IJKLOPQ
2 FLRWXY
3 AJK
4 (C+F ⌂) (H 25/4-30/9) JK**LN** O(Q+T+V ⌂) (W 15/6-15/9) (Y+Z ⌂)
5 **AB**GIJKLMNOPUWZ
6 EGHIJ(N 1km)TV

💬 A level campsite with pitches around various thermal baths. The naturist section is around a small thermal pool with shaded pitches. Swimming pool not included in the CampingCard ACSI rate: 5 euro per person/day. Interesting trips to the famous wine region around Jeruzalem.

🚗 From Graz (Austria) A9/A1 dir. Maribor. Before Maribor A5 dir. Lendava to Vucjavas exit. Turn right dir. Ljutomer to Krizevci. Left dir. Verzej. Right to Banovci after a few km. Follow signs.

**Murska Sobota**

CC

**Ljutomer**

CC € 20 12/5-6/7 1/9-14/9

🗺 N 46°34'22'' E 16°10'20''

---

## Bled, SLO-4260

▲ Camping Bled★★★★★
📧 Kidriceva 10c
☎ +386 45 75 20 00
🗓 1/4 - 15/10
@ info@camping-bled.com

🚹 ♿ 🛜 iD **1109**

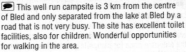

12ha 260T(80-130m²) 16A CEE

1 ABCD**G**IJKLMOPQ
2 DFGJLMNRSVWXY
3 BF**H**IJLNRU**W**Z
4 (A 1/7-31/8) **N** (Q+S+T+U+Y+Z ⌂)
5 **AB**DEFGIJKLMNOPQ**ST**UVW
6 ACFGK(N 3km)RTUVX

💬 This well run campsite is 3 km from the centre of Bled and only separated from the lake at Bled by a road that is not very busy. The site has excellent toilet facilities, also for children. Wonderful opportunities for walking in the area.

🚗 From A2/E61 take exit 3, then drive via Bled along the lake towards Bohinjska Bistrica. Turn right after 1.5 km. You will reach the campsite after about 1 km. Route is clearly signposted.

B91

**Jesenice**

CC **Radovljica**

CC € 20 1/4-15/6 10/9-15/10

🗺 N 46°21'41'' E 14°04'51''

## Bohinjska Bistrica, SLO-4264

�� 📶 **iD** (1110)

🏕 Camp Danica Bohinj★★★★
🏠 Triglavska cesta 60
☎ +386 45 72 17 02
📅 1/1 - 31/12
@ info@camp-danica.si

4,5ha 460T(80-100m²) 12-16A

**1** ABCD**G**IJKLMOPQ
**2** CGRVWXY
**3** AGH**J**L**M**NR**WX**
**4** (**A** 1/5-15/10) (Q 1/6-30/9) (T+Y+Z 🅿)
**5** **AB**EFGIJKLMNOPUW
**6** EGIKL(N 0,1km)TWX

💬 Quiet in low season, between small town and river. Good amenities. Starting point for mountain walks, with cable car to the Alm heights and marked out walks to various mountain cabins in Triglav National Park. Indoor leisure pool/wellness 200 metres away. Payment by credit card not possible with CampingCard ACSI. The Indian summer is beautiful in the autumn-coloured mountains.

🚐 Beyond Bled take dir. Bohinj. 100m past village Bohinjska Bistrica, site is to right of road.

Goreljek

Bohinj  Nemski Rovt

**CC** € **20**  1/1-7/7  25/8-31/12

📍 N 46°16'27'' E 13°56'52''

---

## Bovec, SLO-5230

🔆 📶 **iD** (1111)

🏕 Camping Polovnik★★★
🏠 Ledina 8
☎ +386 53 89 60 07
📅 30/3 - 15/10
@ kamp.polovnik@siol.net

1,2ha 100T(80m²) 16A

**1** ABCD**G**IJKLMO**P**Q
**2** GRSWXY
**3** AHJ**W**
**4** (**A** 1/7-31/8) (T+U+Y 🅿)
**5** **AB**FGIJKLMNO**P**UW
**6** EGK(N 0,2km)

💬 A campsite located on the edge of the Triglav National Park, walking distance to Bovec. Good starting point for excursions into this grandiose natural area. Level campsite, well shaded and with good toilet facilities. Rafting and kayaking. Good restaurant at campsite and in Bovec.

🚐 Northern side of Bovec, follow camping signs. Passo de Predil (between Tarvisio and Bovec) is not recommended for large caravans, please travel via Udine, Cividale (Italy), Kobarid, Bovec.

Soca

Breginj  Kobarid

**CC** € **18**  30/3-1/7  1/9-15/10

📍 N 46°20'10'' E 13°33'30''

---

## Gozd Martuljek, SLO-4282

🔆 📶 **iD** (1112)

🏕 Camping Spik★★★
🏠 Jezerci 15
☎ +386 51 63 44 66
📅 1/1 - 31/12
@ info@camp-spik.si

3ha 200T(80m²) 10A CEE

**1** ACD**G**IJKLOPQ
**2** BKRVWXY
**3** A**F**HJN
**4** (**A** 1/7-31/8) (**F+H** 🅿) **N** (Q+Y 🅿) (Z 15/5-15/9)
**5** **A**EFGIJKLMNOPUW
**6** EGK(N 5km)V

💬 Quiet campsite with shaded and sunny pitches. Lovely view of the mountains. Level grounds. Good toilet facilities. Lovely indoor swimming pool and wellness in Hotel Spik next door with discounts on the entrance price for campsite guests. Restaurant in hotel. Walking and mountain sports.

🚐 Campsite located on E652/1 Podkoren-Jesenice east of Gozd Martuljek village. Arched bridge directly to the north.

A2  B85  A11
B109

Kranjska Gora

**CC** € **20**  1/1-5/7  22/8-31/12

📍 N 46°29'05'' E 13°50'18''

## Kobarid, SLO-5222

🏕 Camping Chalets Koren****
📧 Ladra 1B
☎ +386 53 89 13 11
🔓 1/1 - 31/12
@ info@kamp-koren.si

♿ 🛜 ⚙ **iD** (1113)

2ha 100T(50-140m²) 16A

**1** ABCD**G**IJKLMOPQ
**2** CGJKRTWXY
**3** ABDGHIJKLR**VW**
**4** (**A** 🔓) **N**(Q+R+T+V+Z 🔓)
**5** **AB**CDFGHIJKLMNOPUVWZ
**6** AEI**J**L(N 0,5km)**P**QTV

💬 Kamp Koren is located by the fast flowing Soca river, 200 metres from the picturesque historic town of Kobarid with a WW1 museum and the Napoleon Bridge. There are plenty of tourist opportunities and marked out footpaths with waterfalls. Culture and sports opportunities. Bike hire.

🚗 Road Bovec-Tolmin. Take exit 'Ind. Cora' at Kobarid. Continue between the factory and the supermarket then over the bridge and turn left (40 metres). From Italy: Follow signs Dreznica in Kobarid.

CC € 20 1/1-1/7 1/9-31/12

📍 N 46°15'02'' E 13°35'12''

---

## Lendava, SLO-9220

🏕 Camping Terme Lendava***
📧 Tomsiceva 2a
☎ +386 25 77 44 00
🔓 1/1 - 31/12
@ info@terme-lendava.si

🛜 **iD** (1114)

4ha 90T(60-90m²) 16A CEE

**1** ABCD**G**IJKLMOPST
**2** FGLRVWXY
**3** AJKV
**4** (C 1/5-30/9) (F 🔓)
 (H 1/5-30/9) JK**LNOP**
 (T 20/6-31/8) (Y 🔓)
 (Z 20/6-31/8)
**5** **AB**DGIJKLMNOPUWZ
**6** EGHIKM(N 0,5km)T

💬 A campsite close to the thermal baths. Attractive pitches with gravel base for caravans. Good toilet facilities. Historical sites, vineyards, sports including cycle routes in the area. Entry to the thermal baths included. FKK possible till 23-05 and from 05-09.

🚗 From Graz (Austria) A9/A1 dir. Maribor. Before Maribor A5 dir. Lendava to exit Lendava. Left at roundabout dir. Lendava, 2nd roundabout dir. Terme Lendava. Turn right before hotel, campsite 100m on the left.

CC € 20 7/1-18/4 13/5-15/7 1/9-18/10 1/11-27/12

📍 N 46°33'07'' E 16°27'30''

---

## Ljubljana, SLO-1000

🏕 Ljubljana Resort (hotel & camping)****
📧 Dunajska cesta 270, Jezica
☎ +386 15 89 01 30
🔓 1/1 - 31/12
@ resort@gpl.si

♿ 🛜 **iD** (1115)

3ha 177T(60-90m²) 16A

**1** ABCD**G**IJKLMRT
**2** FGLRVX
**3** BF**K**M**N**RU**VW**
**4** (**C**+**H** 17/6-31/8) **KP**
 (Q 1/6-15/9) (T 1/6-1/9)
 (U 🔓) (Y 1/4-30/9) (Z 🔓)
**5** **AB**DEFGIJKLMNOPUW
**6** CGHIJ**K**M(N 0,7km)RTVW

💬 Ideal for visiting Ljubljana. Direct bus service to the centre. Swimming in the lovely pool of the resort at reduced rates from 17/6. With CampingCard ACSI, cash payments only.

🚗 From the Karawankentunnel: A2 exit 13, Lj-Brod and follow signs. From Maribor: A1 near Ljubljana take H3 exit to Lj-Bezigrad and follow signs. Some signs still show the old name 'Jezica'.

CC € 20 1/4-30/6 1/9-15/10 7=6, 14=11

📍 N 46°05'52'' E 14°31'08''

## Maribor, SLO-2000

⛷ 📶 iD **1116**

🏕 Camping Center Kekec***
✉ Pohorska ulica 35c
☎ +386 40 66 57 32
🔓 1/1 - 31/12
@ info@cck.si

3ha 105T(85m²) 16A

**1** AB**G**IJKLMOPQ
**2** FGKLRUVWX
**3** B**F**H
**5** **AB**DGIJMNOPUWXZ
**6** DEGIJ(N 0,3km)

💬 Small campsite, not far from ski resort. On grassy field with landscaping. Hardened pitches for motorhomes, with wifi. Views of ski slopes and hills. Perfect for visiting Maribor.

🚗 From N on E57/A1 exit dir. Maribor to H2/road 430. Beyond Maribor centre, right at lake then traffic lights. Right dir. Pohorje ski region. From S on E57/A1 or E59 exit dir. Maribor on 430, past Bauhaus (right) to traffic lights. Left to Pohorje ski region. Signposted.

**Pesnica**
**Maribor**
CC

CC € **18** 1/1-30/6 3/9-31/12 📍 N 46°32'10'' E 15°36'12''

---

## Moravske Toplice, SLO-9226

♿ 📶 iD **1117**

🏕 Camping Terme 3000
   Moravske Toplice Spa****
✉ Kranjceva 12
☎ +386 25 12 12 00
🔓 1/1 - 31/12
@ recepcija.camp2@terme3000.si

7ha 230T(80-100m²) 16A CEE

**1** ABCD**G**IJKLMOPST
**2** FLRUVWXY
**3** ABE**J**K**M**NV
**4** (A 🔓) (C 27/4-15/9) (F+H 🔓) IJ**KLN**O**P** (Q 1/4-31/10) (T+U+V+W+X+Y+Z 🔓)
**5** **AB**DFGIJKLMNOPUWZ
**6** EGHI**K**(N 0,5km)RT

💬 A large campsite. Excellent toilet facilities. Leisure pool. Swimming pool not included in CampingCard ACSI rate: 6 Euros per person per day. Hiking, biking and all types of sports are possible in the area. Interesting trips out by car include the wine growing area between Ormoz and Ljutomer.

🚗 From Graz (Austria) A9/A1 dir. Maribor. Before Maribor A5 dir. Lendava as far as Gancani, Moravske Toplice exits. Campsite signposted.

**Murska Sobota**
CC
**Beltinci**

CC € **20** 6/1-12/4 5/5-25/5 16/6-29/6 1/9-29/9 3/11-21/12 📍 N 46°41'05'' E 16°12'57''

---

## Podcetrtek, SLO-3254

🚻 ♿ 📶 iD **1118**

🏕 Camping Terme
   Olimia/Natura*****
✉ Zdraviliska cesta 24
☎ +386 38 29 78 36
🔓 1/1 - 31/12
@ info@terme-olimia.com

4ha 46T(90-100m²) 16A CEE

**1** ABCDGIJKLMPQ
**2** CGLRVWXY
**3** ABF**H**JLN**W**
**4** (A 🔓) (**C+H** 1/5-30/9) **IJK OP** (Q+R+T+V+W+Y+Z 1/5-30/9)
**5** **AB**CGIJKLMNOPUWX
**6** ACEGHK(N 3km)STV

💬 Small site with excellent toilet facilities. Grounds located next to a beautiful swimming pool complex with thermal water. After a stay of more than five days you can use Wellness Termalija and aquapark Aqualuna for free. Site is located in beautiful countryside with great walking and cycling.

🚗 A1 Maribor-Celje, exit Slovenska Bistrica. Then south via Mestinje for ± 30 km. From Celje exit Dramlje and drive via Smarje Pri Jelsah. Follow signs Podcetrtek/Aqualuna.

**Smarje Pri Jelsah**
D207
D206
CC
D229
D205

CC € **18** 7/1-28/6 26/8-23/12 7=6, 14=12 📍 N 46°09'55'' E 15°36'19''

## Podzemelj/Gradac, SLO-8332

👥 🛜 **iD** (1119)

🏕 Camping Bela krajina★★★★
✉ Škrilje 11
☎ +386 73 06 95 72
🔓 19/4 - 29/9
@ info@camping-belakrajina.si

3,5ha 75T(50-100m²) 16A CEE

**1** ABCD**G**IJKLMNOPQ
**2** CKLMRUVWXY
**3** BHJKLN**Q**RV**W**X
**4** (A 1/7-31/8) M**N**(Q 1/6-31/8)
(R 🔓) (X 1/6-15/9)
(Y 1/6-31/8) (Z 🔓)
**5** **A**FGIJKLMNOP**R**STUWZ
**6** DEGHK(N 7km)UV

💬 A natural campsite under deciduous trees by River Kolpa which is nice to swim in. Bungalow section suitable for caravans, the other section is more suitable for tents. Bar, pizzeria and restaurant. Lovely walking and cycling, also from other places in Bela Krajina.

🚗 From Slovenia A2 Ljubljana-Zagreb, exit 27 Novo Mesto. Road 105 to Metlika. Right onto 218 to Podzemelj. From Croatia in Karlovac road 6 to Jurovski Brod and Metlika. Left on 218 to Podzemelj.

**Metlika**

D228

CC

**Crnomelj**

D6

CC € 20 19/4-6/6 1/9-29/9

📍 N 45°36'17'' E 15°16'31''

---

## Ptuj, SLO-2251

♿ 🛜 **iD** (1120)

🏕 Camping Terme Ptuj★★★★
✉ Pot v Toplice 9
☎ +386 27 49 41 00
🔓 1/1 - 31/12
@ kamp@terme-ptuj.si

1,5ha 120T 16A CEE

**1** ABCD**G**IJKLMOPST
**2** FLRVWXY
**3** B**E**JK**M**NOPQV
**4** (**C** 1/5-30/9) (F+H 🔓) IJKNO
**P**(Q 1/6-31/8) (T+U 🔓)
(V 1/7-31/8) (Y+Z 🔓)
**5** **AB**DGIJKLMNOPUWXZ
**6** EGHIK(N 1,5km)RT

💬 Level campsite divided by hedges. Close to a modern thermal centre with 12 swimming pools and many amenities. Swimming pool not included in CampingCard ACSI rate: 6 Euros per person per day. Near one of the most beautiful small Central European towns where culture and nature combine.

🚗 From route 9/E59 Zagreb-Krapina-Maribor take Hajdina-Terme Ptuj exit. To Ptuj/Ormoz. At the roundabout left dir. Ptuj, turn right over bridge at the south west side of the Drava. Signposted.

Starse

**Ptuj**

CC Markovci

CC € 20 6/1-27/4 5/5-25/5 16/6-29/6 1/9-21/12

📍 N 46°25'21'' E 15°51'16''

---

## Recica ob Savinji, SLO-3332

👥 🛜 **iD** (1121)

🏕 Camping Menina★★★★
✉ Varpolje 105
☎ +386 40 52 52 66
🔓 1/1 - 31/12
@ info@campingmenina.com

10ha 210T(100-200m²) 10A CEE

**1** ABCD**G**IJKLMOPQ
**2** BCDLNORTVXY
**3** BGJLNQRU**W**XZ
**4** (A 1/6-20/8) **N**
(V+Y+Z 1/5-31/10)
**5** **AB**DGIJKLMNOPQRUW
**6** AEGIK(N 1km)V

💬 The campsite is located in the middle of Slovenia on the River Savinja and by a small swimming lake. Excellent walking opportunities in the mountains. Perfect location for excursions into Slovenia, organised by owner. Also suitable for seniors. Campsite restaurant with local dishes.

🚗 From A1 Ljubljana-Maribor, take exit Sentrupert/ Mozirje (about 15 km from Celje) and continue north towards the campsite (± 20 km). Take the exit to the campsite in Nizka village.

**Sostanj**

**Mozirje**

CC

CC € 18 1/4-1/7 1/9-15/11

📍 N 46°18'42'' E 14°54'33''

## Sempas, SLO-5261

🛖 Camping Park Lijak
   Active Holidays
🏠 Ozeljan 6A
☎ +386 53 08 85 57
📅 1/1 - 31/10, 1/12 - 31/12
@ info@parklijak.com

1ha 60T(80-100m²) 6-10A CEE

**1** ABCD**G**IJLMOPQ
**2** FGKRWX
**3** A
**4** (Q 1/4-30/9) (X+Z 📷)
**5** **AB**GIJKLMNOPUWY
**6** ABEG**K**(N 0,5km)

💬 5 km from Nova Gorica and Italian Goriza in wine-growing area with mountain views. Mild climate until Oct. Suitable as stopover campsite. Base for trips out (Venice, Postojna Caves and Lipica) or relaxing. Paradise for paragliders. Modern toilet facilities. Grill restaurant.

🚐 From H4 motorway (Ajdovscina-Italian border), exit Vogrsko then drive north. Left at end of road. Campsite further on right. From Bovec and Nova Forica direction Ajdovscina after roundabout (4 km).

**Nova Gorica**
**Gorizia**

€ 18  1/1-23/6  2/9-31/12  1/12-31/12  7=6   N 45°56'31'' E 13°43'05''

## Soca, SLO-5232

🛖 Camp Soca**
🏠 Soca 8
☎ +386 53 88 93 18
📅 1/4 - 31/10
@ kamp.soca@siol.net

3ha 250T(120-160m²) 6A

**1** ABCD**G**IJKLMPQ
**2** CGJKRTWX
**3** AHRU**W**
**4** **N**(Q+T+V+Z 📷)
**5** **AB**DGIJMNOPUVW
**6** ACE**K**(N 8km)V

💬 A peaceful and spacious site in Triglav National Park with large pitches, an open centre and surrounded by greenery. Pebble beach on the banks of the (cold) River Soca. Mountain hiking, white water sailing. Braziers and wood available.

🚐 North of Bovec, exit Trenta/Kranska Gora, 1st campsite in the valley. From the Vrsic Pass at Kranska Gora (not for caravans). 5th campsite in the valley. Alternative route for larger caravans via Italy. Udine and Cividale recommended.

SS54
**Trenta**
Zaga
Kobarid

€ 20  1/4-30/6  1/9-31/10   N 46°20'07'' E 13°38'39''

## Vipava, SLO-5271

🛖 Kamp Tura***
🏠 Gradisce pri Vipavi 14a
☎ +386 31 65 57 76
📅 1/1 - 31/12
@ info@kamp-tura.si

1,5ha 40T(40-120m²) 16A CEE

**1** ACD**G**IJKLOPQ
**2** FJKRVWX
**3** AHJ**M**NU
**4** (**A**+Q+Z 📷)
**5** **AB**DGIJMNOP
**6** GJ(N 2km)V

💬 Campsite Tura is located beneath the natural climbing rock Gradiska Tura in the unspoilt nature of Natura 2000. You will be surprised by the wonderful views of the upper part of the Vipava wine valley. The campsite has extensive sports facilities but there is also a quiet section of the site.

🚐 Take Vipava exit on Ljubljana-Nova Gorica motorway. Campsite signposted on the right in Vipava. Follow these; after 1500 metres campsite.

Crni Vrh
**Ajdovscina**
Vipava

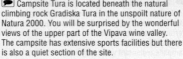

€ 20  1/3-30/6  2/9-30/11   N 45°49'56'' E 13°58'16''

# Croatia

## General
Croatia is a member of the EU.

### Time
The time in Croatia is the same as Amsterdam, Paris and Rome and one hour ahead of London.

### Language
Croatian, but German and English is spoken in many places.

## Border formalities
Many formalities and agreements about matters such as necessary travel documents, car papers, requirements relating to your means of transport and accommodation, medical expenses and taking pets with you do not only depend on the country you are travelling to but also on your departure point and nationality. The length of your stay can also play a role here. It is not possible within the confines of this guide to guarantee the correct and most up to date information with regard to these matters.

We advise you to consult the relevant authorities before your departure about:
- which travel documents you will need for yourself and your fellow passengers
- which documents you need for your car
- which regulations your caravan must meet
- which goods you may import and export
- how medical treatment will be arranged and paid for in your holiday destination in cases of accident or illness
- whether you can take pets. Contact your vets well in advance. They can give you

information about the necessary vaccinations, proof thereof and obligations on return. It would also make sense to enquire whether any special regulations apply to your pet in public places at your holiday destination. In some countries for example dogs must always be muzzled or transported in a cage.

You will find plenty of general information on ▶ *www.europa.eu* ◀ but make certain you select information that is relevant to your specific situation.

For the most recent customs regulations you should get in contact with the authorities of your holiday destination in your country of residence.

## Currency
The currency in Croatia is the kuna (HRK). Approximate exchange rates September 2018: £ 1 = 8.34 HRK. Payments are also accepted in euros in most parts of Croatia.

### Cash machines
There are plenty of cash machines in Croatia.

### Credit cards
All credit cards and travellers cheques are accepted. You can exchange currency in banks and exchange offices.

## Opening times
### Banks
Banks are open Monday to Friday until 19:00, and on Saturday until 13:00.

## Shops

Most shops are open on weekdays until 20:00 and on Saturdays and Sundays until 14:00.

## Chemists

In general chemists are open from 08:00 to 13:00 and 15:00 to 19:00, on Saturdays till 14:00.

# Communication

## (Mobile) phones

The mobile network works well throughout Croatia. There is a 4G network for mobile internet.

## Wifi, internet

You can make use of a wifi network at more and more public locations, often for free.

## Post

Mostly open on weekdays until 18:00. In the most popular tourist destinations and in large towns some post offices are also open on Saturdays.

# Roads and traffic

## Road network

Unpaved roads are only found in rural areas. You are advised not to drive after dark on these roads. If you have breakdown insurance you can make use of the services of the Croatian motoring association HAK, tel. 1987.

## Traffic regulations

Remember, all traffic in Croatia drives on the right and overtakes on the left! Headlight deflectors are advisable to prevent annoying oncoming drivers. Croatia uses the metric system, so distances are measured in kilometres (km) and speeds in kilometres per hour (km/h). Traffic on roundabouts has priority. Ascending traffic on mountain roads has priority over descending traffic.

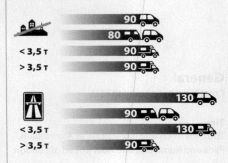

*Maximum speed*

Maximum permitted alcohol level is 0.5‰. Use of low beam headlights is mandatory during the day. Using phones is only permitted hands-free. School buses which have stopped to take on or drop off passengers must not be overtaken. When overtaking you must use your indicators during the entire manoeuvre. Accidents must be reported to the local police. Winter tyres are mandatory during the winter period (early November to end of April). Snow chains are required in mountainous regions.

## Caravans, motorhomes

Vehicles with a trailer or caravan need to be equipped with two emergency triangles. You are advised to take with you receipts for expensive equipment in your caravan or motorhome.

## Maximum allowed measurements of combined length

Height 4 metres, width 2.55 metres and maximum length 18.75 metres (of which the trailer maximum 12 metres).

## Fuel

Petrol and diesel are easily available. LPG is reasonably well available, especially in larger towns and on motorways.

### Filling stations
Filling stations are generally open between 07:00 and 20:00, often till 22:00 in summer. Credit cards are only accepted at a few service stations.

### Tolls
Nearly all motorways in Croatia are toll roads. You can pay in euros or kunas or by credit card. More information on ▸ *www.hac.hr* ◂
You must pay special tolls for the bridge to Krk, the Ucka Tunnel between Rovinj and Rijeka and for the Mirna viaduct between Rovinj and Umag.

### Emergency number
122: the national emergency number for fire, police and ambulance.

## Camping
There is hardly a free pitch to be found in July and August at campsites in Istria or along the northern Dalmatian coast. You are advised to book in plenty of time if you want to camp in high season. Recreational opportunities are numerous compared to the European norm. Entertainment is provided as standard at large campsites. Croatia is very popular with naturists.

The construction of a new motorway between Zagreb and Dubrovnik is making campsites in central and southern parts of the Dalmatian coast more popular. The idyllically situated campsites on the islands are mostly suitable for tent campers. Overnight camping by the roadside is not permitted.

### Practical
- Make sure you have a world adaptor for electrical appliances.
- The tap water is safe.

## Banjole/Pula, HR-52100 / Istra

♿ 🛜 **iD** (1125)

△ Camp Peškera***
🏠 Indije 73
☎ +385 52 57 32 09
📅 19/4 - 6/10
@ info@camp-peskera.com

1,5ha 80T(75-100m²) 6A

**1** ABG**I**JKLMO**P**ST
**2** EKQTWXY
**3** **W**Y
**4** (Y+Z 25/5-15/9)
**5** CGH**I**JKMNOPUV
**6** ACEG**J**(N 0,5km)T

💬 A small, peaceful campsite with good amenities right on the rocky Adriatic coast with shaded and sunny pitches. Panoramic views of the sea and islands. Banjole has many good restaurants. 7 km from the historic town of Pula. CampingCard ACSI rate is valid for B and C pitches. Sea water still warm in september.

🚗 After Pula follow motorway towards Premantura, exit Banjole and continue towards Indije. 50m before Indije campsite. Turn left, Peškera after 100m.

**CC** € **18** *19/4-7/7  24/8-6/10*    📷 N 44°49'22'' E 13°51'04''

---

## Banjole/Pula, HR-52203 / Istra

♿ 🛜 **iD** (1126)

△ Camping Arena Indije**
🏠 Indie 96
☎ +385 52 57 30 66
📅 19/4 - 29/9
@ arenaindije@
   arenacampsites.com

19ha 399T(60-120m²) 10A

**1** ABCD**G**IJKLM**P**ST
**2** EIKOQRTWXY
**3** AR**W**Y
**4** (Q+S+T+U+V+Y+Z 🔑)
**5** **AB**FGIJKMNOPU
**6** AEGK(N 2km)QT

💬 The perfect choice for people in search of a relaxing holiday. Located on a headland in unspoilt countryside with large spacious grounds. The beach is partly rocky and partly pebbles. The campsite is located 7 km from the historic centre of Pula. CampingCard ACSI is not valid on 'Seaside', 'Premium' and 'Superior' zones.

🚗 From the Pula ring road, drive towards Premantura, exit Banjole. Follow the camping signs.

**CC** € **18** *19/4-15/6  13/9-29/9*    📷 N 44°49'26'' E 13°51'03''

---

## Baska (Krk), HR-51523 / Primorje-Gorski Kotar

🏊 ♿ 🛜 **iD** (1127)

△ Bunculuka Camping Resort****
🏠 Kricin 30
☎ +385 51 85 68 06
📅 19/4 - 29/9
@ bunculuka@valamar.com

4,7ha 400T(60-100m²) 10-16A CEE

**1** ABCD**G**IJKLM
**2** EIJKNOQRTVWXY
**3** BGH**M**NQR**W**Y
**4** (A 15/6-20/9)
   (Q+S+U+V+W+Y+Z 🔑)
**5** **AB**DEFGIJKLMNOPTUWX
   YZ
**6** ACEG**I**KLM(N 0,5km)QRTV

💬 A tasteful, quiet naturist campsite, surrounded by beautiful mountainous countryside. Wide pebble beach with panoramic views. Superb restaurant with buffet and regular menu to choose from, and adjacent terrace with designer furniture. Modern and very well-maintained toilet facilities. Discount on wellness facilities at the hotel.

🚗 Keep to the left just before Baska, in the direction of Valbiska and FKK. Then follow the signs to 'FKK Bunculuka'.

**CC** € **20** *28/4-30/5  2/6-7/6  10/6-14/6  6/9-29/9*    📷 N 44°58'09'' E 14°46'01''

## Baska (Krk), HR-51523 / Primorje-Gorski Kotar

♿ 📶 iD **1128**

🏕 Zablace Camping Resort****
📧 Put Zablaca 40
☎ +385 51 85 69 09
🔑 19/4 - 6/10
@ zablace@valamar.com

9ha 493T(80-120m²) 16A CEE

**1** ABCDGIJKLMOPQ
**2** AEGKNRTVWX
**3** AHK**M**NQR**V**W**Y**
**4** (A 15/6-1/9) (C+F+G 🔑) **JK**
  **NP**(Q+R+T+U+V+Y+Z 🔑)
**5** **AB**EFGIJKLMNOPUWXYZ
**6** CFG**I**KLM(N 0,5km)QRTX

💬 The campsite is situated in the beautiful region of Baska and positioned on level grounds. The first section, which is located on the beach has marked out pitches with electricity and water. In section 2 on the other side of the road the pitches are not marked out. Large beach. Guests can make use of the facilities in the adjacent hotel, such as swimming pool and wellness.

🚗 Keep right before Baska. Follow 'Kamp Zablace' signs.

Krk — D102 — D8
Draga Bascanska — Senj
CC

CC € **18** 19/4-30/5 2/6-7/6 10/6-14/6 8/9-6/10

🏖 N 44°58'01'' E 14°44'43''

---

## Biograd na Moru, HR-23210 / Zadar

♿ 📶 ✿ iD **1129**

🏕 Camping Park Soline****
📧 Put Kumenta 16
☎ +385 23 38 33 51
🔑 1/3 - 30/11
@ info@campsoline.com

20ha 550T(90-100m²) 16A CEE

**1** ABCD**G**IJKLMO**P**ST
**2** BENOPTUVWXY
**3** BGJRV**W**Y
**4** (Q 1/6-30/9) (R 1/5-30/9)
  (T+V+Z 🔑)
**5** **AB**FGIJKLMNOPUWXYZ
**6** DGKM(N 2km)RV

💬 A large, coastal campsite under pine trees on level or slightly sloping grounds with partially refurbished toilet facilities. Many Central European campers. Good base for trips to the nearby harbours and nature reserves. Motorboat via Marina! CampingCard ACSI is valid in zones I, II, III and not valid in the extra zone.

🚗 On the A1 Karlovac-Split motorway past Zadar take exit Biograd na Moru. Continue to Benkovac/Biograd and turn left at the first traffic lights. Signposted.

D503 — E65
Sveti Filip I Jakov — D27
D8
CC — Pakostane

CC € **20** 1/3-30/6 1/9-30/11

🏖 N 43°55'42'' E 15°27'20''

---

## Drage, HR-23211 / Zadar

♿ 📶 iD **1130**

🏕 Camping Oaza Mira****
📧 Ul. Dr. Franje Tudmana 2
☎ +385 23 63 54 19
🔑 1/4 - 31/10
@ info@oaza-mira.hr

4ha 192T(120-150m²) 16A

**1** ABCD**G**IJKLMO**P**Q
**2** EJKLNTUVWXY
**3** AGJMNQV**W**Y
**4** (B 1/6-20/9) (Q+R 1/6-30/9)
  (T 1/6-20/9) (Y 1/5-20/9)
  (Z 1/6-20/9)
**5** **AB**EGIJKLMNOP**QR**UWXZ
**6** EGKM(N 9,9km)RTW

💬 New campsite located on a lovely bay with marked out pitches on a fine gravel base. Partially under trees, most pitches are situated on terraces with sea view. Close to Drage. Well away from the crowds. Perfect for campers with a boat. Not all amenities operate if too few guests.

🚗 A1 Karlovac-Split past Zadar, exit Biograd na Moru. Coast road 8 direction Sibenik. Beyond Pakostane in Drage, signposted on the coastal side of the road. Follow signs to Autokamp Oaza Mira.

Sveti Filip I Jakov — A1
Biograd Na Moru
D8
CC

CC € **20** 1/4-30/6 1/9-31/10

🏖 N 43°53'30'' E 15°32'03''

## Duga Resa, HR-47250 / Karlovac

♿ 📶 iD (1131)

🏕 Camp Slapic★★★★
📧 Mreznicki Brig 79b
☎ +385 98 86 06 01
📅 1/4 - 31/10
@ autocamp@inet.hr

2,3ha 100T(100-130m²) 16A

**1** ABCD**G**IJKLMOPQ
**2** CLMRVWXY
**3** AHJK**M**RWX
**4** (Q+Y+Z 🔑)
**5** **AB**EGIJKLMNOP**RS**UWXZ
**6** EGKM(N 3,5km)RTV

💬 Spacious pitches on one of Croatia's most beautiful rivers in the middle of the countryside. Modern toilet facilities, lively bar and small restaurant, children's playground and various sports fields. Has earned the natural campsite label. Train connections to Zagreb and trips out by car to Plitvice.

🚗 From Karlovac D23 direction Duga Resa/Senj. Campsite signposted from Duga Resa.

Karlovac
D6
A1
E71
E65 **Duga Resa**
D3 D1
CC
D23

CC € **20** 1/4-7/7 26/8-31/10 | N 45°25'11'' E 15°29'01''

---

## Fazana, HR-52212 / Istra

♿ 📶 iD (1132)

🏕 Camping Bi-Village★★★★
📧 Dragonja 115
☎ +385 52 30 03 00
📅 20/4 - 13/10
@ info@bivillage.com

25ha 970T(100-120m²) 10A CEE

**1** ABC**G**HIJKLMOPST
**2** EGKLNORVWXY
**3** A**F**J**M**N**Q**RWY
**4** (C+H+Q+S+T+U+V+Y+Z 🔑)
**5** **AB**DEFGIJKLMNOP**RS**TU WX
**6** AEGKM(N 1km)PRTUWX

💬 A modern, large campsite located by the sea with lovely views of the Brionian islands. Close to the charming village of Fazana and the historic town of Pula. The site has every amenity: several swimming pools, restaurants and recreation. There is a surcharge on the CampingCard ACSI rate for Belvedere camping pitches. Lovely in spring and autumn. Seawater is still warm in September.

🚗 A9 exit Vodnjan/Fazana, direction Fazana. Follow the camping signs.

E751
A9 D66
CC
**Pula**
Medulin

CC € **18** 20/4-22/6 31/8-13/10 | N 44°55'03'' E 13°48'40''

---

## Funtana, HR-52452 / Istra

♿ 📶 iD (1133)

🏕 Camping Polidor★★★★
📧 Bijela Uvala 12
☎ +385 52 21 94 95
📅 1/1 - 31/12
@ booking@campingpolidor.com

1,3ha 48T(80-110m²) 16A CEE

**1** ABCD**G**IJKLMOST
**2** JNTVWX
**3** AKUV
**4** (C+H 1/4-31/10) (Q 🔑) (R 1/6-30/9) (Y 1/4-30/9) (Z 🔑)
**5** **AB**DEFGIJKLMNOP**S**U WXY
**6** CEGK(N 1,5km)QRTUV

NEW

💬 Polidor Camping Park is a small 4 star campsite in the vicinity of Funtana. The campsite is open the whole year and can accommodate up to 300 guests. Relax in the shade of pine trees, cooled by a fresh sea breeze, far away from the hustle and bustle of city life. Many bike routes and there are bikes for rent. Restaurant with the best traditional Istrian meals.

🚗 Take coast road from Porec to Funtana/Vrsar. Campsite a few km north of Funtana.

D75
**Porec**
A9
D302 E751
CC
Rovinjsko Selo
**Rovinj**

CC € **18** 1/1-12/4 6/5-6/6 25/6-27/6 1/9-30/10 5/11-20/12 | N 45°11'27'' E 13°35'57''

## Funtana/Vrsar, HR-52450 / Istra

 ♿ 🛜 **iD** (1134)

🏕 Camping Valkanela\*\*\*
☎ +385 52 40 66 40
🗓 19/4 - 29/9
@ valkanela@maistra.hr

55ha 1230T(90-120m²) 10A CEE

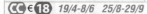

1 ABCD**G**IJKLMO**P**Q
2 EKLNOPQRTVWXY
3 ABJ**MN**Q**R**UW**Y**
4 (B+G 15/5-15/9)
  (Q+S+T+V 💶) (W 1/5-15/9)
  (X+Y+Z 💶)
5 **AB**EFGIJKLMNOP**S**UV
  WXZ
6 ACGHKM(N 1km)RTV

💬 A real family campsite located in a valley between Funtana and Vrsar. The campsite has modern toilet facilities. A lovely long beach invites you to sunbathe or to take a swim. Plenty of sports events for active holiday makers. The CampingCard ACSI rate is based on the standard pitch. There is a lovely big swimming pool, opened in 2016.

🚗 From the road Porec-Vrsar, when south of Funtana turn towards the campsite.

**Porec**
D21
CC
**Rovinj**

**CC** € **18** 19/4-8/6 25/8-29/9    ◪ N 45°09'54'' E 13°36'28''

---

## Glavotok (Krk), HR-51500 / Primorje-Gorski Kotar

 ♿ 🛜 ✿ **iD** (1135)

🏕 Camping Glavotok\*\*\*
✉ Glavotok 4
☎ +385 51 86 78 80
🗓 19/4 - 13/10
@ info@kamp-glavotok.hr

6ha 333T(80-120m²) 10A

1 ABCD**G**IJKLOPQ
2 BEIJKNQRTVXY
3 BHJLNR**WY**
4 (B+G 💶) M
  (Q+R+T+U+V+Y 💶)
  (Z 15/5-10/9)
5 **A**EFGIJKLMNO**P**UVW
6 ACEGI**K**M(N 2,5km)STX

💬 In May wake to the sound of the many birds singing. Perfect surroundings for walking, cycling or swimming. Peace returns in September; swimming, diving or snorkelling become even more enjoyable as the sea still has a very agreeable temperature. Swimming pool with lovely panoramic views.

🚗 Take the main road Toll bridge/Krk. Turn right at the exit Valbiska. Then follow signs Glavotok. The last 2 km are on a narrow winding road with passing places.

Njivice
Dobrinj
CC
Krk

**CC** € **18** 19/4-9/6 23/6-29/6 8/9-13/10    ◪ N 45°05'38'' E 14°26'25''

---

## Grabovac/Rakovica, HR-47245 / Karlovac

🛜 ✿ **iD** (1136)

🏕 Plitvice Holiday Resort\*\*\*
✉ Grabovac 102
☎ +385 47 78 41 92
🗓 1/4 - 31/10
@ info@plitvice.com

5ha 170T(70-180m²) 16A CEE

1 ABCD**G**IJKLMO**P**Q
2 GIJRTUVWXY
3 BHJ**O**QRV
4 (C 1/5-30/9)
  (Q+R+U+V+Y+Z 💶)
5 **AB**EGIJKLMNOPUWXYZ
6 ADEGKM(N 2km)V

💬 Completely renewed, quiet campsite with swimming pool. Partly undulating. Plenty of level and paved pitches. Good location for outings to the Plitvice lakes and for walks in Slunj. Restaurant next to campsite.

🚗 D1 Karlovac-Plitvice. Located 8 km before Plitvice, in Grabovac, opposite the INA service station and next to restaurant ATG-Turist.

Rakovica
CC
D1
D42
Plitvicka
Jezera
D217
D504

**CC** € **20** 1/4-17/6 1/9-30/10    ◪ N 44°58'20'' E 15°38'51''

## Kampor, HR-51280 / Primorje-Gorski Kotar

&#9855; &#128246; iD **1137**

🏕 Camping Lando Resort\*\*\*\*
📧 321
☎ +385 9 96 45 70 00
📅 26/4 - 6/10
@ rab@starturist.hr

0,6ha 10T(80-100m²) 16A CEE

1 ABCD**G**IJKLNO**P**Q
2 AEGLMRSVWX
3 AHJY
4 (C+H 🔲) (T+U 15/5-1/10)
 (Y 🔲)
5 **AB**IJKLMNOPUWXY
6 ACEGIK(N 1km)R

💬 Lando Resort is a recently opened small-scale campsite located on Kampor Mel Bay, directly on a sandy beach about 7 km from the town of Rab. The campsite has a modern and luxurious appearance in a parkland setting. There are two heated swimming pools with sun loungers and parasols, a restaurant, cocktail bar and children's playground.

🚗 Coming from Krk or the mainland direction Rab, then direction Kampor. At Kampor follow signs to Resort Lando.

Supetarska
Draga CC
**Rab**

CC € **20**  26/4-8/6  1/9-6/10  📷 N 44°47'02'' E 14°42'24''

---

## Klimno/Dobrinj, HR-51514 / Primorje-Gorski Kotar

&#9855; &#128246; iD **1138**

🏕 Camping Slamni\*\*\*\*
📧 Klimno 8a
☎ +385 51 85 31 69
📅 19/4 - 6/10
@ info@kampslamni.com.hr

0,7ha 35T(35-80m²) 16A CEE

1 ABCD**G**IJKLMOPQ
2 EGKNUVWX
3 BGHJKRUV**W**Y
4 (C+H 🔲) **K**M
 (Q+R 15/5-30/9)
 (U+V+Y+Z 🔲)
5 **AB**EFGIJKLMNOPUWXYZ
6 CEGIK(N 0,3km)OQRTVX

💬 A campsite with a lovely beach right on the Soline bay. Small campsite with wide range of modern amenities such as a fitness room, beach bar, restaurant and new children's pool. Very suitable for families with toddlers.

🚗 Take Krk bridge from the mainland to Krk island. Continue straight ahead at first roundabout. Turn left after 1300 metres to Dobinj (don't go straight). Route to campsite signposted from there.

D8
**Crikvenica**
CC
Bribir

D102

CC € **18**  19/4-8/6  24/6-30/6  1/9-6/10  📷 N 45°09'13'' E 14°37'02''

---

## Kolan (Pag), HR-23251 / Zadar

&#128246; iD **1139**

🏕 Camping Village Šimuni\*\*\*
📧 Simuni 106
☎ +385 23 69 74 41
📅 1/1 - 31/12
@ info@camping-simuni.hr

40ha 900T(60-140m²) 16A CEE

1 ABCD**G**IJKLMO**P**ST
2 AEGIJKLNTUVWXY
3 ABGJKLM**N**R**S**TUV**W**Y
4 JM(Q 20/4-30/9) (R 🔲)
 (S+T+V 1/5-30/9)
 (W 1/7-1/9) (X 🔲)
 (Y 1/5-1/10) (Z 1/5-30/9)
5 **AB**DEFGIJKLMNOP**RS**UW
 XYZ
6 ADFGHKM(N 9,9km)PTVX

💬 Large partly refurbished site, partly terraced, partly sloping. On a lovely bay in an 'oasis' on Pag headland. Restaurant and small shop. Perfect for beach holidays. CampingCard ACSI only valid for zone C.

🚗 On the M2/E27 (coastal road) follow signs for ferry Prizna-Zigljen. Then take direction Pag. Or take new A1 motorway Karlovac-Split, before Zadar exit in Posedarje to Pag (43 km). Then 11 km further direction Novalja. Signposted.

Novalja
D25
D8
Kolan E65
CC Pag

CC € **18**  1/1-8/6  7/9-31/12  📷 N 44°27'55'' E 14°58'01''

## Krk (Krk), HR-51500 / Primorje-Gorski Kotar

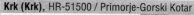

👫 ♿ 📶 **iD** (1140)

🏕 Camping Bor***
✉ Crikvenicka 10
☎ +385 51 22 15 81
🔓 1/1 - 31/12
@ info@camp-bor.hr

2,2ha 160T(70-130m²) 10A

1 **A**GIJKLMNOPQ
2 IJKTVWX
3 AHJ
4 (B+G 15/5-15/9)
  (Q+R 1/5-30/9)
  (Y+Z 1/4-30/10)
5 **A**DEFGIJKLMNOPUWXY
6 ACEG**K**(N 1km)TV

💬 Family campsite within walking distance of Krk town. Plenty of olive, cherry and fig trees. In June the owner will surprise you with delicious cherries, in September with figs. You will be treated to a glass of wine in the restaurant on presentation of your CampingCard ACSI. Renovated toilet facilities and comfort pitches with (waste)water and power connection.

🚗 Before Krk follow signs to 'Centar'. Follow signs 'Autocamp Bor' from the roundabout, 1st turning right.

Vrbnik
Krk  Punat
CC
Cres

**CC** €**20** 1/1-6/7  1/9-31/12  14=13    🏕 N 45°01'21'' E 14°33'44''

---

## Krk (Krk), HR-51500 / Primorje-Gorski Kotar

♿ 📶 **iD** (1141)

🏕 Jezevac Premium Camping Resort****
✉ Plavnicka 37
☎ +385 51 22 10 81
🔓 19/4 - 6/10
@ camping@valamar.com

11ha 525T(70-120m²) 10A CEE

1 ABCD**G**IJKLMOPST
2 EGIJKNPQRTVWXY
3 BGL**M**N**R**W**Y**
4 (C+H 🔓) M
  (Q+R+S+T+U+V+Y+Z 🔓)
5 **AB**EFGIJKLMNOPQ**ST**U
  WXY
6 ACDFG**IK**LM(N 0,5km)QR
  TUV

💬 A large campsite right by a lovely pebble beach with marked out pitches, 40% of which are shaded. Within walking distance of the centre of the town of Krk. Many facilities such as restaurant, beach bar, special beach for dogs, deck chairs, new (2018) heated pool with special paddling pool.

🚗 From Krk follow the Jezevac or autocamp (Jezevac) signs. Campsite is located on the west of the town.

Malinska
D102
Krk
CC
Vrbnik

**CC** €**20** 19/4-30/5  2/6-7/6  10/6-14/6  8/9-6/10    🏕 N 45°01'08'' E 14°34'01''

---

## Krk (Krk), HR-51500 / Primorje-Gorski Kotar

♿ 📶 ✿ **iD** (1142)

🏕 Krk Premium Camping Resort*****
✉ Narodnog Preporoda 80
☎ +385 52 46 50 10
🔓 5/4 - 27/10
@ reservations@valamar.com

5,6ha 310T(80-110m²) 10A CEE

1 ABCD**G**IJKLMOPST
2 EIJKNOPQRTVWX
3 BCHJ**M**NQR**VW**Y
4 (**A**+C+H 🔓) JM**N**
  (Q+R+S+T+U+V+Y+Z 🔓)
5 **AB**CDEFGIJKLMNOPQR**S**
  UWXY
6 BCEGH**I**KLM(N 2km)RST
  UVX

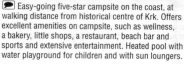

💬 Easy-going five-star campsite on the coast, at walking distance from historical centre of Krk. Offers excellent amenities on campsite, such as wellness, a bakery, little shops, a restaurant, beach bar and sports and extensive entertainment. Heated pool with water playground for children and with sun loungers.

🚗 From Krk drive towards Punat. Turn right before the petrol station (on the left).

Vrbnik
CC  D102
Baska
Cres

**CC** €**20** 5/4-30/5  2/6-7/6  10/6-14/6  8/9-27/10    🏕 N 45°01'28'' E 14°35'30''

## Kuciste, HR-20267 / Dalmatija

⌂ Camping Palme
✉ Kuciste 45
☎ +385 20 71 91 64
🗓 1/1 - 31/12
@ info@kamp-palme.com

1143

1,2ha 122T(50-80m²) 10A

**1** ABCD**G**IJKLMOP
**2** EFJKNTWXY
**3** A**W**Y
**4** (X 1/5-15/10)
**5** **A**GIJKLMNOPUWY
**6** FGHI**K**(N 0,05km)OQTV

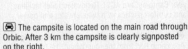

💬 Lovely private campsite with sunny and shaded pitches close to the sea (50m). Ideal for surfers.

🚗 The campsite is located on the main road through Orbic. After 3 km the campsite is clearly signposted on the right.

Orebic
Korcula

CC € ⑱ 1/1-20/6 1/9-31/12      🏞 N 42°58'35'' E 17°07'46''

## Labin, HR-52220 / Istra

⌂ Marina Camping Resort****
✉ Sv. Marina 30 C
☎ +385 52 87 90 58
🗓 12/4 - 27/10
@ marina@valamar.com

1144

5ha 252T(60-110m²) 6-16A CEE

**1** ABCD**G**IJKLOPST
**2** EIJKNPQRTVWX
**3** BR**W**Y
**4** (**C**+Q+R+T+U+V+X+Z 🗝)
**5** **AB**EFGIJKLMNOPUWXYZ
**6** ACEGIJKM(N 0,2km)QRTU

💬 A campsite with a small pebble beach, ideal for people who want a good place to dive. A swimming pool with a fantastic panoramic view and a children's pool guarantee a relaxing holiday. Set in a peaceful bay. CampingCard ACSI rate applies to comfort pitches.

🚗 Go up the hill to the old centre of Labin. Then follow signs to Sv. Marina. The road is often narrow. Beware of cars that cut the corner off.

Labin
Rabac
D66
Rakalj

CC € ⑱ 12/4-1/6 1/9-27/10      🏞 N 45°02'00'' E 14°09'29''

## Lopar (Rab), HR-51280 / Primorje-Gorski Kotar

⌂ San Marino Camping Resort****
✉ Lopar 488
☎ +385 51 77 51 33
🗓 13/4 - 1/10
@ ac-sanmarino@imperial.hr

1145

15ha 584T(80-100m²) 16A

**1** ABCD**G**IJKLMO**PQ**
**2** AEGKRSVWXY
**3** BGH**M**NQR**VW**Y
**4** **JKN**(Q+S 🗝)
   (T+U+V+X+Y+Z 1/5-30/9)
**5** **AB**EFGIJKLMNOP**QRST**U
   WXY
**6** ACFGIM(N 0,5km)OQRTV

💬 Very large campsite with a real sandy beach, recommended for families with children. The perfect low season destination: between mid-July and the end of August it is very busy and very dry. Many amenities provided such as a fitness room, wellness, etc.

🚗 Clearly signposted at the fork in the road at the Lopar Tourist Office.

D8
Rab Palit

CC € ⑱ 13/4-30/5 2/6-7/6 10/6-14/6 1/9-29/9      🏞 N 44°49'24'' E 14°44'14''

## Loviste, HR-20269 / Dalmatija

**1146**

△ Kamp Lupis
🏠 Loviste 68
☎ +385 20 71 80 63
🗓 1/1 - 31/12
@ lupis.djani@amis.net

0,8ha 55T(50-80m²) 16A

1. **AG**IJKLMOT
2. EFGJOQTVWXY
3. A**W**Y
4. (Q+R 🗓)
5. **AB**FGIJKLMNOPRUW
6. EGIJ

💬 A lovely terraced campsite located 50m from the sea with sunny and shaded pitches.

🚗 From Orebic direction Loviste. Lupis campsite clearly indicated at Loviste.

Orebic
Korcula
D118

CC € **18** 1/1-16/6 14/9-31/12

📷 N 43°01'41'' E 17°01'48''

---

## Lozovac, HR-22221 / Sibenik

**1147**

△ Camp Krka***
🏠 Skocici 2
☎ +385 22 77 84 95
🗓 1/3 - 30/11
@ goran.skocic@si.t-com.hr

1ha 40T 16A

1. ABGIJKLMOP
2. FLRTWXY
3. AJ
4. (C 15/4-15/10) (Q 🗓)
   (X 15/4-15/10) (Z 1/4-15/10)
5. **A**GIJKLMNOPUWZ
6. EGK(N 4km)V

💬 A lovely small campsite with plenty of shaded pitches. Clean toilets. Small restaurant with reasonable prices. Well located for visiting the Krka waterfalls, Sibenik and small villages in the area, including Skradin.

🚗 From coast road south of Sibenik direction Skradin/National Park Krka. From A1 exit 21 Skradin/National Park Krka. Campsite signposted a few km from the park.

D56
Skradin
D27    CC    D33
E71
Vodice D8  E65
Sibenik  A1

CC € **16** 1/3-8/7 26/8-30/11

📷 N 43°48'02'' E 15°56'32''

---

## Lozovac, HR-22221 / Sibenik

**1148**

△ Camp Marina (NP. KRKA)**
🏠 Skocici 6
☎ +385 9 53 68 33 23
🗓 1/1 - 31/12
@ predrag.skocic@gmail.com

1ha 37T(40-100m²) 16A

1. ABCDGIJKLMO**P**Q
2. BFGRTUVWXY
3. AJ
4. (B 1/4-1/11) (Q+X 1/3-15/11)
   (Z 🗓)
5. **AB**GIJKLMNOPUWX
6. AEGK(N 3km)V

💬 Camp Marina is close to the Krka National Park (2.5 km) in Lozovac, 5 km from Skradin. A perfect location for stopover campers but also for those who want to visit the tourist attractions in the Šibenik region. Restaurant with Dalmatian dishes. Excursions to Krka National Park.

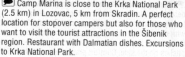

🚗 From coast road south of Sibenik dir. Skradin National Park Krka. From A1 motorway exit Skradin National Park Krka. Site indicated a few km from the park.

D59
D56
Skradin
D27    CC    D33
E65
Vodice
Sibenik  E71
A1

CC € **16** 1/1-8/7 26/8-31/12

📷 N 43°47'59'' E 15°56'39''

**Mali Losinj (Losinj)**, HR-51550 / Primorje-Gorski Kotar ♿ 🛜 iD (1149)

🏕 Camping Cikat****
📧 Cikat 6 A
☎ +385 51 23 21 25
📅 1/1 - 31/12
@ info@camp-cikat.com

6ha 1170T(60-120m²) 10-16A

**1** ABCD**G**IJKLMOPST
**2** BEIJKNPQRTVWXY
**3** ABC**J**KMNRV**W**Y
**4** (A+**B**+**G** 18/5-22/9) **IJ**KMP
(Q+S+T 🔲)
(U+V+X+Y 8/4-21/10) (Z 🔲)
**5** **AB**DEFGIJKLMNOPQR**ST**U
WXZ
**6** CEGKM(N 2km)O**P**QRST
UVW

💬 A campsite on a pebble beach on the north-west of Mali Losinj with its large, lively marina. The campsite has three restaurants and a supermarket. Campsite open all year and has a unique Aquapark. Many lovely plateaus for sun worshipers.

CC Veli Losinj

🚗 When approaching from the ferry cross the islands Cres and Mali Losinj. From the crossroads just past Mali Losinj follow direction Cikat.

CC € 20 2/5-7/6 6/9-1/10 📍 N 44°32'09'' E 14°27'03''

---

**Mali Losinj (Losinj)**, HR-51550 / Primorje-Gorski Kotar ♿ 🛜 iD (1150)

🏕 Camping Poljana****
📧 Rujnica 9a
☎ +385 51 23 17 26
📅 1/4 - 4/11
@ info@poljana.hr

18ha 524T(40-160m²) 10-16A CEE

**1** ABCD**G**IJKLMOPST
**2** BEIJKNQRTVXY
**3** ABK**M**NRW**Y**
**4** (**A** 22/5-30/9)
(Q+S+U+V+Y 🔲)
(Z 25/5-20/9)
**5** **AB**FGIJKLMNOP**QRST**UV
WXYZ
**6** ACDEG**K**M(N 2km)O**P**QRT
VWX

💬 Luxury terraced campsite on the island of Losinj. Has the Adriatic Sea on two sides. With a bit of luck you may see some dolphins swim by. Extensive amenities: a berth for boats and a promenade to Mali Losinj with restaurants, ice-cream parlours, a marina. Excursions to nearby islands. Restaurant and supermarket at campsite.

CC Mali Losinj

🚗 Coming from Nerezine the campsite is on the left side of the road before Mali Losinj.

CC € 20 1/4-8/6 22/6-29/6 2/9-4/11 📍 N 44°33'21'' E 14°26'32''

---

**Martinšcica (Cres)**, HR-51556 / Primorje-Gorski Kotar ♿ 🛜 ✿ iD (1151)

🏕 Camping Slatina****
☎ +385 51 57 41 27
📅 13/4 - 10/10
@ info@camp-slatina.com

15ha 1870T(70-120m²) 16A

**1** ABCD**G**IJKLMOPST
**2** EIJKNPQTVWXY
**3** A**Q**R**W**Y
**4** (Q+S 🔲) (U+V 15/6-1/9)
(Y+Z 🔲)
**5** **AB**EFGIJKLMNOPQ**S**UW
XYZ
**6** ACEGIKM(N 1km)OQRSTU

💬 Terraced campsite with inclines of 20%. Pebble beach with platforms and a pier for swimming. Lovely place for diving and very dog-friendly. Pitches with own water, drainage and power connections. Campsite is divided into avenues with camping pitches on the side. Comfort pitches are available with CampingCard ACSI.

Orlec

CC

Belej

🚗 From Cres, drive in the direction of Osor. Turn right after about 20 km and follow the signs Slatina (8 km). The campsite is located just after Martinscica.

CC € 16 2/5-7/6 6/9-1/10 📍 N 44°49'16'' E 14°20'35''

## Medulin, HR-52203 / Istra

♿ 📶 **iD** (1152)

🏕 Arena Medulin Campsite
✉ Osipovica 30
☎ +385 52 57 28 01
🔑 13/4 - 6/10
@ arenamedulin@
  arenacampsites.com

30ha 946T(60-120m²) 10A CEE

1 ABCD**G**IJKLMO**P**ST
2 AEGIKLORTWXY
3 ABL**WY**
4 **J**(Q+S+T+U+V+Y 🔑)
5 A**BG**IJMNOPUW
6 ACG**I**KM(N 0km)RTW

💬 A family campsite on a wooded level headland surrounded by sea. Small sandy beach with a bay safe for children and a rocky beach. Right next to the lively resort of Medulin. Several toilet blocks of varying quality. CampingCard ACSI is valid in zones L, M, N and R, not in the Seaside, Superior and Premium zones.

🚐 Motorway exit Pula/Medulin. Follow Medulin signs, exit Camps along the boulevard as far as Camping Village Medulin exit.

D66

**Pula**
Medulin
ⒸⒸ

**ⒸⒸ €18** 13/4-15/6 14/9-6/10

🗺 N 44°48'51'' E 13°55'54''

---

## Medveja, HR-51416 / Primorje-Gorski Kotar

👫 🚹 ♿ 📶 **iD** (1153)

🏕 Smart Selection Holiday
  Resort Medveja***
✉ Medveja bb
☎ +385 51 29 11 91
🔑 27/4 - 1/10
@ reservations@liburnia.hr

5,7ha 254T(90-110m²) 10A CEE

1 ABCD**G**IJKLMOPQ
2 EGNRTVXY
3 AHLR**WY**
4 (Q+S+T+U+V+Y+Z 🔑)
5 **AB**EFGIJKLMNOPUW
6 CFGKM(N 2km)QRTV

💬 A campsite on the east coast of Istria, the Croatian Riviera. Mild climate in the early season, ideal for visiting the historic towns. In September the temperature of the sea, nurtured by the summer sun, is a true delight and you can swim in the clear waters. Many activities take place in the outlying villages in September and October.

🚐 Follow the coast road from Opatija towards Pula, through Lovran. Campsite 1 km after Lovran village sign on the right side of the road.

**Opatija  Rijeka**

A8

ⒸⒸ
D66

**ⒸⒸ €18** 27/4-24/6 1/9-1/10

🗺 N 45°16'13'' E 14°15'56''

---

## Moscenicka Draga, HR-51417 / Primorje-Gorski Kotar

👫 🚹 ♿ 📶 **iD** (1154)

🏕 Autocamp Draga***
✉ Aleja Slatina bb
☎ +385 51 73 75 23
🔑 15/4 - 1/10
@ autocampdraga@gmail.com

2,2ha 110T(80-100m²) 10-16A

1 ABCD**G**IJKLMOPQ
2 EGIJNRUVWX
3 AH**WY**
4 (Q+R 1/6-1/10)
5 **A**GIJKLMNOPUWZ
6 CFGK(N 0,1km)RT

💬 A terraced campsite by a main road and near a football pitch. Lush vegetation. About 150 metres from a pebble beach. Toilet blocks are well maintained. Diving lessons possible on the beach. A small harbour with restaurants and cafes along the coast. Wifi on the entire site. Facilities at the Hotel Marina can be used at discounted rates.

🚐 Follow the coastal road from Opatija towards Pula. The campsite is located on the left, exit Moscenicka Draga.

**Veprinac**

ⒸⒸ

**Kozljak** D66
D64

**ⒸⒸ €18** 15/4-10/6 1/9-30/9

🗺 N 45°14'24'' E 14°15'01''

## Nerezine (Losinj), HR-51554 / Primorje-Gorski Kotar

👪 ♿ 📶 iD **1155**

🏕 Camping Lopari***
📧 Lopari 1
☎ +385 51 23 71 27
🔓 20/4 - 14/10
@ lopari@losinia.hr

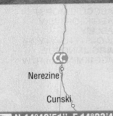

15ha 292T 10-16A CEE

**1** ABCD**G**IJKLMOPST
**2** EKNORTVWXY
**3** BGNRUVY
**4** (Q+S+V+X+Y+Z 🔋)
**5** **AB**EFGIJKLMNOPQUW
**6** CEG**IK**M(N 2km)OQRT

💬 Level campsite on spacious, child-friendly beach. Vegetation mostly consists of deciduous and coniferous trees and bushes with a lovely scent. Two toilet blocks centrally on grounds, one of which is beautifully renovated. Restaurant and supermarket on the site.

🚐 Coming from Osor the campsite is about 1500m on the left of the road to Nerezine.

Nerezine

Cunski

CC € **14** *20/4-22/6  23/8-14/10*

🗺 N 44°40'51'' E 14°23'43''

---

## Nerezine (Losinj), HR-51554 / Primorje-Gorski Kotar

👪 ♿ 📶 iD **1156**

🏕 Camping Rapoca***
📧 Rapoca 21
☎ +385 51 23 71 45
🔓 20/4 - 14/10
@ rapoca@losinia.hr

4,4ha 240T(70-100m²) 16A CEE

**1** ABCD**G**IJKLMOPQ
**2** EGINQTVXY
**3** BR**WY**
**4** (Q+R 🔋) (T+U 15/6-15/9)
    (V 15/6-30/9) (Y 1/6-16/9)
    (Z 15/6-30/9)
**5** **AB**EFGIJKLMNOP**ST**UW
**6** EG**IK**(N 0,2km)QRT

💬 Campsite situated in a village, with a small pebble beach. Largely marked-out pitches. Good options for cycling on Losinj island. Vibrant harbour in Nerezine within walking distance. There is a restaurant at the campsite.

🚐 Coming from Osor the campsite is on the left of the road at the beginning of Nerezine.

Punta Kriza

Cunski

CC € **16** *20/4-22/6  23/8-14/10*

🗺 N 44°39'49'' E 14°23'51''

---

## Nin, HR-23232 / Zadar

📶 iD **1157**

🏕 Camping Ninska Laguna
📧 Put Blata 10
☎ +385 23 26 42 65
🔓 1/1 - 31/12
@ contact@ninskalaguna.hr

1ha 100T(60-90m²) 16A

**1** AB**G**IJKLMO**P**RS
**2** AELRTWXY
**3** **WY**
**5** GI**J**KLMNO**P**UWZ
**6** EJ(N 0,4km)

💬 Very basic site with old-fashioned but clean toilets. Partly under trees for tents and caravans. Half shaded part better for caravans. 150m from lagoon with beach. Perfect for children. Nin town in walking distance.

🚐 Route via A1 motorway Karlovac-Split, before Zadar take the Nin exit on the old coast road A8/E65 direction Zadar. Right after 10 km towards Nin/Privlaka. In Nin direction Vir/Privlaka. Just outside the village, after 400 metres on the right. Signposted.

Povljana

Privlaka

Krneza

CC € **14** *1/4-10/7  1/9-14/10*

🗺 N 44°14'47'' E 15°10'26''

## Njivice (Krk), HR-51512 / Primorje-Gorski Kotar

👫 ♿ 📶 iD (1158)

🔺 Camping Njivice★★
📧 Primorska Cesta 41
☎ +385 51 84 61 68
🔑 5/4 - 5/11
@ reservation@kampnjivice.hr

10ha 429T(80-130m²) 16A CEE

**1** ABCD**G**IJKLMO**P**ST
**2** EIKNOPQRTVXY
**3** BCGHK**MOPQ**RVW**Y**
**4** (A 1/5-29/10) (G 🔑) M
(Q+S+U+V+X+Z 🔑)
**5** **A**DEFGIJKLMNOPUVWXY
**6** ACFG**I**KM(N 2,5km)RTWX

💬 The campsite has shaded fields with touring pitches. Wonderfully quiet in late season and you can swim to your heart's content in lovely warm water. There is an attractive town with lively restaurants and cafes nearby. Supplement required for Premium Mare and Premium pitches. New paddling pool.

🚗 Campsite is 10 km before the toll bridge to Krk. Badly signposted from the main road. Follow sign 'Hotel'.

Crikvenica
D8
Selce
CC

CC € 18  5/4-9/6  7/9-5/11  7=6, 14=12

🏕 N 45°10'10'' E 14°32'49''

---

## Novalja (Pag), HR-53291 / Zadar

👫 📶 iD (1159)

🔺 Camp Navis Novalja
📧 Škuncini stani 100
☎ +385 53 64 84 15
🔑 12/4 - 13/10
@ booking@campnavisnovalja.com

NEW

1,5ha 100T(50-140m²) 16A CEE

**1** ABCD**G**IJKLMO**P**Q
**2** EKLNTUVWX
**3** AJ**W**Y
**4** (Q+T+Z 15/6-15/9)
**5** **A**GIJKLMNOPUWX
**6** EGK(N 3km)TU

💬 New site (100 pitches) far away from everything, around beautiful bay with fine pebble beach. Spacious, partially shaded pitches with water supply and drainage. Bicycle routes. Bar and showers on beach. Ideal for beach lovers and families.

🚗 D8 Rijeka head south to Prizna. Ferry to Zigljen, D106 until before Novalja. Or motorway A1 Zagreb-Split exit 16 Posedarje. Now D106 direction Pag until before Novalja. D107 around Novalja 6.5 km. Now left onto unpaved road. Signposted.

Lun
D8
Cesarica
CC  Novalja

CC € 16  12/4-21/6  1/9-13/10  7=5

🏕 N 44°34'42'' E 14°51'18''

---

## Novalja (Pag), HR-53291 / Zadar

♿ 📶 iD (1160)

🔺 Camping Strasko★★★★
📧 Zeleni put 7
☎ +385 53 66 12 26
🔑 19/4 - 6/10
@ strasko@hadria.biz

57ha 1254T(120-160m²) 10-16A CEE

**1** ABCD**G**IJKLMO**P**ST
**2** EGLNOPRTUVWXY
**3** BCDGJKMN**O**RUVW**Y**
**4** (B+G 🔑) KM(Q+S 🔑)
(T+V+X 1/5-30/9) (Y+Z 🔑)
**5** **A**BEFGIJKLMNOP**QRST**U
WXYZ
**6** CDEGHKM(N 2km)OPRST
UVX

💬 Large, luxury campsite under olive and oak trees with 2 km of mostly pebble beach with entertainment and sports options, clean renovated toilet facilities, restaurants, swimming pools and shops. Small naturist section. Walking distance from Novalja. CampingCard ACSI is not valid on DeLux pitches.

🚗 On M2/E27 Prizna-Zigljen ferryboat is recommended. Turn left before Novalja, signposted, or on A1 in Posedarje exit Pag (43 km), then another 32 km. Turn left before Novalja.

D8
E65
Novalja
CC
Kolan
Simuni

CC € 20  19/4-30/6  1/9-6/10  7=6, 14=12

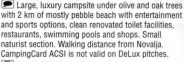

🏕 N 44°32'56'' E 14°53'15''

## Novigrad, HR-52466 / Istra  ♿ 🛜 ✿ iD  **1161**

🏕 Aminess Maravea Camping
Resort★★★★
📧 Mareda bb
☎ +385 52 85 86 80
🔑 19/4 - 29/9
@ camping@aminess.com

22ha 556T(80-140m²) 10-16A CEE

**1** ABCD**G**IJKLMO**P**ST
**2** EGIJNOPQRTUVWXY
**3** ABK**M**N**Q**RUY
**4** (B+G 1/5-29/9)
(Q+S+T+U+V+X+Y+Z 🔑)
**5** **AB**EFGIJKLMNOPUWXY
**6** CEGHIKM(N 3km)RTUV

💬 Friendly campsite. The toilet facilities are well maintained. The friendly town of Novigrad is just a few minutes away by car. Please hand in your CampingCard on arrival. CCA guests will be allocated a place on one of the unnumbered pitches in comfort or standard, or a numbered pitch standard. CampingCard ACSI users cannot make reservations.

🚗 Coming from Novigrad go about 3 km to the north in the direction of Umag. Clearly signposted.

CC €⃝20 19/4-30/6  1/9-29/9   📍 N 45°20'36'' E 13°32'53''

---

## Novigrad, HR-52466 / Istra  ♿ 🛜 ✿ iD  **1162**

🏕 Aminess Sirena Campsite★★★★
📧 Terre 6
☎ +385 52 85 86 70
🔑 22/3 - 2/11
@ camping@aminess.com

10,5ha 426T(80-160m²) 10-16A CEE

**1** ABCD**G**IJKLMO**P**ST
**2** EGIJOPRTVWXY
**3** ABKL**M**N**Q**RWY
**4** (Q 🔑) (S 1/4-30/9)
(T 1/6-31/8) (V 1/6-15/9)
(X+Z 1/5-30/9)
**5** **AB**EFGIJKLMNOPQUWXY
**6** CEGHKLM(N 0,8km)QRT

💬 The campsite is made up of a dense pine wood and a terraced section with hardly any shade. Good toilet facilities. The lively town of Novigrad is within walking distance of the campsite. Please present your CampingCard ACSI on arrival. CCA rates are based on a pitch in the comfort zone. CampingCard ACSI users cannot make reservations.

🚗 The campsite is located directly on the beach; 2 km from Novigrad and 16 km north of Porec.

CC €⃝20 22/3-30/6  1/9-2/11   📍 N 45°18'54'' E 13°34'33''

---

## Okrug Gornji, HR-21223 / Dalmatija  🛜 iD  **1163**

🏕 Camping Labadusa
📧 Uvala Duboka bb
☎ +385 9 19 84 79 59
🔑 1/5 - 1/10
@ camp@labadusa.com

0,6ha 50T(60-80m²) 6A

**1** AGIJKLM**P**ST
**2** EFJKNQTWXY
**3** AWY
**4** (Q+X+Y 🔑) (Z 1/6-1/10)
**5** **A**GIJKLMNOPUW
**6** AEGIK(N 2km)TVX

💬 A terraced campsite with sunny and shaded pitches right by the sea. Good restaurant. Beautiful new toilet block. Shopping within 1 km.

🚗 Follow D8 coast road towards Trogir centre. Left over bridge and follow road. Right at 2nd bridge. After 3 km follow signs. Narrow access road.

CC €⃝18 1/5-14/6  1/9-30/9   📍 N 43°28'55'' E 16°14'41''

## Okrug Gornji, HR-21223 / Dalmatija

♿ 🛜 📱 **1164**

🏕 Camping Rozac***
✉ Setaliste Brace Radic 56
☎ +385 21 80 61 05
📅 23/3 - 6/11
@ booking@camp-rozac.hr

2,5ha 150T(60-100m²) 16A CEE

**1** ACG**G**IJKLMN**P**ST
**2** BEGKNORSXY
**3** BHJKWY
**4** (Q+U+V+X+Y 📅)
(Z 1/5-1/10)
**5** **AB**EFGIJKLMNOPSUW
XYZ
**6** EGKTV

💬 Rozac private campsite. Attractive campsite with plenty of shade, good toilet facilities. Lovely pebble and sandy beach 2 km from Trogir.

🚐 Follow D8 coast road as far as Trogir, towards centre, over the bridge, follow road to the left, right after second bridge. Site 2 km on right.

**Kastela**

**Trogir**
D8   CC

CC € **18**   23/3-8/6   7/9-6/11

🗺 N 43°30'19'' E 16°15'30''

---

## Omis, HR-21310 / Dalmatija

♿ 🛜 ✿ 📱 **1165**

🏕 Camping Galeb***
✉ Vukovarska 7
☎ +385 21 86 44 30
📅 1/1 - 31/12
@ camping@galeb.hr

5ha 231T(70-100m²) 16A CEE

**1** ACD**G**IJKLMOPT
**2** AEGLRSVWXY
**3** AK**M**NRUWY
**4** (B 1/5-31/10) **KN**
(Q 1/6-30/9)
(T+U+V+X+Y+Z 1/4-1/11)
**5** **AB**EFGIJKLMNOPS**UWXY
**6** EGIK(N 0,2km)QRTUVWX

💬 A lovely campsite by the sea with a sandy beach. The site offers plenty of shade and is equipped with every comfort. With CampingCard ACSI you can camp on zones B. Tourist tax and administration costs are not included in the rate.

🚐 From the E65 motorway take exit 25 direction Split, then follow coastal road. On the D8, after sign for Omis, on the right side before petrol station.

**Podstrana**
A1  D62

**Omis**
CC
D8

**Supetar**

CC € **18**   1/1-1/7   31/8-31/12

🗺 N 43°26'26'' E 16°40'47''

---

## Omisalj, HR-51513 / Primorje-Gorski Kotar

🧍‍🧍 ♿ 🛜 📱 **1166**

🏕 Camping Kamp Omisalj*****
✉ Vodotoc 1
☎ +385 51 58 83 90
📅 19/4 - 25/10
@ omisalj@hadria.biz

8ha 180T(100-140m²) 16-A CEE

**1** ABCD**G**IJKLMO**P**ST
**2** EKLNPTUVWX
**3** B**E**KLNQRWY
**4** (B+G+Q+R+S+T+U+V+Y
+Z 📅)
**5** **AB**EFGIJKLMNOPQR**S**
WXY
**6** ADEGKM(N 2km)**P**QRST

NEW

💬 Brand new 5-star campsite, located on the north-western coast of the island of Krk. Near the bridge and the town of Omisalj, the campsite offers sunny, fully equipped plots. Modern toilet facilities, restaurant, shop, swimming pool, mini golf course, playground, entertainment and multifunctional sports field.

🚐 Coming from bridge on island Krk take exit Pusca. Follow road and after about 1 km you will see the campsite.

**Rijeka**
A7  D501
E65
D8
CC

**Crikvenica**
D102

CC € **20**   19/4-30/6   1/9-25/10

🗺 N 45°14'06'' E 14°33'09''

**Orasac**, HR-20234 / Dalmatija    ♿ 📶 iD **1167**

🏕 Auto-Camp Pod Maslinom
🏠 Put Na More bb
☎ +385 20 89 11 69
🗓 1/4 - 1/11
@ bozo@orasac.com

1ha 80T(70m²) 10A

**1** **A**G**IJ**KLM**P**ST
**2** BEFGNSXY
**3** Y
**5** **A**GIJKLMNOPUWZ
**6** EG**IJ**K(N 1km)RT

💬 A private campsite with plenty of shade, the sea is 500m down a steep footpath or 750m via a steep road. Good toilet facilities. Partially terraced. The campsite is ±16 km from Dubrovnik.

🚗 The campsite is on the E27. Turn right 200m past Orasac signn. Campsite clearly signposted.

Dubrovacko Primorje

D8 CC

**Dubrovnik**

CC € **14** 1/4-30/6 10/9-31/10    📍 N 42°41'57'' E 18°00'21''

---

**Orebic**, HR-20250 / Dalmatija    ♿ 📶 iD **1168**

🏕 Lavanda Camping****
🏠 Dubravica bb
☎ +385 20 45 44 84
🗓 15/4 - 31/10
@ info@lavanda-camping.com

2ha 86T(50-120m²) 16A

**1** ABCD**G**IJKLO**P**ST
**2** EFIJKLNOPQTUVWX
**3** AY
**4** (Q 🔌) (T+U+V+Y 1/6-15/10) (Z 🔌)
**5** ABEFGIJKLMNOPUWXY
**6** CDEGK(N 0,5km)QRT

💬 Newly opened (2017) campsite near the picturesque village of Oerbic. An oasis of peace and quiet. Campsite located next to the beach. Fantastic view to the sea and the islands of Kôrcula and Mljet from the spacious pitches. All facilities available.

🚗 On the through road head towards Orebic 2 km before the town. The campsite is on the left.

Orebic CC D415
D414

**Korcula**
D118

CC € **16** 15/4-30/6 1/9-31/10    📍 N 42°58'59'' E 17°12'20''

---

**Orebic**, HR-20250 / Dalmatija    ♿ 📶 iD **1169**

🏕 Nevio Camping****
🏠 Dubravica 15
☎ +385 20 71 39 50
🗓 1/4 - 15/11
@ info@nevio-camping.com

1,5ha 220T(80-100m²) 16A

**1** ACD**G**IJKLMO**P**T
**2** EFGJKNTVWXY
**3** BMN**QW**Y
**4** (B 1/5-15/10) (Q+V 1/6-30/9) (Y 1/4-30/10) (Z 15/6-15/9)
**5** **AB**EFGIJKLMNOP**QR**UW XYZ
**6** CDEGIKM(N 0,2km)OV

💬 A lovely terraced campsite with sunny and shaded pitches. Good toilet facilities, swimming pool and restaurant. Located 200m from the sea and 200m from a large supermarket.

🚗 On through route to Orebic. Campsite signposted 2km before Orebic on the left of the road.

Korcula CC Orebic

CC € **18** 1/4-15/6 15/9-14/11    📍 N 42°58'51'' E 17°11'55''

## Pakostane, HR-23211 / Zadar

♿ 🛜 📱 **iD** **(1170)**

🏕 Autocamp Nordsee
📧 Alojzija Stepinca 68
☎ +385 23 38 14 38
🔓 1/3 - 5/11
@ info@autocamp-nordsee.com

1,7ha 90T(80-100m²) 16A CEE

**1** ABG**I**JKLMOPST
**2** EKNOQTVWXY
**3** **WY**
**4** (T 🔓) (X 1/4-15/10) (Z 🔓)
**5** **A**DGIJKLMNOPUWZ
**6** EG**K**(N 0,4km)TV

💬 Small, friendly and attractive campsite positioned under the trees and by the sea. The German campsite owner is sociable and helpful. Access road is along narrow streets but wide enough for caravans and motorhomes. Pitches in shade or sun.

🚗 Take the Biograd na Moru exit on the A1 motorway Karlovac-Split past Zadar. Then coast road 8 towards Sibenik. Signposted just outside Pakostane (direction Drage) on the right of the road. Now follow Autocamp Nordsee signs.

Sveti Filip I Jakov D503  A1
Biograd Na Moru  D8  CC

**CC** € **18** 1/3-30/6  1/9-4/11

🗺 N 43°54'20'' E 15°30'58''

---

## Pakostane, HR-23211 / Zadar

♿ 🛜 **iD** **(1171)**

🏕 Camp Vransko lake - Crkvine***
📧 Crkvine 2
☎ +385 9 93 32 14 37
🔓 1/4 - 31/10
@ camp@vransko-lake.eu

**NEW**

5,5ha 180T(100m²) 16A CEE

**1** ABCD**G**IJKLMOP
**2** DLRWXY
**3** ABGJNR**WZ**
**4** (Q 🔓) (S+Z 1/6-30/9)
**5** **A**EFGIJKLMNOP**R**UWXYZ
**6** EGK(N 2km)T

💬 Campsite partly under trees in the interior next to inland lake (with lots of fish) with well maintained toilet facilities. Ideal for anglers or cyclists - route along the lake. Centrally located between Zadar and Sibenik.

🚗 On new motorway A1 Karlovac-Split past Zadar take exit Benkovac/Biograd after Moru towards Biograd. Then follow coastal road nr. 8 dir. Sibenik/Split. In Pakostane left to Vransko Jezero. Signposted from here.

D503  A1  E71  E65
Sveti Filip I Jakov  D27
Pakostane  CC
D8

**CC** € **18** 1/4-22/6  1/9-31/10

🗺 N 43°55'49'' E 15°30'35''

---

## Pakostane, HR-23211 / Zadar

🛜 **iD** **(1172)**

🏕 Camping Kozarica****
📧 Brune Busica 43
☎ +385 23 38 10 70
🔓 6/4 - 31/10
@ kozarica@adria-more.hr

6ha 255T(80-110m²) 16A CEE

**1** ABCD**G**IJKLMOP
**2** EGLNOPTUVWXY
**3** BGJR**WY**
**4** (G+Q+S 1/5-30/9)
  (Y 1/6-15/9) (Z 1/5-30/9)
**5** **AB**EFGIJKLMNOP**RS**U
  WXZ
**6** DEG**K**M(N 6km)RTV

💬 A large campsite under pine trees with all types of amenity. Suitable for watersports and diving (diving course). Centrally located between Zadar and Sibenik and for boat trips to the nature parks on the Kornati Islands.

🚗 Take Benkovac/Biograd na Moru exit on the A1 Karlovac-Split motorway past Zadar. Then follow coast road 8 to Biograd. Turn off on the seaward side between Pakostane and Biograd at the Kozarica sign.

D503  E65  A1
Sveti Filip I Jakov  Biograd Na Moru  D27
CC
D8

**CC** € **18** 6/4-15/6  10/9-30/10

🗺 N 43°54'41'' E 15°29'59''

## Podaca, HR-21335 / Dalmatija

♿ 📶 iD (1173)

▲ Camping Uvala Borova***
✉ Lucica 23
☎ +385 21 62 91 11
🔑 1/4 - 30/9
@ camp.uvala.borova@gmail.com

2ha 93T(40-80m²) 16A CEE

**1** ACD**G**IJKLMO
**2** BEFGJKNOTWXY
**3** R**W**Y
**4** (Q+R 15/6-15/9)
   (U+V 1/5-15/9)
   (X+Z 1/5-30/9)
**5** **A**GIJKMNOPUWX
**6** EGI**K**(N 1km)TVX

💬 A friendly terraced campsite by the sea with views of the setting sun. Shaded pitches. Peaceful, child-friendly and clean. Free wifi on the site. Trips out in the surrounding area possible (Dubrovnik, Korcula, Hvar, Medugorje). Restaurant and supermarket. Plenty of watersports opportunities.

🚗 Follow coast road. Turn right after Podaca campsite signs. Campsite clearly signposted.

A1 E65 D62
D512
D8
CC Gradac
**Ploce**

CC € **18** 1/4-29/6 1/9-29/9

📷 N 43°07'52'' E 17°17'16''

---

## Povljana, HR-23249 / Zadar

📶 iD (1174)

▲ Camp Porat***
✉ Put Hrscice 2a
☎ +385 23 69 29 95
🔑 23/4 - 30/9
@ info@camp-porat.com

1,6ha 100T(80-100m²) 16A

**1** ABCD**G**IJKLMO**P**ST
**2** AENPRTVWX
**3** AJ**W**Y
**4** (Q+S+T 📷) (Y 20/5-25/9)
   (Z 📷)
**5** **A**EGIJKLMNOPUWXZ
**6** EGK(N 2km)T

💬 Camp Porat is located in the main centre of the town of Povljana. Surrounded by pine forests the campsite spreads on 16000 m². The nearest grocery store can be reached within 50 metres, as well as restaurants serving international and local cuisine and an ATM.

🚗 A1 exit 16 Posedarje dir. Pag. Left after 30 km to Povljana (6 km). Campsite signposted. From Rijeka via coast road take ferry in Prizna to Zigljen. Past Pag village 7 km on right, road 108 to Povljana.

Pag
8
Baric Draga
CC
Vir

CC € **14** 23/4-30/6 26/8-29/9

📷 N 44°20'58'' E 15°06'19''

---

## Premantura, HR-52205 / Istra

📶 iD (1175)

▲ Camping Arena Runke
☎ +385 52 57 50 22
🔑 19/4 - 29/9
@ arenarunke@
   arenacampsites.com

4,5ha 247T(60-120m²) 10A

**1** ABCD**G**IJKLMO**P**
**2** EGIJKORTWXY
**3** M**W**Y
**4** (Q+R+Y 1/5-18/9)
   (Z 1/7-18/9)
**5** **AB**CEHIKMNOPUVW
**6** EGK(N 1km)T

💬 Camping Runke, with its beautiful views of Medulin Bay is located just a few steps away from the small and picturesque village of Premantura and 10 km from the historic centre of Pula. Plenty of shade with a number of terraced and fairly level pitches sloping down to the beach. There is a small bay for mooring small boats. CampingCard ACSI is not valid for the 'Seaside' zone.

🚗 Signposted from the ring road in Pula.

**Pula**
Medulin
CC

CC € **16** 19/4-15/6 13/9-29/9

📷 N 44°48'28'' E 13°55'00''

## Premantura, HR-52203 / Istra  📶 🆔 1176

🏕 Camping Arena Stupice**
✉ Selo 250
☎ +385 52 57 51 11
🗓 13/4 - 6/10
@ arenastupice@
   arenacampsites.com

26ha 920T(60-120m²) 10A

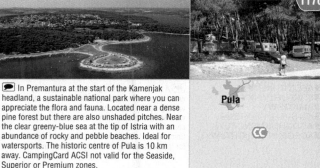

**1** ABCD**G**IJKLMO**P**ST
**2** BEGIKLNORTWXY
**3** AGKMN**W**Y
**4** (Q+S+T+U+V+Y 🖭)
**5** **AB**CFGHIJMOP**R**UVW
**6** ACEGK(N 0,5km)ORT

💬 In Premantura at the start of the Kamenjak headland, a sustainable national park where you can appreciate the flora and fauna. Located near a dense pine forest but there are also unshaded pitches. Near the clear greeny-blue sea at the tip of Istria with an abundance of rocky and pebble beaches. Ideal for watersports. The historic centre of Pula is 10 km away. CampingCard ACSI not valid for the Seaside, Superior or Premium zones.
🚐 Signposted from the ring road in Pula.

**Pula**

CC

CC € 18  13/4-15/6  14/9-6/10          📷 N 44°47'52" E 13°54'50"

---

## Premantura, HR-52100 / Istra 📶 🆔 1177

🏕 Camping Arena Tasalera*
✉ Premantura bb
☎ +385 52 57 55 55
🗓 19/4 - 29/9
@ arenatasalera@
   arenacampsites.com

4ha 100T(90-100m²) 10A

**1** ABCD**G**IJKLM**PQ**
**2** EIJKLORTVWXY
**3** AWY
**4** (Q+S+U+Y+Z 🖭)
**5** **A**CGIJMNOPVW
**6** EK(N 1km)T

💬 Partly level and open, partly sloping and wooded grounds. Right by the sea. Moderate toilet facilities. CampingCard ACSI is not valid for pitches in the 'seaside' zone. Mild climate in spring and autumn. Seawater still warm in September.

🚐 Follow Premantura signs from Pula ring road. Follow camping signs.

E751
**Pula**  Liznjan
CC

CC € 16  19/4-15/6  13/9-29/9          📷 N 44°48'52" E 13°54'42"

---

## Primosten, HR-22000 / Sibenik ♿ 📶 🆔 1178

🏕 Camp Adriatic Cat.1
✉ Huljerat 1a
☎ +385 22 57 12 23
🗓 15/3 - 31/10
@ camp-adriatiq@adriatiq.com

12ha 512T(80-140m²) 10A CEE

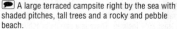

**1** ACD**G**IJKLMOPT
**2** EGIJNOQTVXY
**3** ABCGJ**M**NR**W**Y
**4** (Q+S 1/5-15/10)
   (T+U+V 1/5-30/9)
   (X+Y+Z 🖭)
**5** **AB**EFGIJKLMNOPUWXY
**6** CEGHK(N 2km)QTUV

💬 A large terraced campsite right by the sea with shaded pitches, tall trees and a rocky and pebble beach.

🚐 On the coastal road D8, 20 km south of Sibenik, before Primosten to the right of road. Clearly signposted.

E65
Brodarica Zaboric D58
D8
CC

CC € 18  15/3-29/6  7/9-31/10          📷 N 43°36'23" E 15°55'15"

**Pula,** HR-52100 / Istra ♿ 🛜 📱iD **1179**

🏕 Camping Arena Stoja***
📧 Stoja 37
☎ +385 52 38 71 44
🔓 13/4 - 6/10
@ arenastoja@arenacampsites.com

16,7ha 718T(60-144m²) 10A

**1** ABCD**G**IJKLM**P**ST
**2** EGKLORTVWXY
**3** A**MNQRW**Y
**4** (Q+S+T+U+V+Y+Z 🔓)
**5** A CDGHIJK**L**MNOPUW
**6** ACEGIK(N 3km)QRTVWX

💬 A family campsite right by the sea, partly wooded, partly on open ground with toilet blocks of varying quality. Mostly level ground. 3 km from Pula, with Roman amphitheatre, temples, early Christian churches, castle, daily Mediterranean market. CampingCard ACSI is valid in zones 500 and 600, not for the Seaside, Superior and Premium zones.

🚗 Signposted from the Pula ring road.

CC €**18** 13/4-15/6 14/9-6/10 📍 N 44°51'34'' E 13°48'52''

---

**Punat (Krk),** HR-51521 / Primorje-Gorski Kotar ♿ 🛜 📱iD **1180**

🏕 Camping Pila***
📧 Setaliste i. Brusica 2
☎ +385 51 85 40 20
🔓 20/4 - 30/9
@ camp.pila@falkensteiner.com

11ha 600T(80-100m²) 10A CEE

**1** ABCD**G**IJKLMOPST
**2** EGIKOPRTVX
**3** BN**W**Y
**4** (Q+S+T+U+Y+Z 🔓)
**5** A**B**EFGIJKLMNOPUWXZ
**6** ACFGKM(N 0,3km)QRTV

💬 Campsite situated on the Adriatic Sea and located in the beautiful Punat Bay with its lovely harbour. Part of the campsite is set in the shade of pine trees. Beyond August you can swim in water heated by the radiant sun. You can appreciate the local festivals in the village of Punat within walking distance.

🚗 When approaching from Krk, drive past Punat in the direction of Stara Baska. The campsite is the first one located on the right. Turn right at supermarket.

CC €**18** 20/4-30/6 1/9-30/9 📍 N 45°00'58'' E 14°37'44''

---

**Punat (Krk),** HR-51521 / Primorje-Gorski Kotar ♿ 🛜 📱iD **1181**

🏕 Naturist Camp Konobe***
☎ +385 51 85 40 36
🔓 19/4 - 30/9
@ camp.konobe@falkensteiner.com

20ha 330T(60-100m²) 10A CEE

**1** ABCD**G**IJKLOPST
**2** EIJKNOQRTVWX
**3** **M**NQR**W**Y
**4** (Q+R 🔓) (T+U 1/5-15/9) (Y 1/5-30/9) (Z 1/6-30/9)
**5** A**B**FGIJKLMNOPUVW
**6** ACDEGKM(N 1km)QRT

💬 Next to level grounds (on the left) this is a terraced site with significant differences in height (at least 20% incline). There is a pebble beach in the flat part. Lovely sea views. Very peaceful campsite, situated in the beautiful Konobe bay. The natural environment is maintained.

🚗 When approaching from Krk, drive past Punat in the direction of Stara Baska. The campsite is located to the right after about 3 km.

CC €**18** 19/4-30/6 1/9-29/9 📍 N 44°59'29'' E 14°37'50''

## Rab, HR-51280 / Primorje-Gorski Kotar

🛇 🤝 **iD** (1182)

🔺 Padova Premium
Camping Resort***
🏠 Banjol 496
☎ +385 51 72 43 55
🔑 18/4 - 15/10
@ padova3@imperial.hr

7ha 336T(80-100m²) 16A CEE

**1** ABCD**G**IJKLMOPQ
**2** AEIJKNRTVWX
**3** BCR**W**Y
**4** (Q+S+T+U+V+Y+Z 🔒)
**5** **AB**EFGIJKLMNOPUVWXY
**6** ACFG**I**KM(N 2km)OQRTUV

💬 Medium-sized long-stay campsite within walking distance of the town of Rab (20 min). Slightly sloping grounds. Beach: small pebbles leading into sand. The pitches are separated by hedges and trees which provide shade. Many amenities are available, such as fitness, restaurant, baker and supermarket.

🚗 Drive in the direction of Rab, exit Lopar, take the first road to the left (sharp bend). The campsite is signposted to the right after about 500 metres.

**Rab** D8
**CC** Stinica

**CC** € **18** 18/4-30/5 2/6-7/6 10/6-14/6 8/9-6/10 🏕 N 44°45'10'' E 14°46'27''

---

## Rabac, HR-52221 / Istra

👫 🛇 🤝 **iD** (1183)

🔺 Camping Autocamp Oliva***
🏠 Rabac bb
☎ +385 52 87 22 58
🔑 20/4 - 5/10
@ olivakamp@maslinica-rabac.com

5,5ha 480T(70-100m²) 6A CEE

**1** ABCD**G**IJKLMO**P**Q
**2** ENRVX
**3** BG**M**NQRVW**Y**
**4** (B+G 🔒) **JLNP**(Q+R+S 🔒)
(U 1/5-1/10) (V 1/5-30/9)
(Y 🔒) (Z 1/5-30/9)
**5** **AB**FGIJKLMNOPUVW
**6** CFG**K**(N 1km)RT

💬 Campsite with many olive trees, situated on a beautiful bay with a pebble beach. Many options for water sports, swimming, diving and snorkeling. Centre of Rabac is only a few minutes on foot, via the boulevard. Bringing your own boat is permitted.

🚗 From Labin drive towards Rabac. At the end of the slope turn right. The road to the campsite goes behind the hotels.

Blaskovici D64
**Labin**
**CC**
D66

**CC** € **20** 20/4-21/6 24/8-5/10 🏕 N 45°04'51'' E 14°08'45''

---

## Rovinj, HR-52210 / Istra

🛇 🤝 **iD** (1184)

🔺 Camping Amarin***
🏠 Monsena bb
☎ +385 52 80 21 00
🔑 19/4 - 29/9
@ ac-amarin@maistra.hr

12,5ha 650T(80-120m²) 16A CEE

**1** ABCD**G**IJKLMOPQ
**2** EGILNOPQRTVX
**3** AG**K**M**N**QRUWY
**4** (B+G 🔒) (Q 1/6-15/9) (S 🔒)
(T 18/5-20/9) (U 1/7-31/8)
(V 18/5-20/9) (W+Y+Z 🔒)
**5** **AB**GIJKLMNOPUVW
**6** ACEGJM(N 4km)QRTUVX

💬 Amarin campsite is located just north of Rovinj and has lovely views of the town. It is a real family campsite with a swimming pool. There are plenty of sports activities and children's playgrounds. Toilet facilities are mostly outdated but clean.

🚗 The campsite is located 3.5 km north of Rovinj, signposted.

Vrsar A9
**CC**
**Rovinj**

**CC** € **16** 19/4-8/6 25/8-29/9 🏕 N 45°06'32'' E 13°37'11''

**Rovinj,** HR-52210 / Istra ⬡ ♿ 📶 **iD** **1185**

🏕 Camping Polari***
🏠 Polari 1
☎ +385 52 80 15 01
📅 19/4 - 29/9
@ polari@maistra.hr

60ha 1496**T**(80-120m²) 10A CEE

**1** ABCD**G**IJKLMOPQ
**2** EGIJLNOPQRTVWXY
**3** ABGJK**M**N**Q**RWY
**4** (B+G 20/5-20/9) M(Q+S 🔑)
  (T+U 1/5-26/9) (V+X 🔑)
  (Y 1/5-26/9) (Z 🔑)
**5** **AB**EFGIJKLMNOP**S**UWXY
**6** ACEGHIKM(N 2,5km)QR
  TVX

💬 The expansive Polari campsite is located close to the beautiful town of Rovinj. The grounds have a lovely swimming pool with water playground (open from 20 May) and good toilet facilities. CampingCard guests are entitled to a standard pitch. A small part of the campsite is reserved for naturists.

🚗 3 km south of Rovinj, follow the camping signs.

**Rovinj**  CC   Bale

CC € **18**  19/4-8/6  25/8-29/9   📍 N 45°03'46''  E 13°40'30''

---

**Rovinj,** HR-52210 / Istra ♿ 📶 **iD** **1186**

🏕 Camping Veštar****
🏠 Veštar 1
☎ +385 52 80 37 00
📅 19/4 - 29/9
@ vestar@maistra.hr

15ha 458**T**(60-120m²) 16A CEE

**1** ABCD**G**IJKLMOPQ
**2** EIKLNOQRTUVWX
**3** AJKNRWY
**4** (B+G 15/5-15/9) M
  (Q 1/5-28/9) (S 1/5-25/9)
  (T 15/6-31/8)
  (U+V 15/5-15/9) (X+Y+Z 🔑)
**5** **AB**EFGIJKLMNOP**S**UWXY
**6** ACEGHKM(N 5km)RTV

💬 Quiet, well-maintained campsite. Lovely pebble beach and meadow. Toilet facilities are excellent and clean. The campsite has a pleasant sweet water pool with water playground.

🚗 From Rovinj, drive in the direction of Pula. Turn right after about 4 km and follow the signs.

E751
**Rovinj**  CC  Bale  A9

CC € **20**  19/4-8/6  1/9-29/9   📍 N 45°03'15''  E 13°41'11''

---

**Seget Donji/Trogir,** HR-21218 / Dalmatija 📶 **iD** **1187**

🏕 Kamp Seget
🏠 Hrvatskih zrtava 121
☎ +385 21 88 03 94
📅 1/4 - 20/10
@ booking@kamp-seget.hr

1,5ha 75**T**(80-100m²) 16A CEE

**1** ACD**G**IJKLMPT
**2** EGIJKNORWX
**3** **W**Y
**4** (Q+R 15/5-1/10)
  (X 15/5-15/9)
**5** **A**GIJKLMNOPUW
**6** FG**I**K(N 2km)QTV

💬 Small campsite directly on the seaside, 2 km from Trogir by shuttle boat and 25 km from Split. New toilet block, small shop, lovely pebble beach and traditional Dalmatian restaurant, helpful staff. CampingCard ACSI not valid on front part of campsite by sea.

🚗 On the D8, in Seget Donji, take the old coastal road to the right. Campsite is signposted. 2 km before Trogir.

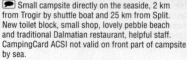

E71 A1
**Kastel Stari**
Marina  D8  CC

CC € **18**  1/4-29/6  1/9-20/10   📍 N 43°31'08''  E 16°13'27''

## Seget Vranjica/Trogir, HR-21218 / Dalmatija

&#9650; Camping Belvedere****
&#9993; Kralja Zvonimira 62
&#9743; +385 21 79 82 22
&#9875; 18/4 - 18/10
@ info@vranjica-belvedere.hr

15ha 381T(80-100m²) 16A

**1** ACD**G**IJKLMO**P**T
**2** EGIJKNOSTVWXY
**3** B**M**R**W**Y
**4** (B+G+Q+S+T+U+V+X+Y +Z &#9992;)
**5** **AB**EFGIJKMNOP**R**UWXYZ
**6** AEGKM(N 4km)QRTV

&#128488; Large terraced campsite with views of the sea and islands. Plenty of shaded pitches and beautiful new pool, bordered by palm trees and a beautiful flower garden.

&#128663; From the motorway E65 take exit 24 direction Trogir. 5 km west of Trogir on the coastal road D8; the road from Sibenik to Split.

Kastela
Trogir
D8 CC

CC € 20 18/4-25/6 1/9-17/10

N 43°30'42'' E 16°11'38''

---

## Sibenik, HR-22000 / Sibenik

&#9650; Camping Resort Solaris****
&#9743; +385 22 36 10 17
&#9875; 18/4 - 18/10
@ camping@solaris.hr

50ha 650T(70-100m²) 6A

**1** ACD**G**IJKLMO**P**ST
**2** EGNOTUVWXY
**3** AG**MN**WY
**4** (B+**F**+G+Q+S+T+U+V+X +Y+Z &#9992;)
**5** **AB**EFGIJKLMNOP**Q**UWXY
**6** ABDFG**I**JM(N 5km)OQRTV

&#128488; Large campsite by the sea with a shingle and concrete beach. Plenty of shade. The campsite offers every comfort. There is water recreation and a swimming pool for young and old. Campsite is part of resort with many amenities.

&#128663; On D8 coastal road from Šibenik-Split, campsite is located 5 km south of Šibenik.

D27 D33
Vodice
Šibenik A1
CC D58
Grebastica
D8

CC € 20 18/4-25/6 1/9-17/10

N 43°41'57'' E 15°52'46''

---

## Stara Baska/Punat (Krk), HR-51521 / Primorje-Gorski Kotar

&#9650; Skrila Sunny Camping***
&#9993; Stara Baska 300
&#9743; +385 51 84 46 78
&#9875; 19/4 - 29/9
@ skrila@valamar.com

5,5ha 291T(70-100m²) 10A CEE

**1** ABCD**G**IJKLMOPST
**2** AEGIJKNQTUVWXY
**3** BHR**W**Y
**4** (Q+R+T+U+V+Y+Z &#9992;)
**5** **AB**FGIJKLMNOPUWXZ
**6** ACDEGKM(N 9km)QRT

&#128488; A terraced campsite close to Stara Baska. Attractive features of the campsite are the beautiful beaches; fine shingle beaches mingling with rock formations. Part of the beach is reserved for naturists. The surrounding countryside is untouched and quite rugged. Good toilet facilities and refurbished restaurant and supermarket.

&#128663; Coming from Krk, drive past Punat towards Stara Baska. Campsite about 9 km on the right. (Last section is 12%).

Krk
Baska
CC

CC € 18 19/4-30/5 2/6-7/6 10/6-14/6 6/9-29/9

N 44°58'00'' E 14°40'26''

479

## Starigrad/Paklenica, HR-23244 / Zadar

🛖 Bluesun Camp Paklenica****
✉ Dr. Franje Tudmana 14
☎ +385 23 20 90 66
🗓 15/4 - 30/10
@ zrinka.katic@bluesunhotels.com

2,5ha 150T(35-80m²) 16A

**1** ABCD**G**IJKLMO**P**
**2** EFGLNOPRTVWXY
**3** ABHJRY
**4** (B+G+Q+S+Y+Z ⊙)
**5** **A**EFGIJKLMNOP**RS**UW XYZ
**6** EGKM(N 0,1km)RTV

💬 By the sea on level grounds and mostly under trees. Close to the village. Camp shop, pool and renovated toilets. Well situated for visits to the Starigrad-Paklenica Nature Park and to Zadar. Entrance near hotel Blue Sun.

🚗 In Starigrad-Paklenica 45 km south of Karlobag on the M2/E27. The campsite is near Hotel Blue Sun. Or via the motorway A1 Karlovac-Split, before exit in Maslenica direction Rijeka. Then follow M2/E27 (coast road) to Starigrad, signposted.

ⒸⒸ €**18** 15/4-30/6 1/9-29/10    🧭 N 44°17'14'' E 15°26'51''

**1191**

---

## Starigrad/Paklenica, HR-23244 / Zadar

🛖 Camping Plantaza***
✉ Put Plantaze 2
☎ +385 23 36 91 31
🗓 1/1 - 31/12
@ plantaza@hi.t-com.hr

1,5ha 100T 16A

**1** ABCD**G**IJKLMO**P**Q
**2** EGINOPTWXY
**3** HJ**WY**
**4** (Q 15/5-30/9) (V 1/4-31/10) (Y 1/4-30/10) (Z 1/4-31/10)
**5** **AB**DEGIJKLMNOP**S**UWZ
**6** EGKM(N 0,5km)V

💬 Situated in the shade of the Mediterranean vegetation directly on the sea coast. Pebble beach, clear sea, immediate vicinity of the Paklenica National Park provides a genuine pleasure and rest far from the modern life.

🚗 From Rijeka follow M2/E27 coast road until 1km north of Starigrad-Paklenica. Signposted. Or via A1 Karlovac-Split, turn off in Maslenica before Zadar towards Rijeka. Then follow M2/E27 (coast road) till past Starigrad. Signposted.

ⒸⒸ €**18** 1/1-30/6 1/9-31/12    🧭 N 44°18'02'' E 15°25'55''

**1192**

---

## Stobrec, HR-21311 / Dalmatija

🛖 Camping Stobrec Split****
✉ Sv. Lovre 6
☎ +385 21 32 54 26
🗓 1/1 - 31/12
@ camping.split@gmail.com

5ha 330T(70-110m²) 16A CEE

**1** ACD**G**IJKLMO**P**ST
**2** EGKNQRSVWY
**3** B**E**RWY
**4** (**B**+**G** 1/5-30/9) (Q+R+S+U+V+X+Y+Z ⊙)
**5** **AB**EFGIJKLMNO**P**UWXYZ
**6** EGIKM(N 3km)ORTVX

💬 Family campsite with both shaded and sunny pitches. Close to a beautiful pebble beach. Good toilet facilities. Located 5 km from Split.

🚗 Turn right 5 km south of Split at the Stobrec sign. Campsite on the left 100 metres further on (from motorway E65 exit 25 direction Split).

ⒸⒸ €**18** 1/1-30/6 1/9-31/12    🧭 N 43°30'15'' E 16°31'34''

**1193**

## Tar, HR-52465 / Istra

♿ 📶 **iD** (1194)

🏕 Lanterna Premium Camping Resort****
📧 Lanterna 1
☎ +385 52 46 50 10
📅 19/4 - 29/9
@ reservations@valamar.com

83ha 1456T(70-120m²) 16A CEE

1 ABCD**G**IJKLMOPQ
2 AEGIJKLNOPQRTUVWXY
3 ABGJK**MNOPQR**S**UY
4 (B+G 1/5-30/9) JKM (Q+S+T+U+V+X+Y+Z 🔋)
5 **AB**EFGIJKLMNOPRUVWXY
6 BCDFGHJLM(N 3km)OQRTVW

💬 Very large, well-equipped campsite, directly on the sea. Ideal for families with children. Many sports facilities and several restaurants on the site. There are several swimming pools, at two campsite locations. Several paddling pools, water slides etc. Specially constructed sandy beach.

🚗 In Istria from the motorway towards Pula, A9, take the exit Nova Vas. Then via Novigrad direction Porec. The campsite exit is signposted.

CC € **18** 19/4-3/6 1/9-29/9

N 45°17'50'' E 13°35'40''

---

## Tisno, HR-22240 / Sibenik

♿ 📶 **iD** (1195)

🏕 Olivia Camping Resort Dalmacija Tisno***
📧 Put Jazine 328
☎ +385 9 16 05 66 52
📅 1/4 - 30/11
@ info@dalmacija-tisno.com

24ha 100T(50-100m²) 16A CEE

1 ABCDGIJKLMOPST
2 EJKLNOPTUVWXY
3 AJ**WY**
4 (B 🔋) (Q 1/6-15/9) (X+Z 1/5-1/10)
5 **A**EFGIJKLMNOPUWZ
6 AEKM(N 1km)T

💬 A campsite with shaded pitches overlooking a beautiful bay. Bar and restaurant with lovely views of the sea and the beach. Tisno is within walking or cycling distance. The picturesque Murter headland with its many beaches and small villages is close by.

🚗 A1 Zagreb-Karlovac-Split, beyond Zadar take exit 20 Pirovac dir. Murter. Cross coast road 8 to the Murter headland. Right after 6.5 km before Tisno village. Before the entrance of Jazina campsite turn left on the gravel road.

CC € **20** 1/4-30/6 1/9-30/11

N 43°48'44'' E 15°37'23''

---

## Tribanj, HR-23244 / Zadar

📶 **iD** (1196)

🏕 Camping Sibuljina**
📧 Tribanj Sibuljina bb
☎ +385 23 65 80 04
📅 1/4 - 31/10
@ info@campsibuljina.com

2,4ha 100T 16A

1 ABCD**G**IJKLMO**P**ST
2 EGOPTWXY
3 AWY
4 (Q+S 🔋) (T+Y+Z 1/6-1/10)
5 **A**EGIJKLMNOPUWZ
6 EGK(N 9,9km)TV

💬 Renovated campsite under pine trees, on the coast. Not far from Starigrad-Paklenica and the nature reserve with the same name. A real paradise for hikers and mountain climbers. 2 euros supplement for the first row by the sea.

🚗 From Rijeka follow the M2/E27 coast road till 1 km north of Starigrad-Paklenica. Then signposted. Or A1 Karlovac-Split, turn off in Maslenica before Zadar towards Rijeka. Follow M2/E27 as far as Tribanj-Sibuljina.

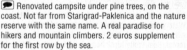

CC € **16** 1/4-30/6 1/9-30/10

N 44°20'16'' E 15°20'28''

## Umag, HR-52470 / Istra

♿ 📶 **iD** (1197)

🏕 Camping Stella Maris★★★★
🏠 Stella Maris 9a
☎ +385 52 71 09 00
📅 18/4 - 29/9
@ stella.maris@istracamping.com

5ha  443T(80-100m²)  10A CEE

**1** ABCD**G**IJKLMO**PQ**
**2** EILNOPQRSTVWXY
**3** BKL**MN**Q**R**WY
**4** (B+G 1/5-27/9)
   (Q+S+T+V+Y+Z 🔒)
**5** **AB**EGIJKLMNOPUWXY
**6** CEG**I**KLM(N 2km)QRSTV

NEW

💬 Its attractive location, modern outdoor swimming pools and sports grounds nearby make Camping Stella Maris an ideal destination for an active holiday, but it is also a nice, quiet place. The campsite was completely renovated in 2018, with a new restaurant and reception, improved and marked-out pitches and a large swimming pool complex.

🚗 From Umag, follow the signs to Stella Maris.

Piran  Izola
CC
Umag
E751
A9
D300
D75
D301

CC € 16  25/4-3/6  1/9-29/9    N 45°27'14'' E 13°31'17''

---

## Umag/Karigador, HR-52474 / Istra

♿ 📶 **iD** (1198)

🏕 Camping Park Umag★★★★
🏠 Ladin Gaj 132 A
☎ +385 52 71 37 40
📅 18/4 - 29/9
@ park.umag@istracamping.com

138ha  1719T(80-120m²)  10A CEE

**1** ABCD**G**IJKLMOPST
**2** EGKLNOPQRTVWXY
**3** ABKL**MN**Q**R**WY
**4** (B 1/5-30/9) (G 1/5-29/9)
   (Q+S 🔒) (T 1/6-29/9)
   (V+Y+Z 🔒)
**5** **AB**EFGIJKLMNOPRUWXY
**6** ACEGHIKM(N 5km)QRS
   TUV

💬 CampingIN Park Umag is one of the largest and best-equipped Mediterranean campsites. The campsite is an ideal destination for the entire family, offering something for everyone, from entertainment and activities to food and shopping. The campsite offers top-quality camping infrastructure and services, beautiful beaches, greenery and walking paths.

🚗 From Umag direction Novigrad. Campsite located 8 km further on, on the coastal side.

Umag
E751
A9
D300
D75
CC
D301
Novigrad

CC € 18  25/4-3/6  1/9-29/9    N 45°22'02'' E 13°32'50''

---

## Vabriga, HR-52465 / Istra

🚻 ♿ 📶 **iD** (1199)

🏕 Camping Santa Marina★★★★★
🏠 Santa Marina 12
☎ +385 52 44 44 11
📅 15/4 - 15/10
@ info@santamarina-camping.com

4,5ha  81T(100-110m²)  16A CEE

**1** ABCD**G**IJKLMPQ
**2** TUVWX
**3** AKLR
**4** (B+G+Q+R+V+Y+Z 🔒)
**5** **AB**EFGIJKLMNOPRSUWX
**6** CEGIKLM(N 1,5km)QRSTV

NEW

💬 An idyllic spot for a perfect family holiday. Spacious shaded pitches with modern toilet facilities. Watery fun is guaranteed in the large swimming pool with water park that is perfect for children. Free bike rental. Beautifully furnished à la carte restaurant, with traditional specialities.

🚗 In Istria from motorway direction Pula, A9, exit Nova Vas. Then via Novigrad towards Porec. Take exit Vabriga and follow signs to campsite.

D75  D301  D44
E751
Novigrad  A9
CC
Porec
D302

CC € 20  15/4-30/6  1/9-15/10    N 45°17'19'' E 13°36'31''

## Vrsar, HR-52450 / Istra

♿ 🛜 ✿ iD **1200**

🔺 Camping Porto Sole***
☎ +385 52 42 65 00
🔓 1/1 - 31/12
@ portosole@maistra.hr

17ha 712T(100m²) 10A CEE

1. ABCD**G**IJKLM**P**ST
2. EIJKLNOPQRTVWXY
3. ABGJK**M**N**Q**RWY
4. (B+G 15/5-30/9) (Q 🔓)
   (S 1/5-30/9) (T 🔓)
   (V+Y 1/5-30/9) (Z 🔓)
5. **AB**DEFGIJKLMNOPUW
   XYZ
6. ACEGIKM(N 1km)RTV

💬 A medium sized family campsite within walking distance of the village. It has a lovely swimming pool. Part of the site is laid out in terraces. The other part is level and offers reasonable shade.

🚗 The campsite is located 1 km south of Vrsar in the direction of Koversada.

Porec

A9
E751

CC

Rovinj

CC € 18 1/1-8/6 25/8-31/12

📷 N 45°08'30'' E 13°36'08''

---

## Zaostrog, HR-21334 / Dalmatija

♿ 🛜 iD **1201**

🔺 Camping Viter
📧 A.K. Miosica 1
☎ +385 98 70 40 18
🔓 1/4 - 1/11
@ info@camp-viter.com

1,3ha 100T 10A CEE

1. A**G**IJKLOPST
2. EFGNOTWXY
3. **W**Y
5. **AB**EGIJMNOPUW
6. EGI**K**(N 0,1km)T

💬 Auto Camp Viter is a family and friendly campsite situated in Zaostrog directly on the shores of a beach on the Adriatic sea. It is located between Split and Dubrovnik. And also very close to the ferry (3 km) that connects us with the islands Hvar, Korcula and Brac. There is a one hour long drive to Mostar.

🚗 Follow Viter signs 600m on the right after the Zaostrog sign.

Vrgorac

A1
D512  E65  D62

Sucuraj

CC  D8

Ploce

CC € 18 1/4-30/6 1/9-14/10

📷 N 43°08'21'' E 17°16'50''

---

## Zaton/Nin (Zadar), HR-23232 / Zadar

🛜 iD **1202**

🔺 Autocamp Peros
📧 Put Petra Zoranica 20
☎ +385 23 26 58 30
🔓 1/3 - 30/11
@ info@autocamp-peros.hr

2ha 60T(60-100m²) 16A CEE

1. ABCD**G**IJKLMO**P**ST
2. AELNTUVWXY
3. AJ**W**Y
4. (B+G 1/5-1/10) (V 1/6-20/9)
   (Z 🔓)
5. **A**GIJKLMNOPUWXYZ
6. ABEGK(N 2km)

💬 Campsite with pool and pitches on gravel and trees with shade. Neat toilet facilities, bar, pizzeria, at 300 metres from the beach. Friendly owners. Good alternative for people looking for a small, quiet and comfortable campsite.

🚗 Best route via motorway A1 Karlovac-Split. Before Zadar exit in Nin. In Nin dir. Zadar. Just outside village right after 2 km. Right before main entrance Zaton campsite. Signposted.

Vir  Razanac

CC

Murvica

Zadar  D8

CC € 18 1/3-10/7 1/9-29/11

📷 N 44°13'48'' E 15°10'20''

## Zaton/Nin (Zadar), HR-23232 / Zadar

🚹 🛜 ✿ **iD** (1203)

🏔 Camping Zaton Holiday Resort★★★★
✉ Draznikova 76t
☎ +385 23 28 02 15
🕐 20/4 - 5/10
@ camping@zaton.hr

100ha 1000T(80-120m²) 16A CEE

**1** ABCD**G**IJKLMO**P**
**2** AELNTVWXY
**3** B**G**JKM**N**OPQRVW**Y**
**4** (C+H 🕐) IM**P**
  (Q+S+T+V+X+Y+Z 🕐)
**5** **AB**EFGIJKLMNOP**R**UW XYZ
**6** CDFGHKM(N 1km)OQRTV

💬 A large, well-equipped luxury campsite by a sand and pebble beach with all types of accommodation. Forms part of a holiday centre. Good base for trips out to Nin and the old centre of Zadar and many old fishing villages (towards the south). CampingCard ACSI valid for zones B and C. Euro2 supplement for zone A.

🚗 Recommended route via motorway A1 Zagreb-Zadar, before Zadar exit Nin/Zadar Zapat. In Nin left dir. Zadar. Signposted on right after 2 km.

Vir — Razanac
Privlaka — Nin
CC
Zadar
D8

**CC** € **20** 20/4-14/6 7/9-5/10 📍 N 44°13'41" E 15°10'09"

# Greece

## General
Greece is a member of the EU.

### Time
The time in Greece is one hour ahead of Amsterdam, Paris and Rome and two hours ahead of London.

### Languages
Greek, but English and German are well understood.

## Border formalities
Many formalities and agreements about matters such as necessary travel documents, car papers, requirements relating to your means of transport and accommodation, medical expenses and taking pets with you do not only depend on the country you are travelling to but also on your departure point and nationality. The length of your stay can also play a role here. It is not possible within the confines of this guide to guarantee the correct and most up to date information with regard to these matters.

We advise you to consult the relevant authorities before your departure about:
- which travel documents you will need for yourself and your fellow passengers
- which documents you need for your car
- which regulations your caravan must meet
- which goods you may import and export
- how medical treatment will be arranged and paid for in your holiday destination in cases of accident or illness
- whether you can take pets. Contact your vets well in advance. They can give you

information about the necessary vaccinations, proof thereof and obligations on return. It would also make sense to enquire whether any special regulations apply to your pet in public places at your holiday destination. In some countries for example dogs must always be muzzled or transported in a cage.

You will find plenty of general information on ▶ *www.europa.eu* ◀ but make certain you select information that is relevant to your specific situation.

For the most recent customs regulations you should get in contact with the authorities of your holiday destination in your country of residence.

## Currency
The currency in Greece is the euro. Approximate exchange rates September 2018: £1 = € 1.12. Take note: some cash machines issue the money before returning your card.

### Credit cards
You can pay by credit card in larger hotels, restaurants, shopping chains and car rental companies. You are advised to take sufficient cash with you.

## Opening times
### Banks
Banks are mostly open on weekdays until 14:00. A number of banks in larger towns and tourist areas are open in the evening and on Saturdays.

### Shops

Shops in Greece have different opening times in winter and summer. In winter the opening times are Monday and Wednesday until 16:30, Tuesday, Thursday and Friday until 14:00 and from 17:00 till 20:00 in the evening. Saturday until 15:00. In summer shops open Monday, Wednesday and Saturday until 14:00, Tuesday, Thursday and Friday until 14:00 and from 17:30 to 20:30 in the evening.

### Chemists

The price of medication is considerably lower than in the UK. Be aware that specialist medical help on the Greek islands is limited. Chemists are open until 14:00. Chemists in larger towns may also be open between 17:30 and 22:00.

## Communication

### (Mobile) phones

The mobile network works well throughout Greece. There is a 4G network for mobile internet.

### Wifi, internet

You can make use of a wifi network at more and more public locations, often for free.

### Post

Greek post offices are called 'tachydromeia'. They are open on weekdays until 19:00 and in rural areas until 14:00.

## Roads and traffic

### Road network

Greek drivers do not always adhere to driving rules! The road system is limited on Greek islands, with the exception of Crete. Driving after dark is not advised outside the towns. If you have breakdown insurance you can call the Greek automobile club (ELPA) for assistance on 10400.

### Traffic regulations

Remember, all traffic in Greece drives on the right and overtakes on the left! Headlight deflectors are advisable to prevent annoying oncoming drivers.

Greece uses the metric system, so distances are measured in kilometres (km) and speeds in kilometres per hour (km/h). Traffic from the right has priority in built-up areas; outside these areas traffic on main roads has priority. Ascending traffic always has priority over descending traffic.

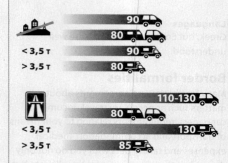

*Maximum speed*

Maximum permitted alcohol level is 0.5‰. The use of dipped headlights during the day is not compulsory. Drivers may only use a phone hands-free. Seatbelts are only mandatory in the front seats. If a child under 12 years is travelling in your car you are not allowed to smoke. Your car does not need to have winter tyres.

### Caravans, motorhomes

Bear in mind that on the Greek islands suitable facilities for caravans and motorhomes are limited. If travelling with a car and caravan you must pay double tolls on motorways. The toll for a motorhome is even higher than for a car and caravan.

### Maximum allowed measurements of combined length
Height 4 metres, width 2.55 metres and maximum length 18 metres (of which the trailer maximum 12 metres).

### Fuel
Lead-free petrol and diesel are readily available. LPG is readily available on the mainland.

### Filling stations
Filling stations in larger towns close at midnight; elsewhere they are usually open from 07:00 to 22:00.

### Tolls
You are required to pay a toll on certain Greek roads. You can only pay in cash, not by credit card.

### Emergency number
112: the national emergency number for fire, police and ambulance.

## Camping
Free camping is not permitted. Most campsites are of a very respectable standard. Toilet facilities are usually well maintained. You will find campsites with marked out pitches on the mainland and the Peloponnesos peninsula. Campsites on the Greek islands are geared mainly towards tent campers. Be aware that in early and late seasons most campsites on the coast are much quieter than in summer. It may occur that not all facilities are in use.

### Ferries
Take note that the number of places for motorhomes on car ferries is limited. If travelling from Italy to Greece in high season it is advisable to book well in advance. It is a good idea to book tickets for ferry services between the Greek islands one day in advance.

### Practical information
- Deep sea diving is possible in specially designated places. It is only permitted under the guidance of a diving instructor.
- Make sure you have a world adaptor for electrical appliances.
- You are advised to drink bottled (mineral) water in preference to mains water.

## Amaliada/Palouki, GR-27200 / Peloponnese

♿ 🛜 **iD** (1204)

🏕 Camping Palouki
☎ +30 26 22 02 49 42
📅 1/4 - 31/10
@ info@camping-palouki.gr

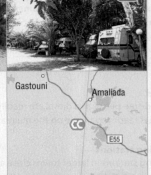

1,7ha 61T(45-80m²) 6A

**1** ACDGIJKLM**P**ST
**2** AEFGRVWXY
**3** RWY
**4** (Q+S 🔑) (Y+Z 1/5-15/10)
**5** **A**GIJKLMNOPUWX
**6** ACDEGIJ(N 6km)TV

💬 Beautifully landscaped campsite, right on the sea, with a large sandy beach. Ideal for families with (small) children.

🚐 Nat. Road Patras-Pirgos. Right at km post 80, at exit Palouki. Campsite 2 km on the left, clearly signposted.

Gastouni — Amaliada

CC — E55

**CC** € ⑳ 1/4-25/6  12/9-30/10    🗺 N 37°45'15'' E 21°18'22''

---

## Ancient Epidavros, GR-21059 / Peloponnese

♿ 🛜 **iD** (1205)

🏕 Camping Bekas
📧 Nikolaou Pitidi
☎ +30 2 75 30 99 93 01
📅 28/3 - 25/10
@ info@bekas.gr

2,1ha 100T(60-120m²) 16A

**1** ACGIJKLMPQ
**2** EINSTWXY
**3** KNUWY
**4** (Q+R 🔑) (Y 18/5-22/9)
**5** **A**FGIJKLMNOPUVZ
**6** ACEGK(N 2km)OVW

💬 Campsite located right by the sea with shaded pitches under high trees. Close to Mycene, Nafplion and the most well-preserved theatre from ancient Greece: Epidaurus. Restaurant and small supermarket on campsite.

🚐 Korinth, direction Epidavros. Take Ancient Epidavros, Kranidi, Portocheli, Galatas, Ermioni exit. Follow road and after ±150m left under the road and left again at small roundabout. Then follow campsite signs.

Nea Epidavros — Epidavros — CC

**CC** € ⑱ 28/3-30/6  1/9-25/10    🗺 N 37°37'07'' E 23°09'23''

---

## Ancient Epidavros, GR-21059 / Peloponnese

🛜 **iD** (1206)

🏕 Camping Nicolas I
☎ +30 27 53 04 12 97
📅 1/4 - 31/10
@ info@nicolasgikas.gr

1ha 90T(20-50m²) 16A

**1** ACGIJKLMPQ
**2** EJLMNOSTVXY
**3** UWY
**4** (Q 🔑) (R+T 15/5-30/9)
(Y 1/4-15/10) (Z 15/4-15/10)
**5** **A**GIJKLMNOPUWZ
**6** AEGK(N 1km)W

💬 Plenty of space for guests and excellent communal facilities, all this in a lavishly green location directly by the sea. Convenient location near some of the most interesting sights dating back to ancient times. Campsite has a meadow with sun loungers.

🚐 Korinth direction Epidavros. Take Ancient Epidavros, Kranidi, Portocheli, Galatas, Ermioni exit. Follow road and after ±150m left under the road and left again at small roundabout. Then follow camping signs.

Nea Epidavros — Epidavros — CC

**CC** € ⑱ 1/4-8/7  26/8-30/10    🗺 N 37°37'49'' E 23°09'26''

## Ancient Epidavros/Argolida, GR-21059 / Peloponnese

⌂ Camping Nicolas II
✉ Nikolaou Pitidi
☎ +30 27 53 04 14 45
⌚ 1/4 - 31/10
@ dimitrisgikas@gmail.com

1,2ha 90T(35-50m²) 16A

**1** AGIJKLMPQ
**2** EJNRSTXY
**3** UWY
**4** (Q ⌚) (R 1/5-30/9)
(Y+Z 15/4-31/10)
**5** **A**FGIJKLMNOPUWXZ
**6** ACEGK(N 3km)OW

💬 A peaceful campsite with a private beach (pebbles) and opportunities for water sports and fishing. With shaded pitches and a restaurant. Ideally situated for visiting Mycenae, Nafplion and Epidaurus theatre.

🚗 Korinth, direction Epidavros. Take Ancient Epidavros, Kranidi, Portocheli, Galatas, Ermioni exit. Follow road and after ±150m left under the road and left again at small roundabout. Then follow camping signs.

CC € 18  1/4-8/7  26/8-30/10

📷 N 37°36'58'' E 23°09'34''

---

## Dassia (Corfu), GR-49100 / Ionian Islands

⌂ Camping Karda Beach
✉ PB 225
☎ +30 26 61 09 35 95
⌚ 23/4 - 7/10
@ campco@otenet.gr

2,6ha 130T(60-120m²) 16A

**1** ACDGIJKLMOPQ
**2** EGLNORTVWXY
**3** ANRWY
**4** (B+G+Q+S+T+U+Y+Z 1/5-30/9)
**5** **A**GIJKLMNOPUVW
**6** EGI**J**(N 0,2km)OTVWX

💬 A luxurious campsite by the sea 12 km from Corfu town in natural surroundings. Marked out shaded pitches on level ground with attractive landscaping. The toilet facilities are extensive and well maintained. Lovely swimming pool with nearby bar and restaurant.

🚗 From Corfu harbour take main road to the right (direction Paleokastritsa). Turn right at the Dassia/Kassiopi sign after about 8.5 km. Campsite located 3.5 km further on the right. Entrance clearly signposted.

CC € 20  23/4-29/6  1/9-6/10

📷 N 39°41'10'' E 19°50'19''

---

## Delphi, GR-33054 / Central

⌂ Camping Apollon Cat.A
☎ +30 22 65 08 27 50
⌚ 1/1 - 31/12
@ apollon4@otenet.gr

2,5ha 120T(30-70m²) 16A

**1** ACDFIJKLM**P**Q
**2** GJKLSVXY
**3** AHKNR
**4** (**A** 1/5-31/8) (B 1/4-15/10)
(Q+R+U+Y+Z 1/5-1/10)
**5** **A**EGIJKLMNOPUWXZ
**6** CDEGI**K**(N 1,5km)OTV

💬 A very good campsite with all modern amenities. Within walking distance of Ancient Delphi. Unforgettable views of Itea bay from the swimming pool and from the restaurant with traditional Greek cuisine.

🚗 Campsite is the first on the Delphi-Itea road.

CC € 20  1/1-30/6  1/9-31/12

📷 N 38°29'02'' E 22°28'32''

## Delphi, GR-33054 / Central ♿ 🛜 iD 1210

🏕 Delphi Camping Cat.A
🚏 Delphi-Itea Road
☎ +30 22 65 08 27 45
🔓 1/4 - 31/10
@ info@delphicamping.com

2,2ha 100T(60-80m²) 10A

**1** ACDFIJKLMPST
**2** GJKLSTVXY
**3** AR
**4** (B 20/4-30/9) (Q+R+Y 🔓)
**5** AEGIJKLMNOPUWZ
**6** CEGIK(N 2km)OTV

💬 Delphi campsite is located on the slopes of the Parnassos, south of ancient Delphi which is 4 km from the campsite. Many archaeological sites are to be found on the road to Athens, 500m past the town of Delphi. The campsite has a terrace and restaurant with views of the Gulf of Corinth.

🚗 Located on the Itea-Delphi road 4 km before Delphi.

**Amfissa**     Arachova
E65    CC

CC €18 1/4-30/6 1/9-31/10          📷 N 38°28'42'' E 22°28'31''

---

## Delphi/Fokis, GR-33054 / Central 🛜 iD 1211

🏕 Chrissa Camping Cat.A
☎ +30 22 65 08 20 50
🔓 1/4 - 31/10
@ info@chrissacamping.gr

1,6ha 65T(80-100m²) 16A

**1** ACGIJKLMPT
**2** GIJKLSTXY
**3** A
**4** (A 🔓) (B+G 1/5-30/9) (Q+R+T 🔓) (U+Y 1/5-30/9)
**5** AGJLMNOPUWZ
**6** CEGIK(N 1km)OQTV

💬 This terraced campsite lies at the foot of the Parnassus mountain range and offers lovely views of the surrounding countryside. Excellent toilet facilities. All pitches have electricity and are shaded. Traditional Greek cuisine in the restaurant. Own organic garden.

🚗 The campsite is 7 km west of Delphi, on the Delphi-Itea road.

**Amfissa**     Arachova
E65    CC
Itea

CC €16 1/4-7/7 24/8-31/10 7=6, 14=11          📷 N 38°28'25'' E 22°27'30''

---

## Drepanon/Vivari, GR-21100 / Peloponnese 🛜 iD 1212

🏕 Camping Lefka Beach
☎ +30 27 52 09 23 34
🔓 1/1 - 31/12
@ info@camping-lefka.gr

1,3ha 68T(25-45m²) 16A

**1** ACGIJKLMP
**2** EIJNSTXY
**3** UWY
**4** (Q 1/5-30/10) (R 1/5-30/9) (T+Y+Z 1/5-30/10)
**5** ABGIJKLMNOPUZ
**6** ACEGJ(N 1km)V

💬 Lovely, agreeable, shaded terraced campsite on Lefka Bay. Beautiful views of the bay from every pitch. The camping pitches and taverna are accessible via a well-surfaced, downhill road. The first row of pitches by the sea are not available to CampingCard ACSI-holders. Visit the antiquities at Epidavros, Ancient Korinthe, Myecne, Argos and Nafplion.

🚗 Situated on the Nafplion-Drepanon-Iria road. About 1 km to the right after village of Vivari. Campsite signposted.

**Nafplio** Asini
CC

CC €18 1/1-30/6 1/9-31/12          📷 N 37°32'02'' E 22°55'54''

## Elafonisos, GR-23053 / Peloponnese

👪 ♿ 📶 **iD**  **1213**

🏔 Simos Camping
☎ +30 27 34 02 26 72
🔑 15/4 - 31/10
@ info@simoscamping.gr

**NEW**

6ha 190T(35-60m²) 16A

**1** ACDGIJKLMOP
**2** AEKUVWXY
**3** AJY
**4** (Q 🔌)
   (S+T+U+V+W+Z 15/5-20/9)
**5** **AB**GIJKLMNOPUWZ
**6** CGIJ(N 4km)TV

💬 Situated on beautiful sandy beach with dunes on idyllic island of Elafonisos, a protected nature reserve. The water is crystal clear blue/green in color. Special marked out pitches for tents and caravans/motorhomes with shade nets and trees. Good facilities and self-service restaurant.

🚐 Take E65 Korinth-Sparta. National road Sparta-Neapolis to Agios Georgios, then head for Pounta. In Pounta, take ferry to Elefonisos and follow campsite signs in direction Lefki.

Elafonisos    Neapoli

CC

**CC** €**18** 15/4-30/6 5/9-30/10    📡 N 36°28'38'' E 22°58'29''

---

## Finikounda, GR-24006 / Peloponnese

♿ 📶 **iD**  **1214**

🏔 Camping Thines
☎ +30 27 23 07 12 00
🔑 1/1 - 31/12
@ thines@otenet.gr

0,8ha 55T(49-56m²) 10A

**1** ACDGIJKLM**P**Q
**2** AEKTVXY
**3** WY
**4** (Q+R+T+U+X+Z 1/5-31/10)
**5** **A**FGIJKLMNOPUZ
**6** CEGIK(N 0,5km)TV

💬 Quiet family campsite with spotless toilet facilities. Situated next to the the wide sandy beach at Finikounda. Swimming, water sports (such as surfing) or taking in the sun. Delicious food in the restaurant, including homegrown regional produce.

🚐 National road Methoni-Koroni. Campsite is located 1 km west of Finikounda and is well signposted.

Pylos    Aipeia

CC    Vasilitsio

**CC** €**18** 1/4-30/6 1/9-31/10 13=12    📡 N 36°48'18'' E 21°47'43''

---

## Glifa, GR-27050 / Peloponnese

♿ 📶 ✿ **iD**  **1215**

🏔 Camping Ionion Beach
☎ +30 26 23 09 68 28
🔑 1/1 - 31/12
@ ionionfl@otenet.gr

3,8ha 210T(50-120m²) 16A

**1** ACDGHIJKLMOPQ
**2** AENRSTVXY
**3** ABNRWY
**4** (C+H 1/4-31/5,1/9-31/10) K
   (Q+R 1/4-30/10)
   (T+V 15/5-15/10)
   (Y 1/4-31/10) (Z 15/5-15/10)
**5** **AB**DEGIJKLMNOPU
**6** ACEGK(N 1km)OTV

💬 A luxurious flower-filled campsite with lovely pitches located on a sandy beach. The A and C pitches on the site right by the sea are not available to CampingCard ACSI-holders. Visit the mountains in the Ilia region. You can sail from Killini to the beautiful island of Zakynthos.

🚐 From national road Patras-Pirgos, turn right via Gastouni and Vartalomia at km post 67 direction Loutra Killini. Left at fork in road towards Glifa Beach. Follow signs.

E55
Gastouni
Vartholomio
CC

**CC** €**20** 1/1-30/6 11/9-31/12    📡 N 37°50'11'' E 21°08'01''

**Glifa/Ilias**, GR-27050 / Peloponnese    ♿ 🛜 ✿ **iD** **1216**

🔺 Camping Aginara Beach***
☎ +30 26 23 09 62 11
🕐 1/1 - 31/12
@ info@camping-aginara.gr

3,8ha 120T(70-100m²) 16A

**1** ACDGIJKLMPQ
**2** AENRSTVY
**3** AWY
**4** (Q+R 20/3-31/10)
  (T 1/5-31/10) (Y 1/4-31/10)
  (Z 1/5-31/10)
**5** **A**GIJKLMNOPQRU
**6** EGIK(N 1,5km)OTV

💬 A campsite located on one of the most beautiful sandy beaches of the Ionian Sea with spacious, idyllic and mostly shaded pitches. Good lively restaurant. Modern, well maintained toilet facilities. Various trees, bushes and abundant plants ensure a wonderful stay.

🚗 Nat. Road Patras-Pyrgos, turn right at 67 km post via Gastouni and Vartholomio. Dir. Loutra Killinis (signed). Direction Glifa Beach at fork in road Follow signs.

E55 Gastouni
Vartholomio
CC

**CC** € **18** 1/1-30/6 26/8-31/12    🏔 N 37°50'18'' E 21°07'47''

---

**Gythion/Lakonias**, GR-23200 / Peloponnese    ♿ 🛜 **iD** **1217**

🔺 Camping Gythion Bay***
🚏 Highway Gythion-Areopoli
☎ +30 27 33 02 25 22
🕐 1/4 - 31/10
@ info@gythiocamping.gr

4ha 300T(30-100m²) 16A

**1** ACDGIJKLMPQ
**2** AEGKLNRTWXY
**3** BJRWY
**4** (B+G 1/5-31/10)
  (Q+S+T+U+Y+Z 1/6-30/9)
**5** **A**FGIJKLMNOPUVW
**6** CDEGJ(N 0,1km)RTV

💬 You will always find a free, shaded pitch under the olive and orange trees. Totally renovated, modern toilet facilities. Located right by the sea with a lovely sandy beach. Also new swimming pool near the restaurant and bar.

🚗 The campsite is located 5 km outside Gythion on the left of the Gythion-Areopolis road, directly by the sea.

E961 Gytheio
CC
Oitylo
Pyrrichos

**CC** € **20** 1/4-30/6 1/9-30/10    🏔 N 36°43'45'' E 22°32'43''

---

**Gythion/Lakonias**, GR-23200 / Peloponnese    ♿ 🛜 **iD** **1218**

🔺 Camping Mani-Beach
🚏 Highway Gythion-Areopoli
☎ +30 27 33 02 34 51
🕐 1/1 - 31/12
@ info@manibeach.gr

2,8ha 238T(40-120m²) 16A

**1** ACDGIJKLMPQ
**2** AEGKNRTUVWXY
**3** **O**RWY
**4** (Q 🕐) (R+T+X+Z 1/5-31/10)
**5** **A**GIJKLMNOPUWZ
**6** CEGJ(N 0,2km)ORTV

💬 Large campsite on the coast with a wide sandy beach. Pitches in almost full shade. Ideal for all types of water sports, particularly windsurfing and kitesurfing.

🚗 The campsite is located about 4 km south of Gythion on the road to Areopolis, directly by the sea.

°Prosilio
E961 Gytheio
CC
Oitylo

**CC** € **18** 1/1-30/6 1/9-31/12    🏔 N 36°43'42'' E 22°32'32''

## Gythion/Lakonias, GR-23200 / Peloponnese    ♿ 🛜 **iD** (1219)

▲ Camping Meltemi
🛣 Highway Gythion-Areopoli
☎ +30 27 33 02 32 60
🔓 1/4 - 21/10
@ info@campingmeltemi.gr

3ha 180T(40-80m²) 16A CEE

**1** ACDGIJKLMPQ
**2** AEGKNRVXY
**3** BMNRWY
**4** (B 10/6-15/9) (Q 🔓)
  (R 15/5-15/9) (S 🔓)
  (T+U+W 15/5-15/9)
  (Z 1/6-10/9)
**5** **AB**EGIJKLMNOPUWZ
**6** CEGJ(N 0,5km)ORTV

💬 The hospitable Camping Meltemi is located in a beautiful olive grove. It has spacious pitches under the olive trees or in the shade of the pine trees on the beautiful and clean sandy beach. The sea and the beach are a protected area for the Caretta sea turtles. Adequate and well-maintained amenities. Close to the towers and Byzantine churches of Mani.

🚐 Campsite is about 3 km south of Gytheio on the left of the road to Areopoli.

E961
Gytheio
Mavrovouni
CC

CC € (20) 1/4-30/6 1/9-20/10     📷 N 36°43'51'' E 22°33'12''

---

## Igoumenitsa, GR-461 00 / Epirus    👫 ♿ 🛜 **iD** (1220)

▲ Camping Drepanos
🛣 Drepanos Beach
☎ +30 26 65 02 69 80
🔓 1/1 - 31/12
@ camping@drepano.gr

5ha 80T(30-100m²) 6-16A

**1** ACDGIJKLMOPST
**2** AEGKTWXY
**3** AJKWY
**4** (Q 🔓) (R 1/6-31/10)
  (U+Y+Z 1/5-30/10)
**5** **A**GIJKLMNOPUWZ
**6** GK(N 4km)TWX

💬 Campsite with a long, child-friendly sandy beach (free sun loungers) on a headland close to Igoumenitsa, next to an extensive nature reserve and bird sanctuary. The toilet facilities have been completely renewed, also for the disabled. Great restaurant and beach terrace. Many of the pitches are shaded under the trees. An ideal spot to relax, cycle or do watersports.

🚐 Take the coast road from Igoumenitsa northwards. After leaving the town follow Drepanos Beach signs.

Smertos
Igoumenitsa
CC
E90 E92
E55

CC € (18) 1/1-30/6 1/9-30/12     📷 N 39°30'37'' E 20°13'16''

---

## Iria/Argolis, GR-21060 / Peloponnese    🛜 **iD** (1221)

▲ Iria Beach Camping
🛣 Paralia Iria
☎ +30 27 52 09 42 53
🔓 1/1 - 31/12
@ iriabeach@naf.forthnet.gr

1,4ha 72T(40-100m²) 16A

**1** AGIJKLMO**P**RS
**2** AEGTXY
**3** AUWY
**4** (B+G 1/5-30/9) (Q 🔓)
  (R+T+Z 1/6-30/9)
**5** **AB**DEFGIJKLMNOPSUWZ
**6** ACEGJ(N 4km)OV

💬 A quietly situated campsite for a cultural or beach holiday. You can visit Epidaurus, Mycenae and Nafplio from the campsite. The lovely sandy beach offers various water sports. Swimming pool on the campsite. Vassilli and Diana Mitsopoulos offer you a warm welcome.

🚐 From Nafplion towards Drepanon, in Drepanon take the road towards Iria, before Iria take exit Iria Beach. After 1.5 km the campsite is left of the road.

Asini
Karnezaiika
CC

CC € (18) 1/1-5/7 25/8-31/12     📷 N 37°29'50'' E 22°59'26''

## Iria/Argolis, GR-21060 / Peloponnese 👫 ♿ 📶 iD ⑴⁲²²

- 🏕 Posidon Camping
- 🏖 Iria Beach
- ☎ +30 27 52 09 40 91
- 📅 30/3 - 31/10
- @ info@posidoncamping.gr

NEW

2ha 81**T**(30-70m²) 10A

1. ACDGJKLMNP
2. AESTXY
3. ARU**WY**
4. (Q+R+Z 📅)
5. **A**GIJKLMNOP**R**UWXZ
6. CEGK(N 4km)OV

💬 The campsite is situated in a quiet area directly by the sea. Trees provide shade on the beach. From the campsite you can visit various ancient sites including Mycenae, Epidavros and Nafplio.

🚗 Nafplio direction Drepanon, in Drepanon take direction Iria. Before Iria take exit Iria Beach, after 0.6 km the campsite is on right of road.

Lefkakia

CC Iria
Salantio

CC € ⑱ 30/3-30/6 1/9-30/10 7=6  📍 N 37°30'19'' E 22°59'14''

---

## Isthmia, GR-20100 / Peloponnese 👫 ♿ 📶 iD ⑴²²³

- 🏕 Isthmia Beach Camping
- ☎ +30 27 41 03 74 47
- 📅 1/4 - 30/10
- @ info@campingisthmia.gr

2,5ha 100**T**(40-50m²) 10A

1. ACGIJKLMO**P**
2. EFNORTVXY
3. ANWY
4. (Q+R 📅) (X+Z 1/7-31/8)
5. **A**GIJKLMNOPUVWZ
6. ACDEGIJ(N 2km)W

💬 A well-maintained campsite right on the coast. Perfect for visiting antiquities in the area, such as Ancient Corinth, the Corinth Channel and the old theatre in Epidavros.

🚗 National Road Patras-Athens or Athens-Patras. Take exit Epidavros. Follow signs.

Loutraki-
Perachora

**Korinthos** E94

E65 CC

CC € ⑳ 1/4-10/7 28/8-30/10 7=6  📍 N 37°53'22'' E 23°00'20''

---

## Kastraki/Kalambaka, GR-42200 / Thessalia Sporades 👫 📶 iD ⑴²²⁴

- 🏕 Camping Vrachos Kastraki
- ☎ +30 24 32 02 22 93
- 📅 1/1 - 31/12
- @ tsourvaka@yahoo.gr

3,5ha 300**T** 16A

1. AGIJLMOPQ
2. GLRTXY
3. ANU
4. (B 15/4-15/9) (Q+R 📅)
   (T+X+Y 1/4-30/10)
5. **A**EGIJKLMNOPUW
6. EGIJ(N 0km)OTV

💬 You can enjoy Greek hospitality at this lovely and well-run campsite at the foot of the Meteora; you will be surprised by a welcome and farewell present. Very high satisfaction ratings by camping guests for the past years. Highly recommended!

🚗 On arriving in Kalambaka take the road to Kastraki. The campsite is located 1 km further on, on the road to the Meteora abbey. The campsite is next to the bus stop.

Tymfaioi

E92 CC Kalampaka
Paralithaioi

CC € ⑳ 1/1-30/6 25/8-31/12  📍 N 39°42'48'' E 21°36'57''

## Kato Alissos, GR-25002 / Peloponnese

&#9855; &#128246; **iD** 1225

🔺 Camping Kato Alissos
☎ +30 26 93 07 12 49
⊙ 1/4 - 31/10
@ info@camping-kato-alissos.gr

1,2ha 60T(60-80m²) 10A

**1** ACDGIJKLM**PQ**
**2** EFGKNRTXY
**3** AWY
**4** (Q+R ⊙─) (T 30/6-31/8)
(U+Y 1/5-30/9)
**5** **A**GIJKLMNOPUWZ
**6** EGK(N 2km)OTV

💬 A natural rural setting. There are olive, lemon, and many other types of trees and plants on the campsite. Wonderful swimming in the sea and sunbathing on the long gravel beach. Sample traditional dishes in the shade of 1000 year old olive trees with views of Patraikos Bay and the town of Patras.

🚐 New Nat. Road Patras-Pirgos. Turn right at km-marker 21, left at end of road onto Old Nat. Road; right after 700 metres, right at end of road. Follow the signs.

Paralia
Dymi CC
E55   Olenia

**CC** € **18** 1/4-30/6  1/9-30/10  7=6
📷 N 38°09'00'' E 21°34'38''

---

## Kato Gatzea (Pilion), GR-37010 / Thessalia Sporades

&#9855; &#128246; **iD** 1226

🔺 Camping Hellas
🏳 Kato Gatzea
☎ +30 24 23 02 22 67
⊙ 1/1 - 31/12
@ info@campinghellas.gr

2ha 120T 16A

**1** ACDGIJKLMOPQ
**2** AEGJKRSTXY
**3** HJWY
**4** (Q+R+T+U+V+Y+Z 1/4-31/10)
**5** **A**GIJKLMNOPUWZ
**6** ACEGIK(N 0,8km)ORTVWX

💬 Located on a lovely sandy beach in a beautiful bay. Andonis and Aristea welcome you to their campsite. Grounds are partly level and partly terraced. Most pitches shaded by olive trees. Modern toilet facilities are well maintained and suitable for the disabled. The campsite has a lively bar and a restaurant on the sandy beach.

🚐 In Volos follow Pilio-Argalasti. 18 km further on between Kato Gatzea and Kala Nera. Well signposted.

Mouresio
Milies
Agria
CC

**CC** € **20** 1/3-30/6  1/9-30/11
📷 N 39°18'40'' E 23°06'33''

---

## Kato Gatzea (Pilion), GR-37300 / Thessalia Sporades

👫 &#9855; &#128246; **iD** 1227

🔺 Camping Sikia
🏳 Kato Gatzea
☎ +30 24 23 02 22 79
⊙ 1/1 - 31/12
@ info@camping-sikia.gr

3ha 120T 16A

**1** ACDGIJKLMOPST
**2** AEGJKORSTVWXY
**3** ANWY
**4** (Q+S+T+U+V+Y+Z 1/4-15/10)
**5** **A**FGIJKLMNOPQRUVWZ
**6** ACEGK(N 0,3km)ORTVWX

💬 A shaded campsite on a lovely sandy beach in a beautiful bay. Many pitches have panoramic views. A warm welcome. Well maintained toilet facilities. Separate facilities for the disabled. Bar and restaurant on the sandy beach. All pitches easily accessible with excellent pitches for less physically able guests. Live Greek music regularly, also in low season. Free wifi.

🚐 Follow Pilion/Argalasti in Volos. Campsite 18 km further in Kato Gatzea, well signposted.

Mouresio
Milies
Agria
CC

**CC** € **20** 1/1-30/6  1/9-30/12
📷 N 39°18'37'' E 23°06'36''

## Korinthos, GR-20011 / Peloponnese ♿ 🛜 iD (1228)

🏕 Camping Blue Dolphin
☎ +30 27 41 02 57 66
🗓 1/4 - 31/10
@ skouspos@otenet.gr

0,8ha 130T(20-50m²) 16A

**1** ACGIJKLM**P**S
**2** EFGNOSTVXY
**3** Y
**4** (Q+Y 1/5-30/9)
**5** **A**GIJKLMNOPUWZ
**6** AEGK(N 6km)TV

💬 A campsite suitable for visiting antiquities in the area. The campsite is situated right by the sea with a pleasant sea temperature. Ancient sights: Ancient Corinth and Corinth canal.

🚗 Athens-Patras exit Anc. Corinthos. Turn right, at roundabout 2nd exit to Lechaio. End of road right, follow signs. Patras-Corinthos exit Anc. Korinthos. At roundabout 3rd exit Lechaio. 2nd roundabout see previous.

CC € 20  1/4-14/7  1/9-30/10    🧭 N 37°56'05'' E 22°51'56''

---

## Koroni/Messinias, GR-24004 / Peloponnese 🛜 iD (1229)

🏕 Camping Koroni
☎ +30 27 25 02 21 19
🗓 1/1 - 31/12
@ info@koronicamping.com

1,3ha 86T(25-80m²) 16A

**1** ACDGIJKLM**P**Q
**2** AEJLRTVWXY
**3** R**V**WY
**4** (B+Q+R+T+U+Y+Z 1/4-15/10)
**5** **A**GIJKLMNOPUWZ
**6** ACDEGIK(N 0,2km)V

💬 The campsite is located near the picturesque town of Koroni. The grounds are largely shaded. There is a cozy restaurant with terrace next to the pool overlooking Koroni. Beach accessible by stairs/path after 50 meters.

🚗 Kalamata to Pylos road, turn left at Rizomylos, continue to Koroni via Petalidi. Campsite on the left 200m before Koroni.

CC € 18  1/1-30/6  1/9-31/12    🧭 N 36°47'58'' E 21°57'00''

---

## Lefkada, GR-31100 / Ionian Islands 👫 🛜 iD (1230)

🏕 Camping Kariotes Beach
🚌 Spasmeni Vrisi
☎ +30 26 45 07 11 03
🗓 15/4 - 1/10
@ info@campingkariotes.gr

0,8ha 75T 16A

**1** AGIJLMO**P**
**2** AEGRTY
**3** Y
**4** (B 20/5-20/9) (G 15/5-20/9)
  (Q+R 1/6-30/9)
  (T+U 15/5-30/9)
  (X 15/5-15/9)
**5** **A**GIKMNOPU
**6** FGK(N 0,5km)ORTV

💬 The campsite is located 2 km from Lefkada town, excellent base for excursions. A small shaded campsite with a lovely swimming pool (open from 1 June) and taverna (open from 15 May). The swimming pool, bar, restaurant and good toilet facilities, together with Greek hospitality offer an enjoyable stay. Welcome!

🚗 Campsite on the main Lefkada to Vasiliki road. Site 2 km south of Lefkada town, on the right of the road.

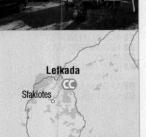

CC € 18  15/4-9/7  27/8-30/9    🧭 N 38°48'16'' E 20°42'52''

## Nea Moudania, GR-63200 / Macedonia

1231

Camping A.Ouzouni s.a.
+30 23 73 04 29 22
1/5 - 15/9
info@campingouzouni.com

0,8ha 60**T**(40-100m²) 6A

1 ACDGIJKLMPQ
2 AEGRVXY
3 AWY
4 (Q+S ) (T+U+Y+Z 1/6-10/9)
5 **A**GIJKLMNOPUV
6 CEGK(N 3,5km)ORTV

This campsite welcomes you into a green surroundings for a comfortable and enjoyable stay. The shop has a very large selection of products. In the restaurant right on the beach you can enjoy your meal with a view over the azure blue sea.

Nat. Road Thessaloniki-Kasandra, exit 2 km south of Nea Moudania. Right at end of road. Then immediate left, follow Local Road beside motorway. Right after 1100m and take campsite on the left at end of road.

Nea Moudania
Nea Fokaia


CC € 16 *1/5-30/6 20/8-15/9 7=6*

N 40°12'57'' E 23°19'06''

## Nea Moudania, GR-63200 / Macedonia

1232

Camping Ouzouni Beach
+30 23 73 04 24 44
1/5 - 30/9
info@ouzounibeach.gr

1,2ha 64**T**(65-85m²) 6A

1 ACDGIJKLMPQ
2 AEGRVXY
3 WY
4 (Q )
5 **AB**EGIJKLMNPUVX
6 ACEGK(N 3,5km)T

Completely renovated campsite with a sandy beach and crystal clear sea on one of Greece's most beautiful coastlines. Very good location for visiting Thessaloniki and the peninsulas Kassandra, Sithonia and Athos with their interesting sites from ancient times.

Nat. Road Thessaloniki-Kasandra, exit 2 km south of Nea Moudania. Right at end of road. Then immediate left, follow Local Road parallel to motorway. Right after 1100m, campsite on the right at end of road.

Portaria
25
Nea Moudania
Nea Fokaia


CC € 16 *1/5-30/6 24/8-30/9*

N 40°12'59'' E 23°19'06''

## Nikiti, GR-63088 / Macedonia

1233

Camping Mitari
+30 23 75 07 17 75
1/5 - 30/9
mitaricamp@hotmail.com

2,5ha 70**T**(65-90m²) 10A

1 ACDFIJKLPQ
2 AEGJKRSTXY
3 WY
4 (Q ) (S 1/6-31/8) (Y+Z 10/6-31/8)
5 **A**GIJKLMO**P**UVX
6 CEGJ(N 8km)QTV

A modern campsite with shaded pitches. The campsite has two sandy beaches and a lively bar with beautiful views.

West coast of Sithonia, 12 km beyond Nikiti.

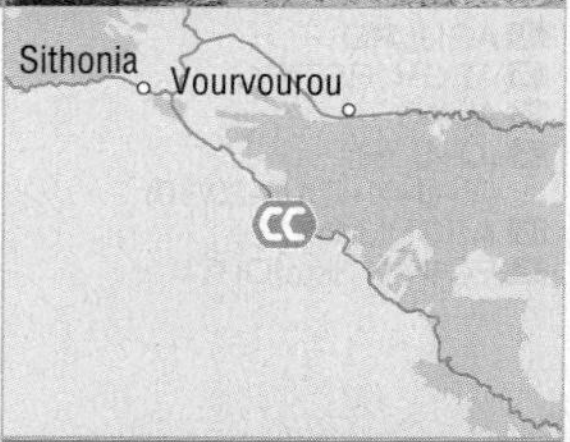

Sithonia
Vourvourou


CC € 18 *1/5-30/6 24/8-30/9 7=6*

N 40°08'36'' E 23°44'08''

## Ouranoupolis (Athos), GR-63075 / Macedonia

♿ ⚡ 📶 🆔 **1234**

⛺ Camping Ouranoupoli
☎ +30 23 77 07 11 71
📅 1/4 - 31/10
@ camping-ouranoupoli@
hotmail.com

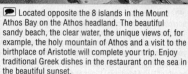

1,1ha 110T(70-110m²) 10A

**1** ACDGIJKLMPQ
**2** AEGRVWXY
**3** AWY
**4** (Q 1/5-15/10)
   (S+Y 1/5-31/10)
**5** AGIJKLMNOPUVXY
**6** CDEGIK(N 1,8km)ORTV

💬 Located opposite the 8 islands in the Mount Athos Bay on the Athos headland. The beautiful sandy beach, the clear water, the unique views of, for example, the holy mountain of Athos and a visit to the birthplace of Aristotle will complete your trip. Enjoy traditional Greek dishes in the restaurant on the sea in the beautiful sunset.

Stagira-Akanthos

CC

🚐 Campsite located on Ierissos-Ouranoupolis road, 1.8 km before Ouranoupolis at the right of the road.

CC €**18** 1/4-15/6 14/9-31/10    🏔 N 40°20'22'' E 23°58'14''

---

## Panteleimon, GR-60065 / Macedonia

📶 🆔 **1235**

⛺ Camping Poseidon Beach
☎ +30 23 52 04 16 54
📅 1/4 - 31/10
@ poseidonbeach@gmail.com

1,7ha 27T(60-120m²) 6-16A

**1** ACDGIJKLPQ
**2** AEFRSVXY
**3** WY
**4** (Z 1/5-10/9)
**5** ABGIJKLMNOPUWZ
**6** CEGIK(N 0,1km)TV

💬 Typical Greek family campsite with many seasonal pitches located by the sea with a wide sandy beach. Newly created pitches with a view of the sea. Many sights in the vicinity, including Olympus, King's Burial Site, Platamon Castle etc.

🚐 From north: A1/E75 Thessaloniki-Athens, exit Skotina. Follow Panteleimon Beach signs. From south: exit Platamon. Follow Panteleimon signs. After 3 km near Platamon Castle direction Panteleimon Beach. Follow road.

Panteleimon
E75
E75

CC €**18** 1/4-9/7 27/8-31/10 7=6    🏔 N 40°00'47'' E 22°35'25''

---

## Parga/Lichnos, GR-48060 / Epirus

📶 🆔 **1236**

⛺ Camping Enjoy Lichnos
☎ +30 26 84 03 13 71
📅 1/4 - 25/10
@ holidays@enjoy-lichnos.net

4,8ha 150T 5-16A

**1** AGIJLPQ
**2** AEGHJRSTXY
**3** AUWY
**4** (Q+S 🚐)
   (T+U+X+Z 1/5-20/10)
**5** AEGIJLMNOPU
**6** EGIK(N 3km)ORTV

💬 A modern, well maintained terraced campsite located on one of the most beautiful bays in Greece. Various watersports. Beautiful views of the Ionian Sea. Taxi boats from the campsite to Parga and back.

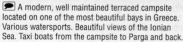

Perdika

Parga CC E55
Fanari

🚐 Take the road from Igoumenitsa to Parga. Take exit Parga and the campsite is on the bay, 3 km before Parga on the left. Or take the new road from Igoumenitsa to Ioannina, exit Parga.

CC €**20** 1/4-20/6 1/9-25/10    🏔 N 39°17'01'' E 20°25'59''

## Preveza, GR-48100 / Epirus

👫 ♿ 🛜 **iD** (1237)

🏕 Camping Village Kalamitsi Beach
☎ +30 26 82 02 21 92
🔑 1/5 - 30/9
@ info@campingkalamitsi.eu

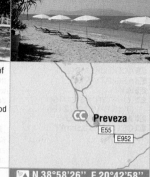

1,4ha 116T 4-10A

**1** ACGIJLMOPQ
**2** AERTXY
**3** AKUY
**4** (B 30/5-30/9)
 (Q+R+T+X 1/6-30/9)
**5** AGIJKMNOPU
**6** EGIJ(N 4km)OQRTV

💬 A very peacefully located campsite with plenty of shade about 4 km from the lively village of Preveza and within walking distance of the sea (100m). Offers a lovely swimming pool and excellent cuisine. Swimming pool/kitchen open 1/6 to 30/9. A very good base for excursions in the surrounding area.

🚐 Follow E55 past Kanaliki (from Parga) and drive towards Preveza (tunnel). Campsite on right 4 km before Preveza (via small road).

**Preveza**
E55
E952

CC € 20 1/5-30/6 1/9-30/9

🧭 N 38°58'26'' E 20°42'58''

## Sarti (Sithonia), GR-63072 / Macedonia

♿ 🛜 **iD** (1238)

🏕 Camping Armenistis
☎ +30 23 75 09 14 97
🔑 26/4 - 23/9
@ info@armenistis.gr

6ha 300T(50-100m²) 10A

**1** ACDFIJKLMNPRS
**2** AEGLRSVWXY
**3** BNWY
**4** (Q+S 🔑) (T 1/6-20/9)
 (U+Y+Z 🔑)
**5** AGIJKLMNOPUV
**6** CEGKMOQRTV

💬 An ideal campsite for young watersports enthusiasts. Well organised. Expert leadership. Separate fields for various (age) categories. Glamping!

🚐 On the east coast of Sithonia. 17 km south of Vourvourou and 13 km north of Sarti. Entrance signposted.

Sarti
Neos Marmaras

CC € 18 26/4-30/6 1/9-23/9

🧭 N 40°09'07'' E 23°54'49''

## Sikia, GR-63072 / Macedonia

🛜 **iD** (1239)

🏕 Camping Melissi
☎ +30 23 75 04 16 31
🔑 1/5 - 30/9
@ info@camping-melissi.gr

1,5ha 70T(54-100m²) 6A

**1** ACDFIJKLMOPQ
**2** AEKRWXY
**3** AWY
**4** (Q+S 1/5-15/9)
**5** AGIJKLMNOPUV
**6** CEGIK(N 7km)T

💬 In the south of the beautiful peninsula Sithonia, you'll find an endless sandy beach and bay with crystal-clear water. Quiet campsite not far from Mount Athos. Pitches among many trees which provide shade and on open field with sea-view for those who enjoy the sun.

🚐 Located to the east of Sithonia, 7 km south of Sarti. Indicated by 'Sikia Beach' signs on the coast road. Then well signposted on the asphalt road beside the beach. Follow campsite signs.

Sykia
Toroni

CC € 18 1/5-30/6 1/9-30/9 10=9

🧭 N 40°02'45'' E 23°59'05''

## Stoupa, GR-24024 / Peloponnese

🏕 Camping Kalogria
📧 Barbezea Nicos 29
☎ +30 27 21 07 73 19
📅 1/4 - 20/11
@ campingkalogria@yahoo.gr

🛜 iD 1240

NEW

2ha 102T(50-120m²) 16A

**1** ACDGIJKLM**P**Q
**2** AEGIRTVWXY
**3** WY
**4** (Q 🔑) (R 1/6-31/10)
   (T 15/6-15/10) (Z 🔑)
**5** **A**GIJKLMNOPUW
**6** CEGK(N 0,25km)V

💬 The campsite is located near the centre of the touristic town of Stoupa. The beautiful bay with a beautiful sandy beach can be reached by a descending path.

🚗 Campsite is located in Stoupa, a village along the Kalamata-Areopolis coastal road, exit Kalogria-Beach, exit Stoupa, Kalogria. Take street opposite UNEP supermarket.

Akrogiali

Lefktro

CC € 18  1/4-16/6  1/9-31/10

📍 N 36°50'58'' E 22°15'32''

---

## Tiros/Arcadia, GR-22029 / Peloponnese

🏕 Zaritsi Camping
☎ +30 27 57 04 14 29
📅 1/4 - 15/10
@ campingzaritsi@gmail.com

🛜 iD 1241

3ha 120T(50-120m²) 16A

**1** ACDGIJKLMNOPQ
**2** EGKNRTUVWXY
**3** NWY
**4** (Q+R 🔑) (T+U 1/5-31/8)
   (X 1/5-15/6,1/9-30/9)
   (Y 16/6-31/8) (Z 🔑)
**5** **A**GIJKLMNOPUXZ
**6** ACEGJ(N 4km)V

💬 The campsite is located on a sun-drenched pebble beach in Zaritsi bay. The site is run by a super-friendly family that wants your stay to be great. Spacious pitches with natural and artificial shade. You can enjoy a delicious meal in the restaurant.

🚗 Drive south from Nafplion towards Astros. Campsite lies 30 km south of Astros and 5 km north of Tiros. Sharp bend towards the sea at campsite sign (800m downhill paved road).

Agios
Andreas

CC
Apollon

CC € 18  1/4-30/6  1/9-14/10

📍 N 37°16'12'' E 22°50'34''

---

## Vourvourou, GR-63088 / Macedonia

🏕 Lacara Camping
📧 Akti Koutloumoussi
☎ +30 23 75 09 14 44
📅 11/5 - 22/9
@ info@lacaracamping.gr

♿ 🛜 iD 1242

7,6ha 196T(40-120m²) 6A

**1** ACDGIJKLMO**P**Q
**2** ABCEFGKLNRSVWXY
**3** AMNWY
**4** (Q+S+T+U+Y+Z 🔑)
**5** **AB**GIJKLMNOPUVW
**6** EGIJK(N 8,5km)RTV

💬 This large family campsite is located in a shaded valley with a lovely sandy beach. Restaurant and beach bar! Good base for walking and hiking in the mountains.

🚗 On the east coast of Sithonia from the north 8,5 km past Vourvourou village. Campsite signposted.

Karydi

CC

Sarti

CC € 18  11/5-30/6  1/9-22/9  7=6

📍 N 40°10'12'' E 23°51'15''

## Vourvourou (Sithonia), GR-63078 / Macedonia

 iD (1243)

🔺 Camping Rea
☎ +30 23 75 09 11 00
🗓 1/5 - 30/9
@ campingrea@gmail.com

2ha 40T(80-100m²) 16A

**1** ACDFIJKLMPQ
**2** AEGRSVWXY
**3** AWY
**4** (Q 🅿) (S+U+Y 15/5-30/9)
**5** AGIJKLMNOPUVWX
**6** EGIJ(N 2km)TV

💬 Quiet campsite in unspoiled natural surroundings with beautiful sandy beaches and an azure blue sea. The spacious pitches offer a lovely view over the island of Diaporos. From the campsite, it's just 4 km to the harbour at Ormos Panagias for a cruise past the monasteries on the holy Mount Athos.

🚗 On the east coast of Sithonia 4 km south of Agios Nikolaos and 2 km north of Vourvourou. Campsite is signposted.

Sithonia
Nikiti
CC

CC € 18 1/5-30/6 1/9-30/6

🗺 N 40°12'24'' E 23°45'46''

CC

You can easily find a campsite that meets your needs on the website. Search using the map, a place name, or amenities.

# www.CampingCard.com

501

# United Kingdom

## General
At the time of printing this guide, the United Kingdom is a member of the EU.

## Time
The time in the United Kingdom is one hour behind Amsterdam, Paris and Rome.

## Language
English.

## Crossings
There are several ferry companies offering crossings from France, Belgium, the

Netherlands and Scandinavia. You can also travel under the English channel with your car on the train through the Eurotunnel.
Take note: if your car is fitted with an LPG tank you cannot take it on the train through the Eurotunnel. There are special regulations for integral gas containers in caravans and motorhomes. Portable gas containers are permitted but you must declare them. See
▶ www.eurotunnel.com ◀

## Border formalities
Many formalities and agreements about matters such as necessary travel documents, car papers, requirements relating to your means of transport and accommodation, medical expenses and taking pets with you do not only depend on the country you are travelling to but also on your departure point and nationality. The length of your stay can also play a role here. It is not possible within the confines of this guide to guarantee the correct and most up to date information with regard to these matters.

We advise you to consult the relevant authorities before your departure about:
- which travel documents you will need for yourself and your fellow passengers
- which documents you need for your car
- which regulations your caravan must meet
- which goods you may import and export
- how medical treatment will be arranged and paid for in your holiday destination in cases of accident or illness
- whether you can take pets. Contact your vets well in advance. They can give you

information about the necessary vaccinations, proof thereof and obligations on return. It would also make sense to enquire whether any special regulations apply to your pet in public places at your holiday destination. In some countries for example dogs must always be muzzled or transported in a cage.

You will find plenty of general information on ▶ *www.europa.eu* ◀ but make certain you select information that is relevant to your specific situation.

For the most recent customs regulations you should get in contact with the authorities of your holiday destination in your country of residence.

## Currency

The currency in Great Britain is the pound sterling. Approximate exchange rates September 2018: £1 = € 1.12. You can exchange money at post offices, banks and exchange offices.

Scotland, the Channel Islands and the Isle of Man have their own notes and coins which cannot always be used outside these areas.

### Credit cards

You can pay almost everywhere by credit card.

## Opening times

### Banks

Open on weekdays until 16:00.

### Shops

Shops are open from Monday to Saturday until 17:30. Shops stay open later on Wednesday or Thursday evenings. Shops in Scotland are open on Sundays more often than in the rest of the UK.

### Pubs

Most British pubs are open Monday to Sunday from 11:00 to 23:00. In cities many open at 09:00 to serve breakfast.

### Chemists, doctors

Doctors are available between 08:30 and 18:00 Monday to Friday. Be sure to make an appointment! Chemists or 'pharmacies' are open Monday to Friday until 18:00, on Saturday until 13:00.

## Communication

### (Mobile) phones

The mobile network works well throughout the United Kingdom except on the west coast of Scotland. There is a 4G network for mobile internet.

### Wifi, internet

You can make use of a wifi network at more and more public locations, often for free.

### Post

Post offices are generally open from Monday to Friday until 17:30. On Saturdays in larger towns until 12:30.

## Roads and traffic

### Road network

There is a breakdown service on major roads that you can contact using the Automobile Association (AA) phones. On minor roads call the AA Breakdown number: tel. 0800-887766.

### Traffic rules

All traffic in the UK drives on the left and overtakes on the right! Where two main roads meet there is no general rule so you need to look at the signs. Main roads have priority, this is shown by 'Stop' or 'Give way' signs. Traffic on a roundabout (coming from the right!) has priority over traffic entering it.
Maximum permitted alcohol level is 0.8‰. Maximum permitted alcohol level in Scotland is 0.5‰. The use of dipped headlights during the daytime is not compulsory in the United Kingdom unless visibility is less than 100 metres.

Phones may only be used hands-free. You can adjust your lights for driving on the left by placing a special sticker on the headlights. You can obtain this sticker on the webshop of
▶ *www.visitbritainshop.com* ◀
There are no regulations concerning the use of winter tyres.

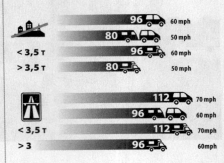

*Maximum speed*

| | |
|---|---|
| 96 | 60 mph |
| 80 | 50 mph |
| < 3,5 т   96 | 60 mph |
| > 3,5 т   80 | 50 mph |
| 112 | 70 mph |
| 96 | 60 mph |
| < 3,5 т   112 | 70mph |
| > 3   96 | 60mph |

### Caravans, motorhomes

You may not drive with a caravan on the outside lane of three-lane roads. Caravans are not permitted on the Isle of Man.

### Maximum allowed measurements of combined length

Height 4 metres, width 2.55 metres and maximum length 18.75 metres (of which the trailer maximum 12 metres). Larger sizes, particularly in width, can lead to problems when entering campsites on narrow roads.

### Fuel

Lead-free petrol, LPG and diesel are widely available.

### Filling stations

Filling stations on motorways are open 24 hours, other service stations are open until 22:00. You can usually pay by credit card.

**Tolls**

A toll must be paid on the M6 north of Birmingham. This also applies to some bridges and tunnels.

Attention! It is no longer possible to pay at a tollbooth at the Dartford Crossing (ring road London M25). Instead, payment needs to be done beforehand or afterwards (within 24 hours) via internet. If you do not do this, you will receive a hefty fine. More information: ▶ *www.gov.uk/highways/dartford* ◀

Low emission zone (LEZ):
The 'low emission zone' (LEZ) has been introduced in London to control the air quality. The LEZ does not apply to cars but it does to motorhomes. If you are planning to visit London with a motorhome you will need to register your vehicle with Transport for London (TfL) on ▶ *www.tfl.gov.uk* ◀. By not registering you are liable to a fine.

'Congestion charge':
In Central London you also need to pay a 'Congestion Charge'. The rates are:
- £ 14 if you pay the next day
- £ 11,50 if you pay on the same day
- £ 10,50 if you pay automatically via CC Auto Pay.

You can pay online, by SMS, telephone or in shops and post offices. You do not need to pay at weekends, during UK holidays or between 18:00 and 07:00. More information about the 'Congestion Charge' ▶ *www.tfl.gov.uk* ◀ (in English and fifteen other languages).

**Emergency number**

112: the national emergency number for fire, police or ambulance.

# Camping

Free camping is allowed in Scotland, in the rest of the UK you need permission from the landowner.

Camping by the side of the road and in car parks is prohibited. On some campsites additional tents will be charged extra.

**'Campsite', 'Touringpark' and 'Caravan Park'**

The main difference between a 'campsite' and a 'touring park' is that the former is larger and has more permanent places for mobile homes. Touring parks are really for people with their own tent or caravan. Tents are not permitted on caravan parks.

It is definitely advisable to reserve in advance if you want to stay on a campsite during a bank holiday or at the weekend.

**Practical**

- Distances are measured in miles (1 mile = 1.609 km, 1 km = 0.621 mile).
- Not all gas bottles from other countries can be filled or exchanged because of different valve types.
- Blue Campingaz 907 bottles are usually available, and sometimes 901 and 904.
- Make sure you have a world adaptor for electrical appliances.
- Tap water is safe to drink.

## Aberystwyth, GB-SY23 4DX / Wales

**1244**

▲ Midfield Holiday &
  Residential Park
🚏 South Gate
☎ +44 19 70 61 25 42
🔓 1/4 - 31/10
@ enquiries@midfield.me

2ha 75T(80-100m²) 1-10A CEE

**1** ACDGIJKLMOPQ
**2** GIJKNRTWX
**3** AFHJ
**5** **AB**GIJKLMNOPUWZ
**6** AEGK(N 0,5km)OT

💬 On the south of the attractive town of
Aberystwyth with fantastic views over town and sea.
Ideal to discover the surroundings, visit the town or
ride through the Rheidol valley in the steam train.
Suitable as a stopover site when travelling over Wales
coastal roads. Two signposted cycling routes at 500
metres.

🚐 On the A4120, between Aberystwyth and Devils
Bridge/Pontarfynach. Site is situated on main road, 300
metres from the junction with the A487 in Aberystwyth.

Aberystwyth

CC € **18** 1/4-17/4 24/4-1/5 8/5-22/5 29/5-1/7 28/8-31/10 7=6, 14=12    N 52°23'52'' W 04°03'59''

---

## Bletchingdon/Oxford, GB-OX5 3BQ / England (South East)

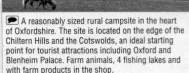

NEW

**1245**

▲ Greenhill Farm C&C
  Leisure Park***
🚏 Station Road
☎ +44 18 69 35 16 00
🔓 2/1 - 22/12
@ info@greenhill-leisure-park.co.uk

2ha 150T(100m²) 16A CEE

**1** ACD**F**IJKLMOPQ
**2** CFKLRTUVWX
**3** AFHNRUW
**4** (R+Z 🔓)
**5** **AB**CDGHIJKLMNOPRUWZ
**6** CDFK(N 5km)OTU

💬 A reasonably sized rural campsite in the heart
of Oxfordshire. The site is located on the edge of the
Chiltern Hills and the Cotswolds, an ideal starting
point for tourist attractions including Oxford and
Blenheim Palace. Farm animals, 4 fishing lakes and
with farm products in the shop.

🚐 M40 exit 9. Then A34 direction Oxford. Then the
B4027 direction Bletchingdon. Site on left-hand side
after leaving the village.

CC € **20** 1/3-18/4 22/4-2/5 7/5-22/5 3/6-5/7 2/9-30/9    N 51°51'24'' W 01°16'59''

---

## Brean Sands, GB-TA8 2RB / England (South West)

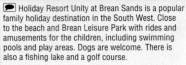

**1246**

▲ Holiday Resort Unity***
🚏 Coast Road
☎ +44 12 78 75 12 35
🔓 15/2 - 17/11
@ admin@hru.co.uk

100ha 446T(100-144m²) 16A CEE

**1** ACD**G**IJKLMOPQ
**2** AEFGRUVW
**3** BC**EF**HJKNQT**U**VWY
**4** (**C** 1/6-1/9) (**F+G** 🔓) JL**N**
  (Q+S 🔓)
  (T+U+V+Y+Z 19/4-7/10)
**5** **AB**DFGIJKLMNPQRTU
  WXY
**6** ACFGH**K**M(N 4km)OTUV

💬 Holiday Resort Unity at Brean Sands is a popular
family holiday destination in the South West. Close
to the beach and Brean Leisure Park with rides and
amusements for the children, including swimming
pools and play areas. Dogs are welcome. There is
also a fishing lake and a golf course.

🚐 Take junction 22 on the M5 and follow the brown
'Brean Leisure Park' signs. Entrance to campsite 200
metres south of entrance to the Leisure Park.

Weston-Super-
Mare

CC € **20** 15/2-19/4 6/5-23/5 31/5-21/6 30/8-26/9 7/10-17/11    N 51°16'50'' W 03°00'46''

## Bude, GB-EX23 9HJ / England (South West)

🚫 ♿ 📶 ✿ **iD** (1247)

🏕 Wooda Farm Holiday Park*****
🏡 Poughill
☎ +44 12 88 35 20 69
🔑 30/3 - 1/11
@ enquiries@wooda.co.uk

6ha 210T(80-120m²) 16A CEE

**1** ACD**G**IJKLMP**Q**
**2** IKRUVWX
**3** BCEH**M**RU**VW**
**4** (Q+S+T+U+W+Z 🔑)
**5** **AB**DFGIJKLMNOPQR**S**U
WYZ
**6** CDEH**K**(N 1km)OSUV

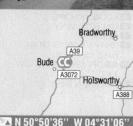

💬 A sunny and pleasant large family campsite with plenty of recreational opportunities, both in and beyond the campsite. The location is most suitable for trips out to Bude.

🚗 A39, north of Bude (direction Bideford). Direction Poughill and Stibb after about 4 km. Campsite clearly signposted.

Bradworthy

A39

Bude **CC**

A3072

Holsworthy

A388

**CC** €**20** 30/3-23/5 2/6-11/7 31/8-1/11    🏕 N 50°50'36'' W 04°31'06''

---

## Corpach/Fort William, GB-PH33 7NL / Scotland

⛷ 📶 ✿ **iD** (1248)

🏕 Linnhe Lochside Holidays****
☎ +44 13 97 77 23 76
🔑 1/1 - 31/10, 15/12 - 31/12
@ relax@
linnhe-lochside-holidays.co.uk

5ha 105T(45-90m²) 10-16A CEE

**1** ACD**G**IJKLMOP**Q**
**2** DEG**J**KNOQRUVWXY
**3** BC**F**JWYZ
**4** (Q+S 1/3-31/10)
**5** **AB**CDFGHIJKLMNOPRU
WXZ
**6** ACEG**J**(N 3km)OTU

💬 Beautiful terraced campsite in a lush garden with a beautiful view over the lochs and the surrounding mountains. Modern facilities. Here, you can relax or have an active holiday.

🚗 Follow the A82 northwards. Take the A830 direction Corpach in Fort William. Campsite on the left after about 8 km. Well signposted.

A830

**CC** Banavie

Fort William

A82

**CC** €**20** 8/1-15/2 4/3-7/4 13/5-23/5 4/6-14/7 1/9-13/10    🏕 N 56°50'51'' W 05°09'39''

---

## Cullompton, GB-EX15 2DT / England (South West)

🧒 ♿ 📶 ✿ **iD** (1249)

🏕 Forest Glade Holiday Park****
🏡 Near Kentisbeare
☎ +44 14 04 84 13 81
🔑 22/3 - 2/11
@ enquiries@forest-glade.co.uk

6ha 81T(120-140m²) 10-16A CEE

**1** ACD**G**IJKLMOP**Q**
**2** B**F**LRTUVWXY
**3** BCH**M**NRU
**4** (F+H 🔑) **N**(Q+S+U 🔑)
**5** **AB**CDEFGHIJKLMNOPQRU
WXYZ
**6** ACDEG**K**M(N 9,5km)OU

💬 Quiet, family-run caravan park in a forest clearing with level, sheltered pitches and free indoor swimming pool. Forest walks from the park, shop with off-licence and take-away food.

🚗 Do not use Satnav! Site accessible from North Honiton, direction Dunkeswell and after ±4.5 km follow brown camping signs. Cars from M5 take exit 28, A373 dir. Honiton, left just past Keepers Cottage Inn. Campsite 4 km up the hill.

A361

Willand

Cullompton

M5

**CC**

A373

Honiton

A30   A35

**CC** €**18** 22/3-19/4 22/4-24/5 2/6-15/7 1/9-2/11 7=6    🏕 N 50°51'31'' W 03°16'41''

## Dalwood/Axminster, GB-EX13 7DY / England (South West) 👬 ♿ 🛜 ⚙ iD **1250**

🔺 Andrewshayes Holiday Park****
☎ +44 14 04 83 12 25
📅 29/3 - 3/11
@ info@andrewshayes.co.uk

4,4ha 35T(90-100m²) 10A CEE

**1** ACD**G**IJKLOP**Q**
**2** IJKLRTUVWXY
**3** A**F**HNRU
**4** (E+H 1/4-28/10) (R 📷)
(U+Z 15/7-31/8)
**5** **AB**DFGIJKLMNPQRUW
XYZ
**6** ADFG**K**(N 5km)OU

💬 A terraced campsite with spacious pitches in the middle of the hilly area of East Devon. Indoor heated pool with sliding roof, play rooms for young and old. Close to the Jurassic Coast, the resorts of Charmouth and Lyme Regis and the English Riviera.

🚗 A35 from Axminster to Honiton dir. Dalwood/Stockland at crossroads after 5 km follow camping sign on right. A35 from Honiton to Dorchester at crossroads after 9 km dir. Dalwood/Stockland, camping sign.

🆑 € 18  29/3-5/4  23/4-2/5  7/5-23/5  3/6-15/7  2/9-3/11  7=6   ◰ N 50°46'59'' W 03°04'10''

---

## Dartmouth, GB-TQ9 7DQ / England (South West) ♿ 🛜 iD **1251**

🔺 Woodlands Grove Car. & Camping*****
🏠 Blackawton
☎ +44 18 03 71 25 98
📅 29/3 - 4/11
@ holiday@woodlandsgrove.com

24ha 326T(100-120m²) 10A CEE

**1** ACD**G**IJKLMOP**Q**
**2** BGJKLTUWXY
**3** ABCD**F**HJNQRU
**4** (G 27/5-31/8) M(Q+R+T 📷)
(U 20/7-31/8) (X 📷)
**5** **AB**DEFGIJKLMNOPQRSTU
WXYZ
**6** ACFGH**K**MOUV

💬 Set in stunning countryside, a few minutes from picturesque Dartmouth, South Devon coastal path and National Trust properties. Hidden in the valley below is Woodlands Leisure Park with Falconry Centre and Zoo-Farm. Families, grandparents and couples love this perfect location.

🚗 Exit A38 southbound Buckfastleigh/Totnes or northbound Brent/Awonwick junction. Follow brown signs to Woodlands Leisure Park, not Sat/Nav. On A3122 road to Dartmouth.

🆑 € 18  29/3-18/4  22/4-2/5  6/5-23/5  2/6-15/7  3/9-4/11   ◰ N 50°21'24'' W 03°40'19''

---

## Dawlish (Devon), GB-EX6 8RP / England (South West) 👬 ♿ 🛜 ⚙ iD **1252**

🔺 Cofton Holidays****
🏠 Church Road
☎ +44 16 26 89 01 11
📅 1/1 - 31/12
@ info@coftonholidays.co.uk

12ha 496T(90-120m²) 10A CEE

**1** ACDGIJKLMOP**Q**
**2** DIJKLRUVWXY
**3** ABC**F**HJNTU**VW**
**4** (C 25/5-16/9) (F 📷)
(H 24/5-15/9) LN
(Q+S+T+U+Y+Z 📷)
**5** **AB**DEFGHIJKLMNOPQRU
WXYZ
**6** ACDEGHJ**K**M(N 5km)OS
TUV

💬 A large campsite with excellent facilities, divided into several separate fields with level and sloping sections in an undulating landscape.

🚗 From Exeter, on M5 exit 30, take the A379 towards Dawlish. 2 km past Starcross service station on the right of the road. Then another 1 km. Campsite located on the left. Signposted.

🆑 € 18  1/1-23/5  1/6-14/7  31/8-31/12   ◰ N 50°36'46'' W 03°27'38''

## Devil's Bridge/Aberystwyth, GB-SY23 3JW / Wales

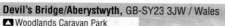

👫 ♿ 📶 **iD** (1253)

🏔 Woodlands Caravan Park
☎ +44 19 70 89 02 33
📅 1/3 - 31/10
@ enquiries@
woodlandsdevilsbridge.co.uk

2ha 60T(80-100m²) 1-16A CEE

**1** ACD**G**IJKLMOP**Q**
**2** KRTUWX
**3** AHJ**W**
**4** (R+T+U+X ⌂)
**5** **AB**DEFGIJKLMNPQRUWZ
**6** AEGJ(N 5km)OSU

💬 An attractive campsite situated in a wooded area close to Devil's Bridge Water Falls and the historic Aberystwyth-Devil's Bridge railway. An ideal base for exploring Central Wales, for walking, mountain biking, bird-watching, fishing or simply enjoying the beautiful landscape. You will camp among lovely pieces of artwork.

🚗 On the A4120 between Aberystwyth and Ponterwyd, near Devil's Bridge. The entrance to the campsite is 500m from Devil's Bridge station (Steam Train).

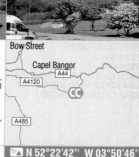

Bow Street
Capel Bangor
A44
A4120
CC
A485

**CC** €**18** 1/3-11/4 30/4-2/5 7/5-23/5 3/6-12/7 4/9-24/10 | N 52°22'42'' W 03°50'46''

---

## East Worlington/Crediton, GB-EX17 4TN / England (South West)

♿ 📶 **iD** (1254)

🏔 Yeatheridge Farm Car. &
Cp. Park****
☎ +44 18 84 86 03 30
📅 15/3 - 8/10
@ info@yeatheridge.co.uk

5ha 117T(80-120m²) 16A CEE

**1** ACD**G**IJKLMOP**Q**
**2** IJKRTVWXY
**3** **A**FHN**O**RUW
**4** (F+H ⌂) J(Q+S ⌂)
(U 15/3-2/10) (X+Y+Z ⌂)
**5** **AB**DEFGIJK**L**MNPQRUWZ
**6** CEJ**K**(N 5km)OSUV

💬 Comfortable farm campsite in undulating landscape of farmland and meadows. With a lovely indoor pool. The small town of Tiverton is nearby and so are the national parks of Devon. The stunning Arlington Court (NT) is about 35 km away.

🚗 Take exit 27 on the M5 then A361 towards Tiverton. Via A396 (south) to B3137 direction Witheridge. B3042 before Witheridge. Campsite 5 km on the left.

A361
Witheridge
A377
CC
North Tawton
Cheriton Fitzpaine
A3072

**CC** €**14** 15/3-5/4 23/4-3/5 7/5-24/5 3/6-14/7 2/9-3/10 | N 50°53'12'' W 03°45'04''

---

## Four Lanes/Redruth, GB-TR16 6LP / England (South West)

📶 ✿ **iD** (1255)

🏔 Lanyon Holiday Park****
✉ Loscombe Lane
☎ +44 12 09 31 34 74
📅 29/3 - 30/10
@ info@lanyonholidaypark.co.uk

5,2ha 105T(100m²) 16A CEE

**1** ACD**G**IJKLMOP**Q**
**2** RTVWX
**3** **A**FHJU
**4** (F ⌂) (U+X+Z 15/7-31/8)
**5** **AB**CDGHIJKLMNOPQR
UWZ
**6** CEGK(N 3km)UV

💬 Beautiful park, views towards St. Ives Bay. Near Falmouth & Penzance. Walk to Great Flat Lode, a historic mine trail, ideal for walkers/cyclists. Beach Portreath 8 km. Indoor swimming pool, 3 sanitary blocks, games room, playground, bar/restaurant, dog walking paddock.

🚗 A30 exit Redruth. Continue towards centre, take B3297 Helston. Enter Four Lanes Village, 2nd right into Loscombe Lane. Park on left. Advice: follow this route, not SatNav.

Camborne
CC
Penryn
A394 Helston

**CC** €**20** 1/4-15/7 1/9-30/10 | N 50°12'10'' W 05°14'44''

## Gristhorpe/Filey, GB-YO14 9PS / England (Yorkshire & Humberside) ♿ 📶 (1256)

🔺 Crows Nest Caravan Park****
✉ Stonepit Lane
☎ +44 17 23 58 22 06
📅 1/3 - 31/10
@ enquiries@
crowsnestcaravanpark.com

7ha 50T(100m²) 16A

**1** CDGIJKLMOQ
**2** AEGIKUV
**3** BFHY
**4** (F+Q+R+S+U+Z 21/4-30/9)
**5** ABDGJLMNPQRSTWXYZ
**6** ABCFGK(N 3km)OSU

💬 Perfectly situated campsite on the Yorkshire coast with well-facilitated pitches. Many facilities for the whole family including a heated indoor swimming pool, playground and supermarket. Good and even award-winning toilet facilities. Beautiful sea views from the campsite. The campsite is only one hour away from Port of Hull. From the cliff you can see the seal colony.

🚗 From Hull take A165 towards Scarborough. Turn right 3 km past Filey. Follow signs 'Crows Nest'.

Scarborough

CC € ⑳ 1/3-16/4 28/4-1/5 7/5-22/5 2/6-4/7 1/9-31/10 📷 N 54°13'52'' W 00°20'13''

---

## Hayle, GB-TR27 5AW / England (South West) ♿ 📶 iD (1257)

🔺 Beachside Holiday Park****
✉ Lethlean Lane
☎ +44 17 36 75 30 80
📅 6/4 - 1/11
@ reception@beachside.co.uk

14,8ha 85T(110m²) 10-16A CEE

**1** ACDEIJKLMOPQ
**2** AEGIKLRVW
**3** ABFGHNRUY
**4** (C+H+Q+S+U+Z 29/4-29/9)
**5** ABCDFGHIJMNPQRUWZ
**6** CEGHJ(N 2,5km)T

💬 This campsite is in the dunes on the bay of St. Ives, 5 minutes from a beautiful sandy beach. With a heated outdoor pool, little shop, and bar and takeaway. No dogs allowed.

🚗 Coming from the north exit A30 in Hayle and head towards the centre. Continue straight on over two roundabouts then take the 1st road on the right. The campsite is signposted there.

Redruth
Penzance

CC € ⑱ 6/4-24/5 1/6-28/6 31/8-1/11 📷 N 50°11'46'' W 05°24'37''

---

## Henlow (Bedfordshire), GB-SG16 6LN / England (South East) ♿ 📶 iD (1258)

🔺 Camping Henlow Bridge
Lakes & Riverside
✉ Bridge End Road
☎ +44 14 62 81 26 45
📅 1/1 - 31/12
@ info@henlowbridgelakes.co.uk

16ha 163T(100-120m²) 10A CEE

**1** ACDFIJKLMOPRS
**2** CDFGRTUVWX
**3** ABFGW
**4** (Q+R 📅)
**5** ABCDEFGHIJKLMNPR
UWX
**6** DFJM(N 4km)OUV

💬 A friendly and well kept campsite with several fields. Heated toilet block with wifi. There are several lakes with carp where you can fish for a charge. London King's Cross station is just 30 minutes by train, the station is within walking distance. Good starting point for trips out to Bedford, Cambridge or Woburn Safari Park. Suitable for larger motorhomes.

🚗 A1 exit 10 direction Bedford. Campsite on the left on the 507 at the roundabout in Henlow.

Wilstead
Baldock
Hitchin

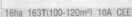

CC € ⑳ 1/1-18/4 23/4-2/5 7/5-23/5 28/5-4/7 10/7-18/7 9/9-31/12 7=6, 14=11 📷 N 52°01'36'' W 00°16'09''

## Horton (Gower), GB-SA3 1LL / Wales

  ♿ 🛜 iD   **1259**

🏕 Bank Farm Leisure, Camp.
    & Car. Park
☎ +44 17 92 39 02 28
📅 1/3 - 31/12
@ enquiries@bankfarmleisure.co.uk

30ha 230T(80-120m²) 10A CEE

1 ACD**G**IJKLO**PQ**
2 AEGIKLOQRW
3 B**F**H**M**NUWY
4 (E+H+Q 🖢) (S 1/3-31/10)
   (T+U+V+X+Z 🖢)
5 **AB**GIJMNPUWZ
6 DEHJ**K**(N 2km)OV

💬 Large campsite on open meadows with lovely views of the sea. If the sea is too cold the heated swimming pool offers plenty of fun in the water. The beautiful countryside around Gower is an invitation to go out for walks.

🚗 On the A4118 Killay-Port Eynon, turn left towards Horton just before Port Eynon and follow the camping signs. This way is better than using SatNav which selects roads that are too narrow.

CC € **18**   1/3-14/4   6/5-23/5   3/6-30/6   1/9-31/12    ⛰ N 51°33'02'' W 04°12'15''

---

## Inverness, GB-IV2 5AA / Scotland

  ♿ 🛜 iD   **1260**

🏕 Ardtower Caravan Park
✉ Culloden Road
☎ +44 14 63 79 05 55
📅 4/3 - 31/12
@ ardtower@outlook.com

2ha 67T(50-80m²) 16A CEE

1 ACD**G**IJKLMOPST
2 GIJKRUVW
3 A**F**
4 (Q+R 🖢)
5 **AB**CDFGHIJKLMNOPU
  WXZ
6 ABCFGK(N 3km)OTU

💬 Excellent base for discovering Scottish highlands. Located only 6 km from Inverness with beautiful view of the Beauly Firth, the Black Isle and the mountains. Hardened pitches and grass for tents, luxury and modern toilet facilities with underfloor heating. Near to Loch Ness, Culloden Battlefield and dolphins.

🚗 Site is ± 6 km east of Inverness centre. From Inverness centre follow D9 south. Exit Culloden Battlefield. Site is on right after ± 3 km.

CC € **20**   4/3-3/4   29/4-16/6   1/9-30/9    ⛰ N 57°28'11'' W 04°09'02''

---

## Llandovery, GB-SA20 0RD / Wales

  ♿ 🛜 ✿ iD   **1261**

🏕 Erwlon Caravan & Camping
    Park*****
✉ Brecon Road
☎ +44 15 50 72 10 21
📅 1/1 - 31/12
@ peter@erwlon.co.uk

4ha 105T(64-90m²) 1-10A CEE

1 ACD**G**IJKLMO**PQ**
2 CGKRTUVWX
3 A**F**HJ**W**
5 **AB**DFGIJKLMNOPQRUW
  XYZ
6 CEKL(N 1km)OTU

💬 A large campsite with very good toilet facilities. Within walking distance of Llandovery. A good central location for visiting the beautiful Brecon Beacons National Park.

🚗 Campsite located on the A40, 1 km east of Llandovery.

CC € **20**   2/1-18/4   23/4-4/5   12/5-23/5   4/6-30/6   4/9-21/12    ⛰ N 51°59'36'' W 03°46'49''

### Looe, GB-PL13 2JR / England (South West) 🏕 ♿ 📶 iD 1262

🔺 Tencreek Holiday Park\*\*\*\*
🏠 Polperro Road
☎ +44 15 03 26 24 47
📅 1/1 - 31/12
@ reception@tencreek.co.uk

5,5ha 250T(100-120m²) 10A CEE

**1** ACD**G**IJKLOP**Q**
**2** AGILQRUVWXY
**3** BFHJNU
**4** (F+H+R 📧)
   (T+U+Y+Z 1/4-30/11)
**5** **AB**DFGHIJKLMNOPQUW
   XYZ
**6** CEGJ**K**M(N 1,5km)OTUV

💬 Large campsite with many amenities. Beautiful surroundings, nice villages like Looe and Polperro. Many activities are organised. The campsite has plenty of indoor space, so there is always entertainment, even when the weather is bad.

🚗 A38 Plymouth-Bodmin, A390 direction St. Austell, then B3359 direction Looe/Polperro to T-junction with A387, then A387 left direction Looe. Indicated at 3 km distance.

CC € **18**  1/1-24/5  27/5-14/7  1/9-20/9  23/9-31/12   📷 **N 50°20'47'' W 04°29'00''**

---

### Lostwithiel, GB-PL30 5BU / England (South West) ♿ 📶 ⚙ iD 1263

🔺 Eden Valley Holiday Park\*\*\*\*\*
🏠 Lanlivery
☎ +44 12 08 87 22 77
📅 1/4 - 31/10
@ edenvalleyholidaypark@
   btconnect.com

5ha 59T(100-130m²) 16A CEE

**1** ACD**F**IJKLM**P**Q
**2** CRSUWXY
**3** BFHJO**R**U
**4** (R 📧)
**5** **AB**DGIJKLMNOPTUWZ
**6** ACDEG**K**(N 2km)OU

💬 A quiet, clean and green campsite. Good value for money. Close to Lostwithiel castle and the old fishing villages Mevagissey and Fowey. Cornwall's main attraction, the Eden Project, is nearby. For cyclists there's the Camel trail, a route from Bodmin to Padstow over an old railway track.

🚗 On the A38 Plymouth-Bodmin, in Dobwalls take the A390 towards St. Austell. The site is located between Lostwithiel and St. Blazey, 2 km SW of Lostwithiel and 3 km NE of St. Blazey.

CC € **16**  1/4-13/7  4/9-31/10   📷 **N 50°24'06'' W 04°41'50''**

---

### Netley Abbey/Southampton, GB-SO31 8GD / England (South East) 🏕 ♿ 📶 iD 1264

🔺 Sunnydale Farm Touring Park
🏠 Grange Road
☎ +44 23 80 45 74 62
📅 1/1 - 31/12
@ enquiries@sunnydalefarm.co.uk

0,9ha 67T(150-200m²) 10A CEE

**1** ACD**G**IJKLMOP
**2** FGRUVWX
**3** F
**4** (R 📧)
**5** **AB**DGIJKLMNPUWXYZ
**6** ABCFK(N 3km)TU

💬 Spaciously appointed family business. Ideal for visits to Southampton, the historic town of Portsmouth and the Isle of Wight. Open all year. With hardened pitches. Close to bus stop, shops, several take-aways and the Royal Victoria Country Park. Security barrier.

🚗 Leave M27 at junc. 8, follow signs to Hamble (B3397) past Tesco on the left then follow A3025. Campsite signposted. Left into Grange Road, campsite 800m on left.

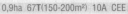

CC € **20**  1/3-4/4  23/4-1/5  7/5-22/5  3/6-15/7  1/9-12/9  24/9-19/10   📷 **N 50°53'09'' W 01°20'30''**

## Newquay, GB-TR8 4NY / England (South West)  ♿ 📶 ✿ **iD** ⑴²⁶⁵

🏕 Hendra Holiday Park*****
☎ +44 16 37 87 57 78
📅 23/3 - 3/11
@ enquiries@hendra-holidays.com

8ha 589T(69-120m²) 16A CEE

**1** ACD**G**IJKLMOPQ
**2** GIJKLRUVWXY
**3** ABC**F**JKNRUV
**4** (C 1/6-15/9) (**F+H** 📅) **IJ**
   (Q+S+T+U+V+Y+Z)
**5** **AB**CDEFGHIJKLMNPRSTU
   WXYZ
**6** CDFGHJ**K**LM(N 2km)OST
   UVX

💬 Large family campsite with lots of entertainment for young and old. Swimming pools, restaurant, entertainment and shops are all next to each other, like in a lively little village. Good toilet facilities on the campsite. All energy is sustainably sourced. The leisure pool is also open to non-campers.

🚗 A30 to exit Highgate Hill. Follow A392 direction Newquay. In Quintrell Downs continue straight ahead at the roundabout. 800 metres further on, Hendra park to the left.

Newquay
CC · A39
Goonhavern · A3058
Foxhole
A3075 · A30

CC € ⑯ 23/3-24/5  3/6-1/7  1/9-1/11      📡 N 50°24'05'' W 05°03'00''

---

## Otterton, GB-EX9 7BX / England (South West)  ♿ 📶 ✿ **iD** ⑴²⁶⁶

🏕 Ladram Bay Holiday Park
☎ +44 13 95 56 83 98
📅 15/3 - 3/11
@ info@ladrambay.co.uk

6ha 90T(49-120m²) 16A CEE

**1** ACD**G**IJKLMOPQ
**2** EIJKLNQRTUVWX
**3** BC**F**HN**QUV**WY
**4** (**F+H** 📅) **LMN**
   (Q+S+T+U+Y+Z 📅)
**5** **AB**CDFGHIJKLMNPQRU
   WXY
**6** AEGH**K**M(N 8km)OTUV

💬 Large terraced campsite on a beach with beautiful views of the sea. Hardened pitches with water and drainage connections. Many amenities and activities including watersports, indoor pool, bowling, disco, adventure playground and supermarket.

🚗 From M5 exit 30, then A3052 dir. Sidmouth. Right at Newton Poppleford onto B3178 dir. Budleigh Salterton. 1.5 km past Colaton Raleigh left towards Otterton. Campsite signposted in Otterton.

A30
A375
A3052
A376
Budleigh
Salterton  CC
Dawlish

CC € ⑱ 15/3-6/4  1/5-24/5  3/6-13/7  2/9-3/11  7=6      📡 N 50°39'37'' W 03°16'50''

---

## Paignton, GB-TQ4 7PF / England (South West)  ♿ 📶 **iD** ⑴²⁶⁷

🏕 Whitehill Country Park
🚏 Stoke Road
☎ +44 18 03 78 23 38
📅 23/3 - 3/11
@ info@whitehill-park.co.uk

80ha 324T(90-120m²) 16A CEE

**1** ACDGIJKLMO**P**Q
**2** GIKLRSTUVWXY
**3** ABC**F**HJRU
**4** (C+H 📅) KM
   (Q+S+T+U+V+X+Y+Z 📅)
**5** **AB**DEFGIJKLMNOPQR**S**T
   UWZ
**6** DEGJ**K**(N 3,5km)OTV

💬 Well-maintained campsite. Various meadows separated by shrubbery. Panoramic views of the surrounding hills. Heated outdoor pool which is open during the entire time the campsite is open.

🚗 Follow A38 Torquay-Paignton. Turn right in Paignton direction Totnes (A385), then immediately left by the 'Parkers Arms'. Then follow signs.

A38 · A384 · Torquay
A385 · Totnes · Paignton
CC
A381
A3122
A379

CC € ⑱ 22/4-3/5  13/5-25/5  2/6-15/7  8/9-19/10      📡 N 50°25'05'' W 03°36'32''

## Porthtowan/Truro, GB-TR4 8TY / England (South West)

♿ 📶 ✿ **iD** `1268`

▲ Porthtowan Tourist Park
🏠 Mile Hill
☎ +44 12 09 89 02 56
🗓 23/3 - 12/10
@ porthtowantouristpark@
gmail.com

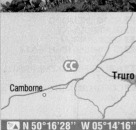

2ha 72T(100m²) 10A CEE

❶ ACD**G**IJKLOP**Q**
❷ QRTUVWXY
❸ A**F**JNRU
❹ (Q+R 🔧)
❺ **AB**DFGHIJKLMNPQRUWZ
❻ CEG**K**(N 2km)OU

💬 Quiet family site with spacious level pitches, clean modern facilities. Surrounded by fields, situated on the outskirts of the village. Close to one of the best surfing beaches, the South West Coast Path and the Coast to Coast Cycle Trail, only 13 km from Truro.

🚗 A30 Bodmin-Penzance, take the Porthtowan turning. Cross over the A30 and continue as far as the T junction through North Country. Turn right after 750 metres, campsite on the left.

CC € **18** 1/4-30/6 1/9-12/10

🗺 N 50°16'28'' W 05°14'16''

---

## Portreath, GB-TR16 4JQ / England (South West)

⊗ ✈ ♿ 📶 ✿ **iD** `1269`

▲ Tehidy Holiday Park
🏠 Harris Mill - Illogan
☎ +44 12 09 21 64 89
🗓 30/3 - 2/11
@ holiday@tehidy.co.uk

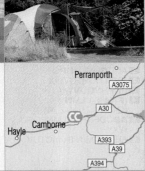

1,8ha 28T(42-100m²) 16A CEE

❶ ACDEIJKLOP**Q**
❷ CGIJRTUVWXY
❸ B**F**HJNRU
❹ (Q+R 🔧)
❺ **AB**CDFGIJKLMNOPQR
UWZ
❻ CEG**K**(N 2km)V

💬 A small, family friendly, four star campsite close to sandy beaches, cycle trails and coastal footpath. David Bellamy Gold Conservation Award. Voted Best Small Site in the UK and Regional Winners of Cornwall for 5 years running. Set in a beautiful wooded valley. Large private pitches. Modern facilities.

🚗 A30 exit Redruth/Portreath, 3rd exit on roundabout. 1st road left through North Country, straight across main road, see sign on left.

CC € **18** 5/4-2/7 1/9-20/10

🗺 N 50°14'42'' W 05°15'11''

---

## Rhuallt, GB-LL17 0AW / Wales

♿ 📶 **iD** `1270`

▲ Rhuallt Country Park
🏠 Holywell Rd B5429
☎ +44 17 45 53 00 99
🗓 1/1 - 31/12
@ info@rhualltcountrypark.co.uk

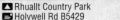

1,6ha 60T(60-120m²) 10A CEE

❶ ACD**G**IJKLMOPQU
❷ FGKRUVW
❸ FHIJ
❹ (U+Y+Z 🔧)
❺ **AB**DGIJKLMNPQRUWXYZ
❻ BDFGJ**K**(N 4km)OTU

💬 Located 3 minutes from the A55 main road. Perfect for exploring Northwest Wales, 30 minutes to Chester or Conwy, 40 minutes to Snowdonia. Fully equipped pitches on firm ground. Free wifi. Stunning area for walking. 5 star restaurant on the campsite.

🚗 A55 exit 28 or exit 29. Follow signs.

CC € **20** 3/1-28/2 4/3-18/4 23/4-2/5 7/5-23/5 28/5-30/6 1/9-23/12

🗺 N 53°15'48'' W 03°23'46''

## Salisbury/Netherhampton, GB-SP2 8PN / England (South West)

iD **1271**

🔺 Coombe Touring Caravan Park
📧 The Race Plain
☎ +44 17 22 32 84 51
🗓 1/1 - 31/12
@ enquiries@
   coombecaravanpark.co.uk

4ha 80T(80-100m²) 10A CEE

**1** AGIJKLOPQ
**2** RTUVWXY
**3** AFR
**4** (R 1/4-30/9)
**5** ABEFGIJLMNPUWZ
**6** EG(N 4km)V

💬 Quiet, beautifully situated site close to Salisbury. Ample panoramic views from campsite. The site is next to the race course (horses). In bad weather there is a building (up to 60 people) where you can cook food, sit, watch television etc.

🚗 M27, exit 2, A36. In Salisbury follow the A36 towards the west and then A3094 exit racecourse. After 1.5 km keep to the right at the fork in the road. The campsite is located after approx. 1.5 km, to the right of the racecourse.

Wylye — A360 — A345 — Wilton — A30 — **Salisbury** — CC — A36 — A354 — A338

CC €20 1/1-18/4 22/4-3/5 6/5-24/5 3/6-1/7 9/9-31/12    N 51°03'15'' W 01°51'40''

---

## Silloth, GB-CA7 4HH / England (Northern)

♿ 📶 iD **1272**

🔺 Stanwix Park Holiday
   Centre*****
📧 Greenrow
☎ +44 16 97 33 26 66
🗓 1/1 - 24/12, 27/12 - 31/12
@ enquiries@stanwix.com

10ha 121T(64m²) 10A CEE

**1** ACDGIJKLMOQ
**2** AGLUVWX
**3** BCFKMQRTUV
**4** (C 1/6-31/8) (F+H 🔒) JKLM
   N (Q+S 8/2-24/11)
   (T+U+X+Z 🔒)
**5** ABCDFGHIJKLMNOPRSW
   XYZ
**6** ABCFGHJKM(N 1,5km)
   OUV

💬 Beautiful, well-designed and maintained campsite with indoor and outdoor pools. Relax in the sauna, the steam bath and the jacuzzi and then have a bite to eat in the self-service restaurant or a drink in one of the bars. There is entertainment for children and adults. There are well-equipped toilet facilities.

🚗 M6 exit 41, via B5305 to Wigton, then via B5302 to Silloth. In Silloth turn left, and then follow the signs to Stanwix.

Anthorn — CC — Wigton — A596 — A595

CC €18 6/5-23/5 3/6-14/7 9/9-19/9 23/9-30/9    N 54°51'41'' W 03°23'13''

---

## Slingsby, GB-Y062 4AP / England (Yorkshire & Humberside)

👫 📶 iD **1273**

🔺 Robin Hood Caravan Park*****
📧 Greendyke Lane
☎ +44 16 53 62 83 91
🗓 1/3 - 3/11
@ info@
   robinhoodcaravanpark.co.uk

4ha 30T(90m²) 16A CEE

**1** ACDFIJKLOPQ
**2** GRUVX
**3** ABF
**4** (R 🔒)
**5** ABFGIJKLMNOPUWXYZ
**6** AEGK(N 1km)OU

💬 Campsite has a beautiful location in the hills in the countryside. Less than 5 km from Castle Howard and less than 30 km from the beautiful town of York. Pitches with pebbles or grass. Plenty of walking and cycling options.

🚗 From York take the A64 towards Scarborough. Take exit Castle Howard/Slingsby. In Slingsby turn right and immediately after 100 metres turn left to the B1257.

Pickering — A170 — A169 — Malton — Norton — A64 — CC

CC €20 1/3-16/4 28/4-1/5 7/5-22/5 2/6-4/7 8/7-11/7 1/9-2/11    N 54°09'44'' W 00°55'45''

## St. Agnes, GB-TR5 0NU / England (South West)

🌐 📶 **iD** (1274)

🏕 Beacon Cottage Farm*****
📧 Beacon Drive
☎ +44 18 72 55 23 47
🗓 1/4 - 30/9
@ jane@
  beaconcottagefarmholidays.co.uk

1,6ha 73T(100-200m²) 10-16A CEE

**1** ACDG**I**JKLNO**P**Q
**2** AIJKQRTUVWXY
**3** B**F**HNW
**4** (R 🔑)
**5** **AB**DEFGIJKLMNOPQRSTU
  WXYZ
**6** ACEG**J**(N 2,5km)OU

💬 An active family farm in a nature reserve. The South West Coast footpath is next to the site with the best views of Cornwall. The site is divided into 6 fields, some overlook the sea, others sheltered by trees.

🚗 A30 Bodmin-Redruth, turn right at Three Burrows roundabout B3277 to St. Agnes. In St. Agnes towards Beacon. Follow the camping signs to a narrow entrance. Coming from Porthtowan through the village, uphill and follow the camping signs.

CC 🔵 A3075
Redruth          Truro
A30          A39

CC € **20**  1/4-24/5  2/6-1/7  8/9-30/9   📡 N 50°18'23'' W 05°13'35''

---

## St. Buryan/Penzance, GB-TR19 6BZ / England (South West)

♿ 📶 **iD** (1275)

🏕 Tower Park
☎ +44 17 36 81 02 86
🗓 25/3 - 27/10
@ enquiries@
  towerparkcamping.co.uk

5ha 142T(100m²) 16A CEE

**1** ACDGIJKLMOPQ
**2** GKRVWX
**3** A**F**HRU
**4** (R+U+V 14/7-31/8)
**5** **AB**FGIJKLMNP**Q**RUWZ
**6** EJ(N 0,5km)OUV

💬 A friendly well maintained campsite with several fields, some shaded, others with lovely views of typical Cornish landscape. Spacious pitches, reading corner and billiards. Good base for Land's End and St Michaels' Mount. Walk to bus stop, post office and supermarket.

🚗 A30 Penzance-Land's End. After ±5 km B3283 dir. St. Buryan. In St. Buryan campsite is indicated. Other route not suitable for caravans.

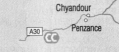

Chyandour
A30          Penzance
CC

CC € **16**  25/3-13/7  1/9-26/10   📡 N 50°04'44'' W 05°37'27''

---

## St. Buryan/Penzance, GB-TR19 6DL / England (South West)

📶 **iD** (1276)

🏕 Treverven Touring C. & C.
  Park***
📧 Coastal Road B3315
☎ +44 17 36 81 02 00
🗓 1/4 - 30/10
@ info@treverventouringpark.co.uk

2,5ha 115T(100-120m²) 16A CEE

**1** ACDGIJKLMOPQ
**2** EIKLQRVWX
**3** A**F**HN
**4** (Q 1/7-31/8) (R 🔑)
  (T+U 15/7-31/8)
**5** **AB**FGIJKLMNOPUWXZ
**6** EK(N 4km)ORU

💬 A panorama campsite with good facilities positioned high above the sea. 10 minutes from the coast, for walks along the cliffs and beaches to the Minack open-air theatre or even Land's End. The Telegraph museum in Porthcurno, southwest Cornwall is also worth visiting.

🚗 Stay on the A30 Land's End. After Penzance take exit to B3283. 2 km past St. Buryan then turn off to Mousehole (B3315). Campsite on the right side just over 1 km.

Pendeen
          Penzance
A30
CC

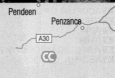

CC € **18**  1/4-8/7  8/9-29/10   📡 N 50°03'29'' W 05°37'06''

## St. Leonards/Ringwood, GB-BH24 2SB / England (South West)

&#x267F; &#x1F4F6; &#x2699; **iD** (1277)

▲ Back of Beyond Touring Park★★★★
✉ 234A Ringwood Rd, East Moors Lane
☎ +44 12 02 87 69 68
⌚ 1/3 - 31/10
@ info@
backofbeyondtouringpark.co.uk

0,6ha 127T(50-72m²) 10A CEE

**1** ACD**G**IJKLMOPU
**2** CDFGRUVWXY
**3** EGHJ**OW**
**4** (Q+R ⌚)
**5** **AB**DGIJKLMNPUWZ
**6** ABCEHK(N 5km)OU

💬 This quiet campsite is situated on the border of Hampshire and Dorset next to The New Forest. The campsite includes a golf course, woods and ponds for fishing. Not far from the beach and historic towns. The campsite is only for campers over the age of 18.

🚗 M27, exit 1. A31 dir. Ringwood. Follow A31. Pass St. Leonards at next roundabout back dir. Ringwood, then immediately turn left into East Moors Lane. Sign saying Back of Beyond. Then drive past Shamba.

Wimborne CC
A31
A341 A338 A35
Upton **Bournemouth** Christchurch

**CC** €**20** 1/3-18/4 24/4-2/5 8/5-23/5 2/6-5/7 15/9-31/10

📡 N 50°49'44'' W 01°51'13''

---

## St. Leonards/Ringwood, GB-BH24 2SB / England (South West)

&#x267F; &#x1F4F6; &#x2699; **iD** (1278)

▲ Camping Shamba Holidays★★★★
✉ 230 Eastmoors Lane
☎ +44 12 02 87 33 02
⌚ 1/1 - 31/12
@ enquiries@
shambaholidays.co.uk

7,6ha 145T(100m²) 16A CEE

**1** ACD**G**IJKLMOQ
**2** FGRSTUVWX
**3** BHJN**O**U
**4** (E+H ⌚) (Q 1/3-31/10)
(S ⌚) (U+Y+Z 1/3-31/10)
**5** **AB**DEFGIJKLMNPQR**S**
UWZ
**6** BCEGH**K**(N 4km)TUV

💬 Private campsite surrounded by tall bushes and trees. Lovely level grounds. Excellent toilet facilities, lovely swimming pool, very friendly and helpful staff. Close to the New Forest, a beautifully natural area.

🚗 M27 exit 1, on A31 direction Ringwood. Follow A31. After St. Leonards at next roundabout back direction Ringwood, then immediately left into East Moors Lane. Signpost marked Shamba.

A31
CC
A338
**Bournemouth Christchurch**

**CC** €**20** 5/1-5/4 4/5-24/5 3/6-15/7 7/9-30/11

📡 N 50°49'28'' W 01°51'13''

---

## Tavistock, GB-PL19 8NY / England (South West)

&#x1F4F6; **iD** (1279)

▲ Camping Woodovis Park★★★★★
✉ Gulworthy
☎ +44 18 22 83 29 68
⌚ 15/3 - 2/11
@ info@woodovis.com

4,8ha 50T(80-120m²) 10-16A CEE

**1** ACD**G**IJKLOPQ
**2** JKRTUVWX
**3** A**F**GHJLRU
**4** (F ⌚) KN(Q+R ⌚)
(U 1/7-30/8)
**5** **AB**DFGIJKLMNOPSUW
XYZ
**6** ACEG**K**L(N 6km)OSU

💬 A luxury campsite close to Tavistock and run by a family. A quiet and rural location. Large pitches. Lovely indoor swimming pool. Close to Plymouth and Dartmoor National Park, an Area of Outstanding Natural Beauty.

🚗 Follow the A390 from Tavistock towards Liskeard and then after approx. 5 km follow the signs to the campsite. At Gulworthy turn right at roundabout. After approx. 1.5 km the entrance to the campsite is on the left.

Launceston
A386
A388
CC Tavistock
A390
Yelverton

**CC** €**20** 15/3-15/7 8/9-1/11

📡 N 50°33'07'' W 04°12'18''

## Torrington, GB-EX38 8PU / England (South West) ♿ 🛜 iD (1280)

🏠 Smytham Holiday Park
📧 Little Torrington
☎ +44 18 05 62 21 10
📅 16/3 - 3/11
@ info@smytham.co.uk

9ha 78T(100-225m²) 16A CEE

**1** ACD**G**IJKLMO**P**Q
**2** GJKLRTUVWX
**3** A**F**HJRU
**4** (C 20/5-1/9) (R+Z 🔑)
**5** **AB**CDFGIJKLMNPQRUW
   XYZ
**6** CEGH**K**(N 5km)UV

💬 Beautifully located in a park-like setting. There are five small lakes. The campsite is situated in a valley with plenty of wildlife. You can walk or cycle from the site to the famous Tarka Trail, an old railway line that has been transformed into one of the loveliest routes in the country.

🚗 Campsite located 3 km from the A386 from Great Torrington to Okehampton. Entrance to the site on the right. ATTENTION: you must use this road.

**CC** € **18**  16/3-19/4  24/4-3/5  8/5-24/5  5/6-30/6  3/9-25/10  📐 N 50°55'37'' W 04°08'58''

---

## Washington, GB-RH20 4AJ / England (South East) 🛜 iD (1281)

🏠 Washington Caravan &
   Camp. Park
📧 London Road
☎ +44 19 03 89 28 69
📅 1/1 - 31/12
@ washingtoncampsite@
   yahoo.co.uk

1,6ha 114T 16A CEE

**1** ACDGIJKLMOPQ
**2** FGIRUWXY
**3** F HJ
**5** **AB**DIJKLMNPUWZ
**6** BE**K**(N 3km)TU

💬 The campsite is located in the countryside in West Sussex and borders on the South Downs National Park, a beautiful nature reserve with good hiking. Easily accessible by car, caravan or motorhome. There are several castles with beautiful gardens nearby. The South Coast is about half an hour away.

🚗 A24, exit A283. Immediately left after the roundabout. The campsite is ± 500 metres north of Washington.

**CC** € **20**  1/1-18/4  23/4-2/5  7/5-23/5  3/6-14/7  1/9-31/12  📐 N 50°54'32'' W 00°24'23''

---

## West Wittering, GB-PO20 8ED / England (South East) 👫 ♿ 🛜 iD (1282)

🏠 Camping Scotts Farm
📧 Cakeham road
☎ +44 12 43 67 17 20
📅 1/3 - 30/10
@ scottsfarm@live.com

10ha 650T(49-120m²) 10A CEE

**1** ACDGIJKLMOQ
**2** AEFGLNRTVW
**3** BFHNW
**5** **AB**GIJKLMNPQUWZ
**6** EK(N 0,3km)OTU

💬 A spacious campsite with a beach within walking distance. Cycling and walking possibilities e.g. 'The Salterns Way'. Excellent toilet facilities. East Wittering less than ten minutes away: a town with a wide choice of (takeaway) restaurants, authentic pubs and shops.

🚗 On the A27, south of Chichester, exit A286. After about 6 km left, B2198 in the direction of East-Wittering. After Lively Lady Pub turn right. The campsite is located after the village, on the right.

**CC** € **18**  1/3-4/4  24/4-30/4  8/5-20/5  5/6-30/6  7/9-30/10  📐 N 50°46'14'' W 00°52'40''

**Wool,** GB-BH20 6HG / England (South West)  ♿ 📶 iD **1283**

🔺 Whitemead Car. Park****
✉ East Burton Road
☎ +44 19 29 46 22 41
📅 14/3 - 31/10
@ book@
  whitemeadcaravanpark.co.uk

2ha  95T(70-120m²)  10A  CEE

**1** ACD**G**IJKL**P**Q
**2** CGRUVWXY
**3** A**F**HJUX
**4** (R 🔲)
**5** **AB**DGHIJKLMNOPUWX
**6** FG**K**(N 0,5km)OT

💬 Jill and Roy welcome you at their attractively laid out site near Wool. Modern toilets, shower facilities, launderette. Wifi. Monkey World and Bovington Tank Museum are a short drive away. Frome is interesting for anglers and swimmers. From station to Norden for nostalgic Swanage Railway. Jurassic Coast is nearby.

🚗 A352 Wareham-Dorchester. Just before level crossing in Wool, turn right and follow signs to campsite. Campsite is on right, 200 metres further on.

CC € 20  14/3-24/5  1/6-14/7  1/9-31/10  ⛺ N 50°40'52'' W 02°13'34''

# Ireland

## General
Ireland is a member of the EU.

### Time
The time in Ireland is one hour behind Amsterdam, Paris and Rome and the same as London.

### Languages
Irish and English.

## Border formalities
Many formalities and agreements about matters such as necessary travel documents, car papers, requirements relating to your means of transport and accommodation, medical expenses and taking pets with you do not only depend on the country you are travelling to but also on your departure point and nationality. The length of your stay can also play a role here. It is not possible within the confines of this guide to guarantee the correct and most up to date information with regard to these matters.

We advise you to consult the relevant authorities before your departure about:
- which travel documents you will need for yourself and your fellow passengers
- which documents you need for your car
- which regulations your caravan must meet
- which goods you may import and export
- how medical treatment will be arranged and paid for in your holiday destination in cases of accident or illness
- whether you can take pets. Contact your vets well in advance. They can give you information about the necessary vaccinations, proof thereof and obligations on return. It would also make sense to enquire whether any special regulations apply to your pet in public places at your holiday destination. In some countries for example dogs must always be muzzled or transported in a cage.

You will find plenty of general information on ▶ *www.europa.eu* ◀ but make certain you select information that is relevant to your specific situation.

For the most recent customs regulations you should get in contact with the authorities of your holiday destination in your country of residence.

## Currency
The currency in Ireland is the euro. Approximate exchange rates September 2018: £1 = € 1.12.

### Credit cards
Credit cards are accepted in many places in Ireland.

## Opening times
### Banks
Banks are open Monday to Friday until 16:30. On Thursdays banks are open until 17:00.

### Shops
In general open until 18:00. In many towns the shops are open on Thursday or Friday until 20:00. Ireland also has Sunday opening.

### Chemists
Chemists are open Monday to Friday until 18:00.

A number of chemists in Dublin open 7 days a week until 23:00.

## Communication

### (Mobile) phones

The mobile network works well throughout Ireland. There is a 4G network for mobile internet.

### Wifi, internet

You can make use of a wifi network at more and more public locations, often for free.

### Post

Open Monday to Friday until 17:30. Post offices are open on Saturdays until 13:00 and in larger towns also from 14:15 to 17:00.

## Roads and traffic

### Road network

Main roads (shown by the letter 'N') and secondary roads ('R') generally have a good surface but are much narrower than the roads you will be used to. Minor roads are so narrow that passing places are provided so that you can pass traffic coming in the opposite direction. The Irish AA patrols major roads night and day: tel. 1800-667788.

### Traffic regulations

All traffic drives on the left and overtakes on the right. Traffic on main roads always has priority at intersections. Vehicles on main roads have priority over vehicles on minor roads. On a roundabout you have priority over vehicles entering the roundabout.

The maximum permitted alcohol level is 0.5‰. Use of dipped headlights during the day is not mandatory. Use of phones is only permitted hands-free. Visitors from other countries are advised to fix headlight deflectors to prevent annoying oncoming drivers. All traffic signs are in English and Irish. There are no regulations concerning the use of winter tyres.

_Maximum speed_

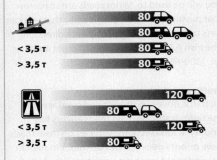

## Maximum allowed measurements of combined length

Height 4.65 metres, width 2.55 metres and maximum length 18.75 metres (of which the trailer maximum 12 metres).

## Fuel

Unleaded petrol and diesel are readily available. There is limited availability of LPG.

## Filling stations

Filling stations are generally open from 07:30 to 22:00. Make sure you have enough fuel in your tank on major roads as filling stations can be a long way from each other.

## Tolls

Tolls are charged on various bridges and roads. You cannot pay in cash on the M50 motorway around Dublin. Cameras register your number plate. You must pay no later than 20:00 the following day. For more information ▶ *www.eflow.ie* ◀

## Emergency number

112: the national emergency number for fire, police and ambulance.

## Travelling through the Channel Tunnel (if driving to Ireland via England)

If your car is fitted with an LPG tank you cannot take it on the train through the Channel Tunnel. There are special regulations for integral gas containers in caravans and motorhomes. Portable gas containers are permitted but you must declare them. See ▶ *www.eurotunnel.com* ◀

## Camping

Most campsites are located in the countryside and along the coast. The majority of sites are small and modest. The narrow twisting coast roads to the campsites will demand quite a bit of your time! Irish campsites often have well maintained grassy areas and there are often hardened pitches for caravans and motorhomes.

## Practical

- Make sure you have a world adaptor for electrical appliances. UK 13A plugs fit electrical sockets in Ireland.
- Tap water is safe to drink.

## Athlone, Leinster

1284

🏕 Camping Lough Ree East CSC
🏤 Ballykeeran
☎ +353 9 06 47 85 61
🗓 1/1 - 30/12
@ athlonecamping@eircom.net

2ha 60T(30-60m²) 6A CEE

**1** GIJKLM**P**Q
**2** CDFILNRTUWX
**3** AHUWZ
**5** **AB**GIJKLMNO**P**UWZ
**6** CEGK(N 3km)

💬 Simple campsite directly on the lake. Swimming, canoeing, fishing, sailing and surfing permitted.

🚗 From Athlone follow N55 to Ballykeeran. When campsite is signposted immediately left in bend and then campsite entrance is on the right after 30m.

CC €20 22/4-30/4 4/5-10/7 26/8-30/8 1/9-22/9    N 53°26'54'' W 07°53'23''

---

## Ballyshannon, Ulster

1285

🏕 Lakeside Caravan & Camping****
🏤 Belleek Road
☎ +353 7 19 85 28 22
🗓 8/4 - 8/10
@ lakesidecentre@eircom.net

2,5ha 98T(30-80m²) 16A CEE

**1** ACDGIJKLMO**P**Q
**2** ADFGKLRUVW
**3** BC**F**HJNUZ
**4** (R+T+U+Z 🗓)
**5** **AB**FGIJKLMNOPUWYZ
**6** CEGHKM(N 0,5km)TUV

💬 The campsite is located by a reservoir and has very good amenities including a pleasant restaurant and various watersports opportunities; motor boats are sometimes not permitted. Live Irish music on some Saturday evenings. Ballyshannon offers plenty of places for a night out.

🚗 On N15 turn onto N3. Follow camping signs on Belleek Rd.

CC € 20 8/4-20/4 23/4-3/5 7/5-24/5 28/5-29/5 5/6-30/6 1/9-8/10    N 54°29'49'' W 08°10'21''

---

## Caherdaniel, Munster

1286

🏕 Wave Crest C. & C. Park****
☎ +353 6 69 47 51 88
🗓 1/1 - 31/12
@ wavecrest@eircom.net

2,2ha 110T(40-80m²) 13A CEE

**1** ACGIJKLM**P**Q
**2** EGIJKNOQRTUVWX
**3** A**O**P**U**WY
**4** (Q 1/6-31/8) (S 1/6-1/9)
  (U+V+X+Z 1/6-31/8)
**5** **AB**GIJKLMNO**P**UWZ
**6** EGH**I**K(N 1,5km)OTV

💬 A large campsite beautifully located on the Atlantic. Extensive reception with plenty of information about the area. Fishing tackle on sale. Cafe/restaurant serving light meals and an extensive shop with provisions and other main requirements.

🚗 Clearly signed on the ring road from Kerry. Coming from Kenmare, 2nd campsite on the left before Caherdaniel. From Cahirciveen 2nd campsite on the left after Caherdaniel.

CC € 20 1/3-30/5 4/6-27/6 2/9-31/10    N 51°45'32'' W 10°05'28''

## Cahir, Munster

⊗ 🐟 ♿ 📶 **iD** (1287)

🏕 Camping The Apple Farm KI.A***
🏠 Moorstown
☎ +353 5 27 44 14 59
🅾 1/5 - 30/9
@ con@theapplefarm.com

1,5ha 32T(100-110m²) 16A CEE

**1** ACDEIJKLMOPQ
**2** FRTUWXY
**3** AFMU
**5** ABGIJKLMNOPUWZ
**6** CEGJ(N 6km)O

💬 A small, atmospheric campsite located in a fruit orchard. Sample the apple juice and enjoy a relaxing walk among the fruit trees. Apple juice, jam and cider are on sale in the shop. Ideal for day trips. Free use of the tennis courts. Drinking water from own source.

🚗 The campsite is along the N24 Cahir-Clonmel, 6 km from Cahir.

**Cahir**
**N24**
**Clonmel**
**Ardfinnan**
CC

CC € **14** 1/5-2/6 1/9-30/9 — N 52°22'35'' W 07°50'33''

---

## Cahirciveen, Munster

📶 **iD** (1288)

🏕 Mannix Point Park***
🏠 N70
☎ +353 6 69 47 28 06
🅾 20/4 - 15/9
@ mortimer@campinginkerry.com

2,8ha 42T(> 80m²) 10A CEE

**1** AGIJKLMPQ
**2** EKNORTUVWX
**3** HJNWY
**5** ABFGIJKLMNOPUWX
**6** DEGIK(N 0,5km)

💬 Mannix Point is located on the furthermost point of Europe and looks out over the bay and island of Valentia. The Gulf Stream ensures it has a mild climate. The campsite has already won 19 prizes and praiseworthy mentions. Come and visit us and see why.

🚗 N70 from Killorglin to Cahirciveen. Through the town of Cahirciveen, right by the sea, ± 500m from the N70.

**Kells**
**Knightstown** CC **N70**

CC € **20** 24/4-2/5 7/5-31/5 4/6-26/6 1/9-15/9 — N 51°56'23'' W 10°14'19''

---

## Cong, Connacht

📶 **iD** (1289)

🏕 Cong Car. & Camp. Park***
🏠 Lisloughrey Quay Road
☎ +353 9 49 54 60 89
🅾 3/3 - 3/11
@ camping@
   congholidaygroup.com

NEW

1ha 40T(30-60m²) 16A CEE

**1** ACGIJKLMPQ
**2** GJLRUWX
**3** ABCFHJKNW
**4** (A 🅾) (Q 17/3-1/11) (R 🅾)
**5** ABDFGIJKLMNPUW
**6** DEGIK(N 1,6km)QUV

💬 Campsite is located next to a castle and at 1,5 km walking distance to the centre of Cong, a historic village. Near the filming location of 'Quiet Man'. Sports activities include fishing and canoeing. Large park and cycling route in the centre.

🚗 From N54 exit to R334 Hereford-Cross. Left R346 to Cong. 1.5 km before the centre turn off at castle. After 300 metres site is on left. Site is well signposted with brown signs.

**Ballinrobe**
**Kilmaine**
CC **N84**
**N59**

CC € **20** 3/3-17/4 24/4-2/5 7/5-30/5 4/6-6/7 24/8-3/11 14=13 — N 53°32'22'' W 09°16'14''

## Garrettstown/Kinsale, Munster

♿ 🛜 **iD** **1290**

🏠 Garrettstown House
Holiday Park★★★★
📧 R604
☎ +353 2 14 77 81 56
📅 3/5 - 28/9
@ denis@garrettstownhouse.com

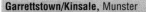

NEW

8ha 60T(40-70m²) 6A CEE

**1** AGIJL**PQ**
**2** AIJRVWX
**3** BC**F**GMNQRU
**4** (Q 3/5-1/9) (R 📅)
   (U 2/7-20/8)
**5** **AB**FGIJKLMNO**P**UWXZ
**6** DEGK(N 2km)OTUV

💬 Large family campsite. Beautiful view. Many facilities are housed in authentic buildings dating from the early 1700s.

🚐 From Kinsale follow the main road to Ballinspittle. Then head towards the beach and follow 'Camping/Garrettstown' signs.

Kinsale
Timoleague
CC

**CC** € **20** 3/5-27/6 31/8-28/9 | 📷 N 51°39'12'' W 08°35'28''

---

## Glen of Aherlow, Munster

🛜 **iD** **1291**

🏠 Camping Ballinacourty
House★★★★
📧 Ballinacourty
☎ +353 8 73 27 85 73
📅 29/3 - 30/9
@ info@camping.ie

3,5ha 45T(80-110m²) 6A CEE

**1** ACDGIJL**PQ**
**2** RUWX
**3** A**F**HIJKMN**Q**RU
**4** (R+Y 📅)
**5** **AB**FGIJKLMNOPQUWX
**6** CDEGK(N 1,5km)OV

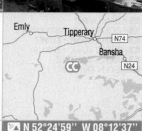

💬 A rural campsite on an ancient estate in a large nature reserve. Plenty of opportunities for walking in the forests and hills. The campsite offers beautiful views of the surrounding area and has a very good restaurant. New in 2015: re-planted Victorian garden with free entry.

🚐 N24 Tipperary-Cahia. In Bansha R663 (westwards) to Gabbally. Right onto side road after about 12 km. Campsite signposted on R663.

Emly
Tipperary
N74
Bansha
N24
CC

**CC** € **18** 5/4-30/5 5/6-28/6 26/8-29/9 | 📷 N 52°24'59'' W 08°12'37''

---

## Kilcornan (Co. Limerick), Munster

**iD** **1292**

🏠 Curragh Chase C.& C.
Park Kilcornan★★★
☎ +353 61 39 63 49
📅 1/3 - 1/11
@ info@
   curraghchasecaravanpark.ie

NEW

6ha 45T(40-80m²) -16A CEE

**1** BCDGIJKLMOPQ
**2** BDKLMRTUVWXY
**3** ABE**HJ**
**4** QR(T 📅)
**5** **AB**FGIJKLMNOPUWZ
**6** ABEGM(N 9km)QTU

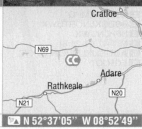

💬 Beautifully situated campsite in the middle of a natural park, facilities could be in better condition. Quietly situated, beautiful surroundings. Numerous opportunities for forest walks. Access to the park costs 5,- euros, but you get that back at the campsite.

🚐 The campsite is located about 20 km west of Limerick in the Curragh Chase Forest Park on the N69. Campsite signposted at entrance of the Forest Park.

Cratloe
N69
CC
Adare
Rathkeale
N20
N21

**CC** € **18** 1/3-30/6 20/8-31/10 | 📷 N 52°37'05'' W 08°52'49''

## Knightstown (Valentia Island), Munster 🛜 📶 1293

🏕 Valentia Island Caravan
& Camping Park
☎ +353 8 79 67 36 73
⊶ 1/4 - 1/10
@ info@valentiaislandcamping.com

43T(> 50m²) 10A CEE

**1** AGIJKLMOPQ
**2** AEFGIJKLNOQTUVW
**3** ACDHJKMUWY
**4** (A+T+U+V+X+Y+Z ⊶)
**5** **AB**FGIJKLMNOPQUWXYZ
**6** DEGK(N 0,4km)PT

💬 Completely new campsite. Exceptionally well-maintained. Run by very friendly, young managers. Just outside the centre. Various options for sports, such as canoeing, walking, cycling and swimming.

🚌 Take ferry to Valentia Island from the mainland on the N70 past Caherciveen. Campsite located 2 km beyond Knightstown. Back to mainland on R565 to Portmagee.

Caherciveen
CC N70

ⒸⒸ €⓴ 1/4-3/5  8/5-31/5  5/6-6/7  1/9-30/9      🏕 N 51°55'21'' W 10°17'47''

---

## Mullingar, Leinster 📶 1294

🏕 Lough Ennell C. & C. Park***
📧 Tudenham Shore Carrickwood
☎ +353 4 49 34 81 01
⊶ 17/3 - 30/10
@ eamon@
caravanparksireland.com

3ha 70T(40-80m²) 7A CEE

**1** AGIJKLM**P**Q
**2** ABCDFIKLMNRSTUVWXY
**3** BD**FH**JKN**OPRT**UW**Z**
**4** (Q+R+T+U+X 1/6-31/8)
**5** **AB**GIJMN**P**UWZ
**6** CEG(N 6km)OV

💬 Welcoming family campsite located in a beautiful forest on the Lough Ennell. Plenty of options for swimming, surfing, sailing, fishing, walking and making excursions to historic places. Toilet facilities are dated, but clean. Campsite has various pitches for tents, motorhomes and caravans. These are located on well-maintained grass fields (with shelter among trees).

🚌 M4, exit 2 to the N4. After 10 km exit Lough Ennell Park. Campsite is clearly signposted.

Mullingar
N4
CC
N52
Rochfortbridge

ⒸⒸ €⓴ 17/3-29/3  3/4-3/5  8/5-31/5  5/6-28/6  24/8-30/10      🏕 N 53°27'58'' W 07°22'30''

---

## Rathdrum (Wicklow), Leinster 🛜 📶 1295

🏕 Hidden Valley Holiday Park****
📧 Rathdrum
☎ +353 8 67 27 28 72
⊶ 15/3 - 29/9
@ info@irelandholidaypark.com

6ha 135T(100-110m²) 16A CEE

**1** ACGIJKLMPQ
**2** BCDGKLNORTUWX
**3** B**F**HJNUW**X**
**4** M(T+U 1/7-31/8)
**5** **AB**DGIJKLMNO**P**UWXYZ
**6** EGHJOT

💬 The campsite is located in a magnificent valley, the Vale of Clara, with waterfalls leading to Avonmore River. In Rathdrum (10-minute walk) you will find pubs with live music, restaurants, cafeterias and shops. Wicklow Mountains and Clara Vale national park are close by and great for a day out.

🚌 Via N11 to Wicklow. At Wicklow follow signs Rathdrum R752. In Rathdrum campsite is signposted.

Laragh
(Glendalough)
Wicklow
CC
N11

ⒸⒸ €⓴ 15/3-11/4  29/4-2/5  7/5-30/5  3/6-30/6  1/9-29/9      🏕 N 52°56'12'' W 06°13'39''

## Tralee, IRL-VG2RW89 / Munster

 ♿ 🛜 iD (1296)

🏕 Camping Woodlands★★★★
📫 Dan Spring Road
☎ +353 6 67 12 12 35
📅 1/2 - 30/11
@ woodlandstralee@gmail.com

6ha 135T(165m²) 10A CEE

**1** ACDGIJKLMPQ
**2** BGRTUVWX
**3** BFHJNU
**4** (Q+R 1/7-31/8)
**5** ABDFGIJKLMNOPQUWXY
**6** CDEGJ(N 0,5km)OTUV

💬 A well maintained and attractive town campsite with views of the woods. Within walking distance of Ireland's largest Aquadome which is open each day until 22:00 (large discounts for campsite guests, almost 50%).

🚗 The campsite is on the N86 Tralee-Dingle, 0,5 km south of Tralee and is also signposted on the N22 from Killarney.

Ardfert

**Tralee** [N69]
CC
[N21]
[N70] [N22]
Castlemaine [N23]

CC €20 1/3-15/3 18/3-18/4 22/4-2/5 6/5-30/5 3/6-23/6 1/9-24/10    📷 N 52°15'49'' W 09°42'11''

---

## Wicklow, Leinster

iD (1297)

🏕 Wolohan Silver Strand
   Caravan Park
📫 Dunbur Upper
☎ +353 40 46 94 04
📅 12/4 - 30/9
@ info@silverstrand.ie

7ha 75T(100-120m²) 10A CEE

**1** ACDGIJKLMOPQ
**2** AEFIKLQRTVWX
**3** EFWY
**4** (Q+R 1/6-31/8)
**5** ABGIJMNOPUW
**6** EMOT

💬 A campsite on a large green field with beautiful views of the Irish Sea. Its own beach, Silver Strand is below. Plenty of peace and space. Close to the town of Wicklow. Rural setting. Less than an hour from Dublin. Rural location.

🚗 Via the N11 to Dublin-Wexford, take Wicklow exit. Through Wicklow towards the Coast Road. The campsite is located on the left after about 3 km and is the 2nd campsite on this road. Both sites are called Silverstrand.

Wicklow
CC
[N11]

CC €20 12/4-30/5 3/6-4/7 26/8-30/9    📷 N 52°57'17'' W 06°01'00''

---

# Place name index

## A

# C

# D

# F

# G

# H

# Naturist camp sites

In this CampingCard guide you will find the following naturist camp sites or camp sites with a naturist section. Be aware that on most of these sites you will need to be a member of a naturist association.

## 🚶 Naturist camp sites

### Germany
**Mecklenburg-Vorpommern**

### Austria

### Hungary

### Croatia

## ☺ Partially naturist camp sites

### Netherlands
**Noord-Holland**

### Germany
**Hessen**

**Mecklenburg-Vorpommern**

**Sachsen**

### Austria

### Slovenia

### Croatia

# Acknowledgements

**2019 · 16th edition**
Print run: 445,000 copies (seven languages)
CampingCard ACSI is an ACSI initiative.
This CampingCard ACSI guide is a publication
of ACSI Publishing BV
PO Box 34, 6670 AA Zetten, the Netherlands
Telephone +31 (0)488 - 471434
Fax +31 (0)488 - 454210

## Questions or comments?

For campers:
www.campingcard.com/customerservice
For campsites:
www.campingcard.com/sales

## Printing

westermann druck GmbH
Braunschweig, Germany

## Maps

MapCreator BV, 5628 WB Eindhoven
mapcreator.eu/©Here/©Andes

ISBN: 978-94-92023-69-8

## Editor-in-chief

Willeke Verbeek

## Editorial staff

Suzanne Bas, Florian van Beem, Peter
Dellepoort, Rein Driessens, Nienke
Groenendijk, Marieke Krämer, Maurice van
Meteren, Ria Neutel, Ton Oppers, Marloes van
der Plaats, Rick Reijntjes, Teunis Roes, Mariëlle
Rouwenhorst-Küper, Thijs Saat, Koen Scholtes,
Esther Schoonderbeek, Erik Spikmans, Rens
Willemsen

## Translation

Interlex Language Services, Nuenen
www.interlex.eu

*ACSI office in
Andelst*